Access™ 2007 VBA
Programmer's Reference

Access™ 2007 VBA
Programmer's Reference

Teresa Hennig
Rob Cooper
Geoffrey Griffith
Armen Stein

Wiley Publishing, Inc.

Access™ 2007 VBA Programmer's Reference

Published by
Wiley Publishing, Inc.
10475 Crosspoint Boulevard
Indianapolis, IN 46256
www.wiley.com

Copyright ©2007 by Wiley Publishing, Inc., Indianapolis, Indiana

Published simultaneously in Canada

ISBN: 978-0-470-04703-3

Manufactured in the United States of America

10 9 8 7 6 5 4 3 2 1

Library of Congress Cataloging-in-Publication Data: Available from Publisher.

I dedicate my work, passion, and energies to my brother. Kirk is an inspiration, mentor, and good friend, and he leads by example in his unstinting support of the Spinal Cord Society's research to cure paralysis. And to my Mom and Papa and my Dad, who encourage me, laugh with me, and share in my joys, struggles, and jubilations as I take on extraordinary challenges such as climbing Mt. Rainier, riding 220 miles on a bike, and even writing this book.

And I dedicate this book to all the people who are just learning about Access and about VBA. Access 2007 has some phenomenal new features that empower users and give Access a more universal appeal. I am privileged to help you on your journey.

— Teresa

To my Mom, for her love and encouragement over the years and for instilling in me the passion to find the things I enjoy. To Karen and Chris, for reminding me where I come from. And in loving memory of my dad Marvin, who continues to drive me in my search for meaning.

— Rob

To my wife Jamie, for all the love and support you have given me. To my family: Mom, Dad, Cara, Sean, Ariana, and Army, for the encouragement, knowledge, and strength you have given me. My deepest gratitude does not even begin to define my love and appreciation for each of you.

— Geoff

To my wife Lori. Our work and interests are often so different, but I couldn't ask for a better partner.

— Armen

About the Authors

Teresa Hennig loves challenges, solving problems, and making things happen. Her company, Data Dynamics NW, reflects her dynamic personality and her innate ability to quickly grasp a situation and formulate a solution.

Teresa is president of both the Pacific Northwest Access Developer Group and the Seattle Access Group, and is host for INETA's monthly webcasts. She was the coordinating author for Access 2003 VBA Programmer's reference, and continues to publish two monthly Access newsletters. In recognition of her expertise and dedication to the Access community, Teresa was awarded Microsoft Access MVP.

Rob Cooper is a test lead on the Access team at Microsoft. He started at Microsoft as a support engineer in Charlotte, North Carolina, in 1998 and joined the Access 2003 test team in Redmond in 2001. During the Access 2007 release, he led the security efforts across the test team and worked on several new features including disabled mode, database encryption, Office Trust Center, and sorting, grouping and totals. Rob also led efforts around the Access object model and continues to provide direction around programmability and security in Access.

A long-time fan of Access, Rob is a frequent speaker at the Seattle Access Group and PNWADG meetings and has written for the Microsoft Knowledge Base and Access Advisor. Aside from writing code in Access and C#, he also enjoys spending time with his family watching movies, going to the zoo and aquarium, and hanging out in and around Seattle.

Geoffrey Griffith is an avid Access user who was raised in the Boulder, Colorado, area. He holds a Bachelor of Science degree in Computer Science from University of Colorado, where he studied software engineering. Now living in the Seattle, Washington, area and employed by Microsoft, he contributed to the Access 2007 product as a Software Design Engineer in Test for the Microsoft Office Access team. He enjoys participating in software community events by attending and speaking for local users groups and helping all those who would seek it.

Armen Stein is a Microsoft Access MVP and the president of J Street Technology, Inc., a team of database application developers in Redmond, Washington. J Street also offers web design, web hosting, and CartGenie, a complete web storefront and shopping cart system. Armen is President Emeritus of the Pacific Northwest Access Developers Group, and has also spoken at Seattle Access and Portland Access Users Group meetings. He has taught database classes at Bellevue Community College, and also developed and taught one-day training classes on Access and Access/SQL Server development. Armen earned a Business Administration/Computer Science degree from Western Washington University, and has been developing computer applications since 1984. His other interests include activities with his family, backgammon, Mariners baseball, and driving his 1969 Ford Bronco in the sun.

Credits

Executive Editor
Robert Elliott

Development Editor
Maryann Steinhart

Technical Editors
Michael Brotherton
Michael Tucker

Production Editor
Angela Smith

Copy Editor
Nancy Rapoport

Editorial Manager
Mary Beth Wakefield

Production Manager
Tim Tate

Vice President and Executive Group Publisher
Richard Swadley

Vice President and Executive Publisher
Joseph B. Wikert

Armen Stein Cover Photo by
Walt Jones

Composition
Maureen Forys, Happenstance Type-O-Rama

Proofreading
Christopher Jones

Indexing
Robert Swanson

Anniversary Logo Design
Richard Pacifico

Acknowledgments

We want to start with a huge thank you to everyone who was pulled into the research and review for the uniquely challenging adventure of writing about Access 2007 while working with the beta versions and using Vista beta. And a very heartfelt hug of appreciation to the families and friends of the authors and tech editors for putting up with our all-nighters as we strove to make this the most technically accurate and comprehensive book in its class. Speaking of tech editors, words alone cannot adequately acknowledge the valuable contributions of our two tech editors, Michael Brotherton and Michael Tucker. We also want to thank the Microsoft Access team for their passion and devotion and for making such revolutionary changes to Access. And, it wouldn't be as good as it is without the people who shared ideas and contributed to this book, including David Antonsen, Tim Getsch, Michael Kaplan, Michael Tucker, and Randy Weers.

We also want to thank Wiley and Wrox for providing the opportunity and infrastructure to reach our audience. We especially want to thank Bob Elliott for guiding us through the process and understanding the challenges of working with two beta systems. And we have a very special vote of appreciation for our development editor, Maryann Steinhart, who did a great job of managing the formatting and editing. Despite numerous delays, Maryann worked with us to incorporate final revisions when 2007 was released. And of course, we want to thank the authors of the 2003 edition, Patricia Cardoza, Teresa Hennig, Graham Seach, Armen Stein, and contributors Randy, Sam, Steve, and Brian.

Writing this book has been a challenging and incredibly rewarding experience. It was only possible because of teamwork and the contributions of others. So, thank you all!

— The Authors

I have to start by saying that is has been an honor and privilege to lead such an amazing team of authors and tech editors. Their combined expertise, experience, and passion for Access is unprecedented. This may have been the most challenging version to write about, and thanks to your devotion and team spirit our book will set a new standard for technical accuracy. As shocking as this may be, I'm at a loss for words to adequately express my heartfelt appreciation.

Of course, I have to thank the Access team for going all out for Access 2007 and for their seemingly tireless dedication to supporting the Access community. It's only through their efforts that we have so many new features. I can hardly wait to feel the excitement as people start to use Access 2007. That being said, I want to thank the members of my Access groups and all of the people who are using our book to get more out of Access. You are my motivation, and our team wrote this book for you.

I want to thank my family and special friends for their understanding and support through the roller coaster ride of writing this book. You were always available to listen to my stories and graciously accepted the many times that I was "unavailable." And, I am so fortunate to have the most amazing clients. Thank you for hanging in there when my time was consumed by the book and I had to defer your projects. You'll recognize Randy from our last book; although he was unable to officially join our team this time, Randy has my undying gratitude for helping me with Chapter 10. And no matter how immersed I became, I could always count on my friends Marc, David, Randy, Andi, and Mike. Ahhh,

Acknowledgments

yes, there it is again, the M word. So yes, my world is still filled with Mikes and Michaels. I wouldn't want it any other way <g>.

To friends, challenges, and opportunities. May we learn to celebrate them all.

— Teresa

First, I'd like to thank my wife Sandi for her support during all of the late nights and weekends. To my children Isabel and Gillian for being so understanding at such a young age while Daddy was working and not playing soccer or hanging out on the weekends. And to my oldest Taryn for being there on many occasions while I was not. The sushi is still better on the left-coast!

Huge thanks to Teresa Hennig for the opportunity to work on this book and for the project coordination efforts. This is something I have always wanted to do and I am truly grateful for the opportunity. Thanks to everyone on the Access team at Microsoft for their amazing work during this release and for answering questions that I came across while writing. I'd also like to thank the following people in particular: Sherri Duran for her encouragement and support while I started on this project, Kumar Srinivasamurthy for the encouragement and for being both a great lead and teacher this release, Adam Kenney for teaching me about the Ribbon, Michael Tucker and Michael Brotherton for agreeing to work on this project and for providing outstanding technical feedback, and Tim Getsch for writing the Foreword and great Access conversation.

— Rob

I'd like to acknowledge my wife Jamie and her family — Ken, Mary and Tammy — for the numerous sacrifices you have made for me; they are far too many to count. To my own family — Mom, Dad, Cara, Sean, Ariana, Army, and all my grandparents, aunts, uncles and cousins — your love and support has been monumental and the foundation of my entire life. To my best friends throughout the years — Mike and Megan, Joe, Rudi, Dylan, the Tom's, Sean, Cody, Ryan, Sammy, Marc, John, Paul, Matt, Elgin, Dave and Lori, Joe, Shinya, Andrew, Scott, and Dee Dee — thanks for all the encouragement and great times. To Sherri, Shawn, and everyone on the Access Team, for answering all of my questions and providing me with tremendous, life-changing experiences. Andrei, Valdimir, Tianru, Richard and Stephanie, thanks for taking a chance on a young kid, teaching me Access, and breaking me into the software industry. The writers and contributors to this book — Teresa, Rob, Armen, Michael, Michael, Maryann, Bob, and David — thanks for the great team and providing me with the magnificent opportunity of working on this book. To the previous authors of this book: Patricia, Teresa, Graham and Armen, as well as the contributing authors Steve, Brian, Randy, and Sam, for laying a powerful foundation for this book and sharing your extensive knowledge and experience in the previous book. To Clayton, Doug, Ed ("Dr. A"), Dr. Tom Lookabaugh, Dr. Michael Main, Jan, Mrs. Best, Jeannie, Yvonne, and all of my other teachers and professors, thanks for helping me learn and grow. Finally, all the hundreds of people who have made a difference in my life, even though you have not been called out by name, I still acknowledge your support and appreciate your contributions. Every last one of you is a Rock Star!

— Geoff

Thanks to my team at J Street Technology for their dedication to quality database applications: Steve, Sandra, Tyler, Matt, Stacey and Jessica. And thanks to my wife Lori and kids Lauren and Jonathan, who always support me in everything I do.

— Armen

Foreword

When I saw the list of authors Teresa brought together for this second edition of the *Access VBA Programmer's Reference*, I was very impressed. I have known each of the authors for several years, and they each have valuable insight. Teresa Hennig and Armen Stein are both Microsoft MVPs who have served the Access community in the Seattle area for many years. Rob Cooper is one of the top testers on the Access team and has a long history with the Access product as a support engineer. Geoffrey Griffith is an up-and-coming tester on the Access team who carries a lot of passion for the product. I have worked closely with him since his first day at Microsoft. Even the technical editors for this book have extremely strong resumes. Both Michael Brotherton and Michael Tucker have worked at Microsoft for more than 10 years and were testers on the Access 2007 team.

Not only was this book written and reviewed by a strong cast of authors, it nicely covers a wide spectrum of topics that you will encounter as you build your solutions in Access. It has topics for people new to Access or new to programming as well as topics that will improve the skills of seasoned veterans. This book teaches about many of the latest innovations as well as illustrating several commonly used techniques.

You will not just learn how to properly use VBA, but you will also see several new features in Access 2007 that eliminate or reduce the need for VBA code. Ultimately, you have a job to get done, and this book shows you the tools that are at your disposal. It is full of sample code that can help you get started, and it teaches you solid techniques that will help your code become easier to maintain in the long run.

This is a great book for anyone wanting to learn the depth and breadth of Access 2007. It is also an excellent reference and something that you will surely want to keep close at hand.

Tim Getsch
Program Manager, Microsoft Access

Contents

Contents

Contents

Contents

Contents

Contents

Contents

Contents

Contents

Contents

Contents

Contents

Introduction

Welcome to *Access 2007 VBA Programmer's Reference*. This release of Access probably has the most dramatic changes for developers and users since Access 97 and arguably since Access 2.0. With changes of this magnitude, you will want to leverage community resources to get up to speed quickly so that you are working smarter and more efficiently. That's where this book comes in.

Why this book? It has an unparalleled team of authors and tech editors who are as devoted to helping fellow developers as they are passionate about the product. Armen and Teresa have both earned Access MVP status in recognition of their expertise and contributions to the Access community, and Rob and Geoff are members of the Microsoft Access test team. They have the level of familiarity with Access 2007 that can only be developed through time and use. Both of the tech editors are testers on the Microsoft Access team, so they too have been working with Access 2007 for more than a year. In addition to editing, they also contributed resources, suggestions, and some of the tips in Appendix M. Every member of the team has been working with Access since 97 or before. Even with this remarkable level of expertise, we took the opportunity to complement our own experiences with contributions from other developers to bring you the best available information on using VBA (Microsoft Visual Basic for Applications) in Access 2007.

Many of the new features in Access 2007 can accomplish tasks that previously required VBA programming. In addition to reducing development time, these features can create better and more professional looking solutions. For many of us, being able to take advantage of the new features, right out of the box, is more than enough reason to upgrade. So although the primary focus of this book is to help you extend the power of Access by adding VBA, we identify the new features of Access 2007. Because many of you are familiar with prior versions of Access, we also point out some of the major changes, particularly if they affect the way that you will be working.

The goal is for *Access 2007 VBA Programmer's Reference* to be your primary resource and tool to help you leverage both Access's built-in functionality and VBA in a manner that helps you to create the best applications that you can imagine. Access 2007 makes it easy to start working as soon as it's installed. With the new UI (user interface), people will be building complex applications using the tools and resources that ship with Access. And, with a little outside guidance, they can work a lot smarter, with more confidence, and avoid several pitfalls. So, this book is for the typical Access user as well as the seasoned programmer. It will help you utilize the power of Microsoft Access more effectively and help you choose when to let the wizards do the work, as well as showing you how to modify and enhance the code that the wizards create. Access builds great forms and reports that can be customized on-the-fly by using VBA code to respond to a multitude of events. Interactive reports, or report browse, may be the ultimate example of the power and potential of Access. And Access now offers invaluable opportunities to integrate with external applications and multiple data sources. It's almost as easy as "a click of a button" to retrieve data from e-mail or to work with SharePoint and other online services. You can even use SharePoint for deployment and version control.

With all the new templates, macros, wizards, and help files, it is easier than ever to open the program and quickly start creating tables, forms, and reports. When you consider how easy it is to get started, you'll realize that it is doubly important to be working smart and in the right direction. Use this book and its online resources as your guide to better programming and more effective solutions.

What Is VBA?

Microsoft Visual Basic for Applications (VBA) enables programmers to develop highly customized desktop applications that integrate with a variety of Microsoft and non-Microsoft programs. For example, all of the Microsoft Office System products support VBA and can be extended even further by employing Visual Studio Tools for Office. In addition, many third-party programs, such as accounting software packages, mapping software, and drafting programs also support VBA. And, if the company provides an integration tool, or SDK (software development kit), it typically requires VB or VBA to work with it.

VBA is actually a subset of the Visual Basic programming language and is a superset of VB Script (another in the Visual Basic family of development tools). VBA includes a robust suite of programming tools based on the Visual Basic development, arguably the world's most popular rapid application development system for desktop solutions. Developers can add code to tailor any VBA-enabled application to their specific business processes. Starting with a blank database or building on a template, you can build complex solutions. For example, a construction company can use VBA within Microsoft Access to develop a sophisticated system covering estimating, ordering, scheduling, costing, and inventory control. The look and operation of the system can be tailored for each group and it can easily limit what data a person can view or change.

The report browse feature in Access 2007 is going to revolutionize the way both developers and users work with data. Developers will create more powerful and informative reports and users will have more options for analyzing and reporting data. It will enable people to make smarter decisions faster. Whatever the industry, Access may be the cost-effective alternative to purchasing an off-the-shelf product. Instead of paying the high cost of a proprietary program that offers limited capability for customization, developers can use Access to build a robust, expandable application that easily integrates with other programs. Once the Access application is in place, it can continue to be enhanced quickly and efficiently.

You might wonder why you should develop in VBA rather than Visual Basic 6.0 or Visual Basic .NET, both robust, popular, and capable programming languages. Using VBA within Access gives you a couple of key benefits. First, you can profit from a built-in Access object library, taking full advantage of a wide variety of Access commands, including executing any command from the Ribbon or custom toolbar in Access. And second, it's cost effective because VBA is included in all Microsoft Office System applications. To develop in Visual Basic, you need to purchase Visual Basic 6.0 or Visual Basic .NET either alone or as part of the Visual Studio or Visual Studio .NET suite. If they are required, they can be cost-effective tools, but it may not be necessary to burden a project with that overhead. And, since VBA is included with the Microsoft Office applications, your code and skills are transferable and it makes it much easier to integrate with other applications.

Despite the advantages of VBA, there are still circumstances where it would be beneficial to use Visual Basic. For example, to deploy an application to a wide variety of computers, especially those without a full installation of Microsoft Access, Visual Basic is a valid option. In fact, this book discusses using the Access Developer Extensions that ship with Visual Studio Tools for Office for that very purpose.

What Does This Book Cover?

Access 2007 VBA Programmer's Reference covers a wide spectrum of programming topics relevant to Access. Although it assumes the reader has some familiarity with VBA programming language, it begins with a brief introduction to VBA. And to help you leverage the tools that Access provides, a chapter highlights the new features in Microsoft Office Access 2007 — including new wizards and GUI (graphical user interface) elements that previously required VBA code, as well as new VBA features.

The book also discusses how to create and name variables, how to use Data Access Object (DAO) and ActiveX Data Object (ADO) to manipulate data both within Access and within other applications, proper error handling techniques, and advanced functions such as creating classes and using APIs. Key new objects such as using Macros and the Ribbon are explored, too, as are forms and reports, the two most powerful tools for working with and displaying data. Working with other applications is covered extensively both in a general nature and for working specifically with Microsoft Office applications, Windows SharePoint Services, and SQL Server. Of course, this book wouldn't be complete without discussing security issues and the Developer Extensions.

The Chapters

Chapters 1–5 provide material that you need if you're new to Access or VBA. After a review of Access 2007's new features, you explore the building blocks of VBA, including objects, properties, methods, and events. And you're introduced to the VBA Editor and its various debugging tools.

Chapters 6 and 7 focus on using VBA to access data. Both DAO and ADO provide methods for accessing data in Microsoft Access and other external data sources such as Informix, SQL Server, and a variety of accounting programs.

Chapters 8 and 9 provide detailed information on executing and debugging VBA code. Every development project needs some debugging, even if you're an expert developer. You'll see some easy ways to debug your code, and get some tips and tricks to make the tedious process of debugging a bit easier. Error handling is for more than just trapping problems and preventing crashes. It provides a powerful tool for interacting with users and adding functionality to programs.

Chapters 10 and 11 tackle forms and reports, two Access objects that can make particularly heavy use of VBA. In many applications, forms and reports control what the user can see and do. With the advent of report browsers, nearly all of the events that were available on forms are now accessible on reports. So, in addition to using code to show or hide sections of reports and to provide special formatting, you can now drill into the data underlying the report. These two chapters are packed with information; you'll see how to use split screens on forms, create professional image controls, format reports based on cross tab queries, enhance interactive reports, alternate row colors, and much more.

Advanced VBA programming information begins in the next four chapters (12–15) — creating classes in VBA, using APIs, and using SQL and VBA. Because the Office Ribbon is new, there is a chapter dedicated to explaining how to customize and work with the ribbon.

Chapters 16–22 provide information about working with other programs, working with Windows, and controlling access to your applications and files. They also discuss some techniques for deploying database solutions. You'll learn to create tasks and e-mail in Outlook, perform a mail merge in Word, export data to an Excel spreadsheet, and take information from Access, create a graph, and insert that graph into PowerPoint. Windows SharePoint services can help your applications share data across the Web. You'll see how new file formats add to network and Access security. In addition, you'll work with client/server development, learn to take advantage of Windows Registry and explore the Access Developer Extensions, essentially a Microsoft add-in, before you tackle macro security.

The Appendixes

As a developer, you can often spend hours going from source to source looking for reference material. The authors have applied the principles of relational databases (doing the work once so it can be used many times in multiple ways) to the appendixes, providing a compilation of data from a myriad of sources.

Appendix A addresses the issues and processes of upgrading, converting, and compatibility. The other 12 appendixes provide lists and tables that complement specific chapters in the book. You'll find detailed lists of objects for both DAO and ADO as well as the Access object model and Windows Registry. The appendixes on naming conventions and reserved words provide invaluable information that not only can strengthen your programming style but can save you from using terms or characters that can cause hours of needless pain and frustration in debugging and correcting. The last appendix is filled with tips and tricks to make it easier and faster for you to develop professional applications, all solicited from MVPs and developers around the world.

How to Use This Book

The initial chapters are written in a tutorial format with detailed examples. True to the Wrox Programmer's Reference standard format, the book includes numerous reference appendixes with details on the various object models you might use when writing VBA code in Access. It also provides a detailed primer on the Windows Registry and a listing of common API functions you might want to use in your code.

Real-world examples are given for many, if not most, of the programming topics covered in this book. These are just of few of the topics and examples that are included:

- ❑ How to control access to data based on database login information.
- ❑ How to create custom reports based on information entered on a form.
- ❑ How to leverage report browse — the new interactive report feature that enables drilling into data on reports.
- ❑ How to summarize and graphically display data using cross-tab reports.
- ❑ How to use VBA to transfer data between Access and other Office programs such as Outlook, Word, and Excel.
- ❑ How to configure custom ribbons, toolbars, and menus for your Access database applications.
- ❑ How to use the image controls for more intuitive and professional looking forms.

Throughout the book, we've also included tips and tricks discovered during the authors' programming experiences.

We recommend that as you go through the book, you download the code and sample databases so that you can see how the code works and experiment with changes. (See the "Source Code" section later in this Introduction for details on downloading the code.) Working with the code is how you take ownership of the concept and start to incorporate it into your work and solutions.

Other Access/VBA Sources

You've heard the saying that there are as many ways to build a solution as there are programmers. Well, there is a lot of history underlying that statement. So, although this book is an excellent reference for all of your Access 2007 programming needs, there just isn't enough time and ink to cover everything — to say nothing about fixes, updates, and add-ons. That's where networking, newsgroups, and other information sites come in. Here are some of the authors' favorites for you to check out:

❑ Microsoft Newsgroups — Microsoft maintains a news server and has a wide variety of Access and VBA newsgroups to choose from. Currently there are more than 18 Access newsgroups for you to choose from. They all begin with `microsoft.public.access`. You can access newsgroups through a newsreader such as Outlook Express or through the Web at `http://support.microsoft.com/newsgroups/default.aspx`.

❑ Microsoft Office Discussion Groups (`http://microsoft.com/office/community/en-us/FlyoutOverview.mspx`) — Microsoft is encouraging users to help each other, and it hosts discussion groups on selected products. There are currently 12 newsgroups listed for Microsoft Access.

❑ MVPS.ORG (`http://mvps.org`) — Your jumping-off point to a number of interesting offerings provided by a few folks associated with the Microsoft Most Valuable Professional (MVP) program.

❑ Microsoft Access Developer Portal (`http://msdn.microsoft.com/office/program/access`) — Provides information about current issues, downloads, updates, and ways to obtain product support. There are links to excellent tutorials and training as well as videos about Access 2007 and links to external sites such as user groups, newsgroups, and other valuable resources.

❑ Microsoft TechNet (`http://microsoft.com/technet`) — Offers quick access to Microsoft Knowledge Base articles, security information, and many other technical articles and tips.

❑ Microsoft Office Online - Access (`http://office.microsoft.com/en-us/FX010857911033.aspx`) — Provides quick tips, and direct links to Access resources such as downloads, templates, training, add-ins, and other pertinent information.

❑ Utter Access (`http://utteraccess.com`) — Currently the leading independent forum for Microsoft Access questions and solutions.

Conventions Used in This Book

Several different styles of text in this book will help you understand different types of information. Some of the styles we've used are listed here:

> **Mission-critical information or tips we've found particularly valuable in development are included in a box such as this.**

Tips, hints, tricks, and asides to the current discussion are offset and placed in italics like this.

As for styles in the text:

❑ New terms and important words are *highlighted* when they're introduced.

❑ Keyboard strokes appear like this: Ctrl+A.

❑ Simple filenames, URLs, and code within the text look like so: `persistence.properties`.

❑ Code is presented in two different ways:

```
In code examples, new and important code is highlighted with a gray background.

The gray highlighting is not used for code that's less important in the present
context, or that has been shown before.
```

Source Code

As you work through the examples in this book, you may choose either to type in all the code manually or to use the source code files that accompany the book. All of the source code used in this book is available for download at `http://www.wrox.com`. Once at the site, simply locate the book's title (either by using the Search box or by using one of the title lists) and click the Download Code link on the book's detail page to obtain all the source code for the book.

Because many books have similar titles, you may find it easiest to search by ISBN; this book's ISBN is 978-0-470-04703-3.

Once you download the code, just decompress it with your favorite compression tool. Alternatively, you can go to the main Wrox code download page at `http://www.wrox.com/dynamic/books/download.aspx` to see the code available for this book and all other Wrox books.

Errata

Every effort is made to ensure that there are no errors in the text or in the code. However, no one is perfect, and mistakes do occur. If you find an error like a spelling mistake or faulty piece of code in one of our books, we would be grateful for your feedback. By sending in errata you may save another reader hours of frustration and at the same time you will be helping us provide even higher quality information.

To find the errata page for this book, go to `http://www.wrox.com` and locate the title using the Search box or one of the title lists. Then, on the book details page, click the Book Errata link. On this page you can view all errata that has been submitted for this book and posted by Wrox editors. A complete book list including links to each book's errata is also available at `www.wrox.com/misc-pages/booklist.shtml`.

If you don't spot "your" error on the Book Errata page, go to `www.wrox.com/contact/techsupport.shtml` and complete the form there to send us the error you have found. We'll check the information and, if appropriate, post a message to the book's errata page and fix the problem in subsequent editions of the book.

p2p.wrox.com

For author and peer discussion, join the P2P forums at p2p.wrox.com. The forums are a Web-based system for you to post messages relating to Wrox books and related technologies and interact with other readers and technology users. The forums offer a subscription feature to e-mail you topics of interest of your choosing when new posts are made to the forums. Wrox authors, editors, other industry experts, and your fellow readers are present on these forums.

At http://p2p.wrox.com you will find a number of different forums that will help you not only as you read this book, but also as you develop your own applications. To join the forums, just follow these steps:

1. Go to p2p.wrox.com and click the Register link.

2. Read the terms of use and click Agree.

3. Complete the required information to join as well as any optional information you want to provide, and click Submit.

4. You will receive an e-mail with information describing how to verify your account and complete the joining process.

   You can read messages in the forums without joining P2P but to post your own messages, you must join.

Once you join, you can post new messages and respond to messages other users post. You can read messages at any time on the Web. If you would like to have new messages from a particular forum e-mailed to you, click the Subscribe to this Forum icon by the forum name in the forum listing.

For more information about how to use the Wrox P2P, be sure to read the P2P FAQs for answers to questions about how the forum software works as well as many common questions specific to P2P and Wrox books. To read the FAQs, click the FAQ link on any P2P page.

Access™ 2007 VBA
Programmer's Reference

Introduction to Microsoft Access 2007

What is Microsoft Office Access 2007? Simply put, it's the newest version of Access, a well-known and widely used relational database management system (RDBMS) for Microsoft Windows designed for building small- to medium-scale database applications. Access 2007 provides a rich set of features and tools for designing, creating, storing, analyzing, and viewing data, as well as the capability to connect to a large variety of other data sources. Access combines ease-of-use features with software development capabilities to support a wide range of user skill sets. Access also provides a Primary Interop Assembly (PIA) to allow other development platforms, such as Microsoft Visual Studio .NET 2005, to manage data using an Access database or even incorporate Access functionality into an external application.

If you're reading this book, you probably already know a good deal about Microsoft Office Access 2007 or a previous version. While this book presents the various aspects of programming Access applications using VBA code, this chapter provides an overview of Access and discusses some of the basics. Although it's possible to create and administer a database application using only code, there are also many tools for creating, designing, and editing database objects. Some of the more common tools are briefly covered in this chapter. If you've used Access before and are familiar with the visual designers and other Access tools, you can easily skip ahead to Chapter 3 to learn about the new features included in Access 2007.

A Brief History of Access

Microsoft Access has been around for nearly 15 years. The first version of Access, Microsoft Access 1.0, was released in November of 1992. Built on top of the Jet Database Engine, Access was designed to enable users to create and manipulate Jet-compatible database applications through a variety of visual designers and a scripting language called Access Basic. Access quickly became one of the most popular database development systems for Windows and the user base started growing rapidly.

With Microsoft Access 95, the fourth release, Access was adopted as a new member of the Microsoft Office product line. This was the perfect move for the product because it allowed Access to integrate and leverage many great features shared among other Office applications, such as Spell Checking or the Format Painter. Access Basic was replaced with the integration of Visual Basic for Applications (VBA) across the Office applications to provide a common programming language for creating solutions using the core Office products.

By the time Access 97 was released, millions of people were using Access routinely to build applications to store and manage their personal and business data. Access 97 is still in use today by many individual and business users and it is widely regarded as one of the best releases of Access ever. Some of the key features for that release were increased Web support, the hyperlink data type, and many new wizards. For developers, the release showcased the introduction of the Object Browser, VBA class modules, source code control, conditional compilations, and programmable command bars. That's a truly compelling set of features for users developing advanced applications.

Access 2003 VBA Programmer's Reference, the predecessor to this book, focused on the Microsoft Office Access 2003 product, the eighth release of Access. By 2003, everyone from individual users to the United States government was using Access. Access 2003 included a number of feature enhancements, as well as new additions. XML support, Data Import, and Data Export were improved in a number of ways, and signed database projects and disabled mode were introduced for added security.

Fast-forward to the present, and you have Microsoft Office Access 2007, the ninth full release of Access. Now shipping in 38 languages, Access is used throughout the world on Windows systems everywhere. For this release, there is a large focus on ease of use, and you'll notice major changes from previous versions as soon as you boot the program. Access 2007 probably has as many new elements and enhancements as the last four releases combined, and there are a number of developer-oriented features as well. One of the largest features is a new database engine called the Access Connectivity Engine (ACE), which supports several new data types, such as Attachment fields and Complex Data. Additionally, there are a number of new form and report designers, which make build Access database solutions even faster than before. After trying out Access 2007, I'm sure you'll see that Microsoft Office Access 2007 is the absolute best release of Access ever.

Is Access the Only Database System?

Some may ask the question, is Access the end-all to database systems? The simple answer is, "No." Access is not the only database product on the market, nor is it the only database product available from Microsoft or for Windows. There are times you might want to use a different type of database system such as SQL Server or SQL Server Express. If you've only used Microsoft Access for your database needs, you might be wondering why you'd ever need another database system. It could be argued that Access can connect to so many different types of data sources that there's no need for other front-end products. Moreover, developers could make a case that an Access database is a perfect solution for data storage for an application developed outside of the Access client, such as a .NET application that stores data in a back-end Access database. Still, there may be several reasons to use other database products, and the following sections discuss Access features, as well as other database system features, to help you choose what is right for your scenario.

Microsoft Office Access 2007

Microsoft Access is the perfect solution for single-user applications. Access provides many built-in features for quickly and easily building forms, reports, charts, and queries to view data. The user interface

(UI) is designed to be simple and intuitive so that even novice users can accomplish their tasks. Developers have the ability to create Macros and write VBA code to support application development. Another key feature of an Access database that is often overlooked is the storage of all database objects in a single file, which makes the database easy to distribute to others. The maximum supported database size is 2GB of data, which provides ample space for almost any personal database.

Multiple-user applications are supported by Access, although there are a number of considerations of which you should be aware. There are record-locking options that affect how data is accessed, and some operations require the database to be opened in exclusive mode, thus locking other users out of the application. The recommendation for multi-user Access applications is to create a distributable front-end database (for each user) that connects to a backend database that stores the data. For example, a front-end application written in Visual Basic can take advantage of DAO or ADO to make calls to retrieve and modify data in the back-end Access database. This type of application works well in a single- or multi-user environment, because the data is only manipulated when DAO or ADO code manipulates the back-end database. Even then, applications that have large numbers of data transactions may encounter performance limitations in the ACE database engine.

SQL Server 2005 Express Edition

The Microsoft SQL Server 2005 Express edition is a scaled-down version of SQL Server 2005. Microsoft provides this product for free and it can be distributed for free as one of many ways to integrate data with .NET applications. It is ideal as an embedded database for small desktop applications that call for a fully functional SQL Server database, but do not require a large number of users. Some of the features in SQL Server Express include new reporting tools and many feature enhancements for data views. SQL Server supports database triggers and stored procedures, which are database features not supported by the ACE database engine, although they can be used by Access in an Access project (ADP) file.

However, database development using SQL Server Express requires fair knowledge and there is no built-in forms package. You would not be able to build a complete Windows database application using only SQL Server Express in the same way you could using Access. Probably the most common scenario for using SQL Server Express is when developing a front-end application using Microsoft .NET Framework technology, in a programming language such as C#, which connects to the SQL Server database engine to manage data. It is worth noting that a fully functioning front-end database application (complete with forms, reports, and charts) easily could be created in Access 2007 and connected to a back-end SQL database on a machine running any version of SQL Server 2005 to enjoy many of the benefits of the SQL Server database engine.

SQL Server 2005

Microsoft SQL Server 2005 is the perfect solution for large-scale database applications. Typically, applications that require a large number of users, many concurrent connections, great amounts of data storage, data transactions, direct data security, or that need routine database backups are ideal for SQL Server. SQL Server is one of the most robust and scalable databases systems available for Windows. But, as with SQL Server Express, SQL Server requires a front-end application to be developed to allow users to access the data stored in the SQL database. All of this power comes with an associated cost. SQL Server is not free, so there is a monetary factor to consider when using it. Additionally, creating database applications with SQL Server also requires rather in-depth knowledge of database design and how to work with SQL Server. Although not the best choice for a small, end-user database solution, Microsoft SQL Server is ideal for very large databases in enterprise systems used for storing critical and sensitive business data.

How Do You Choose?

If you're not sure which type of database to create for your application, ask yourself the following questions:

- ❑   Will your database grow beyond 2GB?
- ❑   Are there security concerns for the data stored and used by your application?
- ❑   Is the data in your application critical or irreplaceable?
- ❑   Does your application require a large number of transactions at any given time?
- ❑   Does your database need to be accessed by a large number of users simultaneously?
- ❑   How will users work with the data from the database in the application?

Even answering these questions won't provide a definitive solution as to which type of database you should use for any given application. Every application's data storage mechanism should be evaluated on a separate basis by gathering storage requirements and researching the application's purpose to determine which type of database management system to use. For example, if the application will need to store 1.5GB of data, store confidential data, and need to be accessed by thousands of users at any given time, you might consider employing SQL Server 2005. However, if an application requires less than 1GB of data, needs to accommodate 20 users with relatively low traffic, and must maintain low development and support costs, Microsoft Office Access 2007 is the perfect choice.

Whatever database management system you choose, be sure to adequately understand the application requirements and research database system options before beginning work. The cost of redeveloping and porting an existing system can be huge, and in many cases, much more expensive than the cost of developing the proper system initially. Doing a little research and choosing the correct system the first time almost always pays off in long-term development and support costs.

Developing Databases Without VBA Code

This book is about automating Access with VBA code, but not everything you need to do with a database solution should be accomplished via code. Part of being a good developer is knowing how to develop an application with the most features, stability, and flexibility at the least possible cost. Access provides a powerful development environment that includes a variety of wizards and built-in tools to help improve efficiency in developing your application.

As soon as you start Access 2007, you will see immediate enhancements when compared to previous versions. Instead of a blank window, you are presented with the new Getting Started interface. It enables you to quickly open an existing database, create a new blank database, or even create a fully functional database application using the new database template feature. If the computer has an Internet connection and is online, links to Office online and its content are also present to help keep you connected to the latest resources available. You may also notice that the old Windows-style menus have been replaced by the new Ribbon user interface—the Office button, which replaces the File menu, exposes the Access Options dialog box for database and applications settings, as well as other common file options.

Access 2007 Database Templates

New to Access 2007, database templates are a great starting point for a simple database solution. Several different types of business and personal database templates are installed with Access and more are available from Office Online. Some of the different types of database applications you can create include:

- ❑ **Assets:** For tracking tangible items.
- ❑ **Contacts:** For tracking people or organizations.
- ❑ **Events:** For tracking important dates.
- ❑ **Issues:** For tracking assignable issues or problems.
- ❑ **Tasks:** For tracking groups of work tasks.

To create a new database using a template, click on one of the categories on the left side of Getting Started. Then click on a template in that category to select it. The template preview pane opens on the right side of the Getting Started window. If the template is from Office Online, you will see a Download button; otherwise, you see the Create button. Go ahead, choose the Business category and click on the Issues template, as shown in Figure 1-1.

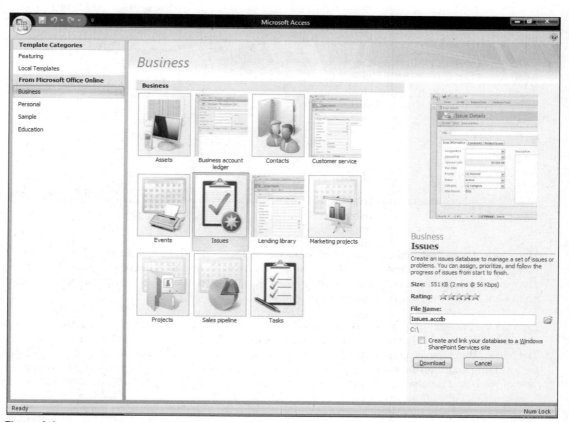

Figure 1-1

Clicking the Download or Create button creates the new database from the template—the Issues template, in this example. Once you start the database creation process, you briefly see the Preparing Template dialog box and then the new database solution opens in the Access client window, as shown in Figure 1-2.

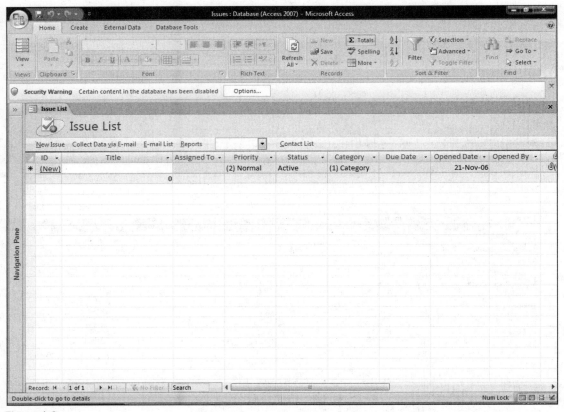

Figure 1-2

Many new Access features can be used in the Issues application just created. Among them is the Navigation pane, which replaces the Database Container window and is the primary interface for accessing database objects in Access. In the Issues database, by default, the Navigation pane is collapsed on the left side of the Access client window.

Click on the Navigation pane to expand it and see the database objects contained in the database application. Notice that the default grouping of objects is much different than in previous versions of Access. The Navigation Pane is a highly flexible and customizable feature that provides a number of methods for grouping and filtering database objects based on various properties of the particular object. In the case of the Issues database, a custom Navigation pane grouping named Issues Navigation is defined;

it's shown at the top of the Navigation pane. Clicking the top of the pane displays the various object grouping options available in the database. Click the text that says Issues Navigation at the top of the Navigation pane and choose the Object Type option. The Navigation pane grouping now shows all of the database objects grouped by their object types, as shown in Figure 1-3.

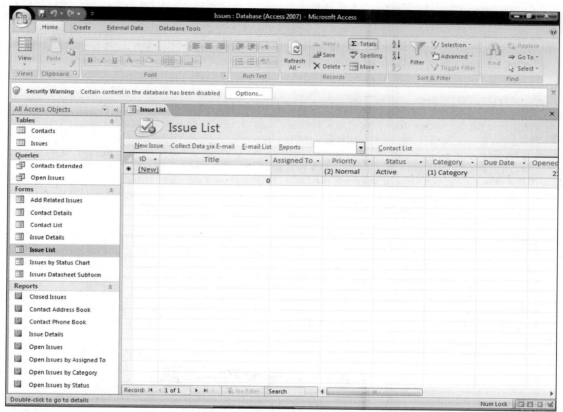

Figure 1-3

The Issues template is the perfect example of a highly flexible, fully functional database application complete with forms, reports, charts, and queries to easily manage data. The beauty of this application is that all of the functionality has been created without your writing a single line of code in the entire application. Moreover, all of the functionality in this application can run without trusting the database itself because of the use of safe macro actions (see Chapter 22 for more information about macro security). Notice the Security Warning between the Navigation pane and the Ribbon denoting that the application has disabled some content, such as unsafe macro actions and VBA code. By default, Access 2007 opens all databases with unsafe macro actions and VBA code disabled, unless the database resides in a user-defined trusted location. Fortunately, the Issues database application leverages known safe macro actions and built-in Access features to support its functionality and is completely usable even with code disabled.

Access Database Objects

With the Navigation pane grouped on Object Type, you can see that there are four different types of database objects included in the Issues database: Tables, Queries, Forms, and Reports. The Access 2007 File Format (ACCDB) actually supports eight types of database objects: Tables, Queries, Forms, Reports, Macros, Modules, Class Modules, and Data Access Pages (DAPs). All of these objects except DAPs can be created through code or through the Access user interface (DAPs are deprecated in Access 2007, but can still be viewed). There are many reasons why you would want to create database objects via DAO or ADO code in an automated fashion, but often, it makes more sense to design database objects via the Access UI. The following sections explain how to create five of the object types via the Access 2007 UI.

Creating Tables

Tables are the backbone of any database. Because they store all of the data, designing them correctly the first time is crucial. The type of data you need to store in any given table is dictated by its purpose in the application. For example, if you need to store the date on which some event occurred, you would use a Date/Time field data type. You could use a Text field type to store a date and there may be cases where that makes sense, but most of the time, the Date/Time type will be more beneficial because it enables you to leverage the comparison operations provided by the ACE database engine, which you could not do with the Text field type.

Creating tables through the Access 2007 UI is quite easy. When a database is open, the Access Ribbon has four tabs—Home, Create, External Data, and Database Tools—by default. In previous versions of Access, you could create new tables through the UI via the Insert menu or the Database Container window. In Access 2007, you create all database objects through the UI via the Ribbon's Create tab.

Click the Create tab. The Ribbon changes to show all of the various entry points for creating Access database objects. There are four options for creating tables: Table, Table Templates, SharePoint Lists, and Table Design. Figure 1-4 shows these options.

Figure 1-4

Click the Table Templates Ribbon button and the template fly-out menu appears. Click the Asset table template and a new table opens in Datasheet View mode, complete with all of the fields found in the Assets table. This is a great starting point for a new table because much of the work of setting up the table structure has already been done for you—and all it took was a few clicks of the mouse.

Now right-click the new table's Document tab and choose Design View to open the new Assets table in design mode. Because the table has not yet been saved, you are prompted for a table name to Save As. In the Save As dialog box, type in the name **Assets** and click the OK button. The Assets table is saved and opened in design mode for editing. Figure 1-5 shows the `Assets` table in the Table Designer.

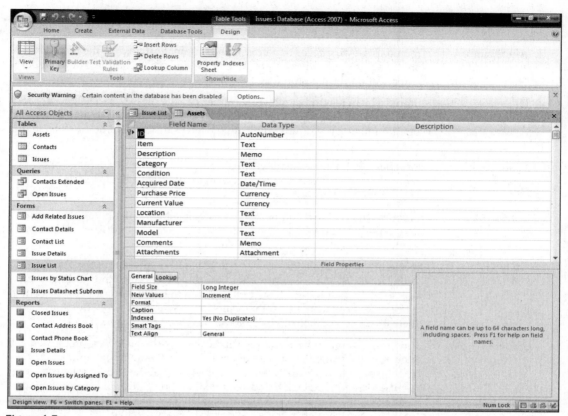

Figure 1-5

In Access 2007, ten different basic field data types are supported by the ACE database engine: Attachment, AutoNumber, Currency, Date/Time, Hyperlink, Memo, Number, OLE Object, Text, and Yes/No. In addition to these field types, ACE, and Jet databases support table field lookups to other tables through either queries or system relationships. Another new feature in Access 2007 is the capability to create complex data from certain data types (but not every data type). Complex data give the user the option to select multiple values from a value list or query for a single record. Additionally, when examining the data in the Complex Data field, all selected options can be taken as the value or each of the individual items (the scalar values) can be examined for the field. The following table provides a brief description of each data type's purpose and whether it supports complex data.

Data Type	Description
Attachment	A field type to store a collection of files for a given record. Stored as a complex data field, the complex scalar fields expose three pieces of data: File Name, File Data (the file itself), and the File Type. Stored as a complex lookup into a hidden complex scalar table.

Table continues on next page

Data Type	Description
AutoNumber	Stored as 4-byte integer that is assigned automatically when the record is created. Can be assigned as consecutive or random values. If the AutoNumber is a Replication ID, it is stored as a 16-byte GUID, instead of an integer.
Currency	Stored as 8-byte number allowing numeric range of: -922,337,203,685,477.5808 to 922,337,203,685,477.5807. The number is scaled by 10,000 to give a fixed-point number, providing 15 digits to the left of the decimal point and 4 digits to the right.
Date/Time	Stored as IEEE 8-byte, floating-point number allowing a date range of 1 January 100 to 31 December 9999. The date may also include a time value range of: 0:00:00 to 23:59:59.
Hyperlink	A combination of text and numbers stored in a Memo field type to be used as a hyperlink address. The hyperlink can have four parts: Text to Display, Address, Sub Address, and Screen Tip.
Memo	Stores any number of characters up to the limit on the size of the database, 2GB. However, text box controls and the datasheet only allow adding or editing up to the first 63,999 characters stored in the field. You need to use code to work with more than 64,000 characters in a Memo field. Only the first 255 of these characters can be indexed or searched.
Number	Provides several numeric data types dictated by the Field Size property for this type. A number field can be either an integer or floating type numbers. Supported data types are Byte (1-byte integer), Integer (2-byte integer), Long (4-byte integer), Single (2-byte scaled floating point), Double (4-byte scaled floating point), Replication ID (16-byte GUID), and Decimal (12-byte scaled floating point). Number fields can be complex data fields.
OLE Object	Stores up to 1GB of OLE object data (such as a bitmap image, Word document, an Excel spreadsheet, or some other binary data) linked to or embedded in the field.
Text	Stores up to 255 characters of text, where the field length is dictated by the Field Size property for the field. The field can be indexed and is fully searchable. Text data type fields can be complex data fields.
Yes/No	Stores a 1-bit value of 0 or −1, but can also be formatted as Yes/No, On/Off, or True/False. The size of this data type is 1 byte.

Each data has its own unique purposes, some of which overlap, so be sure to choose the data types wisely. For example, both Text and Memo field types store text characters. Because both types are searchable up to 255 characters and the memo field can hold much more than 256 characters, you might assume that all strings should be stored in Memo fields. However, if that implementation were the case, database users might encounter performance issues when running queries against large sets of Memo field data, which could be avoided by using a Text field type instead. Be sure to completely analyze the data your application will need to store so that you can plan appropriately when designing the database tables.

If you want to track when a record for the new Assets table is created, you need to add a new field in the table called Created Date. Create a new field at the end of the table by typing **Created Date** in the

Field Name cell in the first empty row in the Table Designer. Then, for the Field Type, click the down arrow to expand the data type options and select Date/Time. Notice the Field Properties grid shown just below the list of Table Fields in the Table Designer. The `Default Value` property is a simple way to set the value for a field automatically when a record is created without having to write any code. For the `Created Date` field, set the `Default Value` property to the expression `Now()` to use the `Now` function (see Figure 1-6). Now, every time a new `Assets` record is created in the table, the `Created Date` value will be set to the current date and time.

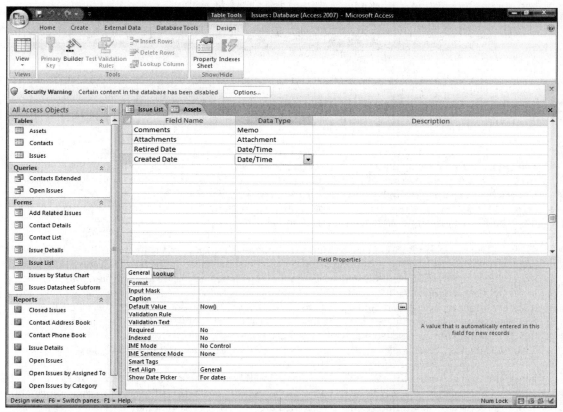

Figure 1-6

Click the Close button in the top-right corner of the table and choose to save the changes. That's an example of how you use the Access Table Designer to create tables.

Creating Queries

Queries can be used for a wide variety of purposes such as filtering data based on certain criteria, calculating values, joining records separated by different tables, deleting records from a table, updating certain records based upon specific criteria, creating new tables, and much, much more. Now that your database has a table to store data in, you probably want to create ways to view that data. One of the greatest tools that Access 2007 provides is the Query Builder, which helps you develop many types of queries. If you have prior database development experience, you've probably had to write SQL statements and already know how complex they can be (and how difficult they can be to get correct). The Access Query Builder provides a graphical interface to help generate the correct SQL statement for many query types, often helping to reduce the complexity of creating accurate SQL statements.

As mentioned earlier, the Ribbon's Create tab shows all of the various entry points for creating Access database objects. In the Other section of the Create Ribbon (all the way to the right—see Figure 1-7), are two options for creating queries: Query Wizard and Query Design.

Figure 1-7

The Query Wizard button launches the Query Wizard, which was included with previous versions of Access. It helps you generate four different types of queries—Select, Crosstab, Find Duplicates, and Find Unmatched queries—through several wizard screens. While these are useful, you will find that there are many other types of queries that cannot be created from the wizard and you will most likely want to use the Access Query designer to help you create those.

Click the Query Design button in the Ribbon to open the Access Query Designer. The Show Table dialog box displays to help add tables to be used in the query. In the Show Table dialog box, click the `Assets` table, the Add button, and the Close button. A field list for the `Assets` table appears in the designer for the new query. In the field list, double-click the * (star) field to add all of the fields in the table to the Query view. Notice that the `Assets.*` field is added to the list of fields in the grid at the bottom of the query designer. In the field list, double-click on the Created Date field to add it to the list of fields. Click the checkbox to uncheck the Show option for the field, so that the Created Date field is not shown twice. For the criteria for the Created Date field, enter `>(Now()-7)`. Figure 1-8 shows what the query should look like at this point.

When this query is run, all `Assets` records created within the last seven days are returned in the result. Criteria values can be any hard-coded values, functions, or expressions that define some information about the records you want to select. Switch the Query to SQL View mode by clicking the SQL View mode button in the bottom-right of the Access window; you'll see the following SQL statement generated by the Access Query designer:

```
SELECT Assets.*
FROM Assets
WHERE (((Assets.[Created Date])>(Now()-7)));
```

You can also create the specific query you need for your application by writing it directly in the SQL View mode.

Now click the Close button in the top-right corner of the new Query object. You will be prompted to save the query, so type in the name **Assets Created This Week** and click OK. The new query is added to the list of query objects in the Navigation pane.

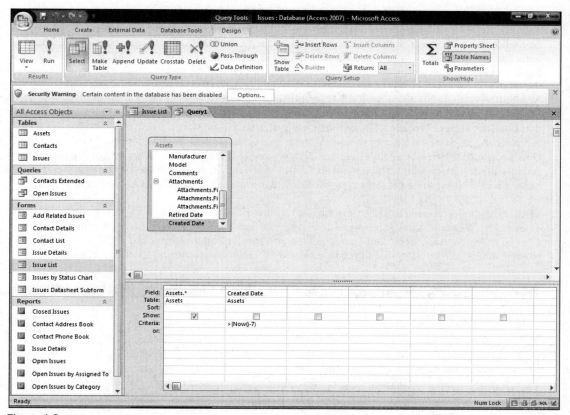

Figure 1-8

Creating Forms

Forms are vital for allowing users to add, modify, and delete data within your database applications. Access 2007 provides an extensive forms package and several designers to afford you robust functionality for your forms. While it is quite easy to create forms via Access automation, often times, it is much more practical to build forms using the Access Form designers.

The Access Ribbon's Create tab has several options for forms (see Figure 1-9) to enable you to reduce development time by quickly creating common form types.

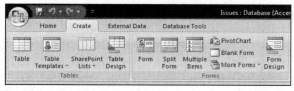

Figure 1-9

The Create Ribbon hosts nine different options for creating various predefined form types: Form, Split Form, Multiple Items Form, Datasheet Form, Pivot Chart Form, Pivot Table Form, Modal Form, Blank Form, and Form Design. An important fact to remember is that the Form, Split Form, Multiple Item Form, Datasheet Form, Pivot Table Form, and Pivot Chart Form options will be created based upon the object that is selected in the Navigation pane. If the Navigation pane does not currently have focus, the form will be based on the open object that does have focus. For example, selecting a query in the Navigation pane and then clicking the Form button creates a new form for that query. This rule applies for Tables Queries, Forms, and Reports that are selected in the Navigation pane. If you select any object that does not support creating one of the quick forms, such as a Macro, some of the buttons in the Ribbon become disabled. Any of the quick forms can be created in Design view mode by using the Form Design option. When all else fails, use the Design view to manipulate the form to just the right settings because all design changes can be made in Form Design mode. If you've used Access previously, you know that this used to be the only view mode available for designing forms and reports.

Click on the `Assets` table to select it in the Navigation pane and then click the Form button. This creates a new form in Layout View mode already populated with controls working with the fields in the `Assets` table. New to Access 2007, Layout View is a view mode for forms and reports that enables you to view data while building the new form. Figure 1-10 shows an example for the new form.

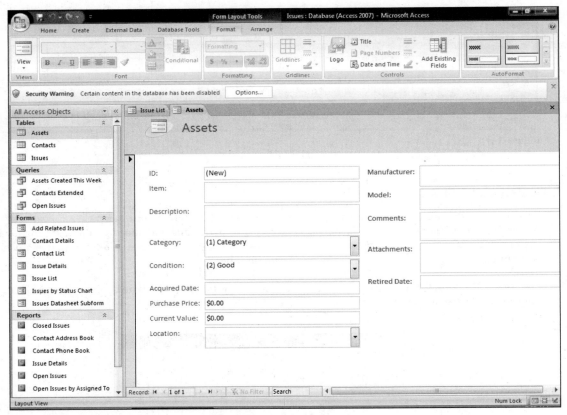

Figure 1-10

Depending on which view mode you have open for forms and reports, you only have a certain set of tools available. Controls and several other features can be added only in Design view mode. However, Layout mode is still quite useful because of the capability to see exactly what the object will look like with real data, while you are creating it. It's also nice to see formatting changes such as image and color changes while in Layout view mode, along with seeing the actual finished form without the design grid.

Click on the Close button in the top-right corner of the form. Once again, a save dialog box displays. Type in the name **Assets Form** and click OK. The new form is added immediately to Navigation pane.

Creating Reports

Reports are probably the most common way that users will view their data, and that's why one of the more robust features in Access is reporting. If you've used previous versions of Access, you'll notice that reporting has had a complete overhaul. Access 2007 has a slew of new reporting features that simplify common tasks to help decrease database development cost. There are two new view modes: an interactive report mode to allow users to use controls on the report and a layout mode to enable the report creator to see the data in the report while it is being created. Also, two new panes have been added: the Grouping and Sorting pane greatly improves grouping, sorting, and filtering tasks in a report, and the Design Task pane provides access to the updated Field List to allow working with more than just the fields in the record source of the form or report. In addition, there are many updates to previously existing features that were becoming archaic, such as the Auto Formats. Reporting in Access 2007 is a brand new experience for any user.

To create a new report, click on the Ribbon's Create tab of the Ribbon. As with forms, there are many options for predefined report layouts available, as show in Figure 1-11.

Figure 1-11

In the case of reports, you have the following options: Report, Labels, Blank Report, Report Wizard, and Report Design. As with forms, the Report and Label options are only available when Tables, Queries, Forms, and Reports are selected in the Navigation pane. If another open database object has focus instead of the Navigation pane, the report will be created based on the object with focus. Also similar to forms, certain design options are only available in Design View mode. For example, if you want to add controls to a report, the report must be open in Design mode. But, as mentioned before, the Layout view mode is extremely useful for viewing data, which helps refine report design and real estate efficiency.

Perhaps you want to create a report based on the Assets Created This Week query that you made earlier in the "Creating Queries" section of this chapter. Click on the Assets Created This Week query in the Navigation Pane to select it. Then, click the Report button in the Ribbon. A new report is created and opened in Layout View mode; it contains controls for all of the fields in the selected query. Because the report is in Layout mode, you are able to change the layout of the controls in it. All of the fields from the Assets Created This Week query are shown, so you may want to remove some of them, so that the data fits in the report all on one page. Go ahead and delete all of the fields in the report except Item, Category, Condition, and Purchase Price by clicking on the column and pressing the Delete key. Then, right-click on the Category field and choose the Group on Category option in the context menu. Notice that the Label and Grouping for the Category field is adjusted automatically (illustrating one of the many powerful grouping options available in Access 2007). Figure 1-12 shows what the report should look like with a few records of data added.

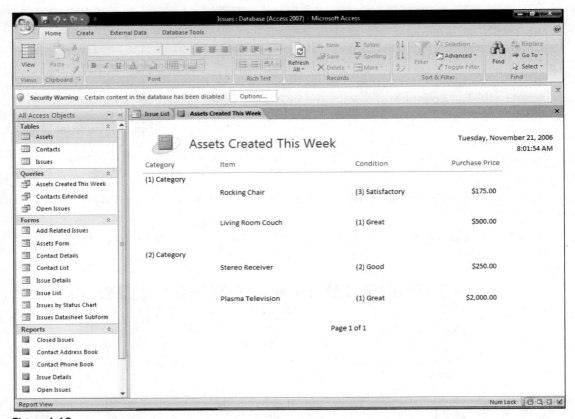

Figure 1-12

Using the quick report option can be one of the biggest time savers that Access 2007 offers. Often, reports (as well as forms) can be very time consuming in setting up and formatting to the desired settings. When used effectively, the quick report option eliminates much of the work to get the controls set on the report. Remember, a developer's time should be spent writing new code and designing systems, not fighting with the design of a report.

Now click on the Close button in the top-right corner of the report. Again, you are prompted to save, so type in the name **New Assets Report** and click OK. The new report is added to Navigation pane.

Creating Macros

The final object type to explore in this chapter is the Macro object. Macros are mostly used by novice and intermediate Access users, and often overlooked by developers. Macros can be powerful when used correctly and Access 2007 has had a number of feature additions and improvements in this area. Macros are common commands that can be selected from a list and named, so that a control can call the macro by name to run the functionality. All of the commands that can be run from macros can be run from code. However, one benefit of using macros is that there are many macro actions that can run when code is disabled in the database, meaning that a user is not required to enable code in the database application to use the functionality within it.

Buried deep within the Create tab, the Macro button can be found all the way to the right in the Other section, just to the right of Query option buttons. Clicking the Macro button here creates a new Macro object in Design view mode. The macro designer enables users to see the macro actions that are available in the Action list control. By default, only safe macro actions are shown in the Actions list, but clicking the Show All Actions button in the Macro Design Ribbon displays all macros. Click on the expander for the Macro actions and choose the OpenForm macro action. In the Action Arguments grid at the bottom, set Form Name to the name Assets Form (the form created earlier in this chapter). Figure 1-13 shows an example of what the macro builder looks like at this point.

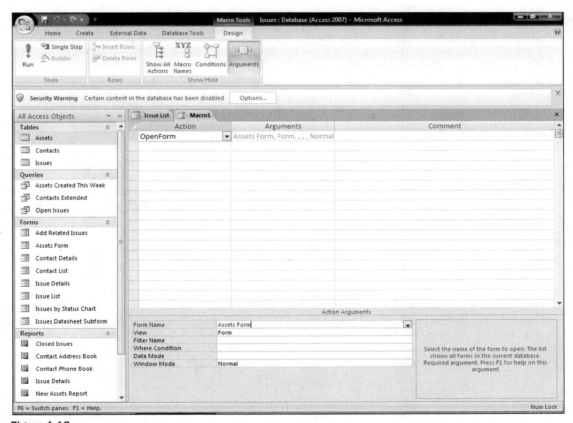

Figure 1-13

One important thing to know about Macros concerns the use of the AutoExec macro. Any macro named AutoExec in a database application is always executed on load of the database as a means of running macros or code on load of the application. It is common for even developers to use this feature and it is probably the most widely used function of macros. If you develop regularly in Access, you are bound to run into this at one point or another. To open a database without allowing this macro (or any other macro, code, or other startup options) to run, here's a little trick: hold down the Shift key and open the application. No code or macros will run.

To see the AutoExec macro work, close the new macro and save it as AutoExec. Now close and reopen the database. Notice that two forms are open. The Issues List form opens because it is set to open on application startup and the Assets Form opens because the AutoExec macro tells the database solution to open it on startup.

One last item to discuss about Macros is that they can have conditions. New to Access 2007 is the [CurrentProject].[IsTrusted] condition. This condition is extremely helpful in determining whether the database has code enabled when it is opened. The Northwind 2007 database uses this macro for just that purpose—to determine if the database has code enabled. If the database is opened and does not have code enabled, a message saying that code needs to be enabled for the database to work properly is shown to the user. That's very helpful for Access developers who use VBA in their applications. For example, you could create a form with a label that says that code needs to be enabled for the database. Then, you could create a macro for the OnLoad event for the form to an OpenForm macro with the condition [CurrentProject].[IsTrusted] set, so that a specific form opens if code is enabled in the database. The form with the OnLoad event macro could be set as the startup form for the database, so that the user is notified if the database must have code enabled to operate correctly. In this way, anytime the database is opened and code is not enabled, the user will see the form and know that he must enable code to use the database.

Summary

This chapter reviewed some of the basics for the Table, Query, Form, Report, and Macro designers for Access 2007. You learned when it is appropriate to use an Access database to store your data, and explored some of the benefits of using the designers to quickly build database objects without writing any code. You've seen that many tasks can be accomplished quickly using the tools built right into the Access product.

Many more features such as these are available, but they are beyond the scope of this book. Wiley Publishing, Inc., offers several books about how to use Access 2007 that are quite useful for learning more about these features. Visit www.wiley.com to read about them.

This book is about Access 2007 VBA, and you're probably wondering when you're going to write some code. Stay tuned. Chapter 2 covers the basics of VBA development. If you're already experienced in VBA you can probably skip that chapter. However, if you are new to VBA development, or you just want a refresher course in some of the basics, be sure to read Chapter 2. The rest of the book breaks VBA in Access into manageable topics, going into specific detail about each.

2

Access, VBA, and Macros

Chapter 1 introduced the various object designers available in Access to add functionality to your database. One of these, the Macro designer, enables you to add automation to your database, but at this point you're still not satisfied. Your database needs more. It is just about time to write some VBA code to work with your Access database. Before you do this, you'll need a basic understanding of VBA and how it is used in Access. This chapter covers the differences between VBA and macros in Access, as well as a bit about using VBA in Access. It also provides information about the differences you'll find between Access VBA and other forms of VBA, such as VBA in Excel or VBA in Word. Finally, this chapter takes a closer look at the new features that have been added to macros in Access 2007. Yes, that's right. New features.

VBA in Access

If you're reading this book, you've made the decision to use VBA in Access to develop your application. VBA in Access can be implemented in several places, such as writing VBA code in modules and behind controls on forms and reports. You take a quick look at both types of code in this section. Later chapters will provide in-depth coverage of VBA in forms and reports as well as the many different uses of VBA in modules.

Writing Code in Modules

A module is a container for code. You can store various subs, functions, and declarations in a module. To view all modules currently available in your Access database, click the Modules group of the Access navigation pane. To view a module, double-click it to open the Visual Basic Editor (see Figure 2-1).

Chapter 4 explores the various components of the VBA Editor in detail, but you'll notice that by default, the VBA Editor contains a Project Explorer, a Properties dialog box, and the main code editor. If you have various modules available in your project, they are listed in the Project Explorer in the upper-left pane. The Properties pane (lower-right) displays the properties for the currently selected object (either the module itself, or a control or form within the module).

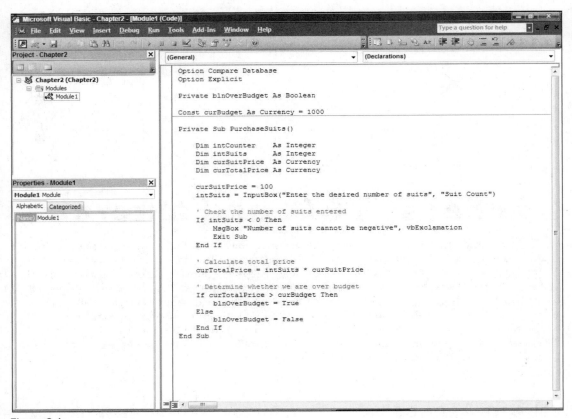

Figure 2-1

Writing Code Behind Forms and Reports

Before you dive head first into VBA, you might want to get your feet wet by writing some basic code in a form. Every object on a form has a number of events you can respond to through VBA. Most objects or controls have a click event, a change event, and enter and exit events, just to name a few. You can add code to any of these events and that code will run in response to a user's actions on your form.

Open an Access database and view a form in design mode. To build code in response to the `Click` event of a command button, click once to select the control and then display the Properties for the control by clicking the Property Sheet icon on the Ribbon or by right-clicking the control and choosing Properties. Once the Properties are visible, click the Event tab. Choose the `On Click` event property in the Property Sheet and click the Ellipses button (...) next to the Event property. Choose Code Builder from the dialog box that appears to display the VBA Editor, as shown in Figure 2-2.

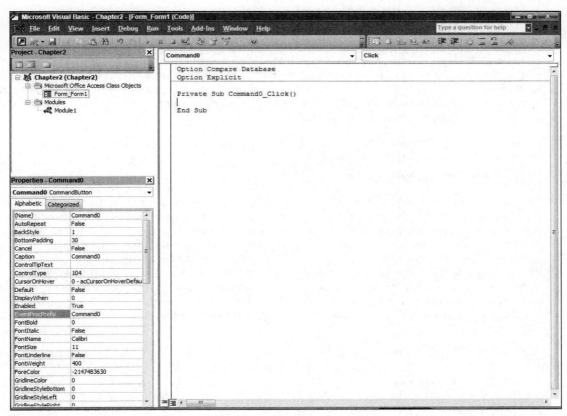

Figure 2-2

You'll notice two differences between Figure 2-1 and Figure 2-2. First of all, the Property Sheet shows all of the properties for the control you selected on your form. From this view you can change any number of properties of the control including size, `ControlTipText`, and `TabIndex`. The second difference is subtle; there's a new heading, Microsoft Office Access Class Objects, in the upper-left corner of the Project Explorer window. Under that heading is the name of the loaded form that contains the control you're currently working with.

The code window displays the name of the control you're working with and the event you choose. Whenever you choose to build code, a subroutine (sub) is created for you automatically. A function, the other main type of code block you'll write, is used when your code needs to return a value. Because you're writing code in response to an event on the form, you're not actually returning a value. You might update the value of the control on the form within the sub, but the actual sub itself doesn't return a value.

Other than the differences listed previously, the VBA Editor used to build code in response to a control's event is identical to that available in a module. The next chapter goes into detail about the various programming components you'll need to work in VBA.

VBA versus Macros in Access

Now that you've seen a little about how VBA works within Access you might be chomping at the bit to get started. However, there's one other item you should consider before jumping into Access programming without looking back: a macro. A macro is simply a saved series of commands. Unlike in Word and Excel, where you can record your own macros, in Access you create the macro yourself, step by step. A macro enables you to perform a variety of operations in Access in response to the click of a command button or any other programmable event on a form or report.

Macros in Word or Excel refer to a piece of VBA code that you would write in a module in Access. In Access, a macro is a separate type of object, one that's made up of a list of actions. Note that Word and Excel also enable you to create your own modules.

If you've programmed in Word or Excel, you know that you can create a macro by starting the macro recorder and performing the desired steps. When you stop the macro recorder, all of the operations you've performed—from mouse clicks to keyboard strokes to menu selections—are recorded and saved in VBA code. You can then run the macro at a later time by selecting it from the Macros dialog box or in response to a keyboard or Ribbon command. After you've recorded your macro, you can examine the VBA code behind the macro by simply choosing Edit from the Macros dialog box. This is one of the easiest ways to learn some VBA code within Word or Excel. For example, if you want to know the VBA code to insert three lines of text at the end of your Word document, just create a Word document, start recording a macro, and type your three lines of text. You'll end up with code that looks similar to the following:

```
Sub InsertNames()
'
' InsertNames Macro
'
    Selection.TypeText Text:="Rob Cooper"
    Selection.TypeParagraph
    Selection.TypeText Text:="Software Design Engineer in Test"
    Selection.TypeParagraph
    Selection.TypeText Text:="Microsoft Corporation"
End Sub
```

As you can see, you need to know some keywords before you can program Word to do what you want in VBA. Recording a macro in Word first, then perusing the commands, can help you to figure out how to write more sophisticated code directly in the VBA Editor. TypeText, for example, is the method of the Selection object that allows you to enter your own text in the document. TypeParagraph inserts a carriage return in the document. These are just two of the many methods you can use with the Selection object. While few programmers ever need to use every method of an object, you can write better VBA code by familiarizing yourself with some of the most frequently used methods of the objects you'll deal with.

While Word and Excel have the capability to record macros, Access does not. To write VBA code in Access, you just jump right in and code. However, if you aren't quite ready for VBA code, you can still create detailed macros using the Macro Editor in Access. The only limitation is that you can't record a macro; you must create it yourself step-by-step. This book is the *Access 2007 VBA Programmer's Reference* so it doesn't cover a lot about macros, but this chapter provides a brief tutorial on creating and using macros in Access. Then you'll explore the new features mentioned earlier.

Creating Macros in Access 2007

Although Access 2007 does not have a macro recorder, there are some pretty interesting additions to macros that you'll see shortly.

You can use macros for a variety of tasks in Access. Even though it might sound a bit crazy, most developers prefer to write code than to create a macro, but that's not always the easiest or most logical method of automation. Access 2007 includes 70 built-in macro commands. Many have additional conditions that can be set. For example, the OpenForm macro action requires you to select an existing form in your database. You can also choose whether to open the form in Form view or Design view. Other macro actions have similar required arguments.

To create a new macro, click the Macro button on the Create tab of the Access 2007 Ribbon. Access displays the new Macro window, as shown in Figure 2-3.

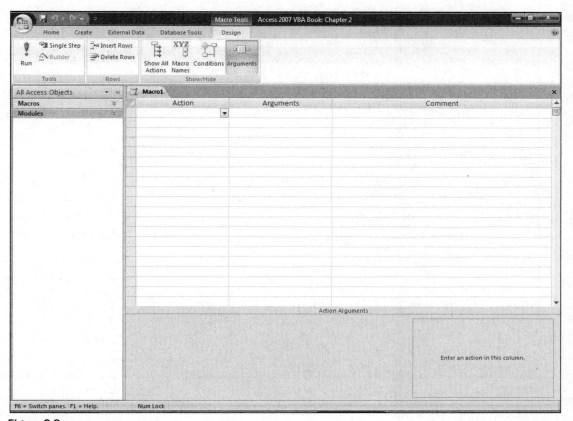

Figure 2-3

The default name for your new macro is Macro1, but you should change the name when you save the macro. There's nothing inherently wrong with naming it Macro1, but it doesn't give you very much of a clue about what the macro is for. It is better to give your macro a descriptive name, such as `mcrOpenForm` (which follows the Reddick naming conventions) or even something as simple as `GoToRecord` (which can be the name of the action the macro performs). Whatever you name your macro, make sure you can easily discern its purpose when you're looking at your Access 2007 database objects.

> *When I started working with Access, I didn't have a book like this to learn from, so I created many queries with the names Query1, Query2, and so on—particularly when creating nested queries. They all worked just fine, but when I had to update those databases years later or hand them off to other users, I couldn't remember what each individual query did. I had to go through every query and rename it all according to its purpose before I could update the database. Don't make the same mistakes I did.*

Now that you've opened up a blank macro, click the first line of the Action column to display the Actions drop-down list shown in Figure 2-4.

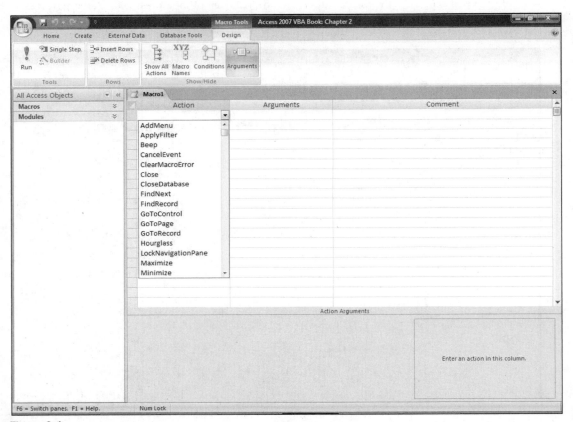

Figure 2-4

To implement an action, click the Action name to add it to your macro. Depending on the action you choose, additional criteria appear in the Action Arguments section of the window. Not all actions have arguments. In particular the `Beep`, `CancelEvent`, `FindNext`, `Maximize`, `Minimize`, `Restore`, `ShowAllRecords`, and `StopMacro` actions don't have arguments. Figure 2-5 shows a macro with several different actions. The Action Arguments section shows the arguments for the selected `OpenForm` action.

For readability, some Access programmers like to group their actions in a macro, leaving a blank line between groups of actions. There's nothing wrong with that practice, but there's no advantage to it either.

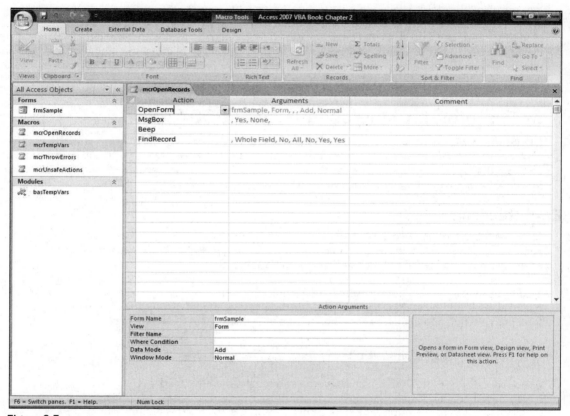

Figure 2-5

Now that you've completed your macro, save you changes and exit. However, what good is a macro if you don't have a way to call it? One of the common uses for a macro and one of the easiest ways to use one is in response to the click event of a command button on a form. To associate a macro with the click event of a command button, use the following steps:

1. Within the design of your form, choose a command button.

2. Click the Property Sheet button on the Ribbon button to display the Property Sheet for the command button.

3. Click the Event tab of the Property Sheet.

4. Click in the `OnClick` line of the Property Sheet to display the drop-down list.

5. From the drop-down list, choose the name of your macro. (All macros in your database are included in the drop-down list.)

6. Save and run your form. Clicking the command button runs each action in the macro sequentially.

You can also call macros from within your code. You might wonder why you would ever do that. After all, you're already writing code—why not just write code to accomplish the steps in the macro? Well, there's no definitive answer to that question, except to say that if you already have a perfectly good macro that does what you need, why not use it? Writing code to duplicate a working macro is like taking two steps backward for every one step forward. On the other hand, sometimes you just want everything in one place. If so, go ahead and duplicate your macro actions in code.

New Features for Macros in Access 2007

Okay, time to discuss those new features in macros that have been mentioned! Mind you, this is still a book about VBA, but these features are worth pointing out. Three features in particular—error handling, embedded macros, and `TempVars`—can certainly make using macros more attractive and even feasible in scenarios that were not possible in the past.

Error Handling

Error handling is often the primary reason that developers shy away from Access macros. In previous versions of Access, error handling in macros was simply not possible. When a macro encountered an error, there was no way to redirect the error to an error handler.

Macros in Access 2007 include error handling using the `OnError`, `SingleStep`, and `ClearMacroError` macro actions, and the `MacroError` object. The `OnError` statement defines the error-handling behavior for a macro action and includes two action arguments described in the following table:

Argument	Description
Go to	Determines how errors are propagated by an action:
	`Next`: Moves to the next line in the macro. This is similar to `On Error Resume Next`.
	`Macro Name`: Jumps to the named macro.
	`Fail`: Aborts the macro and throws the macro error.
Macro name	Name of a macro in the current macro group that handles errors.

Single step was available in macros in previous versions of Access but has been added as an action in Access 2007. By using the `SingleStep` action, you can conditionally step through macros using the Macro Single Step dialog box as shown in Figure 2-6.

Figure 2-6

The `MacroError` object is similar to the Error object in VBA, with the difference being that it is only available in a macro. Figure 2-7 shows the new error handling features in action.

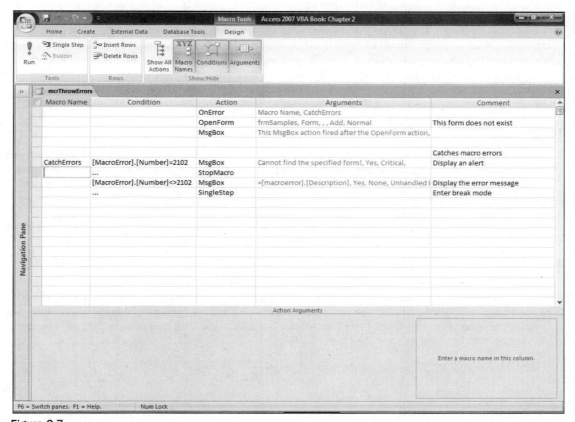

Figure 2-7

In this example, the OnError action redirects macro errors to the macro named CatchErrors in this macro group. This macro tests the Number property of the MacroError object to display a custom error message then clears the error and exits the macro.

Embedded Macros

An embedded macro is a macro object that is stored directly in an event property for a form, report, or control. These macros have two advantages over VBA and macro objects. First, if you have ever copied a control that had code behind it and then wished that the code also was duplicated, this feature is for you! Because these macros are part of a control's properties, the macro that is associated with a control event is also copied.

Second, you no longer need separate macro objects that perform small, simple tasks. Such macros can be associated directly with an event property.

Embedded macros cannot be referenced from other macros. If you need to re-use the actions that are defined by a macro you should use a separate macro object.

To create an embedded macro, choose Macro Builder from an event property's Choose Builder dialog box. Once you create the macro, the event property changes to [Embedded Macro].

Lastly, the wizards in Access 2007 are updated to create embedded macros in the new format database (ACCDB) because code will not execute in Disabled mode, meaning that wizard-generated code will not run unless a database is trusted. The wizards now allow the application to run as much as possible in Disabled mode without failing. For backward compatibility, VBA code is still created using the wizards in the previous file formats (MDB and ADP), but they have been updated to use the RunCommand method where appropriate. That's right—the wizards no longer create code that calls DoMenuItem!

For more information about Disabled mode, please see Chapter 22.

TempVars

Another limitation of macros in previous versions of Access was that they could not declare or reference variables. For such functionality, you have always had to use VBA. Access 2007 adds a new object called TempVar that is contained in a TempVars collection. A TempVar object is simply a name/value pair that can be referenced in macros.

You can use three macro actions to work with TempVars. The first, SetTempVar is used to create a new TempVar. To remove a TempVar, you can use the RemoveTempVar action. Finally, you can clear the TempVars collection by calling the RemoveAllTempVars action.

TempVars are pretty cool on their own, but you can also work with them in expressions in queries, forms, and reports. You can even work with them in VBA, meaning that you can now pass data between a macro and your VBA code. Where you might have used a hidden form or global variables in the past, you can now accomplish using a TempVar. Once you create some TempVar objects, you can use the following code to list the TempVar objects from VBA:

```
' Demonstrates communication between macros
' and VBA using TempVars
Function ShowTempVars()
```

```
    Dim tv       As TempVar
    Dim strVars As String

    ' Build the TempVars string
    For Each tv In Application.TempVars
        strVars = strVars & tv.Name & " = " & tv.Value & vbCrLf
    Next

    ' display
    MsgBox strVars, vbInformation
End Function
```

Don't worry if parts of this code seem out of place for the time being. It'll all be explained throughout the course of the book.

Macro Designer Changes

You may have already noticed a few changes to the Macro Designer in Access 2007. The first is the addition of the Arguments column. This column displays a list of the arguments for a macro action. No longer do you have to jump between the design grid and the action arguments at the bottom of the designer to see all of the arguments!

By default, Access 2007 only shows those macros actions that have been deemed *safe*. Generally speaking, a safe action is one that does not perform any of the following tasks:

- ❏ Change data
- ❏ Create or delete objects
- ❏ Update or alter the Access user interface
- ❏ Access the Windows file system
- ❏ Run a SQL statement
- ❏ Send e-mail

Actions that fall under these categories include TransferText (creates a file), CopyObject (creates a new object), DeleteObject (removes an object), or RunSQL (can be used to add or remove objects, or update or delete data).

To see the list of all possible actions, click the Show All Actions button (new in Access 2007) in the Ribbon. All actions and RunCommand action arguments are then available for choosing. When an unsafe action is selected, the Macro Designer displays a warning icon in the column next to the action name, as shown in Figure 2-8.

It is important to note that some actions can be deemed safe until you change one of their action arguments. In the example in Figure 2-8, the SendObject action is deemed safe until you change the Edit Message action argument to No. That's because it is safe to send e-mail when the e-mail message is opened first.

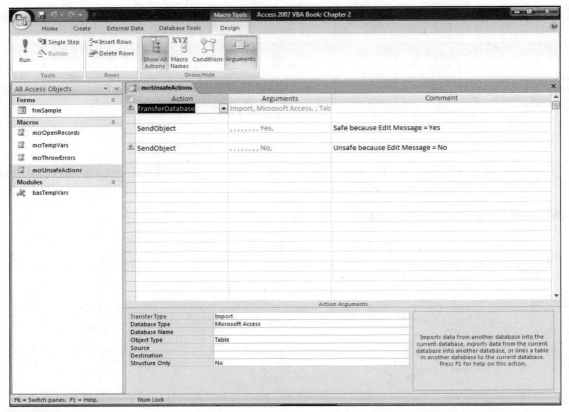

Figure 2-8

Why All the Changes?

You might be asking yourself, "Why did Microsoft make all these changes to macros when they have been relatively unchanged for quite some time?" Good question. The short answer is for Disabled mode. To make applications relatively functional without running code, these changes were required to macros. These combined features make macros more viable than in previous versions, and the templates in Access were designed with Disabled mode in mind. As mentioned in Chapter 1, most of the new templates run using safe macro actions and without code.

Does that mean that you shouldn't use VBA for your solutions? Of course not! But it does mean that in certain scenarios such as where you might not want code to run, or you are looking for simple light-weight solutions, macros might provide a reasonable alternative.

Advantages to Using VBA over Macros

While macros are perfectly acceptable and even recommended in certain situations, there are some key advantages to using VBA. The following is a list of some of the advantages you'll enjoy by using VBA instead of a macro.

- ❑ **Speed:** A one-action macro will probably execute faster than the equivalent VBA code. However, running a complex macro with 10 or 12 actions usually takes significantly longer than the equivalent code. VBA code within Access is fast. If you're designing an end-user application, you definitely need to be concerned with speed. If your users see the hourglass for even more than 5 or 6 seconds, their perception will be that your application is slow.

- ❑ **Functionality:** With 70 macro actions, how could you ever miss functionality? We're being facetious, of course—if all Access programming were limited to 70 actions, there wouldn't be many applications written in Access. How would you play a sound other than the default "beep" or open an HTML file in response to a button click? VBA provides so much more functionality than Access macros do. For example, VBA gives you the capability to interact with other applications. Using VBA, you can open Word or Excel files, send e-mail from Outlook, open an Internet Explorer browser and navigate to a particular Web site, or open almost any file stored on your computer or a network drive. External application access isn't limited to Microsoft products either. You can add a reference to any number of applications through the References dialog box in Access VBA. Once you've added a reference, you can control other applications such as Adobe Acrobat, VMWare, or Yahoo Messenger. You can also take advantage of many Web services, such as MapPoint and CarPoint.

- ❑ **Control:** With VBA, you can exercise almost complete control over your code. Instead of having to let the chosen macro actions perform the work, you can control each step of the process in VBA. Some tasks—such as dynamically creating an ADO connection based on user input— simply cannot be accomplished using macros. Some tasks are possible, but considerably more difficult. Asking for a variety of variables to input into an equation, for instance, can be easily accomplished using VBA, but is rather difficult using a macro (macros would require a `TempVar` or hidden form to store the data). Macros cannot easily run a different set of actions for each user of your application. VBA can accomplish this task with ease.

- ❑ **Interaction with other applications:** When using VBA in Access you're not limited to merely programming Microsoft Access. You can add references to other object libraries such as Word, Excel, Outlook, and even non-Microsoft programs including accounting packages, drafting programs, and even graphics programs.

Summary

This chapter covered the basics of VBA in Access and how to create some basic macros in Access. It also examined the new features for macros in Access 2007. Finally, it discussed why you might want to use VBA instead of a macro within Access. If you're going to use VBA, however, you'll need to understand the various components of VBA programming. Chapter 3 covers what's new in Access 2007. Chapter 4 explains how to work with the VBA Editor. Chapter 5 covers properties, methods, and events, detailing their interactions. If you're an experienced VBA programmer, you can skip Chapter 5. However, if you're a self-taught programmer (and there are many) or just want a refresher course on the basics, take a look at it.

New Features in Access 2007

Some of the key new features in Access 2007 will likely have a big impact on the way that developers think about VBA, macros, and even their approach to database design. With changes of this magnitude, it will take a while to adapt or even to figure out what projects to upgrade and when. The main thing right now is for you to be aware of the opportunities and how you can both enhance your projects and significantly reduce development time.

If you look at the big picture, it appears that the new features in 2007 are designed to benefit just about anybody who has contact with Access. The count of new features ranges from about 50 to more than 100, depending on who is counting and the way that things are grouped and sorted. With so many changes, it would be nearly impossible for a developer to find them all on his own. This chapter describes the highlights of the key new features or feature sets so that you'll know what to look for and can then investigate changes that are relevant to your projects and your clients. It starts with a summary of benefits to the end user, the power user, IT departments, and the developer. Then, it introduces the main improvements grouped into the following areas:

- ❑ Access's new look
- ❑ Development environment
- ❑ Forms
- ❑ Reports
- ❑ Embedded macros
- ❑ Access data engine (ACE)
- ❑ Integration with SharePoint
- ❑ External data sources
- ❑ Security
- ❑ Easy upgrading
- ❑ Access Developer Extensions (ADEs)

There are almost 1,000 commands in Access, but the new user interface is smart about displaying relevant commands in a manner that makes it easy for you to find and select the correct one.

Who Benefits

Access 2007 offers significant benefits to four major user types: the end user, the power user, the IT department, and the developer. When looking at the benefits of upgrading, it's important to focus on what is relevant to the particular audience.

The End User

The new look and feel of Access has an instant appeal to end users, especially if they are familiar with Excel or other Office programs. New users can hit the ground running by selecting from a growing list of templates that provide ready-to-use, customizable solutions. And the combination of the new navigation pane and the Ribbon make it easy to find and use the tools that are germane to the current task. The user interface is context sensitive, displays relevant commands and options, and requires few drop-down menus. It's a dramatic change, so expect to need some time to get used to it. Once you become adept with the new UI, the payoffs make it worth the effort.

In Access 2007, both forms and reports offer WYSIWYG design changes. Split forms enable users to scroll thorough lists in Datasheet view and simultaneously see the details of a selected record in a form. The new column summary allows users to quickly show calculated fields and includes such options as the sum or the minimum or maximum value—no VBA required. And finally, Access has built-in filter, find, and sort capabilities comparable to those found in Excel. With Office 2007, the filtering options change according to the field type, so dates can be filtered for factors such as Yesterday, Last Week, and Next Month.

Report Layout view is probably the biggest change. With a new interface, users see exactly how the report will print as they add and move the fields. Report Browse enables users to click controls and drill into the data—yes, that means that reports are interactive (and are covered in detail in Chapter 11).

Then there's the capability to link to SharePoint sites with just one click. It won't be long before a novice begins to collect data from e-mail and a myriad of other tasks that used to require custom interfaces. End users will initiate processes that previously required assistance from developers.

The Power User

Out-of-the-box features and some of the new field types in the Access data engine (ACE) offer further opportunities for power users. The new complex data type acts like multi-value select boxes and actually creates tables to manage the underlying many-to-many relationship. Users can add preformatted fields to tables as easily as dragging them from a table or field template. Tracking reference material is easier because the attachment field type automatically compresses the file and stores it in the database. Need to track expertise and experience so that you can pick the team for your next project? Your data can store project summaries, notes, schedules, and even photos. Suddenly, creating an impressive proposal package just got a whole lot easier and faster.

A common characteristic of power users is the need to compile and share information from multiple sources. Access 2007 provides many enhancements to support those needs. Access is now smarter about field type recognition when it creates fields for data that is pasted into a table. And, you can finally specify field types and save the import and export specifications for Excel files. Because import and export processes are often done on a regular basis, wouldn't it be convenient to have a reminder? Consider it done—just click the button to schedule the import or export as an Outlook task. Using HTML or InfoPath forms, Outlook can collect and store data directly into Access tables. And you can easily share contact information between Access and Outlook.

For bigger projects and greater reach, there's SQL Server and Windows SharePoint Services (WSS). Because power users are adept at creating their own queries, they may appreciate that by using linked tables to connect to SQL Server they can have the best of both worlds—all the new features provided in the ACCDB file format harnessing the power of SQL Server. Access project files (ADPs) are still an option, but they do not implement many of Access's new features. Data Access Pages (DAPs) are one of the few deprecated features. They can be viewed only through Internet Explorer. (A brief explanation of these and other deprecated features is provided at the end of this chapter.) And now, SharePoint offers even more options for expanding data and file management. Many power users are finding that SharePoint is an extension of their workspace. It facilitates working offline, synchronizing files, collaboration, file backups, and even working with mobile devices. (Chapter 17 discusses Windows SharePoint Services.)

A greater reach and better integration with external data sources means more data to crunch, organize, and report. Access 2007 offers a host of wizards and dialog boxes to help with grouping, sorting, and adding calculations to just about anything that can be displayed in datasheet view. It's easy to insert a calculation row, and you can study and modify the queries and properties created by the wizards. In addition to creating an object, wizards are great tools for learning how to create complex queries, such as queries that include calculations and criteria and that can accept multiple parameters at runtime. The wizards can even create and then expose advanced techniques such as outer joins and correlated subqueries.

Access also provides the capability to create embedded macros for routine tasks. People who like to work with several forms at one time might appreciate tabbed document viewing, which makes it easy to keep track of and switch to any open object. Of course, the flip side is that tabbed documents aren't conducive to side-by-side comparison. Report Browse enables easily customizable reports, and alternating row colors and grid lines add style and make reports easier to read. Along with Report Browse, there is also the capability to drill into data and to create PivotTable views and charts. It is easier to share reports with non-Access users because exporting to PDF is fully supported by a free, easy-to-install download from Microsoft's website. You can also choose to put your report right into a PowerPoint presentation.

The IT Department

Historically, some IT departments have demonstrated resistance to Access based on frustrations with version control, securing data, and managing permissions for file and data updates. The new integration with Windows SharePoint Services (SharePoint) provides solutions for most of those issues. You can download SharePoint from Microsoft or use services available through Office Live that enable users to create websites that can take advantage of these features.

SharePoint can be a valuable collaboration tool when used to track changes to the application or file and to the data. Using SharePoint for version control, IT needs to manage only one location to ensure that people are using the correct front-end file. Data changes are tracked, along with user information. People can download data, work offline, and then synchronize the data when they log back in. IT can use SharePoint to control who may access or edit files, and to implement policies for data protection, backups, and recovery. The SharePoint recycle bin also enables you to recover deleted records.

So far, it looks like SharePoint offers enhanced features that are alternatives to replication, user-level security, version control, and data backups. Chapter 17 covers SharePoint in detail. For now, suffice it to say that IT has reason to see Access in a more favorable light.

The Developer

The capability to rapidly provide better solutions has to be one of the strongest motivations for any developer. With the new features of Access 2007, developers can turn their focus to understanding business rules and providing solutions that enable managers to view and share information in ways that help them make better decisions faster. Access 2007 provides tools that allow faster development, better integration, easier deployment, and better security. But what does that really mean?

In Access 2007, many tasks that previously required add-ins or custom code are just a click away. The navigation pane not only displays the database objects, but it allows related objects to be grouped together. The Ribbon and Record selector and Field List pane are context sensitive and display relevant options. This means that, based on the control that you are working on, you can instantly add features such as the data picker and rich text formatting, have the ability to save a report in PDF format, add groups and totals to data sheets, and even manage many-to-many relationships. If you already have roll-your-own versions of toolbars and search tools, you might wonder why you'd use the built-in features. Think about consistency, compatibility, and expediency. Using built-in functionality makes it easier to collaborate, eliminates the hassles of maintaining additional references and libraries, and avoids security issues related to executable code. Templates are another time-saver. In addition to customizable solutions, there are table and field templates. And, as you'll read in Chapter 21, developers can use ADE—Access Developer Extensions—to create their own templates.

New features such as the Ribbon, the image and text on controls, and the ability to optimize form displays based on screen resolution also afford more professional and polished presentation. And in addition to better management of hyperlinks, you can now save attachments—multiple attachments and attachment types per record—in the database. Access efficiently manages the compression and reduces database bloat.

Working with external data just got a whole lot easier. Automatic field type recognition is just the tip of the iceberg. Because a lot of data comes from Excel, there's the capability to specify field types and then save the import or export specifications. If it is a routine task, it can even be scheduled in Outlook. And speaking of Outlook, contact information can now be updated and sent to and from Outlook. And you have better options for working with SQL Server. Using linked tables with the ACCDB file format, you can connect directly to SQL Server data and leverage the powerful new features of Access 2007 for queries, forms, and reports. Access 2007 also works with InfoPath and XML.

There are also changes to various aspects of security, particularly with the new ACCDB file format. This format does not support user-level security, but it does provide enhanced data security at the file level through data encryption. As explained in the IT section, many deployment and security issues, such as user permissions, can be handled through integration with a SharePoint server. You can also create your own permission control system. Of course, in Access 2007, user- and group-level security is still supported in MDB format databases using the workgroup administrator and MDW file. And then there are macros. These warrant being included in security discussions because embedded macros can run in disabled mode, which means that the database can have significant functionality without being signed or explicitly trusted.

Macros and disabled mode bring us to the new concept of the Trust Center. The Trust Center is the Office 2007 interface for managing security and privacy settings. It allows users to establish the settings for the current application as well as for all Office applications. In Access, users can adjust macro security settings, trusted locations, and trusted publishers. And proper management of the trust center settings (see Chapter 22) can reduce some security nuisances associated with deployment. Macros will become more of a developer tool now that they have error handling and debugging, and support the use of variables.

Some developers have expressed disappointment, believing that the new features in Access 2007 benefit end users more than developers. But the following list of new tools and features should reassure developers:

- ❑ To work with macros, there are three new temporary variables: `SetTempVar`, `RemoveTempVar`, and `RemoveAllTempVars`.

- ❑ To support the new multi-value fields, DAO has three new objects: `ComplexType`, `Field2`, and `RecordSet2`.

- ❑ The Code Project has new properties of `IsTrusted` and `ImportExportSpecification`, and it no longer has the property `AddDataAccessPages`.

- ❑ DoCmd has 10 new methods, including `DoCmd.ExportNavigationPane` and `DoCmd.ClearMacroError`.

- ❑ Controls have 20 new properties, many of which are associated with the grid lines and anchoring, such as `BottomPadding`, `GridlineColor`, and `HorizontalAnchor`.

- ❑ Forms have 14 new properties, including `DatasheetAlternateBackColor`, `DisplayOnSharePointSite`, `NavigationCaption`, and `OrderByOnLoad`.

- ❑ Subforms have 18 new properties, including `FilterOnEmptyMaster` and `LayoutId`, plus several related to anchoring and gridlines.

- ❑ Reports have 32 new properties, including `OnApplyFilter`, `FilterOnLoad`, and `FitToPage` as well as most of the new form properties. Reports also have one new method and 18 new events, including the events from forms, such as `Click`, `GotFocus`, and `Timer`.

- ❑ Report sections have three new properties to support alternating row colors and auto resizing. They also have `Paint`, a new event that fires every time a specified section is redrawn. (You'll see more about `Paint` in Chapter 11.)

- ❑ There are 153 new constants, including `acFormatPDF`, `acFormatXLSX`, and `acFormatXPS`. A few constants such as `acFormatASP` and `acFormatDAP` are no longer supported.

And finally, there is one feature that will go at the top of developers' lists—the mouse scroll wheel works in VBA!

New Look

Access's new user interface is fast, functional, and intuitive. It puts power at your fingertips by displaying commands and options when and where you need them, yet at the same time, leaves you in control with the capability to resize, customize, and hide at will.

Most of the new features fall into more specific categories discussed later in this chapter and book. But there are a few crosscutting features that really help define the new look and feel of Access. Getting Started, the Ribbon, and tabbed windows help set the foundation for the other new features. So let's explore them.

Getting Started

Upon opening Access, users are greeted by an intuitive graphical interface that displays links to a new database, recent files, and the template groups. Clicking on a template group—personal, business, or educational—displays related templates. When a template is chosen, the pane on the right prompts and guides the user through downloading the file or creating the database and linking it to a SharePoint site. There'll be more about SharePoint shortly. For now, suffice it to say that the program walks the user through creating the file and the links, and it prompts you to create a backup copy of the database on the SharePoint site.

If a new database is selected, the user is prompted to save the file. As soon as the file is saved, the database opens to a new table ready to accept data, and the user can immediately start typing input. The Ribbon shows appropriate options, and if needed, it only takes two clicks for the user to add a preformatted field. Clicking New Fields on the Ribbon opens the Field Templates pane. Clicking (or double-clicking) on a field name adds the field to the table. Figure 3-1 shows the Ribbon with the Fields Templates record source.

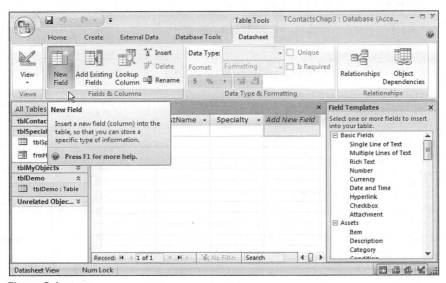

Figure 3-1

The Ribbon

If you're like a lot of developers, the Ribbon takes a little getting used to. It provides the pivotal functionality in Access's new "results-oriented, context-sensitive" interface. Access has nearly 1,000 commands, so it is a benefit that the Ribbon and new UI display only those that are relevant to the task at hand. And, when you want more screen space, the Ribbon can quickly be minimized. If you like custom toolbars and you don't want to give up control of the user environment, you can relax because the Ribbon is customizable and exportable (Chapter 12 covers Ribbon customization). That means that you can create custom ribbons to ship with your solutions. You can even create modal ribbons and toolbars for each form or report—and you can export and take your personalized ribbon to use when working on other applications. `LoadCustomUI` loads the XML markup that represents a customized Ribbon.

If you do nothing else with the Ribbon, take some time to investigate all the resources on the Database Tools tab, shown in Figure 3-2. Open Northwind 2007 and see how easy it is to document and analyze a complex solution, to work with SQL Server, and to protect data using encryption. Being context sensitive, the Ribbon conveniently groups and organizes new tools with familiar favorites.

Figure 3-2

That being said, if you're absolutely stuck on using your custom tool bars, you can avoid displaying the Ribbon altogether. You will need to set the startup options to use a custom main menu bar and to hide built-in toolbars. However, if you include custom menu bars and tool bars without disabling built-in toolbars, the Ribbon will still be displayed and your custom menu bars will be listed under the Add-In tab on the Ribbon.

Tabbed Document

Tabbed controls have proven effective for managing and moving between multiple screens on a form. Access takes tabbed controls that one step farther and displays all open objects in tabbed windows. You can see everything that is open, and just click the tab that you want in full view. No resizing, moving, or minimizing is needed to find another object.

The tabbed windows keep objects in viewable areas, offer users the convenience of knowing what is open, and make it easy for the user to move among the open objects. But, what about those who want to see multiple forms or reports at the same time? Thankfully, it is easy to return to your comfort zone through the Access Options dialog box. Open the Access Options dialog box and choose Current Database ⇨ Document Window Options ⇨ Overlapping Windows. Voilà, you can now view and position multiple objects.

Development Environment

Access 2007 provides a new interface for much of the development experience. Some things may take some getting used to, but that's typical with most changes. Of course, there are things that will have instant appeal, such as being able to scroll through code. (That's right—no add-ins required; the mouse wheel now scrolls through the code window in the VBA editor.) This section explores some of the other key changes.

Navigation Pane

The Navigation pane (commonly referred to as the NavPane) combines the best of the database window and the Object Dependencies feature. The resizable pane makes all of the objects conveniently available yet easy to hide. Think about one of your projects with more than a hundred objects. Say that you're working on a form that can open two reports and has a subform. How nice would it be if Access listed all of the related objects together? You could see, select, test, and update the right queries, reports, and forms. Well, that's the type of functionality that the NavPane provides.

By default, the Navigation pane displays the tables with their related objects, such as the queries and forms that are based on the table. But it takes only two clicks to change the grouping to be by object type (like the database window), by creation date, or by a variety of other standard listings. Of course, developers have the opportunity to control not only their own environment but also what users can see. So, yes, the Navigation pane can be manipulated programmatically to create custom groups. It is even portable, so customized panes can be imported and exported using DoCmd.ImportNavigationPane or Docmd.ExportNavigationPane. You can save the XML file to any folder so it can be easily shared with other databases—as long as they support using a Navigation pane, meaning that they are Access 2007 files. There are also commands to limit changes to the Navigation pane, such as using NavigateTo to control which objects the users can see, and LockNavigationPane to prevent users from deleting database objects.

There is similar functionality and ease of use in the Data Source task pane—*sans* Import/Export features.

Data Source Task Pane

The Data Source task pane is a fast, easy way to manage record sources. It's better than the field list because the task pane shows all of the source fields, and you have the option of viewing source, related, and other tables. That means the pane displays the tables and queries so that you can easily select a field.

If you have a form and you want a combo box for a look-up field, for example, use the source, related, and other tables to select a field and drag it onto the form. Voilà, a combo box is created. Similarly, you can drag a field from one table onto another table to instantly create a look-up field, and the appropriate joins are automatically created.

Table and Field Templates

Development is about creating better solutions. Using built-in features and functionality not only reduces development time, but it lessens problems down the road and allows developers to focus on more complex issues.

When you are building an application that includes a contacts table (that would be just about every application), you can now select one or more tables from the list of template tables and build from there. The five standard table templates are Contacts, Tasks, Issues, Events, and Assets. Once added, the tables can be customized by dragging fields from the Field Template task pane or by creating additional fields of your own. It's also that simple to add fields to tables that were designed from scratch. Chapter 21 explains how to create and share custom templates. Regrettably, even if you create your own table templates, you cannot add them to the ribbon.

Being able to add or delete fields in Datasheet view means that you can add a field and begin using it without switching views. This is essentially what-you-see-is-what-you-get (WYSIWYG) for tables. With that in mind, you can now use Datasheet view to add fields from existing tables or templates. It just takes a few easy steps. With a table in Datasheet view, click the Datasheet tab. The controls for Fields & Columns appear toward the left. Click the New Field command and the Field Templates display in a new pane on the right. There are nine basic fields plus six tables of field templates. That makes it easy to add fields based on their type, such as rich text or attachment, or based on what they will contain, such as a priority status or date.

Using a template does not mean that you are stuck with its properties. Switch to Design view and make all the adjustments you want. From Design view, you can also copy and paste fields between existing tables and even to a table in a different database.

Field Insertion and Automatic Data Type Detection

Just start typing data in a new column and Access will create the field and automatically determine the data type. That isn't just for creating new tables; it also works for adding a column to the Datasheet view of an existing table.

As in the past, you can paste Excel tables into a new datasheet.

Interactive Form and Report Designing

In the WYSIWYG Design views for both forms and reports, you can actually position and adjust controls with the data displayed—no more switching between design and print preview. It gets even better with form auto resizing to help optimize screen real estate and using Report Layout view with tabbed and columnar options. These features are described further in the forms and reports sections later in this chapter.

Field (Column) History

Many of you have created a variety of techniques to track the changes to data stored in a field. Now, Access provides a built-in solution: Column History. Column History is a new property on the Application object that uses an `AppendOnly` field property—which must be set to `True`—on memo fields to add new data with a date stamp. The data is actually stored as multiple entries in a separate table, so it can be filtered and sorted. The options for retrieving the Column History are limited, but it is a start. And, it's probably good to reiterate that this property is available only on memo fields. However, this new structure is supported in SharePoint V3, so Access can track changes to text fields that are stored in a SharePoint list.

SharePoint takes tracking a few steps further with its Revision History feature, which is discussed briefly a little later in this chapter and covered in-depth in Chapter 17.

Rich Text Fields

Access 2007 supports rich text fields better and with more flexibility than was previously available with add-ins. In addition to displaying multiple formats in one text box, the field also supports page breaks, line feeds, and carriage returns—`Chr(12)`, `Chr(10)`, and `Chr(13)`—in both forms and reports. Figure 3-3 illustrates the versatility of the rich text field.

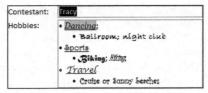

Figure 3-3

Search from the Record Selector

The record selector is beefed up. In addition to navigation controls, the record selector now indicates whether the data is filtered, and it allows quick searches through the open object. So, you can type a word into the record selector search box and the cursor will jump to the next instance. For example, with a contacts form open, type a first name into the search box. The first record containing that name opens. Change the name, and the record changes—no need to add a combo box to your form. Figure 3-4 shows the new record selector used to search for the contestant named Sandra.

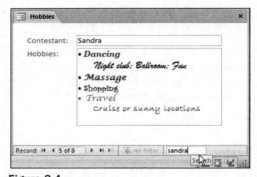

Figure 3-4

This functionality is available in tables, queries and forms. Search is also available programmatically using either `DoCmd` or the `SearchForRecord` method.

Save Database As

Working with multiple versions of Access or Access file types has never been easier. With one or two commands, files can be converted to other file formats (2000, 2002–2003, and 2007) and file types, such as the MDE, ACCDE, and ACCDR.

Click the Office button, and then hover over Save As. You'll see how easy it is to either save the current object or to convert the database to a different format. Because Access creates a copy of the database before converting to a different format, it is that easy to work with both the ACCDB and MDB files. The file types to save as will change based on the type and version of the current database.

Managed Code and Access Add-ins

Changes have been made to the Access 2007 Primary Interop Assembly (PIA) that enable you to listen for events in managed code and respond to them. You also have the option of enhancing your Access applications with add-ins and smart panes based on managed Microsoft .NET code. This could be as little as adding a custom button to the Ribbon to open a custom browse tool that makes it easier for users to store files on the correct network server.

The PIAs for Access, DAO, and Office enable managed code running in these add-ins and smart panes to manipulate Access user interface objects and Access data. A great way to find additional information about using managed code within Access or about using Visual Studio to create add-ins, is to search the Microsoft Developer Network (MSDN), http://msdn.microsoft.com.

Forms

First impressions are lasting, and developers rely on forms to create an instant bond between their solutions and the user. The forms need to be intuitive, readable, and easy to navigate. No matter how good the data structure is, if the user doesn't understand how a form is intended to work, the solution won't fly.

Some of the new features for forms include the split form, alternating row color, auto resizing, context sensitive filtering, and the date picker (calendar control), bound image controls, edit list items, and subform control enhancement. And, since forms are all about looks, you'll really appreciate the new styles or AutoFormats. Using the wizards, you'll have more than twenty styles to choose from for both forms and reports. Chapter 10 provides detailed instructions for working with forms, so we'll only touch on the highlights here.

Split Forms

The split form begs for an imagination that can test its potential. Simplistically, a split form is half Datasheet view and half Form view, as shown in Figure 3-5. You can scroll or search through the datasheet, click on a record, and the Detail view populates. This is remarkably fast and does not require code.

Figure 3-5

The two areas do not have to display the same fields. And you can lock the datasheet to prevent edits. You can also apply some of the nifty new tools for filtering, sorting, and calculating totals. The position of the forms can be set programmatically. For example, you might have 95 percent Datasheet view for scrolling through records and then use a command button to switch to a 50/50 split. And, the placement of the split can be specified with precision of a twip.

A twip is ¼,₄₄₀ of an inch, a mere ⅟₅₆₇ of a centimeter or better known (HA) as ½₀th of a point.

Alternating Row Color

Alternating row color is another coding challenge turned property. And yes, it is now that easy to display alternating row colors. You can set the controls for the datasheet as well as for repeating sections. In a table, the control is conveniently located with the font options. Click the control, and select from the array of color swatches displayed in the standard color pallet or choose More Colors and select whatever you want from the gradient scale. Figure 3-6 shows the color pallet with alternating rows in a table.

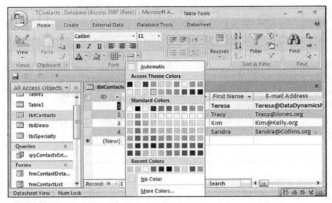

Figure 3-6

This feature is also available for tables, forms, and reports.

Grouped Control

With auto resizing to take advantage of larger screens, controls can now be grouped and anchored. As the form expands, the group of controls moves with its anchor point. This can take a bit of getting used to. It's discussed further in Chapter 10.

If you make design changes to a form that has the AutoResize property set to NO *and the AutoCenter property set to* YES, *switch to Form view before saving the form. Otherwise, the right and bottom edges might be trimmed the next time the form opens.*

New Filtering and Sorting

The new filtering options are context sensitive and list the options in simple English. Figure 3-7 shows an example of filtering a text field by selecting from criteria Begins With, Does Not Contain, and similar easy to understand expressions.

Figure 3-7

Dates have an impressive list of filter options, including today, tomorrow, next quarter, past, future and all dates in a period. And users can still apply a filter to filtered records so they can keep narrowing the list of prospects until they find what they need.

Access added sorting to the filter control to create a powerful tool—no code required, no troubleshooting, and no need for special forms. Empower your users to work with out-of-the-box features and devote more time to complex challenges.

Column Summaries

Forms and reports both take advantage of enhancements to the datasheet, including calculating totals on-the-fly. The totals row is used for calculations such as counts, average, sums, and so on. Basically, the aggregate functions that previously required code are now available when viewing a datasheet—no code required.

Truncated Number Displays

Speaking of totals, how many times have you looked at a form or report and not realized that some of the digits were missing? It could be rather disconcerting, because Access did not provide an indication that the field was too narrow to display all of the digits. With Access 2007, you can retain that default behavior or set a new Access Option to Check for `Truncated Number Fields`. If that is selected, Access will fill the text box with pound signs rather than display a truncated number. This applies to text boxes on both forms and reports.

Date Picker

The calendar control is built into all date fields. You're familiar with it: arrow right or left to scroll through the months, click a day and it populates the field, click "today" and today's date is entered. Of course, you may not want the Date Picker to always be offered. Using the `ShowDatePicker` property, which is on all textbox controls, you can select one of two values. For Dates will display the calendar control when the text box is bound to a DateTime field and Never will totally suppress the calendar control. Again, total convenience and reliability. No add-in, no references—just add the field and set the date.

Bound Image Controls

The bound image control is part of what gives Access 2007 its modern look and feel. Now you can use a transparent background to create controls that combine custom images with text. It just takes a minute to add personality and pizzazz to your solutions by creating a custom control. Keep in mind that graphics may be affected by both hardware and system settings. Figure 3-8 shows four different looks, including the option to use switch to the hyperlink hand and the ability to change the background color with a mouse over event. Bound image controls are also great from building radio buttons that combine icons and relevant text, such as for `First` and `Last`.

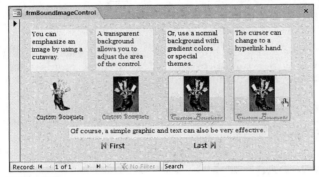

Figure 3-8

The first two controls in the figure appear borderless and have a transparent background. Using a BMP file, you can make the picture background the same color as the form, so that it appears like a cutout, like the first control. Then make the border invisible and resize the control to make the clickable area as large as you want. The second control uses the photo's original background, so users may perceive that the control area is limited to the photo. The third control uses the theme background that changes colors as the cursor moves over the control area, as illustrated by the fourth control.

It's easy to see how nicely these controls can spiff up an application. The effects are great for hyperlinks, too. Bound image controls are also good from building radio buttons that combine icons and relevant text.

Edit List Items

Users can now edit a value list or a combo box on-the-fly. How's that for adding flexibility and meeting a common need? Just about every application has a combo box, and now you have an easy way to allow users to update them with—you got it—no code required.

To allow users to edit or add new items to a value list, set property `Allow Value List Edits` to `Yes`. Users will see an Edit button when they are selecting an item from the list. Then, if they don't see what they want, they click the button and a dialog box prompts them through adding the new value. The list is updated and work proceeds. Chapter 10 has more information about combo boxes and value lists.

SubForm

Access provides great wizards for creating forms, including those with one or more subforms. Between the help files and wizard, it's pretty straightforward to create the relationships, queries, and forms with any combination of one-to-many-to-many relationships. Say a customer has several orders (form-sub-form) and each order can have multiple delivery dates (form-subform with nested subform)—yep, the form wizard can even work with that.

Everything seems peachy keen, right up until the subform's master field is null—meaning that the main form does not have a value in the field that is used in the relationship with the subform. Now, the data tab of the subform Property Sheet includes Filter On Empty Master, which allows the values of Yes or No to stipulate if all or no records are displayed if the subform's master field is null. This can also be set in code using the new `FilterOnEmptyMaster` property.

Remember that these are just the highlights of the new features related to forms. There aren't enough pages to show all the great new things that we can do with forms.

Reports

For the first time, users not only get to view reports, but they can also interact with reports. Now, reports can actually contain controls to open forms, attachments, and other reports. This means that in report browse mode, users can drill into data and search for records from reports as well as from forms. Reports also benefit from most of the new form features, such as alternating row color, grid lines, bound image controls, rich text formatting, and better filtering and sorting.

Layout view saves development time because you no longer have to switch between Design and Report views to see what the final report will look like. You'll still want to use Design view to change the properties of forms and controls, but most of the presentation can be tweaked in Layout view.

Properties, Methods, and Events

There are really too many new properties, methods, and events to cover here, but the key ones are listed here. The descriptions are the same as those for form properties, methods, and events. Chapter 11 provides the details for employing these.

❑ **Properties:** `Filter On Load`, `Fit To Page`, and nearly all the events associated with forms.

❑ **Methods:** `Requery` to update the data. Because it's possible to open a form and update the data underlying the report, it is critical to also provide an easy mechanism to requery, not just refresh the data.

❑ **Events:** `Paint`, `Retreat`, `GotFocus`, `Timer`, `Load`, and `Unload` (after it closes but before it is removed from the screen). The `Paint` event is rather special because it fires every time the specified section of the report is redrawn. The `Retreat` event is used to undo and reset properties when an item has to be moved to the next page. An example is a section with `KeepTogether` set to yes that won't all fit on a page, so the entire section moves to the next page. The alternating line colors, continuous line numbering, and other features would be affected.

❑ **Report** `Section` **properties:** `AlternateBackColor` and `AutoHeight` (adjusts section's height automatically when controls are resized).

Layout View

In Layout view you can design reports while you are viewing your actual data. Many of the tasks of creating a report, such as formatting, sorting and grouping, and adding totals can be accomplished in Layout view while your data is onscreen, so you no longer need to switch between Design view and Print Preview.

Because you're working with actual data in Layout view, there's no need to guess if the controls are properly sized and spaced. Selecting data for the report is also easier, with related tables becoming available for selection automatically after an initial table is chosen.

Much like Form design, Layout view supports working with blocks of controls. You have to switch to Design view to change the grouping or to make other structural changes, but you can change just about any of the format controls in Layout view. And amazingly, that includes adding totals . . . you got it . . . while displaying the real data. We'll mention that again momentarily and include a shot of the new sorting bar. One last comment about Layout view—before deploying your applications, you can set the form's property to not allow Layout view so that users cannot inadvertently open it and make changes.

Report Browse

Now users can browse through reports with the convenience and ease previously associated with forms. The new, robust features for searching, finding and filtering on forms are also available on reports. You can dress up your reports, add the fancy new image controls, and still have total control over the print process.

Maybe you're wondering, why not just build an application of reports? That wouldn't work because you still need forms to edit the data. Reports are powerful tools for finding, analyzing, and disseminating information, but they do not allow data to be edited. As mentioned, the report can have a control to open a form to edit the data; then the report can be updated by using the `requery` method. However, attachments to reports cannot be edited unless they are saved to a new location or name.

Group and Total

The new Group, Sort, and Total pane is an enhanced merger of the Report Wizard and the old Grouping dialog box. It enables you to quickly add totals, counts, and averages to multiple groups as the wizard builds the report.

Adding or changing groups and totals after the fact is also a piece of cake using the Group, Sort, and Total pane. From Report Layout, click the formatting tab and select Group & Sort in the Grouping & Totals controls. A graphical interface (see Figure 3-9) steps you through creating groups, sorting, and adding totals.

Figure 3-9

Because you're working with real data, you can see the effects of your selections and ensure that you're getting the anticipated results. And don't forget that although it is the default location, totals are not stuck in the group footers—they can be moved.

As with other 2007 controls, the grouping options are context sensitive and will coincide with the data type.

Grid Line Controls and Alternating Row Color

Lines and shading not only make a report look better, but they make it easier to read. In addition to interactive status, Access gives reports cool design features. Can you imagine being able to add vertical lines to a report just by clicking a control? Now you can.

You also get the complete set of graphical options to format the lines. Just go to Design view, pick a report section, and customize the grid lines. While you're at it, check out the Conditional Formatting dialog box. It couldn't be made any easier.

PivotTable Views and Charts

Reports are all about communicating information and a chart is about the most concise way there is to convey statistics. You've probably been working with Pivot Tables and charts for a while, but Access 2007 makes them better looking and also makes them easier to create and customize. Chapter 11 will take you through the process.

PDF and XPS Support

Developers invest a lot of time in creating picture-perfect reports and generally want to preserve the layout regardless of how the reports are distributed. Access now provides a way to export reports, complete in their formatted splendor.

With Access 2007, Microsoft offers a free download that enables users to save a report in a Portable Document Format (PDF) or an XML Paper Specification (XPS) format for printing, posting, and e-mail distribution. Anyone who can open a PDF or XPS file can view and print formatted reports. There are several free options for viewing PDF files, including Adobe Acrobat Reader, which is available from

Adobe's website. As for XPS files, for now you'll need Windows Vista, but let's hope that a free viewer will become available. So, say good-bye to Save to Word and Save as Snapshot because who wants plain old reports when you no longer need an add-in to send PDF files?

Embedded Macros

Developers used to campaign loudly against macros because one little error could shut down an entire application. Now, macros can be embedded in events for forms, reports, and controls and are often an effective replacement for some VBA code. An embedded macro becomes part of the parent object and is not visible in the Navigation pane. Embedded macros can run in disabled mode, and they include error handling and debugging, can be combined into groups, and can use temporary variables. Okay, before anyone has a heart attack about perceived risks, I'll add the caveat that unsafe macro actions are blocked in disabled mode, which means that they would not allow embedded macros to run such tasks as File system interactions. But the big picture is that not only can macros save time, but they can avoid a lot of hassles associated with deployment and trusting files.

When you combine embedded macros with the new features in 2007, you can create robust solutions with little or no VBA code. Before you scoff at the potential functionality, realize that Access 2007 templates deliver all their features, program integration, and a polished interface using macros instead of VBA code. Developers need not panic—there's still plenty of need for VBA code. For one thing, somebody needs to create all of the new macros, and who knows the business rules and needs better than a developer? When you think about it, the real purpose of a developer is to understand the business model and to build smart solutions with whatever combination of VBA, macros, add-ins, and integration seems appropriate.

How about allowing a user to add a new item to a combo box list, refresh the list, and then select the new item? Of course, it must be done smoothly, without unnecessary messages or warning. If you use a value list, Access can handle the process with just a couple of questions, as shown in Figure 3-10. Because most combo boxes use a query or table instead of a value list, you've probably been using VBA to manage the process. Now, macros can do all of that without using VBA code. Chapter 10 discusses several ways of working with combo boxes.

The following is a recap of some of the key features and benefits of macros. Chapter 2 included a more detailed discussion.

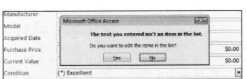
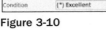

Figure 3-10

Disabled Mode

Disabled mode essentially means that a database will open but the VBA code and unsafe macro actions will not run. The default setting for Access 2007 is to open a database in disabled mode. Because embedded macros run in Disabled mode, the more routine commands that are included in macros, the more functionality an application has when it's opened in a non-trusted location. VBA code is disabled by default, so safe macros (those that consist only of safe macro actions) allow solutions to be deployed without worrying about signatures, certificates, and trusted locations. That means fewer hassles for e-mailing and downloading files. Of course, there will be a tradeoff in functionality. As mentioned before, unsafe macro actions are blocked in disabled mode, so disabled mode would block a macro from doing such things as running an action query, deleting an object, or interacting with the File system.

Macros can be embedded into any event handler, which means that they can be used on forms, reports, and controls. To use macros most effectively, they should be grouped and named, have error handling, go through debugging, and take advantage of temporary variables as appropriate. Chapter 2 provides examples and guidance for using macros.

Error Handling

Macro errors can be trapped, recorded, and researched. Again, the processes are similar to working with VBA code. Macros have an OnError action that can be used to suppress messages, respond to the condition, and maintain the flow of the application or to display a custom message box and allow user interaction. If the OnError action is not used to suppress error messages, the macro stops, and the user sees a standard error message.

Debugging

As with code, macros are most powerful when they accomplish several actions. That's great if everything is working, but if you are building or troubleshooting, it typically works best to break a process into steps. There is a comfortable familiarity to the SingleStep mode, which enables you to go through a macro group one action at a time.

Temporary Variables

TempVar Object and TempVars collections enable developers to manage and exchange data between macros and VBA procedures. There are several factors to remember when working with a TempVar. First, a TempVar is created by using the Add method or the SetTempVar macro action. Second, once created, a TempVar object remains in memory until Access is closed, so it is a good practice to delete it after it has served its purpose. Take a minute to think about this and you'll recognize a tremendous benefit. This means that the TempVar can store a global variable and it will not lose its value if there is an error.

Third, you can delete one TempVar with the Remove method or the RemoveTempVar macro action or you can delete all TempVars with the RemoveAll method or the RemoveAllTempVar macro action. Either approach deletes the specified objects from the TempVars collection. Fourth, the TempVars collection has a limit of 255 TempVars. And finally, a TempVar can be referred to by its ordinal number or by its Name as specified in the property setting.

You spent some time with macros in Chapter 2 and you'll work with them again in the chapters on forms and reports.

Access Data Engine

Access 2007 ships with a custom version called the Access data engine (also known as ACE). In addition to being totally compatible with the Microsoft Jet 2000 and 2002-2003 file formats, the Access data engine introduces the new ACCDB file format, which provides a richer environment and greater reach. "Rich" refers to powerful new features such as multi-value fields (MVF) and attachment field types. The term "reach" refers to more than being specifically designed to integrate with SharePoint. Although that is a huge part of it, reach also refers to better integration with Excel, SQL Server, Outlook, and a multitude of other programs. The Access data engine can use Open Database Connectivity (ODBC) or installable indexed sequential access method (ISAM) drivers to link tables to external data sources.

One of the key features of the ACCDB format is the capability to store multi-valued lookup fields (also referred to as complex data). Storing multi-valued fields requires the presence of a new system table, `MSysComplexColumns`, plus a series of built-in schema tables. The `MSysComplexColumns` table and the built-in schema tables are automatically created whenever a new ACCDB file is created.

Multi-Value Fields

Most database programs, including earlier versions of Access, allow you to store only a single value in each field. In Office Access 2007, however, you can now create a lookup field that enables you to store more than one value. In effect, it creates a many-to-many relationship within the field and hides the details of the implementation using system tables. Users can easily see and work with the data because the items are all displayed in the field, separated by commas.

The easiest and most effective way to create these fields is to use the Lookup Wizard to create a multi-value lookup column. In line with so many other design changes, the Lookup Wizard can be initiated from the table Datasheet view as well as from Design view. In Datasheet view, either select Lookup Column from the Fields & Columns group or drag a field from another table in the Field pane into the current table's field list. (You can edit the field properties in Design view.)

The wizard automatically creates the appropriate field property settings, table relationships, and indexes. You can still create a lookup column manually or modify one that is created by the wizard. Working with multi-value fields is much like working with combo boxes but with additional settings and properties.

When you think about all the work involved with properly structuring tables to manage many-to-many relationships, what goes on under the hood is pretty impressive. And it is nice to know that the data is exposed for your use. In DAO and ADO, the data is a collection and exposed through the `.Value` property. With an MVF field, the `.Value` property contains a recordset that can be enumerated. You can also test if a field is a MVF by seeing if the `IsComplex` property of a `Field` object is true. If the value is true, then the `.Value` property will contain a DAO or ADO recordset. The data is also exposed through the Query Designer using `.Value`, similar to regular combo box settings, or by working with the collection and using the ID. Although the data is exposed, the join field is a system table that is not exposed to developers, so you may still prefer to create your own look-up fields and manage many-to-many relationships using a separate table (often referred to as a linking or xfer table) for the join field.

In support of multi-value fields, DAO uses the `ComplexType` object, `Field2` object, and `Recordset2` object. (See Chapter 6 on DAO to learn more about using code to manipulate these new field types.) The `Field2` object contains several new properties and methods that support multi-value field types:

Property	AppendOnly	Use to create field history for memo fields. For all other datatypes the value is False.
	ComplexType	For multi-value fields.
	IsComplex	For multi-value fields. Returns true if the field is a multi-valued lookup field.
Method	LoadFromFile	For attachments.
	SaveToFile	For attachments.

A `Recordset2` object contains the same properties and methods as the `Recordset` object. It also contains a new property, `ParentRecordset`, that supports multi-value field types.

The Lookup Wizard can do a lot for you. Going back to the example of selecting a team for a project, let's say that in the past each project had one lead. With the growing complexity of development and shared workloads, some projects might now require co-leads. That would be a prime candidate for utilizing a multi-value field. Given that the database has an Employee table and a Project table, you merely drag the employee field from the employee table onto the project table and work with the wizard do the rest. It's critical that on the last page of the wizard, the checkbox "Allow multiple values" is checked. Keep in mind that that if you click Finish before the last page, you won't have the opportunity to check this box and request a multi-value field. When you add the new field type to a form, the list will have a check box beside each name and users can select as many people as they need. When you look at the employee record in the project table, it will display a delimited list of selected names. That's it; no struggling with linking tables and no complicated code for multi-select options.

Access uses multi-value fields for storing attachments within the database. And, you can see that multi-value fields are also excellent for creating your own solution for working with reference material. For example, a construction company might want to store photos of various stages of each project, and it likely has bios for key project personnel. When it's time to bid on a new project, the company could quickly create a proposal that illustrates experience and expertise by including personnel bios and project histories with photos. What a great segue to talking about the attachment field type.

Attachment Field Type

The attachment feature gives developers the opportunity to offer compact and portable solutions to a wide new market. No more trying to keep track of files and update hyperlinks when files are moved or deleted. Using the attachment field type automatically compresses the file and stores it in the database. Multiple files and file types—resumés as Word documents, some JPG photos, an Excel spreadsheet, or even a PowerPoint file—can be stored in a single field or record. Access actually creates system tables to normalize the data. You cannot view or work with these tables, and once the data type is set to attachment, it cannot be changed. This makes sense because it would essentially create orphaned system tables and records. Although you can't work with the system tables, you can programmatically work with the attachments. The `Import RunCommand` macro and the `acCmdImport` have been replaced with the `ImportAttach` command.

The Attachments dialog box makes it easy to add, edit, remove, and save attachments. The dialog box opens directly from an attachment field in a table or when using the attachment control on a form or report. Because a record can have multiple attachments, it is handy to be able so save multiple attachments at one time. It is one or all, but that is still better than being limited to one at a time. If the attachment's parent program is installed on the computer, the attachment can be opened and edited with that program. You can save the edited file back to the database or to a different folder. Because reports do not allow edits, an attachment opened from a report can only be saved to a different location.

You must be wondering about file types and sizes. Suffice it to say that you can attach just about any file created in the 2007 Microsoft Office System as well as log files, text files, zip files, and most image files. There are a few file formats that are blocked and therefore can't be saved as attachments. Because that list is likely change, it is best to check for updated information on Microsoft's MSDN website. Appendix L lists the file types for attachments when discussing naming conventions.

Access still has a maximum file size of 2-gigabytes, so there is plenty of room for photos and just about anything else you can think of. Each attachment can be a whopping 256 megabytes, so there is no need to sacrifice quality. And, as previously mentioned, Access conveniently compresses files as when it creates the attachments (that is unless the file is already compressed in its native format, such as JPEG files).

Unlike previous versions of Access that stored attachments as bitmap images that could be 10 times larger than the actual file, Access 2007 compresses files in their native format. So Access opens attachments and allows them to be edited in their parent program.

XML Tables, Schema, and Data

When combined with SQL Server, InfoPath, SharePoint, Outlook, and other Internet services, Access truly has a global reach. So obviously the need to work with XML (eXtensible Markup Language) has been growing exponentially to keep up.

If you're not familiar with XML, there are plenty of online tutorials that can help you get up to speed. Just search the Internet for XML.

The capability to import and export to XML comes in a variety of sizes and options. It can apply to the entire database or to a specific object. And you can export the structure, the data, or the entire form, complete with rich formatting. Basically, you can choose to export the data as an XML file, the schema of the data as an XSD file, or the presentation of the data as an XSL file, also known as a transformation file. Working with Outlook and HTML forms will make this a little clearer.

XSD is the XML Schema standard approved by the World Wide Web Consortium (W3C) for describing the type and structure of XML documents.

XML and E-mail

You can now use Outlook and InfoPath forms to collect data for surveys, routine reports, and countless other purposes. By using properly constructed forms, the process can be fully automated, eliminating the need for user intervention and thereby reducing the potential for errors. The success of the process is totally dependent on the XML and the XSL.

The XSL file can be generated during the export, and subsequently applied during an import. When you import XML data, the transformation file is automatically applied to the data as soon as the data is imported, before a new table is created or before any data is appended to an existing table, so the user sees only the formatted data.

Integration with Outlook and other programs is covered in Chapter 16.

XML Tables, Schema, and Data

You've had the option for a while now to export a table or form to XML, and you know that you can choose to import or export the data, the structure, or both. But the Access 2007 file format requires some pretty intense behind-the-scenes work to handle the new field types, such as attachments, multi-value fields, and data history.

Well, XML support has kicked it up a notch and can include the complete table schema for the entire database. That's right. 2007 will convert the entire database schema, including custom properties and even the scheme for complex data to fully support the import and export in XML format. Commands are conveniently in the import and export groups of the Ribbon's External Data tab. Of course, that goes hand in hand with being able to fully integrate with SharePoint Services.

Integration with SharePoint

In the past, the default setting was for Access MDB database files to be blocked by SharePoint, Outlook, and most anti-virus programs because unsafe code could be shipped and trigged to run from the database. That isn't the case for the Access 2007 ACCDB file format. Since the code can be either verified as safe or disabled, it is easier to integrate Access databases more fully with SharePoint Version 3 sites and Office Outlook 2007. That also means that it is easier for anti-virus programs to inspect Access database files and verify that they are safe; therefore ACCDB files can generally be e-mailed as is. Hey, it's worked for me so far; they don't even have to be zipped to get past the screening.

Access 2007 has a full host of features that take advantage of SharePoint Services. And now that the Ribbon puts commands at your fingertips, working with SharePoint is almost as easy as point-and-click. You can quickly link your Access application to a SharePoint data source, move data to SharePoint, or link to SharePoint when a file is created. A glance at the External Data tab on the Ribbon (see Figure 3-11) shows just how simple it is to work with SharePoint. Along with Import, Export, and Collect Data commands is an entire group of commands for SharePoint Lists.

Figure 3-11

By working with SharePoint, a file can be backed up, tracked, scheduled, saved, shared, protected, and controlled in just about every way imaginable. Chapter 17 is all about SharePoint, but the following sections point out some of the highlights. Even if your current projects don't lend themselves to globalization, it pays to be aware of the options and benefits.

Working with Data on SharePoint

Working data on a SharePoint server can mean several different things. The options run the gamut from having the entire application on SharePoint, including the front end and forms, to just relying on data backup and revision management features. With the caveat that SharePoint can protect the data and enforce permissions, the following sections focus on two of the most common configurations.

Move Data to SharePoint

Publishing the data file to SharePoint but keeping the application on a local workstation could be perceived as the best of both worlds. Access uses linked tables to connect the data stored on the SharePoint server, and you get to take advantage of Access's rapid development environment to create a flexible user interface. Having the data on the server facilitates collaboration and satisfies a host of security and IT concerns. It provides the reliability of SQL Server combined with the universal access of a website.

When data is published to SharePoint, users can still download lists and have the freedom to work offline. When they reconnect to SharePoint, they can synchronize the data. The process prompts for the resolution of conflicts because of the potential for records to be updated in multiple locations. This functionality is an alternative to replication that is easier to manage. The fact that replication is not supported by the ACCDB file format may be a strong incentive to start working with SharePoint.

Moving the data to SharePoint initiates the Move to SharePoint Site Wizard. The wizard manages moving all of the tables at the same time, and it creates SharePoint lists with the appropriate relationships. It also creates a new front-end file linked to the newly created SharePoint lists. The new front-end file stores the links to the lists on the SharePoint site, and can be distributed without the hassles of relinking tables.

The External Data tab includes a prompt to link to SharePoint lists, making it easy to create a linked table or to import the data from any SharePoint list. Additionally, Access and SharePoint share several templates, so opening the SharePoint lists instantiates the matching template in Access. You can also create Access views on SharePoint.

Access forms, reports, and datasheets can be listed in a SharePoint document library along with other documents. When a user chooses one of these objects, Access opens on the SharePoint site. The user not only gets the current data, but also the correct version of the form or report, and he does not have to run Access on his computer.

Start with a SharePoint List

While it's great to publish an Access data file, what about working with data already contained in SharePoint lists? As you would expect, there's a wizard to handle this, too. Just open the list in SharePoint and select Actions ⇨ Open In Microsoft Access. When you choose to link to the data on the SharePoint site, you can build queries, forms, and reports to work with the SharePoint list as well as with any other data source.

If you publish the database to a SharePoint library, the forms, reports, and other objects are listed on the View menu for others to use.

Publish the Database to SharePoint

Keeping a copy of the database in a SharePoint library is an excellent approach for collaboration. Reports can be published and shared using a documents library or they can be scheduled and automatically e-mailed.

In addition to providing version control on the data, it also offers and easy mechanism to track and control the versions of reports and views.

Additional SharePoint Features

Whether it's the data or the entire application, SharePoint offers some great tools to protect and recover data and to give people more options for staying connected and sharing information. They're introduced in the following sections (Chapter 17 provides in-depth coverage).

Work Offline and Synchronize Data

The capability to add, edit, and delete records and then synchronize the data when you next connect to the SharePoint site is such an important feature that it even has its own control in the SharePoint Lists section of the Ribbon's External Data tab. Right next to Work Offline is the control to synchronize the data the next time you connect.

The complete process not only allows users the freedom to work wherever and whenever they want, it also provides the logic and process for comparing records, identifying differences, and allowing users to make educated decisions about which version to keep. This is a powerful alternative to replication.

Issues Tracking

Access 2007 has an issues tracking template designed to track the progress and resolution of issues. Because the Access template uses the same schema as the SharePoint template, it is a snap to push the data to a SharePoint site. Having a centralized tracking file facilitates assigning responsibilities and tracking completion. Tasks can easily be created and added to an Outlook calendar.

Workflow

Creating a schedule and delivering on time can be a challenge for any project. The bigger the project, the more likely it is to have multiple interdependencies. Knowing the critical path elements and being able to adjust schedules and workloads accordingly can make the difference in the delivery and in the quality. SharePoint Workflow can automatically assign tasks to users and report on project status. Workflow reports can track the status of multiple lists or be expanded to cover multiple workflows or projects. The associated tasks can be viewed in Access 2007 as well as Outlook 2007.

E-mail and RSS Notifications

SharePoint provides a rich set of e-mail and RSS Notifications for changes to data in SharePoint lists. If you have an Access application with linked SharePoint lists, you can configure the SharePoint site to automatically send e-mail notifications whenever records are added, changed, or deleted. Likewise,

SharePoint can be configured to provide RSS subscriptions that are updated automatically whenever linked data is updated in your Access application.

Mobile Connectivity

Because SharePoint lists can be accessed through mobile phones, remote users can stay connected and up-to-date. If your application needs to support mobile devices, going through SharePoint may be the easiest way to create a custom solution.

Security and Permissions

You can use SharePoint to manage which users have access to your data. You can assign limited reading permissions or full editing rights to lists and to published databases. Like the workgroup administrator, you can assign permission levels to groups and then assign individuals to one or more groups. Plus, you can allow or deny access to specific users. The permissions are cumulative, which results in the most restrictive being enforced.

Revision History

SharePoint takes revision tracking to a whole new level for Access. New functionality enables you to track records and see who created, edited, and deleted records. You can also view when the information was modified and roll back data edits if necessary.

Recycle Bin

If the Access database is using SharePoint, data can be recovered from the Recycle Bin. You don't have to replace an entire file; the Recycle Bin allows you to view deleted records and selectively recover the ones that are still needed.

Whether it was your client's data or someone else's, we've all felt that sinking sensation when we realize that there is no way to recover records that were inadvertently deleted. Something as seemingly innocent as using delete instead of a filter to sort through records in a `select` query can result in the sudden elimination of a quarter of the database. That is a real scenario. Thankfully, SharePoint not only provides maximum flexibility to work but it also provides remarkable backup and recovery features. The capability to view and recover deleted records is a definite plus.

Office Live

Many Access developers are independent consultants or work for small companies and don't have the resources or need for a SharePoint server. Of course, there are more and more options and price points for purchasing a SharePoint space from a hosting company. But before investing elsewhere, it is worth checking out the services offered through Microsoft Office Live, a hosted SharePoint Service through which you can create and test applications and solutions. As with many Microsoft services, there are a range of plans—from free to full-featured versions.

Check it out to see what it is like to publish one of your solutions.

If you have a Windows Server 2003 license, the basic Windows SharePoint Services product is a free download from the Microsoft website.

External Data Sources

One of the things that makes Access such a powerful database and user interface is the capability to collect and work with data from multiple, disparate sources. Power users may be adept at crunching numbers in Excel, but they turn to Access for data collection, integration, and reporting. Large organizations may rely on SQL Server or SharePoint to maintain the data, but many departments rely on Access for custom applications and to create ad-hoc queries.

People need to work with data from around the world, and Access supports that reach with tools and integration for XML, InfoPath, Outlook, SQL Server, SharePoint Services, managed code, and mobile devices. There is built-in integration with Outlook, both to collect data from forms and to exchange contact information. Using linked tables to connect with SQL Server, users can leverage the new features in Access 2007. And, when exchanging data with Excel, the Import Wizard now allows changes to field data types so import and export specifications can be properly constructed and saved.

Those are just some of the highlights for improvements in working with Microsoft products. The Access data engine and Jet database engine both support connections using Open Database Connectivity (ODBC) or installable index sequential access method (ISAM) drivers. So, there are plenty of opportunities for creating solutions to interface with accounting programs, Web applications, and a host of other commercial and custom programs.

Excel

When it comes to working with external data, Excel files are among the most common files of external data that you work with in Access, so the new Access capability to specify the data types as you are importing the data is a great benefit and time saver.

Importing and exporting to Excel follows the standard process that you are familiar with for text files. The wizard walks through the steps and provides options for specifying field types and even saving the specifications. This creates an `ImportExportSpecification` object that contains all the information necessary to repeat the process. An import specification contains the link to the source file, the name of the destination database, the table name, and if it is an `append` or `create` function, the primary key information, field names, and all of the details necessary to import the data.

Reusing a specification is fast and easy and avoids the potential for input errors. You can easily schedule these routine processes as Outlook tasks so that they occur on time. That's just one of several opportunities to integrate with Outlook; you'll see more in a moment. First you'll want to know that copy and paste is better than ever as a quick way to add records to a table in Access. You can copy and paste an entire spreadsheet into the datasheet view of a new table, and Access not only creates the fields, but is a lot smarter about field type recognition. You get as many rows and columns as you paste—no more being surprised by missing columns and rows, and you don't need to delete the initial blank rows to get started. Couple that with more design capabilities in Datasheet view, and you have a powerful combination that particularly appeals to power users.

Outlook

In addition to being a robust e-mail client, Outlook often functions as a contact manager, maintains a calendar, and tracks tasks. The new Access file format avoids many security issues and allows Access to leverage these features. As mentioned, routine tasks can be added to Outlook, so that users get reminders and processes are run on schedule. Other new features utilize Outlook to collect data and make it easier to share information about contacts.

Contact information is a significant business asset. Because e-mail is one of the most used channels for communications, it needs to be easy to maintain contact lists, both in Access solutions and in Outlook. Now it's simple to import and export contact records to and from Outlook 2007 and Access 2007.

But there is something even better. With Outlook 2007, you can select contacts from Outlook or from an Access table and use either an HTML e-mail or an InfoPath form to collect data and import it directly into a database. Whether it's a new record or updating an existing record, the entire process can be automated. This is a big benefit for collecting routine reports, such as daily sales totals, inventories, or attendance records, as well as for surveys and other questionnaires. As you can imagine, it's also an excellent tool for collecting error messages and other data about application usage and events.

SQL Server

Access is an agile front end that leverages the power and capacity of SQL Server with its native rapid development environment and intuitive user interface features. By connecting to SQL Server using linked tables, developers and users receive the benefit of most of the new features in Access 2007. However, linked tables do not allow design change. If you need to modify the SQL structure or views, you still have the options of Access project files and ADPs.

Chapter 19 focuses on working with SQL Server.

Security

Security comes in a multitude of wrappers—some are from Access and others are from servers and network settings. For many companies, the best way to protect data is to store it on a server, such as SharePoint or SQL Server and then use the network and server settings to control access.

Access 2007 has additional options for both data and file protection. The ACCDB file format enables data encryption. This form of data protection is far superior to anything previously available in user and group security features. With an ACCDB file, the data, itself, is protected by encryption rather than relying on restricting access to specific users and groups. Access also utilizes trust center settings to determine if a database is trusted or will open in disabled mode. With tighter virus protection controls, trust center use makes it easier for developers to deploy VBA powered solutions. Chapter 18 discusses security measures and options for both MDB and ACCDB file formats. Unless system administrators have established other policies, users still have the opportunity to enable an untrusted database opened from an untrusted location. That's covered briefly later and in more detail in Chapter 22.

Encryption with Database Password

After years of humbly conceding that the security features in Access were more about permissions than protection, developers can finally claim that Access can preserve and protect the data. With the ACCDB file format, Access 2007 uses the Windows System Cryptographic APIs to encrypt data. And like other security measures, 2007 encryption uses a stronger algorithm to scramble the data than prior versions. If you use data encryption, be careful to store the password in a safe location because it cannot be retrieved by Access, Windows, or even Microsoft. Take this seriously because there is no bypass key to magically provide an alternative method for opening the file or extracting the data. However, as with most password requirements, users who can set passwords can also change or remove them.

Being able to encrypt data is a tremendous benefit to many businesses. But as mentioned, one trade-off of switching to the ACCDB file format is having to forego use of the work group administrator to set user and group permissions. True to form, developers have created their own ways to establish and enforce permissions, as you'll see in Chapter 18.

Signed Database Package

Access 2007 has a new way to package and digitally sign a database: Package-and-Sign. It creates a signed Access Deployment file (ACCDC) for ACCDB and ACCDE files. The process starts by compressing the database into a package file (.accdc), which can help reduce transfer times. Then the package file is signed using a code-signing certificate, which indicates that the code has not been tampered with. As with digital signatures, if you trust the publisher, you can extract the contents of the package. Once the database has been extracted, it is no longer associated with the package file, and it opens in disabled mode (unless it is opened from a trusted location).

Because Package-and-Sign works only with the new ACCDB file format, Access 2007 also includes the older tools for signing and distributing MDB file formats. As in the past, databases will open and be enabled if they contain a valid digital signature from a trusted publisher and the user trusts the certificate.

Trusted Locations

Database files that are in trusted locations can be opened and all components will run without warning messages or prompts to enable content. This pertains to the 2007 and earlier file formats, so essentially all ACCDB and MDB file extensions. That does not override the need to trust the publisher of a database with a digital signature for the VBA code to run. (Chapter 18 provides more about digital signatures, running in disabled mode, and related issues.)

Access 2007 uses the Trust Center to create and change security settings for Access and to create and change trusted locations, such as files folders and network shares. The Trust Center also contains the criteria for determining whether a database is safe to open or if it should be disabled. The new security settings are easier to understand and provide more flexibility than working with signed databases in Access 2003. The Access 2007 Trust Center also integrates with the Microsoft Office Trust Center.

The easiest way to make a database trusted is to open it from a trusted folder, providing that the Access Trust Center option is set to Allow Trusted Locations. That option allows any database in the specified folder to open with all code and macros enabled. There are two parts to the process: establishing trusted locations and moving the database to one of those folders.

To create a trusted location, open Access and click the Office Button. Select Access Options ➪ Trust Center ➪ Trust Center Settings ➪ Trusted Locations. Click the Add New Location button to browse to and select the desired folder, check to Include Subfolders if appropriate, and add the new location. Confirm and accept to complete the process. That allows files in the listed folders to open and run without security warnings.

> *Check the box to Allow Trusted Locations On My Network makes it easier to work with files on other computers.*

Message Bar

The Security Warning message bar appears when Access 2007 opens a database from outside of a trusted location. The message bar has a handy Options button that opens the Microsoft Office Security Options dialog box to give users options and information. They can enable the content, be protected from the content (run in disabled mode), and even open the Trust Center and change settings (if they have the necessary permissions).

This sounds totally effective and convenient. There's just one catch. With all the new controls, the security warning has been overlooked by quite a few people, including seasoned developers. You'll want to put "check for security warnings" at the top of your FAQs and user guides. Figure 3-12 shows how well the security warning blends in with the other controls. You definitely want to respond to the warning before starting to work because the code is disabled and the act of enabling the code closes the file— even if you've saved your work, you'll lose your place.

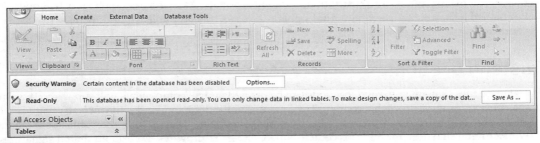

Figure 3-12

> *Did you notice the Read-Only warning? If you open a compressed (zipped) file, you may need to change the database properties to ensure that Read-Only is not checked. This is reminiscent of copying a database from a CD—way back in the 20th century.*

Disabled Mode

If a database is not trusted, the default behavior for Access 2007 is to open the database in disabled mode. Disabled mode allows most of the embedded macros to run, but does not allow actions or events that are driven by Microsoft Visual Basic for Applications (VBA) code or components. If there is any question about the integrity of the database, it is a tremendous benefit to be able to open the file in disabled mode because you can view the data it without the risk of enabling malicious code.

Convert with Confidence

You can convert to the new ACCDB file format as easily as selecting File ⇨ Save As. There's 100 percent compatibility with Access 2000 and 2002 file formats and you can even have an MDB and ACCDB version of the same app open at the same time. One hundred percent compatible? Okay, there is a qualifier. Just because the file formats are compatible doesn't mean that the code converts smoothly or is totally supported, to say nothing about little bugs that have thus far escaped detection.

Appendix A covers the issues and processes associated with converting a variety of file formats, including MDEs, secured, and even replicated databases. For now, the best way to know how your applications will be affected is to install Access 2007, open the file, and save it as an ACCDB file type.

Secured Databases

There's good news and bad news—and it's the same news: Everything related to the MDW and userlever security could be wiped out with just one click. That's fantastic, at least it is for those who don't need or already have an alternate method for enforcing permissions and also have a modicum of restrictions for file access. But the ease of removing the MDW is also risky: Developers and managers especially need to be aware that if someone has Access 2007 and can sign into a secured MDW with sufficient permission, he can merely save the MDB as an ACCDB, instantly removing all related security and permission.

Save as MDB

Once again, Microsoft has made it remarkably easy to share files with older versions of Access. With Access 2007, the File ⇨ Save As command allows files to be saved directly in either the Access 2000 or the Access 2002-2003 MDB file format. Of course, new features are either ignored or handled in their earlier method. For example, when a file is converted to an MDB format, the user has to leave the Ribbon and go back to menus and toolbars, and rich text formatting is ignored so users will see plain text. However, there are some new features, specifically the new field types, that cannot be accommodated in the MDB file format. If the ACCDB contains field types that are not available for MDBs, the file cannot be saved in a prior version. That means files with complex data, offline data, or attachments cannot be saved as MDB files.

But what about the Access 2003 user who receives an ACCDB file? That's not a big problem because there are converters that allow Access 2000 and 2002–2003 users to open ACCDB files. You can download the free converters from the Microsoft website.

ADE and Creating Runtime Files

This may be the gift of the decade. The ADE, or Access 2007 Developer Extensions and the Access 2007 Runtime are *free* downloads. This is a huge bonus for developers because these tools were previously bundled in Visual Studio Tools for Microsoft Office System, which has cost as much as $800. The Access 2007 Runtime will allow developers to deploy Access 2007 solutions on computers that do not have full installations of Access 2007. The Access 2007 Developer Extensions will include the Package Solution,

Save as Template, and Source Code Control. Two features included in previous versions will not be provided with the 2007 ADE: the Property Scanner and the Customer Startup Wizard.

The Runtime and ADE can be invaluable tools for efficiently creating, deploying, and distributing solutions. Having them freely available will open the door to new opportunities for a multitude of developers and companies. Chapter 21 provides explanations and steps for using the ADE tools, so the following is only to pique your interest.

Runtimes

The ADE continues to include the Access redistributable runtime engine. Anyone with the license for the ADE is authorized to package and deploy Access runtime solutions. That means that the end user is not required to own or have Access on his computer. A distributable runtime solution includes and installs a runtime Access client and all supporting files, including the Access database engine, ACE. An additional benefit is that the runtime mode helps lock down the environment and limits user options. It can be invoked even if the full version of Access is installed.

The Access 2007 runtime can be either an MDB/MDE file or an ACCDB/ACCDR file. If your solution uses the new ACCDB file format, then the runtime can be invoked by merely changing the file extension to ACCDR. However, if the application needs to remain in the MDB file format it requires the command line switch /runtime to invoke the runtime engine and environment.

Chapter 21 goes through the process of creating and distributing runtime applications. It also discusses some related issues, such as deployment options and managing multiple versions of Access.

Package Wizard

Whether you use it to distribute runtimes or just the application, the package wizard can guide you through the process of creating a professional delivery for your solution. The package wizard creates the MSI installer, which installs the entire database solution for the user. Among other things, the wizard allows you to include the database files, icons as well as additional files and folders. It can also be used to create short cuts for the user, to set registry keys and more. And, as in the past, the wizard allows you to save a template of a package solution. So, when you need to make modifications, you don't have to start from scratch. Again, I refer you to Chapter 21.

Database Template Creator

The 2007 ADE tools include the Access Database Template creator. It allows developers to take an existing solution and convert it to the Access 2007 template file format (ACCDT). The files that you keep pulling your standard tables from can officially become templates. You can turn a polished solution into a template, place it in the correct folder (such as the Access Template folder), and have it appear as a template in the Access Getting Started experience. The other benefit of template is that it is stored in a safe text file format. So templates can easily be shared, saved, and e-mailed—another way for developers to leverage the tools that they have accumulated.

Chapter 21 walks through the process to create and deploy a template.

Source Code Control Support

Many developers use or would like to have software to provide version control and backups as they work on their projects. There are several source code control (SCC) programs that offer that functionality, but the problem has been that Access itself does not have a mechanism to provide the information needed for a standard SCC. ADE now includes tools that will work with SCC programs to document information about changes to database objects.

To institute a version control process, you'll likely start with the Access SCC support tools and use them in conjunction with a reputable add-in. Chapter 21 explains the process using Microsoft Visual Source Safe 2005, which is available with Microsoft Visual Studio .NET 2005.

What's Gone or Deprecated

Hey, this chapter is about new features, so why are we talking about things that are removed? Well, if you're a developer, you probably want to know up front that you aren't going to find certain things in the new Access. And that would be particularly important if one of your solutions relied on affected functionality.

There comes a time when some things are no longer need. It could be because they have been replaced by something so much better, because other influences have added risks, or because they have slowly become obsolete. Those are the main reasons why some features are not supported by Access 2007. For the most part, there are new and better options. The following sections explain the more common Access features that have been removed or replaced with an alternative.

Data Access Pages

Data Access Pages (DAPs) were primarily used to work with an Access database over the Internet. DAP was essentially a Web form that allowed users to view, enter, edit, and delete data. However, DAPs didn't offer the features and flexibility that users needed; they were based on Active X technology, and they suffered from various security issues. Although you cannot open or work with DAPs in Access 2007, you can open them with Internet Explorer.

Office and Access 2007 offer a variety of solutions that provide the security and flexibility that users expect. Integration with InfoPath, SharePoint, and SQL Server are great examples. There is also new support for managed code, so look for easier integration with ASP and .NET.

Import RunCommand

`Import RunCommand` was briefly mentioned in the discussion about the new attachment field type. `DoCmd.RunCommand acCmdImport` and the `Import RunCommand` macro are not supported in Access 2007. Making either the object model call or macro call generates an error message. The functionality has been replaced by the `ImportAttachment` command.

Snapshot Viewer

The Snapshot Viewer (downloadable from Microsoft) allows computers that don't have Access to view an Access report that was saved as a snapshot—which means that reports were created by Access 2003 or an earlier version. Existing versions will continue to be supported. However, Access 2007 will not save reports as Snapshots, so there is not a Snapshot Viewer for Access 2007. But 2007 has something better. The new capability to save as PDF and XPS provides a superior alternative for sending reports.

> *The Access Snapshot Viewer is a free download, and it will be available for the foreseeable future. It opens snapshot files, which is one of the report export options in Access 2003 and earlier versions. Snapshots remain the only "official" report viewing technology in those earlier versions.*

User Interface: Legacy Export and Import Formats

As technology advances, some specialties are enhanced, new ones are created, and a few are left behind. At some point, it is no longer cost effective to build user interfaces between the new platforms and the legacy programs. A similar logic applies if two technologies are advancing in different directions such that the need for integration is diminished. That is essentially the situation with Access 2007 and it explains why some import and export interfaces were dropped.

Access 2007 does not have a user interface for exporting to ASP or to IDC/HTX. It also does not have a user interface for importing from Lotus 1-2-3/DOS (*.wj*) or from Exchange. However, when you see the lists of files that Access 2007 does work with, these deletions appear to be based on good business decisions to put resources to work where they will provide a bigger overall benefit. In the event that you do come across the need to import or export to one of these formats, you can do so by building a function that uses the object model.

Summary

This chapter was just an appetizer for what's to come. You've seen only the highlights of selected new features—but there are a thousand more pages to help you delve into the details and learn how to incorporate them into your solutions. Access 2007 has taken one of the most powerful tools for rapid solution development and given it a richer developer environment, a more intuitive user interface, and the capability to easily integrate with Web services and other applications. The new out-of-the-box solutions not only save significant development time, but they afford you a huge population of new users and potential clients.

If VBA is a relatively new challenge, you couldn't have picked a better time. Access 2007 provides new options that make it easier and faster to create dynamite applications as you are learning about VBA and macros, and building reliable, expandable applications. Chapters 4 and 5 provide a solid foundation for understanding the material and examples in the rest of the book. Keep in mind that most chapters have sample databases and code available for download from this book's website. Working with a sample file as you read through a chapter will likely make it a lot more fun and easier to learn new material and techniques.

Using the VBA Editor

You'll use the VBA Editor to write almost all of your VBA code. Although you can simply open the VBA Editor and start typing code, knowing a bit about the different components of the editor not only helps you properly structure and debug your code, but saves you time while you're at it. In this chapter, you explore the major structural components of the VBA Editor as well as some basic code debugging techniques.

The topics in Chapters 4 and 5 are so interconnected that it was difficult to decide which chapter to put first. If you get the sense that you are jumping into the middle without having covered the basics, what you think you're missing is likely in Chapter 5.

Anatomy of the VBA Editor

You can access the VBA Editor in several ways. From anywhere in Microsoft Access, press Alt+F11 or choose from several places on Access's new Ribbon: Create, Macros, Modules, Database Tools, or Visual Basic. You can also open the VBA Editor by double-clicking a module name in the navigation pane or from any form or report. From the Properties dialog box, click the Events tab, select the event that you're interested in, click the Ellipses button (. . .), and choose Code Builder. When you first view the VBA Editor, you might be a little overwhelmed by the number of components on the screen. Take a look at the VBA Editor within a user-created module, as shown in Figure 4-1.

The VBA Editor has the following components:

❑ **Three types of modules:** Form or report modules, class modules, and standard modules. Each type of component has its own icon. The Project Explorer in Figure 4-1 contains a class module, a source form, and a standard module. The VBA project carries the same name as the current database. If the Project Explorer isn't visible when you display the VBA Editor, press Ctrl+R to display it.

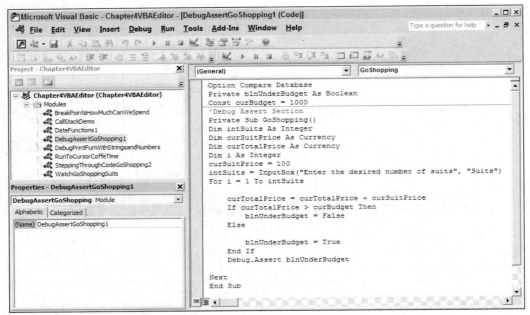

Figure 4-1

❏ **The Properties window:** Typically shown in the bottom-left corner of the VBA Editor, the Properties window lists all properties for the currently selected object. The object could be a module or a class module. The Properties window is quite helpful for working with user forms in Visual Basic, but you probably won't use it very often when writing VBA code in Access. However, it is a handy way to see all the properties for an object, so go ahead and check it out. Click the drop-down list and scroll through the alphabetical listing of the properties for that object.

❏ **The Code window:** This is where you actually write your code. By default, the Code window displays all subs and functions within the current module. You can change the display of the Code window and limit it to only the currently selected procedure by selecting Tools ⇨ Options and, in the Window Settings frame of the Editor tab, clearing the checkbox, Default to Full Module View. Click OK to save your changes. The Code window has several components of its own, including the Object list on the upper left and the Procedure list on the upper right.

❏ **The Object list box:** Enables you to choose from a variety of objects. When you're writing code inside a standard module, the list box contains only the (General) option. When you're writing code in a class module associated with a form or report, the Object list box contains an entry for every object (text box, combo box, label, and so on) within that form or report.

❏ **The Procedure list box:** Displays different items depending on the type of module you're viewing. When viewing a class module associated with a form or report, the Procedure list box contains an entry for every event associated with the selected object. For example, if you choose a combo box on your form, the Procedure list box contains entries for events such as the Click, BeforeUpdate, AfterUpdate, and LostFocus events, among others.

If you're viewing a standard module, the list box contains an entry for every sub or function in your module, even the ones that you write or rename. Using the drop-down list is a quick way to select the specific procedure you need to edit. You can even add a procedure by clicking on its name.

If you have a module with lots of objects and procedures, scrolling through the Code window to find the desired procedure can be a time-consuming task, so simply select the object and then click the Procedure drop-down box to choose and jump to any available procedure you want in the current module or class module. Subs and functions are listed alphabetically, although your code may not keep them that way. You can also use the Procedure drop-down list to jump directly to the General Declaration section.

In addition to these visible components, there are a number of components you can display to help you write your code and work with the Access 2007 objects. Most of these components are available under the VBA Editor's View menu.

Your Database and VBA Project—Better Together

You might wonder about the correlation between a VBA project and your database. Quite simply, the database with forms and reports is what you see, and the VBA project contains the instructions to make it work. Although you won't see a separate file, there is a VBA project for every database created in Access. The objects in the Project Explorer shown in Figure 4-1 are present no matter where the code is used in your database. Whether you are writing code behind a form or report or in a module, you will see the same objects listed in the Project Explorer.

Using the Object Browser

The Object Browser is probably one of the most powerful tools you'll use when writing VBA code. Display it in the VBA Editor by selecting View ⇨ Object Browser or by clicking F2. The Object Browser, shown in Figure 4-2, has a number of components.

When you load the Object Browser, you can still view the Project Explorer and the Properties window. The Object Browser appears directly over the Code window. You can return to the Code window at any time by selecting View ⇨ Code. If multiple code windows are open, you can choose Window from the menu and then select the code window that you want, or you can move the cursor to the code window by clicking on F7. The following are some of the Object Browser's components that you'll use most often:

❑ **The Project/Library box:** Shows all the available type libraries. You can choose *All Libraries* or any available type library from the drop-down box. The type library you choose dictates which objects you can browse with the Object Browser. Later in this chapter, you'll see how to add a type library to your Project.

❑ **The Search box:** Enter search terms and click the Search button (the binoculars icon) to search the selected type libraries for the particular term. Results of your search are displayed in the Search Results pane.

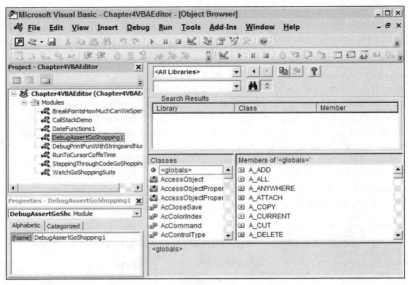

Figure 4-2

❑ **The Search Results pane:** Lists all of the results of your search. You can show or hide the Search Results pane by clicking the Show/Hide icon (two up or down arrows) next to the Search button. The Search Results pane lists the relevant library, class, and member of any object returned by your search. To display more information about any object displayed in the Search Results pane, click the object to display its full information in the Details pane.

❑ **The Classes list:** Displays all of the objects, enums, and collections in the currently referenced library. You can scroll through the Classes list and click to select any of the listed items. After you select an item, its details are displayed in the Members Of list and in the Details pane. You learn more about objects, collections, and enums in Chapter 5.

❑ **The Members of *classname* list:** Displays the properties, methods, events, and constants associated with the object currently selected in the Classes list. Select any of the items in the Members of *classname* list to display details in the Details pane.

❑ **The Details pane of the Object Browser:** Displays information such as the type of object, its data type, the arguments it needs, and the parent library or collection. For example, in Figure 4-3, the Details pane informs you that the constant vbOKOnly is a member of the Enum vbMsgBoxStyle, which is a member of the VBA object library. Its value is 0 and the other members of the Enum vbMsgBoxStyle include vbInformation, vbOKCancel, and vbYesNo.

If a Help file is associated with the currently selected object, you can display a Help topic by selecting the item in either the Classes or Members list, and then pressing F1 or clicking the Help button in the upper-right corner of the Object Browser.

The buttons next to the Project/Library box enable you to scroll through the previous or next members of the current collection.

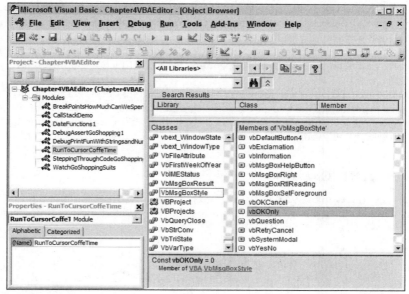

Figure 4-3

One of the advantages of the Object Browser is that you can actually use it to take you to anywhere in the code that the current object is declared. For example, in Figure 4-3 the current database's object library (Chapter4VBAEditor) is searched for the procedure CoffeeTime. The Search Results pane lists the library, class, and member for the CoffeeTime sub. You can click the View Definition button (the fourth button from the left, next to the Project Library drop-down box) to return to the Code window and display the CoffeeTime sub.

The rest of this chapter delves into the other components of the VBA Editor that can help you write and debug VBA code.

Testing and Debugging VBA Code

The Code window is where you actually write your code, including the subroutines, functions, and declarations. In addition to the Code window, you'll use other components of the VBA Editor to test and debug your code. The following sections look at each of those components.

When Should You Debug Your Code?

There are a few schools of thought about when to debug your VBA code, and it's normal for developers to use different approaches in varying situations. You could debug as you write, testing every few lines, although that could be quite time-consuming. You'd have to run your code every few lines (possibly with incomplete procedures) and make heavy use of the tools such as the Immediate window and Watch statements discussed later in this section. The advantage of this method is that you always know the value of your variables, and the likelihood of making or perpetuating a mistake is reduced.

An alternative method is to write all of the code for your application and then debug it. This approach might seem tempting because it doesn't require you to stop your productive code typing to debug your application. However, you can easily end up with numerous errors, some of which could require you to make major changes to your code. Using that technique can be like opening Pandora's Box, particularly as code becomes more complex and interdependent, with one function calling another function.

The best debugging method falls somewhere between those two options. You should definitely debug at the end of each procedure. That allows you to be confident that each procedure produces the appropriate and expected values. Unless you're writing incredibly long procedures, this method should be sufficient to ensure you're not writing code with too many errors.

Immediate Window

The Immediate window in the Visual Basic Editor enables you to enter commands and view the contents of variables while your code is in break mode. Press Ctrl+G or select View ➪ Immediate Window to open the window, as shown in Figure 4-4.

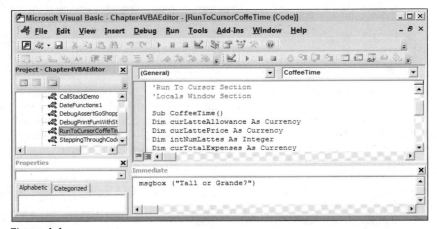

Figure 4-4

In the Immediate window, you can display the value of a variable by using the `? Debug.Print` command. Just type `?` along with the variable name and press Enter. VBA Editor displays the contents of the variable in the Immediate window. For example, typing the following and pressing Enter will display the value of `intNumEmployee` in the Immediate window:

```
? intNumEmployees
```

Seeing the current value of a variable can be helpful when troubleshooting code if you're encountering unexpected results. Simply set a breakpoint in your code and test the value of a variable at any time. This enables you to determine where in the code the value is being incorrectly calculated. The question mark is shorthand for typing `Debug.Print`. Instead of typing `? intNumEmployees`, you can type `Debug.Print intNumEmployees` and press Enter. Both statements produce the same results.

In addition to displaying the value of variables, you can also execute VBA commands in the Immediate window. Just eliminate the ? character and type the entire command, and then press Enter. Typing `msgbox("Tall or Grande?")` and pressing Enter displays the message shown in Figure 4-5.

Figure 4-5

You can even perform calculations in the Immediate window such as:

```
intTotalEmployees = intTempEmployees + intFullTimeEmployees.
```

The Immediate window is also a powerful debugging tool for your applications. For more information about the Immediate window, see Chapter 8.

Using the Immediate window along with other aspects of the VBA Editor detailed in this chapter, such as breakpoints and stepping through code, is the most generally accepted method of debugging your code. However, there are other options. One method that is often used by beginning developers is to place message box code throughout the code to test the values of selected variables or calculations. Although there is nothing technically wrong with this method, it can be messy and cumbersome. After all, when you're done debugging the code, you still need to comment out or remove all of the message box calls. That can be a lot of unnecessary work.

The Debug.Print Statement

As you already know, the ? character is short for `Debug.Print`, and you've seen how easy it is to use both commands directly in the Immediate window. That's not the only place you can use `Debug.Print` statements, The following code illustrates how `Debug.Print` can be used within a module, so you can imagine how it can be helpful for testing and debugging.

```
Sub FunWithStringsAndNumbers()
Dim strBikes As String
Dim strCost As String
Dim strCustomerName As String
Dim intBikes As Integer
Dim curCost As Currency
strBikes = "5"
strCost = "100"
strCustomerName = "The ""W"" Hotel, New York City"
intBikes = 5
curCost = 100
Debug.Print strBikes + strCost
Debug.Print intBikes + curCost
Debug.Print strCustomerName
End Sub
```

This code produces the following results in the Immediate window:

```
5100
105
The "W" Hotel, New York City
```

You can use the `Debug.Print` statement within any procedure to display results of calculations or values of variables in the Immediate window. That's a quick way to confirm that your code is achieving the desired results.

The Debug.Assert Statement

You can just as easily type `Debug.Assert` in the Immediate window. This option conditionally suspends execution of code at the line where `Debug.Assert` appears. For example, the following code uses the `Debug.Assert` statement to stop code execution when a specific condition is met:

```
Option Compare Database
Private blnUnderBudget As Boolean
Const curBudget = 1000

Private Sub GoShopping()
Dim intSuits As Integer
Dim curSuitPrice As Currency
Dim curTotalPrice As Currency
Dim i as Integer
curSuitPrice = 100
intSuits = InputBox("Enter the desired number of suits", "Suits")
For i=1To intSuits
    curTotalPrice = curTotalPrice + curSuitPrice
    If curTotalPrice > curBudget Then
        blnUnderBudget = False
    Else
        blnUnderBudget = True
    End If
    Debug.Assert blnUnderBudget
Next
End Sub
```

The code breaks every time you go over budget on your shopping trip. You can use this statement when testing for specific conditions within your code. Although `Debug.Assert` is a good debugging tool, you probably won't ever use it in live code because it's a rather abrupt way to stop an application. The user would get no warning and because the code stops, you do not get to provide him with a friendly message or explanation.

Breakpoints

Breakpoints are simply places in your code that pause execution of code. For example, to check the value of a variable `curTotalCost` midway through the following procedure, you'd need to use the `Debug.Print` statement (as in the following code) or set a breakpoint.

```
Sub HowMuchCanWeSpend()
Dim curTotalPrice As Currency
Dim curUnitPrice As Currency
Dim intNumSocks As Integer
Dim i As Integer
curUnitPrice = 3.5
intNumSocks = InputBox( _
    "Please enter the number of pairs of socks youwant.", _
    "Pairs of Socks")
For i=1 To intNumSocks
    curTotalPrice = curTotalPrice + curUnitPrice
Next
Debug.Print curTotalPrice
End Sub
```

This code prints in the Immediate window the amount you'll spend for the total sock purchase. That's great, but what if you want to see how your total expense is adding up as you go? You can certainly add a Debug.Print statement within the For...Next loop, but you can also set a breakpoint anywhere in the procedure. Once the breakpoint is reached, you can use the Immediate window to check the value of your variables. You can set a breakpoint on any line of code except for Dim statements and comments.

The simplest way to set a breakpoint is to click in the left margin of the Code window. A brick-colored dot appears in the margin and the corresponding line of code is highlighted. To clear a breakpoint, click the left margin again in the same spot. You can also set and clear breakpoints by placing your cursor in the desired line of code and selecting Debug ➪ Toggle Breakpoint or pressing F9. When you run the code, every time the breakpoint is reached, code execution stops and VBA waits for you to decide what to do next. You can choose from the following options:

❑ Check the value of variables in the Immediate window. When your code reaches a breakpoint, the value of all variables is retained. You can check the value of any variable by using the Debug.Print statement or the ? character within the Immediate window.

❑ Use your mouse to hover over any variable in the current procedure. The value of the variable is displayed close to the mouse cursor.

❑ Press F5 or select Run ➪ Continue to continue code execution. Execution proceeds until the next breakpoint or the end of the procedure.

When VBA encounters a breakpoint, it pauses execution immediately before the line of code is executed. The line of code that contains the breakpoint is not executed unless or until you choose to step through the code using the F8 key.

Stepping Through Code

In most cases, you design code to run with little or no user intervention. However, when you're testing code, sometimes it is helpful to do more than insert a couple of breakpoints or include some Debug.Print statements. If you're running code with several variable changes or some intricate looping, it can sometimes be helpful to step through the code line by line. Doing this allows you to watch the value of variables after each line of code is executed. This can help you pinpoint any errors or mistakes in the logic of the code.

To step through your code, place the cursor at the point that you want to initiate the process and press F8 to begin the procedure (you can also press F8 after the code has entered break mode to step through the remaining code). When you press F8 to begin code execution, the name of the sub or function is highlighted in yellow. Subsequent presses of the F8 key move execution from line to line, highlighting the next executable line in yellow. Comment lines and Dim statements are skipped when stepping through code. As you press F8, the highlighted line is executed.

Stepping through code is an important tool so it is worth reiterating how the process works. The first instance of F8 highlights the next executable code; the subsequent instance of F8 executes the highlighted code. If nothing is highlighted, F8 highlights code; if something is highlighted, F8 runs it.

If the current procedure calls another sub or function, F8 will also execute the called procedure line by line. If you're confident that the called procedure doesn't contain any errors, you can execute the entire called procedure and then return to line-by-line execution of the calling procedure. This is called *stepping over* the procedure, and it is done by pressing Shift+F8. Stepping over the called procedure executes the entire procedure and then returns to the calling procedure, to proceed with code execution one step at a time. If you're within a called procedure, you can press Ctrl+Shift+F8 to *step out* of the current procedure. What's the difference between stepping over and stepping out of the procedure? If you're already in the called procedure, the two are exactly the same. But here's an example that illustrates the difference and gives you some practice with code. Assume you're stepping through the following code (which is in the Chapter 4 download material):

```
Option Compare Database
Private blnUnderBudget As Boolean
Const curBudget = 1000

Private Sub GoShopping()
Dim intSuits As Integer
Dim curSuitPrice As Currency
Dim curTotalPrice As Currency
curSuitPrice = 100
intSuits = InputBox("Enter the desired number of suits", "Suits")
For i=1To intSuits
    curTotalPrice = curTotalPrice + curSuitPrice
    If curTotalPrice > curBudget Then
        blnUnderBudget = False
    Else
        blnUnderBudget = True
    End If
Next
If blnUnderBudget = False Then
    OverBudget
End If
End Sub

Private Sub OverBudget()
Debug.Print "You've gone over budget."
Debug.Print "You need to work some overtime."
Debug.Print "Remember to pay your taxes."
End Sub
```

Use the F8 key to step through the code until you reach the last If...Then loop (If blnUnderBudget = False Then). When the OverBudget line is highlighted in yellow (meaning it hasn't yet been executed), stepping over the OverBudget procedure returns execution to the line after the OverBudget call (in this case the End If line). If you step out of the procedure, the OverBudget procedure runs, and your code returns to the GoShopping procedure and completes the procedure. If, however, you use the F8 key to step through your code until you reach the first line of the OverBudget procedure, stepping out of the procedure returns you to the line after the OverBudget call (the End If line). Use the following table as a cheat sheet and create some simple procedures to test the various debugging techniques shown in this chapter.

Debugging Technique	Description	Keyboard Shortcut
Step Into	Executes the next line of code in your procedure (highlights line in yellow).	F8
Step Over	Executes code one line at a time within the current procedure. If a second procedure is called from within the first, the entire second procedure is executed at once.	Shift+F8
Step Out	VBA executes the remainder of the current procedure. If executed within the second procedure, the entire second procedure is executed and execution returns to first procedure on the line following the line that called the second procedure.	Ctrl+Shift+F8

Call Stack

The Call Stack dialog box displays a list of the current active procedure(s) when you are stepping through code. An active procedure is one that is started but not completed. You can access the Call Stack dialog box in several ways, including from the menu bar (View the Call Stack) or by pressing Ctrl+L. Because the call stack is available only in break mode, access to the call stack is often grayed out (disabled).

The Call Stack dialog box is not a window and therefore cannot be left open when stepping through code. It is opened and closed at each active procedure.

You gain the most benefit from the Call Stack dialog box when one procedure is calling another or if you have nested procedures, whether they are in the same module or being called by other modules. If another procedure is called from the first procedure, the dialog box displays the new procedure at the top of the list with the original (calling) procedure under it, thus stacking them. Figure 4-6 illustrates this stacking process. OverBudget was called by GoShopping, so OverBudget is listed first, and it is highlighted because it is the procedure being run. Once a procedure is finished, it is removed from the stack. In this case, after OverBudget is run, GoShopping will be the only procedure in the stack.

```
(General)                                OverBudget

    Dim curTotalPrice As Currency
    curSuitPrice = 300
    intSuits = InputBox("Enter the desired number of suits", "Suits")
    For i = 1 To intSuits
        curTotalPrice = curTotalPrice + curSuitPrice
        If curTotalPrice > curBudget Then
            blnUnderBudget = False
        Else
            blnUnderBudget = True
        End If
    Next
    If blnUnderBudget = False Then
        OverBudget
    End If
    End Sub

⇨ Private Sub OverBudget()
    Debug.Print "You've gone over budget."
    Debug.Print "You need to work some overtime."
    Debug.Print "Remember to pay your taxes."
    End Sub
```

Call Stack   ×

Project.Module.Function   Show

Chapter4VBAEditor.CallStackDemo.OverBudget
Chapter4VBAEditor.CallStackDemo.GoShopping   Close

Locals   ×

Chapter4VBAEditor.Ca   ...

Expression
⊞ CallStackDemo

Figure 4-6

When stepping through multiple procedures from different modules, or even from the same module, it can be a little confusing as to where a particular procedure is being called. To help find the start of the any active procedure in the call stack, highlight the active (top) procedure in the list and either double-click the item or click the Show button. In the current example, the call stack was opened when OverBudget was called, so two procedures are listed. To find out what line called OverBudget, you can double-click on GoShopping, the calling procedure. This puts a green pointer at the line in GoShopping that called OverBudget. Figure 4-7 shows OverBudget still highlighted in yellow, because that's the current point in stepping through the code, and the green pointer at the call to OverBudget.

```
(General)                                GoShopping

    Dim curTotalPrice As Currency
    curSuitPrice = 300
    intSuits = InputBox("Enter the desired number of suits", "Suits")
    For i = 1 To intSuits
        curTotalPrice = curTotalPrice + curSuitPrice
        If curTotalPrice > curBudget Then
            blnUnderBudget = False
        Else
            blnUnderBudget = True
        End If
    Next
    If blnUnderBudget = False Then
▷       OverBudget
    End If
    End Sub

⇨ Private Sub OverBudget()
    Debug.Print "You've gone over budget."
    Debug.Print "You need to work some overtime."
    Debug.Print "Remember to pay your taxes."
    End Sub
```

Figure 4-7

As you might imagine, the call stack is helpful when you are working with multiple procedures and trying to determine where errant data may be originating. It is also a handy tool when working with someone else's application or even modules.

Run to Cursor

Many times when you're executing code, you don't want to run every line of code line by line, but executing the entire procedure at once doesn't help you isolate the problem. And it is very tedious to execute every line of the loop each time a long loop needs to run. For example, consider the following code:

```
Sub CoffeeTime()
Dim curLatteAllowance As Currency
Dim curLattePrice As Currency
Dim intNumLattes As Integer
Dim curTotalExpenses As Currency
curLattePrice = 3.5
curLatteAllowance = InputBox( _
    "Enter the amount of money you have for lattes.", _
    "Latte Allowance")
While curTotalExpenses < curLatteAllowance
    intNumLattes = intNumLattes + 1
    curTotalExpenses = curTotalExpenses + curLattePrice
Wend
Debug.Print intNumLattes
MsgBox "You can purchase " & intNumLattes & " lattes.", _
    vbOkOnly, "Total Lattes"
End Sub
```

If you have $350 to spend on lattes, the `While...Wend` loop will run 100 times. Pressing F8 to step through that long of a loop can be quite tiresome. Thankfully, there is a shortcut. If you're not worried that the loop is producing incorrect data, you can place your cursor in the `Debug.Print intNumLattes` line and press Ctrl+F8. Your procedure will run until it reaches the `Debug.Print` line, where it halts and is highlighted. You can then press F8 to execute just the highlighted line of code or press F5 to continue execution until the end of the procedure.

Locals Window

Sometimes it can be utterly mind-numbing to test the value of every variable when your code enters break mode. If you're stepping through code and need to test the value of seven different variables every step of the way, that's a lot of `Debug.Print` statements to keep track of in the Immediate window. You can use the Locals window to display all the variables in a procedure and their values. You can watch the variable values change as you step through the code. To display the Locals window, select View ⇨ Locals Window. Figure 4-8 shows the Locals window while stepping through a procedure.

As you step through the procedure, the Locals window shows you the up-to-date values of all variables. The Locals window is not emptied until the last line of code has been executed. In this case, you'd see a message box stating, "You can purchase 100 lattes."

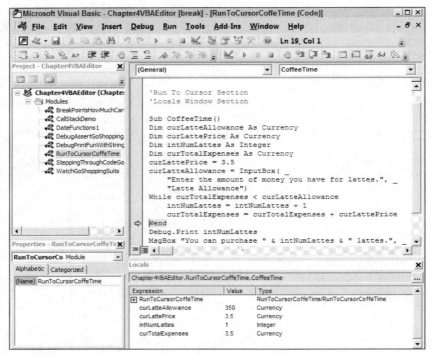

Figure 4-8

Watch Window

The last debugging tool you'll examine in this chapter is the Watch window, which enables you to watch a variable within your procedure. When the value of the variable changes or when the variable is `True`, your code enters break mode. To open the Watch window, select View ➪ Watch Window.

To see how the Watch window works, use `WatchGoShoppingSuits`, a modified version of the `GoShopping` module. Recall that it uses a Boolean expression and message box to let you know if you're over budget. Add a watch on the `blnOverBudget.Start` by right-clicking in the Watch window and choosing Add Watch. The Add Watch dialog box opens (see Figure 4-9).

Enter `blnOverBudget` in the Expression text box. In the Watch Type, the default is to Watch Expression, although you could choose Break When Value is True, or Break When Value Changes. For this example, choose Break When Value Is True, and then click OK to save your watch. When you run the `SteppingThroughCodeGoShopping2` procedure, the procedure enters break mode when the value of `blnOverBudget` becomes true. As soon as the loop executes for the eleventh time, the watch expression is triggered and the code enters break mode.

If you choose to simply watch the expression (rather than break), the Watch window behaves almost exactly like the Locals window except that only watched variables are shown.

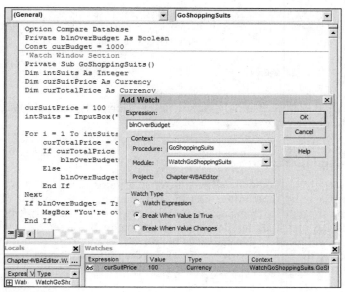

Figure 4-9

If you have a rather long loop to execute and you no longer need your watch, you can delete it while your code is in break mode. Simply right-click the watch and select Delete Watch. You can then press F5 to continue code execution.

```
Option Compare Database
Private blnOverBudget As Boolean
Const curBudget = 1000

Private Sub GoShoppingSuits()

Dim intSuits As Integer
Dim curSuitPrice As Currency
Dim curTotalPrice As Currency

curSuitPrice = 100
intSuits = InputBox("Enter the desired number of suits", "Suits")

For i=1 To intSuits
    curTotalPrice = curTotalPrice + curSuitPrice

    If curTotalPrice > curBudget Then
        blnOverBudget = True
    Else
        blnOverBudget = False
    End If
```

```
    Next
    If blnOverBudget = True Then
        Msgbox "You're over budget!", vbExclamation, "Over Budget"
    End If

    End Sub
```

A shortcut for adding a watch is to right-click the expression and select Add Watch. The expression is filled in automatically, so you avoid the risk of typos.

On-the-Fly Changes

Every once in a while your code will halt because of an error or a breakpoint. The VBA Editor will display the problem line or breakpoint line with an arrow pointing to it. You may discover the problem on that line, make the appropriate changes, and find that the line executes correctly. You can test this simply by pressing the F8 key and stepping through that line of code. If you realize that the problem is several lines before the current location, you can make the correction and easily restart the code from a different location. Just click on the original arrow (pointer) and drag it to the line where you want to start executing the code.

Be aware that depending on what code was executed, you may not get valid results, particularly if it is dependent on earlier code or values. So if you think you've corrected the problem but it still isn't displaying the expected values, it would be prudent to rerun the entire module or function.

Also, code changes during execution may not always be saved when the program ends. Although all the scenarios that might trigger that can't be identified, you can expect it to happen if the code causes the application to shut down. The logic is that you would not want to save modifications that caused the application to crash. But because it can be frustrating to lose other, desirable modifications, it's prudent to save your changes as you go, as usual.

Summary

This chapter explored the VBA Editor, and showed you how to use some of the tools and numerous windows that it provides. As you work with applications and projects, you will find the Immediate window to be an invaluable tool.

Understanding the fundamentals will make it a lot easier and more fun to go through the rest of the book. There are lots of new features and tools to create powerful and professional forms and reports and to make it a breeze to work with other applications.

Remember that you can download the code, databases, and other materials from the book's website. At a minimum, the sample files make it easier to follow along; plus, they'll help you avoid the potential for typos or misreading characters or formatting.

VBA Basics

Now that you know a bit about automating Access, using macros, and how VBA fits into the Access automation picture, you're almost ready to write some code. The next step is to review some VBA basics.

For experienced programmers, this chapter is unnecessary; however, if you're just delving into VBA from another programming language or from VBScript, this chapter contains vital information that will help you to better understand and utilize what you learn in subsequent chapters. Here you'll examine the basic VBA programming objects, learn about variables and how to declare them, and review some additional VBA structures that you'll use in your code. Along the way, you'll build a few procedures, and you will soon gain the skill and confidence to modify those procedures and to create your own.

VBA Objects

You can't program in VBA without understanding how the various VBA components work together. All VBA code is comprised of individual statements. Those statements take objects and manipulate their properties, call their methods, and perform their events. This section introduces the concepts of objects, properties, methods, and events.

VBA is an object-oriented programming (OOP) language. OOP is a type of programming in which programmers define a complete data structure from data types to the operations that can be applied to the data structure. Programmers can create an entire object that contains both data and the operations that the object can perform. They can also create relationships between objects.

There are seemingly countless objects that you can work with using VBA. The collection of objects exposed by a particular application is called an *object library*. You can incorporate multiple object libraries in VBA. For example, you can use VBA to manipulate the Access object library and work with objects such as tables, queries, forms, and reports. You can set references to other object libraries such as Microsoft Outlook, Adobe Acrobat, or Microsoft Word. (Appendix B provides an in-depth discussion of how to set and use references.) Every time you set a reference to another application's object library, you have access to all objects within that library. An object is generally thought of as a physical thing. For example, if you were to set a reference to a car's object library, you could access all the car's objects, such as its tires, roof, carpet, steering wheel, and windows.

Properties

A *property* is a physical attribute of an object. Each property can have multiple values. For example, the properties for a car object include color (silver), doors (four), and cylinders (four). However, the car has objects of its own. The car's tire object has a brand property of Michelin. The car's carpet object has properties of `style` (plush) and `clean` (true).

Some properties of an object can be easily changed. If you want to change the value for the car's property `color`, you take it to an auto detailer and choose another color. With one spilled latte, the carpet's property `clean` is turned to false. However, you can't easily change the number of doors on the car. And, short of completely replacing the engine, you can't change the number of cylinders. Similarly, objects in VBA have some properties that can be changed and some that cannot.

Additionally, every object in Access also has properties. The `form` object, for instance, has many properties including `Border Style`, `Width`, `Height`, and `Caption`. Each of these properties has range of possible values. The `Border Style` property, for example, can be set to `None`, `Thin`, `Sizable`, and `Dialog`—each choice presents the form object with a slightly different look. Before you start manipulating properties in VBA code, take a look at the object and examine some of its properties. In the case of a form, launch the form in design mode and change some of its properties. Then run the form to see how the changes affect not only the display but also the operation of the form. (Forms and controls generally have quite a few properties and options, but they're relatively logical and you typically work with only a few. You'll learn more about forms in Chapter 10.)

Methods

A *method* is an action that can be performed by, or on, an object. When you're in your car, you can invoke the start method of the engine, invoke the release method of the parking break, invoke the shift method of the transmission, and invoke the press method of the gas pedal. Each of these methods causes something to happen. If things work according to your programming, the car goes forward (which can be described as causing the drive method to be executed on the car itself). Generally, an action or event that happens (such as driving) is made up of many other methods performed on multiple objects.

Objects in VBA have methods, as well. For example, you can invoke the `LoadPicture` method on an ActiveX control within an Access form; this causes a picture to be displayed within the control. One of the frequently used methods moves the cursor to the next record in a DAO recordset:

```
rst.MoveNext
```

Events

An *event* is something that happens to an object. The car turns when you turn the steering wheel. The horn blares when you press it. The door closes when you pull it. Turning, blaring, and closing are all events of the car. Events and methods are related in a cause-and-effect way. An event happens when the user does something. The actual doing is the method. So you invoke the move method on the wheel and the car invokes the turn event. It's sometimes difficult to grasp the difference between the two; it'll become clearer as you take a look at the relationship between the methods and events of an Access form.

When you open an Access form, you actually raise (or cause to happen) the OnOpen event. When you close the form, you raise the OnClose event. Within code, however, you can invoke the Open method of the form. Invoking the Open method causes the OnOpen event to fire. So, invoking a method causes an event to happen or fire.

Now that you know a bit more about properties, methods, and events, you're ready for a brief review of the fundamentals of VBA programming.

Variables and VBA Syntax

This section goes over some basics you need to know to program successfully in VBA. Most of them need only to be recapitulated, so if you need more information about any of these topics, you might want to purchase a beginner's guide to VBA programming, such as *VBA For Dummies*, by John Paul Mueller (Wiley Publishing, Inc., ISBN 0764539892). Of course, the help features in Access and VBA also provide guidance on specific tasks or features.

Variables

One of the most important concepts in programming is the use of variables. A *variable* is a location in memory where you can store a value while your code is running. VBA only needs to find an item's location the first time it is used in code; it does not need to look up the location each time. For example, if you need to specify a particular state repeatedly in your code, it can be much faster and cleaner to create a variable strState than to repeatedly use Washington in your code. Not only will the code run faster, but if you ever need to switch states and use California instead, all you have to do is change the value of your variable rather than find all instances of Washington in your code.

Using variables can also make your code easier to interpret. They not only define what VBA allows in the field, but they let you and other developers know what the field can be used for.

Variables hold a variety of types of data including strings, numbers, and objects. As you'll see shortly, a string variable is basically any combination of alpha or alphanumeric data, such as a phrase or name. Although it can store numbers, the numbers will not function as numbers in equations. This is explained a little later, too. The number types store values that can be used in mathematical equations. Objects include database objects and collections.

Properly declaring variables is one of the most important tasks you need to master to program in VBA. It's not hard, but it is a critical skill, and you'll explore the major rules and recommendations for variables in the next few sections.

Variable Data Types

In VBA, you can declare many different types of variables. Variables are named by the type of data that they are designed to hold. Make it a point to declare your variables with the correct type so that your code runs as efficiently as possible and provides more descriptive error messages. If you choose to not declare a data type, the variable is created as a variant. Variant variables are slower then explicitly defined data types and require significantly more space in memory than other types of variables. The following table lists the variable data types, the amount of memory they take, and the range of values that they can store.

Data Type	Size in Memory	Possible Values
Byte	1 byte	0 to 255.
Boolean	2 bytes	True or False.
Integer	2 bytes	–32,768 to 32,767.
Long (long integer)	4 bytes	–2,147,483,648 to 2,147,483,647.
Single (single-precision real)	4 bytes	Approximately –3.4E38 to 3.4E38.
Double (double-precision real)	8 bytes	Approximately –1.8E308 to 4.9E324.
Currency (scaled integer)	8 bytes	Approximately –922,337,203,685,477.5808 to 922,337,203,685,477.5807.
Decimal*	14 bytes	With no decimal places, the range is +/–79,228,162,514,264,337,593,543,950, 335 or with decimal places, the range is +/– 1E–28 (one to the 28th power). The smallest possible non-zero number is 0.000,000,000,000,000,000,000,000,000,1 written +/–1E-28.
Date	8 bytes	1/1/100 to 12/31/9999.
GUID	16 bytes	_2,147,483,648 to 2,147,483,647.
Object	4 bytes	Any object reference.
String – variable length	10 bytes + string length	Variable length: ≤ about 2 billion.
String – fixed length	String length	Up to 65,400.
Variant – Number	16 bytes for numbers	Same as double.
Variant – String	22 bytes + string length	Same as string.
User-defined	Varies	Defined by user.

*The Decimal data type is included in this table although it cannot be used as a variable in a Dim statement. Rather, the Decimal data type can be a Variant subtype using the CDec () function.

Notice that the VBA data types are similar to the data types in an Access table. The major differences between Access data types and VBA data types are that there is no equivalent to the variant or object data types in Access data types, and the Access Number data type has a field size property that enables you to specify the field as Byte, Integer, Long, Single, Decimal, or Double. Access has one other number data type that VBA doesn't: GUID, which can be 16 bytes. It's used for ReplicationId. Properly specifying the field size this way saves memory and improves performance.

Number Data Types

When working with numeric data, you have a choice of seven different data types: Long, Double, Byte, Integer, Single, Currency, and Boolean. This section provides a brief introduction to data types and will provide the information you need to choose the proper data type for your purpose.

Each numeric data type provides a different level of accuracy, and they also use differing amounts of space. You can follow some general rules of thumb when choosing the right data type for your variable:

❑ When creating a variable to store whole numbers, choose the Long data type.

❑ When creating a variable to store fractional numbers, choose the Double data type.

❑ To store a negative value, use Integer, Single, Double, Long, Currency, or Decimal data type.

❑ If you need to store a value outside the range of −32768 to 32767, do not use the Integer data type because it can't handle numbers that large or small.

❑ To control loops, always use an Integer data type.

❑ The Boolean data type is often used in Yes/No or True/False scenarios. Any non-zero number evaluates to True (or Yes).

❑ ReplicationID is used only for replicated databases. Although Access 2007 supports replication using the MDB file format, the new ACCDB file format does not support replication.

There are a few key differences between the Single and Double data types. The Single data type allows you a precision level of 7 digits, whereas the Double data type gives you approximately 15 digits of precision. Both data types allow you to work with numbers larger than 2 billion.

You should never use Double or Single data types to represent fractional numbers. These cannot do so with extreme accuracy. (Although you may not notice the error for a while, those things tend to come back to haunt you at the most inopportune times.) Here's an example of using a Double data type with a fraction in a loop:

```
Sub TestFractionalDivision()
'Do not actually run this code!
'If need be, use Ctrl+Break to stop code execution
Dim dblResult As Double
dblResult = 1 / 5

    'Demonstrates that dblResult will never truly equal 1.
Do Until dblResult = 1

    'The following line is and alternative comparison
    'that will evaluate and stop execution.
    'To test this, comment out the previous Do statement and
    'Remove the comment mark from the following Do statement.

'Do Until dblResult >= 1


    'Do something interesting -
    'In this case, start with 1/5 and keep adding 1/5 to the result.
    dblResult = dblResult + 1 / 5
Loop
End Sub
```

The loop will run forever because the value of `dblResult` never actually equals 1. You'll have to use Ctrl+Break to end this code loop. That's why you're always better off using integers for looping operations.

An alternative is to use a comparison of greater than or equal to one (`>= 1`), as shown in the comment in the preceding example. This approach may result in an extra iteration, but it does stop.

The `Single` and `Double` data types are floating-point data types. So they can handle numbers with the decimal point in a variety of places. The `Currency` data type is a fixed-point number, meaning that there are always four decimal places in a currency number to handle most types of international currency (of course, you don't need to display four decimal places). Just because the `currency` data type is generally used for dealing with dollars and cents, it's not limited to financial transactions. You can use the currency data type for any number with up to four decimal places.

Because the decimal is always in the same place, VBA actually performs a little trick with currency calculations. It removes the decimal points, performs the calculation on the integer numbers, and then puts the decimal points back. This speeds up the calculation while retaining the four-decimal-place accuracy.

Boolean Data Type

In addition to typical numeric data types, you can use a variety of other data types. `Boolean` variables can take only two values, `True` and `False`. If you've ever used VBScript, you're probably familiar with using numeric values to represent true and false. When you refer to a `Boolean` data type in VBScript, 0 is false and –1 is true. You can still use these values with `Boolean` data types. VBA interprets 0 as false, but it is critical to remember that any non-zero value is always interpreted as true. The following two code examples, for instance, produce the same result:

```
Sub TestIsTrue()
Dim blnIsTrue As Boolean
blnIsTrue = True
If blnIsTrue = True Then
    MsgBox "True"
End If
End Sub
```

```
Sub TestIsTrue()
Dim blnIsTrue As Boolean
blnIsTrue = 2
If blnIsTrue = True Then
    MsgBox "True"
End If
End Sub
```

The Date Data Type

Remember the Y2K bug? Computers used to store dates with only two-digit years, which caused a problem when computers needed to start storing dates past the year 1999. After all, 01 could be a two-digit year code for 1901 or for 2001. Programmers scrambled for several years to fix the problem. So now computers store dates with a four-digit year. However, that wasn't the only problem with dates. Different countries represent dates in various formats. For example, the date 4/1/2007 could represent either April 1, 2007, or January 4, 2007, depending on the region of the world in which you live. To work around this challenge, VBA has a nifty way of dealing with dates. All dates are represented as a floating-point number (one with a flexible number of decimal places). When working with a date and time, the date portion is converted to an integer. The time is represented by the decimal portion of the number and is calculated as a percentage of a day. For example, noon would be half of a day and represented by 0.5. To determine the integer value for the date, an initial date is needed for calculations. Access uses December 30, 1899 as day 0, so April 1, 2007 would be represented as 39173, so it follows that 6:00 P.M. on that date is represented as 39173.75.

Rest assured that when you're working with dates in VBA, you do not have to perform conversions between 39173.75 and April 1, 2007, 6:00 P.M. VBA is aware of the regional settings specified in the user's Control Panel Regional Settings applet and converts the date to the proper format. So, if you're in Australia, VBA converts 39173.75 to 01/04/07. If you're in the United States, VBA displays 04/01/07 (or 04/01/2007 depending on your settings). VBA's use of calculated numbers for dates ensures that dates are always calculated correctly regardless of the specific regional settings used on the local computer. And, of course, you can further control how dates and times are displayed through code, as well as with a control's Format property.

Here's a brief example to illustrate how to work with VBA date calculations. As mentioned, a variable declared as a date has an initial value of December 30, 1899 (or 0 when converted to the floating-point decimal value). The following code produces a value of December 31, 1899.

```
Sub AddADay()
Dim dtInitialDate As Date
dtInitialDate = DateAdd("d", 1, dtInitialDate)
Debug.Print dtInitialDate
End Sub
```

You can work with dates directly in VBA by assigning the literal date value to a date variable. To do so, use # to delimit your date. For example, to assign a value of April 1, 2007, to the variable dtInitialDate, use the following code:

```
dtInitialDate = #04/01/2007#
```

That ensures that VBA will recognize the date properly no matter what your regional settings are. However, if you're in a region of the world that enters dates with d/m/yyyy, you'll need to enter the literal date in the format m/d/yyyy when using this method. Otherwise, VBA won't recognize it properly.

The String Data Type

The String data type is fairly straightforward. You use it for all types of alphanumeric data including names, sentences, or phrases. Numbers stored as a string data type respond to sorts and calculations as characters rather than numbers, as illustrated in the following code snippet:

```
Sub FunWithStrings()
Dim strBikes As String
Dim strCost As String
Dim intBikes As Integer
Dim curCost As Currency

strBikes = "5"
```

```
strCost = "100"

intBikes = 5

curCost = 100

Debug.Print strBikes + strCost

Debug.Print intBikes + curCost

End Sub
```

The first operation, `Debug.Print strBikes + strCost` produces a result of 5100. Because these are text values, the operation concatenates the two string variables. The second operation involves numeric data types, so `Debug.Print intBikes + curCost` actually performs the mathematical calculation and produces a result of 105. You'll immediately notice the impact when sorting a string of numbers.

When creating a string variable, the default value of the variable is a zero-length string. It isn't the same as a `Null` value; it's more like an empty value. You can assign pretty much any value to the string variable. The trickiest problem you're likely to encounter while using string variables in VBA is dealing with quotation marks within the content of the string. For example, the following is a valid way to assign a string value to a variable:

```
strCustomerName = "ABC Textiles"
```

The same syntax works if you need to store a value with a single quote in the name, such as the following:

```
strCustomerName = "Johnny's Cycles"
```

What if you need to store a value with a double-quoted character in the name? If you follow the same rules as the previous two examples, you end up with something like the following:

```
strCustomerName = "The "W" Hotel, New York City"
```

It might look like a valid line of code, but when you actually type that into your code, you'll get a compile error before you run the code. The problem is that VBA sees the second double quote and thinks you want to end the string. VBA doesn't quite know what to do with the text that follows that quote. To work around the issue, you use a double set of double quotes within your string, basically quoting the quote, so that your actual assignment statement looks like the following:

```
strCustomerName = "The ""W"" Hotel, New York City"
```

If you enter all strings with double quotes using that method, you'll get predictable results every time.

String Comparisons

You can't have a discussion about string variables without discussing how to work with strings. Keeping in mind that strings are typically text or alpha-numeric, some of the most common tasks you'll perform with strings include comparing two strings, finding matches to a partial string, or determining the length of a string. The next few paragraphs describe some of the tricks you can use to work with string variables.

When comparing two strings, you'll find that VBA is not case sensitive by default. In other words, California and CALIFORNIA are considered to be the same string. You can change this default behavior by editing the first line of your VBA code. When opening a module in VBA, the first line is Option Compare Database. Changing this line to Option Compare Binary has one immediate effect: All string comparisons are now case sensitive. The following table provides a summary of the three options you can select for the Option Compare statement in VBA. Keep in mind that these statements are module specific, so they only affect the module that they are in.

Compare Statement	Definition
Option Compare Database	String comparisons are case insensitive. Local settings of the current database are used.
Option Compare Binary	String comparisons are case sensitive. Local settings of the current database are ignored.
Option Compare Text	String comparisons are case insensitive. Local settings specified in Control Panel are used. This setting is seldom used.

Unless you have good reason to change the Option Compare statement, leave it at the default value of Option Compare Database. (You'll probably find that the default value is used in more than 99 percent of the modules.)

You don't always have to compare entire strings to each other. You can search for strings based on one or more characters in the string. For example, the following code illustrates a couple of types of string comparisons.

```
Sub CompareStrings()
Dim strString1 As String
strString1 = "Microsoft"

If strString1 Like "Micr*" Then
    Debug.Print "True"
End If

If strString1 Like "Mic*t" Then
    Debug.Print "True"
End If

End Sub
```

Both of these comparison operations return True. The first returns True whenever the first four letters of strString1 are Micr. The second comparison returns True whenever the first three letters of strString1 are Mic and the last letter is t.

The following table lists the key wildcards used for string comparisons.

Character	Description
? or _ (underscore)	Single character
* or %	Any number characters
#	One digit, 0–9
[]	One character from the enclosed list
[!]	One character *not* in the enclosed list

Keep in mind that characters are alpha, numeric, and special. The following table shows the variety of comparison operations that you can use in VBA.

Comparison Expression	Strings That Match	Strings That Do Not Match
Like "Mi*"	Microsoft, Michigan	MapPoint, Monochrome
Like "sol*d"	sold, solid	solids
Like "s?t"	sit, sat	seat
Like "177#"	1776, 1777, 1778, and so on	1977, 177, 1077
Like "s[ea]t"	set, sat	sit, seat
Like "s[!ea]t"	sit	set, sat
Like "s[aeio][aeio]t"	seat, soot	set, sat

As you can see from the table, the rules are fairly straightforward. The last three examples are the most confusing. Using two characters (or more) within the brackets tells VBA that any of the characters within the brackets can be used within the string; that means that a match can contain any one of the characters. Putting the exclamation point inside the brackets and before the characters tells VBA that any character except those within the brackets can be used to compare the string. Using two sets of bracketed characters tells VBA to match two characters—one from each set. You can also enclose a range in the brackets—for example, 3–6 would indicate the numbers 3, 4, 5, and 6.

Variants

The Variant data type is probably the most flexible data type within VBA. Unlike other variable types, which can only hold one type of data, the variant data type can hold many different types of data. You can use it to hold text, numbers, dates, and user-defined types. The only type of data a variant data type cannot hold is a fixed-length string. As previously explained, there is a price to be paid for such flexibility. As tempting as it might seem to use variant data types for all of your coding, the practice results in much higher memory use and means a performance hit compared to using the proper data type. For example, using a variant to hold a string of data requires 11 extra bytes of data for every string you store. Over the course of an entire application, these extra bytes can have a significant performance impact.

There are times, however, when you need to use a variant data type. For example, if you're not sure what type of information a variable needs to hold, it is likely best to use the variant data type. Most often, this type of unknown or unpredictable data configuration occurs when users are entering data in a relatively unstructured manner, such as on Web forms. If you're not sure whether users will enter a date, a number, or a string, you can create a `variant` data type and store the input in that variable. Another place to use a variant is for the variable of a function return. Look at this code segment:

```
MyField = DLookup("Lastname", "Employees", "[Lastname] = 'Doe'")
```

Even though you know the answer will be a string, if `Doe` does not exist, DLookup will return a `Null` and an error will be generated if `MyField` is declared as a string. Of course, there are other ways to handle `Nulls`, but this will work and it provided such a good segue.

Nulls

We should discuss another important concept when talking about variables, and that is `Null`. When you first learn programming, you learn that `Null` is the value of a field with no data. If you create a field in a table and don't fill it with any data, the value of the field is `Null`. So what is `Null`? `Null` is nothing, but `Null` is also something. It sounds a bit confusing, because it is. Here's an example to help demonstrate just how mind-boggling `Null` can be.

```
Sub CompareNulls()
Dim varValue1 As Variant
Dim varValue2 As Variant

varValue1 = Null
varValue2 = Null

If varValue1 = varValue2 Then
    Debug.Print "Nulls are equal"
End If
End Sub
```

If you run this code, you'll see that the phrase never prints in the Immediate window. But how can that be? You just set the two variables equal to the same value. Well, you might think you set them to the same value, but really, two `Nulls` never equal each other.

There are two rules to remember when working with `Null`. First, you cannot assign `Null` to anything other than a Variant data type. So, you can never have a `Null` string; instead you have a zero-length string. You cannot have a `Null` single or double (numeric data type); instead you have a variable with value 0. The second rule of `Null` is, as previously demonstrated, that no two `Nulls` match. `Null` doesn't match zero; it doesn't match a zero-length string; it doesn't even match itself. The only comparison operation you can run on `Null` is to determine whether it is `Null`. But, as mentioned previously, `Null` never equals `Null`. If you're thinking, *great*, now what can I do?, you'll be relieved to learn that there are relatively straightforward processes to test for and work with `Null`. And, by slightly modifying the previous code sample, you get a completely different result and the print phrase will appear in the Immediate window, as shown in the following example:

```
Sub CompareNulls2()
Dim varValue1 As Variant
```

```
Dim varValue2 As Variant

varValue1 = Null
varValue2 = Null

If IsNull(varValue1) And IsNull(varValue2) Then
    Debug.Print "Both variables are Null"
End If
End Sub
```

This code sample prints the phrase in the Immediate window. By independently testing each variable for `Null`, you can compare the results. You test for the `Null` condition by using the `IsNull` function, which evaluates to `True` if the value of the variable is `Null` and to `False` if the value of the variable is not `Null`.

Just remember the two basic rules of `Null`. `Null` doesn't equal anything and `Null` equals nothing.

`Null`s also react differently when used in mathematical formulas instead of string operations. To quickly test what happens, enter these simple lines with the question marks in the Immediate window. For illustration purposes, the results are included after each example. Remember that `"5"` is a string.

```
?5 + Null       ' number with a math formula
Null
?"5" + Null     ' string with a math formula
Null
?5 & Null       ' number with a string concatenation
5
?"5" & Null     ' string with a string concatenation
5
```

As you can see, in the math formula using addition (+), `Null` is the result. However, in the string concatenation operation (&), `Null` drops off, which is kind of like adding a zero. Keeping this in mind can be useful when working with strings. Consider the following code that concatenates fields for first, middle, and last names plus tag line, and adds spaces and punctuation:

```
Public Function Which2Use()
Dim strMI As Variant      'Declared as a variant so that you can use a Null value.

    strMI = Null
    Debug.Print "John" & " " & strMI & ". " & "Doe - Null with & (string operator)"
    Debug.Print "John" & " " & strMI + ". " & "Doe - Null with + (math equation)"

    Debug.Print

    strMI = "P"
    Debug.Print "John" & " " & strMI & ". " & "Doe - P with & (string operator)"
    Debug.Print "John" & " " & strMI + ". " & "Doe - P with + (math equation)"

End Function
```

The results are:

```
John . Doe          ' Null with & (string operator)
John Doe            ' Null with + (math equation)

John P. Doe         ' P with & (string operator)
John P. Doe         ' Null with +  P with + (math equation)
```

The first example with `Null` uses a string operator to concatenate the values, so the period and extra spaces print. The second line uses the numeric plus function; `Null` added to a period and space returns `Null`, so the period and space are removed.

In the second set of examples, `Null` is not a factor, so adding and concatenating text yield the same result.

User-Defined Data Type

VBA provides a way to group different data types under one heading. This creates an object with a set of properties. You define the group with the word `Type` on a Module level and by default it is `Public`. You can use the `Private` keyword if you want to restrict it to the module only. Here's an example:

```
Option Compare Database
Option Explicit

Public Type WeatherElements
    Type As String
    Temp As Single
    Protect As Boolean
End Type

Public Function Action()
Dim Yesterday As WeatherElements
Dim Today As WeatherElements

    Today.Type = "Sunny"
    Today.Temp = 64.3
    Today.Protect = False

    Yesterday.Type = "Snow"
    Yesterday.Temp = 31.2
    Yesterday.Protect = True

    Debug.Print "The weather took a turn for the better!"
    Debug.Print "Readings:  Yesterday    Today"
    Debug.Print "Weather:    " & Yesterday.Type & "            " & Today.Type
    Debug.Print "Temperture: " & Yesterday.Temp & "            " & Today.Temp
    Debug.Print "Protection: " & Yesterday.Protect & "           " & Today.Protect

End Function
```

As you can see, several elements (data types) are grouped under the object `WeatherElements` and a new data type is assigned to two different variables. By using the variable name followed by the dot and then the element name, you get the value of that element. When you run the preceding code sample, this is what you should see in the Immediate window.

```
The weather took a turn for the better!
Readings:   Yesterday   Today
Weather:    Snow        Sunny
Temperature: 31.2        64.3
Protection: True         False
```

Using Variables

If you're using a large number of variables in your application, it's easy to forget that the last line of code you just entered contained a new variable. Fortunately, VBA has an option that requires you to declare all of your variables before you use them—it causes VBA to produce an error for every undeclared variable. You'll see what it is in just a minute. Keep in mind that VBA's gentle reminder (error message) occurs when you run your code, not when you are writing it.

As mentioned earlier, it is good programming practice to declare all of your variables. This practice ensures that your variables have the proper types and can speed code execution. Additionally, if you don't declare your variables, they can actually get you into trouble. The following code sample illustrates this:

```
Sub BuyNewBike()
Dim curBikePrice as Integer

curBikePrice = InputBox("Please enter bike price.", "Enter Bike Price")

If curVikePrice > 100 Then

    MsgBox "Don't Buy the Bike! It's too expensive!", _
        vbCritical, "Bike Purchase"Else
Else

    MsgBox "You can buy the bike. It's within your budget.", _
        vbOKOnly, "Bike Purchase"
End If

End Sub
```

This code sample looks simple enough. You enter the price of the bike in the Input box that appears on the screen when you run this code. If the price of the bike is greater than $100, the program tells you not to buy the bike. If the price is less than $100, you can buy the bike.

However, the code won't actually work. Examine it carefully and you'll see that the variable that accepts the price of the bike, `curBikePrice`, isn't the same as the variable used in the `If...Then` statement, `curVikePrice`. A mistake like that is quite easy to make. You're typing along and you hit the wrong key. You probably wouldn't even notice it until you run the code and nothing happens. As it's written, there's actually nothing wrong with the code. It won't produce any errors; it just won't produce the required results.

There is one easy way to prevent this type of mistake, and that's the VBA option mentioned earlier. Just add a single line of code to the General Declarations section of your code: `Option Explicit`. These two words tell VBA that all variables used in your module must be declared before they can be used. If you force variable declaration, then typing the wrong name for a variable causes VBA to display an error when the code is compiled, as shown in Figure 5-1.

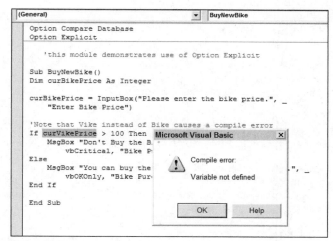

Figure 5-1

Once the error message is displayed, VBA highlights the undeclared variable(s), so that you can quickly see and correct the errors. For this situation, it is to either correct the spelling of the variable to match the declared variable or to add a new line of code to declare the variable used in your code.

Always use `Option Explicit` in your modules. You can configure Access to do this for you. From anywhere in the Access VBA Editor, select Tools ➪ Options. Choose the Editor tab and check the box marked Require Variable Declaration. Click OK to save your changes. Now, whenever you create a new module or build code behind any Access form or report, you'll be prompted to declare your variables. The Editor only adds `Option Explicit` as new modules are created, so you will need to insert that phrase at the top of each existing module.

Declaring Variables

You declare a variable by use of the `Dim` (short for dimension) keyword, and then the variable name, followed by the word `As`, and then the variable type. For example, the following statement declares the state variable in your procedure:

```
Dim strState As String
```

Once you dimension your variable, you can assign it a value anywhere in your procedure. For string variables such as `strState`, use the following statement to assign the value `"Washington"`:

```
strState = "Washington"
```

Now that your variable has a value, you can use it repeatedly within your procedure. Consider the following code segment:

```
Private Sub OpenDatabaseConnection()

Dim objConn As ADODB.Connection
Dim objRST As ADODB.Recordset
Dim strSQL As String
Dim strConn As String
Dim strState As String

'Create the ADODB Connection and Recordset Objects
Set objConn = CreateObject("ADODB.Connection")
Set objRST = CreateObject("ADODB.Recordset")

'Open your ADODB Connection
strConn = "Provider=Microsoft.ACE.OLEDB.12.0;Data Source=c:\Cust.mdb;"
strSQL = "Select * from tblCust WHERE CustState = '" & "Washington" & "';"

objConn.Open (strConn)
objConn.Mode = adModeRead
objRST.Open strSQL, objConn, adOpenForwardOnly, adLockOptimistic
objRST.MoveFirst

'Print relevant customer information

While Not objRST.EOF
    Debug.Print objRST.Fields("CustName")
    Debug.Print objRST.Fields("CustState")
    Debug.Print objRST.Fields("CustCountry")
    objRST.MoveNext
Wend          'while end - closed the while loop

objRST.Close
objConn.Close
    'Release your variables
Set objRST = Nothing
Set objConn = Nothing

End Sub
```

This code opens an ActiveX Data Objects (ADO) connection to an Access database. It then opens a recordset of all customers in Washington and prints their names, state, and country in the Immediate window. This is pretty simple code. You're referencing the state in only one place, so you really do not need to create a variable to hold the state name. If you know without a doubt that you'll never need to change your code and you won't need the same value later in your code, you could just use the actual value. However, consider the situation where users are allowed to input their own state name. If you've hard-coded the state name into the procedure, you have no way to switch states when the user needs to do so. You could adapt the previous code through the use of a variable and input box to allow users to select the state they need. Here's how that code might look:

```
Private Sub OpenDatabaseConnection()

Dim objConn As ADODB.Connection
Dim objRST As ADODB.Recordset
Dim strSQL As String
Dim strConn As String
Dim strState As String

'Create the ADODB Connection and Recordset Objects
Set objConn = CreateObject("ADODB.Connection")
Set objRST = CreateObject("ADODB.Recordset")

'Open your ADODB Connection
strConn = "Provider=Microsoft.ACE.OLEDB.12.0;Data Source=c:\Cust.mdb;"
strState = InputBox("Please enter a state", "Enter State")
strSQL = "Select * from tblCust WHERE CustState = '" & strState & "';"

objConn.Open (strConn)
objConn.Mode = adModeRead
objRST.Open strSQL, objConn, adOpenForwardOnly, adLockOptimistic
objRST.MoveFirst

'Print relevant customer information

While Not objRST.EOF
    Debug.Print objRST.Fields("CustName")
    Debug.Print objRST.Fields("CustState")
    Debug.Print objRST.Fields("CustCountry")
    objRST.MoveNext
Wend

objRST.Close
objConn.Close
    'Release your variables
Set objRST = Nothing
Set objConn = Nothing

End Sub
```

Using the preceding code, users can enter any state in response to the input box and your code will run and return the appropriate records.

There is still a key element missing from this procedure—error handling. As you know, or will soon discover, in addition to trapping for events triggered by code, error handling can help control what users are able to do and how data is handled. For example, if users enter Sacramento as a state, misspell Mississippi, or simply choose a state for which no records exist in your database, the preceding code will generate an error. Chapter 9 focuses on error handling.

Naming Your Variables

There are a few rules to follow when naming a variable:

❏   Use only letters, numbers, and the underscore symbol (_). No other symbols are allowed.

❏ Variable names must start with a letter.

❏ Do not use a reserved word for your variable name.

❏ Variable names must be less than 255 characters.

Special characters and reserved words are discussed in Appendix K.

In addition to the rules you must follow when naming your variables, it's customary to follow some sort of naming convention when creating your variables. While you may choose any convention, the most popular is the Reddick naming convention. Appendix L provides detailed information about this naming convention, and guidelines for creating your own naming conventions. Although developers have the latitude to implement a recognized convention, to modify a convention to fit their style, or even to ignore conventions, it's strongly recommended that you at least create meaningful variable names. Meaningful names not only make it easier to read through the code, but they minimize conflicts and facilitate debugging. If you create variables with names such as var1, var2, and var3, you'll have a hard time keeping track of which variable you need to use for which statement.

This book sticks pretty closely to Reddick's naming conventions. So variables usually contain a prefix that determines their data type. A string variable, for example, will ususally have the str *prefix, such as* strSQL *and* strMsg, *whereas a Boolean variable will have a* bln *prefix, such as* blnUnderBudget *and* blnCurrentMeeting.

In addition to Reddick's naming conventions, some developers like to use an additional convention to make their code easier to interpret: adding a prefix to variable names to denote whether the variable is a global, private, or local variable. The following table describes the prefixes used to denote variable scope and lifetime.

Prefix	Variable Scope	Examples	Usage
g	Global variable	gobj; gcurPrice	Variables declared with the Public keyword
m	Private (module-level) variables	mSalesTotal	Variables declared with the Private keyword
s	Static variables	sintWhileCount	Local variables declared with the Static keyword

Variable Scope and Lifetime

The *scope* of a variable defines where in the program the variable is recognized. The *lifetime* of a variable describes how long it will persist.

If you declare your variable within a sub or function, the variable's scope is limited to that sub or function only. That's why you don't need to worry about variables conflicting with each other if you use the same name for a variable in another sub or function. The lifetime of that variable is the same as the sub or function—the variable lives only while the sub or function is running. As soon as the procedure ends, the variable is destroyed and the memory used by the variable is released. A subsequent call of the procedure creates the variable again and it has no memory of the previous existence.

At times you want your variable to exist outside of a particular sub or function. If you declare the variable in the General Declarations section of the module (located at the top of the module), your variable can have a longer scope and lifetime. You can declare the variable in two ways:

❑   Use the `Private` keyword to make the variable available to any and all procedures within the current module.

❑   Use the `Public` keyword to make the variable available anywhere in the entire application.

The following code sample illustrates how both the declaration and its location affect a variable's scope and lifetime:

```
Option Explicit 'Used to require variable declaration

Public txtCustomerName as String 'Scope is entire application
Private txtVendor as String 'Scope is any procedure in this module
Dim txtSupplier as String 'Scope is the current module

Private Sub GetCustomerName()
Dim txtCustomer as String 'Scope is limited to this sub
End Sub
```

You might be wondering why the two statements that begin with `Dim` have different scopes. Use of the `Dim` keyword in the General Declarations section sets the scope of the variable to the module so it can be used by any procedure in that module. In the previous listing, `txtVendor` and `txtSupplier` are both module-level variables. They can be used anywhere within the module and anytime the module is loaded. `txtCustomerName` is a global variable. It can be used anywhere within any procedure in the application.

Use of the `Static` keyword enables you to create a local variable with an ongoing lifetime. There are several reasons why you might want to do this. If you needed to know how many times a particular procedure was run, you could simply declare a global variable and increment this variable every time the procedure runs. However, it's often easier to track the use of variables when they are declared within the procedure in which they're used. There's one big difference between using the `Static` keyword within the procedure and using the `Public` keyword in the General Declarations section to declare your variables. If you declare the variable with the `Public` keyword in the General Declarations section, you can use the variable anywhere within your application. If you use the `Static` keyword within a procedure, you can only use the variable within that procedure. The key thing is that the variable isn't destroyed when the procedure completes. The variable remains and retains its value for the next time that procedure is called. Keep in mind that the variable is still dedicated to the one procedure, so you cannot use the `Static` keyword to create a variable within Procedure A and use it within Procedure B.

Overlapping Variables

When writing code, be careful to use a variable name only once. If you declare a global variable of `strString` and then declare a variable within your procedure named `strString`, VBA will always use the procedure-level variable. If you are using procedures to call routines in other procedures, you may forget that one has a variable with the same name as a global variable, and that can create unexpected results. Here's an example:

```
Option Compare Database
Option Explicit
    'this module demonstrates that local variables
    'take precedence over global variables.
Public intQuantity As Integer
Public curPrice As Currency



Private Sub FindTotals()
Dim intQuantity As Integer
Dim curTotalPrice As Currency
    'this sub declares the local variable intQuantity
    'but does not give it a value, so the value is 0.

  curPrice = InputBox("Please enter the bike price.",_
  "Enter Bike Price")
  curTotalPrice = intQuantity * curPrice
  MsgBox curTotalPrice, vbOKOnly, "Total Price"

End Sub



Private Sub EnterValues()
    'this is storing the value into the global variable.
  intQuantity = InputBox("Please enter the number of bikes", _
    "you want to buy.", "Total Bikes")
End Sub



Private Sub CalculatePrice()
    'This sub runs the two subs listed below.
    'Although Enter Values stores a quantity in the
    'global Variable, intQuantity, the FindTotals sub will
    'use the local variable intQuantity to calculate curTotalPrice.
  EnterValues
  FindTotals

End Sub
```

These three procedures illustrate how variables can overlap. If you run the CalculatePrice procedure, Access VBA will run the other two procedures, EnterValues and FindTotals. When that code is run, the EnterValues procedure asks you for the total number of bikes you want to buy. This stores the value into the global variable, intQuantity. The FindTotals procedure asks you for the bike price and calculates the total purchase price (quantity of bikes multiplied by the purchase price). However, there's one problem here. The line in the FindTotals procedure—Dim intQuantity as Integer—causes the calculation to return zero. This one line tells Access VBA to create a local procedure-level variable with the same name as the public variable declared in the General Declarations section of the module. Because there is no input for this local variable, it uses the default value of 0. The procedure uses the local variable instead of the global any time `intQuantity`. So the equation `curTotalPrice` yields 0 as its result.

If you want Access VBA to use the global variable, you can add the module's name before the variable name. The following code works as intended:

```
Option Compare Database
Option Explicit
    'this module demonstrates that by explicitly naming a variable
    'with both the module and variable name, value of the global
    'global variable will be used.  mintQuantity would also work.

Public intQuantity As Integer
Public curPrice As Currency

_____


Private Sub FindTotals()
Dim intQuantity As Integer
Dim curTotalPrice As Currency
    'This sub declares the local variable intQuantity
    'but does not give it a value, so the value is 0.
    'replace [ModuleName] with the name of the current module.

  curPrice = InputBox("Please enter the bike price.",_
  "Enter Bike Price")
  curTotalPrice = [ModuleName].intQuantity * curPrice
  MsgBox curTotalPrice, vbOKOnly, "Total Price"

End Sub

_____


Private Sub EnterValues()
  'this is storing the value into the global variable.
  intQuantity = InputBox("Please enter the number of bikes", _
    "you want to buy.", "Total Bikes")
End Sub

_____


Private Sub CalculatePrice()
    'This sub runs the two subs listed below.
    'Although Enter Values stores a quantity in the
    'global Variable, intQuantity, the FindTotals sub will
    'use the local variable intQuantity to calculate curTotalPrice.
  EnterValues
  FindTotals

End Sub
```

Adding the name of the module in front of the variable name is an easy way to tell Access VBA exactly which variable you need. You'll also recall that some developers like to use a prefix to specify the variable scope. Using `mintQuantity` in the General Declarations section would have prevented the overlap. It's best, however, to avoid this situation entirely. Utilize naming conventions and declare your variables with as narrow a scope as you need. If you don't need to declare a public variable, it is better to use a procedure-level variable. For your convenience, these two modules are included in the download code for this chapter.

Other VBA Structures

You'll often use a few other VBA components within your code: comments, constants, and to a lesser extent, enums. This section provides a brief introduction to each and shows you how these components can be helpful within your code.

Comments

VBA programming consists of writing statements and comments. Although comments are not explicitly required, they make it much easier to read the code and figure out what it is intended to do. As you've probably noticed, uncommented code is hard to read and difficult to understand. Comments are especially helpful to someone else who may end up working with your code; of course, if it's been a while since you've worked on a particular project, you'll find that those comments can get you back up to speed quickly.

When working with the VBA Editor in Access, you can add comments by prefacing text with an apostrophe. The default setting is that comments appear in green, so they are quickly recognized when scanning through code. Although you can insert comments at the end of a line of code, they are more commonly used before or after a procedure or function. Comments are ignored during code execution. You can have one or many lines of comments in a procedure, and VBA will ignore them all. Comments don't slow down the execution of your code; so you can use them liberally. At a minimum, your comments should list what the procedure is for and when it was written. Figure 5-2 shows a typical procedure with detailed comments—albeit these comments are primarily for training purposes.

You might be wondering why you need to add comments to code you're writing for your own applications. Well, any time you write code, there's a chance that it will be used for more than one application. It's also possible that someone else will eventually inherit your code. If you choose to take a new job elsewhere, the replacement programmer your company hires might need to make changes to your code. If you haven't added any comments to your code, he'll have a hard time understanding your procedures. If you've ever had to examine another programmer's code and found it without comments, you understand the importance of comments.

Comments help you understand why you might have used a particular piece of code. For example, if you hard coded certain values within your application, you might wonder why you chose to use those particular values. Comments can also provide invaluable notes during development and testing. You can include notes about business rules and when to use one process instead of another. During testing, comments are reminders about a problem created or solved by specific lines of code.

```
(General)                                          ▼   CalculatePrice
   Option Compare Database
   Option Explicit
      'this module demonstrates that by explicitly naming a variable
      'with both the module and variable name, value of the global
      'global variable will be used.  mintQuantity would also work.

   Public intQuantity As Integer
   Public curPrice As Currency

   Private Sub FindTotals()
   Dim intQuantity As Integer
   Dim curTotalPrice As Currency
      'This sub declares the local variable intQuantity
      'but does not give it a value, so the value is 0.
      'replace [PurchaseBikeNamedVariable] with the name of the current module.

      curPrice = InputBox("Please enter the bike price.", _
         "Enter Bike Price")
      curTotalPrice = PurchaseBikeNamedVariable.intQuantity * curPrice
      MsgBox curTotalPrice, vbOKOnly, "Total Price"

   End Sub

   Private Sub EnterValues()
      'this is storing the value into the global variable.
      intQuantity = InputBox("Please enter the number of bikes", _
         "you want to buy.", "Total Bikes")
   End Sub

   Private Sub CalculatePrice()
      'This sub runs the two subs listed below.
      'Although Enter Values stores a quantity in the
      'global Variable, intQuantity, the FindTotals sub will
      'use the local variable intQuantity to calculate curTotalPrice.
      EnterValues
      FindTotals

   End Sub
```

Figure 5-2

Line Continuation

Strategic line breaks also help make code easier to read and understand. Many VBA statements are quite long. Take the following If...Then statement used to fill a variable with a value:

```
If (txtCustomerState = "CA" And txtCustomerZip = "95685") Or
   (txtCustomerState = "WA" And txtCustomerZip = "89231") Then
   txtCustomerRegion = "Western US"
End If
```

As you can see, this code is a bit long. When printed in this book, even the conditional portion of the statement takes up several lines. When you write this code in VBA, all of the code will go on one very long line. Obviously, the line won't all display on the screen, as shown in Figure 5-3. This can make procedures difficult to read, as you need to not only scroll up and down to view the entire procedure but scroll left and right, as well.

A line continuation character (an underscore preceded by a space) is used to break long lines of code into understandable, easy-to-read segments. Although you are inserting characters, they are for visual appearance and do not change the meaning of the code. The space/underscore at the end of a code line indicates that the next line is a continuation of the current line as in the following code snippet, as shown in the second example in Figure 5-3. The benefit of using line breaks is evident.

```
If (txtCustomerState = "CA" And txtCustomerZip = "95685") Or _
    (txtCustomerState = "WA" And txtCustomerZip = "89231") Then
    txtCustomerRegion = "Western US"
End If
```

```
'Chapter 5 Line Continuation Sample with an If THEN statement

'BEFORE - Code below is written without Line Continuation
'Notice that the text only wraps after the word Then.

If (txtCustomerState = "CA" And txtCustomerZip = "95685") Or (txtCustome:
txtCustomerRegion = "Western US"
End If

'AFTER - The same example with line breaks created by adding a space
'and underscore 'at the end of the line. The breaks not only keep the
'code within the viewing pane, but they also follow natural grouping.
'Again, the underscore is not required after the word Then.

If (txtCustomerState = "CA" And txtCustomerZip = "95685") Or _
    (txtCustomerState = "WA" And txtCustomerZip = "89231") Then
    txtCustomerRegion = "Western US"
End If
```

Figure 5-3

Strategic line breaks not only keep the code within the viewing pane, but they also help developers recognize individual steps within a procedure. There's one limitation to the line continuation character, however; you can't use it "as is" within literal strings. If you're using the line continuation character in a string, you must use the & symbol on the continued line and add extra quotation marks—one before the space/underscore at the end of the line and one after &/space at the start of the next line. Figure 5-4 illustrates the following examples. When opening a recordset with an SQL statement, you could end up with a very long SQL statement to include all of the fields you need within your table. The statement might read something like the following:

```
strSQL = "SELECT [CustomerName], [CustomerCode], [CustomerAddress1],
[CustomerCity], [CustomerState], [CustomerZip] FROM Customers WHERE [CustomerState]
Is Not Null;"
```

You can use the line continuation character along with the & symbol to turn that code into the following:

```
strSQL = "SELECT [CustomerName], [CustomerCode], [CustomerAddress1]" _
& ", [CustomerCity], [CustomerState], [CustomerZip] FROM" _
& " Customers WHERE [CustomerState] Is Not Null;"
```

```
'Line Continuation Sample for a SQL statement
'BEFORE - Code below is written without Line Continuation
strSQL = "SELECT [CustomerName], [CustomerCode], [CustomerAddress1], [CustomerCity],

'AFTER - Using Line Continuation makes code easier to read.
' There is a " at the end and beginning of each line of the code.
'Only the part within the quotes is concatentated into the string of code.
'Notice the space after the comma at the beginning of the second line
'and after the " at the beginning of the third line.

strSQL = "SELECT [CustomerName], [CustomerCode], [CustomerAddress1]" _
& ", [CustomerCity], [CustomerState], [CustomerZip] FROM" _
& " Customers WHERE [CustomerState]  Is Not Null;"
```

Figure 5-4

Use line continuation characters any time you have code lines longer than your screen width. Keep in mind that you need to include the space that is used to separate words. It can be placed after the last character at the end of the line but before the underscore, or between the quotation mark and the first character at the beginning of the next line. Without the appropriate spaces, words can run together. So the preceding example, might end up with " ... [CustomerZip] FROMCustomers WHERE..."

Constants

In general, a constant is just what it says, something that doesn't change. It can be a string or numeric value. Constants can be grouped as literal, symbolic, and built-in.

Literal constants are numbers, strings, and dates that are hard-coded in the procedure. They may be used for clarity, by adding a definition (name) to a number that will be used. The following line of code shows how a literal constant makes it easy to recognize that October 23, 2007 is the start date for something.

```
Public dtStartDate as Date = #10/23/2007#
```

A symbolic constant is much like a variable. It is used for fixed values that won't change in your code. They are usually declared at the beginning of your procedure by using the Const keyword instead of the Dim keyword. Specifying a constant for the width of a page is an example of a symbolic constant. Often, the constant name is typed in all capital letters, as in this example:

```
Const PAGE_WIDTH = 80
```

As you're reading and working through the examples, consider developing your own list of conventions to add structure and consistency to the format and layout of your code.

You can declare literal and symbolic constants in several ways, such as in the General Declarations section or within a procedure and declaring it as Public or Private to stipulate the scope. Constants follow many of the same rules that variables do, plus a couple more of their own. They must have a unique name, and not just within the ones you create. You cannot create a constant with the same name as a built-in constant. And once you have created a constant, you cannot change it or its value.

Built-in constants are defined within VBA, either by a program or by the system. They help you code by enabling you to learn the constant name rather than the number associated with the constant's value. For example, VBA provides constants for such uses as defining the types of buttons you see on a message box. Rather than use the number that corresponds to the Yes or No button option in a message box, you can use the constant vbYesNo. Because the constant has a somewhat intuitive name, it is relatively easy to remember. You call a built-in constant by simply using its name. All built-in constants in VBA begin with the letters vb. There are approximately 700 built-in constants in VBA. Thankfully, you don't need to learn about all 700. In fact, you will likely use only a small percentage on a regular basis.

The following table describes some of VBA's built-in constants. As you can see, there are constants for all sorts of VBA operations. If you're curious about the entire list of VBA constants, you can view them in the Object Browser. To open the Object Browser from the VBA window, you can simply use the shortcut key F2 or you can select View ➪ Object Browser.

Constant Name	Value	Purpose
vbFirstFourDays	2	Configures the first week of the year to be the first week with at least four days.
vbFirstFullWeek	3	Configures the first week of the year to be the first full (7-day) week.
vbOkOnly	0	Describes a type of message box with only an OK button.
vbYesNoCancel	3	Describes a type of message box with three buttons: Yes, No, and Cancel.
vbMonday	2	Constant used to specify Monday as the day of the week.
vbWednesday	4	Constant used to specify Wednesday as the day of the week.
vbHidden	2	Used to describe the hidden attribute of a file.

Each object library that is referenced within your code contains its own set of built-in constants. For example, in Microsoft Access there are seven built-in constants to specify a type of form view: acViewDesign, acViewLayout, acViewNormal, acViewPivotChart, acViewPivotTable, acViewPreview, and acViewReport. Using the built-in constants in your code is a lot easier than remembering that you need to specify the number 1 to open a form in design mode. Each object library has its own prefix. All built-in constants in Access use the prefix ac; in Outlook the prefix is ol; and in Word constants begin with wd.

You're probably wondering how to find out if there are constants that you could use in your code. Well, one way is to just start invoking properties, methods, and events. One of the great advantages of VBA is that once you start typing, VBA helps you along by providing IntelliSense, at least for many objects and commands and providing that you use the dot (.), not the bang (!).

When you start typing the message box function, VBA prompts you to choose the proper constant for the type of buttons you need. Figure 5-5 illustrates how IntelliSense provides syntax prompts, as it does with the message box.

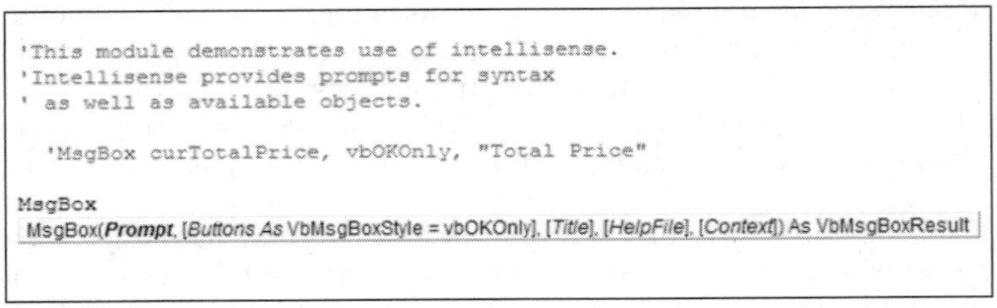

```
'This module demonstrates use of intellisense.
'Intellisense provides prompts for syntax
' as well as available objects.

  'MsgBox curTotalPrice, vbOKOnly, "Total Price"

MsgBox
MsgBox(Prompt, [Buttons As VbMsgBoxStyle = vbOKOnly], [Title], [HelpFile], [Context]) As VbMsgBoxResult
```

Figure 5-5

When working with commands and objects, IntelliSense prompts with available commands, objects, arguments, and syntax. So, when you type the period (dot) after DoCmd—DoCmd.—a drop-down list displays available actions and the list is updated based on the letters that you type. Similarly, if you type forms., you get prompts specific to the forms collection; if you type form., you can scroll through and click to select the correct item from the list of events and properties for a form (see Figure 5-6).

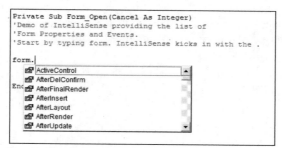

Figure 5-6

Using the spacebar moves the cursor to the next prompt; pressing Enter ends the IntelliSense session and moves the cursor to a new blank line.

Enums

Both Access and VBA contain another structure called an *enum*. Short for enumeration, this structure is essentially a wrapper for a group of built-in constants. It is more of a way to categorize constants than to do anything with them. You won't actually use the enum to do anything; rather, you'll use the constants declared in the enum instead of using their intrinsic values. As you can imagine, Access has a numerous built-in enums. The following enum describes the constants that can be used to specify the view of a form.

```
Enum acFormView
    acNormal = 0
    acDesign = 1
    acPreview = 2
    acFormDS = 3
    acFormPivotTable = 4
    acFormPivotChart = 5
    acFormLayout = 6
End Enum
```

You can browse any of the Access or VBA enums in the Object Browser, which you learned about in Chapter 4.

Summary

In this chapter, you reviewed the basics of VBA and reinforced some of the items covered in Chapter 4. So now you have the basic tools and are ready to start writing code. As you proceed through the book, you'll learn about DAO and ADO, about leveraging the powerful tools that Access provides for customizing forms and reports, and about interfacing with other programs and applications.

Remember that this is a multipurpose reference book. It's a great tool for becoming familiar with fundamental concepts, as well as for learning about advanced techniques.

6

Using DAO to Access Data

As you've seen in previous chapters, VBA is the programming language you use to programmatically interact with the Access object model. You use VBA to manipulate Access-specific objects, such as forms, reports, and so on. But because Access is a Relational Database Management System, you will undoubtedly find yourself also needing to programmatically interact with the data it contains, and indeed with the database design, or schema. Microsoft Access employs two data access object models: Data Access Objects (DAO) and ActiveX Data Objects (ADO).

Chapter 7 covers ADO; this chapter is solely concerned with the DAO model. It begins with a brief history of DAO and an indication of when it might be most appropriate to use DAO in preference to ADO. You'll see the new features in DAO before examining the three most important objects in the DAO object hierarchy: the DBEngine, Workspace, and Database objects. Then you'll explore database properties and how to use them.

Before you start working with DAO objects to access your data, you'll take an in-depth look at how to use DAO to create and modify your database structure, including tables, fields, indexes, and relations. You'll also spend some time looking at the Access Database Engine (formerly JET or Joint Engine Technology) security model, and how you can create and manipulate security objects, such as users, groups, and of course, how to read and assign object permissions. Finally, you'll look at data access in detail using QueryDefs and Recordsets.

Data Access Objects

DAO is the programmatic interface between VBA and Access database engine databases, ODBC (Open Database Connectivity) data stores, and installable ISAM (Indexed Sequential Access Method) data sources, such as Excel, Paradox, dBase, and Lotus 1-2-3.DAO was first released as a part of Visual Basic 2.0 and later released with Access 1.0 in November 1992. Over the years, many changes have been made to both DAO and to the Microsoft Jet database engine to reflect technologies at the time. Support for 32-bit operating systems, ODBC data sources, and Unicode languages were all included in current versions of DAO.

DAO 12.0 is the latest version, shipped with Access 2007, and is the version used by the new ACCDB file format. This new release was written for use with the Access database engine, which is an updated version of the Microsoft Jet database engine and is 100% compatible with Jet. The new features added to DAO and the Access database engine include new objects and properties that support multi-value lookup fields, a new Attachment data type, append-only memo fields, and database encryption using the database password. The filename for the Access database engine is ACECORE.DLL. (With ACE in the name, you may occasionally see the Access database engine referred to as ACE in newsgroups and blogs.)

Why Use DAO?

Visual Basic programmers highly recommend ADO as their preferred object model for accessing databases. Although ADO is an excellent model with its own unique benefits, in the context of Access databases, it doesn't have the benefit of native database connectivity, which is where DAO has the distinct advantage.

Applications written in other programming languages, such as Visual Basic, Delphi, and the like, must explicitly connect to the data source they intend to manipulate, and they must do so every time they need to manipulate the data or underlying schema. That's because, unlike Access, these applications do not have an inherent connection to the data source. When used in Access, DAO enables you to manipulate data and schema through an implicit connection that Access maintains to whichever Access database engine, ODBC, or ISAM data source it happens to be connected to.

Because linked tables are a uniquely Access-specific feature, DAO is quite simply the better alternative for accessing Access databases. In fact, it is impossible to do so natively using any other data access model.

DAO has evolved right alongside Jet and the Access database engine, and has become the best model for accessing and manipulating Access database engine objects and structure. Because of its tight integration with Access, DAO also provides much faster access to Access databases than does ADO or the Jet Replication Objects (JRO). This may all sound like marketing hype, but to qualify the advantages of DAO over other models, consider the following:

❑ ADO connections can only be applied to one database at a time, whereas DAO enables you to link (connect) to multiple databases simultaneously.

❑ Using the OpenRecordset method's dbDenyWrite option, DAO enables you to open a table while preventing other users from opening the same table with write access. The ADO Connection object's adModeShareDenyWrite constant operates at connection level — not at table level.

❑ Using the OpenRecordset method's dbDenyRead option, DAO enables you to open a table while preventing other users from opening the table at all. The ADO Connection object's adModeShareDenyRead constant can only be set at connection level.

❑ You can create users and groups in DAO, but not in ADO, because you can't specify the PID (Personal IDentifier) in ADO.

❑ You can secure Access objects (such as forms, reports, and so on) in DAO, but not in ADO, because there are no suitable ADO constants to specify permissions for execute, read changes, and write changes.

❑ You can dynamically link an updatable ODBC table in DAO, but not in ADO.

❏ DAO enables you to create replica databases that prevent users from deleting records; JRO does not.

❏ In DAO, you can return information about Exchange and Outlook folders and columns using the `TableDef` and `Field Attributes` properties. ADO does not pass this information on.

❏ Using the `DBEngine`'s `GetOption` and `SetOption` methods, DAO enables you to set and change Access database engine options without requiring you to make Registry changes.

❏ DAO enables you to create, change, and delete custom database properties.

❏ You can force the database-locking mode with the `DAO.LockTypeEnum` constants against `CurrentDb`, but you can't do the same thing in ADO using `ADO.LockTypeEnum` against `CurrentProject.Connection`.

❏ Using `AllPermissions` properties, DAO enables you to retrieve an object's implicit permissions, whereas ADO doesn't have an `AllPermissions` property, forcing you to enumerate the groups of each user.

❏ DAO enables you to run a separate session of the Access database engine, using `PrivDBEngine`; ADO does not.

❏ DAO enables you to create multi-value lookup fields using new complex data types. A multi-value lookup field is a single field that can store multiple values in an embedded recordset. You'll explore this new field type in more detail later in this chapter.

❏ DAO enables you to create and insert data in an Attachment field. Attachment fields are a new data type in the Access database engine and will be examined in more detail later in this chapter.

The current version of DAO is a very mature, well-documented, and easy-to-use object model for accessing database services. You can use DAO from any VBA environment such as Word, Excel, and so on, and a variety of other programming languages such as Visual Basic, FoxPro, and C++.

Finally, it's fairly safe to say that DAO will be around as long as Access or Jet databases are used.

New Features in DAO

As mentioned earlier, Microsoft has introduced several new features in DAO for Access 2007. These features are multi-value lookup fields, attachment fields, append-only memo fields, and database encryption. Each of these features is only available in the ACCDB file format so as not to break backward compatibility with the MDB file format.

All of these features, with the exception of database encryption, have been available on Windows SharePoint Services, and were added to Access for feature parity with that platform. (You can find out more about SharePoint in Chapter 17.)

Multi-Value Lookup Fields

When you create a lookup field in Access 2007, you can optionally choose to allow that field to store multiple values. For example, say you have a table of students, and you want to track the classes that the students take. Traditionally, you accomplish this by using three tables: one for Students, one for Classes, and a table in between these two called a junction table. *Multi-value lookup fields*, also known as *complex fields*, can also be used to store the classes for a particular student as a single field in the Students table. A multi-value lookup field can store many related records in a single field value. You can think of them as an embedded or nested recordset in a field for a particular record. In fact, that's exactly how you work with multi-value lookup fields in DAO. Access displays them using a list of values, as shown in Figure 6-1.

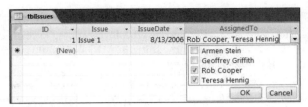

Figure 6-1

You might look at that list and think to yourself, "Isn't that denormalized?" Well, not to worry — the values for multiple-value fields are stored behind the scenes in related tables that are not available for viewing. Access does all of the work to maintain these relationships and lets you, as the developer, focus on data manipulation in a natural manner — by using DAO.

Multi-value lookup fields can be useful for simple one-to-many relationships, but they have one major limitation. The nested recordset for a multi-value lookup field can only contain one column. This is true whether the lookup field is created using the Access interface or DAO. To extend the example a little, it might be nice to know the semester in which a student attended a particular class, and even the grade he received for the class. That is not possible using a multi-value lookup field because those fields store only one field per record.

Attachment Fields

Access has had a means for storing files in the database for some time with the OLE Object data type. However, there are a few problems with this type. The first is that Access stores a wrapper around the data, which can often result in database bloat. This is even true for linked OLE Objects. Once the data was stored in the database, it wasn't easy to retrieve outside of Access. Frequently, a form was required to display data in the field, and using DAO against OLE Object fields was not easy.

Microsoft has solved this problem by adding a new data type called *Attachment*. Attachment fields are a special type of multi-valued field that allow for both multiple fields and multiple values in the nested recordset. The file itself is compressed by Access and stored in the database. As such, Access can store an attachment field without the additional space required by an OLE Object. No more database bloat! A new Attachment control is also available for working with the data inside of Access.

Append Only Fields

Have you ever wanted to track the history for a particular field in a table? As requirements for maintaining data over time become more and more common, scenarios such as this may become more important. Access now enables you to store a history of the data in a memo field, using a new property called

`Append Only`. When this property is set, Access automatically stores the previous version of text in the field as part of the data along with a timestamp. As you might imagine, this data is also stored using a multi-valued field.

Database Encryption

In previous versions of Access, you could assign a password to your database to require users to enter a password when opening a database, but that did not encrypt the data in the file. Database encryption in Access 2007 now uses Windows encryption technologies to encrypt a database when you assign a data-base password. This feature also replaces the *encoding* feature that was available in Jet.

Each of these features is covered in more detail later in the chapter.

Referring to DAO Objects

In code, you refer to objects in the DAO hierarchy by working your way down the object hierarchy. The following format illustrates generally how to reference DAO objects:

```
DBEngine.ParentCollection.ChildCollection!Object.Method_or_Property
```

You might recall from earlier discussion that a collection is a container for a group of objects of the same type. Many DAO object collections contain still other collections, so it is sometimes necessary to drill down through several collections before you get to the object that you want to operate on. This provides a highly structured and predictable method for accessing data and schema.

With the exception of the `DBEngine` object, all DAO objects are contained within their own collections. For example, the `TableDef` object is part of a `TableDefs` collection, and the `Group` object is part of a `Groups` collection. As a way of distinguishing between collections and individual objects, those that are named in the plural (ending with the letter `s`) are collections, whereas those named in the singular are individual objects.

Collections provide an easy way to enumerate their members by allowing you to refer to them by their name or ordinal position. You can also populate a variable with the object's name and use it instead. For example, the following examples show how you can refer to the same object in different ways.

Syntax	Description	Example
`Collection("name")`	Literal string	`DBEngine.Workspaces(0).Databases("myDB")`
`Collection(position)`	Ordinal collection position	`DBEngine.Workspaces(0).Databases(0)`
`Collection(variable)`	String or variant variable	`strVar = "myDB"` `DBEngine.Workspaces(0).Databases(strVar)`
`Collection![Name]`	Object name	`DBEngine.Workspaces(0).Databases!myDB`

> Where the object name contains nonstandard characters, such as spaces, you must enclose the object name in square brackets ([]).

Finally, this chapter uses the convention of capitalizing the first character of object and collection names, to highlight the difference between them and the casual use of the same word for other purposes. The following example illustrates this convention:

The Database object is an instance of a connection to a database or other data source. It is a member of the Workspace object's Databases collection, which is a container for a group of Database objects that represent connections to one or more databases.

Let's say you wanted to retrieve the `DefaultValue` property for a field called `PaymentDate` in a table called `tblPayments`. This is the long way of doing it:

```
DBEngine.Workspaces(0).Databases(0).TableDefs!tblPayments.Fields!PaymentDate↵
.DefaultValue
```

As you can see, referring to objects, properties, and methods can sometimes result in quite long lines of code. This can get pretty tedious after a while, so you can also refer to objects by their parent collection's default item. Assuming `tblPayments` is the first table in the `TableDefs` collection, and `PaymentDate` is the first field in that table's `Fields` collection, here is the shortened version:

```
DBEngine(0)(0)(0)(0).DefaultValue
```

The default item for any DAO object collection is the item that occupies ordinal position 0. This is in contrast to VBA collections, in which the first member occupies position 1 — an important fact to remember.

The following table lists examples of the two ways you can use to refer to DAO collection members.

Collection	Default Member	Example

Containers	Documents	`DBEngine.Workspaces(0).Databases(0)`
		`.Containers(0).Documents(0)`
		
		`DBEngine(0)(0).Containers(0)(0)`

Databases	TableDefs	`DBEngine.Workspaces(0).Databases(0)`
		`.TableDefs(0)`
		
		`DBEngine(0)(0)(0)`

DBEngine	Workspaces	`DBEngine.Workspaces(0)`
		
		`DBEngine(0)`

Groups	Users	`DBEngine.Workspaces(0).Groups(0).Users(0)`
		
		`DBEngine(0).Groups(0)(0)`

Collection	Default Member	Example
QueryDefs	Parameters	DBEngine.Workspaces(0).Databases(0) .QueryDefs(0).Parameters(0) DBEngine(0)(0).QueryDefs(0)(0)
Recordsets	Fields	DBEngine.Workspaces(0).Databases(0) .Recordsets(0).Fields(0) DBEngine(0)(0).Recordsets(0)(0)
Relations	Fields	DBEngine.Workspaces(0).Databases(0) .Relations(0).Fields(0) DBEngine(0)(0).Relations(0)(0)
TableDefs	Fields	DBEngine.Workspaces(0).Databases(0) .TableDefs(0).Fields(0) DBEngine(0)(0)(0)(0)
Users	Groups	DBEngine.Workspaces(0).Groups(0) .Users(0).Groups(0) DBEngine(0).Groups(0)(0)(0)
Workspaces	Databases	DBEngine.Workspaces(0) DBEngine(0)

The DBEngine Object

The DBEngine object is a property of the Access *Application* object, and represents the top-level object in the DAO model. The DBEngine object contains all the other objects in the DAO object hierarchy, yet unlike many of the other DAO objects, you can't create additional DBEngine objects.

The DBEngine object contains two major collections — Workspaces and Errors — which are described in this section because they relate so closely to the DBEngine object.

The Workspaces Collection

A *workspace* is a named user session that contains open databases and provides the facility for transactions and (depending on the database format) user-and group-level security. As you can have more than one workspace active at any time, the Workspaces collection is the repository for all the workspaces that have been created.

You use the Microsoft Access workspace to access Microsoft Access database engine databases (ACCDB files created in Access 2007), Microsoft Jet databases (MDB files created in previous versions), and ODBC or installable ISAM data sources through the Microsoft Access database engine. For a list of the collections, objects, and methods supported by Microsoft Access workspaces, refer to Appendix D.

The `Workspace` object contains three different object collections. These are `Databases`, `Groups`, and `Users`. Note that the `Groups` and `Users` collections are hidden in Access 2007 and you'll need to show them in the Object Browser before they will appear using IntelliSense. Each of these collections is described in later sections.

ODBCDirect

In addition to the Microsoft Access workspace, previous versions of DAO supported a second type of Workspace object called ODBCDirect. ODBCDirect workspaces are used against ODBC data sources such as SQL Server. Beginning with Office 2007, Microsoft is no longer shipping RDO that enabled this type of workspace. As a result, ODBCDirect is no longer supported in DAO. You will see a runtime error if you try to create an ODBCDirect workspace using the `CreateWorkspace` method as shown in Figure 6-2.

Figure 6-2

Subsequently, because you cannot create ODBCDirect workspaces, calling the `OpenConnection` method will cause a runtime error, and the `Connections` collection of the `DBEngine` object will not contain any `Connection` objects.

Creating a Workspace

If you have Microsoft Jet databases that use Jet security to help secure objects, there may be times when you need to provide access to them from unsecured databases. For such an occasion, you can create a new Workspace object to provide the username and password for the secured database.

When you first refer to a `Workspace` object, or one of its collections, objects, methods, or properties, you automatically create the default workspace, which can be referenced using the following syntaxes:

❑   `DBEngine.Workspaces(0)`

❑   `DBEngine(0)`

❑   simply `Workspaces(0)`

The default workspace is given the name #Default Workspace#. In the absence of user- and group-level security, the default workspace's UserName property is set to Admin. If security is implemented, the UserName property is set to the name of the user who logged on.

You don't have to do anything to begin using a Microsoft Access workspace; Access creates one by default.

The basic procedure for creating a new workspace is as follows:

1. Create the workspace, using the DBEngine's CreateWorkspace method.
2. Append the new workspace to the Workspaces collection.

You can use a workspace without appending it to the Workspaces collection, but you must refer to it using the object variable to which it was assigned. You will not be able to refer to it through the Workspaces collection until it is appended.

The following example demonstrates how to create a Microsoft Access workspace, and print the Name property:

```
Dim wsAccess As DAO.Workspace
Dim strUserName As String
Dim strPassword As String

'Set the user name and password
strUserName = "Admin"
strPassword = ""

'Create a new Microsoft Access workspace
Set wsAccess = DBEngine.CreateWorkspace( _
    "myAccessWS", strUserName, strPassword, dbUseJet)

'Append the workspaces to the collection
Workspaces.Append wsAccess

'Print the name of the workspace
Debug.Print "wsAccess.Name: " & wsAccess.Name 'myAccessWS

'Clean up
wsAccess.Close
Set wsAccess = Nothing
```

To use the default workspace, you can either refer to it as DBEngine(0), or create a reference to it in the same way you create references to other Access or DAO objects:

```
'Create a reference to the default workspace
Set wsAccess1 = DBEngine(0)
Debug.Print "wsAccess1.Name: " & wsAccess1.Name '#Default Workspace#
```

Because you're not creating a new workspace object, there is no need to append it to the Workspaces collection.

Finally, there is one other way to create a new workspace. To maintain compatibility with previous versions of DAO, Access 2007 still provides the `DefaultWorkspaceClone` method.

```
'Create a clone of the default workspace
Set wsAccess2 = Application.DefaultWorkspaceClone
Debug.Print "wsAccess2.Name: " & wsAccess.Name '#CloneAccess#
```

The `DefaultWorkspaceClone` method creates a clone (identical copy) of the default workspace, whatever it happens to be. The cloned workspace takes on properties identical to those of the original, with the exception of its `Name` property, which is set to `#CloneAccess#`. You can change this name if you choose.

You would use the `DefaultWorkspaceClone` method where you want to operate two independent transactions simultaneously without needing to prompt the user again for the username and password.

Using Transactions

A *transaction* is defined as a delimited set of changes that are performed on a database's schema or data. They increase the speed of actions that change data, and enable you to undo changes that have not yet been committed.

Transactions offer a great deal of data integrity insurance for situations where an entire series of actions must complete successfully, or not complete at all. This is the all-or-nothing principle that is employed in most financial transactions.

For example, when your employer transfers your monthly salary from their bank to yours, two actions actually occur. The first is a withdrawal from your employer's account, and the second is a deposit into yours. If the withdrawal completes, but for some reason, the deposit fails, you can argue until you're blue in the face, but your employer can prove that they paid you, and are not likely to want to do so again. Similarly, your bank will not be too impressed if the withdrawal fails, but the deposit succeeds. The reality is that the bank will take the money back, and you still end up with no salary. If, however, the two actions are enclosed in a single transaction, they must both complete successfully, or the transaction is deemed to have failed, and both actions are rolled back (reversed).

You begin a transaction by issuing the `BeginTrans` method against the `Workspace` object. To write the transaction to disk, you issue the `CommitTrans` method, and to cancel, or roll back the transaction, strangely enough, you issue the `Rollback` method.

Normally, transactions are cached, and not immediately written to disk. But if you're in a real hurry to get home at five o'clock, and immediately switch off your computer before the cache is written to disk, your most recent changes are lost. In Microsoft Access workspaces, you can force the database engine to immediately write all changes to disk, instead of caching them. You do this by including the `dbForceOSFlush` constant with `CommitTrans`. Forcing immediate writes may affect your application's performance, but the data integrity benefits may outweigh any performance hit in certain situations.

The following code segment demonstrates a typical funds transfer transaction. In this and in other examples in this chapter, the code deviates from the Reddick object-naming convention by varying the names for `Workspace`, `Database`, and `Recordset` object variables, making the code easier to understand. In this example, rather than extend the length of the two `Database` object names, they are named `dbC` and dbX, for the current and external databases respectively. They could just as easily have been named dbsC and dbsX.

```
Public Sub TransferFunds()
    Dim wrk As DAO.Workspace
    Dim dbC As DAO.Database
    Dim dbX As DAO.Database

    Set wrk = DBEngine(0)
    Set dbC = CurrentDb
    Set dbX = wrk.OpenDatabase("c:\Temp\myDB.mdb")

    On Error GoTo trans_Err

    'Begin the transaction
    wrk.BeginTrans

    'Run a SQL statement to withdraw funds from one account table
    dbC.Execute "UPDATE Table1.....", dbFailOnError

    'Run a SQL statement to deposit funds into another account table
    dbX.Execute "INSERT INTO Table22.....", dbFailOnError

    'Commit the transaction
    wrk.CommitTrans dbForceOSFlush

trans_Exit:
    'Clean up
    wrk.Close
    Set dbC = Nothing
    Set dbX = Nothing
    Set wrk = Nothing
    Exit Sub

trans_Err:
    'Roll back the transaction
    wrk.Rollback
    Resume trans_Exit
End Sub
```

In this example, changes to both databases will complete as a unit, or will be rolled back as a unit.

You don't need to use transactions, but if you do, they can be nested up to five levels. It is also important to understand that transactions are global to the workspace — not the database. For example, if you make changes to two databases in the same workspace, and you roll back the changes to one of those databases, the changes made to the other database will also be rolled back.

The Errors Collection

The first thing to remember about the DAO Errors collection is that it is not the same as the VBA.Err object. The VBA.Err object is a single object that stores information about the last VBA error. The DAO Errors collection stores information about the last DAO error.

Any operation performed on any DAO object can generate one or more errors. The DBEngine.Errors collection stores all the error objects that are added as the result of an error that occurs during a single DAO operation. Each Error object in the collection, therefore, contains information about only one error.

Having said that, some operations can generate multiple errors, in which case the lowest level error is stored in the collection first, followed by the higher level errors. The last error object usually indicates that the operation failed. Enumerating the Errors collection enables your error handling code to more precisely determine the cause of the problem, and to take the most appropriate remedial action.

When a subsequent DAO operation generates an error, the Errors collection is cleared and a new set of Error objects is added to the collection. This happens regardless of whether you have retrieved the previous error information or not. So you can see that unless you retrieve the information about an error as soon as it occurs, you may lose it if another error happens in the meantime. Each error obliterates and replaces its predecessor — a bit like politics really.

One last point to note is that an error that occurs in an object that has not yet been added to its collection, is not added to the DBEngine.Errors collection, because the "object" is not considered to be an object until it is added to a collection. In such cases, the error information will be available in the VBA.Err object.

To fully account for all errors, your error handler should verify that the error number returned by both the VBA.Err object and the last member of the DBEngine.Error object are the same. The following code demonstrates a typical error handler:

```
intDAOErrNo = DBEngine.Errors(DBEngine.Errors.Count -1).Number

If VBA.Err <> intDAOErrNo Then
    DBEngine.Errors.Refresh
End If

For intCtr = 0 To DBEngine.Errors.Count -1
    Select Case DBEngine.Errors(intCtr).Number
        Case 1
        'Code to handle error
        Case 2
        'Code to handle error
        '
        'Other Case statements
        '
        Case 99
        'Code to handle error
        End Select
Next intCtr
```

The Databases Collection

Using DAO, you can have more than one database open in Access at any time. If you're using an .accdb or .mdb database file, you already have one database open (called the *current* database). Using the Workspace object's OpenDatabase method, as shown earlier in the example in the "Using Transactions" section, you can open more than one database, and operate on them under the same workspace context. Indeed, if you were to define more than one Workspace object, you could have several databases open, each operating under a different workspace context. The Databases collection contains and manages all databases currently open in the workspace.

The Default (Access) Database

Unless you're working with an Access Data Project, when you create a database in Access, it is automatically added to the Databases collection.

Among its properties and methods, the Database object contains five collections: TableDefs, Containers, QueryDefs, Recordsets, and Relations. Each of these collections and their respective objects and properties are discussed in later sections. In most cases, you will be working with the default Microsoft Access database, which you can refer to using any of the following syntaxes:

```
DBEngine.Workspaces("#Default Workspace#").Databases(0)
DBEngine.Workspaces(0).Databases(0)
DBEngine(0).Databases(0)
DBEngine(0)(0)
CurrentDb()
```

The current user's default database is an object that you will use quite a lot. Although you can work with it using any of the reference methods listed, in most cases it is often more convenient to assign it to an object variable.

```
Dim dbs As DAO.Database
Set dbs = DBEngine(0)(0)
```

But far and away the most common method is to use the CurrentDb() function, described in the following section.

The CurrentDb() Function

Access always maintains a single permanent reference to the current database. The first member of the Databases collection is populated with a reference to the current database at startup. This reference, pointed to by DBEngine(0)(0), is fine under most circumstances, but when, for example, you are working on wizards, it is not always up-to-date. In these circumstances it is possible for the first database collection member to point to something other than the default database. The chance of this occurring in *normal* databases is negligible, but to ensure that you are working with the current database, you need to execute the Refresh method, which rebuilds the collection, placing the current database in the first position in the Databases collection. This can be annoying, of course, , but in addition, your code experiences a huge performance hit every time you want to use the current database.

```
DBEngine(0).Databases.Refresh
Debug.Print DBEngine(0)(0).Name
```

The solution that Microsoft came up with was to provide the CurrentDb() function. CurrentDb (the parentheses are optional) is not an object; it is a built-in function that provides a reference to the current user's default database. Although they do refer to the same database, it is essential that you understand two important concepts.

CurrentDb and DBEngine(0)(0) are not the same objects internally. Access maintains a single perma-nent reference to the current database, but CurrentDb temporarily creates a new internal object — one in which the collections are guaranteed to be up-to-date.

When CurrentDb is executed, Access creates a new internal object that recreates the hierarchy and refers to the current database. The interesting fact is that immediately after CurrentDb executes and returns a pointer, the internal object is destroyed.

For example, the following code generates an error because the reference to the current database is lost immediately after the line containing CurrentDb executes:

```
Dim fld As DAO.Field
Set fld = CurrentDb.TableDefs(0).Fields(0)
Debug.Print fld.Name
```

This is the case for most DAO objects. One notable exception to this is the Recordset object, for which Access tries to maintain the database reference. To use CurrentDb effectively, it is always wiser to assign the reference to an object variable.

```
Dim dbs As DAO.Database
Dim fld As DAO.Field

Set dbs = CurrentDb
Set fld = dbs.TableDefs(0).Fields(0)

Debug.Print fld.Name
dbs.Close
Set dbs = Nothing
```

Of course, nothing is free, and CurrentDb is no exception. The price you pay for the convenience and reliability of a function like CurrentDb is a considerable performance hit. CurrentDb is (in my tests) roughly 60 times slower than DBEngine(0)(0). So why would you use it?

The reason you would use CurrentDb in preference to DBEngine(0)(0) is that you can rely on its col-lections being up-to-date. For the majority of cases, the performance hit experienced using CurrentDb is not an issue because it is highly unlikely that you will ever call it in a loop. The recommended method for setting a reference to the current database is as follows:

```
Private dbC As DAO.Database

Public Property Get CurrentDbC() As DAO.Database
    If (dbC Is Nothing) Then Set dbC = CurrentDb
    Set CurrentDbC = dbC
End Property
```

This Property procedure can be used in both class modules and standard modules, and relies on the existence of a Database object variable declared at module level. If you want, you can change it to a function instead; it will work just the same. The reason it checks dbC is that variables can be erased (and thus the reference lost) when an error occurs somewhere in your application, or if someone hits Stop in the IDE (integrated development environment).

Opening an External Database

Sometimes you need to work with data in another Access database, a dBase IV database, or Excel spreadsheet, but you don't want a permanent link. You can do so by opening a temporary connection to it with OpenDatabase method on the DBEngine object. Although the connection to the external database is temporary, the new Database object is still added to the Databases collection.

The OpenDatabase method is fairly straightforward.

```
Set dbs = DBEngine.OpenDatabase(dbname, options, read-only, connect)
```

The following table describes the OpenDatabase method arguments.

Argument	Description
dbname	A string value that represents the full path and filename of the database you want to open.
options	An optional Boolean true (-1) or false (0) that indicates whether to open the database in exclusive (True) or shared mode (False).
Read-only	An optional Boolean true (-1) or false (0) that indicates whether to open the database as read-only.
Connect	Specifies connection information such as passwords

The following code demonstrates how to open several different databases using various techniques. After opening each database, you'll notice that the code prints the name of the database, and a count of the respective Databases collection.

Specifically, it opens the following databases from the following sources:

❑ Microsoft Access database

❑ dBase IV database using Jet

❑ SQL Server database using ODBC through Jet

```
Public Sub OpenSeveralDatabases(strUsrName As String, strPwd As String)
    Dim wsAccess As Workspace
    Dim dbAccess As DAO.Database
    Dim dbdBase As DAO.Database
    Dim dbODBC As DAO.Database

    'Create the Access workspace
    Set wsAccess = DBEngine(0)

    'Print the details for the default database
    Debug.Print "Access Database "; wsAccess.Databases.Count & _
        "-"& CurrentDb.Name

    'Open a Microsoft Access database -shared -read-only
    Set dbAccess = wsAccess.OpenDatabase("C:\Temp\db1.accdb", False, True)
```

```
      Debug.Print "Access Database "; wsAccess.Databases.Count & _
          "-"& dbAccess.Name

      'Open a dBase IV database -exclusive -read-write
      Set dbdBase = wsAccess.OpenDatabase( _
          "dBase IV;DATABASE=C:\Temp\db2.dbf", True, False)
      Debug.Print "Database "; wsAccess.Databases.Count & _
          "-"& dbdBase.Name

      'Open an ODBC database using a DSN -exclusive -read-only
      Set dbODBC = wsAccess.OpenDatabase( _
          "", dbDriverComplete, True, "ODBC;DATABASE=myDB;DSN=myDSN")
      Debug.Print "Access Database "; wsAccess.Databases.Count & _
          "-"& dbODBC.Name

      'Clean up
      wsAccess.Close
      Set dbAccess = Nothing
      Set dbdBase = Nothing
      Set dbODBC = Nothing
      Set cn = Nothing
      Set wsAccess = Nothing
  End Sub
```

Closing and Destroying Database Object References

There has been a great deal of confusion about whether to explicitly close and destroy object references to the current database. Some of the most highly regarded experts in the field have publicly clarified this issue many times, but many still seem to cling to the fear that doing so will blow their database up. This section attempts to lay that fear to rest once and for all.

The problem stemmed from the fact that in Access 2.0, if you called the Close method against DBEngine(0)(0) or CurrentDb, the call would fail, but problems would occur with any open objects, specifically recordsets. This resulted either in an application hang, or with Access refusing to close. Following the fix to this bug (where the internal "OK to close?" check routine was moved from the end of the method, to the beginning), calls to dbs.Close issued against either DBEngine(0)(0) or CurrentDb now do absolutely nothing to the permanent internal database object. Many people still believe that this long dead bug still exists, and warnings about it still resound in the halls of UseNet. If it gives you a warm fuzzy feeling inside, you can call Close but any attempt to do so against DBEngine(0)(0) or CurrentDb will literally do nothing. Therefore, dbs.Close is redundant.

Some people have experienced bugs with the DAO Recordset object, in particular, the RecordsetClone object, where an orphaned reference sometimes prevents Access from closing. There has never been any such bug with the Database object.

Destroying object references is a different affair. For the present, you still should set Database object variables to Nothing when you have finished with them, as you would with any other object reference. It is perfectly safe to do so, regardless of whether the reference came from DBEngine(0)(0) or CurrentDb.

Setting myObj = Nothing decrements the internal object reference count by one. When the reference count reaches zero, the object is destroyed. But because Access maintains a *permanent* internal reference to the current database, this will not destroy the internal object, and thus will never have any effect on it.

DAO Object Properties

As you're no doubt already aware from previous chapters, every Access object (such as forms and reports) has a collection of properties. This section examines some of those properties, and describes how to use them to change Access and DAO object behavior.

All the properties associated with an Access object exist from the moment you create the object. DAO object properties, however, exhibit quite different behavior. In DAO, depending on the object, not all its properties exist until you set its value. It is quite important, therefore, that you understand the differences between the types of properties used in DAO.

DAO Property Types

In contrast to Access object properties, the three types of object properties are: built-in, system-defined, and user-defined.

❏ Built-in properties exist when the object is created, and like most of their Access counterparts, define the characteristics of the object itself. For example, `Name` and `Type` are examples of built-in properties.

❏ System-defined properties are those that Access adds to the object's `Properties` collection when it needs the property in order to work its magic. These are not Access database engine properties, but are created and used by Access.

❏ A user-defined property can be added to an object's `Properties` collection when you explicitly set a value to it. For example, a field's `Description` property is a user-defined property. Although you can set a value to it when you define the table, Access doesn't recognize that the property exists until after you've done so. In fact, after you've set its value, it appears in the field's `Properties` collection, but you still can't see it in the `Object Browser`, as shown in Figure 6-3.

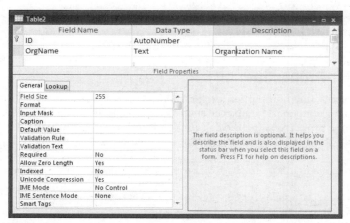

Figure 6-3

Creating, Setting, and Retrieving Properties

Without even thinking about it, you've been setting and retrieving properties for as long as you've been programming. Whenever you check the value of a `TextBox`, or set the `Enabled` state of a command button, you are working with object properties. This section explores how to manipulate Access properties, object properties, and user-defined properties.

You can refer to built-in properties either directly through the object to which they belong or through the object's `Properties` collection. User-defined properties, on the other hand, do not form part of an object's type library, and thus are not available via that route, so you have to refer to them through the object's `Properties` collection.

Setting and Retrieving Built-In Object Properties

The built-in properties that you would be most familiar with are those that affect the way form and report controls work. Even DAO objects have properties that can be manipulated in the same way. For example, to change a `TextBox`'s `Enabled` property, you can refer to it in either of the following two ways:

```
Me!TextBox1.Enabled = False
Me!TextBox1.Properties("Enabled") = False
```

To check the name of a recordset's `Field` object, you retrieve its `Name` property. The following two examples are equivalent ways to check this property:

```
Debug.Print rst.Fields(0).Name
Debug.Print rst.Fields(0).Properties("Name")
```

All objects have a default property, which is the property that is referenced when you call the object itself. For example, when you test a `Field` object directly, you are actually referring to its `Value` property. The following lines of code all refer to the `Field` object's `Value` property:

```
rst.Fields(0)
rst.Fields(0).Properties("Value")
rst.Fields(0).Properties(0)
rst.Fields(0).Value
```

Creating Object Properties

You can create user-defined properties for persistent DAO objects, such as tables and queries. You can't create properties for nonpersistent objects, such as recordsets. To create a user-defined property, you must first create the property, using the `Database`'s `CreateProperty` method. You then append the property using the `Properties` collection's `Append` method. That's all there is to it.

Using the example of a field's `Description` property, the following code demonstrates just how easy it is:

```
Public Sub SetFieldDescription(strTableName As String, _
    strFieldName As String, _
    varValue As Variant, _
)

    Dim dbs As DAO.Database
    Dim prop As DAO.Property
```

```
        Set dbs = CurrentDb

        'Create the property
        Set prop = dbs.CreateProperty("Description", dbText, varValue)

        'Append the property to the object Properties collection
        dbs(strTableName)(strFieldName).Properties.Append prop
        Debug.Print dbs(strTableName)(strFieldName).Properties("Description")

        'Clean up
        Set prop = Nothing
        Set dbs = Nothing
    End Sub
```

You could even create a special user-defined property for a table in the same way, as the following code shows. This approach can be used with all persistent objects.

```
    Public Sub CreateSpecialTableProp(strTableName As String, _
        strPropName As String, _
        lngPropType As DataTypeEnum, _
        varValue As Variant)

        Dim dbs As DAO.Database
        Dim prop As DAO.Property

        Set dbs = CurrentDb

        'Create the property
        Set prop = dbs.CreateProperty(strPropName, lngPropType, varValue, False)

        'Append the property to the object Properties collection
        dbs(strTableName).Properties.Append prop

        Debug.Print dbs(strTableName).Properties(strPropName)

        'Clean up
        Set prop = Nothing
        Set dbs = Nothing
    End Sub
```

For another example, let's say you wanted to create a Yes/No field, but tell Access to make the field a checkbox instead of a text box. You can create the DisplayControl property to specify the type of control for Access.

```
    Public Sub CreateYesNoField(strTableName As String, _
            strFieldName As String)

        Dim dbs As DAO.Database
        Dim tdf As DAO.TableDef
        Dim fld As DAO.Field
        Dim prop As DAO.Property

        Set dbs = CurrentDb
        Set tdf = dbs.TableDefs(strTableName)
```

```
            'Create and append the field
            Set fld = tdf.CreateField(strFieldName, dbBoolean)
            tdf.Fields.Append fld

            'Create the property
            Set prop = dbs.CreateProperty("DisplayControl", _
                dbInteger, acCheckBox)

            'Append the property to the object Properties collection
            fld.Properties.Append prop

            'Clean up
            Set prop = Nothing
            Set fld = Nothing
            Set tdf = Nothing
            Set dbs = Nothing
        End Sub
```

Setting and Retrieving SummaryInfo Properties

When you select Database Properties from the Manage menu under the Office button, Access opens the Properties dialog box. It displays several built-in properties, some you can change, and some you can't. The General tab displays various information about the database, including its file location and size, creation date, and the dates it was last modified and accessed. The Summary tab enables you to enter your own properties, such as the document Title (which is different from the Application Title, because it's set from the Access Options dialog box), Subject, Author, Manager, and so on. These two tabs contain the information the Search facility uses when you want to find a specific file, using File ➪ Open ➪ Find, as shown in Figure 6-4.

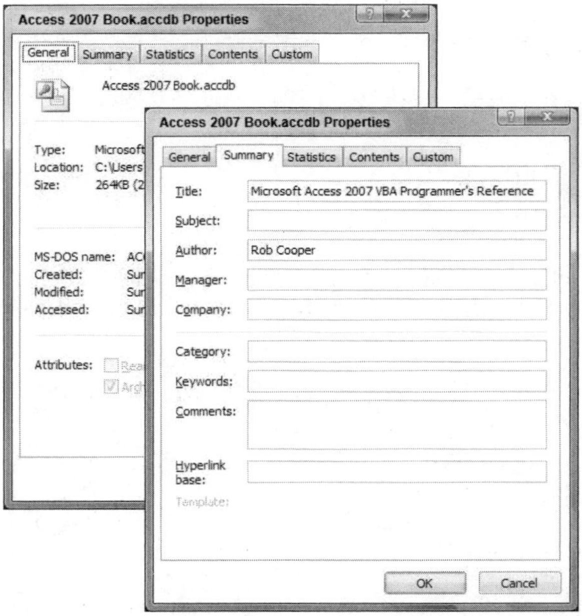

Figure 6-4

In DAO code, you can set and retrieve the value of any of these properties from the SummaryInfo document of the Databases container for the current database. Of course, you don't have to create these properties before using them. Access creates them automatically when you launch the database. The following code line illustrates how to access the `Subject` property shown in the Properties dialog box.

```
dbs.Containers("Databases").Documents("SummaryInfo").Properties("Subject")
```

Setting and Retrieving User-Defined Properties

You can also create and use user-defined properties for other purposes. A lot of developers often use a custom database property to record the database version. As with the example of a field's `Description` property, there are two ways to create a user-defined property: using the user interface, and through code.

To create such a property with the user interface, click the Office button and select Manage ⇨ Database Properties. The Properties dialog box displays, as shown in Figure 6-5. Select the Custom tab. Enter the property name into the Name box, select the appropriate data type, give it a value, and click Add.

Figure 6-5

The following example shows how you can create the same property in code, and retrieve its value using `Debug.Print`:

```
Public Sub SetVersion(strVersion As String)
    Dim prop As DAO.Property
    Dim dbs As DAO.Database

    On Error Resume Next

    Set dbs = CurrentDb
```

```
        'Set the property's value
        'If it doesn't exist, an error 3270 "Property not found" will occur
        dbs.Containers("Databases")("UserDefined").Properties("Version") = _
            strVersion

    If Err <> 0 Then
        'If the property doesn't exist, create it
        Set prop = dbs.CreateProperty("Version", dbText, strVersion)

        'Append it to the collection
        dbs.Containers("Databases")("UserDefined").Properties.Append prop
    End If

        'Now read the property
        Debug.Print _
            dbs.Containers("Databases")("UserDefined").Properties("Version")

        'Clean up
        Set prop = Nothing
        Set dbs = Nothing
    End Sub
```

First you must test that the property exists. In this example, you test it by attempting to set its value. If all goes well, the property must already exist, and its value is set. If an error occurs, you have to create the property — again by using the `CreateProperty` method at database level, and then appending it to the appropriate collection.

Creating Schema Objects with DAO

Sometimes you need to create data access objects on-the-fly. Much of DAO's power lies in its capability to create things such as tables and queries programmatically.

Let's say you inherit a copper-plated widget manufacturing company from an uncle. He never actually sold any because of the absence of an invoicing system, so you decide to implement one. Naturally enough, you'll want to create a database schema to record the details of the invoices you issue to your customers: one table for the invoice header, and one for the line items.

Like the man says, "experience is the best teacher," so to learn how to do it, let's just jump right in and create a table schema in code. Here's the basic procedure:

1. Create the header table (`tblInvoice`), including its fields.

2. Create the line items table (`tblInvItem`), including its fields.

3. Create the indexes for both tables.

4. Create the relationship between the two tables.

Creating Tables and Fields

For the invoicing system, you have two tables to create. The basic procedure for creating a table in code is as follows:

1. Check if the table already exists, and if so, rename it. You could also choose to delete the table instead of renaming it.

2. Create the table object using the Database's CreateTableDef method.

3. Create the Field objects in memory, using the TableDef's CreateField method, setting each field's attributes as appropriate.

4. Append each Field object to the TableDef's Fields collection.

5. Append the TableDef object to the Database's TableDefs collection.

6. Refresh the TableDefs collection to ensure it is up-to-date, and optionally call Application.RefreshDatabaseWindow to refresh the Navigation pane.

The header table stores the basic high-level information about each invoice, such as the invoice number, date, and the customer ID. The following example demonstrates how to create a new table called tblInvoice and add four fields to it. First, declare all the objects needed to create the table:

```
Public Sub CreateInvoiceTable()
    Dim dbs As DAO.Database
    Dim tdf As DAO.TableDef
    Dim fldInvNo As DAO.Field
    Dim fldInvDate As DAO.Field
    Dim fldCustID As DAO.Field
    Dim fldComments As DAO.Field

    Set dbs = CurrentDb
    On Error Resume Next

    'If the table already exists, rename it
    If IsObject(dbs.TableDefs("tblInvoice")) Then
        DoCmd.Rename "tblInvoice_Backup", acTable, "tblInvoice"
    End If
    On Error GoTo 0

    'Create the table definition in memory
    Set tdf = dbs.CreateTableDef("tblInvoice")
```

At this point, you have created the new TableDef, but it exists only in memory. It won't become a permanent part of the database until you add it to the TableDefs collection. Before you do that, however, you need to add one or more fields to the table, because you can't save a table that has no fields. You add the fields like this:

```
    'Create the field definitions in memory
    Set fldInvNo = tdf.CreateField("InvoiceNo", dbText, 10)
    fldInvNo.AllowZeroLength = False
    fldInvNo.Required = True
```

```
        'The InvoiceNo field could also have been specified thus:
        'Set fldInvNo = tdf.CreateField()
        'With fldInvNo
        '    .Name = "InvoiceNo"
        '    .Type = dbText
        '    .Size = 10
        '    .AllowZeroLength = False
        '    .Required = True
        'End With

        Set fldInvDate = tdf.CreateField("InvoiceDate", dbDate)
        fldInvDate.Required = True

        Set fldCustID = tdf.CreateField("CustomerID", dbLong)
        fldCustID.Required = True

        Set fldComments = tdf.CreateField("Comments", dbText, 50)
        fldComments.AllowZeroLength = True
        fldComments.Required = False

        'Append the fields to the TableDef's Fields collection
        tdf.Fields.Append fldInvNo
        tdf.Fields.Append fldInvDate
        tdf.Fields.Append fldCustID
        tdf.Fields.Append fldComments
```

The table still needs to be added to the `TableDefs` collection to make it a permanent fixture. Once you've done that, refresh the `TableDefs` collection to ensure it is up-to-date, because in a multiuser application, the new table may not be immediately propagated to other users' collections until you do:

```
        'Append the TableDef to the Database's TableDefs collection
        dbs.TableDefs.Append tdf

        'Refresh the TableDefs collection
        dbs.TableDefs.Refresh
        Application.RefreshDatabaseWindow

        Set fldInvNo = Nothing
        Set fldInvDate = Nothing
        Set fldCustID = Nothing
        Set fldComments = Nothing
        Set tdf = Nothing
        Set dbs = Nothing
    End Sub
```

Next, you need to create a table to store the invoice line items, including the product ID, the number of items sold, and their individual unit price. Because the total invoice price and tax can be calculated at runtime, you won't violate normalization rules by creating fields for these items.

The following code creates a new table called `tblInvItem`, and adds five fields to it. It is based on the same basic procedure for creating tables, but includes an additional attribute definition, `dbAutoIncrField`, to create an `AutoNumber` field.

```
Public Sub CreateInvItemTable()
    Dim dbs As DAO.Database
    Dim tdf As DAO.TableDef
    Dim fldInvItemID As DAO.Field
    Dim fldInvNo As DAO.Field
    Dim fldProductID As DAO.Field
    Dim fldQty As DAO.Field
    Dim fldUnitPrice As DAO.Field

    Set dbs = CurrentDb
    On Error Resume Next

    'If the table already exists, rename it
    If IsObject(dbs.TableDefs("tblInvItem")) Then
        DoCmd.Rename "tblInvItem_Backup", acTable, "tblInvItem"
    End If

    'Create the table definition in memory
    Set tdf = dbs.CreateTableDef("tblInvItem")

    'Create the field definitions in memory
    Set fldInvItemID = tdf.CreateField("InvItemID", dbLong)

    'Make the field an AutoNumber datatype
    fldInvItemID.Attributes = dbAutoIncrField
    fldInvItemID.Required = True

    Set fldInvNo = tdf.CreateField("InvoiceNo", dbText, 10)
    fldInvNo.Required = True
    fldInvNo.AllowZeroLength = False

    Set fldProductID = tdf.CreateField("ProductID", dbLong)
    fldProductID.Required = True

    Set fldQty = tdf.CreateField("Qty", dbInteger)
    fldQty.Required = True

    Set fldUnitPrice = tdf.CreateField("UnitCost", dbCurrency)
    fldUnitPrice.Required = False

    'Append the fields to the TableDef's Fields collection
    tdf.Fields.Append fldInvItemID
    tdf.Fields.Append fldInvNo
    tdf.Fields.Append fldProductID
    tdf.Fields.Append fldQty
    tdf.Fields.Append fldUnitPrice

    'Append the TableDef to the Database's TableDefs collection
    dbs.TableDefs.Append tdf

    'Refresh the TableDefs collection
    dbs.TableDefs.Refresh
    Application.RefreshDatabaseWindow
```

```
        Set fldInvItemID = Nothing
        Set fldInvNo = Nothing
        Set fldProductID = Nothing
        Set fldQty = Nothing
        Set fldUnitPrice = Nothing
        Set tdf = Nothing
        Set dbs = Nothing
    End Sub
```

Creating Indexes

Just creating the tables and fields isn't enough. Eventually the tables are going to get pretty big, and querying against them will take some time. To provide some measure of performance, you need to create indexes because without proper indexes, the Access engine must scan the entire table to find the records you want. Here's the basic procedure for creating an index:

1. Create the `Index` object using the `TableDef`'s `CreateIndex` method.

2. Set the index's properties as appropriate.

3. Create the index's `Field` objects using its `CreateField` method.

4. Append each `Field` object to the index's `Fields` collection.

5. Append the index to the `TableDef`'s `Indexes` collection.

Before you create your first index, you should be aware of the following three things:

❑ Once an index is appended to its collection, its properties are read-only. Therefore, if you want to change an index's property after you've created it, you must delete the index and re-create it with the new properties.

❑ Although you can give an index any name you like, when you create a primary key using the Access Table Designer, it is automatically named PrimaryKey. To maintain consistency, it is wise to give code-created primary keys the same name.

❑ Access databases do not support clustered indexes, so in Access workspaces and other workspaces that connect to databases that use the Access database engine, the `Index` object's `Clustered` property is ignored.

Start the process of creating indexes by creating the primary key. When you create a primary key, Access automatically creates an index for it. The following procedure creates a primary key index for the specified table, which includes the fields supplied in the `ParamArray` argument. In the case of the invoice tables, that'll be only one field in each.

```
Public Sub CreatePKIndexes(strTableName As String, ParamArray varPKFields())
    Dim dbs As DAO.Database
    Dim tdf As DAO.TableDef
    Dim idx As DAO.Index
    Dim fld As DAO.Field
    Dim strPKey As String
    Dim strIdxFldName As String
    Dim intCounter As Integer
```

```
        Set dbs = CurrentDb
        Set tdf = dbs.TableDefs(strTableName)

        'Check if a Primary Key exists.
        'If so, delete it.
        strPKey = GetPrimaryKey(tdf)

        If Len(strPKey) > 0 Then
            tdf.Indexes.Delete varPKey
        End If

        'Create a new primary key
        Set idx = tdf.CreateIndex("PrimaryKey")
        idx.Primary = True
        idx.Required = True
        idx.Unique = True
```

At this point, the index exists in memory, and remains so until it is added to the `TableDef`'s `Indexes` collection. But before you do that, you must add the fields that make up the key to the index's `Fields` collection, and refresh the collection.

```
        'Append the fields
        For intCouter = LBound(varPKFields) To UBound(varPKFields)
            ' get the field name
            strIdxFldName = varPKFields(intCounter)

            ' get the field object and append it to the index
            Set fld = idx.CreateField(strIdxFldName)
            idx.Fields.Append fld
        Next intCounter

        'Append the index to the Indexes collection
        tdf.Indexes.Append idx

        'Refresh the Indexes collection
        tdf.Indexes.Refresh

        Set fld = Nothing
        Set idx = Nothing
        Set tdf = Nothing
        Set dbs = Nothing
    End Sub
```

The following function is called from the above `CreatePKIndexes` procedure, and returns the name of the primary key if one exists, and `Null` if there isn't one:

```
Public Function GetPrimaryKey(tdf As DAO.TableDef) As String
    'Determine if the specified Primary Key exists
    Dim idx As DAO.Index

    For Each idx In tdf.Indexes
        If idx.Primary Then
            'If a Primary Key exists, return its name
            GetPrimaryKey = idx.Name
```

```
            Exit Function
        End If
    Next idx

    'If no Primary Key exists, return empty string
    GetPrimaryKey = vbNullString
End Function
```

Run the `CreatePKIndexes` procedure to define the indexes for both the `tblInvoice` and `tblInvItem` tables. In fact, you can run this procedure in your own applications to create indexes on any table that doesn't have primary keys defined. Finally, because Access is a relational database, set up relationships between the two tables to tell Access how the information in one table relates to information in the other. This enables you to create related datasets in queries. The following section describes how to create those relationships in code.

Creating Relations

The basic procedure for creating a relation is as follows:

1. Create the `Relation` object using the `Database`'s `CreateRelation` method.

2. Set the `Relation` object's attributes as appropriate.

3. Create the fields that participate in the relationship, using the `Relation` object's `CreateField` method.

4. Set the `Field` object's attributes as appropriate.

5. Append each field to the `Relation`'s `Fields` collection.

6. Append the `Relation` object to the `Database`'s `Relations` collection.

The following code creates a relationship whose name is specified by the `strRelName` argument, specifies its attributes, and adds the tables and fields that make up the relationship. (Note that you can name a relationship any way you like, but when you create a relationship using the Relationships window, Access names the relationship according to the names of the tables involved. For example, if you were to create a relationship between `tblInvoice` and `tblInvItem`, Access would name it `tblInvoicetblInvItem`.)

```
Public Sub CreateRelation(strRelName As String, _
    strSrcTable As String, strSrcField As String, _
    strDestTable As String, strDestField As String)

    Dim dbs As DAO.Database
    Dim fld As DAO.Field
    Dim rel As DAO.Relation
    Dim varRel As Variant

    Set dbs = CurrentDb
    On Error Resume Next

    'Check if the relationship already exists.
    'If so, delete it.
    If IsObject(dbs.Relations(strRelName)) Then
```

```
            dbs.Relations.Delete strRelName
    End If
    On Error Goto 0

    'Create the relation object
    Set rel = dbs.CreateRelation(strRelName, strSrcTable, strDestTable)
```

The `Relation` object now exists in memory, but as with the `TableDef` and `Index` objects, it won't be a permanent part of the database until you append it to the `Database`'s `Relations` collection.

The following code segment defines the relationship's attributes. It uses three `Relation` attribute enum values: `dbRelationLeft`, `dbRelationUpdateCascade`, and `dbRelationDeleteCascade`. These, of course, define a `LEFT JOIN` relationship with referential integrity set to `Cascade Update` and `Cascade Delete`.

When you specify the `Attribute` property, use the sum of the enum values you want to include. This is accomplished using the logical `Or` operator, rather than the unary plus (+) operator.

```
    'Set this relationship to:
    ' LEFT JOIN
    ' Referential integrity = Cascade Update and Cascade Delete
    rel.Attributes = dbRelationLeft Or _
                     dbRelationUpdateCascade Or _
                     dbRelationDeleteCascade
```

Once the `Relation` object has been created and its attributes specified, you then add all the fields that collectively form the relationship. Finally, you add the new relationship to the `Database`'s `Relations` collection to make it permanent, and refresh it.

```
    'Append the field(s) involved in the relationship
    'The Field object represents the left side of the relationship,
    'where the right side of the relationship is set with the
    'ForeignName property.
    Set fld = rel.CreateField(strSrcField)
    fld.ForeignName = strDestField

    'Append the field to the relation's Fields collection
    rel.Fields.Append fld

    'Append the relation to the Database's Relations collection
    dbs.Relations.Append rel

    'Refresh the Relations collection
    dbs.Relations.Refresh

    Set rel = Nothing
    Set fld = Nothing
    Set dbs = Nothing
End Sub
```

When you create your own relationships in code, they will not automatically appear in the Relationships window. To display the Relationships window, click the Relationships button from the Database Tools tab in the Access Ribbon.

To display the new relationships you've created in code, either add the related tables to the Relationships window, or click Show All from the Relationships group.

Putting It All Together

When writing your own procedures to create DAO objects, you should include sufficient error handling code, and perhaps even wrap the whole lot in a transaction, so if any part of it fails, you don't have orphaned objects that you will have to delete manually.

> **Remember that an orphaned object (one that remains alive in Access's memory space, but not in your application) can easily prevent Access from closing. The other side effect of having orphaned objects is that every object consumes system resources; if you have enough orphaned objects unnecessarily consuming resources, you can quite simply run out of memory, and your application will fail without warning.**

You can use the following procedure to manage all the code you just created, to test the creation of invoice tables, indexes, and relationships:

```
Public Sub CreateInvoiceSchema()
    CreateInvoiceTable
    CreatePKIndexes "tblInvoice", "InvoiceNo"
    CreateInvItemTable
    CreatePKIndexes "tblInvItem", "InvItemID"
    CreateRelation "Relation1", "tblInvoice",
        "InvoiceNo", "tblInvItem", "InvoiceNo"
End Sub
```

Creating Multi-Value Lookup Fields

There are new data types in DAO that are used to define a multi-value lookup field. The names of these types begin with dbComplex and contain the name of a type that can be used for the lookup field. In other words, if the related field for the lookup is an Integer, you can use dbComplexInteger for a multi-value lookup field. The valid field types are:

- ❏   dbComplexByte
- ❏   dbComplexDecimal
- ❏   dbComplexDouble
- ❏   dbComplexGUID
- ❏   dbComplexInteger
- ❏   dbComplexLong
- ❏   dbComplexSingle
- ❏   dbComplexText

Let's say that you have a database that tracks students and classes, with respective tables tblStudents and tblClasses. The tblClasses table defines a ClassID field, which is an AutoNumber field and the primary key. The Students table includes a field that is defined as dbComplexLong that is the multi-value lookup field for the tblClasses table. To create a multi-valued field, you must use the new Field2 object defined in DAO.

This code also demonstrates an alternate technique you can use when executing the CreateField method:

```
tdf.Fields.Append tdf.CreateField("FirstName", dbText, 50)
```

Because CreateField returns a DAO.Field2 object, it is passed as the argument to the Append method of the Fields property on the TableDef object. Using this approach reduces the amount of code you have to write and maintain.

Here's the code:

```
' Creates the Classes table
Sub CreateClassesTable()
    Dim dbs As DAO.Database
    Dim tdf As DAO.TableDef
    Dim idx As DAO.Index
    Dim fld As DAO.Field2

    'Get the database
    Set dbs = CurrentDb

    'Create the classes table
    Set tdf = dbs.CreateTableDef("tblClasses")

    'Create the ClassID field
    Set fld = tdf.CreateField("ClassID", dbLong)
    fld.Attributes = dbAutoIncrField
    tdf.Fields.Append fld

    'Create the Primary Key index using ClassID
    Set idx = tdf.CreateIndex("PrimaryKey")
    idx.Primary = True
    idx.Fields.Append tdf.CreateField("ClassID")
    idx.Fields.Refresh

    'Append the index and refresh
    tdf.Indexes.Append idx
    tdf.Indexes.Refresh

    'Create and append the ClassCode field using the abbreviated syntax
    tdf.Fields.Append tdf.CreateField("ClassCode", dbText, 25)

    'Create and append the ClassDescription field
    tdf.Fields.Append tdf.CreateField("ClassDescription", dbMemo)
    tdf.Fields.Refresh

    'Append the table to the database
    dbs.TableDefs.Append tdf
```

```
        'Cleanup
        Set fld = Nothing
        Set tdf = Nothing
        Set dbs = Nothing
End Sub

'Creates the students table
Sub CreateStudentsTable()
    Dim dbs As DAO.Database
    Dim tdf As DAO.TableDef
    Dim idx As DAO.Index
    Dim fld As DAO.Field2

    'Get the database
    Set dbs = CurrentDb

    'Create the Students table
    Set tdf = dbs.CreateTableDef("tblStudents")

    'Create the StudentID field
    Set fld = tdf.CreateField("StudentID", dbLong)
    fld.Attributes = dbAutoIncrField
    tdf.Fields.Append fld

    'Create the Primary Key (Student - AutoNumber)
    Set idx = tdf.CreateIndex("PrimaryKey")
    idx.Primary = True
    idx.Fields.Append tdf.CreateField("StudentID")
    idx.Fields.Refresh

    'Append the index and refresh
    tdf.Indexes.Append idx
    tdf.Indexes.Refresh

    'Create and append the following fields:
    'FirstName, LastName, Address, City, StateOrProvince, Region, PostalCode,
Country
    tdf.Fields.Append tdf.CreateField("FirstName", dbText, 50)
    tdf.Fields.Append tdf.CreateField("LastName", dbText, 50)
    tdf.Fields.Append tdf.CreateField("Address", dbText, 50)
    tdf.Fields.Append tdf.CreateField("City", dbText, 50)
    tdf.Fields.Append tdf.CreateField("StateOrProvince", dbText, 50)
    tdf.Fields.Append tdf.CreateField("Region", dbText, 50)
    tdf.Fields.Append tdf.CreateField("PostalCode", dbText, 50)
    tdf.Fields.Append tdf.CreateField("Country", dbText, 50)

    'Ok, now for the multi-value lookup field.
    'For this, define the field as dbComplexLong since it will
    'perform a lookup to a Long Integer field (ClassID) in the Classes table
    Set fld = tdf.CreateField("Classes", dbComplexLong)

    'Append the field
    tdf.Fields.Append fld
```

```
      'Append the table to the database
      dbs.TableDefs.Append tdf

      'Set Access properties to use the combo box control
      '- DisplayControl: ComboBox
      '- ColumnCount: 2
      '- ColumnWidths: "0"
      '- RowSource: tblClasses - This is the lookup table
      With fld
          .Properties.Append .CreateProperty("DisplayControl", dbInteger, acComboBox)
          .Properties.Append .CreateProperty("RowSource", dbText, "tblClasses")
          .Properties.Append .CreateProperty("ColumnCount", dbInteger, 2)
          .Properties.Append .CreateProperty("ColumnWidths", dbText, "0")
      End With

      'Cleanup
      Set fld = Nothing
      Set tdf = Nothing
      Set dbs = Nothing
  End Sub
```

Database Encryption with DAO

Access 2007 now supports standard encryption algorithms that are included with Windows. To maintain backward compatibility with previous versions of Access, this feature is only available for the new file formats. Database encryption combines two features that have existed in Jet for some time: database passwords and encoding. You can decrypt the database by removing the database password.

You can set the database password using DAO in several ways:

❑   Call the NewPassword method of the Database object.

❑   Compact an existing database and include a password using the CompactDatabase method.

❑   Create a new database using the CreateDatabase method and specify the password.

Using ActiveX Data Objects (ADO), you can run a query that calls ALTER DATABASE PASSWORD, *but this does not work from DAO.*

Setting the Database Password

Let's look at the three ways you can set a database password using DAO:

❑   Using the NewPassword method

❑   Compacting a database

❑   Creating a new database

Setting the database password requires that the database is opened exclusively.

143

Using the NewPassword Method

To change the password for the current database without creating a new database, you can use the NewPassword method on the Database object like this:

```
Sub ChangePassword(strOldPassword As String, strNewPassword As String)
    'Possible errors
    Const ERR_DB_OPENED_SHARED As Long = 3621
    Const ERR_INVALID_PASSWORD As Long = 3031

    On Error GoTo ChangePasswordErrors

    Dim dbs As DAO.Database

    'Get the database object
    Set dbs = CurrentDb

    'Change the password
    dbs.NewPassword strOldPassword, strNewPassword

Cleanup:
    Set dbs = Nothing
    Exit Sub

ChangePasswordErrors:
    Dim strMsg As String

    'Handle errors: invalid password and not opened exclusively
    Select Case Err.Number
        Case ERR_DB_OPENED_SHARED:
            strMsg = "The current database is not opened exclusively"
        Case ERR_INVALID_PASSWORD:
            strMsg = "The specified password is invalid"
        Case Else
            strMsg = "Unhandled Error: " & Err.Description
    End Select

    'Display the message
    MsgBox strMsg, vbCritical, "Cannot Change Password"
    Goto Cleanup
End Sub
```

Compacting a Database

Let's say that you want to compact a database using DAO and add a database password to the newly compacted database. The following code shows you how to include the database password for the CompactDatabase method on the DBEngine object:

```
Sub CompactAndEncrypt( _
        strOldDatabase As String, _
        strNewDatabase As String, _
        strPassword As String)
```

```
    'Make sure the old database exists
    If Dir(strOldDatabase) = "" Then
        MsgBox "Cannot find database: " & strOldDatabase, vbExclamation
        Exit Sub
    End If


    'Make sure the old database is not
    'the current database
    If strOldDatabase = CurrentDb.Name Then
        MsgBox "Cannot compact the currently opened database", vbExclamation
        Exit Sub
    End If


    'Make sure the new password is between 1-20 characters
    If Len(strPassword) < 1 Or Len(strPassword) > 20 Then
        MsgBox "Password must be between 1 and 20 characters", vbExclamation
        Exit Sub
    End If


    'Ok, now compact the database and set the new password
    DBEngine.CompactDatabase _
        strOldDatabase, _
        strNewDatabase, _
        dbLangGeneral & ";PWD=" & strPassword

End Sub
```

Creating a New Database

Finally, you can create a new database that is encrypted to begin with:

```
Sub CreateAndEncrypt(strDatabase As String, strPassword As String)

    'Make sure the database does not exist
    If Dir(strDatabase) <> "" Then
        MsgBox "The specified database already exists: " & strDatabase, vbExclamation
        Exit Sub
    End If


    'Make sure the new password is between 1-20 characters
    If Len(strPassword) < 1 Or Len(strPassword) > 20 Then
        MsgBox "Password must be between 1 and 20 characters", vbExclamation
        Exit Sub
    End If


    'Ok, now create the database and set the new password
    DBEngine.CreateDatabase _
        strDatabase, _
        dbLangGeneral & ";PWD=" & strPassword

End Sub
```

Setting Encryption Options

When you encrypt a database, the encryption is performed by calling into a Cryptographic Service Provider (CSP) that is registered by Windows. The CSP uses a specified encryption algorithm and key length to encrypt the specified data. For additional information about database encryption, please refer to Chapter 18.

By default, Access uses Microsoft Base Cryptographic Provider v1.0 for database encryption. The default encryption algorithm is RC4.

These options can be changed in DAO by executing the SetOption method of the DBEngine object. The three option values for database encryption are:

Option Value	Description
dbPasswordEncryptionAlgorithm	Used to change the encryption algorithm. Access only supports stream ciphers such as "RC4."
dbPasswordEncryptionKeyLength	Key length for the encryption algorithm. Set to 0 to use the default key length for the algorithm as defined by the CSP.
dbPasswordEncryptionProvider	Changes the Cryptographic Service Provider (CSP). Valid CSP names can be found in the registry.

SetOption changes settings for the current session in Access. When Access is closed, the database engine reverts to the default settings. SetOption does not affect the database that is currently open. Instead, the setting is reflected after calling another method on DBEngine.

The following code demonstrates how to change the CSP and encrypt the current database by setting the database password:

```
Sub SetPasswordAndCSP(strOldPassword As String, strNewPassword As String)
    Dim dbs As DAO.Database

    'Get the current database
    Set dbs = CurrentDb

    'Change the CSP
    DBEngine.SetOption dbPasswordEncryptionProvider, _
        "Microsoft Enhanced RSA and AES Cryptographic Provider"

    'Now, set the password
    dbs.NewPassword strOldPassword, strNewPassword

    'You could also choose to compact a database or
    'create a new database once the CSP was set

    'Cleanup
    Set dbs = Nothing
End Sub
```

> You receive a runtime error if you set the `dbPasswordEncryptionProvider` value to an invalid CSP name. The error is displayed when you execute either the `NewPassword`, `CompactDatabase`, or `CreateDatabase` method. The `SetOption` method does not display any errors.

Managing Access (JET) Security with DAO

Security in Access is based on the workgroup model, which is conceptually similar to the user-level security model employed by the Windows operating system. In contrast to database-level security models employed by other desktop database systems, Access workgroup information is stored in a file that can reside on a network share. Using this approach, the same security system can be shared by many databases, rather than having to create a separate security system for every instance of your database. It enables you to simplify security maintenance by adding or removing users and groups, or changing permissions in one centralized file.

Microsoft Access security is always present and always enabled; it is not something that can be disabled. You just don't notice it because of the default workgroup and several default users and groups.

Because DAO acts only as an interface to security in the Access database engine, a detailed discussion of this security model is beyond the scope of this book. For those who want to learn about Access database engine security in greater detail, there are several excellent books on the subject that you can read. This chapter discusses only those aspects of the DAO object model that directly relate to security; specifically how to manage users, groups, and permissions in the Access database engine using code.

> Beginning with Access 2007, user-level security is no longer supported for new file formats. This means that you cannot assign permissions to database objects such as tables and queries, or Access objects such as forms and reports in ACCDB files. User-level security is still supported for MDB files. However, the DAO object model related to users and groups has been hidden. Your code will continue to run, although DAO objects such as `User` and `Group` will not appear in the Object Browser unless you select Show Hidden Members from the browser's context menu.
>
> For additional information about this change, please refer to Chapter 18.

DAO deals with Access security in two ways. First, the `Workspace` object maintains two security-related collections: `Groups` and `Users`. Each `Group` object maintains a `Users` collection that contains information about all the users who belong to that group. Similarly, each `User` object contains a `Groups` collection that lists the groups to which that user belongs. Second, Access and database engine objects (for example, tables, forms, and so on) each have a `Permission` object that stores information about the permissions a user has to that object.

Creating Security Objects

When you create a new user or group account, either through the user interface or via code, you must supply a Personal IDentifier (PID). The PID is a case-sensitive 4–20 character string that Access combines with the user or group name to create a unique Security IDentifier (SID). The SID is a unique identifier, which is similar to a public security key. Once you create the account, you can never view or change the SID. But (and this is why the SID is notable) if you ever delete the user or group account, and later decide to re-create it, you must use the same PID because Access remembers it. If the resulting SID does not match, Access will not allow you to re-create the account. Therefore, whenever you create a new user or group account, save the PID offsite so you don't lose it.

When you create a new user account, you can also include a case-sensitive password of 1 to 20 characters, which the user must enter when logging on. The only user who can change the password is the user who owns it. However, members of the Admins group can clear any user's password.

Passwords and PIDs are encoded and stored in the workgroup file, and thus, cannot be viewed by anyone. The following sections demonstrate how to create and modify user and group accounts, and includes code to add SIDs and passwords.

Managing Users and Groups

The `Workspace` object contains a `Groups` collection and a `Users` collection. The `Groups` collection contains all the `Group` objects used in the workgroup. A `Group`, as its name suggests, is a collection of `Users` to whom you want to assign the same privileges. You can enumerate the users and groups using the following code:

```
Public Sub EnumUsersAndGroups()
    Dim wrk As DAO.Workspace
    Dim grp As DAO.Group
    Dim usr As DAO.User

    Set wrk = DBEngine(0)

    'Enumerate the groups
    Debug.Print "Groups..."
    For Each grp In wrk.Groups
        Debug.Print vbTab & grp.Name
    Next grp

    'Enumerate the users
    Debug.Print "Users..."
    For Each usr In wrk.Users
        Debug.Print vbTab & usr.Name
    Next usr

    Set grp = Nothing
    Set wrk = Nothing
End Sub
```

The preceding code simply lists all the users and groups that exist in the system, but it doesn't show the relationship between them. If you want to find out which users belong to a specific group, you need to enumerate the `Users` collection for that specific group:

```
Public Sub EnumGroupUsers(strGroup As String)
    Dim wrk As DAO.Workspace
```

```
        Dim varUser As Variant

        Set wrk = DBEngine(0)

        Debug.Print "Users belonging to the '" & strGroup & "' group..."
        For Each varUser In wrk.Groups(strGroup).Users
            Debug.Print vbTab & varUser.Name
        Next varUser

        Set wrk = Nothing
    End Sub
```

Similarly, you can list all the groups that a specific user belongs to by enumerating the Groups collection for that user:

```
    Public Sub EnumUserGroups(strUser As String)
        Dim wrk As DAO.Workspace
        Dim varGroup As Variant

        Set wrk = DBEngine(0)

        Debug.Print "Groups to which user '" & strUser & "' belongs..."
        For Each varGroup In wrk.Users(strUser).Groups
            Debug.Print vbTab & varGroup.Name
        Next varGroup

        Set wrk = Nothing
    End Sub
```

The Current User

The current user is defined as the user who is currently logged on to the database application. For most security-related operations, you need to know the name of the current user. DAO provides a convenient way of obtaining this information using the Workspace object's UserName property:

```
    strMyName = DBEngine(0).UserName
```

Using this property, you can create a User object for the current user, without having to know his name, as follows:

```
    Dim usr As DAO.User
    Set usr = DBEngine(0).Users(DBEngine(0).UserName)
```

The Access Application object also provides an easy way of obtaining the name of the user who is currently logged on, using a function appropriately named CurrentUser.

Creating and Deleting Groups

Rather than assign access permissions to individual users, as mentioned earlier, you can create groups to which one or more users can be assigned. Each group can be assigned specific permissions to the database's objects, and every user who is assigned to that group will *inherit* the permissions of that group. In this section, you learn how to use DAO to create or delete Groups in code. The following code shows how to create a new group. The basic procedure is to create the group using the `CreateGroup` method, and then append it to the `Groups` collection:

```
Public Sub CreateUserGroup(strGroupName As String,
strPID As String)
    Dim wrk As DAO.Workspace
    Dim grp As DAO.Group

    Set wrk = DBEngine(0)
    On Error GoTo CreateUserGroupErr

    'Create the new group
    Set grp = wrk.CreateGroup(strGroupName, strPID)
    ws.Groups.Append grp

CreateUserGroupErr:
    Set grp = Nothing
    Set wrk = Nothing

End Sub
```

Deleting a group is even easier. Simply execute the `Groups` collection's `Delete` method, as follows:

```
Public Sub DeleteGroup(strGroup As String)
    On Error Resume Next
    DBEngine(0).Groups.Delete strGroup
End Sub
```

You can't rename a group once it has been created. If you need to rename a group, you have to delete it, and then re-create it. Remember, though, if you need to re-create a user or group, you must supply the same PID that you used to create it in the first place.

Creating and Deleting Users

Using DAO, you can create a new user account that can then be added to one or more groups. The following code shows how to create a new user. The basic procedure is to create the user with the `CreateUser` method, and then append it to the `Users` collection:

```
Public Function CreateUserAccount(strUserName As String, _
    strPID As String, _
    strPassword As String)

    Dim wrk As DAO.Workspace
    Dim usr As DAO.User

    Set wrk = DBEngine(0)
    On Error GoTo CreateUserAccountErr

    'Create the new user
    Set usr = wrk.CreateUser(strUserName, strPID, strPassword)
    wrk.Users.Append usr

CreateUserAccountErr:
```

```
        Set usr = Nothing
        Set wrk = Nothing
    End Function
```

As with deleting a group, deleting a user is quite simple; just execute the `Users` collection's `Delete` method:

```
Public Sub DeleteUser(strUser As String)
    On Error Resume Next
    DBEngine(0).Users.Delete strUser
End Sub
```

To rename a user account, you must delete the account, and then re-create it.

User and Group Operations

Before you can assign permissions that allow users to access any of the Access or database engine objects, you must add the users to one or more groups.

There are two ways you can do this: by adding users to the group, or by adding the group to the users. Although the following two procedures achieve exactly the same end, they demonstrate how to do it:

Example: Adding Users to Groups

```
Public Sub AddUser2Group(strUser As String, strGroup As String)
    Dim wrk As DAO.Workspace
    Dim usr As DAO.User
    Dim grp As DAO.Group

    Set wrk = DBEngine(0)
    On Error Resume Next

    'Create object references
    Set grp = wrk.Groups(strUser)
    Set usr = grp.CreateUser(strUser)

    'Add the group to the user's Groups collection
    grp.Users.Append usr
    grp.Users.Refresh

    Set usr = Nothing
    Set grp = Nothing
    Set wrk = Nothing
End Sub
```

Example: Adding Groups to Users

```
Public Sub AddGroup2User(strUser As String, strGroup As String)
    Dim wrk As DAO.Workspace
    Dim usr As DAO.User
    Dim grp As DAO.Group
```

```
        Set wrk = DBEngine(0)
        On Error Resume Next

        'Create object references
        Set usr = wrk.Users(strUser)
        Set grp = usr.CreateGroup(strGroup)

        'Add the group to the user's Groups collection
        usr.Groups.Append grp
        usr.Groups.Refresh

        Set usr = Nothing
        Set grp = Nothing
        Set wrk = Nothing
    End Sub
```

Similarly, if you want to delete a user from a group, you can delete the user's entry from the Groups collection, or delete the group from the Users collection. Here's one way:

```
    Public Sub DeleteUserFromGroup(strUser As String, strGroup As String)
        Dim wrk As DAO.Workspace

        Set wrk = DBEngine(0)
        On Error Resume Next

        wrk.Users(strUser).Groups.Delete strGroup

        Set wrk = Nothing
    End Sub
```

Determining If a User Belongs to a Specific Group

When determining if a user should have access to a particular object or function, you may need to determine whether the user belongs to a specific group. As with most other functions, this is also fairly easy; simply check if the name of the user exists in the group's Users collection, or if the group exists in the user's Groups collection.

```
    Public Function IsUserInGroup (strUser As String, strGroup As String) As Boolean
        Dim wrk As DAO.Workspace
        Set wrk = DBEngine(0)

        On Error Resume Next

        IsUserInGroup = False

        'Check in the Users --> Groups collection
        IsUserInGroup = _
            (wrk.Users(strUser).Groups(strGroup).Name = strGroup)

        'You can also do it this way...
        'Check in the Groups --> Users collection
        'IsUserInGroup = _
```

```
         (wrk.Groups(strGroup).Users(strUser).Name = strUser)

     Set wrk = Nothing
End Function
```

Managing Passwords

To change a user's password, you execute the User object's NewPassword method. You must provide both the old and new passwords. However, if you are a member of the Admins groups and are changing the password of another user, the old password argument is ignored.

```
Public Sub ChangePassword(strUser As String, _
    strOldPassword As String, _
    strNewPassword As String)

    Dim wrk As DAO.Workspace
    Dim usr As DAO.User

    Set wrk = DBEngine(0)
    Set usr = wrk.Users(strUser)

    'Change the password
    usr.NewPassword strOldPassword, strNewPassword

    Set usr = Nothing
    Set wrk = Nothing
End Sub
```

The issue, of course, is that there is no way to view the password for any user.

Managing Permissions

Computer systems grant or deny access to objects and data based on the rights assigned to users or groups of users. These permissions are granted by the system administrator or owner of an object. Further, specific users can be granted or denied special access in addition to the rights of the group to which they belong.

In Access, you can grant permissions based on a specific user or group. Permissions can be *removed* from a user or group, but you cannot deny permissions in the same manner as you can in Windows or SQL Server. There is no explicit deny for permissions in a database.

In Access, user and group permissions are defined in two places. First, permissions relating to individual objects are stored in the Permissions property of Document objects. Second, permissions for objects that are created later are stored in the Permissions property of Container objects.

Depending on the specific object, different permissions can be granted. The following table describes those permissions and the constants that define them.

Object	Permission Constant	Value	Description
Container	dbSecNoAccess	0	No access to the object
	dbSecFullAccess	1048575	Full access to the object
	dbSecDelete	65536	Can delete the object
	dbSecReadSec	131072	Can read the object's security information
	dbSecWriteSec	262144	Can change the object's security information
	dbSecWriteOwner	524288	Can change the ownership of the object
Table	dbSecCreate	1	Can create new Document objects (valid only with a Container object)
	dbSecReadDef	4	Can read the table definition
	dbSecWriteDef	65548	Can modify or change the table definition
	dbSecRetrieveData	20	Can retrieve data from the Document object
	dbSecInsertData	32	Can add records
	dbSecReplaceData	64	Can modify records
	dbSecDeleteData	128	Can delete records
Database	dbSecDBAdmin	8	Assigns admin rights — can create replicas, change the database password, and set startup properties
	dbSecDBCreate	1	Can create new databases (valid only on the Databases container object in the Workgroup Information File)
	dbSecDBExclusive	4	Can open the database exclusively
	dbSecDBOpen	2	Can open the database
Macro	acSecMacExecute	8	Can run the macro
	acSecMacReadDef	10	Can read the macro's definition
	acSecMacWriteDef	65542	Can modify the macro's definition
	acSecFrmRptExecute	256	Can open the form or report
	acSecFrmRptReadDef	4	Can read the form's or report's definition and its module
	acSecFrmRptWriteDef	65548	Can modify the form's or report's definition and its module

Reading Permissions

As mentioned earlier, object permissions are stored in two main places: the Permissions property of Document objects, and the Permissions property of Container objects, the latter being where the permissions for future objects are defined. But before you get too carried away with this new found knowledge, you might be interested to know that object permissions are stored in a Long Integer bit field. To get at individual permissions, you need to perform a bitwise operation, which is not very difficult.

To determine the permissions that the current user has to Table1, for example, just read the Permissions property of its Document object:

```
Debug.Print dbs.Containers("Tables").Documents("Table1").Permissions
```

Be aware that the Permissions property returns only *explicit* permissions, which are those that are explicitly defined for that particular user. *Implicit* permissions, which are returned by the AllPermissions property, are the sum of all the permissions the user has, whether explicitly granted, or the ones they inherited by virtue of their membership of one or more groups.

For example, suppose that Fred Nurk belongs to a group called Data Entry, and the Data Entry group has dbSecInsertData and dbSecReplaceData permissions to Table1. In addition, the administrator has explicitly granted him dbSecDeleteData permissions, but accidentally revoked his individual dbSecReplaceData permissions to the same table. Because the Data Entry group has dbSecReplaceData permissions, Fred's total permissions are the sum of all permissions — dbSecInsertData + dbSecDeleteData + dbSecReplaceData.

To determine if the current user has particular permissions to an object, you must explicitly test for those permissions. The following example demonstrates this:

```
Public Function HasDeletePermissons(strTableName As String, _
    Optional strUser As String) As Boolean

    'Checks if the current user has Delete permissions to a specific table
    Dim dbs As DAO.Database
    Dim doc As DAO.Document

    Set dbs = CurrentDb

    'Set a reference to the table's Document
    Set doc = dbs.Containers!Tables.Documents(strTableName)

    'Specify the user
    If strUser <> "" Then doc.UserName = strUser

    'Test for explicit permissions only
    HasDeletePermissons = _
    ((doc.Permissions And dbSecDeleteData) = dbSecDeleteData)

    'To test for implicit permissions,
    'uncomment the following line
    'HasDeletePermissons = _
    ((doc.AllPermissions And dbSecDeleteData) = dbSecDeleteData)
```

```
         Set doc = Nothing
         Set dbs = Nothing
   End Function
```

The more observant reader might have noticed that you can, in fact, specify the username. The default setting for the Document object's UserName property is that of the current user. If, however, you set the UserName property prior to reading the Permissions property, you can check the permissions for any user or group in the workgroup.

The following code shows how to determine the exact object permissions for a specific user or group:

```
Public Sub WhichPermissions(strTableName As String, Optional strUser As String)
     'Determines the specific permissions a
     'specific user has to a specific table
     Dim dbs As DAO.Database
     Dim doc As DAO.Document
     Dim lngPermission As Long

     Set dbs = CurrentDb

     'Set a reference to the table's Document
     Set doc = dbs.Containers!Tables.Documents(strTable)

     'Specify the user
     If strUser <> "" Then doc.UserName = strUser

     'Retrieve the permissions
     lngPermission = doc.AllPermissions

     'Determine the user's implicit permissions
     Debug.Print "Permissions granted to " & strUser & " for " & strTable
     If ((doc.AllPermissions And dbSecNoAccess) = dbSecNoAccess) Then
         Debug.Print vbTab & "dbSecNoAccess"
     End If

     If ((doc.AllPermissions And dbSecFullAccess) = dbSecFullAccess) Then
         Debug.Print vbTab & "dbSecFullAccess"
     End If

     If ((doc.AllPermissions And dbSecDelete) = dbSecDelete) Then
         Debug.Print vbTab & "dbSecDelete"
     End If

     If ((doc.AllPermissions And dbSecReadSec) = dbSecReadSec) Then
         Debug.Print vbTab & "dbSecReadSec"
     End If

     If ((doc.AllPermissions And dbSecWriteSec) = dbSecWriteSec) Then
         Debug.Print vbTab & "dbSecWriteSec"
     End If
```

```
        If ((doc.AllPermissions And dbSecWriteOwner) = dbSecWriteOwner) Then
            Debug.Print vbTab & "dbSecWriteOwner"
        End If

        Set doc = Nothing
        Set dbs = Nothing
    End Sub
```

So far you've seen how to check the permissions for existing objects, but what about objects that will be created in the future? DAO provides a facility for this, too. You can retrieve the default permissions that have been set for any new objects by checking the `Permissions` property of the `Document` object's parent — the `Container` object:

```
    Debug.Print dbs.Containers!Tables.AllPermissions
    Debug.Print dbs.Containers!Tables.Permissions
```

Setting Permissions

Setting object permissions is similar to setting any other property. It is worth mentioning that you cannot set only the property, but can also simultaneously set multiple permissions, and add or remove one or more permissions.

To explicitly set the permissions for an object, you simply assign the permission to the object's `Permission` property. For example, to assign the permission for the current user to delete data from `Table1`:

```
    Set doc = dbs.Containers!Tables.Documents!Table1
    doc.Permissions = dbSecInsertData Or dbSecDeleteData
```

To add a permission to an object's existing permissions, use the bitwise `Or` operator with the existing permissions. For example, to add permission for the current user to delete data from `Table1`:

```
    Set doc = dbs.Containers!Tables.Documents!Table1
    doc.Permissions = doc.Permissions Or dbSecInsertData
```

To remove one or more permissions from the object's existing permissions, you make use of the `And` and `Not` operators. For example, to remove two permissions — the capabilities to modify and delete data — from `Table1`:

```
    Set doc = dbs.Containers!Tables.Documents!Table1
    doc.permissions = doc.Permissions And Not ( _
    dbSecReplaceData Or dbSecDeleteData)
```

Data Access with DAO

Accessing data is the reason you use databases, and a large proportion of your programming will usually revolve around manipulating those objects that deal with data: queries and recordsets. In this section, you take a detailed look at how to access and manipulate your database data using DAO objects.

Working with QueryDefs

When you build a query with the graphical Query Designer, you are building a `QueryDef` object in the default Access workspace. When you save the query, you are also appending a reference to it in the `QueryDefs` collection. You can also build a `QueryDef` in code, which is one of the purposes of this section.

You can think of permanent (Access workspace) `QueryDefs` as SQL statements that are compiled the first time they are executed. This is similar in concept to the way code is compiled. Once compiled, permanent queries run marginally faster than their temporary, unsaved counterparts, because Access does not need to compile them before execution. Temporary `QueryDefs` are useful when you don't need to save them, as when you create their SQL statements during runtime. You would normally build and run SQL statements in line with your code when you need to change its clauses depending on current operating conditions or the value of some variable.

Creating a QueryDef

To create a `QueryDef`, execute the `CreateQueryDef` method against the `Database` object.

In Microsoft Access workspaces, if you set a `QueryDef`'s `Name` property to something other than a zero-length string, it is automatically appended to the `QueryDefs` collection, and saved to disk. Omitting the `Name` property, or explicitly setting it to a zero-length string, results in a temporary (unsaved) `QueryDef`.

The following code demonstrates how to create a `QueryDef` in a Microsoft Access workspace:

```
Public Sub CreateQuery (strName As String, strSQL As String)
    Dim dbs As DAO.Database
    Dim qdf As DAO.QueryDef

    Set dbs = CurrentDb

    'Create the QueryDef
    'If the user supplies a name, the QueryDef will be
    'automatically appended to the QueryDefs collection
    Set qdf = dbs.CreateQueryDef(strName, strSQL)

    'If the user supplies a name, refresh the Navigation Pane
    If vbNullString <> strName Then Application.RefreshDatabaseWindow

    Set qdf = Nothing
    Set dbs = Nothing
End Sub
```

You can create a pass-through query to an ODBC data source by setting the `QueryDef`'s `Connect` property to a valid connection string, after the query has been created. Pass-through queries enable you to run SQL statements directly on another database such as SQL Server or Oracle.

```
    qdf.Connect = strConnectionString
```

Parameters

Although you can't append parameters to a `QueryDef` using DAO, you can create them by declaring them in the SQL as shown in the following code:

```
Sub CreateQueryWithParameters()

    Dim dbs As DAO.Database
    Dim qdf As DAO.QueryDef
    Dim prm As DAO.Parameter
    Dim strSQL As String

    Set dbs = CurrentDb
    Set qdf = dbs.CreateQueryDef("myQuery")
    Application.RefreshDatabaseWindow

    strSQL = "PARAMETERS Param1 TEXT, Param2 INT; "
    strSQL = strSQL & "SELECT * FROM [Table1] "
    strSQL = strSQL & "WHERE [Field1] = [Param1] AND [Field2] = [Param2];"
    qdf.SQL = strSQL

    Debug.Print qdf.Parameters.Count
    For Each prm In qdf.Parameters
        Debug.Print , prm.Name, prm.Type
    Next prm

    qdf.Close
    Set prm = Nothing
    Set qdf = Nothing
    Set dbs = Nothing
End Sub
```

You can also specify a query parameter's value in order to specify the value of criteria to filter the query's output, or the selected records on which the query operates. For example, the following procedure sets a reference to an existing query called `myActionQuery`, sets the value of its parameter (`Organization`), and then executes the query:

```
Public Sub ExecParameterQuery()
Dim dbs As DAO.Database
Dim qdf As DAO.QueryDef

Set dbs = CurrentDb
Set qdf = dbs.QueryDefs("myActionQuery")

'Set the value of the QueryDef's parameter
qdf.Parameters("Organization").Value = "Microsoft"

'Execute the query
qdf.Execute dbFailOnError

'Clean up
qdf.Close
Set qdf = Nothing
Set dbs = Nothing

End Sub
```

Modifying a QueryDef

Once you have created a `QueryDef`, you can modify its properties as easily as you modify any other DAO property. Here's an example:

```
Public Sub ModifyQuery(strName As String, strNewSQL As String)
    Dim dbs As DAO.Database
    Dim qdf As DAO.QueryDef

    Set dbs = CurrentDb

    'Modify the QueryDef's properties
    dbs.QueryDefs(strName).SQL = strNewSQL

    Set dbs = Nothing
End Sub
```

Deleting a QueryDef

Deleting a `QueryDef` is simple. Just issue the `Delete` method against the `QueryDefs` collection:

```
dbs.QueryDefs.Delete strName
```

Executing Queries

Queries that insert, update, or delete queries are known as *action queries*. While these types of queries do not return records, it is common to run them using code.

There are three ways to programmatically execute a query: using the `DoCmd.RunSQL` method, the `object.Execute` method, and the `OpenRecordset` method. The query argument for any of the following methods can either be the name of a permanent or temporary `QueryDef`, or a string expression that equates to a query.

DoCmd.RunSQL

Although not part of the DAO object model, you can execute the `RunSQL` method of the `DoCmd` object to run an action query:

```
DoCmd.RunSQL "UPDATE Table1 SET Field1 = 123"
```

Running a query this way displays a message box to confirm that you want to make changes to the database. To eliminate that message box, set the `DoCmd` object's `SetWarnings` property to `False` prior to calling `DoCmd.RunSQL`, but remember to set it back when you've finished, or all warning messages will thereafter be disabled.

```
DoCmd.SetWarnings False
DoCmd.RunSQL "UPDATE Table1 SET Field1 = 123"
DoCmd.SetWarnings True
```

Any errors raised while executing the query will display a message box. You can disable the message box as described previously, and you can trap the error using the `On Error Goto` construct. By default, the query is included in an existing transaction, but you can exclude it by setting the `UseTransaction` property to `False`:

```
DoCmd.RunSQL "UPDATE Table1 SET Field1 = 123", False
```

object.Execute

You can also use the `Execute` method of the `QueryDef` object or the `Database` object to run an action query:

```
qdf.Execute options
dbs.Execute "UPDATE Table1 SET Field1 = 123", options
```

With the `Execute` method, there is no need to call the `SetWarnings` method to disable change confirmation message boxes because none are displayed. The `Execute` method operates directly on its parent object.

There are several major benefits to using the `Execute` method rather than the `DoCmd.RunSQL` method:

❑   `Execute` runs faster than `DoCmd.RunSQL` does.

❑   `Execute` can be included in an existing transaction, like any other DAO operation, without needing to specify an option to do so.

❑   You can specify several options that change the way the method works.

The following table lists the various constants that can be supplied as options for the `Execute` method.

Constant	Description
dbDenyWrite	Denies write permission to other users (Microsoft Access workspaces only).
dbInconsistent	Executes inconsistent updates (Microsoft Access workspaces only).
dbConsistent	Executes consistent updates (Microsoft Access workspaces only).
dbSQLPassThrough	Executes an SQL pass-through query, which passes the query to an ODBC database for processing. (Microsoft Access workspaces only).
dbFailOnError	Rolls back updates if an error occurs (Microsoft Access workspaces only).
dbSeeChanges	Generates a runtime error if another user is changing data that you are editing (Microsoft Access workspaces only).

OpenRecordset

Last, you can execute a query when you open a recordset. To do so, specify the query name in the `Database` object's `OpenRecordset` method to run a select or action query:

```
Set rst = dbs.OpenRecordset("SELECT * FROM Table1")
```

Similarly, you can open a recordset based on a query, like so:

```
Set qdf = dbs.QueryDefs("qryMyQuery")
Set rst = qdf.OpenRecordset(dbOpenDynaset)
```

The following section on recordsets describes this in greater detail.

Working with Recordsets

When you need to access and manipulate data one record at a time, you must use a `Recordset` object. For this reason, *recordsets* are the workhorses of database programming. As you've already seen, four types of recordsets are available in DAO. The one you use depends on where the data comes from, and what you want to do with it.

Creating a Recordset

You can create a recordset by using the `OpenRecordset` method of the `Database`, `TableDef`, or `QueryDef` objects:

```
Set rst = dbs.OpenRecordset( Source, Type, Options, LockEdits )
Set rst = object.OpenRecordset( Type, Options, LockEdits )
```

The `Source` argument specifies the name of a table or query, or a string expression that equates to an SQL query. For recordsets opened using the `dbOpenTable` type argument, the `Source` argument can only be the name of a table.

The default recordset type that is opened if you omit the `Type` argument, depends on the type of table you're trying to open. If you open a Microsoft Access recordset on a local table, the default is a *Table* type. If you open a Microsoft Access recordset against a linked table or query, the default type is dynaset.

The `Type` argument values are specified by a number of constants. These constants and their values can be found in Appendix D. The following code examples demonstrate how to open different types of recordsets.

Opening a Recordset Based on a Table or Query

To open a Table type recordset or dynaset-type recordset, use code such as the following:

```
Dim dbs As DAO.Database
Dim rsTable As DAO.Recordset
Dim rsQuery As DAO.Recordset

Set dbs = CurrentDb

'Open a table-type recordset
Set rsTable = dbs.OpenRecordset("Table1", dbOpenTable)

'Open a dynaset-type recordset using a saved query
Set rsQuery = dbs.OpenRecordset("qryMyQuery", dbOpenDynaset)
```

Opening a Recordset Based on a Parameter Query

Parameter queries accept criteria based on a parameter prompt. The parameter prompt can be a hard-coded name such as the prompt shown in Figure 6-6, or you can supply its value based on a control on a form as illustrated in Figure 6-7.

Figure 6-6

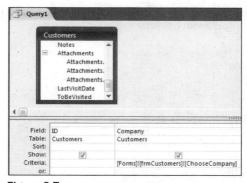

Figure 6-7

You must provide the parameter values before opening a recordset based on this type of query. To do so, you can use the `Parameters` collection of the `QueryDef` object:

```
Dim dbs As DAO.Database
Dim qdf As DAO.QueryDef
Dim rst As DAO.Recordset

Set dbs = CurrentDb

'Get the parameter query
Set qdf = dbs.QueryDefs("qryMyParameterQuery")

'Supply the parameter values
qdf.Parameters("EnterStartDate") = Date
qdf.Parameters("EnterEndDate") = Date + 7

'Open a recordset based on the parameter query
Set rst = qdf.OpenRecordset()
```

Opening a Recordset Based on an SQL Statement

The following code shows how to open a snapshot-type recordset based on an SQL statement:

```
Dim dbs As DAO.Database
Dim rsSQL As DAO.Recordset
Dim strSQL As String

Set dbs = CurrentDb

'Open a snapshot-type recordset based on an SQL statement
strSQL = "SELECT * FROM Table1 WHERE Field2 = 33"
Set rsSQL = dbs.OpenRecordset(strSQL, dbOpenSnapshot)
```

Opening a Recordset That Locks Out All Other Users

The following code opens a dynaset-type recordset using a saved query and specifies the dbDenyRead argument to prevent other users from opening the query.

```
Dim dbs As DAO.Database
Dim rsSQL As DAO.Recordset

Set dbs = CurrentDb

'Open a dynaset-type recordset based on a saved query
Set rsSQL = dbs.OpenRecordset("qryMyQuery", _
    dbOpenDynaset, dbDenyRead)
```

Filtering and Ordering Recordsets

Whenever you work on records in a database, it is rare that you want to carry out an action on the entire table. If you did, you would be best served by using an action query because queries operate much faster on large numbers of rows than do row processing methods (recordsets). However, it is more likely that you'll want to do something with a subset of records, and that means you would need to filter your query to select only those records that you wanted to work on.

With recordsets, you have the additional opportunity to sort the records, so you can operate on them in a specific order, perhaps by ascending date, for example. This section illustrates how to filter your recordsets and order their output.

Filtering Records

Filtering is simply a way of restricting the number of rows returned by a recordset so that you can minimize the amount of data you have to wade through. The additional benefit of filtering is that it also reduces the amount of data that is sent across the network, thereby minimizing bandwidth usage.

As you've already seen, you can filter a recordset using a WHERE clause in a query on which the recordset can be based, or in its Source argument. For example:

```
Set rst = dbs.OpenRecordset( _
    "SELECT * FROM tblCustomers WHERE CustomerNo > 1234")
```

This filters the recordset as it is being created. Of course, you can't do this on table-type recordsets because they load the entire table. You can, however, filter dynaset- and snapshot-type recordsets.

Another method of filtering a recordset as it is being created is to use the `Recordset` object's `Filter` property. You can't filter an existing recordset once it's been created, so the filter won't take effect until you create a new recordset that is based on the first.

For example, if you create a recordset such as the previous one (filtered on `CustomerNo`), you can then further filter its records and place the output into a second recordset. You do this by setting its `Filter` property, by specifying the WHERE clause of an SQL query, without the word WHERE. For example:

```
rst.Filter = "[CustName] LIKE '*parts*'"
```

Once the `Filter` property has been set, you can create a new recordset that will be based on a subset of the rows in the first recordset such as this:

```
Set rstFiltered = rst.OpenRecordset
```

After doing so, `rstFiltered` contains only those rows from `rst` whose `CustName` rows contains the word *parts*. You might think that this is a rather inefficient way of doing things, and under normal circumstances you'd be right; however, there are circumstances in which this approach might be the better way to go.

For example, say you want your sales representatives to visit all the customers in a certain city, based solely on when that city that was last visited. You don't know which city that might be, so the following example code creates a recordset that returns rows for all customers who were last visited between 30 and 60 days ago. Once you have the record for the last customer visited within that time frame, you then extract the name of the city in which they reside, and create another filtered recordset (based on the first), and set their `ToBeVisited` flag to `True`. This lets the sales representatives know to visit them. Of course, there's nothing here that couldn't be done in an action query, but this example demonstrates how you could use this feature.

```
Dim dbs As DAO.Database
Dim rst As DAO.Recordset
Dim rstFiltered As DAO.Recordset
Dim strCity As String

Set dbs = CurrentDb
'Create the first filtered recordset, returning customer records
'for those visited between 30-60 days ago.

Set rst = dbs.OpenRecordset( _
"SELECT * FROM Customers WHERE LastVisitDate BETWEEN Date()-60 " & _
"AND Date()-30 ORDER BY LastVisitDate DESC")

'Begin row processing
Do While Not rst.EOF

    'Retrieve the name of the first city in the selected rows
    strCity = rst!City
```

```
        'Now filter the recordset to return only the customers from that city
        rst.Filter = "City = '" & strCity & "'"
        Set rstFiltered = rst.OpenRecordset

        'Process the rows
        Do While Not rstFiltered.EOF
            rstFiltered.Edit
            rstfiltered!ToBeVisited = True
            rstFiltered.Update
            rstFiltered.MoveNext
        Loop

        'We've done what hat needed. Now exit.
        Exit Do
        rst.MoveNext
    Loop

    'Cleanup
    rstFiltered.Close
    rst.Close

    Set rstFiltered = Nothing
    Set rst = Nothing
```

Notice the ORDER BY clause in this example? It's explained in the next section.

Ordering Records

Ordering is a way of defining how the data returned in the recordset is to be sorted. For example, you might want to see, in ascending order of amount, a list of customers who owe you money.

There are three ways to sort recordsets: using the ORDER BY clause in a query on which the recordset can be based, or in its Source argument; using the Index property; or using the Sort property. You can only use the Index property on table-type recordsets, whereas the ORDER BY clause and Sort property work only with dynaset- and snapshot-type recordsets.

Ordering Using the ORDER BY Clause

When you specify the SQL statement on which a recordset is based, you can terminate the query with an ORDER BY clause. This clause specifies three things: the columns on which the sort will be based, the order of precedence for the sorting of those columns, and the actual order in which the data in those columns will be sorted. For example:

```
SELECT * FROM tblCustomers ORDER BY CustomerNo DESC, CustName
```

In this query, the records returned will be ordered according to the criteria set up for both the CustomerNo and CustName columns. By virtue of their relative positions in the clause (CustomerNo appears before CustName), the recordset will first be sorted according to the criteria for CustomerNo, and then by CustName. As you can see, CustomerNo will be sorted in descending order.

The default order is ascending, so although you can specify ASC, there's no need to explicitly declare it.

Ordering Using the Index Property

Setting the Index property of a table-type recordset is quite simple; however, you are restricted to the sort order already specified by the table's index. For example, the following code will immediately reorder the recordset in CustomerNo order. If the CustomerNo index is defined in ascending order, that is how the recordset will be sorted.

```
rst.Index = "CustomerNo"
```

Ordering Using the Sort Property

As with the Filter property discussed previously, setting the Sort property does not affect the current recordset. Rather, it affects only a new recordset that is based on the current one.

For instance, if you create a recordset, filtered on CustomerNo, you set the recordset's Sort property by specifying the ORDER BY clause of an SQL query, without the words ORDER BY. For example:

```
Set rst = dbs.OpenRecordset( _
    "SELECT * FROM tblCustomers WHERE CustomerNo > 1234")
rst.Sort = "[CustomerNo] DESC, [CustName]"
```

Then you create a new recordset whose sort order is defined by the Sort property, such as this:

```
Set rstOrdered = rst.OpenRecordset
```

Navigating Recordsets

Once you've opened a recordset, you'll probably want to get at its data and you'll probably want to move from record to record.

DAO provides five methods and five properties to help you navigate through your recordsets. The methods are Move, MoveFirst, MovePrevious, MoveNext, and MoveLast. The properties are AbsolutePosition, PercentPosition, RecordCount, BOF (beginning of file), and EOF (end of file).

Navigational Methods

The Recordset object's Move method enables you to move the cursor to another position relative to either the current position, or that specified by a Bookmark. The Move method provides two arguments.

```
rst.Move rows[, start]
```

The rows argument specifies the number of rows to move, and the direction: greater than zero indicates forward, less than zero means backward. The optional start argument specifies where to start the move. When you supply a Bookmark (discussed later in this chapter) for the start argument, DAO moves the cursor the appropriate number of rows from the position specified by the Bookmark. If you omit the start argument, DAO moves the cursor from the current position.

MoveFirst, MovePrevious, MoveNext, and MoveLast are the workhorses of recordset navigation, particularly MoveNext and MovePrevious. As their names suggest, they allow you to move the cursor forward and backward from the current position.

AbsolutePosition, PercentPosition

The `AbsolutePosition` and `PercentPosition` methods enable you to move the cursor to a specific row in the recordset. For example, if you wanted to move to the 127th row, you could issue the following method call:

```
rst.AbsolutePosition = 127
```

Similarly, to move to (roughly) half-way through the recordset, you could issue this:

```
rst.PercentPosition = 50
```

`AbsolutePosition` does not equate to a row number, and although it does return the cursor's current position in the recordset, that position can change as you add or delete rows, or change your filtering and sorting. You can't use `AbsolutePosition` with table-type recordsets.

RecordCount

Given its name, you might assume that the `RecordCount` property actually indicates the number of records returned by a recordset. That assumption is not quite accurate.

Recordsets do not always return their entire dataset immediately; they can take quite some time to populate; the more rows they have to return, the longer they take. DAO returns a pointer to the recordset early, so you can get on with doing whatever it is you want to do, assuming that the later rows will have been returned by the time you get to them.

The `RecordCount` property actually returns the number of rows that the recordset has accessed so far.

Of course, if you issue the `MoveLast` method before checking `RecordCount`, the recordset does not return until all the records have been accessed, in which case `RecordCount` then reports the correct number of rows. In fact, that's how you get an accurate record count, by issuing a `MoveLast`, followed by checking the `RecordCount` property, as the following example shows. Note that this technique does not work with forward-only recordsets.

```
Set rst = dbs.OpenRecordset("SELECT * FROM Table1", dbOpenDynaset)

If rst.AbsolutePosition > -1 Then
    'Move to the last row
    rst.MoveLast

    'Now get the count
    lngCount = rst.RecordCount

    'If you want, you can now move again
    rst.MoveFirst

    '----
    'Continue processing
    '----

End If
```

RecordCount always returns the correct number of rows for table-type recordsets.

In a single-user environment, once RecordCount has the correct number of rows, it stays synchronized when rows are added or deleted. In a multiuser environment, however, things get a little trickier.

For example, if two users are modifying records in the same table, additions or deletions made by one user will not be reflected on the other user's computer until they access *that* record (or the place where a deleted record *used* to be). To ensure you have an accurate record count in a multiuser environment:

- ❑ Use the recordset's Requery method (see the following note); or
- ❑ Use the MoveLast method again.

> *The Requery method is not supported on table-type recordsets. The RecordCount property for snapshot-type recordsets will not change once it has been created, and it certainly won't reflect changes made by other users.*

BOF, EOF

If you move beyond the boundaries of a recordset, an error will occur. To avoid this rather unpleasant side effect of poor programming practice, you should test to see whether you have reached the beginning or end of the recordset. Make sense?

Before using MoveNext or MoveFirst, you should check the value of BOF and EOF.

```
If Not rst.BOF Then rst.MovePrevious
```

or

```
If Not rst.EOF Then rst.MoveNext
```

To help you understand the behavior of these properties, consider the following scenarios:

- ❑ You issue MoveNext while the cursor is on the last row, and EOF returns True. You then issue MoveNext again, EOF remains True, and an error occurs.
- ❑ You issue MovePrevious while the cursor is on the first row, and BOF returns True. You then issue MovePrevious again, BOF remains True, and an error occurs.
- ❑ AbsolutePosition can be used to test for an empty recordset, but it cannot be used on table-type recordsets, so you need another method (discussed in the next section) for determining whether a recordset contains any records.
- ❑ BOF and EOF are widely used when looping through recordsets, when you don't know how many records have been returned. Usually, row processing begins at the first row, and continues unil all the rows have been processed. Sometimes, however, processing begins at the last record, and continues backward until the beginning of the recordset. BOF and EOF allow you to do this.

For example, the following code shows a standard forward looping construct:

```
Set rst = dbs.OpenRecordset("SELECT * FROM Table1", dbOpenDynaset)
```

```
Do While Not rst.EOF
    'Process the rows
    rst.MoveNext
Loop
```

The following example demonstrates a typical reverse-direction loop:

```
Set rst = dbs.OpenRecordset("SELECT * FROM Table1", dbOpenDynaset)
rst.MoveLast

Do While Not rst.BOF
    'Process the rows
    rst.MovePrevious
Loop
```

Testing for an Empty Recordset

As mentioned in the previous section, if you attempt to move beyond a recordset's boundaries, an error occurs. Similarly, if you attempt to execute any other recordset method on an empty recordset (one that has not returned any records), an error occurs.

Whenever you open a recordset, you usually want to do something with the data it returns, so the first thing you need to know is whether it returned any records. If the data is there, you can confidently take whatever actions you had planned. But if, for whatever reason, the recordset doesn't return any records, you have to take some alternative action such as displaying a message to the user or simply exiting the routine.

Testing for an empty recordset can be accomplished in several ways:

❑   Test for `AbsolutePosition`, as described earlier.

❑   Test for `BOF` and `EOF` together. If `BOF` and `EOF` are both `True`, the recordset is empty. For example:

```
Set rst = dbs.OpenRecordset("SELECT * FROM Table1", dbOpenDynaset)
If Not (rst.BOF And rst.EOF) Then
    'The recordset returned records
End If
```

❑   If you need to loop through the recordset, create a condition test that can't be met in the event of an empty recordset. For example:

```
Set rst = dbs.OpenRecordset("SELECT * FROM Table1", dbOpenDynaset)
Do Until rst.EOF
    'The recordset returned records
Loop
```

❑   Check the recordset's `RecordCount` property. If it is zero, you know there aren't any records. For example:

```
Set rst = dbs.OpenRecordset("SELECT * FROM Table1", dbOpenDynaset)
If rst.RecordCount > 0 Then
    'The recordset returned records
End If
```

Navigating Recordsets with Multi-Value Lookup Fields

You've seen the `Recordset` and `Field` objects for accessing data in a table or query. There are, however, new objects in DAO that are used to manipulate and navigate multi-value lookup fields. These objects are appropriately named `Recordset2` and `Field2`. In fact, if you declare a `Recordset` or `Field` object in an ACCDB file, you are actually using a `Recordset2` or `Field2` object. This happens regardless of whether you open a recordset that contains a multi-value lookup field.

Because a multi-value lookup field can store many values, the value of the field is actually a recordset. In other words, you can navigate through the values in a multi-value lookup field in the same manner as other recordsets.

For example, say you are an administrator at a small college and would like to track students and the classes that those students take. You have already created the table of classes that contains information about each class. You start by creating the Students table and adding a multi-value lookup field named `Classes` to store all of the classes taken by a particular student. The following code shows how to print the list of students and the classes they take:

```
Sub PrintStudentsAndClasses()
    Dim dbs As DAO.Database
    Dim rsStudents As DAO.Recordset2    'Recordset for students
    Dim rsClasses  As DAO.Recordset2    'Recordset for classes
    Dim fld As DAO.Field2

    'open the database
    Set dbs = CurrentDb()

    'get the table of students
    Set rsStudents = dbs.OpenRecordset("tblStudents")

    'loop through the students
    Do While Not rsStudents.EOF

        'get the classes field
        Set fld = rsStudents("Classes")

        'get the classes Recordset
        'make sure the field is a multi-valued field before
        'getting a Recordset object
        If fld.IsComplex Then
            Set rsClasses = fld.Value
        End IF

        'access all records in the recordset
        If Not (rsClasses.BOF And rsClasses.EOF) Then
            rsClasses.MoveLast
            rsClasses.MoveFirst
        End If

        'print the student and number of classes
        Debug.Print rsStudents("FirstName") & " " & rsStudents("LastName"), _
            "Number of classes: " & rsClasses.RecordCount
```

```
                 'print the classes for this student
                 Do While Not rsClasses.EOF
                     Debug.Print , rsClasses("Value")
                     rsClasses.MoveNext
                 Loop

                 'close the Classes recordset
                 rsClasses.Close

                 'get the next student
                 rsStudents.MoveNext
             Loop

             'cleanup
             rsStudents.Close

             Set fld = Nothing
             Set rsStudents = Nothing
             Set dbs = Nothing
         End Sub
```

Because the related class data is stored as a recordset, you can use the following line to retrieve the classes for a student:

```
Set rsClasses = fld.Value
```

This creates a `Recordset2` object that contains one field named `Value`. This field contains the value of the bound column as displayed in the multi-valued combo box or list box in Access.

Bookmarks and Recordset Clones

A recordset `Bookmark` is a special marker that you place in your recordset so you can quickly return or refer to it at some later stage. For example, to move from your current position in the recordset to check or change a value in some other part of the same recordset, you could set a `Bookmark`, move to the other spot, make your changes, and then return to where you were in the first place.

In terms of recordsets, a clone is a functional replica of the original. A clone of a recordset points to the same data as the recordset it was copied from. Changes made to the data in the clone are reflected in the original recordset. The difference is primarily in navigation. Using a cloned recordset, you can navigate or search for data without moving the cursor in the original recordset. For example, you might want to search for data in a form without changing the record position of the form. Using a clone, you can perform the search, and then when you find the data you're looking for, save the current `Bookmark` for the clone. Once the `Bookmark` has been set, then set the `Bookmark` in the original recordset to move its cursor.

Using Bookmarks

When you open a recordset, every row is automatically assigned a unique internal `Bookmark`, and as you will soon see, creating a reference to a `Bookmark` is simply a matter of setting the value of a variable. So there is really no practical limit to the number of bookmarks you can set. When you close the recordset, the internal `Bookmarks` are lost, and any `Bookmarks` you have set become invalid.

Although recordsets based entirely on Access tables always support Bookmarks, not all recordset types do. Recordsets based on external data sources may not allow them. For example, recordsets based on linked Paradox tables that have no primary key do not support bookmarks. For that reason, you should always check the Recordset object's Bookmarkable property before attempting to use Bookmarks on non-Access recordsets.

Using Bookmarks is much faster than using the other recordset navigation methods. The following procedure demonstrates how to use Bookmarks for record navigation:

```
Public Sub UsingBookmarks()
    Dim dbs As DAO.Database
    Dim rst As DAO.Recordset
    Dim varBookmark As Variant

    Set dbs = CurrentDb
    Set rst = dbs.OpenRecordset("SELECT * FROM Table1", dbOpenDynaset)

    If rst.AbsolutePosition > -1 Then
        'Force the entire recordset to load
        rst.MoveLast
        rst.MoveFirst

        'Move to the middle of the recordset, and print
        'the current cursor position, for reference
        rst.PercentPosition = 50
        Debug.Print "Current position: " & rs.AbsolutePosition

        'Set the bookmark
        varBookmark = rst.Bookmark

        'Move to the last record, and print its position
        rst.MoveLast
        Debug.Print "Current position: " & rs.AbsolutePosition

        '
        'Do whatever you came here to do
        '

        'Now move back, and verify the position
        rst.Bookmark = varBookmark
        Debug.Print "Current position: " & rs.AbsolutePosition
    End If

    rst.Close
    Set rst = Nothing
    Set dbs = Nothing

End Sub
```

Now What About Those Clones?

As mentioned earlier, a clone is a functional replica of the original. Now let's take a closer look at how to use them. There are two clone methods: Clone and RecordsetClone. Clone is a method of the

Recordset object, whereas RecordsetClone is a property of the Access Form object. Both are identical in function, except that you can't set the Filter or Sort properties for recordsets created using the RecordSetClone property.

> *Microsoft states in the online help that the recordset returned by the* Clone *method has no current position when it is first created. Calling* AbsolutePosition *straight after creating the clone indicates that it does; however, I'm inclined to take Microsoft at its word and not rely on a clone having a current position until after I've executed one of the* Move *methods.*

If you use the Clone or RecordsetClone method to create a copy of the original recordset, all the bookmarks are identical because rather than creating a new recordset from scratch, the two clone methods simply point an object variable at the original set of rows. The clone operates on exactly the same data as the original, so any changes made in one are reflected in the other. But (and here's the nifty part), although the data and bookmarks are identical, you can operate on the clone independent of the original; that is, you can change the cursor position in the clone (by using any of the navigation methods) and have no effect on the cursor position in the original. It is for this reason that recordset clones and bookmarks are usually mentioned together.

Let's say you are designing a data entry form for customers and that you want to allow the users to type in a customer number, and have the form immediately display the record for the customer with that number. There are several ways to do this, not all of them satisfactory.

You could use DoCmd.ApplyFilter or reopen the form using a filter with DoCmd.OpenForm, but at best, they would return only one record, and your form navigation buttons would be useless. At worst, they would return an empty recordset. The solution is to use a bookmark and recordset clone together. In the AfterUpdate event of your Customer Number text box, you could add the following code:

```
Private Sub txtEnterCustNo_AfterUpdate()
    Dim rstClone As DAO.Recordset
    Dim strCustNo As String

    'Remove leading and trailing spaces
    strCustNo = Trim(Me.txtEnterCustNo)

    'Check that the text box contains a value
    If strCustNo <> "" Then
        'Create a clone of the form's recordset
        Set rstClone = Me.RecordSetClone

        'Search for the customer's record
        rstClone.FindFirst "[CustNo] = """ & strCustNo & """"

        'The FindFirst method is explained in the following section
        'Test the result of the search
        If rstClone.NoMatch Then
            'NoMatch returned True (not a match)
            MsgBox "Customer not found."
        Else
            'NoMatch returned False (found)
            'The clone's bookmark is now set to its current position
            'which is the row returned by the FindFirst method
            '
```

```
                'Move the form's current cursor position
                'to the one pointed to by the clone's bookmark
                Me.Bookmark = rstClone.Bookmark
            End If
        End If

        'Clean up
        On Error Resume Next
        rstClone.Close
        Set rstClone = Nothing

    End Sub
```

Examining the code, you can see that the real work is done in no more than four lines.

1. Create a clone of the form's recordset.

```
Set rsClone = Me.RecordsetClone
```

2. Search for the record using the clone (leaves the original recordset untouched).

```
rsClone.FindFirst "[CustNo] = """ & strCustNo & """"
```

3. Check if the search failed. If so, you return a message box to inform the user. If the search passes, you execute line 4.

```
If rsClone.NoMatch Then
```

4. Change the form's `Bookmark`.

```
Me.Bookmark = rsClone.Bookmark
```

Finding Records

As you saw in the preceding section, you often need a way to find a specific record when working with recordsets. DAO provides two ways to find a specific record: `Seek` and `Find`. The one you choose to use depends entirely on the type of recordset you want to use it on.

The Seek Method

The `Seek` method is the fastest way to find a specific record, but it can be used only on table-type recordsets because it specifically relies on the table's indexes. Naturally, the table must have at least one index for it to search on. Trying to call `Seek` against a non–table-type recordset will earn you a runtime error. `Seek` uses the following syntax:

```
rst.Seek comparison, key1, key2. . .key13
```

To use `Seek`, you must specify three things: the name of the index to use (you can specify only one index at a time), a comparison operator string (which can be <, <=, =, =>,or >), and one or more values that correspond to the value of the key you're looking for. You can specify up to 13 different key values.

For example, the following code shows how to search the `tblCustomers` table to find a customer whose `CustomerNo` is `123`:

```
Set rst = dbs.OpenRecordset("tblCustomer", dbOpenTable)
rst.Index = "CustomerNo"
rst.Seek "=", 123
```

You might recall from the section on creating table indexes that the primary key index is called `PrimaryKey` by default, although you can name it anything you like. If you want to use the table's primary key index, you must know its name.

To use `Seek` effectively, you need to understand how it works. If you specify =, =>,or > as the comparison operator, Access starts its search at the beginning of the recordset and works its way to the end. If you use any of the other operators, Access starts at the end of the recordset, and moves toward the beginning. With that knowledge, you can see that using `Seek` within a loop is essentially pointless.

You must specify a key value for each column in the index, particularly if you're using the = comparison operator. The reason is that some of the key fields may default to `Null`, and because nothing can "equal" `Null`, your `Seek` method will usually not find what you're looking for.

The `Seek` method is not supported for linked tables, but all is not lost; the following code demonstrates how to use `Seek` on a linked table:

```
'Open the database that contains the table that is linked
Set dbs = OpenDatabase(strMyExternalDatabase)

'Open a table-type recordset against the external table
Set rst = dbs.OpenRecordset("tblCustomers", dbOpenTable)

'Specify which index to search on
rst.Index = "CustomerNo"

'Specify the criteria
rst.Seek "=", 123

'Check the result
If rst.NoMatch Then
    MsgBox "Record not found."
Else
    MsgBox "Customer name: " & rs.CustName
End If
```

What this does is open the external database that contains the table that is linked in the current database. It then creates a table-type recordset on the table in that database, so that you are operating directly on the table you want to search. The code searches the table and, finally, checks to see if the search failed. Never assume that the search is successful; instead, always use the recordset's `NoMatch` property to determine the result.

Even doing things this way, in most circumstances, the `Seek` method is still faster than the `Find` methods.

The Find Methods

There are four `Find` methods: `FindFirst`, `FindPrevious`, `FindNext`, and `FindLast`. Their purpose is self-evident, given their names, and you can use them on all recordset types.

Because the `Find` methods enable you to specify any field in the criteria, they may not be capable of using a table's indexes to execute a search. Compare this to the `Seek` method, which always uses a table's indexes to execute the search. Without an indexed field, the `Find` methods can just as easily use a table scan to find the right record; it just depends on the type of search, and amount of data being searched. Not surprisingly then, using the `Find` methods is usually far slower than using `Seek`.

A table scan is where the database engine must read each record as a part of a search. This often results in a query or operation that is significantly slower than methods such as `Seek`.

The `Find` methods can be used on filtered dynaset and snapshot recordsets, which minimizes the number of records that have to be searched.

In addition, because you have `FindNext` and `FindPrevious` methods at your disposal, you don't have to start at the beginning or end of the recordset to find subsequent matches; you can just keep searching until you find the record you want.

All four methods use the same syntax:

```
rs.[FindFirst | FindPrevious | FindNext | FindLast] criteria
```

The `criteria` argument can be any valid SQL WHERE clause, without the word WHERE. For example, the following code demonstrates how to find all instances of a customer having the word *parts* in his or her name.

```
Sub FindOrgName()
    Dim dbs As DAO.Database
    Dim rst As DAO.Recordset

    'Get the database and recordset
    Set dbs = CurrentDb
    Set rst = dbs.OpenRecordset("tblCustomers")

    'Search for the first matching record
    rst.FindFirst "[OrgName] LIKE '*parts*'"

    'Check the result
    If rst.NoMatch Then
        MsgBox "Record not found."
        GoTo Cleanup
    Else
        Do While Not rs.NoMatch
            MsgBox "Customer name: " & rst!CustName
            rs.FindNext "[OrgName] LIKE '*parts*'"
        Loop

        'Search for the next matching record
        rst.FindNext "[OrgName] LIKE '*parts*'"
```

```
        End If

Cleanup:
    rst.Close
    Set rst = Nothing
    Set dbs = Nothing
End Sub
```

Once a matching record is found, any subsequent search begins from the *current* cursor position, not the start or end of the recordset like in the Seek method. Again, always follow the search with a check of the recordset's NoMatch property, to determine the result of the search.

Working with Recordsets

So far you've looked at navigating through recordsets, setting and using bookmarks, creating recordset clones, and finding specific records. All this has been done so that you can get to the exact record that you intend to do something with.

So what can you do with recordsets? The following sections answer that question.

Retrieving Field Values

On an open recordset, you return a field value by simply referring to it. There are, of course, several ways to do this.

The first method is to refer to the field by name, as in the following code.

```
Set rst = dbs.OpenRecordset("tblMyTable")
MsgBox rst!CustomerNo
'or
MsgBox rst("CustomerNo")
```

Don't forget that the field name you use depends entirely on the table or query on which the recordset is based. For example, if the customer number is contained in the CustomerNo field, and the recordset gets its data directly from tblCustomers, then rs!CustomerNo would suffice. However, if the recordset gets its data from a query in which the CustomerNo field is renamed (using the As keyword) to CustNo:

```
SELECT CustomerID, CustomerNo As CustNo, CustName FROM tblCustomers
```

then you would use rs!CustNo.

You can also refer to a field by the recordset's Field object, as in the following example:

```
MsgBox rst.Fields!CustomerNo
MsgBox rst.Fields("CustomerNo")
MsgBox rst.Fields(2)
```

Adding, Editing, and Deleting Rows

Not all recordsets are editable, and the same can be said about some rows. Snapshot recordsets are never editable, and user permissions and record locks can result in recordsets or individual rows that you cannot edit. In addition, joins in some recordsets that are based on multiple tables can render the entire recordset uneditable.

Adding Rows

The procedure for adding rows to a recordset is quite simple: Open the recordset, issue the recordset's AddNew method, make the additions, and then issue the Update method. Here's an example:

```
'Open the recordset
Set rst = dbs.OpenRecordset("tblCustomers", dbOpenynaset)
With rst

    'Begin the editing session

    .AddNew
    'Make the additions
    !CustName = "Fred Nurk"
    !DOB = DateSerial(1956, 11, 5)
    !LastVisited = Date()
    '
    'Make other additions if you wish
    '
    'Commit the changes

    .Update
End With
```

If using an Autonumber field, there is no need to specify it as Access will automatically calculate and enter it for you. In fact, if you try to specify a value for an Autonumber field, Access will give an error.

Editing Rows

The procedure for editing recordset data is quite simple: Move to the row you want to edit, issue the recordset's Edit method, make the changes, and then issue the Update method. The following example demonstrates how:

```
'Open the recordset
Set rst = dbs.OpenRecordset("tblCustomers", dbOpenDynaset)
With rst
    'Find the record you want to edit
    .FindFirst "[CustomerNo] = 123"

    If Not .NoMatch Then
        'Begin the editing session
        .Edit

        'Make the change(s)
        !LastVisited = Date()
        '
        'Make other changes if you wish
        '

        'Commit the changes
```

```
        .Update
    Else
        MsgBox "Record not found."
    End If
End With
```

Deleting Rows

Deleting rows is even simpler; you just move to the row you want to delete and issue the `Delete` method.

```
'Open the recordset
Set rst = dbs.OpenRecordset("tblCustomers", dbOpenynaset)
With rst

    'Find the record you want to edit
    .FindFirst "[CustomerNo] = 123"

    If Not .NoMatch Then
        'Delete the row
        .Delete
    Else
        MsgBox "Record not found."
    End If
End With
```

An important point to note when deleting rows is that as soon as you delete one, all the rows above it shift down one position. This is of real consequence only if you are moving up through the recordset (toward the end), deleting rows as you go. For example, if you wanted to delete a contiguous set of rows, you could end up deleting every second row. This is because when you delete the current row, the cursor does not move, but the rows above it move down one position to compensate. So, as Figure 6-8 shows, if you were on row 6 when you deleted it, the cursor hasn't changed position, but you will then be on row 7.

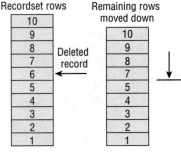

Figure 6-8

180

The recommended procedure for deleting contiguous rows is to move down (from the end to the beginning) through the rows, rather than up.

```
rst.MoveLast
Do Until rst.BOF
    rst.Delete
    rst.MovePrevious
Loop
```

Canceling an Edit

If you change your mind and decide not to continue adding or editing records, you can cancel the update using the CancelUpdate method. You can only the cancel changes between the AddNew...Update or Edit...Update methods. For example:

```
With rst
    .AddNew
    !OrgName = strOrgName
    !Address = strAddress

    'If some criteria is met, update the record
    If IsFinancial(lngOrgID) Then
        .Refund = curRefundAmt
        .Update
    Else
        'If the criteria test fails, cancel the update
    .CancelUpdate
    End If
End With
```

Using Arrays with Recordsets

Sometimes you may choose to populate an array with data from a recordset. Perhaps you're intending to pass the array to a Windows API, and because APIs do not accept recordsets as parameters, this is the only way you can do it. Typically, you would define the array and then loop through the rows, appending data to the array as you went, as the following code illustrates:

```
Dim varMyArray() As Variant
Dim varField As Variant

Set rst = dbs.OpenRecordset("Table1", dbOpenSnapshot)

rst.MoveLast
ReDim varMyArray(rst.RecordCount, rst.Fields.Count)
rst.MoveFirst

Do While Not rst.EOF
    For Each varField In rst.Fields
        varMyArray(rst.AbsolutePosition, varField.OrdinalPosition) = varField
    Next varField
    rst.MoveNext
Loop
```

But DAO provides a nifty little method to do all this for you — `GetRows`. `GetRows` returns a two-dimensional array containing all the column data for the specified number of rows, with the first element specifying the row and the second specifying the column.

```
Dim varMyArray As Variant
Set rst = dbs.OpenRecordset("SELECT Field1, Field2 FROM Table1", dbOpenSnapshot)
varMyArray = rst.GetRows(120)
```

You don't have to define the array's rows; in fact, you don't even have to declare it as an array; just define it as a variant. Access takes care of the rest.

After you call `GetRows`, the recordset's cursor position is set to the next unread row. You can specify the number of rows to return, but if you specify more rows than exist, Access returns only the number of rows actually present in the recordset.

Be a little judicious when using this technique, because Access returns all the recordset columns, regardless of their data type. You could end up with Memo and OLE (object linking and embedding) data in your array. It is wiser to filter the recordset, so you only have the data you actually need.

Working with Attachment Fields

As mentioned earlier, Access 2007 includes a new data type — Attachment — that you can use with ACCDB files in Access. This type can store zero or more files that are associated with an individual record. Remember the students and classes example? Say that you want to store the class syllabus and homework assignments with the class. The Attachment data type enables you to save the file as part of the database without the bloat of an OLE Object.

Attachment fields are a special type of multi-valued field in which multiple fields are included in the nested recordset. The fields defined by the Attachment data type are described in the following table:

Field Name	Description
FileData	The file itself is stored in this field.
FileFlags	Reserved for future use.
FileName	The name of the file in the attachment field.
FileTimeStamp	Reserved for future use.
FileType	The file extension of the file in the attachment field.
FileURL	The URL for the file for a linked SharePoint list. Will be `Null` for local Access tables.

Navigating Attachments

Because attachment fields are a type of multi-valued field, you can navigate them by enumerating through the nested recordset for the field. The following code shows how to print a list of attachments that are included with each record in a table.

```
Sub ListAttachments()
    Dim dbs As DAO.Database
    Dim rst As DAO.Recordset2
    Dim rsA As DAO.Recordset2
    Dim fld As DAO.Field2

    'Get the database, recordset, and attachment field
    Set dbs = CurrentDb
    Set rst = dbs.OpenRecordset("tblAttachments")
    Set fld = rst("Attachments")

    'Navigate through the table
    Do While Not rst.EOF

        'Print the first and last name
        Debug.Print rst("FirstName") & " " & rst("LastName")

        'Get the recordset for the Attachments field
        Set rsA = fld.Value

        'Print all attachments in the field
        Do While Not rsA.EOF
            Debug.Print , rsA("FileType"), rsA("FileName")

            'Next attachment
            rsA.MoveNext
        Loop

        'Next record
        rst.MoveNext
    Loop

    rst.Close
    dbs.Close
    Set fld = Nothing
    Set rst = Nothing
    Set dbs = Nothing
End Sub
```

Adding, Saving, and Deleting Attachments

To load binary data in an Access database in the past, you could either use the OLE Object data type and automate a form by using the Bound OLE Object control or you could use the AppendChunk method of the Field object. Attachment fields make this much more elegant and save space because they are compressed in the database.

Adding Attachments

Using the Field2 object, you can insert or save attachment fields. The Field2 object makes it easy to insert an attachment into a field using a new method called LoadFromFile.

The following code demonstrates inserting a file into an attachment field. The `strPattern` argument in the function enables you to add all files in the directory specified by `strPath` that match a given pattern. This might be useful for loading all `.bmp` files in a folder, but not the `.gif` files.

```
Public Function LoadAttachments(strPath As String, Optional strPattern As ↵
String = "*.*") As Long
    Dim dbs As DAO.Database
    Dim rst As DAO.Recordset2
    Dim rsA As DAO.Recordset2
    Dim fld As DAO.Field2
    Dim strFile As String

    'Get the database, recordset, and attachment field
    Set dbs = CurrentDb
    Set rst = dbs.OpenRecordset("tblAttachments")
    Set fld = rst("Attachments")

    'Navigate through the table
    Do While Not rst.EOF

        'Get the recordset for the Attachments field
        Set rsA = fld.Value

        'Load all attachments in the specified directory
        strFile = Dir(strPath & "\*.*")

        rst.Edit
        Do While Len(strFile) > 0
            'Add a new attachment that matches the pattern.
            'Pass "" to match all files.
            If strFile Like strPattern Then
                rsA.AddNew
                rsA("FileData").LoadFromFile strPath & "\" & strFile
                rsA.Update

                'Increment the number of files added
                LoadAttachments = LoadAttachments + 1
            End If
            strFile = Dir
        Loop
        rsA.Close

        rst.Update
        'Next record
        rst.MoveNext
    Loop

    rst.Close
    dbs.Close

    Set fld = Nothing
    Set rsA = Nothing
    Set rst = Nothing
    Set dbs = Nothing
End Function
```

Saving Attachments

To save an OLE Object field value to the computer required writing code for the Bound OLE Object control on a form. Using an Attachment field, you can now save your attachments to the computer without the need for a form. The `Field2` object includes a new method named `SaveToFile` that makes this easier. The following code demonstrates saving an attachment to a specified location.

```
Public Function SaveAttachments(strPath As String, Optional strPattern As ↵
String = "*.*") As Long
    Dim dbs As DAO.Database
    Dim rst As DAO.Recordset2
    Dim rsA As DAO.Recordset2
    Dim fld As DAO.Field2
    Dim strFullPath As String

    'Get the database, recordset, and attachment field
    Set dbs = CurrentDb
    Set rst = dbs.OpenRecordset("tblAttachments")
    Set fld = rst("Attachments")

    'Navigate through the table
    Do While Not rst.EOF

        'Get the recordset for the Attachments field
        Set rsA = fld.Value

        'Save all attachments in the field
        Do While Not rsA.EOF
            If rsA("FileName") Like strPattern Then
                strFullPath = strPath & "\" & rsA("FileName")

                'Make sure the file does not exist and save
                If Dir(strFullPath) = "" Then
                    rsA("FileData").SaveToFile strFullPath
                End If

                'Increment the number of files saved
                SaveAttachments = SaveAttachments + 1
            End If

            'Next attachment
            rsA.MoveNext
        Loop
        rsA.Close

        'Next record
        rst.MoveNext
    Loop

    rst.Close
    dbs.Close

    Set fld = Nothing
    Set rsA = Nothing
    Set rst = Nothing
    Set dbs = Nothing
```

Deleting Attachments

The following code shows you how to delete an attachment from a table. The `strRemoveFile` argument is the name of the file to remove. Specify the `strFilter` argument to add a filter to the table prior to deleting attachments.

```
Function RemoveAttachment(strRemoveFile As String, Optional strFilter As ↵
String) As Long
    Dim dbs As DAO.Database
    Dim rst As DAO.Recordset2
    Dim rsA As DAO.Recordset2
    Dim fld As DAO.Field2

    'Get the database
    Set dbs = CurrentDb

    'Open the recordset. If the strFilter is supplied, add it to the WHERE
    'clause for the recordset. Otherwise, any files matching strFileName
    'will be deleted
    If Len(strFilter) > 0 Then
        Set rst = dbs.OpenRecordset("SELECT * FROM tblAttachments WHERE " ↵
& strFilter)
    Else
        Set rst = dbs.OpenRecordset("tblAttachments")
    End If

    'Get the Attachment field
    Set fld = rst("Attachments")

    'Navigate through the recordset
    Do While Not rst.EOF

        'Get the recordset for the Attachments field
        Set rsA = fld.Value

        'Walk the attachments and look for the file name to remove
        Do While Not rsA.EOF
            If rsA("FileName") Like strRemoveFile Then
                rsA.Delete

                'Increment the number of files removed
                RemoveAttachment = RemoveAttachment + 1
            End If
            rsA.MoveNext
        Loop

        'Cleanup the Attachments recordset
        rsA.Close
        Set rsA = Nothing

        'Next record
        rst.MoveNext
    Loop

    rst.Close
    dbs.Close
```

```
        Set fld = Nothing
        Set rst = Nothing
        Set dbs = Nothing
    End Function
```

Append Only Fields

As mentioned earlier, you can create an append-only field by setting the AppendOnly property of a Memo field. In DAO, you can set the AppendOnly property of the Field2 object to True. When this property is enabled, the memo field keeps its previous values as the data in the field is changed. This happens regardless of whether you change the value in the Access interface or in DAO. In the Access interface only the current value is displayed.

This can be useful in many scenarios such as:

❑   Call centers tracking correspondence with a customer

❑   Keeping a maintenance history for an asset

❑   Content tracking for a small content management system

While this feature is very powerful, there isn't a way to retrieve the history data for the field using DAO. Fortunately, the Access Application object has a method named ColumnHistory to retrieve this data. This, however, requires that Access is installed to retrieve this information. External applications will not be able to retrieve this data.

Some distinct limitations to the ColumnHistory method exist. First, the combined history is returned as a single string value. That means you have to parse the value to get something meaningful. You'll see an example of parsing this value shortly. Second, all rich formatting is removed. And finally, the date/time value in the string is localized, making it more difficult to write generic parsing code.

For tracking purposes, the column history also includes the date and time that the change was made. This data is stored in the order in which the changes were made and appears in the following format:

```
[Version:  Date Time ] History Data
```

You can also view the column history for a memo field using the Access interface (see Figure 6-9).

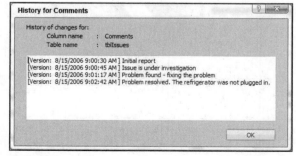

Figure 6-9

Let's say that in the issue tracking example that you would like to see the data sorted in descending order. The following code uses the ColumnHistory method in Access to retrieve the values that were in the column and add them to a list box named lstHistory:

```
Private Sub ShowColumnHistory(strTableName As String, strFieldName As String)
    'History data is in this format:
    '[Version:  Date Time ] History Data
    Const VERSION_PREFIX As String = "[Version:  "

    Dim strHistory      As String
    Dim strHistoryItem  As String
    Dim astrHistory()   As String
    Dim lngCounter      As Long
    Dim datDate         As Date
    Dim datTime         As Date
    Dim strData         As String

    'Get the column history
    strHistory = Application.ColumnHistory(strTableName, strFieldName, "")

    'Make sure there is history data
    If Len(strHistory) > 0 Then
        'Parse the column history into separate items.
        'Each item in the history is separated by a vbCrLf, but
        'if there are carriage-returns in the memo field data
        'you will get unexpected results. Split on the VERSION string
        'in the history data.
        astrHistory = Split(strHistory, VERSION_PREFIX)

        'Adding these lines ensures this code works regardless of
        'how the control is configured on the form
        Me.lstHistory.RowSourceType = "Value List"
        Me.lstHistory.ColumnCount = 3
        Me.lstHistory.ColumnHeads = True

        'Add column headings to the list box
        Me.lstHistory.AddItem "Date;Time;History"

        'Enumerate the history data in reverse
        'to fill the list box in descending order
        For lngCounter = UBound(astrHistory) To LBound(astrHistory) Step -1
            'Parse the history data
            strHistoryItem = astrHistory(lngCounter)

            If Len(strHistoryItem) > 0 Then

                'Parse the date from the history data.
                'This example parse the default US date format.
                datDate = CDate(Left(strHistoryItem, InStr(strHistoryItem, " ") - 1))
                strHistoryItem = Mid(strHistoryItem, InStr(strHistoryItem, " ") + 1)

                'Parse the time from the history data
                datTime = CDate(Left(strHistoryItem, InStr(strHistoryItem, " ] ") - 1))
                strHistoryItem = Mid(strHistoryItem, InStr(strHistoryItem, " ] ") + 3)
```

```
                'Add the history item to the list box.
                Me.lstHistory.AddItem datDate & ";" & datTime & ";" & strHistoryItem
            End If
        Next
    Else
        MsgBox "There is no history information for the specified field"
    End If
End Sub
```

The form with the list box is shown in Figure 6-10.

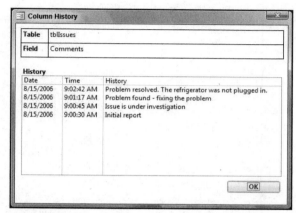

Figure 6-10

Summary

In this chapter, you took a detailed look into the world of DAO including powerful new features that have been added in Access 2007. By now you should have a fairly good understanding of when to use DAO, and how to refer to its objects. You should have a good working knowledge of the main objects in the hierarchy, such as the DBEngine, Workspace, Error, Database, and Recordset objects, and their associated collections. Although very few people can remember every single property and method of every object, you should have gained enough exposure to them by now, to be able to start writing some reasonably sophisticated software. In any case, IntelliSense can help you out when you're unsure.

Now that you've mastered DAO, you're ready to tackle a whole new object model — ActiveX Data Objects.

Using ADO to Access Data

7

Data Access Objects (DAO) was the default data access technology in the early versions of Access. In fact, Access was bound so closely to the Jet database engine by the fact that developers used Access as both the front-end user interface and the back-end data store that they rarely felt a need for anything else. As application designs evolved from standalone solutions into client/server architectures, the need to connect to and access data from disparate data sources became more and more important. Although Microsoft made several attempts at evolving DAO into a remote data access technology, its true strength is accessing data from local Jet databases. So to fulfill the need to connect to external data sources, Microsoft created ActiveX Data Objects (ADO). ADO is designed to provide an ActiveX standard object model for connecting to a wide variety of external data sources.

ADO is a part of Microsoft's data access vision of the future, called *Universal Data Access* (UDA). UDA is a concept in which a single method is used to retrieve data from any data source: relational databases, the mainframe indexed sequential access method/virtual storage access method (ISAM/VSAM) data sources, hierarchical databases, e-mail, disk files, graphical data, and so on. OLE DB (Object Linking and Embedding Databases) is the interface that enables UDA. ADO is a development interface for OLE DB that provides similar functionality to DAO.

OLE DB sees the world in terms of data providers. It acts as an interface between the data source and data consumer. Although OLE DB was written for procedural programming models, ADO sits atop OLE DB, providing programmers with an object-oriented model they can use to access and manipulate the data sources.

When you use Access 2007 to create a standard Jet database (MDB) or standard ACE database (ACCDB), by default, Access uses the ACE OLE DB provider for the connection to the CurrentProject. Any functionality that uses the `CurrentProject` object will go through the OLE DB provider. To confirm this, enter the following line of code into the Visual Basic Editor's Immediate window:

```
?CurrentProject.Connection
```

The return connection string begins with the following:

```
Provider=Microsoft.ACE.OLEDB.12.0;
```

Similarly, Access uses the Access OLE DB provider when you create an Access Data Project (ADP) against the SQL Server or MSDE. The same property call returns a connection string that begins thus:

```
Provider=Microsoft.Access.OLEDB.10.0;
```

While ADPs use the Access OLE DB provider for the `CurrentProject` object, the data provider for an ADP is the SQLOLEDB provider because an ADP is connected to a SQL data source. This chapter explores ADO and how it applies to an Access database solutions.

Ambiguous References

In versions prior to Access 2000, the DAO object library reference was selected by default for new database solutions. This enabled you to write code using DAO without requiring you to realize that your code depended on this object model.

Starting in Access 2000, the ADO object library was referenced by default for new VBA projects (expecting you to use the ADO library for accessing data). Unfortunately, the change generated much confusion. It turned out that average Access developers didn't know the difference between the two object models. Many developers learned the hard way when their applications started generating errors in code that had previously worked.

By the time Microsoft realized the ramifications of adding ADO as the default reference, Access 2002 was already in beta, and the ADO reference remained. The issue was finally resolved in Access 2003 by referencing both object libraries by default. In Access 2007, there is another change to default references in databases:

❑ ACCDB files have a reference to ACE DAO.

❑ MDB files have a reference to DAO 3.6.

Of course, ADP files only have a reference to ADO 2.5 because DAO does not apply to SQL data sources.

Writing unambiguous VBA code has never been more important. There are likely thousands of Access applications that use code that does not reference a specific library when multiple references are present. If this code is run in a different version of Access than the version in which the database was created, you may encounter errors where code had previously worked. Consider the following code:

```
Dim db As Database
Dim rs As Recordset
```

Nothing is terribly strange in this code, but there are two things to consider: First, only DAO has a `Database` object — ADO has none. Second, DAO and ADO both have `Recordset` objects. This begs the question: If both DAO and ADO object libraries are selected, to which library does the `Recordset` object refer?

If you have only one library referenced, Access chooses the only possible `Recordset` object. However, if you have references to both ADO and DAO, Access examines the library list and chooses the first possible reference for the object that it finds. If the reference ordering becomes switched, the database solution may begin behaving in strange ways, causing failures.

Many professional Access developers have written code using DAO and ADO objects interchangeably, and could not understand why the code failed to work. To ensure that Access (and you) knows which object refers to which object library, explicitly specify the object library. The following code illustrates explicit references to ADO and DAO objects:

```
Dim db As DAO.Database
Dim cn As ADODB.Connection
Dim rsDAO As DAO.Recordset
Dim rsADO As ADODB.Recordset
```

Clarifying references also makes the code run a tad faster because Access doesn't have to examine the library list to decide which library to use.

Referring to ADO Objects

When you refer to ADO objects, you do so in the same way you would using DAO. The difference is that ADO does not have a native data connection like DAO in ACCDB and MDB databases.

Recall that in DAO you can use the DBEngine(0)(0) object or the CurrentDb() function to return a reference to the current database. ADO does not have a current database. In fact, it doesn't know anything about datasets in the data source; it only knows about data source through the provider. In ADO, you must always implement a connection to an external data store through a provider before any actions can be executed for the data.

As in DAO, an object's parent collection can have a default member to which you can refer. The following table lists the default members for those ADO objects that have them.

Object Library	Collection	Default Member	Example
ADODB	Command	Parameters	cmd(0)
	Record	Fields	rcADO(0)
	Recordset	Fields	rsADO(0)
ADOX	Catalog	Tables	cat(0)
	Table	Columns	cat.tables(0)(0)

Connecting to a Data Source

The Connection object is considered the top-level object in the ADO object model. Although it doesn't contain all the other ADO objects, as the DAO DBEngine object does, you must specify the connection that the other ADO objects will use to carry out their functions.

The Connection object represents a single connection to an OLE DB provider, but of course you can create several connection objects, each connecting to a different provider. There are two ways to create a connection: implicitly and explicitly.

To create an *implicit* connection, you supply the connection string when creating a child object, such as a `Recordset`. The following example opens the connection implicitly when opening a `Recordset`:

```
Function OpenRecordsetADO() As ADODB.Recordset

    ' Define Variables
    Dim strSQL As String
    Dim rs As New ADODB.Recordset

    ' Set the SQL for the Recordset
    strSQL = "SELECT [CONTACTS].* FROM [CONTACTS];"

    ' Open the Recordset using to Contacts connection
    rs.Open strSQL, CurrentProject.Connection
    Set CreateConnectionADO = rs

End Function
```

This creates a temporary connection that is destroyed when you close the `Recordset` object.

To create an *explicit* connection, you must declare it, instantiate it, supply it with the various properties it needs, and then open it. The following function creates a connection to the current database and returns it to the caller:

```
Function CreateConnectionADO() As ADODB.Connection

    ' Define Variables
    Dim strConnectionString As String
    Dim cn As New ADODB.Connection

    ' Set the Connection Settings
    With cn
        .ConnectionString = CurrentProject.Connection
        .CursorLocation = adUseClient
        .Attributes = .Attributes Or adXactCommitRetaining
    End With

    ' Open the Connection
    cn.Open
    Set CreateConnectionADO = cn

End Function
```

This example uses the `CurrentProject.Connection` property to supply the connection string information for the connection. In DAO, you would have used `DBEngine(0)(0)` or `CurrentDb()`. Because ADO does not have a `Database` object, use the `CurrentProject` object instead.

> The `Open` method for the `Connection` will fail to open an Access database if it is already opened in exclusive mode by another source, such as the current instance of Access that is running the code. This could easily be the case with the previous code sample because it creates the new connection with `CurrentProject.Connection`.

You generally create an explicit connection when connecting to an external data source from an ACCDB, MDB, or ADP. `CurrentProject.Connection` can be called in the VBE Immediate window to see what an actual connection string looks like. Both the Access help file and the section "Rolling Your Own Connection String" later in this chapter also provide some guidance.

Specifying a Cursor Location

In contrast with DAO, when you create an ADO connection, you specify a *cursor*, which is a database element that controls record navigation, data updateability, and the tracking of changes made by other users.

There are two types of cursor: client side and server side. Choose the cursor you want to use by setting the `Command` or `Recordset` object's `CursorLocation` property to one of the following two constants before you open the connection or recordset:

```
rs.CursorLocation = adUseClient ' Use a client-side cursor
rs.CursorLocation = adUseServer ' Default. Use a server-side cursor
```

As with most things in life, the choice comes with a tradeoff. In most cases, server-side cursors are a bit faster; however, client-side cursors offer a little more functionality.

When you set `CursorLocation` at the connection level, you are specifying the location that will be used by default when you create recordsets against that connection. You can override this setting at the recordset level at any point during code execution.

Server-Side Cursors

When using a server-side cursor (the default in ADO), the records contained in the recordset are cached on the server. The major benefit is significantly reduced network traffic thus improving application performance. The downside is that server resources are consumed for every active client — the more clients (and the more data being cached), the more server resources are consumed. It's important to plan ahead to ensure your server has sufficient resources to do the job. Server-side cursors enable you to use both keyset and dynamic cursors, and also support direct positional updates, which are fast and avoid update collisions.

You can also use each connection for more than one operation. For example, you can have a recordset open and still execute multiple update queries without having to open an additional connection. Server-side cursors are best for inserting, updating, and deleting records, and they enable you to have multiple active statements on the same connection.

Client-Side Cursors

If the data source to which you're connecting doesn't support server-side cursors, you have no choice but to use a client-side cursor. With non-keyset client-side cursors, the server sends the entire recordset to the client across the network. Because the client must now provide and manage the resources necessary to cache the records, this places a significant load on both the network and the client. Needless to say, this reduces your application's overall performance.

One benefit of using client-side cursors is that, once the data is cached, subsequent access to the data is much faster than with server side cursors because the data resides locally. A second benefit is that the application is generally more scalable because the resources required to run the application are distributed among many clients, rather than loading down a single server.

Rolling Your Own Connection String

The following is the output of the `CurrentProject.Connection` property for the Northwind 2007 sample database. (To shorten the file paths for this example, the database is moved to a different folder.)

```
Provider=Microsoft.ACE.OLEDB.12.0;
User ID=Admin;
Data Source=C:\Databases\Northwind2007.accdb;
Mode=Share Deny None;
Extended Properties="";
Jet OLEDB:System database=C:\Databases\System.mdw;
Jet OLEDB:Registry Path=
     Software\Microsoft\Office\12.0\Access\Access Connectivity Engine;
Jet OLEDB:Database Password="";
Jet OLEDB:Engine Type=6;
Jet OLEDB:Database Locking Mode=0;
Jet OLEDB:Global Partial Bulk Ops=2;
Jet OLEDB:Global Bulk Transactions=1;
Jet OLEDB:New Database Password="";
Jet OLEDB:Create System Database=False;
Jet OLEDB:Encrypt Database=False;
Jet OLEDB:Don't Copy Locale on Compact=False;
Jet OLEDB:Compact Without Replica Repair=False;
Jet OLEDB:SFP=False;
Jet OLEDB:Support Complex Data=True
```

Note there is one connection option listed that was not available in previous versions of Access. That's the `Jet OLEDB:Support Complex Data=True` option, which explicitly requires that the connection provider support the complex data in Access 2007 for `Multi-valued` and `Attachment` field types.

When creating a connection string, only the following five parameters need to be supplied:

- ❑ Provider (including version)
- ❑ User ID
- ❑ Password or database password (if applicable)
- ❑ Data source
- ❑ System database (if applicable)

In the case of an ADP, the requirements for the connection string are slightly different. You need to supply the provider, security info, data source, integrated security, initial catalog, and the data provider. All the other information is contained in the ADP Data Link for the ADP. Here's an example of an ADP connection string:

```
Provider=Microsoft.Access.OLEDB.10.0;
Persist Security Info=False;
```

```
Data Source=<SQL machine name>;
Integrated Security=SSPI;
Initial Catalog=SampleDB;
Data Provider=SQLOLEDB.1
```

Creating and Using a Data Link

Instead of using `CurrentProject.Connection` to set your connection string, or writing your own, you can use a Data Link. You can specify the Data Link filename as a parameter of the `Connection` object, but you have to create a UDL file first. To create a custom data link, do the following:

1. Open Windows Explorer and select File ⇨ New ⇨ Text Document.

2. Rename the file to something meaningful, and change its file extension to `.UDL`.

3. Click Yes in the message box that Windows subsequently displays to rename the extension.

4. Double-click the new UDL file and the Data Link Properties dialog box opens (see Figure 7-1).

Figure 7-1

5. On the Provider tab, select Microsoft Office 12.0 Access Database Engine OLE DB Provider, and click the Next button.

6. In the Data Source text box, type the name and path to your Access database. For example:

```
C:\Users\<user>\Northwind 2007.accdb
```

7. Click the Test Connection button. If all went well, the message box shown in Figure 7-2 displays.

Figure 7-2

8. Go to the Advanced tab and examine the permissions you can set for this link. For this demonstration, accept the default settings. If you want, the ALL tab can be selected to change the settings manually.

9. Click OK.

The UDL file is now created and should be working properly. You can specify the connection string by supplying the filename and path to the data link file just created. For example, a function could be written to open the connection from the UDL file:

```
Function CreateConnectionUDL() As ADODB.Connection

    ' Define Variables
    Dim strConnectionString As String
    Dim cn As New ADODB.Connection

    ' Open the Conection from the UDL file
    cn.Open "C:\MyConnection.UDL"

    ' Return the Connection
    Set CreateConnectionUDL = cn

End Function
```

Using Transactions

A transaction is a delimited set of changes that are performed on a database's schema or data. These changes increase the speed of actions that change data, and enable you to undo changes that have not yet been committed.

In DAO, transactions operate under the context of a Workspace; ADO transactions operate under the context of a `Connection`. As with a DAO transaction, an ADO transaction is started by calling the `BeginTrans` method against the `Connection` object. To write the transaction to disk, call the `CommitTrans` method. But instead of calling a `Rollback` method as in DAO, for ADO you call the `RollbackTrans` method.

Not all providers support transactions, so you need to verify that the provider-defined property `Transaction DDL` is one of the `Connection` object's properties. The following line entered in the VBE Immediate window checks the value of that property:

```
?CurrentProject.Connection.Properties("Transaction DDL")
```

If no error occurs, the provider supports transactions.

The following code demonstrates how an ADO transaction can be performed. (Some error handling is added here to roll back the transaction if an error occurs.)

```
Public Sub UseTransactions()

    ' Define Variables
    Dim cn As New ADODB.Connection

    ' Open a connection to the current database
    With cn
        .ConnectionString = CurrentProject.Connection
        .Open
    End With

' Set error handling in case there is a problem
On Error GoTo Transaction_Error

    ' Try to complete a transaction.  If an error occurs,
    ' the error handling routine will rollback
    cn.BeginTrans                           ' Begin the transaction
    cn.Execute "UPDATE Table1..."           ' Withdraw funds from one account
    cn.Execute "INSERT INTO Table2..."      ' Deposit funds into another account
    cn.CommitTrans                          ' Commit the transaction

Transaction_Exit:

    ' Clean up
    cn.Close
    Set cn = Nothing
    Exit Sub

Transaction_Error:

    ' An error occurred, rollback the transaction
    cn.RollbackTrans
    Resume Transaction_Exit

End Sub
```

In this example, changes to both tables either complete as a unit or are rolled back as a unit. If an error occurs, the error handling routine rolls back all changes you tried to execute. This means you can be certain that none of the changes were applied if the operation fails.

You can nest ADO transactions, but in contrast with DAO transactions, you can return an ADO transaction's nesting position when you create it. A return value of 1 indicates the transaction occupies the top-level position in a virtual collection. A value of 2 indicates the transaction is a second-level transaction, and so on.

When you call CommitTrans or RollbackTrans, you are operating on the most recently opened transaction. To resolve higher-level transactions, you must close or roll back the current transaction.

When you call CommitTrans or RollbackTrans, the appropriate action is taken, and the transaction is closed. If you set the Connection object's Attributes property to adXactCommitRetaining, a new transaction is created after you issue CommitTrans. If you set it to adXactAbortRetaining (you can set both), the same occurs after calling RollbackTrans.

Data Access with ADO

Storing and retrieving data is the reason databases are employed, and a large proportion of your programming usually revolves around manipulating those objects that deal with data: views, stored procedures, and recordsets. To do this in ADO, you need some understanding of the parts of the ADO Object Model. This section discusses using ADO methods to access data.

Overview of the ADO Object Model

The ADO Object Model contains five main objects: the Connection, Command, Recordset, Record, and the Stream objects. Although you've already explored some examples that use the Connection object to execute actions on a data source, that's really just the beginning of the ADO functionality. These other ADO objects provide much of the rich and powerful functionality of the ADO library.

As already mentioned, the ADO Connection object stores the information that is necessary to describe the connection to an ADO data provider. It provides several methods for working with the connection, such as opening, closing, beginning transactions, committing transactions, executing commands, and so on. In general, but not always, a connection is opened to a data source when a database solution is invoked and is used to execute commands throughout the use of the Access solution.

The ADO Command object provides an interface for you to execute actions on the ADO data source. A command statement is applied to the object's CommandText or CommandStream property and the Execute method is called to run the command. While the supported command statements depend on the data source provider and vary among data sources types, they're typically SQL statements or stored procedures. One of the benefits of working directly with a Command object is that you can use its Parameters collection to specify arguments for parameterized queries or stored procedures.

One of the most commonly used ADO objects, Recordset, provides a container for working with sets of data. The Recordset can be used to store existing data, add new data, and perform actions on that data. Additionally, the Recordset provides the capability to search for specific data contained in the set and even save the data in a disconnected state. The Recordset is used often in this chapter.

The Record object can be seen as a single row of data in a recordset. Although records have limited functionality compared to recordsets, they relieve you of the overhead of having to instantiate the more complex recordset. They also have different properties and methods that can be quite useful. The Record object can manipulate data such as folders and files in a file system, and e-mail messages, meaning the source of data for the Record object can be the current row of a recordset or even a URL. This object is useful when working with just one record from a table.

The Stream object reads, writes, and manages a stream of bytes, which can be text or binary and is limited in size only by the available system resources. You typically use an ADO Stream object to contain the text or bytes of a file or message supplied using a provider such as the Microsoft OLE DB Provider for Internet Publishing. The object's data source can be a file whose location is specified by a URL, a field in a record or recordset that contains a `Stream` object, a resource field containing the URL of a file, a BLOB field in a recordset, or a custom-designed stream that exists in memory.

Unfortunately the full ADO Object Model is far too extensive to discuss every property, object, method, and event it provides, but Access help files and the MSDN library provide hundreds of pages describing the various aspects of the model and examples for working with those objects.

Using the Execute Method

The `Execute` method is used perform actions against the data source using ADO. This is often done by creating a query that carries out some action for a set of data, which may or may not return rows of records. Both the `Connection` and `Command` objects expose an `Execute` method to explicitly execute a command against a given data source. These methods vary slightly depending on the object, so you'll explore using both in this section.

The Connection.Execute Method

The `Connection` object's `Execute` method takes three parameters and returns a recordset object containing any records the command may have returned. The parameters for this method on the `Connection` object are different than the parameters for the `Command` object's `Execute` method. They are described in the following table:

Parameter	Description
CommandText	Required. A String data type containing the command statement to be executed.
RecordsAffected	Optional. A Long data type out parameter that contains the number of records affected by the operation.
Options	Optional. A Long data type value indicating how the command statement should be evaluated by the provider. This is typically specified using a member of the CommandTypeEnum objects.

The `Connection` object's `Execute` is extremely easy to use. Just instantiate a connection and issue its `Execute` method — it's that simple! The following is an example calling the method:

```
Function ExecuteFromConnection(strSQL As String) As ADODB.Recordset

    ' Define Variables
    Dim cn As New ADODB.Connection
    Dim rs As ADODB.Recordset

    ' Open the connection and Execute the command
    cn.Open CurrentProject.Connection
    Set rs = cn.Execute(strSQL)

    ' Return the Recordset as Clean up
    Set ExecuteFromConnection = rs
```

```
        Set cn = Nothing

    End Function
```

The `CommandText` argument can be a SQL statement: the name of a table or a stored procedure, or a provider-specific text or command. The `RecordsAffected` is an out parameter and if supplied, is populated with the number of records affected by the operation when the operation completes.

The `Options` argument can be a combination of the `CommandTypeEnum` values or `ExecuteOptionEnum` values that affect the way the `Execute` method works. Appendix F provides a list and description of all the available `CommandTypeEnum` and `ExecuteOptionEnum` members.

The Command.Execute Method

You can also execute an action query by calling the `Execute` method against a `Command` object. The `Command.Execute` method also takes there parameters and returns a `Recordset` object if the command supports returning records. However, calling `Execute` from the `Command` object is slightly different; the `CommandText` parameter is not passed because it is a property of the `Command` object itself. The `Command.Execute` object takes the following parameters:

Parameter	Description
RecordsAffected	Optional. A Long data type out parameter that contains the number of records affected by the operation.
Parameters	Optional. A Variant array data type that contains a list of parameters used in conjunction with statements stored in the `CommandText` or `CommandStream` properties.
Options	Optional. A Long data type value indicating how the command statement should be evaluated by the provider. This is typically specified using a member of the `CommandTypeEnum` objects.

A common way to execute a command from the `Command` object is to simply set the `Command` object's `CommandText`, `CommandType`, and `ActiveConnection` properties; then call the `Execute` method. The `Parameters` property can be populated by a variant array of parameter values passed with a SQL statement. The `Options` property tells the provider how to evaluate the `CommandText` property. Here's an example of calling `Execute` from the `Command` object:

```
Function ExecuteFromCommand(strSQL As String) As ADODB.Recordset

    ' Define Variables
    Dim cmd As New ADODB.Command
    Dim rs As Recordset

    ' Set the required properties
    With cmd
        .CommandText = strSQL
        .CommandType = adCmdUnknown
        .ActiveConnection = CurrentProject.Connection
    End With
```

```
    ' Exectute the command
    Set rs = cmd.Execute

    ' Return the Recordset and Clean up
    Set ExecuteFromCommand = rs
    Set cmd = Nothing

End Function
```

Specifying Command Parameters

Instead of specifying the Command object's parameters in the SQL statement, you can also set them using the Command object's Parameter object. For example, the following function retrieves the price of a specified Item by calling a Select query in the current database.

```
Public Function GetPrice(strName As String) As Double

    ' Define Variables
    Dim cmd As New ADODB.Command
    Dim rs As Recordset

    ' Build the Command object
    With cmd
        ' Set the connection
        .ActiveConnection = CurrentProject.Connection

        ' Set other properties
        .CommandText = "qryGetPrice"
        .CommandType = adCmdTable

        ' To be able to refer to parameters by name,
        ' you must refresh the parameters collection
        .Parameters.Refresh

        ' Supply the parameter for the query
        .Parameters("[strItemName]") = strName
    End With

    ' Execute the Query and return the price
    Set rs = cmd.Execute

    ' Set the Price
    If rs.RecordCount < 1 Then
        MsgBox "There was no record for the Item Specified"
        GetPrice = 0
    Else
        GetPrice = rs("Price").Value
    End If

    ' Clean up
    Set rs = Nothing
    Set cmd = Nothing

End Function
```

Creating Your Own Parameters

It's quite simple to create your own parameters on-the-fly in code using ADO. To create the parameter for a given query, call the `CreateParameter` method from the `Command` object. The benefit in this case is that you can specify a SQL statement in code and create the parameters for that statement when the code is run. Here's an example of creating parameters using the `Command` object:

```
Public Function GetPriceByCustomParameter(strName As String) As Double

    ' Define Variables
    Dim cmd As New ADODB.Command
    Dim rs As New ADODB.Recordset

    ' Setup the Command object
    With cmd
        ' Set the connection
        .ActiveConnection = CurrentProject.Connection

        ' Set the CommandText
        .CommandText = "SELECT [Prices].* FROM [Prices] WHERE
[Prices].[ItemName]=[strItemName]"
        .CommandType = adCmdUnknown

        ' Create the parameter and set the value
        .Parameters.Append cmd.CreateParameter("[strItemName]", adVarChar,
adParamInput, 100)
        .Parameters("[strItemName]") = strName
    End With

    ' Execute the Query and return the price
    Set rs = cmd.Execute

    ' Set the Price
    If rs.RecordCount < 1 Then
        MsgBox "There was no record for the Item specified"
        GetPriceByCustomParameter = 0
    Else
        GetPriceByCustomParameter = rs("Price").Value
    End If

    ' Clean up
    Set rs = Nothing
    Set cmd = Nothing

End Function
```

Creating ADO Recordsets

Both ADO and DAO provide `Recordset` objects, which are commonly used in code. In fact, many of the code samples in this chapter use recordsets. However, up to now, the recordset has been assigned a value based on the records returned as the result of executing an action.

Using the ADO `Recordset` object, you can implicitly execute an action by calling the `Open` method for the `Recordset`. `Open` retrieves the records from a data source based on the criteria and stores them in the `Recordset` object. It has five parameters, all of which are optional. The following table describes each of those parameters.

Parameter	Description
Source	Optional. The `Source` argument can be a SQL statement, the name of a table, the name of a stored procedure, a URL, or a provider-specific text or command.
ConnectionString	Optional. The `ConnectionString` argument can be a `Connection` object or a `Connection` string.
CursorType	Optional. Specifies the type of cursor to use for the `Recordset`.
LockType	Optional. Specifies the type of lock to use for the `Recordset`.
Options	Optional. Specifies the command option(s) to use for the `Recordset`.

Appendix F contains a list of all the available `CursorType`, `LockType`, and `Options` members and a description of those members. You can supply more than one `Options` value by using the `Or` operator; for example:

```
rs.Options = adCmdStoredProc Or adAsyncFetchNonBlocking
```

Creating a Recordset from a Command Object

Suppose you need to create a recordset that is based on a parameter query. Most often, you won't know what values to supply until you get to that point in your code. The problem, of course, is how to supply those values. The answer is to base your recordset on a `Command` object, which itself is based on the `Parameter` query. Take another look at the `GetPrice` function:

```
Public Function GetPrice(strName As String) As Double

    ' Define Variables
    Dim cmd As New ADODB.Command
    Dim rs As Recordset

    ' Build the Command object
    With cmd
        ' Set the connection
        .ActiveConnection = CurrentProject.Connection

        ' Set other properties
        .CommandText = "qryGetPrice"
        .CommandType = adCmdTable

        ' To be able to refer to parameters by name,
        ' you must refresh the parameters collection
        .Parameters.Refresh
```

```
        ' Supply the parameter for the query
        .Parameters("[strItemName]") = strName
    End With

    ' Execute the Query and return the price
    Set rs = cmd.Execute

    ' Set the Price
    If rs.RecordCount < 1 Then
        MsgBox "There was no record for the Item Specified"
        GetPrice = 0
    Else
        GetPrice = rs("Price").Value
    End If

    ' Clean up
    Set rs = Nothing
    Set cmd = Nothing

End Function
```

Because the `Recordset` object does not have a `Parameters` collection, you can see that the `Command` object is what executes the query and passes its dataset to the `Recordset` when the `Recordset` is created. The `Command` object has a `Parameters` collection, so you can supply the query's parameters to it.

To pass parameters to a stored procedure in an ADP, you need to do two things:

❏ Specify the `CommandType` as `adCmdStoredProc`

❏ Prefix field names with the @ symbol

Here's an example:

```
'Build the Command object for an ADP Stored Procedure
With cmd
    .ActiveConnection = CurrentProject.Connection
    .CommandText = "qryGetPricesProc"
    .CommandType = adCmdStoredProc
    .Parameters.Refresh
    .Parameters("@ItemName") = strName
End With
```

Opening a Shaped Recordset

A useful feature of ADO is that you can create shaped recordsets. *Data shaping* enables you to define the columns of a recordset, the relationships between them, and the manner in which the recordset is populated with data. The columns can contain data from a provider such as Access or the SQL Server, references to another recordset, values derived from a calculation on a row, and so on.

Here's a simple example from the NorthwindCS sample database (in the Chapter 19 code download), which has two tables with a parent-child relationship: Orders, which contains the header information for customer orders, and Order Details, which contains the individual line items for each order.

In the past, to populate a list with the details of a select set of orders, you would have created a recordset based on a query much like the following:

```
SELECT O.OrderID, O.CustomerID, O.OrderDate,
       D.ProductID, D.UnitPrice, D.Quantity, D.Discount
FROM Orders As O
INNER JOIN [Order Details] As D ON D.OrderID = O.OrderID
WHERE Year(O.OrderDate) = 1996
AND OrderID BETWEEN 10248 AND 10250
ORDER BY O.OrderDate DESC
```

This query returns a dataset that contains all the orders in 1996 where the OrderID is between 10248 and 10250, in descending date order. In this case, the columns from the Orders table (OrderID, Customer, and OrderDate) are repeated unnecessarily for every row of data returned from the Order Details table. Wouldn't it be nice if you could return only one row of Orders data for each group of related rows from Order Details? Closely examine the following ADO code, paying particular attention to the SQL statement:

```
Dim cn As New ADODB.Connection
Dim rsOrders As New ADODB.Recordset
Dim rsDetails As New ADODB.Recordset
Dim strSQL As String

' Define and create the connection
cn.CursorLocation = adUseClient

' We have to use this provider
cn.Provider = "MSDataShape"

' Open a connection to SQL Server
cn.Open "Data Provider=SQLOLEDB;" & _
    "Integrated Security=SSPI;Database=NorthwindCS"

' Create the SQL statement that does all the work
strSQL = "SHAPE {SELECT DISTINCT OrderID, " & _
                "CustomerID, OrderDate FROM Orders " & _
                "WHERE Year(OrderDate) = 1996 " & _
                "AND OrderID BETWEEN 10248 AND 10250 " & _
                "ORDER BY OrderDate DESC} " &_
            "APPEND ({SELECT OrderID, ProductID, UnitPrice, Quantity, Discount " & _
                "FROM [Order Details]} " &_
            "RELATE OrderID TO OrderID)"

' Create the recordset for the orders table
rsOrders.Open strSQL, cn
```

Shaped recordsets such as this are called *hierarchical recordsets*. They exhibit a parent-child relationship in which the parent is the container recordset and the child is the contained recordset. The Shape statement enables you to create a shaped recordset, which you can then access programmatically or through a visual control. You issue the Shape statement as you do any other ADO command text.

This simple example demonstrates only a fraction of what can be accomplished using the Shape statement. Although an in-depth examination of SQL Shapes is beyond the scope of this book, the Access help has several informative topics on the subject.

Verifying the Options a Recordset Supports

To check which options a specific recordset supports, use the Supports method. Supports takes a member of the CursorCommandEnum enumeration and returns True if the option is supported, and False otherwise. The following table describes what you can do with the members of the CursorCommandEnum enumeration.

Member Name	Description
adAddNew	Use the AddNew method to add records.
adApproxPosition	Use the AbsolutePosition and AbsolutePage properties.
adBookmark	Use the Bookmark property.
adDelete	Use the Delete method to delete records.
adFind	Use the Find method to locate a specific record.
adHoldRecords	Move the cursor position without committing any changes to the current record.
adIndex	Use the Index property to set an index.
adMovePrevious	Use the MoveFirst, MovePrevious, and Move methods to move the cursor position backward.
adNotify	Determines whether the provider supports receiving notifications.
adResync	Use the Resync method to resynchronize the recordset with its underlying data.
adSeek	Use the Seek method to locate a specific record.
adUpdate	Use the Update method to commit changes to the current record.
adUpdateBatch	Use the UpdateBatch and CancelBatch methods.

Here's an example of how to test for the AbsolutePosition functionality:

```
booResult = rs.Supports(adApproxPosition)

MsgBox "This recordset does " & _
        IIf(booResult = True,"", "not") & _
        "support AbsolutePosition and AbsolutePage"
```

Referring to Recordset Columns

As with DAO recordsets, you can refer to fields in an ADO recordset in a variety of ways. The following are some examples of how a field can be referred to in code:

```
rs.Collect(1)
rs.Collect("myField")
rs!myField
rs(1)
rs.Fields(1)
rs.Fields!myField
rs("myField")
rs.Fields("myField")
```

Filtering and Ordering Recordsets

Also like DAO, you can filter a recordset's output by specifying its source using a WHERE or HAVING clause, or by setting its Filter property. Similarly, setting the ADO recordset's Sort property changes its sort order, just like in DAO.

Navigating Recordsets

SQL queries operate on many records at the same time, but recordsets are designed to enable you to operate on records one at a time. To use recordsets effectively, you must be able to navigate from record to record. The following sections describe the various ways in which you can move around in a recordset.

RecordCount

You might recall that the RecordCount property in DAO returns the number of rows that the recordset has accessed so far. In ADO, the RecordCount property returns the actual number of rows in the recordset, without first having to force a count by moving to the last row. Here's an example:

```
rs.Open "SELECT * FROM Table1", CurrentProject.Connection
If rs.AbsolutePosition > adPosUnknown Then
    'Get the count
    lngCount = rs.RecordCount
    '----
    'Continue processing
    '----
End If
```

AbsolutePosition, AbsolutePage

Assuming the provider supports absolute positioning, the AbsolutePosition property enables you to move the cursor to a specific row in the recordset, just as in DAO. For example, to move to the 127th row, you could issue the following call:

```
rs.AbsolutePosition = 127
```

ADO provides three constants you can use to verify the current cursor position, two of which obviously replace the BOF and EOF properties found in DAO:

❑ adPosUnknown: The recordset is empty, or the provider doesn't support absolute positioning.

❑ adPosBOF: True if the current cursor position is before the first record.

❑ adPosEOF: True if the current cursor position is after the last record.

The ADO-specific AbsolutePage property indicates the page on which the current record resides. For example:

```
lngCurrentPage = rs.AbsolutePage
```

You might also recall that the DAO object model provides a PercentPosition property, with which you can move to a relative position in the recordset by specifying a percentage value. ADO does not support that property, but you can accomplish the same thing by calculating the percentage and supplying it to the AbsolutePosition property. For example, to move to (roughly) halfway through the recordset, you could do this:

```
rs.AbsolutePosition = 0.5 * rs.RecordCount
```

Other Methods

The MoveFirst, MovePrevious, MoveNext, MoveLast, and Move methods work exactly the same way in ADO as they do in DAO. Bookmarks and Recordset clones in ADO are exactly the same as in DAO. (For more details on using Bookmarks and Recordset clones, refer to Chapter 6.)

Finding Records

As you saw in the Chapter 6, you often need a way to retrieve a specific record when working with recordsets. DAO provides two ways to locate a specific record: Seek and Find.

The Seek Method

The ADO Seek method, although a little different from its DAO cousin, is still the fastest way to find a specific record, but it can only be used with server-side cursors on tables that have been opened as adCmdTableDirect because it specifically relies on the table's indexes (and the indexes reside on the server — not on the client). Naturally, the table must have at least one index for it to search on.

To use the ADO Seek method, you have to specify three things: the name of the index key to use, a variant array whose members specify the values to be compared with the key columns, and a SeekEnum constant that defines the kind of Seek to execute. You must set the recordset's index property prior to calling the Seek method. The SeekOption constant can be any of the ones described in the following table.

Constant	Value	Description
adSeekFirstEQ	1	Locates the first key that is equal to the value specified in KeyValues.
adSeekLastEQ	2	Locates the last key that is equal to the value specified in KeyValues.

Constant	Value	Description
adSeekAfterEQ	4	Locates the key that is equal to the value specified in KeyValues, or the key just after it.
aAdSeekAfter	8	Locates the key that is immediately following a match with a value specified in KeyValues would have occurred.
adSeekBeforeEQ	16	Locates the key that is equal to the value specified in KeyValues, or the key immediately after where the desired key would have occurred if it is not present.
adSeekBefore	32	Locates the key that is immediately before the matching key with the value specified in KeyValues would have occurred.

For example, the following code shows how to search the tblCustomers table to find a customer whose CustomerNo. is 123:

```
Set rs = db.OpenRecordset("tblCustomer", dbOpenTable)

rs.Index = "CustomerNo"
rs.Seek 123, adSeekFirstEQ

If rs.EOF Then
    'A matching record was found
Else
    'A matching record was not found
End If
```

Primary key indexes in ACE and Jet databases are called PrimaryKey; primary key indexes in the SQL Server are called PK_tablename by default, but you can name them anything you like. So if you want to use the table's primary key index, you have to know its name.

You must specify a key value for each column in the index. The reason is that some of the key fields may default to Null, and because nothing can equal Null, your Seek method usually does not find what you're looking for.

In contrast with the DAO Seek method where you would check the NoMatch property to see if the search succeeded or failed, the ADO Seek method has no such property. If the method finds a record that matches the criteria, the Recordset object's cursor is moved to that row, and if not, to the end of the recordset. So if no matching record is found, the Recordset object's EOF property is set to True.

The Find Method

Unlike DAO, ADO has only one Find method. It has the following syntax:

```
rs.Find Criteria, SkipRows, SearchDirection, Start
```

The Criteria argument can be any valid SQL WHERE clause for a single column, without the word WHERE. The SkipRows argument is the number of rows to skip when searching for the next or previous match. The `Start` argument is a bookmark that you can use as a starting point for the search. And last, the `SearchDirection` argument can be either `adSearchForward` or `adSearchBackward`, the function of which is fairly obvious.

Unless otherwise specified, all searches begin at the current row, so it's a good idea to issue the `MoveFirst` method before attempting `Find` when you first open a recordset. The following code shows how to find the first and second instances of a customer having the word *parts* in its name:

```
' Move to the first record
rs.MoveFirst

' Search for the first matching record
rs.Find "[OrgName] LIKE '*parts*'", , adSearchForward

' Search for the next matching record
rs.Find "[OrgName] LIKE '*parts*'", 1, adSearchForward
```

The `SkipRows` argument can be specified to skip the current row during the search. Unfortunately, you can specify only a single column name in the search criterion. The `Find` method does not support multi-column search.

Two interesting points to note are that literal string values can be specified either within single quotes or within hash characters. For example:

```
"State = 'NY'" or "State = #NY#"
```

Also, the use of the asterisk as a wildcard character is restricted. You can specify it at the end of the criterion string, or at the beginning *and* end. You cannot use the asterisk at the beginning (without one also being at the end), or in the middle. The following truth table illustrates this point.

State LIKE '*York'	Illegal
State LIKE 'New*'	OK
State LIKE '*ew Yor*'	OK
State LIKE 'New *ork'	Illegal

Once a matching record is found, any subsequent search begins from the current cursor position, not from the start or end of the recordset like the `Seek` method.

Editing Data with Recordsets

As in DAO, you edit data in recordsets using the `AddNew`, `Update`, and `CancelUpdate` methods. Unlike DAO, ADO has no `Edit` method.

In DAO, when you leave a record, any changes are discarded. By contrast, when you leave a record in ADO, the changes are immediately committed. In addition, the ADO `Update` method is optional. You don't need to use it; however, you'll earn yourself a runtime error if you attempt to close a recordset without committing or canceling any changes, so it is recommended that you explicitly use it anyway. For example:

```
With rs
    .Open "Shippers", cn, adOpenDynamic, adLockOptimistic, adCmdTable

    'Check that a record exists
    If .AbsolutePosition > adPosUnknown Then
        'ADO does not have an "Edit" method
        !Phone = "555-5554"
        .Update
    End If

    'Add a new record
    .AddNew
    !CompanyName = "Ollivanders"
    !Phone = "555-5555"

    If booOK2Save = True Then
        .Update
    Else
        .CancelUpdate
    End If
End With
```

Using this technique, you can edit records and send the updates to the database one at a time. Of course, you can edit a bunch of records and send the updates all at once, as follows:

```
With rs
    .Open "Shippers", cn, adOpenDynamic, adLockOptimistic, adCmdTable

    'Check that a record exists
    If .AbsolutePosition > adPosUnknown Then
        'Edit several records
        !Phone = "555-5554"

        .MoveNext
        !Phone = "666-6666"

        .MoveNext
        !Phone "777-7777"
        .Update
    End If
End With
```

In this code, each time you make a update to the data, the MoveNext method automatically commits the record. However, ADO also allows batch updates, which enables you to edit multiple records and then send them all to the OLE DB provider to be saved as a single operation by calling the UpdateBatch method. To use this feature, a client-side cursor must be used and you must be sure to open the recordset using the adLockBatchOptimisticLockType option. Here's an example:

```
With rs
    .CursorLocation = adUseClient
```

```
        .CursorType = adOpenKeyset
        .LockType = adLockBatchOptimistic
        .Open "Customers", cn

        'Find the right record to edit
        .Find "Country = 'USA'"
        Do While Not .EOF
            'Edit the current record
            !Region = "AA"

            'Skip over the current record to
            'find the next matching record
            .Find "Country = 'USA'", 1
        Loop

        'Commit all the changes
        .UpdateBatch
    End With
```

Persistent Recordsets

In DAO, a recordset exists only within the scope of its object variable, after which it is destroyed. The same can be said of ADO recordsets; however, ADO also provides you with a way to save your recordsets to a file on the disk. This enables you to create a recordset, save it to disk, reopen it at some point in the future, make changes to it, and save it again.

To do all this, you use the Recordset object's Save method. The following examples demonstrate how to save, reopen, modify, and then resave a recordset. Not all providers allow you to save a recordset to a file. You're safe with the ACE OLE DB provider, but to be certain with other providers, open the recordset using a client-side cursor.

```
Dim rs As ADODB.Recordset
Dim strADTGFile As String
Dim strXMLFile As String

Set rs = New ADODB.Recordset

'Open the recordset
rs.CursorLocation = adUseClient
rs.Open _
    "Prices", CurrentProject.Connection, adOpenStatic, adLockOptimistic, adCmdTable

'Specify the output files
strADTGFile = "c:\Temp\Customers.adtg"
strXMLFile = "c:\Temp\Customers.xml"
```

You'll get a runtime error if you try to save a recordset to a file that already exists, so you have to delete any existing file first.

Then use the Save method to save the recordset to disk. You have two options for file formats: Advanced Data Tablegram (ADTG), which is a proprietary Microsoft format, or the Extensible Markup Language (XML) format.

Saving the recordset in XML format is great if you intend to exchange data with another application that supports XML, but the ADTG format produces a smaller file size.

```
'Save the recordset to disk as an ADT file
rs.Save strADTGFile, adPersistADTG

'Just to show that it can be done, save
'the recordset to disk as an XML file
rs.Save strXMLFile, adPersistXML

'Clean up
rs.Close
Set rs = Nothing
Set cn = Nothing
```

Leave both files on the disk for now, but you aren't finished with them yet.

If you were to continue working with the recordset, adding and deleting rows, or modifying data, the changes would be reflected in the database, not in the file. Any changes you want reflected in the file must be explicitly saved to the file — remember that this recordset is bound to the database by a connection.

Creating a Recordset Based on a File

The next example shows you how to reopen the recordset that you saved to the disk in the preceding section, make a change to it, and resave it:

When you want to open a recordset using a file as its source, you must do so without specifying a connection. This creates a disconnected recordset (which is explained a bit later). Once the recordset is open, you can work with it as you would any other recordset, but it will be bound to the file and not the database. If you want to bind the recordset to the database, you must set the recordset's `ActiveConnection` property. This example reconnects to the database, but also resaves the recordset to the file:

```
Dim rs As New ADODB.Recordset
Dim strADTGFile As String

'Specify the output file
strADTGFile = "c:\Temp\Customers.adtg"
' Open the recordset with a client-side cursor, but NO connection!
rs.CursorLocation = adUseClient
rs.Open strADTGFile, , adOpenStatic, adLockOptimistic

' Now set the recordset's connection
rs.ActiveConnection = CurrentProject.Connection

' Make a change and save it again
rs!Fax = "555-1234"
rs.Update

Kill strADTGFile
rs.Save strADTGFile, adPersistADTG

' Clean up
```

```
rs.Close
Set rs = Nothing
```

The final example in this section opens the file again to demonstrate that the goal is accomplished — a modified recordset is saved, after which the two output files are deleted because they aren't used any more:

```
Dim rs As New ADODB.Recordset
Dim strADTGFile As String
Dim strXMLFile As String

' Specify the output file
strADTGFile = "c:\Temp\Customers.adtg"

' Open the recordset with a client-side cursor, but NO connection!
rs.CursorLocation = adUseClient
rs.Open strADTGFile, , adOpenStatic, adLockOptimistic

' Clean up
rs.Close
Set rs = Nothing
Kill strADTGFile
Kill strXMLFile
```

Disconnected Recordsets

Ever wanted to use a recordset to store temporary data, but been forced to use a multidimensional array because DAO recordsets are always bound to the database? A disconnected recordset is one that is not bound to a database, file, or other data source. It is completely independent. You can add and delete columns, rows, and indexes — all without affecting the data in your database.

To create a disconnected recordset, just open it without a connection. Here's an example:

```
Dim rs As New ADODB.Recordset

' Append some fields
rs.Fields.Append "CustomerID", adInteger
rs.Fields.Append "CustName", adVarChar, 20
rs.Fields.Append "Phone", adVarChar, 15
rs.Fields.Refresh

' Add some data
With rs
    .Open

    .AddNew
    !CustomerID = 1
    !CustName = "Ollivander"
    !Phone = "555-5555"

    .Update
End With
```

```
'
' Now do whatever you want with this disconnected recordset here, it won't
' affect the original record set.
'

' Clean up
rs.Close
Set rs = Nothing
```

You can also create a disconnected recordset by removing the connection from a bound recordset, like this:

```
Dim rs As New ADODB.Recordset

' Give it a client-side cursor, and set its attributes
rs.CursorLocation = adUseClient
rs.LockType = adLockBatchOptimistic
rs.CursorType = adOpenKeyset

' Open the recordset, getting its data from the database
rs.Open "Customers", CurrentProject.Connection

' Now disconnect the recordset
Set rs.ActiveConnection = Nothing

' Print out the data to prove we still have it
Debug.Print rs!CustomerID, rs!CompanyName

' Clean up
rs.Close
Set rs = Nothing
```

The default cursor in ADO is server-side, so you must use a client-side cursor for this to work because once you disconnect, there is no server. Any changes you make to the data while the recordset is disconnected will not be reflected in the database until you reconnect it and issue the Update or UpdateBatch method (depending on how many records you changed).

```
' Change the data
rs!CompanyName = "who cares"

' Reconnect to the data source
rs.ActiveConnection = CurrentProject.Connection

' Update the data
rs.UpdateBatch
```

If you intend to use UpdateBatch, the recordset's LockType must be set to adLockBatchOptimistic, as shown earlier.

Opening a Recordset Containing More Than One SELECT Query

As in DAO, you can create a recordset containing more than one SELECT query.

The following example demonstrates how to create and use such a recordset. Start by creating a stored procedure to do the job:

```
CREATE PROCEDURE dbo.MultiSelect AS
SELECT * FROM Invoices
SELECT * FROM Customers
```

Or, specify a hard-coded query:

```
strSQL= "SELECT * FROM Invoices SELECT * FROM Customers"
```

The example that follows uses a stored procedure. You might recall from the same section in Chapter 6 that each SQL statement in DAO is separated by a semicolon. As you can see, that's not the case in ADO; just separate the statements by a space (or in the case of a stored procedure, by a line break). Next, a procedure is created to demonstrate how it's done.

```
Dim cmd As New ADODB.Command
Dim rs As ADODB.Recordset

' Setup the Command object
With cmd
    .ActiveConnection = CurrentProject.Connection
    .CommandText = "MultiSelect"
    .CommandType = adCmdStoredProc
End With

'Open the first set of data
Set rs = cmd.Execute
```

When you create the recordset, the initial dataset to be loaded is the one that is specified first in the stored procedure or SQL statement (if hard-coded), and you can cycle through each recordset the same way you would in other recordsets:

```
Do While Not rs Is Nothing
    Do While Not rs.EOF
        Debug.Print rs.Fields(0).Name, rs.Fields(0).Value
        rs.MoveNext
    Loop
```

The `Recordset` object's `NextRecordset` method retrieves subsequent sets of data. The recordset is set to `Nothing` when no more recordsets are available. You can terminate a recordset and move on to the next one by calling the `NextRecordset` method:

```
    'Open the next set of data
    Set rs = rs.NextRecordset
Loop

'Clean up
'There is no need to close the Recordset object
Set cmd = Nothing
```

As with other recordsets, you can flush it with the recordset's `Cancel` method, but remember, that cancels the entire recordset, not just the current dataset.

Creating Schema Recordsets

You're no doubt familiar with using recordsets to access and manipulate data. But ADO also allows you to open recordsets that contain information about your database's tables. Of course, you can get at this information using ADOX, but some details are more readily accessed using ADO schema recordsets.

To open a schema recordset, issue the OpenSchema method against the Connection object. The OpenSchema method has three parameters you can use to specify more options. Here's the syntax:

```
connection.OpenSchema Schema, Restrictions, SchemaID As Recordset
```

The Schema parameter specifies the type of information to return as the result. The available values are defined in Appendix F.

The optional Restrictions parameter allows you to filter the output. For example, you can filter the recordset to return only a single table or view. The available values are listed in Appendix F.

The SchemaID parameter is required only when the Schema parameter is set to adSchemaProvider-Specific, so you must also supply a globally unique identifier (GUID) that identifies the provider schema to return. These are shown as Constants in the example code at the end of this section. For instance, the following code prints the details of every table and view in the current database:

```
Dim rs As ADODB.Recordset
Dim fld As ADODB.Field

' Create the recordset
Set rs = CurrentProject.Connection.OpenSchema(adSchemaTables)

' Loop through the recordset rows
Do Until rs.EOF
    For Each fld In rs.Fields
        ' Loop through the fields in ach row
        Debug.Print fld.Name
        Debug.Print vbTab & Nz(fld.Value, "** Null **")
    Next fld

    rs.MoveNext
    Debug.Print String(20, "-")
Loop

' Clean up
rs.Close
Set fld = Nothing
Set rs = Nothing
```

To restrict the output of the OpenSchema method, you must supply an array of values from the Restrictions list. In other words, where the preceding code prints a list of all the tables and views in the database, the constraint columns for an adSchemaTables recordset are:

❑ TABLE_CATALOG

❑ TABLE_SCHEMA

❑ TABLE_NAME

❑ TABLE_TYPE

The array values must be specified in the same order that they appear in the following code:

```
Array(TABLE_CATALOG, TABLE_SCHEMA, TABLE_NAME, TABLE_TYPE)
```

So, to restrict the output to a single table with a TABLE_NAME of Categories and a TABLE_TYPE of Table, the resulting array would be:

```
Array(TABLE_CATALOG, TABLE_SCHEMA, "Categories", "Table")
```

and you'd end up with:

```
Set rs = CurrentProject.Connection.OpenSchema ( _
adSchemaTables, Array(Empty, Empty, "Categories", "Table"))
```

The ACE provider also supplies eight provider-specific schema recordsets in two broad categories. The following example demonstrates how to use them:

```
'Access object security GUIDs
Public Const JET_SECURITY_FORMS = _
"{c49c842e-9dcb-11d1-9f0a-00c04fc2c2e0}"
Public Const JET_SECURITY_REPORTS = _
"{c49c8430-9dcb-11d1-9f0a-00c04fc2c2e0}"
Public Const JET_SECURITY_MACROS = _
"{c49c842f-9dcb-11d1-9f0a-00c04fc2c2e0}"
Public Const JET_SECURITY_MODULES = _
"{c49c8432-9dcb-11d1-9f0a-00c04fc2c2e0}"

'Jet OLE DB provider-defined schema rowsets
Public Const JET_SCHEMA_REPLPARTIALFILTERLIST = _
"{e2082df0-54ac-11d1-bdbb-00c04fb92675}"
Public Const JET_SCHEMA_REPLCONFLICTTABLES = _
"{e2082df2-54ac-11d1-bdbb-00c04fb92675}"
Public Const JET_SCHEMA_USERROSTER = _
"{947bb102-5d43-11d1-bdbf-00c04fb92675}"
Public Const JET_SCHEMA_ISAMSTATS = _
"{8703b612-5d43-11d1-bdbf-00c04fb92675}"
```

The following code lists all the currently logged-on users:

```
Public Sub WhosOn()
    ' Print the details of all currently logged-on users
    Dim rs As ADODB.Recordset
    Dim fld As ADODB.Field

    ' Create the recordset
    Set rs = CurrentProject.Connection.OpenSchema( _
        adSchemaProviderSpecific, , JET_SCHEMA_USERROSTER)

    ' Loop through the recordset
```

```
        Do Until rs.EOF
            For Each fld In rs.Fields
                ' Loop through the Fields collection
                Debug.Print fld.Name
                Debug.Print vbTab & Nz(fld.Value, "-NULL-")
            Next fld

            rs.MoveNext
        Loop

        ' Clean up
        rs.Close
        Set fld = Nothing
        Set rs = Nothing

    End Sub
```

Using ADO Events

The ADO `Connection` and `Recordset` objects support several events for a variety of operations. These events won't interrupt your code, and can be more accurately pictured as notifications, which are actually a call to an event procedure that you define in your code, much like a text box's `AfterUpdate` event.

ADO object events aren't always so important for synchronous operations because your code waits for the operation to complete before proceeding. They can be important for asynchronous operations, however, because there's no way of telling when the operation will complete.

For example, say you execute the following code to open an asynchronous connection against a SQL Server database that resides on the other side of the country:

```
Dim cn As New ADODB.Connection
Dim rs As New ADODB.Recordset

' Open an asynchronous connection
cn.CursorLocation = adUseServer
cn.Open CurrentProject.Connection, , , adAsyncConnect
rs.Open "vwSomeView", cn
```

Just for fun, say the network runs at 9600 baud. With such a slow network speed, getting connected takes considerable time. Naturally enough, an error will occur when you try to open the recordset, because the connection will not have opened by the time you execute the recordset's `Open` method.

To account for this possibility, you can use the `Connection` object's `ConnectComplete` event. But before you do that, you must declare the `Connection` object using the `WithEvents` keyword.

```
Private WithEvents cn As ADODB.Connection
```

Remember, however, that the `WithEvents` keyword can only be issued in a class module. That being the case, the preceding code could be written as follows:

```
' Open an asynchronous connection
cn.CursorLocation = adUseServer
cn.Open CurrentProject.Connection, , , adAsyncConnect
```

Then you wait for the connection attempt to succeed or fail, as the case may be. You trap the event with the following event procedure:

```
Private Sub cn_ConnectComplete(ByVal pError As ADODB.Error, _
                               adStatus As ADODB.EventStatusEnum, _
                               ByVal pConnection As ADODB.Connection)

    Dim rs As New ADODB.Recordset

    ' Check the connection status and take the appropriate action
    Select Case adStatus
        Case adStatusOK
            'Indicates that the operation succeeded without error
            rs.Open "Invoices", cn

        Case adStatusErrorsOccurred
            'The operation failed due to an error
            'Display the error message
            MsgBox "Error: " & pError.Number, pError.Description
    End Select

    ' Clean up
    rs.Close
    cn.Close
    Set rs = Nothing
    Set cn = Nothing

End Sub
```

Within the event procedure, you can also set `adStatus` to any of the following values to specify certain behaviors:

❑ `adStatusCantDeny`: Specifies that the operation can't request cancellation for a pending operation.

❑ `adStatusCancel`: Cancels the operation.

❑ `adStatusUnwantedEvent`: Does not allow any more notifications for the duration of the event procedure.

The `Connection` object also exposes other events such as `WillConnect`, `ConnectComplete`, and `Disconnect`. The `Recordset` object exposes other events as well. Refer to Appendix F for a list of all the available events for the `Connection` and `Recordset` objects.

Testing the State Property

If you choose not to rely on events, you can always test the object's State property. It returns a value that indicates the status of the operation currently being carried out. For example, the following code segment tests the current state of a Connection object's Open operation.

```
cn.Open CurrentProject.Connection, , , adAsyncConnect
Do Until cn.State = adStateOpen
    DoEvents
Loop

rs.Open "Invoices", cn
```

Not what you'd call a professional approach, but every programmer is different, and you might like to do such things. Of course, the previous code could get into an endless loop if the connection is never opened, so it is usually a good idea to limit the number of loops to a finite number when using an asynchronous connection. The State property can return the following values.

Constant	Value	Description
adStateClosed	0	The object is closed.
adStateOpen	1	The object is open.
adStateConnecting	2	The object is connecting.
adStateExecuting	4	The object is executing a command.
adStateFetching	8	The object is retrieving rows.

Creating Schema Objects with ADOX

So far I've been working with the ADODB library, which is the library to use when you want to work with database data. The ADOX library is the one you use when you want to work with the database schema, such as tables, views (queries), indexes, and so on.

To implement ADOX, you need to add a reference to it. Open any code module by pressing Alt+F11, and select Tools ⇨ References. The References dialog box displays. Locate and select ADO Ext. 2.7 for DDL and Security, and click OK.

The ADOX Object Model

The ADOX model contains one top-level object, Catalog, which contains five collections: Tables, Groups, Users, Procedures, and Views, as illustrated in Figure 7-3.

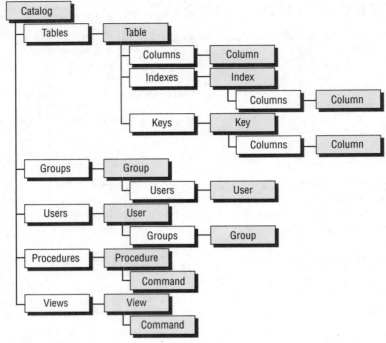

Figure 7-3

Each of the `Table`, `Index`, and `Column` objects also has a standard ADO `Properties` collection, as shown in Figure 7-4.

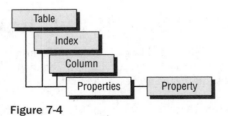

Figure 7-4

Working with Queries (Views)

Because ADO is part of its UDA strategy, Microsoft thought that the term *query* failed to adequately describe the mechanism for retrieving data from a source that could be almost anything. As described earlier, ADO can retrieve data from many different sources, not just the ACE and Jet database engines, so the term "view" was adopted in ADO to more accurately describe a view, or perspective, of the data, regardless of where it came from.

To simplify things while working with the ACE database engine, Microsoft has maintained the existing terminology by referring to them externally as queries; however, this nomenclature changes to views when working with external data sources such as the SQL Server.

If this seems a little confusing, don't worry. Just remember that ADO is a different object model that simply refers to the same objects in a different way, and (sometimes) by different names. When working with queries, just replace the DAO-specific keywords query and QueryDef with the new ADO keyword view. That's all you need to do.

Whenever you work with other data access objects, such as Recordset and Command objects, you can also use a View object to specify the SQL operation that should be used. Exactly how that is done is explained in the relevant sections on Recordset and Command objects.

As with DAO QueryDefs, you can also build ADO views in code.

Creating a View

The process of creating an ADO View is the same as in DAO. To create a view in ADO, follow these steps:

1. Create a Catalog object and define its ActiveConnection property.

2. Create a Command object and define its CommandText property.

3. Append a new View object to the Views collection, using the Command object as its argument:

```
Dim cat As New ADOX.Catalog
Dim cmd As New ADODB.Command

' Open the Catalog
cat.ActiveConnection = CurrentProject.Connection

' Create the Command object that represents the View
cmd.CommandText = "SELECT * FROM tblCustomers"

' Create the View
Cat.Views.Append "AllCustomers", cmd

' Clean up
Set cat.ActiveConnection = Nothing
Set cat = Nothing
Set cmd = Nothing
```

Remember you can set the value of any parameter in code using the Command object. Several examples that demonstrate how to work with the parameters appear earlier in this chapter.

Modifying a View

To modify an existing view, reassign its Command object:

```
' Create the Command object that represents the View
cmd.CommandText = "SELECT * FROM tblCustomers WHERE City = 'Boise'"

' Create the View
Cat.Views("AllCustomers").Command = cmd
```

Deleting a View

Deleting a `View` is simple. Just issue the `Delete` method against the `Catalog` object's `Views` collection:

```
cat.Views.Delete strViewName
```

Creating Tables and Columns

There are many times when you want to create tables from code. ADO fully supports creating tables and columns for those tables. Follow these steps to create a table in ADO:

1. Create a `Catalog` object and define its `ActiveConnection` property.

2. Create a `Table` object.

3. Check if the table already exists, and if so, delete it.

4. Create the table object in memory using the `New` keyword.

5. Create the `Column` objects in memory, using the table's `Append` method, setting each column's attributes as appropriate.

6. Append the `Table` object to the catalog object's `Tables` collection.

7. Refresh the `Tables` collection to ensure it is up-to-date.

The following example creates an invoices table (`tblInvoice`) to store the basic high-level information about each invoice, such as the invoice number, data, and customer ID, and adds four fields to the table:

1. Declare all the objects needed to create the table:

```
Public Sub CreateInvoiceTable()
Dim cat As ADOX.Catalog
Dim tbl As ADOX.Table

' Create and connect a Catalog object
Set cat = New ADOX.Catalog
cat.ActiveConnection = CurrentProject.Connection

On Error Resume Next

' If the table already exists, delete it
cat.Tables.Delete "tblInvoice"
On Error Goto 0

' Create the table definition in memory
Set tbl = New ADOX.Table
tbl.Name = "tblInvoice"
```

2. The new `table` object exists, but only in memory. It won't become a permanent part of the database until you add it to the `catalog` object's collection. Before you do that, however, you need to add one or more columns (called fields in DAO) to the table because you can't save a table that has no columns. Here's how:

```
' Create the new columns
```

```
tbl.Columns.Append "InvoiceNo", adVarChar, 10

' The InvoiceNo column could also have been specified thus:
' Dim col As ADOX.Column
' Set col = New ADOX.Column
' With col
'     .Name = "InvoiceNo"
'     .Type = adVarChar
'     .DefinedSize = 10
' End With
'
' tbl.Columns.Append col

' Create the remaining columns
tbl.Columns.Append "InvoiceDate" adDBDate
tbl.Columns.Append "CustomerID" adInteger
tbl.Columns.Append "Comments" adVarChar, 50
```

3. The columns are added to the table, but the table still needs to be added to the catalog's `Tables` collection to make it a permanent fixture. Then refresh the `Tables` collection to ensure it is up-to-date because in a multiuser application, the new table may not be propagated to other users' collections until you do.

```
' Append the new table to the collection
cat.Tables.Append tbl
cat.Tables.Refresh

' Clean up
cat.ActiveConnection = Nothing
Set tbl = Nothing
Set cat = Nothing
```

4. Create a table to store the invoice line items, including the product ID, the number of items sold, and the individual unit prices. Because the total invoice price and tax can be calculated at runtime, you won't violate normalization rules by creating fields for these items.

```
Public Sub CreateInvItemTable()
Dim cat As ADOX.Catalog
Dim tbl As ADOX.Table

' Create and connect the Catalog object
Set cat = New ADOX.Catalog
cat.ActiveConnection = CurrentProject.Connection

On Error Resume Next

' If the table already exists, delete it
cat.Tables.Delete "tblInvItem"
On Error Goto 0

' Create the table definition in memory
Set tbl = New ADOX.Table
tbl.Name = "tblInvItem"
```

```
With tbl.Columns
    .Append "InvItemID", adInteger
    .Append "InvoiceNo", adVarChar, 10
    .Append "ProductID", adInteger
    .Append "Qty", adSmallInt
    .Append "UnitCost", adCurrency
End With
```

5. After you've appended a column to the table, you can set its Access-specific properties. For example, to make a column (in this case, the `InvItemID` column) the `AutoNumber` column, you first set its `ParentCatalog` property, and then set its `AutoIncrement` property:

```
With tbl.Columns("InvItemID")
    .ParentCatalog = cat
    .Properties("AutoIncrement") = True
End With

' Append the new table to the collection
cat.Tables.Append tbl
cat.Tables.Refresh

' Clean up
cat.ActiveConnection = Nothing
Set tbl = Nothing
Set cat = Nothing
```

Creating Indexes

The basic procedure for creating an index is as follows:

1. Create a `Catalog` object and define its `ActiveConnection` property.
2. Create a `Table` object and instantiate it.
3. Create an `Index` object.
4. Check whether the primary key already exists, and if so, delete it.
5. Create the index using the `New` keyword, and set its attributes as appropriate.
6. Append the index's columns to the `Columns` collection.
7. Append the index to the table's `Indexes` collection.

Remember three things when creating indexes in ADO:

❑   Not all providers support all index attributes. Check the provider's documentation for those it does support.

❑   ACE and Jet databases do not support clustered indexes.

❑   Although you can give an index any name you like, when you create a primary key using the Access Table Designer, it is automatically named `PrimaryKey` for ACE and Jet databases, and `PK_tablename` for SQL Server databases. To maintain consistency, it is wise to give code-created primary keys the same name.

The following sub creates a primary key index for the specified table, which can include multiple fields whose names are supplied in the `ParamArray` argument. In the invoice tables example, there is only one field in each.

```
Public Sub CreatePKIndexes(strTableName As String, _
                           ParamArray varPKColumns() As Variant)
    Dim cat As ADOX.Catalog
    Dim tbl As ADOX.Table
    Dim idx As ADOX.Index
    Dim varColumn As Variant

    ' Create and connect the Catalog object
    Set cat = New ADOX.Catalog
    cat.ActiveConnection = CurrentProject.Connection

    Set tbl = cat.Tables(strTableName)

    ' Check if a Primary Key exists. If so, delete it.
    For Each idx In tbl.Indexes
        If idx.PrimaryKey Then
            tbl.Indexes.Delete idx.Name
        End If
    Next idx

    ' Create a new primary key
    Set idx = New ADOX.Index
    With idx
        .Name = "PrimaryKey"
        .PrimaryKey = True
        .Unique = True
    End With
```

At this point, the index exists in memory, and will remain so until it is added to the table's `Indexes` collection. First, however, you must add the columns that make up the key to the index's `Columns` collection and refresh the collection:

```
    ' Append the columns
    For Each varColumn In varPKColumns
        idx.Columns.Append varColumn
    Next varColumn

    ' Append the index to the collection
    tbl.Indexes.Append idx
    tbl.Indexes.Refresh

    ' Clean up
    Set cat.ActiveConnection = Nothing
    Set cat = Nothing
    Set tbl = Nothing
    Set idx = Nothing

End Sub
```

Run the `CreatePKIndexes` procedure to define the indexes for both `tblInvoice` and `tblInvItem` tables.

Finally, relationships must be set up between the two tables.

Creating Relationships

The basic procedure for creating a relationship is as follows:

1. Create a `Catalog` object and define its `ActiveConnection` property.

2. Create a `Key` object to act as the foreign key (the many side of the relationship).

3. Supply the `RelatedTable` property, which is the name of the primary table (the one side of the relationship).

4. Supply the `RelatedColumn` property (which is the name of the matching column in the primary table) for each column.

5. Set the other key attributes as appropriate.

6. Add the key to the table's `Keys` collection.

The following code creates a foreign key relationship between the `tblInvoice` table and the `tblProducts` table:

You can name a relationship any way you like, but when you create a relationship using the Relationships window, Access names the relationship according to the names of the tables involved. For example, if you were to create a relationship between `tblInvoice` *and tblProducts, Access would name it* `tblInvoicetblProducts`.

```
Dim cat As New ADOX.Catalog
Dim ky As New ADOX.Key

' Create and connect the Catalog object
cat.ActiveConnection = CurrentProject.Connection

' Define the foreign key
With ky
    .Name = "ProductID"
    .Type = adKeyForeign
    .RelatedTable = "tblProducts"
    .Columns.Append "ProductID"
    .Columns("ProductID").RelatedColumn = "ProductID"
    .UpdateRule = adRICascade
End With

' Append the foreign key
cat.Tables("tblInvoice").Keys.Append ky

' Clean up
Set cat.ActiveConnection = Nothing
Set cat = Nothing
Set ky = Nothing
```

Managing Security with ADO

Finally, one very powerful feature ADO provides is the capability to manage database security. Using ADO, you can set a database password and manage users and groups permissions (when supported). Chapter 18, which concerns Access database security, provides in-depth coverage of how to use ADO to manage security in a database solution.

> *ACE databases (ACCDB files) do not support User Level Security. For more information about User Level Security for Jet, please refer to Chapter 18.*

Summary

In this chapter, you learned about the ADO object model, which included both the ADODB library, for manipulating data, and the ADOX library, for manipulating database schema.

By now you have a fairly good working knowledge of creating and using ADO connections and transactions, and can create and execute queries using both `Connection` and `Command` objects. You should be able to confidently create and filter ADO recordsets, navigate your way around their rows, find specific records, and edit their data.

You also explored persistent and disconnected recordsets, and examined the use of multiple SELECT clauses, shaped queries, and schema recordsets. You should be fairly confident of your understanding of ADO events.

In addition, you took a look at creating queries (views), tables and columns, indexes, and relations to help you create and modify entire databases from the ground up. Finally, you learned how to work with the Jet security model in ADO, creating groups and users, and managing object permissions.

In the next chapter, you examine VBA in some detail, which will add a great deal of context to what's been covered in Chapters 6 and 7.

8

Executing VBA

In the old days of programming, procedural languages ruled, meaning that the overall program execution traveled from top to bottom. The main body of any of these programs had to cover every possibility: display a screen to the user, gather input, perform edit checking, display messages, update the database (or simple files in those days), and close when everything was done. The main program also had to deal with every option or side request that the user might make. This made it difficult to understand the entire program, and it was tough to make changes because everything had to be retested when a modification was made. Those lumbering beasts included COBOL, RPG, Pascal, and earlier forms of Basic. Millions of lines of code were written in these languages.

Fortunately, those days are over for VBA programmers. VBA is an *event-driven* language. In every Access form and report there are a variety of events that are waiting for you to use. They are available when the form opens and closes, when records are updated, even when individual fields on the screen are changed. They're all there at your fingertips. Each event can contain a procedure, which is where you get back to your procedural roots. Although each procedure runs from top to bottom, just like in the old days, it only runs when the event *fires*. Until then, it sleeps quietly, not complicating your logic or slowing down your program.

Event-driven programming makes it much easier to handle complex programming tasks. By only worrying about events in your coding when they actually happen, each procedure is simpler and easier to debug.

In this chapter, you'll explore the nature of VBA events and see how the most common events are used, and you'll look at how two different sections of your VBA code can run at the same time. The chapter provides some guidelines about when and how to use Public and Private procedures, class modules, and data types, and also outlines structural guidelines for procedures, shows some common string and date handling techniques, and explains how to prevent rounding errors in your calculations.

When Events Fire

Events are at the heart of event-driven programming — which is no surprise. What can be surprising to novice programmers is the sheer number of events available to use. They all beg to have some code behind them. In reality though, very few events are used on a consistent basis. Most of them have absolutely no code behind them, and never will in normal usage. The trick is to know which ones are important and commonly used, and which ones are obscure and hardly ever used. They all look equally important in Access Help.

Common Form Events

To cut to the chase, here's a list of commonly used events and how you might want to use them. If you know how to use this basic set of events, you're most of the way there to understanding event-driven programming in Access VBA.

Form Event	Description
On Open	Fires before the On Load event (so you can't reference any bound controls on your form yet because they haven't been instantiated) and before the recordset is evaluated for the form. This means you can use this event to change the recordset (by changing the WHERE or ORDER BY clause) before the form continues to load. Cancel this event by setting its intrinsic parameter Cancel = True, so the form will close without continuing to the On Load event.
On Load	Fires after the recordset for the form has been evaluated but before the form is displayed to the user. This offers you an opportunity to make calculations, set defaults, and change visual attributes based on the data from the recordset.
Before Update	To perform some data edits before the user's changes are updated in the database, use this event. All the field values are available to you, so you can do multiple field edits (such as HireDate must be greater than BirthDate). If something doesn't pass your validity checks, you can display a message box and cancel this event by setting the intrinsic parameter Cancel = True. This event also fires before a new record is inserted, so you can place edits for both new and changed records here.
On Double Click	A non-intuitive special-purpose event. If you build a continuous form to display records in a read-only format, your users will expect to drill down to the detail of the record by double-clicking anywhere on the row. But what if they double-click the record selector (the gray arrow at the left side of each row)? The event that fires is the Form's On Double Click event. By using this event, you can run the code that opens your detail form. This gives your user a consistent experience and the confidence that your applications work no matter what.
On Unload	This event can be used to check data validity before your form closes. It can be canceled, which redisplays your form without closing it. It also has another useful behavior. If it is canceled during an unload that occurred because the user is closing Access (using the X button in the window heading), canceling the Unload event also cancels all other form closures and the closure of Access itself. This allows you to prompt the user with an "Are you sure?" message box when the user tries to close Access.

Form Event	Description
On Current	This is one of the most overused events by novice programmers, but it does have some good uses. It fires every time your form's "current" record changes. The current record is the one that the record selector (the gray arrow on the left side of each record) points to. It also fires when your form initially loads and positions to the first record in your recordset. One good place to use On Current is on a continuous form where one of the buttons below is valid for some records but not for others. In the On Current event, you can test the current record and set the Enabled property of the button to True or False as appropriate. Because this event fires so often, it can be hard to control and cause performance issues. Use it only when you need to.
On Delete	Fires after each record is deleted, but before the delete is actually finalized, enabling you to display an "Are you sure?" message. Then the user has an opportunity to decide whether or not to delete this individual record. Use this in conjunction with the Before Delete Confirm event.
Before Delete Confirm	Fires before a group of deletes is finalized. If you cancel this event, none of the records in the group is actually deleted. This event also has a Response parameter; it can be used to suppress the normal Access message asking the user if he wants to delete the group of records.
On Activate	Fires after the form's On Open and On Load events, just before the form is displayed. It also fires whenever the form regains the focus, so it can be used to refresh or requery the data on the form after the user has returned from another form.

Common Control Events

The following table lists some events on form controls (such as text boxes, combo boxes, command buttons, and so on) that are commonly used.

Control Event	Description
On Click	This one is obvious; it fires when the control (most likely a command button) is clicked. This is where you put the code to run when the user clicks a button.
Before Update	Useful for controls that contain values, such as text boxes and combo boxes. It fires just before a change to the control is committed, so you have a chance to validate the new value of the field. If this event is canceled, the control reverts to its previous value. You can ask the user a question in this event using a message box, such as "Are you sure you want to change the Invoice Number?" You can then continue normally or set Cancel = True based on his response.

Table continues on the next page

Control Event	Description
After Update	Fires after a change to the control is made. This is a good time to control the next field to receive the focus, manipulate other fields in response to this one, or perform other actions (these techniques are used in Chapter 15).
On Double Click	Fires when a control is double-clicked. Useful when you want to provide a method of drilling down to a detail form from a read-only index form. Make sure you add the code to open the detail form to every double-click event of every field in the detail section. If your record selector arrow is visible, include your drill-down code to the form's On Double Click event (see previous section).

Common Report Events

The following table lists some report events that are commonly used. These events can run code to customize and display reports so that they are much more flexible for your users.

Report Event	Description
On Open	Fires before the recordset is evaluated for the report. Just as with forms, you can use this event to change the recordset (by changing the WHERE or ORDER BY clause) before the report continues to load. This can be especially helpful when you use a form to prompt the user for selection criteria before the report continues to load (described in detail in Chapter 14). This event can be canceled by setting the Cancel parameter to True, which will prevent the report from continuing to open.
On Activate	Fires after the On Open event, and just as the report window is displayed to the user. The main thing this event is used for is to maximize the Access windows using DoCmd.Maximize. This allows the user to see more of the report. However, you'll probably want to restore the Access windows to their previous sizes when the report closes, which brings us to the On Close event.
On Close	Fires when the report closes. A common line of code to include here is DoCmd.Restore to restore the sizes of your form windows that were maximized in the On Activate event.
On No Data	Fires after the On Open event when the report evaluates the recordset and discovers that there are no records. This can easily happen if you allow users to specify the criteria for the report and they choose a combination of values that doesn't exist in the database. You can display a friendly message box to the user, and then set the intrinsic Cancel parameter to True, which closes the report.
On Load	New in Access 2007. It fires after the On Open event. In this event, the recordset for the report has already been evaluated and data from the first record is available.

Asynchronous Execution

Sometimes, Access runs two areas of your VBA code simultaneously, even though you've placed the code into different events or even in different forms and reports. This ability for Access to start running one procedure of code before another one is finished is called *asynchronous execution*. Most of the time asynchronous execution happens without you (or your user) really noticing, but it can sometimes cause problems, so you should know when it happens and what to do about it.

OpenForm

The most common asynchronous execution you'll encounter is when you open a form using the `OpenForm` command. Most of the time you won't notice it, but here's what really happens: When the `OpenForm` statement runs, the form you ask for starts to open, along with all of its `On Open`, `On Load`, and `On Current` events. However, your code after the `OpenForm` command also continues to run at the same time. Usually, not much happens at this point, so there's no harm done.

There are times, however, when you would like the execution of the code in the calling form to stop until the user is done with the form you open. This can happen when you are prompting the user for selection criteria during the `Open` event of a report (see Chapter 14), or when you open a form to add a new record from an index form.

In this latter case, you normally want to requery the index form to show the record that was just added, but you have to wait for the user to finish adding it. If you perform a requery right after the `OpenForm`, your code will continue merrily along and requery your first form, only within milliseconds after your second form has started to open. No matter how fast your user is, that's not enough time for them to add the new record. So your requery runs before the new record is added, and the new record will not appear on your index form.

There is a simple solution to the normal asynchronous execution of the `OpenForm` command. It's called Dialog mode.

Dialog Mode to the Rescue

To prevent asynchronous execution when a form opens, use Dialog mode. Instead of:

```
DoCmd.OpenForm FormName:="frmMyForm"
```

specify this:

```
DoCmd.OpenForm FormName:="frmMyForm", windowmode:=acDialog
```

Note the use of named parameters in these examples — `FormName:="frmMyForm"`, for instance. Functions and subs in VBA can receive parameters (also often called arguments) using either positions or names. If the names are not specified, VBA assigns parameters based on their position: first, second, and so on. When you see extra commas indicating missing parameters, you know that positional parameters are being used. Named parameters are much clearer to read and understand, and experienced programmers often use them.

Dialog mode accomplishes two things:

❑   It opens the form in Modal mode, which prevents the user from clicking on any other Access windows until they are done with this form.

❑   It stops the execution of the calling code until the newly opened form is either closed or hidden.

This second feature of Dialog mode is what is so helpful in preventing Access from trying to run two areas of your code at once.

Notice that the code stops until the form is closed or hidden. This is the basis for many clever uses of Dialog mode where values from the called form are used elsewhere. If you just hide the form (by setting its `Visible` property to `False`), the values on the form are still there and ready for you to reference, even though the code in the calling form now continues to run. This is the technique for gathering selection criteria and building SQL statements, which is described in Chapter 14.

There is a disadvantage to using Dialog mode. While a form is open and visible in Dialog mode, any report that is opened will appear behind the form and won't be accessible. If you encounter this problem, you can use another technique to control the timing of form requeries. One technique is to open the second form normally and allow the code in the first form to complete. Then, put your requery code in the first form's `On Activate` *event to fire when the focus returns to the first form.*

VBA Procedures

VBA code can be structured clearly and efficiently by breaking up sections of code into logical "chunks" called procedures. In this section, you'll see how to use the different types of VBA procedures and to employ good practices in their design.

Function or Sub?

A common area of confusion among novice VBA programmers is whether to write a function or a sub (short for "subroutine"). Some developers create functions for every procedure they write, in the belief that they are better in some way. They aren't. Functions and subs are just two kinds of procedures, and they both have their purposes. A quick way to determine which one is more appropriate is to ask this question: Does my procedure *do* something or *return* something?

If the purpose of your procedure is to compute or retrieve a value and return it to the calling procedure, then of course you should use a function. After all, functions are designed to return a single value to the calling procedure. They do it efficiently and easily, and they can be used directly in queries and calculated controls on forms and reports. They can even be used directly in macros.

Functions tend to have names that are nouns, like `LastDayOfMonth` or `FullAddress`. For example, a control on a report might have this Control Source property value:

```
=LastDayOfMonth(Date())
```

The field would display the results of calling some function called `LastDayOfMonth` with the parameter value of today's date.

On the other hand, if the main purpose of your procedure is to do some action and there is no clear-cut value to return, use a sub. Many programmers think that they must return something, even if they have to make up some artificial return code or status. This practice can make your code harder for others to understand. However, if you really need a return code or status after the procedure finishes, it is perfectly okay to make it a function.

Subs tend to have names that are verbs like `LoadWorkTable` or `CloseMonth`. In practice, the code looks like this:

```
LoadWorkTable
```

Pretty easy, right? Any developer looking at this line of code can see the obvious: A sub called `LoadWorkTable` is being called, and it doesn't return a value.

It is possible to call a function as if it were a sub, without parentheses around the parameters. In that case, the function runs, but the return value is discarded. This usually is not a good coding practice, but you may encounter it in existing code.

Public or Private?

Another decision that you have to make when you create procedures is whether to make them `Public` or `Private`. By default, Access makes procedures you create `Public`, but that's not necessarily what you want.

If you are working in a standalone module (those that appear in the Modules area of the Access Navigation pane), the rules are a little different than if you are working in code that resides in a form or report. Forms and reports are intrinsically encapsulated as class modules, so their `Public` procedures aren't as public as you might expect. Let's take a look at procedures in standalone modules first.

Public and Private Procedures in Modules

Public functions and subs in standalone modules are just that — public property. Every area of your application can see them and use them. To do that, `Public` procedures in modules must have unique names. Otherwise, how would your code know which one to run? If you have two `Public` procedures with the same name, you'll get a compile error.

`Private` procedures in modules are very shy — they can't be seen or referenced by any code outside their own module. If you try to reference a `Private` procedure from a different module or another form or report, Access insists (at compile time) that no such procedure exists.

The hidden nature of `Private` procedures is their best feature. Because they are hidden, their names need to be unique only within their own module. Therefore, you can name them whatever you want — you don't have to worry about them conflicting with other procedures in your application.

This feature really comes into play when you reuse code by importing modules into other databases, maybe even ones you didn't create. If most of your module procedures are `Private`, you'll have a minimum of naming conflicts because the rest of the application can't see them. The `Public` procedures still need to have a unique name, which is why many procedures that are meant to be imported have interesting prefixes such as the author's initials or the company name.

Public and Private Procedures in Forms and Reports

`Private` procedures in forms and reports behave just like `Private` procedures in modules. They can't be seen or referenced from outside the form or report. The event procedures that Access automatically builds behind your forms and reports are automatically set to `Private`. This makes sense because `Form_Open` and `OnClick` events are useful only inside that particular form or report. Also, these procedures need to have standard names, which could result in a big mess of duplicate names if they were `Public`.

In reality, this problem wouldn't occur. The code behind your forms and reports isn't like the code in normal modules. Access calls them Class Objects, but they behave like class modules, which are covered later in this chapter. You can see this in the Visual Basic Editing window, as shown in Figure 8-1. Note the three headings: Microsoft Office Access Class Modules, Modules, and Class Modules.

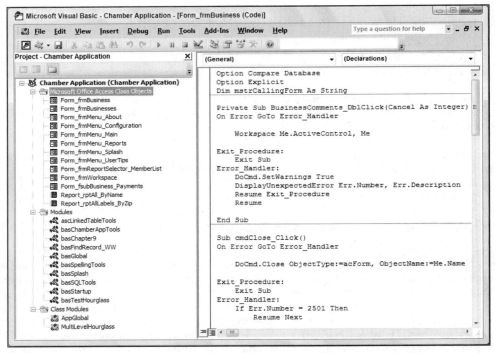

Figure 8-1

It turns out that even a `Public` procedure that you build in the code behind a form can be named the same as a procedure in another form. That's because class modules require that you specify the name of the class object (in this case, the form name) before the name of the procedure if you want to call it from outside the form. However, this is rarely needed. One possible situation might be some form initialization code that you want to run from outside the form, such as `InitializeForm`. If you want to do it, here's the syntax:

```
Form_frmMyFormName.InitializeForm
```

Notice that the prefix `Form_` and the name of the form qualifies the `InitializeForm` procedure name. Because many forms could have the same procedure name, you need to tell the code which form's procedure you want to run.

Coupling and Cohesion

The design of your procedures is important to delivering understandable, readable code. Two principles that guide the logical design of procedures (functions or subs) are *coupling* (bad) and *cohesion* (good). This topic isn't specific to VBA, but it bears mentioning while you're working with procedures.

Uncouple Procedures

Coupling is the tempting tendency to write long, complex procedures that do lots of things; in other words, *coupling* multiple tasks into one procedure. That should be avoided. As a guideline, write procedures that compute just one value or perform just one task. Some signs that you might have coupling in your procedures include:

❑   Procedure names that include multiple ideas, such as `ComputeValuesAndReloadWorkTables`

❑   Procedures with large blocks of code that have section header comments explaining what each section does

❑   Procedures that include "modes," with parameters that tell the procedure what to do

If your procedure couples multiple tasks together, you can run into problems like these:

❑   Your procedure is too complicated, making it harder to write and debug.

❑   The different tasks in your procedure can't be used separately; it's an all-or-nothing deal.

❑   If you make a change to your procedure, the whole thing needs to be retested. You can't trust that your little change didn't mess up other parts of the procedure. Remember the common programmer's lament: "But all I changed was . . .".

If you find yourself writing long procedures with these coupling problems, take a deep breath and step back from it for a minute. Try to identify chunks of code that do something simple and cohesive. As a rule, procedures should do or calculate one thing, and should do so independently using parameters that are passed to them. They can also retrieve information from tables or queries to get the information they need.

You may wonder how to build procedures that must be complex. Sometimes there is no way to avoid complexity, but you can hide a lot of complexity by breaking your logic into smaller functions and subs, then calling them where appropriate. That way, each one of your procedures can be written and debugged separately. If you are working as a team, these can even be written by different developers.

Adhere to Cohesion

Cohesion means that each procedure should perform one function, and should be able to do its thing without a lot of help or knowledge from outside the procedure. It shouldn't rely on global variables or other objects to exist. Some signs of a poor cohesion are:

❑   Procedures that include duplicate blocks of code

- ❑ Procedures that expect forms or reports with specific names
- ❑ Use of global variables, especially when they are expected to retain their value for a long time
- ❑ Hard coding of system environment information such as file paths
- ❑ Hard coding or special handling of certain records or values in tables

Hard coding is the practice of using values in code that would be more appropriate in a configurable lookup table or some other easy-to-change place. For example, many poorly written applications hard code paths to files. The moment those applications are moved to another computer, they break. Another more insidious example is the use of values lists for combo boxes in forms. These seem so easy to set up, but they are just another instance of hard coding that makes your application less robust and more difficult to change over time. A better approach for a list of values that you don't think will change (or that you need to code against) is to put them in a table that doesn't have a maintenance form. This prevents your user from adding or removing the critical values your code depends on, but allows you flexibility over time. If you like, you can use a specific naming convention (as an extension of Reddick naming conventions) for these values list tables, such as `tval` instead of `tlkp` or `tbl`.

To improve cohesion, think of the old black box principle of programming: You should need no knowledge of how a procedure produces its result, only that given valid input, it will produce the correct output. Along the same lines, the procedure should need little knowledge of the world outside to do its job. Each procedure you write should perform one task or calculation and need a minimum of special knowledge from outside its own boundaries. The best way to send information into a procedure is through parameters, not by using global variables or referring to specific forms or reports.

All this being said, cohesion is a spectrum, not a final black-or-white goal. Using VBA in Access sometimes calls for the use of global variables in controlled scenarios, or referring to an open form, or duplicating some code. It's best to be aware of coupling and cohesion principles so that you can make good coding decisions.

Error Handling

All of your procedures should have at least a minimum level of error handling. There are easy ways to implement simple error handling that can help you debug your code and protect your users from errors (both expected and unexpected). This topic is covered in much greater detail in Chapter 9.

Class Modules

Class modules are special modules within VBA that allow you to build code objects that have all the capabilities of built-in Access objects: methods, properties, multiple instances, and data persistence. These special capabilities of class modules are interesting, but they are rarely needed in normal application programming. However, if you're familiar with class modules, you'll find times when they come in very handy. One reason to use class modules is their capability to remember data across multiple times they are called. This can also be done using the `Static` keyword when dimensioning variables in regular modules, or by using Global variables, but using a class module is a cleaner way.

A related benefit to the class module "memory" is that you can set multiple properties of an instance of a class, and then ask it to do something with a method. It sounds technical, but, in reality, a class module uses a property `Let` procedure to merely remember a value in a variable. And a method is really just a procedure that does something — similar to the subs you've already seen. The best way to show how class modules work is with a simple example, but one that you might actually use sometime. If your application has some time-consuming processing, you may want to turn on the Hourglass mouse pointer icon so that the user knows that you're working on something and she should wait patiently.

However, sometimes multiple time-consuming functions and subs have to run in succession or in a nested structure, and sometimes one procedure is run without the others. Keeping track of the Hourglass status can be difficult in these cases. You need to be sure that it is on while the processing is occurring, but also that it is turned off at the end.

A good approach is to keep track of how "on" the Hourglass is. Every time a procedure needs the Hourglass, it increases the hourglass level — 1 means that one procedure turned it on, 2 means that two nested procedures have turned it on, and so on. As each procedure finishes, it decrements the level by 1. When the hourglass level reaches 0, the Hourglass icon itself is turned off.

This class module, called `MultiLevelHourglass`, demonstrates how you can use class modules to remember the state of an object (in this case, the hourglass level) and manipulate it over time. It consists of three procedures:

- ❏ `TurnOn`: Increments the hourglass level and turns the Hourglass on, if necessary.

- ❏ `TurnOff`: Decrements the hourglass level and turns the Hourglass off if necessary, plus an over-ride parameter to force the Hourglass off regardless of level.

- ❏ `IsOn`: A property that returns whether the Hourglass is currently on.

To create a class module, open the Visual Basic editor and select Insert ➪ Class Module.

Here's the code from the class module called `MultiLevelHourglass`. First, note the local module level variable. It keeps track of the current level. Because this is a class module, the variable's value will be retained across multiple uses of the object.

```
Option Compare Database
Option Explicit

Private mintHourglassLevel As Integer
```

The following is the simple property, called a `Property Get` in a class module. It merely sets the `IsOn` property to `True` if the level is greater than `0` or `False` if it isn't.

```
Public Property Get IsOn() As Boolean
  IsOn = (mintHourglassLevel > 0)
End Property
```

The following method turns the Hourglass on, or to be more accurate, increases the level of the Hourglass. If the hourglass level becomes 1 during a call to this procedure, the Access Hourglass itself is turned on. If the level is already greater than 1, there's no need, because the Access Hourglass is already on.

```
Public Function TurnOn()
On Error GoTo Error_Handler
```

```
    'Increment the hourglass level.
    mintHourglassLevel = mintHourglassLevel + 1
    'Turn on the hourglass if the level is exactly 1
    If mintHourglassLevel = 1 Then

        DoCmd.Hourglass True
    End If

Exit_Procedure:
    Exit Function

Error_Handler:
    DisplayUnexpectedError Err.Number, Err.Description
    Resume Exit_Procedure
    Resume

End Function
```

Note the call to `DisplayUnexpectedError`. This procedure displays an error message to the user, and is described in detail in Chapter 9.

Finally, here is the method that lowers the Hourglass level, and actually turns off the Hourglass if level 0 is reached. Note the optional parameter to force the Hourglass icon off. This is just a safety valve — you shouldn't need it if each procedure you run is consistent about decreasing the level using `TurnOff` when it is finished. However, if you know that you are at the end of a long-running process and you want to be sure, you can use `ForceOff:=True` to ensure that the Hourglass icon isn't stuck on.

```
Public Function TurnOff(Optional ForceOff As Boolean)
On Error GoTo Error_Handler

    'Decrement the hourglass level.
    mintHourglassLevel = mintHourglassLevel -1
    'Turn off the hourglass if the level is less than or equal to zero
    'or if it is being forced off regardless of level
    If mintHourglassLevel <= 0 Or ForceOff Then

        mintHourglassLevel = 0
        DoCmd.Hourglass False
    End If

Exit_Procedure:
    Exit Function

Error_Handler:
    DisplayUnexpectedError Err.Number, Err.Description
    Resume Exit_Procedure
    Resume

End Function
```

That's it for the class module called `MultiLevelHourglass`. Now all you need is some code to test it out:

```
Option Compare Database
Global objHourGlass As New MultiLevelHourglass

Public Sub HourglassTest()

objHourGlass.TurnOn
'lots of time consuming code here

objHourGlass.TurnOn
objHourGlass.TurnOn
objHourGlass.TurnOff

objHourGlass.TurnOff
'any called functions should also use .TurnOn and .TurnOff
Debug.Print objHourGlass.IsOn 'just for debugging purposes
objHourGlass.TurnOff ForceOff:=True 'all done

End Sub
```

To use this technique, call `objHourGlass.TurnOn` and `objHourGlass.TurnOff` to control the Hourglass throughout your application. Use `DoCmd.Hourglass` to make sure that no other procedures are controlling the Hourglass directly because that would circumvent this multilevel approach.

Using Variables

When using variables in your VBA code, there are several things to remember to ensure that your code runs smoothly. Choosing the appropriate data type for each variable is critical, and it's also important to use global variables correctly.

Naming conventions for variables are important. The Reddick naming conventions for variables are described in Appendix L. If you get into the habit of naming your variables consistently, your code will be easier to maintain over time, faster to debug, and look more professional.

Using Appropriate Data Types and Sizes

First, make sure that your variable types will handle the size of data they are expected to store. Many overflow errors occur because an AutoNumber key value from a table was stored in a variable defined as an Integer. This may work fine during testing because an integer can store numbers with values up to 32,767. Then, when a user starts adding more data, the application breaks on an overflow error.

It's a good idea to define variables with the maximum size that is possible to occur. AutoNumber fields should be stored in variables defined as Long (which is the same as the Long Integer in Access tables). Defining a variable as String allows it to store very long strings, whether they are defined as Text or Memo in a table.

If a variable can possibly contain a Null, then you must define it as a Variant, in which case it will be able to store just about anything that you throw into it — a messy approach, and one that takes Access a bit longer to process. It's usually better to decide what kind of data each variable is going to hold, then set the appropriate data type so that Access doesn't have to figure out what's in there every time it uses the variable. Sometimes, though, it's useful to allow a variable to contain a Null, especially when there might not always be data to load into the field. If you do use a Variant data type, use it because there's a specific reason that it might contain a Null, not because you don't know what type it should be.

If you don't specify a variable's data type, it is a Variant by default. A common error is to define more than one variable on a single line of code, like this:

```
Dim strCallingForm, strReportTitle as String
```

Many novice VBA programmers think that both variables in this example are defined as Strings, but they won't be. VBA requires that each and every variable has its data type defined. In this example, strCallingForm will be defined as a Variant because its data type wasn't specified.

A correct way to define the two string variables on one line is like this:

```
Dim strCallingForm as String, strReportTitle as String
```

This style is technically correct (both variables are defined as Strings), but the second variable is easy to miss when you are looking at your code. The clearest and most consistent style for defining variables is to give each one its own line:

```
Dim strCallingForm as String
Dim strReportTitle as String
```

This may take an extra line of code, but it is much easier to read and understand.

Using Global Variables

Global variables are variables that retain their value until they are changed or until the application stops. They can be handy, but they should be used in specific ways to avoid problems. To define a global variable, simply use Global instead of Dim, like this:

```
Global gstrCallingForm As String
```

Notice the naming convention: g for Global, str for String, and then the variable name.

A global can be defined in any standalone module; it doesn't matter which one. You can refer to it and set its value from anywhere in your application (that's why it's called global). However, you probably want to designate a module to store all your main reusable application code, which is where you can define your global variables. You could name this module basGlobal or something similar.

Global variables, however, have a problem. If your code is interrupted — after an error, for example — the global variables are cleared out. There are two ways to reduce the impact of this little problem. The best way is to use the value in global variables for a very short time, perhaps a few milliseconds. Globals can be used like parameters for objects that don't accept true parameters, such as forms. For example, the form daisy-chaining logic given in Appendix M uses a single global variable to pass the name of the calling form to the called form, but the called form immediately stores the name in a local module variable for safekeeping.

Another way to work around the problem with global variables is to create a wrapper function that first checks whether the variable has a value. If it does, it merely returns it. If it doesn't have a value (which will happen the first time the function is called, or if the value has been reset), the function then computes or retrieves the value, sets the global variable, and returns the value. This can be a good way to retrieve or compute values that take some time, such as connection string properties or other application-wide values that are retrieved from tables. You get the speed of a global variable and the reliability of computing the values when necessary.

Access 2007 has a new way of storing global values: `TempVars`. This is a collection of values that you can define and maintain, and it won't be reset if you stop your code during debugging. The values are retained as long as the current database is open. `TempVars` are explained in detail in Appendix M.

Evaluating Expressions in VBA

Expressions are one of the basic building blocks of any programming language. There are several ways to evaluate expressions in VBA so that you can control the flow of your procedural logic.

If .. Then

Nearly, every programming language has some way of asking If, and VBA is no exception. The `If..Then` structure is one of the most commonly used in VBA. Its usage is straightforward, but there are a couple of issues that warrant extra attention. First, the expression you are using needs to be formed correctly and completely. One common mistake is to use an expression like this:

```
If intOrderStatus = 1 Or 2 Then
    'some interesting code here
End If
```

The problem here is that a complete Boolean (true or false) expression needs to be on both sides of the `Or`. The literal way to interpret this expression is "if intOrderStatus = 1 or if 2 is True, then," which, of course, makes no sense. The value 2 is not true. In fact, in Access VBA any value other than –1 is false, so the value 2 is always false. This `If` statement has a big problem — the interesting code will run if the order status is 1, but it will never run if it is 2.

The correct way to write this line of code is as follows:

```
If intOrderStatus = 1 Or intOrderStatus = 2 Then
    'some interesting code here
End If
```

It's repetitive, but you have to tell VBA exactly what you want to do.

Instead of using multiple `Or` *operators in SQL statements, you can use a much easier syntax: the* `In` *operator. In SQL, the equivalent to* `Where OrderStatus = 1 or OrderStatus = 2` *is merely* `Where OrderStatus In (1,2)`. *That's much easier to read and understand, and it only gets better the more values you have to compare.*

Checking for Nulls

Another common area of confusion is checking for Null. The following statement is not correct:

```
If varCustomerKey = Null Then
   'even more interesting code here
End If
```

An interesting fact about Null: It never equals anything. It is, by definition, unknown and undefined. A variable containing a null can't "equal" anything, including Null. In this example, the interesting code will never run, no matter how null the customer key field is.

To check for a Null in a field, you must use the IsNull function, like this:

```
If IsNull(varCustomerKey) Then
   'even more interesting code here
End If
```

The IsNull function is the only way VBA can look into a variable or recordset field and determine if there's a Null in there. The = just can't do it. By the way, this is true in Access SQL, too — you need to use IsNull to test for Nulls in the WHERE clauses of queries and recordsets, or you can use the SQL specific syntax WHERE [FieldName] IS NULL.

Sometimes, you want to check to see if a field is either Null or contains an empty string (also known as a zero-length string). Empty strings can creep into your tables if you specify Yes to Allow Zero Length in the field definition during table design. To ensure that you are checking for both, use code such as this:

```
If IsNull(BusinessName) or BusinessName = "" Then
```

What a hassle — you have to type the name of the field twice, and the line is confusing to read. There's a much easier way:

```
If BusinessName & "" = "" Then
```

This technique uses the concatenation behavior of the & operator. The & concatenates two strings, even if one of them is Null (see the section String Handling Techniques later in this chapter). In this case, it concatenates an empty string ("") onto the end of BusinessName. If BusinessName is Null, the result is an empty string. If BusinessName has any string value in it, it remains unchanged by tacking on an empty string. This behavior enables you to quickly check if a field has a Null or an empty string.

Notice that this example uses the & operator to concatenate strings. The + operator also concatenates strings, but there's an important difference: + propagates Null. That is, if either side (operand) is Null, the result is also Null. Concatenation of strings is discussed in more detail later in this chapter.

On the subject of Nulls, the NZ() function converts a Null value to 0 (zero). It's built into VBA and can be helpful in math calculations when you don't want a Null to wipe out the whole result. For example, to calculate a price with a discount you could use this code:

```
NetPrice = ItemPrice - (ItemPrice * DiscountPercent)
```

This works fine as long as `DiscountPercent` has a value. If it is Null, the `NetPrice` will also be set to Null, which is an error. The following code works correctly:

```
NetPrice = ItemPrice - (ItemPrice * NZ(DiscountPercent))
```

Now, if `DiscountPercent` is Null, it is converted to 0 by the `NZ` function, and the `NetPrice` will be set to the full `ItemPrice`.

Select Case

Another way to evaluate expressions and run code based on them is the often under-utilized `Select Case` structure. It enables you to test for multiple values of a variable in a clean, easy-to-understand structure, and then run blocks of code depending on those values. Here's an example of a `Select Case` structure:

```
Select Case intOrderStatus
Case 1, 2
   'fascinating code for status 1 or 2
Case 3
   'riveting code for status 3
Case Else
   'hmm, it's some other value, just handle it
End Select
```

Notice that there is no need for nested and indented `If` statements, and each `Case` block of code doesn't need a beginning or ending statement. Just to show the difference, the equivalent code using plain old `If` statements looks like this:

```
If intOrderStatus = 1 Or intOrderStatus = 2 Then
   'fascinating code for status 1 or 2
Else
   If intOrderStatus = 3 Then
     'riveting code for status 3
   Else
     'hmm, it's some other value, just handle it
   End If
Endif
```

This code is harder to read and understand. If you need to choose among multiple blocks of code depending on an expression's value, then `Select Case` is the preferred method.

Using Recordsets

Recordset operations are one of the cornerstones of Access VBA, enabling you to directly read, update, add, and delete records in Access tables and queries. You'll explore all of this in the following sections.

Opening Recordsets

Opening a recordset is easy, using either DAO or ADO (for more details about DAO and ADO, refer to Chapters 6 and 7). To open a recordset, you first need a reference to the current database, usually named db, and a `recordset` object. Here's how to accomplish that using DAO:

```
Dim db as Database
Set db = CurrentDB
Dim rec as DAO.Recordset
```

Now, you need to actually open the recordset. There are three basic ways to open a recordset: by table, by query, and by SQL statement. Here's the way to use a table directly:

```
Set rec = db.OpenRecordset("tblMyTableName")
```

If you have a query that already has some joined tables, selection criteria, or sort order, you can use it to open the recordset instead of using a table.

```
Set rec = db.OpenRecordset("qryMyQueryName")
```

Finally, you can open a recordset using your own SQL statement instead of using a preexisting query. Access evaluates and runs the query string on the fly.

```
Set rec = db.OpenRecordset("Select * From tblMyTableName")
```

Now, you're probably thinking, "why is that last way any better than opening the table directly?" Your question is justified in this simple example. But using a recordset based on a SQL statement is much more flexible than using a table or query directly because you can modify the SQL statement in VBA code, for example like this:

```
Set rec = db.OpenRecordset("Select * From tblMyTable Where MyKey = " & Me!MyKey)
```

Now you're seeing some flexibility. This example opens a recordset limited to only those records that match the MyKey field on the form that contains this code. You can use values from your open forms or other recordsets as selection criteria, set flexible sort fields, and so on.

Looping Through Recordsets

When your recordset opens, it automatically points to the first record. One of the most common uses for a recordset is to loop through the records, top to bottom, and perform some action for each one. The action could be sending an e-mail, copying records across child tables, or whatever you need to do. Following is some example code to loop through all of the records in tblBusiness:

```
Dim db As Database
Dim recBusiness As DAO.Recordset

Set db = CurrentDb

Set recBusiness = db.OpenRecordset("tblBusiness")

Do While Not recBusiness.EOF
```

```
        'do some code here with each business
        recBusiness.MoveNext
    Loop
```

Notice that the EOF (end of file) property of the recordset object is True when there are no more records in the recordset. It begins with a True value if there are no records in the recordset at all.

Remember to include the .MoveNext method before the Loop statement. If you omit it, your code drops into an infinite loop, repeatedly processing the first record, and not moving to the next one.

Don't use recordset looping and updating to simply update a group of records in a table. It is much more efficient to build an update query with the same selection criteria to modify the records as a group.

If you need to perform an action on some of the records in a recordset, limit the recordset using a Where clause when you open it. Avoid testing the records with If statements inside your loop to determine whether to perform the action. It is much more efficient to exclude them from the recordset to begin with, rather than ignoring certain records in your loop.

Adding Records

To add a record using a recordset, the recordset type needs to be capable of updates. Most recordsets for Access (Jet) tables, such as the one previously described, can be updated. However, if you need an updateable recordset for a SQL Server table opened via ODBC, you may need to also specify the dbOpenDynaset parameter value for the type. There's no harm in specifying it, even if the table is in Jet.

```
Set rec = db.OpenRecordset("tblMyTable", dbOpenDynaset)

With rec
  .AddNew
  !MyField1 = "A"
  !MyField2 = "B"
  .Update

End With
```

The .AddNew method of the recordset object instantiates the new record in the table, and if the table is in Jet, also immediately assigns a new AutoNumber value to the record if the table contains one. Don't forget the final .Update, because without it, your record won't actually be added.

If the table is linked using ODBC (like SQL Server), the AutoNumber/Identity value is not generated immediately when the .AddNew method runs. Instead, the Identity value is set after the .Update. This is discussed in the section "Copying Trees of Parent and Child Recordsets" later in this chapter.

Finding Records

To find a record in a recordset, use the FindFirst method. This is really just a way to reposition the current record pointer (cursor) to the first record that meets some criteria you specify. The criteria is specified like a WHERE clause in a SQL statement, except you omit the word WHERE. It looks like this:

```
rec.FindFirst "CustomerKey = " & Me!CustomerKey
```

After you perform a FindFirst, you can check the NoMatch property of the recordset to determine whether you successfully found at least one matching record. You can also use the FindNext, FindPrevious, and FindLast methods to navigate to other records.

In general, you shouldn't need to use the Seek method of a recordset. It may be slightly faster than FindFirst, but it won't work on a linked table without extra programming to open the table in a separate Workspace.

Updating Records

The code for updating records in a recordset is almost the same as adding them. You may also need to find the correct record to update using FindFirst. If you find it successfully, you can update it. Here's an example:

```
Set rec = db.OpenRecordset("tblMyTable")

With rec
   .FindFirst "CustomerKey = " & Me!CustomerKey
   If Not .NoMatch Then 'we found the record

     .Edit
     !CustomerName = "ABC Construction"
     !CustomerStatus = 1
     .Update

   End If
End With
```

The With statement is purely a programming convenience. Instead of typing the name of the object every single time, you can use With <objectname>. After that, and until you use End With, any references with no object name, just a dot (.) or bang (!), are assumed to belong to the With object. You may want to improve the clarity of your code by not using it when you are trying to keep track of multiple recordsets, as in the next example.

Using Multiple Recordsets

You can easily keep track of multiple open recordsets at once. Each one needs to be defined with a Dim statement and opened using OpenRecordset, and they are kept completely separate by Access. Each recordset has its own current record pointer (often called a cursor), end of file (EOF), and beginning of file (BOF) values, and so on.

This technique is necessary to perform the following trick: Copy a parent record and all of its child records into the same tables.

Copying Trees of Parent and Child Records

Here's a task that can stump an Access programmer trying to tackle it for the first time. The problem is as follows: There are two tables, tblPC and tblSpecification. Each (parent) PC has many (child)

Specifications. Many PCs have almost identical Specifications, but with slight variations. You need to write some code to copy one PC to another, along with all of its Specifications. The user will then manually update the copied PC's Specifications.

At first, you might think that this seemingly simple problem can be performed using only queries. However, you soon run into a problem — you need to know the key of the newly copied PC so that you can assign the copied Specifications to it.

You can solve the problem by using multiple recordsets. Let's say that you have a continuous form showing a list of PCs and a Copy button at the bottom of the form. The desired functionality is to copy the PC record (with "Copy of " as a prefix of the new PC) and also copy over all of its Specification records to the new PC:

```
Dim db As Database
Dim recPC As DAO.Recordset
Dim recSpecFrom As DAO.Recordset
Dim recSpecTo As DAO.Recordset
Dim lngPCKey as Long

Set db = CurrentDb

If Not IsNull(Me.PCKey) Then

    Set recPC = db.OpenRecordset("tblPC", dbOpenDynaset)

    'copy the parent record and remember its key
    recPC.AddNew
    recPC!PCName = "Copy of " & Me!PCName
    recPC.Update
    recPC.Bookmark = recPC.LastModified
    lngPCKey = recPC!PCKey

    recPC.Close
    Set recPC = Nothing

    Set recSpecTo = db.OpenRecordset("tblSpecification", dbOpenDynaset)
    Set recSpecFrom = db.OpenRecordset _
    ("Select * From tblSpecification Where PCKey = " & Me!PCKey)

    Do While Not recSpecFrom.EOF

        recSpecTo.AddNew
        recSpecTo!PCKey = lngPCKey 'set to the new parent key
        recSpecTo!SpecificationName = recSpecFrom!SpecificationName
        recSpecTo!SpecificationQty = recSpecFrom!SpecificationQty
        recSpecTo.Update

        recSpecFrom.MoveNext
    Loop

    recSpecTo.Close
    Set recSpecTo = Nothing
    recSpecFrom.Close
```

```
    Set recSpecFrom = Nothing

    Me.Requery
  End If

Exit_Procedure:
  On Error Resume Next
  Set db = Nothing
  Exit Sub

Error_Handler:
  DisplayUnexpectedError Err.Number, Err.Description
  Resume Exit_Procedure
  Resume
```

This code has several key things to understand:

❑   The variable lngPCKey stores the key of the newly created copy of PC record. It's defined as a Long because this example assumes you are using AutoNumber keys, which are Long Integers.

❑   To find the record that was just created, you can use the LastModified property of the record-set. It returns a Bookmark to the record that was added. You can use this to find the new key.

❑   Setting the Bookmark property of a recordset positions it to that record.

❑   Use Me.Requery to requery the form's recordset so that the newly added record will be shown.

If your backend database is Access (Jet), there's a simpler way to find the AutoNumber key of a newly added record. Anywhere between the .AddNew and the .Update, the AutoNumber key field of the table has already been set, so you can save it into a variable. Using this method, you don't need the Bookmark or LastModified properties. But be careful: If your backend database is SQL Server or another ODBC database, the key won't be set until after the .AddNew, and your code won't work. The technique shown here is more flexible because it works for both Jet and ODBC databases.

Some developers are tempted to find the AutoNumber key with the highest value immediately after adding a record, thinking that this is a good way to find the new record. Don't do it! There are two problems with this approach. First, it fails in a multiuser environment if another user just happens to add a record in the fraction of a second after your code adds a new record but before it finds the "highest" value. Second, you shouldn't write code that depends on an AutoNumber key to have a certain value or sequence. If your database is ever switched to random keys (which can happen if it is replicated), this technique fails.

Using Bookmark and RecordsetClone

In the previous example, there's one annoying behavior. After the form is requeried, the record selector is repositioned to the top of the list. That's disconcerting and can make it difficult to find the record that was just created.

It's easy to reposition the form to the new record — after all, you already know its key. Just after the Me.Requery, you add some code to find the new record in the just-requeried recordset and reposition the form to it.

To reposition the form, you use a `RecordsetClone`. This is a strange concept to developers when they first use it. Think of a `RecordsetClone` as a "twin" of the main recordset that the form is bound to. The nice thing about a `RecordsetClone` is that it has its own record cursor (with separate `FindFirst`, `EOF`, and so on), but it uses the exact same set of records as the form. The way to synchronize the "twin" recordsets is with a `Bookmark`, which is essentially a pointer to an exact record in both recordsets.

If you find a record using a form's `RecordsetClone`, you can use the `Bookmark` to instantly reposition the form to that record. Here's the same code, with the extra repositioning section:

```
Dim db As Database
Dim recPC As DAO.Recordset
Dim recSpecFrom As DAO.Recordset
Dim recSpecTo As DAO.Recordset
Dim lngPCKey as Long

Set db = CurrentDb

If Not IsNull(Me.PCKey) Then

  Set recPC = db.OpenRecordset("tblPC", dbOpenDynaset)

  'copy the parent record and remember its key
  recPC.AddNew
  recPC!PCName = "Copy of " & Me!PCName
 recPC.Update
  recPC.Bookmark = recPC.LastModified
  lngPCKey = recPC!PCKey

  recPC.Close
  Set recPC = Nothing

  Set recSpecTo = db.OpenRecordset("tblSpecification", dbOpenDynaset)
  Set recSpecFrom = db.OpenRecordset _
  ("Select * From tblSpecification Where PCKey = " & Me!PCKey)

  Do While Not recSpecFrom.EOF

    recSpecTo.AddNew
    recSpecTo!PCKey = lngPCKey 'set to the new parent key
    recSpecTo!SpecificationName = recSpecFrom!SpecificationName
    recSpecTo!SpecificationQty = recSpecFrom!SpecificationQty
    recSpecTo.Update

    recSpecFrom.MoveNext
  Loop

  recSpecTo.Close
  Set recSpecTo = Nothing
  recSpecFrom.Close
  Set recSpecFrom = Nothing

  Me.Requery
```

```
'reposition form to new record
Set recPC = Me.RecordsetClone
recPC.FindFirst "PCKey = " & lngPCKey
If Not recPC.EOF Then
  Me.Bookmark = recPC.Bookmark
End If
recPC.Close
Set recPC = Nothing
```

```
End If

Exit_Procedure:
  On Error Resume Next
  Set db = Nothing
  Exit Sub

Error_Handler:
  DisplayUnexpectedError Err.Number, Err.Description
  Resume Exit_Procedure
  Resume
```

You can reuse the recPC recordset object for the repositioning logic because you are finished using it from earlier in the code, and it has an appropriate name. Of course, you need to close it and set it to Nothing again when you're done.

Cleaning Up

Although Access VBA is supposed to automatically clean up local objects when a procedure ends, there is a history of errors and exceptions to this. So, programmers have learned that the safest practice is to clean up everything themselves. It's boring, but it shows an attention to detail that is missing in many novice applications. To clean up recordsets, make sure that you:

❑   Close the recordset using the .Close method.

❑   Release the recordset object by setting it to Nothing.

These two easy steps may prevent strange problems and, more importantly, help you gain the respect of your peers.

Using VBA in Forms and Reports

Much of the power and flexibility of applications built using Access comes from the VBA code that you can use behind your forms and reports. Although code-less forms and reports can provide a lot of good functionality, they really shine when VBA coding techniques are added.

Access Wizards provide a first look at VBA code behind forms and reports. However, Wizard-built code is just scratching the surface. Here are some guidelines and techniques that will help you build extra functionality into your Access applications.

All About Me

Me is a very special word in Access VBA. It is a reference to the form or report that your code is running in. For example, if you have some code behind the form frmBusiness, anytime you use Me in that code, you get a reference to the form object of frmBusiness.

This is a beautiful thing because there are many times that you need a reference to your own form or report, such as when you need to make it visible. You could refer to it directly, like this:

```
Forms!frmBusiness.Visible = True
```

Or, you can use the Me reference instead:

```
Me.Visible = True
```

Obviously, the Me reference is much shorter and easier to type. But there is a far greater reason to use Me: it enables you to move code from one form or report to another, where it automatically adapts to its new home.

The Me object is a full reference to a form object. Not only can you refer to it, but you can also pass it to other functions as a parameter. All you have to do is define a function with a parameter with a Form data type, and you can pass the Me reference to it. You can see that used in the Better Record Finder technique shown in Appendix M, "Tips and Tricks."

It's good that you can pass Me as a parameter because it doesn't work outside the code of the form or report. Remember that Me refers to the form or report that it lives in, not the form or report that's currently active. So Me will not work in a stand-alone module.

Referring to Controls

A control is any object that is placed on a form or report, such as a label, text box, combo box, image, checkbox, and so on. To refer to a control (for example, a bound text box named BusinessName) from the code behind a form or report, you use the following:

```
Me!BusinessName
```

So, if you want to clear out the BusinessName control, you use the following:

```
Me!BusinessName = Null
```

There has long been confusion in the VBA world about when to use a ! (bang) and when to use a . (dot). There are more technical ways to describe it, but for the average VBA programmer there's a quick rule that works most of the time: If you (or any programmer) named it, you can use a bang. If Access named it, you use a dot. (Now, before all the VBA experts reading this get upset, please realize that it's only a general guideline. However, it does help.)

With that said, here's an exception. In the last few versions of Access, you can use either a bang or a dot when referring to controls on forms or reports, even though you named them. That's because of a little trick Access does: it turns all of your controls into properties of the form or report, so they can be referred to with dots. This has a handy benefit: Access uses IntelliSense to prompt you with the possible properties and methods that are available for an object. So, in the `Me!BusinessName`, example, you type `Me` and then `.` (dot), and Access prompts you with every method and property for the object `Me`, including your control `BusinessName`.

> *That little trick about using a dot instead of a bang for controls on forms and reports does not extend to fields in a recordset. To refer to them directly, you still need to use bang, like this:* `recMyRecordset!BusinessName`. *Or you can use other ways, such as the Fields collection:* `recMyRecordset.Fields("BusinessName")`.

Referring to Subforms and Subreports

One of the most common questions about subforms and subreports is how to refer to their controls from the main form or report. Let's say that you have a form named `frmBusiness` and on it you have a continuous subform named `fsubPayments`. Each `Business` record may have many `Payments`. You need to refer to a value of the calculated field `txtSumPaymentAmount` on the subform, but you would like to do it from the main form `frmBusiness`.

The correct way to refer to `txtSumPaymentAmount` from `frmBusiness` is:

```
Me!fsubPayments.Form!txtSumPaymentAmount
```

The following table shows what each of the parts refers to:

`Me`	The parent form where the code is running, which in this example is `frmBusiness`.
`!fsubPayments`	The control that contains the subform (its name usually defaults to the name of the subform object itself, but some programmers rename it).
`.Form`	This is the tricky piece. You need to drill down into the form that's in the control because that's where the controls in the subform live. The control on the main form named `fsubPayments` is just a container — it doesn't contain the control you're looking for, but it does have this Form reference to use to get down into the subform itself.
`!txtSumPaymentAmount`	The control you want. You can even refer to controls that are on subforms on subforms (two levels down).

Remember that you need to use the `Form` reference to get into the form that's in the subform control container. For example, `frmA` contains subform `fsubB` contains subform `fsubC`, which has control `txtC`. The full reference looks like this:

```
Me!fsubB.Form!fsubC.Form!txtC
```

You can also shift into reverse and refer to controls above a subform, using the `Parent` property. If some code in `fsubC` (at the bottom) needed to refer to control `txtA` on `frmA` (at the top), it would look like this:

```
Me.Parent.Parent!txtA
```

Note that you don't need the `Form` reference here because the `Parent` reference is already a `Form` reference.

Sizing Reports

Here's a quick tip about viewing reports. Most of the time you'll want your reports to run maximized inside the Access window because that gives more room to see the report, and the preview mode automatically resizes the report and allows you to zoom in and out.

In Access 2007, reports and forms maximize automatically by default. If you're using Access 2007, you don't need to read the rest of this section. If you would like your reports to maximize automatically in earlier versions of Access, you need a little bit of VBA code. The earlier versions treat all of their child windows (both forms and reports) equally. They're all maximized or they're all restore-sized — mixing isn't allowed. The dilemma is that most developers want to run Access forms in Restore size, so they can control the look of the form and not have extra gray space on the edges of the form. This is a problem especially with modern high-resolution screens with all that extra screen real estate.

The way to solve this problem is to run your forms in Restore size mode, and only switch to Maximized size when you run a report. In the `On Activate` event of each report, add the following line:

```
DoCmd.Maximize
```

In the `On Close` event of each report, add the line:

```
DoCmd.Restore
```

When your report activates (which is the last event that runs before you actually see the report displayed), Access maximizes all open child windows. Although this maximizes all your visible forms, it doesn't matter because your open report hides them from view.

When your report closes, it restores all the Access child windows to their former size just before you see them, so when the report disappears your forms are waiting there as if they had never undergone the indignity of being maximized and restored while you were looking at your report.

Why not maximize the report during the `On Open` event? The reason is timing. During the `On Open` event, the report isn't yet visible, so your forms are still showing. If you maximize everything then, your user will see your forms expand into maximized size for a brief moment before your report obscures them. By waiting until the `Activate` event, you ensure that the report will mask the maximized display of the forms.

Closing Forms

If you want a button to close a form in Access instead of clicking the X button, you need to write VBA code to close the form. The basic way to do that is with the following code:

```
DoCmd.Close
```

This method of the `DoCmd` object closes the active object, like your form. It doesn't get much simpler than that. Unfortunately, there is an obscure situation that will cause this code to fail to close the correct form.

If you read the help documentation on `DoCmd.Close`, you'll see that if you don't provide any parameters, it closes the active form. You might assume that the active form is the one containing this code; after all, you just clicked the Close button, so the form must be active. However, there are situations where another form is the active one.

One case is when you have a hidden form on a timer that periodically does something. This is a technique that is often used in automatic log-off functionality, where a hidden form uses a timer to periodically check a table to determine whether it should shut down the application. The problem is, when that timer fires and the code in the form checks the table, it becomes the active form. If you're unlucky enough for that to happen right when the Close button is clicked, the wrong form (the hidden one) will close instead of the form you intended.

Another situation is when the code in your closing routine reaches out and runs code in another form; this can make the other form active at that moment. The solution is to clarify the `DoCmd.Close` statement, like this:

```
DoCmd.Close ObjectType:=acForm, ObjectName:=Me.Name
```

This specifies that a form be closed, specifically the form to which this code belongs. If you get into the habit of using this syntax, the proper form will always close correctly.

Debugging VBA

Programming in VBA isn't easy. No matter how skilled you are there are times when you need help figuring out what the code is actually doing. Fortunately, VBA provides a rich and powerful debugging environment. You can stop the code at various times and for various reasons, view values of variables (and even change them), and step through your code line-by-line until you understand what's going on.

The main reason you need to debug your code is because Access has displayed an error message. (Hopefully you've put error handling in your code, which can make this activity easier. This topic is covered extensively in Chapter 9.) Let's say you've coded a cool copy routine like the one shown earlier in this chapter. However, when you try it, Access displays an error. If you don't have error handling, a message box displays, as shown in Figure 8-2.

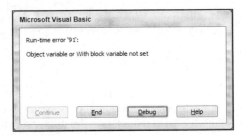

Figure 8-2

If you do have error handling, good job! Your error handling message box will display, as shown in Figure 8-3.

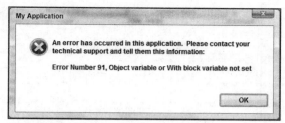

Figure 8-3

When Access displays your handled error message box, your code execution is suspended. To debug your code, press Ctrl+Break to interrupt code execution and display the dialog box shown in Figure 8-4.

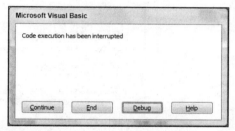

Figure 8-4

Whichever way you get there, you can finally click the Debug button. When you do, your code appears in the VBA code window. If you are not using error handling, the line of code that caused the error is indicated by an arrow and highlighted in yellow. If you are using error handling with the centralized Msgbox text and an extra Resume statement as described in Chapter 9, press F8 to step back to the procedure that contains the error. Then you can reposition to the specific line that caused the error, as shown in Figure 8-5.

Investigating Variables

Now that you can see your code and the line that might be causing the problem, it's time to investigate. The error message — Object variable or With block variable not set — is a clue, but it doesn't tell you exactly what the problem is. The first step is to check the current values of the variables near the line that caused the error. Remember, your code is suspended, so all your variables are intact and able to report their values.

The quickest and easiest way to determine the value of a variable is to hover your mouse pointer over the variable name in the code window when your code is suspended. If the variable is part of a longer phrase, though, hovering may not work. For example, the variable Me.BusinessKey is simple enough to be hoverable (see Figure 8-6).

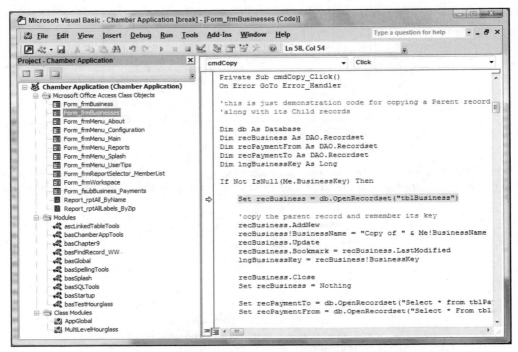

Figure 8-5

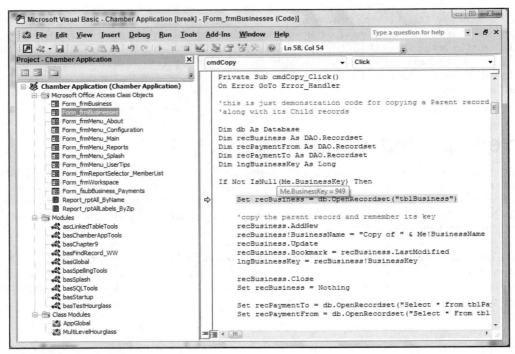

Figure 8-6

Because `BusinessKey` has a reasonable value, it doesn't seem to be the problem. To check variables or objects that are part of a more complex statement, highlight the portion you are interested before you hover over it. In this example, just hovering over the object name `db` doesn't display anything, but after selecting `db`, hovering provides a value, as shown in Figure 8-7.

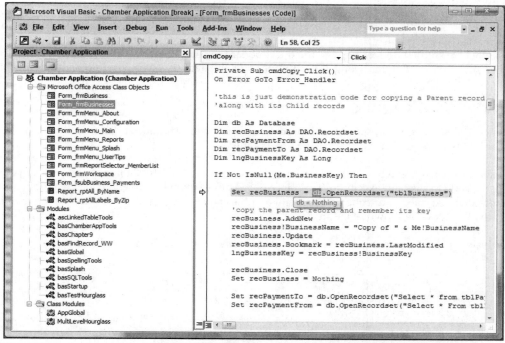

Figure 8-7

By checking the value of `db`, you can see that it is currently set to `Nothing`. This is Access's way of telling you that the `db` object reference hasn't been set to any value yet. Sure enough, when you look at the code, you can see that although you defined `db` using the line `Dim db As Database`, you forgot to include the line `Set db = CurrentDb`. Adding this line before the `OpenRecordset` line resolves the problem.

When Hovering Isn't Enough — Using the Immediate Window

There are times when having the value of a variable pop up by hovering over it isn't sufficient. Perhaps the value doesn't fit in the pop-up, or maybe you need to copy the value to use it somewhere else. Or maybe you just want to look at it longer than the limited time the pop-up value displays. In those cases, you can use the Immediate Window (instead of hovering) to view variable values.

If the Immediate Window isn't already displayed, select View ➪ Immediate Window or press Ctrl+G to open it. Then you can ask Access to display the value of a variable using ?, like this:

```
?Me.BusinessKey
```

When you press Enter, Access returns the value:

```
?Me.BusinessKey
```

```
949
```

The ? in the Immediate window is just a quick way of specifying `Print`.

No matter how long this value is (it could be a very long string, for example), Access displays it here so that you can study it or even copy it into the clipboard to use somewhere else. This comes in handy when the variable contains a long SQL string that you want to try out by pasting it into a new query.

Setting Breakpoints

Sometimes, your code doesn't actually produce an error, but it still doesn't work correctly. In those cases, you need to stop the code yourself using breakpoints.

The easiest way to set a breakpoint is to click the gray area to the left of a line of code where you would like the code to suspend execution. This places a red dot to remind you where the breakpoint is set. Just before that line runs, your code will suspend and the code window will be displayed with that line highlighted in yellow, as shown in Figure 8-8.

At this point, you can investigate variable values as discussed previously in this chapter.

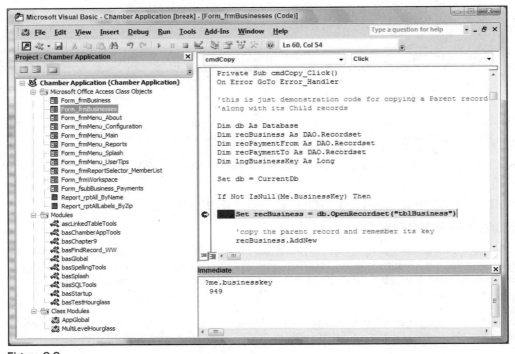

Figure 8-8

Setting Watch Values

Sometimes you have no clue where the problem lies, so you don't know where to set the breakpoint. However, you may want to suspend your code and investigate whenever a certain variable is set to a certain value. To do this you can use a watch value.

A watch value enables you to suspend execution of your code whenever a variable or object (or expression using a variable or object) changes or has a certain value. This is especially powerful in complex code scenarios where you are having trouble finding where your logic is going wrong. You create watch values using the Add Watch window (see Figure 8-9), which you can request using `Debug..Add Watch` or by right-clicking in the Watches window.

Figure 8-9

You can watch a single field, or you can type in an expression that uses multiple variables or values. Also, you can widen the context; it defaults to the procedure you are in, but you can widen it to include all procedures. Finally, you can choose to merely watch the expression, to break (suspend your code execution) when the expression becomes true (for example, when `BusinessKey = 949`), or to break every time your expression changes. After you add your watch, it appears in the Watches window, as shown in Figure 8-10.

When the break condition you specify occurs, your code is displayed in the window. However, now you have an additional window, the Watches window. You can add more watch expressions here, too, and if you specify an object to watch (such as a form, report, recordset, and so on), you can even drill down to all of its properties using the plus sign (+) next to the object name.

Stopping Runaway Code

Everyone has done it. Every developer has created code that created an infinite loop. That's where your Access application just freezes, consuming all available computer power while it runs around the little race track that you accidentally created.

To stop your code in mid-execution, press Ctrl+Break. This suspends your code and drops you into the code window on whatever line that happens to be executing at that moment.

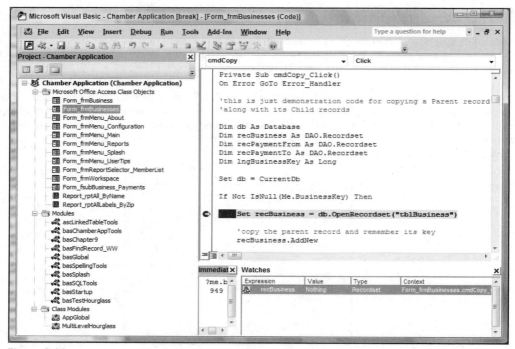

Figure 8-10

Stepping Through Your Code

Sometimes the only way to figure out a problem in your code is to actually run it line-by-line until you see where it goes wrong. You can use any of the preceding methods to stop your code, but there's nothing like getting your mind right into the logic by stepping through the code one line at a time.

You step through code by selecting Debug ➪ Step Into (or pressing F8). This debug command is the most common one to use because it's so basic. It runs the line of code that is highlighted, displays the next line that will be run, and awaits your next command. The Step Into and other Step commands are shown in Figure 8-11.

Sometimes the basic nature of Step Into is a problem. If the highlighted line of code is a call to another procedure (either a function or a sub), Step Into will do just that — it will dive into that procedure and highlight its first line.

Now, maybe that's just what you want. But if you are following good programming practices, such as the coupling and cohesion guidelines presented earlier in this chapter, you have lots of small, fully tested functions that will be supremely boring and laborious to step through. After all, you know the error isn't in one of those, right?

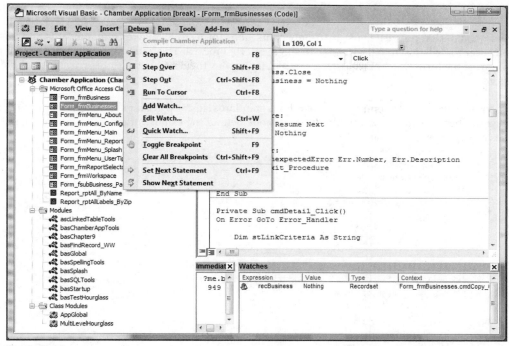

Figure 8-11

The answer to this little problem is to use a cousin of Step Into called Step Over (Shift+F8). Its name isn't quite accurate, because when you use it, the highlighted line of code isn't really stepped over, it's actually stepped through. The line of code that's highlighted will run, even if it is a call to one of your functions or subs, and then the next line will be highlighted. The entire function or sub will run without stopping, so you don't have to step through all that boring code.

Also note that Step Over works exactly the same as Step Into for a normal line of code (not a call to another procedure). This means that you can get into the habit of leaning on the Shift key when you use F8, and you'll never need to step through called procedures unless you want to.

What if you accidentally use Step Into when you meant to use Step Over? Hope is not lost. By using the often-forgotten Step Out (Ctrl+Shift+F8), you can run the remainder of the current procedure without stopping, and automatically stop on the next line after your code returns to the calling procedure.

Common VBA Techniques

Every Access developer will face some common VBA challenges at some point. There are simple and easy ways to handle drilling down to detail records, date math, rounding issues, and tricky string concatenation problems.

Drilling Down with Double-Click

It's a good design practice to use read-only continuous forms to display multiple records and then allow your user to drill down to the detail of a single selected record. This action should have a button at the bottom of the form (called Detail, for example) that opens the detail form for the currently selected record.

For convenience and to comply with Windows standards, it's also good to allow the user to drill down using double-click. Because you already have code behind the Detail button that opens the detail form, you can easily reuse that code:

```vba
Private Sub cmdDetail_Click()
On Error GoTo Error_Handler
    Dim stLinkCriteria As String
    If IsNull(Me!BusinessKey) Then
        EnableDisableControls
        GoTo Exit_Procedure
    End If

    gstrCallingForm = Me.Name
    stLinkCriteria = "[BusinessKey]=" & Me![BusinessKey]
    DoCmd.OpenForm FormName:="frmBusiness", _
        wherecondition:=stLinkCriteria
    Me.Visible = False

Exit_Procedure:
    On Error Resume Next
    Exit Sub
Error_Handler:
    DisplayUnexpectedError Err.Number, Err.Description
    Resume Exit_Procedure
    Resume

End Sub
```

Because this code is already written and tested, you only need to call it by name (`cmdDetail_Click`) when the user double-clicks a record. This is quite simple to do: you just add a double-click event to each textbox on your detail form and add one line of code to each double-click procedure:

```vba
Private Sub txtBusinessName_DblClick(Cancel As Integer)
On Error GoTo Error_Handler

    cmdDetail_Click

Exit_Procedure:
    On Error Resume Next
    Exit Sub

Error_Handler:
    DisplayUnexpectedError Err.Number, Err.Description
    Resume Exit_Procedure
    Resume
End Sub
```

Here's a case where your actual code (1 line) is a lot shorter than all the error handling, but that line allows you to reuse the code you already have behind the Detail button.

Just because Access creates and names an event procedure (cmdDetail_Click in this case) doesn't mean you can't use it yourself. Just call it by typing its name as a statement in VBA.

To support double-click all the way across your row, you need to add the same code to each field's Double-Click event. That way, whichever field your user double-clicks, they'll drill down to the detail record.

Now, there's only one more thing to add. Users will often double-click the Record Selector itself (the arrow to the left of the current record) when they want to drill down to the record's detail. Surprisingly, the event that fires in this case is not related to the detail section of the continuous form; instead, the Form's double-click event will fire. To support double-click the Record Selector, you can use this code behind the Form's On Double Click event:

```
Private Sub Form_DblClick(Cancel As Integer)
On Error GoTo Error_Handler

  cmdDetail_Click

Exit_Procedure:
  On Error Resume Next
  Exit Sub

Error_Handler:
  DisplayUnexpectedError Err.Number, Err.Description
  Resume Exit_Procedure
  Resume
End Sub
```

Date Handling

The way Access stores and manipulates dates can be a source of confusion to developers, especially those who remember the older database methods of storing days, months, and years in date fields. Access handles dates in an elegant, easy-to-use manner.

How Access Stores Dates and Times

Access stores a particular date as the number of days that have elapsed since an arbitrary starting "zero date" (December 30, 1899). You can prove this to yourself by typing the following in the Immediate Window (you can bring up the Immediate Window in Access using Ctrl+G).

```
?CLng(#12/31/1899#)
1
```

The CLng function converts an expression to a Long Integer. To this question, Access will answer with 1, meaning that 1 day elapsed since December 30, 1899. Of course, Access can handle dates before this date; they're stored as negative integers. If you want to see how many days have elapsed since that special zero date, try this:

```
?CLng(Date)
```

Access can perform date math very easily, because internally it doesn't store a date as days, months, and years. It just stores the number of days since the zero date and converts that value to an understandable date format only when the date needs to be displayed. But the date storage technique that Access uses goes even farther. Access can also store the time of day in the same date field. To do this, Access uses the decimal portion (the numbers after the decimal point) to store a fraction of a day. For example, 12 noon is stored as .5(half way through the day), and 6 A.M. is stored as .25. Again, you can see this for yourself by typing this into the Immediate window:

```
?CDbl(Now)
```

There are a couple of things to note here. One is that you now need to use CDbl (Convert to Double Precision Number) so that you can see the decimal portion (the time portion) that is returned by the Now function. The other is that each time you run this command, you'll see that the decimal portion changes because time is elapsing.

> When you're storing the current date in a table, be sure to use the Date function. If you use Now, you'll also get a time component, which may cause incorrect results when you use dates in your query criteria. For example, if your query selects records where a date field is <=4/28/2007, then any records with a date of 4/28/2007 should be returned. However, if they were stored with a decimal time component (by using Now instead of Date), they'll be fractionally greater than 4/28/2007 and won't be returned.

Simple Date Math

To add or subtract calendar time from a date field, use the DateAdd function. For example, to add 1 month to today's date, use:

```
?dateadd("m",1,Date)
```

To subtract, use a negative number for the second parameter, Number. You can use different units of calendar time for the Interval parameter, like "d" for days, "ww" for weeks, "q" for quarters, and so on. Be careful when adding or subtracting years; you have to use "yyyy", not just "y". The interval of "y" is day of year, which acts just like day in the DateAdd function.

Here's an example of date math. It computes the last day of a month by finding the first day of the next month, then subtracting 1 day.

```
Public Function LastDateofMonth(StartDate As Date)

On Error GoTo Error_Handler

  Dim dtNextMonth As Date
  Dim dtNewDate As Date

  'add a month to the start date
  dtNextMonth = DateAdd("m", 1, StartDate)

  'build a date
```

```
   dtNewDate = CDate((DatePart("m", dtNextMonth)) & _
   "/01/" & (DatePart("yyyy", dtNextMonth)))

   'subtract a day
   LastDateofMonth = dtNewDate -1

Exit_Procedure:
   Exit Function
Error_Handler:
   DisplayUnexpectedError Err.Number, Err.Description
   Resume Exit_Procedure
   Resume

End Function
```

Note the use of CDate, which converts any expression that can be interpreted as a date into an actual date data type. You can use the IsDate to check whether an expression can be interpreted as a date. Also note how the DatePart function is used to break up a date into string components for Month, Year, and so on.

Handling Rounding Issues

Rounding problems are among the most difficult to understand and debug. They usually occur when adding up money values, but they can also happen in any math where a series of values is expected to add up correctly.

Rounding of Sums

One basic issue is not Access-related at all, but rather an issue whenever you add up a list of rounded numbers. For example, take a list of numbers that each represent one third of a dollar. If you add them up, you'll get 99 cents because the value of each portion (.33333333...) was truncated to .33.

```
.33
.33
.33
.99
```

A common place for this to show up is in a list of percentages that are supposed to total 100%. They often don't because some precision was lost in the list. Then, you are faced with a decision — add up the actual numbers and show a total that's not 100, or just hard-code 100% so that it looks right. Most of the time you will want to use 100%, even though close observation will show that the numbers don't actually add up to 100. You may need to explain this kind of rounding error to your users.

Rounding Errors Caused by Floating Point Numbers

Another kind of rounding error comes from the way Access stores numbers in floating-point fields. These fields cannot store certain numbers without losing some precision, so totals based on them may be slightly wrong. The best way to avoid these kind of rounding errors is to use the Currency data type for fields when they need to hold money values (as you might expect), or the Decimal type for any other numeric values that you want to use in calculations. The Currency data type is somewhat misnamed; it really can hold any decimal value.

> Access uses the word Currency for both a data type and a format. This is unfortunate because they really are two different things. The Currency data type is a method of storing the numeric values in a table. The Currency format only affects the display of numeric data. The two can be used independently or together.

Access Rounding Functions

Access has a built-in function (Round) to round numbers, but it may not work the way you expect. Most people think that any decimal ending in 5 should round up to the next higher number. However, Access uses a form of scientific rounding that works like this:

- ❑ If the digit to be rounded is 0 through 4, round down to the lower number.
- ❑ If the digit to be rounded is 6 through 9, round up to the higher number.
- ❑ If the digit to be rounded is 5, round up if digit to the left is odd, and round down if the digit to the left is even.

This last rule is what surprises a lot of developers. Using this rule, Round gives the following results:

```
?round(1.5)
2
?round(2.5)
2
```

Yes, that's right. Both 1.5 and 2.5 round to 2 using the built-in Round function in Access VBA, because 1 is odd (round up) and 2 is even (round down). Here's another example:

```
?round(1.545,2)

1.54
?round(1.555,2)

1.56
```

In this example,.545 rounds down, but .555 rounds up, for the same reason. Because this can cause some trouble in business applications, developers have taken to writing their own rounding functions that behave the way business people expect. Here's an example of a function that rounds a trailing 5 upward to a specified number of decimal places:

```
Public Function RoundCurr(OriginalValue As Currency, Optional _
NumberOfDecimals As Integer) As Currency
On Error GoTo Error_Handler

'returns a currency value rounded to the specified number of decimals of
'the Original Value

If IsMissing(NumberOfDecimals) Then
  NumberOfDecimals = 0
End If
```

```
RoundCurr = Int((OriginalValue * (10 ^ NumberOfDecimals)) + 0.5) _
    / (10 ^ NumberOfDecimals)

Exit_Procedure:
    Exit Function
Error_Handler:
    DisplayUnexpectedError Err.Number, Err.Description
    Resume Exit_Procedure

End Function
```

This function can be placed in any module in your application and used whenever you want the business-style rounding that most users expect. Note that if you don't specify the number of decimals you would like, the function will assume that you want none and will return a whole number.

String Concatenation Techniques

Sooner or later, you'll need to join (concatenate) two strings together. The operator for performing concatenation is &. You may be tempted to say "and" when you see this symbol, but it really means "concatenate with." A classic example is joining First Name with Last Name, like this:

```
strFullName = FirstName & "" & LastName
```

This results in the First Name and Last Name together in one string, like "Tom Smith."

The Difference Between & and +

There are times when you may need to concatenate something to a string, but only if the string actually has a value. For example, you may want to include the Middle Initial in a person's full name. If you write code like this:

```
strFullName = FirstName & "" & MiddleInitial & "" & LastName
```

you will have a small problem. People with no middle name (Null in the table) will have two spaces between their first and last names, like this:

```
Tom   Smith
```

Fortunately, there is another concatenation operator: +. The technical explanation of this operator is "concatenation with Null propagation." That's a great phrase to impress your friends with at parties, but an easier explanation is that it concatenates two strings like the & operator, but only if both strings have a value. If either one is Null, the result of the whole concatenation operation is Null.

Using the FullName example, the goal is to have only one space separating First and Last names if there is no Middle Initial. Using +, you can tack on the extra space only if the Middle Name is not Null:

```
MiddleName + " "
```

The whole thing looks like this:

```
strFullName = FirstName & "" & (MiddleInitial + " ") & LastName
```

As shown, you can use parentheses to ensure that the operations happen in the correct order. In this case, the inner phrase — `(MiddleInitial + " ")` — will evaluate to the Middle Initial plus a space, or to Null (if there is no middle initial). Then, the rest of the statement will be performed.

String Concatenation Example

Here is another example that you can use in your code. It concatenates the city, state, postal code (ZIP Code), and nation into one text field. This can be handy if you want to show a simulation of an address label on a form or report.

```
Function CityStZIPNat(City As Variant, State As Variant, ZIP As Variant, _
    Nation As Variant) As Variant
On Error GoTo Error_Handler

CityStZIPNat = City & (", " + State) & (" " + ZIP) & _
(IIf(Nation = "US" Or Nation = "CA", "", (" " + Nation)))

Exit_Procedure:
    Exit Function
Error_Handler:
    MsgBox Err.Number & ", " & Err.Description
    Resume Exit_Procedure
    Resume

End Function
```

You can try it out by calling it in the Immediate window like this:

```
?CityStZIPNat("Seattle", "WA", "98011", "US")

Seattle, WA 98011
```

Notice that this code also tacks on the Nation at the end of the string, but only if it isn't US or CA (the ISO standard nation codes for USA and Canada, respectively). This enables you to use this function for both domestic and foreign addresses.

Summary

The only way to really learn how to execute VBA in your Access applications is to jump in there and try it. Using the techniques explained in this chapter — how to prevent problems with asynchronous execution, how class modules work, how to use recordsets and recordset clones, how to debug VBA, and more — you can tackle many of the common programming tasks that your users will need.

VBA Error Handling

When programmers use the term "error handling," they really mean graceful or planned error handling. After all, Access takes some kind of action for any error that it encounters in your code. *Graceful* error handling includes the following:

- ❑ Quietly absorbing expected errors so the user never sees them.
- ❑ Displaying a "friendly" message to the user for unexpected errors, and closing the procedure properly.

Error handling in Access VBA involves adding code to every procedure — both subroutines (also known as subs) and functions — to take specific actions when Access encounters an error. This is called handling or trapping the error. (Some developers call the encounter with an error *throwing* an error. Error handling is the code that *catches* the error and handles it properly, either by hiding it from the users or by explaining it to them.)

This chapter provides techniques to handle several types of expected and unexpected errors so that your applications look and feel more professional to your users. But first, you'll explore why you should use error handling at all. Many Access developers see it as a mundane chore, but there are good reasons for including error handling in every procedure you write.

Why Use Error Handling?

Without error-handling code, Access treats all errors equally, displaying unfriendly error messages and abruptly ending procedures. Even worse, if you are using the runtime mode of Access, the entire application closes. This is not what you want users to experience.

Figure 9-1 shows an example of an error message that Access displays if you attempt to divide a number by zero in your application. Sure, technically it indicates what happened, but what is the user supposed to do about it? And what if he clicks the Debug button? If he's running an MDB/ACCDB instead of an MDE/ACCDE, he'll be looking at your code!

Figure 9-1

When Access encounters an error, it abruptly ends the procedure. It does not run another line of code; it just terminates the function or sub that contains the error. So, it can often leave things hanging — open objects, open forms, the mouse pointer in hourglass mode, warnings turned off, and so on.

> *Amateur or pro? When your code is being evaluated by another programmer, one of the easiest things for him to check is whether you have proper error handling. No matter how good your code is, without error handling you may look like a beginner. It's worth making sure that every procedure has error handling.*

Now for the good news: Error handling isn't difficult. By using some easy techniques and code templates, you can make sure that your application never suffers an unhandled error. If you establish a standard way to handle errors, you can make it easy to implement in every procedure you write. It may not be fun or glamorous, but it will certainly make your application better.

Two Kinds of Errors: Unexpected and Expected

All errors that your Access application may encounter fall into one of two categories: unexpected and expected. The following sections explain these two categories and what your application should do when errors occur in each of them.

Handling Unexpected Errors

Unexpected errors are ones that you have no way of predicting, and that under normal circumstances should not occur. When your application encounters an unexpected error (for example, divide by zero or a missing object), and no error handling is in effect, Access displays an error message like the one shown earlier and abruptly ends the procedure.

The goal of error handling in this case is not to solve the problem the error is indicating — there's nothing you can do about that now. Your code has tripped on an error and fallen down. The only thing you can do is let the user know what happened calmly and in plain language. Figure 9-2 is an example of what your error message might look like.

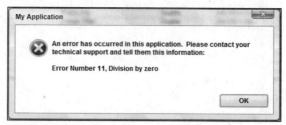

Figure 9-2

There are several differences between the error message Access shows and the "handled" error message you can show:

❑   You can specify the title of the message box instead of displaying "Microsoft Visual Basic" or "Microsoft Access."

❑   You can show an icon to have a stronger impact.

❑   You can add a text explanation. You can even mention your phone number or other contact information.

❑   You can format the error message with blank lines, commas, and so on.

❑   Your user can't enter debug mode and look at your code.

Absorbing Expected Errors

Some errors can be expected during normal operation. One such error happens in your application whenever the On Open event of a report is canceled. This occurs when you display a form to prompt the user for selection criteria during the On Open event, and the user decides to cancel the report. This report criteria technique is described in Chapter 14.

There are other errors that you can expect. Maybe you expect a certain file to be on the hard drive, but it isn't. Maybe you expect a form to be open, but somehow it has been closed. These kinds of errors can be absorbed by your application if possible, never allowing the user to see them.

In these situations, your code should just ignore the error and keep going. Whenever Access encounters an error, it makes an error number available to your code. To absorb an expected error, you add an If statement to check if the error number matches the number you expect. If it matches, you can just Resume Next to continue to the next line of code without bothering the user with an error dialog box. If it doesn't match, you can drop into your normal error handling.

Next, you explore some basic error-handling code that can be used to handle both expected and unexpected errors in your application. Then you'll look more specifically at expected errors in the section "More on Absorbing Expected Errors."

Basic Error Handling

Let's start with the basics. Here's some code that you could add to every procedure to build in easy, no-frills error handling:

```
Public Function MyFunction
On Error GoTo Error_Handler

   'your function code goes here

Exit_Procedure:
   Exit Function

Error_Handler:
   MsgBox "An error has occurred in this application. " _
   & "Please contact your technical support and " _
   & "tell them this information:" _
   & vbCrLf & vbCrLf & "Error Number " & Err.Number & ", " _
   & Err.Description, _
   Buttons:=vbCritical

   Resume Exit_Procedure
End Function
```

Let's take a look at some important lines in the code, beginning with the following:

```
On Error GoTo Error_Handler
```

The `On Error GoTo` statement in VBA tells the code to jump to a particular line in the procedure whenever an error is encountered. It sets up this directive, which remains in effect until it is replaced by another `On Error` statement or until the procedure ends. In this example, when any error is encountered, the code execution jumps to the line named `Error_Handler`.

> In the early days of Basic and other procedural languages, lines were numbered, not named. For example, your code might have a line GOTO 1100. In VBA, you still have the GoTo statement, but instead of numbering the lines, you can give them meaningful names like Exit_Procedure.

If no error occurs throughout the main body of the procedure, the execution of the code falls through to this point:

```
Exit_Procedure:
   Exit Function
```

and the `Exit Function` will run. As its name implies, the `Exit Function` statement exits this function immediately, and no lines after it will be executed. Note that if this procedure is a sub instead of a function, you use `Exit Sub` instead.

This same `Exit_Procedure` line is also executed after any unexpected errors are handled:

```
Error_Handler:
  MsgBox "An error has occurred in this application. " _
  & "Please contact your technical support and " _
  & "tell them this information:" _
  & vbCrLf & vbCrLf & "Error Number " & Err.Number & ", " _
  & Err.Description, _
  Buttons:=vbCritical
```

If an error occurs, execution jumps to the `Error_Handler` line, and a message box is displayed to the user. When the user clicks OK (her only choice), the code execution is redirected back to the `Exit_Procedure` line:

```
Resume Exit_Procedure
```

and your code exits the procedure.

With this technique, execution of the code falls through to the `Exit_Procedure` code and the function exits normally, as long as no errors are encountered. However, if an error is encountered, the execution is redirected to the error-handling section.

> *In early versions of Access, the labels for the `Exit_Procedure` and `Error_Handler` sections had to be unique in the entire module. This forced programmers to use labels like `Exit_MyFunction` and `Error_MyFunction`. In recent versions of Access, these labels may be duplicated in different procedures. This is a great improvement because now you can copy and paste error-handling code into each procedure with almost no modification.*

This is the most basic error handling you can include in your code. However, there's one word that you can add to make your code much easier to debug: `Resume`. Yes, it's just one word, but it can work wonders when you are trying to make your code work just right.

Basic Error Handling with an Extra Resume

One of the problems with basic error handling is that when an error does occur, you have no easy way of knowing the exact line that caused the error. After all, your procedure may have dozens or hundreds of lines of code. When you see the error message, the execution of your code has already jumped to your error handler routine and displayed the message box; you may not be able to tell which line caused the problem. Many programmers rerun the code, using debug mode, to step through the code to try to find the offending line.

But there is a much easier way to find that error-producing line of code: Just add a `Resume` line after the `Resume Exit_Procedure`.

You're probably thinking, "Why would you add an extra `Resume` right after another `Resume Exit_Procedure`? The extra `Resume` will never run!" You're right. It will never run under *normal* circumstances. But it will run if you ask it to. If your application encounters an error, you can override the next line that will run. In debug mode, you can just change the next line to be executed to your extra

Resume. The `Resume Exit_Procedure` statement is skipped entirely. The following code is identical to the basic code shown previously, but with that one extra `Resume`.

```
Public Function MyFunction()
On Error GoTo Error_Handler

  Dim varReturnVal As Variant

  'your function code goes here

Exit_Procedure:
  Exit Function 'or Exit Sub if this is a Sub

Error_Handler:
  MsgBox "An error has occurred in this application. " _
  & "Please contact your technical support and tell them this information:" _
  & vbCrLf & vbCrLf & "Error Number " & Err.Number & ", " _
  & Err.Description, _
  Buttons:=vbCritical, title:="My Application"
  Resume Exit_Procedure
  Resume

End Function
```

Under normal operation, the extra `Resume` never runs because the line before it transfers execution of the code elsewhere. It comes into play only when you manually cause it to run. To do this, you can do something that is rarely done in debug mode: move the execution point in the code to a different statement.

Here's how the extra `Resume` works. Say your code is supposed to open a report, but there's a problem: the report name you specified doesn't exist. Your code might look like this:

```
Private Sub cmdPreview_Click()
On Error GoTo Error_Handler

  If Me!lstReport.Column(3) & "" <> "" Then
    DoCmd.OpenReport ReportName:=Me!lstReport.Column(3),
    View:=acViewPreview
  End If

  'Update the Last Run Date of the report
  DoCmd.SetWarnings False
  DoCmd.RunSQL "UPDATE tsysReport " _
  & "SET tsysReport.DtLastRan = Date() " _
  & "WHERE tsysReport.RptKey = " & Me.lstReport
  DoCmd.SetWarnings True

Exit_Procedure:
  On Error Resume Next
  DoCmd.SetWarnings True
  Exit Sub
```

```
Error_Handler:
  MsgBox "An error has occurred in this application. " _
  & "Please contact your technical support and " _
  & "tell them this information:" _
  & vbCrLf & vbCrLf & "Error Number " & Err.Number & ", " &
  Err.Description, _
  Buttons:=vbCritical, title:="My Application"
  Resume Exit_Procedure
  Resume

End Sub
```

When you run your code, an error message appears, as shown in Figure 9-3.

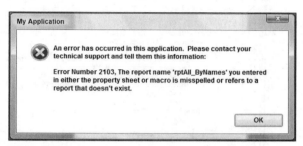

Figure 9-3

Instead of clicking OK as your user would do, press Ctrl+Break on your keyboard. A Visual Basic dialog box appears, as shown in Figure 9-4.

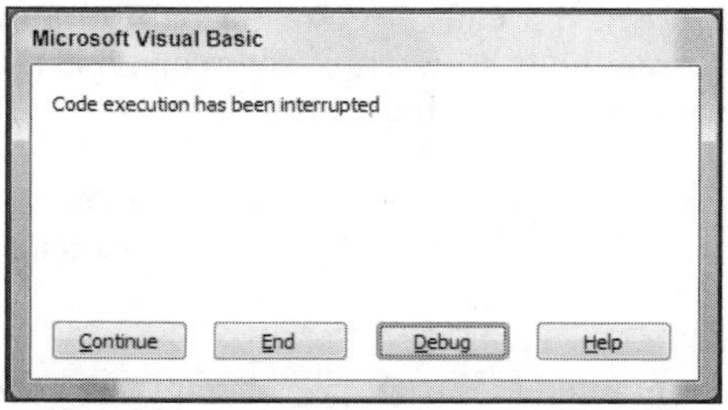

Figure 9-4

This extra Resume *technique won't work in an Access runtime application because in runtime mode no design modes are allowed, including the VBA code editor. It also won't work in an Access MDE or ACCDE because all VBA source code is removed from those applications.*

Now click the Debug button. The code displays in the Code window, as shown in Figure 9-5.

Figure 9-5

The `Resume Exit_Procedure` statement will be indicated by an arrow and highlighted in yellow. This is the statement that will execute next if you continue normally. But instead of letting it run, you take control, using your mouse to drag the yellow arrow down one line to the extra `Resume` line. By doing this, you indicate that you want the `Resume` line to run next.

> *Instead of using the mouse, you can click or arrow down to the `Resume` line, and then use `Debug..Set Next` statement (Ctrl+F9 on your keyboard). As usual in Access, there are several ways to do the same thing.*

Now, the yellow arrow will be pointed at the `Resume` statement, as shown in Figure 9-6.

Now, you want the `Resume` statement to run, in order to retry the statement that caused the error. Press F8 to run the next line of code (your `Resume`) and stop. Or, you can choose `Debug..Step Into` from the menu.

The exact line that caused the error will now be indicated by an arrow and highlighted in yellow, as shown in Figure 9-7. That was easy, wasn't it?

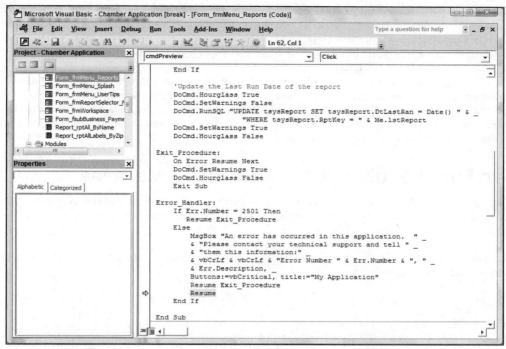

Figure 9-6

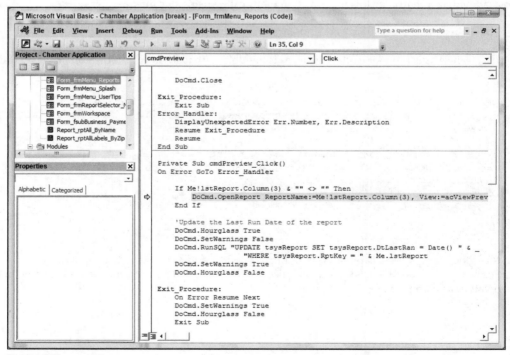

Figure 9-7

Now, admittedly, this is a simple example. You probably could have determined which line caused the error just by looking at the error description. However, when your procedures contain pages of code, often with coding loops, complex logic, and similar statements, this extra `Resume` technique comes in handy. It can save you many hours of time while you are debugging your VBA code.

The extra `Resume` doesn't cause any harm in your code, so you can leave it in every procedure even when you deliver your application. Also, if a technically savvy client encounters an unexpected error and she's running an MDB or ACCDB (not an MDE or ACCDE), you can walk the client through this process to help determine what caused the problem in the client's environment. As you know, what works on your PC doesn't always work when your user is running it.

Basic Error Handling with a Centralized Message

There's one more thing you can do to make your error-handling code even easier to maintain. Instead of repeating the code to display the message box in every procedure, you can move it to a reusable function that handles it consistently every time.

The following code basically tells the user that an unexpected error occurred. It is needed in every procedure in your application.

```
MsgBox "An error has occurred in this application. " _
& "Please contact your technical support and " _
& "tell them this information:" _
& vbCrLf & vbCrLf & "Error Number " & Err.Number & ", " &
Err.Description, _Buttons:=vbCritical, title:="My Application"
```

Instead, you can centralize this in a function that's called using one line:

```
DisplayUnexpectedError Err.Number, Err.Description
```

Much cleaner! This mundane bit of business is handled with just one line. Now you just need the function that it calls, `DisplayUnexpectedError`. Here it is:

```
Public Sub DisplayUnexpectedError (ErrorNumber as String, ErrorDescription as String)
' Note: since this is a universal error handling procedure, it does not have error
handling

MsgBox "An error has occurred in this application. " _
& "Please contact your technical support and " _
& "tell them this information:" _
& vbCrLf & vbCrLf & "Error Number " & ErrorNumber & ", " &
ErrorDescription, _Buttons:=vbCritical, title:="My Application"

End Sub
```

In this code, `Err.Number` is replaced with `ErrorNumber`, and `Err.Description` with `ErrorDescription`. That's necessary because you're calling a different function and sending in those two values as parameters.

This technique cleans up and shortens your code a lot, but there is an even better reason to use it. If you ever want to change the text of the message displayed to the user, you have only to change it in one place — the `DisplayUnexpectedError` function — instead of searching and replacing it throughout all your procedures.

Note that if you use this centralized message technique, you'll have one more step in your code when you debug using the extra `Resume` statement shown earlier. After you click Debug, the `End Sub` statement in the subroutine `DisplayUnexpectedError` will be highlighted. Press F8 (Step Into) once to get back to the procedure that caused the error. (This is a minor inconvenience compared to the benefit of the centralized error message.)

Cleaning Up After an Error

Errors often occur in the middle of a lengthy procedure, when all kinds of things are happening. Many settings or values persist after an error occurs, and it's up to you to make sure they are reset back to their appropriate values. For example, these situations may be true when an unexpected error occurs in your procedure:

❑ Objects are open.

❑ The hourglass is on.

❑ You have set the status bar text or a progress meter.

❑ Warnings are off.

❑ You are in a transaction that should be rolled back if an error occurs.

Although your code may clean up all these settings under normal circumstances, a common mistake is to leave a mess when your code encounters an error. You don't want to leave a mess, do you?

Neglecting to clean up can cause problems, ranging in severity from annoying to serious. For example, if you don't turn the hourglass off, it will remain on while your users continue their work in Access. That's just annoying.

More seriously, if you don't turn `DoCmd.SetWarnings` back to `True`, any action queries (such as an `Update` or `Delete` query) will modify or delete data without any warning. Obviously, that can cause some serious problems that neither you nor your users will appreciate.

> *Have you ever seen an Access application that won't close? Even when you click the X button, or run a `DoCmd.Quit` in your code, Access just minimizes instead of closing. This can be quite mysterious. Many reasons have been identified for this behavior, but one of them is related to cleaning up. Normally, Access automatically closes and releases objects when they fall out of scope, typically when your procedure ends. However, some versions of Access have issues where this normal cleanup doesn't occur. Because Access won't close if it thinks that some of its objects are still needed, it just minimizes instead. To prevent this, make sure you close the objects you open, and then set them equal to Nothing. Although later versions of Access, including Access 2007, do a better job of automatically releasing each object when its procedure ends, it is good practice to clean them up explicitly.*

To prevent these issues, make sure your code cleans everything up even if it encounters an error. Even as it is failing and exiting the procedure, its last actions can save you some trouble. Here's an example:

```
Public Function MyFunction

On Error GoTo Error_Handler

   Dim varReturnVal as Variant

   'your function code goes here

Exit_Procedure:
   Exit Function

Error_Handler:
   On Error Resume Next
   DoCmd.Hourglass False
   DoCmd.SetWarnings True
   varReturnVal = SysCmd(acSysCmdClearStatus)

   DisplayUnexpectedError Err.Number, Err.Description

   Resume Exit_Procedure
   Resume

End Function
```

Note that the first line in the `Error_Handler` section is `On Error Resume Next`. This overrides the normal error handling and forces the code to continue even if an error is encountered.

Programmers have different styles and preferences for cleaning up after an error. For example, some programmers prefer to put all the cleanup code in the `Exit_Procedure` section because they know that section will run whether the procedure ends normally or abnormally. Other programmers prefer to clean everything up as they go along in the main body of the code and then add additional cleanup code in the `Error_Handler` section. Either style is fine. The important thing to remember is that your procedure won't necessarily end normally. Look through your code to see what will happen if an error occurs, and make sure it is cleaned up.

One last point: Don't let your error handling trigger an infinite error loop. When your code is already in an error-handling situation, or if it is just trying to finish the procedure, set your error trapping to `On Error Resume Next`. That way, your code continues, ignoring any errors that occur. If you don't add that statement, you might end up in an infinite loop where an error in your error handler triggers the error handler again and again.

More on Absorbing Expected Errors

As stated earlier in this chapter, sometimes a normal activity in your application results in Access encountering an error. For example, if the code behind a report cancels the `On Open` event, Access displays an error message. Because this is a normal event, your user shouldn't see an error message. Your application should continue as though nothing happened.

The code in the Open event of the report looks something like this:

```
Private Sub Report_Open(Cancel As Integer)
On Error GoTo Error_Handler

   Me.Caption = "My Application"

   DoCmd.OpenForm FormName:="frmReportSelector_MemberList", _
   WindowMode:=acDialog

   'Cancel the report if "cancel" was selected on the dialog form.

   If Forms!frmReportSelector_MemberList!txtContinue = "no" Then
      Cancel = True
      GoTo Exit_Procedure
   End If

   Me.RecordSource = ReplaceWhereClause(Me.RecordSource,
   Forms!frmReportSelector_MemberList!txtWhereClause)

Exit_Procedure:
   Exit Sub

Error_Handler:
   DisplayUnexpectedError Err.Number, Err.Description

   Resume Exit_Procedure
   Resume

End Sub
```

An open selection criteria form is shown in Figure 9-8.

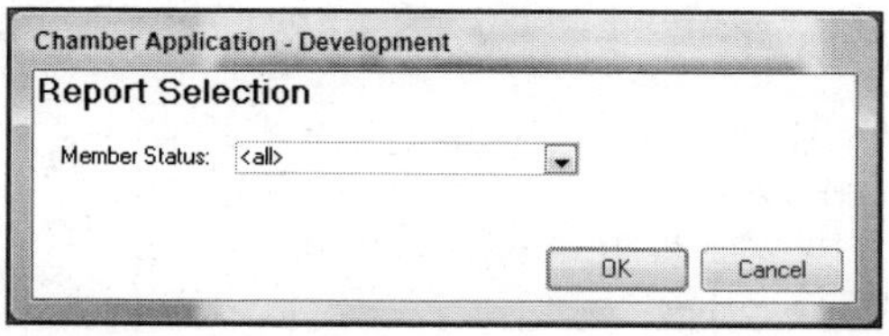

Figure 9-8

If the user clicks OK, the form is hidden and the report's On Open code continues. It adds the selection criteria to the report's RecordSource property and displays the report. However, if the user clicks Cancel, the form sets a hidden Continue text box to no before it is hidden. If the report sees a "no" in this text box, it cancels itself by setting Cancel = True.

If you set the Cancel parameter to True in a report's On Open procedure, an error is returned to the calling code, and if it isn't handled, you see an error, as shown in Figure 9-9.

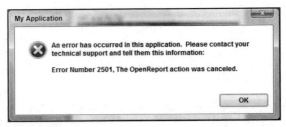

Figure 9-9

Now that is one unnecessary error message! For Access to continue without inflicting it on your poor user, you must check for this particular error (in this case, 2501) and absorb it by doing nothing but exiting the procedure. The following code shows how to absorb the error:

```
Private Sub cmdPreview_Click()
On Error GoTo Error_Handler

  If Me!lstReport.Column(3) & "" <> "" Then
    DoCmd.OpenReport ReportName:=Me!lstReport.Column(3), _
    View:=acViewPreview
  End If

  'Update the Last Run Date of the report
  DoCmd.Hourglass True
  DoCmd.SetWarnings False
  DoCmd.RunSQL _
  "UPDATE tsysReport SET tsysReport.DtLastRan = Date() " & _
  "WHERE tsysReport.RptKey = " & Me.lstReport
  DoCmd.SetWarnings True
  DoCmd.Hourglass False

Exit_Procedure:
  Exit Sub

Error_Handler:
  If Err.Number = 2501 Then
    Resume Exit_Procedure
  Else
    On Error Resume Next
    DoCmd.SetWarnings True
    DoCmd.Hourglass False
    DisplayUnexpectedError Err.Number, Err.Description
    Resume Exit_Procedure
    Resume

  End If
End Sub
```

In this code, you tell Access to ignore error 2501, should it be encountered. Access will not display an error message, and will instead exit the procedure immediately. If errors other than 2501 occur, the code will continue through to the Else statement and use your normal error-handling logic.

If you have several expected error codes that you want to quietly absorb, you can either add them to the `If` statement using `Or`, like this:

```
If Err.Number = 2501 Or Err.Number = 2450 Then
```

or, if you want to take a different action for each error, you can use a `Select Case` statement, like this:

```
Select Case Err.Number
Case 2501 'report was cancelled
  Resume Exit_Procedure
Case 2450 'form is no longer loaded
  Resume Next
Case Else
  ...normal error handling
End Select
```

In this example, when the report is canceled (error 2501), Access will jump directly to `Exit_Procedure`, but if it encounters a form that is not loaded (error 2450), it will use `Resume Next` to ignore the error and continue with the next line of code.

While you are becoming familiar with including error handling in every procedure, or if you aren't sure which error numbers need special handling, just include the basic error handling with the extra `Resume`. As specific expected errors pop up during your development and testing, you can add the code to quietly handle and absorb them.

Issues in Error Handling

Some developers try to enhance their error handling with writing log files or sending e-mail. There are some issues involved with these error-handling techniques, as explained in the following sections.

Don't Use Error Handling with Logging

Some developers write code to insert an error log record into a table or text file when an error occurs. The idea is to be able to analyze when and where errors have occurred by querying this table long after the errors happened. However, this technique has some issues.

❑ Access does not provide a way to determine the name of the procedure that is currently running. Because any error logging routine needs to know which procedure caused the error, you need to manually code the name of the current procedure into each error routine. That is labor intensive and prone to errors.

❑ The benefit of error logging is questionable because few errors should be happening after your code has been tested and delivered. Errors should be rare enough that your users will let you know when they happen. You can always ask them to capture a screenshot if you want to see the details.

❑ Some types of errors cause the attempt to log them to fail. Examples include loss of network connectivity, and disconnected storage hardware. Your user may see additional unrelated errors, or you could be lulled into thinking that all errors are logged, when they may not be.

If your code is running in a managed environment, it may be beneficial to log errors to the System Event Log. For more information on this, refer to Appendix C. The bottom line is that spending the time to log unexpected errors to a table or text file is not recommended. This is one of those cases where the benefits usually don't outweigh the costs.

Don't Use Error Handling That Sends e-mail

Another interesting way to track the errors that are occurring in an application is to add code to the error-handling routines that "phones home" when an error occurs. Specifically, the application builds and sends an e-mail to you (the developer) whenever an unexpected error occurs. This is usually done with the SendObject method, although there are other ways to utilize MAPI (mail application programming interface) directly.

This approach has the same problems listed in the preceding section, plus a few more:

❑ Your code needs to be able to send an e-mail using an installed e-mail client. There is always a possibility that there is no e-mail client installed, or it is not compatible with your e-mailing code.

❑ Some e-mail clients (for example, Microsoft Outlook) have code to protect against viruses using the e-mail program to propagate themselves to other computers. If an outside program (in this case, yours) tries to send an e-mail, a warning message displays alerting the user that a virus may be attempting to send e-mail. That isn't what you want your user to see when your application is running.

As with error handling with logging, this technique is probably more trouble than it is worth.

Summary

Every procedure you write in Access VBA should have error handling. Keep error handling simple and easy to implement, with one basic copy-and-paste code block. Then do a few quick steps if necessary to adapt the error handling to your procedure:

❑ Change Exit Function to Exit Sub if the procedure is a sub.

❑ Add code to quietly absorb expected errors, if any.

❑ Make sure you perform any necessary cleanup if an error occurs.

By following these error-handling guidelines, you'll build VBA code that is easier to debug and maintain, so you can focus on building great features into your application.

Using VBA to Enhance Forms

First impressions are lasting, so be sure that your forms make it a great one. When you are providing a solution, forms are the first things that people see and use. So forms need to be as attractive as they are effective and intuitive.

Access 2007's out-of-the box features and controls replace many of the common tools and functions that required testing, error trapping, and add-ins. This is more than just a time saver; it builds in consistency and motivates you to deliver better solutions. Forms can be dressed up with subtle shading, colorful lines, and sleek new image controls.

Users like being able to scroll through data sheets, instantly see the details, and even update the record. They also appreciate how easy it is to assign a task to several people, particularly because they can add a person to the list without missing a beat. And there are unlimited opportunities for including attachments right in the database.

Those are just some of the features that you'll explore in this chapter.

If something already looks and works this good, then imagine how great your solution will be when you leverage it with VBA. That's what this chapter is all about. In addition to seeing how to use VBA with some of the new features, you'll also examine some of the important mainstays such as working with combo boxes, creating multiple instances of a form, and building a tree view control.

VBA Basics

Before you dive into the wonderful world of forms, take a minute to review the following table, which shows the concepts that are fundamental to working with VBA.

Concept	Definition	Examples
Object	An entity that can be manipulated with code	`Form`, `Report`, `TextBox`, `ComboBox`, `CommandButton`, `DoCmd`, `Debug`
Method	Any intrinsic (built-in) functionality already assigned to an object	`Form.Requery`, `Report.Print`, `TextBox.SetFocus`, `ComboBox.Dropdown`, `DoCmd.OpenForm`, `Debug.Print`
Event	An action associated to an object that executes when triggered by the user	`Form.Open`, `Report.NoData`, `TextBox.AfterUpdate`, `ComboBox.NotInList`, `CommandButton.Click`
Property	An attribute of an object that defines its characteristics (such as size, color, or screen location) or an aspect of its behavior (such as whether it is hidden)	`Form.BackColor`, `TextBox.ControlSource`, `ComboBox.RowSource`, `CommandButton.Picture`, `Report.Recordsource`

Properties

Forms have properties and so do the controls on a form. Although there are a few properties that can only be read or set in VBA, the majority of an object's properties are listed on the Property Sheet. The main four categories of properties are format, data, event, and other. The needs of the customer and users will dictate which of these properties you set and when. Setting the properties in the Property Sheet may be all that is needed for some; however, the majority of your forms will have some kind of programmatic interaction with the user. Being able to respond to user input relies heavily on setting the properties using VBA. Of course, some of the routine functionality can now be provided by embedded macros. But this chapter focuses on VBA, particularly on how to utilize the event properties.

The following table provides examples of properties. Appendix G provides a more extensive list in discussing the Access Object model, and it is complimented by the appendices on ADO and DAO.

Object	Property	Description
Form	`Caption`	A string expression that appears in the title bar of the form.
	`RecordSource`	A string expression that defines the source of data.
	`AllowEdits`	Boolean value that specifies if the user can edit records on the form.
Text box	`ControlSource`	A string expression identifying the name of the field in the Form's RecordSource that the text box should push/pull data; or an expression evaluated to display a calculation or text result.

Object	Property	Description
	Visible	Boolean value that specifies if the control is visible to the user.
	InputMask	A string expression that defines the way data is entered.
	StatusBarText	A string expression displayed at the bottom of the Access window while the cursor is in the control.
Combo box	RowSource	A string expression that defines the source of data.
	LimitToList	Boolean value that restricts the user's selection to only values in the combo box.
	TabIndex	Numerical value that specifies the order in which the cursor should travel from one field to the next.

Event Properties: Where Does the Code Go?

The power of a form is often derived from responding to the user. Typically, a response is based on intentional input. But VBA can also respond to ancillary or inadvertent actions. The most common place to use code is in the event properties of the form or control. This is frequently referred to as the code behind the form.

It isn't enough to have the code right; the code also has to be behind the right event or it may not be triggered. Time and again, the problem of code that "just doesn't work" is solved by moving the code to a different event. So, in addition to being able to write VBA, it is important to be familiar with the timing or order of events as well as what triggers them. After all, the best code in the world isn't going to help if it doesn't get to run. The following table describes what triggers some of the events most commonly used in a form and in the form's objects.

In code, events have no spaces with the first letter of each word capitalized: Open *and* BeforeUpdate.

Events	Triggers When
Open	The form is opened (can be canceled).
Close	The form is closing, but before it is removed from the screen.
Load	The form loads.
Unload	The form unloads before it deactivates and is closed, so criteria in this event can determine if the form should remain open. Because the Close event cannot be canceled, this is the stage in which to include a way to abort the process of closing the form.
Click	A section of the form or a control is clicked once by the mouse.
DblClick	A section of the form or a control is double-clicked by the mouse.

Table continues on the next page

Events	Triggers When
Current	A record gets the focus when a form is opened or focus moves to a different record.
Dirty	The user makes any modification to the current record.
BeforeInsert	User types the first character in a new record. On a form, this actually occurs before the record is created and it can be canceled.
BeforeUpdate	Before the update (new data or change) is committed to the form or control — so the update can be canceled.
AfterUpdate	A form record or an individual control has been updated.
AfterInsert	The record updated is a new record.
Change	A value on a control is modified. It's helpful to note that this applies only to a text box or the text portion of a combo box and to moving between pages on a tab control.
Timer	Regular intervals specified by the TimerInterval property are reached.
NotInList	The user enters a value that is not in a combo box.
MouseMove	The mouse is moved over a section of the form or a control.
Enter	The user physically places the edit cursor into the control. This can be accomplished with the Tab or Enter key or by a mouse click.

As you can see, events are fired or triggered by a specific action or circumstance. Some events occur in sequence, such as when opening or closing a form, and others — Click and NotInList, for example — occur when certain conditions are met. (To understand more about event firing, see Chapter 8.)

Although there isn't a comprehensive list of events and their firing order, you can use Access 2007 Help to get information about a specific event. Office Online typically lists three to five related events, giving a brief explanation. For example, when a form is opened, the events occur in this order: Open → Load → Resize → Activate → Current. And events closely related to closing a form occur as follows: Unload → Deactivate → Close. The Close event can be the mechanism for such things as opening another form or creating a log of who used the form.

Naming Conventions

As you know by now, it is important to adopt and consistently apply naming conventions. In addition to making your code more readable, a good naming convention minimizes the potential for a name to be given to more than one object. The following table shows some of the more common ways to name objects and controls.

Appendix L provides a more extensive list of tags for forms, subforms, and the objects that might be used on them. Note that some items have more than one common tag. Subform, for example, might be represented by fsub, sfrm, or sfr.

Tag	Object	Example
frm	Form	frmContacts
sfr	Subform	sfrContactDetails
cbo	Combobox	cboClientNames
lst	Listbox	lstClientNames
txt	Textbox	txtFName
cmd	Command Button	cmdOpenContacts
qry	Query	qryFavoriteContacts

If your first programming language is VBA, you were probably taught to use cmd for command buttons. When you get into other languages such as VB.NET, ASP.NET, and C#, command takes on a different meaning and refers to commands that talk to a database (OLE DB or SQL Server). With ADO, it was often suggested that Cmd (uppercase C) be used for command and cmd (lowercase) be used for command button. btn has also been used as a generic tag for a button. And now, using btn may become popular as a way to differentiate between command buttons on the Ribbon and controls on a form or report, which use cmd as a tag. That isn't to underplay the benefits of explicit naming, such as tgl for a toggle button, opt for an option button, and, yes, cmd for a command button.

Now let's get on with building custom forms.

Creating Forms the 2007 Way

When you are ready to create a new form, you'll probably have a good idea about its general look and function based on the record source and purpose. Access 2007 gives developers a huge jump-start on form design by providing a good selection of form options on the Ribbon (see Figure 10-1). You can select an item from the Navigation pane, which will become the Record Source of the new form, and then click on one of the Ribbon's form buttons to initiate the process. Thanks to a form wizard, the new form will (instantly) appear in Layout view so that you can begin adding more features and functionality.

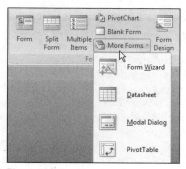

Figure 10-1

Some Form layouts (designs) are new and others just have a new name or new origination point. The following table shows the old wizard/process and new Ribbon command for the various form layouts. All but Modal Dialog and Form Design initially open in Layout view, which is the new WYSIWYG view that enables developers to change the look of a form (or report) with the data displayed. (The wizard uses layout to list the options for the fundamental design of a form, but Layout view is not the design style.)

Previous Wizard/Command Button	Ribbon Command Button
Design	Form Design (no record source by default)
Form Wizard	Form Wizard (located under More Forms)*
AutoForm: Columnar	Form*
AutoForm: Tabular	Multiple Items*
AutoForm: Datasheet	Datasheet (located under More Forms)*
AutoForm: PivotTable	PivotTable (located under More Forms)*
AutoForm: PivotChart	PivotChart*
	Blank Form* (opens with Field List pane)
	Modal Dialog (located under More Forms)
	Split Form*

* Form opens in Layout view

You may be wondering why the Form Wizard is still around even though there seems to be a button on the Ribbon for each of the form layouts. At this point, the biggest benefits of the wizard are that it enables you to specify which fields to include from the selected record source and that it make it so easy to use the new styles (AutoFormats) . When you create a form by clicking one of the layouts on the Ribbon, the form will include all of the underlying fields – which means you'll likely spend extra time deleting and repositioning fields.

Tabular and Stacked Layouts

It is important to understand about tabular and stacked layouts because of the effect that they have on moving controls when designing a form. We'll view examples in a moment, but for now, you might envision that tabular layout is used for what is known as single form view and stacked layout essentially looks like datasheet view. In Access 2007, using a wizard to create a form almost always results in a tabular layout when working in Design view. The normal process for creating a form is to select a record source from the Navigation pane and then use the Ribbon's Create tab to select the desired form. The form opens in Layout view and includes all of the fields in the record source (except, obviously, when you choose a blank form, Form Design, or Form Wizard). Logically, selecting the layout for Multiple Items creates a form with a stacked layout. But selecting one of the other formats, such as Form, places all of the fields on the form in tabular layout. Even the Pivot Chart has a tabular layout if you look at the form in Design view.

One of the key benefits of tabular and stacked layouts is that the controls are pre-grouped so they move together and stay in alignment. The grouping enables you to reorder or remove fields and have controls automatically reposition themselves to the proper spacing and alignment. You can remove the grouping from all controls or from selected controls, and you can even use a combination of tabular and stacked groups along with independent fields all on the same form. The grouping can be changed in Design or Layout view by using the Control Layout options on the Ribbon's Arrange tab (see Figure 10-2). That's where you can also specify the margins within the control (the distance between the control border and the control contents) as well as the padding (space between controls).

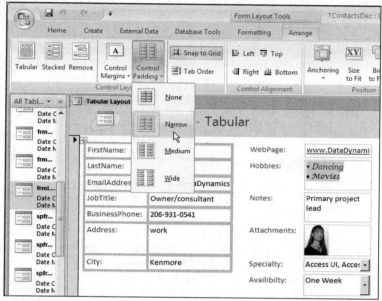

Figure 10-2

Right-click a control within a group to access the shortcut menu for Layout, as shown in Figure 10-3. This menu enables you to quickly remove one control from the group or to work with an entire column or row of controls. (If you can't adapt to working with grouped controls, the grouping can be removed using the same shortcut menu; merely select the group and then right-click to use the shortcut menu and then choose Layout ⇨ Remove.)

The Gridlines option on the shortcut menu is a slick way to add vertical and horizontal lines to a form.

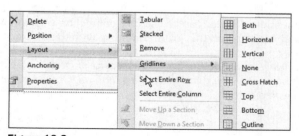

Figure 10-3

Anchoring

Anchoring ties a control or group of controls to a position. Specify the position — top, bottom, side, or corner — and the control moves into place. You do this by using two of the new properties for controls, Horizontal Anchor and Vertical Anchor. (Note, these two properties apply only to controls on forms and are not available on reports.) If two stacks of controls are anchored to opposite sides or corners of a form and the form is resized, the controls automatically move in accordance with their anchor points. Anchoring includes several options that can be selected from the shortcut menu by right-clicking a control. But a better way to see what the options do is to check out the Anchoring section of the Ribbon's Arrange tab as shown in Figure 10-4.

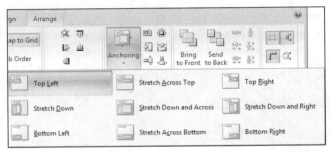

Figure 10-4

The stretch options enable you to maximize the use of available space by expanding the control or group of controls vertically or horizontally, and you can stretch labels as well. For example, you can use stretch across the top to position a heading so that the width of the label grows as the form gets wider. With two stacks of controls, you can anchor the group on the right to the right, put the cursor in a text box of the stack on the left, and select Stretch Down And Across. Then as the form grows, the fields in the left stack get wider and taller. Or, if you know that the data is going to be a fixed width, but would like to give the labels more room, you could designate that column of the stack as the portion to stretch. It is important to know that only one control in a tabular layout can be set to stretch horizontally and that only one control in a stacked layout can be set to stretch vertically.

As in the past, there are several subtleties to perfecting a form's design. For one thing, controls that are not in a group may end up overlapping if the form is stretched. A good illustration is two controls, side-by-side — as they stretch with the form, the control on the left will eventually encroach upon the space for the control on the right. This is also a good example of the type of issues to be alert to, in addition to issues from your other experiences with form design.

The gridline options mentioned earlier can be used in conjunction with groups and anchoring so you can have horizontal and vertical lines that grow and move with the controls.

If you make design changes to a form that has the AutoResize property set to NO and the AutoCenter property set to YES, switch to Form view before saving the form. Otherwise, the right and bottom edges might be trimmed the next time the form opens.

The Modal Dialog Mode

The Modal Dialog form opens as a modal window, which means that the user must respond to and close the form before any other object can have the focus. These are often referred to as modal dialog forms because they typically have the sole purpose of obtaining a specific input or feedback from the user. Once the user has provided the required response, they can close the form and the application can continue its process, whereas a modal form merely needs to be closed before the user can proceed with other processes.

If you have ever created dialog forms, you know how tedious the process can be — setting the same form properties and adding the same command buttons to every form. The Modal Dialog Wizard now does the work and saves you a lot of time. The new form will be essentially blank, except for two command buttons (one labeled OK and the other, Cancel). Both buttons have the Close method for their On Click event, so you will most likely want to change or remove one of the buttons. Because the buttons use an embedded macro, they run in disabled mode. The best part of using the wizard to create a modal dialog form is that the wizard correctly sets the appropriate properties such as the formatting (border style and navigation) and the settings for pop-up and Modal mode.

Creating a new modal form is great, but simple dialog forms aren't the ones that you may want to open in modal mode. Any form or report can be set to open in modal dialog mode by setting the Modal property to Yes or by using code to specify the view as the form is opened. Here are two examples of code that will open a modal form in a modal window:

```
Docmd.OpenForm "frmMyModalForm" , acNormal, ,, acFormEdit, acWindowNormal

Docmd.OpenForm "frmMyModalForm" , acNormal, ,, acFormEdit, acDialog
```

The first line works only when the form properties specify that the form is modal. The second line can be used to open any form in a modal window — providing that you put the correct form name in the quotes. The difference between the two is the last parameter. It is an optional parameter named WindowMode that specifies the window mode in which the form will open. IntelliSense prompts you through the process of writing the command line and shows the options as the cursor gets to each parameter. WindowMode has the options to use the Access enums acDialog, acHidden, acIcon, and acWidowNormal, but only two apply to modal forms. acWindowNormal opens the form to whatever the form properties state as the default view and style. Stipulating acDialog overwrites the property settings and opens the form in a modal window.

Control Wizards — Creating Command Buttons Using VBA or Macros

Control wizards provide a fast, easy process for adding controls, or command buttons, to a form. Wizards provide consistency and write the code. Right? Well, not necessarily anymore — at least as far as writing code. Access 2007 relies heavily on embedded macros. So, instead of code, the control wizards now generate macros when you are working with an ACCDB file. Be assured that the wizards support backward compatibly and will continue to create VBA code in MDB and ADP files. After you complete the wizard process, you can open the Property Sheet (see Figure 10-5) to see the embedded macro listed for the event. You can click the builder button [...] to the right of the property to view or edit the embedded macro. However, if instead of using the newly created macro, you choose something else from the drop-down list (such as Event Procedure), you cannot subsequently select the original embedded macro. The builder button allows you to select the Macro Builder, Expression Builder, or Code Builder. The drop-down list enables you to select Event Procedure or one of the previously created named macros.

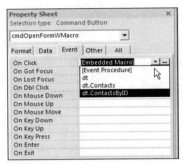

Figure 10-5

If you choose to have the wizard create a macro, you still have the option to change the property from using an embedded macro to using an event procedure. One of the easiest ways to convert a macro to VBA code is to use the Ribbon button Convert Form's Macros to Visual Basic found in the Macro group on the Ribbon's Database Tools tab. Keep in mind that this process will delete the macro; however, it will preserve the functionality by creating the appropriate VBA code. You also need to be aware that if you merely use the control's property sheet to select Event Procedure from the drop-down list, it will erase the macro and leave your event procedure blank.

Command Button Properties

There are several new command button properties, including two that provide fun features that are worth mentioning. Although they aren't specifically called out in the examples in the book, they are used in the sample databases for this chapter. I'm sure you'll want to use them as well:

❏ **Cursor On Hover:** Enables your cursor to change to the hyperlink hand (little hand pointing a finger) when hovering over the button.

❏ **Picture Caption Arrangement:** Enables you to add a caption with a picture and then arrange the caption — well, arrange within the limited options of No Picture Caption, General, Top, Bottom, Left, and Right.

And yes, `Picture Caption Arrangement` means that a caption can be included with an image on a command button. For example, navigation buttons might have Previous and Next juxtaposed with double arrows. As you'll see later, the command buttons that navigate through the attachments on a record in Figure 10-6 display both a caption and an image.

Each new version of Access offers more properties for each object. The following table describes a few of the properties related to the exciting new features for forms.

Feature	Applies To	Benefit
Show Date Picker	Textbox	No more ActiveX controls or lengthy workarounds.
Padding	All controls	Enables you to place content a given distance from the cell border.
Anchoring	All controls	Controls and groups of controls can be anchored to the top, bottom, left, or right. When a form is stretched, the control or group will move accordingly.
Gridline Style	All controls	Similar to cells in an Excel file, each control can have its own border for each side, transparent, solid, dots, or dashes.
Split Form Orientation	Form	You can specify where the datasheet will display: top, bottom, left, or right.

New Attachment Controls

In addition to being a new field data type, the attachment is also one of the new controls that can be found in the Toolbox. The Attachment control enables you to attach a file or collection of files to any record. When you right-click the control, a toolbar provides forward and backward buttons to cycle through the files and a paperclip button that opens the Attachment dialog box. That sounds fairly straightforward, but as a developer, you will likely want to provide a more elegant solution by including navigation controls and displaying the filename on your form. The next set of examples leads you through the process of obtaining the names of the attachments, displaying the count for the number of attachments, and creating radio buttons to move through a record's attachments. After that, you'll create an option group so that the user can choose how attachments will be listed on a form. There is a similar example in the downloadable file for this chapter. It is in the database AttachmentDemo and uses the form frmAttachments and the table tblIssues.

> *For a quick demonstration, you could just add an attachment field to an existing table and create a form based on that.*

This example uses a form called frmAttachments and a table called tblIssues. The table contains several fields, but the critical one in this case is called IssueAttachment with the data type Attachment. With frmAttachments in Single Form view, you'll work with the following objects (the labels are up to you):

❑ **Three unbound text boxes:** txtFileName, txtFileType, and txtNumberFiles.

❑ **Two command buttons:** cmdAttBack and cmdAttForward.

❑ **One attachment control:** MyAttachment with the control source IssueAttachment (a field in tblIssues).

When this process is complete, the form should look similar to Figure 10-6.

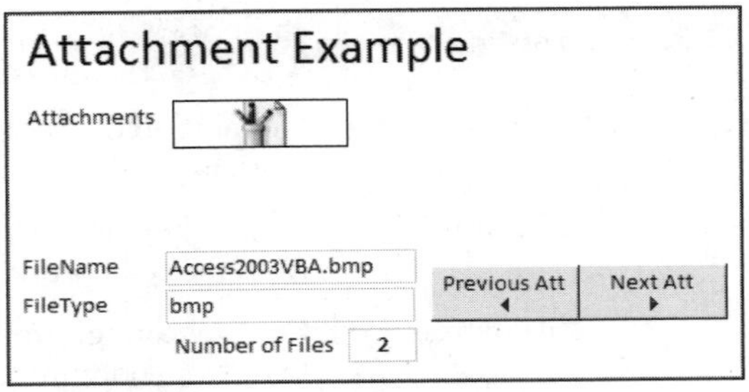

Figure 10-6

For the attachment control, you'll want to change the `Display As` property to `Image/Icon` (rather than the icon as shown here) so that you can see the images as you move through the attachments. That brings you to formatting and providing the code behind the two command buttons. As shown in the figure, the command buttons are formatted to use embedded pictures that have the caption at the top. The code is provided below.

If there are multiple attachments for one record, the code will navigate through them using `Forward` and `Back` methods. The `Click` events should use the code as is. The code also provides for the display of the count for the number of attachments.

> For some of the following functionality to work properly, the form must be in **Single Form or Continuous Form** view. Regrettably, the **Split Form** or **Datasheet** view does not allow the controls to properly display the attachment properties. So, save yourself a lot of time and testing by setting the Default view of your form to **Single Form or Continuous Form** and set the properties to not allow Datasheet or Split form views.

The code behind `frmAttachments` shows attachments as an image or icon. In the database, you'll see that similar code is behind `frmAttachmentsIcon`, which uses only icons to indicate the attachment type. Although you can probably interpret the code, we'll explain some of the reasoning behind the form's `MyAttachment.AttachmentCurrent`.

```
Private Sub cmdAttachForward_Click()
    Me.MyAttachment.Forward
    Me.txtAttMyFiles.Value = Me.MyAttachment.FileName
    Me. txtAttMyFileType.Value = Me.MyAttachment.FileType

End Sub
Private Sub cmdAttachBack_Click()
    Me.MyAttachment.Back
    Me.txtAttMyFiles.Value = Me.MyAttachment.FileName
    Me.txtAttMyFileType.Value = Me.MyAttachment.FileType
End Sub
```

```
Private Sub MyAttachment_AttachmentCurrent()
' update the text boxes for form view where the
' default view is not a split form or datasheet view.
    If (Me.CurrentView = AcCurrentView.acCurViewFormBrowse _
        And Me.DefaultView <> AcDefView.acDefViewSplitForm
        And Me.DefaultView <> AcDefView.acDefViewDataSheet) Then
        Me.txtFileName.Value = Me.MyAttachment.FileName
        Me.txtFileCount.Value = Me.MyAttachment.AttachmentCount
        Me.txtFileType.Value = Me.MyAttachment.FileType
    Else
        Me.txtFileName.Value = Null
        Me.txtFileCount.Value = Null
        Me.txtFileType.Value = Null
    End If

End Sub
```

With this code, you can now view the attachment filenames and file types (extension) as you browse through the attachments. It may seem redundant to explicitly retrieve the file type because it typically shows up in the filename, but the purpose here is to demonstrate how to retrieve the information.

This example code starts by retrieving the values for the attachment only if the form is not displayed in Split Form or Datasheet view (we already learned that lesson). There may be issues or unexpected results when trying to obtain these values from other form views, so the value is set to null for other cases. In specifying the values, the left side of the equation identifies the text box that will display the value retrieved. The right side identifies the source of the data; in this case, it is looking at the control called MyAttachment. Because it's an attachment control, it has some special properties, including FileName, FileType, and AttachmentCount.

❑ FileName: The actual name of the file (MyPicture.jpeg will display as MyPicture.jpeg).

❑ FileType: Refers to file extension or type (JPEG, TXT, BMP, PDF).

❑ AttachmentCount: The number of attachments stored for that record.

The event AttachmentCurrent works similar to the form's OnCurrent event in that it fires when moving the focus from one attachment to another. Within this event you can both extract information and specify the way that attachments will be represented. As the preceding code demonstrated, you can use the AttachmentCount property to list the number of attachments. It is helpful to use this count in conjunction with the icon and image displays since they do not indicate the number of attachments. The attachment control uses an image and has the following three display options:

❑ acDisplayAsIcon: Displays the default icon for that file.

❑ acDisplayAsImageIcon: Displays icons for txt files; actual picture for jpeg's and bmp's.

❑ acDisplayAsPaperclip: The default setting. Although this does not indicate the file type, it is the only option that, by default, displays the AttachmentCount.

In the next example, an option group demonstrates the three different views to display the image. The option group is added to the form, and Figure 10-7 uses the `DisplayAsImageIcon` option in showing the same record and attachment shown in Figure 10-6.

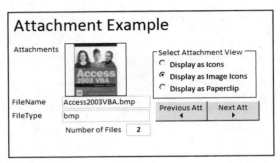

Figure 10-7

The following code allows the user to choose whether the attachment control will display as an icon, icon/image, or paper clip.

```
Private Sub grpAttachView_Click()
Dim OptSelect as Integer
OptSelect = Me.grpAttachView.Value
Select Case OptSelect
    Case 1
        With Me.MyAttachment
            .ControlTipText = "This option displays file Icons only."
            .DisplayAs = acDisplayAsIcon
            .Height = "450"
        End With
    Case 2
        With Me.MyAttachment
            .ControlTipText = "This option displays file Images and Icons."
            .DisplayAs = acDisplayAsImageIcon
            .Height = "1440"
        End With
    Case 3
        With Me.MyAttachment
            .ControlTipText = "This option displays files as a Paperclip."
            .DisplayAs = acDisplayAsPaperclip
        End With
End Select
End Sub
```

For options `acDisplayAsIcon` and `acDisplayAsImageIcon`, you add the `Height` property and set it to `"450"` twips and `"1440"` twips (1 inch), respectively. Why specify the height? Because the default height for an attachment control that is set to `acDisplayAsPaperclip` is only 0.1667 inches. By specifying the height in code, the control can grow or shrink as appropriate for the display type.

I don't know about you, but I certainly am not accustomed to calculating in twips. So, if you are trying to specify image heights, you may appreciate knowing that a twip is $\frac{1}{1440}$ of an inch, which is the equivalent of $\frac{1}{567}$ of a centimeter or $\frac{1}{20}$th of a point.

When using code to specify the height and width in twips, do not use commas as regional settings may cause the comma to be interpreted as a decimal point. Notice that the code uses 1440 not 1,440 and that the numbers are enclosed in double quotes.

While you are at it, you may also want to use the Property Sheet Format tab and change the Picture Size Mode to Zoom, which will preserve the image proportions. If you are concerned about space or presenting a compact look, you may also want to adjust the cell padding around images and icons. Figure 10-8 illustrates the effects of several of these settings.

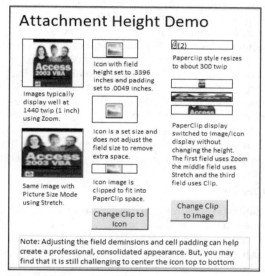

Figure 10-8

The attachment control has its own pop-up menu for adding, removing, opening, saving, and moving through attachments. This is a powerful little control because it works like the OpenFile dialog box but saves the collections of files within the record rather than in a separate table, streamlining the process of saving or attaching files to a record. However, with the built-in control, you must select working with none, one, or all attachments. Unlike a fully functional multi-select group, it does not allow users to select several (but not all) attachments.

Combo Boxes

The combo box is a potent control that can combine the processes to search, select, and populate data into fields (or other objects), as well as limit the values that a user may enter. Many nuances affect how combo boxes work; this section addresses some of the more common ones. It also covers some new features, including two new properties: `Allow Value List Edits` and `List Items Edit Form`.

The combo box and list box have a lot of the same properties and functionality. The primary difference is that the contents of the list box are always displayed on the form, so the list box takes more space. List box values are also limited to the list, which can be updated programmatically by adding values to the row source, but not directly by the user. Combo boxes, on the other hand, generally use the space of a normal text box and employ a drop-down list to display the number of rows specified in the properties. The row source can be set to be updateable or to allow only existing values.

Before continuing, let's clarify the difference between control source and row source. The *control source* is specified if the value selected in the combo box will automatically (rather than programmatically) be stored in a field. The last question in the Combo Box Wizard, for instance, is about remembering or storing the selected value. If you choose to store the selected value in a field, that field becomes the control source. The *row source* provides the values that are displayed and used by the combo box. It can be a table, a query, a value list, or a field list. The row source value can even be an empty string when the form opens and then be set programmatically. For the most part, the row source consists of multiple columns with only one column visible to the user. The other columns can be used to populate other fields or as the link to other record sources. For example, one column could be the field that links the current form to a subform. Again, referring to the wizard provides a quick demonstration of some of the properties related to the row source. When you tell the Combo Box Wizard, for instance, that the combo box will look up values in a table or query, you are specifying the row source. The wizard then goes through the process of selecting the fields for the columns and allowing you to specify the column widths. The wizard automatically adds the primary key if one is available.

The other main element that you'll work with is controlling the values that the user can use or add. But first, you'll tackle an easy example of using a combo box to display existing data.

Combo Box as a Look-Up

An excellent use for the combo box control is to display descriptive information for the user even though the data that's actually stored in the database is the value of some sort of key (primary or foreign). For example, you may have a form in which users allocate sales and you want the users to identify a department. If that form (or even just the combo box) is bound to a table that stores the Department ID rather than the name of the department, you don't want to force the user to remember or figure out which Department ID to enter. Instead, you can use a combo box to display a list of departments (field name `Department`) and let the form manage how the Department ID is stored. The following table lists the combo box settings for this scenario. You will also find this in `frmContactsComboLookUp` in this chapter's database file named `ComboBox.accdb`.

Property	Value
Control Source	Department (this is from the table Contacts)
Row Source	Select DepartmentID and Department from tblDepartment
Row Source Type	Table/Query
Bound Column	1
Limit To List	Yes

Property	Value
Allow Value List Edits	No
List Items Edit Form	No value (leave blank)
Column Count	2
Column Width	0";2"

Two of the properties that are crucial to selecting the value that will be stored in the database are Bound Column and Column Width. Setting Bound Column to 1 means the data for the field that will be stored in the database is in the first column of the Row Source. Setting the Column Width of the bound column to 0 means that the bound column will not be displayed in the combo box.

If you are familiar with coding combo boxes, you probably noticed the new Access 2007 Combo Box properties Allow Value List Edits and List Items Edit Form. These new properties enable you to let users maintain their own set of valid values for the field without requiring you to write code. The next two sections examine those properties.

As in prior versions of Access, if the Limit To List property is set to No, the user is allowed to type whatever he wants as many times as he wants. The combo box only helps the user select previously defined values without restricting him to only those values, and it allows users to enter the same value multiple times and with myriad variations. When Limit To List is set to Yes, the user can select only the values in the list. However, if the user enters a value that isn't in the list, it can trigger a response depending on whether you've captured bad data entry using the On Not In List event and/or based on the settings for the new Allow Value List Edits property along with the List Items Edit Form property. All this is by way of saying you should be aware that the On Not In List event occurs before the settings of the new properties are even considered.

It may seem as though we are hammering on just a few properties, but slight variations in how they are combined can have a big impact on results.

Allow Value List Edits

The Allow Value List Edits property provides a simple way for you to allow the user to change the contents of the list without requiring the user to go into Design view to change the row source or you (the developer) to write code to change the row source. Keep in mind that this property is intended for combo boxes where the Row Source Type property is set to Value List — meaning that it is not designed to work with other row source types, so don't be tempted to misapply this feature.

If Allow Value List Edits is set to No and the user enters a value that isn't in the list, the user will see the standard Access message (see Figure 10-9) advising him to select an item from the list.

Figure 10-9

If `Allow Value List Edits` is set to `Yes` and the user enters a value that isn't in the list, the user will see a message box that asks if he wants to edit the items in the list, as shown in Figure 10-10a. You'll also notice the extra question at the bottom of the message box, "Was this information helpful?" That message will appear if the user has enabled "Help Improve Access." Responding to this query will clear that message without closing the message box, as shown in Figure 10-10b.

Figure 10-10

If the user chooses Yes, to edit the list, the default Access `Edit Items List` form displays (see Figure 10-11). This default form is clearly designed to capture only a simple list of values, and it is intended to be used only when the combo box `Row Source Type` is set to `Value List`, `Inherit Value List` is set to `Yes`, and both the the `Bound Column` and `Column Count` are set to `1`. Keep in mind that this form provides no means for you to control the values that the user might enter, so terms may be entered multiple times with different spellings. In Figure 10-11, you can see that Dance has been added to the list from the combo box labeled "`Value List With Edit:`" even though "Dancing" was already in the list. If you want more control over what the user enters for the list or if you want to provide a multicolumn list, you should set the `Row Source Type` to be `Table/Query` and use the `List Items Edit Form` property to specify a custom form. We will discuss that approach shortly.

Figure 10-11

One thing to note about using this approach to allow value list edits is that the `Row Source` property of the combo box is actually updated, which in turn causes Access to respond as though the design of the form has changed. Because of this, when the user closes the form that contains the (updated) combo box, Access will display a message box to ask if the user wants to "…save changes to the design of the form [*form name*]". This is not a good message for users to see, so you may want to use the `DoCmd.Save` `acForm, Me.Name` statement to save the form in the `Form_AfterUpdate` event. (This is obviously not a desired scenario, and you can hope for a resolution in an early Access update.)

> **When allowing value list edits by using the default Access `Edit Items List` form, it is critical that the `Row Source Type` is `Value List` and `Inherit Value List` is set to Yes. This allows Access to properly handle the update. With other property configurations, users may get a warning and be asked if they want to save changes to the design of the form. After all, a change to a value list behind a control is a change to the form's design.**

List Items Edit Form

As mentioned earlier, the big advantages of the new `Allow Value List Edits` property is that you don't have to write code in the `On NotIn List` event to capture the new value, and it provides a method that allows the user to include the values he wants in the list. But please remember (and this is worth repeating) that the new `Allow Value List Edits` property is intended only for combo boxes and list boxes with a `Row Source Type` of `Value List`. If you are using the `Row Source Type of Table/Query`, you can use the new `List Items Edit Form` property to display an alternate form that allows the user to edit the list.

First you must first create a form that will maintain the data that is displayed from the `row source` of the combo box. Then you set the `List Items Edit Form` property to name of that form. You could get a little fancy with your form by programmatically taking the invalid value that the user entered in the combo box and loading it into the appropriate field on your edit form. That kind of defeats the concept of using this new feature to avoid writing code, but then this book is about code and creating solutions that save time and prevent errors. Coming up is one example of using code to optimize use of a couple of the new "no code required" features.

> *Because users can use the Navigation pane, it might be beneficial to programmatically restrict the capability to open your edit forms, such as by using the `Is Loaded` event (see discussion later in this chapter). After all, you don't want users to get an error message if they open a form from the Navigation pane. (In the database for this section, EditValueList.accdb, the form frmMayorUpdate includes a method to prevent the form from being opened from the Navigation pane.)*

This example uses a form called `frmContactMayor` with combo box `cboCity`, which uses a look-up table to capture the city for the contact, storing the data in the field named `City` in `tblContacts`. For this exercise, assume that the application needs to capture the mayor of every city. Basically, this means that if a user enters a new city, you want the application, through a form, to require him to enter the name of that city's mayor. To accomplish this, the example uses a table of mayors called `tblMayors` and a `frmMayorUpdate` form to update that table. You also want to think about creating an index on city/state and requiring that to have a unique value.

This example is provided in the chapter download file, EditValueList.accdb. To get the process started, you'll create (or modify) the combo box, `cboCity`, to have the key property values shown in the following table.

Property	Value
Control Source	City
Row Source	tblMayors
Row Source Type	Table/Query
Bound Column	2
Limit To List	Yes
Allow Value List Edits	Yes
List Items Edit Form	frmMayorUpdate
Column Count	2
Column Widths	0";2"

To ensure that the mayor's name is provided, the form should use one of the other techniques you've learned in this book. For instance, you could use the Form_BeforeUpdate event to see if the mayor's name field has a value. The example uses Form_Open to check for the value.

Additionally, set the frmMayorUpdate form Pop Up property to Yes, and set the Modal property to Yes, and set Cycle to Current Record (found on the Other tab of the property sheet). You do this so that the Form_Open code in the form frmMayorUpdate always executes. One reason for making this a modal form is to force the user to close the form before he can enter additional data in the form frmContactMayor (or before he can work with other objects, for that matter). If the user is allowed to leave frmMayorUpdate open while continuing to enter data on frmContactMayor, the next invalid entry in cboCity won't fire the Form_Open event in frmMayorUpdate.

At this point, you're about ready to put the following code in the Open event for frmMayorUpdate. First you establish a constant to be used for the "calling form." That makes this snippet more portable. Instead of replacing the name of the calling form throughout the code, you merely change the value for the constant, cFormUsage.

```
Const cFormUsage = "frmContactMayor"
Private Sub Form_Open(Cancel As Integer)
Dim strText As String
Dim rs As Recordset

' Don't let this form be opened from the Navigator
If Not CurrentProject.AllForms(cFormUsage).IsLoaded Then
    MsgBox "This form cannot be opened from the Navigation Pane.", _
        vbInformation + vbOKOnly, "Invalid form usage"
    Cancel = True
    Exit Sub
End If

strText = Forms(cFormUsage)!cboCity.Text
If strText = "" Then
    ' If the City is empty, the user may have opened the form from the navigator
```

```
            ' while the other form is opened (thus it passed the above test)
            MsgBox "This form is intended to add Cities for the '" & ↵
    Forms(cFormUsage).Caption & "' form.", _
                vbInformation + vbOKOnly, "Invalid form usage"
            Cancel = True
            Exit Sub
    End If


    ' If you use the following syntax to insert the new value,
    ' make sure that the user hasn't entered an apostrophe (') in his text.
    ' Of course there are many ways to add the record
    DoCmd.SetWarnings False
    DoCmd.RunSQL "INSERT INTO tblMayors (City) VALUES ('" & strText & "')"
    Me.Requery
    DoCmd.SetWarnings True


    ' Now point to the row just added and set the filter so the user can't scroll
    Set rs = Me.RecordsetClone
    rs.FindFirst "City = '" & strText & "'"
    If Not rs.EOF Then
        Me.Bookmark = rs.Bookmark
        Me.Filter = "[ID] = " & Me.ID
        Me.FilterOn = True
    End If


    Me.Mayor.SetFocus


    End Sub
```

After the user indicates that she wants to edit the items in the list, the process will open frmMayorUpdate because it is the form specified as the value for the List Items Edit Form. The Form_Open event looks at the cboCity field in frmContactMayor and stores the text of that field in strText. The code then inserts the City that doesn't have a value associated with the Mayor's name into tblMayors. With the record inserted, the code makes a copy of the recordset of the form, uses the FindFirst method to locate that record, and moves to it using the Bookmark property. Finally it sets the focus on the Mayor name field, so that it is easy for the user to enter the required data.

Of course, you could accomplish that with a lot less code, as shown in the following snippet:

```
    Private Sub Form_Open(Cancel As Integer)
    DoCmd.RunCommand acCmdRecordsGoToNew ' insert a new record
    Me.City = Forms("frmContactMayor")!cboCity.Text
    Me.txtMayor.SetFocus
    End Sub
```

This code simply goes to a new record on the form and copies the text from cboCity to the City field. An advantage of this method is that you can then define the Mayor name field in tblMayors as required and let Access determine if the data entered by the user is valid. Then you don't need the Form_BeforeUpdate check to make sure the user entered something in the Mayor name field.

Now that you've worked through this example, take a moment to think about related business rules. This scenario has some obvious issues that would have to be addressed, such as the potential to have multiple cities with the same name, the opportunity for people to use different spellings of the same city, and the need to be able to rename a city or mayor. But it does provide a fairly elegant process to allow users to add values.

If you prefer to write code (and most developers do), there is another way to allow the users to update the list of valid values available in a combo box. It provides the means for you to validate the value and saves you from having to create another form. It's the `Not In List` event, which you look at next.

Not In List()

The `Not In List` event is triggered when the `Limit To List` property is set to `Yes` and the user enters data that is not in the list. It occurs independently of the settings for `Allow Value List Edits` and `List Items Edit Form` properties, so you can use it to control how your application responds when invalid data is entered in a combo box.

Because combo boxes are usually based on a look-up table, the following example offers the user a chance to add a value that is not in the list. To provide a friendlier dialogue with the user, it also demonstrates how to create a custom message box such as the one shown in Figure 10-12. As you can see, the user tried to use "Entertainment" as the main category. Because it isn't in the list, he's asked if he'd like to add it.

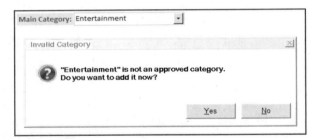

Figure 10-12

As a refresher, you can use the `Limit To List` property to control what happens when a user enters data into a control. If the value is set to No, it places no restrictions on what is entered. If the value is set to Yes, several things can be triggered, including the following:

- ❑ The user is limited to what is in the list.
- ❑ If other data is entered, users are asked to choose from the list.
- ❑ Entering other data can trigger the `NotInList` event.

Because combo boxes are typically based on a look-up table, the following example provides code to offer the user a chance to add a value that is not in the list. It also creates a custom message box.

```
Private Sub cboMainCategory_NotInList(NewData As String, Response As Integer)
On Error GoTo Error_Handler
Dim intAnswer as Integer
intAnswer = MsgBox("""" & NewData & """ is not an approved category. " & vbcrlf _
```

```
                & "Do you want to add it now?", _
                vbYesNo + vbQuestion, "Invalid Category")

    Select Case intAnswer
        Case vbYes
            DoCmd.SetWarnings False
            DoCmd.RunSQL "INSERT INTO tlkpCategoryNotInList (Category) " & _
                "Select """ & NewData & """;"
            DoCmd.SetWarnings True
            Response = acDataErrAdded
        Case vbNo
            Msgbox "Please select an item from the list.", _
                vbExclamation + vbOkOnly, "Invalid Entry"
            Response = acDataErrContinue
    End Select
    Exit_Procedure:
        DoCmd.SetWarnings True
        Exit Sub
    Error_Handler:
        MsgBox Err.Number & ", " & Err.Description
        Resume Exit_Procedure
        Resume
    End Sub
```

The NotInList event comes with two parameters:

❑ NewData As String: Holds the value that is not found in your list.

❑ Response As Integer: Provides three intrinsic constants:

   ❑ acDataErrContinue: Suppresses the standard error message.

   ❑ acDataErrAdded: Suppresses the standard error message, and refreshes the entries in
       the combo box.

   ❑ acDataErrDisplay: Displays the standard error message.

The NotInList event property is literally asking, "This value is not in your table, so what should I do?"
The example starts by telling Access to display a message box notifying the user that the name is not in
the list. You use the vbYesNo constant to provide buttons to get the user's answer and the vbQuestion
constant to display the Question icon in the message box.

The user can choose Yes or No. If Yes (vbYes) is selected, the code adds the new value using the INSERT
INTO SQL command that appends NewData to the specified lookup table. Because it is an append query,
the standard append query warnings are triggered. Docmd.SetWarnings False turns off these warnings, and later you use Docmd.SetWarnings True to turn them back on.

Next, you need to set the Response, one of the intrinsic constants for the message box. If the user has
responded Yes, acDataErrAdded automatically refreshes the combo box. If the user chooses No, Response
is set to equal acDataContinue, which allows the user to continue without adding the item to the list.
Either of those constants (responses) will suppress the default Access message. The point here is that by
creating custom messages boxes you proivde a more informative and professional user interface.

Field List

One of the values for `Row Source Type` that hasn't been mentioned yet is `Field List`. Setting the `Row Source Type` to `Field List` makes the values displayed in the combo box be the actual names of the fields (rather than the data contained in the field) found in the table or query specified in the row source. The `Field List` value is most commonly used when you're going to allow the user to select field names to build a custom filter. Of course, Access 2007 already provides some powerful new ways to filter a form, so they may be a better alternative.

But if your form has several fields, a drop-down field finder might help users quickly get to the fields that they are looking for. To create such a tool, first add an unbound combo box to a form. In the combo box properties, set the `Row Source Type` to `Field List`. Then, in `Row Source`, enter the table or query that is used for your form. In the `AfterUpdate` event of the combo box type the following code:

```
Private Sub cboSearchFields_AfterUpdate()
    Dim strFieldChoice as String
    strFieldChoice = Me.cboSearchFields.Value

    DoCmd.GotoControl strFieldChoice

End Sub
```

The user can select the field from the combo box and be taken straight to that field. This code assumes that the `Name` property of the controls on your form are the same as the names of the fields in your `Row Source`. However, that probably isn't the case because you've implemented good naming conventions so the controls have prefixes such as `txt`; in which case you'll have to interpret the names. The following `Select Case` statement is an example of how to do that:

```
Private Sub cboSearchFields_AfterUpdate()
    Dim strFieldChoice as String
    strFieldChoice = Me.cboSearchFields.Value

    Select Case strFieldChoice
        Case "CustomerFirstName"
            strFieldChoice = "txtCustomerFName"
        Case "CustomerLastName"
            strFieldChoice = "txtCustomerLName"
    End Select

    DoCmd.GotoControl strFieldChoice

End sub
```

The user will see the easy-to-interpret term `CustomerFirstName` but the code in the `Select Case` statement switches the value to equal the actual Name property of the control: `txtCustomerFName`.

Synchronizing Two Combo Boxes Using AfterUpdate()

It has become rather popular to synchronize combo boxes (often called cascading combo boxes). The value selected from the first combo box updates the second combo box so that it contains only records related to the item selected in the first combo box. In the following example (`ComboBox.accdb` in the chapter download), the row source of the first combo box (cboMainCategory) is set to tlkpCategory and the second combo box (cboSubCategory) needs the row source to display the values from tlkpSubCategory where the foreign key for each subcategory matches the values of the MainCategoryIDs. This is a common function when there is a one-to-many relationship between two tables. In other words, each main category can have many subcategories (as one sales rep has many customers) but only certain subcategories are valid for a given main category.

One way to synchronize the combo boxes is to add the following snippet of code to the AfterUpdate event of the first combo box (cboMainCategory):

```
Private Sub cboMainCategory_AfterUpdate()
' bind data to the second combo box based on the value selected
If IsNull(Me.cboMainCategory) Then
    Me.cboSubCategory.RowSource = ""
Else
    Me.cboSubCategory.RowSource = _
        "SELECT  SubCategoryID, SubCategoryName " _
        & "FROM tlkpSubCategory " _
        & "WHERE MainCategoryID = " & Me.cboMainCategory
End If
End Sub
```

While the row source of cboSubCategory is changed dynamically, the initial value of cboSubCategory can be set to equal nothing. This ensures that the user cannot select a value from the second combo box unless there is a value selected in the first combo box. If the user can scroll through records on the form, you'll also want to use this code in the form's On Current event to make sure that the row source of the second combo box is reset every time the record changes. For that, we used the following snippet:

```
Private Sub Form_Current()
' bind data to the second combo box based on the value selected
' leave second combo box empty if there is nothing in the first combo box
If IsNull(Me.cboMainCategory) Then
    Me.cboSubCategory.RowSource = ""
Else
    Me.cboSubCategory.RowSource = _
        "SELECT  SubCategoryID, SubCategoryName " _
        & "FROM tlkpSubCategory " _
        & "WHERE MainCategoryID = " & Me.cboMainCategory
End If
End Sub
```

Of course, there are a myriad other enhancements to add, such as having the drop-down lists display automatically. But for now, we're focused on the functionality of synchronizing combo boxes. Figure 10-13 shows the property configuration for the second combo box, cboSubCategory.

Although only the value of the subcategory is displayed, there are two fields listed in the Row Source. And if you open the Row Source query builder, you will see that all three fields of the table, tlkpSubCategory, are included in the query. You can understand why it is critical for the query to include the foreign key from tlkpCategory because that is the field that links the two combo boxes and provides the filter for the second combo box list. Comparing the SQL statement for the row source to the query behind it is a good way to learn what makes this work so that you can apply the principles elsewhere. You can also use this example to demonstrate that the value for the `Column Count` can be based on the Select statement in the Row Source (2 fields) or on the underlying query (3 fields). The critical part is to ensure that the bound columns and column widths match the field configuration.

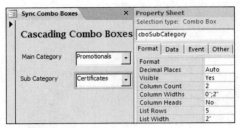 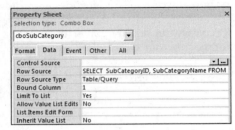

Figure 10-13

An alternative method for handling synchronized combo boxes is to code the row source of the second combo box to point to the value in the first combo box. If the name of the form with the combo boxes is `frmMain`, for example, instead of writing the preceding code, you could just make the `Row Source` of `cboSubCategory` the following:

```
Select SubCategoryID, SubCategoryName From tlkpSubCategories Where ↵
   MainCategoryID = Forms!frmMain!cboMainCategory
```

One of the easiest ways to create that type of `Select` statement is to use the Query Builder for the `Row Source`. After you have the correct properties, the trick is to make sure that the `cboSubCategory` field is refreshed with the new set of valid values. A simple `Me.cboSubCategory.Requery` statement will work. For this example, you would put that code in the `cboMainCategory_AfterUpdate` event and also in the `Form_Current` event.

The downside to this alternative method is that if you rename `frmMain`, you have to remember that you hard-coded the name in the `cboSubCategory` row source and that will have to be updated to use the form's new name.

Regardless of the method, you can use cascading combo boxes for a multitude of purposes. This example was simple, and it can easily be modified and incorporated into complex scenarios. Remember that you can add additional rows to the row source and use them to auto-fill text boxes or as links to other objects. You can also display additional fields in the combo box to assist users in selecting the correct record. Keep in mind that the `List Width` can be wider than the control width, so there is ample room to briefly display data.

Combo boxes are a great way to help speed up the data entry processes for your user. In Access 2007, `Allow Value List Edits` and `List Items Edit Form` enable you to eliminate some of the code that we used to capture data-entry errors. Of course, you can still use the `Not In List` event to trap user input and provide special handling. The combo box is definitely worth spending some time learning about so that you can leverage its versatility and benefits.

BeforeUpdate Event

The `BeforeUpdate` events can be used to validate user input, and as such, they are used most often on the form or record rather than the field. During data entry, users are typically allowed to fill in all the information for one record before they are prompted to resolve erroneous or missing. But that's not always the case, so we'll explain both approaches.

The choice between using the `Form_BeforeUpdate` event or the `field_BeforeUpdate` event is often based on the type of validation that's needed. In general, you use the `field_BeforeUpdate` event for required data or when the field value does not depend on other values that are entered on the form. The following code example shows a test for `FieldOne`, a required field.

```
Private Sub FieldOne_BeforeUpdate(Cancel as Integer)
If Trim(FieldOne.Value & "") = "" Then
    MsgBox "You must provide data for field 'FieldOne'.", _
        vbOKOnly, "Required Field"
    Cancel = True
End If

End Sub
```

The `Cancel = True` statement prevents the user from moving from `FieldOne` to another field until a value is entered in `FieldOne`. By concatenating the empty string to the value of `FieldOne`, and using the `Trim` string function, and then testing to see if the result is equal to the empty string, you take care of the situation in which Access returns a Null value when the user hasn't entered any data in the field as well as the situation where the user may have simply pressed the spacebar.

You'll want to use the `Form_BeforeUpdate` event if your form is structured in such a manner that valid values for one field depend on the value entered in another field. The following code snippet shows a case where the value in `FieldTwo` is required only when a value is entered in `FieldOne`. You'll recognize that this code does not address any aspects of preventing input unless a criterion is met. That is a different business rule — one that is often handled by enabling and disabling controls.

```
Private Sub Form_BeforeUpdate(Cancel As Integer)
If (IsNull(Me.FieldOne)) Or (Me.FieldOne.Value =  "") Then
    ' No action required
Else
    If (IsNull(Me.FieldTwo)) or (Me.FieldTwo.Value = "") Then
        MsgBox "You must provide data for field 'FieldTwo', " & _
            "if a value is entered in FieldOne", _
            vbOKOnly, "Required Field"
        Me.FieldTwo.SetFocus
        Cancel = True
        Exit Sub
    End If
End If

End Sub
```

Because the user may have been on a field other than `FieldTwo` when she attempted to leave or save the record, `SetFocus` is used to move the cursor to the field that has the error. The `Cancel = True` statement prevents the record from being saved. Otherwise, the user may get multiple error messages and be able to address only the last message displayed. The `Exit Sub` statement isn't essential, but it's a good coding technique to include the `Exit Sub` statement at any point where you are reporting an error. And, in many cases, you may come back to this code to add another validation check.

So, your choice of `Form_BeforeUpdate` versus `field_BeforeUpdate` depends on the type of validation performed. Use the `field_BeforeUpdate` when you want to give the user immediate feedback about invalid data. Use the `Form_BeforeUpdate` when you have to perform cross-field validation checks.

The next example uses the `On Click` event of a command button. First you need a simple form for data entry. On the Property Sheet, set the form's properties as shown in the following table.

Property	Value
Allow Data-Entry	Yes
Allow Edits	No
Allow Deletions	No

Make sure that the command button is the last control in the tab order, just before navigating to the next new record. Now add the following snippet of code to the command button's `On Click` event:

```
Private Sub cmdCloseForm_Click()

Dim intAnswer As Integer
intAnswer = MsgBox("Do you want to save this record?", _
    vbYesNo + vbQuestion, "Save or Cancel"

Select Case intAnswer
    Case vbYes ' run through the validation
        If (IsNull(Me.FieldOne)) or (Me.FieldOne.Value = "") Then
            MsgBox "You must provide data for field "FieldOne".", _
                vbOKOnly, "Required Field"
            ' direct user to empty field and exit sub
            Me.FieldOne.SetFocus
            Exit Sub
        End If

        If (IsNull(Me.FieldTwo.Value)) or (Me.FieldTwo.Value = "") Then
            MsgBox "You must provide data for field 'FieldTwo'.", _
                vbOKOnly, "Required Field"
            Me.FieldTwo.SetFocus
            Exit Sub
        End If

    Case vbNo ' give user a way out.
            Me.Undo
End Select

DoCmd.Close acForm, Me.Name

End sub
```

This is similar to the `Form_BeforeUpdate` example. In this case, when the `Close` button is clicked, the user is asked if he wants to save the record. If he selects Yes, the code runs through the steps in the `Select Case` process and stops the form's `Close` operation only if a field is empty. In that case, the focus is set to the field in error and the code exits the procedure (`Exit Sub`). If the user selects No, the changes to the record are undone using `Me.Undo` so that no changes are saved. If the process makes it successfully through the `Select Case` checks or if the changes are undone, the form closes as expected. Keep in mind that if a method other than this `Close` button is used to close the form, this validation process will not occur. Of course, you could institute processes to cover contingencies.

One more point about testing for data in the field: The examples use `IsNull` and a test for the empty string and trimming and concatenating the empty string. Because Access trims spaces off of data entered on the form, you're not required to test for a single space entered in a field. The code used in the `field_BeforeUpdate` example is just a technique used to simplify validations as well as ensure that Access behaves the way you expect it to.

Saving E-mail Addresses Using Textbox AfterUpdate Event

Access 2007 is smarter about the way it stores website and e-mail addresses. Data in a hyperlink field is automatically evaluated and tagged. The value is tagged with `http` for websites or `mailto` for e-mail addresses.

In previous versions, the Hyperlink data type stored e-mail addresses as Web addresses (`http://customeremail@msn.com`, for example), so when you clicked the link, it opened Internet Explorer and tried to find the website — not at all helpful. (One way to fix this is to right-click the link, select Edit Hyperlink, and change `http` to `mailto` by selecting e-mail Address in the dialog box. Be sure to copy the e-mail address first because you have to add it again.)

However, you want the user to add an e-mail address and have it correctly stored so that he can later click the link and open a new email message. The following code ensures that the initial input is stored in the correct format. You can try it with a simple form to add customers and e-mail addresses; add this code to the `AfterUpdate` event of the `EmailAddress` field, `txtEmailAddress`.

```
Private Sub txtEmailAddress_AfterUpdate()

If Not IsNull(Me.EmailAddress) Then
    Me.EmailAddress = Replace(Me.EmailAddress, "http://", "mailto:")
End if

End Sub
```

The first line checks to see if there is an e-mail address. If data is in the e-mail address field, it uses the `Replace` function to replace `http` with `mailto`. The code makes this change on-the-fly without the user even knowing.

This works great for sending e-mail to only one person. What if you need to send one e-mail to many people? Assume there is a Contacts table and that e-mail addresses are stored in a field with a Text data type rather than as a hyperlink. On your form, you can add a list box named `lstContacts`, as shown in Figure 10-14.

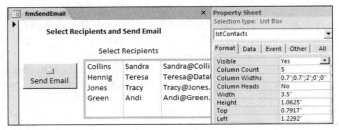

Figure 10-14

The list box `RowSource` would equal `tblContacts`, so the column count and column width need to be set to display the first name, last name, and e-mail address for each record. You'll need to set the list box property named `Multi Select` (on the Property Sheet's Other tab), which has three options:

- ❏ `None`: Select one item at a time from the list.

- ❏ `Simple`: Select blocks of items from the list by selecting one item and then holding down the Shift key while highlighting the other items.

- ❏ `Extended`: Select multiple items by holding down the Ctrl key and then randomly selecting items.

For this example, use `Extended`.

Next, you need a command button named `cmdSendEMail`. Add the following code to its `On Click` event.

```
Private Sub cmdSendEMail_Click()

Dim emName As String, varItem As Variant
Dim emailSubject as String
Dim emailBody as String

emailSubject = "Confirmation Email"
'note the carriage return line feeds to insert a blank line between
'the greeting and the message body. Also, there is no need for the
' & at the beginning of the second and third lines because we used a
' comma after the greeting - just before the close quote on the first line.

emailBody = "Dear Customer, " & vbCrLf & vbCrLf & _
    "We are sending this email to let you know that your request has been " & _
    "confirmed. Please allow 2-3 weeks for shipping."

On Error GoTo cmdSendEMail_Click_error

'if there are no selected items (Contacts) in the list, exit
If Me!lstContacts.ItemsSelected.Count = 0 Then
Exit Sub

For Each varItem In Me!lstContacts.ItemsSelected
    'char(34) adds quotes to Me!lstContacts.
    'Then add a comma to separate the selected items
```

```
        emName = emName & Chr(34) & Me!lstContacts.Column(4, varItem) & Chr(34) & ","
    Next varItem


    'remove the extra comma at the end
    emName = Left$( emName, Len(emName) - 1)


    'send the message
    DoCmd.SendObject acSendNoObject, , , emName, , , emailSubject, emailBody, _
        True, False


    cmdSendEMail_Click_error:
        If Err.Number = 2501 Then
            MsgBox "You just cancelled the Email. You'll have to start over.", _
                vbCritical, "Alert!"
        ElseIf Err.Number > 0 then
            Msgbox "Error sending email." & vbCrlf & Err.Description, _
                vbCritical, "Send Error"
        End If


End Sub
```

This code starts by declaring the e-mail name (emName), subject of the e-mail (emailSubject), and the e-mail body (emailBody) as String, and a variable to use the items in the list as Variant (varItem). Next, it initializes the subject and body variables with string text. The first If statement checks the count of the number of selected items in the list, and if the count is zero, exits the routine.

The For Each loop processes each of the items the user has selected. Because Multi Select is set to Extended, the user can use the Ctrl or Shift keys with the mouse click to select items in sequence or randomly.

With tblContacts as the list box's Row Source, each field defined in tblContacts becomes a column in the list box. You can use the Column property to access the value of each column in the list box. (This applies to multicolumn combo boxes as well.)

> As with most arrays in VBA, the index for the Column property starts at zero; thus the first field in tblContacts is the 0 column in the list box. In this example, the e-mail address is the fifth field defined in tblContacts, so in code this would be referred to as .Column(4).

When building emName, a comma separator is added for each selected item in the list box. That leaves you with an extra comma that you have to strip off after all of the e-mail addresses have been collected.

With all the items collected, use DoCmd.SendObject with the following arguments to create the e-mail:

```
DoCmd.SendObject acSendNoObject, , , emName, , , emailSubject, emailBody, _
    True, False
```

Selecting acSendNoObject means that the e-mail will not have an attachment because there is no object (form/report) to send. After that, the commas are the place markers for the following nine arguments:

```
[ObjectName], [OutputFormat], [To], [Cc], [Bcc], [Subject], [Message], _
[EditMessage], [TemplateFile]
```

As in the example, [ObjectName] and [OutputFormat] can be left blank; [To] will be emName (the selected items from the list box); [Cc] and [Bcc] can be left blank; [Subject] will be the emailSubject variable; [Message] will be emailBody; [EditMessage] is True just in case you need to edit the message; and [TemplateFile] is False.

Your users now have the option to send an e-mail to one contact or many contacts by simply selecting the recipient(s) from the list box. Figure 10-15 shows an e-mail created by this example.

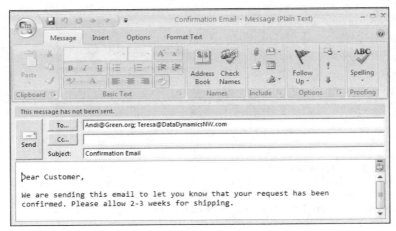

Figure 10-15

You'll recall that this example uses an e-mail address from a text field. That is an important distinction because if you use it with a hyperlink field type, the address line will look something like the following:

```
TO: Teresa@DataDynamicsNW.com#mailto:Teresa@DataDynamicsNW.com#
```

Most mail clients interpret this as one long string, and won't treat it as a valid e-mail address.

Output to PDF

A common challenge for Access developers has been to have a way to send data or output to a PDF file format. Sure, you could do it, but it wasn't easy. Previous versions required the developer to obtain some third-party software (CutePDF, for example) and then to build creative workarounds.

Now Access 2007 has streamlined the process by providing the bridge between Access and PDF utilities, particularly if you download Microsoft's free Add-in "Microsoft Save as PDF or XPS." Instead of working with complicated code, you'll have a Save As PDF button on the Ribbon. Along with PDF, you probably discerned that this add-in also offers the option to save in XML Paper Specification (XPS) file format. To take advantage of this, you'll need to download and install the file SaveAsPDFandXPS.exe. A link to the web is provided in the Access Help files. You can find it by typing **XPS** or **PDF** in the Search text box or by going to Microsoft.com and searching for SaveAsPDFandXPS.exe.

People will still need a PDF viewer to open PDF files. But viewers are commonly available as free downloads, such as the Adobe Reader. Windows Vista is required to view XPS files, but here again, a viewer may become available.

To work with PDF and XPS file formats programmatically, Access has two new constants. They are named in the following table.

File Type	Constant
PDF	acFormatPDF
XPS	acFormatXPS

To see all of the constants, open the Object Browser and search for acFormat.

Both DoCmd.SendObject and DoCmd.OutputTo use these constants in their arguments to define the format. The following code snippets show three different ways to use the PDF file format. There are minor differences in the functionality. For example, you'll notice that using OutputTo allows you to specify the export quality.

```
DoCmd.SendObject acSendReport, "MyFormName", acFormatPDF, [To], [Cc], [Bcc], _
    [Subject], [MessageText]

Docmd.OutputTo acOutputReport, _
    "MyReportName", acFormatPDF, , False, , , acExportQualityScreen

Docmd.OutputTo acOutputReport, _
    "MyReportName", acFormatPDF, , False, , , acExportQualityPrint
```

OpenArgs

What if you want to check for conditions or set certain properties when a form is opening? You can use the OpenArgs property of the form to pass parameters to the form when you open it. The OpenForm method's seventh (last) parameter supplies the value for OpenArgs, as shown in the following statement:

```
DoCmd.OpenForm "FormName", , , , , , "OpenArgs value"
```

In this case, the value of the OpenArgs property would be "OpenArgs value".

Because the Open event triggers whenever a form opens, you can include the OpenArgs parameter on the OpenForm method to provide information that can be used even before the user sees the form.

An excellent application of this is to ensure that the form is opened by code and only under specific conditions. For example, you may have a form that should be opened only by certain users. Because users can open the form from the Navigation pane, it's possible for any user to open a form — unless you have implemented programmatic restriction. One approach is to use the following code in the form's OnOpen event to prevent it from being opened from the Navigation pane.

```
Private Sub Form_Open(Cancel As Integer)

If Me.OpenArgs() <> "Valid User" Then
    MsgBox "You are not authorized to use this form!", _
        vbExclamation + vbOKOnly, "Invalid Access"
    Cancel = True
End If
End Sub
```

If a user opens this form from the Navigation pane, she will see the message, You are not authorized to use this form! The Cancel = True statement prevents the form from opening.

For a user to gain access to this form you must have code in your application that, after the user has been approved, allows the form to open. For example, a form named frmRestricted would need your code to execute the following statement (be sure to specify other parameters as appropriate):

```
DoCmd.OpenForm "frmRestricted", , , , , "Valid User"
```

Another time to use OpenArgs might be when you automatically populate information in the form you're opening. Suppose you have a combo box that requires the user to select a valid value. If the user enters an undefined value, you may want to pop up a form to collect information about the value just entered — you might want to pass the text that the user entered to the form that you're opening so it is populated in the appropriate field on the pop-up form. Clearly you can utilize the OpenArgs property for a variety of purposes.

> *You may prefer the new* List Items Edit Form *property, discussed earlier in the chapter, over writing your own code to pop up a form to collect a new value for the combo box.*

Be aware that once the form is opened, the value of OpenArgs does not change on subsequent executions of the OpenForm method. For that reason, you may want to check to see if the form is open before you execute OpenForm. The form's IsLoaded property can tell you if a form is loaded.

IsLoaded()

There are numerous situations in which you might want to know if a form is open, or loaded. The following scenario will help illustrate when and why to use the IsLoaded property. In this situation, a user may have several forms open, including frmEvent, which lists the names of everyone scheduled to participate in an event. Say that one of the participants cancels, so the user opens a participant form and clicks a command button (cmdCancel) to remove that participant from the event. Because the event form is already open, the data that it displays cannot be updated without some action being taken. One approach is to include code behind cmdCancel on the participant form to see if the event schedule form is open by using the event IsLoaded. If the form, frmEvent, is not open, the regular cancellation process continues. If frmEvent is open, the appropriate actions — such as closing the event schedule form or requerying the event form after canceling the appointment — should also be included in the code behind cmdCancel. The snippet below is an example of code that could be used in this scenario.

```
        If frmEvent.IsLoaded Then
            frmEvent.Requery    ... 'add additional actions
        End If
```

Consider another example: Perhaps you want users to be able to open a form in a specific way, such as only from a specified form, and definitely not from the Navigation pane. In that case, you may also first want to determine if the form is already open. The following example uses the `IsLoaded` property to see if a particular form is open before it continues code execution. In the code, `CurrentProject` refers to the open database and for illustration purposes, `frmEvent` is used again:

```
    Private Sub cmdCancel_Click()
        If Not CurrentProject.AllForms("frmEvent").IsLoaded Then

            Msgbox "Cannot cancel while 'frmEvent' form is open.", _
                vbInformation + VBOkOnly, "Cancel Invalid"
            Exit Sub

        End If
    End Sub
```

As you can see, the `IsLoaded` property is a convenient and useful way to determine if a form is open.

On Timer ()

The `On Timer` event property can identify a process that can be triggered at timed intervals. It is used in conjunction with the `TimerInterval` property, which stipulates the frequency of the event. When specifying the value for the `TimerInterval` property, the time is entered in milliseconds (1/1000 of a second), so entering 5000 will trigger the event at 5-second intervals.

You may be wondering when you might use a timer. How about to close an application's splash screen (a form that displays for a few seconds as the application opens and then is automatically closed) or to close a message that you only want to display for a few seconds? For instance, you could display your company logo and contact number during the few seconds that it takes for an application. Of course, you don't want to leave the splash screen open for too long — four seconds seems like a reasonable time. Let's assume that the application has an AutoExec macro that runs when the database opens and that one of the actions includes a macro to open the splash screen.

To set the timer for any form, open the form's Property Sheet to the Event tab. Scroll down to `Timer Interval`. The property default is 0; for our example, we would change it to 4000, the equivalent of 4 seconds. Then in the `OnTimer` property, select `Event Procedure` and open the IDE to add the following code.

```
    Private Sub Form_Timer()

        DoCmd.Close acForm, Me.Name

    End Sub
```

When the splash screen (our form) opens, the Timer Interval starts counting down. When the timer reaches the specified interval time, 4 seconds, the code runs. In this event, `DoCmd.Close` will close the splash screen. This scenario has worked well in the past, but it can cause problems if the database is opened in disabled mode by Access 2007. If the VBA is disabled, the timer event code never runs and the splash screen is not closed. To avoid risking that situation, you can close a splash screen by using a macro for the OnTimer event. (One of the reasons that I'm mentioning this is because you may work with MDB files that use VBA to close a splash screen. If so, you need to either replace the code or ensure that the databases are opened fully enabled, from a trusted location and/or are digitally signed.)

To create the macro to close the splash screen, set the OnTimer property to a macro by clicking the ellipsis and selecting the Macro Builder. In the Action column, select Close; the lower pane displays the Action Arguments. For the Object Type, select Form; from the Object Name list, select the form that is used as the splash screen; and for Save, select No. From the Close group on the menu bar, select Save As, on the first line enter a name for the macro, and then click OK.

Another example of using the OnTimer event is in a multi-user environment where the users are recording meetings and setting scheduled times for the clients of the Sales staff. Obviously, it is crucial to know when sales people are available and to not book them twice for the same time period. Because several people have the potential to be booking appointments at the same time, the form that displays and records the appointments needs to be requeried constantly. For this situation, the form's Timer Interval is set to 6 seconds (6000) and the form's Timer event contains the following code:

```
Private Sub Form_Timer()

Me.Requery

End Sub
```

That allows the form to update on its own rather than requiring the user to click an update button. Because you need to get additions and deletions, the form uses Requery instead of Refresh, which would retrieve only changes to existing records. As shown in Figure 10-16, the main form consistently displays the appointment time blocks, and the subform uses a continuous form to show the number of available openings for each wave for every scheduled date. The timer event runs a query to refresh the data for the subform. When an appointment is booked, the number for the respective date and wave is decreased. And, thanks to the Timer event, the display will be updated for any user that has the schedule form open. And, to see the details for any day, they merely double-click the record selector to open the appointment schedule to review or change an appointment.

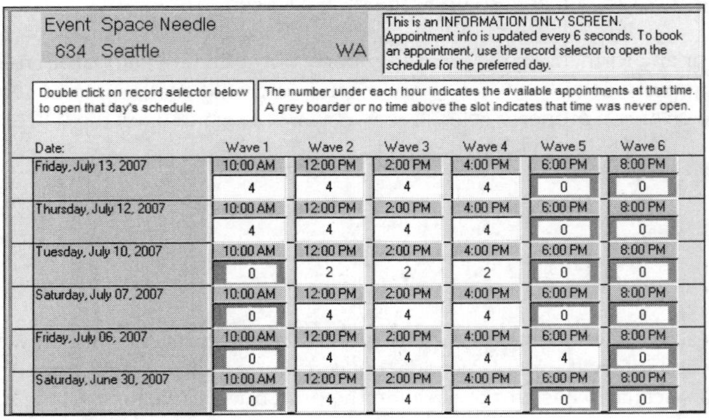

Date:	Wave 1	Wave 2	Wave 3	Wave 4	Wave 5	Wave 6
Friday, July 13, 2007	10:00 AM	12:00 PM	2:00 PM	4:00 PM	6:00 PM	8:00 PM
	4	4	4	4	0	0
Thursday, July 12, 2007	10:00 AM	12:00 PM	2:00 PM	4:00 PM	6:00 PM	8:00 PM
	4	4	4	4	0	0
Tuesday, July 10, 2007	10:00 AM	12:00 PM	2:00 PM	4:00 PM	6:00 PM	8:00 PM
	0	2	2	2	0	0
Saturday, July 07, 2007	10:00 AM	12:00 PM	2:00 PM	4:00 PM	6:00 PM	8:00 PM
	0	4	4	4	0	0
Friday, July 06, 2007	10:00 AM	12:00 PM	2:00 PM	4:00 PM	6:00 PM	8:00 PM
	0	4	4	4	4	0
Saturday, June 30, 2007	10:00 AM	12:00 PM	2:00 PM	4:00 PM	6:00 PM	8:00 PM
	0	4	4	4	0	0

Figure 10-16

Keep in mind that the timer event can create a significant performance hit. And, if users are manually entering data, there are likely better alternatives — 2 seconds wouldn't be adequate for data entry. However, in situations where you are merely displaying information, such as the number of appointments or openings in a time slot, then a short timer interval can be an effective mechanism to udpate data in open forms.

Late Binding

Another timing issue that can have significant impact on performance is whether the form is using early or late binding. Basically, this refers to when the record (or recordset) is created for a form or other object. Late binding typically involves filtering, which reduces the size of the recordset and also allows the developer greater control of the record source.

When you add fields to your form, the text boxes that are created become bound text boxes. That is, the table or query fields are bound to those text boxes and when the form opens, the data from your table or query binds to the controls on your form to display data. If the form has only a few controls or is a lightweight form, you might not notice a performance hit when the form loads. But loading all the possible records behind a complex form that has numerous controls, combo boxes, subforms, and complicated criteria can create a drastic slowdown.

One option is to load the controls on demand or after receiving criteria to filter the data rather than when the form opens. The following code snippet uses the `Form_Open` event to set the `RowSource` and `SourceObjects` of a combo box, list box, and subform to an empty string (`""`). Obviously, if the intent is for these to be unbound objects, it is better to save the form without record sources for those controls. But a form may inadvertently have been saved with values stored for the controls, so the following example demonstrates how to remove the values. Speaking of saving the form, a technique commonly used with subforms is to save the `SourceObject` as an empty string to prevent the subform from attempting to acquire data as the form opens.

```
Private Sub Form_Open()
Me.cboMyComboBox.RowSource = ""
'Or
Me.lstMyListbox.RowSource = ""
'Or
Me.fsubMySubform.SourceObject = ""
End sub
```

After the form opens, you will need a way to fill the `RowSource`. Common techniques are to initiate the process from a command button or by selecting a value from a combo box or list box.

Another method is to use the Option Group control to load data to other controls. The Option Group contains controls that include radio buttons, check boxes, and toggle buttons. Each radio button, check box, or toggle button (depending on the type of Option Box controls you chose) can be assigned a value that is set whenever that control is selected. That numeric value can be used in a `Select Case` statement to populate the list box or subform.

In the next example, you'll populate the list box with a list of forms and reports in your database by selecting a numeric value from the Option Group. You can use the lists for several purposes, even as the basis for a switchboard (menu form), as shown in Figure 10-17. To get started, you need a table to hold the names of the forms and reports that are in the database. Some developers use the hidden system tables that store the object names. Although that's functional, it isn't pretty because they return the actual object names, which the user might not recognize. It is much better to provide the user with concise yet descriptive names rather than have them decipher terms that starts with tags such as frm or rpt.

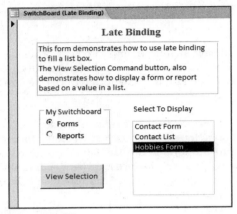

Figure 10-17

So, create table tblMyObjects with the following fields:

- ❑ userObjectName: The name of the form or report that the user will see.

- ❑ devObjectName: The actual name of the form or report.

- ❑ devObjectCode: The code number (created by you) assigned to that object. For this example, 1 = forms and 2 = reports.

Your table should resemble the one used in the query shown in Figure 10-17. Then, you'll need to populate the table with data. (That will be a manual process, unless you just want to follow along using the LateBinding.accdb file that's included with the download for this chapter.)

Next, create two queries using all of the fields in tblMyObjects. Name the first query qryFormName, where devObjectCode = 1, and name the other query qryReportName, where devObjectCode = 2. Based on those criteria, qryFormName will retrieve all the forms and qryReportName will retrieve all the reports. Sicne the first row contains the ID field, you need to clear the Show check box so that userObjectName to be the first visible field. To display the names alphabetically, set Sort order for this field to be Ascending. Each query has the same four fields; the critical differences are the name of the query and the criteria. Because these queries are the foundation for several more steps, it might be prudent to confirm that your query looks similar to the example in Figure 10-18.

You'll use these queries to populate a list box to display forms and reports that a user might want to use. Although the queries use all four fields, only the userObjectName field will be displayed. The devObjectCode is used for selecting the items and the devObjectName can be used to programmatically open the object. You'll start the process by creating an unbound form named frmSwitchboard with an option group and a list box. (Figure 10-17, above, showed the switchboard form with the Option Group named `grpSwitchboard` labeled My Switchboard and the list box displaying user-friendly names of selected forms.)

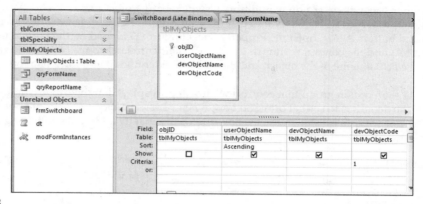

Figure 10-18

Begin by adding an option group to the form. The Option Group Wizard prompts for label names. On the first line type **Forms** and on the second line type **Reports**. Next, select Forms as the default option. You then can assign values that match the criteria from the queries that you created: `Forms` is assigned the value of 1 and `Reports` a value of 2. You'll use these values to write code for the Option Group's `AfterUpdate` event. You can create additional buttons for other types of actions, or create custom groups of forms and reports, such as by department. The final question from the wizard is what to name the caption for the group. Call it My Switchboard.

Now, open the control's Property Sheet and change the name from `frame0` to `grpSwitchboard`. You need to add code to the `AfterUpdate` event, but first create an unbound list box that the code will populate. So, add a list box to the form but close the wizard without answering any questions. That creates an unbound list box. Use the Property Sheet to rename this `lstItems` and to add the following code to the `grpSwitchboard` `AfterUdpate` event.

```
Private Sub grpSwitchboard_AfterUpdate()
Dim strRST as String        'RowSourceType
strRST = "Table/Query"
Me.lstItems.RowSourceType = strRST

Select Case Me.grpSwitchboard.Value
    Case 1
        Me.lstItems.RowSource = "qryFormName"
    Case 2
        Me.lstItems.RowSource = "qryReportName"

End Select

End Sub
```

This code sets the row source type to Table/Query for the list box lstItems, which enables you to use queries to populate the display. If grpSwitchboard has value 1 selected, the results from qryFormName are shown. If the value 2 is selected, the data from qryReportName is displayed. If additional objects or options are added, they need similar code. This is great for viewing a list of forms or reports, but it lacks the capability to open them as you would from a switchboard. Before that can work, you'll need to set some column properties on the list box so that the values from the query (row source) are available to the command button. Again, open the Property Sheet for lstItems and on the Format tab, set the column count to 3 and the column widths to 1";0";0". This correlates to the columns for the name the user sees, the actual name of the object, and the code that identifies it as a form or a report.

Now, you have an option group that controls what will be displayed in the list box, and you've also stipulated that the default is to select Forms. So now, when frmSwitchboard opens, it appears that Forms are selected, but nothing is listed in the list box. You rectify that by adding the following code to the form's Open event.

```
Private Sub Form_Open(Cancel As Integer)
 'When the form opens, load the list box with information
 'based on the default option group selection.
Call grpSwitchboard_AfterUpdate
End Sub
```

And finally, you add functionality to open a form or report by creating a command button that will open whichever object is selected. Add the command button to the form and close the wizard without answering any questions (because this will open both forms and reports, you'll write your own code). Use the Property Sheet to rename it cmdOpenObject. For the On Click event of cmdOpenObject, add the following code:

```
Private Sub cmdOpenObject_Click()
Dim varCode as Variant
Dim varObjName as Variant

' Make sure that an item is selected before attempting to display it.
If Me.lstItems.ItemsSelected.Count = 0 Then
    MsgBox "Please select items to display.", vbInformation + vbOKOnly, _
        "List Items Required."
    Exit Sub
End If

varCode = Me.lstItems.Column(2)
varObjName = Me.lstItems.Column(1)

Select Case varCode
    Case 1 'open the form
        DoCmd.OpenForm varObjName
    Case 2 'open the report in preview mode
        DoCmd.OpenReport varObjName, acPreview
End Select

End Sub
```

The process is predicated on an item being selected from the list, so this code starts with the IF statement and message box. Once the item is selected, you can extract the data necessary to display a form or report. To do that, start by declaring two variables — one for the devObjectCode (varCode) field and one for the devObjectName (varObjName) field (the actual name of the object). Once those variables are set, you evaluate varCode with a Select Case statement and use DoCmd to open a form or report using the name from the varObjName variable. You would also want to include additional error trapping, such as for reports with no data. Figure 10-19 shows the form in Design view with the lstItems Property Sheet open. (This chapter's download code includes this example, LateBinding.accdb.)

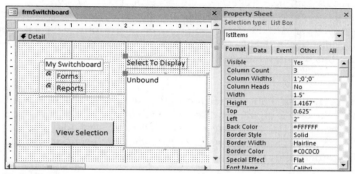

Figure 10-19

On Click(): Open a Form Based on a Value on the Current Form

Opening a form based on a value stored on another form is a common practice. The functionality applies to a myriad of tasks, from listing all of the orders for one customer to gaining a bigger picture by comparing the total purchases of one customer to other customers in the region. It also works well for drilling into details, such as searching a contact list and then clicking a record to see the detail information about that person.

For this example, you drill into data to get information about the orders of one customer. You'll use two forms, frmCustomer and frmOrder, which display information about customers and orders respectively. You may want to use the Northwind database to work through this exercise. For now, just say that you already have the two forms, so you just need a way to integrate their operations. All it takes is a command button (cmdShowOrders) on frmCustomer and some VBA code.

The pieces that have to be tied together are the field names that correspond between frmCustomer and frmOrder. Typically, the table for each of these entities contains the field called CustomerID with an AutoNumber data type. You also need the name of the control that is bound to the CustomerID field on frmCustomer; in this case, that's called txtCustomerID. On frmCustomer, add a command button. Close the command button wizard when it opens and use the Property Sheet to name the button cmdShowOrders. For the On Click event, include the following code snippet:

```
Private Sub cmdShowOrders_Click()
If Not Me.NewRecord Then
    DoCmd.OpenForm "frmOrder", _
```

```
            WhereCondition:="CustomerID=" & Me.txtCustomerID
    End If
    End Sub
```

If the tables do not follow good naming conventions, you may need to include brackets around the field names. Such is the case with the Northwind database, where the space in the field name requires brackets, so the line would look like to the following:

```
    DoCmd.OpenForm "frmOrder",_
        WhereCondition:="[Customer ID]=" & Me.txtCustomerID
```

Using this process, you can add that code configuration to any form to have it open another form to the related record(s). Again, the critical factor is the dependency or relationship between the record sources. You will recognize this type of relationship on the subform Property Sheet, using the Link Child Fields and Link Master Fields.

The line If Not Me.NewRecord Then references the NewRecord property, which is a Boolean value. It signifies whether the user is on the New Record of the form. NewRecord is more than just a new record — it is the form's property, because in Access, all records are added on the New Record. You check the NewRecord property because when a customer is just being entered there obviously should not be any existing orders; thus there is no need to open the Orders form.

The OpenForm method opens the form called frmOrder and issues a Where clause to specify which records to display in the form. That clause is often called a filter or a query because it limits the form's record source to only those records that meet the criteria. In this example, the criteria restrict the data to those with customer IDs that match the value in the text box called txtCustomerID. For clarification, the field name on the left of the equal symbol (=) refers to the field on the opened object. The field name on the right refers to a field on the calling object. In plain English this says to open the Order form to show the orders for the current customer on the Customer form.

Suppose that each order has one invoice printed for it. When you are viewing the Order record, you can print the invoice for the order. The code is nearly identical, except that a Report is being opened in Print Preview:

```
    Private Sub cmdShowInvoice_Click()
    If Not Me.NewRecord Then
        DoCmd.OpenReport "rptInvoice", WhereCondition:="OrderID=" & Me.txtOrderID
    End If
    End Sub
```

Another way to open a form to a specific record is to use the approach *query by form*; that is, to use a query as the record source of the form that is being opened. *Query by form* is a common method by which the criteria for any particular field in your query is set to a control on the main form. It's done by adding criteria to the query using the syntax Forms!frmName!FieldName. The first part of that expression stipulates the Forms collection, the second specifies which object to use (a form, in this case), and the last part is the control name that will have the criteria. Now you see how important it is to follow naming conventions — if you don't rename text boxes, they will likely have the same name as the field that is in the record source.

Figure 10-20 shows the portion of the query grid with the criteria used to filter the records as you did previously with the command button cmdShowOrders. The query is saved as qryCustomerOrders. You could use it as the record source of the form `frmOrder` and it would open to display the orders for the customer selected on the form `frmCustomer`.

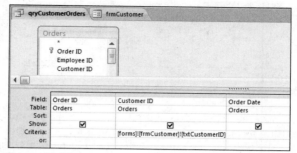

Figure 10-20

The following code shows two ways to use queries to filter data (with one table) using one form.

```
Docmd.OpenForm "frmOrder", "qryCustomerOrders", , acFormPropertySettings,
acWindowNormal
```

or

```
' use the FilterName instead of WhereCondition
Docmd.OpenForm "frmOrder", FilterName:= "qryCustomerOrders"
```

The first line of code leaves the record source for `frmOrder` set to `tblOrders` (set in the form properties). It then uses the saved query named `qryCustomerOrders` as the `WhereCondition`. `qryCustomerOrders` is based on `tblOrders`, and includes all of the fields. In `qryCustomerOrders`, the `CustomerID` field needs the criteria `Forms!frmCustomer!txtCustomerID`. That field is the critical link between the customer and the order.

The second example uses the `Docmd.OpenForm` string but instead of using the `WhereCondition` argument, it uses the `FilterName` argument. Using a query (`qryCustomerOrders`) for the `FilterName` actually overrides a form's record source (in this case `tblOrders`).

Multiple Form Instances

There are situations in which the user needs to compare two or more records from the same table. For example, you may need to compare Order 1 to Order 2 or Supplier1 to Supplier 2 or Supplier1 to Supplier2 and to Supplier3. This can be accomplished by opening the same form multiple times.

Let's say a database consultant is creating an Access solution for a client. The consultant is in a bind and needs to subcontract parts of the project to one of her fellow developers. She checks her database to view her contact list. She opens the contact list form (`frmContactList`, Figure 10-21) and selects two of the records (or contacts) from her list so that she can compare their specialties to find the best match for both the client and project.

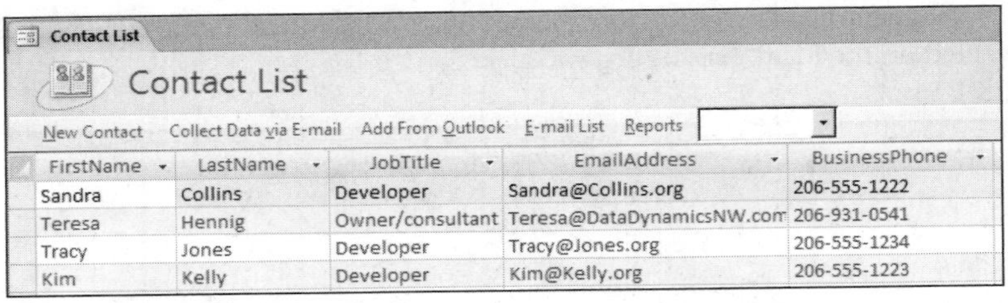

Figure 10-21

The form that's used to view the details is named `frmContactDetails` and it is opened twice so that the consultant can do a side-by-side comparison of the candidate's strengths as relayed by the Notes field (see Figure 10-22). (The figure looks a bit crowded, but most screens display two complete records.)

Figure 10-22

Opening the same form multiple times is referred to as *multiple instances* because every time the same form is opened, Access has to create or instantiate a new instance of the form. The default process is to allow one instance of a form and merely change the record source, so it requires a little code and some preplanning to show multiple instances of the same form.

For this example, use the file `TContacts.accdb` (in the download for this chapter). The exercise starts with a split form, but you can achieve the same functionality using a regular form. The critical part is to have two forms, one for your list and the other to open multiple times to show and compare details. This example also demonstrates using a drill-through procedure to open the details form. Again, this works equally well for opening forms or reports.

The code can be used wherever you require this type of functionality. First you create a new module and a global variable to hold the form objects in a collection:

```
Option Compare Database
Option Explicit

Private mcolFormInstances As New Collection
```

In the collection name, mcolFormInstances, m is for module level and col represents collection.

The collection will hold the forms as they are created. Next, you create a function that allows the user to open the same form multiple times:

```
Function OpenFormInstance(FormName As String, Optional WhereCondition As String)
'Declare the form name
Dim frm As Form
Select Case FormName
    Case "frmContactDetails"
        Set frm = New Form_frmContactDetails
    Case Else
        Debug.Assert False
End Select

If WhereCondition <> "" Then
    frm.Filter = WhereCondition
    frm.FilterOn = True
End If
'make the form visible
frm.Visible = True
' Need to add a reference to the form so that it doesn't
' immediately close when the form variable goes out of scope.
mcolFormInstances.Add frm

End Function
```

The function begins by declaring two parameters, FormName and WhereCondition. FormName will hold the name of the form you need to create. WhereCondition will contain a string expression that allows the form to display the correct record. You'll call the function from the Contact form frmContactList and fill these parameters later.

A variable is declared for the form object:

```
Dim frm as Form
```

The Select Case statement evaluates the value in the FormName variable. If the value equals frmContactDetails, then the variable frm is set to equal a new Contact Details form. To use this function for another form, such as to review details about the projects that a contact has worked on, just insert another case in the Select Case statement before the Case Else.

An `If..Then` statement evaluates the value of the `WhereCondition` parameter. Because there's always a value for the `WhereCondition`, the form's filter property equals its value. With a value being supplied to the filter property, you need to turn on the filter with the following line of code:

```
frm.FilterOn = True
```

Adding the form to the module level collection is how you will continue to display the record after another record is selected — in other words, add the form to the collection or it will revert to displaying a single instance of the form. That's because when the `frm` variable goes out of scope, it loses its value, and the initial instance of the form and its record are gone. So you make the form visible and add it to the collection:

```
frm.Visible = True
mcolFormInstances.Add frm
```

Let's go to `frmContactList` and examine the `OpenFormInstance` function. With `frmContactList` open in Design view, you use the ID field's `On Click` event to place the `OpenFormInstance` function. You also use the ID field in the expression for the `WhereCondition` parameter. There are at least four ways to make this function work. Three of the possibilities use code, as the following examples show, and the fourth uses an embedded macro.

```
Private Sub ID_Click()
'1st example
Dim FormName As String
Dim WhereCondition As String
FormName = "frmContactDetails"
WhereCondition = "[ID]=" & Me.ID
'Or
'WhereCondition = "[ID]=" & Screen.ActiveControl
Call OpenFormInstance(FormName, WhereCondition)

'2nd example
'Call OpenFormInstance("frmContactDetails", "[ID]=" & Screen.ActiveControl)

'3rd example
'Call OpenFormInstance("frmContactDetails", "[ID]=" & Me.ID)

End Sub
```

All three code examples are basically the same in that the `FormName` equals the Contact Details form (`frmContactDetails`) and the `WhereCondition` gets its value from the ID field.

The code shows two options for the `WhereCondtion` expression. The first says, "Let the ID field of the Details form equal the ID field from the main form." The second is slightly different: "Let the ID field of the Details form equal the value from the Active control (ID field) from the main screen (main form)." Use the style of `WhereCondition` and `Call` that is appropriate for your scenario. You need to use only one.

Notice that you don't use the `Docmd.OpenForm` to open the details form. Instead, the form is instantiated by declaring the form object and setting it to equal the form specified in `FormName`. The Filter properties are set to accept the expression from the `WhereCondition`, the form is made visible, and the form instance is added to the collection that was created to hold each instance of this form.

As mentioned, the fourth method uses a macro. This example uses the same function, `OpenFormInstance`, to open multiple instances of the forms. To create a new macro, select Macro on the Ribbon's Create tab. You should have a macro object tab named Macro1. Right-click that tab and select Save. Change the name to `dt` (for drill-through). With the blank macro still open, click the buttons `Conditions` and `Macro Names` in the Ribbon. Those columns, which are hidden when you first open a new macro, now display, as shown in Figure 10-23.

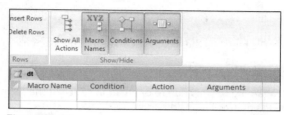

Figure 10-23

Start with the Action column and select `StopMacro`. That will stop the macro from running once a condition is met. Next, create named macros for each of the forms you want to drill to. (The process and details are coming up in a moment, but at the end of the exercise, your macro should look similar to the one in Figure 10-24.)

Macro Name	Condition	Action	Arguments	Comment
		StopMacro		
Contacts	Not IsNull([Screen].[ActiveControl])	RunCode	OpenFormInstance("frmContactDetails","[ID]=" & [	
ContactsByID	Not IsNull([ID])	RunCode	OpenFormInstance("frmContactDetails","[ID]=" & [	

Action Arguments	
Function Name	OpenFormInstance("frmContactDetails","[ID]=" & [Screen].[ActiveControl])

Figure 10-24

Briefly, you start by naming the next macro `Contacts`. In the Condition column, supply an expression that, when evaluated, will equal `True`. If the condition is `True`, then perform the action specified in the Action column (`RunCode`). `RunCode` requires arguments or action arguments to run the code. In this case, you provide the function name `OpenFormInstance` and fill in the parameters just like the ones in the code behind.

With the following steps, you create macros that provide two approaches to drill into the details.

1. The first example uses the active control as the record ID to drill into data. In the Macro Name column, type **Contacts**. For the condition, type:

```
Not IsNull([Screen].[ActiveControl])
```

2. The Action column has a drop-down list; select RunCode.

3. The lower pane will help prompt for action arguments. Click on the ellipsis to open the Expression Builder and then select the function that you created, OpenFormInstance.

4. The Code Builder assists with syntax, but the key is to include the where clause as you did in VBA. Alternatively, you can type the arguments directly into the Arguments field. The completed argument will look like this:

```
OpenFormInstance("frmContactDetails","[ID]=" & [Screen].[ActiveControl])
```

5. The second example matches the record ID, so name the macro ContactsByID. The condition is:

```
Not IsNull([ID])
```

6. The action will again be to run code to open an instance of the form frmContactDetails where the ID fields match. Here's the argument:

```
OpenFormInstance("frmContactDetails","[ID]=" &[ID]
```

The great thing about the macro is that you can have many sub-macros under one roof. You could have dt.Contacts, dt.Orders, dt.Products, and so on, all living in the same macro named dt. Because each of the arguments uses the OpenFormInstance function, it's easier to use the macro to organize or keep track of all the forms needing that functionality. Instead of opening the code behind, you only need to set the Property Sheet for that event to the sub-macro name. Just remember that for every form that is added to the macro, you must change the Select Case statement in the OpenFormInstance function to add a case statement for the new form, as shown in Figure 10-25.

```
'Declaring global variable to create collection
'to hold multiple instances of a form
' the same module is used for several forms.
Private mcolFormInstances1 As New Collection

Function OpenFormInstance(FormName As String, Optional WhereCondition As String)
'Declare the Form Object
    Dim frm As Form
    Select Case FormName
    Case "frmContactDetails"
        Set frm = New Form_frmContactDetails
    Case "fsubOrderDetails"
        Set frm = New Form_fsubOrderDetails
    Case "ThirdFormName"
        Set frm = New Form_ThirdFormName
    Case Else
        Debug.Assert False
    End Select

    'set the filter properties on the form.
    If WhereCondition <> "" Then
        frm.Filter = WhereCondition
        frm.FilterOn = True
    End If
    'Now make the form visible.
    frm.Visible = True

    ' Need to keep a reference to the form so that it doesn't immediately
    ' close when the frm variable goes out of scope.
    mcolFormInstances.Add frm
End Function
```

Figure 10-25

The macro name identifies each macro within the macro group. In the Property Sheet for the ID field's On Click event, select the name of the macro instead of selecting Event Procedure. The Property Sheet offers auto-complete for macro names so as soon as you type dt, you get a list of all the named macros in the dt macro group. See Figure 10-26.

> *Remember that a macro group often contains several macros but it's still called a macro; each named action or series of actions in the group is also called a macro. The terminology can be a bit confusing, but macros are still likely to evolve into popular developer tools.*

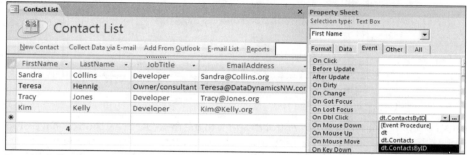

Figure 10-26

Displaying Data in TreeView and ListView Controls

One powerful feature of Access development is the capability to add an ActiveX control to a form or report. ActiveX controls are additional components that provide their own user interface, properties, and methods. Adding a control such as TreeView, ListView, or Calendar is a great way to add functionality to your applications with minimal effort on your part. ActiveX controls are not without cost, however. They must be installed on each computer to use them. In many cases, this means you must have a license to distribute a particular control to other computers.

The TreeView control is used to display data that exists within a hierarchy of information. A hierarchy can involve any data contained within a one-to-one or one-to-many relationship. For example, in the Northwind database, Customers have Orders, and Orders have line items that are known as Order Details. In this section, you'll see how to add a TreeView control to a form and how to populate and display the information based on user interaction with it. You'll also take a look at the ListView control, and see an example of responding to an event in the TreeView control to fill the ListView control.

Let's say that you are tracking students and classes for a small college. Classes at the school are categorized into departments. In this example, you display the departments along with their classes in a TreeView control, and the students in a given class in a ListView control.

To begin, create a new blank form. The form does not need to be bound to a table or query because you will populate data in the TreeView control. Once you create the form, click the Insert ActiveX Control button on the Ribbon. The Insert ActiveX Control dialog box displays, as shown in Figure 10-27. For this example, you use the TreeView and ListView controls from Visual Basic 6, SP 6. Name the controls tvwClasses and lvwStudents respectively.

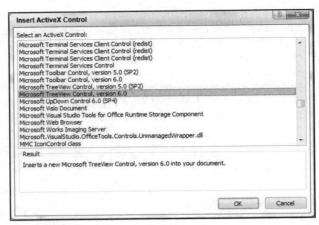

Figure 10-27

In the dialog box, select the desired control to add it to the form. ActiveX controls have properties that are displayed in the standard Access properties window, but many also have another set of custom properties that were added by the author of the control. Figure 10-28 shows the custom property dialog box for the `TreeView` control.

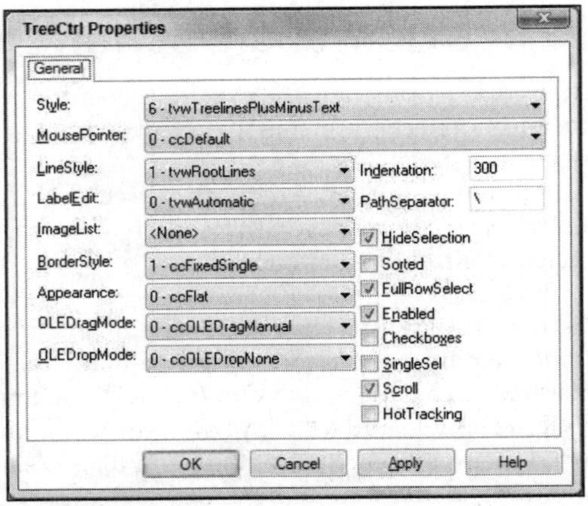

Figure 10-28

You can include images in a `TreeView` or `ListView` control by using another ActiveX control called `ImageList`. `ImageList` is a storage area for pictures that the `TreeView` uses when it displays the data. You won't use images in this example.

The next step is to populate the data in the `TreeView` control. Each item of data in a `TreeView` is called a node and is stored in the `TreeView` `Nodes` collection. The following code demonstrates the addition of a data node to the collection of `TreeView` nodes:

```
tvx.Nodes.Add Key:="C105", Text:="Acme Supply Co.", Image:= 1, SelectedImage:=2
```

The node is defined with a unique key of C105, a display name of Acme Supply Co., and is set to use the image with the key of 1 by default, and the image with the key of 2 when selected. If you use images, the image indexes are defined in a corresponding ImageList control.

The Key property of every node is of type Text, it must start with a letter, and it must be unique.

Filling the TreeView Control

During the Form_Load event procedure in this example, the TreeView is populated with one node for every department in the Departments table, along with the classes that are in the department. Here's how. First you declare object variables for the TreeView and ListView controls. You use these objects to work with the controls on the form.

```
Dim objTree       As TreeView
Dim objList       As ListView
Dim objItem       As ListItem
Dim objParentNode As Node
Dim objChildNode  As Node
```

Next, create the Form_Load event procedure and add the following code to use the controls on the form and provide some formatting.

```
Private Sub Form_Load()
    ' fill the treeview
    Dim rsDept As DAO.Recordset
    Dim rsClasses As DAO.Recordset

    ' get the controls
    Set objTree = Me.tvwClasses.Object
    Set objList = Me.lvwStudents.Object

    ' format the controls
    With objTree.Font
        .Size = 9
        .Name = "Segoe UI"
    End With
    With objList.Font
        .Size = 9
        .Name = "Segoe UI"
    End With
```

Note the use of the .Object property. It is defined by Access to return the object for the control. This property enables you to use *early binding* for the object model in an ActiveX control. Binding works the same here as it does for other objects. Essentially, early binding loads the data when a form loads and late binding delays attaching to the data, which typically allows for a smaller recordset and takes less time to process.

If you've used the ListView or TreeView controls in the past, you may notice that some tabs are missing from the custom property dialog box for the TreeView control. Access 2007 no longer includes the components that provide the Font property sheet, which is why you added code to format the control.

Now loop through the departments and add a node to the `TreeView` control:

```
' get the departments
Set rsDept = CurrentDb.OpenRecordset( _
    "SELECT * FROM tblDepartments ORDER BY Department")

' loop through the departments
While (Not rsDept.EOF)
    ' add the department node
    Set objParentNode = objTree.Nodes.Add(, , _
        "DPT" & rsDept("DepartmentID"), rsDept("Department"))
```

Here you're adding a node for each department with a key value of `DPT` & `rsDept("DepartmentID")`. Each node on the `TreeView` control needs to have a unique key value. By concatenating the value of a primary key field (`DepartmentID`) with a unique abbreviation for the table (`DPT`), you can ensure that each node has a unique key value. You'll re-use this key later to build relationships with other nodes. For this example, `tblDepartments` is the parent table. The relationships are based on the primary and foreign key relationships of the tables as shown in the `WHERE` clause of the next snippet of code.

It's time to add the related classes. You loop through another recordset to get the classes for the current department, and add a new node that is a child of `objParentNode` by specifying the `tvwChild` relationship argument to the `Nodes.Add` method:

```
        ' get the classes in the selected department
        Set rsClasses = CurrentDb.OpenRecordset( _
            "SELECT * FROM tblClasses WHERE Department = " & _
            rsDept("DepartmentID") & " ORDER BY ClassName")

        ' add the classes to the treeview
        While (Not rsClasses.EOF)
            Set objChildNode = objTree.Nodes.Add(objParentNode, tvwChild, _
                "CLS" & rsClasses("ClassID"), rsClasses("ClassName"))
            rsClasses.MoveNext
        Wend
        rsDept.MoveNext
    Wend
```

The only thing left to do now is some cleanup:

```
    rsClasses.Close
    rsDept.Close
    Set rsDept = Nothing
    Set rsClasses = Nothing
End Sub
```

In this example, you're working with a small number of departments and classes so you're filling everything when the form is loaded. If you have a lot of nodes to add to the `TreeView`, filling all the data when the form loads might take a while. To resolve that, you might choose to load the classes for a department when a node is selected, which is known as *delay loading* or *loading on-demand*.

Along with properties and methods, ActiveX controls can also provide events such as `NodeClick` for the `TreeView`. Access does not know anything about these events, so they must be added using the Visual

Basic Editor. To delay loading the classes in the `TreeView`, add the following event, which will then be called when you click a node in the `TreeView`:

```
Private Sub tvwClasses_NodeClick(ByVal Node As Object)
    Dim objNode     As Node

    ' get the node object
    Set objNode = Node

    If (objNode.Children = 0 And objNode.Parent Is Nothing) Then
        ShowClasses Node
    End If

End Sub
```

This code makes sure that the selected node does not already have any children. It also checks the `Parent` property of the `Node` object to make sure that classes are added only when a department is selected. For root or parent nodes that do not have a parent node of their own, the `Parent` property will be set to `Nothing`.

Here's the `ShowClasses` procedure:

```
Private Sub ShowClasses(pNode As Node)
    Dim rsClasses As DAO.Recordset
    Dim lngDept    As Long

    ' parse the department ID from the selected node
    lngDept = CLng(Mid(pNode.Key, 4))

    ' get the classes in the selected department
    Set rsClasses = CurrentDb.OpenRecordset( _
        "SELECT * FROM tblClasses WHERE Department = " & _
        lngDept & " ORDER BY ClassName")

    ' add the classes to the treeview
    While (Not rsClasses.EOF)
        Set objChildNode = objTree.Nodes.Add(pNode, tvwChild, _
            "CLS" & rsClasses("ClassID"), rsClasses("ClassName"))
        rsClasses.MoveNext
    Wend

    rsClasses.Close
    Set rsClasses = Nothing
End Sub
```

Filling the ListView Control

Once you've filled the `TreeView` control, you want to display the students in a given class. To accomplish this, use the `ListView` control that you added to the form earlier. But first, you need to configure the `ListView`. Begin by opening the property sheet for the `ListView` control, and change the View property to `lvwReport`.

The values for the View property probably look familiar. That's because the list of files in a Windows Explorer window is a ListView. *The Explorer's Details view is called the Report view in the* ListView *ActiveX control. The Report view enables you to add your own columns to the* ListView *control.*

Now add the following columns on the Column Headers tab of the ListView property dialog box. Use the Insert Column button in the dialog box (see Figure 10-29) to do so.

Index	Text	Width
1	Class	2160.00
2	First Name	1440.00
3	Last Name	1440.00
4	Major	1440.00

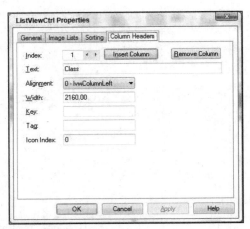

Figure 10-29

To fill the ListView, add the following code in the NodeClick event for the TreeView. If a department is selected, the names of all the students in all classes for that department will display. If a class is selected, the names of its students display.

```
Private Sub tvwClasses_NodeClick(ByVal Node As Object)
    Dim rstStudents As DAO.Recordset
    Dim objNode     As Node
    Dim strSQL      As String
    Dim lngID       As Long

    ' get the node object
    Set objNode = Node
```

```
' parse the ID from the node Key property
lngID = CLng(Mid(objNode.Key, 4))
```

Earlier you saved the ID field along with a table abbreviation in the Key for the node. The preceding code parses the value of the primary key field from the Key so that you can use it in a WHERE clause to get the classes for the selected class or department. Next, you look at the key to determine whether a department or class was selected and create the appropriate SQL statement:

```
' get the students in the selected class or department
If (objNode.Key Like "DPT*") Then
    strSQL = "SELECT * FROM qryStudents WHERE DepartmentID = " & lngID
ElseIf (objNode.Key Like "CLS*") Then
    strSQL = "SELECT * FROM qryStudents WHERE ClassID = " & lngID
End If


' open the recordset
Set rstStudents = CurrentDb.OpenRecordset(strSQL)
```

Time to fill the ListView. For this, use the ListItems collection of the ListView. To create an entry in the ListView, use the ListItems.Add method. This returns a ListItem object that you'll use to add ListSubItems. The Add method of the ListItems collection is used to add the first column to the ListView. Subsequent columns are added to the ListSubItems collection.

```
' fill the listview
With objList
    .ListItems.Clear
    While (Not rstStudents.EOF)
        Set objItem = .ListItems.Add(, , rstStudents("ClassName"))
        objItem.ListSubItems.Add , , rstStudents("FirstName")
        objItem.ListSubItems.Add , , rstStudents("LastName")
        objItem.ListSubItems.Add , , Nz(rstStudents("Major"), "Undeclared")
        rstStudents.MoveNext
    Wend
End With

' cleanup
rstStudents.Close
Set rstStudents = Nothing
Set objNode = Nothing
End Sub
```

When this is all said and done, you should have something that looks like the form in Figure 10-30.

Although the task of creating the TreeView control is completed, many other features could be added to create a more robust tool. For example, using drill through, you could open a Students detail form when you select a student in the ListView. You could add an e-mail control using the check boxes in the ListView to facilitate e-mailing grades or sending information about an upcoming exam or lecture. You can also write code to sort the items in the ListView control. With minimal programming, adding ActiveX controls to an application can give it an extra level of professionalism and pizzazz that many users will appreciate.

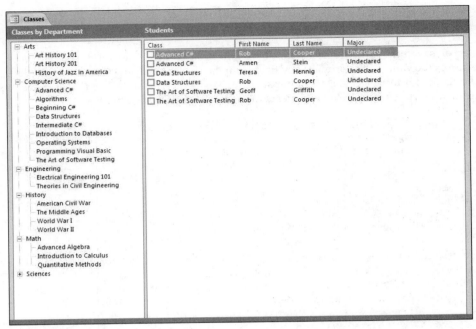

Figure 10-30

Summary

The new features in Access 2007 make it so much easier and faster to create complex solutions. In this chapter, you explore many facets of VBA programming within the form environment. You examined new features and investigated examples of how they might be used and how to leverage them with VBA. And you walked through examples of creating and implementing complex scenarios, such as showing multiple instances of a form and using the `TreeView` control.

Forms are exciting because they are the primary user interface. They are your primary tool in helping users enter, search, and report data. Access 2007's interactive reports are also winners, and you tackle them in the next chapter.

11

Enhancing Reports with VBA

Because of their rich printed view, reports have long been one of the more widely used features in Access. This chapter takes an in-depth look at reports in Access 2007. It starts from the beginning, so if you're already familiar with creating reports in Access, you might want to skip to the section "New in Access 2007."

The chapter also looks at several ways that you can enhance your reports by adding VBA behind them. You'll explore the various events that are available for reports and sections, and then move into some common uses for those events. Along the way, you'll see some issues that you should look out for as you're designing reports. Finally, you'll examine several new features in reports in Access 2007, including Layout view and Report view.

When you write code behind a form, there are certain things to consider, such as the flow of the application, searching for data, data entry, and validation. While reports in Access 2007 are still read-only, they have been greatly enhanced to allow for some of the form-type scenarios that you might have created in the past such as search, sorting, and filtering.

Introduction to Reports

Reports in Access are designed to provide a view of data in a table or query whose initial purpose is to be printed. That said, Access 2007 takes reports to the next level and provides interactivity that was not available in previous versions.

How Reports Are Structured

Several different components make up a report. Perhaps the most important are the various sections and group levels that are defined in a report.

Sections are used to display data and other controls such as labels or combo boxes. The following table describes the types of sections in order.

Section Type	Description
Report Header	Typically displays report titles or similar information. Prints once at the top of the report.
Page Header	Prints at the top of each page.
Group Header	Typically displays unique data for a group or aggregate data such as a Sum or Average. Prints at the top of each group level. This section can be repeated when the data in a group spans multiple pages. (You can have a maximum of 10 groups in a report.)
Detail	Displays records in a report.
Group Footer	Displays summary information for a group level. Prints at the bottom of each group level.
Page Footer	Prints at the bottom of each page. Often used to display page numbers.
Report Footer	Prints once at the end of the report.

One thing that sets reports apart from forms is the capability to group data. Grouping lets you create aggregates or to view related data in a hierarchical fashion using group levels. Let's say you are tracking sessions for a conference and the attendees for each session. Using a report, you can group by the session as well as the time of the session, and display the attendees for each session.

Reports also support sort levels in the hierarchical data. A sort level is the same as a group level, but without a header or footer section. Data within a group or across the report is sorted by the specified field. You can create a maximum of ten group and sort levels in a report. These levels are stored in GroupLevel objects in the GroupLevel property of the report.

> The GroupLevel property of the Report object is not a collection; it's an indexed property. Because it includes an index parameter, it acts like a collection, but does not have methods normally associated with collections such as Add, Item, Count, and Remove.

You can add a subreport to a report. A subreport can show related data in a hierarchy, or you can use subreports to build dashboard-style reports. You'll take a closer look at building dashboard reports later in this chapter.

How Reports Differ from Forms

Naturally, you usually think of using reports for read-only, printed views, and of using forms for inputting data, but what are some other differences? As mentioned earlier, reports have the capability to create groups that provide a hierarchical view of data. Group levels and their related sections are not available in forms. Reports also differ from forms in that they:

❑ **Have better support for printing:** The primary job for a report is to be printed. Sure, you can print a form, and forms even support the page setup features that are supported in reports such as multiple columns and margins. Reports, however, make it easier to add page breaks (per section), and support the CanGrow and CanShrink properties. These properties dynamically control the height of a control when a report is printed to avoid taking up extra space or worse, not enough space. These properties do not work in forms. You take a closer look at the `CanGrow` and `CanShrink` properties later in this chapter.

❑ **Provide running sums:** Because reports are often tabular in nature, they also have the capability to accumulate totals over records using the `RunningSum` property. This property is not available for controls in forms. You can use running sums to create totals across the entire report or over groups in the report. When you set the `RunningSum` property to `Over Group`, the totals in the running sum are reset at the start of a new group.

❑ **Display multiple columns:** Reports also enable you to display multiple columns when printed, so you can create views such as a newsletter, or mailing labels.

As mentioned, forms also support multiple columns when printed, but not in their normal view which is Form view. The normal view for a report by definition is to the printer.

With the introduction of Report view, many events that have been available in forms in previous versions of Access are now available in reports, including the `Load`, `Current`, and `Timer` events. Because reports are still read-only by nature, not all events are available. For example, using a form, you can handle the `AfterUpdate` event when a record has been updated. This event does not fire on a report because you cannot update data. Likewise, the `Delete` event is not available because you cannot delete records using a report.

New in Access 2007

Reports are among the most improved areas in Access 2007. Several new features have been added to make reports both easier to create and more powerful. For starters, *Layout view* allows you to design reports while you are viewing your actual data. Many of the tasks of creating a report, such as formatting, sorting and grouping, and adding totals handled in Layout view while your data is onscreen. As a result, you can accomplish many design tasks without having to switch between Design view and Print Preview.

A report opened in Print Preview is really just an image, so you cannot easily search for data or sort or filter content. Access 2007 introduces *Report view*, which provides a new view of the data in a report that rivals that of forms.

Sorting and grouping is another area that has been enhanced in Access 2007. The sorting and grouping dialog box used in previous versions of Access has been replaced with the new Group, Sort, and Total pane. It enables you to quickly create group levels and sort levels, as shown in Figure 11-1.

Creating reports has also been made easier using the Layout feature. Layouts are groups of aligned controls that resize and move in conjunction with one another. There are two types of layouts: stacked and tabular. Stacked layouts are useful for grouping controls in a stack, where controls are aligned vertically as shown in Figure 11-2. These are also particularly useful for forms.

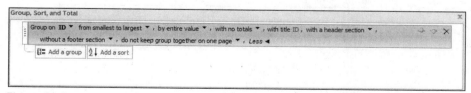

Figure 11-1

Report1

ID	1
Company	Microsoft
First Name	Rob
Last Name	Cooper
ID	2
Company	Data Dynamics NW
First Name	Teresa
Last Name	Hennig
ID	3
Company	J Street Technologies
First Name	Armen
Last Name	Stein
ID	4
Company	Microsoft
First Name	Geoff
Last Name	Griffith

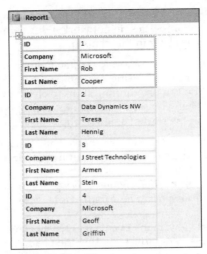

Figure 11-2

A tabular layout is used to group controls that are aligned horizontally, such as a table (see Figure 11-3).

Report1

ID	Company	First Name	Last Name
1	Microsoft	Rob	Cooper
2	Data Dynamics NW	Teresa	Hennig
3	J Street Technologies	Armen	Stein
4	Microsoft	Geoff	Griffith

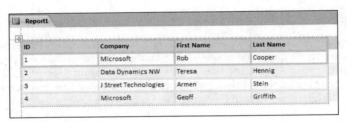

Figure 11-3

Layouts also enable you to add gridlines that grow or shrink with the data. These are much easier than creating lines in previous versions of Access. The Line and Rectangle controls are still available if you require more control over the placement of lines. Figure 11-4 shows a report with a tabular layout that has gridlines.

rptTabularLayout

ID	Company	First Name	Last Name
1	Microsoft	Rob	Cooper
2	Data Dynamics NW	Teresa	Hennig
3	J Street Technologies	Armen	Stein
4	Microsoft	Geoff	Griffith

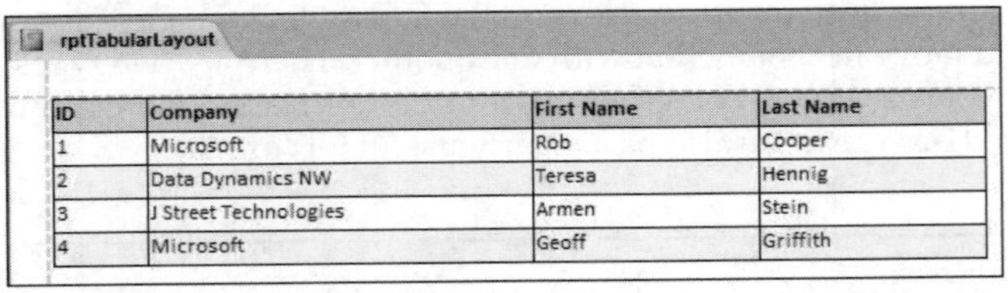

Figure 11-4

Creating a Report

There are many ways to create a report in Access 2007, including the following:

- ❑ **Using Report Wizard:** The Report Wizard walks you through a report creation process with a number of options from which to choose. The options include data settings such as data source, grouping, and sorting, and formatting options such as layout, orientation, and style. Using the wizard is also an easy way to create reports using multiple tables.

- ❑ **Using Report Designer:** Using the Report Designer gives you the most control over report creation. You can place any type of control on the design surface and bind the report to a table or query. The Report Designer also enables you to add VBA code behind the report.

- ❑ **Programmatically:** You can create reports with code. Access provides a method on the `Application` object appropriately called `CreateReport`, which can be used to create a report. This method is largely used when you want to create reports using your own mechanism for gathering input from the user.

- ❑ **Using Layout view:** The Report Designer offers a powerful way to create reports. However, as you design your reports, you may frequently need to switch between Print Preview and report design because data from the tables is not shown at design time. Layout view, as mentioned earlier, was created to solve this. With it, you can make changes such as sorting and grouping, adding totals, or applying formatting while viewing the actual data from a table or query.

- ❑ **Using Quick Reports:** Click the Report button in the Ribbon's Create tab to create a new report with a tabular layout. The report includes common elements such as header and footer sections, and a count of the number of records.

You'll see more about working in Layout view later in this chapter.

Working with VBA in Reports

This is a book about VBA, so let's talk about code. More specifically, you'll explore some examples that use specific events and properties such as `CanGrow` and `CanShrink`, and then move into some of the more common types of reports that you can create with just a little VBA. Let's start with some of the basics.

To add a module to a report, simply add an event handler for an event such as `Open`, or set the `HasModule` property of the report to Yes.

Control Naming Issues

As you add controls, or even when you name fields, there are a few things to keep in mind that make the process of creating queries, forms, and reports much easier. The first is to avoid the use of spaces or punctuation in field and control names. Spaces may make your field names easier to read, but they are not user-friendly when it comes to queries or code. Consider a field named `Last Name` with a space in the middle. This field name must be bracketed when used in a query. Without the space, brackets are not required. It turns out that brackets are also required when you refer to the field in code, so instead of referring to the field like this:

```
Me!LastName
```

you must refer to it like this:

```
Me![Last Name]
```

As you can see, using the space in the name makes it harder to read and write in code. Instead, don't use spaces in names; use the `Caption` property of a field or label control to change the displayed text.

Another issue that causes problems is circular references. A circular reference occurs when a control uses itself in an expression. Say, for example, you drag a field named `LastName` to a report, and then decide to change the `ControlSource` property for the control to:

```
=Left([LastName], 1)
```

Unless you rename this control, the `LastName` control will try to use `LastName` in the expression, which is itself an expression — in other words, a circular reference. To avoid circular references, be sure to rename the control when you modify the `ControlSource`. In this example, you might consider renaming `LastName` to `txtLastName`.

The Me Object

The `Me` keyword is used in class modules in VBA. For forms and reports, `Me` returns the current form or report object. For a standalone class module, the `Me` object returns the current running instance of the class. This is particularly useful for writing generic code. For example, if you have a procedure that changes the caption of a report based on the user who is currently logged on, and you want to write the routine so it can be used on any report, you might write this:

```
Public Sub SetReportCaption(objReport as Report)
    ' Set the report caption to the user name
    objReport.Caption = Environ$("USERNAME")
End Sub
```

To pass a `Report` object from the report that is currently opened, pass the `Me` keyword as the parameter for the procedure. The following example uses the new `Load` event for a report to set the caption:

```
Private Sub Report_Load()
    SetReportCaption Me
End Sub
```

Important Report Events and Properties

The following sections examine the most common events on reports that you will need to use in the course of developing your applications. These events occur when opening a report, when you work with sections and controls, and when you close a report. You can find a more comprehensive list of report events and the order in which they fire in Appendix G.

Opening a Report

The `Open`, `NoData`, `Load`, and `Current` events are important events that are necessary to implement many Access solutions. The `Load` and `Current` events are new to reports in Access 2007.

Open Event

`Open` is the first event that fires when you open a report. It's fired before Access fetches the data for the report, which means that you can dynamically create or alter the query for the report based on user input or the state of controls on another form or report in the database.

You can also cancel the `Open` event. If you set the `Cancel` argument of the event to true, Access stops loading the report, no further events fire, and the report is not displayed on screen. This is useful when you want to ensure that the application is in a certain state before opening the report. For instance, you might want a particular user logged in or a particular form open before opening the report.

If you have a report and you want it to display data from the last 30 days of sales, for example, you can modify the report's `RecordSource` property when the report is opened to restrict the data:

```
Private Sub Report_Open(Cancel As Integer)
    Me.RecordSource = "SELECT * FROM [Orders] WHERE [Order Date] > Date()-30"
End Sub
```

That can be more efficient than changing the `Filter` property of the report.

Other cases where you might use the `Open` event include:

❑ Creating a query for the report based on data from a table or displayed on a form

❑ Setting the sort order of a report based on the selection in a form

❑ Filtering the data in the report based on the user who is currently logged on to the computer

NoData Event

If the report is not cancelled in the `Open` event, Access runs a query specified in the report's `RecordSource` property to fetch the data needed by the report. If that query returns no records, either because data has not been entered or because the `WHERE` clause in the query resulted in no rows being returned, Access fires the `NoData` event. If the query does return data, the `NoData` event is not fired.

You can create an event handler that tells Access what to do if there is no data for your report. Often, you'll want to display a message to the user telling him that no data was found. Alternatively, you may want to open a form to allow the user to change the filter or to add new data to a table.

To not display the report if there is no data available, set the `Cancel` argument of the event to `True`. That tells Access to stop loading the report. The report is closed, and only the `Close` event fires.

For example, let's say that you have a report that lists the customers who have ordered a particular product during the current month. You want to notify users if they run the report but no customers ordered the product this month. The following code displays a message and then cancels the report:

```
Private Sub Report_NoData(Cancel As Integer)
    ' Add code here that will be executed if no data
    ' was returned by the Report's RecordSource
    MsgBox "No customers ordered this product this month. " & _
            "The report will now close."
    Cancel = True
End Sub
```

Load Event

After Access has fetched the data and created the controls on your report, the `Load` event fires. It enables you to interact with controls on your report before the report is displayed. The `Load` event is new to reports in Access 2007.

Unlike the `Open` event, the `Load` event is not cancelable. You can perform actions inside the `Load` event, but Access continues to load the report regardless of any logic in your event handler.

Some suggested uses for the `Load` event include:

❑ Display calculated values in unbound controls using the data in your report's recordset.

❑ Change default values for controls on your report.

Now that reports support both the `Open` and `Load` events, the question comes up as to which one to choose. To create or modify the query on which your report is based, use the `Open` event handler. This event fires before the query does, giving you a chance to customize the data provided to the report.

To interact with a control on your report, you must use the `Load` event handler. When the `Open` event fires, Access has not yet created the controls on your report.

Current Event

Forms in Access have always had a `Current` event. Every time you move to a new record, the `Current` event fires to notify your form that it has moved. You can use the `Current` event to apply custom formatting to a field, or to hide or show controls based on data in the form.

Until Access 2007, reports were not interactive. You could open a report, view it on the screen, and print it, but you couldn't interact with it, and you certainly couldn't move from record to record. Access 2007 adds the capability to interact with report data. You can browse from record to record, click in individual rows in your report, and drill down into the data. With the new interactivity, Microsoft added the `Current` event so that your code can know when a user has clicked into a row on your report.

There is one difference between the `Current` event in a report and the `Current` event in a form. When you open a form, the `Current` event fires toward the end of the opening sequence of events because controls receive focus in forms and records are activated as a result. That is not the case with reports. Controls do not receive focus by default when you open a report, and the `Current` event does not fire. You can use the `Load` event of the report to set focus to a control, which will cause the `Current` event to fire when the report is opened. Naturally, because this event fires when a record on the report receives focus, it does not fire in Print Preview.

Use the `SetFocus` method of a control to set focus to it in the `Load` event.

Section Events

Each section in an Access report has many events that may be fired. You probably won't use most of these events in your applications, but it's great to have them all available if you need them.

Here you'll explore the `Format`, `Retreat`, `Paint`, `Print`, and `Page` events. You can find a more comprehensive list of report events and the order in which they fire in Appendix G.

Format Event

The Format event is fired when Access is laying out a section for a printed page. It fires after Access has determined that the data in the section will begin on a given page, but before the section is actually formatted.

Because the event fires before formatting occurs, you can add code to the Format event that changes the way Access formats the section. You can test the contents of the controls in the section, and you can set values into unbound controls.

The Format event is cancellable, which means you can tell Access to not display a report section.

> *This event is not fired when laying out a section for display on the screen.* Format *is fired only when Access is preparing to interact with a printer driver. In other words, it does not fire in Report view or Layout view.*

You can use the Format event to customize section properties and controls. Suggested uses for the Format event handler include:

- ❑ Dynamically displaying page numbers
- ❑ Creating dictionary-style headers

For example, let's say you have a report that lists all products that are available for ordering. You want to ensure that items that are out of stock are not listed in the report. You add code to the Format event handler for the Detail section to cancel formatting the item, like this:

```
Private Sub Detail_Format(Cancel As Integer, FormatCount As Integer)
    ' Add code here to affect the formatting of the section
    If Me!ItemStatus = "Out Of Stock" Then
        Cancel = True
    End If
End Sub
```

When you cancel the Format event, the section is not printed. Cancelling the Format event also prevents the Print event from firing for the section.

Retreat Event

The Retreat event is a partner to the Format event; if you don't have a Format event handler, you do not need a Retreat event handler. Retreat fires whenever Access determines that a formatting operation needs to be undone. It is not commonly used, but it's a bit tricky.

Retreat is fired for a section when the Format event has already been fired for the section, and Access determines that the content for the section will not fit on the current page.

For example, you may have set the KeepTogether property on a section to true, to request that the entire section be placed together on the same page. If, while formatting the section, Access determines that the entire section cannot fit on the page, it fires the Retreat event to notify your code that the formatting needs to be done all over again. This enables you to undo any actions you may have performed in the Format event (remember, Format is fired before the actual formatting is done).

This is important if you have code in the Format event handler that assumes a linear progression. You can put code into the Retreat event handler to undo whatever you did in the Format event handler.

Here's an example that shows how this works. You have a report that sequentially numbers each detail section item in the report. Access fires the Format event to notify your code that a new detail section is being formatted. Your Format event handler increments a variable and then sets that value into an unbound text box in the section. The first 50 items fit fine on page one: The Format event has been fired 50 times and you have not yet seen a Retreat event because everything fits.

The 51st time through, Access again fires the Format event to tell your code that it will begin to format a new item. Your Format event handler increments the variable to 51, and sets the unbound text box, just as it has successfully done 50 times before. When your event handler finishes, Access begins actually formatting the section, and that's when it discovers that the section doesn't fit on page one, and needs to be placed on page two instead. Access fires the Retreat event to notify your code that this section is being "unformatted."

Access now knows that this section needs to appear on the next page. So what does it do? When it's time to put the section on page two, Access fires the Format event again! Access doesn't know what you may want to do during formatting, so it always tells you when it begins formatting a section. If you don't have code to handle the Retreat event, what's going to happen? When the Format event is fired for this section for page two, the line counter is incremented (this time from 51 to 52), and 52 is dutifully put in the unbound text box on the report. Yikes! Your user will look at the report and wonder what happened to row 51.

To fix this, all you need to do is handle the Retreat event. You can put code into the Retreat event handler to decrement the page number variable. When Access figures out that row 51 doesn't fit on page one, it fires the Retreat event; in the event handler, you subtract one from the line counter variable, setting it back to 50. Now you are prepared for the Format event that Access will fire when formatting the item for page two.

> **If you do something in the Format event handler, do the opposite in the Retreat event handler.**

Paint Event

The Paint event is new to Access 2007 and is fired whenever a section needs to be drawn on the screen. Access paints various items in a given section at different times. For example, the background and foreground colors and items are painted separately. Calculated controls are also painted separately, and each section paints its own calculated controls. As you might imagine, the Paint event fires multiple times for a given section.

The Paint event applies to the screen, not the printer. Paint events fire when paging through a report on the screen, not Print Preview.

Because the Format event does not fire in Report view, the Paint event can be used for conditional formatting of controls in that view.

Print Event

The `Print` event is fired after Access has finished formatting a section for printing, but before it is sent to the printer. The `Print` event handler is passed two parameters:

- ❑ `Cancel`: Set to `True` to cancel sending the section to the printer.
- ❑ `PrintCount`: Reports how many times the `Print` event handler has been called for the section item. Typically, this is set to 1, meaning this call is the first time the handler has been called by the layout engine.

The following code shows you how to accumulate totals at the bottom of each page:

```
Dim curTotal As Currency

Private Sub Detail_Print(Cancel As Integer, PrintCount As Integer)
    If PrintCount = 1 Then
        ' accumulate the total for the page
        curTotal = curTotal + Me!ItemAmount
    End If
End Sub

Private Sub PageHeaderSection_Print(Cancel As Integer, PrintCount As Integer)
    ' reset the total at the beginning of the page
    curTotal = 0
End Sub

Private Sub PageFooterSection_Print(Cancel As Integer, PrintCount As Integer)
    ' Display the total at the bottom of the page
    Me!txtPageTotal = curTotal
End Sub
```

Suggested uses for the `Print` event handler include:

- ❑ Printing totals such as a count at the bottom of each page
- ❑ Printing a record more than once
- ❑ Tracking when reports are printed

Page Event

The `Page` event is fired after a page has been formatted for printing, but before the page is actually sent to the printer. You can place code in the `Page` event handler to adorn a page with borders or watermarks.

To draw a border around the pages of your report and display a "Confidential" watermark, for example, you add code to the `Page` event handler to use the `Line` method of the report to draw a line for the border, and use several report properties to draw the watermark text in the center of the page, like this:

```
Private Sub Report_Page()
    Dim strWatermarkText As String
    Dim sizeHor As Single
    Dim sizeVer As Single

    With Me
```

```
                    ' Print page border
                    Me.Line (0, 0)-(.ScaleWidth - 1, .ScaleHeight - 1), vbBlack, B

                    ' Print watermark
                    strWatermarkText = "Confidential"

                    .ScaleMode = 3
                    .FontName = "Segoe UI"
                    .FontSize = 48
                    .ForeColor = vbRed

                    ' Calculate text metrics
                    sizeHor =.TextWidth(strWatermarkText)
                    sizeVer = .TextHeight(strWatermarkText)

                    ' Set the print location
                    .CurrentX = (.ScaleWidth / 2) - (sizeHor / 2)
                    .CurrentY = (.ScaleHeight / 2) - (sizeVer / 2)

                    ' Print the watermark
                    .Print strWatermarkText
            End With
        End Sub
```

Closing a Report

The Unload and Close events are necessary to implement many Access solutions.

Unload Event

The Unload event is fired when someone (your user, VBA code, or a macro) attempts to close the report. It is the first event fired during the shutdown sequence, and report data and report controls are still available to your code in this event handler.

Because the Unload event is cancellable, you can add code to the event handler to decide whether you want to allow the user to close the report. If you do not want the report to close, simply set the Cancel argument to True. Most likely you will also want to display a message box or some other form of user feedback to let your user know why you are prohibiting the report from closing.

Close Event

The Close event is the last event fired by a report. It allows you to clean up after the report, or prepare another object that you want to work with after the report is closed. This event is fired after the report has closed. You cannot interact with any report controls or data from this event. If you need to work with report controls, use the Unload event handler instead.

Report Properties

There are many properties on a report you can use to add some interesting features to your reports. Let's look at a few of these properties and some scenarios for using them with VBA. You can find a more comprehensive list of properties for reports and sections in Appendix G.

Section Properties

As you might expect, the properties on the Section object include members such as CanGrow and CanShrink and formatting properties such as AlternateBackColor. They're interesting, but there are a few properties that are not available in the property sheet that you'll want to look at a little closer.

WillContinue

A section's WillContinue property indicates whether the section will break onto the next page. It's useful for displaying a string such as "Continued on the next page" in a label at the bottom of the page.

This property is not available to reports opened in Report view or Layout view.

HasContinued

The HasContinued property is the opposite of the WillContinue property. It indicates whether a section has continued from the previous page. This is useful for displaying a string such as "(continued)" in a section at the top of the page.

This property is not available to reports opened in Report view or Layout view.

ForceNewPage

The ForceNewPage property sets page breaks on a report. You can use it to force a page break after a group level to keep related data on a single page. A good example of this is invoices, where you want the invoice for a single customer to print on a single page.

KeepTogether

You are already aware of two KeepTogether properties: one for the Section object and one for the GroupLevel object.

The KeepTogether property of a Section object attempts to prevent a section from printing across multiple pages. Keep in mind that some sections are so large that this is not always possible. This property is a Boolean value. If it is set to Yes, and the section cannot be completely printed on the current page, printing starts at the top of the next page. If it is set to No, the section is allowed to break across pages as needed to fill the entire page.

The KeepTogether property for a GroupLevel object controls how sections within a group are kept together. This is not a Boolean property, but instead has three values: No, Whole Group, and With First Detail. The default value is No, and it does not attempt to keep any of the sections that make up a group on the same page. With First Detail will make sure that the group header will print on the same page as the first Detail section in the group, while any other Detail sections and the group footer are allowed to be on the following pages. The Whole Group setting attempts to keep all sections in the entire group on the same page. Obviously, with larger groups that may not be possible, but in those cases; the group header would always start on a new page. That may not be the case if you have multiple small groups that will fit onto the same page.

The KeepTogether property for a GroupLevel object controls how sections within a group are kept together. This is not a Boolean property, but instead has three values:

❑ No: The default value. No attempt is made to keep any of the sections that make up a group on the same page.

❑ Whole Group: Attempts to keep all sections in the entire group on the same page. Obviously, that's not possible with larger groups, but in those cases the group header would always start on a new page. That may not be the case if you have multiple small groups that will fit onto the same page.

❑ With First Detail: Ensures that the group header prints on the same page as the first Detail section in the group, while any other Detail sections and the group footer are allowed to be on the following pages.

RepeatSection

When a group header section prints its controls, the data in the section is not displayed on more than one page. If the group extends to more than one page, this may be confusing for users reading the report. To solve this problem, use the RepeatSection property. It repeats the group header section on each page the section spans. A good example of this is a company directory where you want to list employees grouped by department. By using the RepeatSection property, you can display the department information at the top of each page if the entire group does not fit on a single page. This property applies only to group header sections.

Control Properties

Most of the built-in Access controls have two properties that are used by Access to customize how the control is displayed on a report: CanGrow and CanShrink. Report sections also have these properties, except for the Page Header and Page Footer sections, which are always displayed.

Memo fields can store a large amount of data — up to 65,535 characters in the Access user interface, and up to 1GB if you use DAO! While you probably won't have that much to display on a report, the pure fact that they can vary greatly in size can cause some design challenges for display. One record may contain a large amount of data in a memo field, and the next record may contain a very small amount of data. So how do you design report controls to accommodate for something that is not a fixed size?

Enter the CanGrow and CanShrink properties. These properties have been around for some time, and are very useful in designing reports.

The CanGrow property, as its name suggests, determines whether a control can grow (in height) to fit its data. Controls that are below a control that has grown are pushed down to follow the larger control. The CanShrink property determines whether a control can shrink (in height) to fit its data. Width of a control is not affected by these properties.

Working with Charts

Charts are useful tools for both forms and reports. They enable you to visually display aggregate data in trends or compared with other data. There are two types of charts you can use on reports. The first is created using the Microsoft Graph OLE Object and can be inserted using the Insert Chart button on the Design tab in the Report Designer. The other is a PivotChart, which can be created using a form. That form can subsequently be used as a subreport on a report to display the chart. The PivotChart object is more flexible and contains a rich object model that you can use from Access. While a discussion of this object model is beyond the scope of this book, there are some useful things you can do using PivotCharts such as display a chart in a group for a subset of records in a hierarchy.

Both types of charts can display related data using the `LinkChildFields` and `LinkMasterFields` properties.

Common Report Requests

There's a lot that you can do with some imagination and a little VBA code behind your reports. Let's take a look at some of the more common types of reports you can create by adding VBA.

Gathering Information from a Form

There may be times when you want to retrieve some information from a form to provide data to a report. For example, you may want to provide the user with a form to create a filter for the report. You can use the `OpenForm` method with the `acDialog` argument to open the form in the report's `Open` event. `acDialog` opens the form in a modal view and stops subsequent code from executing. This also prevents the report from opening until the form is closed.

The following is an example of this technique. The code opens a form that contains a unique list of company names in a combo box. When a company is selected, the form is hidden, which runs the remainder of the code in the report. This example also shows how you can change the record source for a report at runtime.

```
Private Sub Report_Open(Cancel As Integer)
    Dim strCompany As String

    ' open the form
    DoCmd.OpenForm "frmFilterReport", acNormal, , , , acDialog

    ' get the company
    strCompany = Nz(Forms("frmFilterReport")!cboCompanies, "")

    ' set the recordsource for the report
    If (Len(strCompany) > 0) Then
        Me.RecordSource = "SELECT [Last Name], [First Name], Company " & _
                          "FROM tblAttendees " & _
                          "WHERE Company = '" & strCompany & "'"
    Else
        Me.RecordSource = "SELECT [Last Name], [First Name], Company " & _
                          "FROM tblAttendees"
    End If

    DoCmd.Close acForm, "frmFilterReport"
End Sub
```

Changing the Printer

The `Printer` object was introduced in Access 2002 and greatly simplified changing printer settings or the printer itself for reports. To change the printer for a report, you must open the report in Print Preview, and then change the report's `Printer` property. You cannot change the `Printer` property from the `Open` event of a report, so you'll have to create a form that allows the user to select a printer, and then select a list of reports to send to the printer.

Start by creating a form with two list boxes, named `lstPrinters` and `lstReports`. Set the following properties of `lstReports`:

Property Name	Value
Row Source	SELECT Name FROM MSysObjects WHERE Type=-32764 ORDER BY Name;
Multi Select	Extended

For this example, you use the `MSysObjects` system table to retrieve the list of reports in the database. There are other ways to accomplish that task, but this will suffice.

Before getting into the bulk of the code, you need a variable declaration. Add the following line of code to the declarations section of the form:

```
Private objPrinter As Printer
```

Next, fill in `lstPrinters`, the list box that will contain the list of installed printers on the computer. To do so, add the following code to the `Load` event of the form:

```
Private Sub Form_Load()
    ' fill the list of printers
    For Each objPrinter In Printers
        Me.lstPrinters.AddItem objPrinter.DeviceName
    Next
End Sub
```

This code uses the `Application` object's `Printers` collection property. This property contains a collection of all printers installed on the computer. When you run this code, `lstPrinters` should contain the list of all printers on your computer.

Now, you need to be able to print the selected reports. Add a command button to the form named `cmdPrint` with the following code. Also add a checkbox named `chkSendToPrinter`.

```
Private Sub cmdPrint_Click()
    Dim varItem   As Variant
    Dim strReport As String

    ' loop through the selected printers
    For Each varItem In Me.lstReports.ItemsSelected
        ' open the report in print preview
```

```
        strReport = Me.lstReports.ItemData(varItem)
        DoCmd.OpenReport strReport, acViewPreview

        ' set the printer
        If (Not IsNull(Me.lstPrinters)) Then
            Set objPrinter = Application.Printers(Me.lstPrinters.Value)
            Set Reports(strReport).Printer = objPrinter

            ' if the check box on the form is checked,
            ' send the report to the printer
            If (Me.chkSendToPrinter) Then
                DoCmd.OpenReport strReport, acViewNormal
            End If

            ' close
            DoCmd.Close acReport, strReport
        End If
    Next
End Sub
```

This code iterates through the `ItemsSelected` property of the `lstReports` list box and opens each report in Print Preview. It gets a `Printer` object for the printer that was selected in `lstPrinters`. Then, it sets the `Printer` property of the `Report` object to `objPrinter` and conditionally sends it to the printer. Finally, you close the report for cleanup.

Dictionary-Style Headings

Phone books and dictionaries typically add the first entry and last entry at the top of the page to make it easier to find information. You can accomplish this on your reports by adding some code in several different sections. The code uses the `Format` event to create listings at the top of each page. Because this event does not fire for reports open in Report view, you'll need to open the report in Print Preview to see the effect.

The report you'll create is a listing of the attendees for the conference. It is grouped by the first letter of the last name. Figure 11-5 shows part of the report.

	Last Name	First Name	Company
A			
	Angel Paolino	Miguel	Tortuga Restaurante
	Accorti	Paolo	Franchi S.p.A.
	Anders	Maria	Alfreds Futterkiste
	Afonso	Pedro	Comércio Mineiro
	Ashworth	Victoria	B's Beverages
B			
	Buchanan	Steven	
	Braunschweiger	Art	Split Rail Beer & Ale
	Bertrand	Marie	Paris spécialités
	Bergulfsen	Jonas	Santé Gourmet
	Berglund	Christina	Berglunds snabbköp
	Batista	Bernardo	Que Delicia
	Brown	Elizabeth	Consolidated Holdings
	Bennett	Helen	Island Trading

Figure 11-5

You'll modify the report to add two text boxes to the Page Header section. The first control, named txtFirst, will be hidden and store the first entry on each page by setting the ControlSource property to the last name of the attendee. The second control, named txtLast, will be visible and display the attendee entries.

The trick is to force Access to do two passes on the report because you need to determine the last attendee on the page and subsequently display it on the top of the page. To do this, use the Pages property in the Page Footer. To calculate the number of pages in the report, Access will format the report twice. You also need a report footer section to run some code. Add a text box to the page footer with the following expression:

```
="Page " & [Page] & " of " & [Pages]
```

Now you'll start adding the code. First, add two variables. The first is a flag to indicate whether you are on the first or the second pass. The second will be used to store the last name of the attendee when you get to the bottom of each page.

```
Dim blnFirstPass As Boolean
Dim astrLastNames() As String
```

Next, add code to the Open event of the report. It sets up the array and initializes the flag.

```
Private Sub Report_Open(Cancel As Integer)
    ' start the first pass
    ReDim astrLastNames(0)
    blnFirstPass = True
End Sub
```

Save the last name of the last attendee on the page. This is the value you want to display at the top of the page. For this, add the following code in the Format event of the Page Footer section:

```
Private Sub PageFooterSection_Format(Cancel As Integer, FormatCount As Integer)
    ' Resize the array
    ReDim Preserve astrLastNames(UBound(astrLastNames) + 1)
    ' Save the Last Name of the last attendee on the page
    astrLastNames(Me.Page - 1) = Me![Last Name]
End Sub
```

Now you need to display the first entry and the last entry on the page in the Page Header section. Add the following code to the Format event of the section:

```
Private Sub PageHeaderSection_Format(Cancel As Integer, FormatCount As Integer)
    ' Make sure we are not on the first pass
    If (Not blnFirstPass) Then
        Me.txtLast = Me.txtFirst & " - " & astrLastNames(Me.Page - 1)
    End If
End Sub
```

Finally, you set the first pass flag to False to indicate that the first pass is complete. Add the following code to the Format event of the Report Footer section. The Report Footer is the last formatted section in the report so it's a good place to reset the flag.

```
Private Sub ReportFooter_Format(Cancel As Integer, FormatCount As Integer)
    ' first pass is complete
    blnFirstPass = False
End Sub
```

When you run the report, it should look something like the one shown in Figure 11-6.

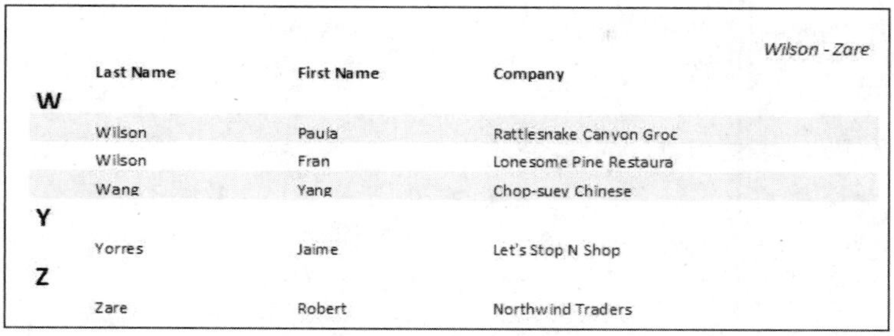

	Last Name	First Name	Company	Wilson - Zare
W				
	Wilson	Paula	Rattlesnake Canyon Groc	
	Wilson	Fran	Lonesome Pine Restaura	
	Wang	Yang	Chop-suev Chinese	
Y				
	Yorres	Jaime	Let's Stop N Shop	
Z				
	Zare	Robert	Northwind Traders	

Figure 11-6

Shading Alternate Rows

Access 2007 includes the capability to set a section's alternate back color so the technique explored here is no longer required for many scenarios. However, you might choose to shade the alternate row color based on the current group level, and for that you still need code. The following example shows how to combine different section events to provide custom shading based on the group level.

With the sessions and attendees example in mind, imagine you are creating a report brochure that is grouped by day so that you can quickly see the sessions on a given day. In the brochure, you want to shade the presentations on Monday in gray, Tuesday in blue, and Wednesday in yellow. You can accomplish this as follows.

Start by declaring a variable to store the shaded color:

```
Private lngShadingColor As Long
```

Next, add code to the Format event of the GroupHeader section to set the color based on the day:

```
Private Sub GroupHeader0_Format(Cancel As Integer, FormatCount As Integer)
    ' Set the alternate row color based on date
    Select Case Weekday(CDate(Me.txtSessionDate))
        Case vbMonday
            lngShadingColor = &HECECEC
        Case vbTuesday
            lngShadingColor = &HD6DFEC
        Case vbWednesday
            lngShadingColor = vbYellow
    End Select
End Sub
```

Finally, add the following code to the `Format` event of the `Detail` section to shade the rows. You use a `Static` counter variable to count the rows and then use the `Mod` operator to determine whether the counter value is divisible by two. When it is not divisible by two, you apply the shading.

```
Private Sub Detail_Format(Cancel As Integer, FormatCount As Integer)
    Static intCounter As Integer

    ' reset the counter
    If (Me.Detail.BackColor <> lngShadingColor And _
        Me.Detail.BackColor <> vbWhite) Then
        intCounter = 1
    Else
        intCounter = intCounter + 1
    End If

    If (intCounter Mod 2 = 1) Then
        Me.Detail.BackColor = lngShadingColor
    Else
        Me.Detail.BackColor = vbWhite
    End If
End Sub
```

A last note about this code: In Access 2007, you can just set the `AlternateBackColor` property for the `Detail` section instead of adding code to the `Format` event of the `Detail` section. Access defines the alternate row as the second row. The preceding code defines the alternate row as the first row for a slightly different effect, as shown in Figure 11-7.

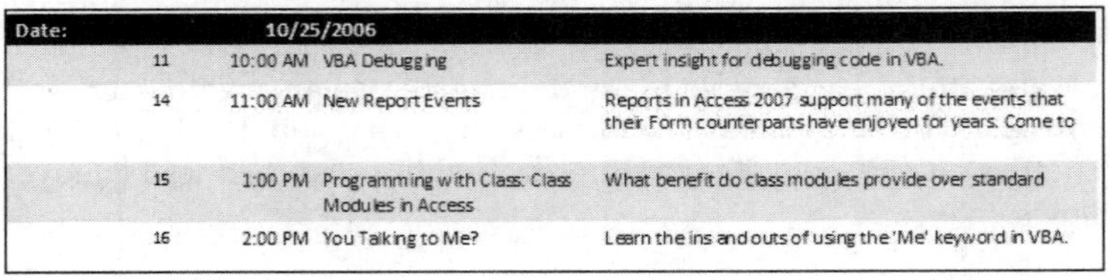

Figure 11-7

The Format and Print events do not fire in Report view. There you must use the new Paint event for a section.

Conditional Formatting of a Control

Access includes a feature called Conditional Formatting that enables you to change formatting properties of a control based on an expression. This is a powerful feature, although you can create only up to three conditions for a given control. If you need to test more than three conditions, you have to use code. The following example sets the `BackColor` property for a control called `AvgOfRating` based on its value. It calls a routine from the `Paint` and `Format` events to achieve the same effect in Report view or Print Preview.

```
Private Sub SetControlFormatting()
    If (Me.AvgOfRating >= 8) Then
```

```
        Me.AvgOfRating.BackColor = vbGreen
    ElseIf (Me.AvgOfRating >= 5) Then
        Me.AvgOfRating.BackColor = vbYellow
    Else
        Me.AvgOfRating.BackColor = vbRed
    End If
End Sub

Private Sub Detail_Format(Cancel As Integer, FormatCount As Integer)
    ' do conditional formatting for the control in print preview
    SetControlFormatting
End Sub

Private Sub Detail_Paint()
    ' do conditional formatting for the control in Report view
    SetControlFormatting
End Sub
```

Dashboard Reports

Dashboard reports are cool. They display several pieces of disparate data to give an overview or describe a story. Take the conference application, for example. A dashboard report for it could contain any number of summaries, including the following:

- ❑ Today's sessions
- ❑ Speaker requests
- ❑ Ratings for today's sessions
- ❑ Attendance per session
- ❑ Item sales
- ❑ Attendee feedback
- ❑ Registration numbers
- ❑ Many, many more

Dashboard reports are often created using an unbound main report with one or more subreports to display the separate pieces of data. One area that can get tricky is the positioning of different subreports to fit on a page or two pages.

Creating a Progress Meter Report

Progress meter reports are an interesting way to display status as a percentage of a given value. In the conference application, for example, you could ask the attendees to rate each session on a scale of one to ten, and enter the data in a table called tblSessionRatings. Aggregate the data using the following query:

```
SELECT tblSessionRatings.Session,
    tblSessions.Title,
    CDate(CLng([Start Time])) AS SessionDate,
    Avg(tblSessionRatings.Rating) AS AvgOfRating
```

```
FROM tblSessions
RIGHT JOIN tblSessionRatings ON tblSessions.ID=tblSessionRatings.Session
GROUP BY tblSessionRatings.Session, tblSessions.Title, CDate(CLng([Start Time]))
ORDER BY tblSessions.Title,
    CDate(CLng([Start Time])),
    Avg(tblSessionRatings.Rating) DESC;
```

Figure 11-8 shows the query's result.

rptSessionRatings	qrySessionRatings		
Session	Title	SessionDate	AvgOfRating
3	Creating Forms and Reports	10/23/2006	3.5
7	Creating Forms and Reports	10/24/2006	7
1	Introduction to Microsoft Access	10/23/2006	7
5	Introduction to Microsoft Access	10/24/2006	8.5
2	VBA Debugging	10/23/2006	6
6	VBA Debugging	10/24/2006	4.5
11	VBA Debugging	10/25/2006	8
4	What's New in Access 2007	10/23/2006	4.5

Figure 11-8

This data is valuable, but you can make it stand out by using a report. Because you're working with a fixed scale (1–10), you can display the rating as a percentage of 10. To do so, you create the report based on the query and add two rectangle controls to the Detail section of the report. Name the rectangles boxInside and boxOutside and position boxInside inside boxOutside as the names suggest. For each average rating, you'll resize the width of boxInside to a percentage of the width of boxOutside.

You cannot resize controls in Report view, so you'll add code to the Load event of the report to hide the rectangles if the report is not opened in Print Preview. Add the following code to the Load event:

```
Private Sub Report_Load()
    If (Me.CurrentView = AcCurrentView.acCurViewPreview) Then
        Me.boxInside.Visible = True
        Me.boxOutside.Visible = True
    Else
        Me.boxInside.Visible = False
        Me.boxOutside.Visible = False
    End If
End Sub
```

Next, to resize the width of boxInside, add the following code to the Detail section's Format event:

```
Private Sub Detail_Format(Cancel As Integer, FormatCount As Integer)
    Dim lngOffset As Long

    ' Calculate the offset between boxOutside and boxInside for effect
    lngOffset = (Me.boxInside.Left - Me.boxOutside.Left) * 2

    ' size the width of the rectangle and subtract the offset
    Me.boxInside.Width = (Me.boxOutside.Width * (Me.AvgOfRating / 10)) - lngOffset
End Sub
```

This code divides the average rating by the maximum rating (10) to get a percentage, and then multiplies that percentage by the width of the outside rectangle to set the width of the inside rectangle. For effect, `boxOutside` is slightly offset from `boxInside` so that it looks like there is a border around `boxInside`. Therefore, you calculate this offset and multiply it by 2 to achieve the padding on both sides. The offset represents the difference between the `Left` property of `boxInside` and the `Left` property of `boxOutside`. Figure 11-9 shows the report.

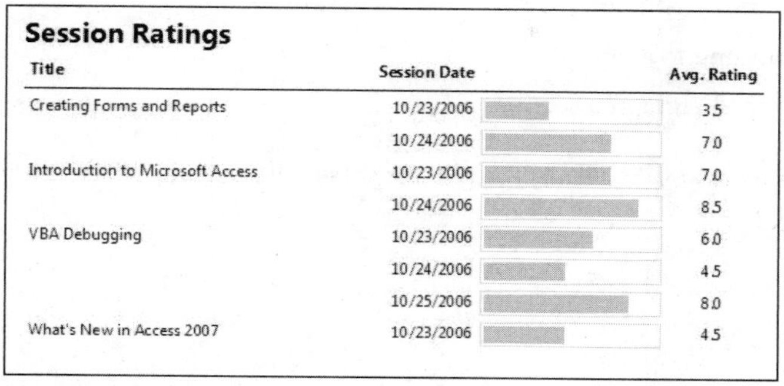

Session Ratings

Title	Session Date		Avg. Rating
Creating Forms and Reports	10/23/2006		3.5
	10/24/2006		7.0
Introduction to Microsoft Access	10/23/2006		7.0
	10/24/2006		8.5
VBA Debugging	10/23/2006		6.0
	10/24/2006		4.5
	10/25/2006		8.0
What's New in Access 2007	10/23/2006		4.5

Figure 11-9

Layout View

If you've designed reports in Access in the past and found that you had to frequently switch between Design view and Print Preview, then Layout view is for you. The primary advantage of using Layout view is its speed in creating something that gives you a sense of how the report will look onscreen or in print. That's because Layout view is a combination of Design view and Browse view, giving you a live view of the data while you perform certain design type tasks, including the following:

- ❑ Grouping and sorting
- ❑ Adding totals
- ❑ Formatting controls and sections
- ❑ Changing the AutoFormat
- ❑ Inserting labels and image controls
- ❑ Adding new fields
- ❑ Adding controls to layouts and formatting layouts
- ❑ Binding the record source to a table
- ❑ Changing the record source
- ❑ Changing many other properties

As you can see, there's a lot that can be accomplished in Layout view, all while viewing the live data in the record source to give you a better perspective of the end result. There are, however, a few tasks that cannot be accomplished using Layout view:

❑ Adding code or setting the `HasModule` property

❑ Inserting unbound controls such as text boxes or combo boxes

❑ Changing the orientation

❑ Initially binding to a query

❑ Changing the height of a section

Even with these few tasks, Layout view is still a valuable time-saver when it comes to creating reports in Access 2007.

Report View

As mentioned at the beginning of this chapter, Access 2007 introduces a new interactive view for reports called Report view. It is the default view for new reports created in Access 2007 and gives you much of the same functionality that you've enjoyed with forms, including the capability to search, sort and filter, and even copy! Let's look at some ways you can use all that new functionality.

Considerations When Designing for Report View

Before you start switching all of your existing reports to use Report view, there are a few things to consider. The following sections explore those factors.

Where Are All My Pages?

The first thing you'll notice about Report view is that there aren't any pages. A report open in Report view is really one big page that you scroll like a continuous form. Because of this, calculations that depend on the `Page` or `Pages` properties of the report may return unexpected results.

Events

As mentioned earlier, the `Format` and `Print` events don't fire in Report view. That's because those events are used with individual sections as a report is printed.

Because reports opened in Report view are not printed, there is a new `Paint` event to use with sections in Report view. As you learned earlier in the "Paint Event" section, `Paint` fires multiple times for a single section because of the way that controls are drawn on reports. When a section is being painted, it is too late to hide it, so you cannot dynamically hide sections on a report open in Report view. That's why the `Paint` event handler does not include any arguments.

Controls

With this newfound interactivity, you might be tempted to add other controls you wouldn't normally add to a report such as a command button. To maintain the rich printed view, you'll want to hide those controls when the report is printed. To do so, check the `CurrentView` property of the report, or change the `DisplayWhen` property of the control to `Screen Only`. That displays the control in Report view but hides it in Print Preview.

Text box and combo box controls have a new property called `DisplayAsHyperlink`. It's similar in concept to the `DisplayWhen` property in that it determines how information or data is displayed for screen versus print. `DisplayAsHyperlink` can be used to format data as a hyperlink in screen views such as Report or Layout, but not printed views. The result is that fields displayed as hyperlinks include formatting such as underlines and link colors onscreen, but print without those embellishments.

See the table that follows for the values of this property.

Value	Description
If Hyperlink	Formats text as a hyperlink if it is recognized as a hyperlink. This is the default.
Always	Text is formatted as a hyperlink in all views.
Screen Only	Text is formatted as a hyperlink, but not in printed views.

Interactivity

The capability to search, sort and filter, and copy data makes reports much easier to use than in previous versions. In addition to the standard Access functionality, you can add your own interactivity in reports that has only been available in forms in the past. Using some of these features, it is possible to create great reports that act in much the same way as read-only forms, but have the additional benefit of a great printed view.

Hyperlinks

Now that reports are interactive, you can click on hyperlinks in a report to open a Web browser or another object in the database. For instance, you can use a report to list information about one of the conference sessions from earlier examples, and include the link on the report to more information on the session's website.

Drill-Down/Click-Through

By using a hyperlink or the `Click` event of a text box or command button, you can provide drill-down functionality in a report to view detailed information. The templates in Access 2007 frequently use this technique. For example, when you click on the name of a session on a report, you can open a form or another report that shows the attendees for the session and their ratings. The "Query by Report" section coming up includes an example of this.

Multiple Report Instances

Sometimes you might want to show multiple instances of a report to display different pieces of data. A common example is to change the filter or sort for a given report. Because modules behind forms and reports are class modules, you can create new instances of them using syntax such as this:

```
Dim objMyReport as Report_rptMyReport
Set objMyReport = New Report_rptMyReport
objMyReport.Visible = True
```

With interactive reports, you can enable this scenario in your solutions as a part of the drill-down/click-through scenario. Using multiple report instances is another way to enhance the user experience to provide different views of the same report.

You can find more information about using forms as class modules in Chapters 10 and 13. The concepts introduced for forms also apply to reports.

Query by Report

Another feature that forms have always enjoyed is the capability to create a query that uses a control on a form as criteria in the query. The technique is known as *query by form*, and much has been written about it over the years. With the advent of Report view in Access 2007, reports also can take advantage of this useful feature. Because controls on reports can also receive focus (in Report view), you can now refer to controls on reports as criteria in a query.

Consider the conference tracking application. You have a report that lists the attendees and you want to open another report that you can print as an invoice for the items they purchased. By clicking on an attendee's name, you can run a query something like this:

```
SELECT tblAttendeeSales.Attendee,
       tblAttendeeSales.Quantity,
       tblItems.ItemName,
       tblItems.NormalPrice,
       tblItems.ConferenceDiscount
       tblAttendees.Company,
       tblAttendees.Address,
       tblAttendees.City,
       tblAttendees.[State/Province],
       tblAttendees.[ZIP/Postal Code]
FROM tblAttendees
INNER JOIN (tblItems INNER JOIN tblAttendeeSales ON tblItems.ItemID =
tblAttendeeSales.ItemID) ON tblAttendees.ID = tblAttendeeSales.Attendee
WHERE tblAttendeeSales.Attendee = [Reports]![rptAttendeesDirectory]![ID] OR
[Reports]![rptAttendeesDirectory]![ID] Is Null
```

This query uses the data from three tables to create the invoice. Note the WHERE clause of the query that uses the reference to the ID control on the report called rptAttendeesDirectory. The invoice report is bound to this query so all you have to do from the directory report is open the invoice report as follows:

```
Private Sub Last_Name_Click()
    ' open the invoice
    DoCmd.OpenReport "rptSalesInvoice", acViewReport
End Sub
```

The query uses the ID for the current record to display a single invoice record, as shown in Figure 11-10.

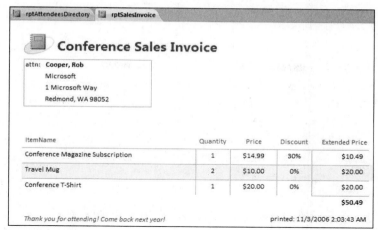

Figure 11-10

Summary

This chapter provided a closer look at reports and some of the features that make them different from forms. You saw various methods for creating reports and some of the different events you can use with reports and sections. In addition, you learned some ways to extend reports by adding just a small amount of VBA code — in many cases, it doesn't take much code to make reports more interesting, just a solid knowledge of how reports work and when events fire.

The chapter also presented an in-depth look at some of the new features for reports in Access 2007, and how you can use these features to make report creation easier and to extend the user experience around working with reports.

12

Customizing the Ribbon

The first time you open Access 2007, you'll notice that things are different. The familiar menu bar and toolbars have been replaced with the Ribbon. The new interface may appear a bit daunting, but it's only a matter of time until you've learned where commands are located and are more comfortable with it.

This chapter provides a brief look at the Ribbon in Access 2007 and discusses some of the design goals of the Ribbon that you can apply to your applications. Then comes the fun stuff: customization. You start by examining the types of objects you can create in a custom ribbon, and then use what you learn to create two sample applications with different design goals: a Ribbon that integrates with the Access Ribbon, and another to replace the Access Ribbon. As you'll soon see, the Ribbon is highly customizable, which can help you create new and exciting interfaces for your own applications.

Ribbon customizations are written in XML. Even if you've never written XML or are just getting started with XML, don't worry — it's straightforward and easy to understand. This chapter affords you the information and tools you need to customize the Ribbon (and learn a little about XML at the same time).

Ribbon Overview

The Ribbon, the new interface that appears at the top of the large majority of the applications in Office 2007, is designed to provide easier access to those tools that you use most. No longer are the most common commands buried under several layers of menus or hard-to-discover toolbars. Microsoft has added a Home tab in each of the Office applications that support the Ribbon, and it contains the most commonly used tools in that application.

The Ribbon is currently supported in the following applications:

- ❑ Access
- ❑ Excel

❑   Outlook (in object inspectors)

❑   PowerPoint

❑   Word

Figure 12-1 shows the Home tab in Access 2007.

Figure 12-1

Each group of controls in a tab in the Ribbon is, appropriately enough, called a *group*. The Home tab in Access contains a group to change views (Views), a group to access the clipboard (Clipboard), groups for work with formatting (Font and Rich Text), and groups to work with data (Records, Sort & Filter, and Find).

The Access 2007 Ribbon includes three additional default tabs:

❑   **Create:** Replaces the Insert menu in previous versions of Access. Use it to create the different types of objects in your database such as Forms and Reports.

❑   **External Data:** Replaces the Get External Data and Import menu items on the File menu in previous versions. It contains the tools that enable you to import and export data.

❑   **Database Tools:** Replaces much of the Tools menu in previous versions of Access.

You may also notice that there seem to be fewer controls or items available in the Ribbon when compared to previous Access menus and toolbars. That's because many of the tools are available only in a particular mode. These tools are said to be *contextual* — that is, they only apply under the context of a particular task.

Custom Menu Bars and Toolbars

If you built custom menu bars and toolbars in previous versions of Access, you might wonder what happens to those in Access 2007. Well, don't worry — you can still use them in Access 2007, although their appearance may be different than what you are used to.

Custom Menu Bars

Custom menu bars that you created in previous versions of Access will appear as a menu bar as long as you have set the `Allow Full Menus` property to No. In previous versions of Access, this property appears in the Startup dialog box under the Tools menu. If you have not set this property, custom menu bars will appear on a separate tab in the Ribbon called Add-Ins.

Shortcut Menu Bars

The shortcut menu bars that you created for forms in previous versions of Access will continue to work in Access 2007. They will appear on the context menu, not in the Ribbon. However, the tools for creating toolbars and menu bars have been removed. Unfortunately this means there is no way to create a new shortcut menu bar unless you write code or use a previous version of Access.

The following code (which requires a reference to the Microsoft Office 12.0 Type Library) creates a shortcut menu with two button controls. For more information about the CommandBar object model, please visit the MSDN website at http://msdn.microsoft.com.

```
Public Sub CreateShortcutMenu(strName As String)
    Dim objCommandBar As Office.CommandBar
    Dim objCommandBarControl As Office.CommandBarControl

    ' create the shortcut menu
    Set objCommandBar = Application.CommandBars.Add(strName, msoBarPopup)

    ' create a control
    Set objCommandBarControl = objCommandBar.Controls.Add(msoControlButton)
    objCommandBarControl.Caption = "Button1"
    objCommandBarControl.OnAction = "=MsgBox('Button1')"

    ' create another control
    Set objCommandBarControl = objCommandBar.Controls.Add(msoControlButton)
    objCommandBarControl.Caption = "Button2"
    objCommandBarControl.OnAction = "=MsgBox('Button2')"

    ' Cleanup
    Set objCommandBarControl = Nothing
    Set objCommandBar = Nothing

End Sub
```

Ribbon Customization

Because you could customize your applications by creating custom menu bars and toolbars in previous versions of Office or Access, you want similar functionality for the Ribbon. Microsoft has created a rich customization model that enables you to create your own Ribbons for use in your applications. Ribbon customizations are written in XML, and must conform to a specified schema that can be downloaded from the Microsoft website. To find the download, search http:// microsoft.com/downloads for "2007 XML Schema Reference."

Saving a Custom Ribbon

Because you'll probably want to test your custom ribbon as you build it, let's start by talking about how to use ribbon customizations in Access. The primary way to use a custom ribbon is with a special table named USysRibbons. This section explains how you can create this table.

Access loads ribbon customizations from a `USysRibbons` table, which contains the fields shown in the table that follows:

Field Name	Data Type	Description
RibbonName	TEXT	Contains the name of a Ribbon that you use in your application. You can specify the name of a Ribbon for a form, report, or database.
RibbonXml	MEMO	Contains the XML definition for the ribbon customization.

Alternatively, you can create this table using the following SQL statement in a DDL query:

```
CREATE TABLE USysRibbons
(
    RibbonName TEXT (255) PRIMARY KEY,
    RibbonXml MEMO
);
```

You can also create application-level Ribbons using a COM Add-in. Appendix C provides more information about writing a COM Add-in to customize the Ribbon.

To define multiple Ribbons in your application, simply add a new record to the `USysRibbons` table.

There is yet another way to create the `USysRibbons` table for use in your databases: by creating a database called `Blank12.accdb`. When you create a new blank database in Access 2007, Access first looks for a file named `Blank12.accdb` in the Office\Templates directory. If it finds one, it creates a copy of the file for your new Blank Database. If this file contains a `USyRibbons` table, your new database automatically includes the table.

The `USysRibbons` table should be local to the database you are customizing. Ribbon customizations are not loaded if the `USysRibbons` table is linked in another database.

Specifying the Custom Ribbon

Once you write a ribbon customization, you need some way to display it for your database, form, or report. That's where the new `Ribbon Name` property (in the Current Database group of the Access Options dialog box) comes in. To set the Ribbon for a database, you just set this property to the name of a ribbon in the `USysRibbons` table. Your custom ribbon displays when you re-open the database.

For form and report Ribbons, set the `Ribbon Name` property on the Other tab of the form or report property sheet.

Defining a Ribbon Using XML

Before jumping in to write the XML, there is one change to make to your Access environment. By default, any errors that may be caused by the XML are not displayed. Instead, the customization may fail without warning and not load. To see the errors, you must enable the Show Add-In User Interface Errors option in the General section of the Advanced group of the Access Options dialog box.

You can write XML using a text editor such as Notepad, or an integrated development environment (IDE) such as Visual Studio or XML Spy. The examples in this chapter use Microsoft Visual Web Developer 2005 Express Edition, which at the time of this writing is freely available for download from the Microsoft website, `http://msdn.microsoft.com/vstudio/express/vwd`.

Many IDEs such as Visual Web Developer provide auto-completion, or IntelliSense, when an XML Schema (XSD) is available. Because the XML you write here is based on a schema, the process is greatly simplified.

Using the Ribbon Schema

The schema file for ribbon customizations is called `customui.xsd`. Using Visual Web Developer, the first thing to do is create a new XML file. Once the file is created, click the button in the Schemas property to open the Schemas dialog box. Click the Add button at the bottom of the dialog box to browse to the `customui.xsd` XML schema that is included in the 2007 Office System: XML Schema Reference. Figure 12-2 shows the schema file added to the dialog box.

Figure 12-2

You can save the step of adding the schema by copying customui.xsd to %programfiles%\Microsoft Visual Studio 8\Xml\Schemas.

Writing the XML

Once you point Visual Web Developer to the schema, you're ready to start writing. The *root node* of a ribbon customization is:

```
<customUI xmlns="http://schemas.microsoft.com/office/2006/01/customui">
```

A root node is the node at the top of an XML document. There is one and only one root node in any given document.

The namespace specified by the `xmlns` attribute is known as the default namespace. It defines the elements and attributes used when you write a ribbon customization. Within a customization, you can create a Ribbon, modify commands in the Quick Access Toolbar, or modify the Office Menu. You'll create a Ribbon here and look at the other options later in this chapter.

Next, tell the XML that you are creating a Ribbon by adding the `ribbon` tag to define it:

```
<ribbon startFromScratch="true">
```

The `startFromScratch` attribute tells Access whether to display the built-in Ribbon. Use the following XML to create an empty Ribbon for your database as shown in Figure 12-3.

```
<customUI xmlns="http://schemas.microsoft.com/office/2006/01/customui">
    <ribbon startFromScratch="true"/>
</customUI>
```

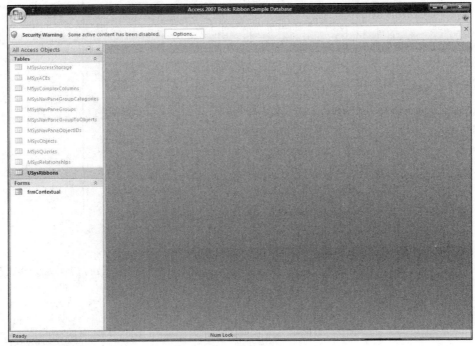

Figure 12-3

When you create a Ribbon from scratch, the Office menu is also modified as shown in Figure 12-4. The Office menu contains many commands that are central to the application itself.

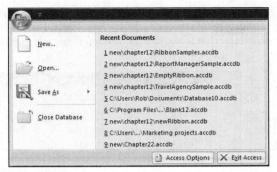

Figure 12-4

Later in this chapter, you'll build two solutions — one that is incorporated into the Access Ribbon and one that you build from scratch.

Adding Tabs and Groups

Controls such as buttons, drop-downs, and checkboxes are organized into tabs and groups in the Ribbon. Tabs appear at the top of the Ribbon and contain groups. You can define your own tabs and groups, or you can incorporate controls from existing tabs and groups. Tabs are defined using the `tab` element and groups are defined using the `group` element.

Here's an example. Say you want to add a tab with one group to the existing Ribbon. The following XML adds a new tab called `My Tab` at the end of the existing tab set. Start with the `customUI` node and the `ribbon` node that you saw in the previous section:

```
<customUI xmlns="http://schemas.microsoft.com/office/2006/01/customui">
    <ribbon startFromScratch="false">
```

To define tabs, you first add a `tabs` node under the `ribbon` node to say that you are defining a tab set:

```
        <tabs>
```

Next, add the tab using the `tab` node as follows:

```
            <tab id="tabMyTab" label="My Tab">
```

Add the group below the tab:

```
                <group id="grpMyGroup" label="My Group"></group>
```

Now, finish the XML by adding the end nodes:

```
            </tab>
        </tabs>
    </ribbon>
</customUI>
```

Notice that the `tab` and `group` nodes include attributes named `id` and `label`. All controls that you add to your Ribbon including tabs and groups must have an ID attribute, which is a string that is unique throughout the Ribbon and cannot contain spaces. Add this XML to the `RibbonXml` field of the `USysRibbons` table. Assign the XML the name **My First Ribbon** in the `RibbonName` field and then set the `Ribbon Name` property in the Access Options dialog box to the same name: My First Ribbon. When you've completed these steps, you should have something that looks like the Ribbon shown in Figure 12-5.

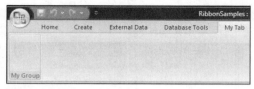

Figure 12-5

Congratulations! You've just written your first custom ribbon!

> *For the remainder of this section, the* `customUI` *and* `ribbon` *nodes are omitted in the XML. Except where noted, each of the following examples should include these nodes.*

If you are using an IDE that provides IntelliSense, you may have noticed an attribute in the tab node called `insertBeforeMso` or `insertAfterMso`. You can use these attributes to set the position of a tab relative to an existing tab in Access. For example, here's the XML that will move the My Tab tab to the beginning of the Ribbon instead of the end:

```
<tabs>
    <tab id="tabMyTab" insertBeforeMso="TabHomeAccess" label="My Tab">
        <group id="grpMyGroup" label="My Group"/>
    </tab>
</tabs>
```

The first tab always receives the focus after a tab is switched. Imagine that your My Tab appears before the Home tab, and you open a form in Design view. Forms and reports in Design view display a contextual tab that enables you to work with the design surfaces. When you close the form, focus is given back to the first tab — in this case, the custom My Tab. You'll see more about contextual tabs shortly.

> Any attribute that ends with `Mso` refers to items provided by Office. For example, `imageMso` refers to images that are included in Office. This attribute is discussed later in the chapter.

It is also possible to add a new group to an existing tab by specifying the `idMso` attribute. You can use this attribute to refer to tabs, groups, and even controls that are provided by Office. (More on re-using groups and controls later.)

The following XML adds the group called My Group after the Clipboard group in the Home tab:

```
<tabs>
  <tab idMso="TabHomeAccess">
    <group id="grpMyGroup" label="My Group" insertAfterMso="GroupClipboard"/>
  </tab>
</tabs>
```

Figure 12-6 shows the result.

Figure 12-6

Fun, huh? Wait, it gets better!

You can also choose to include an existing group in another tab. For example, the Clipboard group contains the familiar controls for Cut, Copy, and Paste, which are pretty useful, so say you want to include that group in your tab. The following XML adds the Clipboard group and two custom groups to My Tab:

```
<tabs>
  <tab id="tabMyTab" label="My Tab">
    <group id="grpMyGroup1" label="First Group"/>
    <group idMso="GroupClipboard"/>
    <group id="grpMyGroup2" label="Second Group"/>
  </tab>
</tabs>
```

The result of this Ribbon is shown in Figure 12-7.

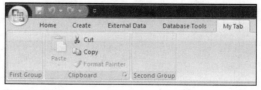

Figure 12-7

Now let's take a look at contextual tabs.

Contextual Tabs

As mentioned earlier, a contextual tab is designed to appear for a specific task. For example, contextual tabs are used in Access for designing objects, setting margins on a report, or working with relationships. You can define contextual tabs for forms and reports by setting the Ribbon Name property of the form or report.

Contextual tabs work slightly different from regular tabs. To define a contextual tab, you use the `contextualTab` node, which contains a `tabSet` node. The tab set for contextual tabs is defined by Access and must be specified using the `idMso` attribute `TabSetFormReportExtensibility`.

Here's what it looks like:

```
<customUI xmlns="http://schemas.microsoft.com/office/2006/01/customui">
    <ribbon startFromScratch="false">
        <contextualTabs>
            <tabSet idMso="TabSetFormReportExtensibility">
                <tab id="tabMyCTab" label="My Contextual Tab">
                    <group id="grpMyGroup" label="Group1"/>
                </tab>
            </tabSet>
        </contextualTabs>
    </ribbon>
</customUI>
```

Contextual tabs receive the focus when the object is opened, and are hidden when the object loses focus. They are not given focus when you switch back to the form or report.

You design contextual tabs to give context or meaning to specific forms or reports. Use a tab if you have functionality that you want to be available throughout your application. The `Caption` property of a form or report is used as the title of the tab set in the window as shown in Figure 12-8.

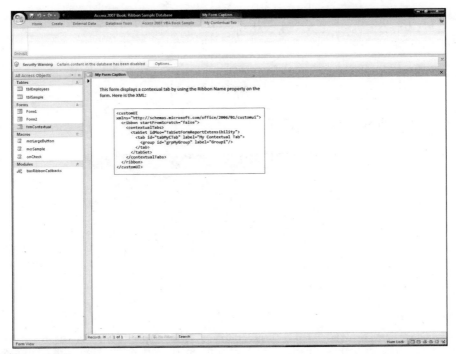

Figure 12-8

Adding Controls

There is a wide range of controls that you can use in your customizations. Because you've already examined tabs and groups, the XML that follows only describes the controls. To use these controls in the Ribbon you need to include `tab` and `group` nodes in addition to the `customUI` and `ribbon` nodes.

The solutions that you build later in this chapter will use these controls, including two of the more interesting controls: galleries and dynamic menus.

Menus and Menu Separators

A menu control is a container for other types of controls and is specified using the `menu` node. You can specify the size of the menu control in the Ribbon using the `size` attribute. You can also specify the size of items in the menu using the `itemSize` attribute. Possible values for both attributes are `normal`, shown in Figure 12-9, and `large`, shown in Figure 12-10.

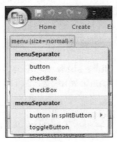

Figure 12-9

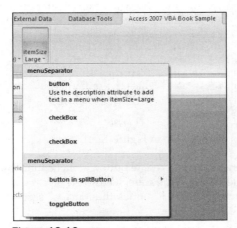

Figure 12-10

The following XML defines a large menu with three buttons and two menu separators:

```
<menu id="mnuSample" label="Sample Menu" size="large" itemSize="large">
    <menuSeparator id="msep1" title="Separator 1"/>
    <button id="btnSample1" label="Button1"/>
    <button id="btnSample2" label="Button2"/>
    <menuSeparator id="msep2" title="Separator 2"/>
    <button id="btnSample3" label="Button3"/>
</menu>
```

You can use the `menuSeparator` node inside a `menu` node to add a menu separator. The `title` attribute of the `menuSeparator` sets the text for the menu separator.

Buttons, Toggle Buttons, and Split Buttons

The vast majority of controls you use will be buttons. As with menus, buttons are available in two sizes: `normal` and `large`. To create a button in your customization, use the `button` node as shown in the following XML:

```
<button id="btnSample" label="Sample Button"/>
```

You can use a toggle button to reflect a state such as on or off, or true or false. An example of the toggle button in Access is the Bold button. To create a toggle button, use the `toggleButton` node as shown in the following XML:

```
<toggleButton id="tglNormal" label="toggleButton (size=normal)"/>
```

Split buttons are a new control that you can use in Office 2007. They contain a menu and either a button or a toggle button. The effect is similar to that of a menu, but there is a button that is included in the Ribbon as well. The following XML shows how to create a split button with a button:

```
<splitButton id="sb1">
    <button id="b2" label="button in splitButton"/>
    <menu id="mnu2" label="menu in splitButton">
    <button id="b3" label="splitButton > menu > button"/>
    <button id="b4" label="splitButton > menu > button"/>
    </menu>
</splitButton>
```

The different types of buttons are shown in Figure 12-11.

To run your own code when a button or toggle button is clicked, handle the `onAction` callback. To get the pressed state for a toggle button using code, handle the `getPressed` callback. Callback actions are discussed later in the "Writing Callback Routines and Macros" section.

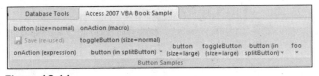

Figure 12-11

Check Boxes

As with a toggle button, a checkbox is used to show true or false, or on or off. To create a checkbox in your customization, use the `checkBox` node as shown in the following XML:

```
<checkBox id="chkSample" label="Sample Checkbox"/>
```

You can use a checkbox control by itself or inside of a menu control. The appearance of a checkbox in a menu is different from a checkbox outside of a menu, as shown in Figure 12-12.

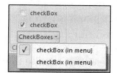

Figure 12-12

To run your own code when a checkbox is checked, handle the `onAction` callback. To get the checked state for a checkbox using code, handle the `getPressed` callback.

Combo Boxes and Drop-Downs

The Ribbon offers two types of controls for listing multiple items — the combo box and the drop-down. There are a couple of differences between these two controls. First, you can type text into a combo box control but not into a drop-down. Also, although both combo box and drop-down controls contain `item` nodes for their items, the drop-down control can also contain buttons, as shown in Figure 12-13.

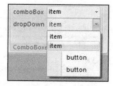

Figure 12-13

The `size` attribute is not available for these controls, but you can set their width using the `sizeString` attribute. The width of the control is set to the width of the text specified in this attribute. For example, if you set the `sizeString` to WWWWW, the width of the control is sized to fit the literal string WWWWW.

To create a combo box in your customization, use the `comboBox` node as shown in the following XML:

```
<comboBox id="cboSample" label="Sample Combo Box"/>
```

To create a drop-down in your customization, use the `dropDown` node:

```
<dropDown id="ddnSample" label="Sample Drop Down"/>
```

The following XML shows a combo box control with three items:

```
<comboBox id="cboSample" label="comboBox">
    <item id="item1" label="item1"/>
    <item id="item2" label="item2"/>
    <item id="item3" label="item3"/>
</comboBox>
```

Drop-downs and combo boxes in ribbon customizations can be very useful. For example, to provide a mechanism to log in to your application, you can create a drop-down control to display a list of user names that the user can select. Or, you might want to list the days of the week for a filter. Because that list is static, the drop-down control in a Ribbon might be a good place to display it. You'll see an example of the latter when you build your first solution.

To run your own code when an item is selected, handle the onAction callback. You can fill the items in a combo box or drop-down using three callback functions: getItemCount, getItemLabel, and getItemID.

Edit Boxes and Labels

Edit boxes also allow text to be typed in the Ribbon. You create an edit box using the editBox node. The control enables you to limit the amount of text that is typed in the edit box using the maxLength argument as shown in the following XML:

```
<editBox id="txtEditSample" label="editBox" maxLength="5" onChange="onEditChange"/>
```

Figure 12-14 shows what the Ribbon looks like when too much text is typed in an editBox control.

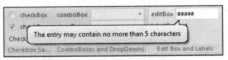

Figure 12-14

As the name implies, the labelControl node is used to display static text in the Ribbon. You might use this control to display messages to your users, such as status information, or the current date. The following XML uses the labelControl node to display static text:

```
<labelControl id="lblSample" label="Sample Label"/>
```

To run your own code when the text is updated in an edit box control, handle the onChange callback. To dynamically get the text for a label control, handle the getLabel callback.

Separator

A separator node is used to provide separation between controls. The separator control appears as a vertical line between controls in the ribbon and is created with the following XML:

```
<separator id="sepMySeparator"/>
```

DialogBoxLauncher

Let's say that you have many choices or options to display to the user — perhaps user settings that are part of your application — but you don't necessarily want to show them all in the Ribbon. You might choose to use a form to collect all the related information from the user, and still decide to show the more common options in the Ribbon. To make it easy to get to the full set of options, you can use a dialog box launcher in the Ribbon to open a form in your database. By using the dialog box launcher, you can avoid having a separate `button` node in the group to open the form.

Use the `dialogBoxLauncher` node to create a launcher in a `group`. It requires a `button` node that is used to handle the click action taken by the user. The dialog box launcher adds a small button in the bottom of the Other Controls group label as shown in Figure 12-15.

Figure 12-15

The following XML shows a dialog box launcher that displays a message box when clicked:

```
<dialogBoxLauncher>
    <button id="btnDlgLauncher" onAction="=MsgBox('Open a dialog here')"/>
</dialogBoxLauncher>
```

Grouping Controls

There are a few additional types of controls that can be used to group other controls. A `box` control is used to group controls together either horizontally or vertically. A `buttonGroup` control is used to group button type controls and adds some style to the group. Buttons inside a `buttonGroup` do not support the size attribute for large buttons. You also can use a `separator` to display a vertical line between controls for separation. Each of these controls is shown in Figure 12-16.

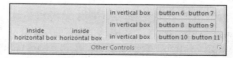

Figure 12-16

Here's the XML for the grouping control Ribbon:

```
<group id="grpMiscSample" label="Other Controls">
    <box boxStyle="horizontal" id="boxHorizontal">
       <button id="boxButton1" label="inside horizontal box" size="large"/>
       <button id="boxButton2" label="inside horizontal box" size="large"/>
    </box>
    <separator id="sep1"/>
    <box boxStyle="vertical" id="boxVertical">
        <button id="boxButton3" label="in vertical box"/>
        <button id="boxButton4" label="in vertical box"/>
        <button id="boxButton5" label="in vertical box"/>
    </box>
```

```
        <separator id="sep2"/>
        <buttonGroup id="bgrp1">
            <button id="boxButton6" label="button 6"/>
            <button id="boxButton7" label="button 7"/>
        </buttonGroup>
        <buttonGroup id="bgrp2">
            <button id="boxButton8" label="button 8"/>
            <button id="boxButton9" label="button 9"/>
        </buttonGroup>
        <buttonGroup id="bgrp3">
            <button id="boxButton10" label="button 10"/>
            <button id="boxButton11" label="button 11"/>
        </buttonGroup>
        <dialogBoxLauncher>
            <button id="btnDlgLauncher" onAction="=MsgBox('Open a dialog here')"/>
        </dialogBoxLauncher>
    </group>
```

Writing Callback Routines and Macros

Now that you've looked at the different types of controls you can create in a ribbon customization, it's time to make them do some work! Callbacks were mentioned with nearly every control, but what is a callback? A callback is nothing more than a routine that is called when the Ribbon asks for information, or when an action is performed.

Callbacks enable you to respond to actions, such as when a button is clicked or when an item is selected in a drop-down. In addition, they enable you to update controls in the Ribbon itself.

In Access, you can handle a callback in three ways: using a macro, an expression, or VBA code. Naturally, using VBA provides the most flexibility and control and you'll want to use that in most cases. The following sections explore each of these in the context of clicking a button in the Ribbon.

Using Expressions

The easiest way to respond to the onAction callback is to use an expression, but the choices for the expressions you can call are a bit limited. We show using an expression for the onAction callback here for completeness. Use the following XML to display a message box when the user clicks on a button:

```
<button id="btnOnActionExpression" label="Expression"
        onAction="=MsgBox('onAction-Expression')"/>
```

Using Access Macros

As an alternative to using an expression, you can call an Access macro from the onAction callback. Using macros, you can create portions of the application that are available when the database is disabled. For more information about disabled mode, please see Chapter 22.

To specify an Access macro, simply use the name of the macro in the onAction attribute, as shown in the following XML:

```
<button id="btnMacro" label="onAction (macro)" onAction="mcrLargeButton"/>
```

Using VBA

You'll probably want to write most of your callbacks using VBA. As you would expect, you have much more control and flexibility over the Ribbon by writing code than by using a macro.

To use VBA in the onAction callback, you simply give the name of the subroutine in the onAction attribute, but there are some extra steps. In VBA (or other languages such as C# or C++), the callback routine must match a particular *signature*. A signature is the declaration of the routine including its parameters and return type. The onAction callback for a button control has the following signature:

```
Public Sub MyRoutine(ctl As IRibbonControl)
```

In this example, MyRoutine is the name of a sub procedure that you specify in the onAction attribute. The IRibbonControl parameter is passed to your code by the Ribbon, and represents the control that was clicked. To use this parameter, you need to add a reference to the Microsoft Office 12.0 Object Library.

The IRibbonControl object has three properties: Context, Id, and Tag. The Context property returns the Application object for the application that contains the Ribbon. In this example, that is Microsoft Access. The Id property contains the Id of the control that was clicked. The Tag property is like the Tag property for a control in Access — it can be used to store extra data with a Ribbon control. The value of the Tag property is specified using the tag attribute for a control.

Say, for example, that you have two buttons in a Ribbon. The first button opens a form named Form1, and the second button opens a form named Form2. One way to open these forms is to use a separate onAction callback for each button. In this case, you just want to open forms, so you'll take a different approach.

Because the Ribbon gives you both the Id and Tag property for a control, you can open the form using the data that you're given. One method is to determine the Id of the control and open the appropriate form as shown in the following code:

```
Sub DoOpenForm(ctl As IRibbonControl)
    Select Case ctl.Id
        Case "btnForm1": DoCmd.OpenForm "Form1"
        Case "btnForm2": DoCmd.OpenForm "Form2"
    End Select
End Sub
```

As you can see, if you reuse this code for many buttons, it can quickly grow quite large. But, by using the tag attribute, you can specify the name of the form to open with the control as illustrated in the following XML:

```
<button id="btnForm1" label="Open Form1" onAction="onOpenForm" tag="Form1"/>
<button id="btnForm2" label="Open Form2" onAction="onOpenForm" tag="Form2"/>
```

This means you can write the following code to open a form:

```
Public Sub DoOpenForm(ctl As IRibbonControl)
    DoCmd.OpenForm ctl.Tag
End Sub
```

Of course, there will be times when you want to pass extra data or perform extra tasks while opening a form that might require additional code. By combining these techniques, you could use the name of the form as the control Id, and pass an OpenArgs value to a form in the tag attribute, like this:

```
Public Sub DoOpenForm2(ctl As IRibbonControl)
    DoCmd.OpenForm FormName:=ctl.Id, OpenArgs:=ctl.Tag
End Sub
```

The Ribbon allows this type of flexibility depending on the needs of your application.

More Callback Routines

Determining when a button is clicked is useful, but there are many other callbacks that you can use in your customizations to provide a rich experience for your users. As mentioned in some of the other control types, the onAction callback is used to notify you that something has happened. In many of those cases, the signature for the routine you write with that callback is different from the signature for a button. You'll take a look at these in a moment.

If you've looked through the schema or the attributes of the controls, you may have noticed that there are a lot of attributes that begin with the word "get." These attributes are also callbacks. When the Ribbon needs to determine the state of a control or the items in a control, it asks your database for that information if you have implemented the appropriate callback. The information is relayed back to the Ribbon using the callbacks. Take a closer look, starting with the onAction callback for a checkBox.

Checking a Checkbox

The signature for the onAction callback for a button provides only the control that was clicked. For a checkbox, you also want to know whether it was checked. Because the IRibbonControl object does not provide a property for this, the signature for this callback is different. To take an action when a checkbox is checked (or *pressed* as the Ribbon refers to it), use the following callback signature:

```
Sub OnPressed(ctl As IRibbonControl, pressed As Boolean)
```

In this case, if the checkbox is pressed, the pressed argument will be True. Otherwise, it will be False. You might use this callback to show or hide portions of your user interface.

Determining Whether to Preselect a Checkbox

Let's say that you want to determine whether a checkbox is pressed when the Ribbon is loaded. To do this, you can handle the getPressed callback. The signature for that callback is the same as the onAction callback for a checkbox:

```
Sub OnGetPressed(ctl As IRibbonControl, ByRef pressed As Boolean)
```

ByRef is the default modifier for a parameter in Visual Basic and VBA, meaning that even if you don't specify ByRef, this modifier is implicitly defined. In effect these two signatures are identical. To set the pressed state of a checkbox, set the pressed argument before leaving the routine as shown in the following code:

```
Sub OnGetPressed(ctl As IRibbonControl, ByRef pressed As Boolean)
    If ctl.Id = "chkMyCheckBox" Then
        ' Code to determine whether the check box should be pressed
        pressed = True
    End If
End Sub
```

> **Most of the** get **callbacks follow this pattern — they return a value using a** ByRef
> **parameter rather than using a function procedure.**

Filling a Combo Box or Drop-Down

The comboBox and dropDown nodes enable you to add items using XML, but there may be times when you need to fill them dynamically. To display a list of employees from a table called tblEmployees in a dropDown, for example, you want a way to fill the control at runtime because the data in an employee table may change. The sample Employees table is shown in Figure 12-17.

tblEmployees			
ID ▾	FirstName ▾	LastName ▾	Add New Field
3	Teresa	Hennig	
4	Rob	Cooper	
5	Geoff	Griffith	
6	Armen	Stein	
* (New)			

Figure 12-17

To do this, there are three callback attributes to handle. The first is called is getItemCount. It determines the number of items in the combo box or drop-down. The next one that is called is getItemLabel. It sets the label for a given item that appears in the combo box or drop-down. The last callback is getItemID. It sets the unique ID for an item in the list. Note that these callbacks are called when the tab containing the drop-down receives focus. They may not necessarily run when the Ribbon loads.

These last two callbacks are called once for each item that is created when you set the count in getItemCount. So if getItemCount returns four items, then getItemLabel and getItemID are called four times. The following XML defines these attributes:

```
<dropDown id="ddnEmployees" label="Employees"
        getItemCount="OnGetItemCount"
        getItemLabel="OnGetItemLabel"
        getItemID="OnGetItemID">
</dropDown>
```

To fill the drop-down list, you want to read data from the Employees table. For that you need a Recordset — more specifically, you need a Recordset that is available from all three callbacks. So, start with a module-level Recordset declaration:

```
Dim rst As DAO.Recordset
```

The first callback that's called is `getItemCount`, so open the Recordset from there:

```
Public Sub OnGetItemCount(ctl As IRibbonControl, ByRef Count As Variant)
    If ctl.ID = "ddnEmployees" Then
        ' open the Recordset and return the count
        Set rst = CurrentDb.OpenRecordset("tblEmployees")
        Count = rst.RecordCount
    End If
End Sub
```

Now you need to set the label and the ID in that order. First, the label:

```
Public Sub OnGetItemLabel(ctl As IRibbonControl, index As Integer, _
    ByRef Label As Variant)

    If ctl.ID = "ddnEmployees" Then
        If Not rst.EOF Then
            ' set the label text
            Label = rst("FirstName") & " " & rst("LastName")
        End If
    End If
End Sub
```

Next, the ID. Because this is the last routine called before getting the next item, you'll move to the next record in the Recordset here. When you reach EOF, you'll close the Recordset and destroy the object.

```
Public Sub OnGetItemID(ctl As IRibbonControl, index As Integer, _
    ByRef ID As Variant)

    If ctl.ID = "ddnEmployees" Then
        ' make sure you are not at EOF
        If Not rst.EOF Then
            ' set the id using the ID field in the table
            ID = "EmployeeID" & rst("ID")

            ' get the next employee
            rst.MoveNext

            ' cleanup when you are at EOF
            If rst.EOF Then
                rst.Close
                Set rst = Nothing
            End If
        End If
    End If
End Sub
```

The drop-down created using this code and XML is shown in Figure 12-18.

Use an ID that is relevant for the item being added. As you'll see in the next section, you are not given the text for the item that is selected, only its ID.

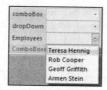

Figure 12-18

Selecting an Item in a Combo Box or Drop-Down

The callback specified by the `onAction` attribute is called when an item is selected in a combo box or drop-down. Its signature is as follows:

```
Public Sub DoSelectedItem(ctl As IRibbonControl, selectedId As String, _
                          selectedIndex As Integer)
```

As you can see from the signature, you are given the ID for a selected item and its index in the list, but not its value. Therefore, you should use an ID value that pertains to the selected item so that you can infer the item given its ID. In other words, if you are displaying a list of employees in a combo box in the Ribbon, consider including the ID of the employee as part of the ID attribute for the item in the combo box. This will help you determine which employee was selected later.

For the Employees example, you first want to modify the XML to specify the `onAction` attribute:

```
<dropDown id="ddnEmployees" label="Employees"
          getItemCount="OnGetItemCount"
          getItemLabel="OnGetItemLabel"
          getItemID="OnGetItemID"
          onAction="OnSelectItem">
</dropDown>
```

Next, you write the callback routine, as follows. Because you used the ID value from the table in the ID string for the item, the code just needs to parse it out of the `selectedId` argument.

```
Public Sub OnSelectItem(ctl As IRibbonControl, _
        selectedId As String, _
        selectedIndex As Integer)

    Dim lngID        As Long
    Dim strFirstName As String
    Dim strLastName  As String

    ' parse the ID from the ID string
    lngID = CLng(Replace(selectedId, "EmployeeID", ""))

    ' get the first and last name
    strFirstName = DLookup("FirstName", "tblEmployees", "ID = " & lngID)
    strLastName = DLookup("LastName", "tblEmployees", "ID = " & lngID)

    ' Display a message to the user
    MsgBox "Welcome, " & strFirstName & " " & strLastName
End Sub
```

If you use the items from a table that has an `AutoNumber` *field where the values are sequential, you can probably just use the* `selectedIndex` *argument.*

Disabling a Control

Disabling a control is similar to setting the checked state of a checkbox. To disable a control, use the `getEnabled` attribute, like this:

```
<button id="btnForm1" label="Open Form1" tag="Form1"
  onAction="onOpenForm" getEnabled="OnGetEnabled"/>
```

Here's the code to handle the callback:

```
Public Sub OnGetEnabled(ctl As IRibbonControl, ByRef Enabled As Variant)
    Select Case ctl.Id
        ' disable the Form3 button
        Case "btnForm3": Enabled = False
        Case Else: Enabled = True
    End Select
End Sub
```

You might disable a control depending on the specific user, application state, state of data, or any number of reasons.

You can hide a control using the `getVisible` *callback, but the Office guideline is to disable a control rather than hide it. This is to prevent the Ribbon from jumping around as controls are shown or hidden.*

Displaying Images

The Ribbon is graphical in nature so it makes sense that there are a few ways you can load images into your controls. Images can be an important part of an application. They can be used to provide status or state, or help give it a polished look. Perhaps, more importantly, images provide visual cues to users that may help make an application easier for them to use.

You can use three techniques to load images in your application's Ribbon, and they're discussed in the following sections.

imageMso Attribute

The easiest way to use images in your application is to use those provided by Office. The `imageMso` attribute on a control specifies an image that is provided by Office. You can use any images provided by any application in Office. For example, here's how you might include images from Outlook in your application:

```
<group id="grpOutlook" label="Outlook">
    <button id="btn17" label="FollowUpComposeMenu" imageMso="FollowUpComposeMenu"/>
    <button id="btn18" label="CalendarInsert" imageMso="CalendarInsert"/>
    <button id="btn19" label="ChartInsert" imageMso="ChartInsert"/>
    <separator id="sep4"/>
    <button id="btn20" label="NewTaskNumbered" imageMso="NewTaskNumbered"/>
    <button id="btn21" label="NewContactNumbered" imageMso="NewContactNumbered"/>
</group>
```

You can download the list of control IDs from the Microsoft website or get them from inside an Office application (as explained in the section "More Ribbon Tips" at the end of the chapter).

Figures 12-19, 12-20, 12-21, and 12-22 show some of the `imageMso` attributes you can specify in your Access applications. This is only a small subset of what is available to you.

Figure 12-19

Figure 12-20

Figure 12-21

Figure 12-22

loadImage Callback

Using images that are included with Office is an easy way to use images in your applications. But if you are developing an application, there are likely many more times where you want to use your own images. To do so, the Ribbon provides a callback called `loadImage`, which is called whenever an image is requested via the `image` attribute. To provide a single function for this task, the attribute is defined on the custom UI node as demonstrated in the following XML:

```xml
<customUI xmlns="http://schemas.microsoft.com/office/2006/01/customui"
    loadImage="OnLoadImage">
  <ribbon startFromScratch="true">
    <tabs>
      <tab id="tabLoadImageSamples" label="loadImage Samples">
        <group id="grpBMP" label="BMP">
          <button id="btnLoadImage1"
                  label="News"
                  image="news.bmp"
                  size="large"/>
          <button id="btnLoadImage2"
                  label="Reminder"
                  image="bell.bmp"
                  size="large"/>
        </group>
      </tab>
```

```
    </tabs>
  </ribbon>
</customUI>
```

The `image` attribute is the name of an image file that is passed to the `loadImage` callback. You can use BMP, GIF, or JPG files for your images. The following code implements the `loadImage` callback to load images in an `Images` subdirectory of the directory from which the database is currently opened. This means you can distribute images as a part of your application and load them dynamically.

```
Public Sub OnLoadImage(imageName As String, ByRef image)
    Dim strPath As String
    strPath = CurrentProject.Path & "\images\" & imageName

    ' return the image
    Set image = LoadPicture(strPath)
End Sub
```

In this case, the `image` argument must return an object of type `IPictureDisp`. The easiest way to create one is to use the `LoadPicture` function.

getImage Callbacks

If you have a table in your database that stores the names of images for your application, you might choose not to implement the `loadImage` callback because you want to read it from a table. To load the image for this scenario, you can use the `getImage` callback for a control. The sample table of images is shown in Figure 12-23.

tblImages

id	ControlId	ImageFileName	Add New Field
1	btnGetImage1	ReportCard.gif	
2	btnGetImage2	News.gif	
3	btnGetImage3	Bell.gif	
(New)			

Figure 12-23

Using this table, let's define a few buttons to display images.

```
<group id="grpGetImage" label="getImage Samples">
    <button id="btnGetImage1" label="Test" getImage="OnGetImage" size="large"/>
    <button id="btnGetImage2" label="News" getImage="OnGetImage" size="large"/>
    <button id="btnGetImage3" label="Bell" getImage="OnGetImage" size="large"/>
</group>
```

Now, implement the `getImage` callback to read from the table as follows. For demo purposes, the `DLookup` function is used. If you had a lot of images in this scenario, a `Recordset` would probably give better performance.

```
Public Sub OnGetImage(ctl As IRibbonControl, ByRef Image)
    Dim strPath As String
    Dim strImageName As String
```

```
      ' get the image name from the table
      strImageName = Nz(DLookup("ImageFileName", "tblImages", _
          "ControlId = '" & ctl.Id & "'"), "")

      ' build the path
      strPath = CurrentProject.Path & "\images\" & strImageName

      ' make sure the file exists
      If Len(Dir(strPath)) = 0 Then
          Exit Sub
      End If

      ' return the image
      Set Image = LoadPicture(strPath)
End Sub
```

The size of an image displayed in the normal *size is 16 × 16 (pixels) while* large *images are 32 × 32.*

Refreshing Ribbon Content

The Ribbons that you've built so far have been fairly static in nature. You were able to read data from tables and display dynamic content, but upon making selections, you took actions in forms and reports. But perhaps you'd like to update other content in the Ribbon itself upon selection — to provide a welcome message to a user, to show status information about a particular piece of data, or even to show something fun like a clock. The following sections describe how to update items in the Ribbon itself.

onLoad Callback

When the Ribbon loads, it calls the onLoad callback if one has been specified. This callback gives you a copy of an IRibbonUI object that can be used to refresh content in the Ribbon itself. Once you have stored a copy of the Ribbon object, you can refresh content using either its Invalidate or InvalidateControl method.

The onLoad callback has the following signature:

```
Public Sub OnRibbonLoad(ribbon As IRibbonUI)
```

Dynamically Setting Text for a Button Control

There have been lots of solutions for building a clock on a form over the years. Most involve using a Timer event of a form and a label or text box to display the current time. To update that example for the Access 2007 Ribbon, use a button node to display an image. While the button won't do anything in particular, you might use it to stop the Timer or to open the Windows Date and Time applet in the Control Panel.

Start with the XML for the USysRibbons table:

```
<customUI xmlns="http://schemas.microsoft.com/office/2006/01/customui"
          onLoad="OnRibbonLoad">
  <ribbon startFromScratch="false">
    <tabs>
      <tab idMso="TabHomeAccess">
        <group id="grpClock" insertBeforeMso="GroupViews" label="Clock">
```

```
            <button id="btnClock" getLabel="OnTick" size="large"
                imageMso="StartAfterPrevious"/>
          </group>
        </tab>
      </tabs>
    </ribbon>
  </customUI>
```

The `onLoad` attribute for the `customUI` node stores a copy of the Ribbon. Also notice that you are going to implement the `getLabel` callback for the button because you want the label text to change with each `Timer` event.

Next, implement the callbacks. First, the `onLoad` callback. To store a copy of the Ribbon, declare a `Public` module level variable of type `IRibbonUI`:

```
' This should appear in the declarations section of a module
Public gobjRibbon As IRibbonUI

Public Sub OnRibbonLoad(ribbon As IRibbonUI)
    Set gobjRibbon = ribbon
End Sub
```

Then implement the `getLabel` callback (named `OnTick`). This routine sets the `Label` argument to the current time using the `Now()` function. It also makes sure that the form that contains the `Timer` event is open. In this case, the form is bound to the `USysRibbons` table.

```
Public Sub OnTick(ctl As IRibbonControl, ByRef Label)
    ' timer form
    If (Not (CurrentProject.AllForms("frmUSysRibbons").IsLoaded)) Then
        DoCmd.OpenForm "frmUSysRibbons", , , , , acHidden
    End If

    ' label
    If ctl.ID = "btnClock" Then
        Label = Now()
    End If
End Sub
```

Finally, because this is a clock, you need a timer, so create a form named `frmUSysRibbons` with a `TimerInterval` property of `1000`. That fires the `Timer` event every second. Then, create the `Timer` event for the form as follows:

```
Private Sub Form_Timer()
    ' Invalidate the clock every second to update the ribbon
    gobjRibbon.InvalidateControl "btnClock"
End Sub
```

By calling the `InvalidateControl` method, you're asking the `btnClock` control to redraw itself. Because this button implements the `getLabel` callback, the `OnTick` routine is called every time the `Timer` event fires for the form. That gives you the clock tick effect and creates the Ribbon shown in Figure 12-24.

Figure 12-24

Use the `Invalidate` method to refresh all controls in the Ribbon.

Creating an Integrated Ribbon

You've examined the different ways in which you can define ribbon customizations using tabs, groups, and controls. Now let's take a look at two scenarios for which you'll customize the Ribbon.

First, you'll create a Report Manager that integrates with the Access Ribbon. The Report Manager provides users with a nice way to view a list of reports that are in the database and provide them with a means to open a report. Second, you'll create your own contextual tab that you can use from a report to add some custom filtering.

Let's get started!

The sample database that implements the report manager is available with the code download for this chapter.

Building the Report Manager

The first scenario has two parts — the Report Manager and the custom filtering for the report. The Report Manager consists of a table to store information about reports, the XML for the Ribbon, and two callback routines.

Creating the Reports Table

To manage your reports, you'll create a table that contains the name and a friendly name for each report. To prevent the user from seeing the actual names of the reports, you'll show the friendly names in the menu. Both fields are defined as Text fields. Figure 12-25 shows the sample reports table named `tblReports`.

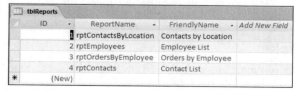

Figure 12-25

Using dynamicMenu

Next, write the XML that will fill the menu. Because the number of reports may change throughout development, use the dynamicMenu control in the Ribbon. If your users create their own reports in the application, this allows their reports to appear in the menu as well, as long as they add an entry to tblReports.

Content for the dynamicMenu control is provided using the getContent callback, which is a required attribute. Here's the XML for the report manager control:

```xml
<customUI xmlns="http://schemas.microsoft.com/office/2006/01/customui">
  <ribbon startFromScratch="false">
    <tabs>
      <tab idMso="TabDatabaseTools">
        <group id="grpReportManager" label="Report Manager"
               insertBeforeMso="GroupMacro">
          <!-- Report manager button -->
          <button id="btnReportManager"
                  label="Report Manager"
                  size="large"
                  tag="frmReportManager"
                  onAction="DoOpenForm"
                  imageMso="FormulaMoreFunctionsMenu"/>
          <separator id="sep1"/>
          <!-- Dynamic report menu to view reports -->
          <dynamicMenu id="dmnuReports" label="Reports"
                       getContent="OnGetReportList"
                       imageMso="ViewsReportView"
                       size="large"
                       invalidateContentOnDrop="true"/>
        </group>
      </tab>
    </tabs>
  </ribbon>
</customUI>
```

The dynamicMenu node also defines an attribute called invalidateContentOnDrop. This attribute tells the Ribbon to call the getContent callback when the user opens the drop-down menu. Setting it to true ensures that the control always has the latest content.

Notice that comments in the XML help make it more readable. XML comments appear between the <!-- and --> characters. This XML also includes a button to open a form that is bound to tblReports. This makes it easy to add reports to the report manager.

Writing the Callbacks

Finally, add the callback routines. Implement the getContent callback to fill the dynamicMenu. Start by declaring the routine with the following signature:

```vba
Public Sub OnGetReportList(ctl As IRibbonControl, ByRef content)
```

Next, add the declarations and open a Recordset for the reports table:

```
Dim rst As DAO.Recordset
Dim strMenu As String
Dim strID   As String

' open the reports table
Set rst = CurrentDb.OpenRecordset("SELECT * FROM tblReports ORDER BY FriendlyName")
```

Then start to build the XML for the dynamicMenu. This XML should contain a menu node, which can subsequently include items such as buttons, checkboxes, split buttons, and toggle buttons. You also need to include the namespace for the Ribbon, as shown in the following code:

```
' build the menu
strMenu = "<menu xmlns='http://schemas.microsoft.com/office/2006/01/customui'>"
```

Now, loop through the reports and add button nodes for each report in the Recordset.

```
' loop through the reports
While Not rst.EOF
    ' get the ID for the button by replacing any spaces with empty spaces
    strID = Replace(rst("ReportName"), " ", "")

    ' Append the button node
    strMenu = strMenu & GetButtonXml(strID, _
              rst("FriendlyName"), _
              "OnOpenReport", _
              rst("ReportName"))

    ' Get the next report in the table
    rst.MoveNext
Wend
```

Close the menu node, do some cleanup, and return the menu content:

```
' close the menu node
strMenu = strMenu & "</menu>"

rst.Close
Set rst = Nothing

' return the menu string
content = strMenu
End Sub
```

The callback refers to a helper function called GetButtonXml which is defined as follows:

```
Private Function GetButtonXml(strID As String, _
      strLabel As String, _
      strAction As String, _
      Optional strTag As String = "")

    ' builds the XML for a button
```

```
        GetButtonXml = "<button id='" & strID & "'" & _
        "           label='" & strLabel & "'" & _
        "           onAction='" & strAction & "'"

     ' add the tag attribute
     If Len(strTag) > 0 Then
         GetButtonXml = GetButtonXml & "           tag='" & strTag & "'"
     End If

     ' close the node
     GetButtonXml = GetButtonXml & "/>"
End Function
```

To use the `OnOpenReport` callback that is called when you click a button in the menu, add the following code:

```
Public Sub OnOpenReport(ctl As IRibbonControl)
    ' opens the report in report view
    DoCmd.OpenReport ctl.tag, acViewReport
End Sub
```

Great! You are ready for testing. Add the XML you created earlier to a `USysRibbons` table and set the Ribbon Name property for the database. When you select the Database Tools tab, you should have a Ribbon that looks like the one shown in Figure 12-26.

Figure 12-26

If you add or remove reports from `tblReports`, the menu should grow or shrink accordingly.

Building the Custom Filter Interface

Access 2007 includes a new Report View. It provides interactive reports that allow sorting and filtering like never before. In previous versions of Access, you might create a form to provide custom filtering for a report. In this section, you'll create a contextual tab in the Ribbon to provide a different filtering experience for a specific report.

Creating the Report

For this report, use a simple contacts report that includes the company name and the last name for a given contact. The easiest way to create this table is to use the Contacts table template on the Create tab of the Ribbon. The sample table is named `tblContacts` and has fields named `Company` and `Last Name`. These are the fields that you'll use for the filter.

Building the Contextual Tab

This filter only applies to the contacts report, so you'll use a contextual tab that will appear in the Ribbon when the report is opened and has focus. Inside the tab, you'll include two dropDown controls — one for the Company field, and one for the Last Name field. To make the callbacks as flexible as possible, store the name of the field that is filtered with the appropriate drop-down in the tag attribute. Create the following XML to define the Ribbon.

```xml
<customUI xmlns="http://schemas.microsoft.com/office/2006/01/customui">
  <ribbon startFromScratch="false">
    <contextualTabs>
      <tabSet idMso="TabSetFormReportExtensibility">
        <tab id="tabReportFilter" label="Filter Report">
          <group id="grpReportFilter" label="Filter Report">
            <!--
              Company dropdown: The tag attribute is the field that
              will be filtered
            -->
            <dropDown id="ddnCompany" label="Company" tag="Company"
                      getItemCount="OnGetItemCount"
                      getItemLabel="OnGetItemLabels"
                      getItemID="OnGetItemIDs"
                      onAction="OnReportFilter"
                      sizeString="Microsoft Corporation">
            </dropDown>
            <!--
              Last Name dropdown: The tag attribute is the field that
              will be filtered
            -->
            <dropDown id="ddnLastName" label="Last Name" tag="LastName"
                      getItemCount="OnGetItemCount"
                      getItemLabel="OnGetItemLabels"
                      getItemID="OnGetItemIDs"
                      onAction="OnReportFilter"
                      sizeString="Microsoft Corporation">
            </dropDown>
            <!-- Toggle Filter button -->
            <separator id="sep1"/>
            <toggleButton idMso="FilterToggleFilter" size="large"/>
          </group>
        </tab>
      </tabSet>
    </contextualTabs>
  </ribbon>
</customUI>
```

The filtering interface gives the user the capability to choose the company name or last name for a given contact to filter the report. To make it easy to turn the filter on or off, the Toggle Filter button from Access is included. The idMso attribute for this button is FilterToggleFilter.

Writing the Callbacks

To provide the data for the drop-downs, you implement the `getItemCount`, `getItemLabel`, and `getItemID` callbacks you saw earlier. For this, you need a recordset. Start by declaring a `Recordset` object in the declarations section of the module:

```
Private rst As DAO.Recordset
```

Now, implement the callbacks. Because the `tag` attribute stores the name of the field, you can use that in your callback code:

```
Public Sub OnGetItemCount(ctl As IRibbonControl, ByRef Count)
    Dim strSQL As String

    ' get the unique data from tblContacts
    strSQL = "SELECT DISTINCT [" & ctl.tag & "] FROM tblContacts"

    Set rst = CurrentDb.OpenRecordset(strSQL)
    Count = rst.RecordCount
End Sub

Public Sub OnGetItemLabels(ctl As IRibbonControl, Index As Integer, ByRef label)
    If Not rst.EOF Then
        label = rst(ctl.tag)
    End If
End Sub

Public Sub OnGetItemIDs(ctl As IRibbonControl, Index As Integer, ByRef id)
    If Not rst.EOF Then
        id = "id" & rst(ctl.tag)
        rst.MoveNext

        If rst.EOF Then
            rst.Close
            Set rst = Nothing
        End If
    End If
End Sub
```

Figure 12-27 shows the Ribbon when you open the Company drop-down.

Figure 12-27

Finally, you need to filter the report when the item is selected. For that, you implement the `onAction` callback:

```
Public Sub OnReportFilter(ctl As IRibbonControl, _
        selectedId As String, _
```

```
            selectedIndex As Integer)

      Dim strFilter As String
      Dim strName   As String

      strName = Mid(selectedId, 3)
      strFilter = "[" & ctl.tag & "] = '" & strName & "'"

      ' filter the report
      Screen.ActiveReport.Filter = strFilter
      Screen.ActiveReport.FilterOn = True
   End Sub
```

The resulting Ribbon should look like Figure 12-28. When you select an item in either drop-down, the report is filtered accordingly. This filter is not cumulative — that is, it does not append criteria to use the AND or OR operators. To refresh the controls when new contacts are added, you can implement the onLoad callback for the Ribbon and invalidate the drop-down controls as demonstrated later in the section "Refreshing Ribbon Content."

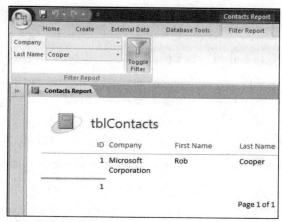

Figure 12-28

Creating a Ribbon from Scratch

In this second scenario, you'll design a ribbon customization for an application to be used in a travel agency. The application provides tools that are useful for someone working in a travel agency, and the users are not concerned with building databases. As such, the goal for this application is to provide a more off-the-shelf experience. As with any application of this nature, your Ribbon should replace the Access Ribbon.

By now, the techniques for building the Ribbon should be familiar. You'll build the XML and write the necessary callbacks. Along the way, you'll examine the design decisions made for the application and see some cool stuff such as filling a dropDown control with a list of months and a gallery control.

> *The sample database (TravelAgencySample.accdb) that implements the travel agency application is part of the download code for this book.*

Defining the Tabs and Groups

Start the Ribbon by defining the tabs and groups that you want to build. That provides some organization to the Ribbon and helps you fill in the controls in the coming sections. The application will have the following tabs:

- **Home:** Contains the most common functionality in the application such as travel information.
- **Destinations:** Contains galleries of the different destination packages offered by the agency.
- **Customers:** The travel agency wouldn't be what it is without customers! This tab provides entry points to customer-related forms.
- **Reports:** Contains a report manager like the one you built earlier. Provides an easy way to view reports in the application.
- **Settings:** Provides a way to change application settings. This is an alternative to the traditional options form.
- **Administration:** Contains administrative tasks for the agency such as employee management. This tab will only be available for certain users.

Now let's flush out the groups in each tab:

Tab	Group Label	Group Description
Home	Flight	Contains controls that work with flight travel such as booking, schedules, and delays.
	Cruise	Provides controls to book a cruise and a destination gallery.
	Hotel	Provides controls to find or book a hotel.
	Rental Cars	Contains controls to book a rental car.
	Login	Provides a means to log in to the travel agency.
Destinations	Location	Contains galleries that display destination packages.
	Activity	Provides tools to look for destinations by activity.
Customers	Customer	Provides controls to view customer information.
	Marketing	Contains controls that send marketing materials such as e-mail or brochures to a customer.
Reports	Report Manager	Contains the report manager group that you just created.
Settings	Setting	Provides a way to change application settings directly from the Ribbon.
Administration	Employee	Contains tools that manage employees.
	Data	Provides tools to re-link tables or export data.
	Security	Provides custom and built-in security tools for the application.

Not listed here is an additional group called Home. It is the first group in each tab and provides an easy way to get back to the startup form for the application.

Define the tabs and groups with XML:

```xml
<customUI xmlns="http://schemas.microsoft.com/office/2006/01/customui"
 loadImage="onLoadImage">
  <ribbon startFromScratch="true">
    <tabs>
      <tab id="tabHome" label="Home">
        <group id="grpHomeHome" label="Home">
          <button id="btnHomeHome" size="large" label="Home"
                  imageMso="BlogHomePage" tag="frmHome"
                  onAction="OnOpenForm"/>
        </group>
        <group id="grpTravelFlight" label="Flight"></group>
        <group id="grpTravelCruise" label="Cruise"></group>
        <group id="grpTravelHotel" label="Hotel"></group>
        <group id="grpTravelCar" label="Rental Cars"></group>
        <group id="grpHomeLogin" label="Login">
          <button id="btnLogin" size="large" label="Login"
                  imageMso="Lock"/>
          <button id="btnLogout" size="large" label="Logout"
                  imageMso="PrintPreviewClose"/>
        </group>
      </tab>
      <tab id="tabDest" label="Destinations">
        <group id="grpDestHome" label="Home">
          <button id="btnDestHome" size="large" label="Home"
                  imageMso="BlogHomePage" tag="frmHome"
                  onAction="onOpenForm"/>
        </group>
        <group id="grpDestLocations" label="Location"></group>
        <group id="grpDestActivity" label="Activities"></group>
      </tab>
      <tab id="tabCustomers" label="Customers">
        <group id="grpCustHome" label="Home">
          <button id="btnCustHome" size="large" label="Home"
                  imageMso="BlogHomePage" tag="frmHome"
                  onAction="onOpenForm"/>
        </group>
        <group id="grpCustomer" label="Customer"></group>
        <group id="grpMarketing" label="Marketing"></group>
      </tab>
      <tab id="tabReports" label="Reports">
        <group id="grpReportsHome" label="Home">
          <button id="btnReportsHome" size="large" label="Home"
                  imageMso="BlogHomePage" tag="frmHome"
                  onAction="onOpenForm"/>
        </group>
        <group id="grpReportManager" label="Report Manager"></group>
      </tab>
      <tab id="tabSettings" label="Settings">
        <group id="grpSettingsHome" label="Home">
```

```
                    <button id="btnSettingsHome" size="large" label="Home"
                            imageMso="BlogHomePage" tag="frmHome"
                            onAction="onOpenForm"/>
                 </group>
                 <group id="grpSettings" label="Settings"></group>
              </tab>
              <tab id="tabAdmin" label="Administration">
                 <group id="grpAdminHome" label="Home">
                    <button id="btnAdminHome" size="large" label="Home"
                            imageMso="BlogHomePage" tag="frmHome"
                            onAction="onOpenForm"/>
                 </group>
                 <group id="grpEmployees" label="Employees"></group>
              </tab>
           </tabs>
        </ribbon>
     </customUI>
```

The `loadImage` callback is included on the `customUI` node to define a single function to retrieve all images in the `image` attribute. Add the code for the `OnLoadImage` callback as follows:

```
Public Sub OnLoadImage(imageName As String, ByRef image)
    Dim strPath As String
    strPath = CurrentProject.Path & "\images\" & imageName

    ' return the image
    If Dir(strPath) <> "" Then
        Set image = LoadPicture(strPath)
    End If
End Sub
```

This XML also includes the Home group and button as well as the Login and Logout buttons.

Building the Home Tab

With your tabs defined, it's time to start filling them in with controls. Use the Home tab in Access as the design principle for the application's first tab, also called Home. This tab contains the tools that might be used commonly in a travel agency.

Building the Flight Group

The Flight group contains controls to book or search for flights as well as other flight-related data such as airport information, flight delays, or weather. For this project, each of these controls will be implemented as a `button`. While they do not include the `onAction` or `tag` attributes, you could add those to open a form defined in the application as demonstrated earlier.

Here's the XML for the Flight group:

```
<group id="grpTravelFlight" label="Flight">
    <button id="btnBookFlights" label="Book Flight" size="large"
            imageMso="OutlookGlobe"/>
    <button id="btnFindFlights" label="Find Flight" size="large"
```

```
                    imageMso="ZoomClassic"/>
     <button id="btnFlightSched" label="Flight Schedules" size="large"
             imageMso="CalendarInsert"/>
     <button id="btnFlightDeals" label="Today's Deals" size="large"
             imageMso="AccountingFormat"/>
     <separator id="s1"/>
     <button id="btnAirportInfo" label="Airports" imageMso="RmsNavigationBar"/>
     <button id="btnFlightDelays" label="Flight Delays" imageMso="Risks"/>
     <button id="btnTravelWeather" label="Travel Weather"
             imageMso="PictureReflectionGalleryItem"/>
   </group>
```

Notice that you're using images that were built into Office for each of the controls. The Ribbon defined by this XML is shown in Figure 12-29.

Figure 12-29

Building the Cruise Group

The Cruise group contains three controls. A `button` to book a cruise, a `gallery` that displays the cruise destinations, and a `dropDown` that lists the months of the year (although you could use it to display a list of cruises that are sailing in a particular month).

You'll fill both the `gallery` and `dropDown` controls using callbacks.

You might wonder why you'd use code to fill the list of months instead of a static list of months in the XML. The reason is so that you can fill the list using the MonthName *function in VBA. That function returns the localized name of the month depending on the user interface language for Microsoft Office. Using it enables you to build applications that display well in other languages.*

Writing the XML

Here's the XML for the Cruise group:

```
<group id="grpTravelCruise" label="Cruise">
    <button id="btnBookCruise" label="Book Cruise" size="large"
            image="cruise6.bmp"/>
    <gallery id="galCruiseDestinations" label="Destinations"
             size="large" imageMso="PictureReflectionGallery"
             columns="3" rows="3" itemHeight="80" itemWidth="80"
             getItemCount="onGetItemCount"
             getItemLabel="onGetItemLabel"
             getItemImage="onGetItemImage"
             getItemID="onGetItemID"
             onAction="onSelectDestination">
    <button id="btnCruiseDestinations" label="All Cruise Destinations"/>
        </gallery>
```

```
            <dropDown id="ddnFindByMonth" label="Find by Month"
                      getItemCount="onGetItemCount"
                      getItemLabel="onGetItemLabel">
        </dropDown>
    </group>
```

Gallery controls provide a few additional attributes of which you should be aware. The first are the columns and rows attributes. They define the number of columns and rows in the gallery when it is dropped down. Next are the itemHeight and itemWidth attributes. These define the height and width of images in the gallery.

Filling the gallery is similar to filling the dropDown control that you saw earlier. In addition to the getItemCount, getItemID, and getItemLabel callbacks, you also use the getItemImage callback to fill the images from a table.

A button node is included in the gallery. It will display a single button at the bottom of the gallery control.

Writing the Callbacks

To fill both the gallery and the combo box, add the following callbacks. First, the getItemCount callback. Here, you're returning a hard-coded value of 12 for the number of months for the drop-down while the number of destinations for the gallery comes from a query called qryDestinations.

```
Public Sub OnGetItemCount(ctl As IRibbonControl, ByRef Count)
    Dim strSQL As String

    Select Case ctl.id
        Case "ddnFindByMonth": Count = 12 ' number of months
        Case "galCruiseDestinations":
            ' Open the recordset for cruises. Use a query because
            ' you store a relative path to the image in the table.
            strSQL = "SELECT * FROM qryDestinations" ' WHERE DestinationType = 2"
            Set rstDestinations = CurrentDb.OpenRecordset(strSQL)

            ' return the recordcount
            rstDestinations.MoveLast
            rstDestinations.MoveFirst
            Count = rstDestinations.RecordCount
    End Select
End Sub
```

Next, the getItemLabel callback. Note the use of the MonthName function for the drop-down.

```
Public Sub onGetItemLabel(ctl As IRibbonControl, Index As Integer, ByRef Label)
    Select Case ctl.id
        Case "ddnFindByMonth"
            Label = MonthName(Index + 1)
        Case "galCruiseDestinations"
            ' return the label from tblDestinations
            Label = rstDestinations("Destination")
    End Select
End Sub
```

Then, the `getItemImage` callback. You aren't concerned with images for the drop-down so you only return an image for the gallery.

```
Public Sub onGetItemImage(ctl As IRibbonControl, Index As Integer, ByRef Image)
    Select Case ctl.id
        Case "galCruiseDestinations"
            ' return the image
            If Dir(rstDestinations("ImagePath") <> "" Then
                Set Image = LoadPicture(rstDestinations("ImagePath"))
            End If
    End Select
End Sub
```

Finally, return an ID for the gallery using the `getItemID` callback.

```
Public Sub onGetItemID(ctl As IRibbonControl, Index As Integer, ByRef id)
    Dim strID As String

    Select Case ctl.id
        Case "galCruiseDestinations"
            ' use the ID field in the control id
            strID = "qryDestinationsID" & rstDestinations("DestinationID")

            ' return the ID
            id = strID

            ' get the next destination
            rstDestinations.MoveNext

            ' cleanup when you reach the end
            If rstDestinations.EOF Then
                rstDestinations.Close
                Set rstDestinations = Nothing
            End If
    End Select
End Sub
```

When the Ribbon loads, it calls these callbacks to fill the gallery and the drop-down. The drop-down contains the list of months; the gallery is displayed in Figure 12-30.

Figure 12-30

The image files for this project are included in the download code for this chapter.

Galleries are cool! There's an onAction callback when an item is selected in the gallery. In this case, you'll open a form that is filtered to the item that was clicked. The onAction callback is implemented in the following code:

```
Public Sub onSelectDestination(ctl As IRibbonControl, selectedId As String, _
selectedIndex As Integer)
    Dim lngID As Long

    ' parse the ID number from the ID string
    lngID = CLng(Replace(selectedId, "qryDestinationsID", ""))

    ' open the destinations form
    DoCmd.OpenForm "frmDestinations", , , "DestinationID = " & lngID
End Sub
```

Selecting an item in the gallery opens the form shown in Figure 12-31.

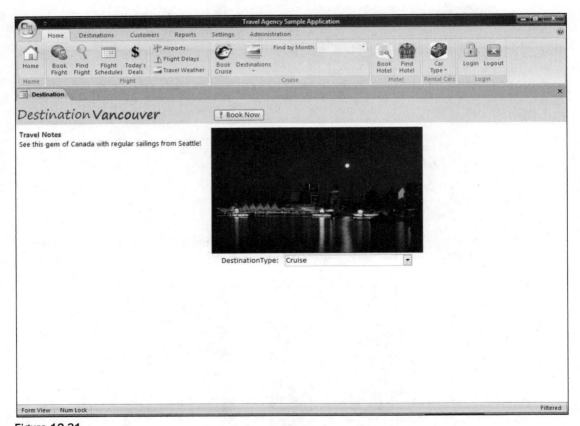

Figure 12-31

Building the Hotel Group

The Hotel group contains only two buttons: one to book a hotel, and one to find a hotel. Here's the XML for the group:

```
<group id="grpTravelHotel" label="Hotel">
    <button id="btnBookHotel" label="Book Hotel" size="large"
            image="HotelKey.bmp"/>
    <button id="btnFindHotel" label="Find Hotel" size="large"
            image="Dublin 43.bmp"/>
</group>
```

Building the Rental Cars Group

The Rental Cars group contains a single gallery control. This one is filled using item nodes as shown in the following XML:

```
<group id="grpTravelCar" label="Rental Cars">
    <gallery id="galRentalCars" label="Car Type" size="large"
             rows="3" columns="1" itemHeight="80" itemWidth="80"
             image="SportsCar3.bmp">
        <item id="itemCar1" label="Sports Car" image="SportsCar1.bmp"/>
        <item id="itemCar2" label="Sports Car" image="SportsCar2.bmp"/>
        <item id="itemCar3" label="Sports Car" image="SportsCar3.bmp"/>
        <item id="itemCar4" label="Camper" image="Camper1.bmp"/>
        <item id="itemCar5" label="Van" image="Van1.bmp"/>
        <item id="itemCar6" label="Mustang" image="Mustang.bmp"/>
    </gallery>
</group>
```

This XML creates the Ribbon shown in Figure 12-32.

Figure 12-32

Building the Settings Tab

For the Destinations and Customers tabs, you've implemented button controls so let's skip the details of building those tabs. (For the full implementation of those tabs, see the USysRibbons table in the sample database that's included in the code download for this book. The Reports tab contains the report manager you built in the previous solution.)

This brings you to the Settings tab. For this project, you want to store application settings in a table called `tblSettings`. The table has two fields — `SettingName` and `SettingValue` — both of which are defined as `Text`. In this table, you'll add one option for demonstration: to determine whether today's flight deals are displayed when the application opens. You might use this option to open a form at startup to show the flight deals for the day.

> *If the custom Ribbon is active, you may need to close the database and re-open it to create the table. You can return to the Access Ribbon by holding down the Shift key when opening the database.*

Start by creating the table and adding one record. Figure 12-33 shows the table with the setting added.

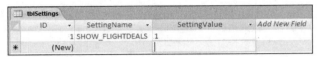

Figure 12-33

Next, add the XML for the Settings group. As you might expect, you're storing the name of the setting in the `tag` attribute of the check box. You're also including a `dialogBoxLauncher` control as described earlier in the chapter.

```xml
<group id="grpSettings" label="Settings">
    <checkBox id="chkSettingFlightDeals" label="Show Flight Deals"
            getPressed="OnGetSetting"
            onAction="OnChangeSetting"
            tag="SHOW_FLIGHTDEALS"/>
    <dialogBoxLauncher>
        <button id="btnSettingsLauncher" tag="frmSettings" onAction="OnOpenForm"/>
    </dialogBoxLauncher>
</group>
```

Now implement the callbacks. Use the `OnGetSetting` callback to read from the table to determine whether the checkbox should be pressed.

```vb
Public Sub OnGetSetting(ctl As IRibbonControl, ByRef pressed)
    ' get the setting value from tblSettings
    Dim varValue As Variant
    varValue = DLookup("SettingValue", "tblSettings", _
        "SettingName = '" & ctl.Tag & "'")

    If varValue = -1 Then
        pressed = True
    Else
        pressed = False
    End If
End Sub
```

You also implement the `OnChangeSetting` callback to update the setting in the table when the checkbox value is changed:

```
Public Sub OnChangeSetting(ctl As IRibbonControl, pressed As Boolean)
    ' Update tblSettings with the new value. The setting name
    ' is stored in the tag attribute.
    Dim strSQL As String

    ' build the SQL statement
    strSQL = "UPDATE tblSettings SET SettingValue = " & pressed
    strSQL = strSQL & " WHERE SettingName = '" & ctl.Tag & "'"

    ' update the table
    CurrentDb.Execute strSQL
End Sub
```

As you click the checkbox, the value in the table should be updated. If you leave it checked, then close and re-open the database, it should be checked when you switch to the Settings tab.

Building the Administration Tab

Although you generally want to disable items rather than hide them, the Administration tab brings up an exception. In this case, you want to completely hide the Administration tab if the user is not a Manager. The setup is straightforward: a table of users named `tblUsers` that contains three fields: `ID`, `UserName`, and `RoleName`. Start by creating the table and entering some data in it. Next, create a login form as shown in Figure 12-34. The combo box on the form should contain all three fields with only the `UserName` column displayed.

Figure 12-34

To change visibility at runtime depending on the role name, you also need to implement the `onLoad` callback on the `customUI` node. Start by changing the `customUI` node in the XML as follows:

```
<customUI xmlns="http://schemas.microsoft.com/office/2006/01/customui"
        loadImage="onLoadImage" onLoad="onRibbonLoad">
```

Update the declaration for the Administration tab as shown:

```
<tab id="tabAdmin" label="Administration" getVisible="OnGetVisible">
```

Next, implement the `onLoad` callback routine to store a copy of the Ribbon.

```
' This should appear in the module declarations section
Public gobjRibbon As IRibbonUI

Public Sub onRibbonLoad(ribbon As IRibbonUI)
    ' save a copy of the ribbon for future invalidation
    Set gobjRibbon = ribbon
End Sub
```

To determine whether the tab should be made visible, implement the `getVisible` callback as shown. This code uses the `Column` property to check the third column in the combo box to determine whether the user is a `Manager`.

```
Public Sub OnGetVisible(ctl As IRibbonControl, ByRef Visible)
    If ctl.id = "tabAdmin" Then
        ' check the login form to determine visibility.
        ' if the form is closed, just return false.
        If Not CurrentProject.AllForms("frmLogin").IsLoaded Then
            Visible = False
            Exit Sub
        End If

        ' The combo box on the login form contains the role:
        ' this can be either Manager or Employee. Show the tab
        ' if it is Manager, otherwise hide it.
        If Forms!frmLogin!cboUsers.Column(2) = "Manager" Then
            Visible = True
        Else
            Visible = False
        End If
    Else
        Visible = True
    End If
End Sub
```

Finally, add code to the `Login` button on the form to invalidate the Administration tab.

```
Private Sub cmdLogin_Click()
    ' invalidate the admin tab to determine visibility
    gobjRibbon.InvalidateControl "tabAdmin"
End Sub
```

To test the callbacks, select different users from the combo box to show and hide the tab.

Customizing the Office Menu

As mentioned earlier, the Office menu is updated when you create a new Ribbon from scratch. In addition to the changes made by the Ribbon, you can also customize the Office menu to suit your needs. In Office 2007, the Office menu is intended for options that affect an entire document or application.

To customize the Office Menu, use the `officeMenu` node, which is a child of the `Ribbon` node as shown below.

```
<customUI xmlns="http://schemas.microsoft.com/office/2006/01/customui">
    <ribbon startFromScratch="true">
        <officeMenu>
            <button idMso="FileNewDatabase" visible="false"/>
            <button idMso="FileOpenDatabase" visible="false"/>
            <button idMso="FileCloseDatabase" visible="false"/>
            <splitButton idMso="FileSaveAsMenuAccess" visible="false"/>
        </officeMenu>
    </ribbon>
</customUI>
```

This XML hides the built-in buttons for New, Open, Close, and the Save As group in the Office menu in Access. You should provide another means of closing your application gracefully if you choose to hide the Close button.

Let's look at another scenario for which you might customize the Office menu. Say you have a list of links you want to provide in your application. In the case of the travel agency application, you might maintain a list of links to travel sites, airline websites, or mapping sites. You can display this list in the Office menu so that it is available from anywhere in the application.

The following XML includes a `menu` node in the Office menu.

```
<customUI xmlns="http://schemas.microsoft.com/office/2006/01/customui">
  <ribbon>
  <officeMenu>
    <button idMso="FileNewDatabase" visible="false"/>
    <button idMso="FileOpenDatabase" visible="false"/>
    <button idMso="FileCloseDatabase" visible="false"/>
    <splitButton idMso="FileSaveAsMenuAccess" visible="false"/>
    <button idMso="ApplicationOptionsDialog" visible="false"/>
    <!-- Links menu -->
    <menu id="mnuLinks" label="Links" imageMso="HyperlinkInsert">
      <menuSeparator id="mnuLinksSep1" title="Travel Sites"/>
      <button id="btnLink1" label="http://www.travelocity.com"
       tag="http://www.travelocity.com" onAction="OnSelectLink"/>
      <button id="btnLink2" label="http://www.expedia.com"
       tag="http://www.expedia.com" onAction="OnSelectLink"/>
      <button id="btnLink3" label="http://www.orbitz.com"
       tag="http://www.orbitz.com" onAction="OnSelectLink"/>
      <menuSeparator id="mnuLinksSep2" title="Mapping Sites"/>
      <button id="btnLink4" label="http://local.live.com"
       tag="http://local.live.com" onAction="OnSelectLink"/>
      <button id="btnLink5" label="http://maps.google.com"
       tag="http://maps.google.com" onAction="OnSelectLink"/>
      <menuSeparator id="mnuLinksSep3" title="Airline Sites"/>
      <button id="btnLink6" label="http://www.alaskaair.com"
       tag="http://www.alaskaair.com" onAction="OnSelectLink"/>
      <button id="btnLink7" label="http://www.delta.com"
       tag="http://www.delta.com" onAction="OnSelectLink"/>
      <button id="btnLink8" label="http://www.usair.com"
```

```
            tag="http://www.usair.com" onAction="OnSelectLink"/>
        <button id="btnLink9" label="http://www.aa.com"
         tag="http://www.aa.com" onAction="OnSelectLink"/>
        <button id="btnLink10" label="http://www.jetblue.com"
          tag="http://www.jetblue.com" onAction="OnSelectLink"/>
      </menu>
    </officeMenu>
   </ribbon>
</customUI>
```

Because the URL for the website is stored in the `tag` attribute, you can use the `FollowHyperlink` method to open the link as shown in the following callback routine:

```
Public Sub OnSelectLink(ctl As IRibbonControl)
    FollowHyperlink ctl.Tag
End Sub
```

This XML creates the Ribbon shown in Figure 12-35.

Figure 12-35

Customizing the Quick Access Toolbar

The Quick Access Toolbar, or QAT, is the small group of controls that appears next to the Office button. You can also use this space to add buttons to your application. The QAT provides fast access to those controls that are used most frequently. Add controls to the QAT for your application by adding the `qat` node as a child of the `Ribbon` node.

The following XML adds a button to the QAT. The `documentControls` node adds controls only for the current database.

```
<qat>
    <documentControls>
        <button id="btnHello" onAction="=MsgBox('Hello!')"/>
    </documentControls>
</qat>
```

More Ribbon Tips

Here are a few tips to keep for writing ribbon customizations. They can help you in creating your applications, as well as in providing additional polish to your solutions.

❏ **Prevent the Ribbon from loading:** You want to prevent the Ribbon from loading when testing or developing. For instance, when you are developing a Ribbon from scratch but you are also developing forms and reports. With a custom ribbon, the form design tools are not available. You can hold down the Shift key as you would to prevent the startup form from loading to prevent your custom ribbon from loading.

❏ **Find existing controls:** Office provides a lot of controls that you can use in your applications. So many in fact it begs the question, how do you find them all? You can download the List of Control IDs from the Microsoft website, but it turns out that Office provides this information for you in the `Customize` group of the Options dialog boxes. To get the control ID for the Toggle Filter button, simply hover over an item in the list as shown in the Access Options dialog box in Figure 12-36. The ID for the control appears in parentheses.

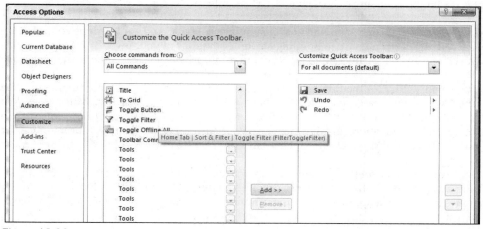

Figure 12-36

❏ **Use** `screenTip`, `superTip`, **and** `description`: Use these additional attributes for controls to customize the tooltip or descriptive information for a given control. The `description` attribute is only valid for controls in a `menu` node with the `itemSize` attribute set to `large`.

❏ **Set keyTips:** A keyTip is the accelerator key or keys for a given control. If not set, the Ribbon assigns keyTips for you such as `Y01` or `Y02`. For keyTips that are more user friendly, set the `keyTip` attribute. You can also implement the `getKeyTip` callback for many controls, which would enable you to create a mapping table for control IDs, and keyTips.

Additional Resources

There has been a lot of excitement generated about customizing the Ribbon, and Microsoft has provided an incredible amount of documentation, including an entire MSDN developer center dedicated to the

Ribbon! There are examples, documentation, tools, and videos all related to building custom ribbons. Here are some of the resources that the authors have found to be indispensable when writing customizations (all of these are available from the Ribbon Developer Center):

❑   Office Ribbon Developer Center: `http://msdn.microsoft.com/office/tool/ribbon/default.aspx`

❑   List of Control IDs: Provides the list of Office controls that you can use in the `imageMso` attribute

❑   2007 Office System: Schema Reference: Contains the XML Schema used by the Ribbon

❑   UI Style Guide for Solutions and Add-Ins

Summary

You can completely customize the Ribbon to suit the needs of your solutions. The tools described in this chapter take full advantage of the new Ribbon user interface in Office 2007.

This chapter provided an in-depth look at customizing ribbons. You explored the controls that are available, as well as put them to use in building a couple solutions of your own. By customizing the Ribbon, you can create new, innovative interfaces for your applications that are in line with today's standards.

The extensibility story for the Ribbon is quite large, and there are several pieces to it. For Access, it starts with the `USysRibbons` table, and the XML that you store in there. From there, you can implement callback routines that give you the power of VBA that you've had in the past with controls and command bars. You also learned how to display images in your customizations to give your interface a fresh look, and how to dynamically use data from tables in a database to provide content to the Ribbon.

Now you can take some of these techniques and create reusable objects to encapsulate Ribbon controls by using class modules. The next chapter provides an insight to working with objects, as well as new techniques that you can apply to your programming style to help create reusable, extensible applications of your own.

13

Creating Classes in VBA

The capability to create self-contained software objects was first conceived in about 1970 with the development of SIMULA 67 (SIMUlation LAnguage), an extension of the scientific ALGOL 60 computer language.

It took quite a while before the programming community realized the implications of the breakthrough that SIMULA represented. When they did, object-oriented programming (OOP) quickly became the new buzzword, relegating structured programming to the realm of the lesser-informed code cutters.

With the release of languages such as SmallTalk, C++ and, later, Java, OOP earned its place in the software hall of fame as the new panacea to all your programming ills. When Visual Basic 4 was released in 1993, Basic developers were tantalized by a new toy: the class module.

Long snubbed by C++ developers who had been using class modules for years, Basic developers were finally able to hold their heads high with the new found capability to create fully self-contained and reusable *objects*.

In OOP parlance, an *object* is a unique *instance* of a data structure, called a *class*, that has both *properties* (which define its characteristics), and executable procedures called *methods* (which define its behavior in modifying those properties).

The properties of a class are completely isolated from the outside world and can be modified internally only by its own methods. This doesn't mean that the programmer can't do anything to them, but that he can't do anything to them *directly*; he must use those methods that are exposed for that purpose. The properties and methods you create are termed its *implementation*, whereas the methods it exposes to the programming environment constitute its *interface*. Thus, an object is a completely self-contained programmatic entity, in that it contains both its own data and the program code necessary to implement its own behavior.

This chapter examines VBA classes and class objects. You learn what a class actually is and the difference between it and a class object. Then you create your first class and figure out how it works. After that, you learn to identify classes and then how to get them to communicate with the rest of your application, before diving into the more advanced topics, such as building collection classes. Some object-oriented theory concludes the chapter.

Classes are not as daunting as you might first think, and it's my hope that after reading this chapter, you will cast off any fears you may have had and happily find many uses for your new found skills.

There are many ways to do a single task in Access, and the examples in this book are intended to provide new perspective on programming with classes. Class modules in Access can be useful when applied to complex problems, and the code examples reinforce that theory.

A Touch of Class

Classes have been likened to rubber stamps, cookie-cutters, and a raft of other everyday items in an attempt to make the concept more easily understandable. Because you are reading a book on software development, it seems fairly safe to assume that you understand the concept of a template, such as a Microsoft Word template. That analogy succinctly describes the role of class modules and the distinction between them and class objects.

Just as a class module is equivalent to a Word template, a class object is equivalent to a Word document that is based on that template. Of course, with VBA class modules, you don't define styles or boilerplate text, but you do define a set of properties that includes their data types and read-write attributes. You also define the methods of a class, the data types they return (if any), and the events the class exposes to the calling procedure. It is these properties and methods that constitute the object's interface to the programming environment.

Each unique class object will be exactly the same as the class module it was based on, except of course, for the data it contains. In fact, the class module never gets instantiated and never contains any data because you don't actually work on it. You can, however, create as many instances of it as you like, in the form of class objects, each identified by a different name. To make a change to all the class objects, you need change only the class module. Probably the easiest way to describe a class is to compare it to a standard VBA module.

VBA modules can contain many procedures, such as subs and functions, all of which were explained in Chapter 2.

For instance, you may have a VBA module called modClassroom that contains procedures to implement a single property of a classroom — the number of students in the class:

```
Option Compare Database
Option Explicit

Private mintStudents As Integer

Public Sub AddStudent()
    mintStudents = mintStudents + 1
End Sub

Public Function GetStudents() As Integer
    GetStudents = mintStudents
End Function
```

Your property, the number of students, is stored in a module-level variable called mintStudents. To add a student to the classroom, you call the AddStudent() procedure, and to retrieve the current count you call the GetStudents() function. The potential problem with this approach is illustrated by Figure 13-1.

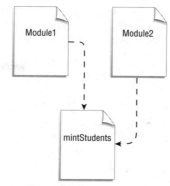

Figure 13-1

What if you have another module somewhere that also uses the AddStudent() procedure? It would change the value of mintStudents. To ensure you can change the number of students for different classrooms, you would have to either create multiple AddStudent procedures, or implement some other way of doing it, such as arrays.

This is where class modules come in. Take a look at the following class module called clsClassroom. Don't worry if you don't quite understand it; all will be explained as you go along.

```
Option Compare Database
Option Explicit

Private mintStudents As Integer

Public Sub AddStudent()
    mintStudents = mintStudents + 1
End Sub

Public Property Get Students() As Integer
    Students = mintStudents
End Property
```

This class is virtually the same as modClassroom. The nifty part about it is the fact that the code used to define the class is essentially a template that you can use to create as many classroom objects as you wish. Further, if you had two different procedures that each called AddStudent(), they would each operate on a different copy, or *instance*, of the clsClassroom class illustrated by Figure 13-2.

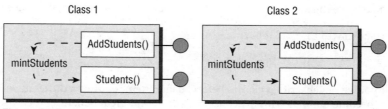

Figure 13-2

For example, the following VBA module contains two procedures, each of which creates a classroom object called myClassroom. The first one, TestClassroom1, adds one student to the classroom then calls TestClassroom2, which creates a second classroom instance and adds two students.

```
Option Compare Database
Option Explicit

Public Sub TestClassroom1()
    Dim MyClassroom As clsClassroom
    Set MyClassroom = New clsClassroom

    MyClassroom.AddStudent
    MsgBox "I have " & MyClassroom.Students & " student in my class."
    TestClassroom2
    MsgBox "I still have only " & MyClassroom.Students & " student in my class."
End Sub

Public Sub TestClassroom2()
    Dim MyClassroom As clsClassroom
    Set MyClassroom = New clsClassroom

    MyClassroom. AddStudent
    MyClassroom. AddStudent
    MsgBox "I have " & MyClassroom.Students & " students in my class."
End Sub
```

Both instances of the clsClassroom class are exactly the same in form and function, but are completely different entities. Thus, the properties of each are completely distinct from each other.

Why Use Classes?

From a coding perspective, the only real difference between using the built-in Access or VBA objects and the ones you write yourself, is that you have to *instantiate* your custom objects. Other than that, there's no difference at all.

There is a learning curve associated with creating your own class objects, but once learned, the major benefit is much simpler and more manageable code. Let's say you are using API functions in your application. You can create your own interface that hides the complexity of the API functions with a class. By this same token, classes are also very useful if you are writing code that will be used by other developers.

Also, while you can instantiate the built-in objects, using the Dim construct, you don't always have to. For example, to expose the Name property of a Table object, either of the following examples will work.

```
MsgBox DBEngine(0)(0).TableDefs(1).Name

Set tdf = DBEngine(0)(0).TableDefs(1)
```

Admittedly, if you've never written classes before, using them requires a different way of thinking at first. Once you become familiar with the concepts, you'll find great benefit in their usage. Once written, classes provide increased reusability and a layer of abstraction that enables you to focus more on business logic or rules. The end result is code that is easier to use. The `Recordset` class in DAO is an example of a class that is used quite frequently. So why not write your own?

Now having just expounded the virtues of adopting modern OOP techniques, I most certainly wouldn't recommend writing a collection class where a simple array would suffice. You should still apply the right tool to the right job! If a standard module is all you need, use one! In other words, don't over-engineer a project, just so you can use the latest technology.

Creating a Class Module

Everyone learns best by doing, so to learn the basics of creating a class module, you'll create one. The class module will model a classroom at a school. You'll see this example throughout the chapter, showing the different parts of a class module and how to model its relationships with other classes.

Adding a Class Module to the Project

The easiest way to add a new class module to your project is to press Alt+F11 to open the Visual Basic Editor. Then, in the Visual Basic designer window, select Insert ⇨ Class Module. You can also right-click anywhere in the Project Explorer and select Insert ⇨ Class Module from the context menu. In addition, you can also create a class module from within Access by selecting Class Module under the Macro split button in the Other group in the Ribbon's Create tab.

VBA opens a new class module and adds a reference to it in the Project Explorer. Copy the `clsClassroom` code into the module as shown in Figure 13-3. That's it! You've created your first class module!

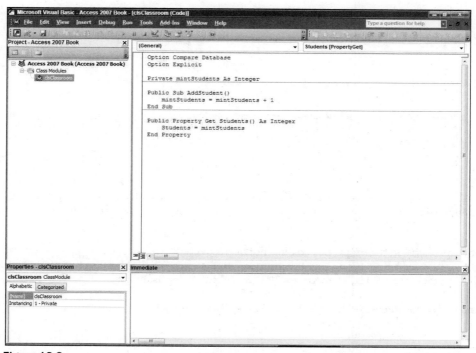

Figure 13-3

A Brief Word on Naming the Class

All things have names, and class modules are no different. The name you give a class module, however, is the name that is shown in both the Project Explorer and the Object Browser, so it should be something relevant and meaningful. A more in-depth discussion on naming objects comes later in this chapter.

Open the Object Browser by selecting View ⇨ Object Browser, or by pressing F2.

To name your class, display the Properties window by selecting it from the View menu, or by pressing F4. Then enter a name in the (Name) property.

Access also enables you to create a hidden class (or module) by prefixing the name of your module with an underscore. Figure 13-4 shows a class named `clsHidden` that appears as hidden in the Object Browser when Show Hidden Members is enabled.

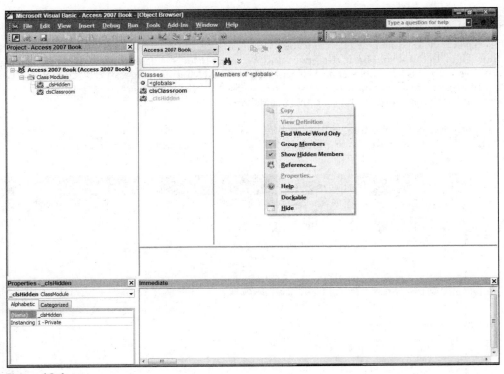

Figure 13-4

Another property in the Properties box has not been covered: `Instancing`. There are several other concepts to introduce before discussing this property, but later in the chapter you'll explore it and look at a trick using the `Instancing` property to allow for additional reusability.

Figure 13-5 shows the `clsClassroom` class in the Object Browser.

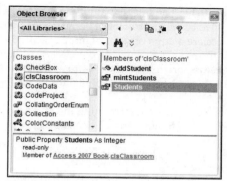

Figure 13-5

Notice that details of the selected property or method are displayed under the Classes pane. You can filter the Classes pane by selecting a project or library from the Project/Library combo box, as shown in Figure 13-6.

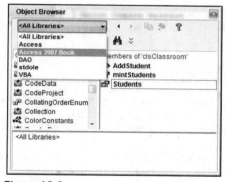

Figure 13-6

A more detailed explanation of the Object Browser is given in Chapter 4. You can't do any damage by experimenting in the Object Browser, however, so feel free to look around and click all the buttons.

Instantiating Class Objects

In Chapter 5, you saw how to declare and instantiate object variables, such as the `Recordset` object, using the `Set` keyword. Class objects are brought into existence in exactly the same way. The following code segment demonstrates how to declare and instantiate an object variable.

```
Dim myClassroom As clsClassroom
Set myClassroom = New clsClassroom
```

As mentioned earlier, once you instantiate a class, it is referred to as an object *instance* of that class.

If you were declaring a variable to hold an integer value, you would declare it as an Integer data type using the `Dim intMyVariable As Integer` construct. But because you are declaring a variable to contain an *instance* of a class object, you declare it as an object, but more specifically as an object of the `clsSomeClass` type, where `clsSomeClass` is the name you gave to your class. So when you declare a variable of that type, Access allocates sufficient memory to hold a *pointer* to an *instance* of your object. That's right, when you instantiate the class object, the variable doesn't contain the object itself, just a pointer to it.

Of course, you could save a line of code by instantiating the object on one line using the `New` keyword, but it's not the recommended way of doing things. For example,

```
Dim myClassroom As New clsClassroom
```

The reason that using the `New` keyword isn't a good idea is that although you might save a line of code, programmers often need to know exactly when an object is instantiated, particularly when debugging someone else's code. By using one line to declare the variable and one to instantiate the object, it is quite clear when things happen. The performance impact is negligible.

Using the `Dim myObject As New clsSomeClass` construct, the object is not actually instantiated until the first property or method of the object is accessed. Given the following example, the object is instantiated on the call to `AddStudent`.

```
Dim myClassroom As New clsClassroom
myClassroom.AddStudent
```

Creating Class Methods

Class modules have subs and functions, but to give the impression that they're somewhat special, they're called *methods*. It makes some sense when you consider that a class's procedures carry out actions on its properties, and therefore, constitute the *method* by which those actions are executed.

In the same way that methods are executed against objects in the Access object model, class methods are executed against class objects. For example, to move a DAO recordset cursor to the next record, you are actually using a method exposed by the `Recordset` class.

```
rst.MoveNext
```

There are three types of methods: sub(routine)s, functions, and properties. Subs and functions you know about, but properties, which will be introduced a little later, are special types of methods that can exhibit the characteristics of both.

> *Subs, functions, and properties of a class are also known as members of the class.*

To create an external interface for your class, you need to add subs, functions, and properties. Let's take a closer look at the `clsClassroom` class.

```
Option Compare Database
Option Explicit

Private mintStudents As Integer
```

```
Public Sub AddStudents(intHowMany As Integer)
    'Make sure we don't receive a negative number
    If intHowMany > 0 Then
        mintStudents = mintStudents + intHowMany
    End If
End Sub

Public Function GiveTest() As Boolean
    'Code to implement the GiveTest action.
    If AllStudentsPresent() = True Then
        'code to administer a test
        GiveTest = True
    End If
End Function

Private Function AllStudentsPresent() As Boolean
    'Code to determine if all students are present.
    'For our example, we'll just return True.
    AllStudentsPresent = True
End Function

Public Property Let Students(intNewValue As Integer)
    mintStudents = intNewValue
End Property

Public Property Get Students() As Integer
    Students = mintStudents
End Property
```

In this class module, you have a private integer variable called `mintStudents`, declared at module-level so all your procedures can access it. You also have a public sub procedure called `AddStudents`, a public function called `GiveTest()`, a private function called `AllStudentsPresent()`, and two Property Procedures, both called `Students` (I'll explain in a moment).

The `AddStudents` method takes a single integer argument that specifies the number of students to add to your classroom. Nothing special there. The `GiveTest` method takes no arguments, but returns a `Boolean` value indicating success or failure. You might also notice that `GiveTest` executes some code to actually administer the test, but only if the `AllStudentsPresent()` function returns `True`. Once the students have had their test, `GiveTest` returns `True` to the code that called it.

You've probably already noticed that you seem to have duplicate procedure names. You do, but property procedures are a special type of procedure for which duplicate names are allowed. But before you explore property procedures, it's appropriate to first understand a term that is often used to describe the object properties and methods that are visible and accessible to the VBA code that instantiated the object: the interface.

Having already mentioned the class *interface*, it may be worthwhile digressing a little to offer an explanation before you proceed with property procedures. Simply put, an *interface* is the set of `Public` properties and methods in a class. Much like any VBA procedure, the `Public` members of the class are available to other code running outside the class, whereas `Private` members are only available inside the class. In the example shown in the preceding section, the interface is defined by those methods and procedures declared as `Public`. Code outside the class cannot see private members, and therefore, cannot execute them. Therefore, properties and methods declared as `Private` are not part the interface of your class.

In the following example, the `PrintPayraise()` procedure is part of the object's interface, while `GivePayraise()` is not. It's that simple!

```
Public Sub PrintPayraise()
    'Public methods are part of the object's interface.
End Sub

Private Sub GivePayraise()
    'Private methods are not part of the object's interface.
End Sub
```

When creating classes, it is very important that you maintain the integrity of its interface. That is, you should avoid changing the names of properties, methods, or any arguments. Also, avoid changing the number of arguments or their data types. Programmers go to a great deal of trouble to write VBA code to instantiate and use a class object that has a specific interface, so if you change that interface, you *break* the very thing that VBA code needs to make it all work.

On large software projects, where many developers are working on different parts of the system, a single changed interface can result in many weeks of lost time while everyone changes their code. Rarely does this make for a happy team.

The rule in most software development houses is *"never break an interface!"* If you need to make changes that will result in the need to change large sections of VBA code, either create a new class or add new methods to the existing one. Existing code continues to use the existing interface, whereas newer code that needs to take advantage of any new or modified functionality can use the new ones.

Creating Property Procedures

A person's name, height, weight, age and so on, can all be considered *properties* of the object known as *humans*. That is, they are the attributes or defining characteristics of the object. In object-oriented programming, this definition also holds true of class properties.

In a programming environment, it is unwise to allow a user to change the properties of an object without validating the value, a task that is best left in the object's capable hands. Additionally, other actions may need to be taken when a property is changed. It is for these reasons that property procedures were invented.

Property procedures come in three flavors: `Property Get`, `Property Let`, and `Property Set`. They provide a standardized way of setting and retrieving the properties of an object.

Property procedures are the only procedures that can share the same name within the same module.

The `Property Get` procedure returns (or gets) the value of the property of the class. Alternatively, the `Property Let` and `Property Set` procedures set (or change) their values. The difference between them is that `Property Let` procedures set scalar values (such as integers, strings and so on), whereas `Property Set` is used for objects.

In the `clsClassroom` class example, `mintStudents` is the actual property, and the two `Students` methods are its property procedures. The property itself is declared as `Private`, to ensure that VBA code must access the property through one of the defined property procedures. In this way, your class can always be assured of controlling how students are added to the classroom and knowing when a property changes.

Using Property Get

The `Property Get` procedure retrieves the value of a class property. Its declaration is much the same as a standard VBA function, but with the addition of the `Get` keyword. As with a function, you declare its return data type to that of the class property it returns. Whatever receives the return value of the procedure must be declared with the same data type.

For example, the following code is the `Students Property Get` procedure from the `clsClassroom` class example.

```
Public Property Get Students() As Integer
    Students = mintStudents
End Property
```

The name `Students` defines the name of the property of the class as far as VBA code is concerned. Its return data type is declared as an integer, and when VBA code calls the property like so:

```
intNumberOfStudents = myClassroom.Students
```

VBA calls the procedure just as any standard function, and the code inside returns the privately declared variable `mintStudents`. Property procedures can do anything a standard procedure can do, even accept arguments, but in practice, that is rarely done. Because methods act on data in ways that often depend on other values or conditions, they tend to be used to accept arguments. Referring to an argument declared in a `Property Get` procedure is simple enough. For example, if you declare your procedure like so:

```
Public Property Get Students(strStreet As String) As Integer
    ' Code that uses the strStreet argument
    Students = mintStudents
End Property
```

You can refer to it like this:

```
intSomeVariable = myClassroom.Students("Main Street")
```

Using Property Let

Whereas the `Property Get` retrieves the value of a class property, the `Property Let` procedure sets the value. For example, the following code is the `Students Property Let` procedure from the `clsClassroom` class example. It is constructed in the same way as the `Property Get` procedure, but using the `Let` keyword.

```
Public Property Let Students(intNewValue As Integer)
    If intNewValue > 0 Then
        mintStudents = intNewValue
    End If
End Property
```

You can declare the data types of its arguments according to your needs, and you can even rename the argument as you would with any other procedure argument. In fact, you can declare more than one argument if you need to — just as with any other procedure.

`Property Let` procedures work differently than standard procedures, and it may take a little getting used to. When VBA code assigns a value to the property, like so:

```
myClassroom.Students = intSomeVariable
```

The code inside passes the argument to the privately declared property `mintStudents`. As with the `Property Get` procedure, you can declare more than one argument in `Property Let`. For example, if you declare your procedure like so:

```
Public Property Let Students(strStreet As String, intNewValue As Integer)
    ' Code that uses the strStreet argument
    mintStudents = intNewValue
End Property
```

you can refer to it like this:

```
myClassroom.Students("Main Street") = intSomeVariable
```

Notice that the property value being passed must be the last argument in the list.

Using Property Set

The `Property Set` procedure is similar to `Property Let`, in that it sets the value of properties. But where `Property Let` populates scalar properties (integer, date, string, and so on), `Property Set` populates *object properties*, that is, properties that are actually pointers to other objects!

For example, in the following `clsClassroom` class module, the `Property Set` procedure sets the value of the `Teacher` property so the `Property Get` procedure can return a new `clsTeacher` object (for clarity, the other properties and methods have been removed):

```
Option Compare Database
Option Explicit

'Private variable that will contain a reference
'to an instance of the clsTeacher object.
Private mobjTeacher As clsTeacher

Public Property Get Teacher() As clsTeacher
    'Return an instance of the mobjTeacher object that
    'was instantiated by the Property Set procedure
    Set Teacher = mobjTeacher
End Property

Public Property Set Teacher(objTeacher As clsTeacher)
    'Instantiate the module-level object variable
    'using the object passed to the procedure
    Set mobjTeacher = objTeacher
End Property
```

To use this construct, external VBA code must pass the `clsTeacher` object to the `Property Set` procedure in a `Set` statement, after which it can access its properties and methods through `myClassroom`'s `Teacher` property.

```
Set myClassroom.Teacher = New clsTeacher
myClassroom.Teacher.Name = "Rob Cooper"
myClassroom.Teacher.GiveHomework
```

Although `Teacher` is a property of the `myClassroom` object, it has been instantiated as a `clsTeacher` object in its own right. Because `clsTeacher` has its own properties and methods, they can now be accessed through the object chain just created. This facility allows you the ability to create a basic object model.

The data type you pass as the argument to the `Property Let` *or* `Property Set` *procedure must be the same as the data type returned by the* `Property Get`.

Declaring Property Read-Write Attributes

To declare an object's property as readable (as far as external VBA code is concerned), you expose its associated `Property Get` procedure to the interface of the class. This makes the procedure visible and accessible to VBA once the object is instantiated. You do this by declaring the property using the `Public` keyword.

To declare the property writable, you expose its `Property Let` or `Property Set` procedures to the interface in a similar fashion. If you want to make a property read-only, declare its `Property Let` or `Property Set` procedures as `Private`, or simply eliminate those procedures entirely. To make a property write-only, do the same thing to the `Property Get` procedure.

A balance on a bank account is a good example of a read-only property. True, you could create a `Property Let` procedure that performs the necessary validation on the account. Using the `Property Let`, you would have to pass a positive number to deposit money into the account and a negative number to withdraw funds. In this example, separate methods such as `Withdraw` or `Deposit` might be a more natural approach to carry out these actions.

A password is a good example of when you might consider a write-only property. It is common practice to be able to set the password using code, but not read it.

Using Enumerated Types with Properties and Methods

You often need to create a set of related constants, and Chapter 5 discussed using enumerated types, or *enums* for that purpose. In class modules, you often use enumerated types in property procedures and methods.

Recall that in the `clsClassroom` class, provision was made for a `clsTeacher` class — after all, it wouldn't be much of a classroom if it didn't have a teacher. To assign the grade level that a teacher will teach and to provide some measure of automation and consistency in the assignment process, you'd set up some enumerated types for specifying the grades to which you may want to assign the teachers.

```
Public Enum GradeLevel
    glFreshman
    glSophomore
    glJunior
```

```
        glSenior
End Enum
```

Notice that in the previous example, no values were specified for any of the constants. This is perfectly acceptable because VBA automatically assigns a Long Integer value to each of them starting at zero and incrementing by one for each member specified. Therefore, glFreshman will have a value of 0, glSophomore is 1, and so on. If you want to explicitly declare values, you can, like so:

```
Public Enum GradeLevel
    glFreshman = 0
    glSophomore = 1
    glJunior
    glSenior = 3
End Enum
```

In this code, the constants for which a value is specified will have that value, but notice that one of them (glJunior) has no value specified. Its value is determined by the value of its preceding member, so in this case, glJunior will have a value of 2. Try changing the value of glSophomore to 123 and test it to see what glJunior's value will be.

Once you've defined the constants you need, simply use the enum as you would any other data type. As you type your definition into the editor, IntelliSense displays your enum as one of the data type options, as shown in Figure 13-7.

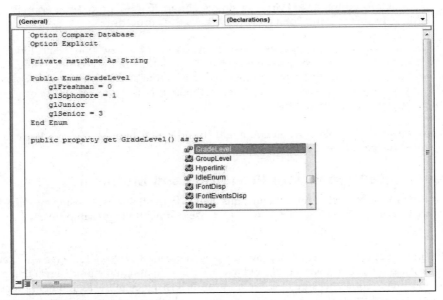

Figure 13-7

To use an enumerated value in your code, just begin typing the value assignment statement and IntelliSense will do the rest, as shown in Figure 13-8.

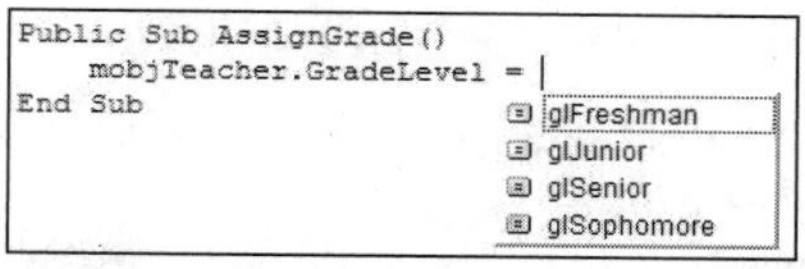

```
Public Sub AssignGrade()
    mobjTeacher.GradeLevel = |
End Sub                        glFreshman
                               glJunior
                               glSenior
                               glSophomore
```

Figure 13-8

Keep in mind that VBA allows you to specify values other than those listed by IntelliSense, so your code needs to account for that possibility, perhaps using `If..Then` or `Select Case..End Case` constructs. For example,

```
Public Property Let GradeLevel(lngLevel As GradeLevel)
    Select Case lngLevel
        Case glFreshman, glSophomore, glJunior, glSenior
            mlngLevel = lngLevel
        Case Else
            ' Do something when the wrong grade is assigned
    End Select
End Property
```

Because enum values are numbers, you can also perform numeric comparisons using named values. For example:

```
Public Property Let GradeLevel(lngLevel As GradeLevel)
    If lngLevel >= glFreshman And lngLevel <= glSenior Then
        mlngLevel = lngLevel
    Else
        ' Do something when the wrong grade is assigned
    End If
End Property
```

Creating Flags

Let's say that you are designing a class named `clsAccount` to model a bank account. In this class, you want to know whether an account has certain features. For example, you might want to know whether an account has overdraft protection, includes free checks, includes a debit card, or offers direct deposit. You could use separate Boolean properties for each of these or you can use *flags*.

A flag is a combination of numeric values that can be used to determine whether one or more attributes is set. Because these values are numbers, enumerations provide an excellent mechanism for working with flags. The trick is to use a power of 2 for the flag values. For example:

```
Private mlngFeatures As AccountFeatures

Public Enum AccountFeatures
    None = 0                    ' no flags set
    OverdraftProtection = 1     ' 2 ^ 0
    FreeChecks = 2              ' 2 ^ 1
    DebitCard = 4               ' 2 ^ 2
    DirectDeposit = 8           ' 2 ^ 3
End Enum
```

Let's add a property that uses this enum:

```
Public Property Get Features() As AccountFeatures
    Features = mlngFeatures
End Property

Public Property Let Features(lngFeatures As AccountFeatures)
    mlngFeatures = lngFeatures
End Property
```

To determine whether a flag has been set in the enum value, use the And operator. To set a flag in an enum value, use the Or operator. To remove a flag from an enum value, use the And Not operators. The following example demonstrates:

```
Public Sub TestAccountFeatures()
    ' Create a clsAccount object
    Dim myAccount As clsAccount
    Set myAccount = New clsAccount

    ' Set some features on the account
    myAccount.Features = (myAccount.Features Or OverdraftProtection)
    myAccount.Features = (myAccount.Features Or FreeChecks)

    ' Determine whether the account offers direct deposit
    If (myAccount.Features And DirectDeposit) = DirectDeposit Then
        Debug.Print "The account offers direct deposit"
    Else
        Debug.Print "This account does not offer direct deposit"
    End If

    ' Remove the free checking feature
    myAccount.Features = (myAccount.Features And Not FreeChecks)

    ' Verify that it was removed
    If (myAccount.Features And FreeChecks) = FreeChecks Then
        Debug.Print "The account offers free checking"
    Else
        Debug.Print "This account does not offer free checking"
    End If

    ' cleanup
    Set myAccount = Nothing
End Sub
```

Because flags are simply enums, which are simply Long Integer values, you might use a helper routine in a standard module to determine whether a flag is set:

```
Function IsFlagSet(Flag As Long, Flags As Long) As Boolean
    IsFlagSet = ((Flags And Flag) = Flag)
End Function
```

If you're working with many flags, you could create a wrapper function to set flag values as well:

```
Sub SetFlag(Flag As Long, Flags As Long)
    Flags = (Flags Or Flag)
End Sub
```

And, to remove a flag:

```
Sub RemoveFlag(Flag as Long, Flags As Long)
    Flags = Flags And Not Flag
End Sub
```

Another approach would be to combine the use of flags and Boolean properties. You can use Boolean properties to determine whether a feature is included on the account, but use the value in mlngFeatures to make the determination. Here's what that might look like:

```
Public Property Get HasOverdraftProtection() As Boolean
    HasOverdraftProtection = IsFlagSet(OverdraftProtection, mlngFeatures)
End Property

Public Property Let HasOverdraftProtection(blnProtect As Boolean)
    If blnProtect Then
        SetFlag OverdraftProtection, mlngFeatures
    Else
        RemoveFlag OverdraftProtection, mlngFeatures
    End If
End Property
```

As you can see, you can design a lot of flexibility into your classes. Thinking about how you would want to use the class can be helpful when you are designing your classes.

Exiting Property Procedures

In Chapter 4, you exited a procedure using the Exit Sub and Exit Function constructs. Similarly, you can exit a For..Next loop or Do..While loop, using the Exit For and Exit Do constructs respectively. When your property procedure has done what it was supposed to do, there is no need to continue executing any more code. You can use the Exit Property construct to immediately stop processing any more code and exit the property procedure.

As with other procedures, it is always better to have a single point of exit, so use Exit Property sparingly.

Procedure Attributes

When declaring class properties and procedures, you can set a number of attributes that modify the procedure's behavior. These attributes are declared on the same line as the property or procedure declaration. The following examples demonstrate the possible declarations:

```
[Public | Private | Friend] [Static] Sub name [(arglist)]
[Public | Private | Friend] [Static] Function name [(arglist)] [As type]
[Public | Private | Friend] [Static] Property Get name [(arglist)] [As type]
[Public | Private | Friend] [Static] Property Let name ([arglist,] value)
[Public | Private | Friend] [Static] Property Set name ([arglist,] reference)
```

The `Static` keyword ensures that all the procedure-level variables retain their values between calls. Variables declared outside the procedure are unaffected. For more information on `Static`, refer to Chapter 5.

You're already familiar with `Public` and `Private` attributes, so the following section focuses on `Friend` attributes.

Friendly Procedures

Let's say you wanted to create a teacher management system that others will reference in their databases. Of course, you want your own database to be able to see and execute its own class properties and methods, but you don't want consumers of your database to execute them directly.

To protect the properties and methods of your class, you can declare them using the `Friend` keyword. Procedures declared as `Friend` are public within the project in which they are defined, but invisible to other projects. The `Friend` keyword can only be used in class modules, and can't be late bound. Because modules behind Access forms and reports are also class modules, you can use the `Friend` keyword there as well.

For example, suppose you want to prevent other databases from changing the salary for your teachers; the following code illustrates the principle. The `mcurSalary` property is accessible to all consumers of the class; any procedure that instantiates the object can read the property's value, but only code within the project can assign a value to it.

```
Private mcurSalary As Currency

Public Property Get Salary() As Currency
    Salary = mcurSalary
End Property

Friend Property Let Salary(curNewValue As Currency)
    mcurSalary = curNewValue
End Property
```

Naming Objects

In the early days of programming, you were limited in the number of characters you could use to name objects and variables. Thus, you gave such meaningful names as *x*, *cbw*, or *A1*. Thanks to long filenames in 32-bit Windows, you are now able to identify objects using truly meaningful names, which in Access 2007 means 64 characters: plenty for most purposes. With such flexibility comes a dilemma: How do you name a class?

The name you assign to *any* database object will have an impact on its perceived purpose, and ultimately, its usability. It doesn't much matter whether it's a form, table, control, or class method; programmers will respond differently to it according to the name you give it. Ultimately it's up to you, but this section seeks to provide a few guidelines to help in the decision-making process.

What Does the Object Do?

Probably, the most important aspect of object naming is to describe what it is or what it does. For example, Access has many built-in objects that are, in my opinion, aptly named. These include the `Database` object, `TableDef`, `Collection`, `Error`, and so on. These names unambiguously describe the object to which they refer.

Other names describe the object's purpose, such as the `Add`, `Count`, and `Remove` methods; and let's not forget the `OpenRecordset` method. Fairly obvious what they do, wouldn't you say?

It is always good practice to keep the names as short as possible. The reason is that really long names are difficult to read and make for terribly difficult and painstaking coding. The worst thing, in my opinion, is writing SQL against long table and field names.

```
SELECT tblTheStudentsInThisClassroom.FirstNameOfStudent,
tblTheStudentsInThisClassroom.FreshmanSophomoreJuniorOrSenior,
tblTheStudentsInThisClassroom.FirstAndLastNameOfStudentsParent,
tblTheStudentsInThisClassroom.TheStudentsPermanentAddress
FROM tblTheStudentsInThisClassroom
WHERE tblTheStudentsInThisClassroom.FirstNameOfStudent <> "Rob Cooper" AND ↵
tblTheStudentsInThisClassroom.FirstAndLastNameOfStudentsParent <> "Rob Cooper"
```

With just a little thought, this could have been simplified like so:

```
SELECT tblStudents.Name, tblStudents.GradeLevel, tblStudents.ParentName,
tblStudents.Address
FROM tblStudents WHERE tblStudents.Name <> "Rob Cooper"
AND tblStudents.ParentName <> "Rob Cooper"
```

A great deal easier to read! You can make good use of abbreviations, acronyms, numbers, and so on, but ensure they are meaningful, rather than cryptic. What may be meaningful or obvious to you, may not mean a thing to someone else.

I frequently do not use the `cls` prefix when naming a class object. Because the classes you create become part of the object model for the database, leaving off the prefix seems more natural.

Verbs, Nouns, and Adjectives

As mentioned earlier, using names that describe an object's purpose and function is arguably the best strategy, but the decision about whether to use verbs, nouns, or adjectives is equally important.

Most programmers use nouns and adjectives to describe properties, and use verbs to describe functions and methods. For example, typical properties might be called `Color`, `Name`, and `Width`, whereas functions and methods might have names like `Add`, `Calculate`, `Show`, and so on.

Naming variables is often a confusing decision, but they should follow the same naming strategy as property names. An exception might be variables of the `Boolean` data type. Because they denote a true or false condition, you can use one of two stratagems. You can prefix them with "Is" or "Has" (for example, `IsOpen` or `HasPermissions`), or where they are used to indicated an authority to carry out some action, use verbs, for example, `ShowDialog`.

Events are often named in two ways. First, name events by using verbs to denote the fact that some action has or is about to occur, for example, `BeforeUpdate` or `Finished`. Second, as is done in Web applications, name events by prefixing the name with `on`, as in `onupdate` or `onopen` (Web projects often exclusively use lowercase for event names).

Whichever strategy you choose, try to be consistent throughout the application.

Case

The judicious use of case can be a highly effective means of naming an object. Traditionally, many objects are named with sentence case, that is, the first character of every word is uppercase. For example:

```
AddNewObject
```

Often to distinguish them from other objects, constants (described in Chapter 5) are named using all uppercase, for example:

```
ERR_NOT_FOUND
```

Underscores

Underscores (_) can also be used to great effect and clarity when naming objects. For example:

```
ERR_NOT_FOUND
```

A word of caution, however: Access and other applications sometimes prefix built-in objects with an underscore, so be aware of potential conflicts when naming your objects.

Prefixes and Suffixes

The Reddick object-naming convention is used throughout this book. It involves prefixing object names with acronyms that describe their type and attributes. Refer to Appendix L for a complete list.

Plurality

In code, and particularly with regard to classes, plural object names are best reserved for collections, such as the `TableDefs` collection. Singular objects are therefore named in the singular, as with the `TableDef` object. This strategy unambiguously describes the *actual* state of the object.

Many people apply a plural naming convention to tables. Although this may make some sense in terms of the fact that tables can contain many records, my preference is to use the singular, for example, `tblAddress` and `tblPerson`. This is just personal preference; you can use plural if you like — just be consistent.

Except in the case of collections, applying plural names to some objects and singular to others of the same type is a definite no-no. Consistency is important, as object names are sometimes all a programmer has to determine the purpose and function of objects in the applications you create.

Using Class Events

Unlike standard modules, class modules can raise their own events. This is a very powerful feature of VBA, because it not only gives your code the ability to know what's going on inside the class instance, it provides the opportunity to take whatever actions you deem necessary based on those events.

Another very important benefit of using class events is that that you can keep User Interface (UI) functionality separate from the class implementation, making the class truly independent and reusable. You can then use your class in many places without worrying about specific UI implementation. This section focuses on getting your class to talk to the rest of your application through events.

Initialize and Terminate Events

Every class module has two built-in events that fire automatically: `Initialize` and `Terminate`. The `Initialize` event fires when the class instance is first created. You can use the `Initialize` event to set default property values and create references to other objects. The `Terminate` event fires before the object is destroyed, and is normally used to clean up local object references.

To define code for these events, select Class from the Object drop-down and then select the event from the Procedure drop-down, as shown in Figure 13-9.

Figure 13-9

The following example shows what the `Initialize` and `Terminate` events might look like for the `clsClassroom` class.

```
Option Compare Database
Option Explicit

'Declare the Teacher object
Private mobjTeacher As clsTeacher

'Declare the Student object
Private mobjStudent As clsStudent

'Declare the room number
Private mlngRoomNumber As Long

Public Property Get RoomNumber() As Long
    RoomNumber = mlngRoomNumber
End Property

Private Sub Class_Initialize()
    mlngRoomNumber = 302

    Set mobjTeacher = New clsTeacher
```

```
        Set mobjStudent = New clsStudent
    End Sub

    Private Sub Class_Terminate()
        Set mobjTeacher = Nothing
        Set mobjStudent = Nothing
    End Sub
```

Creating Custom Class Events

You can, of course, create your own events. Once you've decided on the specific events you want to expose, you declare them in the class's declarations section. Let's say you have a class called clsTest that implements a test given by the teacher. You may want to provide events that notify your code before and after a test is given.

```
Public Event BeforeTest(Cancel As Integer)
Public Event AfterTest()
Public Event Pass(Score As Byte)
Public Event Fail(Score As Byte)
```

Events are declared Public by default, but for clarity, you might want to explicitly declare scope. In any case, nothing outside the class would ever know about an event that was declared Private. Event names can be alphanumeric, but must begin with a non-numeric character, and they can only be raised in the module that declared them.

To fire an event in your class, you issue the RaiseEvent keyword. For example, the following code demonstrates a typical use.

```
Private Const PASSING_SCORE As Byte = 70

Public Sub SubmitTest()
    Dim bytScore As Byte

    ' fire the AfterTest event
    RaiseEvent AfterTest

    ' calculate the test score
    ' for demo purposes, this returns a random number
    bytScore = TestScore

    ' determine pass/fail and return the test score
    If bytScore >= PASSING_SCORE Then
        RaiseEvent Pass(bytScore)
    Else
        RaiseEvent Fail(bytScore)
    End If
End Sub

Private Property Get TestScore() As Byte
    ' get a random score between 0 and 100
    Const MIN_SCORE = 0
    Const MAX_SCORE = 100
```

```
         TestScore = CInt(Int((MAX_SCORE - MIN_SCORE + 1) * Rnd() + MIN_SCORE))
End Property
```

Just like VBA procedures, you can declare event arguments using the `ByVal` and `ByRef` keywords. By default, event arguments are passed `ByRef`, which means that the code that's listening for the event can change its value, and that change is passed back to the class procedure.

Responding to Events

Now that you know how to create custom events in your object, you might want to know how to listen and respond to them in your code. It's actually quite simple. All you need to do is declare the object variable using the `WithEvents` keyword. Unfortunately, however, you can only use `WithEvents` for object variables declared at module-level and only in class modules.

Remember that the code behind forms and reports are class modules too, so you can also use the `WithEvents` keyword in forms. The following declaration example demonstrates how easy it is.

```
Private WithEvents myTest As clsTest
```

Once you declare an object variable using the `WithEvents` keyword, select the object from the Object drop-down, and the event becomes available from the Procedure drop-down, as shown in Figure 13-10. VBA creates the procedure stub based on the arguments you supplied when you defined the event.

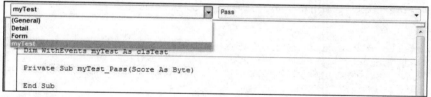

Figure 13-10

Defining custom class events enables you to implement different behavior for different scenarios based on the same outcome. In the `clsTest` example, for instance, the class defines an event named `Fail`, which is raised if the passing score is less than 70 percent. If you have two applications that use this class, you might simply choose to format a text box in one to indicate that the student did not pass the test. In the other application, you might choose to send an e-mail to the student with the results. By raising an event, the `clsTest` class separates user-interface code from business logic code.

> *An example database is included in the download code for this chapter.*

The only thing that might be considered a drawback to class events is that the object that raises the event must wait until the event code is responded to before it can continue processing.

Now let's see how you might be able to use the `WithEvents` keyword in a way that makes practical sense in your day-to-day application development. Let's say you have several text boxes on several different forms whose `BeforeUpdate` and `AfterUpdate` events contain exactly the same code. Normally, you would simply write the same code over and over in the event procedures for each control. But what if you were able to write the code once and have *every* control implement that code. You can accomplish this using a technique known as *subclassing*.

You're probably wondering why you wouldn't just write a public procedure in a standard module. That might work in many cases, but some built-in events have parameters, like the BeforeUpdate event's Cancel parameter. Access won't let you replicate that in a standard module!

You start by creating your class module (clsTBox in this example). Notice that you set the BeforeUpdate and AfterUpdate properties of the textbox because Access won't respond to an event unless the corresponding event property is set to [Event Procedure]. To simplify this, you set the event property when the Textbox object property is set.

```vba
'Declare the class instance
Private WithEvents mtxtTextbox As TextBox

Public Property Get MyTextbox() As TextBox
    Set MyTextbox = mtxtTextbox
End Property

Public Property Set MyTextbox(objTextbox As TextBox)
    Set mtxtTextbox = objTextbox

    ' Access requires that event properties are set
    ' to [Event Procedure] to respond to events.
    ' Set the event properties when the textbox object is set.
    mtxtTextbox.BeforeUpdate = "[Event Procedure]"
    mtxtTextbox.AfterUpdate = "[Event Procedure]"
End Property

Private Sub mtxtTextbox_AfterUpdate()
    'Set the text to normal weight.
    Me.MyTextbox.FontBold = False
End Sub

Private Sub mtxtTextbox_BeforeUpdate(Cancel As Integer)
    'Test for the textbox's value.
    Select Case Me.MyTextbox.Value
        Case "Fred", "Mary"
            'The value is OK.
            'Change the text to black.
            Me.MyTextbox.ForeColor = vbGreen
        Case Else
            'Wrong value! Undo the changes,
            'and change the text to bold red.
            Cancel = True

            Me.MyTextbox.ForeColor = vbRed
            Me.MyTextbox.FontBold = True

    End Select
End Sub
```

As you can see, this code implements the BeforeUpdate and AfterUpdate events for textboxes that can be anywhere in the project. The BeforeUpdate event checks the value of the textbox and turns its text green if it equals "Fred" or "Mary", otherwise it turns it bold red. The AfterUpdate event only fires (setting the text weight to normal) if the text is correct.

Now let's create the form, as shown in Figure 13-11.

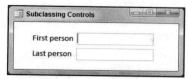

Figure 13-11

Add two text boxes named txtFirst and txtLast (it doesn't really matter what their captions read), and then add the following code to the form's module.

```
'Declare a reference to the class module
Public FirstTB As New clsTBox
Public LastTB As New clsTBox

Public Sub Form_Load()
    'Instantiate the class object for each control
    Set FirstTB.myTextbox = Me.txtFirst
    Set LastTB.myTextbox = Me.txtLast
End Sub

Private Sub Form_Unload(Cancel As Integer)
    'Clean up
    Set FirstTB = Nothing
    Set LastTB = Nothing
End Sub
```

Open the form and type **Fred** into the first textbox. It turns green. Now enter **John** into the second text box, as shown in Figure 13-12.

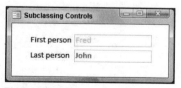

Figure 13-12

Quite simply, here's how it works:

1. When the form class module is instantiated, clsTBox is immediately instantiated into FirstTB and LastTB (notice you use early binding). When the form loads, the two textbox instances are created in separate instances of clsTBox through the MyTextBox property.

2. The `mtxtTextbox` variable stores the instance of the textbox object on the form. When the property is set, you set the event property to `[Event Procedure]` to let Access know that the textbox will respond to events.

3. Once that happens, the linking is complete, and all the textbox events that are exposed in the form, are now available in `clsTBox`.

4. When the `BeforeUpdate` or `AfterUpdate` events occur for either textbox, they actually fire in the instance of `clsTBox` created for it.

5. Try placing breakpoints in the form's `Load` event, and `clsTBox`'s `BeforeUpdate` and `AfterUpdate` events to see what happens.

This is just a small example of how to subclass form controls using the `WithEvents` keyword. You can do the same thing with other controls and events, and also with forms and report events with the exception of the `Open` event.

Handling Errors in Classes

A large part of developing software is trapping and handling errors, and all but the simplest procedure should include some form of error handling. Programmers can save some face by blaming many errors on the users of their brilliantly written software. Although they do have to account for their own mistakes (or those of other programmers), much of error handling is either responding to *status conditions* or protecting data from the users.

Status conditions are errors generated by conditions in other objects. For example, the following code shows one way to instantiate an Excel application object, using a status condition returned as an error.

```
Dim xlApp As Object
On Error Resume Next

'If Excel is already open, get a handle to
'the existing instance.
Set xlApp = GetObject(, "Excel.Application")

'Test for an error condition.
If Err <> 0 Then
    'Excel is not currently open, create an
    'instance.
    Set xlApp = CreateObject("Excel.Application")
End If

xlApp.Quit
Set xlApp = Nothing
```

In this example, a `GetObject` error indicates that an Excel instance is not currently running, in which case, the code then creates an instance using `CreateObject`. You might ask, "Why not just create the instance with `CreateObject`?" The reason is that you often don't want two or more instances of the same object, so you try to use an existing instance where possible.

In any case, this kind of error is more an indication of the current status of the Excel object, rather than an actual error. It should be handled within the procedure in which it occurred, for obvious reasons.

Most other types of errors are unexpected, or at least undesirable. Not only do you have to trap and respond to them, but you need to understand how to work with them in class modules.

Trapping VBA Errors

Chapter 9 discusses trapping errors in standard modules, including using the On Error and If Err constructs.

You might recall that when there is no error handler in the procedure in which the error occurs, VBA passes the error to the next highest procedure in the call chain. VBA continues passing the error up the call chain until it either finds an error handler or reaches the top level, in which case it then displays the standard run-time error dialog box. If you don't handle the errors, VBA will, but you may not like the idea that it resets all your variables when it does. Certainly, the users of your application won't be too impressed either.

Error trapping in class modules is exactly the same, however, you also need to consider the runtime Error Trapping setting in the IDE's Options dialog box, as shown in Figure 13-13.

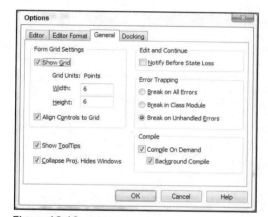

Figure 13-13

The Error Trapping settings control how Access handles runtime errors. The default setting, Break on Unhandled Errors, causes Access to display the standard Windows runtime error dialog box in the absence of any error handlers in the call chain. This is the desired behavior because it enables your error handlers to do their job.

Break on All Errors causes Access to override all your error handlers and display the runtime error dialog box whenever an error occurs in any module (including class modules). Finally, the Break in Class Module option overrides your class module error handlers, but not those in standard modules.

Raising Custom-Defined Errors

The descriptions for a great many error messages must have been written by programmers whose native language was something other than English. Some of them make for interesting reading, but there are quite a few that don't go too far towards educating you about the reason for the problem (or its resolution). Raising your own errors provides the flexibility of displaying more user-friendly or user-specific error messages.

The VBA `Err` object provides a `Raise` method, which enables you to construct and to fire your own custom errors. You must supply everything the `Err` object needs to return anything useful, which includes the error number, description, source, optional path to a help file and the `ContextID`, which identifies a specific topic in the help file.

The syntax for the `Err.Raise` method is as follows:

```
Err.Raise Number, Source, Description, HelpFile, HelpContext
```

To avoid conflicts with errors that are built in to Access or other components, you should add `vbObject?Error` to your error number. The system reserves errors through `vbObjectError + 512`, so user-defined errors in class modules should begin with `vbObjectError + 513`.

For example, the following procedure demonstrates the typical method for trapping errors and raising your own:

```
Const MyContextID = 1010407 ' Define a constant for ContextID

Private Sub ErrorTest()
    Dim xlApp As Object
    On Error Goto ErrorTest_Err

    ' If Excel is already open, get a handle to
    'the existing instance.
    Set xlApp = GetObject(, "Excel.Application")

    ' Other code

ErrorTest_Exit:
    On Error Resume Next
    xlApp.Quit
    Set xlApp = Nothing
    Exit Sub

ErrorTest_Err:
    Select Case Err.Number
        Case 429 ' ActiveX component can't create object
            ' Raise the error.
            strErrDescr = "Unable to open Excel. It may not be installed."

            Err.Raise vbObjectError + 513, TypeName(Me), _
                strErrDesc, _
                "c:\MyProj\MyHelp.Hlp", MyContextID
        Case Else
            ' Something else went wrong.
            Err.Raise Err.Number, Err.Source, Err.Description
    End Select
End Sub
```

You might have noticed the `TypeName` function. `TypeName` returns information about a variable, for example:

❑   `TypeName(strMyString)` returns `String`.

- ❑   `TypeName(intMyInteger)` returns `Integer`.

- ❑   `TypeName(CurrentDb().TableDefs("Table1"))` returns `TableDef`.

But when passed an instance of a class object, it returns the Name property of the class module.

Passing Errors in Class Modules

Although class objects can respond to errors that occur within them, they should not because doing so forever binds the object to a specific implementation.

Class objects don't spontaneously leap into existence; they must be instantiated by other code. The code that creates the class is what implements the broader function. It calls the class only for a smaller part of it, and so *this code* should be what responds to errors that occur within the class object. By definition, any error in the class object is an error in the broader function. This is shown in Figure 13-14.

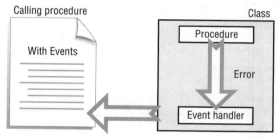

Figure 13-14

So what do you do? Your class must pass the error back to the calling code using the `Err.Raise` method. Whether it's a VBA error or a custom-defined error, your class procedures must trap it and pass it along. All the calling code has to do is test for it. The following examples show how to do this.

Example 1

```
Public sub TestErrors()
    Dim obj As clsMyClass

    On Error Resume Next
    Set obj = New clsMyClass
    Obj.SomeMethod

    If Err <> 0 Then
        ' Handle the error
    End If
    On Error Goto 0
End Sub
```

Example 2

```
Public sub TestErrors()
    Dim obj As clsMyClass
    On Error Goto TestErrors_Err

    Set obj = New clsMyClass
    Obj.SomeMethod 'Error occurs in here

TestErrors_Exit:
    On Error Resume Next
    Set Obj = Nothing
    Exit Sub

TestErrors_Err:
    'Handle the error
    Resume TestErrors_Exit
End Sub
```

Forms as Objects

By now you should have a fair grasp on how to create classes and class objects in Access 2007. Something you might not be aware of is the fact that because form and report modules are also class modules, you can instantiate and use them in exactly the same way as any other class object. The greatest benefits of this are that you can create and operate on more than one instance of the object at any one time, and you can use its events by declaring their object variables using the WithEvents keyword.

Let's say you have a form called Form1. You would, of course, be familiar with the tried and true method of displaying a standard form.

```
DoCmd.OpenForm "Form1"
DoCmd.Close acForm, "Form1"
```

Copy the following code into a standard module and try stepping through it using the F8 key.

```
Public Sub TestFormClass()
    Dim frm As Form_Form1
    Set frm = New Form_Form1

    frm.Visible = True
    Set frm = Nothing
End Sub
```

Then try the same thing with a report.

```
Public Sub TestReportClass()
```

```
        Dim rpt As Report_Report1
        Set rpt = New Report_Report1

        rpt.Visible = True
        Set rpt = Nothing
    End Sub
```

Often, you may want to display a data selection dialog box while editing data in a form, and to return the selected value from the dialog box to the original form. For example, in Microsoft Word, you select Date and Time from the Insert menu. This displays the Date and Time dialog box, from which you select the format of the date you want to insert into your text. You're about to see a mechanism for returning the value selected by the user from the dialog box to the form whose code instantiates it. More often than not, the data selection dialog box must be used in different places throughout the application, so it must be completely independent of specific UI implementation. Past techniques for passing a value to another form included using the OpenForm method's OpenArgs argument:

```
DoCmd.OpenForm "Form1", , , , , strSomeValue
```

Passing multiple values involved stuffing OpenArgs with multiple values separated by some arbitrary character such as the vertical bar (|), and parsing Me.OpenArgs when the data selection dialog box opens, as shown in the following code:

```
Private Sub Form_Open()
    Dim varArgs As Variant
    Dim intCounter As Long

    'Extract all the values from OpenArgs that are separated
    'by the vertical bar character, and put them into varArgs.
    varArgs = Split(Me.OpenArgs, "|", -1, vbTextCompare)

    'Print out the resulting array.
    For intCounter = LBound(varArgs) To UBound(varArgs)
        Debug.Print varArgs(intCounter)
    Next
End Sub
```

Passing values back to the calling form usually involved either setting a global variable with the name of the calling form, adding the form name to OpenArgs so the dialog box can pass the value directly to the calling form, which meant hard-coding the value-passing code into the dialog box itself. None of which could be classified as a professional object-oriented approach.

In the following example, you create a reusable data selection dialog box that is completely independent of other forms. You use the techniques discussed in this chapter, including form properties and events. Yes that's right — forms can have property procedures, and expose their events to the VBA environment.

It might be worth noting here that, unlike other classes, forms and reports don't have `Initialize` and `Terminate` events. Instead, forms and reports both have `Open` `Load`, `Unload`, and `Close` events. The `Open` event fires before the `Load` event, and the `Unload` event fires before the `Close` event.

1. Create a new form, and set its properties, as shown in the following table:

Property	Value
Name	DlgMyDialog
Caption	My Dialog
BorderStyle	Dialog
RecordSelectors	No
NavigationButtons	No
DividingLines	No
Modal	Yes

2. Add the following controls, and set their properties, as shown in this table:

Control Type	Property	Value
Combo Box	Name	cboCombo1
	RowSourceType	Value List
	RowSource	"Value 1"; "Value 2"; "Value 3"
	Enabled	No
Combo box	Name	cboCombo2
	RowSourceType	Value List
	RowSource	"Value 4"; "Value 5"; "Value 6"
	Enabled	No
Rectangle	Left	
	Top	
	Width	
	Height	Place as shown
Command Button	Name	CmdOK
	Caption	OK
Command Button	Name	CmdCancel
	Caption	Cancel

Figure 13-15 shows how the form should look.

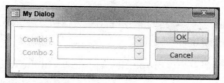

Figure 13-15

3. Copy the following code to the form's class module:

```
'Declare the event to notify the calling form
'that the dialog has finished
'We could also have used the dialog's Close or
'Unload events
Public Event Finished(varReturn As Variant)

'Declare the dialog properties
Private varValueSelected As Variant
Private intWhichOne As Integer

Private Sub cboCombo1_Change()
    varValueSelected = Me.cboCombo1
End Sub

Private Sub cboCombo2_Change()
    varValueSelected = Me.cboCombo2
End Sub

Private Sub cmdCancel_Click()
    varValueSelected = Null
    DoCmd.Close acForm, Me.Name
End Sub

Public Property Get WhichOne() As Integer
    WhichOne = intWhichOne
End Property

Public Property Let WhichOne(ByVal iNewValue As Integer)
    intWhichOne = iNewValue

    'Enable the appropriate combo
    Me.cboCombo1.Enabled = (intWhichOne = 1)
    Me.cboCombo2.Enabled = (intWhichOne = 2)
End Property

Private Sub cmdOK_Click()
    DoCmd.Close acForm, Me.Name
End Sub
```

```
Private Sub Form_Unload(Cancel As Integer)
    'Raise the Finished event so the calling
    'form knows what's happened
    RaiseEvent Finished(varValueSelected)
End Sub
```

4. Create a new form, and set its properties, as shown in the following table:

Property	Value
Name	frmMyMainForm
Caption	My Main Form
BorderStyle	Sizable
Modal	Yes

5. Add the following controls, and set their properties, as shown in the following table:

Control Type	Property	Value
Option Group	Name	optMyOptionGroup
Option Button	Name	[Default]
	OptionValue	1
	Caption (of it's label)	Select from combo 1
Option Button	Name	[Default]
	OptionValue	2
	Caption (of it's label)	Select from combo 2
Text Box	Name	txtMyTextBox
	Caption (of it's label)	Value selected
Button	Name	cmdSelect
	Caption	Select
Button	Name	cmdClose
	Caption	Close

Figure 13-16 shows how the form should look.

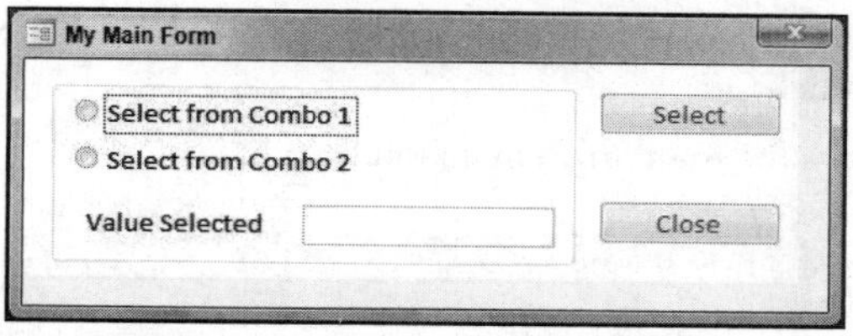

Figure 13-16

6. Copy the following code to the form's class module:

```vba
'Declare the object variable using WithEvents
Private WithEvents dlg As Form_dlgMyDialog

Private Sub cmdClose_Click()
    DoCmd.Close acForm, Me.Name
End Sub

Private Sub cmdSelect_Click()
    'Instantiate the dialog
    Set dlg = New Form_dlgMyDialog

    'Enable the appropriate combo
    dlg.WhichOne = Me.optMyOptionGroup

    'If we had declared dialog properties, we
    'could pass their values here:
    'dlg.Property1 = 123
    'dlg.Property2 = "some value"
    'etc...

    'Show the dialog
    dlg.Visible = True
End Sub

Private Sub dlg_Finished(varReturn As Variant)
    Me.txtMyTextBox.Enabled = (Not IsNull(varReturn))

    If Not IsNull(varReturn) Then
        Me.txtMyTextBox = varReturn
    End If
End Sub

Private Sub Form_Unload(Cancel As Integer)
    'Clean up
    Set dlg = Nothing
End Sub
```

7. Now open `frmMyMainForm`, select one of the options, and click Select. Pick a value from the combo box, and click OK.

Figure 13-17 shows the main form in action.

Figure 13-17

You can call this dialog box from anywhere in your application, without having to specify the name of the form that calls it, and you can also keep all the form-specific functionality in the main form where it belongs.

Variable Scope and Lifetime

Variables declared within class modules exhibit the same scope and lifetime as those declared within standard modules. For example, Private module-level variables are only available to procedures within the same module, and are destroyed when the class instance is destroyed. Public module-level variables are visible to any code that has access to the class instance. Public variables in a class are an easy way to create properties for the class, but lack the ability to perform validation.

Class variables declared at procedure-level remain accessible only to code within that procedure and are destroyed when the procedure exits; unless of course the variable is declared using the `Static` keyword. In such a case, the variable is destroyed along with the module-level variables when the object is destroyed.

Although the variables used to hold pointers to objects obey the normal scope and lifetime rules as described previously, they demand special consideration, as you will soon see.

To demonstrate how variable scope and lifetime works, create the following two class modules.

clsClass1

```
Private obj As clsClass2

Public Property Set Link(objMyObject As clsClass2)
    'Create a link from this object to the other one
    Set obj = objMyObject
    Debug.Print "Creating reference to clsClass2 from clsClass1"
End Property
```

```
Private Sub Class_Initialize()
    Debug.Print "Instantiating clsClass1"
End Sub

Private Sub Class_Terminate()
    Debug.Print "Terminating clsClass1 instance"
End Sub
```

clsClass2

```
Private obj As clsClass1

Public Property Set Link(objMyObject As clsClass1)
    'Create a link from this object to the other one
    Set obj = objMyObject
    Debug.Print "Creating reference to clsClass1 from clsClass2"
End Property

Private Sub Class_Initialize()
    Debug.Print "Instantiating clsClass2"
End Sub

Private Sub Class_Terminate()
    Debug.Print "Terminating clsClass2 instance"
End Sub
```

Then add the following procedure to a standard module.

```
Public Sub TestClassLifetime()
    Dim objMyObject1 As clsClass1
    Dim objMyObject2 As clsClass2

    'Instantiate the two object variables
    Set objMyObject1 = New clsClass1
    Set objMyObject2 = New clsClass2

    'Create a link to one object from the other
    Set objMyObject2.Link = objMyObject1

    'Destroy the local object references
    Set objMyObject1 = Nothing
    Set objMyObject2 = Nothing
End Sub
```

Take a look at the TestClassLifetime procedure. If you step through the procedure line by line (by successively pressing F8), the debug window tells the real story.

The procedure begins by creating the two class objects, objMyObject1 and objMyObject2. The code then sets a second pointer to objMyObject1 in objMyObject2, as shown in Figure 13-18.

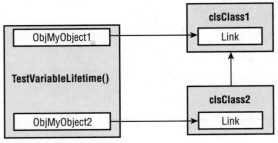

Figure 13-18

Despite the fact that the first local pointer to clsClass1 (objMyObject1) is then set to Nothing, you see that the object itself is not destroyed until after objMyObject2 passes away. Why? Because the second pointer still exists after the demise of the first pointer, so the object itself remains alive.

When the pointer to clsClass2 is destroyed, its pointer to clsClass1 is also destroyed, thereby releasing the clsClass1 object. But that's not the worst that can happen! If you change TestClassLifetime() by setting a reference to clsClass2 from clsClass1, a circular reference is created.

```
'Create a link to one object from the other
Set objMyObject2.Link = objMyObject1
Set objMyObject1.Link = objMyObject2
```

Run the procedure to see what happens. Neither object is destroyed! Why? Because each object maintains a reference to the other, as shown in Figure 13-19. Once such code is executed, both objects remain in memory until the application is shut down; there is no way to programmatically terminate them.

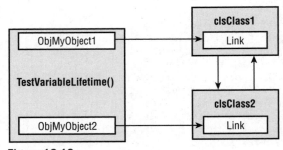

Figure 13-19

So how do you avoid such circular references? You must explicitly terminate each inner reference before destroying the outer reference. You can do so by adding the following method to each class:

```
Public Sub TerminateLink()
    'If the object exists, destroy it
    If Not obj Is Nothing Then
        Set obj = Nothing
    End If
End Sub
```

Then you add the following two lines to `TestClassLifetime()`:

```
objMyObject1.TerminateLink
objMyObject2.TerminateLink
```

The Me Property

The `Me` keyword is an implicitly declared variable that is automatically available to every procedure in a class module. When a class can have more than one instance, `Me` provides a way to refer to the specific instance of the class where the code is executing. Using `Me` is particularly useful for passing information about the currently executing instance of a class to a procedure in another module.

The `Me` keyword contains an object reference to the current class instance, and can be used by code written in forms, reports, and user-defined classes. It returns faster than a fully qualified object reference, and is useful when you have several instances of a class. For example, either of the following code fragments can be executed from the Employees form to refer to the value of the LastName text box on that form.

```
strLastName = Forms!Employees.LastName
strLastName = Me!LastName
```

You can also use `Me` to pass information about the current class instance to a procedure in another module or class. The code in the following sections demonstrates a class that subclasses a form, and binds to the subclass instance from the form.

Subclassing the Form

This class defines a portion of the subclass named `clsFormSubclassed`. Because the subclass stores an instance of an Access `Form` object, all properties of the form are available in the subclass.

```
Private WithEvents mfrmMyForm As Form

Public Property Get FormObject() As Form
    Set FormObject = mfrmMyForm
End Property

Public Property Set FormObject(objForm As Form)
    Set mfrmMyForm = objForm
```

```
        Debug.Print "clsFormSubclassed is bound to the form: " & _
            mfrmMyForm.Name
End Property
```

Creating the Subclassed Form

The following code represents a form named `frmSubclasedForm` that is subclassed by
`clsFormSub?classed`. Note the use of the `Me` keyword that is passed to the `FormObject` property.

```
Private objSubclass As clsFormSubclassed

Private Sub Form_Open(Cancel As Integer)
    'Create an instance of the class
    Set objSubclass = New clsFormSubclassed

    'Use the Me keyword to pass the current form
    'to the subclass
    Set objSubclass.FormObject = Me
End Sub
```

Creating a Parent Property

To create a relationship between a parent class and a derived class, the parent class needs code such
as this:

```
Option Compare Database
Option Explicit

Private mobjTeacher As clsTeacher

Private Sub Class_Initialize()
    'Create a new instance of the derived class
    Set mobjTeacher = New clsTeacher

    'Create the relationship between the parent and child classes
    Set mobjTeacher.Parent = Me
End Sub
```

Of course, you would also need `Parent` property procedures in the child class:

```
Option Compare Database
Option Explicit

Private mobjClassroom As clsClassroom

Public Property Set Parent(objClassroom As clsClassroom)
    'Check that the property hasn't already been set
    If mobjClassroom Is Nothing Then
        Set mobjClassroom = objClassroom
    End If
End Property
```

In these examples, the derived class has one property procedure, `Property Set`. This procedure accepts an object (of the type `clsClassroom`) as its argument, and uses it to store the instance of the parent object.

When a copy of the parent object is stored locally (in `mobjClassroom`), it can act on the parent object by invoking its properties and methods through the `Parent` property.

The parent object instantiates the derived object and simply passes itself (`Me`) to the derived `Parent` property procedure of the object.

If the `Instancing` property of the parent class is `Private`, you cannot pass it as an argument to the child class. You must set `Instancing` to `PublicNotCreatable` to successfully compile the Parent property.

Creating a Clone Method

Let's say you want to create a separate copy of a class object. It might be tempting to write something like this:

```
Dim objTeacher1 As clsTeacher
Dim objTeacher2 As clsTeacher

Set objTeacher 1 = New clsTeacher
Set objTeacher 2 = objTeacher1
```

On the surface, this looks as if it would create a new object named `objTeacher2` that has the same property values as `objTeacher2`, and that is true. However, these objects actually point to the same data. If you change a property for `objTeacher2`, `objTeacher1` also reflects the same value. The following code demonstrates:

```
Sub TestCopy()
    Dim objTeacher1 As clsTeacher
    Dim objTeacher2 As clsTeacher

    ' create the first instance
    Set objTeacher1 = New clsTeacher
    objTeacher1.Name = "Steven Buchanan"
    Debug.Print "Before: " & objTeacher1.Name

    ' create the second instance
    Set objTeacher2 = objTeacher1

    ' set the second name, then print the first
    objTeacher2.Name = "Nancy Davolio"
    Debug.Print "After: " & objTeacher1.Name

    ' Verify that the objects point to different locations
    Debug.Assert ObjPtr(objTeacher1) <> ObjPtr(objTeacher2)

    ' cleanup
```

```
        Set objTeacher1 = Nothing
        Set objTeacher2 = Nothing
    End Sub
```

The first time the Name is printed, the code prints Steven Buchanan. Then after changing the name of objTeacher2, objTeacher1 has been changed to Nancy Davolio.

Note the use of the ObjPtr function. This is a hidden function in VBA that returns the memory address of an object variable. You use this function in a Debug.Assert statement to make sure that the two objects are not equal. If the Assert fails, then the two objects are pointing to the same location in memory.

To create a proper Clone method, you need to create a new instance of the class, and then copy the private data in the first instance to the new instance. Add the following code to the clsTeacher class to add a Clone method:

```
Public Function Clone() As clsTeacher
    Set Clone = New clsTeacher

    ' Copy individual property values to the cloned instance
    With Clone
        .Name = Me.Name
        .GradeLevel = Me.GradeLevel
        .Salary = Me.Salary
        Set .Parent = Me.Parent
    End With
End Function
```

Change the test code that creates the copy to:

```
Set objTeacher2 = objTeacher1.Clone()
```

Now, the Debug.Assert should succeed and you should have a new clsTeacher object that has the same initial properties as objTeacher1. Furthermore, changing the name of objTeacher2 does not change the name of objTeacher1.

Creating and Using Collection Classes

So far, this chapter has dealt with situations where the relationship between objects is one-to-one. Although that's often the case in real-world programming, it is also quite often the case where the relationship is one-to-many. A group of related objects is called a *collection*, and a collection class is simply a class that contains a list, or collection of related classes. VBA provides a neat little object for creating and handling object collections, oddly enough called a Collection object.

The Collection Object

You are familiar with using object collections; VBA is full of them. The TableDefs and QueryDefs collections are examples you use almost every day. These collections maintain a list of pointers to the individual objects they control, in fact collection objects are also referred to as *Controllers*.

To access an individual object within an object collection, you refer to its collection name and either the name of one of the objects it contains, or its ordinal position within the collection. For example, to check the date a table was created, you could use either of the following constructs.

```
Debug.Print CurrentDb.TableDefs("Table1").DateCreated
Debug.Print CurrentDb.TableDefs(1).DateCreated
```

Most collection objects implement the Add, Remove, and Item methods, and the Count property. Unfortunately, the name given to the Add method can vary from application to application, and even from object to object, but they essentially do the same thing. Figure 13-20 shows an example of a collection class.

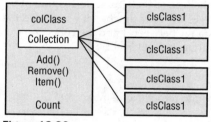

Figure 13-20

For example, to add a worksheet to an Excel workbook, you use the Add method of the Worksheets collection. By contrast, to add a table to the Access TableDefs collection, you create the new table object using CreateTableDef() and append it to the collection using the collection's Append method.

The VBA Collection object uses the Add method. Aren't standards a wonderful thing!

The Add Method

The Add method adds a member to the collection, and has the following syntax:

```
Collection object name.Add (Item, [Key], [Before], [After])
```

The method parameter arguments are:

❑   Item: As you can store almost anything in a collection, the Item parameter is an expression of any type that represents the member to add to the collection. In the case of object collections, this is where you supply a pointer to the object instance.

❏ `Key`: An optional unique string expression that specifies a key that can be used to identify the collection member, instead of using its ordinal position in the collection. The `Key` parameter must be a unique string, otherwise an error occurs.

❏ `Before`: An optional parameter that enables you to specify that the new member is to be added at the position immediately preceding an existing member in the collection. The parameter you supply can be the ordinal numeric position of the existing member, or the `Key` that the existing member was saved with when it was added to the collection. If specifying a number, it must be in the range between 1 and the collection's `Count` property. You can specify a `Before` or `After` position, but not both.

❏ `After`: Similar to the `Before` parameter, the `After` parameter specifies that the new member is to be added at the position immediately following an existing collection member. The parameter you supply can be either the ordinal numeric position of the existing member, or the `Key` that the existing member was saved with when it was added to the collection. If specifying a number, it must be in the range between 1 and the collection's `Count` property. You can specify a `Before` or `After` position, but not both.

The Remove Method

The `Remove` method allows you to remove a member from the collection, and uses the following syntax.

```
object.Remove(index)
```

The `Index` argument specifies the position of an existing collection member. The argument you supply can be the ordinal numeric position of the existing member, or the `Key` that the existing member was saved with when it was added to the collection. If specifying a number, it must be in the range between 1 and the collection's `Count` property.

Note that this is in contrast to the built-in Access collections (such as the `TableDefs` collection) which are zero-based (start at zero).

The Item Method

The `Item` method provides a way for you to specify an object by its ordinal position in the collection. It uses the following syntax:

```
object.Item(index)
```

The `Index` argument specifies the position of an existing collection member. The argument you supply can be either the ordinal numeric position of the existing member, or the `Key` that the existing member was saved with when it was added to the collection. If specifying a number, it must be in the range between 1 and the collection's `Count` property.

Note that this is in contrast to the built-in Access collections (such as the `TableDefs` collection) which are zero-based (start at zero).

As you add and remove members from the middle of the collection, the Item numbers of all the members around it are renumbered to maintain continuity. For example, if you remove item 2 from a 4-member collection, item 3 is renumbered to 2, and item 4 is renumbered to 3. It is for this reason that you should not rely on an object's ordinal position in the collection.

The Count Property

The Count property returns a Long Integer containing the number of objects in a collection, and is read-only.

Collection Class Basics

To demonstrate the basic concepts and techniques used to create a collection class, you extend the classroom example to add students. You create an interface that mirrors the members provided by the VBA Collection object, but by creating your own collection class, you can create an object that is strongly typed. Your collection class can be used to create students and only students.

First, let's flush out a few members of a class that models a student.

clsStudent

Start by creating a class named clsStudent. It will model a student that you'll store in a collection of clsStudent objects.

```vba
Option Compare Database
Option Explicit

Private mstrName     As String
Private mdatDOB      As Date
Private lngStudentID As Long

Private Sub Class_Initialize()
    'Generate the unique key for this object.
    lngStudentID = CLng(Rnd * (2 ^ 31))
End Sub

Public Property Get ID() As Long
    'Return the object's unique key.
    ID = lngStudentID
End Property

Public Property Get Name() As String
    Name = mstrName
End Property

Public Property Let Name(strName As String)
    mstrName = strName
End Property

Public Property Get DOB() As Date
    DOB = mdatDOB
End Property

Public Property Let DOB(datDOB As Date)
    mdatDOB = datDOB
End Property

Public Sub TakeTest()
    ' Code to implement taking a test
End Sub
```

Let's stop for a minute and talk about the ID property. The calculation in the `Initialize` event of the class returns a random number between 215 and 2,147,483,433. This is the largest number that will fit into a Long Integer data type, and offers sufficient range to minimize the risk of duplicates. You'll see why you are generating the random number in a few minutes.

clsStudents

The `Collection` object is declared at module-level and instantiated in the Initialize event. Following best practice, the `Terminate` event destroys the `Collection` instance and any objects it may still contain.

```
Option Compare Database
Option Explicit

Private mcol As Collection 'Declare the collection object

Private Sub Class_Initialize()
    'Instantiates the collection object.
    Set mcol = New Collection
End Sub

Private Sub Class_Terminate()
    'Destroys the collection object.
    Set mcol = Nothing
End Sub
```

The `Add` method adds a pointer to a new `clsStudent` object to the collection class-`clsStudents`. You'll get to the actual implementation of the `Add` method in a moment, but first take a look at usage. There are a couple ways you can implement this method depending on how you want to use it. The `Add` method of the VBA `Collection` object is a `Sub` procedure — that is, it does not return a value. If you choose this implementation, you might pass a `clsStudent` object to the method like this:

```
' Sample usage for the Add method as a Sub
Dim myStudents As clsStudents
Dim myStudent  As clsStudent

' Create the collection class
Set myStudents = New clsStudents

' Create and add a student
Set myStudent = New clsStudent
myStudent.Name = "Rob Cooper"
myStudents.Add myStudent
```

Some implementations of the `Add` method are created as `Function` procedures to return the instance of the object they are adding. In this case, you would need to pass the minimum amount of information, such as the name, to the `Add` method to create the student.

```
' Sample usage for the Add method as a Function
Dim myStudents As clsStudents
Dim myStudent As clsStudent

' Create the collection class
Set myStudents = New clsStudents
```

```
' Create and add the student
Set myStudent = myStudents.Add("Rob Cooper")
```

Whichever approach you choose, you should be consistent in your designs and choose the approach that is best suited for your application. Often, the amount of input you have and when you elect to create the object are deciding factors.

> *Add methods, when implemented as function procedures, are known in OOP parlance as Factory methods. They create an instance of the object they encapsulate.*

Okay, time to implement the Add method. For this example, you use the factory method approach and implement Add as a function. One benefit is that you have less test code as a result.

As mentioned, the Add method adds a pointer to a new clsStudent object and then returns it. Because you are creating a collection of clsStudent objects, you use the ID property that was defined in clsStudent. If an optional Before or After parameter is included in the call, the Add method inserts the object before or after the object that occupies the position specified by the varBefore or varAfter parameter.

The following examples use a routine named ThrowError to display error messages coming from the collection class. The routine is defined later.

```
Public Function Add(strStudentName As String, _
        Optional varBefore As Variant, _
        Optional varAfter As Variant) As clsStudent
    'Adds a member to the collection.

    ' create a temporary student object
    Dim objStudent As clsStudent
    Set objStudent = New clsStudent

    ' set the student name
    objStudent.Name = strStudentName

    If Not IsMissing(varBefore) Then
        mcol.Add objStudent, CStr(objStudent.ID), varBefore
    ElseIf Not IsMissing(varAfter) Then
        mcol.Add objStudent, CStr(objStudent.ID), , varAfter
    Else
        mcol.Add objStudent, CStr(objStudent.ID)
    End If

    ' return the object
    Set Add = objStudent
    On Error Resume Next
    If Err.Number <> 0 Then
        ThrowError Err.Number, Err.Description, Err.Source
    End If
    OnError Goto 0

End Function
```

The following procedure removes the member specified by `strKey`, from the collection, but does not return anything to the calling code.

```vba
Public Sub Remove(strKey As Variant)
    'Removes a member from the collection.

    mcol.Remove strKey

    On Error Resume Next
    If Err.Number <> 0 Then
        ThrowError Err.Number, Err.Description, Err.Source
    End If
    On Error Goto 0
End Sub
```

The `Item` property is interesting (you'll see why shortly), but for the moment the explanation is that it returns a pointer to the object whose `Key` matches that supplied by the `strKey` parameter.

```vba
Public Property Get Item(strKey As String) As clsStudent
    Set Item = mcol(strKey)
End Property
```

The following procedure simply returns a number that represents the number of objects contained in the collection.

```vba
'Returns the number of items in the collection
Public Property Get Count() As Long
    Count = mcol.Count
End Property
```

The `ThrowError` method takes all the errors that occur within the class and packages them up before passing them back up the error chain to the calling procedure.

```vba
Private Sub ThrowError(lngError As Long, strDescr As String, strSource As String)
    'Procedure used to return errors
    Dim strMsg As String

    Select Case lngError
        Case 5
            strMsg = "Member not found."
        Case 9
            strMsg = "Subscript out of range."
        Case 457
            strMsg = "Duplicate member."
        Case Else
            strMsg = "Error " & lngError & vbCrLf & strDescr
    End Select

    Err.Raise vbObjectError + lngError, strSource, strMsg
End Sub
```

Because you're writing your own collection class, you can extend the functionality of the VBA `Collection` object! What follows is only a subset of the additional functionality you could add to your collection classes. For example, you might also choose to add methods that search or sort items in the collection.

The `FirstStudent` property returns a pointer to the object that occupies the first position in the collection, but it doesn't remove it from the collection. Note that you use 1 for the first item in a VBA `Collection`, not 0 as in Access collections such as `TableDefs`.

```
Public Property Get FirstStudent() As clsStudent
    'Returns the first member added to the collection,
    'but does NOT remove it from the collection.

    'Get the first member.
    Set FirstStudent = mcol(1)

    If Err.Number <> 0 Then
        ThrowError Err.Number, Err.Description, Err.Source
    End If
End Property
```

Similarly, the `LastStudent` property returns a pointer to the object that occupies the last position in the collection.

```
Public Property Get LastStudent() As clsStudent
    'Returns the last member added to the collection,
    'but does NOT remove it from the collection.

    'Get the last member.
    Set LastStudent = mcol(mcol.Count)

    If Err.Number <> 0 Then
        ThrowError Err.Number, Err.Description, Err.Source
    End If
End Property
```

The `Clear` method destroys the collection and thus all objects it contains, and then re-instantiates the collection. Although you could have iterated through the collection, removing and destroying objects as you went, destroying the `Collection` object is faster.

```
Public Sub Clear()
    'Clears the collection and destroys all its objects.
    'This is the fastest way.
    Set mcol = Nothing
    Set mcol = New Collection
End Sub
```

Setting Unique Object Keys

The `Collection` object requires that each Key value is unique in the collection. Setting unique `Collection` object keys is not always easy. You can't easily use incrementing numbers because the Key parameter requires a `String` data type, and once you set it, it can't be changed without removing the object and reinserting it.

The best method is to use a property of the object being added (if it has one), but isn't hard to implement. This is the approach you used in your Add method, where you used the ID property of the Student object, but there are other ways to generate unique values as well:

❑ Timestamp values (current date and time)

❑ Network MAC addresses

❑ Telephone numbers

❑ Combination of name and date of birth

❑ Cryptographic random numbers

Okay, perhaps that last one might be a bit of overkill. The point is that you can use whatever means you like to generate a key, but however you do it, ensure the key is unique in the collection.

Testing the clsStudents Class

To test the functionality of the clsStudents class, you can run the following code in a standard module. This test code adds four clsStudent objects to the clsStudents object (the Collection class), and then starts removing them using two different methods: Remove and the Clear method. All the while accessing the clsStudent object's ID property through the collection object. The first Debug.Print statement shows how to access the clsStudent object's Name property through the Students Collection class instance. To begin, create the collection:

```
Public Sub TestCollectionClass()
    Dim myStudents As clsStudents
    Dim obj As clsStudent
    Dim strKey1 As String
    Dim strKey As String

    On Error Resume Next
    Debug.Print "Begin test"

    ' Create the collection
    Set myStudents = New clsStudents
```

Now add code to add a student to the collection using the Add method:

```
    ' Add a student to the collection
    Set obj = myStudents.Add("Teresa Hennig")
    strKey1 = CStr(obj.ID)
    Set obj = Nothing
```

Do the same thing three more times, to add another three students:

```
    ' Add another student to the collection
    Set obj = myStudents.Add("Armen Stein")
    Set obj = Nothing

    ' And another one...
    Set obj = myStudents.Add("Geoff Griffith")
    strKey = CStr(obj.ID)
```

```
        Set obj = Nothing

        ' And the final student
        Set obj = myStudents.Add("Rob Cooper")
        Set obj = Nothing
```

Now print the Name of the student that occupies the first position in the collection:

```
    Debug.Print "The student with ID [" & strKey1 & "] = " & _
        myStudents.Item(strKey1).Name
```

To start removing students from the collection, use the `Remove` method:

```
    'Start removing objects from the collection
    Debug.Print , "There are now " & myStudents.Count & " students."
    Debug.Print , "Removing student: " & strKey1
    myStudents.Remove strKey1

    Debug.Print , "There are now " & myStudents.Count & " students."
    Debug.Print , "Removing student: " & strKey
    myStudents.Remove strKey

    Debug.Print , "There are now " & myStudents.Count & " students."
```

Take advantage of the fact that you issued the `On Error Resume Next` line to trap an error:

```
    'Create an error (key was already removed)
    myStudents.Remove strKey
    If Err <> 0 Then Debug.Print ,"***ERROR " & Err.Number
```

Now, remove the remaining students from the collection, without causing any errors:

```
    'Now do it properly
    myStudents.Clear
    Debug.Print , "There are now " & myStudents.Count & " students."
    Debug.Print "End test"

    Set myStudents = Nothing
End Sub
```

Specifying the Default Procedure

There are two major drawbacks to using custom `Collection` classes; one of them is that Access treats them as normal objects rather than true collections. As such, you do not have access to a default property or procedure. For example, using VBA, the following two statements are equivalent (to test it, ensure you have at least one form open).

```
Debug.Print Forms.Item(0).Name
Debug.Print Forms(0).Name
```

The default property of the `Forms` collection is the `Item` property, which means if you want to, you can omit the `Item` keyword.

Using a custom Collection class, you are forced to explicitly use the Item property, as you did in the previous example. But all is not lost! There is a way to tell Access which procedure to use as the default, but of course, things are never straightforward.

You have to export the procedure to a file, manually add a line of code to the procedure definition and then import it back into Access. The procedure for doing so is as follows:

1. From the Project Explorer window in code view, right-click the module and select Remove.

2. When asked if you want to export the module before removing it, click Yes. The Export File dialog box is displayed.

3. Browse to a convenient folder and change the file name to ***modulename*.txt**, where *modulename* is the name of the module you're exporting.

4. Click Save. The class is removed from the project and saved to disk as a text file.

5. Using Windows Explorer, browse to the appropriate folder and double-click the text file to open it in Notepad.

6. Locate the procedure (in this case the Item property), and add a single line of text such as the one that's highlighted here:

```
Public Property Get Item(strKey As String) As clsStudent
Attribute Item.VB_UserMemId = 0
    Set Item = mcol(strKey)
End Property
```

7. Ensure the procedure or property name appears in the attribute statement and that the attribute is set to zero.

8. Save the file and exit Notepad.

9. In Access code view, right-click anywhere in the Project Explorer and select Import File from the context menu. The Import File dialog box is displayed.

10. Browse to the appropriate folder, select the file you just edited, and click Open. The class is added to the Project Explorer.

You can check the Object Browser (see Figure 13-21) to see that a small blue ball is shown above the procedure's icon, indicating that it is now the default procedure.

The test code previously accessed the clsStudent object's Name property through the myStudents object like this:

```
myStudents.Item(strKey1).Name
```

It can now be accessed like this:

```
myStudents(strKey1).Name
```

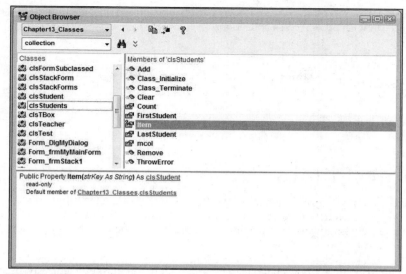

Figure 13-21

Enumerating Collection Classes

A second drawback to using custom `Collection` objects is that you can't enumerate through its members. For example, consider the following code.

```
Public Sub TestEnumeration()
    Dim tdf As TableDef

    For Each tdf In CurrentDb.TableDefs
        Debug.Print tdf.Name
    Next tdf
End Sub
```

This code enables you to enumerate, or iterate, through the collection by declaring an enumeration type. To accomplish the same thing with your custom `Collection` class, you need to go back to Notepad as you did to specify the default procedure, only this time, add an entire public procedure.

Export the class as before and open it in Notepad. Now add the procedure *exactly* as shown here (the only change you can make is the name of the `Collection` object you're using — in this case, `mcol`):

```
Public Function NewEnum() As IUnknown
Attribute NewEnum.VB_UserMemId = -4
    Set NewEnum = mcol.[_NewEnum]
End Function
```

Save the file and re-import it into Access as you did before. Now you can enumerate the collection objects as you can with other Access collections.

```
Dim mbr As Object 'or clsStudent
For Each mbr In myStudents
    Debug.Print mbr.ID
Next mbr
```

Pretty cool stuff, huh?

The Three Pillars

So far, you've examined how to create class modules that are complete with their own properties and procedures. You've seen how to develop their implementation code, instantiate them as objects, link them to other objects singly and in collections, and finally, use them in the application. For most cases, this is all you need to know.

But if you want to create a lot of related classes, and do it in the most efficient way, then you need to understand a few principles of object-oriented programming.

The three pillars of object-oriented theory are:

- ❏ Encapsulation
- ❏ Inheritance
- ❏ Polymorphism

These things have different meanings to different people, and the extent to which they apply to an object-oriented language differs according to which language you happen to prefer. There are other factors like operation overloading, parameterized constructors, and class-level attributes, but their discussion is largely irrelevant because they are not implemented in Access 2007.

Encapsulation

A major advantage of object-oriented programming is the capability to *encapsulate*, or contain data and functionality within simple programmatic entities. That is, every instance of a class object contains exactly the same properties and methods as the class module it was based on. You've seen this in the classes you've created in this chapter.

Another way to describe encapsulation is data hiding. When you create a set of properties and methods to form a class's interface, external code can use that interface to implement its behavior without ever knowing what goes on inside — you don't need to understand the physics of the internal combustion engine to drive to the corner store for milk. This means you can package up data and functionality into a black box that represents some thing, and operate on that thing's interface using standard VBA code, without concerning yourself with how it implements its behavior.

The interface to objects of the same class is well defined, and allows the internal code implementing its methods to be changed as necessary, as long as the interface to the programmer's world remains unchanged. This enables you to execute long or complex operations using simple metaphors provided by the class's interface. For example, if your class implements the mechanics of the human body, and includes all the nerve-muscle-bone interactions, then a programmer using your class would need only issue commands such as:

```
Person.Turn "right"
Person.Walk 10
Person.Stop
Person.Sit
```

Such reliable structure means that an organization can implement its business rules and processes in a class, and then change those rules and processes at will without affecting any code that was written around it — provided of course, that the class's interface remains unchanged.

A side benefit of this is that encapsulation also offers a way of hiding specific business rules and behavior from other developers. For example, suppose you have created a class that determines certain properties of a proprietary chemical formula. You wouldn't want your employees knowing the details of the formula, so you encapsulate it in a custom class and expose only the interface to it. What's an interface? Read on, all will be revealed.

Inheritance

In a nutshell, inheritance is the capability to create new classes from existing ones. A derived class, or subclass, inherits the properties and methods of the class that instantiated it (called the base class, or superclass), and may add new properties and methods. New methods can be defined with the same name as those in the superclass, in which case, they override the original one.

There are two types of inheritance: interface and implementation inheritance. Interface inheritance has been available to Access since VBA 6 introduced the `Implements` keyword. Implementation inheritance is now available in Visual Basic .NET through the `Inherits` keyword, but unfortunately not in Access 2007.

The essential difference between the two forms of inheritance is that interface inheritance specifies only the interface. It doesn't actually provide any corresponding implementation code. For example, suppose you have a `Bike` object that wants to ask the `Wheel` object for its part number. The `Wheel` object wants to borrow the functionality from its superclass, `Parts`. The `Bike` object might implement the following functionality:

```
Private myWheel As Wheel

Private Function GetPartNo() As String
    GetPartNo = myWheel.PartNo()
End Function
```

The implementation of this behavior is in `Part`'s `PartNo()` method. Because VBA 6 doesn't support implementation inheritance, you would need to put some code into the `Wheel` class.

```
Implements Part
Private MyPart As New Part
```

```
Private Function Part_PartNo() As String
    Part_PartNo = myPart.PartNo()
End Function
```

VBA 6 allows the interface, in this case `Part`, to implement the actual behavior. `Wheel` retains an instance of `Part` (a behavior called *containment*), and then asks that reference to carry out some action for it (called *delegation*). This isn't true interface inheritance because it allows you to add code to `Wheel` to provide the actual behavior, but it's close enough.

Polymorphism

Polymorphism is the capability for different object types to implement the same method, thereby allowing you to write VBA code without concerning yourself about what type of object you're using at the time. Another way of looking at it is that objects can be more than one type of thing.

There are two types of polymorphism: *ad-hoc* polymorphism (called *overloading* in VB.NET) and *parametric* polymorphism. Parametric polymorphism is not implemented in Access 2007, and so will be ignored in this book.

Ad-hoc polymorphism provides the capability to use the same calling syntax for objects of different types. For example, say you have `bikes` and `cars` classes, each having its own methods to implement its own unique properties and behaviors, but because both need their tires pumped up occasionally, they would both have a `pump_tires` method. The actual code to implement this behavior would perhaps differ, but as long as their interface remained the same, your VBA code could simply call the `pump_tires` method for both, confident that each class knows how to pump up its own tires.

Okay, it's true that VBA doesn't demonstrate some of the characteristics of a true object-oriented language like C#, but it doesn't pretend to. Applications where you would need polymorphism or inheritance would not be written in VBA, so VBA doesn't need to implement them.

Inheriting Interfaces

Inheritance is an object-oriented concept that allows one class to *inherit* the public properties and methods (the interface) of another class. This section illustrates how you can implement that in your own Access object models.

The `Implements` keyword in VBA allows you to implement interface inheritance, giving programmers access to a form of polymorphism.

For example, suppose you have two objects: `Object1` and `Object2`. If `Object1` inherits the interface exposed by `Object2`, you can say that `Object1` *is a kind of* `Object2`, which is polymorphism in a nutshell.

Often interfaces are referred to as a *contract* because there is an agreement between the creator of the object and its user that the object will provide all the properties and methods that form its interface. The internal implementation may vary, but the object's signature (its property and method names, parameters and data types) may not.

You can use interfaces and polymorphism in any number of ways, but to understand how it all works, examine the most common — categorizing objects on the basis of common traits. Employees are a good example because you can implement different types, such as Programmer, Tester, or Manager.

Each employee has their own attributes and behaviors, such that they each merit their own class. They all share common traits — such as they all work for the same company, have a date of birth, hire date, salary, and so on. All do work, take lunch, and take telephone calls. If you put all the common traits into a single interface (IEmployee), you have a generic way of dealing with all employees at once. For example, you can pay each employee like so:

```
Dim Employee As IEmployee

For Each Employee In Company
    Employee.Pay
Next Employee
```

Although all employees receive pay, they all receive different amounts of pay and may receive pay in different ways. For example, some employees may receive paychecks, whereas others may receive payment through direct deposit. Therefore, the code to pay each employee must be in that employee's class, and will certainly differ from employee to employee.

Additionally, the members of an implemented interface do not automatically become part of the default interface for a class. That is, if a Manager had only one public method, GivePayRaise, you would have to get at the GivePayRaise method like this:

```
Dim Employee As clsManager

Set Employee = new clsManager
Employee.GivePayRaise
```

Traditionally, interface class names are distinguished from other types of class by prepending their names with an uppercase I.

You could copy the IEmployee interface into the default interface, and have both point to a common private procedure that contains the code that makes the employee give a raise. You could also make it simple and just use the Implements keyword in each employee's class:

```
Implements IEmployee
```

By so doing, every employee whose class definition included the Implements keyword would inherit the public properties and methods exposed by the IEmployee interface. So you can begin to understand how interface inheritance works, start by defining two Employee classes based on the type of employee: Programmers and Managers. Before you do that, create an interface class that defines the characteristics that all employees have in common (naturally, you call this class IEmployee):

```
Option Compare Database
Option Explicit
```

```
Public Property Get Salary() As Currency
End Property

Public Property Let Salary(curSalary As Currency)
End Property

Public Property Get Name() As String
End Property

Public Property Let Name(strName As String)
End Property

Public Property Get HireDate() As Date
End Property

Public Property Let HireDate(datHireDate As Date)
End Property

Public Sub DoWork()
End Sub

Public Sub TakeLunch()
End Sub

Public Sub Pay()
End Sub
```

The first thing you notice is that it doesn't have any code to implement an employee's attributes or behavior. That's because you're inheriting the *interface*, not the *implementation*. As discussed at the beginning of the chapter, a class module is like a template. An implementation class is also like a template, but where the template provided by "standard" classes includes interface and implementation, an interface class only provides an interface template.

Next you can create your new `Employee` classes: the first being the `Programmer` class. If you create a basic `Employee` class, with (for simplicity) only one method and one property procedure of its own:

```
Option Compare Database
Option Explicit

Public Property Get KnowsVBA() As Boolean
    ' Code to determine whether the programmer knows VBA
End Property

Public Sub DoCodeReview()
    ' Code to perform a code review
End Property
```

Now you add the `Implements` keyword, after which you can select the `IEmployee` class from the `Object` drop-down list (see Figure 13-22).

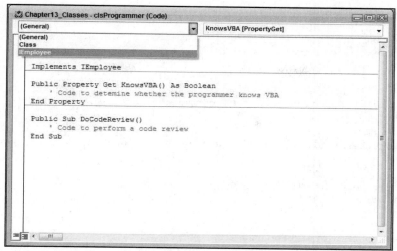

Figure 13-22

Selecting all the IEmployee class's interface procedures from the Procedure drop-down list, you can see that they've all been inherited as Private members. This is because, although all IEmployee's public properties and procedures are inherited (in fact, an error is generated if you don't inherit all of them), you may not want to expose all of them to consumers of the Programmer class.

```vba
Private Sub IEmployee_Pay()

End Sub

Private Sub IEmployee_DoWork()

End Sub

Private Property Let IEmployee_HireDate(RHS As Date)

End Property
```

You can now implement the unique behavior for this employee, without affecting the implementation of any other employee. Add a local variable to store the employee's salary and you end up with the following class definition. First, you declare the objects and variables you need, and issue the Implements keyword.

```vba
Option Compare Database
Option Explicit

Implements IEmployee

Private mcurSalary As Currency
```

Then, create some custom procedures to perform a range of employee-specific actions:

```
Private Sub IEmployee_DoWork()
    ' Code to implement doing work
End Sub

Private Sub IEmployee_Pay()
    ' Code to implement paying a Programmer
End Sub
```

Finally, add a property and a sub procedure to carry out what might be termed Standard Operations, for all employees.

```
Private Property Let IEmployee_Salary(RHS As String)
    mcurSalary = RHS
End Property

Private Sub IEmployee_TakeLunch()
    ' Code to implement a Programmer taking lunch
End Sub
```

You can then create any number of classes for any number of employees, to which you can link an unlimited number of Employee classes, to track individual employees.

Interface inheritance isn't terribly difficult; making sure it doesn't get out of hand is the hard part!

Instancing

Earlier, you were introduced to the Instancing property. Now it's time to explore it. Figure 13-23 shows the available values for the Instancing property for a class module in Access.

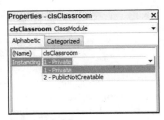

Figure 13-23

A class's Instancing property defines whether the class is private or public, and whether it can be created from external code.

Setting a class's Instancing property to Private means that the class can be used only within the application in which it is defined. As you saw earlier in the section Creating a Parent Property, it can also determine whether instances of the class can be passed as arguments.

Setting it to `PublicNotCreatable` means that although other applications can access type library information about the class, they can use it only after your application has created it first; they can't create instances of it. This can be accomplished by using helper methods in standard modules, such as:

```
Public Function GetNotCreatableInstance() As clsPublicNotCreatable
    Set GetNotCreatableInstance = New clsPublicNotCreatable
End Function
```

Classes that have their `Instancing` property set to `PublicNotCreatable` are referred to as *dependent objects*, and typically form part of more complex objects. Using the Classroom/Teacher/Student example, you might want to allow an external application to create multiple `clsClassroom` objects, but only allow `clsStudent` objects to exist as a part of a `clsClassroom`. To do that, you make the `clsStudent` class `PublicNotCreatable` and let the user add new `Students` by adding a `Students` collection to the `clsClassroom` class. That way, they can only create new `Students` using the collection's `Add` method.

There are situations where you might want to be able to create new instances of a class from another application. The classic example is where you are developing a class library in a database and would like to use it in multiple applications. For this, there is one additional value you can use for the `Instancing` property that does not appear in the Properties window.

Remember that VBA has its roots in VB, which actually supports *six* values for the `Instancing` property! Access supports one of these values called `GlobalMultiUse`, the value of which is 5. Setting the `Instancing` property to 5 allows you to create new instances of your classes, even when used as a reference in another application. To set the property, run this code in the Immediate Window:

```
VBE.ActiveVBProject.VBComponents("clsMyClass").Properties("Instancing") = 5
```

Remember to select the correct VBA project in the Project Explorer before running this code.

Summary

This chapter took you on a whirlwind tour of the object-oriented programming techniques that are made available in Access 2007. If you had any trouble understanding the concepts, just remember that it may just take a little practice. Before long, you'll be writing quite complex OOP code that will make your application development and maintenance a joy to behold.

Specifically in this chapter, you looked at class modules, how they differ from object instances, and when you would use OOP techniques in your applications. You created several classes of your own, designed their properties and methods, and instantiated the classes as objects to investigate how they work and how to use them.

You learned about the object naming strategy, and then you examined class events and errors, to understand how classes communicate with the outside world. You also practiced using forms and reports as objects, and explored collection classes, which are the basis for building your own object models. Finally, you looked at some basic OOP theory and saw how to implement some of it in code.

You have now gone as far as standard VBA can take you. Chapter 14 starts you on the next leg of your programming journey by introducing the Windows API and the many built-in functions that the Windows operating system can offer in terms of advanced programming functionality.

14

Extending VBA with APIs

Microsoft Visual Basic for Applications (VBA) is a full-featured software development language that offers a vast array of built-in functions so that many Access developers never require anything else.

However, when you start developing more and more complex applications in Access, you may find yourself needing to do things for which VBA does not have a built-in function. Moreover, you'll sometimes need to do things that VBA simply can't do. That's not to say that VBA is incomplete, but, like every other programming language, it does not include every function you're ever likely to need. A line has to be drawn somewhere, and Microsoft drew that line at the functions provided by the API.

The Windows operating system provides a large library of functions that you can access using VBA to extend what you're able to do in your applications. But because the API is inherently VBA-unfriendly, you must first understand what it is, and what special considerations you must take into account to use it from VBA.

This chapter explores what the Windows API is, and why you might want to use it. It describes the libraries that make up the API and how to link them into your application. Then you'll see how to declare API functions to use them with VBA and examine the differences between the data types used in APIs and those used in VBA, learning techniques and formulas to convert between them.

Finally, the chapter introduces the VBA LastDLLError method for dynamic-link library (DLL) error handling and explains how to deploy and install applications that contain references to API or other libraries.

Introducing the Win32 API

An API — application programming interface — is simply a group of standard functions that are packaged together and made available to application programmers. There are quite a few APIs, but the one that you've probably heard the most about is the Win32 API, also known as the 32-bit Windows API. The Windows API consists of many DLLs that make up the Windows operating system and ensure that every application that runs under Windows behaves in a consistent manner.

What this actually means is that standard Windows operations such as saving files, opening forms, managing dialog boxes, and so on are all handled by the Windows APIs. For example, the standard Windows File Open dialog box is an API function called `GetOpenFileName` found in `comdlg32.dll`. Similarly, the `GetTempPath` function in `Kernel32.dll` returns the name of the folder where temporary files are stored.

> *The File dialog boxes found in Office applications are customized versions of the Windows dialog boxes. To use these dialog boxes, use the `FileDialog` object in the Office 12.0 Object Library.*

All Windows-based applications interact with the Windows APIs in some way, whether they are opening a file, displaying time, putting text on the screen, or managing computer memory while you play *Flight Simulator*.

When you program in Microsoft Access, you use the built-in VBA functions, which you could loosely refer to as an API. Similarly, when you use the Access Add-in Manager or References dialog box to link to an external DLL, OCX, MDB, and so on, you are linking to something that is essentially an API.

Know the Rules, Program with Confidence

There's no need to feel intimidated by the API, despite the fact that it has the reputation of being highly complex. Because the Windows APIs are written in C/C++, VB programmers must be aware of certain rules, but other than that, the APIs can pretty much be used in the same way as any other function.

For example, enter the following example into a standard module and run it:

```
Private Declare Function GetUserName _
Lib "advapi32.dll" Alias "GetUserNameA" _
(ByVal lpBuffer As String, _
nSize As Long) As Long

Private Const MAXLEN = 255

Function GetLoginName() As String
    Dim strUserName As String
    Dim lngSize As Long
    Dim lngReturn As Long

    lngSize = 256     strUserName = Space(MAXLEN) & Chr(0)

    If GetUserName(strUserName, lngSize) <> 0 Then
        GetLoginName = left(strUserName, lngSize -1)
    Else
        GetLoginName = ""
    End If
End Function
```

This code returns the domain login name of the current Windows user. At this point, the `Declare` function part may be a bit of a mystery, but the rest is a standard VBA function. In Visual Basic, using most APIs is just that simple.

The following table describes just a few of the DLLs that contain APIs to use in VBA applications. For more information about the Windows API, refer to Appendix H.

API	Basic Description
KERNEL32.DLL	Low-level operating system functions, such as memory and task management, resource handling, and so on.
USER32.DLL	Window management functions, including messages, menus, cursors, carets, timers, communications, and most of the nondisplay functions.
GDI32.DLL	The Graphics Device Interface Library. Device output, including most drawing functions, and display context, metafile, coordinate, and font functions.
COMDLG32.DLL	Windows common dialog boxes.
LZ32.DLL	File compression.
VERSION.DLL	Version control.
MAPI32.DLL	Electronic mail.
COMCTL32.DLL	Implements a new set of Windows controls and dialog boxes, including the tree view and rich text edit controls.
NETAPI32.DLL	Network access and control.
ODBC32.DLL	Implements ODBC (Open Database Connectivity), providing functions to work with databases.
WINMM.DLL	Multimedia.
ADVAPI32.DLL	Advanced Win32 Base API. Includes functions to read and write to the Windows Registry, and to retrieve the username.

32-bit Windows packs its APIs into function libraries called DLLs, but before we get too far into the details of how to use them, here is some historical background to help understand how they work.

Why You Need the API

VBA is a powerful language, but you can control only a small part of the operating system with its built-in functions. One of the best features of VBA is its extensibility; that is, you can extend its capabilities in a variety of ways — one of which is by using the API.

For example, VBA provides several built-in functions for manipulating the Windows Registry, but these functions let you use only one small part of the Registry set aside for VBA. To access the remainder of the Registry, you need to use the API.

Similarly, to retrieve and manipulate a disk drive, printer, or system resource settings, you need the API. If you want your Access applications to do more than just beep, the sndPlaySound API function enables you to play sound effects or music. You can even control the transparency of your Access forms using several API functions in conjunction.

Here's an example that puts an icon in a form's title bar; something you can't do using standard VBA. Place the following code into a standard module:

```vba
Public Declare Function LoadImage Lib "user32" _
    Alias "LoadImageA" (ByVal hInst As Long, _
    ByVal lpsz As String, ByVal un1 As Long, _
    ByVal n1 As Long, ByVal n2 As Long, _
    ByVal un2 As Long) As Long

Public Declare Function SendMessage Lib "user32" _
    Alias "SendMessageA" (ByVal hWnd As Long, _
    ByVal wMsg As Long, ByVal wParam As Long, _
    LParam As Any) As Long

'Image type constants
Public Const IMAGE_ICON = 1

'un2 Flags
Public Const LR_LOADFROMFILE = &H10

'Message parameters
Public Const WM_SETICON = &H80
Public Const ICON_SMALL = 0

'Default image size for the Access Titlebar
Public Const IMG_DEFAULT_HEIGHT = 16
Public Const IMG_DEFAULT_WIDTH = 16

Public Sub SetFormIcon(hWnd As Long, strIcon As String)
    Dim hIcon As Long
    Dim lngReturn As Long

    hIcon = LoadImage(0&, strIcon, IMAGE_ICON, IMG_DEFAULT_WIDTH, _
        IMG_DEFAULT_HEIGHT, LR_LOADFROMFILE)

    If hIcon <> 0 Then
        lngReturn = SendMessage(hWnd, WM_SETICON, ICON_SMALL, ByVal hIcon)
    End If
End Sub
```

Then create a new form and add the following code to the form's Load event, making sure to change the C:\myIcons\myIco.ico path to that of an icon file that exists on your computer. You may also have to change the Document Window Options setting to Overlapping Windows in the Current Database group of the Access Options dialog box.

```vba
Private Sub Form_Load()
    SetFormIcon Me.hWnd, "C:\myIcons\myIcon.ico"
End Sub
```

Now open the form to see the icon appear in the form's title bar.

With the APIs at your disposal, you can control a significant portion of the Windows operating system and almost everything within it. Let's begin by discussing how the API works.

Introducing Linking

As previously mentioned, function libraries can be linked or incorporated into applications when required. Libraries are linked using a tool called a *linker*. It takes objects created by a compiler and puts them together into a single executable file. There are two types of linking: *static* and *dynamic*. Static linking occurs at design time, when you create the application. Dynamic linking occurs at runtime.

Static Linking

Most programming languages provide the capability to access some operating system functions. They also usually enable you to create and store your own custom functions, which you can compile into library (*.lib) files and then merge into your applications.

When an executable program is compiled, the linker scans the application for references to external functions and libraries, and then copies them into the final executable, thereby linking them to your application. This is called *static linking* because the addresses your program uses to access these functions are fixed into the executable and remain unchanged (static) when the program runs. Figure 14-1 illustrates how static linking works.

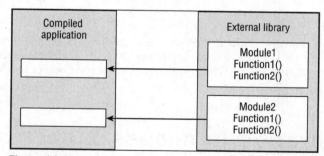

Figure 14-1

Although newer compilers enable you to copy individual functions, older ones typically copied the entire module to the application when linking a library. This meant that all the library's functions were merged into the executable, regardless of whether they were needed.

Of course, copying the entire module to the application increased the resulting file size. While the size increase was usually small, it started to actually mean something if there were 20 executables, each containing a copy of the same library. In a multitasking environment such as Windows, all 20 programs could conceivably be running simultaneously, so a great deal of memory would be in use at any one time.

Dynamic Linking

Instead of grouping functions into libraries, later versions of Windows grouped these functions into a special type of executable called a DLL. When you link a DLL, you specify which function you want to include in your application, and instead of copying in the entire contents of the DLL, the linker/compiler records the name of each externally referenced function along with the name of the DLL in which it resides.

When your application runs, Windows loads the required library so that all its functions are exposed, and it is then that the address of each function is resolved and dynamically linked to the application. That's why it's called *dynamic linking*. Figure 14-2 shows how dynamic linking works.

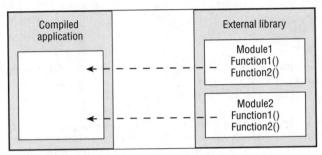

Figure 14-2

Only one copy of the library needs to be stored on disk. All the applications that use its functions access the same physical copy.

Dynamic linked libraries typically have the same file extension (`*.dll`), but that isn't an absolute requirement. Custom controls such as those created in Visual Basic and C++ can have file extensions like `*.ocx`. Device drivers and some Windows system libraries sometimes use file extensions such as `*.drv` and `*.exe`.

Linking Libraries in Access 2007

There are two ways to link a library to an Access 2007 database: by referencing the library or by declaring it.

Referencing a Library

When you set a reference to an external library in Access 2007, you can use its functions as though they were built-in to Access. You can reference type libraries, object libraries, and control libraries.

For example, because the Microsoft Excel Object Library is itself a library of functions, you can reference (link to) it in Access and use its functions as though they were part of Access. To reference a library, select Tools ⇨ References in the Visual Basic Editor. The References dialog box opens, as shown in Figure 14-3.

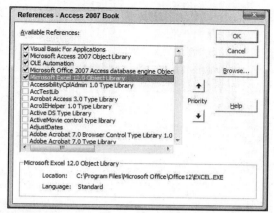

Figure 14-3

Browse the list to see a large range of libraries. Some typical libraries are:

- ❑ Microsoft Office 12.0 Object Library
- ❑ Microsoft Excel, Word, and the other members of the Office suite
- ❑ Microsoft ActiveX Data Objects 2.8 Library
- ❑ Microsoft Office 2007 Access database engine Object Library
- ❑ Microsoft Scripting Runtime
- ❑ Microsoft SQLDMO Object Library

Of course, many of the libraries you'll find listed in the References dialog box are from suppliers other than Microsoft, and depend on the applications you have installed on your computer. You might find such things as:

- ❑ Adobe Acrobat 7.0 Type Library
- ❑ Crystal Reports Common Object Model Library 10.2

To reference a library, browse the list and check the box next to the library you want to use; then click OK. If you don't find the one you are looking for, click Browse and locate the file.

It's worth noting that not all of the libraries can be used without purchasing a license from the supplier. Others are specifically written for C++ or Visual Basic and cannot be used in Access. Check the documentation that was included with the library if you are unsure.

Reference control libraries by selecting Insert ActiveX Control from the Design tab in Form Design View. Figure 14-4 shows the Insert ActiveX Control dialog box.

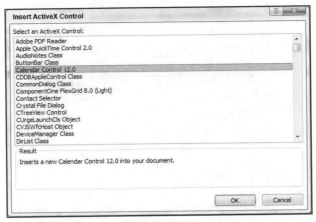

Figure 14-4

When you add a custom control (OCX) to a form in this way, Access adds a reference to it in the References dialog box. For example, adding the Microsoft Calendar Control adds a reference to `C:\Program Files\Microsoft Office\Office12\mscal.ocx`.

How Microsoft Access Resolves VBA References

When Access needs to use the file you've referenced, it does so in the following sequence:

1. It checks the location indicated in the References dialog box.

2. It checks to see if the file is already loaded.

3. It checks the `RefLibPaths` Registry key for a value in the name of the referenced file.

4. If the `RefLibPaths` key does not exist, or doesn't contain the required value, Access checks the Search Path in the following order:

   a. Application folder (where `msaccess.exe` is located)

   b. Current folder

   c. System folder (System and System32 folders, located in the Windows or WinNT folder)

   d. WinDir system variable (the folder where the operating system is running, usually the Windows folder)

   e. `PATH` environment variable (contains a list of folders accessible by the system)

   f. File folder (the folder that contains the ACCDB, ACCDE, MDB, MDE, ADP, or ADE file, and any subfolders

If Access still can't find the referenced file, it generates an error. When you check the References dialog box, you may see a reference marked `MISSING`, as shown in Figure 14-5.

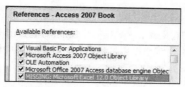

Figure 14-5

Although Access warns you about broken references when you display the VBA Editor, the following property returns `True` if a reference is broken, and `False` otherwise. Run this code in the Immediate window to test:

```
?Application.BrokenReference
```

You can also use the `IsBroken` property of a `Reference` object to determine if a specific reference is broken. This property, issued in the Immediate window, returns `True` if the reference to DAO is broken, and `False` otherwise:

```
?Application.References("DAO").IsBroken
```

Appendix B fully explains creating and managing references.

Once a library is linked, you can use its functions as easily as you would a built-in Access function. For example, after linking Excel, the following code demonstrates how to access Excel's `InchesToPoints()` function, which, as you would expect, converts inches to points:

```
Public Sub Linking2Excel()
Debug.Print Excel.Application.InchesToPoints(1)
End Sub
```

Declaring APIs

The other way to link an external library is to declare it, naturally enough by using the `Declare` keyword. The `Declare` statement typically consists of eight parts, and supports both functions and sub-procedures (subs). You can only declare a procedure at module level (in the Declarations Section).

Declare Syntax for a Sub Procedure

```
[Public | Private] Declare Sub name Lib "libname" [Alias "aliasname"]
[([arglist])]
```

Declare Syntax for a Function Procedure

```
[Public | Private] Declare Function name Lib "libname" [Alias "aliasname"]
[([arglist])] [As type]
```

The Declare Keyword

The Declare keyword alerts VBA that what follows is the definition for a procedure stored in a DLL. The Declare statement also defines the type of procedure being declared: Function or Sub.

As you've already discovered, you can specify that the procedure be either Public or Private, depending on whether you want the procedure to be available to the entire project or only to the module in which it appears. Declare statements made in class modules can only be Private. In fact, you will get a compile error if you omit the Private keyword in a class module.

Naming the Procedure

The name that follows Declare Function or Declare Sub is the name you use to call the procedure from VBA. There is a degree of flexibility here because the name need not be the actual name of the procedure in the DLL.

As in the following example, you can rename the procedure to almost anything, provided you use the Alias keyword to specify the actual name of the API procedure.

```
Private Declare Function MySillyProcedureName Lib "advapi32.dll" _
Alias "GetUserNameA" (ByVal lpBuffer As String, _
nSize As Long) As Long
```

The Alias keyword specifies the actual name of the procedure as it appears in the API. You cannot change this, but as you've seen, you can change the Name argument in the procedure declaration.

There are several reasons for renaming an API procedure:

❑   Some API procedures begin with an underscore character (_), which is illegal in VBA. To get around this, rename the procedure and use the Alias keyword.

❑   API procedure names are case sensitive, and terribly intolerant of programmers who forget that. VBA, on the other hand, doesn't care one way or the other, so by renaming the procedure, you build in a level of forgiveness.

❑   Several API procedures have arguments that can accept different data types. Supplying a wrong data type to such a procedure is a good way to get the API angry because VBA does not check the data types of the arguments you supply. The kind of response you are likely to get by using a wrong data type can range from erroneous data, unexpected application behavior, application hang, or system crash. To avoid type problems, declare several versions of the same procedure, each with a different name and each using arguments of different data types.

❑   Some Windows APIs have names that are the same as the reserved keywords in Access, such as SetFocus and GetObject. Using those keywords results in a compile error. Because you can't rename the Access keywords, you can give the API a unique name in the Declare statement and use the Alias keyword to refer to the API as defined by Windows.

❑   Most API procedures that can take string arguments come in two flavors: one for ANSI and one for Unicode. The ANSI version is suffixed by an A, as in the GetUserNameA example. The Unicode flavor has a W suffix (for wide). VBA uses Unicode internally and converts all strings to ANSI before calling a DLL procedure, so you generally use the ANSI version. But if you need to use both versions in the same project, renaming one or both of them makes sense.

❑   Finally, you can create procedure names that conform to your object naming standards.

What Is Unicode?

Unicode is one of the three distinct character sets supported by the Win32 API:

❏ **Single-byte:** 8 bits wide, and provides for 256 characters. The ANSI character set is a single-byte character set.

❏ **Double-byte (DBCS):** Also 8 bits wide, but some of its byte values are called DBCS lead bytes, which are combined with the byte that follows them to form a single character. DBCSs provide a sufficient number of characters for languages such as Japanese, which have hundreds of characters.

❏ **Unicode:** 16 bits, which provides for up to 65,535 characters; enough to support all the characters in all the languages around the world.

If you make a mistake when declaring the `Alias`, VBA won't find the procedure in the DLL and will present runtime error 453 (`Can't find DLL entry point GetUserNameB in advapi32`), which your error-handling code can trap.

Specifying the Lib(rary) and Argument List

The `Lib` keyword specifies the filename of the library that contains the procedure you're declaring. You declare the filename as a string inside quotes. If VBA can't find the file, it generates a runtime error 53 (`File not found`), which your error handler can also trap.

The API argument list is specified in much the same way as it is in standard VBA subs and functions. However, there are a few rules that you must understand and adhere to when calling API procedures, including knowing when to pass arguments `ByRef` or `ByVal`, how to translate data types, and how to use values that are returned from an API. (You'll get a closer look at data types you might encounter when reading API documentation in the "Understanding C Parameters" section later in the chapter.)

Passing Values

To understand how to pass values to an API function, take a look at the declaration of the `GetUserName` function as defined on MSDN. This declaration is defined in C++:

```
BOOL GetUserName(
  LPTSTR lpBuffer,
  LPDWORD lpnSize
);
```

Two arguments are passed to the `GetUserName` function: `lpBuffer`, a fixed-width string storage area that contains the value returned by the procedure, and `lpnSize`, which is the width of the string Basically, the declaration tells the API where to find the string in memory, and its width. Returning values from API functions is discussed in the next section.

Here's how the `GetUserName` arguments work in VBA:

```
Private Declare Function GetUserName Lib "advapi32.dll" Alias "GetUserNameA" _
(ByVal lpBuffer As String, _
```

```
    nSize As Long) As Long

Private Const MAXLEN = 255

Function GetLoginName() As String
    Dim strUserName As String
    Dim lngSize As Long
    Dim lngReturn As Long

    lngSize = 256

    strUserName = Space(MAXLEN) & Chr(0)

    If GetUserName(strUserName, lngSize) <> 0 Then
        GetLoginName = left(strUserName, lngSize -1)
    Else
        GetLoginName = ""
    End If
End Function
```

The function is declared with two arguments: `ByVal lpBuffer As String` and `nSize As Long`. You might be thinking, "Hang on, `ByRef` passes a pointer, not `ByVal`." Normally that's true, but VBA is somewhat inconsistent in the way it deals with strings. By default, it passes variables `ByRef`; that is, it passes a pointer to the value's location in memory, allowing the procedure to modify the actual value. To test this behavior in VBA, create the following two procedures in a standard module.

TestByRef Procedure

```
Public Sub TestByRef()
    Dim intMyValue As Integer
    intMyValue = 1

    Debug.Print "Initial value: " & intMyValue
    ChangeMyValue intMyValue
    Debug.Print "New value: " & intMyValue
End Sub
```

ChangeMyValue Procedure

```
Private Sub ChangeMyValue(ByRef intSomeValue As Integer)
    intSomeValue = 3
End Sub
```

Run `TestByRef()` and you'll see that the value of `intMyValue` changes. If you modify the `ChangeMyValue()` procedure to pass `intSomeValue ByVal`, and re-run `TestByRef()`, the value doesn't change. In VBA, this is true of strings as well. But when you pass strings to an API, the reverse happens. The reason is that because a string variable is itself a pointer, passing it to an API `ByRef` actually passes a pointer to an OLE 2.0 string (a `BSTR` data type). Generally, the only APIs to use this type of string are those that are part of the OLE 2.0 API. Other APIs don't take too kindly to it. Windows API procedures expect strings to be passed as a pointer to a *null-terminated string*, that is, the string ends with an ASCII zero character. This is a C language convention. When you pass a string ByVal, VBA converts the string to C language format by appending a null-termination character. Because the value is a pointer, the DLL can modify the string even though the ByVal keyword is used.

If you fail to specify the ByVal or ByRef keyword, you run the risk of an error 49, Bad DLL calling convention. Also, if you pass a value ByRef when ByVal is expected, or vice versa, the procedure can overrun memory that it shouldn't, and the system can crash.

Returning Values

Even subprocedure APIs can return values, and the values returned by many API procedures can be quite different from those returned by VBA procedures. You may have noticed that the GetUserName function defined earlier returns a Long Integer, not a String. This is commonplace with many API functions, particularly those declared in Windows. There are two main reasons for this. First, API functions were initially designed to be used by C programmers who are accustomed to checking for an error code after calling a function.

Second, strings in C and C++ are different from those in VBA. VBA has a native data type called String that you can use to assign or refer to character data. C and C++ do not have this intrinsic type; their strings are usually created as an array of characters. As a result, DLLs often cannot return strings directly. Instead, they modify strings that you pass as one of their parameters. When you pass a string parameter to an API that will modify it, you must preinitialize the string with sufficient characters to take the value that will be returned. The API function provides another parameter to accept a number that represents the length of the string. You preinitialize the string using the VBA Space() function, and the Len(strMyString)+1 construct can be used to specify its length. The +1 accounts for the terminating null character in the return string.

> *What all of this really means is that strings in VBA are not really strings. The actual storage for a String in VBA is in an array of bytes. As a result, you can directly assign a string value to a variable that is declared as a Byte array and vice versa.*

The other set of rules that must be followed when passing values to or receiving values from API procedures is that of data types, which are discussed in the next section.

Understanding C Parameters

Most APIs were written by C programmers, so most APIs are written specifically for the C language. Consequently, there are many APIs that are completely unusable by VBA because VBA does not support some of the data types required by those APIs. Of those APIs that are accessible to VBA, most require consideration with regard to the data types used. Use a wrong data type and your computer will quickly let you know all about it.

The following sections describe the C data types often specified for API parameters, the VBA data types that should be used with them, the recommended calling conventions, and, where applicable, the technique that converts signed integer values from unsigned integer values and vice versa.

Signed and Unsigned Integers

First, the C language uses something that is unknown to VBA: *unsigned numbers*. VBA uses only *signed numbers*. An unsigned number is a positive number; that is, it does not have a sign. A signed number can be either positive or negative because of the sign. VBA does actually support one unsigned data type: Byte. For example, Figure 14-6 shows an 8-bit byte. Having a binary 1 in the most significant bit (the eighth bit) signifies that the number contained within the byte is a negative number. A 0 in the same position indicates that the number is positive.

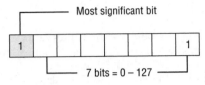

Figure 14-6

Sometimes you'll run across numeric parameters that require an unsigned value. The general algorithm for supplying that value is to convert the value to its next highest data type, subtract the maximum value that the data type can carry, and then convert it back to the original data type.

The following table shows how to convert values from unsigned to signed, and vice versa, for the bit widths of values supported by VBA.

Type	Convert Unsigned to Signed	Convert Signed to Unsigned
8-bit	signed = CByte(unsigned - 255)	unsigned = (CInt(signed) And 255)
16-bit	signed = CInt(unsigned - 65535)	unsigned = (CLng(signed) And 65535)
32-bit	signed = CLng(unsigned - 1.79769313486232E308)	unsigned = (CDbl(signed) And 1.79769313486232E308)

Numeric Parameters

As with VBA, there are many types of numeric data you might come across when working with APIs. The following table outlines the numeric types defined in C/C++ along with their VBA equivalents. Also included are the data type prefixes often found in Windows API declarations on MSDN.

Size (bits)	Data Type	Prefix	Description	VBA Equivalent
8	char	ch	8-bit signed integer	Byte
8	byte, uchar	ch	8-bit unsigned integer	Byte
8	TCHAR	ch	8-bit or 16-bit signed (depending on whether you're using ANSI or Unicode)	Byte or Integer

Size (bits)	Data Type	Prefix	Description	VBA Equivalent
16	short	c	16-bit signed integer	Integer
16	unsigned short, WORD	w	16-bit unsigned integer	Integer
16	TCHAR	ch	8-bit or 16-bit signed (depending on whether you're using ANSI or Unicode)	Byte or Integer
32	int	n	32-bit signed integer	Long
32	long	l	32-bit signed integer	Long
32	unsigned int, UINT	n	32-bit unsigned integer	Long
32	unsigned long, DWORD	dw	32-bit unsigned integer (also referred to as a double-word)	Long

Let's take a closer look at these types of parameters.

8-Bit Numeric Parameters

The 8-bit (1-byte) parameter types are char, uchar, BYTE, and (if using the ANSI character set) 8-bit TCHAR. Although it is unlikely that you will run across them under Win32, they should be explained just in case.

Signed 8-bit values range between –128 and 127, whereas unsigned values range between 0 and 255. VBA supports only unsigned Byte values, regardless of size.

If you do ever have to use unsigned 8-bit parameters, the VBA Byte data type works just fine. Supplying 8-bit signed values is not as straightforward and requires a small algorithm (explained in the preceding section) to produce the required value.

16-Bit Numeric Parameters

The 16-bit (2-byte) numeric parameter types are short, unsigned short, WORD, and, if using the Unicode character set, 16-bit TCHAR. Beginning with 32-bit versions of Windows, you won't likely run into these parameters often, but they are worth explaining. The VBA Integer data type can be used to supply values for the signed parameters (short and 16-bit TCHAR) because VBA Integer values range from –32,768 to 32,767.

To supply unsigned values to unsigned short and WORD parameters, you must first convert the value to something that the API will recognize as an unsigned value. (Refer to the conversion formula shown earlier in the section "Signed and Unsigned Integers.")

32-Bit Numeric Parameters

The six 32-bit (4-byte) numeric parameters are int, unsigned int, long, unsigned long, and DWORD.

The range for the `Long Integer` data type in VBA is between –2,147,483,648 and 2,147,483,647 and is equivalent to the signed C Integer types (`int` and `long`). As such, it can be used anywhere they appear. The unsigned type must be converted; see the conversion formula in the section "Signed and Unsigned Integers."

Currency Parameters

The Win32 API does not use a `Currency` data type. You should generally not use this data type when using API functions.

Floating-Point Parameters

A few APIs use the `Single` (`float` in C/C++) or `Double` data types.

`Single` values are 32 bits (4 bytes) wide and range between –3.402823E38 and –1.401298E–45 for negative values, and from 1.401298E–45 to 3.402823E38 for positive values. `Double` values are 64 bits (8 bytes) wide, and range from –1.79769313486231E308 to –4.94065645841247E–324 for negative values and from 4.94065645841247E–324 to 1.79769313486232E308 for positive values.

If you are supplying values to DLLs that use floating-point parameters, you must ensure that those functions are compatible with VBA because not all are.

Boolean Parameters

The VBA `Long Integer` data type can be used to supply a value for the `BOOL` parameter type. However, both C and VBA define the Boolean `False` as 0. By default, that means all nonzero values must not be false, and are thereby true.

The C language defines a Boolean `True` to be 1, whereas VBA defines `True` as -1.

Supplying a VBA `True` value can sometimes lead to problems when using some API functions because of the way in which Boolean values are interpreted in the C language — some APIs return any nonzero value as `True`.

The C language includes both logical and bitwise operations. A logical operation is a standard Boolean operation that you're familiar with, such as AND, OR, and NOT. A bitwise operation is performed on the individual bits in a number. C's bitwise `not` operation is distinguished by a tilde preceding the number or variable (`~myvar`). The logical `not` operator is distinguished by an exclamation mark (`!myvar`).

If you perform a logical NOT operation on the `True` value (`~1`) in C, you get 0. If you do the same thing for the VBA `True` (`~-1`), you get 0. No problem, as long as both values are nonzero. Because VBA doesn't have a logical Not operator, performing a NOT against both values returns -2 and 0, respectively.

To get around that problem, specify `Abs(booMyVar)` when supplying a Boolean parameter, and `Not (booMyVar = False)` when checking a return value.

The C/C++ `BOOL` data type is a 32-bit Boolean value; 0 is false and 1 is true (although any nonzero VBA value equates to true). Prefixes are `b` and `f` — you'll see both used in C/C++.

Handle Parameters

A Windows handle is a 32-bit (4-byte) number that identifies the memory location where the definition of a Windows object, such as a window, can be found. Handles come in different flavors, including HAN-DLE, HWND, and hDC. More specifically, HWND refers to a handle to a window, and hDC refers to a handle to a device context.

For example, the hwnd of the Access application is a window handle that can be discovered using VBA code. The following table illustrates how to find the hwnd for familiar Access objects.

For Access Object	Do This
Application	`Application.hWndAccessApp`
Form	`Me.Hwnd`
User control on a form	`Private Declare Function GetFocus Lib "user32" () As Long Function GetCtrlhWnd(ctrl As Control) As Long 'Set the focus to the control ctrl.SetFocus 'Get the hwnd from the API GetCtrlhWnd = GetFocus End Function`

Because handles are all 32 bits wide, the VBA Long data type suits this purpose nicely.

Object Parameters

As far as the Windows API is concerned, the Object data type has no meaning. However, the OLE 2.0 API set does support parameters of this type, namely, LPUNKNOWN and LPDISPATCH, which are pointers to COM interfaces.

Therefore, if you ever have to specify an Object pointer, use the VBA Object data type. The following table describes these data types.

Data Type	Prefix	Description	VBA Equivalent
LPUNKNOWN	lp	32-bit pointer to an IUnknown OLE 2.0 interface	Object
LPDISPATCH	Lp	32-bit pointer to an IDispatch OLE 2.0 interface	Object

String Parameters

There are several different data types used to represent strings in C/C++. One of the most common is the LPWSTR data type, which is a pointer to the memory location where the string begins. Most DLLs require null-terminated strings, which VBA can pass ByVal. Some C-language DLLs might return LPSTR pointers that can be copied to VBA strings using API functions. Only those APIs that were specifically written for VB (like `APIGID32.dll`) actually accept or return VBA strings.

A null-terminated string is one that ends in an ASCII Null character. To form such a string, append an ASCII zero or use the `vbNullChar` constant. These two lines of code are equivalent:

```
param = "abc" & Chr$(0)
param = "abc" & vbNullChar
```

A null string, on the other hand, is an empty string, which is formed using a pair of quotes or the `vbNullString` constant. The following lines of code are equivalent:

```
param = ""
param = vbNullString
```

For example, to find the Windows folder (the one that contains most of the Windows application and initialization files), use the following:

```
'Declare the function
Private Declare Function GetWindowsDirectory _
Lib "kernel32" Alias "GetWindowsDirectoryA" ( _
ByVal lpBuffer As String, _
ByVal nSize As Long) As Long

Private Const MAXLEN = 255

Public Function WindowsDir() As String
    Dim strDirectory As String
    Dim lngSize As Long
    Dim lngReturn As Long

    'Pre-initialize the string
    strDirectory = Space(MAXLEN) & Chr(0)
    'Initialize the string length
    lngSize = MAXLEN + 1

    'Retrieve the length of the string returned by the function
    lngReturn = GetWindowsDirectory(strDirectory, lngSize)

    If lngReturn <> 0 Then
        'Return the string containing the Windows directory,
        'using lngReturn to specify how long the string is.
        WindowsDir = left(strDirectory, lngReturn)
    Else
        WindowsDir = ""
    End If
End Function
```

The following table shows some of the more common string data types used by APIs.

Data Type	Prefix	Description
LPWSTR	lpsz	32-bit (long) pointer to a C null-terminated wide string. A wide string is typically a double-byte character.
LPSTR	lpsz	32-bit (long) pointer to a C null-terminated string
LPCSTR	lpsz	32-bit (long) pointer to a constant C null-terminated string
LPTSTR	lpsz	32-bit (long) pointer to a C null-terminated string
LPCWSTR	lpsz	32-bit (long) pointer to a constant C null-terminated wide string

Variant Parameters

VBA `Variant` data types are not supported under the core Win32 APIs. The only APIs to use it are those of the OLE 2.0 specification, in which case the VBA `Variant` data type can be used without conversion.

Pointers to Numeric Values

Pointers are used frequently in the C language. A pointer is simply a memory address that points to a piece of data. Pointers to numeric values, such as LPINT and LPSHORT, can be passed by VBA simply by using the `ByRef` keyword (or just by omitting the `ByVal` keyword).

You must ensure, however, that the data type you pass matches what is required. For example, if a 32-bit data type is required, pass a `Long Integer`, not an `Integer` (16-bit). If you pass an `Integer` when a `Long Integer` is required, the DLL will write not only into the 16 bits of the `Integer`, but also into the next 16 bits, which can cause all sorts of problems, from erroneous data to a system crash.

The following table shows some of the common pointers to numeric data.

Data Type	Prefix	Description
LPSHORT	lps	16-bit (short) pointer to a 16-bit signed integer
LPINT	lpi	32-bit (long) pointer to a 32-bit signed integer
LPUSHORT	lpu	16-bit (short) pointer to a 16-bit unsigned integer
LPUINT	lpu	32-bit (long) pointer to a 32-but unsigned integer

Pointers to C Structures

C-language structures are essentially the same as VBA user-defined types (UDTs), which were described in Chapter 5. You pass a UDT as a DLL parameter `ByRef`, specifying the name declared using the `Type` keyword, but you must also ensure that all the UDT's members consist of data types that are compatible with the API, as described in this chapter.

For example, following is a RECT structure as defined in C. It's used frequently by API functions to refer to a rectangle on the screen.

```
typedef struct _RECT {
  LONG left;
  LONG top;
  LONG right;
  LONG bottom;
} RECT, *PRECT;
```

And here's the VBA equivalent:

```
Public Type RECT
    Left As Long
    Top As Long
    Right As Long
    Bottom As Long
End Type
```

You cannot pass a UDT ByVal.

Pointers to Arrays

Passing arrays to APIs not specifically written for VBA is accomplished by ByRef because those APIs expect a pointer to the first array element. Such APIs also expect a parameter that indicates the number of elements in the array.

There are three issues you should be aware of when passing arrays:

❑   You cannot pass entire string arrays. You can pass single array elements, just not the entire thing.

❑   To pass an entire array, specify the first array element in the call:

    myArray(0)

❑   When denoting the number of elements in an array, you must specify UBound(strMyArray)+1 because UBound() returns only the maximum numeric bound of the array, not the actual count of its elements. Remember also that specifying Option Base 1 will affect the number returned by UBound(). You can, of course, specify a number; just make sure it reflects the actual number of array elements.

C-style APIs don't care much whether you're telling the truth about the number of elements in the array. If you tell it you have ten elements when you have only five, C happily writes to the space required for ten, regardless of whether they actually exist. Naturally this is going to have interesting side effects, which you may not be too happy about.

You can also pass array elements either singly or as a subset of the array. For example, if you have an array that contains a number of xy coordinates, you can get the hwnd of the window within which a specific xy coordinate exists by calling the WindowFromPoint API like this:

    Myhwnd = WindowFromPoint(lngPtArray(2), lngPtArray(3))

Arrays that were written specifically with VBA in mind (and they are rare) expect an OLE 2.0 SAFEAR-RAY structure, including a pointer that is itself a pointer to the array. Therefore, you simply pass the VBA array. That makes sense if you consider a string variable as a single-element array.

Pointers to Functions

FARPROC and DLGPROC are examples of pointers to functions. These pointers are supplied so the API can execute a function as part of its own functionality. Such functions are referred to as *callback functions*.

You specify the memory address of a callback function using the VBA AddressOf operator, which has certain limitations:

❑ It can only be specified in a standard module — you can't use it in a class module.

❑ It must precede an argument in an argument list, and the argument it precedes must be the name of a procedure (sub, function, or property).

The procedure whose location it returns must exist in the same project, so it can't be used with external functions declared with the Declare keyword, or with functions referenced from type libraries.

You can pass a function pointer to an As Any parameter (discussed in the next section), and also create your own callback functions in DLLs compiled in Visual Basic or C++. To work with AddressOf, these functions must use the _stdcall calling convention when working with C or C++.

You can pass a function pointer to an As Any parameter (discussed in the next section), and also create your own callback functions in DLLs compiled in Visual Basic or C++. To work with AddressOf, the functions must use the _stdcall calling convention.

FARPROC and DLGPROC are 32-bit (far) pointers to functions or procedures in VBA. Their prefix is lpfn.

The Any Data Type

Some DLL function parameters can accept different data types. Such parameters are declared using the As Any data type. Calling a DLL function with parameters declared As Any is inherently dangerous because VBA doesn't perform any type checking on it. That is, VBA doesn't check that the data type you supply matches that which is required by the function. Therefore, you need to be absolutely certain that the data type you are supplying to the function is correct.

To avoid the hazards of passing such arguments, declare several versions of the same DLL function, giving each a unique name and a different parameter data type. You can give each version the same Alias to point to the same function in the DLL.

Err.LastDLLError

Like the VBA procedures you write, API procedures can also generate errors. These can be the result of bad or missing data, invalid data type assignments, or a variety of other conditions or failures. This section describes how to trap and retrieve API-generated errors so you can take remedial or other action to shield the user from their adverse effects.

`LastDLLError` is a property of the VBA `Err` object. It returns the error code produced by a call to a DLL, and always contains zero on systems that don't have DLLs (like the Macintosh).

DLL functions usually return a code that indicates whether the call succeeded or failed. Your VBA code should check the value returned after a DLL function is called and, on detecting a failure code, should immediately check the `LastDLLError` property and take whatever action you deem necessary. The DLL's documentation will indicate which codes to check for.

Because no exception is raised when the `LastDLLError` property is set, you cannot use the `On Error Goto` construct, so use `On Error Resume Next`.

The `Err` object's `Description` property will be empty because the error is DLL-specific. However, for many error messages you can use the `FormatMessage` API to get the error message returned by a DLL. Add this code to the module containing the `SetFormIcon` procedure:

```
Private Const FORMAT_MESSAGE_FROM_SYSTEM = &H1000

Private Declare Function FormatMessage Lib "kernel32" Alias _
    "FormatMessageA" (ByVal dwFlags As Long, lpSource As Long, _
    ByVal dwMessageId As Long, ByVal dwLanguageId As Long, _
    ByVal lpBuffer As String, ByVal nSize As Long, Arguments As Any) _
    As Long

Public Function GetAPIErrorMessage(lngError As Long) As String
    Dim strMessage As String
    Dim lngReturn  As Long
    Dim nSize      As Long

    strMessage = Space(256)
    nSize = Len(strMessage)
    lngReturn = FormatMessage(FORMAT_MESSAGE_FROM_SYSTEM, 0, _
        lngError, 0, strMessage, nSize, 0)

    If lngReturn > 0 Then
        GetAPIErrorMessage = Replace(Left(strMessage, lngReturn), vbCrLf, "")
    Else
        GetAPIErrorMessage = "Error not found."
    End If
End Function
```

Next, modify the `SetFormIcon` procedure to generate a DLL error by passing an empty string as the icon path (this shows the `LastDLLError` property in action):

```
Public Sub SetFormIcon(hWnd As Long, strIcon As String)
Dim hIcon As Long
Dim lngReturn As Long

On Error Resume Next

'Pass an empty string as the icon path
hIcon = LoadImage(0&, "", IMAGE_ICON, IMG_DEFAULT_WIDTH, _
IMG_DEFAULT_HEIGHT, LR_LOADFROMFILE)
```

```
'Now check for an error
If hIcon <> 0 Then
lngReturn = SendMessage(hWnd, WM_SETICON, ICON_SMALL, ByVal hIcon)

Else
'Display the error
MsgBox "The last DLL error was: " & GetAPIErrorMessage(Err.LastDllError)

End If
End Sub
```

The `FormatMessage` API will not return error messages defined by applications.

Distributing Applications That Reference Type Libraries and Custom DLLs

It is a bit trickier to deploy applications if they contain references to some type libraries and DLLs. You can't always just drop a database file onto a disk and expect it to work because the target system may not already contain the required type libraries and DLLs.

To ensure that the database functions correctly on every platform, you may have to include additional libraries or DLLs in an installation package you create using the Package and Deployment Wizard that comes with the Access Developer Extensions (ADE).

The Package and Deployment Wizard scans the application for external references and includes the referenced files in the setup package it creates. When run on the target system, the setup program copies all the required files onto the hard disk, and usually registers the type libraries and DLLs. For more information about the ADE, refer to Chapter 21.

Summary

In this chapter, you looked at what APIs and DLLs are and why you might want to use them. You explored the concept of static versus dynamic linking and learned how to reference APIs in Access projects. You also tackled the anatomy of an API call, learning how to use the correct data types when calling API functions. And you examined trapping errors generated by DLLs and the considerations in distributing an application that references Type libraries and custom DLLs.

15

SQL and VBA

You may be familiar with SQL; after all, it's inside every query you create. SQL (Structured Query Language) is the language of queries and recordsets; it's how you retrieve, update, insert, and delete records in your database tables.

When you use the query Design view in Access, you are actually building a SQL statement under the covers. Most of the time, you won't actually need to look at the SQL code, but you can see it using the SQL view if you're curious.

Conversely, you can take most SQL statements, paste them into the SQL view of a new query, and then switch over to Design view to see how they work. There are a few types of SQL statements for which this won't work — union queries and pass-through queries, for example, cannot be viewed using Design view.

Even if you're comfortable using SQL in queries, you may not be familiar with building SQL statements in VBA. If you're not, you're missing out! Using SQL in VBA is a powerful technique that can enable many great features in your Access applications. By using VBA, you can build custom SQL statements for combo boxes, forms, and reports. For example, you'll be able to change the sorting and selecting of records on continuous forms, control the record selection on reports, and limit the drop-down lists of combo boxes based on other combo boxes.

Let's begin by exploring how to build SQL statements using string variables in VBA.

Working with SQL Strings in VBA

To build SQL statements in VBA, you usually load them into string variables by concatenating various phrases together. Some of the phrases are exact SQL text that you supply, while others are the contents of variables in VBA or controls on forms or reports. When the SQL statement is complete, you can use it in queries, in the RecordSource of forms or reports, or in the rowsource of combo boxes or list boxes. This enables you to deliver power and flexibility in your Access applications.

Building SQL Strings with Quotes

The first thing to learn about building SQL statements in VBA is how to handle concatenation and quotes. They may seem simple, but many programmers have stared at VBA strings with multiple nested quotes and struggled to make them work.

Consider a SQL string that selects a record for a particular business from a table of businesses:

```
Select * From tblBusiness Where BusinessKey = 17
```

In actual usage, you replace the 17 in this statement with the BusinessKey that the user is currently working with. To build this SQL statement in VBA, using the BusinessKey from the current form, you would use something like this:

```
strSQL = "Select * From tblBusiness Where BusinessKey = " _
& Me!BusinessKey
```

One reason this is so simple is that BusinessKey is a numeric value. In SQL, numeric values are just stated, without quotes around them. This is great for primary key values, which are often AutoNumbers (that use the Long Integer data type).

However, consider a SQL statement that selects businesses in a particular city:

```
Select * from tblBusiness Where BusinessCity = "Seattle"
```

This is where it starts to get complicated. As you can see, Seattle must be in quotes because SQL expects quotes around text values. The VBA to create this statement, again assuming that BusinessCity is on the current form, is as follows:

```
strSQL = "Select * From tblBusiness Where BusinessCity = """ _
& Me!BusinessCity & """"
```

At first glance, all those quotes seem a little extreme. But if you break them down, they make sense. The first thing to remember is that to have a quote (") inside a string, you need to type two quotes in a row. That lets VBA know that you aren't closing the string with a quote — you actually want a quote *inside* the string. So, the string

```
"Select * From tblBusiness Where BusinessCity = """
```

results in a string that contains:

```
Select * From tblBusiness Where BusinessCity = "
```

Notice that last quote? It's a result of the two quotes after the equal sign (=) "collapsing" into just one quote. The idea of *collapsing quotes* in the interior of your strings is crucial to understanding how to build complex SQL strings in VBA. You may even want to print out your VBA code and circle the interior quote pairs with a pen. Each of these circles represents a quote that will be included inside your string.

Now, for the rest of this simple example . . . After the first phrase (the one that ends with a quote), you tack on the value of `BusinessCity` (Seattle) and then finish it off with a final quote. Concatenating the `BusinessCity` is easy:

```
& Me!BusinessCity
```

But what about that final quote? Here's how it is added:

```
& """"
```

Yes, that's four quotes in a row. Remember that the interior pairs of quotes are collapsed into a quote inside the string. In this case, the result is a string containing merely one quotation mark, which is exactly what you need at the end of `Seattle` in your final SQL string:

```
Select * from tblBusiness Where BusinessCity = "Seattle"
```

In quote collapsing, remember that whenever you see three quotes in a row, you can be sure that one quote mark is being included at the beginning or end of some other text, like this:

```
"Select * From tblBusiness Where BusinessCity = """
```

And whenever you see four quotes in a row, you are seeing just one quote mark being concatenated to the string, as in this example:

```
Me!BusinessCity & """"
```

Now that you know how to build SQL strings with text, values from variables and forms, and double quotes, there's one little side topic to cover: the use of single quotes (') instead of double quotes (").

Using Single Quotes Instead of Double Quotes

Some programmers use a mixture of single quotes (') and double quotes (") when they are building SQL strings. This can be a good technique because you don't need to do any "quote collapsing" as described previously. However, to some people it can be confusing to see the different types of quotes mixed together. It's a style thing — there isn't a right or wrong way.

VBA remembers what kind of quote started a string, so if you use the other kind in the middle of the string, it won't get confused and try to close the string. Access Wizards often use this technique to build SQL strings. For example, here's how the Access Wizard generates the `WhereCondition` phrase when you ask to open a form filtered to a specific value:

```
stLinkCriteria = "[City]=" & "'" & Me![txtCity] & "'"
DoCmd.OpenForm stDocName, , , stLinkCriteria
```

Notice the mixture of single and double quotes in the string loaded into `stLinkCriteria`. The double quotes are used to indicate to VBA where the text phrases start and stop. The single quotes are built into the `stLinkCriteria` field itself. The single quotes work because the Access query processor recognizes either single or double quotes around text values. Therefore, the following two statements are identical to Access SQL:

```
Where City = 'Seattle'
Where City = "Seattle"
```

Also notice that the technique to build the string is a little more complicated than necessary. To generically handle either text values (with quotes) or numeric values (without quotes), the Access Wizard concatenates the first single quote separately. If you are building it yourself, you can tack the single quote right after the equal sign, like this:

```
stLinkCriteria = "[City]='" & Me![txtCity] & "'"
```

> If you build SQL strings to use in SQL Server, remember that only single quotes are valid there — double quotes will not work. This isn't an issue if you're querying linked tables in Access because Access translates the syntax for you. But you must use SQL Server syntax if you're using a pass-through query or are opening a SQL Server recordset directly in code.

The rest of the examples in this chapter use the "collapsing quotes" method described previously. That method works whether you use all single quotes (') or all double quotes (").

Concatenating Long SQL Strings

To keep your VBA readable, break your long statements onto multiple lines. While this is true any time, it's especially helpful when building long SQL strings. If you do not break them into multiple VBA lines, you have to scroll far to the right to read it all. There are two ways to break up those long statements: by building up the string variable in multiple steps, or by using the VBA line continuation character.

Many programmers still use the build-up method for storing long SQL strings into a string variable. It might just be habit left over from the days when there wasn't a line continuation character, or maybe they just like the way it looks. Here's what the method looks like:

```
strSQL = "Select * From tblBusiness"
strSQL = strSQL & " Where BusinessCity = """ & Me!BusinessCity & """"
strSQL = strSQL & " And BusinessActiveFlag = True"
```

Notice how the second and third lines concatenate more text to the same variable, which is why it's called "building up" the string. This method has a slight advantage during debugging because you can see your string's value step by step as it is being built.

The VBA line continuation character is a space and underscore together, right at the end of the code line:

```
strSQL = "Select * From tblBusiness" & _
" Where BusinessCity = """ & Me!BusinessCity & """" & _
" And BusinessActiveFlag = True"
```

Some developers indent the subsequent lines for clarity:

```
strSQL = "Select * From tblBusiness" & _
    " Where BusinessCity = """ & Me!BusinessCity & """" & _
    " And BusinessActiveFlag = True"
```

This method runs the entire concatenation as one line in VBA, even though it is visually spread across multiple lines in your code.

Breaking your VBA onto multiple lines is another area that's really a style choice — all these methods work just fine. The build-up method offers slightly slower performance than using line continuation characters, but on modern PCs it isn't be noticeable. Whichever method you choose, break the statement where it makes sense. Start each new VBA line with a keyword such as Where, And, Or, or Join, so that others can read along more easily.

Be careful to add the extra spaces around the keywords like Where and And. If you don't, your words will run together in the final string, the syntax will be incorrect, and the SQL statement won't run. Many programmers add spaces to the beginning of each section of text instead of the end so that they really stand out, as shown in the preceding examples. Remember that extra spaces between words aren't a problem in SQL; they're ignored by both Access and SQL Server.

Now you're ready to use quotes and build long SQL strings in VBA to enhance Access forms and reports.

Using SQL When Opening Forms and Reports

Whenever you use the Access Wizard to build a command button to open a form or report with a filter to limit the records that are displayed, you are actually using SQL in VBA. The wizard builds VBA code to open the form with a WhereCondition, like this:

```
Private Sub cmdCityBusinesses_Click()
    On Error GoTo Err_cmdCityBusinesses_Click
    Dim stDocName As String
    Dim stLinkCriteria As String
    stDocName = "frmBusiness"
    stLinkCriteria = "[City]=" & "'" & Me![txtCity] & "'"
    DoCmd.OpenForm stDocName, , , stLinkCriteria
Exit_cmdCityBusinesses_Click:
    Exit Sub
Err_cmdCityBusinesses_Click:
    MsgBox Err.Description
    Resume Exit_cmdCityBusinesses_Click
End Sub
```

The WhereCondition on the OpenForm command (it's the fourth parameter, using a variable named stLinkCriteria) is used to filter the form being opened to a set of records that meet some criteria. It's usually used to drill down to a specific single record, so the criterion is merely the primary key value of the record. As in this example, however, it can be used to open a form to a set of multiple records that meet the specified criterion (in this case, the City).

When you use the `WhereCondition`, *you don't include the word* `Where` *at the beginning of the string. It's assumed, so you'll see an error if you specify it.*

This is a simple example of using a fragment of SQL in your code; after all, the wizard will build it for you. The wizard to open a report works much the same way. However, there are many other more compelling reasons to use SQL in your VBA code.

Using SQL to Enhance Forms

Using SQL, you can enhance your forms in many ways. You can allow quick and easy record sorting, the capability to narrow a list of records by applying selections, and the use of combo box values to limit the drop-down lists for other combo boxes. These are all powerful tools that help your user get more value from your application.

Sorting on Columns

Users often expect the capability to sort on columns, similar to other Windows applications such as Outlook and Excel. For example, if you have an index form of businesses, your user may want to sort on either the Business Name or Contact Name column, as shown in Figure 15-1.

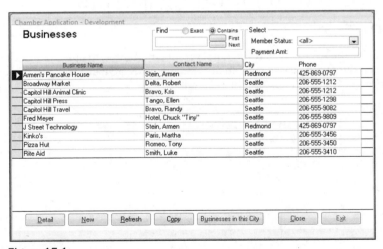

Figure 15-1

The two toggle buttons (Business Name and Contact Name) are in an option group control called `optSort`, which has an `After Update` event that contains the following code:

```
Private Sub optSort_AfterUpdate()
    On Error GoTo Error_Handler
```

```
        Dim strOrderBy As Variant
        strOrderBy = Null

        Select Case Me!optSort
            Case 1 'Business Name
                strOrderBy = " tblBusiness.BusinessName," &_
                "tblBusiness.LastName, tblBusiness.FirstName"
            Case 2 'Contact information
                strOrderBy = "tblBusiness.LastName," &_
                "tblBusiness.FirstName, tblBusiness.BusinessName"
        End Select

        strOrderBy = " ORDER BY " + strOrderBy

        Me.RecordSource = ReplaceOrderByClause(Me.RecordSource, strOrderBy)
        'Me.Requery  'may be needed for earlier versions of Access

Exit_Procedure:
    On Error Resume Next
    Exit Sub

Error_Handler:
    MsgBox Err.Number & ": " & Err.Description
    Resume Exit_Procedure
    Resume

End Sub
```

This technique takes advantage of the fact that you can change the record source of a form while it is already open, and then re-query the form. When you do, the form is reloaded with the records from the new record source, including the sort order.

You build a new Order By clause based on the button that is clicked. To swap the new Order By clause into the RecordSource, you use a function named ReplaceOrderByClause. The code for this function and its cousin ReplaceWhereClause are at the end of this chapter. For now, just assume that the Order By clause will be magically "cut and pasted" into the SQL string in the RecordSource property of the form.

> To replace part of the SQL string in a RecordSource property, start with a SQL string! To use this technique, you can't have just the name of a query or table in the RecordSource. It needs to be a real SQL statement. To make one, just take the query name, say qryBusinesses, and turn it into a SQL string such as "Select * From qryBusinesses". Then you can manipulate it with new Where and Order By clauses.

When your user clicks a column heading, the records are instantly re-sorted by that column. This is much more intuitive and Windows-standard than right-clicking or selecting menu options. Your user will appreciate how easy it is to sort records this way.

Note the Me.Requery in the preceding code. Recent versions of Access automatically requery the form if you change its RecordSource property. If you are using an older version of Access and you don't see the form reflect your sort and select changes, try uncommenting the Me.Requery to force Access to do it.

Sorting isn't the end of the story. You can also provide instant record selection.

Selections on Index Forms

One of the most effective features you can offer your users is the capability to narrow a set of records so that they can more easily find the information they're looking for. By enhancing your index forms with selection criteria, you add a lot of power to your application with only a little work.

Easy Selection Criteria on an Index Form

Simple selections are the most common. Your user would like to narrow the recordset by selecting a criterion for a particular field. However, you also need to provide the capability to open the selection up again to include all records, as shown in Figure 15-2.

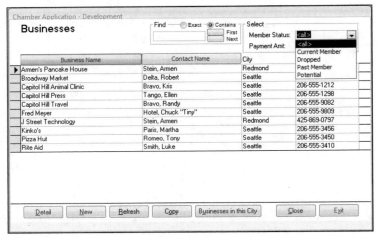

Figure 15-2

First of all, the default selection criterion for a field is `<all>`. To include this in the drop-down list for your criteria combo box, you must use a `UNION` query. An easy way to understand a Union query is to think of it joining tables vertically instead of horizontally; a Union query adds records to the result instead of columns. In this case, you just want to add one additional record: the `<all>` value.

A `UNION` query cannot be built directly using the Query Designer, but fortunately it isn't difficult to create it using SQL. In this case, the `RowSource` for the combo box looks like this:

```
SELECT tblMemberStatus.MemberStatusKey, tblMemberStatus.MemberStatusName
FROM tblMemberStatus
UNION
SELECT "<all>", "<all>" FROM tblMemberStatus
ORDER BY tblMemberStatus.MemberStatusName;
```

Note that `UNION` is really just patching together two `SELECT` statements. The first one returns the actual member statuses from `tblMemberStatus`. The second one is "fake" — it just returns the values `"<all>"` and `"<all>"`. The field names of the resulting set of records will be those from the first `SELECT` statement in your `UNION` query.

To more easily create your UNION *query, build the first part (which retrieves records from a table) using the Query Designer. Then, switch to SQL view and add the* UNION *and second* SELECT *phrase. In fact, whenever you are building a* UNION *query, you can use the Query Designer to build each* SELECT *statement, and then copy its SQL code from SQL view and paste it into your query. Just "glue" each* SELECT *statement together with the* UNION *keyword.*

The Order By clause specifies that the records should be sorted in an ascending order by MemberStatusName, so the <all> value appears at the top of the list because < is a lower value than any alphabet letter. The code to process the user's criteria selection is in the After Update event of the Combo box:

```
Private Sub cboMemberStatusKey_AfterUpdate()
    On Error GoTo Error_Handler

    SelectRecords
    ' cboMemberStatusKey.Requery  'needed for Access versions prior to 2007

Exit_Procedure:
    On Error Resume Next
    Exit Sub

Error_Handler:
    MsgBox Err.Number & ": " & Err.Description
    Resume Exit_Procedure
    Resume

End Sub
```

This code calls another procedure in this form: SelectRecords. You don't want to actually rebuild the SQL statement here because you may add other selection criteria fields later. By rebuilding the Where clause in a central procedure, you can easily add the new criteria fields with a simple procedure just like this one.

Notice that there is a Requery *of the combo box after* SelectRecords *runs, but it is commented out. That's there to handle a little bug that was in the last several versions of Access, including Access 2003, but has been fixed in Access 2007. The bug causes the text in an unbound combo box to become invisible if the recordset of the form contains no records. Requerying the combo box (just the control itself, not the whole form) causes the mysterious invisible text to appear again.*

The SelectRecords procedure is where the SQL statement is rebuilt and the form requeried:

```
Public Sub SelectRecords()
    On Error GoTo Error_Handler

    Dim varWhereClause As Variant
    Dim strAND As String

    varWhereClause = Null
    strAND = " AND "

    If cboMemberStatusKey & "" <> "<all>" Then

        varWhereClause = (varWhereClause + strAND) & _
```

```
            "tblBusiness.MemberStatusKey = """ & _
        cboMemberStatusKey & """"

    End If

    varWhereClause = " WHERE " + varWhereClause

    Me.RecordSource = ReplaceWhereClause(Me.RecordSource,
    varWhereClause)
    Me.Requery

EnableDisableControls

Exit_Procedure:
On Error Resume Next
Exit Sub

Error_Handler:
MsgBox (Err.Number & ": " & Err.Description)
Resume Exit_Procedure
Resume

End Sub
```

If the combo box contains `"<all>"`, no Where clause is built. The ReplaceWhereClause function is designed to just remove the Where clause (and therefore return all records) if a Null is passed in for the WhereClause parameter.

All this code runs immediately when the user chooses a different criterion in the drop-down list, and the records meeting the criteria are displayed. If there are any records that match the selection criteria, they are displayed and the command buttons are enabled, as shown in Figure 15-3.

Using some simple techniques, you can handle multiple selections of different types on the same form.

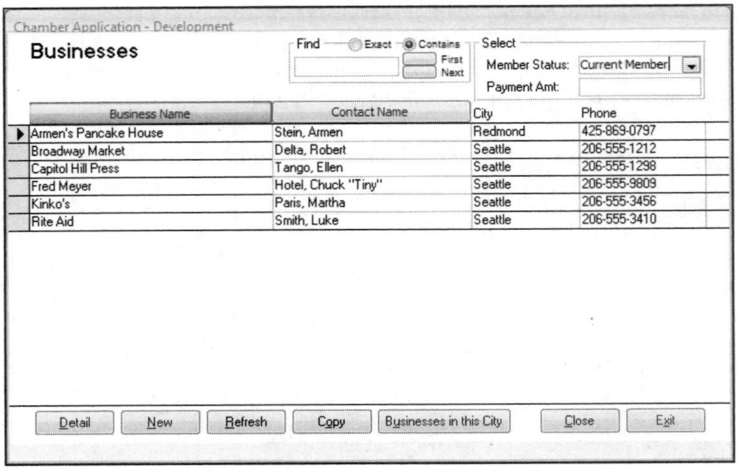

Figure 15-3

The Amazing Expandable SelectRecords Procedure

The code in `SelectRecords` to build the `Where` clause may seem overly complex, but there are good reasons: expandability and flexibility. It is all ready for you to add more criteria fields. For example, to add another selection for `District`, you just need to add the following:

```
If cboDistrictKey & "" <> "<all>" Then

    varWhereClause = (varWhereClause + strAND) & _
    "tblBusiness.DistrictKey = """ & _
    cboDistrictKey & """"

End If
```

The key to this expandability is the concatenation of `varWhereClause` and `strAND`. When the procedure starts `varWhereClause` is Null. And it continues like that until the code discovers a specified selection criterion. When it does, the phrase `(varWhereClause + strAND)` performs its magic. The first time it runs, `varWhereClause` is still Null, so the null-propagating + operator (see Chapter 8) does not add the word AND.

However, the second time it runs (because the user has specified another selection criterion), things are different. Now, `varWhereClause` has a value in it, so the + operator successfully concatenates the AND onto the string before the next part of the `Where` clause is added.

When all the pieces have been built, the final step is to add the word WHERE onto the front of the newly built `Where` clause. However, you don't need it if there are no selection criteria, so it's + to the rescue again. If `varWhereClause` is still Null, you have the following statement:

```
varWhereClause = " WHERE " + varWhereClause
```

That appends WHERE to the front of `varWhereClause`, but only if `varWhereClause` has a value. If it doesn't, it will remain Null. Regardless of the order in which you build the parts of the `Where` clause, this logic works. This extra effort up front makes the `SelectRecords` procedure easy to change and expand later.

Now take a look at a couple of other selection scenarios you might encounter.

Selection Criteria Using Numeric Keys

The previous selection examples assumed that you were using text fields. If your combo box contains a numeric value (such as an `AutoNumber` key), the UNION query looks a little different. Say the `DistrictKey` is an `AutoNumber` primary key:

```
SELECT tblDistrict.DistrictKey, tblDistrict.DistrictName
FROM tblDistrict
UNION
SELECT 0, "<all>" FROM tblDistrict
ORDER BY tblDistrict.DistrictName;
```

The first `<all>` value has been replaced with a 0 to match type with the other numeric key values. Because 0 is never generated by Access as an `AutoNumber` key, it won't be confused with a real record from the District table.

The code in the `SelectRecords` procedure is a little different, too:

```
If cboDistrictKey <> 0 Then
    varWhereClause = (varWhereClause + strAND) & _
    "tblBusiness.DistrictKey = " & cboDistrictKey
End If
```

Note that you are checking to see if the combo box value is 0 instead of <all>. Also, with a numeric value you don't need all the nested quotes — you can just concatenate that number right after the equal sign.

Selection Criteria in Child Records

Sometimes, your users want to search for records that contain a value not in those records, but in their child records. In the example, they might want to find all Businesses that made one or more Payments of a certain amount, say $150, as shown in Figure 15-4.

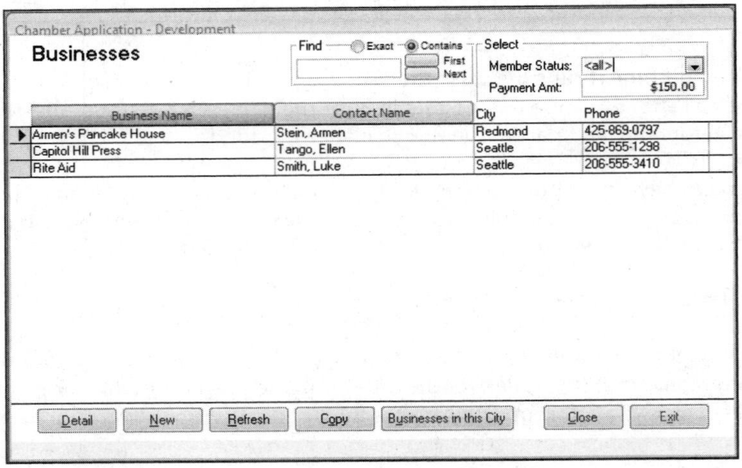

Figure 15-4

In this case, you do not want to apply selection criteria to the Business records themselves. Instead, you want to display all Businesses that have one or more records in the Payment table that are for the desired dollar amount. To perform that kind of selection, you use a *subquery*. A subquery is a query inside another query, and in this example it is used to select Businesses that appear in another query: a list of payments of a certain dollar amount. As with Union queries, subqueries cannot be represented directly in the graphical Design view. However, they are easy to build using SQL view.

For example, when you want the Businesses that have made one or more payments of $150, the desired WHERE clause would be:

```
WHERE tblBusiness.BusinessKey IN (Select BusinessKey

From tblPayment Where PaymentAmount = 150)
```

The key thing is the SQL operator IN, which enables you to determine if a value appears anywhere in a recordset from another Select statement. Here you want all Businesses whose BusinessKeys appear in a list of Payments that equal $150.

The code in the SelectRecords procedure looks like this:

```
If Not IsNull(txtPaymentAmt) Then

    varWhereClause = (varWhereClause + strAND) & _
    "tblBusiness.BusinessKey IN (" & _
    "Select BusinessKey From tblPayment Where" & _
    " PaymentAmount = " & Me!txtPaymentAmt & ")"

End If
```

Because the Payment Amount is a numeric value, you don't need the nested quotes. However, you do need to build the inner subquery with its own Select statement and wrap it in its own set of parentheses: " () ".

With all these selections going on, you should take a look at what happens if the user specifies criteria that omit all of the records.

Disabling Buttons if No Records Are Displayed

When you give your users the capability to narrow a list of records, they might figure out a way to omit all of them! The subroutine EnableDisableControls is called just in case no records meet the criteria. Otherwise, users would get an error if they clicked the Detail button because there wouldn't be a key with which to open the detail record. To prevent that, the Detail button is disabled, as shown in Figure 15-5.

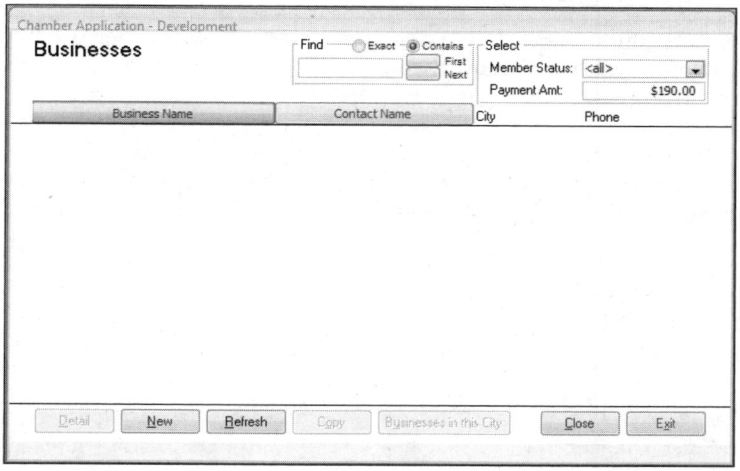

Figure 15-5

The code to disable or enable the appropriate buttons looks like this:

```
Public Sub EnableDisableControls()
    On Error GoTo Error_Handler

    If Me.RecordsetClone.RecordCount = 0 Then
        Me!cmdDetail.Enabled = False
        Me!cmdCityBusinesses.Enabled = False
        Me!cmdCopy.Enabled = False

    Else
        Me!cmdDetail.Enabled = True
        Me!cmdCityBusinesses.Enabled = True
        Me!cmdCopy.Enabled = True

    End If

Exit_Procedure:
    On Error Resume Next
    Exit Sub

Error_Handler:
    MsgBox Err.Number & ": " & Err.Description
    Resume Exit_Procedure
    Resume

End Sub
```

The next section explains how to enhance forms with cascading combo boxes.

Cascading Combo Boxes

Sometimes you want your users to choose a value of a combo box and then use that value to limit the selections in another combo box. Because the upper combo box affects the lower, this is sometimes called *cascading* the combo boxes.

To accomplish this, you need the SQL statement building techniques described earlier in this chapter. Say that you have two combo boxes, one for County and one for City. Each County can have many Cities and each City is in one County. The table design would look something like this:

```
tblCounty
CountyKey AutoNumber
CountyName Text 255

tblCity
CityKey AutoNumber
CityName Text 255
CountyKey Long Integer
```

When you present the selection form, you want the County to be selected first, and then the City list to be limited to those found in that County.

The control `cboCounty` will start off enabled in Design view, but `cboCity` will be disabled. In the `After Update` event for `cboCounty`, you'll include the following code:

```
Me!cboCity = Null

If IsNull(cboCounty) Then
  Me!cboCity.Enabled = False

Else
  Me!cboCity.Enabled = True
  Me!cboCity.Rowsource = ReplaceWhereClause(Me!cboCity.Rowsource, _
  "Where CountyCode = " & Me!cboCounty)
  Me!cboCity.Requery
End If
```

Let's examine this code section by section.

First, you clear out the City combo box by setting it to `Null`:

```
Me!cboCity = Null
```

You do that because you are in the `After Update` event of the County combo box, so you know it's just been changed. If the whole County has been changed, then any value that was in the City combo box is no longer valid, so you just wipe it out.

You are about to disable the City combo box, which won't be possible if it has the focus. Just in case it does, you set the focus back to `cboCounty`:

```
If IsNull(cboCounty) Then
  Me!cboCounty.SetFocus
```

Now, if the user just deleted the value for County (setting it to `Null`), you need to disable the City combo box because the user must choose a County before he can select a City.

```
Me!cboCity.Enabled = False
```

Alternatively, if the user changed the County to another value, the City combo box can be enabled so the user can select a City:

```
Else
  Me!cboCity.Enabled = True
```

But now you need to limit the cities in the drop-down list to those that are in the selected County. To do this, you modify the `Rowsource` property for the City combo box using your old friend `ReplaceWhereClause`:

```
Me!cboCity.Rowsource = ReplaceWhereClause(Me!cboCity.Rowsource, _
"Where CountyCode = " & Me!cboCounty)
```

Although you have changed the `Rowsource` property of the City combo box, it won't take effect until you requery it:

```
    Me!cboCity.Requery
    End If
```

At this point, the user can select from a list of cities that are in the selected County. The cascading selection is complete.

Using SQL for Report Selection Criteria

Many developers build Access reports so that their users can quickly view and print out their data. Consider a report to list businesses from the database, as shown in Figure 15-6.

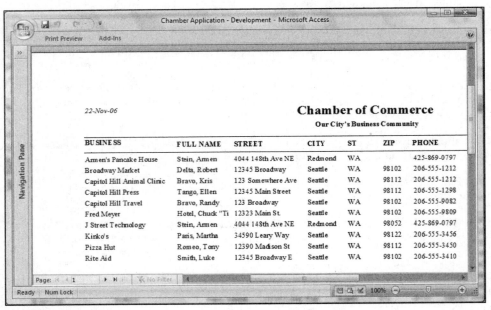

Figure 15-6

Some reports are designed to show all the records in a table or query. However, your user will often want to print only some of the records, based on selection criteria. You can create a different report for each selection criteria, but that approach will result in duplication of report code and difficulty in handling combinations of selection criteria.

When novice Access developers want to allow their users to specify the selection criteria for reports, they often use parameter queries to prompt the user to enter the values. Unfortunately, parameter queries have a few problems:

❑   They prompt the user with a separate dialog box for each value.

❑ They don't allow any formatting or validation of the values.

❑ They often require the user to know key values instead of descriptions for lookups.

❑ They are awkward in handling `Null` or `<all>` values.

A better way to prompt for report selection criteria is to display a form to gather them in easy-to-use fields and combo boxes. This way, you can handle null values, multiple criteria, and validation checking.

For the business list report, your user wants to select whether to see all the businesses in the table (as in Figure 15-7), or just those with a particular Member Status.

Figure 15-7

After he makes his selection and clicks OK, the report is displayed (see Figure 15-8).

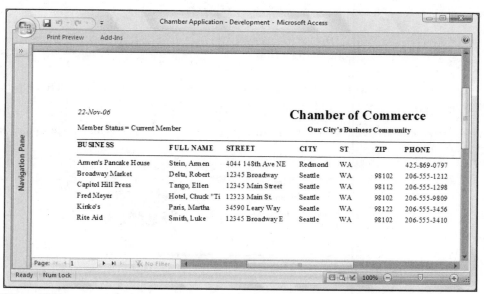

Figure 15-8

The first thing to note is that the order of events might be different than you expect. Many programmers would think that the selection form is opened first, which then opens the report when the OK button is clicked. In fact, it's just the opposite. First, the report is opened. During its `On Open` event (before the report is displayed to the user), the report calls the selection form in Dialog mode, which halts the report code until the selection form is hidden. Here is the code in the On Open event of the report:

```
Private Sub Report_Open(Cancel As Integer)

    On Error GoTo Error_Handler

    Me.Caption = "My Application"

    DoCmd.OpenForm FormName:="frmReportSelector_MemberList", _
    Windowmode:=acDialog

    'Cancel the report if "cancel" was selected on the dialog form.

    If Forms!frmReportSelector_MemberList!txtContinue = "no" Then
        Cancel = True
        GoTo Exit_Procedure
    End If
    Me.RecordSource = ReplaceWhereClause(Me.RecordSource, _
       Forms!frmReportSelector_MemberList!txtWhereClause)

Exit_Procedure:
    Exit Sub

Error_Handler:
    MsgBox Err.Number & ": " & Err.Description
    Resume Exit_Procedure
    Resume

End Sub
```

During the report's Open event, its recordset has not been evaluated yet, so you still have a chance to change it.

Now it's time to see what the selection form really does. It has a few fields that are normally hidden, as shown in Figure 15-9.

Figure 15-9

The extra fields above the OK button are normally set to Visible = No. They hold three pieces of information:

- ❏ The Where clause to use in the report's RecordSource
- ❏ Some selection title text to use in the report's heading

❑ A field to indicate whether the report should continue (OK was clicked) or not (Cancel was clicked)

It's a good idea to mark normally invisible fields in some special way so that you can easily see them if you forget to hide them. One technique is to make the background color of a hidden field red (BackColor = 255). *That way you'll notice it if you forget to hide it!*

Here's the code in the form that builds the Where clause and the selection title, both stored in the hidden fields:

```
Sub RebuildWhereClause()
On Error GoTo Err_RebuildWhereClause

'This subroutine builds an SQL WHERE clause based on the choices
'made by the user on the form. It can be used as the WHERE parameter
'in the OpenReport command. The invisible text box Me![txtWhereClause]
'displays the completed WHERE clause.
'
'SelectionTitle string that contains a title to place at the top
' of the report, which specifies the selection made.
' Stored on form in invisible text box
Me![txtSelectionTitle].

Dim varWhereClause As Variant
Dim strWhereAnd As String
Dim strSelectionTitle As String
Dim strComma As String

varWhereClause = Null
strWhereAnd = ""
strSelectionTitle = ""
strComma = ""

'Member Status Combo Box
If Not (Me!cboMemberStatus & "" = "") And Not _
  (Me!cboMemberStatus = 0) Then

  varWhereClause = (varWhereClause + strWhereAnd) _
  & " (tblBusiness.MemberStatusKey = """ & _
  Me!cboMemberStatus.Column(0) & """) "
  strWhereAnd = " AND "
  strSelectionTitle = strSelectionTitle & strComma _
  & "Member Status = " & Me!cboMemberStatus.Column(1)
  strComma = ", "

End If

If strWhereAnd = "" Then
  varWhereClause = Null
Else
  varWhereClause = " WHERE " + varWhereClause
End If

Me![txtWhereClause] = varWhereClause
```

```
Me![txtSelectionTitle] = strSelectionTitle

Exit_RebuildWhereClause:
  Exit Sub

Err_RebuildWhereClause:
  MsgBox (Err.Number & ": " & Err.Description)
  Resume Exit_RebuildWhereClause
  Resume

End Sub
```

Because it contains the key value, Column(0) of the combo box is used to build the Where clause. However, to build the selection title, you use Column(1) because it contains the more friendly description of the Member Status record from the lookup table.

This code runs when OK is clicked. It rebuilds the Where clause and tells the report to proceed:

```
Sub cmdOK_Click()
On Error GoTo Err_cmdOK_Click

RebuildWhereClause
Me!txtContinue = "yes"
Me.Visible = False

Exit_cmdOK_Click:
  Exit Sub

Err_cmdOK_Click:
  MsgBox (Err.Number & ": " & Err.Description)
  Resume Exit_cmdOK_Click
  Resume

End Sub
```

After the RebuildWhereClause procedure builds the first two hidden fields, only two more things have to happen. First, the third hidden field, txtContinue, is set to Yes. It's the field that the report will check to see if it should continue to open or just cancel.

Finally, the current form's Visible property is set to False. Remember that this form was opened in Dialog mode, so hiding it causes the report code to continue running.

Because the selection form is always hidden, not closed, the selection criteria is retained each time the form is used while the Access database remains open. That makes it easier for your user to re-run reports with the same selection criteria or to adjust the criteria slightly instead of typing it all again each time.

If the user clicks Cancel, the following code runs instead. It tells the report to stop opening.

```
Sub cmdCancel_Click()

On Error GoTo Err_cmdCancel_Click
```

```
    Me!txtContinue = "no"
    Me.Visible = False

Exit_cmdCancel_Click:
    Exit Sub

Err_cmdCancel_Click:
    MsgBox (Err.Number & ": " & Err.Description)
    Resume Exit_cmdCancel_Click
    Resume

End Sub
```

The only difference between this code and the OK code is that you don't bother to rebuild the Where clause because the user is canceling anyway, and you set txtContinue to No so that the report will cancel itself before it even gets a chance to display anything.

When the report is canceled it generates Error 2501, which you should handle so that your user doesn't see an ugly error message. See Chapter 9 for a description of how to handle expected errors like this one.

By adding more fields to your selection form and building the Where clause to apply them to the report's recordset, you can deliver a report to your user that is both flexible and easy to use.

Altering the SQL Inside Queries

Sometimes it can be advantageous to alter the SQL inside a saved query. That's especially common when you are using pass-through queries to another database like SQL Server, but it can also come in handy when you need to nest Access queries several layers deep. Because the queries a few layers down can't be modified directly in a report or form's RecordSource, you may need to change them directly.

*Remember that if you use this technique for a pass-through query, you must use the SQL Server syntax of the backend database, not Access syntax. For example, the wildcard in SQL Server is %, not *. Also, SQL Server expects string values to be surrounded by single quotes ('), whereas Access doesn't care whether you use single quotes (') or double quotes (").*

First, realize that this technique will work only if your user is using the front-end application database exclusively. Because you're changing an actual saved query in the application, you must make sure that you aren't causing problems for other users. A good practice is to have each user run a copy of the front-end application on her local computer, not share it on the network. If you follow this recommendation, altering saved queries in your front-end Access application will work just fine.

To change the Where clause in a saved query, use code like the following:

```
Dim qdf as QueryDef
Dim db as Database
Set db = CurrentDB
Set qdf = db.QueryDefs("YourQueryName")
qdf.SQL = ReplaceWhereClause(qdf.SQL, strYourNewWhereClause)
set qdf = Nothing
set db = Nothing
```

The SQL property of the query definition contains the actual SQL statement of the query; it's the same SQL statement that you see in the SQL view in the Query Designer. You don't have to do anything else to change it; the SQL is replaced instantly.

Will this bloat your database? Database bloating is a problem because Access doesn't reclaim unused space until the database is compacted, so the database size can increase dramatically if you (or your code) creates and deletes objects in the front-end database. However, merely replacing the SQL statement inside an existing query doesn't cause significant bloating.

The ReplaceOrderByClause and ReplaceWhereClause Functions

It's often necessary to "cut and replace" the Where and Order By clauses of a SQL string using VBA. Throughout this chapter, the ReplaceWhereClause and ReplaceOrderByClause functions are used to do that. This section shows you the code that's been doing all that hard work!

This first procedure ParseSQL does the "heavy lifting" of the SQL handling functions. It breaks up the original SQL string into components, so that individual pieces can be replaced. Although ParseSQL is Public, it's rarely called from anywhere other than the ReplaceWhereClause and ReplaceOrderByClause functions that follow it.

Please note that you don't have to type all this code into your application! It's in the Chamber Application file included with this chapter's download code.

```
Option Compare Database
Option Explicit
Public Sub ParseSQL(strSQL As Variant, strSELECT As Variant, strWhere A
Variant, strOrderBy As Variant, strGROUPBY As Variant, strHAVING As Variant)


On Error GoTo Error_Handler
'
'This subroutine accepts a valid SQL string and passes back separated
'SELECT, WHERE, ORDER BY, and GROUP BY clauses.


'
'INPUT:

' strSQL valid SQL string to parse

'OUTPUT:
' strSELECT    SELECT portion of SQL (includes JOIN info)
' strWHERE    WHERE portion of SQL
' strORDERBY ORDER BY portion of SQL
' strGROUPBY GROUP BY portion of SQL
' strHAVING  HAVING portion of SQL
```

Access queries have a semicolon (;) at the end of their SQL statements. While the subroutine accepts the trailing ; character in strSQL, *there is no ; character passed back at any time.*

This subroutine takes in only one parameter (the original SQL string), but modifies and outputs five parameters — one for each portion of the parsed SQL string.

```
Dim intStartSELECT As Integer
Dim intStartWHERE As Integer
Dim intStartORDERBY As Integer
Dim intStartGROUPBY As Integer
Dim intStartHAVING As Integer
Dim intLenSELECT As Integer
Dim intLenWHERE As Integer
Dim intLenORDERBY As Integer
Dim intLenGROUPBY As Integer
Dim intLenHAVING As Integer
Dim intLenSQL As Integer
```

The following code determines the starting location of each clause in the SQL statement by finding the position in the string of the corresponding keywords:

```
intStartSELECT = InStr(strSQL, "SELECT ")

intStartWHERE = InStr(strSQL, "WHERE ")

intStartORDERBY = InStr(strSQL, "ORDER BY ")

intStartGROUPBY = InStr(strSQL, "GROUP BY ")

intStartHAVING = InStr(strSQL, "HAVING ")

'if there's no GROUP BY, there can't be a HAVING
If intStartGROUPBY = 0 Then

  intStartHAVING = 0
End If

If InStr(strSQL, ";") Then 'if it exists, trim off the ';'
  strSQL = Left(strSQL, InStr(strSQL, ";") -1)
End If

intLenSQL = Len(strSQL)
```

Next, the code calculates the length of the Select clause of the SQL statement. Basically, it starts by assuming that the Select clause is the entire remaining length of the SQL statement and then tries shorter and shorter lengths by testing against the starting positions of the other SQL clauses:

```
' find length of Select portion

If intStartSELECT > 0 Then
   ' start with longest it could be
   intLenSELECT = intLenSQL -intStartSELECT + 1
   If intStartWHERE > 0 And intStartWHERE > intStartSELECT _
     And intStartWHERE < intStartSELECT + intLenSELECT Then

      'we found a new portion closer to this one
```

```
      intLenSELECT = intStartWHERE -intStartSELECT
    End If
    If intStartORDERBY > 0 And intStartORDERBY > intStartSELECT _
      And intStartORDERBY < intStartSELECT + intLenSELECT Then

      'we found a new portion closer to this one

      intLenSELECT = intStartORDERBY -intStartSELECT
    End If
    If intStartGROUPBY > 0 And intStartGROUPBY > intStartSELECT _
      And intStartGROUPBY < intStartSELECT + intLenSELECT Then

      'we found a new portion closer to this one

      intLenSELECT = intStartGROUPBY -intStartSELECT
    End If
    If intStartHAVING > 0 And intStartHAVING > intStartSELECT _
      And intStartHAVING < intStartSELECT + intLenSELECT Then

      'we found a new portion closer to this one
      intLenSELECT = intStartHAVING -intStartSELECT
    End If
End If
```

Then the code does the same thing for the Group By clause, determining its length by finding the beginning of the next clause:

```
' find length of GROUPBY portion

If intStartGROUPBY > 0 Then
  ' start with longest it could be
  intLenGROUPBY = intLenSQL -intStartGROUPBY + 1
  If intStartWHERE > 0 And intStartWHERE > intStartGROUPBY _
    And intStartWHERE < intStartGROUPBY + intLenGROUPBY Then

    'we found a new portion closer to this one

    intLenGROUPBY = intStartWHERE -intStartGROUPBY
  End If
  If intStartORDERBY > 0 And intStartORDERBY > intStartGROUPBY _
    And intStartORDERBY < intStartGROUPBY + intLenGROUPBY Then

    'we found a new portion closer to this one

    intLenGROUPBY = intStartORDERBY -intStartGROUPBY
  End If
  If intStartHAVING > 0 And intStartHAVING > intStartGROUPBY _
    And intStartHAVING < intStartGROUPBY + intLenGROUPBY Then

    'we found a new portion closer to this one
    intLenGROUPBY = intStartHAVING -intStartGROUPBY
  End If
End If
```

The following code does the same thing for the `Having` clause:

```
' find length of HAVING portion

If intStartHAVING > 0 Then
  ' start with longest it could be
  intLenHAVING = intLenSQL -intStartHAVING + 1
  If intStartWHERE > 0 And intStartWHERE > intStartHAVING _
    And intStartWHERE < intStartHAVING + intLenHAVING Then

    'we found a new portion closer to this one

    intLenHAVING = intStartWHERE -intStartHAVING
  End If
  If intStartORDERBY > 0 And intStartORDERBY > intStartHAVING _
    And intStartORDERBY < intStartHAVING + intLenHAVING Then

    'we found a new portion closer to this one

    intLenHAVING = intStartORDERBY -intStartHAVING
  End If
  If intStartGROUPBY > 0 And intStartGROUPBY > intStartHAVING _
    And intStartGROUPBY < intStartHAVING + intLenHAVING Then

    'we found a new portion closer to this one
    intLenHAVING = intStartGROUPBY -intStartHAVING
  End If
End If
```

And this code does the same thing for the Order By clause:

```
' find length of ORDERBY portion

If intStartORDERBY > 0 Then
  ' start with longest it could be
  intLenORDERBY = intLenSQL -intStartORDERBY + 1
  If intStartWHERE > 0 And intStartWHERE > intStartORDERBY _
    And intStartWHERE < intStartORDERBY + intLenORDERBY Then

    'we found a new portion closer to this one

    intLenORDERBY = intStartWHERE -intStartORDERBY
  End If
  If intStartGROUPBY > 0 And intStartGROUPBY > intStartORDERBY _
    And intStartGROUPBY < intStartORDERBY + intLenORDERBY Then

    'we found a new portion closer to this one

    intLenORDERBY = intStartGROUPBY -intStartORDERBY
  End If
  If intStartHAVING > 0 And intStartHAVING > intStartORDERBY _
    And intStartHAVING < intStartORDERBY + intLenORDERBY Then
```

```
        'we found a new portion closer to this one
        intLenORDERBY = intStartHAVING -intStartORDERBY
    End If
End If
```

Finally, the length of the Where clause is determined:

```
' find length of WHERE portion

If intStartWHERE > 0 Then
    ' start with longest it could be
    intLenWHERE = intLenSQL -intStartWHERE + 1

    If intStartGROUPBY > 0 And intStartGROUPBY > intStartWHERE _
      And intStartGROUPBY < intStartWHERE + intLenWHERE Then
        'we found a new portion closer to this one
        intLenWHERE = intStartGROUPBY -intStartWHERE

    End If
    If intStartORDERBY > 0 And intStartORDERBY > intStartWHERE _
      And intStartORDERBY < intStartWHERE + intLenWHERE Then

        'we found a new portion closer to this one

        intLenWHERE = intStartORDERBY -intStartWHERE
    End If
    If intStartHAVING > 0 And intStartHAVING > intStartWHERE _
      And intStartHAVING < intStartWHERE + intLenWHERE Then

        'we found a new portion closer to this one
        intLenWHERE = intStartHAVING -intStartWHERE
    End If
End If
```

Now that all the starting positions and lengths of the five SQL clauses have been determined, the output parameters can be set:

```
' set each output portion
If intStartSELECT > 0 Then
    strSELECT = Mid$(strSQL, intStartSELECT, intLenSELECT)
End If
If intStartGROUPBY > 0 Then
    strGROUPBY = Mid$(strSQL, intStartGROUPBY, intLenGROUPBY)
End If
If intStartHAVING > 0 Then
    strHAVING = Mid$(strSQL, intStartHAVING, intLenHAVING)
End If
If intStartORDERBY > 0 Then
    strOrderBy = Mid$(strSQL, intStartORDERBY, intLenORDERBY)
End If
If intStartWHERE > 0 Then
    strWhere = Mid$(strSQL, intStartWHERE, intLenWHERE)
End If
```

```
Exit_Procedure:
  Exit Sub

Error_Handler:
  MsgBox (Err.Number & ": " & Err.Description)
  Resume Exit_Procedure

End Sub
```

The next two functions merely use the `ParseSQL` procedure to break up the SQL statement into its five clauses, and then they replace the appropriate clause with the new clause that was passed in:

```
Public Function ReplaceWhereClause(strSQL As Variant, strNewWHERE As Variant)
On Error GoTo Error_Handler

'This subroutine accepts a valid SQL string and Where clause, and
'returns the same SQL statement with the original Where clause (if any)
'replaced by the passed in Where clause.
'
'INPUT:
' strSQL valid SQL string to change
'OUTPUT:
' strNewWHERE New WHERE clause to insert into SQL statement
'
Dim strSELECT As String, strWhere As String
Dim strOrderBy As String, strGROUPBY As String, strHAVING As String

Call ParseSQL(strSQL, strSELECT, strWhere, strOrderBy, _
strGROUPBY, strHAVING)

ReplaceWhereClause = strSELECT &""& strNewWHERE &""_
& strGROUPBY &""& strHAVING &""& strOrderBy

Exit_Procedure:
  Exit Function

Error_Handler:
  MsgBox (Err.Number & ": " & Err.Description)
  Resume Exit_Procedure

End Function


Public Function ReplaceOrderByClause(strSQL As Variant, strNewOrderBy As Variant)
On Error GoTo Error_Handler
'
'This subroutine accepts a valid SQL string and Where clause, and
'returns the same SQL statement with the original Where clause (if any)
'replaced by the passed in Where clause.
'
'INPUT:
' strSQL valid SQL string to change
'OUTPUT:
```

```
' strNewOrderBy New OrderBy clause to insert into SQL statement
'
Dim strSELECT As String, strWhere As String
Dim strOrderBy As String, strGROUPBY As String, strHAVING As String

Call ParseSQL(strSQL, strSELECT, strWhere, strOrderBy, _
strGROUPBY, strHAVING)

ReplaceOrderByClause = strSELECT &""& strWhere &""& strNewOrderBy

Exit_Procedure:
  Exit Function

Error_Handler:
  MsgBox (Err.Number & ": " & Err.Description)
  Resume Exit_Procedure

End Function
```

These SQL handling procedures can be added to all of your Access applications in their own module, such as basSQLTools. By using `ReplaceWhereClause` and `ReplaceOrderByClause`, you can take a lot of the hassle out of manipulating SQL strings in your VBA code.

Summary

VBA and SQL are both powerful tools for you to use in your Access applications, and they work very well together. The techniques explained in this chapter enable you to add instant sorting to column headings, provide easy record selection on continuous forms, build smart cascading combo boxes that change their drop-down lists based on other selections, prompt your user for report selection criteria without using parameter queries, and change the SQL statement inside saved queries. With these features, your Access applications will be more flexible and easy to use.

16

Working with Office Applications

Designing complete, fully functioning database solutions in Microsoft Access is done quite often without the need for working with any another Microsoft Office application. After all, you can use Access forms to enter data, Access reports to view and print data, and the `SendObject` method to send Access information via e-mail. On the other hand, it is not only possible, but extremely useful to leverage the features of other Office applications to enhance an Access solution with very few lines of code. For example, you might want to use Outlook to generate a customized e-mail with information from an Access table. If the Access solution offers a method for users to export data to Excel, those users can leverage Excel features to customize data in their own way without unwanted interaction with your application. Exporting data to Microsoft Word gives users the capability to add their own text, perform mail merges, customize documentation, and much more in a practically universal file format. This chapter illustrates methods for employing other Office applications directly in your Access database solution.

You'll use code examples for working with the other Office programs, and take a look at some real-world situations that illustrate how interaction with other Office programs can enhance your application. Please download the sample database code files for this chapter to see the code included in this chapter.

Sharing Information Is a Two-Way Street

When sharing information between multiple Microsoft Office programs, you can write code two ways:

❑   Write the code within Access to "push" the data into the other Office programs.

❑   Write code within those other programs to "pull" data from Access into them.

Because this book is about Access 2007 VBA, most of the discussion covers the push scenario, but don't worry — there are examples of the pulling data into other applications as well. Many of the examples in this chapter are based on a hypothetical Inventory Control application for pallets of material from a manufacturing plant, included in the sample code for this chapter.

The sample Inventory Control application is an example of a database solution that allows users to store asset information for their business. A series of forms, reports, tables, and queries enable users to work with the data. In addition, there are a number of more advanced tasks users might want to tap into, which require other components in the Microsoft Office System. Leveraging the other Office 2007 programs, such as Outlook, Word, and Excel, is a powerful way to enhance your Access database application.

Working with Outlook

In today's high-tech world, one of the most common forms of communication is e-mail. Allowing users to send e-mail messages via your application that contains customized data provides a powerful feature to any database application. Access 2007 makes it extremely easy and inexpensive to implement this functionality, using just a few lines of VBA code

Open the sample database and click the Material Order Form button. The Frame Material Order Form opens. Assume that the current record shown in this form contains important information that the user needs to communicate via an e-mail. Click the Alert button and the new e-mail is created. Notice that the e-mail contains the order number, the original order due date, expected material receipt date, and the required Action information that is contained in the current record in the form. Although this message is fairly simple, it is extremely easy to continue customizing the data to your preference, or better yet, let the user do it herself to add a personal touch.

The programmatic creation of e-mails, as found in the Material Orders form in the sample database, is made possible by the Outlook Object Model. To write the VBA code to export the data from Access to Outlook, open the Frame Material Order Form in Design mode and view the code behind the Click event of the Alert button. In working with the Outlook Object Model, you must set a reference to the Microsoft Outlook 12.0 Object Model option in the References dialog box, found under the Tools menu in the Visual Basic Editor. That allows the objects, properties, and methods available in Outlook to be manipulated directly from VBA in the Access application. In the sample database, this reference has already been set in the VBA project and if Outlook 2007 is not installed on the machine, an error describing a missing reference will be shown when the database solution is opened.

Following is the code in the Click event of the Alert button. It first declares the required object variables to work with Outlook and a few Outlook objects necessary to set up a new e-mail message.

```
'Reference the Outlook Application
Dim olApp As Outlook.Application

'The NameSpace object allows you to reference folders
Dim olNS as Outlook.NameSpace
Dim olFolder as Outlook.MAPIFolder

'Create a reference to the email item you will use to send your email
Dim olMailItem As Outlook.MailItem
```

Next, you create the `Outlook.Application` object. Any time you need to automate an Office application, you must create an application object using one of two methods. The first is the `CreateObject` method, which creates a brand new instance of the application class for COM objects (including Office applications, which are themselves COM objects). The second is `GetObject`, which gets an existing instance of the object that is already running on the system.

In this example, you use the `CreateObject` method to get an instance of the `Outlook.Application` object. Outlook is unique among the Microsoft Office applications in that there can be only one instance of Outlook running at any given time. If `CreateObject` is called for an `Outlook.Application` object and Outlook is already running, the application is smart enough to return the current instance of the Outlook program. If it is not already running, Outlook will be invoked.

Call the `CreateObject` method to create the Outlook application. Then, add some code to reference the `NameSpace` object, setting a reference to the Inbox folder, and adding a new e-mail message (IPM.Note) to your code:

```
Set olApp = CreateObject("Outlook.Application")
Set olNS = olApp.GetNamespace("MAPI")
Set olFolder = olNS.GetDefaultFolder(olFolderInbox)
Set olMailItem = olFolder.Items.Add("IPM.Note")
```

The Outlook `Mail` object has several properties that can be manipulated. The following is a complete code example that changes the `Subject`, `To`, `Priority`, and `Body` properties when creating a new e-mail message:Dim strBodyText As String

```
'Reference the Outlook Application
Dim olApp As Outlook.Application

'The NameSpace object allows you to reference folders
Dim olNS As Outlook.NameSpace
Dim olFolder As Outlook.MAPIFolder

'Create a reference to the email item you will use to send your email
Dim olMailItem As Outlook.MailItem

'Create the Outlook object
Set olApp = CreateObject("Outlook.Application")
Set olNS = olApp.GetNamespace("MAPI")
Set olFolder = olNS.GetDefaultFolder(olFolderInbox)
Set olMailItem = olFolder.Items.Add("IPM.Note")

'Create the body of the message from the data in the form
strBodyText = "Material for Order #" & Me.OrderNumber & vbCrLf & _
    "Order Due Date: " & Me.OrderDate & vbCrLf & _
    "Action: Inform customer it will be late"

'Update the new mail object with your data
With olMailItem
    .Subject = "Material Delay for Order #" & Me.OrderNumber
    .To = "OrderEntry@AbraxisCorporation.com"
    .Body = strBodyText
```

```
      .Display
End With

'Release all of your object variables
Set olMailItem = Nothing
Set olFolder = Nothing
Set olNS = Nothing
Set olApp = Nothing
```

This code creates the e-mail message using only a few lines of VBA code. It builds the message text, stored in the `strBodyText` variable, from the `OrderNumber` and `OrderDate` data from the record currently in focus on the form. Then the `To` line, `Subject`, and `Body` of the message are set through their corresponding properties on the olMailItem Mail object. While the message in the example contains all of the basic information a user might need to communicate, you can enhance the code just a bit to add a follow-up flag and a high priority distinction to the message. Simply add the following lines of code into the preceding `With` block:

```
.Importance = olImportanceHigh
.FlagStatus = olFlagMarked
'Set the flag reminder date for two days in advance
.FlagDueBy = Date + 2
```

Finally, calling the `Display` method shows the e-mail message on the screen, allowing the user to manually edit and send it at his convenience. However, a common, and often desired, scenario is to just send the mail message without forcing the user to directly interact with the e-mail itself. The following code shows how the message can be sent automatically using the `Send` method and can replace the `With` code block in the preceding code.

```
With olMailItem
    .Subject = "Material Delay for Order #" & Me.OrderNumber
    .To = "OrderEntry@AbraxisCorporation.com"
    .Body = strBodyText
    'Call the send method to send the mail automatically
    .Send
End With
```

In Outlook 2003 and later, if the message is sent automatically and not shown to the user, the user receives a security dialog box with a message explaining that an e-mail is being sent via Outlook and giving her a chance to stop the operation from happening. This security feature was added to help stop the spread of rampant e-mail viruses, but unfortunately, it is often looked on as more of a nuisance from a developer standpoint. However, there are available methods for working around this dialog box, which are described in the next section.

Working with Outlook's Security Features

If you've previously implemented code similar to the preceding example, you've encountered the security dialog box that pops up when the `Send` method is called, as described in the preceding section. This is actually the second of two dialog boxes Microsoft added to Outlook 2003 in an attempt to prevent potentially malicious e-mails from spreading without user knowledge or intervention. The first dialog box appears when code tries to manipulate addresses in the Contacts folder.

Sending an e-mail programmatically displays the dialog box warning that a program is trying to send an e-mail message. The user has to wait 5 seconds before choosing to send the e-mail message. However, in trusted computing environments, there may be times when it is more desirable to bypass these security dialog boxes. There are at least two possibilities for achieving this goal: configuring security through Exchange Server or using Redemption. These options are examined next.

Using an Exchange Server to Configure Security

First, if the users are working in an Exchange environment (or your application will be used with an Exchange Server), you have the capability to configure the Administrative Options Package for Exchange Server to allow mails to be sent automatically without security dialog boxes. The package allows users to permit programmatic sending of e-mail through configuration of a public folder and custom form stored on the Exchange Server. The advantage of this system is that you don't need to touch the client machines at all. Once the form is installed in the public folder on the server, all you need to do is decide which types of programmatic access are needed. This package provides options to access the address book, use the Send method, and a variety of other types of settings (such as attachment blocking). The major disadvantage to this method is that unless you're writing code within a COM add-in for Outlook, allowing programmatic sending is an all-or-nothing proposition. That is, if you allow one application to send e-mails without discretion, you allow *all* applications using the Outlook Object Model to send e-mail without security warnings. Enabling these features on Exchange removes security restrictions that block potential viruses that propagate via e-mail sent from Outlook, so it is important to be extremely careful when choosing to modify the Exchange Server security settings. If you choose to use the Administrative Options package, make sure that users have virus software for both the client machines and the Exchange Server machine.

Using Redemption to Work with Outlook Security

Another option for preventing the Outlook security dialog boxes involves downloading a third-party DLL called Redemption. The Redemption .dll serves as a wrapper for Extended MAPI, another method of creating and sending e-mail messages. Extended MAPI isn't affected by the Outlook security features. The advantage to Redemption is that it can be specifically targeted to a defined application, so merely having the Redemption DLL present on a system poses no security risk. The major disadvantage is that it must be registered on all machines using the applications that reference it. For single users, Redemption is free. A redistributable Redemption license costs around $100. More information about Redemption can be found on its website at dimastr.com/Redemption.

Redemption is easy to use. Once the DLL has been registered on the system, create a reference to the Safe Outlook Library. Then you need to make just a few key changes to the preceding code and users will no longer be presented with the security dialog box. The following code sample takes the previous example and modifies it to use Redemption. The changes in the code are highlighted.

```
Dim strBodyText As String
Dim olApp As Outlook.Application
Dim olNS As Outlook.NameSpace
Dim olFolder As Outlook.MAPIFolder
Dim olMailItem As Outlook.MailItem

'Add a reference to the Redemption Safe Mail item
Dim objSafeMail as Redemption.SafeMailItem

'Create the Outlook object
Set olApp = CreateObject("Outlook.Application")
Set olNS = olApp.GetNamespace("MAPI")
```

```
Set olFolder = olNS.GetDefaultFolder(olFolderInbox)
Set olMailItem = olFolder.Items.Add("IPM.Note")

'Create the body of the message from the data in the form
strBodyText = "Material for Order #" & Me.OrderNumber & vbCrLf & _
    "Order Due Date: " & Me.OrderDate & vbCrLf & _
    "Action: Inform customer it will be late"

'Update the new mail object with your data
With olMailItem
    .Subject = "Material Delay for Order #" & Me.OrderNumber
    .To = "OrderEntry@FramesRUs.com"
    .Body = strBodyText
    'remove the "Send" method to avoid security dialogs
End With

Set objSafeMail = new Redemption.SafeMailItem

'No need for the Set statement here
objSafeMail.Item = olMailItem
objSafeMail.Send

'Release all of your object variables
Set objSafeMail = Nothing
Set olMailItem = Nothing
Set olFolder = Nothing
Set olNS = Nothing
Set olApp = Nothing
```

Creating Other Types of Outlook Objects from Access

Creating e-mail messages in Outlook isn't the only way to use VBA and Outlook to enhance your database solution. Meetings, appointments, tasks, and journal items can be managed via Outlook using VBA. For example, it is common for business users to schedule tasks in Outlook to remind them to complete an action by a certain date and time. It is very easy to create these tasks, as well as other Outlook items, with just a few lines of code.

View the code behind the Create Task button's Click event on the sample database's Material Order Form. The initial portion of the code is very similar to the code used to create an e-mail message. However, instead of referencing the Inbox folder, set a reference to the Task folder, as shown in the following code.

```
Dim olApp As Outlook.Application
Dim olNS As Outlook.NameSpace
Dim olFolder As Outlook.MAPIFolder
Dim olTaskItem As Outlook.TaskItem

Set olApp = CreateObject("Outlook.Application")
Set olNS = olApp.GetNamespace("MAPI")

'Get the Outlook "Tasks" folder
Set olFolder = olNS.GetDefaultFolder(olFolderTasks)
```

```
'Add the new task
Set olTaskItem = olFolder.Items.Add("IPM.Task")

'Update the new task object with your data
With olTaskItem
    .DueDate = Date + 2
    .Subject = "Confirm Material Receipt for Order #: " & Me.OrderNumber
    .ReminderTime = Date + 2
    .ReminderSet = True
    .Categories = "Material Order"
    .Save
End With

'Release all of your object variables
Set olTaskItem = Nothing
Set olFolder = Nothing
Set olNS = Nothing
Set olApp = Nothing
```

This code is similar to the example code for creating e-mail messages through Outlook, with a few minor differences. Instead of a `MailItem` object, it employs the `TaskItem` object, and instead of getting the Inbox folder by specifying `olFolderInbox`, the code specifies the Tasks folder with the `olFolderTasks` enumeration option. The `TaskItem` object is created and added to the folder by specifying the `"IPM.Task"` string to the `Add` method. `TaskItem` has several properties corresponding to data for the task, including `DueDate`, `ReminderTime`, and `ReminderSet` to supply the details for the task. Finally, calling the `Save` method propagates the changes to the Task in the users Outlook folder, without requiring any user intervention or settings whatsoever.

Creating Outlook objects programmatically is easy and can provide rich functionality to almost any Access database solution. The only requirement is that the user must already have Outlook installed on his local machine.

Sending Information from Access to Excel

Access 2007 provides the capability to create forms and reports, which include graphs and tables. However, you may want to leverage some of the powerful Excel features, such as the new Charting and Conditional Formatting features new to Office 2007. Also, users may find it useful to be able to export their data in an Excel spreadsheet. The code samples for working with Excel can be found in the code behind the Export Report Manager form in the sample database. As with Outlook, using Excel features from VBA in an Access database solution requires a VBA reference to the Microsoft Excel 12.0 Object Model in the Visual Basic Editor's References dialog box.

Working with Data in Excel

A common scenario in any company is to communicate public data via charts, tables, and graphs through periodic reports. By allowing users to export data directly to Excel, you empower them to leverage the rich set of Excel features to create their own charts and tables at a whim, without having to modify the data or design of the architecture of your Access database solution.

The first example here utilizes a form with a list box control that exposes Queries within the application. The Row Source type of the list box control in Access is Table/Query by default, but you can fill your list box in several different ways. If you want users to be able to choose any Report to export, it is pretty easy to add a few lines of code to populate the list box programmatically. The following code loops through each of the Query objects in the application and adds their names to the list box. The code could then be added to the form's OnLoad event (as is done for the OnLoad event for Export Report Manager on the form):

```
Dim qdQueryName As QueryDef

'Clear the list if it is already filled
lstExport.RowSource = ""
lstExport.RowSourceType = "Value List"

'Add all of the Query names to the List Box
For Each qdQueryName In Application.CurrentDb.QueryDefs
    If (InStr(1, qdQueryName.Name, "~") = 0) Then
        Me.lstExport.AddItem qdQueryName.Name
    End If
Next
```

This same functionality can be accomplished by querying the MSysObjects system table. If you leave the Row Source Type as Table/Query for the list box, users can query the MSysObjects system table to get all of the names for any given database objects. A SQL statement can be created to query the MSysObjects system table for a list of all of the queries and place the SQL in the Row Source property for the list box.

```
'Create the SQL Statement
Dim strSQL As String
strSQL = _
    "SELECT MSysObjects.Name " & _
    "FROM MSysObjects " & _
    "WHERE (((MSysObjects.Name) Not Like ""~"") AND ((MSysObjects.Type)=5));"

'Set the Row Source with the SQL Statement
Me.lstExport.RowSourceType = "Table/Query"
Me.lstExport.RowSource = strSQL
```

This shows all of the Query object names in the list box that are not temp queries created by the system — those are denoted by starting with a tilde (~) character. If you don't want users to be able to choose every Query in the database, the names of the object can always be hard-coded into the Row Source property for the list box. Now that there is a list of queries in the list box control, code can be created to export the results of one of those queries to an Excel workbook.

Exporting to Excel can be completed in several different ways, two of which are presented here. The first involves opening Excel, creating a new workbook with a new worksheet, and transferring the data into the worksheet. The second utilizes the SaveAs method of the RunCommand object to automate this process. Additionally, the OutputTo method can be used to export to Excel, which is covered later in the code examples of working with Word.

Using the Excel OM to Create a New Workbook

To create a new worksheet in Excel, you will build the code in a few steps. To start you create an Excel application object. Then, you create a new worksheet object, as shown in the following code:

```
'Define variables
Dim xlApp As Excel.Application
Dim xlWorkbook As Excel.Workbook

'Create the Excel Application object
Set xlApp = CreateObject("Excel.Application")
xlApp.Visible = True

'Create a new workbook
Set xlWorkbook = xlApp.Workbooks.Add
```

After creating the new worksheet, you'll want fill that worksheet with data. The next example uses a Recordset object (from DAO, see Chapter 6) to gather the data from an Access query in the database. The Recordset object enables you to get the data from any table or row returning a query for the desired records to be exported to Excel. The following code creates a new Recordset based on the selected query in the list box and uses that query's name as the name for the Excel worksheet.

```
'Define Variables
Dim objRST As Recordset
Dim strQueryName As String
Dim strSheetName as String

'Create the Recordset
strQueryName = Me.lstExport
Set objRST = Application.CurrentDb.OpenRecordset(strQueryName)

'Create a Sheet Name - Must be 31 chars or less
strSheetName = Trim(Left(strQueryName, 31))
```

Once the Recordset object has been created, Excel's CopyFromRecordset method can be used to copy data from the Recordset to the Cells object of the new worksheet. The following code shows how to accomplish that task (it can be concatenated to the previous two code examples):

```
Dim xlSheet As Excel.Worksheet

'Use code to fill the Excel Sheet
Set xlSheet = xlWorkbook.Sheets(1)
With xlSheet
    .Cells.CopyFromRecordset objRST
    .Name = strSheetName
End With

'Clean up all Variables
Set objRST = Nothing
Set xlSheet = Nothing
Set xlWorkbook = Nothing
Set xlApp = Nothing
```

The preceding code creates a plain Excel worksheet, without any special formatting. However, the spreadsheet might look better to the user if it had column headers. It is easy to add a few lines of code to create column headings and to shade those column headings. Because this code uses a DAO `Recordset` object, you have the properties and methods of the `Recordset` object at your disposal. To add column headings, simply loop through the `Fields` collection of the `Recordset` and add a heading for each field (column) in the data set. This task is completed by adding the following lines of code to the previous example:

```
'Add headings to each of the columns
Set xlSheet = xlWorkbook.Sheets(1)
For lvlColumn = 0 To objRST.Fields.Count - 1
    xlSheet.Cells(1, lvlColumn + 1).Value = _
    objRST.Fields(lvlColumn).Name
Next
```

The preceding code loops through every column in the worksheet and places the appropriate field name in that column. Just placing field names isn't very exciting, however. Why not add some color? For some added pizzazz, you can also add a cell border and a bold font. The following code does the job:

```
'Change the font to bold for the header row
xlSheet.Range(xlSheet.Cells(1, 1), _
xlSheet.Cells(1, objRST.Fields.Count)).Font.Bold = True

'Add a border to header row cells
With xlSheet.Range(xlSheet.Cells(1, 1), _
xlSheet.Cells(1, objRST.Fields.Count)).Borders(xlEdgeLeft)
    .LineStyle = xlContinuous
    .Weight = xlThin
    .ColorIndex = xlAutomatic
End With

With xlSheet.Range(xlSheet.Cells(1, 1), _
xlSheet.Cells(1, objRST.Fields.Count)).Borders(xlEdgeTop)
    .LineStyle = xlContinuous
    .Weight = xlThin
    .ColorIndex = xlAutomatic
End With

With xlSheet.Range(xlSheet.Cells(1, 1), _
xlSheet.Cells(1, objRST.Fields.Count)).Borders(xlEdgeBottom)
    .LineStyle = xlContinuous
    .Weight = xlThin
    .ColorIndex = xlAutomatic
End With

With xlSheet.Range(xlSheet.Cells(1, 1), _
xlSheet.Cells(1, objRST.Fields.Count)).Borders(xlEdgeRight)
    .LineStyle = xlContinuous
    .Weight = xlThin
    .ColorIndex = xlAutomatic
End With
```

This code sets each border (top, bottom, left, and right) to a thin line by calling the `Borders` object with the appropriate edge option and setting the `LineStyle`, `Weight`, and `ColorIndex` properties with the desired values. Now, you're ready to return to the code to fill the sheet with data. In this case, you need to make one minor alteration to the previously listed code. If you add the code to fill and format the column headings, and then try to execute the previously listed code as is, you'll end up with no header row and the first row of data formatted with bold font and borders. To start the data in the second row of the spreadsheet, change this code from the previous example:

```
With xlSheet
    .Cells.CopyFromRecordset objRST
    .Name = strSheetName
End With
```

to the code:

```
With xlSheet
    .Range("A2").CopyFromRecordset objRST
    .Name = strSheetName
End With
```

Once this code has been added, the field names for each of the columns will be in the first row of the Excel spreadsheet and the data from the `Recordset` will start on the second row. This provides not just data, but information about the data to the user who wants to utilize the new worksheet. As the example shows, building spreadsheets in Excel based on `Recordsets` from an Access database solution is simple and requires only a small amount of code.

> In some circumstances the previous code may fail. If the query referenced by the `Recordset` object is an action query (`Update`, `Insert`, `Delete`, and so on), this code will fail. For the `OpenRecordset` method to succeed, the query must return a set of records.

Using TransferSpreadsheet to Create a New Worksheet

If you prefer not to use the `CopyFromRecordset` method, you can also use the `TransferSpreadsheet` method from the `DoCmd` object. There are a few distinct advantages to the `TransferSpreadsheet` method. One advantage is that you can export an entire table to a spreadsheet with one simple command. For example:

```
'Use Transfer Spreadsheet to create an Excel Spreadsheet
DoCmd.TransferSpreadsheet acExport, acSpreadsheetTypeExcel9, "Skids", ↵
"c:\skids.xls"
```

This code is all you need to export the Skids table to a spreadsheet called `skids.xls` to the C drive. This method enables you to export both tables and queries stored in your database. Another advantage to the method is that you don't actually invoke the Excel object model, which requires more code and more overhead, as Excel is loaded into memory.

A noticeable side effect of using the `TransferSpreadsheet` method is that if you already have a file called `skids.xls` in the specified location, with the same sheet name and named data range, the preceding code will fail silently. The code runs, but the existing spreadsheet is not replaced by the new spreadsheet. As a workaround, you could change the named range or delete the original sheet, so that the new sheet will be created. Alternatively, it's easy to add some code to check for the existence of the file before this line of code runs, and if so, delete the workbook before creating the new one. That logic can be accomplished with the following code:

```
Dim strFilePath As String

'Check to see if the file already exists
strFilePath = "C:\skids.xls"
If (Dir$(strFilePath) <> "") Then
    'Delete the file since it already exists
    Kill strFilePath
End If

'Use TransferSpreadsheet to create an Excel Spreadsheet
DoCmd.TransferSpreadsheet acExport, acSpreadsheetTypeExcel9, "Skids", strFilePath
```

Still, this code seems a little inflexible. Ideally, the user should be able to specify the name and location of the new Excel workbook. Adding a reference to the Microsoft Office 12.0 Object Library enables you to leverage the `FileDialog` object in your VBA code so that you can reuse four common dialog boxes built into Office: Open File, Save As, File Picker, and Folder Picker. The Save As dialog box would be perfect, except for one thing: It does not allow the dialog box file type filters to be set. So, instead, using the File Picker dialog box and switching the text of the Title and Button properties to Save As will serve the purpose. The following code implements this scenario:

```
Dim strFilePath As String

'Default Location
strFilePath = "C:\skids.xlsx"

'Use the FileDialog to choose the file location
With Application.FileDialog(msoFileDialogFilePicker)
    .Title = "Save As"
    .ButtonName = "Save As"
    .AllowMultiSelect = False
    .Filters.Add "Excel", "*.xlsx; *.xls", 1
    .Filters.Add "All Files", "*.*", 2
    .InitialFileName = strFilePath

    'Show the dialog and if the dialog returns
    'True, then create the new Spreadsheet
    If .Show = True Then 'The user clicked "Save"
        strFilePath = .SelectedItems(1)
    Else 'The user canceled the dialog so exit
        MsgBox "Save As canceled! Spreadsheet has not been saved."
        Exit Sub
    End If
End With

'Check to see if the file already exists
```

```
If (Dir$(strFilePath) <> "") Then
    'Delete the file since it already exists
    Kill strFilePath
End If

'Use TransferSpreadsheet to create an Excel Spreadsheet
DoCmd.TransferSpreadsheet acExport, acSpreadsheetTypeExcel9, "Skids", strFilePath
```

In this code, the `Application.FileDialog` object is chosen by passing the enumeration option corresponding to the desired dialog type. For the File Dialog, the Title and Button text, set the desired strings to the `Title` and `ButtonName` properties of the `FileDialog` object. Additionally, for the default filename and folder path as well as the selection model for the dialog box are set by specifying the desired settings to the `InitialFileName` and `AllowMultiSelect` properties. Custom the Filters can be created by calling the Add method on the Filters object and passing the filter string. Finally, the Show method is called to show the dialog box to the user, which returns true if the user clicks the action button for the dialog box (in our case named Save As); otherwise, false is returned if the user chooses Cancel or the Close button on the dialog box. The Show method can be wrapped in an `If` statement to provide some feedback to the user, should they decide not to save the file.

One other consideration when using the `TransferSpreadsheet` method is that you do not have the capability to manipulate the look and feel of the spreadsheet when it is created. The new worksheet will be a plain table without any formatting but, fortunately, it will contain column headers. You'll need to decide whether your project requires the formatting and flexibility of the first method or the ease of use of the second method. Both work equally well for their basic task, transferring data between Access and Excel.

Exchanging Data with Microsoft Word

Access 2007 provides a robust set of reporting features for building breathtaking reports. You can sort, group, filter, total, and even employ and manipulate almost every reporting feature using VBA. But even with all of the flexibility supplied by Access, there are still a number of tasks you cannot complete with Access alone and other tasks where you may want to leverage the rich text editing features of Microsoft Word. As such, this section highlights some code samples illustrating how to work with Word using VBA code.

The following code example explores creating a mail merge in Word using application data. While you can create a letter in Access using reports, it may be cumbersome to allow the user to customize the letter once the report has been generated. Fortunately, it is simple to provide users with a boilerplate mail merge document in Word and allow them to customize the mail merge document to suit their needs.

The mail merge code can be written in two ways. The first, and simplest way, is to use Access VBA to define the data source and open the merge document. The second way is to use VBA to perform every step of the mail merge process. You'll examine both methods.

Automate Word to Start Your Merge

If your users are fairly technically savvy with Microsoft Word, they may want to create their own mail merge document. This example uses the Word Object Model to initiate the mail merge using a preexisting Word document. Any project automating Word requires a reference to the Microsoft Word 12.0

Object Model for the VBA project. The sample database already has this reference set, and the code samples for this section can be found in the Form module for the Customer Information form in the sample. The following short code segment assumes the user has already created a mail merge template and saved it to his hard drive (please see the sample Word file mail merge document included in this chapter's download code). This code allows the user to select a Word Mail Merge template and initiate the merge to generate a set of Word documents:

```
'Define Variables
Dim strFilePath As String
Dim objWord As Word.Document

'Allow the user to select the Word document
With Application.FileDialog(msoFileDialogOpen)
    .Title = "Select Word Document"
    .AllowMultiSelect = False
    .Filters.Add "Word Documents", "*.docx; *.doc", 1
    .Filters.Add "All Files", "*.*", 2

    'Show the dialog and if the dialog returns
    'True, then open the selected document
    If .Show = True Then 'The user clicked "OK"
        strFilePath = .SelectedItems(1)
    Else 'The user canceled the dialog so exit
        MsgBox "A Word Document was not selected! Choose a mail merge document."
        Exit Sub
    End If
End With

'Create the Word instance and make it visible
Set objWord = GetObject(strFilePath, "Word.Document")
objWord.Application.Visible = True

'Open the data set from this database
objWord.MailMerge.OpenDataSource _
    Name:=Application.CurrentProject.FullName, _
    OpenExclusive:=False, _
    LinkToSource:=True, _
    Connection:="TABLE Customers", _
    SQLStatement:="SELECT Customers.* FROM Customers;"

'Execute the Mail Merge
objWord.MailMerge.Execute
objWord.Close (0)

'Release variables
Set objWord = Nothing
```

This code completes several operations to make the mail merge work. First, `FileDialog` object code allows the user to select the Word Mail Merge template via the UI of the application from the previous section. Once the document is selected, use the `CreateObject` method to create a new instance of the Word application and set the `Visible` property to true to show the application to the user. With the Word application created, call the `OpenDataSource` method of the `MailMerge` object to get the data in the table in the given database. The `OpenDataSource` method takes parameters for the database path, connection, and any SQL statement needed to gather the proper records. Finally, calling the `MailMerge` object's Execute method actually runs the merge and the data from the records returned from the `OpenDataSource` call are populated into the fields.

If the specified database is locked exclusively, calling the `OpenDataSource` method causes an error and fails. Access sometimes needs to lock the database when certain events occur, such as saving new database objects or, on occasion, when modifying data. There are several ways to work around this issue, such as closing and reopening the database in Shared mode or even creating a new, separate connection to the database. However, error handling does not help in this case because the error actually occurs in the Word object.

One key component is missing in this code: merge fields. If you have a standard merge document already set up with merge fields, then opening this document attempts to requery the data source and fill the document with data. As you may have already considered, it might be more practical to start with a blank document and manually set up the merge using the Word Object Model. The next section examines how to set up the merge document with content and merge fields using the object model.

Using VBA to Set Up Your Merge Document

Creating the mail merge using the Word Object Model really isn't that difficult, but it does require a little more code behind your form. Consider that automating the creation of the Mail merge document in Word through code may be easier and more practical for users because they won't have to create the merge document manually. The following code sample creates the merge document from a blank document, adds the merge fields, and finally, merges the data.

```
'Define Variables
Dim objWordApp As Word.Application
Dim objWord As Word.Document
Dim oSel As Word.Selection

'Create the instance of the new document and show Word
Set objWordApp = CreateObject("Word.Application")
Set objWord = objWordApp.Documents.Add
objWord.Application.Visible = True

'Open the data set from this database
objWord.MailMerge.OpenDataSource _
    Name:=Application.CurrentProject.FullName, _
    OpenExclusive:=False, _
    LinkToSource:=True, _
    Connection:="TABLE Customers", _
    SQLStatement:="SELECT Customers.* FROM Customers;"

'Add fields to the mail merge document
With objWord.MailMerge.Fields
    Set oSel = objWord.Application.Selection

    oSel.TypeText vbNewLine & vbNewLine
    .Add oSel.Range, "CompanyName"
    oSel.TypeParagraph
    .Add oSel.Range, "Address"
```

```
           oSel.TypeParagraph
           .Add oSel.Range, "City"
           oSel.TypeText ", "
           .Add oSel.Range, "Country"
           oSel.TypeParagraph
           oSel.TypeParagraph
           oSel.TypeText "Dear "
           .Add oSel.Range, "ContactName"
           oSel.TypeText ","
           oSel.TypeParagraph
           oSel.TypeParagraph
           oSel.TypeText "We have created this mail just for you..."
           oSel.TypeParagraph
           oSel.TypeParagraph
           oSel.TypeText "Sincerely," & vbNewLine & "John Q. Public"
     End With

     'Execute the mail merge
     objWord.MailMerge.Execute
     objWord.Close (0)

     'Cleanup Variables
     Set oSel = Nothing
     Set objWord = Nothing
     Set objWordApp = Nothing
```

This code is somewhat similar to the last example. In this case, however, instead of opening a pre-existing mail merge template, the Add method of the Documents object is called to create a new document in the instance of Word. To create the mail merge document, a series of text and data from the database is added to the document. The Add method of the Fields object, which is a part of the MailMerge object, can be used to populate the document with data from the records returned by the OpenDataSource method. When populating the Word document with the message text, know that the TypeParagraph method of the selection object inserts a carriage return in the document. The TypeText method simply adds the specified text to the document. The entire letter can be built this way line by line. To give your users the ultimate flexibility, put a text box on the form and allow them to type any custom text right into the form and then insert the data into the document when it is created. This method of creating a mail merge document is extremely flexible and easy to create.

Sending Access Objects to Word

In addition to using VBA to create a mail merge, you can export data in an Access database to Word using VBA and the Word Object Model. The following code, for example, allows a user to export an Access report to a specific Word document. This feature is extremely useful when users need to modify the report or need to perform other operations on the document, such as including external documentation or e-mailing the report to others in an editable format.

```
     'Define Variables
     Dim objWordApp As Word.Application
     Dim objWord As Word.Document
     Dim strFilePath As String
```

```
'Output the Report to RTF format
strFilePath = "C:\Skids.doc"
DoCmd.OutputTo acOutputReport, "Skids", acFormatRTF, strFilePath

'Create a new instance and show Word
Set objWordApp = CreateObject("Word.Application")
Set objWord = objWordApp.Documents.Open(strFilePath)
objWord.Application.Visible = True

'Release COM Objects
Set objWord = Nothing
Set objWordApp = Nothing
```

To accomplish the task, you call the OutputTo method. A member of the DoCmd object, OutputTo enables you to quickly output any Access database object supported in the AcOutputObjectType enumeration to any of the supported data formats in the AcFormat enumeration. This example uses the acFormatRTF option to output a report to the RTF format and then opens the new file in an instance of Microsoft Word. Similarly, consider that you can output database objects to Excel using the acFormatXLS option. In this code, OutputTo outputs the data from the Skids table to a new RTF file. A new instance of Word is created, but in this example, the Open method of the Word application object is called to open the new RTF document created by OutputTo.

With just ten lines of code, the data in the table was output to an RTF document and opened in Word. What other programming environment provides that much power for a developer?

Sending Data to PowerPoint

There are often times when Office users want to convey statistical data during a presentation via the use of graphs and charts. Most of the time the users probably want to build a presentation themselves, but someone who gives many lectures might want to update an existing presentation with the latest data from her Access database. It is worth noting that PowerPoint also provides a rich object model for building presentations on-the-fly. The following example illustrates how to update a presentation with an Excel chart created programmatically with data from an Access report.

This procedure is a little complicated, so let's break it down into three easy steps. First, TransferSpreadsheet is used to export a Recordset into an intermediate Excel file, as was shown previously in this chapter.

```
'Define variables
Dim strExcelFile As String
Dim strQueryName As String

'Use TransferSpreadsheet to create an Excel spreadsheet
strExcelFile = "C:\MiscAssets.xlsx"
strQueryName = "MiscAssetsReport"
DoCmd.TransferSpreadsheet acExport, acSpreadsheetTypeExcel12, strQueryName,
strExcelFile
```

The second step is to create VBA code in your Access application to automate the creation of the chart using the Excel Object Model. To save space in this example, the code uses an existing chart object included the sample code files, but easily could have been created via the Excel Object Model. Here, the newly created workbook in Excel is opened and a chart is created based on the data exported from the query. Then you call the `CopyPicture` method to make a copy of the chart to export to PowerPoint.

```
'Define variables
Dim xlApp As Excel.Application
Dim xlWorkbook As Excel.Workbook
Dim xlSheet As Excel.Worksheet

'Create the Excel application and open the spreadsheet
Set xlApp = CreateObject("Excel.Application")
xlApp.Visible = True
Set xlWorkbook = xlApp.Workbooks.Open(strExcelFile, , ReadOnly:=False)
Set xlSheet = xlWorkbook.ActiveSheet

'Create the Excel chart and copy it
With xlSheet
    xlApp.Charts.Add
    xlApp.ActiveChart.ChartType = xlColumnClustered
    xlApp.ActiveChart.SetSourceData Sheets(strQueryName).Range("A2:B11"), xlRows

    With xlApp.ActiveChart
        .HasTitle = True
        .ChartTitle.Text = "Misc. Assets Count"
        .Axes(xlCategory, xlPrimary).HasTitle = True
        .Axes(xlCategory, xlPrimary).AxisTitle.Text = "Locations"
        .Axes(xlValue, xlPrimary).HasTitle = False
        .CopyPicture
    End With
End With
```

The third step is to use VBA to create a PowerPoint presentation and add a slide (note that you could also reference an existing slide). Then you paste the chart onto the new slide and *voilà*, the PowerPoint presentation is instantly updated. Use the `Top` and `Left` properties of the `Shape` object to adjust the position of the new chart to make sure it is set correctly:

```
'Define variables
Dim pptApp As PowerPoint.Application
Dim pptPresentation As PowerPoint.Presentation
Dim pptSlide As PowerPoint.Slide

'Create the PowerPoint instance and open the presentation
Set pptApp = CreateObject("Powerpoint.Application")
Set pptPresentation = pptApp.Presentations.Add(msoTrue)
pptApp.Visible = True

'Add a new slide and paste the chart
Set pptSlide = pptPresentation.Slides.Add(Index:=1, Layout:=ppLayoutBlank)
pptPresentation.Shapes.Paste

'Adjust the Chart's position
pptSlide.Shapes(1).Left = 18
pptSlide.Shapes(1).Top = 18
```

The following is a complete set of code, with a few little additions to make this operation work smoothly without prompts and to clean up intermediate objects along the way. (You release all of the COM object variables by setting them to nothing in your code.) To see the procedure in action, click the Send Data to PowerPoint button on the Customer Information form in the sample database.

```
'Define Variables
Dim xlApp As Excel.Application
Dim xlWorkbook As Excel.Workbook
Dim xlSheet As Excel.Worksheet
Dim pptApp As PowerPoint.Application
Dim pptPresentation As PowerPoint.Presentation
Dim pptSlide As PowerPoint.Slide
Dim bFileExists As Boolean
Dim strExcelFile As String
Dim strQueryName As String

'Check to see if the file already exists
strExcelFile = "C:\MiscAssets.xlsx"
bFileExists = Dir$(strExcelFile) <> ""
If bFileExists Then
    Kill strExcelFile
End If

'Use TransferSpreadsheet to create an Excel Spreadsheet
strQueryName = "MiscAssetsReport"
DoCmd.TransferSpreadsheet acExport, acSpreadsheetTypeExcel12, strQueryName,
strExcelFile

'Create the Excel instance and open the Spreadsheet
Set xlApp = CreateObject("Excel.Application")
xlApp.Visible = True
Set xlWorkbook = xlApp.Workbooks.Open(strExcelFile, , ReadOnly:=False)
Set xlSheet = xlWorkbook.ActiveSheet

'Create the Excel Chart and copy it
With xlSheet
    xlApp.Charts.Add
    xlApp.ActiveChart.ChartType = xlColumnClustered
    xlApp.ActiveChart.SetSourceData Sheets(strQueryName).Range("A2:B11"), xlRows

    With xlApp.ActiveChart
        .HasTitle = True
        .ChartTitle.Text = "Misc. Assets Count"
        .Axes(xlCategory, xlPrimary).HasTitle = True
        .Axes(xlCategory, xlPrimary).AxisTitle.Text = "Locations"
        .Axes(xlValue, xlPrimary).HasTitle = False
        .CopyPicture
    End With
End With

'Close the Workbook and quit Excel
xlApp.Workbooks(1).Close SaveChanges:=False
xlApp.Quit
```

```
'Delete the SpreadSheet
Kill strExcelFile

'Create the PowerPoint instance and open the presentation
Set pptApp = CreateObject("Powerpoint.Application")
Set pptPresentation = pptApp.Presentations.Add(msoTrue)
pptApp.Visible = True

'Add a new slide and paste the chart
Set pptSlide = pptPresentation.Slides.Add(Index:=1, Layout:=ppLayoutBlank)
pptPresentation.Slides(1).Shapes.Paste

'Adjust the Chart's position
pptSlide.Shapes(1).Left = 18
pptSlide.Shapes(1).Top = 18

'Cleanup
Set xlApp = Nothing
Set xlWorkbook = Nothing
Set xlSheet = Nothing
Set pptApp = Nothing
Set pptPresentation = Nothing
Set pptSlide = Nothing
```

The true beauty of this code is that it uses several different Office programs in harmony to complete a number of advanced tasks, all in one simple subroutine. There are literally countless scenarios where you could implement code to perform tasks moving data between any of the Office programs. In all of the examples up to this point in the chapter, you have used data from an Access database and pushed the data into another Office application by automating it in an Access database solution. However, it is just as easy to automate the Access Object model from another Microsoft Office application to pull data from the database. The next example implements pulling data from an Access database into an Excel spreadsheet from VBA code written in the Excel Workbook's VBA project.

Pulling Data from Access

There are unlimited opportunities to use VBA in an application to manipulate an instance of Access to utilize data in a database solution. The Access Object Model can be managed from other applications that support VBA to enhance those applications with Access functionality. This example gathers data from an Access database into an Excel spreadsheet, which is included with the sample files for this chapter. As with all other Office applications, adding a reference to the Microsoft Access 12.0 Object Model via the VBA References dialog box in Excel's Visual Basic Editor is required to begin employing the Access feature set in a database solution.

In this example, you use Excel to start an Access database application via a button click. Open the Use Access Excel workbook file included with the sample code for this chapter. Notice that a Form button on it is opened automatically. Excel has some lightweight forms, called UserForms, which can be used much like an Access form. Although they don't have all of the properties of Access forms, they are handy and provide quite a bit of functionality. To create one of these forms and add code behind it, simply open VBE for Excel by right-clicking on a tab for any spreadsheet and selecting View Code. In this case some code is added to the Open event for the Workbook module to open the form when the Workbook is opened. Of course, the Excel workbook must have code enabled for the Open event code to run when the workbook is opened. To open the form when the Workbook is opened, add the following code to the Workbook's VBA module:

```
Private Sub Workbook_Open()

    frmAccess.Show False

End Sub
```

The form is shown to the user by simply calling the Show method of the UserForm object. In this example, the form contains a button called Start Inventory Application that, if clicked, opens the sample inventory application that lives in the same directory as the Excel workbook. The code is as follows:

```
'Create the instance of Access and show it
Set accApp = CreateObject("Access.Application")
accApp.Visible = True

If Not (accApp Is Nothing) Then
    'Open the database
    accApp.OpenCurrentDatabase accApp.CurrentProject.Path & "\Inventory.mdb"
Else
    MsgBox "The Access instance could not be created."
End If
```

This code calls the CreateObject method to create a new instance of Access and shows the client window by setting the Visible property to True. If this code is placed behind the click event of a button on a form, a click would start the Access application.

In addition, other actions can be performed from Excel, such as opening a form or report, exporting data in a table as an XML file, or even completing a Compact and Repair of a database application. The following code shows some common examples:

```
'Open a Report
accApp.DoCmd.OpenReport "Customer Addresses"

'Export table as XML data
accApp.ExportXml _
    ObjectType:=acExportTable, _
    DataSource:="Customers", _
    DataTarget:="C:\Customers.xml", _
    Encoding:=acUTF8, _
    OtherFlags:=acEmbedSchema

'Compact and Repair the database
accApp.CompactRepair "C:\Inventory.mdb", "C:\InventoryRepaired.mdb"
```

There are full examples of each of the features mentioned in the previous code samples for this chapter, but we hope you understand where this is leading. Anything that can be done from VBA within an Access application can also be done by automating Access from another application.

Probably a more common scenario would be to gather data from an Access database and pull it into an Excel application, directly from inside the Excel application. The following code creates an ADO connection to an Access database, pulls data into a `Recordset` object, creates a new worksheet, and copies the data from the `Recordset` into the worksheet. In addition, you could just as easily alter the code to utilize DAO to execute a query to gather this data to pull it into the Excel workbook. This example is a complete set of code to implement this scenario:

```
'Define Variables
Dim xlApp As Object
Dim xlWorkbook As Object
Dim xlSheet As Object
Dim oAdoConnect As Object
Dim adoRecordset As ADODB.Recordset
Dim lngColumn As Long
Dim strNewFile As String
Dim strFilePath As String
Dim strSQL As String

'Always have a way to handle errors
On Error GoTo Handler

'Establish your ADO connection
Set oAdoConnect = CreateObject("ADODB.Connection")
oAdoConnect.Provider = "Microsoft.ACE.OLEDB.12.0"
oAdoConnect.Open = Application.ActiveWorkbook.Path & "\Inventory.mdb"

'Create the SQL statement
strSQL = _
    "SELECT Customers.* " & _
    "FROM Customers " & _
    "WHERE (((Customers.ContactName) Like ""M*""));"

'Create and open your Recordset
Set adoRecordset = CreateObject("ADODB.Recordset")
adoRecordset.Open strSQL, oAdoConnect, adOpenStatic, adLockReadOnly

'Create your Excel spreadsheet
Set xlApp = Application
Set xlWorkbook = xlApp.Workbooks.Add

'Add the new Worksheet
With xlWorkbook
    Set xlSheet = .Worksheets.Add
    xlSheet.Name = "Customers"
    For lngColumn = 0 To adoRecordset.Fields.Count - 1
        xlSheet.Cells(1, lngColumn + 1).Value = adoRecordset.Fields(lngColumn).Name
    Next

    xlSheet.Range(xlSheet.Cells(1, 1), _
        xlSheet.Cells(1, adoRecordset.Fields.Count)).Font.Bold = True
    xlSheet.Range("A2").CopyFromRecordset adoRecordset
End With

'Close the Recordset
```

```
adoRecordset.Close

'Cleanup variables
Set adoRecordset = Nothing
Set oAdoConnect = Nothing
Set xlSheet = Nothing
Set xlWorkbook = Nothing
Set xlApp = Nothing
Exit Sub

Handler:
MsgBox _
    "An Error Occurred!" & vbNewLine & vbNewLine & _
    "Error Number: " & Err.Number & vbNewLine & vbNewLine & _
    "Error Message: " & vbNewLine & Err.Description & vbNewLine & vbNewLine & _
    "Error Source: " & Err.Source, vbOKOnly, "Error"
Exit Sub
```

Most of the code in this example should look pretty familiar because it was used earlier in this chapter. The only major difference is that in this case, an ADO `Recordset` is used to gather the data from the database. Although the ADO `Recordset` is similar to the DAO `Recordset` used previously, a connection to the ADO `Recordset` can be created by calling the `CreateObject` method, just like when creating an instance of one of the Office application objects. (To learn mode about ADO, please refer to Chapter 7.)

No matter how you choose to utilize other Office applications in your VBA code, it is sure to dazzle users with the rich feature set afforded from any Access application.

Summary

Throughout this chapter, a variety of examples that use VBA to transfer information between Microsoft Access and other Office applications were covered. This chapter outlined sending information to Outlook, creating a mail merge in Word, and exporting a query to an Excel spreadsheet. Additionally, some code utilizing multiple Office applications was presented to show the ease of working with data through several applications, such as Access, Excel, and PowerPoint as the same time. Using all three applications together to accomplish a seemingly impossible task is done easily and with very few lines of code. Although this code might not perform the exact operations desired for your application, the concepts, methods, and code samples included within this chapter provide a starting point for further development.

These code samples make extensive use of the Object Models of each Office application. The key to making these models work is to understand the various objects and methods needed for the target application. Fortunately, along with all of the powerful functionality discussed in this chapter, Office 2007 also provides a comprehensive set of Help files with more information about all of the objects that can be manipulated through VBA code. Do not be afraid to explore the elaborate functionality for each of the Office 2007 programs, I think you'll find they can be extremely advantageous in any Access application.

17

Working with SharePoint

The fastest growing business software product in the Microsoft family, Windows SharePoint Services is one of the hottest technologies for digital team site management available today. Flexible and easy to use, SharePoint provides users with simple site creation and design, robust content management, and powerful security for business data. Microsoft Office 2007 contains a myriad of new features that integrate with SharePoint to help users communicate information, and one of the pillars of the Access 2007 release is to provide seamless integration with SharePoint.

Access has added new features that fit into two basic categories: features that work from the server and features that work from within the Access client. Starting with the 2003 release, the Microsoft Office teams began a campaign to support content management on SharePoint for site design, online documents, and list data. In many cases, that could be done directly from within the Office application, such as from an Access database, a Word document, or an Excel workbook. Users of Office System 2003 may remember some of the features that Access offered to users, such as Edit in Datasheet or Access Linked Tables. While both of these features are powerful, they pale in comparison to the new features in Microsoft Office Access 2007.

This chapter describes how features of Microsoft Windows SharePoint Services 3.0 integrate with Access 2007. Interestingly, most of the features are so tightly coupled with SharePoint that you do not even need code to leverage them within your Access database solution. All of the SharePoint features in Access 2003 are still available in 2007. While there is not a lot of new VBA code available for working with the SharePoint features programmatically, a number of method and property additions and a few updates to existing OM methods are of interest.

If you don't already have access to a Windows Server with SharePoint Services 3.0, get access to one! SharePoint 3.0 has a number of system requirements, the heaviest of which is that it can be deployed only on Windows Server 2003 or Windows Vista Server. If you do not have a copy of either version of Windows Server, evaluation copies are available at `http://microsoft.com/windows/default.mspx`; those will allow full access to the product for evaluation purposes for 180 days. Once you have access to a Windows Server machine, Windows SharePoint Services can be deployed. Note that Microsoft Office Server System 2007 is a different product, which provides rich server features and additional enterprise-level applications that are built on top of the SharePoint technology. For more information and content downloads for SharePoint, go to: `http://office.microsoft.com/en-us/sharepointtechnology/default.aspx` and `http://microsoft.com/technet/windowsserver/sharepoint/default.mspx`. This chapter focuses on the base SharePoint product features and how they relate to Access. Fortunately, all of the Access 2007 features work just as well with other applications built on top of other SharePoint technologies.

Overview

At its highest level description, a SharePoint site is nothing more than a Web site designed to help users collaborate and communication information. In reality, a SharePoint site is much more than that. A SharePoint site is more like the framework for a living digital library that allows users to create many different Web interfaces to share information such as new sites, pages, lists, data views, charts, document libraries, blogs, applications, and much, much more. Users can store and retain information as well as quickly build new sub-sites, lists, views, charts, document libraries, and so on, with, in most cases, just a few clicks and a couple of keystrokes. Using Office integration, supported document types such as Word documents and Excel workbooks can be edited and even versioned, directly on the server, using the Web interface provided by SharePoint. As for Access 2007, some of the most powerful database applications can be built and integrated directly into SharePoint with extremely minimal effort from the developer.

The Access 2007 features for SharePoint 3.0 break out into two categories: features available on the SharePoint Server and the features used from within an Access application. Some of these features were available in the Access 2003, but many are all new in Access 2007. The following table provides a brief description of the Access 2007 features for SharePoint 2007 that you'll explore in this chapter.

Feature	Description
Access Web Datasheet	Enables the user to edit SharePoint lists in the Access Datasheet in the Internet browser window. Also provides the Datasheet task pane for interacting with both Access and Excel.
Open with Access	When Access 2007 is installed, the Open with Access button on the Actions menu of a SharePoint list enables the user to quickly open the list in a new instance of an Access database. The list can be either imported or linked. Access 2007 also provides three Access application templates for select SharePoint list types.
Access Views on SharePoint	When an Access application has been migrated and published, you have the option to publish the views (Forms and Reports) as links in the SharePoint View menu for the list. When the user selects one of the Access view links from the View menu, the published Access application is invoked and the view opens.
Importing from SharePoint	SharePoint lists and data can be imported into tables in a database. In Access 2007, the Access Connectivity Engine (ACE) fully supports complex data, attachment fields, and even append-only memo fields imported from SharePoint. There are several methods for importing tables, both in the GUI and via code.

Feature	Description
Linked Tables to SharePoint	The SharePoint ISAM (Indexed Sequential Access Method) allows Access to create connections to specific lists on the site. These tables can be linked full time, or even taken offline, modified, and then resynchronized at a later time. Linked SharePoint lists can be the heart of robust client-server applications.
SharePoint Table Templates	Enables the user to create standard Access Table templates that are immediately linked to SharePoint when created.
Migrate Data to SharePoint	Can be applied to an Access application to migrate the tables and data to a SharePoint server. This creates linked tables in the application to the migrated lists and removes the original tables from the database. It is typically used when an application is ready to be upsized to a server environment.
Publish Database to SharePoint	Enables the user to upload Access databases to a document library on the SharePoint server. Then the application can be opened from the library and used in an online fashion, so that users can read and modify data in Access forms and view data in reports.
Workflow Integration	New in Access 2007 is direct access to SharePoint workflow configuration UI, providing the capability to start workflows from within the Access client and will display a list of all active tasks for an owner. However, because this feature is mainly UI-related, it isn't discussed further in this chapter.

Access Web Datasheet, Open with Access, Importing from SharePoint, and Access Views on SharePoint are all Access features that are available from the SharePoint user interface. The last five features detailed in the preceding table — Linked Tables to SharePoint, SharePoint Templates, Migrate Data, Publish Database, and Workflow — are all features that can be used directly from the Access application. The remainder of this chapter tackles both entry points.

To get the code and support files, please see the sample files for this chapter of the book. This chapter has several examples of database applications with tables that are linked to SharePoint. In these cases, the lists will be taken offline so that the sample applications can still be used, although you will not have access to the SharePoint site to which the applications are linked.

You'll find the samples for this chapter in the chapter's download file.

Access Features on SharePoint

Access 2007 has four features for SharePoint that have entry points from within the SharePoint user interface: the Access Web Datasheet, the Open with Access button on SharePoint list Actions menu, Import from SharePoint, and Access Views on SharePoint. While Open in Access and Access Views from SharePoint are new to Access 2007, the Access Web Datasheet and Importing from SharePoint were both available in Access 2003, although the features were somewhat more limited in scope.

Access 2003 was the first release of Access to support any SharePoint integration. This SharePoint support was provided by the owssupp.dll, which is installed and registered on the default installation of Microsoft Office System 2003. Once this DLL was installed, the Access Web Datasheet could be used from within Internet Explorer to edit SharePoint lists. Importing from or linking to a SharePoint List could be completed by using the Access Web Datasheet Task Pane options.

The same is true with Access 2007. By default, the owssupp.dll is installed in the Office program files directory when Microsoft Office 2007 Professional is installed. However, if desired, you can choose not to install the owssupp.dll component during the installation process by selecting the Not Installed option in Office 2007 installer ⇨ Office Tools node ⇨ Windows SharePoint Services components ⇨ Microsoft Office Access Web Datasheet Component.

There is no Install on First Use option — the owssupp.dll *component is either installed or it is not. Of course, if not installed, the DLL can always be added at a later time.*

Access Web Datasheet

Probably one of the most well-known Access features on SharePoint, the Access Web Datasheet allows users to edit SharePoint lists in a datasheet gird on the Web form. Users can add, modify, or delete data stored on the SharePoint server directly from their Internet browsers. The benefits to the user are a rich data editing experience and the capability to add, modify, and delete multiple records at the same time, in a single view. The Access Web Datasheet feature has two components: the Access Web Datasheet and the Access Web Datasheet Task pane.

Edit in Datasheet

Edit in Datasheet is a feature that will be used by people editing a list through the SharePoint user interface. In SharePoint 3.0, clicking the Actions menu reveals a button called Edit in Datasheet (if Access 2007 is installed on the machine). When that button is clicked, the page is refreshed and the list is displayed in the Access Web Datasheet grid. For a Windows SharePoint Services version 2.0 site, the Edit in Datasheet button is on the Lists button bar.

While Edit in Datasheet is a user feature that is integrated directly into the SharePoint site, a developer can still force the datasheet to be used when a SharePoint page is navigated to. In the SharePoint Create View page for any list is an option called Datasheet View. When creating a view from that option, the results are shown in the Access Web Datasheet. That means anyone navigating to the view will see his results in the datasheet and he can use the Access Web Datasheet's rich editing capabilities. Of course, this requires that the user have Access installed on his machine; otherwise, he'll be required to navigate to another view for the list to view the data.

Additionally, any view created on SharePoint can be set as the default view for any given SharePoint list. A standard list is created with All Items as the default view. The All Items view is simply a list of all of the items stored in the list, hence its name. However, any view — datasheet or otherwise — can be specified as the default view for any SharePoint list. Setting a datasheet view as the default view means anyone who navigates to the page will see the SharePoint list in the Access Web Datasheet.

Datasheet Task Pane

One feature tied directly to the Access Web Datasheet is the Access Web Datasheet Task pane. Collapsed by default, the pane can be found on the right side of the Web Datasheet for any SharePoint List. It exposes three entry points for features related to Access — importing, linking, and creating Access views for the SharePoint list — as well as four entry points for Excel features for creating: charts, pivot tables, querying a list, and printing a list. Only the Access-related features are discussed in this section, but it's definitely worth noting the Excel features provided by the Task Pane — just another way Microsoft Office provides seamless integration between applications.

Track this List in Access

The Track this List in Access feature is a quick link that enables the user to open the list in a new or existing database. Choosing this option always creates a SharePoint linked table to the list in the database. This feature is designed as an easy way to create a SharePoint linked table in an Access database, directly from the SharePoint list.

Introduced in Access 2003, the Track this List in Access link, was originally called Create Linked Table In Access. Access 2003 users will see the Create Linked Table In Access link in the task pane for both SharePoint 2003 or 2007 lists. However, Track this List in Access and Create Linked Table In Access perform the same functionality: a linked table is created in a new or existing database.

When a SharePoint list is created in an Access database using Track this List in Access, Access uses the credentials of the user who is logged into the SharePoint site. If the SharePoint site uses NT Authentication, the next time the SharePoint linked table is accessed in the database, the current Windows user's credentials are needed to retrieve or update the data in the list. If the credentials are not valid, the user is prompted for a username and password. In cases when the list is linked to an external SharePoint site that uses credentials different than the current Windows user's, the user is always required to input credentials for the SharePoint site containing the list for the linked table.

Export to Access

The Export to Access link in the Web Datasheet Task pane provides the user with a quick interface for exporting SharePoint list data to a database file. As with Track this List in Access, the Export to Access link enables the user to choose either a new or an existing database file. This is one of many entry points for the Importing from SharePoint feature in Access, the details of which are discussed later in this chapter. For now, just be aware that the Export to Access link is an entry point for importing data into an Access database.

Report with Access

The Report with Access link in the Web Datasheet Task pane provides the user with an entry point for quickly creating Access views. As with the preceding two links in the task pane, the user has the option to create a new or choose an existing database. Once the database file has been selected, a new linked table is created in the database for the SharePoint list. In addition, a new report is created and opened in Layout view mode for the user to work with. Clicking the Report with Access link is equivalent to creating a link to a SharePoint table, selecting it in the Navigation pane, and then creating a new report based upon the linked table.

Open with Access

New to Microsoft Office 2007, the Open with Access button is available on the Actions menu, now available in SharePoint 3.0 lists. The Open with Access feature enables the user to create a linked table to a SharePoint list or to simply import the list directly. Choosing Open with Access for specific types of SharePoint lists, Access will create a database application template based upon the SharePoint list. As you will see shortly, these templates provide a nice simple example of exactly how an Access application can be created against a SharePoint server. The Open with Access button provides a highly visible entry point for creating linked tables in an Access database to the SharePoint list.

It's important to understand the differences between linking to the list and importing the list. When the tables are linked to a SharePoint list, which is the default behavior for Open with Access, any changes made to the data in the table are pushed up to the SharePoint server. On the other hand, because an imported table resides in the new database, changes to the imported table or its data remain in the local database, and the SharePoint list remains unaffected. You'll examine linked and imported tables for SharePoint a little later in the chapter.

Windows SharePoint Services 2.0 does not have the concept of a dynamic Actions menu, so Open with Access is not available for older versions of SharePoint, which means that Open with Access is not available on SharePoint 2.0 when Microsoft Office 2007 is installed on the machine, even though the Access Web Datasheet and associated features are available. The Windows SharePoint Services 2.0 button bar has been replaced by the Actions menu in SharePoint 3.0. In addition to Open with Access, the Actions menu also provides entry points to several features integrated with other Office applications, such as Excel and Visio. The Actions menu is an extremely useful feature that is available only in SharePoint 3.0.

Access Application Templates for SharePoint

As part of the new Access database template features, Access 2007 provides three custom application templates that correspond to three distinct SharePoint list templates. Specifically, these Access applications map the SharePoint Contacts, Tasks, and Issues Tracking lists. When Open with Access is invoked for any of these standard SharePoint lists, and the linked tables option (the default) is chosen, the new database is created as a fully functioning Access application, complete with forms and reports. These templates are designed to provide an example, as well as a starting point, for creating rich Access applications that are tightly bound to a SharePoint data source.

The three Access SharePoint applications are fairly uniform, each with some subtle differences. The beauty of these applications is that they are fully functioning, even when Access is in high macro security mode and all code and unsafe macros are disabled. That is because they rely on safe macros and other built-in Access features to provide all functionality.

When the Open with Access button is clicked for one of these SharePoint list types, the Open in Microsoft Access dialog box is invoked, requesting the name and path for the database, as well as whether the SharePoint tables should be linked or imported. If the linked table option is selected and a new database name is entered (which is the default), then the Access SharePoint template will be invoked and the Access application will be created. However, if an existing database is chosen for the linked tables, only the tables and data will be linked into the existing database and the Access template will not actually be created. For the import option, with either a new or existing database name, only the tables and data for the SharePoint list will be imported, so the template will not be created in this case either.

Access SharePoint Contacts Template

Probably the simplest of the three Access SharePoint templates, the Contacts template complements the SharePoint contacts list very well. The Contacts application has two tables: the contacts table (which is actually the name of the SharePoint list the database was created from) and the User Information List, which is discussed later in the chapter. The User Information Table is not really used in this template, but it is pulled down automatically because of the way Access creates Linked Tables to SharePoint . In addition to the two tables linked to the SharePoint site, the Contacts application also includes a query, two forms, and two reports.

When the Contacts template is created, the Contact list form opens and shows all of the Contacts in the SharePoint list in a list view, by using the Split Form feature that is also new to Access 2007. Notice the various buttons along the top of the list: New Contact, Collect Data via e-mail, Add From Outlook, e-mail List, Reports, Site Recycle Bin, and Open Default View. Each of these buttons enables the user to work with data contained in the list. For example, Add From Outlook allows the user to add contacts from an Outlook Address book directly into the template, one at a time or in bulk. Similarly, the Collect Data via e-mail button leverages the Data Collection feature, also new to Access 2007, to send a specialized data collection e-mail to gather data for the SharePoint list.

> *The Data Collection feature requires that the database not be open in Exclusive mode when Outlook tries to add or update the records in the database. When a template is created in Access, the session will be opened in Exclusive mode; thus the database will need to be closed and reopened in Shared mode before the data collected from e-mail responses can be updated by Outlook.*

Double-clicking on any contact's name in the list opens the Contact Details form. That form exposes the fields in the contacts table so that the user can see all of the default fields in the standard contacts list. If the creator of the contacts table on the SharePoint site has modified the schema of the original list created from the template, the fields on this form may not map correctly to the actual fields in the resulting table and will need to be manually updated by the user.

Finally, the two reports included in the Contacts template provide two different views of the Contacts data. The reports, Address Book and Phone List, as their names suggest, provide an address list for the Contacts, grouped by the first letter of the contact's last name and a list of phone numbers, also grouped by the first letter of the contact's last name. The Access SharePoint Contacts template is easy to use and provides some conventional elements for a commonly used SharePoint data schema.

Access SharePoint Tasks Template

Slightly more complex than the Contacts template, the Access SharePoint Tasks template enables the user to work with the standard SharePoint Tasks list and data in a simple Access database application. One of the major differences between the Tasks and the Contacts templates is that Tasks employs the User Information List as a lookup table for the Assigned To field in the list. That means the users of the SharePoint site can be assigned to the task, which, if configured for that list, automatically sends the user an e-mail informing him of the new task assignment. The Tasks template is a great example of creating an application that works with multiple SharePoint lists that have a relationship to one another.

> *The User Information List cannot be updated from an Access database because that would modify the users of the SharePoint site itself. All users must be added through interfaces available via the SharePoint site.*

The Tasks application has several more forms and reports, such as a User Information List form and a Tasks List form, which function like the Contact List form discussed earlier. Double-clicking any Task or User opens the respective Details form for the record, providing the user with access to all of the fields in the SharePoint list. The User Information Details form has a second tab for showing all of the tasks assigned to the specific user.

Access SharePoint Issue Tracking Template

The Access SharePoint Issue Tracking template is the most complex of the three templates, and it shows what some of the new features are capable of in Access 2007. This template is much like the standalone Issues database template that is included with Access, except that it is linked to a SharePoint site and instead of having a Contacts table, it uses the User Information List for the contact information. This tightly binds the users of the site to the issues that have been entered in the list, much like the Tasks template. Additionally, the Issue Tracking template demonstrates working with Multi-Valued Lookup, Append Only, and Column History fields. The Issue Tracking database application is robust and feature rich.

Take a closer look at the Related Issues field in the Issues table. It is nothing more than a multi-valued field with a lookup back to the table's ID field; essentially the table contains a lookup field back to itself. This allows any record in the table to be related to multiple other records in this same table.

Using the AppendOnly Property

Append-only fields are available in SharePoint linked tables as well as native Access tables. To provide the append-only functionality, the Issue Tracking application simply employs the `AppendOnly` property on the Memo field type. When the `AppendOnly` property is set to `True`, any change to the data is concatenated on the previous value, instead of replacing the previous value. This property is an excellent way to ensure that the history of the data in a table's field is preserved in the database.

In either the SharePoint Issues template or the standalone Issues template, type a few words into the New Comment box on the Comments tab of the Issues Details form and close the form. Repeat this several times. You should notice that there are a bunch of different values stored in the History field in this form. If the Comments field in the Issues table is viewed directly, the user sees only the most recent entry for the fields and no previous entries. The same is true when the field data is retrieved via code — only the most recent data entered into the field will be returned.

Using the ColumnHistory Method

The `ColumnHistory` method is a member of the Application object. It enables you to retrieve the full data history for an Append Only field. The `AppendOnly` field property is available only for the Memo data type and can be set to `True` in the table properties. The `ColumnHistory` method takes three parameters: `TableName`, `ColumnName`, and `QueryString`, each of which is required.

`TableName` obviously takes the name of the table that contains the Append Only field and the `ColumnName` is the name of the Append Only field itself. However, the `QueryString` parameter is really the where condition for the SQL statement, without the WHERE SQL keyword. This type of parameter is common in functions throughout the Access Object Model and is often referred to as the filter string. Using the `ColumnHistory` function requires all three parameters to be passed to the function, which means that the field data history can be returned for only one record at a time.

For example, the `ColumnHistory` method could be called to retrieve the `ColumnHistory` string of a given record in the Comments field of the Issues table:

```
Function GetCommentHistoryForRecord(iRecordId As Integer) As String

    ' Return the ColumnHistory data for the "Comments" field
    GetCommentHistoryForRecord = _
        Application.ColumnHistory( _
            "Issues", _
            "Comments", _
            "[ID]=" & iRecordId)

End Function
```

As in the SharePoint Issues database case, the `ColumnHistory` function can be tied directly to the `RecordSource` property of a Text Box control in a form or report. Because the function is marked as a Safe Macro, `ColumnHistory` will run when tied to the `RecordSource` for the control, without requiring code be enabled in the application. In the Issue Details form, the `TableName` parameter actually is passed as the `RecordSource` property for the form. The `TableName` parameter accepts any table or query that returns a Memo field type. The `ColumnHistory` method is quite powerful when working with Append Only fields in either a SharePoint list or native Access tables.

Creating SharePoint Templates with the NewCurrentDatabase Method

One of the updates to the existing Access Object Model is to the `NewCurrentDatabase` method. In previous versions of Access, `NewCurrentDatabase` was used to create a new database and open it in an instance of the Access client that did not already have a database currently open. In Access 2007, `NewCurrentDatabase` supports a number of new scenarios.

The `NewCurrentDatabase` method is a member of the Application object. In previous versions of Access, this method took only one parameter — the filename and path to the new database that is to be created. In Access 2007, `NewCurrentDatabase` takes five parameters. In addition to creating a new database, you can also create a database from an application template, a database linked to a SharePoint list, or even one of the built-in SharePoint templates linked to a SharePoint site. The following table describes each of the parameters available for `NewCurrentDatabase` in Access 2007.

Parameter	Description
`filePath`	Required. The full name and path for the database that will be created. If the database already exists, the `NewCurrentDatabase` method will fail.
`FileFormat`	The version of database that will be created, as defined by the `AcNew-DatabaseFormat` enumeration. Three database version types are available: Access 2007 file format (ACCDB), Access 2002-2003 file format (MDB), and Access 2000 file format (MDB). Optional; if not supplied, the database created will be the default file format selected in the Access Options on the Popular tab. The same is true if the Default Format member of the enumeration is passed. However, in Access 2007, the database templates can be created only in the ACCDB file format.

Table continues on the next page

Parameter	Description
Template	The full file path to the Access 2007 Database Template (ACCDT) file. This can be either a standalone database template or a template for an application linked to SharePoint. Optional, but if supplied, a new database from the template will be created in the instance of Access.
SiteAddress	Specifies the URL path to the SharePoint site that a new database or template will be created and linked to. The parameter should be passed in the format http://MySharePointSite. Optional; if passed with the Template and ListID parameters, it will create a SharePoint database template linked to the new database.
ListID	Specifies the GUID list ID for the list on the SharePoint site. Optional; if passed with the Template and SiteAddress parameters, it creates a SharePoint database template linked to the new database. The format should be a string like: {5604F321-4F9F-481B-AF53-C1D795EE2398}.

These parameters provide all of the information needed to create new databases, databases with linked tables, and databases from templates. Here's an example of creating the Access SharePoint Issue tracking templates linked to a SharePoint site:

```
Sub CreateSharePointLinkedTemplate()

    ' Define Variables
    Dim accessApp As New Access.Application

    ' Create a new instance of the Access SharePoint Issues template
    accessApp.Visible = True
    accessApp.NewCurrentDatabase _
        "C:\SharePointTemplate.accdb", _
        acNewDatabaseFormatAccess2007, _
        "C:\Program Files\Microsoft Office\Templates\1033\Access\WSS\1100.accdt", _
        "http://MySharePointSite/", _
        "{5604F321-4F9F-481B-AF53-C1D795EE2398}"

    ' Clean up
    accessApp.CloseCurrentDatabase
    Set accessApp = Nothing

End Sub
```

Of course, the URL and the GUID used in the last two parameters of this NewCurrentDatabase call need to be updated to the specific SharePoint site settings before the code works with your site.

A quick method for getting the GUID for a given SharePoint list is to decipher it from the URL. The list's List Settings page shows the GUID for the list in the Address bar for Internet Explorer. However, the non-hexadecimal characters are encoded in the URL, and you will need to reconstruct the GUID, removing any encoded characters.

Although the Access SharePoint templates can be created with Linked Tables To SharePoint sites, only specific templates corresponding to the specific list types will work in this case — the `1100.accdt` file corresponds to the SharePoint Issue Tracking list, the `107.accdt` corresponds to the SharePoint Tasks list, and the `105.accdt` corresponds to the SharePoint Contacts list. Although these template filenames seem arbitrary, the numbers actually correspond to the SharePoint list template ID for which they will be created. That's how the Open with Access feature maps the particular list type to the correct Access database template. Aside from these three SharePoint lists, linking database templates to other SharePoint lists is not supported by `NewCurrentDatabase`.

As noted in the chapter for the Access Developers Extensions, the standalone Access database templates can be created by a developer using the Save as Template feature. Unfortunately, creating templates that are linked to SharePoint is not supported by Save as Template or by Access 2007.

Open with Access for Non-Template Linked Lists

Using Open with Access for any SharePoint list types other than the Issue Tracking, Tasks, and Contacts lists and choosing linked tables will simply create new linked tables in a new database or, if chosen, an existing database. When completing this operation, the user always gets two lists: the primary list from which the Open with Access option was invoked and the User Information List, which describes information about the users of the SharePoint site. These linked tables are standard SharePoint linked tables and are discussed further later in this chapter.

As noted earlier, the `NewCurrentDatabase` object model allows creation of a database with tables linked to a SharePoint site. To do this, simply call `NewCurrentDatabase` without the `Template` parameter. The following code illustrates the creation of a new database with tables linked to SharePoint:

```
Sub CreateSharePointLinkedDatabaseTemplate()

    ' Define Variables
    Dim accessApp As New Access.Application

    ' Create a new instance of the Access SharePoint Issues template
    accessApp.Visible = True
    accessApp.NewCurrentDatabase _
        "C:\SharePointTemplate.accdb", _
        acNewDatabaseFormatAccess2007, , _
        "http://MySharePointSite/", _
        "{5604F321-4F9F-481B-AF53-C1D795EE2398}"

    ' Clean up
    accessApp.CloseCurrentDatabase
    Set accessApp = Nothing

End Sub
```

As with the first `NewCurrentDatabase` code example, the URL and the GUID need to be updated to the specific SharePoint site and list settings before this code will work with your SharePoint site.

Notice that an ACCDB file format database was created. Creating these linked tables in an MDB file format is supported by Access 2007 as well. However, certain features, such as Complex Data, Attachments,

Append Only fields, and any other feature not supported in the MDB file format, will be treated differently. Creating linked tables to an MDB file is discussed later in this chapter.

Importing from SharePoint

An exceptionally useful feature in Access is the capability to import table data and schema directly from a SharePoint list. There are a number of methods for importing this information, such as the Export to Access link in the Web Datasheet Task pane and the Open in Access feature, as noted earlier. Using VBA code, it's easy to import data from a SharePoint list programmatically. Also, there are a couple of approaches for importing data directly from SharePoint within the Access client. This section explores importing SharePoint 3.0 list schema and data into an Access database.

Importing from SharePoint 3.0 into an ACCDB

Fortunately, Access supports most of the data types that SharePoint 3.0 supports, such as Complex Data and Attachment fields. However, there are some differences about how data is imported for certain types of fields, such as Lookup or Person or Group type fields. Additionally, there are a number of fields that are not shown in either the Default View or the Column Settings page that are imported along with the rest of the fields in the list. When importing lists from SharePoint, it is important to understand how these fields are treated by Access and exactly what fields in the table are created.

Because there are a couple of SharePoint data types that are converted during import, take a look at how Access treats each of the types. The following table describes the data types for SharePoint and the Access type that the SharePoint type is imported as.

SharePoint 3.0 Data Type	Access Data Type After Import into an ACCDB
Single Line of Text	Text — No change.
Multiple Lines of Text	Memo — The standard Rich Text setting is persisted into the imported table. However, SharePoint provides two types of rich text: Rich Text and Enhanced Rich Text. Enhanced Rich Text fields support some HTML tags that are not supported by Rich Text fields in Access. The normal Rich Text fields are recommended when creating a SharePoint list that will be used with an Access database solution.
Choice	Text — The values for the choices are imported into the Row Source property for the imported field, and the RowSourceType property is set to Value List.
Number	Number — Double precision; no change.
Data and Time	Date/Time — No change.
Currency	Currency — The Format and DecimalPlaces properties are persisted.
Lookup	Memo — The display values for the lookup are inserted into the imported table instead of a second lookup table being created.

SharePoint 3.0 Data Type	Access Data Type After Import into an ACCDB
Yes/No	Yes/No — No change.
Person or Group	Memo — The display values for the lookup are inserted into the imported table instead of a second lookup table being created.
Hyperlink or Picture	Hyperlink — The data is imported as a link to the image file.
Calculated	Dependent upon the type that the column returns. Once the field has been imported, only the display values for the Calculated field are imported and the table in Access no longer calculates this field.
Multiple Value Fields	Complex Data fields of the same type.
Attachment Fields	Attachment — No change.
Append Only Fields	Memo — With the `AppendOnly` property set to False. Only the value for the last edit is persisted during the import.

In addition to any tables created by the user, a standard custom template includes a number of additional fields that are imported automatically: ID, Encoded Absolute URL, Item Type, Path, URL Path, and Workflow Instance ID. The ID field is imported as an AutoNumber field and can be used for the primary key for the table. The rest are imported as Text fields.

The ACCDB file format supports importing the schema and data from SharePoint well. Almost every SharePoint field type is supported, except for Enhanced Rich Text and Calculated field type, in the same format in which it's stored on SharePoint. While MDB database files also support importing tables from SharePoint 3.0, a developer should be aware of several more data conversions when importing a SharePoint list.

Importing from SharePoint 3.0 into an MDB

While the Access MDB file formats do support importing SharePoint 3.0 lists, there are a few more field types that will be converted when imported. For example, complex data and attachments are not supported in the MDB file format and therefore cannot be imported into an MDB as those data types. The following table compares the SharePoint 3.0 data types to the Access data types after conversion when importing into an MDB file.

SharePoint 3.0 Data Type	Access Data Type After Import into an MDB
Single Line of Text	Text — No change.
Multiple Lines of Text	Memo — Rich Text setting is not persisted in to the imported table because it is not supported in the MDB file format.

Table continues on the next page

SharePoint 3.0 Data Type	Access Data Type After Import into an MDB
Choice	Text — Values for the choices are also imported into the Row Source property for the imported field.
Number	Number — Double precision; no change.
Data and Time	Date/Time — No change.
Currency	Currency — The `Format` and `DecimalPlaces` properties will be persisted.
Lookup	Memo — Display values for the lookup are inserted into the imported table instead of a second lookup table being created.
Yes/No	Yes/No — No change.
Person or Group	Memo — Display values for the lookup are inserted into the imported table instead of a second lookup table being created.
Hyperlink or Picture	Hyperlink — Data is imported as a link, or a link to the image file.
Calculated	Dependent upon the type that the column returns. Once the field has been imported, only the display values for the Calculated field are imported and the table in Access no longer calculates this field.
Multiple Value Fields	Memo — Because Complex Data is not supported in the MDB file format, the data is imported as a comma-separated list for each of the values selected.
Attachment Fields	Yes/No — Because Attachment fields are not supported in am MDB, the field is converted to a Yes/No field. The value of this field corresponds to whether the record had an attachment in the original SharePoint list.
Append Only Fields	Memo — With the `AppendOnly` property set to False. Only the value for the last edit is persisted during the import.

When importing into an MDB from a SharePoint 3.0 list, multiple value fields are converted to Memo data type fields and there is a loss in granularity for each individual option that was selected. Still, the full data set that was stored in the original multiple value field is present, only it is groups in the new Memo field and each individual value is separated by commas. Probably the biggest loss in functionality when importing into an MDB is the Attachment field conversion, because that particular field is converted to a Yes/No field type in Access. Otherwise, there is not much of a difference between importing into an ACCDB file and an MDB file. Even with these field conversions, importing data from SharePoint into an MDB file is extremely easy.

TransferSharePointList Object Model

Aside from being able to import data into Access from the SharePoint entry point, a developer can also leverage some Access Object Model functions available for importing data from SharePoint. Specifically, the `TransferSharePointList` method allows a developer to either import or link to a SharePoint list programmatically. `TransferSharePointList` is a method of the `DoCmd` class, which is a member of the `Application` object. `TransferSharePointList` takes up to six arguments, three of which are required. The following table describes each of these arguments.

Parameter	Description
TransferType	Requires a member of the enumeration type `AcShare-PointListTransferType`. Two options are available: `acImportSharePointList` and `acLinkSharePointList`.
SiteAddress	The full URL path to the SharePoint site. This parameter is required.
ListID	The Name or the GUID of the list to be transferred. This parameter is required.
ViewID	The GUID of the view that should be imported. This means that imported data can be pre-filtered by a specific list view on SharePoint before pulling the data into Access. This parameter is optional and not available for when the `acImportShare-PointList` option is chosen for the Transfer type. If not specified, all of the fields on the SharePoint site will be retrieved.
TableName	The name of the new linked table in the database. This parameter is optional and not available for when the `acImportSharePointList` option is chosen for the Transfer type. If not specified, the name of the SharePoint list will be used for the new table in the database.
GetLookupDisplayValues	When false, any lookup fields will contain the IDs to the list to which the lookup is tied. When `True`, the actual display values will be imported. This parameter is optional and not available for when the `acImportSharePointList` option is chosen for the Transfer type.

Importing SharePoint data into an Access database is extremely easy to do. Just remember that when importing data, only the first three parameters (the non-optional parameters) to the `TransferSharePointList` method can be supplied; otherwise, an error message is raised when the code runs. Here's an example of a simple subroutine for importing a list from SharePoint:

```
Sub ImportSharePointList()

    ' Call TransferSharePointList to import the data
    Application.DoCmd.TransferSharePointList _
```

```
            acLinkSharePointList, _
            "http://MySharePointSite/", _
            "Tasks"

End Sub
```

Writing code for a single import operation may not be cost effective or the easier way for a user to import SharePoint lists into a database. In addition to the entry points for creating an import table in Access from the SharePoint site, there is also a user interface for importing a SharePoint list from within the Access UI.

Importing Through the Access User Interface

Although this section of the chapter is devoted to discussing operations that are available on a Share-Point site, let's briefly discuss the import options available directly in the Access client. Importing data into Access is simple and fast, and the import operation parameters can even be saved for future imports. When any database is open in the Access 2007 client window (and the standard Ribbon options have not been disabled), the user sees a tab called External Data. That tab allows the user to work with all different kinds of Import (and Export) options and provides a collection of all of these entry points. Importing a SharePoint list can be done with just a few simple clicks using the features that the Access user interface provides.

To import a SharePoint list, click the External Data tab on the Ribbon. The fourth button from the right is the SharePoint List button, which invokes the Get External Data Wizard. The wizard enables you to import or link data from SharePoint in three easy steps. Its first page shows both the Link and Import options that are available as well as any sites from which lists have previously been imported. By default, the Linked Table option is selected, so be sure to switch this when importing. The user can select one of the previously imported lists, or provide the full URL path to a new site. The URL should be entered in the following format:

```
http://www.MySharePointSite.com/
```

Once a site has been selected, click Next. The second page of the wizard simply allows you to select any lists on the site to import or link. Then click OK, and the list is imported or linked. The wizard's last page enables you to save the import steps if desired. Otherwise, click the Close button and focus returns to the Access client window. The new tables are imported from the specified SharePoint site.

So far you've looked at the various Access 2007 feature available from a SharePoint 3.0 site. The Access Web Datasheet, Open with Access, and the Import features for Access 2007 have all been discussed. While each of these features is powerful and easy to use, the true developer features are those that can be utilized continuously in an Access database solution, such as Linked Tables To SharePoint. The rest of this chapter focuses on the SharePoint features available from within the Access client and an Access database application.

SharePoint Features in Access

Microsoft Office Access 2007 features a slew of new toys for working with SharePoint lists. The introduction of multi-valued lookups and attachment field support allows Access to work with

SharePoint Multiple Value and Attachment columns much more seamlessly. Several new features have been added, such as Published Databases and Access Views on SharePoint to allow database applications to quickly and easily integrate with SharePoint. There are a number of Object Model updates and feature additions for developers to leverage in an Access database solution, some of which have already been discussed. Access 2007 database applications can finally leverage SharePoint as it was meant to be used.

Linked Tables to SharePoint

Linked Tables to SharePoint is probably the most commonly used SharePoint feature in Access database solutions. It provides the database with virtual tables, which update data on the specified SharePoint site, directly from within the database solution. The SharePoint ISAM provides the interface for Access to connect directly to SharePoint. SharePoint linked tables can be used just like native Access tables, except that the Schema cannot be modified in Access or through VBA code, and the actual data in the table is stored on the SharePoint site. When the tables are in offline mode, the data is copied to Access local storage. SharePoint linked tables can be extraordinarily useful in building Access applications for groups that collaborate using a SharePoint site.

There are several methods for creating linked tables to SharePoint. You've already examined the entry points for creating linked tables directly from a SharePoint site: Open in Access, Track this List in Access, and the Access Views features. In addition, you can create linked tables through the Access UI in much the same way as importing SharePoint lists in the Get External Data Wizard. For developers, there is an object model for dynamically creating linked tables to a SharePoint list, which is done through the `TransferSharePointList` function. Before exploring all of the ways to create a table linked to a SharePoint site, you should first examine the repercussions for linked tables in both the ACCDB and the MDB file formats.

While both ACCDB and MDB files support linked tables to SharePoint, there are some differences between the two formats in how certain SharePoint field types can be used. If you're using the MDB file format, take great care when designing SharePoint List schema because several SharePoint data types are unsupported.

SharePoint Linked Tables in an ACCDB

The ACCDB file format has improved Linked Tables To SharePoint to an unmatched level of support compared to any other database product. Linked tables in Access support all SharePoint data types, including multiple value fields, attachment fields, append-only fields, and rich text fields.

Probably the biggest difference between importing and linking tables to SharePoint lists is that all Lookup tables are automatically created as linked tables when the primary linked table is created. Additionally, Person or Group types on SharePoint are treated as lookup fields to their corresponding list. For that reason, whenever linking tables to SharePoint, the database always gets the User Information List (which is discussed shortly). Calculated fields continue to be calculated, which is also different than importing. Take a look at how SharePoint data types map to Access data types. The following table explains the mapping between SharePoint Data 3.0 and ACCDB.

SharePoint 3.0 Data Type	Access Data Type (for an ACCDB)	Modification Description
Single Line of Text	Text	No change.
Multiple Lines of Text	Memo	Rich Text setting is persisted into the imported table. Enhanced Rich Text is not fully supported.
Choice	Text	Values for the choices are also imported into the Row Source property available for the field.
Number	Number	Double precision; no change.
Data and Time	Date/Time	No change.
Currency	Currency	The `Format` and `DecimalPlaces` properties are persisted.
Lookup	Number	Lookup Tables are automatically pulled down.
Yes/No	Yes/No	No change.
Person or Group	Number	Treated as a Lookup field to the Person or Group list.
Hyperlink or Picture	Hyperlink	Data is imported as a link to the image file.
Calculated	Varies	Dependent upon the type that the column returns. The field continues to be calculated, even when in offline mode.
Multiple Value Fields	Varies	Complex Data fields of the same type. The values for the choices (if a static list) are also imported into the Row Source property for the available for the field. If the choices are a lookup, then the lookup table is pulled down as well.
Attachment	Attachment	No change.
Append Only Fields	Memo	With the `AppendOnly` property set to `True` (the opposite of when importing). The column history is persisted in the linked table and the `ColumnHistory` function can be used against this field.

Using linked tables to SharePoint in an ACCDB database solution allows users the richest SharePoint experience possible.

SharePoint Linked Tables in an MDB

While MDB files support SharePoint linked tables very well, the MDB file format does have a few limitations, as mentioned in the "Importing from SharePoint into an MDB" section above. For one thing, the MDB file format does not support complex data and attachment fields in the same manner that as the ACCDB file format. The following table describes how SharePoint data types map to Access data types when linked.

SharePoint 3.0 Data Type	Access Data Type (for an MDB)	Modification Description
Single Line of Text	Text	No change.
Multiple Lines of Text	Memo	The Rich Text setting is persisted in to the imported table and supported when using Access 2007 with the MDB file.
Choice	Text	The values for the choices are also imported into the Row Source property for the available for the field.
Number	Number	Double precision — No change.
Data and Time	Date/Time	No change.
Currency	Currency	The `Format` and `DecimalPlaces` properties are persisted.
Lookup	Number	Lookup Tables are automatically pulled down.
Yes/No	Yes/No	No change.
Person or Group	Number	Treated as a Lookup field to the Person or Group list.
Hyperlink or Picture	Hyperlink	The data is imported as a link to the image file.
Calculated	Varies	Dependent upon the type that the column returns. The field continues to be calculated.
Multiple Value Fields	Memo	Since Complex Data is not supported in the MDB file format, the data is imported as a comma-separated list for each of the values selected.

Table continues on the next page

SharePoint 3.0 Data Type	Access Data Type (for an MDB)	Modification Description
Attachment	Yes/No	Since Attachment fields are not supported in am MDB, the field is converted to a Yes/No field. The value of the field corresponds to whether the record had an attachment in the original SharePoint list.
Append Only Fields	Memo	Since there is no AppendOnly property in an MDB table field, there is nothing in the Access UI for the user to see. However, the AppendOnly property is enforced when data is edited, and thus the column history is also persisted in the linked table. The ColumnHistory function is available when using Access 2007, although the function call fails in previous versions of Access.

When used with Access 2007, Linked Tables To SharePoint still provides an ample amount of functionality in an MDB, although using the ACCDB file format is preferred.

Creating Linked Tables Via Code

While creating linked table in the Access UI is quick and easy, as described earlier in the "Importing Through the Access User Interface" section, you may find it more useful to create linked tables to SharePoint tables via VBA code. Fortunately, Access supports creating linked tables programmatically through the TransferSharePointList function, which was discussed earlier in this chapter. Because a few more options are available for creating linked tables programmatically, let's examine the TransferSharePointList method a little more.

Recall that the TransferSharePointList method is a member of the DoCmd object, which is part of the Application object. TransferSharePointList accepts up to six parameters, all of which are supported when using this function to link to SharePoint, unlike importing. These parameters are described in the "TransferSharePointList Object Model" section earlier in the chapter.

The following code illustrates a subroutine that links a table from a SharePoint site:

```
Sub LinkSharePointList()

    ' Call TransferSharePointList to link to SharePoint
    Application.DoCmd.TransferSharePointList _
        acLinkSharePointList, _
        "http://MySharePointSite/", _
        "Tasks", _
```

```
            "{E3908E5d-C32A-4D60-9D55-24A2761E5450}", _
            "LinkedTasksList", _
            False

    End Sub
```

As this code shows, it is as easy to create linked tables programmatically as it is to import data from a SharePoint site. Of course, your code will need to use the specific URL, GUID, and List name for the SharePoint list to be imported. When tables are linked to a SharePoint list, remember that when viewing data or updating data, the data will have to be pulled down from the SharePoint site and then pushed back up again if a change or addition occurs. This presents the possibility for performance problems in an Access application because in most cases, query processing needs to be done on the Access client.

Query Processing for SharePoint Data

The client-server chapter outlines several common performance problems that can occur when linked tables are used in an Access application. SharePoint applications are no stranger to performance issues. Unfortunately, because SharePoint uses an ISAM to read and write data, queries created in Access are processed locally, which can lead to possible performance issues. There is no support for making the SharePoint site process Access queries on the server to increase performance. Fortunately, there is one saving grace in the fact that any table can be linked to a specific view for the SharePoint list.

As you'll see in the client-server chapter (Chapter 19), there are many cases when Access needs to pull down all of the data in a table from the data source when processing queries locally. If a large number of users are using the SharePoint server or if the lists contain large amounts of data, processing a query may result in huge network bandwidth consumption. One method of reducing this traffic is creating views that reduce the data set and linking to those directly, instead of the full list. That way, the SharePoint server processes the query to create a particular view locally, and only the data contained in the view — not the entire data set — is transferred across the network. When possible, linking to SharePoint views helps reduce network traffic and improves the overall application performance.

Offline Mode for SharePoint Linked Tables

Another commanding feature new to Access 2007 is Offline mode for SharePoint linked tables. Offline mode enables users of an Access solution that is linked to a SharePoint server to move the tables and data into an offline state where they can interact, modify, add, and delete data in the SharePoint list, without having to actually remain connected to the SharePoint server. Once the table is synchronized, all of the modifications are persisted to the SharePoint site. The Offline feature is exceedingly useful when a user needs access to SharePoint data, even when no Web or network connection is available. Essentially, the Offline feature enables a SharePoint-linked Access application to run in any environment, regardless of a connection to the SharePoint site.

When a table is linked to a SharePoint list, all of the data stored in the list resides on the SharePoint site. When a linked table is taken offline, all of the data in the list is brought down and stored in the database locally. If the user adds, modifies, or deletes data within the list while it is offline, a record of the changes is stored in the Access database. When a solution is switched back into online mode with the SharePoint site again, the data is synchronized and all of the changes are propagated to the list there. However, the data is never removed from the Access database file. The only way to remove the data stored in the file when the database was taken offline is to compact and repair the database file.

One item to consider is multiple users working with the same SharePoint list in different offline database solutions. The model for synchronizing data is: When the linked table is synchronized or moved back into an online state, its current data is synchronized, and any records containing different data will overwrite the existing data on the SharePoint list. That is, the last changes synchronized are always the current data stored on the SharePoint site, overriding any previous data. This may cause a problem when many people are using the same list, and a previous record is overwritten by another person. Fortunately, if a record is modified while an application is offline, the person synchronizing the list is presented with the conflict resolution dialog box. If nothing else, this forces users to make a conscious decision about which data to use when synchronizing the SharePoint list data.

Using Offline Mode Via the Access UI

The External Data tab on the Ribbon makes it easy for users to work with Offline mode options for a database through the Access user interface. The Work Online/Work Offline button simply toggles the tables in the database between online and offline mode.

In addition to online and offline modes, a couple of other useful features are worth noting here. When a list has been taken offline and the user of the application has modified the data in the offline table, all of the changes made can be discarded before synchronizing the data for the list again by using the Discard Changes button on the Ribbon's External Data tab. However, it is important to realize that discarding the changes to a list is an all-or-nothing operation. If the user chooses to discard changes, all additions, modifications, and deletions are undone and then removed from the database completely. There is no way for the user to choose to discard only selected changes in the list.

The Cache List Data button is available on the External Data tab as well. When the list data is cached locally, the table still behaves as though it were online and any changes made are immediately persisted to the SharePoint site. The major difference here is that when data is pulled down from the SharePoint site, it is cached locally, so that queries made against the linked table don't always need to pull down the full data set from the server. Caching list data in the local database file can substantially improve application performance, especially when working with lists that contain large amounts of data and when data in a particular list is frequently queried. Once the application has the data cached locally, it continues to behave this way until the Do Not Cache List Data button is clicked. The Cache List Data and Do Not Cache List Data are actually the same button on the Ribbon, but the text on the button changes depending on the data caching mode.

Using Offline Mode Via Code

Access 2007 also provides the capability to toggle between online and offline modes through VBA code. The RunCommand method now exposes a command to toggle both the Offline status for a list and data caching, making it easy to invoke either of these features.

The acCmdToggleOffline is a member of the AcCommand enumeration. The RunCommand method accepts AcCommand members to perform specific operations in the Access user interface. Here's an example of a simple function to take the SharePoint lists offline:

```
Sub ToggleOffline()

    ' Toggle the tables between online and offline modes
    Application.RunCommand acCmdToggleOffline

End Sub
```

acCmdToggleCacheListData is another member of the AcCommand enumeration. As its name suggests, the acCmdToggleCacheListData option enables a developer to programmatically control whether the list data is cached. The following example is similar to the last, except the cached data mode is being toggled instead of the online mode:

```
Sub ToggleCacheData()

    ' Toggle the Cached Data mode for Online lists
    Application.RunCommand acCmdToggleCacheListData

End Sub
```

Using either the Access UI or code to work with Offline mode is simple. The Offline mode feature is handy when application users cannot access the SharePoint site. But for users to be able to use all of these new Offline features, the application must first be set up on the SharePoint site.

Migrate to SharePoint

While users of previous versions of Access had the capability to link tables to SharePoint lists, creating the links could be time consuming. In addition, if the application already existed, the developer had to do a lot of manual work to get it SharePoint-ready: manually create the SharePoint lists, create linked tables in the application, move the data to the SharePoint list, and then remove the old, local tables. The more complex the database being moved, the more time-consuming the process. Fortunately, Microsoft has greatly simplified the process for migrating Access solutions to a SharePoint site with the Access 2007 release.

Using the Move to SharePoint Feature

Access 2007 includes a brand new Move to SharePoint Site Wizard. For existing applications, this wizard can be invoked by clicking the Move to SharePoint button on the Ribbon's External Data tab. When an application is migrated, the user has the option to publish the database to the SharePoint site in a document library so that it can be shared with other users. The forms and reports of the database solution have the option of being advertised on the View menu for the SharePoint list, discussed later in this chapter. Finally, any features in an Access application that do not support being moved to a SharePoint site are written out to the Move To SharePoint Issues table that is created when the application is migrated.

The Move to SharePoint Site Wizard is basically a one-step process. The user inputs the full URL path to the SharePoint site and clicks the Next button. The Access application moves to the SharePoint site and the last page of the wizard enables the user to see the details that occurred during the upsize process. When the Access solution is upsized, a backup copy of the original database is created automatically, in case there are any problems during the operation. The Move to SharePoint Site Wizard makes migrating an existing database to SharePoint as smooth as it can be.

Getting Started allows users to create any database application template as a SharePoint linked application. From the Getting Started window in the Access client, select any database template. The preview pane displays and just below the filename is a check box to create the database on a SharePoint site. Checking this box and clicking the Create button invokes the Create on SharePoint Site dialog box. The dialog box is really the Move to SharePoint Site Wizard with a different title bar. Navigating this wizard is exactly the same.

When migrating an existing application to a SharePoint site, you must understand that some data type conversion happens because Access data types do not map directly to the SharePoint data types. Additionally, certain Access features are not supported when an application has tables linked to SharePoint. You need to be aware of both of these items before moving an application because they can cause data type conversion and data precision loss, and they can modify application architecture in some cases.

Data Type Conversion

Access 2007 offers a wide variety of data types for table fields. When developing a database solution, you need to take into consideration the type of data that will be stored in each table field. The type of data is typically determined by the known range in values for the data and the format the data will need to be stored in. For example, if a particular database field is used to store the rating for a hotel or restaurant, which accepts integers 0 through 10, the developer may choose the Number data type with the Field Size property set to Byte. While setting the Field Size property to Double would work just as well here, it requires that each field be 8 bytes in size instead of 1 byte and the database field would take more physical disk space than is really necessary.

When designing applications that will be used on SharePoint, you also need to consider the SharePoint data types. When a database is pushed up to SharePoint and the tables in the database are converted to lists that reside on the SharePoint server, some Access data types do not map directly to SharePoint data types and may not be supported. The following table describes the Access data types and how they map to SharePoint when migrated.

Field Type	SharePoint Type	Conversion Information
AutoNumber	Number or Text	AutoNumber fields are not supported on SharePoint. Long Integer AutoNumber fields are converted to a Number field. Replication ID AutoNumber fields are converted to Text. One field required by SharePoint, called ID, is added to each table and is the primary key for the list. It is automatically populated with sequential numbers for each record, much like an Access AutoNumber field.
Attachment	Attachment	No change.
Currency	Number	Converted to a Number with the `FieldSize` property set to Double. The Format property is persisted in the linked table. However, because Currency is a scaled integer whereas the Double is a floating-point number, some records may be modified because of rounding when the conversion is performed. It's always best to start with a Double if it is known that the database will be migrated to SharePoint.
Date/Time	Date/Time	No change.
Hyperlink	Hyperlink	No change.

Field Type	SharePoint Type	Conversion Information
Lookup (Number)	Number	No type conversion is made. However, lookup values may be regenerated because the lookup field may be switched to the SharePoint lists ID field if the lookup is to the Primary key for the table before it is upsized.
Memo	Memo	No change.
Number	Number or Text	Byte, Integer, Long Integer, Single, Double, and Decimal field sizes are all converted to a Double field size when pushed up. The Replication ID number is converted to a Text field type. There may be a loss of data when moving a Decimal field to Double because Decimal fields can hold 12 bytes of data and a Double can hold only 8 bytes. Additionally, a Decimal field is a scaled number field, and a Double is a floating-point number. Some records may be modified because of rounding when the conversion is performed.
OLE Object	Not Migratable	OLE fields are not supported for migration to SharePoint and the field and data are not included in the linked table.
Text	Text	The Field Size property is set to 255.
Yes/No	Yes/No	No changes are made to Yes/No fields.

Probably the most important data type conversions are Decimal and Currency. Because there is no concept of any number type larger than a Double on SharePoint, Decimal format numbers are converted to Double format. Decimal fields have a higher precision than Double fields because they have 4 additional bytes in which to store numbers. Decimal and Currency fields types are both scaled integers, but a Double is a floating-point number. Even though the Double type can store a wider range of numbers, a Double loses precision as the numbers get very large or very small. The Decimal and Currency field types are specifically designed to be more precise and to not lose precision as they get larger or smaller. While there are some cases when a Decimal or Currency field size is necessary, most of the time the Double field size is sufficient to store the data that is required.

The Data Type Conversion aspect of migrating a database solution to SharePoint is important to consider before migration takes place. In most cases, there should not be too many problems with converting data types, but you must remember AutoNumber, Currency, Decimal numbers, OLE Object, and Replication ID field data types can cause problems, not only with the data stored in the table, but also in how the field is used in code. Be sure to fully understand the implications of data conversion on migration to SharePoint for both the table fields and the code that uses these fields.

Database Changes When Migrating to SharePoint

In addition to the modification of the data types in table fields, a few other changes are made to a database when upsized to SharePoint. As mentioned previously, some fields cannot be upsized at all, which results in a linked table without the field added, which can cause problems in the application. Similarly, there are some other changes made to tables and relationships to consider when upsizing your Access solutions.

When a native Access table is migrated to a SharePoint list, some new fields are added to the table. They are used by SharePoint in one way or another and every list on SharePoint must have these fields. The following table describes the fields that are added to the table when migrating.

Field Name	Field Type	Description
ID	AutoNumber	Added as the primary key for the field. This is the only AutoNumber field allowed in the table and is required by SharePoint. The field is Read-Only.
Content Type	Text	Used by SharePoint to describe the content for internal information. The field is Read-Only.
File Type	Text	Used by SharePoint to describe the file type for internal information. The field is Read-Only.
Attachments	Attachment	Stores any attachments that are added to the record. This is the only Attachment field that can be in a list. Any other attachment fields in table are removed.
Workflow Instance ID	Text	Stores the information used by the workflow feature to describe the workflow information tied to the record. The field is Read-Only.
Modified	Date/Time	Stores the time for when the record was last modified. The field is Read-Only, but updated automatically whenever the record is modified.
Modified By	Number	A lookup into the User Information List to the site user who last modified the record. The field is Read-Only, but updated automatically whenever the record is modified.
Created	Date/Time	Stores the time for when the record was created. The field is Read-Only.
Created By	Number	A lookup into the User Information List to the site user that created the record. The field is Read-Only
URL Path	Text	Relative path from the site to the record used by SharePoint internally. The field is Read-Only.
Path	Text	The relative path from the site to the list used by SharePoint internally. The field is Read-Only.
Item Type	Text	Type of SharePoint item the record represents. The field is Read-Only.
Encoded Absolute URL	Text	Full URL path to the record used by SharePoint internally. The field is Read-Only.

The ID field is the interesting addition to the table. If the table already has an ID field, the original field is renamed to _ID and converted to a number field. The new ID field will be the new primary key field in the table and the old _ID field will no longer be the primary key, if it was the key previously. One might assume this operation would cause a problem if the table had fields that were lookups to the original ID field because when the records are pushed up to SharePoint, they may get renumbered when the new values for the ID field are generated, if there is a system relationship between the primary key and foreign key fields. Fortunately, Access is smart enough to take care of this before it becomes a problem. When lookup tables are pushed up to a SharePoint site, the new primary key values are updated for the foreign key fields. Thus, the data in the original database will be consistent when pushed up, although the original values may be different. The important thing here is that the relationship between the two tables is not broken when migrated to a SharePoint site, although it may be modified slightly, as you see in the next section.

Features That Do Not Upsize to SharePoint

Some features cannot be migrated when the application is upsized to a SharePoint site, including field properties, enforced relationships, and other linked tables. Some of these features are extremely common, so it is important for you to be aware.

When a feature cannot be upsized to SharePoint, Access tries to discard the feature. Any item that is discarded has a record added to the Move to SharePoint Site Issues table. This errors table contains several fields, each of which describes information about the problematic feature. The following table describes the purpose of each of the fields in the Move to SharePoint Site Issues table.

Field Name	Description
Issue	Problem that may be caused by the feature not being migrated.
Reason	Explanation of why the feature cannot be moved to SharePoint.
Object Type	Type of object the feature belongs to.
Object Name	Name of the database object.
Field Name	Name of the field affected.
Property Name	Property name for the field, if it exists.

When the Move to SharePoint Wizard completes the migration process, the last page of the wizard denotes whether any errors occurred by showing an error icon. Simply open the Move to SharePoint Site Issues table to see more information about each of the errors that occurred.

There are also several table-related features that cannot be migrated. Some field properties cannot be migrated, referential integrity is not supported, and linked tables to other data sources are not supported. The following is a list of features that cannot be pushed up to a SharePoint list:

Binary table fields

AutoNumber table fields

Referential integrity — cascading updates of deletes

Join types between tables (although they can be recreated once the table is upsized)

Read-only tables

Linked tables to other data sources

Default Value table field property

Input Mask table field property

Validation Rule table field property

Validation Text table field property

Unicode Compression table field property

Unique indexes for indexed fields

Smart Tags table field property (although it can be recreated once the table is upsized)

Text Align table field property (although it can be recreated once the table is upsized)

Several of these features are common to Access solutions, but most of the time they are not critical to the application. The impact of data type conversion is minimal in most applications. Any changes made to the database are practically negligible. Overall, the Move to SharePoint feature is incredibly powerful yet simple to use. Access 2007 makes migrating database applications to SharePoint much easier than ever before.

Publish Database to SharePoint

Another cutting-edge feature added to Microsoft Office Access 2007 is Publish to SharePoint. It enables you to move the physical Access database file into a Document Library on the SharePoint site. Once the database has been published, you can share the Access solution with other users of the site. The Publish to SharePoint feature enables you to better collaborate with your team, using SharePoint as the platform for distribution.

The publish feature allows both applications with linked tables as well as native Access tables to be stored in a SharePoint document library, but with some minor differences. An Access solution can be published by checking the box on the first page of the Move to SharePoint Site Wizard when being upsized or at any other time from File ➪ Publish. When a database has been published to a SharePoint site, the database knows that it has been published because its PublishURL database property is set with the URL to the SharePoint location.

PublishURL Property

Once a database has been published and a local copy of the database is opened, the user sees the Publish option in the message bar. This option enables the user to quickly republish a database when changes have been made to it. The PublishURL database property is used to determine if and where the database is published and can easily be accessed with a single line of VBA code. The following is an example function that returns PublishURL if it exists:

```
Function GetPublishURL() As String

On Error GoTo errFailed
```

```
        ' Return the PublishURL
        GetPublishURL = CurrentDb.Properties("PublishURL").Value
        Exit Function

errFailed:

        ' If there is an error, the PublishURL does not exist
        GetPublishURL = ""
        Exit Function

End Function
```

You can programmatically add, modify, or remove this property just as easily. For example, you may not want the user to see the publish bar when the database is opened, so you could add some code to automatically clear this property when the database is opened.

Opening in Read-Only Mode

When a database is opened from a SharePoint document library, the user is prompted to open in either Read-Only or Edit modes. If Read-Only mode is chosen, Access behaves in one of two ways, depending on whether the application's tables are local or linked. This can mean major differences in how the application functions in Read-Only mode and should definitely be considered when publishing.

If the tables are local to the database file, opening the database in Read-Only mode does not allow the user to add, modify, or delete any data in the application. Because the file is read-only, local tables cannot be written to, which is why the data cannot be changed. The application can still be used in other ways — for example, the user can still perform other operations such as running code, viewing forms and reports, or exporting objects; he just is not able to make any changes to the data.

This behavior is totally different if the application has linked tables to another location. If the published Access solution has linked tables to a data source that is writable, such as linked tables to the SharePoint site, data modification is possible in Read-Only mode. This is often counterintuitive at first because people tend to associate the Read-Only status with being able to change nothing. In reality, although the database file is Read-Only, the data store is not, so modifications can easily be made. Keep this in mind when publishing Access solutions so that you do not inadvertently allow or disallow users to modify data in an application.

Opening in Edit Mode

The other option from a SharePoint site is to open the database in Edit mode. Edit mode enables the user to make any changes to the database objects or data, but requires that the physical database file be downloaded to the local machine. Once the file has been downloaded, the user can make any desired changes and quickly republish the database using the publish bar.

In some cases, you may want to deter the user from republishing the database to the SharePoint site. As mentioned earlier, you can remove the PublishURL property. Here's a quick example of a subroutine to remove that property:

```
Sub ClearPublishURL()

On Error GoTo errFailed
```

```
        ' Remove the PublishURL property to deter users from publishing
        CurrentDb.Properties.Delete "PublishURL"
        Exit Sub

errFailed:

        ' There was an error, the property was not present
        Exit Sub

End Sub
```

These two code examples both do some error checking to ignore errors if the PublishURL property does not exist in the database. Of course, you can add your own error-handling code for these situations.

Opening Published Databases Via Code

Access provides the OpenCurrentDatabase method to open a database, including databases that have been published to SharePoint or other types of websites. OpenCurrentDatabase is a member of the Application object and takes three parameters, two of which are optional. The following table describes those parameters.

Parameter Name	Parameter Description
filePath	The full name and path or URL string to the database to be opened. Required.
Exclusive	The Boolean value which determines whether the database should be opened in exclusive mode. Optional, and if not specified, the default value is False.
bstrPassword	The password string on the database that is to be opened. Optional, and if not specified, it is an empty string. If the database does have a password, the user is still prompted if this parameter is not passed through.

OpenCurrentDatabase can be useful for spawning another application via code. The following is one example of how a database can be opened from a SharePoint site:

```
Sub OpenDatabaseFromSite()

    ' Define variables
    Dim accApp As New Access.Application

    ' Open the database from the SharePoint site
    accApp.Visible = True
    accApp.OpenCurrentDatabase "http://MySharePointSite/Database.accdb"

    ' Clean up
    Set accApp = Nothing

End Sub
```

You can also perform that operation via code using the `FollowHyperlink` method. It's also a member of the `Application` object and takes a single parameter, which is the full URL to the page or other object to open. Here's an example of a subroutine to open a database using `FollowHyperlink`:

```
Sub FollowLinkToDatabase()

    ' Open the database from the SharePoint site
    Application.FollowHyperlink "http://MySharePointSite/Database.accdb"

End Sub
```

No matter which method you choose, Access is sure to make writing code to open a published database easy for you.

Access Views on SharePoint

The final new Access feature for working with SharePoint is the Access View on SharePoint. An Access view is a form or report that is advertised on the SharePoint view menu for any given list. These views are invoked from the SharePoint list and open the database object in the Access client when selected. Views are a great way to show off an application that is linked to a SharePoint list.

There are two methods in the SharePoint UI for opening the Create View page for a list:

❑ Select View ➪ Create View on the list's main page.

❑ Select Setting ➪ Create View.

The Create View page is the starting point for making any view for a SharePoint list. When Access 2007 is not installed on the machine, there are four options for creating new views on the Create View page: Standard View, Calendar View, Datasheet View, and Gantt View. The Datasheet view utilizes the Access Web Datasheet. It does not work when users try to open the view until Access 2007 (or 2003) is installed on the client machine. All other view options on the Create View page should be viewable when created, even if Office or Access is not installed.

When Access 2007 is installed on the machine, the Create View page shows one additional option: Access View. When that option is selected, a new instance of Access opens, prompting the user to choose a save location for a new database. Then the Create Access View dialog box opens, enabling the user to choose a specific form factor for a new form or report for the view. The option he chooses has a link created from the SharePoint view menu to the view in the database. Whenever the user selects the view, his machine launches the Access database and opens the particular form or report.

If the default view for a list is set to an Access view, the Access database is launched automatically any time a user navigates to the list. That's a good way to force people to use a particular Access application to view and modify data for a SharePoint list. However, users of the site who do not have Access 2007 installed may have problems viewing the list, so be sure to use this trick cautiously.

Because the database created from the Access view option is saved on the local machine, it is always a good idea to republish the database to a document library on the SharePoint site so that other users have access to the database. When the list is published, a dialog box asks if the view links in the SharePoint views menu should be updated. If these are updated when the list is published, the view link redirects the user to the database stored in the document library. Views are a powerful way to provide users with the rich view options that Microsoft Office Access 2007 offers.

Advertising Access Views in the SharePoint View Menu

Creating an Access view from the SharePoint View menu is extremely easy, although it is somewhat cumbersome if the user wants to create multiple views for the list. In most cases, it is far more likely that the database creator wants to design the views for the application long before the SharePoint list has even been created. Fortunately, Access provides developers with the capability to create these views programmatically.

When a database application is migrated to a SharePoint site using the Move to SharePoint Site Wizard, each table in the database has a corresponding SharePoint list created if the check box to publish and create shortcuts is selected on the first page of the wizard. Additionally, all of the forms and reports in the database have the chance to be advertised on the View menu for the new SharePoint lists. The form or report will be shown if the `RecordSource` property contains a reference to the list and the `DisplayOnSharePointSite` property is set correctly.

Using the DisplayOnSharePointSite Property

As mentioned, one of the conditions for advertising the view on SharePoint is that the `Display-OnSharePointSite` property is set correctly. That property is available for both forms and reports and can be set directly through the Property sheet in Access. There are two possible values: Follow Table Setting and Do Not Display, which are pretty self-explanatory. If the Follow Table Setting option is chosen, the view displayed is dependent on the table's `DisplayViewsOnSharePointSite` property setting.

Much like the `DisplayOnSharePointSite` property for forms and reports, each table has a `DisplayViewsOnSharePointSite` property. It also has two possible settings: Follow Database Setting and Do Not Display. Needless to say, the Do Not Display option causes any form or report tied to the list not to be displayed automatically. Otherwise, there is a database property setting to have these views displayed on SharePoint.

The `DisplayAllViewsOnSharePointSite` property is the database property that determines if the forms and reports in the database are advertised in the SharePoint list's View menu. This property is not shown in the normal database properties of the `CurrentDb` object. To see it, choose the Access client File ⇨ Manage ⇨ Database Properties. If the `DisplayAllViewsOnSharePointSite` property is set to 1, all of the views for forms and reports will be advertised if the corresponding properties for the form or report object and the table object are set to display the views.

The `DisplayAllViewsOnSharePointSite` property setting can also be determined by using a bit of VBA code. As mentioned previously, this property cannot be retrieved from the `Properties` object from the `CurrentDb` object. To get the object's value, you need to do something slightly different: Retrieve the value from the `UserDefined` properties in the database document. The following function is an example of how the `DisplayAllViewsOnSharePointSite` property can be retrieved in code:

```
Function GetSharePointPropertySetting() As String

On Error GoTo errHandler

    ' Define Variables
    Dim db As DAO.Database
```

```
      Dim doc As DAO.Document
      Dim prp As DAO.Property

      ' Get the property from the custom properties
      Set db = Application.CurrentDb
      Set doc = db.Containers!Databases.Documents!UserDefined
      Set prp = doc.Properties("DisplayAllViewsOnSharePointSite")

      ' Return the value
      GetSharePointPropertySetting = prp.value
      GoTo CleanUp

  errHandler:

      ' If an error is encountered, the property was not present
      GetSharePointPropertySetting = "0"

  CleanUp:

      ' Clean up
      Set prp = Nothing
      Set doc = Nothing
      Set db = Nothing
      Exit Function

  End Function
```

Similarly, if the database does not already have this custom property set, or if the property needs to be set programmatically, a subroutine can be created to set it. Here's an example of how `DisplayAllViewsOnSharePointSite`, or any custom property, can be set programmatically:

```
  Sub SetSharePointPropertySetting(iValue As Integer)

  On Error GoTo errHandler

      ' Define Variables
      Dim db As DAO.Database
      Dim doc As DAO.Document
      Dim prp As DAO.Property

      ' Get the property from the custom properties
      Set db = Application.CurrentDb
      Set doc = db.Containers!Databases.Documents!UserDefined
      Set prp = doc.Properties("DisplayAllViewsOnSharePointSite")

      ' Return the value
      prp.value = iValue
      GoTo CleanUp

  errHandler:

      ' If an error is encountered, the property was not present, so create it
      Set prp = db.CreateProperty( _
          "DisplayAllViewsOnSharePointSite", dbLong, iValue)
```

```
        doc.Properties.Append prp

CleanUp:

    ' Clean up
    Set prp = Nothing
    Set doc = Nothing
    Set db = Nothing
    Exit Sub


End Sub
```

This code is easy to create if you need custom document properties for the database. Whether you're using the Access UI or VBA code to set the `DisplayAllViewsOnSharePointSite` property, it is sure to be simple and quick.

Summary

Microsoft Windows SharePoint Services is one of the fastest growing group collaboration tools in the world, and Microsoft Office 2007 provides a slew of new features for working directly with SharePoint. Access developers now have the capability to leverage much of the rich tool set that SharePoint provides by developing Access applications that harness the SharePoint technology. As you've seen in this chapter, most of those features are simple to incorporate into almost any Access application.

The Access Web Datasheet enables users to edit multiple records in the SharePoint list directly from their Web browsers. They can export or link SharePoint list data to an Access database quickly with features such as the Open with Access button or the Web Datasheet task pane. Access 2007 also supports importing and linking to more SharePoint data types than ever before, and these new entry points are much more discoverable. Developers creating or migrating existing Access solutions can easily perform this operation using the Move to SharePoint functionality. Users can publish databases to a SharePoint site, allowing them to be used in Access applications in the same manner as working with other Office documents on a SharePoint server. And last, but not least, you can create Access Views that invoke Access applications automatically when the view is selected from the SharePoint site.

With all of these features, running Microsoft Windows SharePoint Services 3.0 with Microsoft Office 2007 Professional is a compelling business scenario. Both developers and users can take advantage of the integration between SharePoint and Access 2007 at a very low cost. Be sure to consider using SharePoint technologies to leverage your Access database solution when it is a viable option for your customers.

18

Database Security

Microsoft Office Access 2007 provides a range of security features to meet the needs of most database applications. These security features break down into two categories: database security for the ACCDB file format, which is discussed in the first part of this chapter, and database security for the MDB file format, which is the focus of the rest of the chapter. This chapter discusses the various methods available to secure your Access database applications using VBA code in either file format.

Be aware that several of the security features available in the MDB file format are not available in the ACCDB file format, and vice-versa. For the ACCDB file format portion of this chapter, you'll examine databases encrypted with passwords and code secured by either compiling the database or locking the modules. For the MDB file format portion, you'll explore shared-level security, user-level security, database encoding, MDE files, and using VBA to manipulate security. There's also a discussion about user-level security and the detachment between the MDW file and the secured database application file.

It is important to understand all of the various types of security in both file formats to fully comprehend the implications of the security model being employed by the database. The recommendation is to read this entire chapter before deciding which method of security is best for the database application.

> Microsoft Office Access 2007 provides security features that protect computers from databases that contain malicious code designed to attack or infect machines. In addition, Access 2007 also provides a format for securely transferring database files. These particular security enhancements are covered in Chapter 22.

Security for the ACCDB File Format

One of the new features of Microsoft Office Access 2007 is a file format: ACCDB. The security features available for it are somewhat different than those provided for the MDB file formats in a number of ways. This section discusses the security available for ACCDB files.

The five different forms of database security for the ACCDB file format are as follows:

❏ **Shared-Level Security:** There is one simple form of shared-level security provided by the Access Connectivity Engine for ACCDB: Encrypt Database with Password. Access 2007 uses a password in combination with the RC4 encryption standard to encrypt the contents of a database file. When this security is enabled, the user is required to enter the password before he can open the database and read the contents. In addition, the data in the database is encrypted so that opening a file with a text editor does not reveal the raw data contained in the database. This type of security works well in small workgroups where it isn't necessary to know who opened the database or to restrict users from altering any objects in the database. This feature is new to Access; it replaces both database passwords and database encoding, effectively combining them into one package.

❏ **Compiled Database Code:** Compiling the VBA code project for the database application produces an Access Compiled Database (ACCDE) file. When a database is compiled, the code is compiled to a binary format, removing the readable code from the database file, which means that forms, reports, and modules cannot be modified or exported to another database. This method can be used to protect intellectual property rights, as well as to prevent users from modifying the code in the VBA project in the database. The compiled database security method is commonly used when you want to block users from changing the application's code.

❏ **VBA Project Passwords:** Placing a password on the VBA project can prevent unauthorized users from opening or modifying the code in the database, while still enabling you to distribute the complete code in the application, allowing authorized personnel to make changes to the code. This protection method includes modules, classes, and code behind forms and reports. Be aware that a VBA password in no way secures or abstracts the data in the database, nor does it deter users from interacting with application data in any way. It only protects the VBA code and the code project in the database.

❏ **Package Database as Signed Cab:** The Package as Signed Cab file feature allows users to create a signed database package file for the purpose of securely transferring the database to another user. The receiver of the database package can be assured that the database has not been tampered with and that the database is authentic via the use of a digital signature. This can be used only as a means to verify the database file after it has been transferred. Because it isn't a security feature for use when the database is loaded, its full description is covered in Chapter 22.

❏ **Disabled Mode:** When Access is open in disabled mode, all code and unsafe macros in a database are disabled by default and cannot be run until the database is trusted by the user in one of two ways:

  ❏ Users can trust the database and enable code in any given, non-trusted database on an individual basis, by enabling the database from the Options button on the message bar.

  ❏ A user can flag directories as trusted locations on the machine and, in that case, any database in a flagged directory is enabled by default with full code and macros execution.

This feature is new to Access and replaces macro security from Access 2003. It is also fully discussed in Chapter 22.

In some cases, more than one security method may be applied to a database at the same time to enhance database security. The first three of these security features are discussed in this chapter (the last two are covered in Chapter 22). The Access 2007 security features enable you to provide a fairly robust security model for your database solution. Altogether, these features substantially improve database and application security for both you and the user.

If you are familiar with previous versions of Access security, you may have noticed that one of the major security features in the MDB file format is missing. User-level security has been deprecated and is not available for the ACCDB file format. Fortunately, it's still supported for MDB file formats using Access 2007. User-level security is explored later in this chapter.

Shared-Level Security for ACCDBs

Securing a database application with a password allows a collection of application users to have a shared password to access the data within the database. This model works well for small groups, where all users are allowed to have access to any and all of the data contained in the database file. For example, the Marketing department may need to communicate data statistics through a series of reports created in an Access database solution, in which all of the Marketing employees have full access to the database. Because several departments in the company share the same network resources, though, Marketing wants to prevent unauthorized users, such as Development department employees, from viewing this data until it is released publicly. The shared-level security model is perfect for this situation because all data in the database is okay to be viewed by the entire authorized user group. Meanwhile, this model prevents unauthorized users from seeing the data.

However, simply adding database password is not quite enough security to ensure full data protection. The ACCDB format is similar to its predecessor, the MDB file format, in that the raw data is stored in almost plain text. This means that if the database file is opened in a text-editing program such as Windows Notepad, it is likely that most of the data can be deciphered with ease, especially if the intruder is familiar with the format. Fortunately, the solution to this problem is already built into the shared-level security feature for Access 2007.

Data Encryption Is Key

The missing piece to this security puzzle is data encryption. If the database is encrypted, an intruder will not reap any benefit from opening the file and viewing the raw data. By definition, encryption obscures data files in such a way that they appear to be incomprehensible, random sets of information, and decoding the data without the proper security key is virtually impossible. Data encryption is critical to making this model work correctly; without it, the model is totally flawed.

Fortunately, Microsoft Office Access 2007 supports both passwords and encryption in one easy-to-use feature: Encrypt Database with Password. When applying a password to an ACCDB file, Access encrypts the data contained within the file, using the password as the key for the encryption. Moreover, the key is not contained anywhere within the database file, and only people in possession of the password have access to the data.

Once a password is chosen and the encryption is applied, any user of the database solution is required to supply the password to open the database file. Only a single password can be set for any given database, so there is no way to distinguish which user has opened the database or which objects the user is accessing, only that the user has possession of the password. Be aware that it is extremely easy for an individual to transfer a password to other parties and may be impossible to know exactly all the users who are in possession of the password. Because there is no requirement to provide evidence of identity in any other way, potentially anyone with network access to the file could view the database, provided the password is known.

Although some may consider the feature somewhat limited, shared-level security is still quite effective when used properly. Even better, implementing it in a database application requires only a few clicks of the mouse. The cost/benefit ratio of implementing and using Access 2007 is extremely high because adding the feature is so quick and easy to apply.

Using Access to Encrypt and Password Protect

Setting up a database password via the Access user interface (UI) is probably the fastest method of applying a password to an Access application. Once the database has been opened in exclusive mode, shared-level security is added to a database from the Database Tools tab on the Ribbon. Simply click the Encrypt with Password button to invoke the Set Database Password dialog box. Enter a password from 6 to 20 characters long, then re-enter the same password in the Verify text box to ensure it was typed correctly. Click OK to set the password and encrypt the database and the shared level security feature in Access is applied.

> It is highly recommended that you completely back up the database and store the password in a safe location before applying the database password, if there is a problem with the database or the password is lost at a later date.

The next time the encrypted database file is opened in Access, the user is prompted to enter the database password in the Password dialog box. In addition to the initial time required to encrypt the database, there may be a slight decrease in performance when using the database because data contained in the database needs to be decrypted when read, and then re-encrypted when data is added or modified. However, that's a small price to pay for the added security that is provided by the Encrypt with Password feature.

To decrypt the database, reopen the ACCDB file in Exclusive mode. Enter the current database password to gain access to the database. From the Database Tools tab of the Ribbon, click the Decrypt Database button. The Unset Database Password dialog box prompts you for the database password one last time. Enter the current database password and click OK. The file is decrypted and the password protection is removed.

Although adding a database password is extremely easy to do from the Access UI, there may be cases for which you want to use other methods to change these passwords. Fortunately, Access provides other options for setting the database password.

Using DAO to Set the Database Password

Creating VBA code to use DAO to add, modify, or remove a database password is easy and it can be done with just a few lines of code. DAO provides the NewPassword method, which can be called from the Database object to set the database password. As with the Access UI, the database must be opened in exclusive mode to complete this operation. Notice that the DAO code used in Access 2007 is exactly the same as setting the database passwords for the MDB file format. The following SetDatabasePasswordDAO subroutine is a short example of a procedure you could write to employ DAO to change the database password:

```
Public Sub SetDatabasePasswordDAO( _
    strDatabasePath As String, _
    strNewPassword As String, _
    strOldPassword As String)
```

```
        ' Define Variables
        Dim db As DAO.Database
        Dim wrk As Workspace

        ' Open the database
        Set wrk = CreateWorkspace("myWorkspace", "admin", "", dbUseJet)
        Set db = wrk.OpenDatabase(strDatabasePath, True, False, _
            "MS Access;PWD=" & strOldPassword)

        ' Set the Password
        db.NewPassword strOldPassword, strNewPassword

        ' Clean up variables
        db.Close
        Set db = Nothing
        wrk.Close
        Set wrk = Nothing

    End Sub
```

Using ADO to Set the Database Password

In addition to using the Access UI and DAO, you can create VBA code to call into ADO to add, modify, or remove a database password. To modify the password, open the database in exclusive mode in ADO and execute the following command:

```
ALTER DATABASE PASSWORD [newpassword] [oldpassword]
```

The password is case sensitive and must be specified between square brackets ([ ]). When setting a password on a database that does not currently have a password use NULL without the brackets as the old password. When removing a password from a database use NULL without the brackets as the new password.

The following code is an example of how you can implement a SetDatabasePassword function to add, update, or remove a database password via code calling ADO. Notice that if either the new or old password is not specified (IsMissing) when calling SetDatabasePassword, the word NULL is substituted for the password. If the password is specified, SetDatabasePassword encloses the value in square brackets ([ ]). Also notice that if the old password is specified, the ADODB Connection Properties uses the password without square brackets. Finally, some error handling is included to show how to handle some common errors that can occur when calling this function.

```
Public Function SetDatabasePasswordADO( _
    strDatabasePath As String, _
    Optional pNewPassword As Variant, _
    Optional pOldPassword As Variant) As String

On Error GoTo report_error

    ' Define Variables and Constants
    Const cProvider = "Microsoft.ACE.OLEDB.12.0"
    Dim cnn As ADODB.Connection
    Dim strNewPassword As String
    Dim strOldPassword As String
```

```
       Dim strCommand As String
       Dim strResult As String

       ' If a password is not specified (IsMissing),
       ' the string is "NULL" WITHOUT the brackets
       If IsMissing(pNewPassword) Then
           strNewPassword = "NULL"
       Else
           strNewPassword = "[" & pNewPassword & "]"
       End If
       If IsMissing(pOldPassword) Then
           strOldPassword = "NULL"
       Else
           strOldPassword = "[" & pOldPassword & "]"
       End If

       ' Define the string to change the password
       strCommand = _
           "ALTER DATABASE PASSWORD " & _
           strNewPassword & " " & _
           strOldPassword & ";"

       ' Open a connection to the database
       Set cnn = New ADODB.Connection
       With cnn
           .Mode = adModeShareExclusive
           .Provider = cProvider
           If Not IsMissing(pOldPassword) Then
               .Properties("Jet OLEDB:Database Password") = pOldPassword
           End If
           .Open "Data Source=" & strDatabasePath & ";"
           .Execute strCommand
       End With

       strResult = "Password Set"

exit_SetDatabasePassword:

       ' Clean up on exit
       On Error Resume Next
       cnn.Close
       Set cnn = Nothing
       SetDatabasePassword = strResult
       Exit Function

report_error:

       ' Handle some common errors with passwords
       If Err.Number = -2147467259 Then
           strResult = "An error occured"
       ElseIf Err.Number = -2147217843 Then
           strResult = "Invalid password for database"
       Else
           strResult = Err.Number & " " & Err.Description
```

```
        End If

        ' Exit as an error has occured
        Resume exit_SetDatabasePassword

End Function
```

Using the Access OM to Set the Database Password

The Access 2007 Object Model also provides the capability to open the Set Database Password dialog box through VBA code. You could call the RunCommand object with the acCmdSetDatabasePassword parameter, which opens the Set Database Password dialog box in the instance of Access, so that the user can simply enter the password and click OK. This will not work for a database that is currently open in the instance of Access calling the RunCommand function, though, because applying a password requires that the database be opened in exclusive mode. However, it is plausible that a user wants to create another application that applies security to many different database files. The benefit to using RunCommand is that it allows the user to add the password when the procedure is invoked and that it employs the Access UI, so you do not have to create any UI for this operation. The following code creates a new instance of the Access application class, opens the specified database, and then opens the Set Database Password dialog box:

```
Sub SetDatabasePasswordRunCmd(strSourcePath As String)

    ' Define Variables
    Dim accApp As New Access.Application

    ' Open the Source database in Exclusive mode
    accApp.OpenCurrentDatabase strSourcePath, True

    ' Invoke the "Encode Database As" dialog
    accApp.DoCmd.RunCommand acCmdSetDatabasePassword

    ' Cleanup Variables
    accApp.Quit acQuitSaveNone
    Set accApp = Nothing

End Sub
```

Also, it is worth noting that there are two possible errors that could occur from the last block of code. The first is that the user could click the Cancel button on the dialog, which would cause an error to be generated. The second is that the database could be in Read-Only mode or locked by another source. If you plan to use this code, or other code listed further throughout this chapter, please consider adding some basic error handling, as most of the examples in this chapter only provide a basic outline of the required code to complete the functionality, but not necessarily to handle any error that could occur.

There are two recommended procedures when adding shared-level security to an application:

❑ Always make a backup copy of the database before modifying the password. If the database is corrupted or some other catastrophic error occurs, a backup copy will be useful to have on hand.

❑ Store the new password in a safe location. If you lose the password to a database, the database is not recoverable.

The few previous examples illustrate how to set a database password either programmatically, using ADO or DAO, or through the Access UI. No matter which method you use, adding shared-level security to any database is quite easy and is a great way to improve data security.

Securing VBA Code in ACCDB

Developers generally want to secure their code for a multitude of reasons, from protecting intellectual property to preventing hackers from modifying the original code. Fortunately, Access 2007 provides two methods for protecting the VBA code contained in an ACCDB file. The first is password protecting the VBA Project for the database from the Visual Basic Editor. The second is creating an ACCDE file that compiles the code to a binary format and removes the source code completely from the file. You'll examine both methods in this section.

Locking the VBA Project

The Visual Basic Editor (VBE) application built into Access provides a password protection feature to block the code from being viewed by unauthorized users. This protection allows you to leave the original code in the database file while concealing the code by preventing it from being viewed without the password. It also protects the code from being modified, which ensures consistent application behavior and prevents code tampering by unauthorized users.

The project password can be set while viewing the VBA Project in VBE. When a project has a password and is secured for viewing, the password must be entered in the VBE before the Visual Basic code can be opened. The password is requested only once each time that database is opened, and it is only requested if there is an attempt to access the code using the VBE.

Setting a password for the VBA Project prevents changing the Has Module property on forms and reports until the password has been entered in the VBE because Access needs to open the VBA Project before it can add or remove code.

> Setting a password and locking the project from viewing does not prevent users from changing event properties on Forms or Reports. Specifically, a user can remove the [Event Procedure] setting from a form's event, causing the code to not be executed. Obviously, this could be disastrous if the code executes a critical action when that event occurs. Although users are able to clear the [Event Procedure] setting, they cannot add any new code to the form, reports, or modules. However, they can re-route events, because the [Event Procedure] can be specified as another method and if the procedure already exists, it will be called.

To prevent users from making form or report changes or changing the properties on events, you can generate an ACCDE file from the database and distribute it instead of an ACCDB file. Another way to prevent changes is to institute user-level security and not grant modify permissions for selected users or user groups, but is only supported for the MDB file format, which is discussed later in this chapter. Both of these methods are discussed later.

Password Protecting the VBA Project

You can lock the project from viewing and set a module password for the VBA Project via the options available in the VBE. Here's how:

> Be sure to fully back up the database solution before the password is added. In addition, the password should be kept in a protected location. If the password is lost, the VBA Project can never be opened again from VBE.

1. Open VBE and select the database application's VBA Project in the Project Explorer (the task pane on the top, left side of the VBE window).

2. Select Tools ⇨ *project-name* Properties (*project-name*) is the name of the project in the specific database, which will be unique to the application). The project's Project Properties dialog box is invoked.

3. Select the Protection tab. Check the Lock Project For Viewing checkbox control.

4. Specify a password in the Password text box, and re-enter the password in the Confirm Password text box control.

5. Click OK to save the password and apply the protection to the VBA project.

To verify the module password has been set, close the database and then reopen it. If you try to open VBE and select the project, the Password dialog box is invoked, requesting the password to view the code and project.

Removing Password from the VBA Project

To remove the password protection on the VBA Project, simply clear the Lock Project For Viewing checkbox in the Project Properties, that was checked when the project was initially locked. Here's how:

1. Select Tools ⇨ *project-name* Properties option (*project-name* is the name of the project in the specific database, which is unique to the application). You are prompted for the password to the project; enter it and click the OK button.

2. The project's Project Properties dialog box is invoked. Select the Protection tab.

3. Uncheck the Lock Project For Viewing checkbox control.

4. Clear the data from both the Password and Confirm Password text box controls.

5. Click OK to apply and save the changes and remove the protection to the VBA project.

It isn't necessary to remove the project password to allow the VBA code to remain unlocked. Setting the password, but not checking the Lock Project For Viewing checkbox, will provide password protection to the VBA project properties settings only. Anyone using the database will still be able to view and modify the code without being prompted for the VBA project's password.

Compiling the Database into an ACCDE File

The second (and safer) method for protecting the code in an Access database solution is to create an ACCDE file to distribute to users, instead of the original database file. Creating an ACCDE file compiles the VBA project and creates a binary module, removing all of the source code from the resulting ACCDE database file. Another benefit to compiling is that the code gets optimized and can provide faster execution in some cases. The compile process also compacts the database automatically. An ACCDE database file prevents users from ever seeing the code in the application or modifying the code without the developer's explicit permission.

To make an ACCDE file from an ACCDB file using Access 2007, the database must be opened in exclusive mode. It is important to understand that when the ACCDE file is created, it will not be possible to import, export, create, modify, or rename any forms, reports, pages, or modules in the ACCDE file itself. Therefore, the original ACCDB database used to create the ACCDE file should be retained in a secured location, if the application requires changes in the future. In that circumstance you will need to make changes to the ACCDB file and then create a new ACCDE file to distribute to the users of the application.

If your project has references to other databases, you must make ACCDE files for the referenced databases and update the References to them in the primary application's VBA project before an ACCDE file can be made from the current project.

To create the ACCDE file, click the Make ACCDE button on the Ribbon's Database Tools tab The Save As dialog box opens; enter the name and path to the file to be created and click Save. The Access database solution is compiled and the new ACCDE file is created at the specified location.

Using VBA to Create an ACCDE

Although making an ACCDE through the Access UI is fast and easy, there are times when the developer may want to automate the process through a button click. Perhaps the application is updated constantly and once regular modifications are complete, the developer wants to click a button to create the new ACCDE file that will be distributed to users. Fortunately, there are three methods available for making ACCDE files in various ways programmatically.

Using SysCmd 603 to Create an ACCDE

More savvy Access developers may recall the undocumented SysCmd option 603, which, in previous versions of Access, creates an MDE from an MDB file. Although still officially undocumented by Microsoft, Access 2007 will create an ACCDE file using system command 603. The SysCmd object takes three parameters: the command option and then two arguments that are dependent on the specified command option. In the case of system command 603, the second parameter is the full name and path to the ACCDB database file and the third parameter specifies the path to where the new ACCDE file is to be created. The following code is an example of a single function to create an ACCDE file programmatically using the SysCmd 603 method:

```
Sub MakeACCDESysCmd(strACCDBPath As String, strACCDEOutputPath As String)

    ' Create a new instance of Access
    Dim app As New Access.Application

    ' Set the Automation Security to Low
    app.AutomationSecurity = MsoAutomationSecurity.msoAutomationSecurityLow

    ' Call SysCmd with option 603 to create an ACCDE
    app.SysCmd 603, strACCDBPath, strACCDEOutputPath
    MsgBox "The ACCDE file is ready."

End Sub
```

Using RunCommand to Create an ACCDE

You can also use the RunCommand function to assist in creating an ACCDE. You may have noticed that the AcCommand enumeration for the RunCommand object exposes the acCmdMakeMDEFile option, used for creating MDE files from MDB database in previous versions in Access. Fortunately, Access 2007 supports creating ACCDE files using acCmdMakeMDEFile. Calling RunCommand with this option actually just launches two dialog boxes and has to be run in an instance of Access without a database already open. The first dialog box, Database To Save As, allows a user to select the ACCDB file that will be used to create the ACCDE. The second, Save As, allows the user to choose the output location for the ACCDE file.

Using the RunCommand is desirable when you want to allow the user to choose the ACCDB database when creating the ACCDE. However, the Save As dialog box still defaults to the MDE file extension, so the user must manually change the file extension to ACCDE before clicking the Save button. The following is a snippet of code illustrates how to implement Make ACCDE using RunCommand:

```
Sub MakeACCDERunCommand()

    ' Create a new instance of Access
    Dim app As New Access.Application

    ' Set the Automation Security to Low
    app.AutomationSecurity = MsoAutomationSecurity.msoAutomationSecurityLow

    ' Call RunCommand with the "Make MDE File" option
    app.RunCommand acCmdMakeMDEFile

End Sub
```

Automating the Access UI to Create an ACCDE

The third solution to creating an ACCDE file is to programmatically simulate a button click to the Make ACCDE menu option in the Access UI. Code can be created to automate the Access UI to give you the capability to programmatically open the Save As dialog box for an ACCDB file currently opened exclusively in an instance of Access. This functionality is desirable when the database to make the ACCDE is already known and the user just wants to select the output ACCDE file location. To implement this in VBA, the Access.Application object exposes the CommandBars collection, which enables you to work directly with the menus available in Access UI, including the old menus that are hidden in Access 2007 by default. Note that using the CommandBar and CommandBarPopup objects in code requires a VBA Reference be set to the Microsoft Office 12 Object Library in Access 2007. The following is a short example of creating a Make ACCDE function by simulating a click to the Make ACCDE button on the menu:

```
Sub MakeACCDECommandBars(strSourceACCDBPath As String)

    ' Define variables
    Dim cbp As CommandBarPopup
    Dim cbACCDE As CommandBarButton

    ' Create a new instance of Access
    Dim app As New Access.Application

    ' Enable low security and open the database in exclusive mode
```

```
        app.AutomationSecurity = MsoAutomationSecurity.msoAutomationSecurityLow
        app.OpenCurrentDatabase strSourceACCDBPath, True

        ' Get the "Database Utilities" menu object
        Set cbp = app.CommandBars("Menu Bar").Controls("Tools").Controls↵
("Database Utilities")

        ' Get the "Make ACCDE" CommandBar option
        Set cbACCDE = cb.Controls("Make ACCDE")

        ' Execute the command to open the "Save As ACCDE" dialog
        cbACCDE.Execute

    End Sub
```

This concludes the discussion about security in the ACCDB file format. So far you've learned about: Database Encryption with a Password, Locking the VBA Project, and Compiling and Removing the VBA source code by creating an ACCDE file. These three database security methods provide a good level of protection when used appropriately. The VBA code in a database solution can be secured by locking the VBA project or fully compiling and removing the VBA code by creating an ACCDE. This protects your code from being viewed or stolen, and deters code tampering. Shared-level security uses a password as a key for encrypting the database file to protect the data in the application. Password protecting the database blocks unauthorized users from viewing the database within Access. By encrypting the ACCDB file, an unauthorized user cannot view the contents of the database file using as Text or Binary reader. Combining these methods provides robust security for any database application.

There is still one important security feature missing here, which, in Access 2007, is available only in the MDB file format: user-level security. User-level security enables you to create granular permissions to individual database objects and allows discrimination of database object access based on defined user or group accounts. Although still supported by the MDB file format, user-level security has been deprecated for the ACCDB file format because there are tools that claim they can break the user-level security feature effortlessly. You can still choose to implement user-level security, but you must know that creating database solutions that employ user-level security are restricted to the feature set supported by the legacy MDB file format. The rest of this chapter is devoted to security in the MDB file format.

Security for the MDB File Format

To provide legacy support for the MDB file format, Access 2007 and the Access Connectivity Engine continue to maintain the security features available in previous versions of Access and the Jet Database Engine. With so many types of security features in Access, it is easy to become overwhelmed when deciding which method to choose. Following is a synopsis of MDB security features.

There are generally two common scenarios used when designing a database application:

❑ Standalone databases that contain all of the objects necessary to maintain the desired data, including tables, forms, reports, modules, and so forth. These databases are self-contained and consist of only one database file. These are generally used by a single user at any one time.

❑ Linked databases in which the database application uses two or more database files to fulfill its purpose. In this case, one database typically contains all of the forms, reports, and code and is usually defined as the front-end application. The other databases customarily contain the tables and data and are often defined as the back-end. This more complex model is typically reserved for multiple-user scenarios, where many people need to access data at any one time.

For the Access legacy MDB file formats, there are six security methods that can be used to secure a database. In most cases, several different methods can be applied to the same database to secure the Access solution in multiple ways.

❑ **Shared-Level Security** (also known as database passwords): Access 2007 supports creating database passwords for MDB files, as previous versions of Access did. It's important to understand the differences between setting a password on an MDB file and an ACCDB file. As with ACCDB files, the database password for an MDB is established by setting a password on a database and after it is applied, the user must enter the password before the database can be opened in Access. However, in contrast to an ACCDB, an MDB file will not be encrypted, so the data contained in the file is not obscured in any way, leaving it susceptible to Text or Binary readers. Fortunately, shared-level security in MDB files can be combined with database encoding and/or user-level security to provide additional security protection.

❑ **User-Level Security:** User-level security is established by defining user or group permissions in a Workgroup Information File (an MDW file) and defining database object permissions based on those users or groups. User-level security enables you to grant permissions to database objects based on a specific user and/or group. This can be useful when you have a number of users working in the application and each user needs specific permission to some objects, but must be locked out of other objects. Types of object-level access include adding, deleting, or updating table data, each of which can be established independently of other permissions, based on the credentials supplied by the user at login. Permissions to the database, queries, forms, reports, and pages can also be applied to specific users. This method requires much more planning and possibly more long-term maintenance than other methods, so be sure to have a clearly defined plan for how users are to interact with the application.

❑ **Database Encoding:** Encoding a database morphs the data in the file such that it cannot easily be read using a file explorer/browser tool (Windows Notepad, for example). This type of security is useful when the folder that contains the database file can be opened by anyone with network access to the system, but you need to restrict the data contained in the database to authorized users. Encoding a database does not require or apply a password to the database file. This method is typically combined with shared-level security or user-level security to enhance database security. Don't confuse Database Encoding with Database Encryption, which is only available for ACCDBs. With Database Encryption a user can be assured that the contents of the file are properly obscured; with Database Encoding, there is no guarantee of complete security.

❑ **Compiled Database Code:** As with the ACCDB file format, the VBA code project for the MDB file format database can be compiled and have the source code removed to produce an Access Compiled Database (MDE) file. When the database is compiled, the code is stored in a binary format and the readable source code is removed from the database file completely. Additionally, forms, reports, or modules cannot be modified or exported. This method for securing VBA code protects intellectual property rights and prevents users from making modifications to the code, forms, reports, pages, or modules contained in the MDE file. Be aware that creating an MDE file does not secure the data stored in the tables in the database. It is highly recommended that you adequately back up and retain a development MDB file to create distributable MDE files for users. It is also a good idea to fully test the MDE file to ensure that all scenarios are covered, so that you do not inadvertently lose any functionality or code when compiling the database. The compiled database security method is commonly used on a front-end database to block the users from modifying the database solution.

❑ **VBA Project Passwords:** VBA Passwords for MDB files are exactly the same as for ACCDB files. This method is commonly used on a front-end database to help protect the code while permitting authorized personnel to make changes to the code in the database, if necessary.

❑ **Digital Signatures:** Digital signatures enable you, the application developer, to digitally sign the code project so that users can trust and enable code in the database without having to set Macro Security to Low for all Access applications. You must sign the database with one of two types of digital certificates, and distribute the public key certificate to users who need to trust the database application. The Microsoft Office System includes a tool that enables you to create a Self-Cert, which is a certification that can be issued by the developer to the user to allow the user to trust specific database files. Access VBA Projects can also be signed certificates issued by a third-party known as a Certificate Authority (CA). Certificate Authorities specialize in researching and affirming the identity of the developer issuing the certificate and these are considered the most secure types of certificates. However, obtaining a CA certificate may be expensive and time consuming, and the company applying must make guarantees about its identity and how the certificate will be used. Digital signatures are discussed in depth in Chapter 22.

Most of these security methods can be applied to a standalone, a front-end, or a back-end database without discretion. In most cases you'll want to use a combination of these security features to get the desired level of protection. The security requirements for any database solution need to be decided when the requirements for the application design are being gathered.

Remember, it is always better to plan security from the beginning than to add it at the end. A security flaw found after the solution is implemented is much more costly to fix than had the application been initially designed to deal with the problem. The security requirements help dictate the application design as well as help uncover weak areas in the solution.

A common multi-user, secured database application scenario, which we'll call the linked database scenario, has a front-end database that contains code, forms, reports, queries, and macros, and a back-end database that contains the tables and data used within the Access solution. The front-end database is typically distributed to multiple users, so that each machine has a separate copy. The front-end application contains all of the user interface and business logic for the application and typically contains little or no data. All (or the majority) of the data that is used by the front-end application is stored in tables that are contained in the back-end database, which typically resides on the network file share, so that all users of the front-end application are sharing the same data store. Figure 18-1 shows an example of this scenario.

Linked Table Database Solution Model

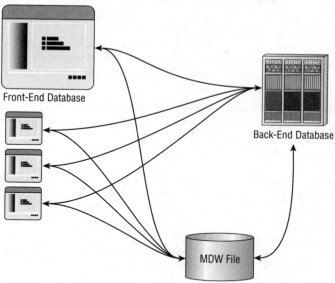

Figure 18-1

The front-end application is usually secured with user-level or shared-level security as well as having either the VBA project locked or converting the front-end database into an MDE file. Because the back-end database does not typically contain any forms, reports, or code, it generally isn't necessary to apply either method to secure code. It normally has user-level or shared-level security, or both, as well as encoded data to help abstract the raw file. All of the application data resides in the back-end database and it is typically exposed on a network file share. Encoding the data prevents it from being viewed with any normal text or binary reader. The following is a brief description about how each security method can be applied and some consideration about using each of them.

❑   **Shared-Level Security:** Shared-level security is set by applying a password to the database. Setting a password on a database requires that a password be entered before the database can be opened. The password for the front-end database does not have to be the same as the password as the back-end database. To establish a link to a table in a back-end database that has a password, the password must be entered at the time the link is created and it will be stored with the linked table connection information.

This method is easy to implement, but it has some security concerns. One is that the password to the back-end database is stored in the Access database system tables in the front-end database. An experienced user could easily determine the password to the back-end database. For that reason, it's best to have a separate password for the front-end database. Password protecting the front-end database prevents people who do not have that password from easily obtaining the back-end database password. Of course, having a password on the front-end does not prevent users who know that password from determining the password to the back-end database. Remember, the password to the back-end database will be stored in the connection properties for the linked tables in the front-end database, so a user with access to the front-end database can gain the password to the back-end database.

Another security concern with shared-level security is that a password is easy to transfer between users, and it is impossible to know who has made changes from within the application. It's often more desirable to define specific permissions for classes of users, based on the particular user's credentials. For example, you may want to have some Administrative users with access to all database objects and some Read-Only users who can only view, not modify, data. This is not possible in the shared-level security model. Fortunately, the legacy MDB file format supported by ACE still has this user-level security model available.

> **Changing the password on the back-end database requires that the table links in a front-end database be reattached. The Linked Table Manager cannot automatically re-link the tables without the new password.**

❑ **User-Level Security:** Much more complex to implement, user-level security entails creating users and groups and assigning specific permission to the database objects that the user/group needs to use. There must be a common Workgroup Information File (an MDW file) for both the front-end and the back-end databases because Access can use only one MDW at any given time. The tables in the back-end database are secured with the proper permissions, and all other objects are secured in the front-end database. The user of the application has a copy of the front-end database and MDW, plus a username and password, which are supplied at login to the application.

User-level security enhances the security in a database application, but there are tools that claim they can break these security features. If you need to ensure 100% data security, look into using Microsoft SQL Server or other high-security database products that can guarantee data security.

❑ **Encoded Tables:** Encoding the tables obscures the data in the physical database file from being easily read through the use of a text or binary reader. Because the back-end database has to be accessible to application users, you can take measures to obscure the data in the MDB file by encoding it. This deters network users who have read access to the back-end database file, but do not have permission to open the database in Access, from gathering vital or sensitive application data by opening the database file in a text reader, such as Notepad, and viewing the data.

❑ **Compiled Front-End:** Compiling the front-end database to an MDE file removes the source code, so that it cannot be read or modified by a user of the database solution. This operation is easy to complete and simply compiles the code and converts the database file to the MDE file format. (In this example, it isn't necessary to compile the back-end database because it does not include any code.)

This scenario is an everyday example of a secured Access database application. While the application is not 100% secure, it provides considerable security features that protect application and business data. You'll examine each of these security features in more detail and explore the methods available for applying them to any MDB file throughout the rest of this chapter.

Keep in mind that several of the security features are only available in the MDB file format and not the ACCDB format. Be sure to adequately plan for and consider all of the security concerns before beginning the implementation of any of these methods. Mistakes and bad assumptions about how the application will be used and what data needs to be stored can be extremely costly to repair once the initial implementation is completed.

Shared-Level Security

The Access Connectivity Engine and the Jet Database Engine only support one form of shared-level security for an MDB file: a database password. Setting a database password is a simple solution to protect a database from being opened by any network user who has access to the location of the database file. Theoretically, this method of security is most effective in situations where any person in possession of the password is permitted to insert, delete, or update the data in the database, as well as update any of the objects (forms, reports, and so forth) in the database, without discretion.

When shared-level security is applied to an MDB file format database, the user is prompted for a password each time the database is opened. In addition, any code or process trying to access the database is required to supply a password to connect to the database. Shared-level security only protects the MDB file on which the password is set and is considered a database-wide setting. When the correct password is entered, the user gains full access to the database file, including all data and all objects contained in that database.

> User-level security (discussed later in this section) does not override the database password. User-level security requires the user to log on to use a database in Access. However, if the database the user opens is also password protected, the user has to enter the shared-level password after entering the username and password for the user-level security settings.

Remember, the Access UI is identical for applying a password to either an ACCDB or an MDB, but the feature itself is very different between the two file formats. In the ACCDB file format, applying a password also automatically encrypts the data in the file. That's not the case in an MDB; adding a password only prompts the user for the password when opening the file in Access, but the data stored in the file remains unaffected, so any person with physical access to the file can still open it in a text or binary file reader and view the data stored with little effort. If you plan to apply a password to a MDB file, it is recommended that you encode the data to help obscure it.

In addition, it is highly recommended that you make a complete backup of the database before setting the database password, in case there is a problem later. Although adding a database password is easy to do via the Access UI, there may be cases where you want to use programmatic methods to change the passwords. Access provides several options for setting the database password using VBA code.

Shared-Level Secured Back-End Databases

When the front-end application links to tables in a password-protected back-end database, the password must be supplied to create the links to the back-end tables. After the tables are linked, the link and the password are stored in plain text in the database. This is true whether you link from another Access Database, create an ODC linking file, or connect to the database via any ODBC connection to access the secured database. After the link has been established, any person in possession of the front-end database can open the protected database and view any of the linked data in the back-end database, without having to supply or even know the password because the back-end database's password is stored in the information for the linked table definition.

ODC is an Office Data Connection. These connections use HTML and XML to store the connection information. Users can view and edit the data in a database through the ODC using Word, Excel, and other text editors.

This may be undesirable for your security model because it makes it quite easy for users to gain the password to the back-end database. It is extremely important to understand the security implications of creating table links to a password-protected, back-end database.

Because user-level security does not expose passwords in this manner, it is preferred for databases that utilize linked tables. At the very least, any front-end database that connects to a password-secured back-end database should also have a password applied. Finally, be sure to consider that a database must always be opened in exclusive mode to modify the password, which means all connections to a database will need to be severed to update the password.

Using the Access UI to Set the Database Password

Much like setting a database password for an ACCDB, the password for an MDB can also be applied through the Access UI. Shared-level security is added to a database from the Ribbon's Database Tools tab. The Set Database Password option is available if the database does not already have a password. The Unset Database Password option is available if the database has a shared-level password applied.

Using VBA Code to Set the Database Password

There are three possible ways to automate the process of adding or modifying a database password. The password can be set using DAO code, ADO code, or the Access OM. Fortunately, the code for setting the password for an ACCDB file is exactly the same as for an MDB file. Please consult the shared-level security section for the ACCDB file format for code examples for setting the database password programmatically.

Encoding an MDB File

To enhance data security for MDB databases, the Access Connectivity Engine and Jet support data encoding for MDB files. As previously stated, encoding the data in the database obscures the data such that it will be much more difficult to decode the data in the database and the raw file data will not show plain text data in the database. However, encoding does not come without a cost.

Aside from the initial cost of time to encode the entire database, performance when reading and writing data may decrease by as much as 15 percent. This is due to the overhead of encoding/decoding the data when making changes, or even just reading data. The Access Connectivity Engine and Microsoft Jet 4.0 data engines both read and write memory in one "page" at any given time. Each page is 4,096 bytes of data and is encoded as its own entity. When the page is loaded up, it must be decoded and if a modification is made to the data, the page must be re-encoded. All of this data processing requires extra calculations be made by the CPU when the data is encoded, which could have an impact on the overall performance of the database application. In most cases, the performance decrease is nominal from the user standpoint, but is more noticeable when the database contains large amounts of data.

Using the Access UI to Encode a Database

Encoding a database from the Access UI is easy and can be done with just a few button clicks. To encode a database, it must be opened in Exclusive mode to start. If the database is secured with user-level security, the person encoding the database must either be the owner of the database or must be a member of the Admins group.

In the Access 2007 UI, the database can be encoded through the entry points on the Ribbon. From the Database Tools tab on the Ribbon, click the Encode/Decode Database button. In the Encode Database As dialog box, choose a name for the new encoded database file that will be created, and click the Save button. Note that the original database is left open in the Access UI and a new encoded database is created as a separate file.

After the database has been encoded, do one of two things:

❑ Delete the original database file.

❑ Move the original database to a secured location where it has adequate protection from unauthorized users.

Remember, all of the raw data in the original, unencoded database file is still readable by any user who has network or other physical access to that file.

Using VBA to Encode a Database

While encoding and decoding a database is fast and easy to do through the Access UI, there are times when you want to provide the user with the capability to encode and decode the database through, say, a button click in the application. If, for example, you are developing an application that's going to be used to manage other database files, you probably want to provide an option for encoding/decoding known databases.

Unfortunately, there is no direct `EncodeDecodeDatabase` method available that takes the original database path and the new database path. You may have noticed the `acCmdEncryptDecryptDatabase` option for the `RunCommand` method. Although most `RunCommand` options bring up the necessary dialog boxes to allow the user to walk through the operation, the `acCmdEncryptDecryptDatabase` option does not seem to be usable for this situation. Fortunately, you can use the `CommandBar` objects to automate the Access UI in the same manner as shown in the previous scenario to create ACCDE files.

The workaround solution to encoding the database file programmatically is to simulate a button click to the Encode/Decode Database menu option in the Access UI. Code can be created to automate the Access UI to give you the capability to programmatically open the Encode Database As dialog box for an MDB file currently open exclusively in an instance of Access. Although there is still some user intervention required with this method, it at least gets the user part of the way there to encode the database, and can be stitched into other code if necessary.

To implement this in VBA, the `Access.Application` object exposes the `CommandBars` collection so you can work directly with all of the menus available in Access UI. Using the `CommandBar`, `CommandBarPopup`, and `CommandBarButton` objects in code requires a VBA Reference be set to the Microsoft Office 12 Object Library in Access 2007. Here's a brief example of creating an Encode Database function by simulating a click to the Encode\Decode Database button in the Access menu bar:

```
Public Sub EncodeMDBCommandBars(strSourceMDBPath As String)

    ' Define variables
    Dim cb As CommandBarPopup
    Dim cbEncode As CommandBarButton

    ' Create a new instance of Access
    Dim app As New Access.Application
```

```
' Enable low security and open the database in exclusive mode
app.AutomationSecurity = MsoAutomationSecurity.msoAutomationSecurityLow
app.OpenCurrentDatabase strSourceMDBPath, True

' Get the "Security" menu object
Set cb = app.CommandBars("Menu Bar").Controls("Tools").Controls("Security")

' Get the "Encode/Decode Database" CommandBar option
Set cbEncode = cb.Controls("Encode/Decode Database...")

' Execute the command to open the "Encode/Decode Database" dialog
cbEncode.Execute

End Sub
```

Decoding an Encoded Database

Decoding a database is as easy as encoding a database. To decode a database that has been previously encoded, the database must be opened in Exclusive mode as described earlier. Then, again, select the Encode/Decode Database option on the Ribbon's Database Tools tab. If the database has been previously encoded, the Decode Database As dialog box opens. Choose a location and click the Save button. A new, decoded copy of the database is created.

Securing VBA Code for MDBs

As with the ACCDB file format, the MDB file format supports protecting the VBA source code in an Access database solution. The methods for securing VBA code in an MDB file format in Access 2007 are locking the VBA Project or compiling the database to an MDE file. These methods are exactly the same as those for securing the VBA project in an ACCDB file, with the exception of some naming. The information applying to the ACCDB file format also applies to the MDB file format, with a few minor differences. The following sections discuss the differences between securing the code in an MDB and an ACCDB, so it may be useful to consult the earlier "Securing VBA Code for ACCDBs" section in conjunction with them.

Locking the VBA Project

As with an ACCDB file, locking the VBA project is a good way to protect the code within the Access database solution, while allowing the developer to retain the code in the actual distributed database. Locking the VBA project will deter unauthorized users from making modifications to the code, without the explicit permission of the developer. This operation is the same in either the ACCDB or the MDB file formats. For more information about locking the VBA project in Access 2007, please consult the ACCDB file format section.

Compiling the Database into an MDE file

The predecessor of the ACCDE compiled database solution was the MDE file format. The MDE and ACCDE file formats are essentially the same from a compiled code standpoint. The VBA code in the database is compiled to a binary format and the source code is removed from the VBA project in both cases. However, the ACCDE format supports the database features in the ACCDB file format and the MDE file format is used to support the legacy MDB file formats. For example, an ACCDE file supports Attachment fields, but Attachment fields are not supported by MDB file formats.

To create an MDE file from an MDB file using Access 2007, the database must be opened in exclusive mode. Also, if the database file format is older than the Access 2002 format, the database will have to be converted forward. Access 2002 and 2003 share the same database format, but neither was the default file format for Access XP or Access 2003. Access 2007 provides an even newer file format (ACCDB), which is the default format for Access. For more information about compiling the VBA Project in an Access 2007 file format database, see the "Security for the ACCDB File Format" section earlier in the chapter.

If your project has references to other databases, you must make MDE files for the referenced databases and update the references to them in the primary application's VBA project before an MDE file can be made from the current project.

Converting a Database to the 2002-2003 File Format

As mentioned above, to make an MDE file, the database must first be in the 2002-2003 MDB file format. A quick way to determine the file format of a given database in Access 2007 is by looking at the title bar for the Access client window. The title bar indicates the database file format at the end of the title bar text, inside the parenthesis. For example, the end of the text in the title bar might say "(Access 2000 file format)." In previous versions of Access, this information could be found by looking at the text in the title bar of the Database Window inside of the Access client window. If the application title is set or the MDI window mode is turned on, the file format in the title bar of Access may not be visible. Another way to quickly find the file format is to read from the tooltip on the task bar item for the instance of the database solution.

To set the Access new database file to always create databases in the 2002-2003 file format, change the default file format in the Access Options dialog box on the Popular tab, which can be found by clicking on the Office button to show the File menu.

To convert a database to the 2002-2003 MDB file format, click the Office button on the Ribbon. The Office menu will be opened. Then hover the mouse over the Save As option and a flyout menu will be shown that contains several different file format options. Choose the Access 2002–2003 Databases option and the Convert Database Into dialog box displays options for you to specify the new destination file. Enter the name of the destination file and click the Save button. The conversion will complete and a new database file will be created for the database application.

After the database has been converted to the 2002-2003 file format, users with Access 2000 or older versions will no longer be able to use the new database.

Compiling an MDB to an MDE file

Once the database application is in the 2002-2003 MDB file format, the MDE file can be built. Once the MDE file is created, it is not possible to import, export, create, modify, or rename any forms, reports, pages, or modules in the MDE file itself. Therefore, the original database that the MDE was created from should be retained in a secured location, if the application requires changes in the future. In that circumstance, you'll make the changes to the original MDB file and then create a new MDE file to distribute to the users of the application.

To create the MDE file, click the Make MDE button on the Ribbon's Database Tools tab. The Save As dialog box opens. Enter the name and path to the file to be created and click Save. The Access application is compiled and the new MDE file is created at the specified location.

> Remember: Once an MDE, always an MDE! An MDE file cannot be converted back to an MDB file format. Therefore, the original MDB file from which the MDE was created must be properly backed up and stored securely for future use.

Using VBA to Make an MDE

As discussed previously, there are three methods that can be used to programmatically create ACCDE files: Using System Command 603, Using the RunCommand acCmdMakeMDEFile option, or by automating the Access UI. In every case, you can use the identical code to create an MDE file — you simply change the name of the output file to MDE when necessary. Because the code is the same, please see the earlier section "Using VBA to Create an ACCDE" for programmatically creating MDE file. The samples for the MDB file format included with this book's download code contain examples illustrating how to automate the creation of MDE files. Of course, any conversion that may be necessary will need to happen before the MDE file can be created.

User-Level Security

The most robust form of security provided for the MDB file format is user-level security. It enables you to grant permissions to groups of users and/or to specific users for each object in a database. Objects include tables, queries, forms, reports, and macros, as well as the database itself. Because user-level security provides such granular permissions to database objects, implementing this security can be quite complex. Thorough planning and documentation will be invaluable to set up and maintain user-level security over the lifetime of a database solution. It's important to get the design right the first time — it will be costly to change the model during implementation or after development is complete.

User-level security does not override shared-level security. User-level security requires the user to log on to use a database in Access. However, if the user opens a shared-level protected database, the user also must have the password to that database. As with shared-level security, user-level security does not prevent the data from being viewed using tools other than Access. So again, consider the option of encoding the database to prevent viewing the data from other text reader tools.

There are two main database components in the user-level security model:

1.   The MDW file, also known as the Workgroup Information File.

2.   The Access database solution files (MDBs) that are to be secured.

With those two main components, there are two primary steps necessary to secure a database with user-level security.

1.   Create or update the MDW file to define user groups and users.

2.   Set up the database to grant user groups or individual users of the MDW file specific permissions to objects in the database.

The distinction, detachment, and dependency between the MDW file and the secured database will be clarified by the following discussion.

The MDW File

The workgroup information for each of the users and groups is stored in the MDW file. Every ACE database session requires loading some workgroup information for any given database file. By default, Access has a blank SYSTEM.MDW file with two groups (Admins and Users) and one user account (Admin). (The Admin user's password is set to blank by default.) Access automatically tries to log into all databases as the Admin user whenever a new Jet/ACE session is started, unless directed to login with different credentials. If Access cannot log in as the Admin user using a blank password, the Login dialog box is displayed to request user credentials. ACE loads/denies object permissions based on the User/Group Security ID's defined for each entity in the workgroup, which stored in the MDW file. The permissions applied to each specific database object for each Security ID is stored in the MDB database file.

The information stored in the MDW uniquely identifies an individual Access user and the user groups to which a given user belongs. New users and groups can be added to the MDW, but the file itself does not contain any information about the database that is being secured, it only stores the Security IDs for each User and Group. The secured database knows nothing about the users or groups defined in the workgroup, it only knows what permissions are defined for any given Security ID. Because of the distinction between the MDW and the secured database, a single MDW can contain many different user and group Security IDs that can be used for multiple database solutions.

When implementing the security model, you can define both groups and users for those groups. It is preferred, but not required, to apply specific database object permissions only to groups and not to individual users. Ideally, groups are designed around the roles and tasks a user will have in the database solution. For example, one group might handle accounting activities whereas another group maintains customer contacts. The most common method is defining all of the various group types that should have access to each database object, so that the permissions can be set for the group from the tasks a user of that group would need to perform. Once the database solution is in use, a database administrator can add specific users to each of those groups.

Users can be assigned to one or more user groups. If a user handles only accounting activities, that user can be initially assigned to the accounting group. Later, if the user becomes involved with customer contacts (through organizational changes or additions to his responsibilities), the user can be assigned to the customer contacts group in addition to the accounting group. Permissions are cumulative, meaning that the user will have the maximum permissions allowed by combining the permissions rather than restrictions of each group that the user belongs to. There will be more on the cumulative effect a bit later.

Granting permissions to a database and the objects within it is best done through groups rather than individual users. This enables you or the database administrator to change the permissions for large groups of users by simply modifying the group(s) to which those users belong, which is stored in the MDW file. Any User/Group changes are picked up the next time the user logs into the updated MDW file. On the other hand, if permissions are granted to the specific users and groups are not assigned, the administrator would need to change the permissions for each user manually, which can become quite cumbersome when there are a large number of users and/or objects in the database that need to be updated.

When you create an MDW file, you specify an internal name (separate from the file name), an organization, and a Workgroup ID (WID). These three values provide the unique information used to authenticate the MDW file. Because almost anyone could recreate an MDW file from this information, be sure to keep it secure; you'll also want to back it up if you have to recreate the MDW.

Each user in the workgroup is assigned his own Personal ID (PID) number, which is also stored in the MDW file. Any user can belong to one or more user groups. Each group is assigned its own Group ID (GID). The authentication information in the MDW file, along with the username and PID, uniquely identifies an Access user.

> **Usernames in the MDW file are in no way associated with the Windows user information or NT Domain Authentication. The user and group information contained in the MDW is completely independent of the Windows User Account. Any Windows User Account can log in to the database, provided the user supplies the correct database and MDW username and passwords.**

To identify users with the MDW file, the database engine running the application receives a set of identification credentials, considered a pass code. Each pass code has a unique characteristic based on the authentication information in the file plus the username and PID, or the authentication information in the file plus the group name and GID. The actual secured database application (not the MDW file) will use these pass codes to determine whether to grant a user permission to the objects in that database.

As previously mentioned, every ACE and Jet database session requires information from an MDW file. A default system MDW file is created for each Windows User Account when a database is opened if there is no default SYSTEM.MDW file present. The default location for this file is C:\Users\user name\AppData\Roaming\Microsoft\Access\System.mdw on Windows Vista or C:\Documents and Settings\user name\Application Data\Microsoft\Access\System.mdw for previous versions of Windows. The Access application is joined to this MDW by default if no other MDW is explicitly specified, meaning that the information contained in SYSTEM.MDW is used when databases are opened. By default, the Admin password in the default SYSTEM.MDW is set to blank, which is why there is no password prompt when opening normal, non-secured databases in Access. For this reason, it is extremely important to understand that if the default SYSTEM.MDW file is modified, and users and groups are added to the default SYSTEM.MDW file, the user for that Windows User Account will always be prompted to log on when opening *any* database, which can become extremely confusing. It is highly recommended that you never modify the default SYSTEM.MDW file. It's always preferable to create a new MDW file and to use a Windows shortcut to open a secured database with the specific MDW file, which will be discussed shortly.

Though not recommended, the Access client can also be joined to a different MDW than the default MDW file created for the Windows user account. To join the Access application to a different pre-existing system.mdw file, use the Workgroup Administrator dialog box. In previous versions of Access, the Workgroup Administrator dialog box could be invoked by selecting Tools ➪ Security ➪ Workgroup Administrator. In Access 2007, the Workgroup Administrator option is no longer available through the Access UI to discourage changing the default joined MDW file. However, you can still use this dialog box; launch it by calling the RunCommand object with the acCmdWorkgroupAdministrator parameter. But remember, if you do decide to modify the permissions in the default system MDW file, the Access user for that Windows account may be prompted to enter a password for his account for every database opened, not just one specific database solution.

If you decide to manipulate the information in the default joined MDW file, it is critical that you create a backup copy of the current MDW. The default MDW file name is SYSTEM.MDW. The current default location is defined in the Workgroup Administrator dialog box.

The Database To Be Secured

The second component of user-level security is the database that is secured at the user-level by granting permissions to each object in that database. Permissions authorize the actions that can be taken on an object. They are granted to Access users based on the pass codes in the MDW file that are in use when user-level security is set up.

> *An Access user does not use the MDW file until he opens a database. If no MDW file is explicitly specified, the default joined MDW file is used. However, the /wrkgrp command line switch can be used when Access is started to specify the path to the MDW file to use for the particular database. These techniques are discussed later.*

The object types that can have permissions set include the database, tables, queries, forms, reports, and macros. Each object, regardless of type, has its own set of permissions. That is, each table in a database has a set of permissions distinct from other tables in the database. Therefore, it is possible to permit a particular user group to have read-only access to some tables while allowing the group to update data in other tables. For example, the database owner could grant database administrators permission to add, modify, or delete values in lookup tables, but deny them permission to change records that refer to those lookup tables.

Permissions are granted to a group or an individual user based on the pass codes previously mentioned. Remember that the pass code consists of the MDW file authentication information plus the group name and Group ID or the MDW file authentication information plus the username and Personal ID. If a user selects the wrong MDW file, even if he is defined in the MDW file that he's selected, he will not be granted the intended permissions because the pass codes will not be the same. This is another reason why it is important to maintain backups of your MDW file and adequate documentation for each of the groups and users contained in it.

> *Microsoft Support provides additional information regarding Access Security and the MDW file. For an alternative explanation of security visit* http://support.microsoft.com/default.aspx?scid=kb;EN-US;305542. *You can search the Microsoft Knowledge base for more answers at* http://support.microsoft.com/default.aspx?pr=kbhowto.

As mentioned earlier, permissions are granted to the user cumulatively. Members of a group receive all of the permissions granted to the group, as well as their own specific set of permissions. If a user is granted permissions that exceed any of the permissions of the groups that the user belongs to, that user receives the additional individual permissions, as well as the most permissive authority from each of the groups to which the user belongs.

To put this cumulative permission effect another way, when users identify themselves to Access through an MDW file, they receive pass codes as follows: one for the username and then one for each group to which they belong. For each of those pass codes, ACE/Jet grants the users all of the permissions that have been granted for the pass code in the secured database. For example, if a user belongs to a group that has read-only permission on the Customer's table, but the individual user is also given update permission for the Customer table, any request to update data in the Customer's table is granted for that user, but not for the group.

The cumulative effect shows why it is important to define the appropriate user groups when designing the database solution, prior to creating the MDW file. Theoretically, it should be possible to create the application so that there is no need for any user to be granted specific permissions outside of the set of permissions available in any group. If the user changes groups, the database administrator need only change the group to which the user belongs, rather than re-analyze and update all of the user's individual permissions for each object. Also, if another user starts working under a role that has already been defined in the MDW file, the user only needs to be assigned to the group that has the correct permission set and removed from the previous group. The bottom line is that assigning permissions to groups appropriately when the application is designed means less cost, work, and headaches for long-term database solution maintenance.

If a database consists of many objects, many user groups, and multiple users, implementing user-level security can be a time-consuming process. If permissions are maintained at the group level and not the user level, there may be additional cost for the initial implementation because each user account needs to be set up, instead of just assigning permissions to each group. Following is a table of different types of permissions provided by ACE and Jet for the MDB file format.

The Owner of the database or of an object in a database always has all permissions to that database or object in the database, regardless of any other permissions.

Permission	Objects	Actions
Open/Run	Database, Form, Report, Macro	Open a database, form, or report, or run a macro in a database.
Open Exclusive	Database	Open a database with exclusive access.
Read Design	Table, Query, Form, Report, Macro	View tables, queries, forms, reports, or macros in Design view.
Modify Design	Table, Query, Form, Report, Macro	View and change the design of tables, queries, forms, reports, or macros; or delete them.
Administer	Database, Table, Query, Form, Report, Macro	For databases, set a database password, replicate a database, and change startup properties. For tables, queries, forms, reports, and macros have full access to these objects and data, including ability to assign permissions.
Read Data	Table, Query	View data in tables and queries.
Update Data	Table, Query	View and modify, but not insert or delete, data in tables and queries.
Insert Data	Table, Query	View and insert, but not modify or delete, data in tables and queries.
Delete Data	Table, Query	View and delete, but not modify or insert, data in tables and queries.

Methods To Create User-Level Security

The three methods for securing a database application with user-level security are as follows:

❑ Use the User-Level Security Wizard to help build the security model.

❑ Use the Access UI to set database permissions manually.

❑ Use the support provided in VBA, including using DAO, ADO, or ADOX or some combination thereof.

These are all fairly large topics that you'll tackle in the following sections.

Using the User-Level Security Wizard

The User-Level Security Wizard is perhaps the easiest method for implementing user-level security. The wizard walks through all the steps necessary to secure the database, including setting up user and group accounts. The wizard automatically creates everything necessary for securing the database, greatly reducing the cost in time to set up the database security manually. The wizard is also a good way to get the hang of using user-level security.

> *The User-Level Security Wizard cannot be used while a database has shared-level security or if the project has been locked from viewing (both discussed earlier). Both need to be disabled prior to running the wizard. These options can easily be added after the wizard has completed its work.*

The wizard is self-explanatory and quite useful, but after user-level security has been established and if it becomes necessary to modify the security settings for a database, the multi-step process of the wizard can be cumbersome. Nevertheless, the wizard provides tools for making changes to security. For example, it has the capability to set passwords for users, provide random Personal IDs, and even create a new MDW file and the necessary Windows shortcut files to open the secured database. Other Access user interface options do not support these features.

Before starting the wizard, consider that it provides a defined set of default groups that include common permission settings based on the group type. These groups can be useful if the permissions types fit the roles of users in your secured database solution. You want to ensure that the design of the group permissions is consistent with the structure of the database solution's design and purpose. Carefully analyze the database objects and their dependencies to define groups before running the wizard. It will be helpful to draw out a representation of the database objects, what those objects depend on, and the groups/users that will need access to each database object.

The User-Level Security Wizard

The User-Level Security Wizard is a great way to set up security on a database. The wizard can secure the database so that:

❑ The creator is the owner of the database and each object in the database.

❑ The owner user has full access to the database.

❑ The Admin group has full access to the database.

❑ The default Admin user has no access to the database.

❏ Permissions are applied to database objects for specific users and groups.

❏ The Users group has no access to the database.

❏ The database itself is encoded (see the earlier "Encoding an MDB File" section).

To start the wizard, click the User-Level Security Wizard button on the Database Tools tab. (Ironically, if you start the wizard with the database open exclusively, you are prompted to reopen the database in shared mode. With the database open in shared mode, the wizard dialog box is invoked.)

Creating an MDW File

The first step in the wizard is to select or create the MDW file that will contain the group and user information to be defined in the database solution. As mentioned earlier, this can be a new file or the default file provided when Access is first used. The recommended approach is to always create a new MDW file for each database application and a custom Windows shortcut to invoke the application. This discourages Access users from accidentally locking themselves out of databases. The User-Level Security Wizard will not permit you to modify the original default SYSTEM.MDW file.

> To enable the option to Modify My Current Workgroup Information File on the first page of the wizard, create a new MDW file through the Workgroup Administrator dialog box and join Access to the new MDW as the default. But remember, this may result in Access prompting for a password anytime that Windows users log in and will apply permissions to all new databases automatically from the new default MDW file.

The second page of the wizard displays the objects that exist in the database, separated into groups under each tab of the named object types. The wizard sets permissions for the objects that are selected, but only for the predefined groups it provides. It also sets ownership for the selected objects. Because this is the first time through the wizard, select all objects using the All Objects tab, click Select All, and then click Next.

On the third page of the wizard, you select groups to receive permissions on the previously selected object. (If you have defined your own set of groups, they are displayed in the list. Also, the wizard provides a set of default groups from which to choose. The wizard doesn't know how to set up permissions for custom groups, though, so do not select your own groups.) Select a group by checking the box next to it. A description of the permissions to be set for that predefined group is then displayed to the right. The advantage to using the default groups is that default permissions are set up. A disadvantage is that any user signed in through Access has the same default groups and permissions. The wizard does not remove any groups from the MDW file. When you have selected all of the predefined groups for the application, click Next.

The wizard's next page enables you to set permission for the Users group. Recall that every user must belong to the Users group. This means that anyone who logs on receives the permissions assigned to the Users group. Therefore it is strongly recommended that you select the No, The Users Group Should Not Have Any Permissions option to prevent unwanted access to the database. Click Next.

The wizard's fifth page enables you to create new users and assign passwords. If you created users when the MDW file was set up, this step can be skipped. If the users were not created earlier, add them now. Be sure to record the PID (Personal ID) for users that are added, especially if the MDW file needs to be re-created later.

Sometimes it is effective to use the same PID for all users. Because the PID cannot be changed by the user, having a standard PID for the database can make it easier to recreate a MDW file if that becomes necessary.

Once all of the user accounts have been created, click Next.

On the wizard's sixth page, you assign groups to users or users to groups, depending on which option is selected. If you created new users on the previous page, be sure to assign them to the appropriate group or groups. Once all users have been assigned to their respective groups, click Next.

The wizard's seventh and last page enables you to specify a backup file location for the database about to be protected with user-level security. The backup file will remain unsecured and should be saved in a safe location. Keep it at least until the security in the database application has been verified to be working correctly. Click Finish to complete the wizard.

You now have all of the pieces necessary to use user-level security in the database application, except the specific permissions each group will have for each object. By default, all groups have their specific permission set applied to all of the database objects. However, you often want to deny permissions to certain database objects for some groups. To modify permissions for specific database objects for users and groups, use the User and Group Permissions dialog box, which is discussed shortly.

Using the Access User Interface

There are many steps involved in creating and using user-level security using the Access user interface. Although it can be much more cumbersome to set up user-level security using the Access UI, it does provide two pieces that the wizard does not: Fine-grained control about how to define users and groups and the capability to assign specific database objects to users and groups. To help explain all of the components of user-level security, this section covers the options available to maintain security from the Access UI options, without using the User-Level Security Wizard.

Creating an MDW File

The first step in setting up user-level security is to select or create the MDW file that will contain the user groups and users to be defined.

As mentioned earlier, this can be a new file or the default file provided when Access is first used. The recommended approach is to always create a new MDW file. To deter users from accidentally locking themselves out of Access, the User-Level Security Wizard will not permit you to use the default SYSTEM.MDW file.

> **If you corrupt the default MDW file, you will have to manually recover that file from another source. Whenever modifying or changing the default MDW file, make a backup and store it in a safe location. Of course, users and groups will also need to have the same ID as well for the permissions to be granted properly.**

Many developers prefer to create application-specific MDW files with names that indicate the underlying application, making it easy to keep track of the MDW associations. It also makes creating (or reading) shortcuts and target paths a bit more obvious.

As previously mentioned, the Workgroup Administrator dialog box is used to create new MDW files, as well as join to a different default MDW. In Access 2007, you invoke this dialog box by calling the RunCommand object with the acCmdWorkgroupAdministrator parameter. This can be called from VBE in the immediate window with the following code:

```
RunCommand acCmdWorkgroupAdministrator
```

While this also works in previous versions of Access, there was also a UI option available, which has been deprecated in Access 2007 to discourage the use of modifying the default system MDW file. In previous versions of Access, to create or select the MDW file, choose Tools ➪ Security ➪ Workgroup Administrator. Calling either the RunCommand or selecting the menu option invokes the Workgroup Administrator dialog box. The Workgroup Administrator dialog box displays the path to the MDW file that is currently joined, as well as options to create a new MDW file or join to a different existing MDW file.

To create a new MDW file, click the Create button. The Workgroup Owner Information dialog box opens. Supply values for the Name, Organization, and Workgroup ID. This information uniquely identifies the authenticity of the MDW file. The Workgroup ID can be from 4 to 20 characters, and should be treated much the same as a password to prevent anyone from guessing it. Once the information has been entered in the Workgroup Owner Information dialog box, click OK. The Workgroup Information File dialog box displays.

The default location is in the C:\Documents and Settings\<user name>\Application Data\Microsoft\Access *folder with the default name of* SYSTEMx.MDW. *On Windows Vista, this path will be like* C:\Documents\<user name>\Application Data\Microsoft\Access.

Enter the name and location for the Workgroup file and click OK. The Confirm Workgroup Information displays all the settings for the new MDW file. Be sure to keep a record of the Name, Organization, and Workgroup ID, as these three items can be used to re-create the MDW if the original is lost or somehow rendered unusable. You also need each of the user and group names and IDs as well to re-create the specific user accounts. Then click OK to complete the creation of the new MDW file. It is recommended that you make a backup copy of this new MDW file in case the file becomes corrupted at a later time.

When the MDW file is created through the Workgroup Administrator dialog box, it is automatically joined as the new default MDW file. The MDW file that was last joined is automatically selected the next time Access is invoked under the same Windows user profile on the computer.

Joining an MDW File

Although it is not recommended, users can join an MDW file to set the default access to the correct set of pass codes for the databases they will use. Refer to the previous MDW file discussion for more information about pass codes.

To join an existing MDW file, open the Workgroup Administrator dialog box (as explained earlier). In the Workgroup Administrator dialog box, click the Join button to display the Workgroup Information File dialog box. This dialog box enables the user to enter the MDW filename and path (or browse to the desired MDW file). Click OK to join that MDW file.

It is not recommended to join to a different MDW file than the user default because the next time the user starts a new Jet/ACE session, the user will be prompted to enter his user credentials. Instead, create a Windows shortcut that points to the specific MDW file for the database application. This can be accomplished using the /wrkgrp *command-line option. The command-line specified MDW will override the default joined MDW file for that instance of the Access database solution.*

Finally, if the original system MDW file is modified and you want to restore the default system MDW file created by Access, simply delete the currently joined MDW file. The next time Access starts, it will try to open the default system MDW, see that it does not exist, and re-create a new, blank system MDW. This can be helpful if usernames or passwords are lost for a non-default joined MDW file.

Updating the MDW File

When a new MDW file is created, it contains one user (Admin) and two groups (Admins and Users). The Admin user is initially assigned to both groups. An MDW file must have at least one user that belongs to the Admins group. All users must belong to the Users group.

The first recommended action for an MDW file is to create a new user to administer the MDW file. Later, you will remove the Admin user from the Admins group and change the ownership of the database to the new administrator, which is necessary because all MDW files have the Admin user and Admins group. If these changes are not made, a default MDW file could be used to gain access to the database. (Learn more about this in the "Setting Permissions on Database Objects" section later in the chapter.)

To create a new user as the administrator, click the User and Group Accounts button on the Ribbon's Database Tools tab. The User and Group Accounts dialog box opens. Select the Users tab and click the New button to display the New User/Group dialog box.

Enter the name for the user to be set as an administrator and a Personal ID number. The Personal ID must be 4 to 20 characters and digits in length. (Follow the same general rules for specifying a password.) Record the Personal ID so that this can be communicated to the new administrator later. This information is critical in the event that the MDW file needs to be recovered.

Click OK to save the new user information. In the User and Group Accounts dialog box, be sure the user created is selected in the Name field. In the Group Membership section of the form, in the Available Groups list, select the Admins group and click the Add >> button to add the Admins group to the new user's assigned groups. (If you need to remove it at some time, select the Admin user in the Name field, and in the Member Of list, select the Admins group and click the << Remove button.)

The Login Dialog Box

By default, the password for the Admin user account is blank. When Access loads a new session of the ACE/Jet database engine, it automatically tries to log in as the Admin user account with a blank password, unless explicitly specified to do otherwise. When it cannot load the database engine with those credentials, Access prompts the user for a username and password via the login dialog box. This means that once the Admin account password has been set, anytime an ACE/Jet database session is started without supplying the user credentials, the Access UI will present the logon dialog box. Furthermore, if the user does not supply a known set of credentials, he will not be able to open the database. This is one of the main reasons we recommend that you don't modify the default joined MDW file and that you always create a new file to distribute with the application.

The logon prompt occurs only once per ACE/Jet session. For example, the first time a database is opened from the Access client causes a new session ACE/Jet engine session to be started. If the user joins another (or rejoins the current) MDW file, a new session also starts for the current database.

Once a password has been applied to a user in the workgroup, the settings will be enabled the next time the MDW file is opened. When creating a new MDW file, always apply a password to the Admin user account. That prevents another user from setting it without permission and also ensures that the password is set appropriately; that's important because this account has the highest set of permissions in the database.

A quick way to verify a change to an MDW file is to rejoin the MDW file. To do this, open the Workgroup Administrator dialog box and choose the Join option previously discussed. This will cause Access to close the current session and create a new session for the database that is currently opened. Of course, if a database session has not been previously started, you will need to open a database to start an ACE/Jet session to verify the MDW modifications.

To assign passwords to new users, you must log on as that user or use VBA code.

Setting Permissions on Database Objects

After the workgroup information has been established and all of the groups have been created, the database object for the particular MDB file needs to have permissions applied. The User and Group Permissions dialog box can be used to add permissions to any database currently opened in Access, based on the workgroup information loaded for that session. Of course, the person modifying the permissions is required to have the proper permissions to modify those objects.

If the database were created with a different MDW file than the one loaded for the session, you may have to log on as the Admin user to set permissions using the new MDW file. This happens because the default owner of a database created under the MDW file is Admin, as noted previously. If new administrative user ownership has not been given any of the database objects, the user will not have permissions to administer the database.

The best way to avoid this particular problem is to recreate the database while logged in as a member of the Admins group in the new MDW file. Once logged in as this user, you can create a new database and import all objects from the original database (be sure not to import linked tables, create new links to those tables). This will ensure that the owner of the database and all objects in the database are set to the expected user and tied to the correct MDW file.

Because administrative permissions are granted by the database, and not by the MDW file, a user who belongs to the Admins group of the MDW file may not be able to administer the database. The user can administer the database only if the user or the user's group has been given administrative permissions or if the user is the database owner. Some permissions, such as setting a new owner of an object, can be set only by the owner of the database.

To begin setting permissions for database objects, select User and Group Permissions on the Ribbon's Database Tools tab. The User and Group Permissions dialog box displays. To remove the permissions for the Users group, click the Groups radio button option. A list of the groups in the MDW file displays under the User/Group Name list box. Click Users to select the Users group. The form shows a list of all of the objects under the Object Name list for the type of object selected in the Object Type combo box. To add permissions to the object for the user or group, click the user or group to select it, click the database object(s) to select them, and then check the appropriate permission type checkboxes in the permissions section on the form.

You can select multiple objects from the Object Name list using the click-and-drag-over — Ctrl+click or Shift+click — methods.

To revoke all permissions from the selected objects, clear the checkboxes for each permission type listed in the Permissions group at the bottom of the dialog box.

Removing the check from the Read Design permission removes all permissions except the Open/Run permission.

When the desired permissions are set or unset, be sure to click Apply before selecting another Object Type or user or group. Continue to remove permissions from the user group Users by selecting each of the other object types: Database, Query, Form, Report, and Macro. Permissions do not change until a user has logged into the database after the updated settings have been saved.

In some instances, removing the permissions from <New Tables/Queries> does not prevent a user from creating a new table. All security settings should be independently verified for each user. (Using the User-Level Security Wizard for the initial setup can prevent this problem.) If there are problems removing permissions using the Access UI, use VBA code to change the permissions. Additionally, removing permissions from <New Form>, <New Report>, and <New Macros> objects does not always prevent a user from attempting to create a new object. However, if the user does not have permission to open the database exclusively, she will not be able to save the object.

As noted earlier, the owner of the database and the owner of each object in the database always have administrative permissions for their respective objects. Permissions cannot be revoked from these owners, even if the permission settings are changed to deny. For that reason, use the User-Level Security Wizard to perform the initial security setup. The wizard changes ownership of all of the selected objects to the user who is logged on when the wizard is run.

To change the owner for objects other than the database itself, select the Change Owner tab on the User and Group Permission dialog box. Then select the objects to set permissions on using the click-and-drag-over, Ctrl+click, or Shift+click method. You may choose to assign ownership to a user group or a specific user. Because any user who belongs to the Admins group probably needs full access no matter what permissions are set, setting the owner to Admins group is desirable. Select the Groups radio button option for the list, which is found just below the New Owner combo box. Select the Admins group in the New Owner combo box, and then click the Change Owner button. As with setting permissions, each object type can have a different owner. Be sure to set the ownership for each object type.

> New groups are not granted any permissions by default. When creating a new group, be sure to grant Open/Run permission for the Database object type for that group; otherwise that group's users will not be able to open the database.

The Database Owner Account

As explained previously, the owner account always has full permissions to the database or any object in the database. This presents a bit of a problem. The first consideration is that the user Admin owns a database if that database was created using the default MDW file. That means that this particular database can be accessed through the Admin user of any MDW file, even after removing all permissions from the Admin user, and even if the MDW is not the file used to set up user-level security.

The second consideration is that the Access UI only allows changing object ownership using the User-Level Security Wizard. The upside to this is that the wizard also adjusts other permission settings quickly. See "Using the User-Level Security Wizard" earlier in the chapter for more information.

If you do not want the Admin user to be the owner of a given database, log in to Access as the user who will be the owner, and then create a new database and import all the objects. That prevents the Admin from another MDW file having ownership rights to the database object itself.

Encoding a User-Level Secured Database

Securing a database with user-level security does not prevent anyone from exploring the database using a tool other than Access. As mentioned previously, much of the physical data contained in the MDB file is in plain text and readable to many different tools. For instance, Windows Notepad could be used to look at the data contained in the database simply by opening an un-encoded database file.

If there is a need to secure a database with user-level security, it is likely that the data in the database is somewhat sensitive in nature. As such, allowing any network user to open the file and read the contents is unacceptable. So, it is recommended that any database secured with user-level security also be encoded to help further protect the data in the database. Fortunately, the User-Level Security Wizard encodes the database automatically.

Linking to a User-Level Secured Database

Unlike shared-level security, linking to tables in a user-level secured database does not store security information in the front-end database file. The front-end application and linked back-end application must use the same MDW file because ACE can have only one workgroup file per session. When the ACE session starts, it loads the Workgroup Information and uses that data to authenticate the user information. When accessing data in a back-end database, ACE uses the information loaded for the current session and there is no way for you to specify a second MDW file. That means the user must use the MDW associated with the database for both the front-end and back-end database files.

If different MDW files are used for the front-end and back-end databases, the user may automatically be logged in as the Admin account (if there is no password set) or prompted for a username and password, which won't ever work if the Workgroup Information in the current session is different than the MDW file used to create the database file. Recall that the identity of the user in the MDW file provides a set of pass codes to access objects within the database. With the wrong pass codes, a user is denied access to the back-end database.

User-Level Security Using DAO

User-level security can be modified using DAO code. Users and Groups are collections of the Database Engine Workspace. The procedures defined here work with users and groups on the open workspace in the current database engine, so the current session must use the correct MDW file to use these procedures. Additionally, these example procedures set permissions in the database that is open (returned by the CurrentDB object). Calling these methods in the current database will result in modifying the MDW file used when the sample database is opened.

The DAO.PermissionsEnum enumeration defines the appropriate numeric values for setting a permission. The ShowSampleDAO procedure later in this section demonstrates how to use this enumeration.

The following declarations are used in the procedures that show how to use DAO to set up user-level security. Note that the cUser and cPW variables should be the username and password for the current user of the database solution, and not the admin username and password, so that the proper permissions are maintained throughout the use of the application.

```
' Define Global Constants
Const cUser = "Admin"
Const cPW = ""
```

Maintaining Groups with DAO

The AddGroupDAO procedure adds groups to the MDW file. The RemoveGroupDAO procedure drops groups from the MDW file. Adding groups to the MDW file does not modify the original database in any way, only the MDW file.

To add a group, create an object of type Group, set the properties for it, and then append the group to the Groups collection for the workspace:

```
Public Sub AddGroupDAO(strGroupName As String, strGID As String)

    ' Define variables
    Dim ws As Workspace
    Dim grp As New Group

    ' Create a workspace object for the database
    Set ws = DBEngine.CreateWorkspace("DAOWS", cUser, cPW)

    ' Set Group properties
    grp.Name = strGroupName
    grp.PID = strGID

    ' Append the Group to the Groups Collection
    ws.Groups.Append grp

    ' Clean up
    ws.Close
    Set ws = Nothing

End Sub
```

To drop a group, simply delete it from the Groups collection of the Workspace:

```
Public Sub RemoveGroupDAO(strGroupName As String)

    ' Define variables
    Dim ws As Workspace

    ' Create a workspace object for the database
    Set ws = DBEngine.CreateWorkspace("DAOWS", cUser, cPW)

    ' Delete the Group from the Collection
    ws.Groups.Delete strGroupName
```

```
    ' Clean up
    ws.Close
    Set ws = Nothing

End Sub
```

Maintaining Users with DAO

The `AddUserDAO` and `RemoveUserDAO` procedures add and drop users from the MDW. As with groups, adding users to the MDW does not modify the original database in any way, only the MDW file.

To add a user, create an object of type User, set the properties for it, and then append the user to the Users collection of the Workspace:

```
Public Sub AddUserDAO(strUserName As String, strPassword As String, strPID As
String)

    ' Define variables
    Dim ws As Workspace
    Dim usr As New User

    ' Create a workspace object for the database
    Set ws = DBEngine.CreateWorkspace("DAOWS", cUser, cPW)

    ' Assign the properties to the user
    usr.Name = strUserName
    usr.Password = strPassword
    usr.PID = strPID

    ' Append the User to the Users Collection
    ws.Users.Append usr

    ' Add the user to the "Users" group - Access requirement
    AddUserToGroupDAO strUserName, "Users"

    ' Clean up
    ws.Close
    Set ws = Nothing
    Set usr = Nothing

End Sub
```

Notice that the `AddUserDAO` procedure also calls the `AddUserToGroupDAO` subroutine, which is defined shortly. This forces the developer to keep the data in the MDW file consistent with the Access rule that all users must belong to the Users group.

To drop a user, simply delete it from the Users collection of the Workspace:

```
Public Sub RemoveUserDAO(strUserName As String)

    ' Define variables
    Dim ws As Workspace
```

```
' Create a workspace object for the database
Set ws = DBEngine.CreateWorkspace("DAOWS", cUser, cPW)

' Delete the User from the collection
ws.Users.Delete (strUserName)

' Clean up
ws.Close
Set ws = Nothing

End Sub
```

The `AddUserToGroupDAO` subroutine called earlier in the `AddUserDAO` subroutine adds a specified user to a specified group. To do this, the code gets a new workspace instance, gets the specified user and groups objects in that workspace, and then appends the user to the group. Here's an example of how to perform this operation:

```
Public Sub AddUserToGroupDAO(strUserName As String, strGroupName As String)

    ' Define variables
    Dim ws As Workspace
    Dim grp As Group
    Dim usr As User

    ' Create a workspace object for the database
    Set ws = DBEngine.CreateWorkspace("DAOWS", cUser, cPW)

    ' Get the User object for the specified user
    Set usr = ws.Users(strUserName)

    ' Get the Group object for the specified group
    Set grp = usr.CreateGroup(strGroupName)

    ' Append the Group changes Groups Collection
    usr.Groups.Append grp

    ' Clean up
    Set usr = Nothing
    Set grp = Nothing
    ws.Close
    Set ws = Nothing

End Sub
```

To drop a user from a group, delete it from Users collection of that group:

```
Public Sub RemoveUserFromGroupDAO(strUserName As String, strGroupName As String)

    ' Define variables
    Dim ws As Workspace
    Dim usr As User
```

```
' Create a workspace object for the database
Set ws = DBEngine.CreateWorkspace("DAOWS", cUser, cPW)

' Delete the User from the Group in which it belongs
ws.Groups(strGroupName).Users.Delete strUserName

' Clean up
ws.Close
Set ws = Nothing

End Sub
```

Maintaining Permissions with DAO

Understanding the detachment between the MDW file and the file that is being secured (as discussed in the "User-Level Security" section), consider that although users and groups are maintained through the DB Engine Workspace, permissions are applied to the current database.

The following procedures demonstrate setting permissions for containers (SetPermissionsOnContainerDAO) and objects (SetPermissionsOnObjectDAO).

Setting permissions for containers (database, tables, queries, forms, reports, macros) sets the permissions for the New object (shown as *New Table/Query* in the Access UI):

```
Public Sub SetPermissionsOnContainerDAO( _
    strContainer As String, _
    strUserName As String, _
    lngPermissions As Long)

    ' Define Variables
    Dim db As Database
    Dim con As Container

    ' Get the current database object
    Set db = CurrentDb()

    ' Get the Container object
    Set con = db.Containers(strContainer)

    ' Set the User name for the container
    con.UserName = strUserName

    ' Set the user's permissions for the container
    con.Permissions = lngPermissions

    ' Clean up
    Set con = Nothing
    db.Close
    Set db = Nothing

End Sub
```

Applying permissions to a database object adds the permissions only to that object. The `SetPermissionsOnObjectDAO` function requires you to specify the container of the object (that's because a form and a table, for instance, could have the same name):

```
Public Sub SetPermissionsOnObjectDAO( _
    strContainer As String, _
    strDocument As String, _
    strUserName As String, _
    lngPermissions As Long)

    ' Define variables
    Dim db As Database
    Dim doc As Document

    ' Get the current database object
    Set db = CurrentDb()

    ' Get the specified Document in the Container
    Set doc = db.Containers(strContainer).Documents(strDocument)

    ' Set the User name for the Document
    doc.UserName = strUserName

    ' Set the user's permissions for the Document
    doc.Permissions = lngPermissions

    ' Clean up
    Set doc = Nothing
    db.Close
    Set db = Nothing

End Sub
```

Working with the DAO.Permission Enumeration

In DAO, the permission object is nothing more than a long integer which stores a set of bits representing the various permission settings. Multiple permission types can be set for a single permission object by OR-ing the permissions types together. Using the OR logic to mask the bits together *preserves all* "1" bits in the both of the enumeration values being operated on, producing a cumulative effect for the permissions. Do not confuse OR logic with AND logic, which only preserves the "1" bits *common to both* values, a common mistake developers can make. The following is an example function which will combine two permission objects into one permission object, preserving both permission settings applied:

```
Public Function CombinePermissions( _
    lngInitialPermissions As Long, _
    lngPermissionToCombine As Long) As Long

    ' Combine the Permissions together
    CombinePermissions = lngInitialPermissions Or lngPermissionToCombine

End Function
```

In contrast to combining permissions together, it is conceivable that a developer wants to write procedures to revoke permissions. This can be not by using the AND NOT operators for the permission to remove. In the case, the NOT operator flips the bits in the permission to be removed, and then AND logic removes the specific permission type. The following is an example of how a function could be created to remove a specific set of permissions form the permission value:

```
Public Function RevokePermissions( _
    lngInitialPermissions As Long, _
    lngPermissionToRemove As Long) As Long

    ' Combine the Permissions together
    RevokePermissions = lngInitialPermissions And Not lngPermissionToRemove

End Function
```

The ChangeOwnerDAO procedure is included with the permissions section because owners always have full permissions. Notice that it is only possible to change ownership on documents (that is, tables, forms, reports, pages, and macros), not on the database or the containers.

```
Public Sub ChangeOwnerDAO( _
    strContainer As String, _
    strDocumentName As String, _
    strOwner As String)

    ' Define variables
    Dim db As Database
    Dim doc As Document

    ' Get the current database object
    Set db = CurrentDb()

    ' Get the Document object
    Set doc = db.Containers(strContainer).Documents(strDocumentName)

    ' Change the Owner of the Document
    doc.Owner = strOwner

    ' Clean up
    Set doc = Nothing
    db.Close
    Set db = Nothing

End Sub
```

Sample Setup Code Using DAO

The following example shows various calls to the preceding DAO procedures:

```
Public Sub RunSampleDAO()

    ' Define variable
    Dim strReturnValue As String
    Dim bHasPerms As Boolean
```

```
        Dim db As Database
        Dim doc As Document


        ' Show initial information
        strReturnValue = "Initial Settings: " & vbNewLine & GetCurrentUserGroupInfo &
vbNewLine & vbNewLine


        ' Add a New User and Group
        AddGroupDAO "TestGroup", "12345"
        AddUserDAO "TestUser", "", "1234"
        AddUserToGroupDAO "TestUser", "TestGroup"
        strReturnValue = strReturnValue & "After Adding a User and Group: " & vbNewLine
& GetCurrentUserGroupInfo & vbNewLine & vbNewLine


        ' Set Read and Write Permissions for the "Tables" container
        Call SetPermissionsOnContainerDAO( _
            "Tables", _
            "TestUser", _
            CombinePermissions(dbSecReadDef, dbSecWriteDef))


        ' Set Permissions for a specific "Form" object
        Call SetPermissionsOnObjectDAO("Forms", "frmMain", "TestUser", dbSecFullAccess)


        ' Verify the user has permission on the object
        Set db = CurrentDb
        Set doc = db.Containers("Forms").Documents("frmMain")
        bHasPerms = HasPermission(doc.Permissions, dbSecFullAccess)
        strReturnValue = strReturnValue & "Check to make sure the permissions " & _
            "have been applied (Should be 'True'): " & bHasPerms & vbNewLine & vbNewLine


        ' Remove the New User and Group
        RemoveUserFromGroupDAO "TestUser", "TestGroup"
        RemoveUserDAO "TestUser"
        RemoveGroupDAO "TestGroup"
        strReturnValue = strReturnValue & "After Removing the User and Group: " & _
                    vbNewLine & GetCurrentUserGroupInfo & vbNewLine & vbNewLine


        ' Show the results
        MsgBox strReturnValue

End Sub
```

The following GetCurrentUserGroupInfo procedure creates a string of the users and groups in the database, which can be useful when there's a need to validate the users and groups that have been set in the MDW file.

```
Public Function GetCurrentUserGroupInfo() As String

    ' Define variable
    Dim strReturnValue As String
    Dim grp As DAO.Group
    Dim usr As DAO.User

' Create a workspace object for the database
```

```
        Dim ws As Workspace
        Set ws = DBEngine.CreateWorkspace("DAOWS", cUser, cPW)


        ' Output the User and Group information
        strReturnValue = "Groups: "
        For Each grp In ws.Groups
            strReturnValue = strReturnValue & grp.Name & ", "
        Next
        strReturnValue = strReturnValue & vbNewLine & "Users: "
        For Each usr In ws.Users
            strReturnValue = strReturnValue & usr.Name & ", "
        Next

        ' Return the information
        GetCurrentUserGroupInfo = strReturnValue

    End Function
```

User-Level Security Using ADO

In addition to DAO code, the Microsoft ACE Database Engine can employ ADO code to set up groups and users and to set up permissions for user-level security.

Groups and users are set up using the SQL statements CREATE, ALTER, and DROP, which, as their names suggest, create, alter (or modify) and drop (or delete) user groups and users. The GROUP and USER keywords indicate whether the action is for a user group or user. The ADD and DROP statements add users to a group or remove them from a group.

GRANT and REVOKE statements grant permissions to or remove permissions from a specific object for a group or individual user. The SELECT, INSERT, UPDATE, and DELETE keywords indicate which permissions are granted or revoked. The table near the end of this chapter defines the meaning of these keywords and additional keyword options.

These routines do not provide any error trapping, which is usually recommended for full implementations of subroutines. Handling basic problems to suit your specific needs enables you to present custom error messages that users can easily understand. For the purpose of this exercise, however, code is concise. The following declarations are used in the procedures that show how to use ADO to set up user-level security. Also, you define a SetGlobals subroutine to quickly set these sample database settings for the VBA code examples.

```
    Dim strDBPath As String
    Dim strMDWPath As String
    Dim strAdminUser As String
    Dim strAdminPass As String

    Enum eObjectTypes
        Database = 1
        Container = 2
        Table = 3
        Other = 4
    End Enum
```

```
Sub SetGlobals()

    strDBPath = CurrentProject.Path & "\SampleMDB.mdb"
    strMDWPath = CurrentProject.Path & "\SampleMDW.mdw"
    strAdminUser = "Admin"
    strAdminPass = ""

End Sub
```

Opening an ADO Connection

Every ADO command must be executed on a specific ADO Connection object. Before any ADO commands can be executed for a database, a connection to the database must first be established. The following is an example `OpenConnectionADO` function that returns a connection for the specified database.

```
Function OpenConnectionADO( _
    strDatabaseNamePath As String, _
    strMDWNamePath As String, _
    strUserName As String, _
    strPassword As String) As ADODB.Connection

    ' Define variables
    Dim cnn As ADODB.Connection

    ' Open a connection to the database
    Set cnn = New ADODB.Connection
    With cnn
        .Provider = "Microsoft.ACE.OLEDB.12.0"
        .Properties("Jet OLEDB:System database") = strMDWNamePath
        .Open "Data Source=" & strDatabaseNamePath _
            & ";User ID=" & strUserName _
            & ";Password=" & strPassword
    End With

    ' Return the new connection
    Set OpenConnectionADO = cnn

End Function
```

Procedures throughout this section establish a connection to the database using the `OpenConnectionADO` subroutine. The provider for the connection is Microsoft.ACE.OLEDB.12.0. The database path to be opened by the connection is specified when calling the `Open` command with the string `"Data Source = your database"`. You can choose a specific MDW file by setting a value for the `Jet OLEDB:System database` connection property. When setting permissions using the GRANT and REVOKE options, it's only necessary to specify the database that will be secured. Otherwise, the data source can be any database. Calling the `Open` method opens the new connection. Be sure to include the User ID and Password parameters for the `Open` method.

The `Execute` method executes the SQL statement. After the statement has run, the connection is closed and the object destroyed.

The SQL statements in these examples cannot be executed from an Access Query.

Maintaining Groups with ADO

The following two procedures demonstrate techniques for adding a group (`AddGroupADO`) and dropping a group (`DropGroupADO`). Notice that when a group is added, the Group ID can be specified. A group must be added to the MDW before a user can be added to the group.

To add a group name that contains an embedded space, enclose the name in square brackets (`[]`). (It might be desirable to always add the brackets because the brackets won't cause any problems if there's no space in the name.) This is true throughout the "User-Level Security with ADO" section.

```
Sub AddGroupADO(strGroupName As String, strGID As String)

    ' Define variables
    Dim cnn As ADODB.Connection
    Dim strCommand As String

    ' Open a connection to the database
    Set cnn = OpenConnectionADO(strDBPath, strMDWPath, strAdminUser, strAdminPass)

    ' Build the command to create the Group
    strCommand = "CREATE GROUP " & strGroupName & " " & strGID & ";"

    ' Execute the command
    cnn.Execute strCommand

    ' Clean up
    cnn.Close
    Set cnn = Nothing

End Sub
```

When a group is dropped, users are dropped from the group but are not dropped from the MDW file, which means those users can still be used for other groups. The code to implement the `DropGroupADO` subroutine is the same as the code for `AddGroupADO`, except that you change the command string to drop instead of add and the Group ID is not required. Here's an example of implementing a `DropGroupADO` subroutine:

```
Sub DropGroupADO(strGroupName As String)

    ' Define variables
    Dim cnn As ADODB.Connection
    Dim strCommand As String

    ' Open a connection to the database
    Set cnn = OpenConnectionADO(strDBPath, strMDWPath, strAdminUser, strAdminPass)

    ' Build the command to drop the Group
    strCommand = "DROP GROUP " & strGroupName & ";"

    ' Execute the command
    cnn.Execute strCommand

    ' Clean up
```

```
        cnn.Close
        Set cnn = Nothing

    End Sub
```

The next two procedures demonstrate how to add users to (AddUserToGroupADO) and drop users from a group (DropUserFromGroupADO).

```
Sub AddUserToGroupADO(strUserName As String, strGroupName As String)

    ' Define variables
    Dim cnn As ADODB.Connection
    Dim strCommand As String

    ' Open a connection to the database
    Set cnn = OpenConnectionADO(strDBPath, strMDWPath, strAdminUser, strAdminPass)

    ' Build the command to add the user to a group
    strCommand = "ADD USER [" & strUserName & "] TO " & strGroupName & ";"

    ' Execute the command
    cnn.Execute strCommand

    ' Clean up
    cnn.Close
    Set cnn = Nothing

End Sub
```

Dropping a user from a group does not remove the user. The user can be assigned to another group, or the user can be dropped using the procedure DropUserADO.

```
Sub DropUserFromGroupADO(strUserName As String, strGroupName As String)

    ' Define variables
    Dim cnn As ADODB.Connection
    Dim strCommand As String

    ' Open a connection to the database
    Set cnn = OpenConnectionADO(strDBPath, strMDWPath, strAdminUser, strAdminPass)

    ' Build the command to drop the user from a group
    strCommand = "DROP USER [" & strUserName & "] FROM " & strGroupName & ";"

    ' Execute the command
    cnn.Execute strCommand

    ' Clean up
    cnn.Close
    Set cnn = Nothing

End Sub
```

Maintaining Users and User Passwords with ADO

The next three procedures demonstrate techniques for adding a user (AddUserADO), dropping a user (DropUserADO), and setting a user password (AlterUserPasswordADO).

When a user is added, the Personal ID must be specified. The AddUserADO procedure automatically adds the user to the group Users with a call to AddUserToGroup function. This keeps the MDW file consistent with the ACE/Jet database engine rule requiring that all users belong to the Users group.

As with groups, the ADO code to add users is identical to the other subroutines, except the command string is slightly different. Instead of the group, this time you specify the user in the command string. Incidentally, to create a username or password that contains an embedded space, enclose that name in square brackets ([]). For that reason, it may be desirable to always use the brackets automatically, so that calls to the AddUserADO function do not fail when there are embedded spaces. This is true throughout the "User-Level Security with ADO" section for both user and group names.

```
Sub AddUserADO(strUserName As String, strPID As String, strPassword As String)

    ' Define variables
    Dim cnn As ADODB.Connection
    Dim strCommand As String

    ' Open a connection to the database
    Set cnn = OpenConnectionADO(strDBPath, strMDWPath, strAdminUser, strAdminPass)

    ' Build the command to create the user
    strCommand = "CREATE USER [" & strUserName & "] [" & strPassword & "] " & _
                 strPID & ";"

    ' Execute the command
    cnn.Execute strCommand

    ' Add the new User to the User Group, per Access integrity rules
    Call AddUserToGroupADO(strUserName, "Users")

    ' Clean up
    cnn.Close
    Set cnn = Nothing

End Sub
```

This code is probably looking very familiar now and you may have guessed that dropping a user also only requires a small modification to the ADO command string. Dropping a user from a group removes only that user with no impact on the group or permission settings for the group that user belonged to.

```
Sub DropUserADO(strUserName As String)

    ' Define variables
    Dim cnn As ADODB.Connection
    Dim strCommand As String

    ' Open a connection to the database
```

```
        Set cnn = OpenConnectionADO(strDBPath, strMDWPath, strAdminUser, strAdminPass)

        ' Build the command to drop the user
        strCommand = "DROP USER [" & strUserName & "];"

        ' Execute the command
        cnn.Execute strCommand

        ' Clean up
        cnn.Close
        Set cnn = Nothing

End Sub
```

The `AlterUserPasswordADO` procedure and the `ALTER USER PASSWORD` SQL statement seem to suggest that the password must be known to alter a user's password. However, if the password is not known, the password parameter can be specified as an empty string. Using the square brackets ([]) in the command to change the password allows the caller to specify an empty string for one of the password strings without discretion. The caller can use an empty string to set the new password to nothing (that is, to clear the password). Here's an example of how the `AlterUserPasswordADO` procedure could be implemented:

```
Sub AlterUserPasswordADO( _
    strUserName As String, _
    strNewPassword As String, _
    strOldPassword As String)

    ' Define variables
    Dim cnn As ADODB.Connection
    Dim strCommand As String

    ' Open a connection to the database
    Set cnn = OpenConnectionADO(strDBPath, strMDWPath, strAdminUser, strAdminPass)

    ' Build the command to change the password
    strCommand = "ALTER USER [" & strUserName & "] PASSWORD [" & strNewPassword & _
            "] [" & strOldPassword & "];"

    ' Execute the command
    cnn.Execute strCommand

    ' Clean up
    cnn.Close
    Set cnn = Nothing

End Sub
```

Maintaining Database Permissions with ADO

The procedures in this section demonstrate techniques for granting permissions to users or groups (`GrantPermissionsOnTableADO` and `GrantPermissionsToObjectADO`) and revoking permissions from users or groups (`RevokePermissionsFromTableADO` and `RevokePermissionsFromObjectADO`).

Permissions can be granted to either user groups or individual users, which you specify through the strUserOrGroupName parameter. As mentioned earlier, the ideal scenario is to grant permissions to groups and then add users to groups so they can have the required permissions. Unlike the procedures that update user group and user information, the correct database must be specified in Data Source to grant permissions to the correct objects.

For these procedures, the strPermissions parameter can be one permission type or many permission types separated by commas, which is different than the method you used to combine permissions for DAO parameters.

> *While not generally recommended, using* PUBLIC *for the group/username (*strUserName*) will set permissions for the default Users group account such that every user will be the assigned the specified permissions. The best use for this would be to grant* CONNECT *permission to the database because that would permit all users access to the database but not necessarily to all objects in the database.*

```
Sub GrantPermissionsOnTableADO( _
    strUserOrGroupName As String, _
    strTableName As String, _
    strPermissions As String)

    ' Define variables
    Dim cnn As ADODB.Connection
    Dim strCommand As String

    ' Open a connection to the database
    Set cnn = OpenConnectionADO(strDBPath, strMDWPath, strAdminUser, strAdminPass)

    ' Build the command to grant permissions
    strCommand = "GRANT " & strPermissions & _
                " ON TABLE " & strTableName & " TO " & strUserOrGroupName & ";"

    ' Execute the command
    cnn.Execute strCommand

    ' Clean up
    cnn.Close
    Set cnn = Nothing

End Sub
```

Permissions are revoked from the user or group depending on the value of strUserOrGroupName. Revoking permissions from a user does not affect the permissions of the group to which that user belongs.

```
Sub RevokePermissionsFromTableADO( _
    strUserOrGroupName As String, _
    strTableName As String, _
    strPermissions As String)

    ' Define variables
    Dim cnn As ADODB.Connection
```

```
          Dim strCommand As String

          ' Open a connection to the database
          Set cnn = OpenConnectionADO(strDBPath, strMDWPath, strAdminUser, strAdminPass)

          ' Build the command to revoke permissions
          strCommand = "REVOKE " & strPermissions & " ON TABLE " & _
                       strTableName & " FROM " & strUserOrGroupName & ";"

          ' Execute the command
          cnn.Execute strCommand

          ' Clean up
          cnn.Close
          Set cnn = Nothing

      End Sub
```

GrantPermissionsToObjectADO is a more generic form of the GrantPermissionsToTableADO procedure. It is used for object types other than tables and easily replaces the table-specific procedure. The GrantPermissionsToObjectADO employs the ObjectType enumeration globally defined previously to allow the caller of the subroutine to choose the database object type to modify.

```
      Sub GrantPermissionsToObjectADO( _
          strUserOrGroupName As String, _
          otObjType As eObjectTypes, _
          strObjectName As String, _
          strPermissions As String)

          ' Define variables
          Dim cnn As ADODB.Connection
          Dim strCommand As String

          ' Open a connection to the database
          Set cnn = OpenConnectionADO(strDBPath, strMDWPath, strAdminUser, strAdminPass)

          ' Build the command to grant permissions
          strCommand = "GRANT " & strPermissions & " ON "
          Select Case otObjType
              Case eObjectTypes.Database:
                  strCommand = strCommand
              Case eObjectTypes.Container:
                  strCommand = strCommand & "CONTAINER"
              Case eObjectTypes.Table:
                  strCommand = strCommand & "TABLE"
              Case eObjectTypes.Other:
                  strCommand = strCommand & "OBJECT"
              Case Else
                  MsgBox "Object Type Not Recognized"
          End Select
          strCommand = strCommand & " " & strObjectName & " TO " & ↵
      strUserOrGroupName & ";"
```

```
' Execute the command
cnn.Execute strCommand

' Clean up
cnn.Close
Set cnn = Nothing

End Sub
```

RevokePermissionsFromObjectADO is a more generic form of the
RevokePermissionsFromTableADO procedure. It is used for object types other than tables and can easily replace the table-specific procedure.

```
Sub RevokePermissionsFromObjectADO( _
    strUserOrGroupName As String, otObjType As eObjectTypes, _
    strObjectName As String, strPermissions As String)

    ' Define variables
    Dim cnn As ADODB.Connection
    Dim strCommand As String

    ' Open a connection to the database
    Set cnn = OpenConnectionADO(strDBPath, strMDWPath, strAdminUser, strAdminPass)

    ' Build the command to revoke permissions
    strCommand = "REVOKE " & strPermissions & " ON "
    Select Case otObjType
        Case eObjectTypes.Database:
            strCommand = strCommand
        Case eObjectTypes.Container:
            strCommand = strCommand & "CONTAINER"
        Case eObjectTypes.Table:
            strCommand = strCommand & "TABLE"
        Case eObjectTypes.Other:
            strCommand = strCommand & "OBJECT"
        Case Else
            Debug.Print "Object type incorrect"
    End Select
    strCommand = strCommand & " " & strObjectName & " FROM " & ↵
            strUserOrGroupName & ";"

    ' Execute the command
    cnn.Execute strCommand

    ' Clean up
    cnn.Close
    Set cnn = Nothing

End Sub
```

Sample Setup Code Using ADO

The following procedure (RunSampleADO) shows various ways to call the previous ADO procedures. Comments have been embedded in the code to explain how it works.

```
Sub RunSampleADO()

    ' Set the Global Paths
    SetGlobals

    ' Add a user with a Personal ID and Password
    AddUserADO "User1", "User1ID", "User1Pass"

    ' Change the Password -
    ' If you don't know the Password, specify the empty string
    AlterUserPasswordADO "User1", "NewPass", ""

    ' Give the user the usual permissions but don't allow INSERT
    ' (Prefer not to do this. But show as a sample anyway.)
    GrantPermissionsOnTableADO "User1", "tblTable1", "SELECT, DELETE, UPDATE"

    ' Add a group
    AddGroupADO "Group1", "Group1ID"

    ' Give permissions to the group
    GrantPermissionsOnTableADO "Group1", "tblTable1", "SELECT, DELETE, UPDATE"

    ' Add a user to the group
    AddUserToGroupADO "User1", "Group1"

    ' Since the user has the same permissions as the group, revoke permissions
    ' from the user
    RevokePermissionsFromObjectADO "User1", Table, "tblTable1", "SELECT, " & ↵
                            "DELETE, UPDATE"

    ' More samples setting permissions
    GrantPermissionsToObjectADO "PUBLIC", Database, "Database", "CONNECT"
    GrantPermissionsToObjectADO "Group1", Container, "Tables", "SELECT"
    GrantPermissionsToObjectADO "User1", Container, "Forms", "SELECT"
    GrantPermissionsToObjectADO "User1", Other, "qryQuery1", "DROP"

    ' Drop everything
    ' Users are automatically dropped from the group when the group is dropped
    DropGroupADO "Group1"
    DropUserADO "User1"

End Sub
```

The following table provides a detailed description of the privileges.

Privilege	Applies To	Allows a User to
SELECT	Tables, Objects, Containers	Read the data and read the design of a specified table, object, or container.
DELETE	Tables, Objects, Containers	Delete data from a specified table, object, or container.
INSERT	Tables, Objects, Containers	Insert data into a specified table, object, or container.
UPDATE	Tables, Objects, Containers	Update data in a specified table, object, or container.
DROP	Tables, Objects, Containers	Remove a specified table, object, or container.
SELECTSECURITY	Tables, Objects, Containers	View the permissions for a specified table, object, or container.
UPDATESECURITY	Tables, Objects, Containers	Allows a user to change the permissions for a specified table, object, or container.
UPDATEIDENTITY	Tables	Change the values in auto-increment columns.
CREATE	Tables, Objects, Containers	Create a new table, object, or container.
SELECTSCHEMA	Tables, Objects, Containers	View the design of a specified table, object, or container.
SCHEMA	Tables, Objects, Containers	Modify the design of a specified table, object, or container.
UPDATEOWNER	Tables, Objects, Containers	Change the owner of a specified table, object, or container.
ALL PRIVILEGES	All	Have all permissions, including administrative, on a specified table, object, container, or database.
CREATEDB	Database	Create a new database.
EXCLUSIVECONNECT	Database	Open a database in exclusive mode.
CONNECT	Database	Allows a user to open a database.
ADMINDB	Database	Administer a database.

User-Level Security Using ADOX

The previous section showed you how to maintain user-level security programmatically using ADO and either the Access Connectivity Engine or the Jet Database Engine. Another method to maintain security through VBA code is to use Microsoft ADO Extensions (ADOX) for DDL and Security.

ADOX uses an object model that supports the Catalog, Group, and User objects. Using those objects, you can perform most of the tasks previously described in ADO. Because of the object model, developing VBA procedures to maintain security can be easier. That is, rather than having to learn all of the SQL syntax, you can use the IntelliSense in VBE to help build the right VBA statements in code.

ADOX also attempts to do some of the work for you. For example, ADOX provides the Personal ID automatically. In this case, because you won't know what the PID is, using ADOX may make it difficult to recreate an MDW file if necessary.

For more information about ADOX you can visit the Microsoft Developers Network library. See the article `http://msdn.microsoft.com/library/default.asp?url=/library/en-us/ado270/htm/admscadoxfundamentals.asp`.

Summary

In most business environments, it is good practice — even essential — to institute some level of security for an Access database application. There are several factors that help determine what is appropriate for the situation, but typically the result is a combination of methods that will provide the most cost-effective solution for the business needs. Simply implementing Access security alone is not always sufficient. Environmental factors play a large part in the security puzzle. Adding firewalls, network security, and strong business rules must complement the security features that Access can provide.

This chapter reviewed the three major security features available in the ACCDB file format. Shared-level security password protects and encrypts the database so that the raw data contained in the file is protected from intruders. Locking the VBA project enables you to distribute the code with the database while not allowing unauthorized users to view or make changes to it. Compiling the database to an ACCDE file enables you to remove all source code from the database and prevent any modification to the code in the database solution. Used separately or in combination, these features enable you to provide a robust security model for ACCDB database solutions.

This chapter also discussed the security features available for MDB file format databases. MDB supports applying a password to the database to implement shared-level security. Creating an MDE database file compiles and removes the source code from the database, preventing users from making changes to the database solution code. Encoding the database prevents (or at least seriously challenges) unauthorized users from viewing or manipulating the physical data stored in the MDB file. Implementing user-level security can help enforce business rules and regulate which actions users and groups can perform for any given database object independently. Although user-level security can be complicated and costly to set up and to maintain, it is typically worth the effort in a controlled business environment where many users have access to a particular database file. But remember, there are products that can overcome user-level security, so it is important to be aware that anyone in possession of the secured database may be able to retrieve the data it houses. In many cases, with the proper network security, a user could open, copy, or even delete the database.

There are also several options for working with security. Many developers may want to use a combination of the User-Level Security Wizard and code. The wizard is excellent for establishing users and groups for user-level security. However, many developers may want to use code to make changes after the initial permissions have been set. And it's certainly handy to use code to generate custom documentation about user-level security. Either way, you are sure to find that Access provides powerful solutions for developing secure applications.

The Access help files, knowledge base articles, and MSDN all provide useful instructions and guidance about various aspects of Access security and how to secure data and code. Chapter 22 covers more information about macro security how Access enhances protection for machines from malicious database attacks that use code in database files.

Understanding
Client-Server Development
with VBA

Access makes it easy to create applications that interact with other database formats and enterprise-level database servers. Unfortunately, the easiest methods are not always the best, and incorrect choices can have serious long-term effects on the design, stability, maintenance, and overall success of a project. A thorough understanding of how Access interacts with other databases and the various alternatives available for developers is critical to making the best design decisions for any given application.

In a typical business environment, Access database applications tend to sprout up because some individual or small group needs functionality and creates an Access database to implement a viable solution. Other people or groups notice the application's usefulness and decide to use the solution as well. Someone may even split the data tables into a backend database and link the tables in the front-end application so that large numbers of users can use a local copy on their machines and connect to the tables stored on a central server. Before long, what began as a personal database application is now shared on the network server, contains hundreds of megabytes of business data, is used on a daily basis by 50 or so people, and requires 2 or 3 people just to maintain and administrate the database. The application has become an unintended, albeit critical, piece of the company's business process.

The solution is cost effective. So another database is created for a different problem, and then a third database, and so on until there are hundreds of applications all over the network, some in use, some dead, and maybe some that were never even completed. Many IT workers cringe at a mere whisper of the words "Access database" because these applications become difficult and expensive to track, maintain, and support. Where does all this data come from? Who has access to the data? Who backs up the data? Who developed this application? Who is maintaining and supporting this database? These are just some of the questions to ask when thinking about how to deal with large numbers of Access databases in a business environment.

Fortunately, there are some easy answers to these tough questions that allow users the flexibility of creating Access applications and save IT the headache of having to support and maintain all of the data. If the data is stored in a controlled, centralized location, an IT department can effectively manage the database and control which users can view/modify the data. A more ideal solution would be using a database server as the centralized location, enabling both developers and administrators to leverage the server's features to help them with their tasks. Fortunately, Access provides the capability to create front-end applications to connect to separate, back-end data sources of many different types. Being able to connect to remote data sources is the basis of the database application architecture often referred to as a client-server application, which we will discuss in the next section.

Client-Server Applications

An Access application with only local tables is a file-server application, where all processing occurs on the local client machine regardless of where the file is physically stored. The idea is that the local machine's or network server's file system will accept commands from the Access Connectivity Engine — ACE database engine — that are made from Access on the local machine during use of the application. This is the key difference between a file-server and a client-server application.

In the client-server application model, an application residing on the local machine retrieves data from a data source that is completely separate from the client application. Often there are many copies of the client application retrieving data from a single or a few remote data sources, which are typically stored in a network location, so that the data can be shared among all clients. At a minimum, the term client-server implies the design of the application is separated into at least two components: a client-side application that allows the user to interact with the data stored in the database, and a server that is responsible for maintaining data and executing requests from the client application. This architectural difference in an application can yield great performance and maintenance benefits, especially when large numbers of users are frequently interacting with the data.

Although it's tempting to think that simply moving the application's tables to a Microsoft SQL Server 2005 database server will make the program a client-server application, in reality, that's only the beginning. It is more accurate to say: moving the data to SQL Server provides the potential for a client-server application. The application still needs to take advantage of that potential for all of the benefits to be realized. Depending on the application, making client-server applications may also yield a few drawbacks. For reasons discussed later in this chapter, it is not uncommon for an application to be slower immediately after migrating the data from the local file to a SQL Server (or other server) database. Regardless of the client format chosen, significant performance, security, maintenance, and storage benefits can be realized through careful planning of the design of the database solution.

Using the Sample Files

This chapter defines techniques for creating client-server applications that, in some cases, store data in a SQL Server database. These SQL Server-specific examples use Microsoft SQL Server Express Edition 2005 as the database server, installed on the local machine. If you do not have SQL Server Express 2005 installed, you can download it for free from Microsoft. SQL Server Express binaries and samples can be found at `http://microsoft.com/sql/editions/express/default.mspx`. In addition, the database used for the examples in this chapter is included with the download files for the book. Find the `Sample.SQL` script, which will build the SQL database when invoked in SQL Server.

SQL Server Express Edition 2005

If you do not have SQL Server installed, but want to use the sample files or try the examples in this chapter, Microsoft SQL Server Express Edition 2005 can be downloaded and installed for free. Just navigate to `http://microsoft.com/sql/editions/express/default.mspx` and follow the links. Be sure to download SQL Server Management Studio Express as well because it provides a visual interface for working with the SQL Server toolset.

Installing SQL Server Express 2005 requires that the .NET Framework 2.0 or greater be installed on the machine prior to the server installation. You can download SQL Server 2005 Express Edition SP1, which is used in the examples, onto your Windows Vista machine.

Follow the installation instructions provided on the websites.

After you've installed SQL Server, you may want to make a few modifications to the server's configuration. By default, network connections from the TCP/IP connections are disabled.

1. From the Windows Start menu, invoke the SQL Server Configuration Manager. The configuration manager will be invoked. In the left pane in the manager, select SQL Server 2005 Network Configuration ➪ Protocols for SQLEXPRESS.

2. Notice that TCP/IP connections are marked as disabled. This means that incoming connection requests from the network will be denied. To enable network connections, right-click the TCP/IP option on the right-side of the screen and select Enabled. A message tells you that changes will take effect after the server is restarted. Click OK and you return to the configuration manager.

   In addition to enabling the TCP connections in SQL Server Express, the Windows Firewall setting may also need to be configured to accept incoming TCP connections. Consult Windows Firewall help if this is the case.

3. In the left pane, select the SQL Server 2005 Services option again and in the right pane, right-click SQL Server and choose Stop. This stops SQL Server. Right-click the SQL Server option again and choose Start to restart the server, applying the changes for network connections. Then exit the configuration manager program, as the SQL Server is now configured correctly.

Installing the Sample Database

Once the SQL Server has been installed and configured, the machine is ready to add the sample database to the system.

1. From the Windows Start menu, navigate to the Microsoft SQL Server 2005 folder and click on the SQL Server Management Studio Express option.

If the SQL Server has been installed on a machine running Windows Vista, Management Studio Express may need to be run as an administrator before any changes can be made to the server. To run the application as an administrator, right-click the icon for Management Studio Express and choose Properties. The properties dialog box opens. On the Compatibility tab, check the Run as Administrator option and apply the setting. Now, every time the application is run from the icon, it will run in administrator mode.

2. The Connect to Server dialog box will be invoked. By default, the name of the SQL Server is *machine name*\SQLEXPRESS. Input the Server Name and click the Connect button. Management Studio Express is connected and you are ready to create the sample database.

3. In Object Explorer, right-click the Databases folder and choose New Database. Type **NorthwindCS** for the Database name in the New Database dialog box and then click OK. A new empty database with the name NorthwindCS is created. Now you're ready to import all of the objects and data in the `Sample.SQL` file included in this chapter's download files.

4. From the File menu, choose Open and browse to `Sample.SQL`. This action prompts you to connect to SQL Server again, so click the Connect button again.

5. `Sample.SQL` will be open for viewing in the main document window of Management Studio. Click the Execute button on the SQL Editor's toolbar to create the sample database. The script runs and the new database table schema, data, and other objects are created. The sample database is ready for use on the new SQL Server. Now you can get down to business.

Choosing the Correct File Format

Many misconceptions exist regarding the differences between the Access Project (ADP) file format and the various Access database (ACCDB and MDB) file formats. Even before ADP files were available (introduced in Access 2000), many developers did not fully understand how MDB files worked or how to optimize their usage in a client-server environment. Although even serious design mistakes can still provide acceptable performance when there is not a large amount of data in the database, as the data grows, the inefficient design becomes more and more detrimental to the application's performance and reliability.

Microsoft Office Access 2007 features a brand new database engine: the Access Connectivity Engine (ACE) — also called the Access database engine. If you've used previous versions of Access, you are probably very familiar with ACE's predecessor, the Jet database engine. ACE is a privatized version of the Jet database engine with a number of feature enhancements. Using ACE, Access 2007 supports creating the following file formats: ACCDB (Access 2007 file format), MDB (Access 2000 and 2002-2003 file formats), ADP (Access Data Project), MDE (Access Complied MDB database), ACCDE (Access Complied ACCDB database), MDA (Access MDB Add-in), ACCDA (Access ACCDB Add-in), and ACCDC (Access Signed CAB file). This section discusses some of the differences between the ACCDB/MDB and ADP file formats.

What Are ACCDB and MDB Files?

Since its inception in 1992, the Jet (Joint Engine Technology) database engine has been the backbone for every Access version until the Access 2007 release. One of the main reasons Jet has been so successful is that it has been available since Microsoft Windows 3.0. Originally released as a part of Access, it was eventually separated and shipped with Microsoft Windows as a system component. This meant that any ODBC or compatible development environment could employ the Jet database engine without requiring that Access be installed on the system. For example, a Microsoft Visual Basic application could make use of a Jet MDB file format database without requiring Access be installed — and many did!

As mentioned earlier, one of the highlights of the Access 2007 release is the introduction of ACE, the Access database engine. Fortunately, ACE supports all of the features that Jet provided in the 2000 and

2002-2003 MDB file formats. While data in certain legacy formats can still be edited via Access 2007, it should be noted that 2000 and 2002-2003 MDB files are the only two legacy MDB file formats still fully supported for database design by Access 2007. To support much of the new feature work, such as Complex Data or Attachment fields, Microsoft has introduced a new Access 2007 file format called ACCDB. While ACCDB is essentially the MDB file format plus a few more system tables, there are some key differences. The following is a list of features that the ACCDB file format supports, but are unsupported for MDB files:

❑ Complex Data and Attachment fields for tables

❑ Complex Data fields for linked tables to SharePoint lists

❑ Append-Only Memo fields

❑ Database file encryption

❑ The Access 2007 Import/Export specifications

Additionally, there are several features supported in MDB, but not in ACCDB, including:

❑ User-level security and the Workgroup Database (MDW) files

❑ Database file encoding

❑ Digital Signatures (2003 MDB file format only)

On the other hand, MDB and ACCDB file format databases are similar in that they store all of the data, database objects, VBA modules, and database properties directly in a single file structure. Starting with Access 2000, all non-data objects are stored in a single record of a database system table used by Access. Upon opening a database file, Access searches for this record and loads the VBA project and all other objects employed by the database application.

In addition to storing the table data directly within the file, the MDB and ACCDB file formats support linking tables to external data sources such as ODBC, SQL server tables, SharePoint lists, other MDB/ACCDB files, Excel Workbook files, and so on. The Microsoft Office Access Object Model, DAO, and ADO components all support working with linked tables to develop robust application feature sets for database applications. However, simply creating an MDB with linked tables to a SQL Server table does not make it an ADP file, as you will see shortly. First, let's explore a little more about linked tables and MDB and ACCDB files.

Linking to External Data

Access 2007 supports connecting to a wide variety of different types of data sources; although some are read-only, many are fully updatable from an Access application. This is because different data source types use separate, but distinct methods to connect to the data. Indexed Sequential Access Method (ISAM) drivers are generally used for connecting to other desktop or file-based data sources, such as Excel, text, and HTML. On the other hand, Open Database Connectivity (ODBC) data source vendors typically supply connection utilities for use with their specific database products. In most cases, the client machine needs to have a specific database product's relevant utilities installed before an application can connect to the data source. For example, even though Access ships with an ODBC driver for Oracle, the Oracle client utilities still need to be installed on the machine for the ODBC driver to be of any use to an Access application.

Fortunately, Access makes linking many different data sources extremely easy. The following steps outline a common method for creating a connection to a SQL Server Express database:

1.   To create a link to an external data source from an Access ACCDB file, select External Data tab on the Ribbon. In the Import section, click the More button on the Ribbon and choose the ODBC database option. This opens the Get External Data Wizard, as shown in Figure 19-1.

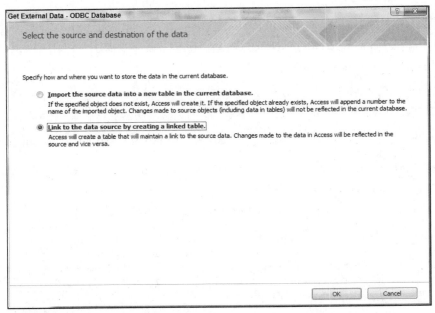

Figure 19-1

2.   In the wizard, choose Link To The Data Source By Creating A Linked Table (the second radio button in the list) and then click OK. This invokes a Select Data Source dialog box that looks similar to the one shown in Figure 19-2. The Select Data Source dialog box enables you to create links from the current database to other supported ODBC databases.

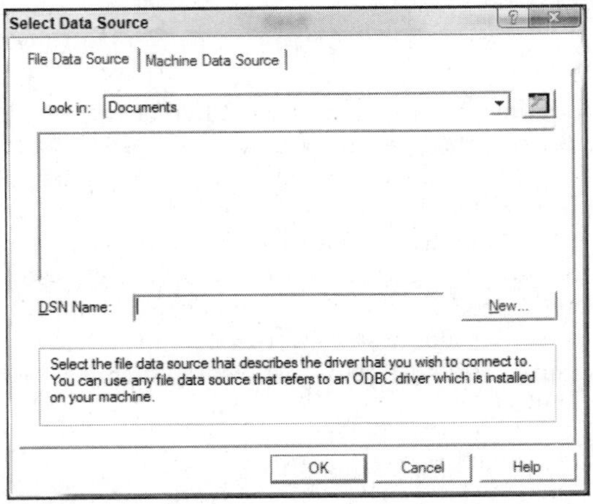

Figure 19-2

3. You can select a pre-existing data source name (DSN) connection or create a new data source. For now, open the Machine Data Source tab and click the New button. The Create New Data Source dialog box opens (see Figure 19-3).

On Windows Vista, you may get a warning that you are not able to create system DSN connections because of how Access is run and/or the permission level of the Windows account. The warning should provide instructions so that you can create a user DSN.

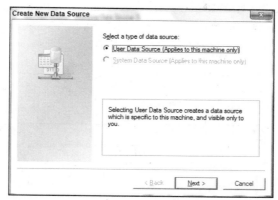

Figure 19-3

The path contained here determines the location in the Registry where the connection information will be stored. User-specific data source locations are stored to the following registry key and are available only to the current user:

```
HKEY_CURRENT_USER\Software\ODBC\ODBC.INI
```

Machine data sources are available for all user profiles and are stored to the following registry location:

```
HKEY_LOCAL_MACHINE\SOFTWARE\ODBC\ODBC.INI
```

Odd but true: HKCU has a proper case Software *node, while HKLM has an uppercase* SOFTWARE *node. The registry is case insensitive, so it would be okay to make these consistent, although you will see the different cases when you open the registry editor UI.*

4. To create a system DSN connection on Windows Vista, you must be logged into an Administrator account or Access will need to be run as an administrator. For now, choose User Data Source, and click the Next button. The next Create New Data Source page opens, as shown in Figure 19-4.

5. At this point, the screens and options presented vary depending on what drivers are present on the machine and which drivers you choose. For now, select SQL Native Client option from the list, click Next, and then click Finish to bring up the dialog box information specific to SQL Server, as shown in Figure 19-5.

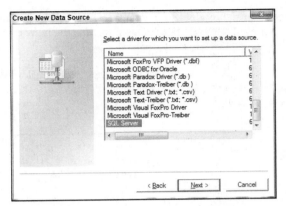

Figure 19-4

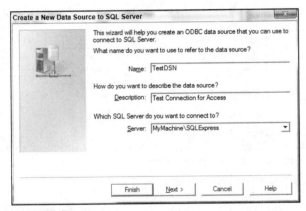

Figure 19-5

6. Enter **TestDSN** for a name and, optionally, the description for the connection. You can type in the name of your SQL Server or you can select it from the list box. The name of the SQL Server is typically *machine name\database server* (for example, MyMachineName\SQLServerExpress). Also, a default SQL Server can be configured for the machine, and in that case, you can enter (local) to reference the default instance of the SQL Server on the machine. Click Next. The page shown in Figure 19-6 opens.

7. Enter the necessary security credentials to log into the server. The credentials will depend on how the particular SQL Server is configured. If the steps shown earlier were used to install the SQL Server, choose the option to use NT Authentication for the Windows User Account. If your server administrator has specified users using SQL Server authentication, select the proper option and type in the username and password. Click Next to continue.

8. The last setting to change is the default database (see Figure 19-7).

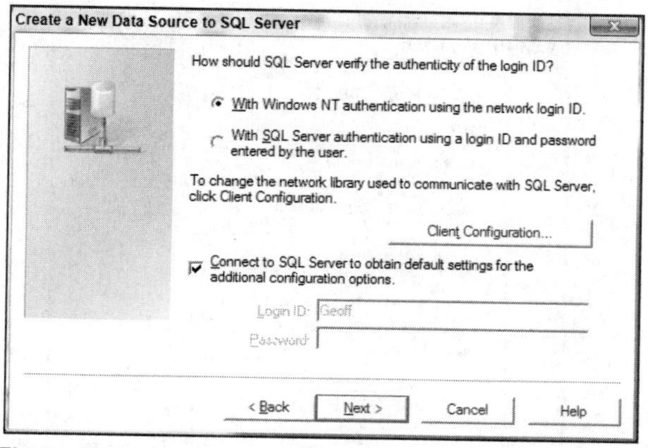

Figure 19-6

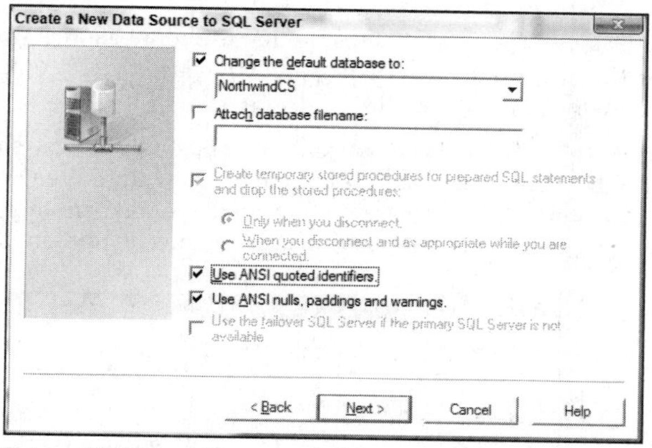

Figure 19-7

The default database can be selected on a per-connection basis and different connections can reference different databases on the same server. The default database selection determines the database context for which commands are issued against the server. For example, if code is called to select records from a table in the NorthwindCS database, but the default database is the master database used by SQL Server, the query results in an error because the table doesn't exist in the master database. Always specify a default database other than the master database to help prevent any accidental, unwanted modifications to the database.

9. For this example, select the NorthwindCS database (which you created earlier) from the default database list and then click Next. The remaining default option settings should be fine, so click Finish to complete the wizard. All of the options selected for the new connection are displayed, as shown in Figure 19-8.

Figure 19-8

10. Click the Test Data Source button to ensure that the connection is working correctly. If the connection is working, the dialog box displays the message TESTS COMPLETED SUCCESSFULLY. Click OK to close the dialog box.

11. You are returned to the Select Data Source dialog box, which now shows a new data source called TestDSN, the connection you just created. If new links are needed for this connection in the future, the existing DSN can be used instead of creating another one from scratch. Select the TestDSN option from the Select Data Source dialog box, as shown in Figure 19-9.

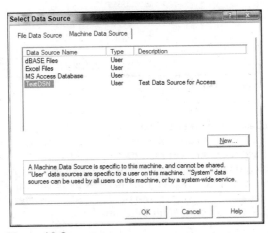

Figure 19-9

12. Click OK. The Link Tables dialog box opens showing all of the available objects in the database for the DSN connection that was just created. The names and types of objects depend on the data source, but in this case, assuming you are using the NorthwindCS database provided in the sample files, the dialog box should look similar to Figure 19-10.

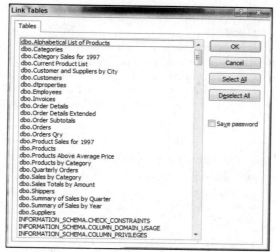

Figure 19-10

13. Select the dbo.Orders table object and click OK. A link to the dbo.Orders table is created and is shown in the Navigation pane. This new link is created directly to the NorthwindCS database on SQL Server and any changes made to the data are reflected in updates to the data on the server. At this point, the new linked table is available to view, bind to a form or report, reference in code, or use in any other way a normal table can be used, except for modifying the schema of the table.

Because the table is linked and the actual structure and data reside on the SQL Server, changes to the schema, or design, of the table must be completed from the SQL Server database. This does not change the data in any way, only the schema. However, if the user credentials supplied to the DSN connection do not have permission to modify the data in the table, no user can make changes to the data. When the Access application connects to the SQL Server, it only has as much permission as the user's account has to the SQL Server.

What Type of DSN Should Be Used?

There are two primary DSN (data source name) connection types available in a Windows platform: file and machine. A DSN file is a text file that contains all of the relevant connectivity information (including the username and optionally, the password) for the data source and can be easily moved around from machine to machine or deployed with an installation package. A machine DSN stores the connectivity information in the registry, and therefore is specific to only that machine, which may prove much more difficult to setup without direct access to the machine itself.

Access handles links differently depending on which type is chosen. With a file DSN, Access stores the connectivity information in the MDB file and does not need to requery the DSN each time the table is opened. With a machine DSN, Access must query the registry to retrieve the connectivity information with each new connection to the DSN.

How ACE and Jet Interact with ODBC Data Sources

Because ACE and Jet send information across the network to the data source, it's important to consider when and how much data is being transferred. The bandwidth of the network connections, load on the SQL Server, and amount of data being transferred across the network directly affect the performance of a client-server application. Before delving into the intricacies of how ACE and Jet deal with sending and retrieving data from SQL Server, consider employing the SQL Server Profiler to help determine when and how much data is being transferred across a network. The profiler provides a breakdown of the command and data sent to and from the SQL Server.

Use the SQL Server Profiler to Spy on Access

If the full version of Microsoft SQL Server 2005 is installed, the SQL Server Profiler can be used to watch commands that are sent to the SQL Server. The profiler allows creation of a Trace Session, which logs every command sent to the server, along with a variety of performance data.

A new session of the SQL Server Profiler can be started from the SQL Server Management Studio. Choose Tools ➪ SQL Server Profiler to launch the program. Once the profiler is invoked, choose File ➪ New Trace to create a new tracing session. You are prompted to connect to the SQL Server that contains the database to which your Access application is linked, and to enter custom properties. If you just want to view the SQL commands that Access issues to the server, accept all the default values and choose Run to start the profiler session.

After a tracing session to the database has been established, every command sent from Microsoft Access to the SQL Server is listed in the trace window, along with a variety of performance information.

To view the results of a SQL command that's listed in the trace window, simply highlight that command and copy the SQL text from the lower half of the trace window. You can then paste the SQL into a new query in SQL Server Management Studio, or create a SQL Pass-through query in your Microsoft Access database. Run the query to see the results that Access received when it ran the query.

When a linked table is opened in the Access application, Access retrieves the primary key information for the table as well as a few records, if any exist. For example, double-click the dbo.Orders table in the Navigation pane, and Access sends the following query to the NorthwindCS database:

```
SELECT "dbo"."Orders"."OrderID" FROM dbo_Orders;
```

This query provides Access with a full list of the unique record identifiers for the existing records contained within the table. Once Access has this information, each of the records contained in the table can be retrieved for viewing or data processing. To gather a few of the records from the table, the next query sent to the SQL Server from Access would be similar to the following:

```
declare @P1 int
set @P1=3
exec sp_prepexec @P1 output, N'@P1 int,@P2 int,@P3 int,@P4 int,@P5 int, ↵
@P6 int,@P7 int,@P8 int,@P9 int,@P10 int', N'SELECT "OrderID", "CustomerID", ↵
"EmployeeID", "OrderDate", "RequiredDate", "ShippedDate", "ShipVia", ↵
```

```
"Freight", "ShipName", "ShipAddress", "ShipCity", "ShipRegion", ↵
"ShipPostalCode", "ShipCountry"
FROM "dbo"."Orders"
WHERE "OrderID" = @P1 OR "OrderID" = @P2 OR "OrderID" = @P3 OR "OrderID" = ↵
@P4 OR "OrderID" = @P5 OR "OrderID" = @P6 OR "OrderID" = @P7 OR "OrderID" = ↵
@P8 OR "OrderID" = @P9 OR "OrderID" = @P10', 10249, 10251, 10258, 10260, ↵
10265, 10267, 10269, 10270, 10274, 10275;
select @P1
```

The `sp_prepexec` stored procedure prepares a SQL statement for use by subsequent queries and accepts parameter input to retrieve the first few rows (those with OrderID 10249-10275). After that statement runs, Access can use the `sp_execute` procedure to retrieve small batches of rows at a time:

```
exec sp_execute 3, 10280, 10281, 10282, 10284, 10288, 10290, 10296, 10309, ↵
10317, 10323
```

The exact query text used is specific to the back end database server and is handled by the ODBC driver for the DSN. Although the specifics are different, Access (ACE/Jet) uses the same overall process for retrieving the primary key information first and then retrieving batches of rows based on the key information.

When opening a query instead of a table, these actions are performed for each table in the query. In this situation, Access usually does the following:

1. Request primary key data for each table separately.
2. Join the key data locally on the client machine.
3. Request all needed field data from each table separately based on the key field.
4. Join the requested data together in a local recordset and display it to the user.

If a query has compound primary keys defined for each table, Access may end up pulling down a lot of data that needs to be joined locally before it even begins to retrieve the data that will eventually be returned in the query result. If the application has a table with thirteen fields, but twelve of these fields comprise a compound primary key, Access will end up bringing down the twelve primary key fields twice: once to get the primary key data by itself and again for a second time to get data to be returned in the query result. Needless to say, using compound key fields in ODBC data sources can force the Access application to have a lot of overhead, but there is still hope for reducing the expense of compound keys.

Under certain circumstances, Access will have the primary key joining done on the server. Unlike the previous example where Access retrieved all the primary key data for each table and joined it locally, if *all* the tables in a particular query are based on the same DSN, Access can sometimes pass a WHERE clause to join the data on the server. For example, if you create a local query in an ACCDB file based on linked Products, Suppliers, and Categories tables from the NorthwindCS database on the SQL Server, and all three tables are based on the same DSN, a query similar to the following is executed:

```
SELECT "dbo"."Products"."ProductID","dbo"."Categories"."CategoryID", ↵
"dbo"."Suppliers"."SupplierID"
FROM "dbo"."Categories","dbo"."Products","dbo"."Suppliers"
WHERE(("dbo"."Products"."CategoryID" = "dbo"."Categories"."CategoryID") AND ↵
("dbo"."Products"."SupplierID" = "dbo"."Suppliers"."SupplierID"))
```

This allows the join for `CategoryID` and `SupplierID` to be created and executed on the server instead of the client machine. The benefit is that only the primary key data that is necessary for the join will be passed over the network and brought down to Access. Although this is not as ideal as having all query processing happen on the server, it can dramatically improve performance depending on how the tables in the application are structured and joined.

The most important element here is that all tables must be based on the exact same DSN connection. Even if two tables are from the same SQL Server database, but one table uses a file DSN and the other uses a different DSN, the less efficient process is used. The more efficient processing is not guaranteed and depends on other factors but it won't happen at all if there is more than one DSN. Always create linked tables from the same database, using the same DSN when possible.

The scenario discussed here uses a robust database server, but much of the processing can still happen locally, depending on the design of the application, and some cases are worse than others. The benefit to this design is that ACE and Jet make it easy for you to create queries that can join multiple remote data sources, in the same manner as if they were querying local tables. The price of ease of use is inefficiency in many cases, causing increased network traffic and more requests to the server.

How Can Performance Be Improved?

When dealing with a client-server environment, the most important factor to remember is to bring data across a network only if it is needed. The best way to accomplish this depends on what the application is designed to do and where any performance problems may be present. There are three main contributors to performance degradation in a client-server environment:

❑   The time consumed processing a query on the server

❑   The time consumed processing a query on the client

❑   The time and bandwidth consumed moving records across the network

All three areas should be examined closely to detect bottlenecks or other performance degradation issues in a client-server application.

Insufficient server resources are rarely the cause of a problem for Access applications. In most cases, it is far more likely that shifting more processing to the server can increase performance. If query processing time on a server seems longer than expected, make sure that the application's table indexes are properly set and optimized. If locking issues occur, changing to the optimistic locking model may help improve performance as well.

Unlike server resources, insufficient client resources are frequently the source of performance issues. When joins are performed locally, queries can cause Access to bring down a lot of records simply to create a join before the requested data is retrieved and tend to be slow if there are inadequate resources on the local machine. All other considerations being equal, the more RAM on the client machine, the faster the query is likely to run locally.

An all too common problem occurs when the tables for an ODBC data source are linked to a local table, or a table from a different data connection. When queries containing joins between multiple tables from different sources are processed, the data for the join fields is always pulled down from the remote table and joined locally; then Access issues another request to fetch the records for the final result. The same is true with data sources that use an ISAM interface for the connection, such as linking to an Excel worksheet, text file, or other supported ISAM data source. Links to ODBC data sources that use ISAMs to manipulate data always consider each table a separate connection, even if they are contained in the same file object, such as two separate sheets in an Excel workbook. In the case of SharePoint, the ISAM has no way to link tables, even if they are on the same SharePoint server, because each table is considered a separate ODBC connection. Always try to minimize queries that use joins between different data sources and use server-side processing when possible to help reduce network traffic and improve application performance.

Finally, networks are often the cause of the bottlenecks for a client-server application because of the vast amount of data Access may retrieve for local joining. When the table contains large amounts of data and the keys need to be joined locally, Access can pull down tens or even hundreds of megabytes of data before returning results that may consist of only a few records. In an environment where network bandwidth is low, such as a WAN or a dial-up environment, joining locally can be devastating to the application's performance.

Pass-Through Queries

Often overlooked, pass-through queries are an easy way to improve performance of a front-end application. Pass-through queries are processed entirely on the server and, as such, are a good technique for transferring data processing to the server. Unfortunately, there is no graphical user interface for creating the SQL statements of a pass-through query in Access and the data they return is read only. However, SQL Server 2005 and many other products have built in tools that are similar to the Query Builder and can generate SQL statements just as Access would. It is important to note that in Access 2007, SQL pass-through queries require that the database have code enabled before they can be run, but because this is a book about VBA, the application most likely requires code anyway!

Because pass-through query data is not updatable, those queries are not as useful for forms. On the other hand, pass-through queries are perfect for list boxes, combo boxes, and reports. Because report data does not need to be updatable, and tends to be based on multiple tables that potentially require local join work, report record sources that have been converted from local queries to pass-through queries can realize dramatic benefits.

Creating a pass-through query is extremely simple if you know how to write the proper SQL. On the Ribbon's Create tab, click the Pass-Through button in the Query menu. Because there is no graphical user interface, the SQL text is specific to the ODBC data source the query will run against. In this case, which uses SQL Server Express 2005, you can use the following SQL as a pass-through query against the NorthwindCS sample database:

```
SELECT dbo.Orders.OrderID, dbo.Customers.CompanyName, dbo.Customers.ContactName,
  dbo.Orders.OrderDate, dbo.Products.ProductName, dbo.[Order Details].Quantity
FROM dbo.Orders
  INNER JOIN dbo.Customers ON dbo.Orders.CustomerID = dbo.Customers.CustomerID
  INNER JOIN dbo.[Order Details] ON dbo.Orders.OrderID = dbo.[Order Details].OrderID
  INNER JOIN dbo.Products ON dbo.[Order Details].ProductID = dbo.Products.ProductID
```

Access does not parse or validate the SQL text of a pass-through query in any way. Instead, the SQL text is sent (passed through) to the specified ODBC data source as-is and Access attempts to create a record-set from whatever results are returned.

Note that when opening a SQL pass-through QueryDef in Access, the user is prompted to select the DSN connection unless you set the query's connection property (through the Property Sheet in Query Design mode). But remember, there is a security issue to consider because the connection information is stored in plain text in this property. If the connection does not use NT Authentication, the User Name and Password for the ODBC connection are visible to anyone with access to the query.

Pass-through queries should be used whenever possible to help reduce network traffic and shift query processing to the server. Pass-through queries can result in huge improvements in the efficiency of Access applications that use linked tables to ODBC data source in an ACCDB/MDB file format.

What Is an ADP?

Unlike Access ACCDB and MDB database files, Access project (ADP) files are client-server applications by definition. ADPs were created specifically for working with SQL Server-based data sources, while still providing the rich features and flexibility of an Access application. The ADP file itself only contains the forms, reports, and other non-data objects like the VBA project. The tables and queries for the application are stored on the SQL Server. Instead of opening a database and retrieving the VBA project stored in it, the VBA project is opened directly and then Access connects to the SQL Server described by the connection properties stored in the file.

ADPs neither use nor depend on the ACE or Jet database engines. Instead, ActiveX Data Objects (ADO) tools are used to connect to the Microsoft SQL Server (or SQL Server Express edition), which is used as the database engine and all table and query objects, as well as all of the data, is stored on SQL Server. After opening an ADP and connecting to the SQL Server, Access retrieves a list of server objects that the user has permission to view or execute and then displays the names in the Tables or Queries tabs in the Navigation Pane.

When you double-click on a table or query in an ADP, Access sends a simple SELECT statement to retrieve all of the object's records. Data processing happens on the server, and Access handles only the set of records returned and the presentation processing on the client side. If a SQL statement is specified as the Record Source for a form, report, or control, the SQL statement is sent as-is to the server.

Although ADP files make it easier to shift processing to the server, this won't help performance much if an application is repeatedly bringing down whole tables of data from the server. It is important to limit the amount of data that is being pulled down by the application and the frequency with which the data is retrieved or updated. One common way to limit the data is to use Recordsets and retrieve and modify records only when necessary. When a form or report is tied to a table or query, Access issues a command to the database server to modify the records and retrieve the data again every time the object is opened or modified. The Recordset object can be applied to the form or report and updates or requeries to the data source can be completely controlled by the application's developer. Of course, this requires more application design, coding, and testing, but the increased performance may be well worth the effort.

How Access Projects Link to External Data Sources

ADP files are specifically designed to work with SQL Server and cannot be bound directly to any other data source. They are tightly bound with and optimized for use with SQL Server, so that all data processing is done on the server, which can greatly improve performance. Fortunately, SQL Server has strong capabilities that allow linking to many other data sources.

Access projects rely on the linked server capability of SQL Server. Although architecturally different than linked ODBC tables in an MDB file, similar functionality is obtained. Comparable to how a machine

DSN stores connection information in the registry that can be referenced by using the DSN name, SQL Server can store connection information (linked servers) in a system table in the SQL Server Master database. An alias defined when the linked server is created can be used to reference the server's connection details. The alias can be used from other SQL Server objects such as views, functions, and stored procedures.

Views based on linked servers can be created programmatically or through the user interface in an ADP. Any version of SQL Server supports creating a linked server, so there is no need to worry about having the correct version for a given machine. Linked servers can be created directly through one of the SQL Server client tools, such as SQL Management Studio Express, or through the Access UI.

Creating Linked Server Data Sources Through Access

To create a new linked-server view connection to a SQL Server, open the `SampleADP.adp` file included with the download files for this chapter, and follow these steps:

1. Go to the Select File ➪ Server ➪ Link Tables to invoke the Link Table Wizard. The wizard opens, as shown in Figure 19-11.

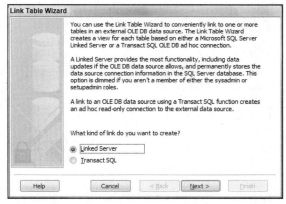

Figure 19-11

2. The Linked Server option should be selected by default if `MSAccess.exe` is set to Run as Administrator, otherwise you will need to set Access to run as administrator to enable this option. (The Transact SQL option stores the connection information in the query instead of creating a linked server. That is useful when you do not have permissions to create a linked server or when the resulting view is run on an infrequent basis.) To continue, select Linked Server and click Next. The Select Data Source dialog box opens, as shown in Figure 19-12.

3. From this point, the pages of the wizard vary depending on which data source you choose. To create a new link to another SQL Server, select `+New SQL Server Connection.odc` and click Open. The Data Connection Wizard opens. Choose the SQL Server option and click Next. The wizard requests the name of the SQL Server, as shown in Figure 19-13.

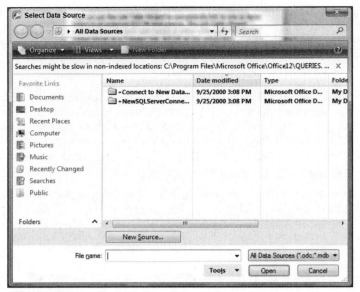

Figure 19-12

Figure 19-13

4. Enter the name of the SQL Server to be linked, enter the necessary security credentials (in this case, you are using NT Authentication), and click Next to continue. A dialog box opens showing the databases and tables on the SQL Server, as in Figure 19-14.

5. Select the NorthwindCS database from the list of databases on the SQL Server in the Data Connection Wizard dialog box. Click Finish and the new SQL Server is linked. The dialog box closes, returning you to the Linked Table Wizard dialog box.

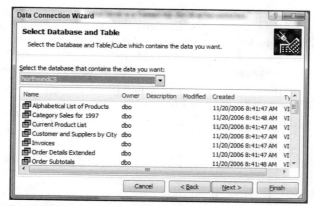

Figure 19-14

At this point, Access needs to know which view to use, so select the objects to create views against. In this case, select the `Table:Orders` table from the left list, click the > button to move the table to the right list, and click Finish. A new view data source file is created in your My Data Sources folder in My Documents.

Unfortunately, the wizard does not always function as well as one might like. It's generally good for creating links to other SQL Server data sources, but less reliable with other data sources. Sometimes Access creates the linked server but not any views that use it and sometimes Access won't even be able to create the linked server. Fortunately, it is not too complicated to create the linked servers programmatically, if needed.

Creating Linked Server Data Sources Programmatically

You can create a linked server by writing some ADO code to execute a SQL command to create the link. The `CurrentProject` object is the instance of the code project that is currently loaded in the Access instance. It exposes the `Connection` object that can be used to specify the SQL Server to which the ADP is connected. The `Connection` object's `Execute` method can be used to execute commands accepted by the SQL Server on the SQL Server. This way, an application can link to a SQL Server by calling `Execute` with the proper SQL statement. Here's an example of linking to a SQL Server data source:

```
Dim strCommand As String

' Create the command to link to the SQL Server
strCommand = _
   "EXEC sp_AddLinkedServer " & _
   "@server='RemoteServerAlias', " & _
   "@srvproduct='', " & _
   "@provider='SQLOLEDB', " & _
   "@datasrc='<Machine Name>\<Instance Name>'"

' Execute the SQL command
CurrentProject.Connection.Execute strCommand
```

`RemoteServerAlias` is the name to use when referencing the linked server in queries. Then `RemoteServerName` is the actual name of the remote network server that is being linked to. In the case of a SQL Server Express edition installation (created at the beginning of this chapter), the format is `<machine name>\sqlexpress`. After creating the linked server, you can execute another SQL statement to create the other database objects by writing a few lines of code, such as the following:

```
Dim strCommand As String

' Create the SQL Statement to create a view object on the server
strCommand = _
    "Create View ViewName as " & _
    "Select ShipperID, CompanyName, Phone " & _
    "From RemoteServerAlias.NorthwindCS.DBO.Shippers;"

' Execute the SQL command
CurrentProject.Connection.Execute strCommand
```

This code uses a standard SQL statement to create a new view object. Because all processing occurs on the server, the statement that is passed as the parameter for `Execute` is passed directly to SQL Server and not executed on the client machine. Therefore, any statement that can be processed on the SQL Server can be issued through the `Execute` method.

Understanding Query Options in SQL Server

The three types of query objects in SQL Server that can be used from an ADP are views, stored procedures, and functions. Each of these types has its own unique strengths that can be leveraged in an Access application.

Views

Views can be thought of as virtual tables. Views can be used in the same manner as regular tables in query objects. The benefit of views is that they can be based on more than one source table and can be limited to include only the fields needed for a particular action. In general, views are similar to an Access Query database object.

Although you can generally update, delete, and insert records into a view, if the view is based on multiple tables, there may be limitations on the type of actions a view can be used for. An example is when a SQL statement attempts to insert a record into a view based on multiple tables. The SQL statement generates an error because SQL Server doesn't always know what needs to be done to add a record to a view with multiple underlying tables.

This behavior can be modified on the SQL Server side by adding *triggers*. A trigger is conceptually similar to having a VBA event procedure for a table or other SQL Server object. Instead of running VBA code, triggers are written in SQL Server–specific Transact-SQL (T-SQL) query syntax. For instance, it's possible to define a trigger for a view so that the actual inserts are handled by the trigger and don't generate a SQL Server error. Although the creation of SQL Server triggers is outside the scope of this book, you should be aware of their existence and know there is plenty of documentation on the Web about working with them.

Additionally, Access projects have a built-in mechanism for adding records to views based on two tables by adding the new records to the source tables directly and bypassing the view. This can sometimes have unexpected side effects for developers who are used to the regular SQL Server behavior. Even if a view is updatable (perhaps because a trigger has been added), Access attempts to update the view's source tables. If a user has permissions to a view, but not the view's source tables, a permissions error is generated when Access attempts to update the underlying table.

Fortunately, changing a view property can modify this behavior. While in Design mode for a view, right-click the background in the upper half of the design area and select Properties. To allow Access to update the view directly, instead of attempting to update source tables, select the Update using view rules checkbox, as shown in Figure 19-15.

Figure 19-15

Stored Procedures

Unlike views, stored procedures are not updateable directly and can't be used as a data source by other query objects. However, they can be used to run update queries and can contain somewhat complicated logic that regular views cannot. Although the data returned from stored procedure objects is read-only, it can appear to be updateable from the user interface of an ADP. Fortunately, Access is capable of working around the read-only restriction by updating the source tables directly. In contrast to a normal view, there is no method for having Access update the stored procedure directly.

Functions

Functions are a sort of cross between views and stored procedures. Unlike stored procedures, functions can be used as a data source in another query object, in the same manner as a view. Unlike a view, the data set returned by a function is not updateable. When opening a function from the user interface, Access can update the data in some cases by updating the source tables directly, similar to the method used to update a stored procedure. Functions tend to be useful in situations that call for returning a single value or a read-only recordset as part of another query.

Choosing Between ACCDB/MDB and ADP

ACCDB, MDB, and ADP formats all have benefits and tradeoffs when connecting to SQL Server or other data sources. It is important to consider these tradeoffs while designing the application before implementation occurs. It is not uncommon for an Access application to start out as an MDB and then eventually have the tables, queries, and data migrated to a SQL Server once the application reaches critical mass. Along with this migration comes the cost for completing this work, which is dependent on the initial design of the application. The following topics provide some information to consider before choosing one format over the other.

Recordset Differences

ACCDB and MDB files use a Dynaset recordset by default. Dynaset-type recordsets have the ability to see changes by other users in near real time. However, it's an expensive recordset to maintain in terms of resource and network usage. If a user moves to the first record in a given table, then to the last record, and then back to the first, Access requeries the first record from the back-end database for updated values. In addition, updates to the recordset are committed immediately. While this may be useful for applications that have multiple users constantly accessing the same records, it means that a lot of data is pushed across the network. In effect, ACE and Jet maintain a rolling recordset that contains just the records being viewed, along with a small buffer of records outside the current viewable set.

With an ADP, Access maintains an updateable snapshot recordset. The user can scroll through the records and make changes, but those changes are not committed to the server until the query is rerun. The main benefit to this approach is that there is much less network traffic and, once the records are brought down, the user can quickly walk them without having to constantly requery large amounts of data. However, if an application is required to have many records in a datasheet type mode and needs to see continuous changes by other users, then ACCDB/MDB files may be preferred. Although there are ways to see streaming changes by other users in an ADP, it requires more custom code.

The other difference in the recordset is that ACCDB and MDB files use ACE or Jet, which is tightly bound with DAO objects. For ADP files, using ADO code is preferred because ADO objects are used to connect to the SQL Server. Although DAO can be used in an ADP in some cases, ADO is much more natural to use and is universal between an ACCDB/MDB and an ADP, as well as other true ODBC data sources. Some database developers make the argument that all Access database code should be done in ADO, so that when the ACCDB grows large enough to be upsized to a SQL Server, very little code has to be changed to update the application. Still, many people have a personal preference for using one object library over the other (usually because they are more familiar with one than the other) and will base their format choice on that preference.

Security Differences

With MDB files, Access developers are able to enforce user-level security using the Jet database engine on almost all database objects, including forms and reports. However, there are tools available that claim to be able to break this security model and it is known to have security issues (see Chapter 18 on database security). Additionally, the ACCDB file format does not support the user-level security feature at all; the best you can get is shared-level security, but that does not allow for granular database object control. This is not the case for the ADP file format.

Using an ADP, you can leverage many of the powerful security features of SQL Server for the tables, views, and data in the database. Once tables and queries have been moved, SQL Server becomes the primary enforcer of security for those objects. Additionally, there is no User-level security at the ADP file level for controlling permission to forms or reports. Instead, data access is controlled at the server level. However, the primary security mechanism at the ADP file level is to add a VBA project password or to convert the file to an ADE file, which strips away the source code. If the application is properly designed, there is no need for user-level security because logging in can be controlled through SQL Server permissions.

Local Data Storage

The inability to store tables and query objects in an ADP file is probably the biggest complaint developers have when moving from an ACCDB/MDB file format to the ADP environment. Unlike the ACCDB/MDB file format, every table and view in an ADP is stored on the SQL Server, and there is no way to have these stored locally in the ADP file itself. This is not as big a limitation as it may seem at first because there are still methods for storing data on the local machine if that's truly necessary.

The three primary methods to utilize local machine storage for tables, views, and data connected to an ADP are the following:

❑ Run SQL Server on the local machine. SQL Server can store tables, views, and data locally and can link to other SQL Server databases across the network.

❑ Have a separate ACCDB/MDB file on the local machine. As mentioned earlier, Access does support ADO, so the database can be accessed programmatically.

❑ Store XML (Extensible Markup Language) data locally. The XML data source could be connected to via code as well. Even in an ADP, it is possible to store data on the local machine, just not in the ADP file itself.

Each of these primary options involves tradeoffs, but each can be a suitable solution in the proper scenarios. The best option for a given scenario usually depends on how the locally stored data needs to be used. For serious local number crunching, using SQL Server on the local machine provides a powerful database server for the application, but at the expense of more resource usage requirements. Alternatively, XML files consume few processor resources, but are more difficult to update and manipulate and may require large amounts of file space and consume lots of RAM, depending on how the XML is loaded. Additionally, XML file security is limited to the security of the network, so anyone with access to the directory can view the data. Using ACCDB/MDB files to store local data for an ADP uses fewer system resources than using SQL Server does, and can be easier to update than XML. It still requires more code in the application to connect and manipulate the database.

Sharing Application Files

For Access applications designed to support multi-user scenarios, it is usually recommended that a front-end database file be installed on each user's local machine and that data be linked to a back-end ACCDB/MDB file stored on the network location. Access does support opening ACCDB/MDB files over the network, and applications are often shared in this manner from a central network location. Sharing ACCDB/MDB files over the network usually works well when only a small number of users are working with the database and they are not using it simultaneously. This greatly reduces the complexity added when creating an application that has both a front-end and back-end database. This functionality is made possible through the use of the ACE and Jet database engines, which can issue commands that are accepted by network file storage interfaces.

Because ADP files don't use the ACE or Jet engines, the same instance of an ADP file cannot be opened by multiple users over a network. You can work around this limitation by flagging the ADP file as read only, but that it is neither recommended nor supported by Microsoft and can potentially corrupt or cause problems with your ADP file. A copy of the master ADP files should always be used locally and never shared across a network.

Controlling the Logon Process

The elegant way to handle logon errors when starting a client-server application is to control the logon process to the back-end database. Undoubtedly the client-server application will run into network or database server connectivity issues at some point in its lifecycle. If the connection process is not controlled at startup, users may get an unpleasant and confusing error message, and it will be difficult to control reconnection in the same session if the network/server becomes disconnected. Controlling the logon process from the beginning makes it is quite easy to store the supplied username and password information for connecting to the data store subsequently without having to re-ask the user for security credentials. However, the process and code needed to log in can vary depending on whether an ADP or an ACCDB/MDB file format is used.

Using Linked Tables in ACCDB/MDB Files

A graceful way to control the login process is to create a startup form in the application to prompt the user for his credentials. If the application uses SQL Security and does not store user credentials explicitly, users may be prompted for credentials from the server when trying to read or manipulate objects in the application when Access first tries to use the table or view. Fortunately, it is easy to create a custom startup login form that looks similar to the one shown in Figure 19-16 and prompts for username and password.

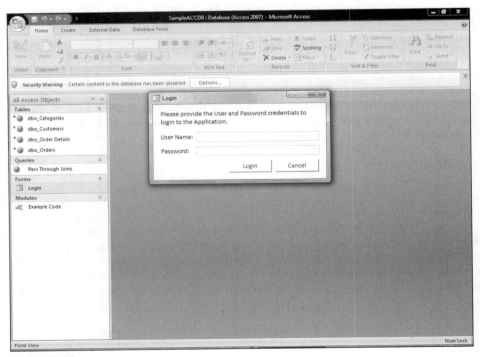

Figure 19-16

The form in Figure 19-16 is simple to create and can execute code when the Login button is clicked to refresh the table links and save the username and password information to global variables. In the case of linked tables, you will likely need code at some point to create a DSN to store connection information for the tables. The following code illustrates how to programmatically create a DSN:

```
Public Sub CreateNewDSN()

    ' Define Variables
    Dim strDSNName As String
    Dim strDriverName As String
    Dim strDescription As String
    Dim strServer As String
    Dim strDatabase As String

    ' This is the DSN name to use when
    ' referencing the DSL in your code
    strDSNName = "TestDSN"

    ' The name of the ODBC Driver used for the connection
    strDriverName = "SQL Server"

    ' This is the optional description to use
    ' in the ODBC Driver Manager program
    strDescription = "Test DSN Description"

    ' In the case of SQL Server, use the following
    ' line of code to specify the SQL Server to connect to
    strServer = "<machine name>\<sqlexpress>"

    ' Then name of the Default database on the server
    ' used for this DSN. If not specified, then SQL Statements
    ' may end up getting executed against the master database
    strDatabase = "NorthwindCS"

    ' Create the DSN
    DBEngine.RegisterDatabase _
        strDSNName, strDriverName, _
        True, "Description=" & strDescription & _
        Chr(13) & "Server=" & strServer & _
        Chr(13) & "Database=" & strDatabase

End Sub
```

Once the DSN has been created, it can be referenced in code to create and refresh linked tables. The following code demonstrates how to create linked tables based on the DSN just created:

```
Public Sub CreateLinkedTable()

    ' NOTE: This code requires the DAO object library to work.
    ' If you are using the SampleACCDB.accdb sample file, then this
    ' reference should already be present. When unsure, check the
    ' VBA project references under Tools -> References menu option
```

```
' in the VBA editor and make sure a reference is set to:
' 1. Access 2007: Microsoft Office 2007 Access database engine Object Library
' 2. Access 2003 and older: Microsoft DAO 3.6 Object library

' Define Variables
Dim strConnection As String
Dim daoTableDef As DAO.TableDef

' This must reference an existing DSN
Const strDSNName = "TestDSN"

' The application name can be used for tracing and
' troubleshooting the source of problems on the server.
' This can be anything, but usually the more specific the better.
Const strAppName = "Microsoft Office Access 2007"

' The database where the table resides on SQL Server
Const strDatabase = "NorthwindCS"

' User name for logging into the database server. This could be
' captured by a logon form and stored in a global variable.
Const strUserName = "sa"

' Password for logging in to the database server. This could
' be captured by a logon form and stored in a global variable.
Const strPassword = "password"

' Then name of the table on the remote server
Const strRemoteTableName = "Customers"

' The name of the table we want create in the local file
' that links to the Remote Table
Const strLocalTableName = "dbo_Customers"

' This will build the ODBC connection string for our new table
strConnection = _
  "ODBC:" & _
  "DSN=" & strDSNName & ";" & _
  "APP=" & strAppName & ";" & _
  "DATABASE=" & strDatabase & ";" & _
  "UID=" & strUserName & ";" & _
  "PWD=" & strPassword & ";" & _
  "TABLE=" & strRemoteTableName

' This creates a new table object and adds it to the local
' database.  If your tables already exist, then you would
' skip this code and use code to refresh the links, instead
Set daoTableDef = CurrentDb.CreateTableDef( _
            strLocalTableName, _
            dbAttachSavePWD, _
            strRemoteTableName, _
            strConnection)
```

```
    CurrentDb.TableDefs.Append daoTableDef

    ' Clean up
    Set daoTableDef = Nothing

End Sub
```

Alternatively, if the tables already exist in the database and the links only need to be refreshed, the DAO `TableDef` object exposes the `RefreshLink` method to easily refresh any linked tables. The following code could be used to refresh a linked table:

```
Sub RefreshTable()

    ' Define Variables
    Dim daoTableDef As DAO.TableDef

    ' The name of the local linked table to refresh
    strLocalTableName = "dbo_Customers"

    ' This will build the ODBC connection string for our new table
    strConnection = _
        "ODBC:DSN=TestDSN;APP=Microsoft Office Access 2007;" & _
        "DATABASE=NorthwindCS;UID=sa;PWD=password;TABLE=Customers"

    ' This code assumes that the linked table object have
    ' already been created and only need to be refershed.
    Set daoTableDef = CurrentDb.TableDefs(strLocalTableName)
    daoTableDef.Connect = strConnection
    daoTableDef.RefreshLink

    ' Clean up
    Set daoTableDef = Nothing

End Sub
```

Using Access Projects

Because Access projects don't store tables in the ADP file, it is only necessary to reconnect the ADP to the SQL Server database that is used for the Access application. The code is similar to the startup form that was suggested earlier for an ACCDB/MDB to collect a username and password, or just run code automatically if the NT Authentication security model is employed. You can call the `OpenConnection` method to connect an ADP application to a specific SQL Server. The first parameter of the `OpenConnection` method takes a standard OLEDB connection string, specifying the server, database name, security option, and optionally, the username and password. The following code illustrates reconnecting the ADP to the SQL Server:

```
Public Sub ConnectADP()

    ' Define Variables
```

```
    Dim strConnect As String

    ' Required - This is the network name of the SQL Server.
    ' "(local)" can be used to reference a default SQL Server
    ' installation on the local machine.
    Const strServerName = "<machine name>\sqlexpress"

    ' Required - This is the database you want the ADP to be based on.
    Const strDBName = "NorthwindCS"

    ' Optional - The SQL Server user name.
    ' Not required if using NT Authentication.
    Const strUserName = "sa"

    ' Optional - The password for the user.
    ' Not required if using NT Authentication.
    Const strPassword = "password"

    ' Use this flag to signify whether the connection string should
    ' contain a username and password or use integrated security.
    Const boolUseIntegratedSecurity = True

    ' This is the full connection string for the ADP. The Provider,
    ' Data Source, and Initial Catalog arguments are required.
    strConnect = _
      "Provider=SQLOLEDB.1" & _
      ";Data Source=" & strServerName & _
      ";Initial Catalog=" & strDBName

    'Add the necessary argument if using NT Authentication
    If boolUseIntegratedSecurity Then
      strConnect = strConnect & ";integrated security=SSPI"

    Else ' Add the user and password arguments if using SQL Server Security
      strConnect = strConnect & ";user id=" & strUserName & _
        ";password=" & strPassword
    End If

    ' Open the connection. If there is already an existing connection
    ' open then this will change it.
    Application.CurrentProject.OpenConnection strConnect

End Sub
```

Unfortunately, one of the limitations of the OpenConnection method is that the advanced connection properties, such as Application Name or Connect Timeout, cannot be set programmatically. In addition, because Access does not expose these properties, there is no convenient method for changing them after the connection is made either. The properties that can't be specified are the properties located on the Advanced and All tabs of the Data Link Properties dialog box. To open the Data Link Properties dialog box (see Figure 19-17), open an ADP file, and choose File ➪ Server ➪ Connection.

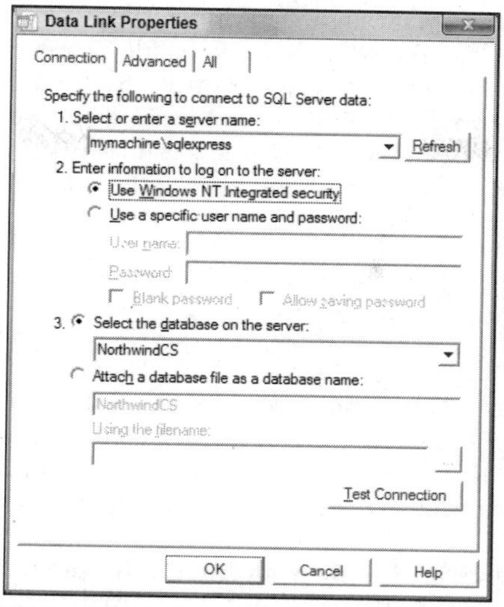

Figure 19-17

What happens if the Server is down when calling the OpenConnection method? If a connection cannot be established with the normal server and the code generates an error, it would be useful to have a convenient way to specify an alternate server, which may not be known when the application was developed. One way to establish a different connection is to use a Universal Data Link (UDL) file to store the connection information about the SQL Server. However, the OpenConnection method does not accept UDL files as a parameter directly, so code is needed to retrieve the connection information by using a regular ADO Connection object to open the UDL file:

```
Sub ConnectToAlternateServer()

    ' Define Variables
    Dim cnnTest As ADODB.Connection

    ' Open the connection from the UDL file
    Set cnnTest = New ADODB.Connection
    cnnTest.Open CurrentProject.Path & "\AlternateConnection.udl;"

    ' Now pass the connection string of the ADO connection to the ADP.
    Application.CurrentProject.OpenConnection cnnTest.ConnectionString

    ' Test the connection
    If CurrentProject.IsConnected = False Then
        ' Error - Failed to Connect
    End If

    ' Clean up
    cnnTest.Close
    Set cnnTest = Nothing

End Sub
```

It's easy to make a custom UDL file through the Windows interface. Simply create a new blank text file, rename the extension to .udl and then double-click the file to open it. Because the file does not contain any UDL data, the Data Link Properties dialog box opens. Set all of the desired properties for the data source and then click OK to store the UDL string in the file. The connection string in the UDL file is identical to the connection string used in the previous code samples, only it is prefixed with the [oledb] string to denote the data source provider. An example of this string is as follows:

```
[oledb]
; Everything after this line is an OLE DB connection string
Provider=SQLOLEDB.1;Integrated Security=SSPI;Persist Security Info=False;Initial
Catalog=NorthwindCS;Data Source=<machine name>\SQLEXPRESS
```

You could even type this directly into a blank text document and then rename the extension to .udl to create the UDL file. The benefit to using the UDL file is that it is easy to transfer from one machine to another, and is independent of any application that uses it. The application could even create a UDL file by parsing the ADP's connection string and writing the data to a local file in the proper structure.

There is one more step to make the UDL file work seamlessly with the application. If the ADP is closed in a normal fashion, the connection information is stored in the ADP file and Access will attempt to reconnect the next time the ADP is opened. Access attempts to reconnect before any code in the ADP has a chance to run, so it is impossible to trap any errors that occur. Fortunately, you can prevent an ADP from trying to connect on startup by clearing the connection string when the ADP is closed. Calling OpenConnection with an empty string kills the existing connection, so place the following line of code on the close event for the last form to be closed in the application:

```
CurrentProject.OpenConnection ""
```

Calling the OpenConnection method with an empty string not only closes the current connection, but it also clears the connection information from the file so that the ADP will open in a disconnected state the next time around. This enables you to run code and reconnect the ADP in your own fashion.

One trick that some developers employ is to run the code from the close event of the initial logon form. If you hide the logon form once the user has logged in, instead of closing it, this guarantees that the code will run no matter how the ADP was closed. The only exception to this is when a power failure or abnormal close of the application occurs, perhaps because the application froze or crashed. In such cases, the previous connection information will still be present in the ADP because the database was not shut down through the normal processes. However, this causes only two logon prompts the next time the ADP is open: the default Access prompt and then the one presented by the application's code. If the application is using integrated security, the user will likely not even notice any difference.

Binding ADODB Recordsets

Built-in table and view links do not provide enough flexibility for controlling the recordset for a form. Often it is extremely useful to build a recordset in code and then bind it to the desired object. Recordsets can be bound to combo boxes, list boxes, forms, and reports in ADP files. This section explores how to create and bind Recordsets in ADO.

Binding to a Form, ComboBox, or ListBox

The code and methods used for binding forms, combo boxes, and list boxes are basically the same. They all have a `Recordset` property that can be assigned an active ADO `Recordset` object. Typically, the recordset is bound to the form during the `Form_Open` event, but can be set at any time while the form is open. The following is an example of binding a form to a `Recordset` object:

```
Sub BindRecordset()

    ' Define Variables
    Dim rsRecordSet As New ADODB.Recordset
    Dim cnConnection As New ADODB.Connection
    Dim frmForm As New Form
    Dim strConnection As String

    ' Create the Connection string
    strConnection = _
        "Provider=SQLOLEDB.1;Data Source=<machine name>\sqlexpress" & _
        ";Initial Catalog=NorthwindCS;user id=sa;password=password"

    ' Open the connection
    cnConnection.Open strConnection

    ' Open the Recordset
    rsRecordSet.Open "Products", cnConnection, adOpenKeyset, adLockOptimistic

    ' Bind the Recordset to the form
    Set frmForm.Recordset = rsRecordSet

    ' Clean up
    rsRecordSet.Close
    Set rsRecordSet = Nothing
    cnConnection.Close
    Set cnConnection = Nothing

End Sub
```

The code for binding a `Recordset` to controls such as a `ComboBox` or a `ListBox` control is virtually the same as this, except you set the Record Source property of the control rather than of the form.

Binding to a Report

Reports are not nearly as easy to dynamically bind to an active `Recordset` as forms, list boxes, and combo boxes. It is also not possible with ACCDB and MDB files. The key difference is that the `Recordset` has to be a shaped recordset, using the Microsoft Data Shaping services for OLEDB (MSDataShape) provider or the Microsoft Client Data Manager (Microsoft.Access.OLEDB.12.0) provider.

For example, the Invoice report in the `SampleADP.adp` file is based on the Invoices view stored on SQL Server. However, if you try to bind a simple ADO Recordset based on the Invoices view to the Invoice report in the same manner as for a form, an error is raised or some unpredictable behavior occurs.

Instead, you need to get a starter shape by calling the Shape object for the report. For instance, you can get the SQL statement for the shape by calling this code from the immediate window:

```
?reports![Invoices].shape
```

Remember, the report must be open in the Access client window, or this call will fail. The result that should be returned will look something like the following SQL statement:

```
SHAPE (SHAPE (SHAPE (SHAPE {SELECT "CustomerName", "OrderDate", "OrderID", ↵
"ShippedDate", "Salesperson", "ProductName", "UnitPrice", "Quantity", ↵
"ExtendedPrice", "Discount", "Freight" FROM "dbo"."Invoices"} APPEND ↵
CALC((Year(OrderDate)*4+(Month(OrderDate)-1)\3)\1) AS __G0) AS rsLevel0 ↵
COMPUTE rsLevel0, ANY(rsLevel0.OrderDate) AS __COLRef1, ANY(rsLevel0.OrderID) ↵
AS __COLRef2, ANY(rsLevel0.ShippedDate) AS __COLRef3, ANY(rsLevel0.Salesperson) ↵
AS __COLRef4, ANY(rsLevel0.Freight) AS __COLRef5, Sum(rsLevel0.[ExtendedPrice]) ↵
AS __Agg0 BY CustomerName AS __COLRef0, __G0) AS rsLevel1 COMPUTE rsLevel1 BY ↵
__COLRef0) AS RS_9229
```

There's one more step to take before the report will render correctly. Although the previous SQL is valid, if you use this code to bind a shaped recordset to the Invoices report, the report generates an error and some fields may display as #Name? or #Error. The reason is that fields are aliased as names such as __COLRef1 in the SQL statement but the textbox bound to the field in the report is expecting the actual field name for the control. Because field names are not defined in the SQL, the error is generated. Why doesn't this work is a good question because you are using the same SQL given to you by Access for the same report. Under the hood, Access must account for this discrepancy in some way and coordinate the two values dynamically. However, there are two ways to fix the problem:

❑ Modify the Control Sources for the broken fields in the report. In this case, the developer would change the Control Source property of the text boxes with aliased fields to something such as __COLRef1. This fixes the problem by using the alias defined in the SQL statement, instead of the original field name the control was bound to.

❑ Modify the SQL statement to use the correct field names. In this case, you would change the references to field aliases like __COLRef1 to the proper field names that the control sources reference in the report. This is the preferred method because using this method does not force the report to be modified in any way. In this case, you would modify the SQL statement to:

```
SHAPE (SHAPE (SHAPE (SHAPE {SELECT "CustomerName", "OrderDate", "OrderID", ↵
"ShippedDate", "Salesperson", "ProductName", "UnitPrice", "Quantity", ↵
"ExtendedPrice", "Discount", "Freight" FROM "dbo"."Invoices"} APPEND ↵
CALC((Year(OrderDate)*4+(Month(OrderDate)-1)\3)\1) AS __G0) AS rsLevel0 COMPUTE ↵
rsLevel0, ANY(rsLevel0.OrderDate) AS OrderDate, ANY(rsLevel0.OrderID) AS ↵
OrderID, ANY(rsLevel0.ShippedDate) AS ShippedDate, ANY(rsLevel0.Salesperson) ↵
AS Salesperson, ANY(rsLevel0.Freight) Freight, Sum(rsLevel0.[ExtendedPrice]) ↵
AS __Agg0 BY CustomerName AS CustomerName, __G0) AS rsLevel1 COMPUTE rsLevel1 ↵
BY __COLRef0) AS RS_9229
```

Now if you run code to bind this SQL statement to the invoices report, the names will match and the report will display as expected.

Once the proper shape SQL is known, it can be used to bind the shaped Recordset to the Invoices report. Using the previous SQL, bind the shaped Recordset by clearing the report's Record Source property and adding the following code to the report's Open event procedure:

```vba
Private Sub Report_Open(Cancel As Integer)

    ' Define Variables
    Dim rsRecordSet As New ADODB.Recordset
    Dim cnConnection As New ADODB.Connection
    Dim strSQL As String
    Dim strConnect As String

    ' Create the connection string
    strConnect = _
        "Provider=Microsoft.Access.OLEDB.10.0;Data Provider=SQLOLEDB.1" & _
        ";Data Source=<machine name>\SQLEXPRESS;Initial Catalog=NorthwindCS" & _
        ";integrated security=SSPI" ' or use ";user id=sa;password=password"

    ' Open the connection
    cnConnection.Open strConnect

    ' Create the SQL statement for the shape
    strSQL = _
        "SHAPE (SHAPE (SHAPE (SHAPE " & _
        "{SELECT ""CustomerName"", ""OrderDate"", ""OrderID"", " & _
        """ShippedDate"", ""Salesperson"", ""ProductName"", " & _
        """UnitPrice"", ""Quantity"", ""ExtendedPrice"", " & _
        """Discount"", ""Freight"" FROM ""dbo"".""Invoices""} " & _
        "APPEND CALC((Year(OrderDate)*4+(Month(OrderDate)-1)\3)\1) " & _
        "AS __G0) AS rsLevel0 COMPUTE rsLevel0, ANY(rsLevel0.OrderDate) " & _
        "AS OrderDate, ANY(rsLevel0.OrderID) AS OrderID, " & _
        "ANY(rsLevel0.ShippedDate) AS ShippedDate, ANY(rsLevel0.Salesperson) " & _
        "AS Salesperson, ANY(rsLevel0.Freight) AS Freight, " & _
        "Sum(rsLevel0.[ExtendedPrice]) AS __Agg0 BY CustomerName " & _
        "AS CustomerName, __G0) AS rsLevel1 COMPUTE rsLevel1 " & _
        "BY CustomerName) AS RS_9229"

    ' Open the new Recordset based upin the shape
    rsRecordSet.Open strSQL, cnConnection, adOpenKeyset ', adLockReadOnly

    ' Set the Recordset to the Report
    Set Me.Recordset = rsRecordSet

    ' Clean up
    Set rsRecordSet = Nothing
    Set cnConnection = Nothing

End Sub
```

As you have probably figured out, binding recordsets to reports is usually more trouble than it is worth. If you have a lot of reports, you should bind the reports' Record Source property and let Access do the shaping. For forms and combo or list boxes, binding recordsets can be an effective means of quickly connecting to remote data sources on-the-fly without relying on linked tables or queries.

Using Persisted Recordsets

While bound recordsets can be useful, sometimes an application needs the same recordset data in multiple forms and thus the data must be retrieved multiple times. When the data usage is read-only and seldom changes, a quick and easy method for caching the data locally can be useful. This also improves overall performance and reduces network traffic because the data is temporarily stored locally and isn't pulled down every time the data is requested. Persisting recordsets can be quite useful when read-only data is frequently accessed.

With an ACCDB/MDB file, you have the option of storing data locally in tables. Even though local tables are easy to populate by appending data from a linked ODBC table, it is not as convenient as when the data has been retrieved via an ADO Recordset. Moreover, storing the data in a local table cannot be done in an ADP file because all of the tables, views, and data must reside on the SQL Server.

Fortunately, the ADO object model allows for a simple method of saving data to a local XML file and quickly recreating it as an ADO Recordset when needed. This often overlooked and underutilized feature of ADO can dramatically reduce network traffic and increase application performance when used correctly. The best scenarios for using locally persisted recordsets is when data is read-only, rarely changes, and is used in multiple locations throughout an application.

For example, an application may employ a states table to store the names and abbreviations for the 50 states in the USA. This table is a good candidate for storing the data locally because states rarely change, state names rarely need to be added or modified, and the data is most likely used in several places. For example, a state field may be used in a Customers form when adding the customer, a Vendors form when adding vendors, and an Orders form when entering shipping addresses. With persisted recordsets, once the data is brought down locally and cached, it can be used in forms and reports without retrieving it from the server again.

Persisting the Data to XML

Creating a persisted Recordset can be done very easily. To create an ADO Recordset (using ADO 2.6 or later) and call the Save method to persist the data to an XML file. The Save method for the ADO Recordset object enables you to save the current structure and data in the recordset to two different file formats, defined by the PersistFormatEnum. The following code is an example of saving a recordset for the Invoices table as XML:

```
Sub SaveRecordSetAsXML()

    ' Define Variables
    Dim rsRecordSet As New ADODB.Recordset

    ' Create the recordset. A seperate ADO connection object can be created,
    ' but the following code uses the current ADP connection for simplicity.
    ' Use a keyset cursor and adLockBatchOptimistic locking when possible
    rsRecordSet.Open "Invoices", CurrentProject.Connection, adOpenKeyset, ↵
adLockBatchOptimistic

    ' The save the Recordset structure and data to an XML file
    rsRecordSet.Save CurrentProject.Path & "\Invoices.xml", adPersistXML

    ' Clean up
    rsRecordSet.Close
```

```
    Set rsRecordSet = Nothing

    End Sub
```

Once saved, the XML file can be opened in notepad or a Web browser such as Microsoft Internet Explorer, and should look similar to Figure 19-18.

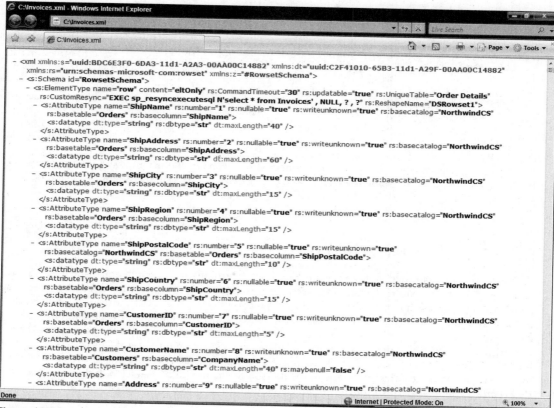

Figure 19-18

Notice that the XML file contains the table's structure and data. This XML could be used by other applications if needed, and calling Save from the ADO Recordset object can be a great way to create custom XML files.

Loading the XML Data

Loading an XML file into a Recordset object is just as easy to do. The Open method for the ADO Recordset accepts the path to an XML file as the first parameter. This is convenient for reloading a Recordset quickly, with little code. The following example illustrates how this can be done:

```
Sub LoadRecordSetWithXML()

   ' Define Variables
   Dim rsRecordSet As New ADODB.Recordset

   ' The save the Recordset structure and data to an XML file
   rsRecordSet.Open CurrentProject.Path & "\Invoices.xml"

   ' Open the Invoices report
   DoCmd.OpenReport "Invoices", acViewReport

   ' Set the Recordset
   Set Application.Reports("Invoices").Recordset = rsRecordSet

   ' Clean up
   rsRecordSet.Close
   Set rsRecordSet = Nothing

End Sub
```

Saving a Recordset as XML and reloading it when needed can be an efficient way to reduce network traffic, lighten the server processing load, and store data locally for an ADP file. Using persisted data can be a great way to improve the overall performance of a client-server application.

Using Unbound Forms

Probably in more cases than not, you want to directly control the way users manipulate data on any given form. It can be extremely useful for security and data control to automatically disallow the manipulation of data, unless it is done explicitly through the application's UI. The most common way to do this is to use unbound forms and manually bind the Recordset to the form as needed. Because recordset modifications are not persisted to the server until you explicitly call it, the data that a user sees in a form is a copy, and if modified, does not result in a change in the data on the server. This differs from a form that has its Record Source set to a database object. A bound form is a one that has the Record Source set to a Query or Table. Any changes made to the data on the form will be persisted to the server, as soon as the record is committed. In simple terms, an unbound form is nothing more than a form that has an empty Record Source property.

Why Use Unbound Forms?

There are a lot of reasons to use unbound forms in Access for both ADP and ACCDB/MDB files. Sometimes there is just no other easy way to get the fine-grained control of data without writing tons of code behind the form and carefully developing a model for the events in the form. Using an unbound form and setting the Record Source to a Recordset object can be much easier for controlling the data in the form. Typical scenarios include the following:

❑ The ADO Recordset is updateable directly but becomes read-only when bound to a form.

❑ There is a trigger on a multi-table SQL Server view to allow insertion of new records.

❑ SQL Server application role security for data access is implemented.

❑   You need to use DAO Recordset objects in an ADP.

❑   You need updateable ADO Recordset objects in an ACCDB/MDB.

❑   Server-side Recordset objects need to be utilized.

❑   You desire finer control over the Recordset behavior.

For example, an ADO Recordset is completely updateable when using the Recordset directly, but it becomes read-only when bound to a form. Another example is a trigger for a multi-table view to handle insertions, but errors are raised when trying to insert a new record from a form or you simply want to completely disallow insertion from that form. In such cases, using an unbound form can provide the necessary flexibility and data control for the application.

The primary drawback to using unbound forms is that there is no built-in method for displaying data automatically, without having to write code to explicitly set the Record Source in the form. It's possible to add ActiveX controls to an Access form that will allow datasheet-type functionality. It is much more difficult, however, to replicate the functionality of some types of forms, such as datasheets, using an unbound form and tying it to a Recordset object. Fortunately, for forms that display single records at a time, unbound forms can be very effective.

Although it takes more code to have an unbound form than a bound one, the code itself is not that complicated. Once a basic unbound form is created and some simple, reusable code is written, it can be copied and pasted for easy reuse in the future. As a general rule, DAO is used in an ACCDB or MDB file and ADO would be used for an ADP.

Creating Unbound Forms

It is usually easier to create a normal form and then convert it to an unbound form than it is to create an unbound form from scratch. When the form is bound, you can use built-in form design tools to drag-and-drop fields to build the forms to the desired layout. This technique minimizes the chance for misspelling a field name and decreases creation time. Once the controls for displaying the data have been added to the form, you can easily convert it to an unbound form by setting the Record Source property for the form to an empty string.

To keep things simple, you'll create a form based on the Customers table in the NorthwindCS SQL Server database. Because the forms are unbound, an ADO Recordset can be used and the code will be the same for both the ADP and ACCDB/MDB files. The following sections lead you through the creation of a simple regular Access form in an ADP and its conversion to an unbound form connected to a SQL Server table.

Modify the Design of the Form

There are several properties that you set for a form when switching it to an unbound form. Because the record selectors and navigation buttons won't be usable when the form is unbound, those properties should be set to No on the Format tab of the Form Properties dialog box. Also, the Record Source property, which can be found on the Data tab of the form's Property Sheet, needs to be cleared.

Because you are going to simulate the behavior of a bound form with your unbound form, you need to add some buttons to provide an interface with which the user can interact. In this case, adding nine command buttons to the form with the following names and captions exposes the functionality that will be replicated in the unbound form:

Name	Caption
btnEdit	Edit
btnSave	Save
btnCancel	Cancel
btnNew	New
btnFirst	First
btnPrevious	Previous
btnNext	Next
btnLast	Last
btnExit	Exit

At this point, if the form is opened in Form view, the text boxes are blank because there is no record source defined for the form. Next, you define the methods needed to make the form work in the way that the user would want to interact with the data in the report.

Creating the Recordset

Now that the basic form is created, code can be added to give it functionality. This section discusses modifications that allow the form to display specific data, one record at a time. Add the following code to the General Declarations section of the form's code module:

```
Option Compare Database
Option Explicit

' Global Variables
Const g_strTableName = "Customers"
Dim g_rsFormSource As ADODB.Recordset
Dim g_cnSQLServer As ADODB.Connection
Dim g_bAddNewMode As Boolean

Private Sub PopulateFields()

    ' Check to be sure the recordset is not in a BOF or EOF state.
    ' If it is then do nothing
    If Not g_rsFormSource.BOF And Not g_rsFormSource.EOF Then
        Me.txtCompanyName.SetFocus
        Me!txtCompanyName.Text = g_rsFormSource.Fields("CompanyName")
        Me.txtContactName.SetFocus
        Me!txtContactName.Text = g_rsFormSource.Fields("ContactName")
        Me.txtContactTitle.SetFocus
        Me!txtContactTitle.Text = g_rsFormSource.Fields("ContactTitle")
        Me.txtCustomerID.SetFocus
```

```vba
      Me!txtCustomerID.Text = g_rsFormSource.Fields("CustomerID")
      Me.txtFax.SetFocus
      Me!txtFax.Text = g_rsFormSource.Fields("Fax")
      Me.txtPhone.SetFocus
      Me!txtPhone.Text = g_rsFormSource.Fields("Phone")

      ' Lock the fields on the form
      Me!txtCompanyName.Locked = True
      Me!txtContactName.Locked = True
      Me!txtContactTitle.Locked = True
      Me!txtCustomerID.Locked = True
      Me!txtFax.Locked = True
      Me!txtPhone.Locked = True
   Else
      ' Throw an error
   End If

   ' Set focus to the Exit control
   Me.btnExit.SetFocus

   ' Reset the buttons on the form
   Me.btnCancel.Enabled = False
   Me.btnEdit.Enabled = True
   Me.btnExit.Enabled = True
   Me.btnFirst.Enabled = True
   Me.btnLast.Enabled = True
   Me.btnNew.Enabled = True
   Me.btnNext.Enabled = True
   Me.btnPrevious.Enabled = True
   Me.btnSave.Enabled = False

   ' Reset the g_bAddNewMode flag
   g_bAddNewMode = False

End Sub
```

The `PopulateFields` subroutine will be used in several events to populate the fields on the form. Next, add the following to the `Open` event of the Form:

```vba
Private Sub Form_Open(Cancel As Integer)

   ' For simpilicity, we will use the built-in connection of the ADP.
   ' If connecting to a different SQL Server or an ACCDB/MDB,
   ' then the connnection string will need to be supplied here.
   Set g_cnSQLServer = New ADODB.Connection
   g_cnSQLServer.ConnectionString = CurrentProject.BaseConnectionString
   g_cnSQLServer.Open

   ' Create the Recordset and move to the first record
   Set g_rsFormSource = New ADODB.Recordset
   g_rsFormSource.Open g_strTableName, g_cnSQLServer, adOpenDynamic, adLockOptimistic
   g_rsFormSource.MoveFirst

   ' Populate the text boxes on the form with data
```

```
    PopulateFields

  End Sub
```

When the form is opened now, data should be seen in the form.

Adding Code to Walk the Recordset

Although the form can now display custom data from a Recordset, it does not yet have much functionality because there is no method to allow users to walk through records or to change any data. You're ready to add code to some of the buttons created earlier to cover that. Add the following code to the btnFirst button:

```
Private Sub btnFirst_Click()

    ' Move to the first record
    g_rsFormSource.MoveFirst
    PopulateFields

End Sub
```

Add the following code to the btnPrevious button:

```
Private Sub btnPrevious_Click()

    ' Check to see if the recordset is already before the
    ' beginning. If so, then do nothing.
    If g_rsFormSource.BOF Then
      Exit Sub
    End If

    ' Moce to the previous record
    g_rsFormSource.MovePrevious

    ' Test for BOF again after moving the recordset
    ' If it is, then reverse the move and do nothing
    If rsTest.BOF Then
      rsTest.MoveNext
      Exit Sub
    End If

    ' Repopulate the controls with data from the previous
    PopulateFields

End Sub
```

Add the following code to the btnNext button:

```
Private Sub btnNext_Click()

    ' Check to see if the recordset is already beyond the
    ' end of the Recordset. If so, then do nothing.
    If g_rsFormSource.EOF Then
```

```
      Exit Sub
   End If

   ' Move to the next record
   g_rsFormSource.MoveNext

   ' Test for EOF again after moving the recordset
   ' If it is, then reverse the move and do nothing
   If g_rsFormSource.EOF Then
     g_rsFormSource.MovePrevious
     Exit Sub
   End If

   ' Repopulate the controls with the next record
   PopulateFields

End Sub
```

Add the following code to the btnLast button:

```
Private Sub btnLast_Click()

   ' Move to the Last record in the set
   g_rsFormSource.MoveLast
   PopulateFields

End Sub
```

After adding this code, the form's user should be able to click the Next, Previous, First, and Last buttons to scroll through the records without generating any errors. However, the text boxes are locked so the user can't make any changes at this point.

Enabling Records for Editing

Although an edit-type button is not absolutely necessary, it simplifies the coding necessary to keep track of changes. Otherwise, code would be needed each time the Recordset is moved to compare values and see if anything needs to be updated. With this method, nothing is updated until the user clicks the Save button.

To enable modifications, add the following code to the Edit button's click event:

```
Private Sub btnEdit_Click()

   ' Only allow edits if there is a current record.
   ' Note that the CustomerID Field does not get unlocked,
   ' because it is a Primary Key Field.
   If Not g_rsFormSource.BOF And Not g_rsFormSource.EOF Then
     Me!txtCompanyName.Locked = False
     Me!txtContactName.Locked = False
     Me!txtContactTitle.Locked = False
     Me!txtCustomerID.Locked = True
     Me!txtFax.Locked = False
     Me!txtPhone.Locked = False
```

```
    End If

    ' Sets focus to the Company Name field
    Me.txtCompanyName.SetFocus

    ' Enable and disable buttons accordingly
    Me.btnSave.Enabled = True
    Me.btnCancel.Enabled = True
    Me.btnEdit.Enabled = False

End Sub
```

To enable saving the modifications, add the following code to the btnSave button:

```
Private Sub btnSave_Click()

    ' Check if this is for new Record or change to existing
    If g_bAddNewMode = True Then
        g_rsFormSource.AddNew
    End If

    ' Update the recordset with the new data
    ' Be prepared to handle any errors that may occur
    g_rsFormSource.Fields("CompanyName") = Me!txtCompanyName.Text
    g_rsFormSource.Fields("ContactName") = Me!txtContactName.Text
    g_rsFormSource.Fields("ContactTitle") = Me!txtContactTitle.Text
    g_rsFormSource.Fields("Fax") = Me!txtFax.Text
    g_rsFormSource.Fields("Phone") = Me!txtPhone.Text

    ' Update the Recordset
    g_rsFormSource.Update

    ' This command refreshes the newly added record
    If g_bAddNewMode = True Then
        g_rsFormSource.MoveLast
    End If

    ' Repopulate the data and lock fields
    PopulateFields

End Sub
```

To allow for canceling a pending modification without saving it, add the following code to the btnCancel button:

```
Private Sub btnCancel_Click()

    ' Check if the recordset is in an add new state,
    ' and ask the user to save the record
    If g_bAddNewMode Then
        ' Prompt to save
    End If
```

```
    ' Repopulate the data and lock fields
    PopulateFields

End Sub
```

Once all of this code has been added, users should be able to modify existing records and have them updated. The last button that needs to be enabled to new record creation is the New Record button. To enable adding new records, add the following code to the click event of the btnNew button:

```
Private Sub btnNew_Click()

    ' Set the boolAddNewMode flag to true
    g_bAddNewMode = True

    ' Clear the current data from the controls and unlock
    ' In this case the CustomerID is autogenerated
    Me.txtCompanyName.SetFocus
    Me!txtCompanyName.Text = ""
    Me.txtContactName.SetFocus
    Me!txtContactName.Text = ""
    Me.txtContactTitle.SetFocus
    Me!txtContactTitle.Text = ""
    Me.txtCustomerID.SetFocus
    Me!txtCustomerID.Text = "(New)"
    Me.txtFax.SetFocus
    Me!txtFax.Text = ""
    Me.txtPhone.SetFocus
    Me!txtPhone.Text = ""

    ' Unlock all of the text controls (except txtCustomerID)
    Me!txtCompanyName.Locked = False
    Me!txtContactName.Locked = False
    Me!txtContactTitle.Locked = False
    Me!txtFax.Locked = False
    Me!txtPhone.Locked = False

    ' Set focus to a field
    Me.CompanyName.SetFocus

    ' Enable the save/cancel buttons
    Me.btnSave.Enabled = True
    Me.btnCancel.Enabled = True
    Me.btnEdit.Enabled = False

End Sub
```

Additionally, it's often helpful to supply a button that allows the user to check if any data has been modified before the form is closed and the changes are lost. Add some code to the btnExit button to close the form and enable the close logic:

```
Private Sub btnExit_Click()

    ' Check if the recordset is in an add new state,
```

```
    ' and ask the user to save the record
    If g_bAddNewMode Then
        ' Prompt to save
    End If

    ' Close the form
    DoCmd.Close acForm, Me.Name, acSaveNo

End Sub
```

By now, the form should be fully functional for the user and behave as a normal single record form created in Access would work, except this one uses code to control the records instead of a query or table tied to the Record Source property. This difference allows you to control all data in the form and protect it by limiting what the user is allowed to do. None of this code is overly complex and it can be modified to behave differently depending on the particular needs, but I hope you get the general idea.

Controlling program and data flow can be essential to building an application that protects the data in the database. Controlling data in an application is also a powerful tool for improving overall application performance, not just for client-server applications, but for standalone database applications as well. Not only is it simple, but it requires only a few lines of code, and can be done in such a way that the user gets the same functionality provided by normal Access forms. The Recordset object provides enough rich functionality that you can easily protect and manipulate data at desired intervals.

Summary

Client-server applications are especially useful when they will be used by a large number of users, or the data needs to be stored on a server. Through careful planning and design, client-server applications can perform splendidly in the right environment.

This chapter discussed how linked tables to ODBC data sources work in Access. You saw several methods for improving performance. One of the largest problems for performance is network bandwidth and local processing of data and queries. Processing joins on the server whenever possible reduces the network bandwidth required for the application and help improve overall performance.

You also examined the major differences between the ACCDB/MDB file formats and the ADP file format. ADP files are specifically designed for working directly with SQL Server and using this file format enables you to leverage many of the rich SQL Server features. Though there are some drawbacks, using ADO provides much of the functionality in an ACCDB or MDB file format.

Whatever file format is chosen for your application, you are sure to find that client-server applications can be extremely useful for multi-user scenarios, data protection, and application scaling. Using SQL Server as the back-end for the client-server application enables you to leverage features and security that SQL Server offers, while providing the flexibility and ease-of-development that Access affords. Using the ADP file format, you can even create and use SQL stored procedures, triggers, and functions directly in your Access application. Microsoft Office Access 2007 truly provides a robust environment for developing powerful client-server database solutions.

20

Working with the Win32 Registry

The Registry is the heart and soul of the 32-bit Windows operating system. It maintains information about the hardware and software installed on a computer, configuration settings, user settings, and information that the system needs to function. In fact, 32-bit Windows can't operate without it.

The capability to access and edit the information contained in the Registry is essential to all but the most basic software developer, and, if you plan to do any serious programming, understanding the Registry is critical.

As you'll see, VBA supports only four native Registry functions, which allow you to store, retrieve, and delete values from one specific area of the Registry. To do anything more advanced, you need to use the Windows Registry APIs. If you don't feel confident with API programming, you should first peruse Chapter 14, which provides the background you'll need to understand the more advanced topics in this chapter.

Although it's true that you can't damage anything by simply reading the Registry, it's also true that making changes to Registry entries when you don't know what you're doing is like randomly pressing buttons in the control room of your local nuclear power station — press the wrong button and everything will melt into a bubbling fluorescent ooze at your feet.

This chapter is not intended to provide highly detailed information about every key, subkey, and value in the Registry; to do so would require a book far larger than you could carry. Instead, the aim is to afford you enough information so you can confidently find your way around the Registry and can write basic VBA code to create, retrieve, edit, and delete Registry values. To get started, here's a basic look at what the Registry is, what's in it, how it is structured, how it works, and, finally, how programmers can make best use of it.

About the Registry

The Registry first appeared in Windows 3.1, in a file called `Reg.dat`, and was used mainly to store OLE object information. At that time, several files — namely, `Win.ini`, `System.ini`, and other INI files that were application-specific — carried out the bulk of what is handled by today's Registry.

`System.ini` maintained information and settings for the hardware (disk drives, memory, mice, and so on). `Win.ini` controlled the desktop and the applications that were installed. Changes to device drivers, fonts, system settings, and user preferences would all be recorded in the INI files, and new applications added their information to the INI files, too.

This all worked pretty well until the number of applications grew and their complexity increased because each installed application added a raft of information to the Registry to the point that it was obvious its 64KB file size limit would be reached. Additionally, everyone made additions to the INI files, but no one ever deleted anything, even if an application was upgraded or uninstalled. So `System.ini` and `Win.ini` grew and grew, and as they grew, performance degraded.

To counter this problem, software vendors started supplying INI files of their own, and instead of the Windows .INI files containing application-specific information and settings, they contained only pointers to the custom INI files. This seemed like a good idea at the time; however, good ideas sometimes create problems of their own. In this case, it was the fact that a large number of INI files began appearing throughout the system, and because an application's .INI settings could override those of `Win.ini`, there was no systemwide setting that had priority. Anything could happen!

In 32-bit Windows, Registry's role was expanded to include all the operating system and application settings and preferences, doing away with the necessity for INI files.

As it is today, the Registry is a set of files, called *hives*, which control all aspects of the operating system and how it interacts with the hardware and software that operate within it. It brings together all the information previously held in `Reg.dat` and all the INI files. It was designed to work exclusively with 32-bit applications, and there is no limit to the size of the Registry on Windows XP, Windows Server 2003, and Windows Vista. With the exception of the hive that controls hardware (which is re-created each time you log on), you can find a list of hive files in the following Registry key:

```
HKEY_LOCAL_MACHINE\System\CurrentControlSet\Control\hivelist
```

What the Registry Does

Without the Registry, Windows does not have enough information to run. It certainly doesn't have enough information to control devices, to run, and to control applications, or to respond to user input. The Registry essentially performs the following functions:

❏ **Hardware and device driver information:** For the operating system to access a hardware device, it gets the location and settings of the driver from the Registry, even if the device is a basic input/output system (BIOS)–supported device. Drivers are independent of the operating system, but Windows still needs to know where to find them and how to use them. So information such as their filename, location, version, and configuration details must be accessed; otherwise they would be unusable.

❏ **Application information:** When you launch an application, the Registry supplies all the information the operating system needs in order to run it and manage it.

The Registry also contains information such as file locations, menus and toolbars, window status, and other details. The operating system also stores file information in the Registry, such as installation date, the user who installed it, version number, add-ins, and so on.

Often, applications store temporary or runtime information in the Registry, such as the current position of a window, the last document opened by a user, or the value of a `Don't display this` check box.

What the Registry Controls

The Registry doesn't control anything, but it does contain information that is used by the operating system and applications to control almost everything. The type of information that the Registry stores is about users and machines (computers). That's why there are only two persistent Registry hives: `HKEY_LOCAL_MACHINE` and `HKEY_USERS`.

Every Registry entry controls either a user function or a computer function. User functions include customizable options, while computer functions include those items that are common to all users, such as the printers and the software installed on a computer.

Some other examples of user functions controlled by the Registry include:

- ❑ Control panel
- ❑ Desktop appearance
- ❑ Network preferences
- ❑ Explorer functionality and features

Some of these functions are the same regardless of the user, while others are user-specific.

Computer-related items are based on the computer name, without regard to the specific user — for example, installing an application. Availability and access to the application are constant, regardless of the user; however, icons to launch the application are dependent on the user. Network protocol availability and priority are based on the computer, but current connections are based on user information.

Some examples of computer-based control items in the Registry include:

- ❑ Access control
- ❑ Log-in validation
- ❑ File and print sharing
- ❑ Network card settings and protocols
- ❑ System performance and virtual memory settings

The Windows Registry is much more complex than the older INI files, but then 32-bit Windows is also far too complex for them now. It is time, then, to acquire an understanding of how the Registry works, what it does, and how to work with it. The remainder of this chapter is devoted to just that.

Accessing the Registry

You can access the Registry with a built-in Windows utility called the Registry Editor. There are two flavors of Registry Editor: `RegEdit.exe` and `Regedt32.exe`.

RegEdit.exe

Prior to Windows NT, `regedit.exe` was a 16-bit application for editing the Registry on 16-bit Windows platforms. It was originally included in Windows NT and 2000 for backward compatibility, but because of its limited functionality in the 32-bit environment, Microsoft recommends that you use `regedit.exe` only for its search capabilities on Windows NT 4.0 and Windows 2000. There is no limited functionality in `regedit.exe` on Windows XP, Windows Server 2003, or Windows Vista.

On x64-based versions of Windows, you will find both a 32-bit version and a 64-bit version of `regedit.exe`. The 64-bit version is the one that is launched by default.

Microsoft rewrote `RegEdit.exe` *as a 32-bit application for Windows XP, Windows Server 2003, and Windows Vista, so on those platforms,* `regedit.exe` *is the preferred 32-bit Registry Editor.*

Regedt32.exe

Prior to Windows XP and Windows Server 2003, `Regedt32.exe` was the preferred 32-bit Registry Editor for Windows NT and 2000. But, of course, nothing is perfect, and Regedt32.exe had limitations — for example, it could not import or export Registry entries (`.reg`) files.

Now, under Windows XP, Windows Server 2003, and Windows Vista, Regedt32.exe is a simple wrapper program that runs `Regedit.exe`. On Windows NT and 2000, you should use `Regedt32.exe`; whereas on Windows XP, Windows Server 2003, and Windows Vista, you can use either `Regedt32.exe` or `RegEdit.exe`.

Launching and Using the Registry Editor

You won't find the Registry Editor on the Start menu because it's not something that Microsoft wants the average user to fool around with. The only way to launch it is via the Run dialog box. Here's how:

1. Click the Start button and select Run, or press the key combination Windows+R. The Run dialog box displays.

2. Type **regedit** or **regedt32**, and then click OK. The Registry Editor opens.

To launch the 32-bit version of `RegEdit.exe` *on x64-based versions of Windows, type* **%windir%\SYSWOW64\regedit** *in the Run dialog box.*

Figure 20-1 shows the Registry Editor with the HKEY_CURRENT_USER hive (discussed in the following section, "Registry Organization") expanded to show some of its keys, subkeys, and values.

You can think of keys and subkeys as being like the hierarchy of folders and subfolders in the Windows file system. As its name suggests, a value is a named container for a single piece of information, such as the width of a menu. The Registry Editor's right pane shows the values contained within the subkey selected in the left pane. With the exception of a default value that is present in every subkey, each value has its own unique name. The icon to the left of each value indicates its data type.

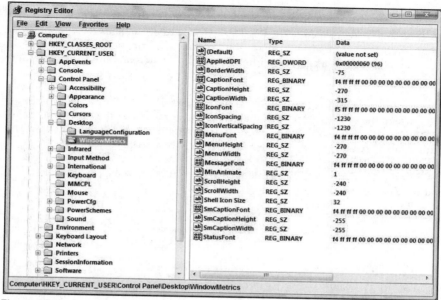

Figure 20-1

Registry Organization

The Registry tree is divided into five sections:

- ❑ HKEY_CLASSES_ROOT
- ❑ HKEY_CURRENT_USER
- ❑ HKEY_LOCAL_MACHINE
- ❑ HKEY_USERS
- ❑ HKEY_CURRENT_CONFIG

These major sections are called Root Keys, much like C:\ is the root directory of your hard disk. Because the Registry can differ greatly from one operating system version to another, you'll examine the most common keys, and for the sake of simplicity, they're listed in the order in which they appear in the Registry Editor (see Figure 20-2).

The following sections examine each of the Root Keys.

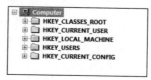

Figure 20-2

HKEY_CLASSES_ROOT

The HKEY_CLASSES_ROOT branch of the Registry tree is actually an alias for HKEY_LOCAL_MACHINE\Software\Classes, and contains information about file associations, documents, and OLE objects. It is a very large branch, containing several thousand entries at the first level alone.

The first group contains subkeys that look like file associations, and they are. Each of these subkeys contains a reference to the second group that makes up the remainder of the first-level subkeys. These are the class definitions associated with the relevant document. The class definitions contain information that includes the following:

❏ A descriptive name for the document type (as you might see in the Windows Explorer–type column). See Figure 20-3.

Name	Date modified	Type	Size
esent.dll	5/18/2006 6:52 PM	Application Extension	1.36 MB
esentprf.dll	5/18/2006 6:52 PM	Application Extension	32.5 KB
esentutl.exe	5/18/2006 6:52 PM	Application	90.0 KB
esrb.rs	5/18/2006 2:05 PM	RS File	35.5 KB
eudcedit.exe	5/18/2006 6:52 PM	Application	202 KB
eventcls.dll	5/18/2006 6:52 PM	Application Extension	20.5 KB
eventcreate.exe	5/18/2006 6:52 PM	Application	36.0 KB
EventViewer_EventDetails.xsl	4/21/2006 11:45 AM	XSL Stylesheet	13.8 KB
eventvwr.exe	5/18/2006 6:52 PM	Application	14.5 KB
eventvwr.msc	4/21/2006 11:45 AM	Microsoft Common Console Document	90.6 KB
evr.dll	5/18/2006 6:52 PM	Application Extension	403 KB
exe2bin.exe	4/21/2006 11:52 AM	Application	8.22 KB
expand.exe	5/18/2006 6:52 PM	Application	39.0 KB
ExplorerFrame.dll	5/18/2006 6:52 PM	Application Extension	37.5 KB
expsrv.dll	5/18/2006 6:52 PM	Application Extension	372 KB
extmgr.dll	5/18/2006 6:52 PM	Application Extension	131 KB
extrac32.exe	5/18/2006 6:52 PM	Application	50.0 KB
f3ahvoas.dll	5/18/2006 6:50 PM	Application Extension	7.00 KB
fastopen.exe	4/21/2006 11:52 AM	Application	882 bytes

Figure 20-3

❏ A pointer to the default icon.

❏ Information about how the application handles the documents as OLE objects.

❏ Information about how the documents are manipulated from the Windows shell (what context menu actions can be taken). See Figure 20-4.

HKEY_CLASSES_ROOT is updated every time an application is installed or removed.

HKEY_CURRENT_USER

The HKEY_CURRENT_USER branch is built during logon and is an alias for the current user's subkey in the HKEY_USERS branch; it contains user-specific information. Twelve major subkeys are in this branch, but depending on your system setup and what's installed, you might find some extra ones.

Figure 20-4

The following table describes the major subkeys.

Subkey	Description
AppEvents	Contains information about the sound files that are specified for individual system and application events, such as the Windows Logon sound and the MailBeep sound. It has two subkeys of its own: EventLabels, which contains the event names, and Schemes, which contains references to the actual sound files organized by the application.
Console	Contains all the user options for the MS-DOS Windows, including layout, screen color, and font settings.
Control Panel	Contains many other subkeys for all the Control Panel settings, such as color schemes, screen savers, keyboard repeat rate, mouse speed, and so on.
Environment	Contains the environment settings, specifically the temporary file locations. It contains the environment variables that you would see in DOS when you typed SET at the command line. Much of the information contained in this key is connected to the System applet in the Control Panel.
Identities	Is present only if Outlook Express 5.x (or later) is installed. It contains subkeys for an Outlook Express account, e-mail, and newsgroup settings, and the MSN Messenger, if installed.
Keyboard Layout	Contains three subkeys that hold information about the current keyboard layout, which you can set using the Control Panel's Keyboard properties. The Preload subkey contains a value for each installed keyboard layout. These values point to keys in HKEY_LOCAL_MACHINE\System\CurrentControlSet\Control\Keyboard Layouts, which contains references to the keyboard drivers.

Table continues on the next page

Subkey	Description
Network	Contains two subkeys that describe the mapped network drives, including persistent connections and recent connections. These subkeys contain values for the connection type and the provider name of each connection.
Printers	This subkey contains information about the current user's installed printers. There may also be a subkey for each remote printer, if installed.
RemoteAccess	Contains address and profile subkeys for the user's dial-up and networking connections. The subkey itself contains global connection details, such as the area code and the number of redial attempts, whereas the `Address` and `Profile` subkeys contain settings for specific connection.
SessionInformation	Contains the number of programs currently running on the computer.
Software	Easily the largest key in the Registry, and one of the two Registry keys that are intended to be used for applications (the other is `HKEY_LOCAL_MACHINE\Software`). It contains vendor-specific subkeys that describe the current user's software settings and a raft of application-specific information that was previously stored in the `Win.ini` or custom vendor `INI` files under Windows 3.x. Each vendor subkey contains a separate subkey for each software application supplied by that vendor. The subkeys and values below them are completely determined by the vendor, but typically contain user preferences, histories, and so on.
Volatile Environment	Contains environment variables related to the current logon session.

Of particular interest to VB and VBA programmers is `HKEY_CURRENT_USER\Software\VB and VBA Program Settings`, which has been set aside specifically for them. Naturally, you will find this key mirrored in `HKEY_USERS\current user subkey\Software\VB and VBA Program Settings`.

HKEY_LOCAL_MACHINE

The `HKEY_LOCAL_MACHINE` branch contains all the computer-specific settings, including hardware configuration and any computer-specific settings for installed software. In Windows XP, there are five major subkeys in this branch, which are described in the following table.

Subkey	Description
Hardware	Contains profiles for all the hardware that has been installed on the computer, such as device drivers, resources like IRQ assignments, and other details. All the information contained is built during startup and deleted during shutdown. That being the case, use this subkey only for viewing, not for writing.

Subkey	Description
SAM	Contains all the user and group account information for the Security Account Manager (SAM). The information in its subkeys is maintained in User Manager. It is also mapped to HKEY_LOCAL_MACHINE\Security, so changes to either are immediately reflected in the other. Do not attempt to change anything in here unless you want to reformat your hard disk afterward.
Security	Contains all the security information for the computer, such as password policies, user rights and permissions, and the groups to which each user belongs. The information in its subkeys is maintained in User Manager. Do not attempt to change anything in here either.
Software	Contains specific configuration information about the software installed on the computer. The entries under this subkey apply to all users, not just the current user, and contain information about what software is installed, and also define file associations and OLE information. Notice that this key has a subkey called Classes, which is an alias for HKEY_CLASSES_ROOT. In x64-based versions of Windows, there is a subkey called WOW6432Node, which stores 32-bit program settings on 64-bit Windows. Organization of the Registry on x64-based versions of Windows is discussed later, in the section "Registry Organization on x64-Based Windows."
System	Contains other subkeys that contain the persistent information about devices and parameters that the system needs to start up, including control sets that contain information like the computer name, subsystems that need to be started, hardware configuration for devices and drivers that the operating system loads, specific hardware profile information when multiple hardware profiles are configured, file system services, and so on.

HKEY_USERS

The HKEY_USERS branch contains the settings for all registered users and the default user. The number of subkeys depends on the number of users registered on the system. The following sections briefly explain the two major kinds of subkeys: .DEFAULT and security identifiers.

.DEFAULT

The settings in the .DEFAULT key constitute the default template that is applied when new users are added to the system, and includes user profiles, environment, screen, sound, and other user-related settings. If you change any of the settings in this subkey, those changes will take place for all new users because they inherit the same settings. Existing users will retain their existing settings, however.

Security Identifier Keys

You may also see several subkeys such as this:

```
S-1-5-21-1475383443-718524000-196120627-1006
```

Each represents a user who has logged on to the system. The number is the user's SID (security identifier). Every user on the network is assigned a unique SID by User Manager for domains. The information changes, therefore, depending on who is currently logged on.

The information for the key is gleaned from the NTUSER.DAT file, found in the user's profile directory. This subkey carries the same data as HKEY_CURRENT_USER\Software\Classes:

```
S-1-5-21-1475383443-718524000-196120627-1006_Classes
```

HKEY_CURRENT_CONFIG

The HKEY_CURRENT_CONFIG branch contains all of the details for the profiles that are current in the system, and is taken from HKEY_LOCAL_MACHINE at system startup.

Registry Organization on x64-Based Windows

With the introduction of Windows XP Professional x64 Edition, a separate view was added to the Registry for 32-bit applications to prevent data in 64-bit Registry keys from being overwritten by keys and values installed by 32-bit programs. Program settings for 64-bit programs are still stored in HKEY_LOCAL_MACHINE\Software, while settings for 32-bit programs run are now stored in a new key called HKEY_LOCAL_MACHINE\Software\WOW6432Node.

> *The Microsoft documentation frequently uses the term "WOW64" which stands for "Windows32-on-Windows 64-bit."*

Let's take a look at three important aspects of the Registry on x64-based Windows.

Registry Redirection

When a call is made to the Registry, it is forwarded to either the 32-bit Registry branch or the 64-bit Registry branch, depending on whether a 32-bit or 64-bit application is making the request. This process is known as *Registry redirection*. For example, if you run a 32-bit application that attempts to read a value from HKEY_LOCAL_MACHINE\Software\MyApplication, the value is actually read from HKEY_LOCAL_MACHINE\Software\WOW6432Node\MyApplication. A 64-bit application that reads this key does not require redirection.

> *For more information about Registry Redirection, please see the "Registry Redirection" article in the Platform SDK, which is available at*
> `http://msdn.microsoft.com/library/default.asp?url=/library/en-us/win64/win64/registry_redirector.asp.`

The following keys participate in redirection by default:

- ❑ HKEY_LOCAL_MACHINE\Software\Classes

- ❑ HKEY_LOCAL_MACHINE\Software\COM3

- ❑ HKEY_LOCAL_MACHINE\Software\EventSystem

- ❑ HKEY_LOCAL_MACHINE\Software\Ole

- ❑ HKEY_LOCAL_MACHINE\Software\Rpc

❑   `HKEY_USERS\*\Software\Classes`

❑   `HKEY_USERS\*_Classes`

(An asterisk (`*`) indicates that redirection occurs for all user security identifiers (SID) under `HKEY_USERS`.)

Registry Reflection

Naturally, certain keys and values should be available to both 32-bit and 64-bit applications. A good example of such a key is the registration for a COM application. Imagine that you have a 32-bit COM library that was registered on an x64-based computer. In order for a 64-bit application to use the library, it needs to be registered in both the 32-bit and 64-bit Registry branches. This is accomplished using Registry reflection.

As the name suggests, *Registry reflection* is a process used by Windows to maintain a mirror between certain 64-bit and 32-bit Registry settings. This mirroring keeps the settings synchronized in real time. On the x64-based Windows editions, there are Registry API functions that enable you to define how keys are reflected. The API functions that work with Registry reflection are listed in Appendix I.

For more information about Registry reflection, please see the white paper "Registry Reflection in Microsoft Windows," which is available at `http://microsoft.com/whdc/system/platform/ 64bit/RegReflect.mspx`*.*

Using the Built-In VBA Registry Functions

Many programmers use global variables to hold values that are used throughout the application. There are two problems associated with this approach. First, if an unhandled error occurs, all your global variables are reset. Second, you have to reassign their values every time the application is launched. An alternative is to store this type of value in the database, but if you're storing the connection string to the remote data store, it might be a little difficult to get at if your application doesn't know where to look.

Another alternative, one that is used in most professional applications, is to store such information in the Registry. You can store all sorts of information in the Registry, from simple values that your applications use from time to time, to connection strings, to user preferences, such as the position and color of forms, and so on.

VBA provides four native functions for manipulating the Registry within VB and VBA. The sole drawback to these functions (if you want to call it a drawback) is that they operate on only one part of the Registry — one that has been specifically allocated to VB and VBA.

The `HKEY_CURRENT_USER\Software\VB and VBA Program Settings` key has been set aside for our exclusive use. As mentioned earlier in the chapter, this key is mirrored in `HKEY_USERS\current user subkey\Software`. This key is created the first time you call the `SaveSetting` function, as shown in the next section.

As application-specific Registry entries are stored using the *application-name, section, key* construct, it makes sense that VBA should do the same. The remainder of this section describes the native VBA Registry functions and how to use them.

SaveSetting

`SaveSetting()` enables you to store a single value in the `HKEY_CURRENT_USER\Software\VB and VBA Program Settings` hive. Its syntax is as follows:

```
SaveSetting appname, section, key, setting
```

The arguments — all required — are described in the following table.

Argument	Description
appname	A string expression that contains the name of the application or project whose key is being set.
section	A string expression that contains the name of the section under which the key is to be set.
key	A string expression that contains the name of the key you are setting.
setting	An expression of any data type that defines the value to which the key will be set.

You can store as many values as you like, in as many keys and subkeys as you like. All VB/VBA applications will have access to the values you store, as long as they know the correct `appname`, `section`, and `key` names.

To standardize your Registry entries, you would normally use the `CurrentProject.Name` *property as the* `appname` *argument, although you are free to use any expression you like.*

The following code demonstrates two calls to the `SaveSetting` function:

```
SaveSetting CurrentDb.Properties("AppTitle"), "Settings", "myStringKey", "123"
SaveSetting CurrentDb.Properties("AppTitle"), "Settings", "myNumericKey", 123
```

Notice that a string value 123 is used in the first example, and a numeric example in the second. This is acceptable; however, you must remember that `GetSetting` always returns a string and `GetAllSettings` always returns a variant.

You can set the `Application Title` *property in the Current Database page in the Access Options dialog box.*

GetSetting

You can use the `GetSetting()` function to retrieve a string value from a single Registry key that you have previously saved. It returns the value specified by the default argument if the key is empty or doesn't exist. `GetSetting()` has the following syntax:

```
GetSetting(appname, section, key, [default])
```

The function arguments are explained in the following table.

Argument	Description
appname	A required string expression that contains the name of the application or project whose key is being sought.
section	A required string expression that contains the name of the section under which the key is found.
key	A required string expression that contains the name of the requested key.
default	An optional default expression to be returned if the key is empty. If you omit this argument, it is assumed to be a zero-length string (" ").

The following code demonstrates the GetSetting function:

```
?GetSetting(CurrentDb.Properties("AppTitle"), "Settings", ↵
"SomeSetting","myDefault")
```

GetAllSettings

The GetAllSettings() function retrieves all the key values that exist under the specified section, as a two-dimensional variant array. It has the following syntax:

```
GetAllSettings(appname, section)
```

The GetAllSettings() function returns an uninitialized (empty) variant if either appname or section does not exist. The arguments are described in the following table.

Argument	Description
appname	A required string expression that contains the name of the application or project whose key is being sought.
section	A required string expression that contains the name of the section under which the key is found.

The following two calls to GetAllSettings() are equivalent:

```
?GetSetting(CurrentDb.Properties("AppTitle"), "Settings", "myKey")
```

To use this function, you must declare a standard variable that will hold the return values. That's right, a standard variable — not an array. If there are values to return, the function redimensions the variable as an array. For example, the following code segment saves several values to the Registry using SaveSetting and retrieves them into a variant using GetAllSettings():

```
Dim varMySettings As Variant
```

```
Dim intCtr As Integer

SaveSetting "myapp", "mysection", "mykey1", "my first setting"
SaveSetting "myapp", "mysection", "mykey2", "my second setting"
SaveSetting "myapp", "mysection", "mykey3", "my third setting" varMySettings = ↵
GetAllSettings("myapp", "mysection")

For intCtr = LBound(varMySettings, 1) To UBound(varMySettings, 1)
    Debug.Print varMySettings(intCtr, 0) & "-" & varMySettings(intCtr, 1) Next ↵
intCtr

DeleteSetting "myapp", "mysection"
```

Notice that the first dimension contains the key name, and the second contains the actual value.

DeleteSetting

The last of the native VBA Registry functions is `DeleteSetting()`. As its name suggests, `DeleteSetting` deletes a section or key, depending on whether the optional key is supplied. It has the following syntax:

```
DeleteSetting appname, section, [key]
```

The `DeleteSetting()` arguments are described in the following table.

Argument	Description
appname	A required string expression that contains the name of the application or project whose key is being sought.
section	A required string expression that contains the name of the section where the key is being deleted. If only appname and section are provided, the specified section is deleted, along with its keys.
key	An optional string expression that contains the name of the key to be deleted.

The following code demonstrates using the `DeleteSetting` function to delete the specified key:

```
DeleteSetting CurrentDb.Properties("AppTitle"), "Settings",
    "myKey"
```

Similarly, the following `DeleteSetting` call deletes the entire specified section and all its keys:

```
DeleteSetting CurrentDb.Properties("AppTitle"), "Settings"
```

Typical Uses for the Built-In VBA Registry Functions

Now that you have a fundamental understanding of the Registry, you might still be wondering how you would use it and what values you would want to store there. In short, why bother?

It all comes down to functionality. As programmers, we are already disciplined enough to know not to use a particular technology, function, or facility unless it is necessary. For example, you wouldn't build a complex procedure where a built-in one exists. But by the same token, you should employ things that enable you to provide the functionality the application requirements demand.

Implementing a Daily Reminders Screen

A typical example might be the humble Daily Reminders screen implemented in many applications. This screen usually pops up when the application starts up, to remind users of overdue accounts, tasks they need to perform that day, or any number of things of which they need to be made aware.

Having such a facility can be of great benefit to both the organization and the user, but some users prefer to display this screen when they want to. Having the screen pop up every time they start the application can be a real nuisance, particularly if it takes some time to process and sort the information that's displayed. The resolution here is to offer the user the capability to have the screen pop up or not.

To do this, you need to store a Boolean value somewhere. You can store it in a table, but if your database is built on a client/server model, with the tables stored on a server share, the setting would affect all users. Storing the value in a local table would mean all users of that particular computer would similarly share the same setting. The answer is to store the value in the Registry so each user can set his own preferences.

To implement that behavior, start by creating an `Overdue Accounts` form containing a list box, command button, and check box, as shown in Figure 20-5. (This example simply adds the company names and amounts to the list box's `RowSource` property, but a real form would probably populate it using a recordset.)

Figure 20-5

Then, add the following code to the check box's `Click()` event.

```
Private Sub chkShowAtStartup_Click()
    Dim strApp As String

    'Assuming you have set the Application Title property in the Access Options
dialog
    strApp = CurrentDb.Properties("AppTitle")

    'Save the new checkbox setting.
    SaveSetting strApp, "Settings", "Show at Startup", _
        Me.chkShowAtStartup
End Sub
```

In this code, it doesn't matter if the user doesn't click the check box because the form displays whether the setting exists or not. But if he does click it, the appropriate setting will be immediately saved to the Registry.

Of course, you need to set the initial value of the check box when the form displays, so add the following code to the form's `Load` event.

```
Private Sub Form_Load()
    Dim strApp As String

    'Assuming you have set the Application Title property in the Access Options
dialog
    strApp = CurrentDb.Properties("AppTitle")

    'Set the checkbox value.
    'If the setting doesn't exist, assume a default True.
    Me.chkShowAtStartup = GetSetting(strApp, "Settings", "Show at Startup", True)
End Sub
```

Then all you have to do is modify your startup code to decide whether to show this form:

```
Dim strApp As String
Dim booShowForm As Boolean

'Assuming you have set the Application Title property in the Access Options dialog
strApp = CurrentDb.Properties("AppTitle")

booShowForm = GetSetting(strApp, "Settings", "Show at Startup", True)

'If the setting doesn't exist, it is probably the
'first time the user has launched the application,
'so show the form.
If booShowForm = True Then
    DoCmd.OpenForm "frmOverDueAccts"
End If
```

Storing and Retrieving Connection Strings

Where several temporary databases, spreadsheets, and files are frequently connected, you can store their connection strings in the Registry to save time and memory. For example, the following function retrieves the connection string for one of several external data sources:

```
Public Function GetConnString(strSourceName As String) As String
    Dim strApp As String
    Dim strCon As String

    strApp = CurrentDb.Properties("AppTitle")

    strCon = GetSetting(strApp, "Settings", strSourceName, "")
    GetConnString = strCon
End Function
```

Storing User Preferences

The VBA Registry functions are often used to store user preferences, such as the following:

❑   Default values, such as the default date to enter into a text box

❑   Sort orders, such as whether to display the delinquent customers list by value or by due date

❑   Menus and toolbars that the user wants displayed

❑   Form colors

❑   Sound effects on/off

❑   Report opened last

❑   Language settings

Storing a Last Used List

Like the Documents list on the Windows Start menu (stored in
`HKEY_CURRENT_USER\Software\Microsoft\Windows\CurrentVersion\Explorer\RecentDocs`),
you can store your own lists in the Registry. For example, a list of the last 10 forms or reports that a user visited, the last six files opened, or the last one that the user changed.

Using the Win32 Registry APIs

This section describes the Win32 Registry API functions you can use to access and manipulate a wider range of Registry keys than you can with the built-in VBA functions. Before attempting this section, however, we strongly advise that you read Chapter 14.

The Win32 API provides all the functions you need to access the Registry. Of course, the scope of some functions is restricted for purely commonsense reasons; after all, there is little point in making changes to the temporary areas.

But, this begs the question: Where do you find information about all these constants and functions? Welcome to the wonderful world of programming! Unfortunately, Microsoft has not published a definitive text on the Registry, or indeed the Win32 API, so you need to rely on the various books, Web pages, and third-party software utilities that deal with these topics.

This section provides a real-world example of how to use the Registry API functions. For example, if you wanted to add your company name under the HKEY_CURRENT_USER\Software key instead of storing Registry settings under Software\VB and VBA Program Settings, you could use the Registry APIs to do so. Appendix I makes available a complete list of all Registry functions, along with declarations of the Registry-related constants and user-defined types.

To make sense of all the information presented in the preceding sections, you need to see how the Registry APIs are used. To do that, you'll create a module that performs the five most widely used functions: create a key, set a key value, read that value, delete the value, and, of course, delete the key.

Getting Started

Create a new standard module and add the following declarations to it (you can find a complete list of declarations, constants, and types related to the Registry in Appendix I):

```
'Key declarations
Public Const HKEY_CLASSES_ROOT As Long = &H80000000
Public Const HKEY_CURRENT_CONFIG As Long = &H80000005
Public Const HKEY_CURRENT_USER As Long = &H80000001
Public Const HKEY_DYN_DATA As Long = &H80000006
Public Const HKEY_LOCAL_MACHINE As Long = &H80000002
Public Const HKEY_PERF_ROOT As Long = HKEY_LOCAL_MACHINE
Public Const HKEY_PERFORMANCE_DATA As Long = &H80000004
Public Const HKEY_USERS As Long = &H80000003

'Root key Enum
Public Enum w32Key
    w32CLASSES_ROOT = HKEY_CLASSES_ROOT
    w32CURRENT_CONFIG = HKEY_CURRENT_CONFIG
    w32CURRENT_USER = HKEY_CURRENT_USER
    w32DYN_DATA = HKEY_DYN_DATA
    w32LOCAL_MACHINE = HKEY_LOCAL_MACHINE
    w32PERF_ROOT = HKEY_PERF_ROOT
    w32PERF_DATA = HKEY_PERFORMANCE_DATA
    w32USERS = HKEY_USERS
End Enum

'Parameter declarations
Public Const REG_NOTIFY_CHANGE_ATTRIBUTES As Long = &H2
Public Const REG_NOTIFY_CHANGE_LAST_SET As Long = &H4
Public Const REG_NOTIFY_CHANGE_NAME As Long = &H1
Public Const REG_NOTIFY_CHANGE_SECURITY As Long = &H8
Public Const REG_CREATED_NEW_KEY As Long = &H1
Public Const REG_OPENED_EXISTING_KEY As Long = &H2
Public Const REG_OPTION_BACKUP_RESTORE As Long = 4
Public Const REG_OPTION_VOLATILE As Long = 1
Public Const REG_OPTION_NON_VOLATILE As Long = 0
```

```
    Public Const STANDARD_RIGHTS_ALL As Long = &H1F0000
    Public Const SYNCHRONIZE As Long = &H100000
    Public Const READ_CONTROL As Long = &H20000
    Public Const STANDARD_RIGHTS_READ As Long = (READ_CONTROL)
    Public Const STANDARD_RIGHTS_WRITE As Long = (READ_CONTROL)
    Public Const KEY_CREATE_LINK As Long = &H20
    Public Const KEY_CREATE_SUB_KEY As Long = &H4
    Public Const KEY_ENUMERATE_SUB_KEYS As Long = &H8
    Public Const KEY_NOTIFY As Long = &H10
    Public Const KEY_QUERY_VALUE As Long = &H1
    Public Const KEY_SET_VALUE As Long = &H2

    'Key value types
    Public Const REG_BINARY As Long = 3
    Public Const REG_DWORD As Long = 4
    Public Const REG_DWORD_BIG_ENDIAN As Long = 5
    Public Const REG_DWORD_LITTLE_ENDIAN As Long = 4
    Public Const REG_EXPAND_SZ As Long = 2
    Public Const REG_LINK As Long = 6
    Public Const REG_MULTI_SZ As Long = 7
    Public Const REG_NONE As Long = 0
    Public Const REG_RESOURCE_LIST As Long = 8
    Public Const REG_SZ As Long = 1

    'Key value type Enum
    Public Enum w32ValueType
        w32BINARY = REG_BINARY
        w32DWORD = REG_DWORD
        w32DWORD_BIG = REG_DWORD_BIG_ENDIAN
        w32DWORD_LITTLE = REG_DWORD_LITTLE_ENDIAN
        w32EXPANDSz = REG_EXPAND_SZ
        w32LINK = REG_LINK
        w32MULTISz = REG_MULTI_SZ
        w32NONE = REG_NONE
        w32RESLIST = REG_RESOURCE_LIST
        w32REGSz = REG_SZ
    End Enum

    Public Const KEY_READ As Long = (( _
        STANDARD_RIGHTS_READ _
        Or KEY_QUERY_VALUE _
        Or KEY_ENUMERATE_SUB_KEYS _
        Or KEY_NOTIFY) _
        And (Not SYNCHRONIZE))

    Public Const KEY_WRITE As Long = (( _
        STANDARD_RIGHTS_WRITE _
        Or KEY_SET_VALUE _
        Or KEY_CREATE_SUB_KEY) _
        And (Not SYNCHRONIZE))

    Public Const KEY_EXECUTE As Long = (KEY_READ)

    Public Const KEY_ALL_ACCESS As Long = (( _
```

```
        STANDARD_RIGHTS_ALL _
        Or KEY_QUERY_VALUE _
        Or KEY_SET_VALUE _
        Or KEY_CREATE_SUB_KEY _
        Or KEY_ENUMERATE_SUB_KEYS _
        Or KEY_NOTIFY _
        Or KEY_CREATE_LINK) _
        And (Not SYNCHRONIZE))
```

Note the addition of two enums: w32Key *and* w32ValueType. *These enums are useful when actually writing the procedures, so you don't have to remember all the constant declarations. Notice also that all the declarations are now* Public *so that they can be accessed from anywhere in the application. If you were to create a class to wrap all your Registry functions, the declarations would still need to be in a standard module, and they would still need to be declared* Public. *You can prevent direct use of the declarations by moving them to the class module and marking them as* Private, *while leaving the enums* Public.

Then add the following constant, which is used to test success or failure of each API function. In your applications, you can test for any of the other return codes for specific errors and conditions, but this example tests only for success or failure.

```
'API return codes
Public Const ERROR_SUCCESS As Long = 0&
```

Next, add the following API declarations. Note that this is not the complete list; it includes only those that are needed by the procedures that will follow.

```
Private Declare Function RegCloseKey Lib "advapi32.dll" _
    (ByVal hKey As Long) As Long

Private Declare Function RegCreateKeyEx Lib "advapi32.dll" _
    Alias "RegCreateKeyExA" ( _
    ByVal hKey As Long, _
    ByVal lpSubKey As String, _
    ByVal Reserved As Long, _
    ByVal lpClass As String, _
    ByVal dwOptions As Long, _
    ByVal samDesired As Long, _
    ByVal lpSecurityAttributes As Long, _
    phkResult As Long, _
    lpdwDisposition As Long) As Long

Private Declare Function RegDeleteKey Lib "advapi32.dll" _
    Alias "RegDeleteKeyA" ( _
    ByVal hKey As Long, _
    ByVal lpSubKey As String) As Long

Private Declare Function RegDeleteValue Lib "advapi32.dll" _
    Alias "RegDeleteValueA" ( _
    ByVal hKey As Long, _
    ByVal lpValueName As String) As Long
```

```
Private Declare Function RegOpenKeyEx Lib "advapi32.dll" _
    Alias "RegOpenKeyExA" ( _
    ByVal hKey As Long, _
    ByVal lpSubKey As String, _
    ByVal ulOptions As Long, _
    ByVal samDesired As Long, _
    phkResult As Long) As Long

Private Declare Function RegQueryValueEx Lib "advapi32.dll" _
    Alias "RegQueryValueExA" ( _
    ByVal hKey As Long, _
    ByVal lpValueName As String, _
    ByVal lpReserved As Long, _
    lpType As Long, _
    lpData As Any, _
    lpcbData As Long) As Long

Private Declare Function RegSetValueEx Lib "advapi32.dll" _
    Alias "RegSetValueExA" ( _
    ByVal hKey As Long, _
    ByVal lpValueName As String, _
    ByVal Reserved As Long, _
    ByVal dwType As Long, _
    lpData As Any, _
    ByVal cbData As Long) As Long
```

Now add the following variable declaration, which is used to store the result of the API function calls. You could declare this variable in each procedure that uses it, but for the purposes of a convenient example, it's declared at module level.

```
'Return value for most procedures
Private lngReturn As Long
```

Add the following procedures to the same module as the preceding declarations. Some of them may look a bit complicated, but if you strip out the error handling, you see they are actually quite simple.

The Function to Create a Key

The first procedure, CreateKey(), wraps the RegCreateKeyEx function to create a new subkey. After the call, it checks that the call completed successfully, and if not, raises a custom error. If the call is successful, it returns the name of the newly created subkey.

```
Public Function CreateKey(lngRootKey As w32Key, _
        strSubKey As String, _
        lngValueType As w32ValueType) _
        As String

    Dim hKey As Long
    Dim hSubKey As Long
    Dim strClass As String
    Dim lngSize As Long
    Dim lngDisposition As Long
```

```
        On Error GoTo CreateKey_Err

        'Create the key
        lngReturn = RegCreateKeyEx(lngRootKey, _
                            strSubKey, _
                            0&, _
                            vbNullString, _
                            0&, _
                            KEY_WRITE, _
                            0&, _
                            hSubKey, _
                            lngDisposition)

        'Check that the call succeeded
        If lngReturn <> ERROR_SUCCESS Then
            Err.Raise vbObjectError + 1, , "Could not create key."
        End If

        'If successful, return the name of the new subkey
        CreateKey = strSubKey

CreateKey_Exit:
    On Error Resume Next
    'Close the key
    lngReturn = RegCloseKey(hKey)
    Exit Function

CreateKey_Err:
    CreateKey = ""
    DoCmd.Beep
    MsgBox "Error " & Err.Number & vbCrLf & _
        Err.Description, vbOKOnly + vbExclamation, _
        "Could not save the key value"

    Resume CreateKey_Exit
End Function
```

The Function to Set a Key Value

The next procedure, `SetKeyValue()`, wraps both `RegOpenKeyEx` and `RegSetValueEx` functions to open the subkey and set its value, respectively. After each function call, it checks that the call completed successfully, and if not, raises a custom error and returns a Boolean `False`. If the call completes successfully, it returns a Boolean `True`.

```
Public Function SetKeyValue(lngRootKey As w32Key, _
        strSubKey As String, _
        strValueName As String, _
        strNewValue As String) _
        As Boolean

    Dim hKey As Long
```

```
    Dim lngSize As Long

    On Error GoTo SetKeyValue_Err

    'Open the key and get its handle
    lngReturn = RegOpenKeyEx(lngRootKey, strSubKey, _
        0&, KEY_WRITE, hKey)

    'Check that the call succeeded
    If lngReturn <> ERROR_SUCCESS Then
        Err.Raise vbObjectError + 2, , "Could not open key."
    End If

    'Initialize the size variable
    lngSize = Len(strNewValue)

    'Set the key value
    lngReturn = RegSetValueEx(hKey, _
                            strValueName, _
                            0&, _
                            REG_SZ, _
                            ByVal strNewValue, _
                            lngSize)

    'Check that the call succeeded
    If lngReturn <> ERROR_SUCCESS Then
        Err.Raise vbObjectError + 3, , "Could not save value."
    End If

SetKeyValue_Exit:
    On Error Resume Next

    'Return success or failure
    SetKeyValue = (lngReturn = ERROR_SUCCESS)

    'Close the key
    lngReturn = RegCloseKey(hKey)
    Exit Function

SetKeyValue_Err:
    DoCmd.Beep
    MsgBox "Error " & Err.Number & vbCrLf & _
        Err.Description, vbOKOnly + vbExclamation, _
        "Could not save the key value"

    Resume SetKeyValue_Exit
End Function
```

The Function to Get a Key Value

The GetKeyValue() procedure wraps both RegOpenKeyEx and RegQueryValueEx functions, which open the subkey and retrieve its value, respectively. Again, after each function call, it checks if the call completed successfully, and if not, raises a custom error and returns a Null value. If the call does complete successfully, it returns the current value.

```vba
Public Function GetKeyValue(lngRootKey As w32Key, _
        strSubKey As String, _
        strValueName As String) _
        As Variant

    Dim hKey As Long
    Dim strBuffer As String
    Dim lngSize As Long

    On Error GoTo GetKeyValue_Err

    'Open the key and get its handle
    lngReturn = RegOpenKeyEx(lngRootKey, strSubKey, _
        0&, KEY_READ, hKey)

    'Check that the call succeeded
    If lngReturn <> ERROR_SUCCESS Then
        Err.Raise vbObjectError + 2, , "Could not open key."
    End If

    'Initialize the variables
    strBuffer = Space(255)
    lngSize = Len(strBuffer)

    'Read the key value
    lngReturn = RegQueryValueEx(hKey, _
                                strValueName, _
                                0&, _
                                REG_SZ, _
                                ByVal strBuffer, _
                                lngSize)

    'Check that the call succeeded
    If lngReturn <> ERROR_SUCCESS Then
        Err.Raise vbObjectError + 4, , "Could not read value."
    End If

    'Return the key value
    GetKeyValue = Left(strBuffer, lngSize -1)

GetKeyValue_Exit:
    On Error Resume Next
    'Close the key
    lngReturn = RegCloseKey(hKey)
    Exit Function

GetKeyValue_Err:
    GetKeyValue = Null
    DoCmd.Beep
```

```
        MsgBox "Error " & Err.Number & vbCrLf & _
            Err.Description, vbOKOnly + vbExclamation, _
            "Could not retrieve the key"

        Resume GetKeyValue_Exit
End Function
```

The Function to Delete a Key Value

The DeleteValue() function wraps both RegOpenKeyEx and RegDeleteValue functions to open the subkey and set its value, respectively. If both calls complete successfully, a Boolean True is returned, otherwise a Boolean False is returned.

```
    Public Function DeleteValue(lngRootKey As w32Key, _
            strSubKey As String, strValueName As String) _
            As Boolean

        Dim hKey As Long

        On Error GoTo DeleteValue_Err

        'Open the key and get its handle
        lngReturn = RegOpenKeyEx(lngRootKey, strSubKey, _
            0&, KEY_ALL_ACCESS, hKey)

        'Check that the call succeeded
        If lngReturn <> ERROR_SUCCESS Then
            Err.Raise vbObjectError + 2, , "Could not open key."
        End If

        'Delete the key value
        lngReturn = RegDeleteValue(hKey, strValueName)

    DeleteValue_Exit:
        On Error Resume Next

        'Return success or failure
        DeleteValue = (lngReturn = ERROR_SUCCESS)

        'Close the key
        lngReturn = RegCloseKey(hKey)
        Exit Function

    DeleteValue_Err:
        DoCmd.Beep
        MsgBox "Error " & Err.Number & vbCrLf & _
            Err.Description, vbOKOnly + vbExclamation, _
            "Could not retrieve the key"

        Resume DeleteValue_Exit
    End Function
```

The Function to Delete a Key

The `DeleteKey()` function is the last of this example's action procedures. It wraps both `RegOpenKeyEx` and `RegDeleteKey` functions to open the subkey and delete it. If both calls complete successfully, a Boolean `True` is returned; otherwise a Boolean `False` is returned.

```
Public Function DeleteKey(lngRootKey As w32Key, strSubKey As String, _
        strKillKey As String) As Boolean

    Dim hKey As Long

    On Error GoTo DeleteKey_Err

    'Open the key and get its handle
    lngReturn = RegOpenKeyEx(lngRootKey, strSubKey, _
        0&, KEY_ALL_ACCESS, hKey)

    'Check that the call succeeded
    If lngReturn <> ERROR_SUCCESS Then
        Err.Raise vbObjectError + 2, , "Could not open key."
    End If

    'Delete the subkey
    lngReturn = RegDeleteKey(hKey, strKillKey)

DeleteKey_Exit:
    On Error Resume Next

    'Return success or failure
    DeleteKey = (lngReturn = ERROR_SUCCESS)

    'Close the key
    lngReturn = RegCloseKey(hKey)
    Exit Function

DeleteKey_Err:
    DoCmd.Beep
    MsgBox "Error " & Err.Number & vbCrLf & _
        Err.Description, vbOKOnly + vbExclamation, _
        "Could not retrieve the key"

    Resume DeleteKey_Exit
End Function
```

Testing the Function Wrappers

Finally, the following procedure is the one you can use to test the preceding API function wrappers. Copy this code to a standard module and step through it using the F8 key.

```
Public Sub TestReg()
    Dim strBaseKey As String
    Dim strSubKey As String
    Dim strMsg As String
```

```
Dim varReturn As Variant

'For convenience only, initialize variables with
'the subkey names.
strBaseKey = "Software\VB and VBA Program Settings\myapp\Settings"
strSubKey = "Software\VB and VBA Program Settings\myapp\Settings\myNewKey"

'=== Create a new subkey.
varReturn = CreateKey(w32CURRENT_USER, strSubKey, w32REGSz)

'Check for success or failure.
'If success, continue with the remaining procedures.
If Not IsNull(varReturn) Then
    strMsg = "Created a new key '" & varReturn & "'."
    MsgBox strMsg, vbOKOnly + vbInformation, "Test Registry functions"

    '=== Set a new subkey value.
    varReturn = SetKeyValue(w32CURRENT_USER, strSubKey, _
        "myValue", "11123")

    'Check success or failure.
    If varReturn = True Then
        strMsg = "Set a new key value to '11123'."
    Else
        strMsg = "Failed to set new key value."
    End If

    MsgBox strMsg, vbOKOnly + vbInformation, "Test Registry functions"

    '=== Retrieve the value we just set.
    varReturn = GetKeyValue(w32CURRENT_USER, strSubKey, _
        "myValue")

    'Check success or failure.
    If Len(varReturn) > 0 Then
        strMsg = "The current value of key '" & strSubKey & _
            "' is '" & varReturn & "'"
    Else
        strMsg = "Failed to read key value."
    End If

    MsgBox strMsg, vbOKOnly + vbInformation, "Test Registry functions"

    '=== Now delete the key value
    varReturn = DeleteValue(w32CURRENT_USER, strSubKey, "myValue")

    'Check success or failure.
    If varReturn = True Then
        strMsg = "Deleted the key value."
    Else
        strMsg = "Failed to delete the key value."
    End If
```

```
        MsgBox strMsg, vbOKOnly + vbInformation, "Test Registry functions"

        '=== Lastly, delete the subkey itself
        varReturn = DeleteKey(w32CURRENT_USER, strBaseKey, "myNewKey")

        'Check success or failure.
        If varReturn = True Then
            strMsg = "Deleted the key."
        Else
            strMsg = "Failed to delete the key."
        End If

        MsgBox strMsg, vbOKOnly + vbInformation, "Test Registry functions"
    Else
        strMsg = "Failed to create the new key."
        MsgBox strMsg, vbOKOnly + vbInformation, "Test Registry functions"
    End If
End Sub
```

Summary

In this chapter, you considered the evolution of the Win32 Registry, what it does, how it works, and how it is used, and looked at the tools you can use to examine and modify the Registry.

You explored the Win32 Registry structure and perused the built-in VBA functions you can use to manipulate that portion of the Registry specifically set aside for VBA programmers. Finally, you built your own modest Registry module.

Having reached the end of this chapter, you've now acquired enough information and experience to develop some fairly sophisticated database applications. All you have left to do then is to package it all up, so you can distribute it to your many users. Chapter 21 focuses on using the Access Developer Extensions to help you on your way.

21

Using the ADE Tools

The Access Developer Extensions (ADE) is a combination of tools designed to aid in the development of Access applications. If you've used the ADE tools in the past, you'll be glad to hear that there are some new features for Access 2007. This chapter examines the ADE tools, shows you how to use them, and discusses how using the ADE can improve Access applications. The ADE package contains several tools for application development and deployment, including the following:

❑ **The Access Redistributable Runtime:** The Access Runtime allows database applications to run on Windows machines, even when Access itself is not installed. The redistributable license allows developers to freely distribute the Access Runtime, in unlimited quantity, without infringing on any Microsoft licensing requirements. Although the Runtime does not allow customers to use the Access program itself, distributing the Access Runtime with your database application will reduce the cost impact for customers who do not already have Access 2007 installed.

❑ **The Package Solution Wizard:** The Package Solution Wizard is an Access add-in that allows developers to quickly and easily build a setup package for production database applications. The wizard bundles the database, any user specified files, and a few other optional files (such as the Access Runtime) into a single package to be used for deployment on the client machines. The resulting package file is a standard Microsoft Windows Installer (MSI) file for installing, repairing, or uninstalling a custom Access application using the conventional Windows installation tools.

❑ **The Access Database Template Creator:** New to the ADE for Office 2007, the Access Database Template creator allows developers to convert existing database applications into the Access 2007 template file format (ACCDT). This provides Access developers with the capability to easily transfer database solutions in a safe text file format, which can be used over and over to generate new database applications. If placed in the proper location on the user's machine, these templates will even show up in the new Getting Started interface, along with the other templates installed with Access 2007.

❑ **Source Code Control program support:** Finally, the ADE includes some tools for working the Source Code Control (SCC) programs to allow developers to version database objects. The SCC support is a set of interfaces to work with standardized source code control programs to retain change information about database objects within an Access application. While the ADE does not include a specific source code control program, there are many programs available (such as Microsoft Visual Source Safe 2005) that will work very well with the ADE SCC interfaces.

Using the ADE tools to enhance Access application development can be extremely effective in reducing development cost and time. They can be an integral part of application development, especially when the application is designed to be deployed to outside customers. These tools are extremely lightweight and can be used separately or in unison, without a huge learning curve.

One last item: The ADE tools are not included with Microsoft Access 2007 or even Microsoft Office System 2007 release disk. In the Microsoft Office 2007 release, the ADE tools are available as a separate download from `http://office.microsoft.com`. Also, as with Microsoft Office 2003, the ADE is included with the Visual Studio Tools for Office (VSTO) product (on a separate installation CD included in the product box). For versions prior to Access 2003, the ADE tools were included in the Developer Edition of Microsoft Office.

The Redistributable Access Runtime

Any computer with a full version of Microsoft Access installed can run any Access-based application, assuming the database version is compatible with the version of Access installed. Simply copy the database application and other necessary files to that computer, invoke the application, and the user is off and running. However, if a computer does not have Access installed, using the database application on that specific machine presents a dilemma. Often, it may not make sense to purchase a full version of Access just to run a few specific database applications on a given machine if the Access program itself won't be used for any other purpose. In cases where the user does not want to purchase a full version of Access for each machine where the application will run, redistributing the Access Runtime can greatly reduce the overall cost of the running those applications.

Consider the following question: Why do you want to deploy an Access application on another computer? An all-too-common scenario is someone in a workgroup creates a database to fill a need or solve a problem that the group frequently encounters. Other members of the group hear about the application and want to use it as well. Pretty soon, 20 or so people are using the application and maybe even requesting additional features or reporting problems with the database. At this point in the application's lifecycle, the developer begins to consider what the minimum requirements are to run the application on other computers. What happens when users do not have Access installed? The lowest common denominator necessary to run an Access-based application on a computer is the Access Runtime. Fortunately, the Redistributable Runtime License allows the developer to distribute the Access Runtime to an unlimited number of machines, at no additional cost! Best of all, the Redistributable Runtime License is included with the ADE, which is free of cost in Access 2007.

There are several ways to transfer the Access Runtime to a client machine:

❑　The user can simply copy the Runtime install package and install it manually.

❑　The developer can write his own custom setup script and include the Access runtime along with the application.

❑　You can use the Package Wizard to create the setup script for the particular application and include the Runtime along with the package.

All of these are feasible, but the wizard is the preferred method.

Creating Runtime Databases

When the Access Runtime is installed on a machine without a full version of Access installed, it is used by default whenever the application is invoked. However, if Access is already installed on the machine, Access — not the Runtime — is used to open the application. This means that users may have the capability to make changes to the application that they would not be able to do if the Runtime had been used. And, of course, the developer of the application may not always know which machines have Access already installed when the application is installed.

To help solve both of these problems, the developer can force the Runtime to be used when the application in invoked. There are a couple of ways to do so. The first, and new in Access 2007, is the ACCDR file format. Any ACCDR file automatically uses the Access Runtime when it is invoked. The second is to invoke the database with the Runtime command-line switch. That is typically done through the use of a Windows shortcut, which is normally created when the application is installed. However, triggering the Runtime can be done by invoking the application from the command line and tacking the /runtime switch to the end of the database path. Using any of these methods to invoke an application with the Runtime should be extremely simple to implement for any Access developer.

The ACCDR File Format

The ACCDR file format is nothing more than a renamed ACCDB file format. If a .accdb database file extension is changed to .accdr, any time the database is opened, the Access Runtime will open the database solution. Although switching the extension for an MDB to ACCDR may work in most cases, it is not guaranteed to work in all cases. When using the ACCDR extension for MDB file format database, it is always best to test the solution to make sure that it is working correctly. Renaming a database application extension to ACCDR is a quick way to use the Access Runtime for your database solution.

The /Runtime Command-Line Switch

Using a command-line switch to invoke a database solution is extremely easy to implement. Typically, this method is accomplished by creating a Windows shortcut pointing to the database that has /runtime enabled as the last parameter of the command. For example, a developer could create a shortcut that has the Target property set to the following:

```
"%ProgramFiles%\Microsoft Office\Office12\MSAccess.exe" C:\Sample.accdb /runtime
```

Notice the %ProgramFiles% environment variable in the path to the msaccess.exe executable program file. The developer may not always know where Access has been installed on the machine, but a good bet is in the Microsoft Office directory in the machine's Program Files directory, which is where Office programs are installed by default. However, during the installation of Access, the user has the capability to choose almost any directory to install Access to, so the ProgramFiles environment variable may not always work. Unfortunately there is no environment variable that guarantees the path of MSAccess.exe. When that's the case, the user may need to manually update the shortcut's path to MSAccess.exe to make it work correctly.

What's the Difference Between Access and the Runtime?

You might be wondering why the Access Runtime should be used. Recall that earlier in this chapter we discussed that one of the major benefits of redistributing the Access Runtime is reducing the overall cost of the application. The Runtime can be deployed on any supported machine without having to purchase another Access license for the machine and at no additional cost to the developer. This can be a huge cost saver when the application is deployed on many machines that do not have Access. But cost savings is not the only benefit to using the Access Runtime.

Using the Access Runtime can also deter the user from making unwanted changes to an Access application. When a database is invoked from the Runtime, there are two other major differences in how the Access client window behaves. First, the Navigation pane will not be available to the user (for applications using a Runtime prior to 2007, this applies to the database container window as well), so the user can't use it to navigate through the application. When using the Runtime, do not forget the user needs to be able to navigate through the entire application using other means, such as clicking buttons included in the forms of the applications. The second major difference is that the Ribbon and most of the options available on the File menu will not be available to the user either. Fortunately, the developer has the capability to create custom ribbon menus for the application, using the Access Ribbon Extensibility features. Both of these differences can be highly effective in locking the application's control flow and deterring users from making unwanted changes to the database.

However, if the user has Access installed on his machine, neither of these methods will stop him from simply opening the database file in the Access client directly. But this is yet one more way to help obscure the database application to the user. If the shortcut option is used, the developer could always rename the database file to some extension other than an extension that is registered as an Access default extension, such as .dat. Still, an experienced user may figure out that the application is powered by Access and open the file manually in his copy of Access and make any changes without intervention from the Runtime. Starting in Runtime mode is only a way of invoking an Access application; it does not directly affect the database file itself. For more information about methods for securing an Access application, see Chapter 18.

The Package Solution Wizard

The Package Solution Wizard is an extremely handy tool for building Access application installation programs. It creates a standard Microsoft Windows Installation package (MSI) file that can perform a number of useful setup tasks, such as deploying Access Runtime and developer-specified application files, adding Windows System Registry keys, and even including digital certificates for the client machine. Employing this wizard greatly reduces the cost and headache of building a streamlined setup process for almost any Access application. And best of all, because the output of the wizard is an MSI file, other commonly used setup editors can make modifications to the package.

The Package Solution Wizard is a standalone application that is invoked from the Windows Start menu. It is a seven-step process that walks you through a series of tasks to build the MSI setup file. Once a setup routine has been created, it can be saved for future use. Keep in mind, however, that if the files for the application change, the setup script may need to be modified as well.

Step 1: Starting the Package Wizard

To start the Package Wizard for Access 2007, click the Office button in an instance of Access and select Developer. Click the Package Solution button and choose the Package Solution Wizard option.

Target System Requirements

Be sure to note the system requirement remarks in the second paragraph on the welcome page warning that the target system for the MSI file to be installed needs to be Windows XP SP2 or higher. The true requirement here is that the target system must have the Microsoft Windows Installer 2.0 or later. The versions of Microsoft Windows Installer included with Windows XP, Windows 2003 Server, and Windows Vista are sufficient.

Starting New or Choosing an Existing Template

The first step in the Package Solution Wizard is to identify whether to create a new template or use an existing template. If an existing template is selected, it can be run without modification. If there is an existing template available, you can apply the template by selecting Load Wizard Settings From Saved Template File. Choosing an existing template sets all of the options that are defined by that particular template. Still, most people prefer to make a custom template for their particular database solution, although it is not required because any template can be applied to any database solution.

Templates created by the wizard are nothing more than XML files containing all of the settings used for the application, with the file extension .adepsws. Once a template is added to the store, you can select it and click Run Template to immediately apply the template. Because the template file contains all of the settings as well as the path to the original database the compiled database file will be created from, applying a template is about a three-click process.

For a new application or an application that does not already have a template, you may want to create a new template for the specified database. The Save Wizard Setting button on the bottom left of the wizard can be clicked at any time to save a template for the current settings of the wizard. This button is on every page of the wizard, so a new template can be created at any time when using the wizard.

Choosing a Destination Location for the MSI File

The last thing to do on the wizard's first page is choose the location where the wizard will output all of the files it creates. A default folder is preselected under your documents folder, and if not pre-existing, will be created. You have the option to select any folder by simply inputting the path in the desired folder or using the Browse dialog box to browse to the folder you want to use.

Click Next to continue.

Step 2: Database Solution Installation Options

The second page of the wizard enables you to specify the details about the installation options for your database solution, including the path to the database solution that will be packaged and the location where the solution will be installed on the target system. You also can specify whether the Redistributable Access Runtime package is to be included or required with this installation. The last preference on this page enables you to specify is the shortcut installation options for the solution.

Installation Options

The installation options enable you to create the settings for how the database solution will be deployed by the MSI file on the target system. The following table describes the options available in this section of the wizard:

Option	Description
File to package	Name and path to the database solution that will be packaged into the final MSI file. You can use the Browse button to specify the location.
Root Installation Folder	Root folder where the application file will be installed. This combo contains common options for the installation location on the machine and defines which users have access to those options.
Installation Subfolder	Subfolder within the root folder for the application. This is optional, but recommended. Typically, it will be a directory name denoting the database solution's name.
Pre-Installation Requirements	Specify the requirements for the database solution in regard to the Access Runtime Package.

The table that follows shows the three options for the pre-installation requirements. Choose the appropriate option for your application by selecting the radio button next to your choice.

Option	Description
Require that Microsoft Office Access 2007 be installed.	The installer checks that Microsoft Office Access 2007 is installed on the user's system before allowing the database solution to be installed.
Require the Access Runtime to be downloaded and installed if Access is not already installed.	When the user tries to install the database solution using the installer, he is prompted to download and install the Access Runtime from the Office Online download site. This ensures that the user has the capability to run the application if he does not already have Access installed on his system. However, he will be required to install the Runtime manually.
Require nothing and install the Access 2007 Runtime if not already installed.	The MSI automatically installs the Access Runtime if Access is not already on the system. Also, the target solution for the database will have the ACCDR file extension to ensure the Runtime is used when the application is run. With this option, the package creator has to supply the installer for the Access Runtime, which will be included with the MSI install package for the Access database solution.

Once you've selected your options, the MSI file can be created, but there are many other useful options still available. It is good to be familiar with the rest of the options because they can be quite useful in creating a professional installation package.

Shortcut Options

The shortcut options specify which shortcuts should be created automatically when the database solution is installed, as well as any functionality for the shortcuts, such as custom icons, startup macros, and command options. The following table describes each of these options.

Option	Description
Install Location	Provides the option of creating Windows shortcuts to the database solution on the Start menu, the Desktop, or both.
Shortcut Name	Name that will be used for the shortcut that is created.
Icon	Icon that will be used for the application as well as the shortcut.
Startup Macro	Name of the macro that will be run when the database solution is launched from the shortcut.
VBA Command values	Command-line arguments to be specified with the database solution.

The following table describes the available command-line switches for Access. To use these, place the switch and any required parameters in the VBA command value field. Placing text in the Startup Macro field automatically adds the /x switch and the macro's name to the command line.

Switch	Description
/runtime	Forces the application to always open in runtime mode. If both Access and the Access Runtime are installed on the machine, then, by default, the application opens in the full version of Access. This is not required if the database solution is installed as an ACCDR file.
/excl	Forces the application to always open in exclusive mode. By default, the application opens in the shared mode without the switch.
/ro	Forces the application to always open in Read-Only mode.
/user	Specifies the user name for a database that is secured by User Level Security. This must be followed by the particular user's name string, such as BackupUser. This setting has no effect for an ACCDB file because User Level Security in not supported in ACCDB file format.
/pwd	Specifies the password for a particular user of a database that is secured by User Level Security. This must be followed by the particular password string, such as Password. This setting has no effect for an ACCDB file because User-Level Security is not supported in ACCDB file format.
/x	Executes a named macro on startup of the application. The switch must be followed by the name string of a macro that exists in the Access application. Note: Another way to run a macro when the application is invoked is to use the AutoExec macro. Any macro named AutoExec in the database is executed automatically when the database is launched and does not require this switch to be set.

Table continues on the next page

Switch	Description
/wrkgrp	Specifies a custom System.MDW file for the Workgroup file to be used for the MDB file format database solution. If this is set for the shortcut, you most likely need to include a custom System.MDW file with the application, which can be done on the third page of the wizard. Setting this switch has no effect for an ACCDB file, which doesn't support User-Level Security.
/cmd	Specifies any command-line arguments that the application needs during startup. All strings that come after this switch on the command line are passed into Access and can be used from VBA code at any time.

Click Next to continue.

Step 3: Additional Files and Registry Keys

The third page of the wizard enables you to include additional files in the database package, as well as specify any registry keys that should be created when the installation package is run.

Additional Files

Use the Additional files option to package other files, such as custom System.MDW files, images, or other files that the database solution needs to function properly. To add a file, click the Add button in the additional files section. The Open File dialog box displays and you can select files to be added to the package. Once a file has been added, you can specify a subfolder of the install root in which to install the file. Clicking the Remove button removes the selected file in the Additional Files group.

Additional Registry Keys

Use the Additional Registry Keys group to create specific registry keys when the package is installed. Clicking the Add button creates a new record for the registry key. You can set the following values for custom registry keys:

- ❏ Root: The key's root in the registry.
- ❏ Key: The registry key that will be created.
- ❏ Name: Name of the key to be created.
- ❏ Type: Data type of the key's value.
- ❏ Value: Value of the key that will be created.

Selecting an existing key in the Additional Registry Keys group and clicking Remove will remove the key from the installation package options.

Once all of the Additional Files and Additional Registry Keys have been selected, click Next to continue.

If your application requires a lot of additional files or keys, it might be a good idea to make a template for the wizard so that you do not have to recreate all of the settings in this page of the wizard the next time an MSI installer is created.

Step 4: Additional MSI File Settings

The fourth and final page of the wizard enables you to specify the final settings for the database solution. It has five categories of additional settings — General Properties, Feature Information, Add/Remove Program Information, MSI File Properties, and Advanced Options — that are explained the following sections.

General Properties

In the General Properties section you can specify three properties of the MSI package that the client will use when the package is created:

❑ **Product Name:** The name that will appear in the installation dialog windows.

❑ **Install Language:** The target language for the package.

❑ **End User License Agreement (EULA):** Specifies a specific EULA file in the RTF format that the user will be required to agree to when the package is installed.

The Product Name and EULA options are not required, but are a nice touch to personalize your application's installation package.

Feature Information

Use the Feature Information section to specify a custom feature title and description for the feature. This information will be shown in the Custom Installation Options screen of the installation dialog box, where the installation options are broken down by component. The information isn't required, but it will make your installation package look more professional.

Add/Remove Programs Information

The Add/Remove Programs Information section enables you to specify data that will be used by the Windows System Add/Remove Programs feature. Although not required, this can be very useful to the end user of the application, in case she wants to remove the database solution in the future using the Add/Remove Programs dialog box. Here are the options:

❑ **Publisher:** Name of the publisher of the software to be shown in the Add/Remove Program properties for the install solution.

❑ **Product Version:** Provide the capability to specify the version of the package being installed by the wizard. This version can include the Major, Minor, and Build numbers for the package.

❑ **Contact Person:** Name of the Person or Entity to contact for more information about the database solution that has been installed.

❑ **Help/Support URL:** The URL to any help information available for the product.

❑ **Product Updates URL:** The URL to the location where updated versions of the product will be published.

❑ **Additional Support Info:** Provide any additional support information that you want to the client to see in the Add/Remove Program properties for this installer package.

These options are simple, but they can be quite useful to the consumers of your installation package and they also make your product more compliant to Windows technology standards. Including this information in the package is recommended.

MSI File Properties

In the File Properties for the Windows Installation Package section, you can set the specific file properties for the MSI file that will be created. These are the standard properties you see when viewing the file properties in Windows. There are five options:

- ❏ **Title:** Title of the MSI package.
- ❏ **Subject:** Subject matter for the MSI package.
- ❏ **Author:** Name of the person or company that created the MSI package.
- ❏ **Keywords:** Keywords for the MSI package.
- ❏ **Comments:** Comment information about the MSI file stored in the file properties.

Although these properties are also not required, setting them adds to the personalization of your installation package.

Advanced Options

Use the Advanced Options section to provide three last options for the MSI file:

- ❏ **Background Image:** The file path to a custom image to be displayed in the MSI installation wizard pages, instead of the default image. The standard size for this image should be 500×400 pixels.
- ❏ **Product Code:** A GUID that uniquely defines the installation package. A default GUID is generated for a new database solution, but you can add a custom value by typing it into this field of the wizard.
- ❏ **Upgrade Code:** A GUID that uniquely defines the upgrade package for this installation package. Again, a default GUID is generated for a new database solution, but you can add a custom value in this field.

For more information about any of these options, MSI files in general, or the Windows Installer 2.0 product, be sure to visit the start page for this product at:

```
http://msdn2.microsoft.com/en-us/library/aa367449.aspx
```

This resource provides tons of useful information about creating and maintaining MSI installer packages. Best of all, it won't cost you a dime to access this plethora of information.

Finishing the Wizard

Once all of the pages of the wizard have been completed, it is probably a good idea to create a Package Wizard template for the application to save all the settings you have created. Otherwise, click OK to create the MSI package. If the data has not been previously saved to a template file, the wizard prompts you about saving the template before creating the MSI file. After you decide, the new MSI file is created and the new installation package for your application will be ready for distribution.

It is always a good idea to test new installation packages every time a new MSI package is created. This ensures that the application is still working as expected and gives you a chance to catch any errors before the file is distributed, greatly reducing the added cost of customer support that might be required.

Additional Information About MSI Files

The MSI file format has been around for quite some time and is well known in the Windows community. As such, lots of information is available on the Web about creating and modifying these files. In addition, many tools are available, free or otherwise, for creating custom installation packages, such as the Custom Package Wizard just discussed. The following sections explore a couple of these tools.

MSI Editing Tools

If you're going to tweak the MSI file, you need an MSI editor. Microsoft provides a tool called Orca.exe, an MSI editor that's free with the Windows Installer SDK. For more information about the Orca tool, including download location information, go to:

    http://msdn2.microsoft.com/en-us/library/aa370557.aspx

Install Chaining

One more action an MSI installation package can perform is called *install chaining*. Install chaining is part of the Office Setup Bootstrap. It is the capability to cause additional installation packages to run at the completion of an installation package. For example, an MSI file could be modified to install a service pack or component update after your application has been installed. Similarly, the package could use install chaining to install an ActiveX control or other auxiliary programs (such as DLLs) that your database solution needs. Install chaining can be extremely useful when other MSI packages need to be installed with your solution. For more information about install chaining, consult the MSI editors help information or the Microsoft website.

Save as Template

Access 2007 has a brand new model for creating database templates, known as the Access Database Template (ACCDT) file format. The new template features replace the database wizards found in Access 2003 and prior versions. These templates offer a great deal more flexibility to developers, who can now create their own templates by using the Save as Template tool included in the ADE — that could not be done with the database wizards. This means you can now create standardized databases to allow users to create a new instance of an application with just a few clicks of a button. ACCDT files are collections of text files that are compressed into single files and, when invoked, require user intervention to create a new copy of a database. They are composed of text, XML, and image files, so the templates are considered to be safe files and can be transferred between users easily. This section explores how templates work, which features are supported, and how they can be created using ADE.

Creating ACCDT Files

One of my favorite new features in Microsoft Access 2007 is the support for database templates, which allows you to create your own custom templates. The ADE provides a nice tool for creating a template using almost any existing database. Most features in the ACCDB file format are supported by the new ACCDT file format. Because everything in the application is contained in one physical file, deployment is no problem because it's all done through user input from the Getting Started window. You could even imagine creating these template files for wide distribution to customers via e-mail or a website, allowing the template file to be reused time after time without the need to keep a blank copy of the database around. No matter what the purpose, creating template files using the ADE is quick and easy!

Once the ADE has been installed, there's a new button — Save as Template — available on the Database Tools tab of the Ribbon. When clicked, it opens a single dialog box in which you specify the required information for the template file. The database must be open in the current instance of Access and must have all of the desired settings applied for the template. Because Access is going off of the instance of the database that is currently opened in Access, any setting that is in effect for that database becomes part of the template file, and is applied to any database created from the template. The fields in the Save as Template dialog box specify the information shown in the table that follows.

Option Name	Description
Save As File Name	Name and full path to the template file that will be output from the tool. If the full path is not specified, and only the template filename is given here, the default database folder is used and is specified as an application-wide setting in the Access options. Clicking the folder button next to this text field opens a browse dialog box to allow the user to choose the filename and path for the new template file. Specifying a name for the ACCDT file is required to create the template.
Preview	Name and full path to the preview image to be used for the template file. The image is displayed in the preview pane in Getting Started when the template is invoked. In Access 2007, the PNG, JPG, GIF, and BMP image file formats are supported. The file browse dialog box for the preview image filters on those file types automatically. Specifying a preview image is optional.
Category	A template's category is also shown in the Preview pane in Getting Started when the template is invoked. In addition, the Category string is added to the category's name tab in Getting Started if the template is stored in the proper location on the machine (discussed later in the "Deploying ACCDT Files" section). The text is simply any string the developer wants. Specifying a category is optional.
Template Name	Name of the template as it will be shown in Getting Started in two places: in the Preview pane when the template is opened in Access, and on the category tab, just below the preview image, if the template is stored in the proper location (discussed later in the chapter). Additionally, it is used as the default name of the resulting database when the template is opened in the Preview pane. Finally, the text string is shown as the Title for the template when the template file itself is hovered over with the mouse cursor in Windows. Specifying a template name is optional.

Option Name	Description
Description	Specifies the description for the template file itself. This text is also shown in the Preview pane in Getting Started to provide the user with information about what the resulting database will do. It is also shown as the Description for the template when the template file itself is hovered over with the mouse cursor in Windows. Specifying a description for the template is optional.

As noted, the only parameter that is required by the Save as Template tool is the actual name for the template to be created. But using all of these options is a nice way to polish the database templates and give the user information about the template. Not only are these properties used by Access, they are shown in the Windows client as well for the information balloons when the template file is hovered over by the mouse.

There are some additional template types that are also supported by Access, but are not creatable by using the ADE's Save as Template tool:

❏ **SharePoint templates:** Created when specific SharePoint List types opened in Access, using the Open in Access button on the SharePoint Actions menu. The only SharePoint list types supported in Access for creating these templates are Issues, Tasks, and Contacts. Those lists have a custom mapping directly to the ID of the list on the WSS Site and no methods are exposed to you for manipulating the mappings.

❏ **Table templates:** Found on the Ribbon's Create tab. Unfortunately, they are not customizable because they are mapped to specific options in the Ribbon. The ACCTB file installed with Access that contains the data for these templates can be customized in a hacky sort of way, but that is beyond the scope of this book and not recommended.

❏ **Field templates (ACCFL files):** These new templates provide support for user extendibility by creating a new table, exporting its XSD file, renaming the extension to .accfland saving the file in the templates folder. While unsupported, creating new custom field templates is quite easy.

The last item to consider when creating a template from an existing database is the features in Access that are not supported by the ACCDT file format. As a general rule, any feature supported in the ACCDB file format is also supported in the ACCDT file format, with a few exceptions. Here are the database features that are not supported in ACCDT:

❏ Creating database file format other than the ACCDB file format

❏ Creating multiple database files from a single instantiation of an ACCDT file

❏ Data Access Page database objects

❏ Object-Level Security (also not supported in ACCDB files)

❏ Database passwords

❏ Replication Information or any replication features

❏ Linked tables to any other data sources

❑   VBA Project property settings (other than the defaults in a new database)

❑   VBA Project passwords

❑   Database encryption or database encoding

❑   Custom command bars (although custom ribbons are supported when the USysRibbons table is used)

❑   PivotTable and PivotChart definitions for tables and queries (PivotChart definitions are supported for forms)

❑   Import and export specifications (new or older formats)

This list is not really that long considering all of the features available in a database. It means almost every feature in Access is available in the ACCDT format and can be applied when a new database is created from the template file. That opens a realm of new scenarios to both Access developers and users. You can easily create and distribute template files to users, who can create entire customized database applications on-the-fly, without having to know virtually anything about using Access.

Deploying ACCDT Files

Once an ACCDT file has been created, the next step is to deploy the new template file. There are several ways to accomplish this, but simply distributing the ACCDT file is quite easy to do. As mentioned earlier, the ACCDT file can be transferred via e-mail or even placed into a setup routine using the Package Wizard.

Once a user is in possession of the ACCDT template file on his local machine, he has several options available for creating new databases from the template:

❑   Double-clicking the ACCDT file to invoke Access and show the template information in Getting Started.

❑   Choosing the template file from the File Open dialog box on the Office menu.

❑   Placing the ACCDT file into one of the recognized template folders so that it shows up in Getting Started automatically with the rest of the templates included with Access.

❑   Using the NewCurrentDatabase Object Model method to create the database from template.

Using any of these methods to create a template is quite simple to do, as you see next.

Opening a Template Using the Access UI

Probably the easiest way to create a database from a Access template is to have the user open the template file in Getting Started and then click the Create button on the Preview pane. The user can open a template file in the Getting Started Preview pane in three ways.

❑   Double-click the ACCDT file

❑   Browse to the ACCDT from the Open File menu.

❑   Select a template from Getting Started's Template Categories.

Double-Click

Users can open a template by navigating to the template file using Windows Explorer, and then double-clicking the ACCDT file. That file format is registered as a known file type and associated with Access, so the default command is to open the file in Access. When the file is invoked, Access opens to the Getting Started menu, with the template information shown in the Preview pane on the left side of the window. A user need only click the Create button, and a new instance of the database is created from the template. This is equivalent to invoking the template from a Windows command line. For example, the user could call the command:

```
"C:\Program Files\Microsoft Office\Office12\MSACCESS.EXE" "C:\test.accdt"
```

Use Open Dialog Box

The second method for opening a template in the Preview pane is to browse to the template by clicking the Office menu button at the top left of the Access client window and select Open. As you probably already know, this invokes the Open dialog box, but it is important to notice that the dialog box is not filtered on the ACCDT file format by default. In the Files of Type list control for the file filter, click the down arrow and choose the Microsoft Office Access Database Templates (*.accdt) filter option. Once this filter is set, the ACCDT files in any given directory display in the open dialog, and when chosen, the template opens in Getting Started's database Preview pane.

Select from Template Categories

Getting Started is shown in the Access client window by default. The Template Categories pane is on the left side of the Access window. By default, there are two template categories: Featuring and Local Templates. These are separate from the Office Online Categories list just below the default categories, but it should be noted that the templates listed in Featuring are from Office online. Select the Local Templates category, and the templates that are installed on the local machine display. Click on any template and the Preview pane shows the template information. A user only needs to click the Create button and a new database for the template is created. Best of all, you can leverage these new features to show your own custom templates in Getting Stared for the user to see.

Showing Custom Templates in Getting Started

Of the Office programs, Access is considered to have one of the steepest learning curves. With the Microsoft Office Access 2007 release, extra attention has been given to help decrease that curve for new users in a number of areas and to entice new customers into using the product. The idea is that using the Save as Template tools in the ADE, both users and developers will be able to make templates for every type of personal database. Users will see these templates and use the applications generated from them as the needs for tracking data arise. The benefit to users is that they are able to create a complete, fully functioning database application in several seconds, without ever having to do one bit of development work. Additionally, one of the best ways to find out how to use the Access program is starting with a pre-built application and playing around with each piece of the application, as you may have done with the Northwind sample application in the past.

You can leverage the template features by showing custom templates in Getting Started's Template Categories. That's a good way to provide a nice professional look and feel to your template. And it's easily done by placing the ACCDT file into either of two directories on the local machine:

❑ Access template folder is where all of the templates included in the product box are placed when the Access program is installed. If the default installation of Access 2007 is completed, those templates can be found in the following location:

```
%ProgramFiles%\Microsoft Office\Templates\1033\Access
```

Typically, this maps to the location `C:\Program Files\Microsoft Office\Templates\1033\Access directory`.

❑ The user's application data directory for Access templates, which is a hidden by default for the user's profile. On versions of Windows prior to Vista, this directory is something like:

```
C:\Documents and Settings\<user name>\Application Data\Microsoft\Templates
```

On Windows Vista, this directory is:

```
C:\Users\<user name>\AppDate\Roaming\Microsoft\Templates
```

The last thing to consider when showing a custom template in the Getting Started Template Categories is the name of the category that will be displayed. By default, the Local Templates category shows all of the templates that are included on the local machine. A custom template can be given a category when it is created. The template's category will be shown in Getting Started when the Access program is invoked. The category displays directly beneath the Local Templates category in Getting Started and, when clicked, shows all templates with that category name. Leveraging the template category is a really nice way to expose your template to users in a manner that integrates directly into the Access client.

Using the Access Object Model to Create Templates

Updated in the Access 2007 product release, the NewCurrentDatabase object model method now provides you with the capability to create new databases from a template in an automated fashion. Previously, NewCurrentDatabase could be used only to open an instance of a new database in the Access client window. Now, a new database can be created from the blank default database in one of three formats or from a template file.

Creating a new blank database in Access is probably the most common way to create a new database. For Access 2007, there are three possible formats to use: the Access 2007 file format (ACCDB), the Access 2002-2003 file format (MDB), and the Access 2000 file format (MDB). The database version to use is passed as the FileFormat parameter (the second parameter) to the NewCurrentDatabase method and is an AcNewDatabaseFormat enumeration object type. This parameter is optional and if not specified, the default database type is used when creating the new database. The default database file format that is set when Access is installed is the Access 2007 File Format (ACCDB), but this can be changed by selecting another supported file format in the Access Options dialog, on the Popular tab in the Access Options dialog. To create a database from VBA code, try the following routine:

```
Application.NewCurrentDatabase _
    "C:\test.accdb", _
    acNewDatabaseFormatAccess2007
```

This opens a new instance of a blank database in the Application object of Access in the ACCDB file format. One thing to keep in mind, however, is that when calling `NewCurrentDatabase`, there must not be any database currently opened in the instance of Access or you will get a runtime error. Of course, you can always call the `CloseCurrentDatabase` method first to close any open database.

In the case of creating a database from a template file, you add a third parameter — `Template` — in the call to `NewCurrentDatabase`. It specifies the template from which the new database will be created. This parameter can simply be passed a string that is the full file path to the custom template's location. As mentioned earlier, templates can only create ACCDB file format databases, so the second parameter to the `NewCurrentDatabase` call will be ignored if it is any file format other than ACCDB. The following is an example of some code to create a database from a custom template:

```
Application.NewCurrentDatabase _
    "C:\test.accdb", _
    acNewDatabaseFormatAccess2007, _
    "C:\my custom template.accdt"
```

The `Template` parameter is of Variant type, not string type. That's because there is support to create templates linked to a SharePoint list using the last two parameters in the `NewCurrentDatabase` method call (discussed in Chapter 17). When creating a database from a SharePoint template, the user can pass the ID number of the template instead of the path to the template file.

Because you can use the ADE tools to create the format, let's examine the specifics of the ACCDT file format next.

The ACCDT File Format

The structure of the Access 2007 ACCDT file format is different from any Access database file formats. The new Office Open XML file format schema defines the ACCDT structure. ACCDT files are collections of text, XML, and image files packaged into a single file that is consumable by Access. When a user invokes a template, Access retrieves the database objects and settings from the ACCDT file, creates a new database, and then builds the database objects that are specified in the ACCDT file. This section discusses the structure for the Access 2007 ACCDT database template file format in depth.

Essentially the ACCDT file format is a hierarchical structure that contains a set of files describing how the data files contained in the file package are related, as well as a collection of data files that store the actual data. That structure is then compressed into a single file using the ZIP file format and its extension is renamed `.accdt`. Figure 21-1 provides a diagram of the file structure hierarchy for the Access 2007 ACCDT file format.

The ACCDT format stores all of the supported objects that can be created from a template, but unfortunately, not all Access features are supported. Before you look at which features are not supported, explore how each of the objects in the file relates to the template. Understanding the parts of the file format will help you discern why certain features aren't supported in a custom template.

Decompressed, the ACCDT file can be thought of as having four levels of data within the file. The root, or the first level, contains data about the types of files contained in the file, metadata about the specific template, and the location of the actual data in the file. The second level, which could be considered the dataroot level, stores the template's preview image, the template settings, a folder containing the objects in the database, as well as a description of how the parts of the database are defined.

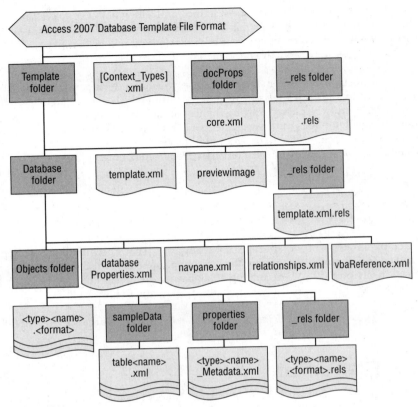

Figure 21-1

The third level, considered the database level settings, contains all of the information about the database properties, the Navigation pane settings, the system relationships, and the VBA project references as well as a folder containing all of the database object information. The last level contains all of the information about the database objects defined in the database solution, as well as any sample data that those objects contain. Each of these files plays an integral role in describing how the resulting database will be created when the template is invoked. The following sections examine each of these files in greater depth.

The Template's Root Folder

The files contained directly in the root of the template's folder are used to describe the metadata about the template file itself. These are the file-level properties for the template and contain information about the template itself. All of the files listed in the root level of the structure are required to be in the template. The following table describes each of these in more detail.

Object Name	Description
`[Content_Types].xml`	Describes the types of data files that are stored within this template file. More accurately, the content types XML file knows the extensions of all of the files stored within the template the file itself. For example, viewing the contents of the file reveals XML nodes like this:
	`<Default Extension="txt" ContentType="text/plain" />`
	Certain file types, such as .exe, are not allowed in an Office Open XML file format. When the package is opened, the extensions are verified and if there are any additional or undefined extension types in the file that are not described by the content types, the entire package is invalidated for security purposes.
docProps folder	Contains the `core.xml` file that describes the template's file-level properties. It can contain any nodes that a developer wants to include, but three specific nodes are reserved for string data about the template. When the template file is opened in Getting Started, the following properties stored in `core.xml` are shown:
	`dc:title`: The name of the template, which will be shown in the Preview pane. It's also the default database name when the template is opened in Getting Started.
	`dc:decription`: A short description about the template, which is also shown to the user in the Preview pane.
	`cp:category`: This is the category of the template, which will be defined by the individual developer. This string will be displayed in the preview pane. Additionally, this is the string used for the category name of the template for getting started (which will be discussed below in the information for deploying templates).
template folder	Contains all of the files used to create the particular database from the template. Everything in this folder is specific to the database that will be created. This is the second level of the structure and will be discussed further in the following section.

Table continues on the next page

Object Name	Description
_rels folder	Contains all of the `.rels` files that describe the relationships of the files within this file package. The root level of the template file structure hierarchy is a single file called `.rels` that relates the other three objects:
	The `CoreDocumentProperties` metadata for the file, which maps to `core.xml`.
	The `PreviewImage` property for the file, which maps to the preview image stored in the template folder. (Remember, the types of file for this image must be defined in the `[Content_Types].xml` file.)
	The Template data for the file, which maps to `template.xml` in the template folder.
	All `*.rels` files always describe the relationships of the objects contained within the file package. Although the root of the template file contains only one RELS file, deeper levels of the file may have multiple RELS files for describing each of the different database objects, which you will see shortly.

Each of these objects is pretty straightforward and should be easy to understand. Each is required for the ACCDT file format and if any are missing, the template file will be invalidated. Although this metadata is required for the file, none of the information defines anything about the database created from the template. The real meat of the resulting database is based on the objects contained in the template folder.

The Template Folder

The template folder, found in the root of the template file structure, holds all of the data that will be used to create the new database. Once again, there is a _rels folder for describing the relationships to the files in the template folder hierarchy. In addition, the `template.xml` file contains information about how the database should be created, and the database folder itself contains all of the information about the database objects that will be created. The following sections briefly describe these objects.

Probably the most pertinent file here is `template.xml` because it contains settings that affect the database. The settings in this file mainly affect localization, and need to be changed only if the raw files contained in the ACCDT file are changed after the file is generated by the Save as Template feature. That means if you always use Save as Template to create your template files, there will never be a need to modify any of the settings in any of the files contained here or elsewhere within the ACCDT file.

Preview Image

Although it is not directly used by the template to create a database, the preview image is stored in the template folder. It is usually named something like `preview.jpg`, but that name is not required. Remember, the preview image name and path is defined by the file in the _rels\.rels file contained in the root for the template. Also, the type of the preview image must be described in the content types XML file. For Access 2007, the JPG, BMP, GIF, and PNG image file formats are supported for the preview image in templates.

template.xml

The `template.xml` file contains metadata about the format of the template file itself. There are six supported tags in this XML file:

❑ `TemplateFormat`: The version number of the ACCDT file format. Because this is a new feature to Access 2007, the only supported value is `1`.

❑ `RequiredAccessVersion`: The minimum version of Access that is supported for the template. This number corresponds to the major build of Access. The lowest value this number can be is `12`. This tag differs from the `TemplateFormat` tag because the major build of Access will be a number higher than 12 and it may contain new features that are not supported in Access 2007.

❑ `FlipRightToLeft`: By default, the Right-To-Left (RTL) setting is turned off (set to `0`). However, for some languages, like Arabic, the standard is to read from the right to the left and users prefer to use computer applications that way as well. Setting this tag to `1` turns on the RTL setting in the database created from the template, and all of the controls on forms and reports are reversed.

❑ `PerformLocalizationFixup`: Because these templates are text files, it is possible to modify them (changing the text for a form's label control, for example) after they have been created. The problem is that the text in the label may then be clipped because the size of the label may not have been updated. If `PerformLocalizationFixup` is set to `1`, the fixup features during template instantiation are executed, and all of the labels in the database will be resized, along with some other actions as well. This setting affects two different features:

    ❑ **Name Maps in the template:** Fixup updates all controls, tables, and fields so that the controls still map to the proper objects.

    ❑ **Label controls:** The Size-to-Fit feature is applied to all of the labels in forms and reports, except when the label is in a tabular layout or when the `Tag` property for the label includes `;DoNotResize;` (note that the label is wrapped in semicolons).

❑ `PerformFontFixup`: When this value is set to `1`, the font fixup is run when the database is created. It simply resizes labels in case the template's font settings were modified after the template was created. Font fixup resizes labels to make sure that they are the correct size for the new font and that no text gets cut off. If this tag is set to `0`, font fixup will not run.

❑ `VariationIdentifier`: Defines the ID of the variation of the template and is used internally by Microsoft. Variations are used to create different versions of a template object for a specific locale, based on the language settings for the target database.

Database Folder

The Database folder contains all of the information about all of the database objects and settings that will be set when the new database is created. It is really the next major piece to the template and it's covered in detail a little later in the chapter.

_rels Folder

You have already seen the _rels folder, which can be found in the root of the template file itself. As mentioned before, the rels files describe the relationships to the objects contained within the template. In this particular _rels folder, you'll find the `template.xml.rels` file, which describes information about the template object relationships to the files contained in the ACCDT file package. For each relationship tag in this XML file, there are three attributes:

❏   `Target`: Contains the path, starting from the template folder as the root, to the particular object in the ACCDT file.

❏   `Id`: Contains information about the name of the object that the relationship is pointing to.

❏   `Type`: The namespace of the object in the relationship that is being referenced.

The rels file can be thought of as describing information about the structure of the ACCDT file format. Each database object file in the Database folder, whether text or XML, needs to be defined in `template.xml.rels` contained in the _rels folder.

The Database Folder

The Database folder is where most of the database settings and properties are stored. It has five objects — four XML files and the objects folder. These XML files describe the database properties, VBA project references, the table relationships, and the Navigation pane settings. The objects folder contains the rest of the information about the template, which will be discussed in depth a little later in this chapter. The following sections describe each of the XML files in detail.

databaseProperties.xml

The `databaseProperties.xml` file is used to store all of the database-level properties that need to be set on the database when it is created. Any properties that are set when a new database is created will be there, but if additional properties need to be set or to override the default database settings, nodes can be added to this file. For example, the startup form of a database is commonly set to provide an interface to a user when the database is loaded. When this is the case for the database, a property called Startup is set at the database level. The name of a database-level property can be retrieved in VBA code and seen in the immediate window by calling:

```
?Application.CurrentDb.Properties(X).Name
```

For each Property node contained in the `databaseProperties.xml` file, there are three attributes that can be set:

❏   `Name`: The name of the property as it is in the database property's `Name` object.

❏   `Type`: The type of the value of the property as it is in the database property's `Type` object.

❏   `Value`: The actual value setting for the property as in the database property's `Value` object.

These attributes are all required for any property setting contained at the database level or otherwise.

navpane.xml

The `navpane.xml` file contains most of the information about the Navigation pane settings and is probably one of the most complex files in the template. It contains all of the structure and data for the four

Navigation pane tables that can be found in any database created or opened by Access 2007. These system tables are called MSysNavPaneGroupCategories, MSysNavPaneGroups, MSysNavPaneGroupToObjects, and MSysNavPaneObjectIDs. All of the data in these tables is required for the database. If navpane.xml is not included or incorrect for the database, there will be a warning that the database's Navigation pane settings need to be updated when the template is created and will be created automatically.

Trying to read and understand the data contained in navpane.xml is quite difficult because of its complexity. Instead, a quick code sample for creating navpane.xml is included at the end of this section. It contains all of the data necessary for the Navigation pane tables in the database, which can be applied to the template to create the desired effect.

There are still several Navigation pane settings that are not contained in the database's system tables. Instead, there are six database-level properties that contain setting information for the Navigation pane. They're described in the following table.

Property	Description
NavPane Category Name	Sets the text shown at the top of the Navigation pane when the grouping is set to Custom. Not required in the database.
NavPane Category	The default category setting for the Navigation pane in the database. If not specified, it is created when the database is created from the template file.
NavPane Closed	Sets whether the Navigation pane is expanded or collapsed in the database. If not specified, the pane is expanded by default.
NavPane Width	The width of the Navigation pane within the Access client. The default width for a new database is used if this property is not specified.
NavPane View By	The View By settings, which can be accessed from Navigation pane header's context menu.
NavPane Sort By	The Sort By settings, which can be accessed from Navigation pane header's context menu.

The only reason navpane.xml would need to be changed is if the settings were updated after the template is created. The Save as Template feature creates the Navigation pane settings based on the current settings of the database instance that is opened in Access at the time the command is executed.

The Access.Application object provides the ExportNavigationPane method to manually create the navpane.xml file described earlier. ExportNavigationPane takes one parameter, the full file path to the output XML file that will be created. Here's an example of calling this method:

```
Sub CreateNavigationPaneXML(strFilePath as string)

    ExportNavigationPane strFilePath

End Sub
```

The complement of ExportNavigationPane is the ImportNavigationPane method, which consumes the XML data created by ExportNavigationPane and loads the new data into the current database open in Access. ImportNavigationPane takes two parameters. The first is the file path to the XML file containing the Navigation pane XML, which is required. The second, which is optional, is a Boolean value of False if the data should replace the current Navigation pane data or True if the data should be appended to the Navigation data. Here's an example of importing the Navigation pane data:

```
Sub CreateNavigationPaneXML(strFilePath as string)

    ImportNavigationPane strFilePath

End Sub
```

relationships.xml

The relationships.xml file describes all of the system relationships that need to be created when the new database is created. It represents all of the data that is found in the MSysRelationships system table that is stored in the master database. The schema for this XML is not required — it's already known by Access because the structure of the MSysRelationships table is known to Access.

If you want to modify this file, you can do so easily by creating the desired relationships in the Access client with the database open. Then call the ExportXML() method to create an XML file containing the data for this table. Here's an example of creating a database's system relationships XML file:

```
Sub CreateRelationshipsXML(strFilePath as string)

    Application.ExportXML acExportTable, "MSysRelationships", strFilePath

End Sub
```

vbaReferences.xml

The vbaReferences.xml file contains all of the data required for the VBA project references that will be set when the template is created. There is no way to package or create new files to be registered when the template is created, so any project references included in the template must already be available on the machine. For example, if there is a reference to the Outlook 12 Object Library in the VBA Project, then Outlook must be installed on the machine before databases created from the template can be used. Otherwise, the project will have broken references when the template is created.

There are two ways a database reference can be set in a template, by GUID or by Path. Each VBA Reference node can have one of two XML subnodes:

❑   **GUID:** The GUID of the reference as listed in the VBA Project properties. This node looks something like this:

```
<GUID>{9CE720EF-0000-0000-1000-ABCA1020FFED}</GUID>
```

❑   **Path:** The full path to the DLL or other referenced file, as listed in the VBA Project properties. This node will look something like this:

```
<Path>C:\Windows\System32\anyold.dll</Path>
```

These XML nodes correspond to the value of the reference that is to be created. Either one or both properties can be present, but the GUID always overrides the Path when the reference is created in the database. Also, references to other MDB or ACCDB files don't provide a GUID, so they must be referenced by Path.

To retrieve the value of either the GUID or Path property for a VBA Project Reference, call either of the following code examples in the VBE immediate window:

```
?Application.References("Access").Path
?Application.References("Access").GUID
```

These calls will return the path and GUID for the Access reference in the VBA project of a given database. If the Access reference does not exist, this code will throw an error.

The Objects Folder

The final piece to the ACCDT file format puzzle is the objects folder. The objects folder contains all of the rest of the information about the database objects in the template file as well as any sample data that may be included as XML data in the sampleData folder. Once again, there will be a _rels folder to describe the structure and a properties folder storing some metadata about each of the objects contained in the database. Each of the file objects in the folder represents a different database object.

Depending on the complexity of the database the template is created for, the object folder most likely contains a fair number of files. The file objects in it will be one of two types: text or XML Schema Document (XSD). Each file represents a different and separate database object for the template. Each of these files uses the naming convention `object typeobject name.file format` — formContactsList.txt, for example. For forms, reports, queries, macros, and modules, these files are in a text type file format. For instance, an ACCDT file might contain a file named `formContacts.txt` that provides information for a form in the database. You can create a text file containing data for any one of these objects using the `SaveAsText` method, which is hidden in the OM. Here's an example:

```
Application.SaveAsText acForm, "Contacts", "C:\formContacts.txt"
```

Although tables can be saved as text using the `SaveAsText` method, they need to be exported differently to work with the ACCDT file. For tables, the file exported will be of type XSD to define the schema of the table. For example, there might be a file called `tableContacts.xsd` included in the template file. An XSD file is a standard way of describing schema in a database table. Still, you can use the `ExportXML` method to export the schema only for a table, by using the following code:

```
ExportXML acExportTable, "Contacts", , "tableContacts.xsd"
```

In this call to `ExportXML`, instead of using the `DataTarget` parameter to specify the output XML file location, the output location to the `SchemaTarget` parameter was passed. (It is possible to pass both parameters simultaneously to output both XML data and schema to two different files.)

This is a more subtle example of how templates created by later versions of Access may support new features without changing the file format itself (that is, the `TemplateFormat` property in `template.xml` still equals 1, but the `RequiredAccessVersion` property may be something like 20). If the `SaveAsText` method supports exporting the feature to text, then the feature is supported by the ACCDT file format.

Aside from the database object files themselves, this objects folder contains several other objects as noted earlier in this section. The following sections describe each of those objects in more detail:

Database Object Files

As mentioned earlier, the `object typeobject name.file format` files in the objects folder are the actual database objects that will be created in the database when the template is invoked. The naming convention is the database object type string, followed by the database object's name string, with the extension listed as the file format for the particular objects. The text files represent all the database objects except tables, and the XSD files represent the table schemas in the template.

sampleData Folder

The sampleData folder contains any sample data that is to be included with the template for redistribution. The files contained are in the XML file format, have the naming convention `tabletable name.xml`, and relate directly to the corresponding table XSD file found in the objects folder. These files do contain the XSD information for the table as well, but the XML files will not add data or build schema if the corresponding XSD file is not present in the objects folder.

One last item to keep in mind: Data that is contained in value lists in controls on Forms or Reports is not included in the sampleData folder. This is because value list data (other than in a table) is stored directly along with the control definition. In this case, the data stored in the corresponding text file will contain information about the control and any value list that is part of its properties.

Properties Folder

The Properties folder holds more XML files that contain more metadata about each of the database objects included along with the template. The naming convention for these files is `object typeobject name_Metadata.xml` and by viewing the file, it is quite easy to understand. Each of these files must correspond to a database object contained in the Objects folder and every database object in the objects folder must have a corresponding metadata file in the properties folder.

The two supported properties are listed as subnodes of the AccessObject XML node that is defined in this file. They are:

❑ `Name`: The name of the object as it will be when the new database is created.

❑ `Type`: The database object type of the corresponding database object that will be created when the template is instantiated.

These metadata files are required to be present in the ACCDT file format.

_rels folder

As mentioned before, the rels files describe the relationships to the objects contained in the template. In this particular rels folder, you'll find a rels file that corresponds to each of the database objects contained in the objects folder. These files describe information about the template object relationships to the files contained in the ACCDT file package. They have the naming convention of `ACCDT object file name.rels`, where the `ACCDT object file name` parameter corresponds to the object in the template with the naming convention `object typeobject name.file format`. For each relationship tag in this XML file, there are four attributes, which are described in the following table.

Attribute	Description
Target	Contains the path, starting from the object folder as the root, to the particular properties XML file in the ACCDT file.
Id	Contains information about the type of relationship the Target path leads to. In this case, the relationship should be metadata because the files in the properties folder are metadata about each of the database objects.
Type	The schema namespace for the metadata object in the relationship that is being referenced.
xmlns	Defines the XML namespace for the relationship schema.

The rels file can be thought of as describing information about the structure of the ACCDT file format. Each database object properties file in the objects folder, whether it be text or XML, needs to be defined by one of the files included in this _rels folder.

Source Code Control Support

The last ADE tool we'll discuss here is the support for standard Source Code Control programs. In this day and age, from single-person shops to huge corporations, the use of source code controls to version and backup software under development is widespread and has been adopted as an industry standard. Source code controls can be effective for versioning and protecting software and any changes made to it, especially when there are multiple users accessing and updating the same code for long periods of time. While there is no mechanism built into Access to version a database or the objects within it, installing the ADE adds the Source Code Control add-in, which can be used to systematically version an Access database development project.

Unfortunately, the ADE does not include a Source Code Control (SCC) program itself, but it does give the user the capability to use Access with a standard SCC program. The standard SCC program is defined as any SCC provider that is registered to Windows as a standardized source code control provider. While many different source code control applications are available on the market, the following examples use the SCC add-in with Microsoft Visual Source Safe 2005 (MS VSS), the latest release of the MS VSS available with the Microsoft Visual Studio .NET 2005 product.

Install the Source Code Control Program

If there is already an SCC program such as Microsoft Visual Source Safe installed on the machine, then once the ADE has been installed, you should be ready to start using the SCC tools. If that's your situation, skip to the next section. However, if a source code control program is not installed on the system, there are a few steps necessary to set up the SCC control program so that it can be used with Access 2007 using the SCC tools in the ADE.

If the ADE is installed prior to installing a source code control program, every time Access is invoked, an error message — "you don't have a source code control program installed" — will be shown. The message asks if Access should continue to show the message when Access is started. Clicking the No button suppresses the message and you will not lose any functionality such as the capability to associate an SCC program with Access.

To begin setting up MS VSS, run the setup program included along with the product disks in Microsoft Visual Studio .NET 2005. Using the default install options for VSS is fine; it needs only to be installed on the system and registered as the default SCC program. Once VSS is installed, there are a couple of setup items to take care of before the SCC can be used.

Register a Database

First you need to register an SCC database for VSS. Start the Visual SourceSafe Administrator program from the Windows Start menu. If you have a preexisting database, choose File ⇨ Open SourceSafe Database; otherwise, select File ⇨ New Database. Either option invokes the Add SourceSafe Database Wizard, which you'll use to create (or add) a database for your source code to be saved into. Complete the following steps for the wizard:

1. Click Next on the first page of the wizard.

2. The second page requests the location of the SCC database. If one already exists, supply the full name and path of the database. Otherwise, choose a new location for the new database, and click Next.

3. On the third page, enter a name for the new database and click Next.

4. The fourth page requests the source code control model to use for the project. Either model can be used, so choose the model that works best for your situation, and then click Next. (More information about either model can be found in the MS VSS help files.)

5. You're at the last page of the wizard — it was just that easy! Click Finish and the new database is set up and ready to go.

Add Users

The second item of business is to add users to the database if the SCC project will be used by multiple people. By default, the user of the account that installed the VSS program is added to the users list automatically. To add other user accounts for the database, simply select Users ⇨ Add User to invoke the Add User dialog box. Add any desired users to the database and then the setup of the database will be complete and you are ready to begin adding Access database applications to the SCC project.

Be sure to note that any users added to the database will also need network access to the database created by the wizard, as described earlier. Each of the users needs to set up VSS on his local machine and then add the database to his VSS client.

After the users have been added, you can close the Visual SourceSafe Administrator program, and you're ready to begin using the SCC tools included in the ADE with your Access applications.

Using the Source Code Control

Once Visual SourceSafe or other SCC control program is installed, a database for the code project has been configured, and users have been added, you're ready to begin using the SCC tools included in the ADE. The SCC add-in has a new, custom Ribbon tab, Source Control, which is added to the Access client when a database is open. This tab is the user interface for working with the SCC features. In this section, you'll see how each of the Source Control options works with the VSS source control database.

Adding a Database to the SCC

To begin using the source control features for any given database, you first add the database to the source code control project. The following steps add a database to the SCC:

1. On the Ribbon's Source Control tab, click the Add Database to SourceSafe button to invoke the Log On To Visual SourceSafe Database dialog box. Use your user name and password. (Note: Your default user name is your Windows user account name and a blank password.) Then click OK to log in and continue.

2. You're prompted for a location to add the database to. Each database that is checked into the SCC database should be separate from all other databases, and it's recommended that you choose a location folder to help separate the projects in a logical manner. Click OK when you're done.

3. The Add Objects to SourceSafe dialog box opens. By default, all objects in the database are selected, so just click OK and the entire database will be added. Of course, you could easily deselect any database objects that are not to be stored in the SCC database.

You are ready to begin using the SCC to version your database project. From now on, when the database is opened in the Access client, you can check out, check in, modify, and sync the database project with just a few button clicks.

Modifying Source Code–Controlled Databases

Now that the database has been added to the SCC database, notice that all of the objects in the Navigation pane have a lock icon to denote that they are checked-in and locked by the SCC database. Right-click any of these objects and you'll see some new options added to the context menu for that database object. These allow the user to work with the various options available for the SCC project.

The user cannot modify the database objects until they are checked-out to him. To check out an object, right-click on the object in the Navigation Pane and choose the Check Out option. The object is checked out and can now be modified. Once all changes have been completed, the object can be checked in from the corresponding option on the Navigation pane's context menu.

Note that there is an Undo Check-Out option available. If it is selected, all of the current changes for the database object will be discarded and the currently Checked-In version of the object will be restored to the local database. This undo option is provided to enable you to disallow any changes that have been made. However, this is an all-or-nothing proposition; there is no way to undo only specific changes made to the database object using the Undo Check-Out option.

Creating a Database from Files in the Source Code Control

If you do not have a copy of a database that's checked in to your source safe project to work on, you can create one from the SCC project. Just open the Office menu and select the Create from SourceSafe option. The Log On To Visual SourceSafe Database dialog box opens. Enter a user name and password and click OK. The Create Local Project Form SourceSafe dialog box is invoked. Navigate to the database you want to create a local copy of, select it, and click OK. A new database registered to the SCC project is created and you are ready to begin working with the database project.

The Source Code Control Options

To work with the features supplied by the SCC provider and the SCC add-in for Access, go to the Source Control Ribbon tab. Because the database is already registered in an SCC project, all of the options on this tab should be enabled, except for the Add Database to SourceSafe for obvious reasons. When working with a database object, for actions such as checking out and checking in changes, click the object name in the Navigation pane and then click the desired action in the Ribbon. The Navigation pane is the interface for selecting database objects to use to work with in the Source Code Control program. Each of the available options for the SCC add-in is described in the following table.

SCC Option	Description
Add database to SourceSafe	Allows you to add the database open in Access to the source code–controlled database. If the current instance of the database is already checked into the SCC database, this option is disabled. The database must be checked into the SCC database before the source control options can be used for the objects of the application.
Create from SourceSafe	Once a database application has been checked into an SCC database, the database project can be restored using the Create from SourceSafe option. It closes the database that is currently open in the Access client, creates a new database based on the objects in the SCC database, and reopens the new database in the current instance of Access. Note: A Create from SourceSafe option is available on the Office menu, which is added when the ADE is installed. When opening a new instance of Access without opening a specific database, a new database can be created from the SCC project by clicking this button on the Office menu. This is important to know because the Source Control Ribbon is not available when there are no databases open in the Access client.
Check In	After a database object has been checked out and modified, you have to check the object back into the SCC project to version and propagate the changes to the object. To check in an object, simply select the object in the Navigation pane and click the Check In button in the Ribbon. (This option is also available in the context menu for the object in the Navigation pane.) The Check In Objects dialog box opens; it enables you to check in one, many, or all database objects that are checked out.
Check Out	Before any change can be made to an object, a database object must be checked out of the SCC project. Fortunately, Access is smart enough to prompt you to do that automatically when you try to make changes to the object. To manually check out an object, select the database object in the Navigation pane and click the Check Out button on the Ribbon. This option is also available for the database objects context menu in the Navigation pane.

SCC Option	Description
Undo Check Out	The equivalent of a standard Revert code option. If a database object is checked out and, possibly, has modifications, Undo Check Out discards all of the current changes, restores the object to the current version in the SCC project, and marks the object as checked in. This can be used if changes are made that do not need to be saved in the project. It also can be used to ensure that the version of the database that the developer is working on is a version that was actually checked in to the SCC project.
Latest Version	Enables you to synchronize your database to the get all of the currently checked-in versions of the database objects. You have the option to get one, many, or all of the current project items. However, if any items in the project are already checked out, you can't get the latest version of them until the file is either checked-in to the project or the changes are reverted. This option is also available on the context menu for the database object in the Navigation pane.
Add Objects to SourceSafe	Some objects, such as modules, are not automatically added to the SCC project when they are saved. If a database object has been added, but has not ever been checked in to the SCC project, click Add Objects to SourceSafe to add the new database object to the project. This is the only way an object can be added to the SCC project if it is not automatically added when the object is created.
History	One of the more powerful features of any source code control program is the capability to see how previous versions of the object were structured and at which date and time. This can be useful if the recent changes to the object do not include some code or other information that was previously included in the database project. To view the history for an object, select the object in the Navigation pane and click the History button. The History Options dialog box opens; to see the full history, simply click OK. The full history of the changes displays in the History dialog box and you can view each version using the SCC program.
SourceSafe Properties	Describes some of the basic details about the object settings in the SCC database. The path to the object, type of object, and current status of the object are described here.
Share Objects	Used to share the current version of a project to create a new subproject or branched version of the project. If a branch of the project is created, changes made in one branch are not propagated to other branches or versions of the SCC project. This can be particularly helpful when trying to lock down changes made to a project for a specific release version, while still allowing changes to be made to the main project, without worrying about them affecting the locked down code.

Table continues on the next page

SCC Option	Description
Differences	Probably the most important feature included with any SCC program is the capability to view the differences between two objects in the SCC database. This is useful in analyzing changes and in comparing how objects have changed over time. To view the differences between two objects, select the object in the Navigation pane and click the Differences button. The Differences Options dialog box opens, and you can select which two files should be compared. This option is also available on the context menu for the database object in the Navigation pane.
Run SourceSafe	Enables you to invoke MS VSS from the instance of Access directly. This opens the SCC database for the current code project in the VSS Explorer window for you to gather data and make changes to.
Refresh Status	Updates the status of all of the objects in the SCC database. If new changes have been made from another user of the SCC project, those changes are propagated to the current instance of Access.
Options	Invokes the Source Code Control Options dialog box for the SCC add-in, which is explained next.

The Source Code Control Options dialog box enables you to set five basic options for the SCC add-in and it exposes an entry point into the SouceSafe Options dialog box. The five options allow the user to do the following:

❑ Choose to automatically get the latest versions of objects when a database is checked in

❑ Specify if the database objects should be automatically checked in when the database is closed

❑ Specify if the objects should be added to the SCC database when they are created in Access

❑ Automatically remove objects from the SCC database when they have been deleted in the Access client

❑ Automatically get the updated status of all objects when the database is opened

Clicking the Advanced button on this dialog box provides you with some of the more granular options provided for the SCC add-in, via the SourceSafe Options dialog box. If you want to add a custom object editor for the SCC add-in, for example, it can be chosen from this SourceSafe Options dialog box. This dialog box also provides a few more options for the SCC database settings.

Even if a program other than Microsoft Visual SourceSafe 2005 is used, the options available should be similar to the items discussed here because the SCC must be registered as a Windows SCC provider.

Summary

The Access Developers Extensions (ADE) for Microsoft Access 2007 provides several very useful tools for building Access applications. In this chapter, you explored four useful features included in the ADE for Access developers: the Access Redistributable Runtime, the Package Wizard, Save as Template, and Source Code Control support. Versions of Microsoft Office XP and lower afforded Access developers permission to distribute the Access Runtime only by purchasing the Developer edition. With the release of Microsoft Access 2003 and introduction of the ADE, the Visual Studio Tools for Office (VSTO) product included several new features for Access developers. For Microsoft Office Access 2007, the ADE includes even more great tools than ever before. These tools can greatly enhance your capability to quickly produce professional, high- quality software products.

Before you go off to build and deploy Access database solutions around the world, be sure you understand all of the options available in the ADE for making your solutions perfect. A little research, planning and experimentation with the ADE tools will pay off in long-term development cost savings and reduce potential problems down the road. Not only does the ADE help build professional, easily deployable Access database solutions, but it also helps improve the overall Access development experience by providing source code control support. The ADE is truly a nice tool set for Access developers of any experience level.

22

Protecting Yourself with Access 2007 Security

Now more than ever, you have to concern yourself with the security of your computer systems. One form of security — securing the information contained in and the intellectual property built into your databases — was discussed in Chapter 18.

Another form of security has to do with preventing malicious attacks on your computers — attacks that can delete files, spread viruses, or otherwise disrupt your work. This chapter focuses on the security enhancements built into Access 2007, which help you protect your computer systems and your users' computer systems.

In Microsoft's efforts to make sure everything is secure, it had to deal with the fact that an Access database has a lot of power (something Access developers have known all along). And because of this power, someone who chooses to use Access maliciously can make an Access database perform destructive operations. In fact, that is the reason that Outlook does not allow Access MDB files to be sent as attachments. From a security perspective, an MDB file is essentially an executable.

To curb this power, Microsoft made changes to Access 2003 that mean that developers must do a little more work to make databases as easy to use as they have been with prior versions of Access. But face it: If your users use Access to open a database from someone else and that database then attacks their computer, they're more likely to blame Access rather than the database they opened. Their confidence in Access would be right out the window. So, really, the security changes weren't all bad.

But this book is about Access 2007. New security features have been added that significantly improve the user experience over that of Access 2003. This chapter explains what the new security features are and why they were added. Perhaps more important, it describes the things you can do to make it easy for your users to use your databases in Access 2007. The existing solutions of using a digital signature and Visual Basic scripts still apply, but additional features such as trusted locations have been added to make it even easier. These are not difficult solutions. And once you learn them, they become second nature.

You'll also take a look at Expression Service and sandbox mode, which are part of the Access database engine. If you installed Access 2003 and found that you had to upgrade to the Jet Engine Service Pack 8, you'll be glad to know that no additional download is required to use wizards or add-ins with sandbox mode in Access 2007. Because Access 2007 includes the Access database engine, everything you need is already there.

The Office Trust Center

The Trust Center is a new security feature that has been implemented across all applications in Office, including Access. It is not the first feature you'll see when you launch Access 2007 (you'll likely come across Disabled mode first), but it provides several of the key concepts you'll want to know before you explore Disabled mode in more detail.

What Is the Trust Center?

The Trust Center is a centralized feature that you can use to manage security settings for an Office application. In Access, you get to the Trust Center by clicking the Access Options button from the Office menu, then selecting the Trust Center page. On the Trust Center page, click the Trust Center Settings button to open the Trust Center, shown in Figure 22-1.

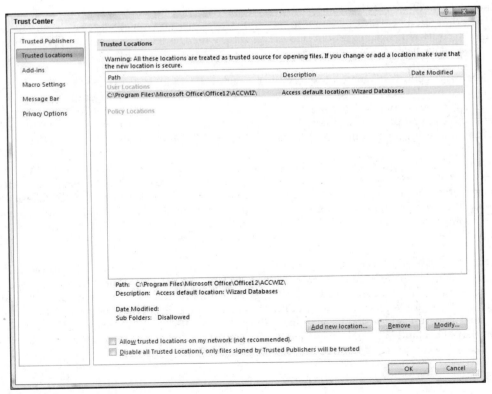

Figure 22-1

Trust Center Features

The Trust Center combines several security and privacy features from previous versions of Office into a common place. Those features include trusted publishers and macro settings. The following sections survey each group in the Trust Center.

Trusted Publishers

The Trusted Publishers page (see Figure 22-2) lists the certificates that are installed to the Trusted Publishers certificate store in Windows. Trusted publishers are added when you choose the option to Trust All Documents From This Publisher when opening a database that is signed with a digital signature.

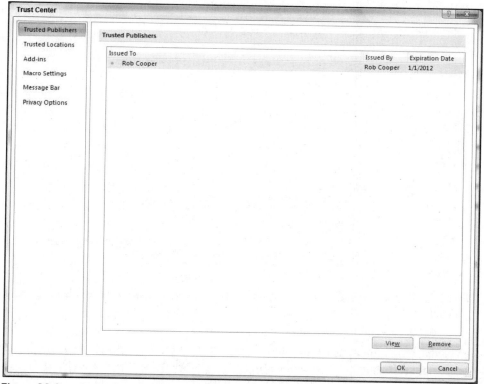

Figure 22-2

When you trust a certificate from a given publisher, you trust all content for any document or database that you receive from that publisher. You should be certain that you really trust the individual or company before choosing to trust a certificate.

Trusted Locations

Trusted locations are the most exciting new feature in the world of security for Office. Having realized some of the issues facing developers and administrators with regard to digital signatures, Microsoft created the concept of a trusted location. A trusted location is exactly what the name suggests — a location that you can designate as trusted for content to execute. You can create a trusted location for local, remote server (UNC), or Internet/intranet paths. To create a trusted location for a UNC or Internet/intranet path, you must select the Allow Trusted Locations On My Network (Not Recommended) option at the bottom of the Trusted Locations page as shown in Figure 22-3.

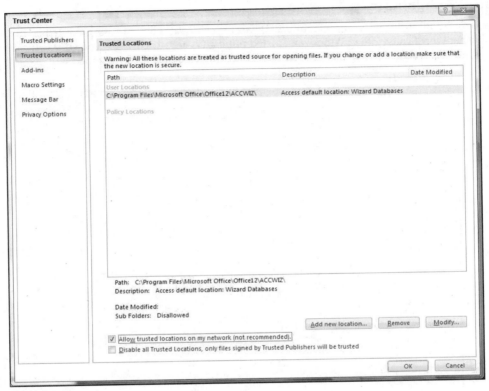

Figure 22-3

Opening a database from a trusted location trumps all other security settings, including macro settings. Databases opened from a trusted location always open enabled. Because of this, you must make sure that the locations you mark as trusted really are secure.

By default, Access 2007 includes one trusted location: the `Microsoft Office\Office12\ACCWIZ` directory. The wizards in Access have been moved to this new directory in Access 2007 and this directory is trusted by default to ensure proper operation.

To add a trusted location, click the Add New Location button. That opens the Trusted Location dialog box as shown in Figure 22-4. You can also choose to trust subfolders of the location. A description can be added that appears in the Trusted Locations group in the Trust Center.

Root folder locations such as `C:,` `\\ServerName\C$,` *or* `http://WebServerName` *cannot be added as trusted locations.*

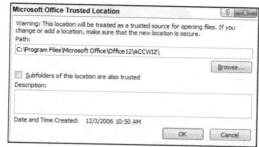

Figure 22-4

You can also choose to disable all trusted locations. Doing so forces all databases to open in Disabled mode unless they are digitally signed.

Add-ins

Add-in security settings in the Trust Center were also available in Access 2003. New in Office 2007 is the capability to disable all add-ins. This also includes the Access wizards, but remember that the trusted location trumps this setting as well. If you check the option to Require Application Add-ins to be signed by Trusted Publisher and also Disable all Trusted Locations, you are prompted to run Access wizards. Figure 22-5 shows the prompt when you launch the Form Wizard in this configuration.

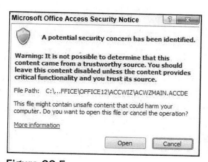

Figure 22-5

If you click Cancel when prompted, you see an error message, as shown in Figure 22-6.

Figure 22-6

Macro Settings

The macro security settings Low, Medium, and High have been replaced with the new Macro Settings in the Trust Center, as shown in Figure 22-7.

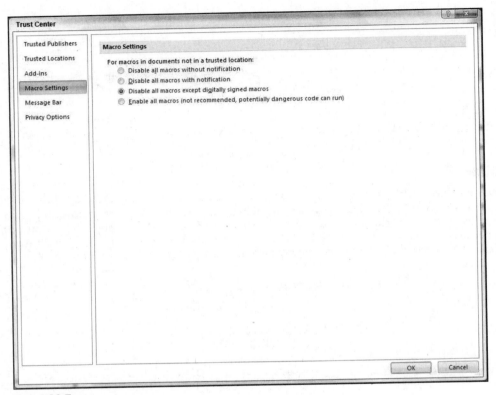

Figure 22-7

The default setting for Access 2007 is Disable All Macros With Notification. With this setting, the Message Bar is displayed for all databases that are not digitally signed or in a trusted location. This is synonymous with the Medium macro security setting in Access 2003.

The most secure setting is Disable All Macros Without Notification, which is similar to the Very High macro security setting from Office 2003. This setting was not available in Access 2003 because there was no way to disable code when a database was opened. With this setting, all databases that are not in a trusted location open disabled. The Message Bar is not displayed.

What was High security in Access 2003 is now Disable All Macros Except Digitally Signed Macros. With this setting, all databases that are not digitally signed or in a trusted location open disabled.

The least secure setting is Enable All Macros. This is synonymous with Low macro security in Access 2003. To reinforce the fact that all code will execute, Microsoft includes a warning next to this setting that reads "(not recommended, potentially dangerous code can run)." If you are sure that all the files and add-ins you open are safe, you can select this option, although it is extremely risky.

I earnestly recommend against using the Low setting. I consider myself a pretty savvy computer user. I have firewalls and virus software, and a pretty good idea of what to download and whether to open a file that has been downloaded for me. But I won't use this setting myself. I would rather have just made the decision to open something that hosed my computer than have it be the result of some setting I chose months ago and then forgot about.

The macro setting for Access is independent of the macro setting for the other Office applications.

Message Bar

By default, the Message Bar appears in the Access window when a database is disabled. The Message Bar page contains one setting titled Never Show Information About Blocked Content. You can choose not to see the Message Bar when a database is opened by this setting. This setting trumps the Macro Setting: Disable All Macros With Notification.

There is check box at the bottom of the page called Enable Trust Center Logging. With Trust Center logging enabled, Office will log all activity related to the Trust Center to a folder called `%LocalAppData%\Microsoft\Office\TCDiag`. For Access, information will be logged to a file called `ACTCD.LOG`. On Windows Vista, this file was created in `C:\Users\<UserName>\AppData\Local\Microsoft\Office\TCDiag`. The log file includes the following information about each file that is inspected by the Trust Center:

```
---
File Name: "C:\Users\Rob\Documents\Database1.accdb"
Date/Time Opened: 9/6/2006 6:59 AM
Content Type: VBA Macro
Certificate: None
Certificate Signature: None
Certificate Status: None
Trust Center Decision: Block Content
User Decision: Enable Content
```

The User Decision entry is added if you make a trust decision about the file in the trust dialog box. More information about the trust dialog box appears later in this chapter.

Privacy Options

Last, the Privacy Options group in the Trust Center includes options to use online content such as help or links. It also provides the opportunity to participate in Microsoft's Customer Experience Improvement Program.

Disabled Mode

If you have opened an existing database in Access 2007, you have probably already seen Disabled mode. It is a new security feature in Access 2007 that prevents certain content in the database from executing. It's designed to let users securely inspect the content of a database without the possibility of running potentially malicious objects. What is a potentially malicious object? Generally speaking, it is any object that can be used to alter database content, the file system, Registry, or network. In Access, this means VBA code, certain types of queries (action queries, SQL Pass-Through, and Data Definition Language), certain macro actions, and ActiveX controls.

If you used digital signatures in Access 2003 you'll recognize this as the list of objects that were signed in Access 2003.

It's pretty easy to notice when code fails to execute. A large piece of functionality in your application doesn't work. As shown in Figure 22-8, the Message Bar is the other way to determine that the database is disabled.

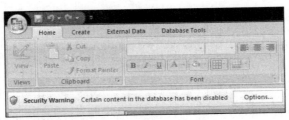

Figure 22-8

Unless you change the macro settings, it's worth noting that unless they are digitally signed or in a trusted location, all databases open in Disabled mode. Even empty databases fall into this category.

Disabled mode is new in Access, but is not new to Office. Other Office applications such as Word and Excel have been capable of opening documents without running VBA code for some time.

Why Do We Have Disabled Mode?

Cognizant that we live in a time when computer security is becoming more and more critical. Microsoft added the capability to inspect a database without the risk of malicious code running. As a result, if you used Access 2003, you'll immediately see that all of the prompts you received when opening a database have been removed. Even in Access 2003, opening a database is all or nothing — there is no way to open the database in a secure manner such that code does not execute. (Of course, you could hold down the Shift key or import the tables to view content, but by and large, code could still execute.) That is what Disabled mode is all about.

Why all this concern over opening a database, even an empty one? Well, with all the capabilities in Access, add-ins and wizards and whatnot, there must be a way for someone to choose to give you a malicious MDB file. And if there is a way, someone will find it and exploit it.

Take the following lines of code for example:

```
DoCmd.SetWarnings False
DoCmd.RunSQL "UPDATE msysaccessobjects " _
& "SET data = Shell(""c:\windows\system32\notepad.exe"");"
```

Entered in the VBE Immediate window using Access 2000, the `RunSQL` command has to execute the VBA Shell function to determine what the value of the field data should be, and Windows Notepad (`c:\windows\system32\notepad.exe`) starts.

Of course, Notepad is not likely to cause problems that would result in destroying your computer. But there are a lot of destructive programs on your computer — format.com, for example — as well as destructive commands such as DEL that could be run using such a technique.

Those code lines could have been written in an Access macro. That macro could have been named AutoExec, which automatically runs when a database is opened. If the Shell function had called a destructive program instead of Notepad, or if the SQL had contained a destructive command like DEL, data could be destroyed on the computer that opened the database, or worse yet, data could be destroyed on other computers networked to the computer that opened the database. So if you're not paying attention to the databases you open, or worse yet, your users aren't paying attention, well, you have heard about the countless hours spent recovering from viruses. That is nothing compared to the value of data that can be deleted if a hard disk drive is reformatted. And malicious code can do just that.

Enabling a Database

When Access opens a database, it gives certain information, known as *evidence*, to the Trust Center. For Access, the evidence includes the location of the file and the digital signature of the database if it has one. The Trust Center takes the evidence and makes a trust decision based on certain logic. The decision is then given to Access, which opens the database in either Disabled or Enabled mode as needed.

Figure 22-9 illustrates the logic for determining whether a database will open in Disabled mode.

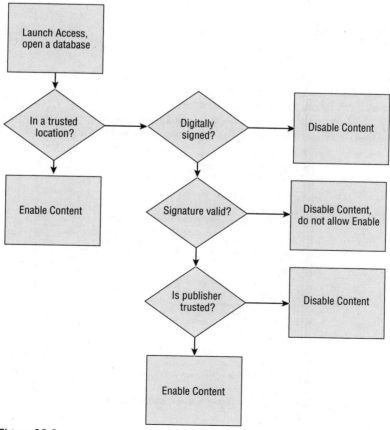

Figure 22-9

When a database is disabled, there are a few different ways to enable it. First, you can click the Options button in the Message Bar. That opens the Office Security Options dialog box, as shown in Figure 22-10.

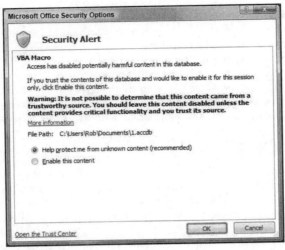

Figure 22-10

To enable the database, select Enable This Content, and click OK. The database will close and then re-open in enabled mode.

If the database is signed, you can view the details of the source by clicking the Show Signature Details link, as shown in Figure 22-11. Additionally, you can select Trust All Documents From This Publisher, which will open them automatically (if the signature is valid). Obviously, whenever you open that database or any database from the same publisher, it will automatically open without prompting. So signing your database is one option to avoid making your users respond to the prompt.

Figure 22-11

Modal Prompts

Certain types of files always prompt the user to open them, unless they are opened from a trusted location or are digitally signed. These include ACCDE, MDE, ADP, and ADE files. Those files are opened with a modal prompt for security reasons. ADP and ADE files connect directly to SQL Server, and code executed in these files can also be executed on the server in the form of stored procedures and functions. One primary goal for Disabled mode is to allow you to view the code in a solution without running it. Because VBA source code is removed from ACCDE and MDE files, these files cannot be opened in Disabled mode. For more information about ACCDE and MDE files, please read Chapter 18.

You are also prompted when opening a database in the Access Runtime or with the /runtime command-line switch, as shown in Figure 22-12. That's because the Trust Center is not available to users in Runtime mode. There's no way to inspect a database for its safety, so users are given the explicit choice to open the file. This isn't necessarily the optimal solution; after all, when you put your database in front of users, you don't particularly want them to have to respond to this warning every time they open your database. In addition to using trusted locations, we'll describe some options to prevent this, including Visual Basic scripts and digital signatures later in this chapter.

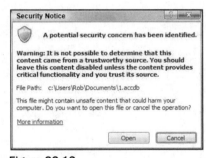

Figure 22-12

For security purposes, you can revert to the Access 2003 behavior where you are prompted to open every file if you so choose. Adding the following value in the Registry makes Access 2007 prompt you to open every file. You need to create the ModalTrustDecisionOnly DWORD value because it does not exist by default.

```
HKEY_CURRENT_USER\Software\Microsoft\Office\12.0\Access\Security\↵
ModalTrustDecisionOnly = 1
```

AutomationSecurity

The AutomationSecurity property was added to the Access Application object in Access 2003. It determines how Access behaves when running under automation. The following sections show you how to use the AutomationSecurity property to open your Access applications without user interaction.

Opening Remote Databases Programmatically

Disabled mode and trusted locations are a major improvement over the warnings in Access 2003. That said, it would still be nice if your users didn't have to deal with prompts or disabled content or trusted locations when opening a database. If you work in an environment where you are opening remote data-bases from VBA code, you'll want (and essentially need) those remote databases to open without issues.

To solve this, you can create a Visual Basic Script file (type VBS) to open a database without getting the security prompt or opening in Disabled mode. The following code temporarily disables security (actu-ally, it effectively enables all code or macros) while the database is being opened. When the script ends, control is turned over to Access and the AcApp object is released. Because the security setting is persist-ent only while the AcApp object exists, the macro setting in Access returns to whatever setting was cho-sen using the Trust Center.

```
Const DATABASE_TO_OPEN = "C:\<FileToOpen>.mdb"
On Error Resume Next

Dim AcApp
Set AcApp = CreateObject("Access.Application")

If AcApp.Version >= 11 Then    ' Set to 11 because this works in Access 2003 as well
    AcApp.AutomationSecurity = 1 ' Enable content (Low security)
End If

AcApp.Visible = True
AcApp.OpenCurrentDatabase DATABASE_TO_OPEN

If AcApp.CurrentProject.FullName <> "" Then
    AcApp.UserControl = True
Else
    AcApp.Quit
    MsgBox "Failed to open '" & DATABASE_TO_OPEN & "'."
End If
```

Similar code can be used in VBA to open and access a remote database. That is, depending on the reason you are opening the remote database, you may or may not want to switch control to the user (AcApp.UserControl = True).

Of course, if you use this VB script for databases that your users open, you cannot specify command-line parameters — for example, /wrkgrp to specify a Workgroup Information file (MDW). If you don't need to specify parameters, this gets around Disabled mode quite easily.

Other Uses for AutomationSecurity

There are several scenarios in VBA code where Access opens a database behind the scenes and can dis-play a prompt to open a database. This is often not desirable because you don't want a dialog box to open while code is running. Examples of this scenario include database conversion using the ConvertAccessProject method, and exporting objects using the TransferDatabase method. To pre-vent the prompt from appearing, you can set the AutomationSecurity property to 1 (Enable Content) prior to calling the specified method.

The following code demonstrates using the AutomationSecurity property prior to converting a data-base using the ConvertAccessProject method.

```
Sub ConvertWithoutPrompt()
```

```
     Const SOURCE_DB As String = "\Database8.accdb"
     Const DEST_DB   As String = "\Database8.mdb"

     ' Set AutomationSecurity. This code requires a reference to the
     ' Office 12.0 Object Library
     Application.AutomationSecurity = msoAutomationSecurityLow

     ' Convert an ACCDB to MDB in 2002-2003 format
     Application.ConvertAccessProject CurrentProject.Path & SOURCE_DB, _
         CurrentProject.Path & DEST_DB, _
         acFileFormatAccess2002
 End Sub
```

Macros in Access 2007

Similar to the way that expressions are evaluated for safety in Access, macros in Access 2007 now run in a sandboxed environment. This means that Access has a list of those macro actions that are safe to execute in Disabled mode. As mentioned in Chapter 2, a safe macro is one that does not perform any of the following tasks:

❑ Change data

❑ Create or delete objects

❑ Update or alter the Access user interface

❑ Access the Windows file system

❑ Run a SQL statement

❑ Send e-mail

Unsafe Actions

Following is a list of actions that are blocked in Disabled mode in Access 2007. If you run any of these actions, an error is displayed while the database is disabled.

CopyDatabaseFile	RunSavedImportExport
CopyObject	RunSQL
DeleteObject	Save
Echo	SendKeys
OpenDataAccessPage	SetValue
OpenDiagram	SetWarnings
OpenFunction	ShowToolbar
OpenModule	TransferDatabase
OpenStoredProcedure	TransferSharePointList
OpenView	TransferSpreadsheet
PrintOut	TransferSQLDatabase
Rename	TransferText
RunApp	

Nine safe actions are blocked when you set an action argument to a specific value. These are described in the following table.

Macro Action	Action Argument	Unsafe Argument Value
Close	Save	No and Yes.
OpenForm	View	Design and Layout.
OpenQuery	View	Design.
OpenReport	View	Design, Layout, and Print.
OpenTable	View	Design.
OutputTo	Output File	Any. When a filename is specified, this action becomes unsafe.
Quit	Options	Exit and Save All.
RunCommand	Command	See the list of commonly used RunCommand action arguments following this table.
SendObject	Edit Message	No.
SendObject	Template File	Any value specified.

The following commonly used RunCommand action arguments are blocked:

        InsertObject

        PasteAppend

        PasteSpecial

        Relationships

        Cut

        Copy

        Paste

        WorkgroupAdministrator

While the list does not include all RunCommand arguments, only a small subset of macro actions are blocked in Disabled mode. Several of the safe actions revolve around navigation, so the actions that remain can still allow an application to be relatively useful. In fact, the majority of the functionality in the new Access templates is implemented using embedded macros so that they can function successfully in Disabled mode. Naturally, for more complex applications you will need to enable the database.

CurrentProject.IsTrusted

If code is blocked in Disabled mode, how do you start your application? Well, you can have an autoexec macro that calls the OpenForm action, or you can set the StartupForm property to the name of a form to open, but what if that form has code? After they upgrade to Access 2007, your users might be left scratching their heads, wondering why your application doesn't work! To help with this, Microsoft has added a new property on the `CurrentProject` object called `IsTrusted`.

As its name suggests, this property determines whether the database is enabled. Naturally, if code is disabled, you cannot check this property using code. If code is running, `IsTrusted` returns `True`. You can, however, use it as the condition in a macro to determine a course of action to take when the application opens. Figure 22-13 shows a macro that uses this property to open one form if the database is enabled, and another form if disabled.

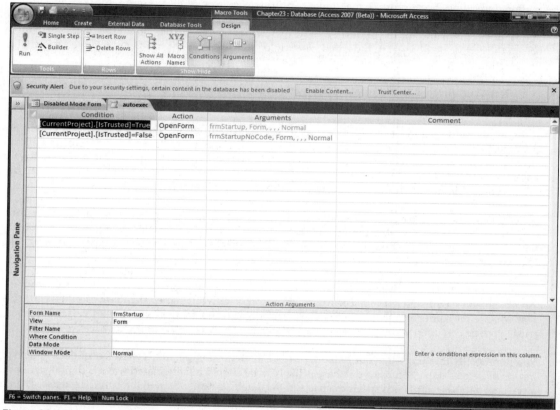

Figure 22-13

Digital Signatures and Certificates

As you now know, databases with digital signatures are exceptions to the macro setting checks. That is, if a database is digitally signed, it can be opened regardless of the macro setting.

Before you tackle creating and using digital signatures, however, let's briefly review ACCDB files. Access 2007 introduces a new file format called ACCDB. These files include additional features for the

Access database engine and are the default file format created in Access 2007, but they do not support digital signatures — at least not in the sense that you were becoming accustomed to in Access 2003. For ACCDB files, Microsoft has introduced a new feature called Signed Packages that enables you to compress a database and sign the compressed file. You'll see more about this feature later in the chapter.

Okay, back to digital signatures. So, what is a digital signature and how do you create one?

You have probably seen various forms of digital signatures or digitally signed programs while browsing the Internet or installing software. Typically you see a security warning dialog box that contains information describing the purpose of the digital certificate used to sign the program, the date and time the certificate was published, and who published it. Some certificates permit you to obtain more information about the program and/or the publisher. After reviewing the information about the certificate, you can accept the certificate or reject it. If desired, you can choose to have that certificate accepted automatically by selecting the Always Trust Content From This Publisher check box.

So a digital certificate is an electronic attachment applied to a program, database, or other electronic document.

A digital signature is a means to apply a digital certificate to programs, databases, or other electronic documents so that a user of that program, database, or document can confirm that the document came from the signer and that it has not been altered. If the program, database, or document is altered after it has been digitally signed, the signature is invalidated (removed). This feature means that you can be assured that nobody can introduce viruses after the signature is applied.

All of this means that you have to obtain a digital certificate to give your database a digital signature. In a moment, you'll see more about how to obtain a digital certificate, and later, how to sign your database with the digital certificate. But first, a bit more explanation about how digital certificates and digital signatures work with Access.

Microsoft Office 2007 uses Microsoft Authenticode technology to enable you to digitally sign your Access database by using a digital certificate. A person using your signed database can then confirm that you are the signer and that your database has not been altered since you signed it. If that person trusts you, he can open your database without regard to his Access macro security level setting.

You're probably thinking that your database will be altered. After all, that's what a user does when he inserts or deletes data. Because a database is likely to be altered in anticipated ways, a digital signature for an Access database applies to specific aspects of the database rather than to the entire database. Therefore, a database can be updated in the ways you would expect without the signature being invalidated.

More specifically, a digital signature on an Access database covers only objects that could be modified to do malicious things. These objects include modules, macros, and certain types of queries, for example, action queries, SQL pass-through queries, and data definition queries. The signature also applies to the ODBC connection string in queries and properties of ActiveX controls. If any of these types of objects are modified after you sign your database, the digital signature is invalidated (removed).

Types of Digital Certificates

There are two types of digital certificates: commercial and internal. Commercial certificates are obtained through a commercial certification authority (CA) such as VeriSign, Inc. Internal certificates are intended for use on a single computer or within a single organization and can be obtained from your organization's security administrator or created using the `Selfcert.exe` program, which is described a little later.

Commercial Certificates

To obtain a commercial certificate, you must request (and usually purchase) one from an authorized commercial certificate authority vendor. The vendor sends you a certificate and instructions about how to install the certificate on your computer and how to use it with your Access application.

> *The certificate you need for your Access databases is called a code-signing certificate. Also look for certificates that are suitable for Microsoft Authenticode technology.*

The commercial certificate provides full protection of your database for authenticity. Because the digital certificate is removed if the file or VBA project is modified, you can be sure that your database will not be authenticated if anyone tampers with it.

Likewise, commercial certificates provide protection for users. In the event someone obtains a certificate and uses it for malicious purposes, the commercial authority will revoke the certificate. Then anyone who uses software that is signed with that certificate will be informed of its revocation by the CA.

> *The computer opening a digitally signed program, database, or other electronic document must have access to the Internet to verify the authenticity and status of a commercial certificate.*

Internal Certificates

An internal certificate is intended for use on a single computer or within a single organization. An internal certificate provides protections similar to a commercial certificate in that if the file or VBA project is changed, the certificate is removed, and the database does not automatically open unless Enable All Macros is selected as the macro setting.

Internal certificates can be created and managed by a certificate authority within your organization using tools such as Microsoft Certificate Server. You can create a certificate for your own computer using the `Selfcert.exe` tool.

Obtaining a Digital Certificate

As mentioned earlier, you can obtain a certificate from a commercial authority such as VeriSign, Inc. For internal certificates you can turn to your security administrator or Digital Certificate group, or you can create your own certificate using the `Selfcert.exe` tool.

Be aware that if you create your own certificate, Access still opens a database in Disabled mode when your signed database is opened on a computer other than the one where the certificate was created. This happens because Microsoft considers it to be a self-signed database.

The trouble with self-certification is that the certificate isn't trusted because it is not in the Trusted Root Certification Authorities store. That is, your certificate isn't registered and Microsoft Authenticode technology cannot determine its authenticity — the certificate gets a crosswise look. And the reason for this is that a digital certificate you create can be imitated: Someone can mimic your certificate and sign a database with it. If you have trusted a digital certificate that has been mimicked, a database signed with that certificate will open, and if that database contains malicious code, it could execute that code. This brings up two important issues:

❑ If a certificate you create can be imitated, what kind of security do you really get?

❑ If your certificate won't be trusted on another computer, why bother creating your own certificate?

A certificate is nothing more than a digital document. As with any digital document it can be copied, replicated, or otherwise imitated. However, Microsoft's Authenticode technology is able to determine authenticity of the certificate if, and only if, it is in a Trusted Root Certification Authorities store.

Using self-certification is a solution that should be considered only if your databases will just be used behind the security of a firewall, with virus software, for protection. If your database, and therefore your certificate, will be made publicly available, such as through the Internet, you will be putting your certificate out where someone could copy it. They could then attach the copy to a database with malicious code and send that database back to you, or worse yet, on to other users who could think the database is from you. If the certificate has been on the computer that is opening the database, that database will be trusted, it will open, and the malicious code will be executed.

If you are interested in acquiring a commercial certificate, the Microsoft Developer Network (MSDN) has list of root certificate program vendors at `http://msdn.microsoft.com/library/default.asp?url=/library/en-us/dnsecure/html/rootcertprog.asp`. When you are looking for a vendor to supply a certificate, you need one that provides a certificate for code signing or that works with Microsoft Authenticode technology.

Using Self-Certification

Now that you have been sufficiently warned about the pitfalls of self-certifying, take a look at how you can self-certify in situations that you believe are secure from hacker attacks.

The question asked in the previous section was: If your certificate isn't going to be trusted on another computer, why bother creating one? The answer is that the certificate isn't trusted unless it is installed on the computer that is opening the signed database. Therefore, the solution is to install your certificate on that computer so that it will be trusted.

Only a few steps are necessary to self-certify and use the certificate for your database as well as use that database on any computer. Some of the steps have to be done only once, and some have to be repeated for each computer that will use your certificate to open your database. First you need to run `Selfcert.exe` to create a certificate on your computer.

Creating a Self-Certification Certificate

To create a certificate for yourself, simply run the `SelfCert.exe` program. This is available from Start ➪ All Programs ➪ Microsoft Office ➪ Microsoft Office Tools ➪ Digital Certificate for VBA Projects. You can also run this from the Office12 folder. For example, mine is located in `C:\Program Files\Microsoft Office\OFFICE12\SELFCERT.EXE`.

If `SelfCert.exe` is not installed on your computer, use the Microsoft Office 2007 installation disk to install it.

When `Selfcert.exe` starts, the Create Digital Certificate window opens, as shown in Figure 22-14.

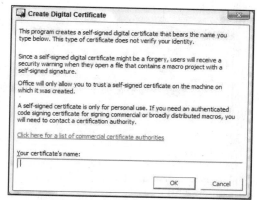

Figure 22-14

Enter a name for your certificate and click OK. This creates a certificate and adds it to the list of certificates for this computer only.

With the certificate created, there are two requirements to use your database on another computer:

1. Sign your database.

2. Create a file from your certificate and install it on the target computer.

Signing your database is done through the Visual Basic Editor. Creating a file from your certificate can be accomplished many ways, usually while viewing the certificate details. Installing the certificate on the target computer can be done from Windows Explorer.

> *Keep in mind these steps apply only to self-certification. If you use a commercial certificate, you won't have to install your certificate on each computer.*

Adding a Certificate to Your Database

To digitally sign your database, you add a certificate to it using the Visual Basic Editor. In the Visual Basic Editor, select Tools ⇨ Digital Signature. The dialog box shown in Figure 22-15 opens.

Figure 22-15

To pick a digital signature to sign your database, click Choose. The Select Certificate dialog box (see Figure 22-16) opens, showing all the code signing certificates on this computer.

Figure 22-16

Select the certificate you want to use to sign this database and click OK. The name of the selected certificate displays in the Digital Signature dialog box, and a Detail button appears, as shown in Figure 22-17.

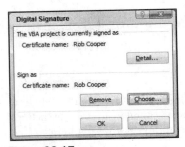

Figure 22-17

You use the Detail button to get access to an option to create a file from your certificate so you can copy that certificate to another computer. To sign your database now, click OK.

Unlike Access 2003, Access 2007 no longer automatically re-signs files when a digital signature has been removed. Regardless of whether you have the certificate that was used to sign the database, you will need to re-sign the database if the signature is broken.

Using a Self-Signed Certificate on Another Computer

Because self-signed databases won't be trusted on another computer, you need to add your self-signed certificate to other computers that will be accessing your databases. You do that by exporting the certificate to a (CER) file, copying the file to the other computer, and adding the certificate to that computer.

One way to create the Certificate (CER) file is to view the details of the certificate from the Visual Basic Editor. Select Tools ⇨ Digital Signature to open the Digital Signature dialog box, and click the Detail button. That displays the Certificate Information, as shown in Figure 22-18.

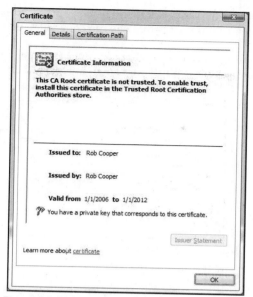

Figure 22-18

The bottom of the form shows you have a private key that corresponds to this certificate. The private key is your personal piece of data associated with the certificate and is required to digitally sign a file. For a self-signed certificate, the private key cannot be exported. When you export the certificate, what you are exporting is the public key. The public key is used to uniquely identify a certificate as having been signed by you.

To get to the option that enables you to save the certificate to a file, click the Details tab, shown in Figure 22-19. (Your tab shows actual values in the Value column; they are omitted here for privacy.)

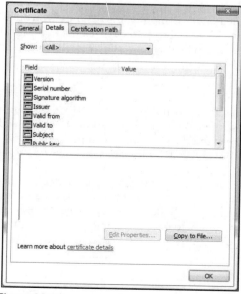

Figure 22-19

Click the Copy to File button at the bottom of the page to start the Certificate Export Wizard, which will lead you through the process to create a file that you can copy to another computer.

After you create the file, you can take it to another computer and open it. A file of type CER is known to Windows and will show the certificate details, as shown in Figure 22-20.

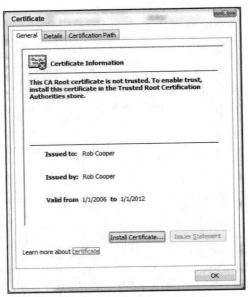

Figure 22-20

Click Install Certificate to start the Certificate Import Wizard.

After the certificate is installed on the computer, the first time you open a database signed with that certificate, the Message Bar appears with the option to trust the publisher. If you select the option to always trust the publisher, databases signed with that certificate will open in Enabled mode.

Signed Packages

As mentioned earlier, Access 2007 does not allow you to digitally sign an ACCDB file using the Digital Signature dialog box, as described in the previous section. Doing so will result in an error message. Instead, you can package the entire database into a compressed file, which is subsequently signed. The process creates a new file with an ACCDC file extension known as a *signed package*.

Signed package files can be used as a security feature and a deployment feature. As a security feature, they provide a mechanism to digitally sign a file that can be used to help identify the publisher of the file- just like digital signatures on MDB files. As a deployment feature, they create a file that is smaller than the original with the capability to be opened in Access and verify the publisher of the file.

Creating the Signed Package

Open any ACCDB database file, click the Office button, and select Publish ⇨ Sign and Package. The Select Certificate dialog box opens. After you select the certificate you wish to use to sign the package and click OK, you will be asked to provide a location for the package file as shown in Figure 22-21. (Remember the location for the signed package; you'll use it in the next section.)

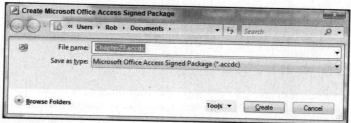

Figure 22-21

Click the Create button to save the package file. Access takes the database file and compresses it into a package with an ACCDC file extension. Then it signs the package file using the certificate you selected in the first step.

> Because the entire database is packaged, including the data, an ACCDC file repre-sents a digitally signed snapshot of the data at a certain point in time.

Creating the signed package file is only half of the process. The rest is to extract the database from the signed package.

Extracting the Signed Package

Once you have created the signed package, you can extract it simply by double-clicking it or by opening it in Access. When you do so, you see a familiar dialog box, as shown in Figure 22-22.

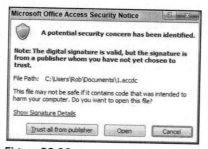

Figure 22-22

If you click Open or Trust All From Publisher, Access asks you to save the ACCDB file inside the package. This database file is not digitally signed, so will open in Disabled mode unless you extract it to a trusted location. The database file is no longer associated with the package file. If you change anything in the database, it will not be updated in the package.

Once the database is open, you can use it as you would any other database.

Access Database Engine Expression Service

The Expression Service has been a part of the Jet database engine for a long time. It is used whenever and wherever expressions are evaluated in Access and also it communicates with the VBA expression service. If you think about all the places in Access that can accept an expression, that's a lot! In terms of security, the surface area for expressions is quite large, so it was not feasible for Microsoft to add expressions to the digital signature for a database. The performance implications of scanning each entry point for an expression would have brought a database to its proverbial knees. (Databases don't really have knees.)

Microsoft takes security very seriously, and it's looking at its software for anything that provides an opportunity for someone to exploit it and maliciously attack your computer. You've seen how the Shell function could be used maliciously. So, how do you protect against an expression that can be misused?

The answer is by enhancing the sandbox mode for the Expression Service. Sandbox mode was first introduced in Jet 3.5 Service Pack 3 and Jet 4.0 Service Pack 1. That's right — for Access 97 and 2000. The enhancements made to the Expression Service for Access 2003 actually made expressions more usable than in previous versions. An enhanced sandbox mode was half of the overall security story for Access 2003. But this book is about Access 2007.

Sandbox Mode in Access 2007

When sandbox mode is enabled in the Registry, certain expressions cannot be executed from SQL queries or from expressions in controls, forms, reports, or macros.

The changes made to sandbox mode in Access 2007 are again by way of an improved user experience. The Expression Service is now installed to run in sandbox mode by default. In addition, interaction with sandbox mode has been simplified in that there is no longer a way to change it using the Access user interface. (It was tied to the macro security level in Access 2003.) Sandbox mode is still set in the Registry under HKEY_LOCAL_MACHINE, which means you must be an administrator on the computer to change the setting.

In addition to the other security enhancements already mentioned, Access 2007 always runs in sandbox mode unless the database is trusted. Even if you change the sandbox mode value in the Registry to turn it off, unsafe expressions are blocked unless the database is opened from a trusted location or has been explicitly enabled. The idea is that when a database is trusted, all content of the database is trusted including its expressions; until then, potentially malicious content, including expressions, is disabled.

Sandbox Mode Limitations

Sandbox mode blocks VBA functions or commands that could be harmful to a computer. (They're blocked by the Access database engine when they are executed from a SQL query or other expressions in controls, forms, reports, or macros.) Here's a list of functions that are blocked when sandbox mode is enabled:

AppActivate	GetAttr
Beep	GetObject
Calendar	GetSetting
CallByName	Input
ChDir	Input$
ChDrive	InputB
Command	InputB$
Command$	Kill
CreateObject	Load
CurDir	Loc
CurDir$	LOF
DeleteSetting	Randomize
DoEvents	Reset
Environ	SaveSetting
Environ$	Seek
EOF	SendKeys
Err	SetAttr
FileAttr	Shell
FileCopy	Spc
FileDateTime	Tab
FileLen	Unload
FreeFile	UserForms
GetAllSettings	Width

The Microsoft Knowledge Base has an excellent article that describes the sandbox mode as well as expressions that are blocked when the Sandbox is enabled at http://support.microsoft.com/kb/294698/. The article also describes how to adjust the sandbox mode by changing a setting in the Windows Registry, but note that the Registry key for Access 2007 has changed to:

```
HKEY_LOCAL_MACHINE\Software\Microsoft\Office\12.0\Access Connectivity
Engine\Engines\SandboxMode
```

If you decide to adjust the sandbox mode, be aware that the Access database engine may be used by services other than Access.

In addition to the functions listed in the table, some properties of ActiveX controls are also blocked. Standard properties such as Name, Value, and Tag are not blocked, but custom properties specific to the control — Day and Month on the Calendar control, for example — may be blocked.

Workarounds

The following sections describe some ways to work around the limitations imposed by sandbox mode in the Access database engine expression service.

Blocked Functions

If you attempt to call one of the functions in the preceding list from an SQL query, you receive a runtime error indicating that you have used an Unknown Function Name. Calling one of these functions from a control on a form or report displays a #Name? error.

The functions listed are not blocked when executed from your VBA code. So if it is necessary for you to execute one of these functions, you can define a Public function in your VBA code to call from your query, provided that code is enabled in the database.

For example, if you use the CurDir function as shown in this SQL statement:

```
SELECT CurDir() AS src FROM Customers;
```

you can write a Public function like this:

```
Public Function CurDir ()
    CurDir = VBA.CurDir()
End Function
```

Blocked Custom Properties of ActiveX Controls

If you need to access custom properties of an ActiveX control through the Access database engine, you can create a function as previously described. Alternatively, you can add the ActiveX control to a list of safe controls when your database is loaded or at any time before accessing the property of the control.

To register the control, call SysCmd 14, <ActiveX Control GUID>. Be careful to register only ActiveX controls that you are certain cannot do anything malicious.

Summary

Microsoft takes security seriously, and as a result it's created some nuisances for you to deal with. However, the nuisances aren't difficult. Sandbox mode helps protect you from malicious attacks on your computer by blocking some functions from SQL queries and other expressions. Because sandbox mode doesn't affect VBA, you can work around these protections by defining Public functions to execute from queries where necessary. You can also use `Public` functions or register ActiveX controls if the properties of those controls are blocked.

You can use the Office Trust Center and Disabled mode to protect you from malicious databases. Both features provide the capability to protect your users and yourself. Because of the power of Access and its increasingly widespread usage, this added protection is a good thing.

You can work around the security warnings in a variety of ways, including trusted locations, using Visual Basic scripts to start your databases or digitally signing the databases you publish. Yes, all this means more effort. But what price do you put on security? It's really a small price to pay for some very effective insurance.

Upgrading to Access 2007

This appendix is a compilation of data gleaned from a couple dozen papers, hours of testing with several versions of Access, and several years of experience — as well as information from other developers. It highlights some of the key considerations in making informed decisions and plans for converting to and working in mixed environments with Access 2007. It also provides some steps for embarking on a conversion process, and deals with concerns for special circumstances such as work group security or replication. It touches on some of the issues users face when converting from 2007 to earlier formats.

With the most dramatic addition of features and power in more than a decade, Access 2007 is designed to appeal to a wide spectrum of users and developers. The new user interface (UI) is more intuitive and can automate many of the tasks that previously either required programming or weren't practical to do. The new features empower users to easily gather and analyze data from multiple sources, including SQL Server, Excel, e-mail, and websites, and make it easier for developers to automate processes and to provide unprecedented flexibility for user-customized reports. It is now feasible to include attachments in the database, and the new file format (ACCDB) offers security through encryption of the data file. Those are just a few of the innovative features that will lure people to 2007.

What about the individuals, businesses, and enterprises that have existing applications? They need to develop a plan to address the issues related to migrating to 2007 and potentially for working in a mixed environment.

In the past, it was easier to be a slow adapter because the advantages of upgrading might not have compelled everyone to make the move. But now, when one leads, the masses quickly follow. As soon as one person begins to leverage the new features available with the ACCDB format, co-workers want (or demand) an equal opportunity. The bottom line is that the new features will enable people to make better decisions quicker. They not only will save time and money, but also will provide an entire new spectrum of methods for people to work with, integrate, and analyze data. And, thanks to the new wizards, managers, and objects, developers can design and deploy incredibly powerful custom solutions faster and more efficiently.

Because the most powerful new features are available only with the new ACCDB file format, there is a strong incentive for users to migrate their applications to 2007 `.accdb` files. But of course it isn't always feasible to move everyone at the same time. Even with a uniform deployment of Access 2007, people still need to know how to work with files from prior versions. Whether it is to work with others, link to data sources, or to pick up new code, there are a multitude of reasons to know how to safely open and use files of different versions and formats.

This appendix discusses converting and enabling Access applications so that you can work with multiple versions of Access; it isn't intended to be a technical reference for addressing the issues that are involved with running multiple versions of Access on the same computer.

To Convert or To Enable

You have several things to consider when deciding whether to convert an application to the new Access 2007 ACCDB format. The primary reason to convert is to take advantage of the powerful new features that require the ACCDB file format, such as the ability to work with complex data, the ease of collecting data from e-mail forms, and better integration with the web and SharePoint Services. To store complex data, Access 2007 includes a new system table, called MSsysComplexColumns, and a series of built-in table schema to automatically manage look-ups that would otherwise be many-to-many relationships. However, the ACCDB format cannot be linked to by an .mdb file, does not support replication (but offers an alternative), and does not work with group-level security (as implemented using the .mdw file. Access 2007 .mdb files will work with these features. So in a mixed version environment, keep in mind that although an .accdb file can link to or import from an .mdb file, the opposite is not true.

Speaking the Same Language

Before we delve into the decision criteria, let's be sure that we are speaking the same language. Words such as "upgrade," "migrate," "convert," and "enable" are sometimes used interchangeably. To make the discussion easier, here's how those words should be interpreted for the purposes of this appendix:

❑ **Upgrade:** You have Office and Access 2007 instead of some prior version. And, with purchases, "upgrade" is often associated with a discount based on owning a prior version. With this release, some of the documentation uses "upgrade" synonymously with "converting." But that isn't uniformly applied, so to avoid confusion, this appendix will limit the use of the term "upgrade."

❑ **Migrate:** The process of converting or enabling applications so that they can be used with newer versions of Access — in this case, Access 2007. It applies to scenarios in which you will be using Access 2007 and have some Access applications that were created in previous versions.

❑ **Convert:** The specific process that Access runs to change the database format from one version to another. Obviously, this appendix focuses on converting to the Access 2007 ACCDB format. Converting allows you to work with the database objects and to utilize the features of the specified version of Access, so by converting to the ACCDB format, your older applications can be enhanced to take advantage of the new complex data types, among other things.

❑ **Enable:** Enabling allows a newer version of Access to open a database created by a previous version of Access, but it does not change the file format. Because Access 2007 can work directly with Access 2000 and 2002 file formats, and pre-97 formats must be converted, only Access 97–format databases will be enabled. In some situations, the need to have older versions of Access using the database makes enabling the practical choice. For the purposes of this appendix, the term *enabling* refers to the fact that Access 2007 can open an Access 97 database without converting it. But if the file is enabled, users can only view and update data, they cannot modify objects, create new database objects, and so on.

Key Decision Factors

Now that we have established some common terminology, we can focus on the key factors for making the decisions about whether, when and how to enable and/or convert. A pivotal factor is whether the situation involves multiple versions of Access sharing the same data file or using the same application. Other key issues to consider include:

- ❑ Will any new features from Access 2007 be incorporated into the application and will they need to be instantly available to all users? This was specifically worded to prompt consideration of a staged migration that allows strategically timed deployment of the Access 2007 version by groups or by selected individuals.

- ❑ What file type do you have and what do you need? Keep in mind that an .mde file cannot be converted or enabled, so you will need to work with the original .mdb file.

- ❑ Are you working with user and group level security and an .mdw file?

- ❑ What version is the original application in, and what version is the data file?

- ❑ What time and resources are required to test and convert the applications? A quick cost/benefit analysis can help determine if it is appropriate, let alone necessary, to convert.

For the most part, it is very straightforward to either enable or convert a database to an Access 2007 ACCDB format. Of course, replacing user-level security will require extra steps. But if the situation warrants a secured database, it is well worth the effort because for the first time, Access offers data encryption. Special situations, such as replication, are handled differently. The Access 2007 ACCDB file format does not support replication; however, an easier and more robust alternative is available using the ACCDB format and SharePoint Services. If the current approach to user-level security and/or replication is critical to the operation, Access 2007 still supports those features when working with MDB file formats. Chapter 17 explains the new approach to both replication and user-lever security, and it is an excellent reference for working with Windows SharePoint Services. A few other features are not supported in Access 2007, such as working with Data Access Pages (DAPs). And, with the advent of the Ribbon, toolbars are not available unless specifically configured in the startup options. These types of issues are covered in more detail later in this appendix.

Barring the reliance on the few features that are no longer supported by Access 2007, an evaluation of the tradeoffs typically endorses the effort to convert. If you are considering some of the costs and time associated with rolling out a new version over a vast network, it can be very handy to have several options that include a mix of status quo, enabling, and converting. And, if you are responsible for making the decision about migrating or staying with earlier versions of Access, we strongly recommend that you focus on how Access 2007's new features can quickly recover the initial investment and improve the bottom line by enabling developers and users to accomplish work much more efficiently. So, managers, end users, and developers will all recognize the benefits of converting to 2007.

Before converting, you will definitely want to spend some time getting familiar with the various security features incorporated in Access 2007. Again, special consideration needs to be taken to address secured applications and replication. Although this appendix refers to various security features, it does not delve into the details. For help with security issues when upgrading, you should review the new security features that are highlighted in Chapters 18 and 22for both the 2007 .MDB and .ACCDB formats. There is also additional information available online, such as through MSDN and Microsoft Access Online Help.

Microsoft has also provided a tool to help evaluate and plan the migration process, the Office Migration Planning Manager (OMPM). The OMPM identifies and provides information about the databases on a network. It lists the files, their locations, format, size, and even the number of objects. If you are converting from Access 97, the OMPM will also identify some of the common issues that may be encountered. To get more information about the OMPM, visit Microsoft's TechNet site or search on Microsoft.com.

Feature Sets and File Extensions: What's New, What's Replaced, What Happens

Obviously, in a controlled environment where everyone will be using Access 2007, it would be a shame to not convert so that everyone can take advantage of the new features of the 2007 ACCDB format. If you think that the current application does everything that people are asking for, you may be wondering why you should bother converting. This might describe the ideal scenario for observing what has been called the "Oh" factor; one of the favorite reactions for developers to witness. Just wait until you see a user's astonishment the first time he clicks on a report control and has a form display the underlying data. "Oh, my gosh. What else can I do?" Users aren't asking for more because it wasn't available. But, give users the opportunity to utilize these tools and suddenly they are empowered to become true knowledge workers. If they are already using the new Office Ribbon in Word and other programs, they will appreciate the consistency of using it in Access as well. However, as we mentioned earlier, there are a few features from earlier versions that are not supported in Access 2007. For the most part, a better alternative has been provided. But, if an application is heavily dependent upon user/group permissions and security, on replications, or on working with selected legacy file types, it is best to establish and test a migration plan before attempting to convert in-service applications.

A brief discussion about deprecated features appears later in this appendix.

In addition to Access 2007's capability to open and even make design changes to 2000 and 2002-2003 .mdb files, it can also convert an .accdb to an .mdb file. With 2007, you can specify the file type so that it will work with the version of Access that will be opening it. However, Access will provide an error message and will not convert an .accdb that contains multi-value lookup fields, offline data, or attachments. With dozens of new features, it is reassuring to know that .mdb files will, for the most part, work as expected. The majority of the new features will be quietly ignored or will not appear when an Access 2007 .mdb file is opened with an earlier version of Access. Chapter 3 provides a rather extensive list of what's new in Access 2007. However, for the purposes of this appendix and discussion, you need to know the features that are available only with the 2007 ACCEB file format.

File Extensions

Office Access 2007 introduces a few new file extensions to work with the new file format. For backward compatibility, Access 2007 also works with the file extensions of .mdb, .mde, .ldb, and .mdw. The following table describes the Access file extensions for both ACCDB and MDB file formats.

Extension	Description
ACCDB	The extension for the new Access 2007 file format. This is the only file format that allows multi-value fields, attachments, data encryption, and some of the other new features. It's essentially the new version of the MDB file extension.
ACCDE	The extension for Access 2007 files that are "execute only". All VBA source code has been removed, so users can execute VBA code but not modify it, so they cannot make design changes to forms or reports. ACCDE is the new format that replaces the MDE file format.
ACCDT	The file extension for Access 2007 database templates. With the ADE, developers will be able to create their own database templates.
ACCDR	A new file extension that enables a database with an ACCDB format to open in runtime mode, You can essentially "lock-down" a database by simply changing the file extension from .accdb to .accdr,.And, you can restore full functionality just by changing the extension back to .accdb.
LACCDB and LDB	The Access 2007 .accdb format locking file. Access 2007 creates an .ldb file when opening an .mdb or .mde file.
MDW	The workgroup information file that stores information for secured databases with an MDB file format. Access 2007 .mdw files have the same file format as those created by Access 2000, 2002, and 2003, so the .mdw files created with any of these versions can be used with all four versions of Access .mdb and .mde files. The ACCDB file format does not recognize .mdw files.
MDB	The Access file format that allows previous versions of Access to open the file. Access 2007 can create or save as an .mdb file in either a 2000 or 2002-2003 format. Access 2007 also works with or converts files from Access 95 and Access 97.
MDE	"Execute Only" mode for the MDB file format. Access 2007 can work with MDEs that are in an Access 2000 or 2002-2003 file format. It can also create a .mde file from a .mdb file.

New Features Available Only with ACCDB File Format

The following features are available when using the 2007 ACCDB file format, but they are not accessible in MDBs. If an .mdb file is converted to an .accdb file, these features become available:

❑ **Multi-valued lookup fields:** Also referred to as complex data fields.

❑ **Attachment Date type:** Compresses data for storage within the database.

❑ **Compressed image storage for any Picture property:** Files are automatically compressed and do not cause database bloat.

❑ **Append Only Memo fields:** Provides history of changes to memo field data; also integrates with the append-only text fields in a SharePoint list.

❑ **Linked tables to files in an ACCDB format.**

❑ **Encrypt with database password:** This uses the Windows Crypto API to encrypt data, which provides stronger security than the work group administrator.

❑ **TempVars:** A new collection for storing global variables and unlike working with global variables in the past, the value of a TempVar is preserved even if the application triggers an error.

❑ **e-mail database as an attachment:** Code can be verified as safe or disabled so databases can integrate more fully with Outlook and SharePoint.

❑ **Built-in integration with Microsoft Office SharePoint Server 2007:** This includes the following:

   ❑ Full support for Linked tables

   ❑ Offline support for Linked tables, which allows for synchronizing data and can be a replacement for replication

   ❑ Leveraging SharePoint workflow management features

Features Not Available with Access 2007

There are only a few features that the Access 2007 ACCDB file format does not support. Typically a more robust alternative has been provided. Although some are still available if using a 2007 .mdb file, others can be achieved only programmatically or not at all. If you are relying on one of the deprecated features, it is likely that workarounds are or soon will be available.

The following features are no longer available in Access 2007:

❑ **Data Access Pages (DAPs):** Access 2007 will list DAP files in the Navigation Pane, but it will default to use Internet Explorer to open a DAP. Even that will require that the correct version of Web Components is also installed. Access 2000 DAPs require that you have Office 2000 Web Components installed and Access 2002 and Access 2003 DAPs require Office XP Web Components. Because DAPs utilize Active X technology, they did not provide the features that customers needed and they could expose users to undue security risks. It is now much easier and more secure to exchange data over the Internet and intranet using SharePoint, InfoPath, Outlook, and other services.

❑ **Microsoft Office XP Web Components:** These components are not installed with Office Access 2007. Forms in PivotTable or PivotChart view still function correctly, but you may need to set the references or download and install the Microsoft Office XP Web Components. Databases with references to OWC10.DLL will automatically point to the new OFFOWC.DLL, which does not support all of the functionality in OWC10.DLL.

❑ **Replication:** Replication is not supported by the ACCDB file format. However, SharePoint Services offers more flexibility and options for both synchronizing data and version control. Access 2007 can replicate an .mdb file.

❑ **MDW:** The work group administrator and MDW files are not supported by theACCDB file format. However, Access 2007 MDB files work with MDW files from Access 2000 through 2003. As an alternative, user and group permissions can be derived through SharePoint Services when working with the new ACCDB file format. User and group permissions can also be managed through add-ins and custom coding, such as by integrating the user with the Windows sign-on. Although it does not provide user-level permissions, the ACCDB file format offers a strong security option that provides data encryption and uses a database password.

❑   **The UI for import and export in older formats:** The UI has been removed, but the existing code and macros should continue to work and new interfaces can be created programmatically. The import and/or export UI has been removed for Lotus 1-2-3/DOS (*.wj*), Exchange, ASP, and IDC/HTX. Import and export options have been added for more current programs and the user has more control over the import specifications.

What Happens When a 2007 MDB Is Opened by 2000+

Access 2007 has a multitude of new features for both the MDB and ACCDB file formats. When working with multiple versions of Access, trying to keep track of what will work can get rather confusing. The following table lists the new features and how they will behave in prior versions of Access. New features for Access 2007 .mdb filess are also available for .accdb files, but the reverse is not always true; features that are available for 2007 .accdb files but not for 2007 .mdb files are denoted by the statement "Not available to .mdb files; only available in ACCDB file format."

2007 New Feature	Behavior in Access 2000, 2002, and 2003
ACCDB file format	Cannot be opened.
Access security and the Trust Center	Prompts with security warnings and does not have the capability to trust a file based on its location.
Alternating row color (alternate Back Color property)	All rows appear the same color as the first row. Alternate Back Color property is ignored.
Append-only memo fields	Not available to .mdb files; available only in ACCDB file format.
Attachments	Not available to .mdb files; available only in ACCDB file format.
Complex data	Not available to .mdb files; available only in ACCDB file format.
Control auto-resize and anchoring	Controls do not automatically resize or move.
Control layouts (stacked and tabular)	Behave like independent controls.
Create data collection e-mail	Older versions have no option to create or manage data collection e-mail.
Creating schema in the datasheet	Schema must be created in table design.
Custom groups in the navigation pane	Navigation Pane converts to the database window, but custom groups are lost.
Customizable caption for the record navigation user interface	Always appears as Record.
Data Source task pane	Field list floating dialog box.
Database templates	Cannot be opened.
Datasheet user interface enhancements	Record selectors and selection.

Table continues on next page

2007 New Feature	Behavior in Access 2000, 2002, and 2003
Date picker	Does not appear.
Design in browse mode for forms and reports	Design via the property sheet only.
Edit list items command for combo boxes and list boxes	Does not appear.
Editable value lists	Value lists do not have a user interface for editing and are not automatically inherited from the table.
Encrypt with database password	Not available to .mdb files; available only in ACCDB file format.
Filtering and sorting improvements	Previous filtering and sorting user interface.
Getting Started experience	Getting Started task pane.
Gridlines on layouts	No gridlines appear.
Improved accessibility	Datasheet, forms, and reports do not have the same support for accessibility aides.
Linked tables to ACCDBs	Cannot link to .accdb files. Available only in ACCDB file format.
Linked tables to Excel 12 files	Linked tables to Excel 12 cannot be opened.
Linked tables to Windows SharePoint Services V3	Not all data types are fully supported. Some columns may be read-only or might not appear.
Macros embedded in event properties	Event properties appear to be blank.
Manage data collection replies	Does not appear.
Navigation pane	Database container.
New Sorting and Grouping task pane	Sorting and grouping dialog box.
Office Center for Options	Separate dialog boxes for Options, Startup, and AutoCorrect.
Offline support for Linked Tables to Windows SharePoint Services	MDBS cannot link to SharePoint tables. This is available in ACCDB file format only.
Property Sheet task pane	Property sheet floating dialog box.
Report Browse mode	Print Preview only.
Ribbon	Command bars.
Ribbon customizations	Does not appear.
Rich text	Appears as plain text with HTML tags.
Save Database As	Can convert to and from older file formats, but cannot convert to a 2007 file format.

2007 New Feature	Behavior in Access 2000, 2002, and 2003
Saved imports and exports	Only the import and export specifications supported in the older format will be converted and available.
Search box in record navigation user interface	Does not appear.
Share database on SharePoint	Does not appear.
SharePoint Site Manager	Does not appear.
Split views	Appears as a single item form.
Tabbed document mode (SDI)	Multiple windows (MDI).
Tables and Views mode	Does not appear.
Upsize database to SharePoint	Does not appear.

Other Things to Consider

As with most projects, there are a lot of incidentals that you'll need to consider, such as converting a functional app, maintaining references, sharing data files, splitting databases, locking files, running multiple versions of Access, and working with SQL Server in new ways. Before a file is converted, the code should be compiled, so those steps are included below

If It Ain't Broke

Everyone seems happy with what they have, so why rock the boat? Users weren't asking for more because it wasn't available. But, give them the opportunity to customize their reports and drill into the underlying data, and suddenly you have empowered them to become true knowledge workers. If they are already using the new Office Ribbon in Word and other programs, then they will appreciate the consistency of having it available in Access as well.

Of course, there are those limited situations in which an application uses a feature that is not available with the ACCDB file format. If the replacement feature isn't an acceptable alternative, then enhancing may be the appropriate solution. Keep in mind that it is acceptable to convert some applications and enhance others. It is also feasible to convert an application for some users while others work with an original version of the same application. In that situation, the shared data files would need to remain in an .mdb file or in a compatible format.

VBA References

As in the past, it is best to have the VBA references match the version of Access that is opening the application and match the version of the programs that they are referencing. However, if the application will be opened by multiple versions of Access, it is a good practice to set references and test the database on the oldest version of Access, Office, and Windows that will use it. It's that backwards compatibility issue. Although newer versions can work with previous versions of a type library, older versions may not recognize new type libraries, which may cause an error message. When that happens, you have to manually set the references to the version of Office applications that are installed on the particular computer.

> When working with multiple versions of Office, it is a good practice to set references and test the database on the oldest version of Access, Office, and Windows that will use it.

Keep in mind that when you make design changes in an application, the references will automatically be updated to the version of Office that is installed on the computer. So, if an application references other Office applications and design changes are made in an Office 2007 environment, the references will need to be changed before the application will work for Office 2003 and earlier version. Be aware that depending on the references, the version of Windows might also require a reference fix. Thankfully, that isn't always the case because many Access applications do not reference other Office programs.

If an application contains VBA using DAO, it may be necessary to check the references and ensure that DAO (typically DAO3.6 Object Library) is listed above ADO (ActiveX Data Objects). ADO and DAO are covered extensively in Chapters 6 and 7 with reference material in other appendixes. You'll recall the benefits of including the Option Explicit statement at the beginning of your code modules to avoid ambiguity.

Shared Data Files

A 2007 .accdb application can open and work with multiple data files and file formats, including those with ACCDB and MDB file formats. But that is fairly standard for backwards compatibility. When linking to tables, it is important to remember that the data file must have the file format of the oldest version of Access that will open it. For .mdb files that could be 2000, 2002-2003 or 2003 file formats — 95 and 97 are special cases. Access 2007 allows users to open previous files and save them in a specified file format.

Splitting a Database

Speaking of shared data files prompts a discussion of splitting the database, or moving the tables to their own file. It's not uncommon to initiate the database design with the tables in the same file as the other objects. And although it works fine to keep it that way for small, single-user applications, it isn't advisable for larger applications or for shared files. Although an application can allow simultaneous use by multiple users, that can lead to significant performance and corruption issues. The easy way to avoid this is to split the database and have multiple front ends sharing one back-end data file.

Access 2007 will split database files with Access 2000 and Access 2002-2003 formats. Be sure to create a copy of the file before initiating this process. The newly created back-end file will be in the same format as the original file, so if all users are moving to a newer version of Access, it can be helpful to convert the database first. However, if the data file will need to support an older version of Access, it is important to separate the tables before converting. The tables need to be in the format of the oldest version of Access that will use them. Splitting the database will not preserve password protection, so that would need to be added to the newly created back-end file if a password is desired.

> Splitting your databases is strongly recommended under all but the most simplistic single-user situations.

Here's how to split a single database into front-end (UI) and back-end (data) files:

1. Open the database with Access 2007.

2. On the menu bar, click Database Tools.

3. From the Move Data group, click Access Database to initiate a wizard.

4. Follow the instructions of the wizard as it offers the opportunity to browse to the desired folder location and to name the new back-end database.

After the database has been converted, it is reassuring to confirm that the tables are correctly linked. You can do this by hovering over the tables and reading the path from the fly-out sheet or by using the Linked Table Manager.

Now, if you want to create multiple versions of the database, you will be converting only the front end. You can convert the front-end file to whatever versions of Access that users will need. All of the front-end files can be linked to the back-end (data) file that was just created.

> If multiple versions of Access will be linking to the resulting data file, the data file should be created in or converted to the oldest file format.

Locking Files

When a database is opened, it uses a separate locking file to control file and record locking. The locking files specific to a database is shared by all users that open that database file. The filenames are the same as the original file, but the filename extension will start with an "l." Access creates an .1db file for .mdb and .mde files and creates an .1accdb file for .accdb, .accde, and .accdr files. Locking files are deleted automatically when the last user has closed the database file.

As in the past, it is possible for Access 2007 to have multiple applications open at the same time. In fact, it can also open both the .mdb and .accdb version of the same application. In other words, if db1.accdb has been converted to db1.mdb and both files are on the same computer, both files could be open simultaneously and they could even run exclusively because they would create two different locking files, db1.1accdb and db1.1db. Logically, it follows that there would be only one data file, db1Data.mdb and the associated locking file db1Data.1db would be shared by both front-end applications.

Having multiple users sharing the same data file is the basis for some of the most powerful benefits that Access provides. It is a best practice, however, to not share front-end applications. This is an important point that is worth reiterating. An application (the front-end file) with simultaneous multiple users will suffer both in performance and reliability and it has an increased risk of experiencing data corruption.

Working with SQL Server

Access 2007 offers more power and flexibility for connecting with SQL server files. If you are working with SQL Server, this benefit alone might warrant migrating. Access 2007 can connect to SQL Server data by linking and by using Access Data Projects (ADPs). Because both 2007 file formats (MDB and ACCDB) can create read/write linked tables to SQL Server tables or views, linking is typically the preferred method for connecting to SQL Server. Linking allows the full flexibility of using local tables and queries for record sources while leveraging the capacity of SQL Server.

Most of the new features for Access 2007 are available in both MDB and ACCDB file formats; however, ADP files benefit from only a few of the new features. So, there are a few key factors to consider when determining whether to use linked tables or ADP files when you enable or convert. Linking provides the ability to connect to multiple SQL Servers, .mdb and .accdb files, and local tables, along with other data sources, such as SharePoint and Excel. Linking also allows the use of local and ad hoc queries, which Jet will optimize so that SQL Server will do as much of the processing as possible. On the flip side, linking does not allow table modification. It requires an ADP file or SQL Server's Enterprise Manager to make schema or design changes to SQL Server files.

This discussion is intended only to highlight decision factor criteria. If you are working with SQL Server, you'll want to review Chapter 19 on client server development.

Compiling the Code

Along with making a copy of the file, it is a good practice to be sure that code is compiled before initiating major changes. Not all applications or files have code, but most front-end applications do. Compiling will essentially clean up and compact the code. It identifies but does not fix errors. So if there are problems, you may need to debug the code before proceeding.

Use the Visual Basic Editor (VBE) to compact the code:

1. Open the VBE (press Alt+F11 or click the Visual Basic button on the Database Tools tab).
2. On the menu bar, click Debug.
3. Click the first option, which is Compile *(current filename)*.

Ideally, everything works fine and there is nothing to debug. With small files it can be so fast that you don't know anything happened until you again click on the Debug menu and see that Compile is grayed out, indicating that the code is compiled. In addition to compiling the code, closing the windows can help improve performance. In complex applications, there can be dozens or even hundreds of windows.

Installing Multiple Versions of Access on One PC

As a developer, you are likely to need to work with multiple versions of Access at the same time and even for the same application. In the past, it was typical to use a different PC for each version. Although this avoided conflicts with DLLs, it took a toll on resources and space. Thankfully, reliable options are now more affordable. Two of the popular options are to use Virtual PC or to have side-by-side installations of selected programs.

With the new processors and hard drives, many machines have the space and capacity to run multiple versions of software. Of course, now that Virtual PC is free, it's usually recommend that you use that for loading temporary or test software. Virtual PC reduces the risk to the production environment, but it can be a bit of a resource hog. So we recommend *Actual PC*. Because we seem to routinely upgrade and replace hardware, it's a great way to put the old boxes to use. Both of those approaches essentially isolate the operating systems and software so the various versions do not conflict with each other.

There are some general guidelines for installing multiple versions of Access directly onto one computer, also known as running side-by-side. First, be sure to install the oldest version first, and although some people recommend that you not skip versions, others are successfully working with only the versions to be used. Second, if you are installing from an Office Suite instead of a standalone copy of Access, select a custom Office installation and install only Access — and while you're at it, install all of the features that might be used. It can be rather frustrating to have to stop in the middle of a process to get the CD and install more features.

> *Be aware that because Access 2007 is brand new, there may be some glitches in running it side-by-side with previous Access versions.*

After installing the versions of Access that you need, you may want to set up shortcuts with icons that clearly denote which version it opens. Oh, and a lot of developers would recommend making an image of the OS and software configuration. This makes it fast and easy to re-install and get back to work, be it from a test configuration, a crash, or just a change in preferences.

Changing File Formats

Before actually converting or enabling older files, it would be good to know how to work with the various file types in Access 2007. A good place to start is to specify the default file format. And, since we all agree that the data should not be in the front-end or application file, we'll also tell you how to split the database. Because earlier files could be .mde files or runtime applications, we figured it would also be handy to have the steps for creating these file types in Access 2007.

Selecting the Access 2007 Default File Format

For Access 2007, the default file format is ACCDB. But, if most of the files will be used by prior versions of Access, it might be best to specify a 2000 or 2002-2003 MDB as the default file format. It is easy to set the default file format. And, if you need to specify a different file type, it takes only a couple of extra clicks to override the default selection.

Setting the default file format is accomplished in a few easy steps.

1. Open Access 2007, but don't open a file.
2. On the Ribbon, click the Microsoft Office Button.
3. Click Access Options, a button at the bottom right of the fly-out.
4. In the left pane of the Access Options dialog box, click Popular.
5. Under Creating Databases, in the Default File Format box, select the preferred default file format.
6. Click OK.

Of course, you probably want to confirm that the settings were saved as expected. One quick verification is to initiate the process for creating a new database. That opens a pane on the right and provides a default name for the file. Clicking the folder to the right of the filename opens the New Database File dialog box. The line Save As Type will display the default file format, including the version and extension, such as 2002-2003 format (*.mdb).

Overriding the Default File Format

Say the default is to create `.accdb` files, but you want to create a new `.mdb` file. This is easily done by specifying the file format when the database is created. By selecting the correct format before doing the design work, you can minimize the possibility for conflicts later on.

To override the default file format when creating a new database, choose to create a `New Blank Database`. That opens a pane on the right to get the database name and file type.

1. Type a name for the new database in the File Name box.

2. Click the yellow folder next to the File Name box to open the New Database File dialog box.

3. Accept or select a different folder location and filename.

4. Select the file format that you want in the Save As Type drop-down list. Specify 2000 mdb, 2002-2003 mdb, 2007 accdb, or adp.

5. Click OK.

That's essentially all it takes to save a file in both the `.accdb` and `.mdb` file formats. Of course, when going from `.accdb` to `.mdb`, some features will not be available. And if the file has multi-value fields, SharePoint offline data, or attachments, Access will provide an error message and not convert the file.

ACCDE and MDE Files

Access 2007 will create either an `.mde` or an `.accde` file, depending on which file type is open. Both files compile and lock down the code, so it cannot be viewed or modified. Any future changes have to be made to the originating `.mdb` or `.accdb` file and then a new `.accde` or `.mde` file will need to be created. Because the steps are essentially the same, this section will only provide the steps for creating an `.accde` file.

It takes just six steps to create an ACCDE file in Office Access 2007.

1. Use Access 2007 to open the database that you want to save as an `.accde` file.

2. On the Database Tools tab, select the Database Tools group.

3. Click Make ACCDE.

4. In the Save As dialog box, browse to the folder to save the file.

5. In the File Name box, type the filename.

6. Click Save.

ACCDR Runtime Files

Access 2007 will also support runtime mode. This "locked down" version limits users' access to commands and to make design changes. In the past, a command line switch would tell Access to open in runtime mode. With the new Jet and the ACCDB file format, switching to a runtime format is even easier, because all it requires is changing the file extension to `.accdr`. To return to the full-feature environment, merely change the file extension back to `.accdb`. Of course, this still requires either a full installation of

Access 2007 or a runtime installation. And, now that the Access Runtime is a free download from Microsoft, we may see a lot more deployments using a runtime file instead of the requiring the full version of Access.

Steps for Converting or Enabling

For the most part, this section will focus on migrating to Access 2007. However, if an Access 2007 application will be used by prior versions of Access, it will also be important to know how to create a compatible file. Access 2007 makes this relatively easy and straightforward. Note the qualification, *relatively*, which based on the inclination to include a caveat about references and VBA. These steps do not check or fix broken references, they don't test and debug code, they don't replace custom menus and toolbars, and they don't do a lot of other things that you will need to manage when converting your Access solutions. However, they do provide important guidance about the issues to consider and they guide you through the steps for converting a database.

File Conversion Using Access 2007: A One-Stop Shop

Access 2007 has essentially one process to manage database conversion. With just a few clicks, a copy of a database can be created to be compatible with and used by multiple versions of Access. This is definitely a time to appreciate simplicity because the process is as easy as changing a picture from a 5MB BMP to a 300KB JPG.

In addition to converting to and from the `.ACCDB` file format, Access 2007 will convert to and from `.mdb` files with 2000 and 2002-2003 formats. There are extra steps and considerations for working with 95 and 97 file formats. Because Access creates and converts a copy of the original file, you will be ready to work with both applications. When converting a database, all database objects need to be closed. If any are open, Access prompts for them to be closed — and even to save changes — before creating a copy of the database.

After you resolve support issues such as feature deprecation, ribbons and toolbars, references, and code, it is time to make the switch. As in the past, we recommend that you compile the database before you convert it. This extra step is certainly worth the time because it reduces the possibility of errors during conversion. Keep in mind that conversion is a low-risk process because Access creates a copy of the file. So the original is preserved and you can quickly start again. If you have an existing database that you want to convert to a different format, you can choose a format under the Save Database As command. Just follow these steps:

1. Use Access 2007 to open the database that you want to convert.

2. Click the Microsoft Office button.

3. Hover over Save As to view and select from the fly-out menu, which has options to save objects or databases. In the section Save The Database In Another Format, select the desired file format.

4. The Save As dialog opens. Enter the filename in the File Name text box (or use the existing name). To save the file in a different location, browse to the folder you want. The file type is already specified.

5. Click Save; Access creates a copy as specified. Depending on the size of the file, this can take a few moments.

6. When the conversion is completed, a dialog box advises you that the file cannot be shared with prior versions of Access. Click OK.

7. The new file opens in Access 2007.

Other Considerations When Converting

Keep in mind that saving to a different file format is only a small part of the process. As already discussed, there may be issues involving code, references, macros, security, and integrating with other applications. Moving to newer versions is certainly easier than moving backward. Newer features may be lost or have only part of their functionality. Custom features may not be recognized or implemented as expected. Despite those concerns, it is certainly handy to have the ability to save a file in an older format when it's needed.

And, what about times that only some of objects are needed? Instead of converting an entire database, there is also the option of importing database objects into an Access 2007 file, either an .mdb or .accdb format. This process does not automatically import references to libraries, so the references may need to be set in the new Access file.

When converting a database that contains linked tables, it is a good practice to ensure that the linked tables are still in the location specified in the Table *properties. Using the Linked Table Manager to relink to the current tables is a fast, easy way to refresh or update the links. After the database has been converted, the tables can be moved and the Linked Table Manager can be used to relink to the tables in their new location.*

To convert a database, it must be closed, meaning that no users can be accessing the database, and you essentially need to have the equivalent of Administrator permissions for the database. Fortunately, the default mode for an unsecured database is for users to have these permissions. There will be more about permissions in the section on converting a secured database, which is discussed later in this appendix.

Converting to Access 97 Is a Two-Version Process

Rather than converting a 2007 file to work with Access 97, consider converting all Access 97 applications to the 2002-2003 file format if at all possible. If the situation demands that the files be converted to Access 97, keep in mind two import factors:

❑ Microsoft no longer supports Access 97, although technical support is still available from a dwindling percentage of developers.

❑ Access 97 does not support Unicode, so there will be issues if the databases contain Unicode data, including Asian and Complex Script languages.

To convert an Access 2007 database to Access 97, you first need to convert it to an intermediate version (2000 or 2002-2003) and then use that file and version to convert to an Access 97 file. Since we've already covered converting from 2007 to 2003, you can use the following steps to convert from Access 200 to Access 97.

1. Convert the file to 2003, as described earlier in the section "File Conversion Using Access 2007: A One-Stop Shop." And because it's a good practice, make a copy of the new MDB file.

2.   Open Access 2003.

3.   Log on to the new database with Open/Run and Open Exclusive permission for the database and Read/Design permission for all of the database objects.

4.   If the code is password protected, remove that protection before initiating the conversion process. The fastest way is to use Alt+F11 to open the IDE to the VBE window. On the Visual Basic menu, select Tools ⇨ Properties. The password dialog box opens. Enter the password, and click OK. The Project Properties dialog box opens. Click the Protection tab, clear the Lock Project For Viewing checkbox, and remove the password from the Password and Confirm Password lines. Click OK to close the dialog box. Close the VBE window and return to Access.

5.   Select Tools ⇨ Database Utilities ⇨ Convert Database, and then select To Access 97 File Format.

6.   In the Convert Database Into dialog box, enter a new name for the converted (97) database, and click Save.

Access 2007 will be able to open the new 97 database and users may enter data. However, all design changes will require Access 97. Additionally, the data file will also need to be converted to Access 97.

Converting a Secured Database

The Access 2007 ACCDB file format offers data encryption using a database password, but it does not support user-level security and using the workgroup information manager. User-level security will be removed as the file is converted to the 2007 ACCDB file format. So, if the application has complex user-level security features that you need to continue using, the database must remain as an .mdb or .mde file. In that case you're home free, at least as for this part.

As security issues have become more critical and complex, new ways have been developed to protect the data and the application while making it easier for users to work with diverse and remote sources. To learn more about Access security features and options, please read Chapter 18, which provides detailed information about creating and working with workgroup information files (WIFs). You'll also benefit from understanding macro security and trust centers, which are covered in Chapter 22.

So after considering the options, you've decided to shed the user/group security (.mdw file)and take advantage of the benefits offered by the ACCDB format. Switching to the new format removes user-level security from the file(s). Access will automatically remove the security settings so you can start clean when applying security and interface controls to the new .accdb or .accde file. Keep in mind that if user-level security were controlling the capability to enter, change, or view certain information, those controls are not provided in the new .accdb file.

> *It's almost scary that it is so easy to remove user-level security, which not only limited who could open a file, but what data they could see or change. It will be important to have a plan for replacing the security and control features before converting a database relying on user-level security.*

To convert the database, use Access 2007 to log in to the database as a user with full administrative permissions for all database objects. Then, follow the steps in the "Changing File Formats" section earlier in the appendix. After the file is converted, close the application and Access. The new .accdb file will open without requiring a password. However if the application has custom user login features, those will still be enabled. And, if macros weren't already addressed, they will need to be enabled. It can be quite a surprise to think that a file is open but nothing shows up. If that occurs, look for an information bar regarding enabling macros. One click may have everything working smoothly.

Chapter 22 is all about macro security.

Converting a Password-Protected Database

If a database is password protected, the password protection must be removed before the database can be converted. Here's what to do:

1. Open Access 2007 and click the Microsoft Office button.

2. Click Open and browse to the target database.

3. Select the target database.

4. Click the drop-down arrow to the right of the Open button.

5. Select Open Exclusive.

6. In the Password Required dialog box, provide the database password and click OK. The database opens in exclusive mode, which enables you to remove the database password requirement.

7. In the Database Tools Group on the Database Tools tab, select Unset Database Password.

8. Type the password into the dialog box and click OK.

The password has been removed and the database can now be converted:

1. Click the Microsoft Office button,

2. Click Convert. The Save As dialog box opens.

3. Provide the folder location and filename, and click Save. A message box indicates that the file has been converted and can no longer be shared with earlier versions of Access.

Keep in mind that unless other measures have been implanted, the file no longer has security so anyone who opens it has full access to the data and to the database objects themselves.

Converting a Database with Password-Protected VBA

Password protection on the VBA does not affect logging in to the database itself, so the conversion process follows the same steps listed earlier in the section "File Conversion Using Access 2007: A One-Stop Shop." Unlike the experience using Access 2003 to convert a database with password-protected VBA, the password is not required to convert to 2007. With 2007, the file is converted and the password preserved. The password will still be required to view or work with code. However, even if the VBA is secured, you will still be able to work with macros because they are in the Access file instead of in the VBA project.

There are mixed opinions about using a password to protect the code. Many developers think that such password protection is more prone to corruption or being locked out of the code, and they prefer to use an .mde *file (now an* .accde *file).*

Converting a Replicated Database

Replication is not supported in the ACCDB file format. Instead, a more powerful and versatile alternative is offered using SharePoint services. Because Access 2007 will work with replicated Access 2000 and 2002–2003 .mdb files, there's no need to convert the files to essentially maintain a status quo. In some cases, however, the benefits of converting to the ACCDB file format will outweigh the benefits derived from replication. The following outlines the process for essentially creating a new database. (Before making any changes, save copies of the files and datasets.)

> *It's best to work with a copy of the Design Master after it has been fully synchronized, but the same process could be used with a replica. The key is that only the data and projects that are in the file that you convert will be in the new* .accdb *file. That should have set off an alert for how important it is to use the fully synchronized Design Master.*

Here are some guidelines to note before you begin:

❑ Hidden and System objects in the replica must be visible so you can access the fields when you are re-creating the database.

❑ Creating a copy of the database requires both Access 2007 and the version of Access that created the replica.

❑ Make interim copies as you proceed and allow plenty of time and patience for testing and adding features.

In general, the process is to use the original version of Access to display the hidden and system objects in the replica file, and then use Access 2007 to create the new application by importing the objects, except for the tables. The tables will be created using Make Table queries.

You will need to use the original version of Access to follow these steps.

1. Open the replica, preferably the Design Master.
2. Select Tools ➪ Options on the menu bar. The Options dialog box opens.
3. On the View tab, be sure Hidden Objects and System Objects are both selected (checked).
4. Click OK to save the changes.
5. Close the database and Access. The file is now ready for the objects to be imported into a new container.

Open Access 2007 and ensure that the default file format is ACCDB. Follow these steps to create a copy of the replica:

1. Create a new blank database by selecting Blank Database and providing a filename. Be sure to accept or select the ACCDB format, and then click Create.
2. Delete the default Table1 by closing it.
3. In the Import group on the External Data tab, click Access. The Get External Data dialog box opens.
4. Browse to the folder containing the prepared replica file and select it by either double-clicking or selecting the file and then clicking Open. This returns you to the Get External Data dialog box.

5. Ensure that that you have selected: Import Tables, Queries, Forms Reports, Macros And Modules In The Current Database, and then click OK. The Import Objects window will then open.

6. On each tab, select the objects that you want to import. (If you want all of the objects, use the Select All button on each tab.) When all of the desired objects are selected, click OK. The wizard will import the objects and then offer the opportunity to save the import steps.

   Selecting Yes enables you to give the process a name and description. If this import process will be repeated on a regular basis, it could even be scheduled as an Outlook task. After filling in the information, click Save Import. The Import Objects window will then close.

7. All the objects except for the tables are imported. Name and save the database.

8. Open another instance of Access 2007 and open the prepared replica database.

9. In the Other group on the Create tab, click Query Design. This opens a new query in Design view.

10. Select the first table from the list, and click Add and then Close. The table is added to the query design window. Double-click the table's title bar to select all the fields, and then drag and drop the fields into the query grid. Although you don't want the s_Lineage and s_Generation fields in the new tables, the most efficient way to accomplish the task is to drag all of the fields into the query grid and then delete these two fields.

11. Click Make Table Query. In the Make Table dialog box, select the current table's name and then select Another Database. Browse to and select the newly created .accdb. Click OK.

12. Click Run to create the table in the new database.

   If s_GUID is the primary key and it is referred to by other tables' foreign keys, then the s_GUID must be included in the new tables. If s_GUID is not used to establish relationships between tables, it is not needed in the new tables.

The new tables do not inherit the field properties or the primary key settings from the original database. Those need to be manually re-created:

1. Open a table in Design view. In the field list, select the field that should be the primary key, and then click Primary Key in the Tools group.

2. In the field list, select the field that requires an index. In the field's Properties pane, click the Indexed drop-down and select either YES (Duplicates OK) or YES (No Duplicates). Continue this procedure through all the tables.

Finally, establish the table relationships as they were in the replica:

1. Click Relationships on the Database Tools tab.

2. Add the appropriate tables to the relationships window.

3. Drag a field from one table to another to create the relationship between the tables based on those two fields. The Edit Relationships dialog box enables you to enforce referential integrity and to specify a join type. When the relationships are established, click Close to close the window and return to the database objects.

4. Save and close the database. Make a copy and start testing.

It is a good practice to split the database, either now or as soon as it is functioning properly.

Enabling a Database

As mentioned earlier, Access 2007 can work with Access 95 and 97 files. Basically, there are two options for working with the file: convert it or enable it. Converting creates a copy of the file in a newer format, as discussed earlier. To work with the file without converting it requires enabling the database.

There are some logical limitations when working with an enabled database. Considering that databases are not forward compatible, it makes sense that although you can use Access 2007 to work with an Access 97 file, you cannot use an Access 97 file to link to a table in an Access 2000 or newer database. Access 2007 will not convert a file to an Access 97 or 95 format. However, you can export the tables to an Access 97 file. You can also move or copy data from a table and paste it directly into a table in a prior-version database.

Other concerns deal with the file format, mostly because features of the new file formats were not available or supported in Access 97. For example, data that relied on Unicode compression may not convert correctly. And because Access 97 had a 256-character set, it may not have equivalent characters for some of the characters in the new format. Also, the `Decimal FieldSize` property for `Number` fields was not available in 97. This property must be changed prior to conversion. Typical alternatives include `Single` or `Double` or changing the data type to `Currency`.

Enabling the Experience: Opening 95 or 97 Files with Access 2007

When Access 2007 opens an Access 95 or 97 file, it displays the Database Enablement dialog box. This might be perceived as a polite way of encouraging users to convert (termed upgrade in this dialog box) the database so that it can take advantage of the new features. If you choose to Proceed With Enablement, Access 2007 will convert the file to the specified file format. Considering the age of the file, it is likely that it would benefit from a thorough review of the code and some additional features. If the database is not enabled, Access 2007 can still open the file and update records, but users will not be able to make any design changes. Remember that a data file cannot be converted if older applications (front-end files) will be using it.

To enable the database, follow these steps:

1. Open Access 2007 and then click on a 95 or 97 `.mdb` file. The Database Enablement dialog box opens.

2. Click Yes, and the Save As dialog box opens.

3. Accept the default file location and filename or select the ones desired.

4. The enablement process will convert files to the default file format. However, the file format can easily be changed after the new file has been saved.

If errors are encountered, a message box will advise you that a table of conversion errors has been created. Here's an example of what you might see:

```
-3831: The current file format no longer supports user-level security. The
conversion or compaction process has removed any user-level permissions.
```

For those rare situations in which users still require a 95 or 97 file format, the only option is to enable the file. Enabling the database will let Access 2007 use the file but is the file will still compatible with Access 95 and 97. It is remarkably easy, just:

1.   Open Access 2007 and select a 95 or 97 .mdb file. The Database Enablement dialog box opens.

2.   Click No. The file will open in the Access 97 file format.

This works well for entering data and for connecting to a data file used by Access 97. The objects can be seen in Design view and the VBE will display the code. Users can even make temporary modifications to objects, such as adding a text box to a form. However, when the object is closed, the design changes will not be saved.

References for Projects

Throughout this book you have seen type libraries or object libraries, such as those described in Chapter 16, used to enhance functionality through VBA code. You know how libraries can provide access to functions that manipulate the Windows System Registry or retrieve and send data to other applications.

In addition to using libraries supplied with Microsoft Office, you can acquire type libraries to help simplify a variety of programming tasks. Like Microsoft Office libraries, other vendors' libraries provide classes to manipulate objects — the QuickBooks libraries provided in QuickBooks Software Development Kit (SDK), for example. These libraries provide classes you can use to create objects that contain data that is returned from a QuickBooks data file through an XML access method.

Acquiring libraries can be a cost-effective way to get more work done in less time. Of course, there's always the tradeoff between what you pay for a library and the exertion that may be required to learn how to use it, and the time and effort you spend writing your own functions. And don't forget the effort you have already put into writing your own code. After all of the "bold, test, and swears" you put into your routines, you really must consider creating code libraries from your code.

This appendix describes techniques for using references to libraries in your projects, including how to reference libraries provided by others and why the order of your reference list can be important. It also discusses the types of libraries available (DLLs and ActiveX controls, for example).

This appendix also discusses procedures for referring to the `References` class and why you would want to. It describes some correct techniques for writing code that will go into your own code libraries. And it suggests ways to avoid getting missing libraries and what to do when they go missing.

Types of References

You can add references to many types of libraries from your Access projects. Library types include the following: type or object libraries (OLB, TLB, and DLL), ActiveX controls (OCX) and references to other Access databases (ACCDB, ACCDE, MDB, and MDE), Access add-ins (ACCDA and MDA), and Access projects (ADP and ADE).

An object library or type library generally provides functionality for access to other applications or adds functionality to use in your Visual Basic code. For example, Microsoft Office exposes its Component Object Model (COM) through the Microsoft Office Object Library DLLs. These include the Microsoft Access 12.0 Object Library, Microsoft Excel 12.0 Object Library, and Microsoft Word 12.0 Object Library, to name just a few.

ActiveX controls usually include controls that you can add to your user interface. They can display data on forms or provide an access method to data through a form with little or no extra programming. For example, DBI Grid Tools 2.0's ctGrid control displays a grid of data, a two-dimensional table that looks similar to Access's datasheet view. It has properties to indicate which data to display, adjust colors of cells, and add icons and much more, all without programming. The control also enables more functionality through Visual Basic when a reference is made to the Grid Tools DLL.

Access add-ins afford enhanced functionality to Access as a whole. For example, the New Form Wizard provided with Access is an add-in. By creating an ACCDA or MDA file from Access, you can create your own add-ins for Access.

By setting a reference to an Access database or project, you can access routines to create your own code library. Those routines can then be used with all of your applications. This is discussed more in the "Building Code Libraries" section later in this appendix.

Adding References to Your Projects

You know that you can automate Office applications by adding a reference to one of the libraries that comes with Microsoft Office, such as Microsoft Office 12.0 Object Library. Here are the steps necessary to add a reference, as well as what it means when you do:

1. Press ALT+F11 to open the Visual Basic Editor and select Tools ➪ References to display the References dialog box, shown in Figure B-1.

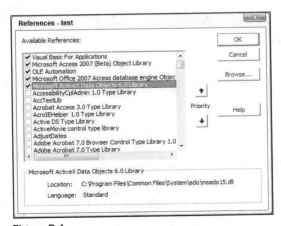

Figure B-1

2. The Available References list includes items that have been registered to the Windows System Registry. To add one of these libraries to references for your project, check the box to the left of its name. When you close and reopen the References dialog box, any libraries you have checked are listed above all unselected libraries.

3. Many application installation packages handle registering libraries for you. If the library you want to use does not appear in the list of Available References, there are two ways to use the library:

❑ **Use the Browse button.** Click the Browse button to open a file selection dialog box. Select the type of library you want from the drop-down list for Files Of Type. Browse to the folder that contains that library and select the library.

❑ **Register the library yourself.** If the library is a 32-bit library (most are), use REGSVR32 to register it. To run REGSVR32, select Run from the Windows Start menu. In the Open box, enter **REGSVR32** followed by the full file specification of the library you want to register. For example:

```
REGSVR32 "C:\Program Files\Common Files\Microsoft\Office11\MSOCFU.DLL"
```

After you register a library, you need to close and reopen the References dialog box to get the library to display in the Available References list.

Reference Order Is Important

One of the reasons for adding references to your project is to make additional classes available so you can declare variables in your code and manipulate objects of those classes. But you must be aware that the name of a class in one library does not have to be unique from the names of classes in other libraries.

A classic example of this occurs when you include references to both DAO (Data Access Objects) and ADO (ActiveX Data Objects,). Both libraries have a Recordset class. (You can use the Object Browser, which is discussed in the next section, to see when a class occurs in more than one library.)

In situations in which there is a duplication of class names, Access determines which class to use by searching sequentially down the list of libraries listed in the Available Libraries list. Unfortunately, the compiler won't always tell you that you have the wrong reference. If you refer to a property or method that is not available for the class you have used in your variable declaration, the compiler will report the problem. Otherwise, you'll discover the problem only when you test your code.

If you have libraries that have classes with the same names, you can get Access to choose the class you want by changing the Priority of the library in the list. Use the Priority buttons (to the right of the Available References list) to move the selected library up or down in the list. Move the library containing the class you want higher than libraries containing the same class name.

You can also avoid problems with duplicate class names by making a specific reference to the library that contains the class you want to use. For example, if you reference both the ADO and DAO libraries, and you want to declare a variable for the Recordset class of ADO, you can declare your variable using the following syntax:

```
Dim rsADO as ADODB.Recordset
```

To declare a variable for the DAO `Recordset` class, you can use the following syntax.

```
Dim rsDAO as DAO.Recordset
```

Using this syntax does not eliminate the need to have the reference to the library in your Reference list, but it prevents any confusion about which library you are referring to in your variable declaration. In addition, it has the added benefit of ensuring that code continues to use the correct library if a new library with a duplicate class name is added later in the development cycle.

The Object Browser

After you have added a reference to a library, the classes contained in that library are available for viewing in the Object Browser. To see the Object Browser in the Visual Basic Editor, select View ⇨ Object Browser or press F2. The Visual Basic Editor displays the Object Browser as shown in Figure B-2.

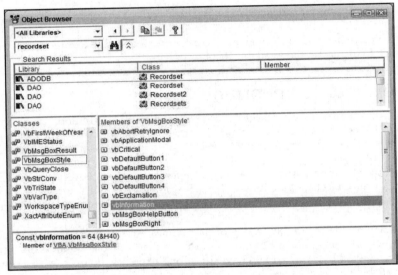

Figure B-2

When you select an item in the Classes list, its properties and methods (its "members") display in the right pane. Select an item in the right pane and more specific information about that item displays in the bottom pane. For example, Figure B-2 shows that `vbTextCompare` is a constant with a value of 1 and is a member of `VBA.VBCompareMethod`.

You can specify which of the referenced libraries you want to browse by selecting it from the libraries drop-down list at the top of the Object Browser (see Figure B-3). That list starts with `<All Libraries>`.

If you are looking for a particular class, property, method, or declared constant, you can specify a portion of the string to search for in the text box below the libraries drop-down, and then click the Search icon (the binoculars) to find it. Figure B-4 shows the results of searching for `recordset`. Because `<All Libraries>` is selected, the class `Recordset` appears in both the DAO and ADO libraries.

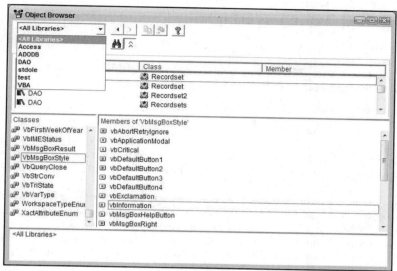

Figure B-3

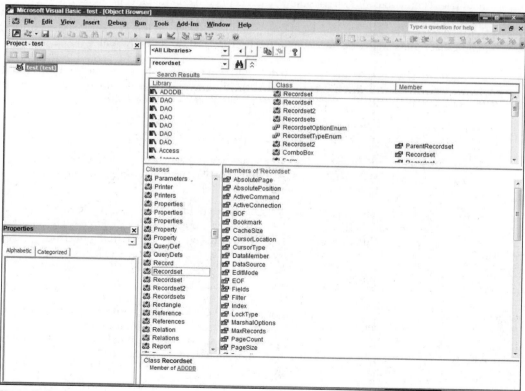

Figure B-4

Building Code Libraries

In addition to the four types of reference libraries (OLB, TLB, DLL, and OCX), a set of library types is often overlooked. These types include:

❑ **MS Access databases:** ACCDB, ACCDE, MDB and MDE

❑ **MS Access add-ins:** ACCDA and MDA

❑ **MS Access projects:** ADP and ADE

With these types of references, you can develop your own code libraries that contain routines to share in all of your applications. An example might be something like a common error handling routine.

Because you can use these routines over and over, you can justify putting a little more effort into them. Take error handling, for example. Generally, you develop code to display a message to the user requesting that the user report the error to you. Have you ever seen a user use your application and expose an error you hadn't found in testing? He clicks OK on the message without giving it a second thought. You ask why he didn't wait to review the message, and he says, "Oh, that happens all the time. I was told to just ignore it."

Suppose that instead of depending on the users to call in report errors, you write routines to track the errors in a table. Then you could investigate what is happening. Perhaps your tables could even maintain some trace data to help discover what causes the problem. Suppose you also realize that the main reason errors don't get reported is that it is too difficult for the user to report them. So you add some functionality that builds an e-mail message for the user to send through Outlook.

Of course, there are always so many things to do when building the current application that you don't have time for tasks like these. But if you could find the time to write these routines and then reuse them in all of your applications, wouldn't that be worthwhile? That's what code libraries are for.

Security

To prevent other users from reading your source code, you can compile the database into an ACCDE or MDE. That removes all the editable code and compresses the database. See Chapter 18 for more information.

If you are going to make an ACCDE or MDE from a database that uses a reference to your code library databases, those databases must be made into ACCDEs or MDEs as well. Remember that if you create an ACCDE or MDE file, you *must* hold on to the ACCDB or MDB file that was used to create the file. You cannot recover source code from an ACCDE or MDE file.

Office XP Developer edition included a component called Code Librarian to help manage the code libraries. However, Office 2007 does not include that component. It's a good program but it can be installed only if you install the full Office XP package. So unless you want to buy Office XP, you won't be able to try it. For those who have Code Librarian installed on their machines, the good news is that it is compatible with Office 2007, so don't remove it.

Using CurrentDB versus CodeDB

One thing to consider when developing code libraries is that `CurrentDB` refers to the database that is open in the Access user interface. If you want your code library project to refer to objects that are in its own database, you need to use `CodeDB`. Likewise, there are the `CurrentProject` and `CodeProject` properties and `CurrentData` and `CodeData` properties, so be sure that you are setting a reference to the correct objects.

For a more detailed explanation about the differences between `CurrentDb` and `CodeDb`, please refer to Appendix G.

Working with References Programmatically

There are a few techniques that make working with Access references easier. And there are a few techniques that you should be aware of to avoid problems when using references to your own code libraries. These techniques are discussed in this section.

The Reference Object

The Access `Application` object includes the References collection, which can be easily used for a number of purposes. The References collection contains the list of references in the database. You can determine the number of references in the project using the following:

```
Application.References.Count
```

You can determine if a reference is missing by checking the `BrokenReference` property of the Access Application object. This property returns `True` if there is a missing reference. From there, you can walk through the References collection to find the missing reference:

```
Dim ref As Reference

If Application.BrokenReference Then
    For Each ref in Application.References
        If ref.IsBroken then
            Debug.Print ref.name & " is broken."
        End if
    Next Ref
End If
```

You can add references using the `AddFromFile` or `AddFromGUID` methods. For `AddFromFile`, you simply specify the full path to the library file. For `AddFromGUID`, the reference library must be registered in the Windows System Registry and you must know the exact GUID for that library, in addition to the major and minor version. The simplest way to find the GUID is to manually add the reference, and then check the `GUID` property of the Reference object for the specified reference.

Running a Procedure from a Library Database

Say you have an `Errors.mdb` file that contains the `HandleError` procedure. You can call that procedure using the `Call` statement in Visual Basic like this (depending on the parameters needed in the routine, of course):

```
Call Errors.HandleError _
(Err. .Number, Err.Description, Err.Source)
```

You can also use the `Application.Run` method:

```
Application.Run("Errors.HandleError", _
Err.Number, Err.Description, Err.Source)
```

The qualifier does not have to be the same as the name of the MDB. In this example, `Errors` was used to qualify where the `HandleError` procedure is located. You can change the name of the qualifier by changing the `Name` property of the project. To change the project name, open the Properties dialog box using the Tools menu in the Visual Basic Editor.

Compiling to Validate References

An easy way to be sure that the references in your project are not broken is to use the Debug ➪ Compile menu option. It quickly finds declarations that use classes that are not available to your project.

For best results with this technique, use `Option Explicit` for every module to be sure that you are declaring all variables. The compiler will tell you if you have not declared a variable even before you attempt to run the code. And, because all variables must be declared, if any variables reference classes or object types from a library that has gone missing, the compiler lets you know.

> **To include the Option Explicit statement for new modules that you create, check Require Variable Declaration in the Options dialog box in the Visual Basic Editor.**

Be aware that because Access uses late binding, types are not checked until the code is executed. That means that until a procedure is run, you may not know that a variable has been defined using a class from a missing library. You can avoid having the users find these problems later by checking the `IsBroken` property of the references in your application during startup. That would be a good routine to write and put into your code library so that you can use it with all of your applications.

Fixing Broken References

If your code suddenly stops working after you have installed your database on another computer, it's a good idea to inspect the references. One of the first things to check for is the `MISSING` referenced type library. As you can see in Figure B-5, `MISSING` stands out at the left of any missing type library.

To fix the missing references, open the Visual Basic Editor's References dialog box and update the references.

You typically run into two problems here. First, if you have delivered the database as an ACCDE or MDE, you cannot modify references. And second, the library you are referencing doesn't exist on the computer. In either case, the most likely solution is to get the library into the right place on the computer. For that, see the section "Avoiding Broken References."

When you have fixed missing references, it's a good idea to compile the module using Debug ➪ Compile — that is, if you're not working with an ACCDE or MDE. Compiling helps ensure that the library on the new computer matches the one on the computer where you did your testing by indicating that the library has the same classes and type definitions you used in your code.

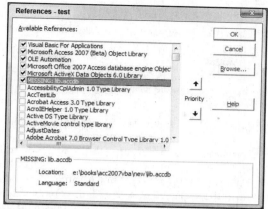

Figure B-5

If you have a broken or missing reference, compiling may report an error incorrectly. In particular, you may find that Visual Basic functions (for example, `Right` or `UCase`) are reported as undefined. If this occurs, fix the missing references first, and then proceed with other fixes.

Avoiding Broken References

Can you claim that you've never had a problem delivering an application to one of your users? Then you've probably never used references. Either that, or you are one of the fortunate developers who develops on a machine with a configuration that is identical to your users'. But even if the machine is identical, you can still run into problems if you have taken the time to develop a code library. You know what we mean — the one you forgot to take with you when you went to the user's machine to install your database.

Of course the first thing to do to avoid broken references is to be sure that you are delivering all of the components that go with your application. And don't forget those DLLs that you acquired from a vendor to improve the features in your application. And just delivering them isn't all that there is to it; you need to be sure you've installed those DLLs in the right folder and that they are registered properly.

So how do you know what the right folder is? When Access searches for referenced libraries, it first searches based on the file specification provided when the library was added. If the library is not found, it follows these steps:

1. Access searches for a `RefLibPaths` key in the following location in the Microsoft Windows Registry: `HKEY_LOCAL_MACHINE\Software\Microsoft\Office\12.0\Access`.

2. If the key exists, Access checks for the existence of a value name that matches the name of the referenced file. If it finds a matching value name, Access loads the reference from the path specified in the corresponding value data.

3. If Access doesn't find a `RefLibPaths` key, it searches for the referenced file in the following locations in order:

    ❑   Application folder containing the application (the folder where `Msaccess.exe` is located).

❑   Current folder.

❑   System folders (the System and System32 folders located in the Windows or WINNT folder).

❑   Windows or WINNT folder.

❑   PATH environment variable. For more information about environment variables, see Windows Help.

❑   The folder that contains the Access file, and any subfolders located in that folder.

If Access still can't find the reference after performing this search, you must fix the reference manually.

When running your code, classes from referenced libraries are not checked until the procedure that declares a variable using one of those classes is executed. In your start up procedure, you can walk through the References using the technique previously mentioned and use the IsBroken property to find broken references. If you find a broken reference you can inform your user with a meaningful message instead of letting an error pop up from Visual Basic.

Resources

A number of commercially available products provide libraries for you to reference from your Access projects. You can also find many shared libraries or libraries that are available as shareware. Here are a few resources to get you started. We have not tried all of the controls and libraries found, so we can't endorse all of them.

❑   **Access Advisor** (http://accessadvisor.net): Search for "ActiveX Control" or search for "DLL." This is a great site for other information, too.

❑   **The Access Web** (www.mvps.org/access/resources/products.htm): With many resources including ActiveX controls and beyond.

❑   **DBi Technologies Inc.** (www.dbi-tech.com): Solutions::PIM, Solutions::Schedule, and many more, tested with Microsoft Access.

❑   **FMS Inc.** (www.fmsinc.com/products): Quite a number of ActiveX controls and add-ins for Microsoft Access.

❑   **ID Automation** (www.idautomation.com/activex): Barcode ActiveX control and DLL designed for Office programs.

❑   **Intuit Developer Network** (www.developer.intuit.com): Software Development Kit (SDK) to work with data in QuickBooks.

You should also be aware that many libraries and ActiveX controls that are designed for Visual Basic programming languages can be used by Access. Contact the vendor to find out.

Calling Managed Code

This appendix provides information about how to call managed code from Access. It begins with an explanation of what managed code is and why you might consider using it in your Access applications. In the process, it defines some commonly used terminology that you might come across while working with managed code. Finally, you'll look at two ways you can use managed code in Access — using class libraries and COM add-ins.

The managed code examples in this appendix are written in both Visual Basic and Visual C#. In this appendix, Visual Basic refers to Visual Basic .NET. This matches the conventions used by Visual Studio and the documentation on MSDN.

A Quick Overview of Managed Code

Code that is managed is code that is running under the auspices of the Common Language Runtime (CLR). The term *managed* most notably refers to memory that is utilized by the application. With unmanaged code written using C/C++ or even Visual Basic and VBA, the programmer is responsible for releasing memory when it is no longer needed. In VBA, you do that by setting an object to `Nothing`. In C++, you do it by deleting a pointer and setting its memory address to `NULL`.

Managed code uses a process called *garbage collection* that does this cleanup for you. In both Visual Basic and Visual C#, objects that you create are tracked by the garbage collector. When the garbage collector determines that an object is no longer needed, the object's resources are automatically freed.

In addition, the CLR provides a common type system (CTS), and code-access security (CAS). Furthermore, because managed code runs through the CLR, it is possible to mix and match languages in a given project. If you want to write your UI using Visual Basic for its RAD capabilities, but write middle-tier objects using C# for its ability to use pointers and some lower-level constructs, the runtime enables you to do this. Want to call a C# class library from a managed C++ application? No problem.

However, it is important to realize that managed code is not immediately compiled. Code written using Visual C# or Visual Basic is actually compiled to intermediate language (IL). This code is then compiled at runtime using the Just-In-Time (JIT) compiler.

When Should You Use Managed Code?

It's true that many things that you can do in managed code can be accomplished using VBA. So why should you use it? After all, this is a major change in the way that applications are developed and executed.

Well, for starters, the base class library in the .NET Framework provides a lot of functionality that would require using Windows API functions. Some examples of this include:

❏ Using Windows common dialog boxes

❏ Retrieving system paths

❏ Determining the amount of memory on the machine

❏ Determining the screen resolution

❏ Retrieving the version number of a file

❏ Working with the Windows Registry

In Visual C#, everything is an object, which makes managed code pretty easy to write and understand. This is also true for classes created in Visual Basic.

Managed code also provides easy deployment. Once the .NET Framework is installed on a computer, deploying an application is often a matter of copying the file. That is the case whether the application is an executable file (.exe), or a class library (.dll).

Later in this appendix, you'll see that there are additional steps for using managed code from an unmanaged application such as Access.

Wow, That Sounds Cool!

Managed code is really cool, but there are a few things to consider before you decide to use it with your Access applications:

❏ Writing a separate library for your application increases the number of files that you must install.

❏ A separate library requires an additional reference in your application.

❏ Running managed code requires the .NET Framework. Version 2.0 of the .NET Framework is included with Windows Vista and is available for download from the Microsoft website.

❏ Writing managed code requires additional tools. You can write class libraries using the Visual Basic 2005 or Visual C# 2005 Express Editions. These are also available for download from the Microsoft website.

❏ Managed code is compiled to intermediate language (IL), not binary code. As such, it can be disassembled using a tool such as .NET Reflector. (Once disassembled, however, anyone can see your source code, so you may want to take advantage of tools that are available to perform obfuscation of source code in the IL.)

But First, a Few Terms

You've seen some good cases for using managed code, but before we get into the details of using it with Access, take a look at the following terms, which are commonly used when referring to managed code:

❑ **Assembly:** A versioned piece of compiled managed code. Code that you write is usually compiled into a single-file assembly such as a DLL or EXE. Assemblies are also self-describing using a technique known as *reflection*. (They are said to be self-describing because they contain metadata that describes each member declared in the assembly.)

❑ **Global Assembly Cache (GAC):** A directory on the machine where managed code can be shared by multiple components. The directory installed by the .NET Framework to `%windir%\ Assembly`. Different versions of the same assembly can exist in the GAC because of the way that assemblies are versioned.

❑ **Common Language Runtime (CLR):** The base of the .NET Framework. All managed languages target features in the CLR including a common type system, garbage collection, and improved security over unmanaged applications. For a language to be managed by the CLR, it must adhere to the Common Language Specification (CLS).

   Because the CLS defines a common type system that must be supported by all managed languages, the CLR enables you to use multiple languages in a particular project. For example, you can use a DLL written in Visual C# in a Visual Basic Windows Forms application. Or, you can consume a Web Service written in Visual C# in a managed C++ application. Some languages, such as C#, define additional types that are not defined within the CLS.

❑ **Base Class Library (BCL):** A key component of the .NET Framework. It supplies managed classes that provide the functionality for Windows Forms, ASP.NET, and other components in the Framework. Also included in the BCL are many classes and methods that implement functionality that has traditionally existed in the Windows API.

❑ **Namespace:** A logical grouping of classes in an assembly. Namespaces are optional, but provide a nice mechanism for organizing similar functionality within your assemblies. The BCL includes many namespaces of its own, such as `System.IO`, `System.Runtime.InteropServices`, and `System.Text`.

❑ **Class:** A class in Visual Basic managed code essentially means the same as it does in Access. In OOP parlance, it defines the blueprint for an object. In Visual C#, all code must be defined inside of a class. Visual Basic supports both class modules and standard modules.

   Use the following code to define a namespace and class inside in your code:

Visual Basic

```
Public Namespace YourNamespace
    Public Class YourClass
        ' Your code goes here
    End Class
End Namespace
```

Visual C#

```
namespace YourNamespace
{
    public class YourClass
    {
        // your code goes here
    }
}
```

❑ **Interface:** Defines a contract that a class must adhere to. A class that derives from an interface is said to *implement* that interface. Properties and methods defined in an interface must be implemented in any class that derives from it. Because interface members must be implemented by these classes, an interface does not contain any implementation.

The following code is an example of an interface definition and a class that implements it:

Visual Basic

```
Public Interface IEmployee
    ' Defines an interface for a class that defines an employee
    Property HireDate () As Date
    Property Name() As String
    Sub DoWork()
End Interface

Public Class Manager : Implements IEmployee
    Private m_hireDate As Date

    Public Sub DoWork() Implements IEmployee.DoWork
        ' Add code to do work

    End Sub

    Public Property HireDate() As Date Implements IEmployee.HireDate
        Get
            Return Me.m_hireDate
        End Get
        Set(ByVal value As String)
            Me.m_hireDate = value
        End Set
    End Property

    Public Property Name() As String Implements IEmployee.Name
        Get
            Return Me.m_name
        End Get
        Set(ByVal value As String)
            Me.m_name = value
        End Set
    End Property
End Class
```

Visual C#

```csharp
public interface IEmployee
{
    // Defines an interface for a class that defines an employee
    DateTime HireDate { get; set; }
    string Name { get; set; }
    void DoWork();
}

public class Manager : IEmployee
{
    private DateTime m_hireDate;
    private string m_name;

    public void DoWork()
    {
        // Add code to do work
    }

    public DateTime HireDate
    {
        get { return m_hireDate;}
        set { m_hireDate = value;}
    }

    public string Name
    {
        get { return m_name;}
        set { m_name = value;}
    }
}
```

By convention, the name of an interface typically begins with the letter I.

❑ **Constructor:** A special method that is called when you create an instance of a class. The constructor is the same name of the class and does not specify a return type.

Use the following code to define a constructor in your code:

Visual Basic

```vbnet
Public Class MyClass
    ' Define the Sub New method in a class to implement
    ' a constructor in Visual Basic
    Public Sub New()
        ' Your constructor code goes here
    End Sub
End Namespace
```

Visual C#

```
public class MyClass
{
    public MyClass
    {
        // your constructor code goes here
    }
}
```

- ❏ **Intermediate Language (IL):** Intermediate Language (IL) is used by .NET compilers such as the Visual C# and Visual Basic compiler. By default, these languages compile to IL instead of machine code. Because the IL produced is essentially the same, you are able to use multiple languages in your managed code projects.

- ❏ **Primary Interop Assembly (PIA):** A managed code assembly that binds to a type library in COM. PIAs are typically provided by the author of a type library and can be referenced like other assemblies in a managed code project. Microsoft Office installs a number of primary interop assemblies such as `Microsoft.Interop.Access.dll` and `Microsoft.Interop.Excel.dll`.

More information about these terms can be found in the MSDN Library, `http://msdn.microsoft.com`.

Writing Managed Code

To write managed code for use in Access, you can use one of the Visual Studio editions such as Visual Studio 2005, Visual Basic 2005 Express Edition, or Visual C# 2005 Express Edition. There are two distinctly different approaches you can take when writing managed code for use in Access:

- ❏ Write a class library that defines classes that you can reference from your Access application.
- ❏ Write a COM add-in that contains user interface code and allows you to launch it when Access starts.

The following sections explore both of these approaches.

Class Libraries

When you write a class library using managed code, Visual Studio creates a DLL for you that contains the classes you have defined. However, the DLL is actually an *assembly* managed by the CLR. Because the DLL contains managed code, referencing it in Access produces an error, as shown in Figure C-1.

Instead, the .NET Framework allows you to create a type library that you can reference from VBA. These type libraries are compatible with COM applications such as Access.

If you want to extend your Access application to write to the Windows event log, for example, you could use the Windows API or the `EventLog` class in the .NET Framework, which is much simpler to write.

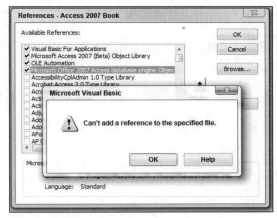

Figure C-1

The examples in this appendix were created using Visual Studio 2005, but can also be created using the Visual C# 2005 or Visual Basic 2005 Express Edition.

First, create a new class library project in Visual Studio 2005:

1. Select File ➪ New ➪ Project.

2. Select Class Library under the Visual C# or Visual Basic language, as shown in Figure C-2.

3. Type **EventLogger** for the name for your project, and then click OK.

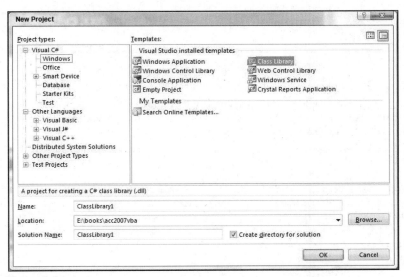

Figure C-2

Once the project is created, you should have an empty class file open, as shown in Figure C-3.

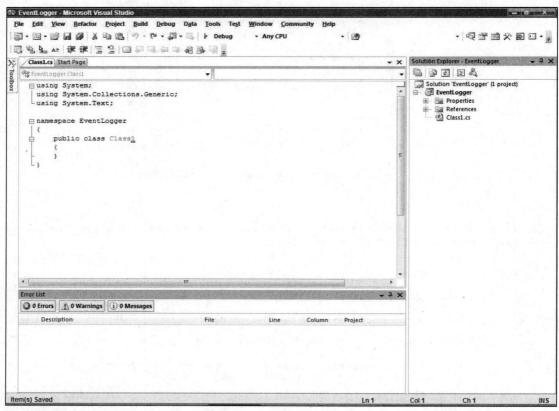

Figure C-3

Now it's time to add some code. Start by changing the name of the class. Because you'll refer to it in Access, the name should be something meaningful. Change the name of the class to EventLogger (in Visual Basic, add the Namespace as shown):

Visual Basic

```
Namespace EventLogger
    Public Class EventLogger
    End Class
End Namespace
```

Visual C#

```
namespace EventLogger
    public class EventLogger
    {
    }
}
```

The `EventLog` class in the .NET Framework will help with your event logging. The class is defined in the `System.Diagnostics` namespace. You need to tell the class how to behave when used by a COM application such as Access. For that, you need the `System.Runtime.InteropServices` namespace.

You could use the .NET classes in your code by typing the full name of the namespace along with the class name, but that would result in a lot of typing! Visual Basic and Visual C# include keywords — `Imports` and `using` — that tell the compiler where to look for class names. Add these namespaces to your class (they should appear at the top of the source file):

Visual Basic

```
Imports System.Diagnostics
Imports System.Runtime.InteropServices
```

Visual C#

```
using System.Diagnostics;
using System.Runtime.InteropServices;
```

Next, define an interface for your class. By default, managed code is available to VBA using late-binding, which means that you cannot use IntelliSense when you are using the code in VBA because there is not enough type information. An interface provides the information needed by IntelliSense in VBA. Define an interface named `IEventLogger` and implement it. The type library will include a custom `Enum` so you'll define that as well. Add the following code above the `Class` declarations:

Visual Basic

```
<ComVisible(True)> _
Public Enum EventLevel
    LevelInformation = EventLogEntryType.Information
    LevelWarning = EventLogEntryType.Warning
    LevelError = EventLogEntryType.Error
End Enum

<ComVisible(True)> _
Public Interface IEventLogger
    Property Level() As EventLevel
    Property EventId() As Integer
    Property SourceName() As String
    Sub WriteEntry(ByVal Message As String)
End Interface
```

Visual C#

```
[ComVisible(true)]
public enum EventLevel
{
    Information = EventLogEntryType.Information,
    Warning = EventLogEntryType.Warning,
    Error = EventLogEntryType.Error
}

[ComVisible(true)]
public interface IEventLogger
{
    EventLevel Level { get; set; }
    int EventId { get; set; }
    string SourceName { get; set; }
    void WriteEntry(string Message);
}
```

Now tell the class to implement the `IEventLogger` interface. To further support IntelliSense, you also need to change the way that the class will be exposed to VBA. That's done by adding an attribute to the class. (Attributes are very useful in both Visual Basic and Visual C#, but are beyond the scope of this book.) Change the class declarations to:

Visual Basic

```
<ComVisible(True)> _
<ClassInterface(ClassInterfaceType.None)> _
Public Class EventLogger : Implements IEventLogger

End Class
```

Visual C#

```
[ComVisible(true)]
[ClassInterface(ClassInterfaceType.None)]
public class EventLogger : IEventLogger
```

So far, so good. The `EventLogger` class needs to be implemented to do the work. First, add the properties, which will be used when you write to the event log. The class will write to the `Application` log in the Windows Event Viewer:

Visual Basic

```
' constants
Private Const LOGNAME As String = "Application"
Private Const ERR_SOURCENAME_NOT_SET = _
    "SourceName argument has not been set"
```

```vb
    ' private data
    Private m_log As EventLog
    Private m_level As EventLevel
    Private m_source As String
    Private m_eventId As Integer

    ' constructor
    Public Sub New()
        ' open the Application event log
        m_log = New EventLog(LOGNAME)
    End Sub

    Public Property EventId() As Integer Implements IEventLogger.EventId
        Get
            Return m_eventId
        End Get
        Set(ByVal value As Integer)
            m_eventId = value
        End Set
    End Property

    Public Property Level() As EventLevel Implements IEventLogger.Level
        Get
            Return m_level
        End Get
        Set(ByVal value As EventLevel)
            m_level = value
        End Set
    End Property

    Public Property SourceName() As String Implements IEventLogger.SourceName
        Get
            Return m_source
        End Get
        Set(ByVal value As String)
            m_source = value
        End Set
    End Property
End Property
```

Visual C#

```csharp
// constants
private const string LOGNAME = "Application";
private const string ERR_SOURCENAME_NOT_SET =
    "SourceName argument has not been set";

// private data
private EventLog    m_log;
private EventLevel m_level;
private string      m_source;
private int         m_eventId;
```

```
// constructor
public EventLogger()
{
    // open the Application event log
    m_log = new EventLog(LOGNAME);
}

public int EventId
{
    get { return m_eventId; }
    set { m_eventId = value; }
}

public EventLevel Level
{
    get { return m_level; }
    set { m_level = value; }
}

public string SourceName
{
    get { return m_source; }
    set
    {
        m_source = value;

        // register the source name
        if (!EventLog.SourceExists(m_source))
            EventLog.CreateEventSource(m_source, LOGNAME);
    }
}
```

Great! Now add the `WriteEntry` method. This is the code that actually writes to the event log:

Visual Basic

```
Public Sub WriteEntry(ByVal Message As String) _
    Implements IEventLogger.WriteEntry

    Dim myLevel As EventLogEntryType = m_level

    ' make sure the SourceName has been set
    If (String.IsNullOrEmpty(m_source)) Then
        Throw New InvalidOperationException(ERR_SOURCENAME_NOT_SET)
    End If

    ' set the EventLog Source and  write to the event log
    m_log.Source = m_source
    m_log.WriteEntry(Message, myLevel, m_eventId)
End Sub
```

Visual C#

```csharp
public void WriteEntry(string Message)
{
    // make sure the SourceName has been set
    if (string.IsNullOrEmpty(m_source))
        throw new InvalidOperationException(ERR_SOURCENAME_NOT_SET);

    // set the EventLog Source and  write to the event log
    m_log.Source = m_source;
    m_log.WriteEntry(Message,
        (EventLogEntryType)m_level,
        m_eventId);
}
```

Finally, build the project so that it can be used in VBA. To do so, register the library for COM Interop:

1. Click EventLogger Properties from the Project menu.

2. For a Visual Basic project, select the Compile options page. For a Visual C# project, choose the Build options page.

3. Check the setting that says Register for COM Interop, as shown in Figure C-4.

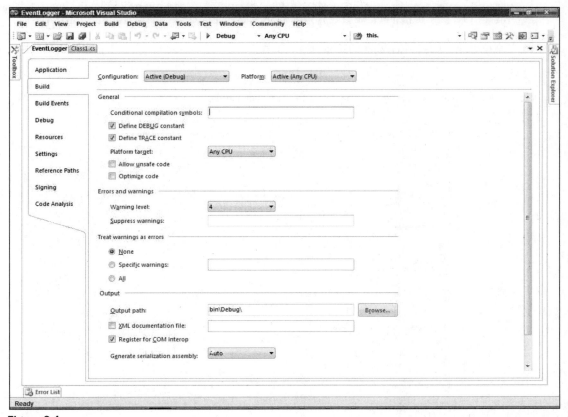

Figure C-4

To create the managed code assembly and the type library, select Build ➪ Build Solution. By default, this creates files in the `bin\Debug` subdirectory below your project directory. If you are constructing a release build, the files will be in the `bin\Release` subdirectory. Remember the path for later. You'll come back to this file in the section "Using Managed Code in Access" later in this chapter

COM Add-ins

The Office Developer Edition for Office 2000 and Office XP allowed you to create COM add-ins using the Visual Basic Editor. This functionality remains in Visual Studio 2005. The Express Editions of Visual Studio do not include the required project type to create COM add-ins.

COM add-ins offer several additional features over a class library:

❑   They enable you to run code when Access starts.

❑   They enable you to run code when Access shuts down.

❑   A COM add-in is given an instance of the Access `Application` object so you can interact with Access or the database that is currently opened from your add-in.

❑   COM add-ins can be used to extend the Ribbon.

As discussed in Chapter 18, the entry point for the Workgroup Administrator tool has been removed from the Access user interface. Because the tool is still available in Access and can be invoked using code, you can write a COM add-in that extends the Access Ribbon to display the Workgroup Administrator.

Start by creating the add-in project using Visual Studio:

1.   Launch Visual Studio, and then select File ➪ New ➪ Project.

2.   Select Extensibility projects under Other Project Types.

3.   Select Shared Add-in from the list of projects, as shown in Figure C-5 and click OK. This launches the Shared Add-in Wizard. Click Next to continue.

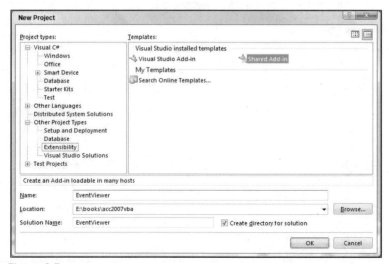

Figure C-5

4. In Page 1 of the wizard, select either Visual C# or Visual Basic for your programming language.

5. In Page 2, clear the checkboxes for all Application hosts with the exception of Microsoft Access, as shown in Figure C-6.

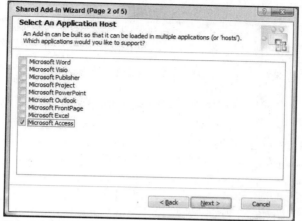

Figure C-6

6. In Page 3, type **Display Workgroup Administrator** for the name of the add-in.

7. In Page 4, select both checkboxes. That tells the add-in to load when Access is launched and that it should be available to all users. You'll load the add-in when Access starts to add an entry point to the Access user interface.

8. In Page 5, click Finish.

Creating an Add-in project actually creates two Visual Studio projects. The first is the add-in, and the second project is a Setup project that creates a setup.exe and an MSI file for the Windows Installer. The MSI file can be used to install the add-in on other computers.

Before you start writing code, there's one more thing to do. As mentioned earlier, the COM add-in receives an instance of the Access Application object. Because COM add-ins are generic in the sense that they can run against a number of host applications, the Application object is given to you as an object type and is not strongly typed. Working with a strongly typed object would be easier, so cast the object type to an instance of the Access Application object in the Access PIA. Start by adding a reference:

1. Select Project ➪ Add Reference.

2. Select Microsoft Access 12.0 Object Library from the list of components in the COM tab. This will include PIA references to DAO, ADODB, and VBIDE.

Ready to start coding? Begin by storing a strongly typed instance of the Application object. First, add the following statements to the top of the class file. This code will include the Access PIA and the Office PIA that you will use later to expose the custom ribbon.

Visual Basic

```
Imports Microsoft.Office.Core
Imports Access = Microsoft.Office.Interop.Access
```

Visual C#

```
using Microsoft.Office.Core;
using Access = Microsoft.Office.Interop.Access;
```

*You add an alias (*Access*) in the* Imports *and* using *statements to avoid conflicts or to clarify which class is being used.*

Next, change the applicationObject declaration from object to Access.Application in the class file:

Visual Basic

```
Dim applicationObject As Access.Application
```

Visual C#

```
private Access.Application applicationObject;
```

If you ever created a COM add-in in VBA, the next steps should look familiar to you. The add-in creates a new class called Connect that implements the IDTExtensibility2 interface. This interface defines five events that are used by COM Add-ins to communicate with host applications. The OnConnection method is called when Access starts. One of the arguments to OnConnection is the Application object. Change the code in this method to use a strongly typed Application object by adding an explicit cast to Access.Application:

Visual Basic

```
applicationObject = CType(application, Access.Application)
```

Visual C#

```
applicationObject = (Access.Application)application;
```

To support extending the Ribbon, you need to implement one more interface in the class named IRibbonExtensibility. Add this interface to the class declarations:

Visual Basic

```
Public Class Connect
    Implements Extensibility.IDTExtensibility2
    Implements IRibbonExtensibility
```

Visual C#

```csharp
public class Connect : Object,
        Extensibility.IDTExtensibility2, IRibbonExtensibility
```

Before adding the code to implement the interface, define the XML that will be used to display the entry point in Access. The XML adds a group and one additional button named Workgroup Administrator to the Database Tools tab in the Access Ribbon. (See Chapter 12 for more information about building custom ribbons.)

```xml
<customUI xmlns="http://schemas.microsoft.com/office/2006/01/customui">
  <ribbon>
    <tabs>
      <tab idMso="TabDatabaseTools">
        <group id="grpWrkGadm" label="Workgroup Administrator">
          <button id="cmdWrkGadm"
                  label="Workgroup Administrator"
                  size="large"
                  onAction="showWrkGadm"
                  imageMso="DatabasePermissionsMenu"/>
        </group>
      </tab>
    </tabs>
  </ribbon>
</customUI>
```

There are a few ways to include the XML for the ribbon. In this example, you'll use a resource file that will provide IntelliSense for the items named in the file. You could also include an XML file as an embedded resource.

1. Select Project ➪ Add New Item.

2. Choose Resources File from the list of templates and click Add. Name the file `RibbonXML.xml`.

3. Add an item in the String table, as shown in Figure C-7. Define the name of the item in the string table as `rbnWrkGadm`. Use the preceding XML as the value in the string table.

Back to the code. The `IRibbonExtensibility` interface defines one other method, named `GetCustomUI`, which you need to add to your class. It is called when the host application asks for XML for the ribbon. Add the following method:

Visual Basic

```vb
Function GetCustomUI(ByVal RibbonID As String) As String _
    Implements IRibbonExtensibility.GetCustomUI
    Return My.Resources.Resource1.rbnWrkGadm
End Function
```

Visual C#

```csharp
public string GetCustomUI(string RibbonID)
{
    return Resource1.rbnWrkGadm;
}
```

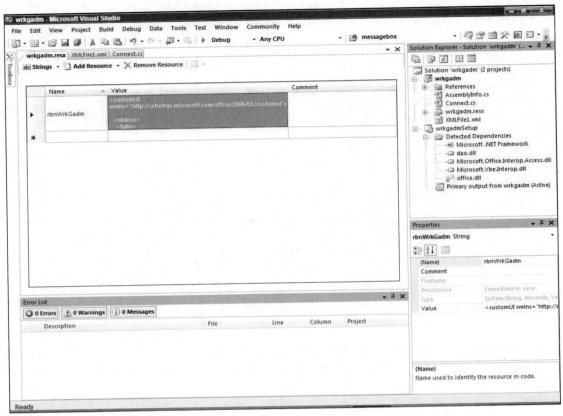

Figure C-7

You're almost done. The XML defined an `onAction` attribute for the button. It tells the button to call the named routine when clicked. For your add-in, show the Workgroup Administrator by calling the `RunCommand` method of the Access `Application` object. Add the following code to the `Connect` class:

Visual Basic

```vb
Public Sub showWrkGadm(ByVal control As IRibbonControl)
    applicationObject.RunCommand(Access.AcCommand.acCmdWorkgroupAdministrator)
End Sub
```

Visual C#

```csharp
public void showWrkGadm(IRibbonControl control)
{
    applicationObject.RunCommand(Access.AcCommand.acCmdWorkgroupAdministrator);
}
```

With that, select Build ⇨ Build Solution and you are ready to test.

Using Managed Code in Access

There are two uses for the managed code you created. First, you want to be able to write to the Windows event log in your Access application. Second, you want to use the COM add-in to add the Workgroup Administrator to the Access Ribbon. To use these components from other computers, you'll need to take a few extra steps to properly register the control.

Registering Managed Code

When you build and run assemblies for COM Interop on a development machine, Visual Studio takes care of the registration for you. However, unless you use a setup package such as the one generated when you create a COM add-in project, there are a few steps you have to take to use managed code on a different machine.

To make an assembly available to all applications on the machine, you can install an assembly to the GAC. That requires that you use the Strong Name utility and sign the assembly. Once the assembly is installed to the GAC, it can be used by other managed code on the machine.

To use the Strong Name utility to generate a key file, enter the following at the command line:

```
sn  -k "YourFileName.snk"
```

To sign the assembly, check Sign The Assembly in the Properties dialog box for the project in Visual Studio and browse to the .snk file that was created using the Strong Name tool.

If you don't want to install your assembly into the GAC, you can use the regasm utility as follows (these steps require the Microsoft .NET Framework on the target machine):

1. Copy the managed class library (.dll) to the target computer.
2. Launch a command window on the machine.
3. Use the regasm utility to register the assembly with the /codebase command-line switch.
4. Use the regasm utility to register a type library on the machine by specifying the /tlb command-line switch. That creates the necessary COM registration on the machine. The command line for regasm might look something like this:

   ```
   regasm "<PathToDLL>\FileName.dll" /tlb:"<PathToTLB>\FileName.tlb"
   ```

   Creating COM registrations creates registry keys in HKEY_LOCAL_MACHINE, so you will need administrative privileges on the machine to run regasm /tlb.

Referencing a Managed Class Library

To use the type library you created earlier using managed code, you need only to add a reference. Here's how:

1. Create a new database in Access. Make note of where the database is located; you'll use it again later in the "Debugging Your Libraries or COM Add-ins" section.

2. Add a module to the database.

3. Select Tools ⇨ References.

4. Select EventLogger in the list of references, and then click OK.

Once the reference has been added, you can use it as you would any other class. Figure C-8 shows that IntelliSense is available for the class. It was enabled by defining the interface in the "Class Libraries" section earlier in this appendix.

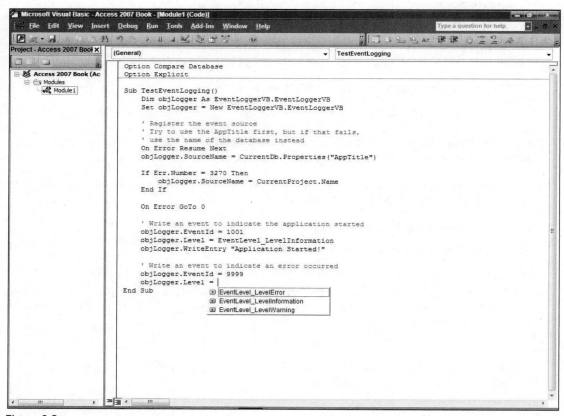

Figure C-8

To test the `EventLogger` class, add a new module in the database and enter the following code:

```
Sub TestEventLogging()
    ' Maximum value for an event ID
    Const MAX_EVENT_ID As Long = 65535

    Dim objLogger As EventLogger.EventLogger
    Set objLogger = New EventLogger.EventLogger

    ' Register the event source
    ' Try to use the AppTitle first but if that fails,
    ' use the name of the database instead
    On Error Resume Next
    objLogger.SourceName = CurrentDb.Properties("AppTitle")

    If Err.Number = 3270 Then
        objLogger.SourceName = CurrentProject.Name
    End If

    On Error GoTo 0

    ' Write an event to indicate the application started
    objLogger.EventId = 1001
    objLogger.Level = EventLevel_LevelInformation
    objLogger.WriteEntry "Application Started!"

    On Error Resume Next

    ' Raise an error to simulate an error in the application
    Err.Raise MAX_EVENT_ID - 513, "Module1", "The expected form was not open"

    ' Write information about the error to the event log
    objLogger.Level = EventLevel_LevelError
    objLogger.EventId = Err.Number
    objLogger.WriteEntry "An unexpected error has occurred. " & _
        "Details of the error are:" & vbCrLf & vbCrLf & _
        "Number = " & Err.Number & vbCrLf & _
        "Source = " & Err.Source & vbCrLf & _
        "Description = " & Err.Description

    On Error GoTo 0

    ' Cleanup
    Set objLogger = Nothing
End Sub
```

Check the event log after running the sample code. There should be an entry, as displayed in Figure C-9.

Logging events may require administrative privileges on the computer.

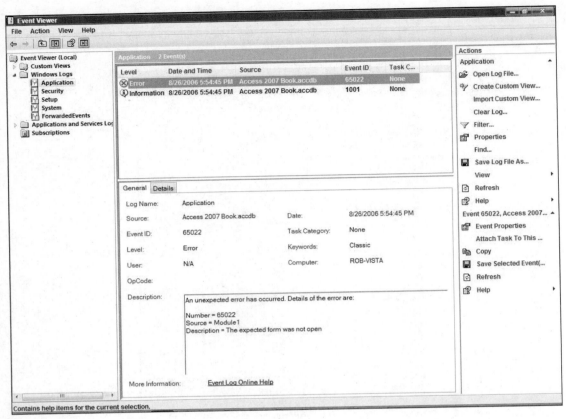

Figure C-9

Installing a COM Add-in

Now you can simply launch Access to load the add-in. Because the ribbon you created adds a group to an existing tab, you need to open a database. Figure C-10 shows the Workgroup Administrator button in the Ribbon once a database is open.

You can also install a COM add-in using the COM Add-ins dialog box (shown in Figure C-11), which is available through the Access Options dialog box on the Add-Ins tab.

Debugging Your Libraries or COM Add-ins

Using Visual Studio, you can debug your class libraries while they are running inside of Access. You cannot directly run a class library (.dll), so the trick is to tell Visual Studio to launch Access while debugging. Then, you simply need to call code in your class library that will be reached inside your Visual Studio project.

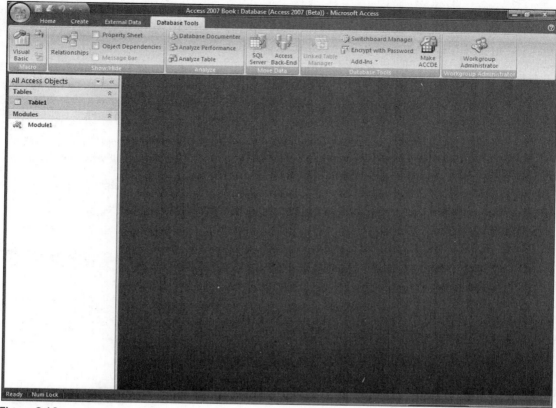

Figure C-10

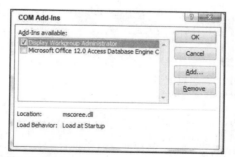

Figure C-11

To debug the `WriteEntry` method in the `EventLogger` class, for example, the following steps tell Visual Studio to launch Access while debugging:

1. Select Project ⇨ EventLogger Properties.
2. Select the Debug options page.

3. Choose the option Start External Program from the Start Action group.

4. Enter the path to `MSACCESS.EXE` on your machine. Access is installed to `C:\Program Files\Microsoft Office\Office12` by default.

You can also specify the database to open in the Command Line Arguments entry in the Debug options. Set a breakpoint on the `WriteEntry` method in the `EventLogger` class by pressing F9 on the method name. Press F5 to start debugging. Open the database you created earlier and run the code. When you reach the `WriteEntry` method in VBA, you should hit the breakpoint, as shown in Figure C-12.

In certain keyboard mapping schemes in Visual Studio, debugging is different than debugging in VBA, as the following table indicates. You can use the more familiar VBA function keys by using the Visual Basic 6 keyboard mapping scheme in Visual Studio 2005.

	Visual Studio	*VBA*
Step into code	*F11*	*F8*
Step over code	*F10*	*Shift+F8*

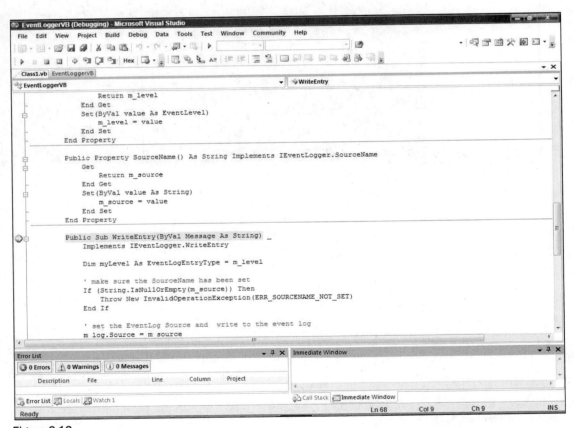

Figure C-12

DAO Object Method and Property Descriptions

This appendix provides a detailed alphabetical list of all the objects that DAO supports, including descriptions of their methods, properties, and collections. These descriptions are for reference purposes only, and you should consult the online Help for more in-depth descriptions.

DAO-Supported Objects

This section outlines the objects that are available in DAO. There have been some changes made to DAO in Access 2007, and they're reflected in the descriptions.

ODBCDirect

In addition to the Microsoft Access workspace, previous versions of DAO supported a second type of Workspace object called ODBCDirect. ODBCDirect workspaces are used against ODBC data sources, such as SQL Server. Beginning with Office 2007, Microsoft is no longer shipping RDO that enabled this type of workspace. As a result, ODBCDirect is no longer supported in DAO.

User-Level Security

Beginning with Access 2007, user-level security is no longer supported for new file formats. Thus, you cannot assign permissions to database objects such as tables and queries, or Access objects such as forms and reports in ACCDB files. User-level security is still supported for MDB files. The DAO object model related to users and groups, however, has been hidden. To view hidden members in an object model, right-click in the Object Browser and choose Show Hidden Members.

Containers Collection

The Containers collection contains all of the Container objects that are defined in a database (Microsoft Access databases only).

Method	Description
Refresh	Refreshes the collection

Property	Description
Count	Returns a count of Container objects in the collection

Container Object

The Container object contains a collection of Document objects that are of the same type. The Containers you are likely to work with the most are Databases, Tables (which also include query objects), Forms, Reports, Scripts (macros), and Modules.

The Container object has no methods.

Property	Description
AllPermissions	(Hidden) Returns a bit field that contains all the permissions that apply to the current user (as identified by the UserName property) of the Container object, including user-specific and inherited (from group membership) permissions (Microsoft Access workspaces only).
Inherit	(Hidden) Sets/returns a flag that specifies whether new Document objects will inherit the default permissions (Microsoft Access workspaces only).
Name	Sets/returns a user-defined name for a DAO object. For an object not appended to a collection, this property is read/write.
Owner	(Hidden) Sets/returns the Container's name (Microsoft Access workspaces only).
Permissions	(Hidden) Returns a bit field that contains the permissions that specifically apply to the current user (or group) of the Container object, as identified by the UserName property (Microsoft Access workspaces only).
UserName	(Hidden) Sets/returns the name of the user, group, or the owner of the Workspace object.

Collections

❑   Documents

❑   Properties

DBEngine

The DBEngine object is the top-level object in the DAO object model.

Method	Description
BeginTrans	Begins a new transaction.
CommitTrans	Ends the current transaction and saves the changes to disk.
CompactDatabase	Copies and compacts a closed Access database.
CreateDatabase	Creates a new Database object and saves it to disk.
CreateWorkspace	Creates a new Workspace object.
Idle	Suspends data processing to allow Access to complete any pending tasks such as memory optimization or page timeouts.
ISAMStats	(Hidden) Returns disk statistics (refer to Chapter 6).
OpenDatabase	Opens an existing database.
RegisterDatabase	Enters ODBC data source connection information in the Registry.
Rollback	Ends the current transaction and cancels any changes made to DAO objects in the workspace.
SetOption	Temporarily overrides Access database engine values in the Registry.

Property	Description
DefaultPassword	Sets the password used to create the default workspace, when it is initialized. Write-only.
DefaultType	Sets/returns a value that defines the type of workspace that will be used by the next Workspace object to be created. ODBCDirect workspaces are no longer supported.
DefaultUser	Sets the user name that is used to create the default workspace when it is initialized.
IniPath	Sets/returns information about the Registry key that contains values for the Access database engine.
LoginTimeout	Sets/returns the number of seconds before an error occurs when you attempt to log on to an ODBC database.
SystemDB	(Hidden) Sets/returns the path to the Workgroup Information File (Microsoft Access workspaces only).
Version	Returns the current DAO version in use.

Collections

- ❏   Errors
- ❏   Properties
- ❏   Workspaces

Databases Collection

The Databases collection contains all open Database objects opened or created within a Workspace object.

Method	Description
Refresh	Refreshes the collection.

Property	Description
Count	Returns a count of Database objects in the collection.

Database Object

The Database object is an open database. Using installable indexed sequential access methods (ISAM) such as Text or Excel, it is possible to open a Database object that points to data sources other than Microsoft Access. Many properties or methods listed here apply only to a Database object that has been opened against a Microsoft Access database. These members are noted as such.

Method	Description
Close	Closes the database.
CreateProperty	Creates a new user-defined Property object (Microsoft Access workspaces only).
CreateQueryDef	Creates a new QueryDef object.
CreateRelation	Creates a new Relation object (Microsoft Access workspaces only).
CreateTableDef	Creates a new TableDef object (Microsoft Access workspaces only).
Execute	Runs an action query.
MakeReplica	Creates a new database replica from another replica (Microsoft Access workspaces only).
NewPassword	Changes the password of an existing database (Microsoft Access workspaces only).
OpenRecordset	Creates a new Recordset object.
PopulatePartial	Synchronizes changes between a full and partial replica.
Synchronize	Synchronizes two replicas (Microsoft Access databases only).

Property	Description
CollatingOrder	Returns the text sort order for string comparisons and sorts (Microsoft Access workspaces only).
Connect	Sets/returns a value for the source of an open database or a database used in a pass-through query.
DesignMasterID	Returns a 16-byte value that uniquely identifies the database as being the design master in a replica set (Microsoft Access workspaces only).
Name	Sets/returns the database's name.
QueryTimeOut	Sets/returns the number of seconds before an error occurs when a query is executed against an ODBC data source.
RecordsAffected	Returns the number of records affected by the most recent Execute method.
Replicable	Sets/returns a value that defines whether a database can be replicated (Microsoft Access workspaces only).
ReplicaID	Returns a 16-byte value that uniquely identifies a database replica (Microsoft Access workspaces only).
Transactions	Returns a value that indicates whether the database supports transactions.
Updatable	Returns a value that indicates whether you can change the Database object.
Version	Returns the version of the ODBC driver currently in use.

Collections

- ❑ Containers
- ❑ Properties
- ❑ QueryDefs
- ❑ Recordsets
- ❑ Relations
- ❑ TableDefs
- ❑ Transactions

Documents Collection

The Documents collection contains all of the Document objects for a specific type of object (Microsoft Access databases only).

Method	Description
Refresh	Refreshes the collection.

Property	Description
Count	Returns a count of Document objects in the collection.

Document Object

The Document object contains information about an instance of an object. The object can be a database, saved table, query, or relationship (Microsoft Access databases only).

Method	Description
CreateProperty	Creates a new user-defined Property object (Microsoft Access workspaces only).

Property	Description
AllPermissions	(Hidden) Returns a bit field that contains all the permissions that apply to the current user (as identified by the UserName property) of the Document object, including user-specific and inherited (from group membership) permissions (Microsoft Access workspaces only).
Container	Returns the name of the Document object's parent Container (Microsoft Access workspaces only).
DateCreated	Returns the date and time that the Document object was created (Microsoft Access workspaces only).
LastUpdated	Returns the date and time of the most recent change that was made to the document (Microsoft Access workspaces only).
Name	Returns the document's name. This property is read-only.
Owner	(Hidden) Sets/returns a value that specifies the document's owner (Microsoft Access workspaces only).
Permissions	(Hidden) Returns a bit field that contains the permissions that specifically apply to the current user (or group) of the Document object, as identified by the UserName property (Microsoft Access workspaces only).
Replicable	Sets/returns a flag that specifies whether the document can be replicated (Microsoft Access workspaces only).
UserName	(Hidden) Sets/returns the name of the user, group, or the owner of the Document object.

Collection

❏   Properties

Errors Collection

The Errors collection contains all stored Error objects.

Method	Description
Refresh	Refreshes the collection.

Property	Description
Count	Returns a count of the current Error objects.

Error Object

The Error object contains details about data access errors. It has no methods. Each Error object relates to a single DAO operation.

Property	Description
Description	Default. Returns a descriptive string associated with an error.
Help Context	(Hidden) Returns a context ID for a topic in a Help file.
Help File	(Hidden) Returns a fully qualified path to the Help file.
Number	Returns an error number.
Source	Returns the name of the object that generated the error.

Collections

None

Fields Collection

The Fields collection contains all stored Field objects of an Index, QueryDef (Microsoft Access workspaces only), Recordset, Recordset2, Relation, or TableDef. Note that the Fields collection of a Recordset2 object contains the collection of Field2 objects.

Method	Description
Append	Appends a new `Field` object to the collection.
Delete	Deletes a `Field` from the collection.
Refresh	Refreshes the collection.

Property	Description
Count	Returns a count of `Field` objects in the collection.

Field Object

The `Field` object is a column of data.

Method	Description
AppendChunk	Appends data from a string expression to a Memo or Long Binary Field object in a `Recordset`.
CreateProperty	Creates a new user-defined `Property` object (Microsoft Access workspaces only).
GetChunk	Returns all or some of the contents of a Memo or Long Binary Field object in the `Fields` collection of a `Recordset` object.

Property	Description
AllowZeroLength	Sets/returns a flag that indicates whether you can enter a zero-length string ("") in a Text or Memo field object (Microsoft Access workspaces only).
Attributes	Sets/returns a value that indicates a `Field`'s characteristics.
CollatingOrder	Returns a value that specifies the sort order for string comparison and sorting (Microsoft Access workspaces only).
DataUpdatable	Returns a flag that specifies whether the data in the field can be updated.
DefaultValue	Sets/returns the default value of a `Field` object. Read-only for `Field` object in the `Fields` collection (Microsoft Access workspaces only).
FieldSize	Returns the number of bytes actually stored in a Memo or Long Binary Field object in a `Recordset` object's `Fields` collection.

Property	Description
ForeignName	Sets/returns the name of the foreign table involved in a relationship with the field (Microsoft Access workspaces only).
Name	Sets/returns a `Field` object's name. Read-only for `Field` objects in the Fields collection.
OrdinalPosition	Sets/returns the relative position of a `Field` object within the `Fields` collection. Read-only for `Field` objects in the `Fields` collection.
Required	Sets/returns a flag that indicates whether data in the `Field` must be non-Null.
Size	Sets/returns a value that indicates the maximum size, in bytes, of the data for a `Field`.
SourceField	Returns the name of the field that is the original source of the data for a `Field` object.
SourceTable	Returns the name of the table that is the original source of the data for a `Field` object.
Type	Sets/returns a value that indicates the field's data type.
ValidateOnSet	Sets/returns a flag that specifies whether the value of a `Field` is immediately validated when data is entered (Microsoft Access workspaces only).
ValidationRule	Sets/returns an expression that validates the data in a field as it is changed or added to the table (Microsoft Access workspaces only).
ValidateText	Sets/returns a value that specifies the text of the message that displays if the data entered in a Field doesn't satisfy the validation rule (Microsoft Access workspaces only).
Value	Default. Sets/returns the field's actual value.

Collection

❑ Properties

Field2 Object

The `Field2` object is a column of data. The `Field2` object was added in Access 2007 and includes support for multi-value lookup and attachment fields. You can use a `Field2` object anywhere you would normally use a `Field` object, including multi-value lookup and attachment fields, although you won't be able to call the additional properties or methods that are available on the `Field2` object.

Appendix D: DAO Object Method and Property Descriptions

Method	Description
AppendChunk	Appends data from a string expression to a Memo or Long Binary Field object in a Recordset.
CreateProperty	Creates a new user-defined Property object (Microsoft Access workspaces only).
GetChunk	Returns all or some of the contents of a Memo or Long Binary Field object in the Fields collection of a Recordset object.
LoadFromFile	Loads the data in an Attachment field from the specified filename. You get runtime error 3259 (Invalid field data type) if you call this method on a non-attachment field.
SaveToFile	Saves the data in an Attachment file to the specified filename.

Property	Description
AllowZeroLength	Sets/returns a flag that indicates whether you can enter a zero-length string ("") in a Text or Memo field object (Microsoft Access workspaces only).
AppendOnly	Sets/returns a flag that indicates whether a memo field is an append-only field.
Attributes	Sets/returns a value that indicates a Field's characteristics.
CollatingOrder	Returns a value that specifies the sort order for string comparison and sorting (Microsoft Access workspaces only).
ComplexType	Contains a property that returns the collection of Fields for a multi-value lookup field.
DataUpdatable	Returns a flag that specifies whether the data in the field can be updated.
DefaultValue	Sets/returns the default value of a Field object. Read-only for Field object in the Fields collection (Microsoft Access workspaces only).
FieldSize	Returns the number of bytes actually stored in a Memo or Long Binary Field object in a Recordset object's Fields collection.
ForeignName	Sets/returns the name of the foreign table involved in a relationship with the field (Microsoft Access workspaces only).
IsComplex	Determines whether a field is a complex field. Returns True for multi-value lookup fields and Attachment fields.
Name	Sets/returns a Field object's name. Read-only for Field objects in the Fields collection.
OrdinalPosition	Sets/returns the relative position of a Field object within the Fields collection. Read-only for Field objects in the Fields collection.

Property	Description
Required	Sets/returns a flag that indicates whether data in the Field must be non-Null.
Size	Sets/returns a value that indicates the maximum size, in bytes, of the data for a Field.
SourceField	Returns the name of the field that is the original source of the data for a Field object.
SourceTable	Returns the name of the table that is the original source of the data for a Field object.
Type	Sets/returns a value that indicates the field's data type.
ValidateOnSet	Sets/returns a flag that specifies whether the value of a Field is immediately validated when data is entered (Microsoft Access workspaces only).
ValidationRule	Sets/returns an expression that validates the data in a field as it is changed or added to the table (Microsoft Access workspaces only).
ValidateText	Sets/returns a value that specifies the text of the message that displays if the data entered in a Field doesn't satisfy the validation rule (Microsoft Access workspaces only).
Value	Default. Sets/returns the field's value. In the case of a multi-valued lookup field, this property actually returns a DAO.Recordset2 object that contains the data in the lookup field. You can determine if a field is a multi-valued lookup field by checking the IsComplex property.

Collection

❑   Properties

Groups Collection

The Groups collection contains all stored Group objects of a Workspace or User object (Microsoft Access workspaces only). A group is one or more users in the Access security model. Assigning permissions based on groups is often easier than managing permissions to individual users.

This collection is hidden in Access 2007, but can still be used if you are working with an MDB file.

Method	Description
Append	Appends a new Group object to the collection.
Delete	Deletes a Group from the collection.
Refresh	Refreshes the collection.

Property	Description
Count	Returns a count of Group objects in the collection.

Group Object

The Group object is a group of User objects that have common access permissions when a workspace operates in a secure workgroup. This object is hidden in Access 2007, but can still be used if you are working with an MDB file.

Method	Description
CreateUser	Creates a new User object (Microsoft Access workspaces only).

Property	Description
Name	Sets/returns the group's name. Read-only if the group has already been added to the collection.
PID	Sets the group's personal identifier (PID) (Microsoft Access workspaces only).

Collections

❑ Properties

❑ Users

Indexes Collection

The Indexes collection contains all stored Index objects of a TableDef object.

Method	Description
Append	Appends a new Index object to the collection.
Delete	Deletes an Index from the collection.
Refresh	Refreshes the collection.

Property	Description
Count	Returns a count of Index objects in the collection.

Index Object

The Index object specifies the order in which records are accessed from a table and whether duplicate records are allowed.

Method	Description
CreateField	Creates a new Field object (Microsoft Access workspaces only).
CreateProperty	Creates a new Property object (Microsoft Access workspaces only).
Clustered	Sets/returns a flag that specifies whether the index is clustered. The Microsoft Access database does not support clustered indexes, so this property is ignored. ODBC data sources always return False because it does not detect if ODBC data sources have clustered indexes.
DistinctCount	Returns the number of unique values (keys) that exist in the table for the index (Microsoft Access workspaces only).
Foreign	Returns a flag that specifies whether the index is a foreign key in another table (Microsoft Access workspaces only).
IgnoreNulls	Sets/returns a flag that specifies whether records that have Null values also have indexes.
Name	Sets/returns the index's name.
Primary	Sets/returns a flag that specifies whether the index is the primary key.
Required	Sets/returns a flag that specifies whether a Field object (or the entire index) can accept Null values. Read-only if the index has been appended to the collection.
Unique	Sets/returns a flag that specifies whether the index keys must be unique.

Collection

❑ Fields

Parameters Collection

The Parameters collection contains all the Parameter objects of a QueryDef object.

Method	Description
Refresh	Refreshes the collection.

Property	Description
Count	Returns a count of Parameters objects in the collection.

Parameter Object

The Parameter object is a defined value supplied to a query. It has no methods.

Property	Description
Name	Returns the parameter's name. Read-only.
Type	Sets/returns a value that indicates the parameter type.
Value	Default. Sets/returns the parameter value.

Collection

❑ Properties

Recordsets Collection

The Recordsets collection contains all open Recordset objects in a Connection or Database.

Method	Description
Refresh	Refreshes the collection.

Property	Description
Count	Returns a count of Recordset objects in the collection.

Recordset Object

The Recordset object represents the records in a base table, or those that result from executing a query.

Method	Description
AddNew	Begins a recordset editing session that creates a new record for an updatable Recordset object.
CancelUpdate	Cancels any pending updates for a Recordset object.
Clone	Creates a new Recordset object that is a duplicate of the original Recordset object.
Close	Closes an open Recordset object.

Method	Description
CopyQueryDef	Creates a new QueryDef object that is a copy of the original QueryDef that was used to create the Recordset object (Microsoft Access workspaces only).
Delete	Deletes the current record in an updatable Recordset object.
Edit	Begins a recordset editing session.
FillCache	Fills all or a part of a local cache for a Recordset object that contains data from a Microsoft Access-connected ODBC data source (Microsoft Access-connected ODBC databases only).
FindFirst	Locates the first record in a dynaset- or snapshot-type Recordset object that matches the specified criteria and makes that row the current row (Microsoft Access workspaces only).
FindLast	Locates the last record in a dynaset-or snapshot-type Recordset object that matches the specified criteria and makes that row the current row (Microsoft Access workspaces only).
FindNext	Locates the next record in a dynaset- or snapshot-type Recordset object that matches the specified criteria and makes that row the current row (Microsoft Access workspaces only).
FindPrevious	Locates the previous record in a dynaset- or snapshot-type Recordset object that matches the specified criteria and makes that row the current row (Microsoft Access workspaces only).
GetRows	Retrieves the specified number of rows from a Recordset object.
Move	Moves the recordset's current cursor position to the specified row.
MoveFirst	Moves the Recordset's current cursor position to the next row in the recordset and makes that row the current row.
MoveLast	Moves the Recordset's current cursor position to the last row in the recordset and makes that row the current row.
MovePrevious	Moves the Recordset's current cursor position to the previous row in the recordset and makes that row the current row.
OpenRecordset	Creates a new Recordset object.
Requery	Refreshes the data in a Recordset object by requerying its data source.
Seek	Locates the record in an indexed table-type recordset that matches the specified criteria for the current index and makes that row the current row (Microsoft Access workspaces only).
Update	Saves all data changes made via a recordset during an editing session.

Property	Description
AbsolutePosition	Sets/returns a recordset's relative row number.
BOF	Returns a flag that indicates whether the current record position is before the first record in a `Recordset` object.
Bookmark	Sets/returns a bookmark that uniquely identifies the current record in a recordset.
Bookmarkable	Returns a flag that indicates whether a `Recordset object` supports bookmarks.
CacheSize	Sets/returns the number of ODBC data source records will be locally cached.
CacheStart	Sets/returns a value that specifies the bookmark of the first record in a dynaset-type `Recordset` object that contains data to be locally cached from an ODBC data source (Microsoft Access workspaces only).
Collect	(Hidden) Returns a field's actual value.
DateCreated	Returns the date and time that the `Recordset` object was created (Microsoft Access workspaces only).
EditMode	Returns a value that indicates the current recordset editing state for the current record.
EOF	Returns a flag that indicates whether the current record position is after the last record in a `Recordset` object.
Filter	Sets/returns a value that specifies the records that will be included in a recordset that is created from the current `Recordset` object (Microsoft Access workspaces only).
Index	Sets/returns the name of the current `Index` object in a table-type `Recordset` object (Microsoft Access workspaces only).
LastModified	Returns a bookmark that specifies the most recently added or changed record.
LastUpdated	Returns the date and time of the most recent change that was made to the recordset or to a base table on a table-type recordset (Microsoft Access workspaces only).
LockEdits	Sets/returns a value indicating the type of locking that is in effect while editing the recordset.
Name	Returns the first 256 characters of the recordset's SQL statement.
NoMatch	Returns a flag that indicates whether one of the find methods (`FindFirst`, `FindPrevious`, `FindNext`, `FindLast`, or `Seek`) found the record it was looking for (Microsoft Access workspaces only).
Parent	Hidden. Returns a `Database` object against which the recordset was created.

Property	Description
PercentPosition	Sets/returns a value that indicates the current row's approximate position, based on a percentage of the records in the recordset.
RecordCount	Returns the number of records accessed (so far) in a recordset or the total number of records in a table-type recordset.
Restartable	Returns a flag that indicates whether a Recordset object supports the Requery method.
Sort	Sets/returns the sort order for records in a recordset (Microsoft Access workspaces only).
Transactions	Returns a flag that indicates whether the recordset supports transactions.
Type	Sets/returns a value that indicates the recordset type.
Updatable	Returns a flag that indicates whether you can change the recordset's definition.
ValidationRule	Sets/returns an expression that validates the data in a field as it is changed or added to the table (Microsoft Access workspaces only).
ValidationText	Sets/returns a value that specifies the text of the message that displays if the data entered in a Field doesn't satisfy the validation rule (Microsoft Access workspaces only).

Collections

❑ Fields

❑ Properties

Recordset2 Object

The Recordset2 object represents the records in a base table, or those that result from executing a query. The Recordset2 object was added in Access 2007 to support multi-valued lookup fields and attachment fields.

Method	Description
AddNew	Begins a recordset editing session that creates a new record for an updatable Recordset object.
CancelUpdate	Cancels any pending updates for a Recordset object.
Clone	Creates a new Recordset object that is a duplicate of the original Recordset object.
Close	Closes an open Recordset object.

Table continues on the next page

Method	Description
CopyQueryDef	Creates a new QueryDef object that is a copy of the original QueryDef that was used to create the Recordset object (Microsoft Access workspaces only).
Delete	Deletes the current record in an updatable Recordset object.
Edit	Begins a recordset editing session.
FillCache	Fills all or a part of a local cache for a Recordset object that contains data from a Microsoft Access-connected ODBC data source (Microsoft Access-connected ODBC databases only).
FindFirst	Locates the first record in a dynaset- or snapshot-type Recordset object that matches the specified criteria and makes that row the current row (Microsoft Access workspaces only).
FindLast	Locates the last record in a dynaset- or snapshot-type Recordset object that matches the specified criteria and makes that row the current row (Microsoft Access workspaces only).
FindNext	Locates the next record in a dynaset- or snapshot-type Recordset object that matches the specified criteria and makes that row the current row (Microsoft Access workspaces only).
FindPrevious	Locates the previous record in a dynaset- or snapshot-type Recordset object that matches the specified criteria and makes that row the current row (Microsoft Access workspaces only).
GetRows	Retrieves the specified number of rows from a Recordset object.
Move	Moves the recordset's current cursor position to the specified row.
MoveFirst	Moves the recordset's current cursor position to the next row in the recordset and makes that row the current row.
MoveLast	Moves the recordset's current cursor position to the last row in the recordset and makes that row the current row.
MovePrevious	Moves the recordset's current cursor position to the previous row in the recordset and makes that row the current row.
OpenRecordset	Creates a new Recordset object.
Requery	Refreshes the data in a Recordset object by requerying its data source.
Seek	Locates the record in an indexed table-type recordset that matches the specified criteria for the current index and makes that row the current row (Microsoft Access workspaces only).
Update	Saves all data changes made via a recordset during an editing session.

Property	Description
AbsolutePosition	Sets/returns a recordset's relative row number.
BOF	Returns a flag that indicates whether the current record position is before the first record in a Recordset object.
Bookmark	Sets/returns a bookmark that uniquely identifies the current record in a recordset.
Bookmarkable	Returns a flag that indicates whether a Recordset object supports bookmarks.
CacheSize	Sets/returns the number of ODBC data source records will be locally cached.
CacheStart	Sets/returns a value that specifies the bookmark of the first record in a dynaset-type Recordset object that contains data to be locally cached from an ODBC data source (Microsoft Access workspaces only).
Collect	(Hidden) Returns a field's actual value.
DateCreated	Returns the date and time that the Recordset object was created (Microsoft Access workspaces only).
EditMode	Returns a value that indicates the current recordset editing state for the current record.
EOF	Returns a flag that indicates whether the current record position is after the last record in a Recordset object.
Filter	Sets/returns a value that specifies the records that will be included in a recordset that is created from the current Recordset object (Microsoft Access workspaces only).
Index	Sets/returns the name of the current Index object in a table-type Recordset object (Microsoft Access workspaces only).
LastModified	Returns a bookmark that specifies the most recently added or changed record.
LastUpdated	Returns the date and time of the most recent change that was made to the recordset or to a base table on a table-type recordset (Microsoft Access workspaces only).
LockEdits	Sets/returns a value indicating the type of locking that is in effect while editing the recordset.
Name	Returns the first 256 characters of the recordset's SQL statement.
NoMatch	Returns a flag that indicates whether one of the find methods (FindFirst, FindPrevious, FindNext, FindLast, or Seek) found the record it was looking for (Microsoft Access workspaces only).

Table continues on the next page

Property	Description
Parent	Hidden. Returns a `Database` object against which the recordset was created.
PercentPosition	Sets/returns a value that indicates the current row's approximate position, based on a percentage of the records in the recordset.
RecordCount	Returns the number of records accessed (so far) in a recordset or the total number of records in a table-type recordset.
Restartable	Returns a flag that indicates whether a `Recordset` object supports the `Requery` method.
Sort	Sets/returns the sort order for records in a recordset (Microsoft Access workspaces only).
Transactions	Returns a flag that indicates whether the recordset supports transactions.
Type	Sets/returns a value that indicates the recordset type.
Updatable	Returns a flag that indicates whether you can change the recordset's definition.
ValidationRule	Sets/returns an expression that validates the data in a field as it is changed or added to the table (Microsoft Access workspaces only).
ValidationText	Sets/returns a value that specifies the text of the message that displays if the data entered in a `Field` doesn't satisfy the validation rule (Microsoft Access workspaces only).

Collections

❑   Fields

❑   Properties

The Fields *collection of the* Recordset2 *object contains* Field2 *objects, not* Field *objects as in the* Fields *collection of a* Recordset *object.*

Properties Collection

The `Properties` collection contains all of the `Property` objects associated with a DAO object.

Method	Description
Append	Appends a new user-defined `Property` object to the collection.
Delete	Deletes a user-defined `Property` object from the collection.
Refresh	Refreshes the collection.

Property	Description
Count	Returns the number of items in the Properties collection.
Item	Default. Returns an individual Property object, either by name or numeric index.

Property Object

The Property object is an attribute that defines an object's characteristics or behavior. It has no methods.

Property	Description
Inherited	Returns a flag that specifies whether a Property object is inherited from an underlying object.
Name	Sets/returns a property's name. Read-only for built-in properties.
Type	Sets/returns a value that indicates the property's data type.
Value	Default. Sets/returns the property's actual value.

Collection

❑ Properties

QueryDefs Collection

The QueryDefs collection contains all QueryDef objects of a Database (Microsoft Access workspaces).

Method	Description
Append	Appends a new QueryDef object to the collection.
Delete	Deletes a QueryDef from the collection.
Refresh	Refreshes the collection.

Property	Description
Count	Returns a count of QueryDef objects in the collection.

QueryDef Object

The QueryDef object is a stored definition of a query in a Microsoft Access database.

Method	Description
Close	Closes an open QueryDef object.
CreateProperty	Creates a new user-defined Property object (Microsoft Access workspaces only).
Execute	Runs an action query.
OpenRecordset	Creates a new Recordset object.

Property	Description
CacheSize	Sets/returns the number of records retrieved from an ODBC data source that will be cached locally.
Connect	Sets/returns a value that indicates the source of an open database used in a pass-through query or a linked table. Read-only.
DateCreated	Returns the date and time that the QueryDef object was created (Microsoft Access workspaces only).
KeepLocal	Sets/returns a flag that specifies whether you want to replicate the query when the database is replicated (Microsoft Access workspaces only).
LastUpdated	Returns the date and time of the most recent change that was made to the QueryDef (Microsoft Access workspaces only).
LogMessages	Sets/returns a flag that specifies whether the messages returned from a Microsoft Access–connected ODBC data source are recorded (Microsoft Access workspaces only).
MaxRecords	Sets/returns the maximum number of records to return from a query against an ODBC data source.
Name	Sets/returns the QueryDef name. Read-only.
ODBCTimeout	Returns the number of seconds to wait before a time-out error occurs when a QueryDef is executed against an ODBC data source.
RecordsAffected	Returns the number of records affected by the most recent Execute method.
Replicable	Sets/returns a value that defines whether a query can be replicated (Microsoft Access workspaces only).

Property	Description
ReturnsRecords	Sets/returns a flag that specifies whether an SQL pass-through query to an external database returns records (Microsoft Access workspaces only).
SQL	Sets/returns the SQL statement that defines the query.
Type	Sets/returns a value that indicates the type of QueryDef.
Updatable	Returns a value that indicates whether you can change the QueryDef object.

Collections

❑ Fields

❑ Parameters

❑ Properties

Relations Collection

The Relations collection contains stored Relation objects of a Database object (Microsoft Access databases only).

Method	Description
Append	Appends a new Relation object to the collection.
Delete	Deletes a Relation from the collection.
Refresh	Refreshes the collection.

Property	Description
Count	Returns a count of Relation objects in the collection.

Relation Object

The Relation object is a defined relationship between fields in tables or queries (Microsoft Access databases only).

Method	Description
CreateField	Creates a new Field object (Microsoft Access workspaces only).

Property	Description
Attributes	Sets/returns a value that defines the relation's characteristics.
ForeignTable	Sets/returns the name of the foreign table in a relationship (Microsoft Access workspaces only).
Name	Sets/returns the relation's name. Read-only if the relation has already been added to the collection.
PartialReplica	Sets/returns a flag that indicates whether that relation should be considered when populating a partial replica from a full replica (Microsoft Access databases only).
Table	Sets/returns the name of a `Relation` object's primary table (`TableDef` name or `QueryDef` name). Read-only if the relation has already been added to the collection (Microsoft Access workspaces only).

Collections

❏ Fields

❏ Properties

TableDefs Collection

The `TableDefs` collection contains all stored `TableDef` objects in a database (Microsoft Access workspaces only).

Method	Description
Append	Adds a `TableDef` object to the collection.
Delete	Deletes a `TableDef` object from the collection.
Refresh	Refreshes the objects in the collection.

Property	Description
Count	Returns a count of `TableDef` objects in the collection.

TableDef Object

The `TableDef` object is the stored definition of a table, linked or otherwise (Microsoft Access workspaces only).

Method	Description
CreateField	Creates a new `Field` object (Microsoft Access workspaces only).
CreateIndex	Creates a new `Index` object (Microsoft Access workspaces only).
CreateProperty	Creates a new user-defined `Property` object (Microsoft Access workspaces only).
OpenRecordset	Creates a new `Recordset` object.
RefreshLink	Refreshes the connection for a linked table (Microsoft Access workspaces only).

Property	Description
Attributes	Sets/returns a value that defines the `TableDef`'s characteristics.
ConflictTable	Returns the name of the conflict table that contains details about the records that conflicted during synchronization (Microsoft Access workspaces only).
Connect	Sets/returns a value that indicates the source of a linked table. This setting is read-only on base tables.
DateCreated	Returns the date and time that the `TableDef` object was created (Microsoft Access workspaces only).
KeepLocal	Sets/returns a flag that specifies whether you want to replicate the table when the database is replicated (Microsoft Access workspaces only).
LastUpdated	Returns the date and time of the most recent change that was made to the table (Microsoft Access workspaces only).
Name	Sets/returns the table's name. This property is read-only on linked tables.
RecordCount	Returns the number of records in the table.
Replicable	Sets/returns a flag that specifies whether the table can be replicated (Microsoft Access workspaces only).
ReplicaFilter	Sets/returns a value within a partial replica that specifies which subset of records will be replicated to the table from a full replica (Microsoft Access databases only).
SourceTableName	For linked tables sets/returns the name of the remote table to which the table is connected (Microsoft Access workspaces only). This property is read-only for base tables.
Updatable	Returns a flag that indicates whether you can change the table definition.

Table continues on the next page

Property	Description
ValidationRule	Sets/returns an expression that validates the data in a field as it is changed or added to the table (Microsoft Access workspaces only).
ValidationText	Sets/returns a value that specifies the text of the message that displays if the data entered in a Field doesn't satisfy the validation rule (Microsoft Access workspaces only).

Collections

- ❏ Fields
- ❏ Indexes
- ❏ Properties

Users Collection

The Users collection contains all stored User objects of a Workspace or Group object (Microsoft Access workspaces only). This collection is hidden in Access 2007, but can be used when working with MDB files.

Method	Description
Append	Appends a new User object to the collection.
Delete	Deletes a User from the collection.
Refresh	Refreshes the collection.

Property	Description
Count	Returns a count of User objects in the collection.

User Object

The User object is a user that has access permissions when a workspace operates in a secure workgroup (Microsoft Access workspaces only). This object is hidden in Access 2007, but can be used when working with MDB files.

Method	Description
CreateGroup	Creates a new User object (Microsoft Access workspaces only).
NewPassword	Changes the password of an existing User object (Microsoft Access workspaces only).

Property	Description
Name	Sets/returns the user's name. Read-only if the user has already been added to the collection.
Password	Sets the password for a User object (Microsoft Access workspaces only).
PID	Sets the personal identifier (PID) for a User object (Microsoft Access workspaces only).

Collections

- ❑ Groups
- ❑ Properties

Workspaces Collection

The Workspaces collection contains all active, unhidden Workspace objects of the DBEngine object.

Method	Description
Append	Appends a new Workspace object to the collection.
Delete	Deletes a persistent object from the collection.
Refresh	Refreshes the collection.

Property	Description
Count	Returns a count of Workspace objects in the collection.

Workspace Object

The Workspace object defines a named user session.

Method	Description
BeginTrans	Begins a new transaction.
Close	Closes a workspace.
CommitTrans	Ends the current transaction and saves the changes to disk.
CreateDatabase	Creates a new Database object and saves it to disk.

Table continues on the next page

Method	Description
CreateGroup	(Hidden) Creates a new Group object (Microsoft Access workspaces only).
CreateUser	(Hidden) Creates a new User object (Microsoft Access workspaces only).
OpenDatabase	Opens a specific database in a Workspace.
Rollback	Ends the current transaction and cancels any changes made to DAO objects in the workspace.

Property	Description
IsolateODBCTrans	Sets/returns a value that specifies if multiple transactions involving the same Access-connected ODBC data source are isolated (Microsoft Access workspaces only).
LoginTimeOut	Sets/returns the number of seconds before an error occurs when you attempt to log on to an ODBC database.
Name	Sets/returns the workspace name.
Type	Sets/returns a value that specifies the type of workspace being used.
UserName	(Hidden) Sets/returns the name of a user, group, or the owner of a Workspace object.

Collections

- ❏ Connections
- ❏ Databases
- ❏ (Hidden) Groups
- ❏ Properties
- ❏ (Hidden) Users

Undocumented Tools and Resources

Several Access-specific utilities and object methods are shipped with Microsoft Access 2007. These utilities and methods are not very well documented by Microsoft or are not documented at all. Nonetheless, you can use them to help you develop and maintain your DAO applications.

Utilities ISAMStats

Microsoft Access 2007 contains an undocumented DBEngine method called ISAMStats, which returns various internal statistics. You use ISAMStats to get statistics about different operations. For example, to determine which of several queries will run faster, you can use ISAMStats to return the number of disk reads performed by each query.

Each of the ISAMStats options maintains a separate statistics counter that records the number of times its metric occurs. To reset the counter, set the Reset argument to True. The syntax is as follows:

```
lngReturn = DBEngine.ISAMStats(StatNum [, Reset])
```

where StatNum is one of the following values:

StatNum Value	Description
0	Number of disk reads.
1	Number of disk writes.
3	Number of reads from cache.
4	Number of reads from read-ahead cache.
5	Number of locks placed.
6	Number of locks released.

You must call ISAMStats twice: once to get a baseline statistic and once (after the operation to be analyzed) to get the final statistic. Then you subtract the baseline statistic from the final one to arrive at the statistic for the operation under test. The following examples demonstrate two ways to use ISAMStats:

Method 1

```
Call DBEngine.IsamStats(0, True)
Set rs = db.OpenRecordset("qryGetOverdueAccts", dbOpenSnapshot)
Debug.Print "Total reads: " & DBEngine.IsamStats(0)
```

In this example, the first call resets the ISAMStats counter. The code then opens a recordset using a query you want to test. The last line retakes the statistics and prints it.

Method 2

```
lngBaseline = DBEngine.IsamStats(0)
Set rs = db.OpenRecordset("qryGetOverdueAccts", dbOpenSnapshot)
lngStatistic = DBEngine.IsamStats(0)
Debug.Print "Total reads: " & lngStatistic -lngBaseline
```

In Method 2, ISAMStats is not reset, but its return value is stored in a variable. The code then opens the recordset. The third line retakes the statistic after the operation, while the fourth and final line calculates the actual statistic.

Methods DAO.PrivDBEngine

The unsupported `PrivDBEngine` object enables you to connect to an external database that uses a different Workgroup Information File to the one currently being used. You can open an Access database without having to create another instance of Access. `PrivDBEngine` only allows access to DAO objects, such as `TableDefs`, `QueryDefs`, `Recordsets`, `Fields`, `Containers`, `Documents`, `Indexes`, and `Relations`.

```
Dim dbX As PrivDBEngine
Dim wsX As Workspace
Dim dbe As Database

'Return a reference to a new instance of the PrivDBEngine object
Set dbe = New PrivDBEngine

'Set the SystemDB property to specify the workgroup file
dbe.SystemDB = strWIFPath

'Specify the username (this could be any valid username)
dbe.DefaultUser = strUserName

'Specify the password
dbe.DefaultPassword = strPassword

'Set the workspace
Set wsX = dbe.Workspaces(0)

'Open the secured database
Set dbe = ws.OpenDatabase(strDBPath)
```

The `PrivDBEngine` object does nothing more than create a new instance of the Access database engine. You can get the same functionality by doing the following:

```
Dim dbe As DAO.DBEngine
Set dbe = CreateObject("DAO.DBEngine")
```

The following table lists the `CreateObject` argument for different versions of the Jet or Access database engine.

Jet/Access Version	Argument	Example
3.0	DAO.DBEngine	Set dbe = CreateObject("DAO.DBEngine")
3.5	DAO.DBEngine.35	Set dbe = CreateObject("DAO.DBEngine.35")
3.6	DAO.DBEngine.36	Set dbe = CreateObject("DAO.DBEngine.36")
12.0	DAO.DBEngine.120	Set dbe = CreateObject("DAO.DBEngine.120")

Recordset.Collect

The DAO `Recordset` and `Recordset2` objects expose a hidden, undocumented property named `Collect`. Although `Collect` is a property, it behaves like the `Recordset` object's `Fields` collection, but it's faster because it doesn't need a reference to the `Field` object. Be aware that `Recordset.Collect` only returns a field's value; it doesn't expose any other properties. You can use this property by passing it a numeric item number, or a field name, just like the `Fields` collection. For example:

```
Set rs = db.OpenRecordset("tblCustomers")
Debug.Print "CustID: " & rs.Collect(0)
Debug.Print "CustomerNo: " & rs.Collect("CustomerNo")
```

Recordset.Parent

The undocumented `Recordset.Parent` property is an object reference to the database to which the recordset belongs. This may be especially useful in situations where you have several `Database` objects in the same application.

DAO Field Types

The following table lists the constants in the DAO `DataTypeEnum` and their corresponding data types in the Access Table designer.

DAO DataTypeEnum	Constant Value	Access Field Type
dbAttachment	101	Attachment
dbBigInt	16	Cannot create in Access, but can be used by linked tables
dbBinary	9	Cannot create in Access designer but can be created in DAO
dbBoolean	1	Yes/No
dbByte	2	Number, Field Size=Byte
dbChar	18	Cannot create in Access, but can be used by linked tables
dbComplexByte	102	Number, Field Size=Byte
dbComplexDecimal	108	Cannot create in DAO but can create in Access designer
dbComplexDouble	106	Number, Field Size=Double
dbComplexGUID	107	Number, Field Size=Replication ID
dbComplexInteger	103	Number, Field Size=Integer
dbComplexLong	104	Number, Field Size=Long Integer

Table continues on the next page

DAO DataTypeEnum	Constant Value	Access Field Type
dbComplexSingle	105	Number, Field Size=Single
dbComplexText	109	Text
dbCurrency	5	Currency
dbDate	8	Date/Time
dbDecimal	20	Cannot create in DAO but can create in Access designer
dbDouble	7	Number, Field Size=Double
dbFloat	21	Cannot create in Access, but can be used by linked tables
dbGUID	15	Number, Field Size=Replication ID
dbInteger	3	Number, Field Size=Integer
dbLong	4	Number, Field Size=Long Integer
dbLongBinary	11	Number, Field Size=OLE Object
dbMemo	12	Memo
dbNumeric	19	Cannot create in Access, but can be used by linked tables
dbSingle	6	Number, Field Size=Single
dbText	10	Text
dbTime	22	Cannot create in Access, but can be used by linked tables
dbTimeStamp	23	Cannot create in Access, but can be used by linked tables
dbVarBinary	17	Cannot create in Access, but can be used by linked tables

OpenRecordset Constants

You'll use a variety of constants when writing VBA code. The following tables list just a few of the constants you might use when opening a DAO recordset.

A runtime error occurs if you attempt to use dbOpenTable in the following Microsoft Access workspace situations:

When the recordset is based on a QueryDef

When the Source argument refers to an SQL statement or TableDef that refers to a linked table

The following table lists the constants that can be specified for the `Type` argument.

Constant	Description
dbOpenTable	Returns an editable dataset consisting of records from a single local table only. Cannot be used with linked tables (Microsoft Access workspaces only).
dbOpenDynaset	Returns an editable dataset consisting of pointers to records in a table or query. Can be used on multiple local and linked tables (Microsoft Access workspaces only).
dbOpenSnapshot	Returns a read-only dataset consisting of a copy of records in a table or query. Can be used on multiple local and linked tables (Microsoft Access workspaces only).
dbOpenForwardOnly	Returns an editable dataset consisting of records in a table. Use this option when you only need to move through the dataset in one pass and in one direction — forward (Microsoft Access workspaces only).

The following table lists the constants that can be specified for the `Options` argument.

The `dbInconsistent` *and* `dbConsistent` *constants are mutually exclusive. Similarly you cannot supply a* `LockEdits` *argument on a recordset whose* `Options` *argument is set to* `dbReadOnly`. *If you attempt to do so, a runtime error occurs.*

Constant	Description
dbAppendOnly	Signifies that you can add new records, but not edit or delete them (Microsoft Access dynaset recordsets only).
dbSQLPassThrough	Signifies that the SQL statement will be passed directly to a Microsoft Access-connected ODBC data source for processing (Microsoft Access snapshot recordsets only).
dbSeeChanges	Triggers a runtime error if another user attempts to change data that you're currently editing (Microsoft Access dynaset recordsets only).
dbDenyWrite	Locks all the underlying tables so other users can only view the data. They cannot add, edit, or delete records while the lock is in place (Microsoft Access recordsets only).
dbDenyRead	Completely locks all the underlying tables so other users cannot even view the data (Microsoft Access table recordsets only).
dbForwardOnly	Creates a forward-only recordset (Microsoft Access snapshot recordsets only). This option is provided for backward compatibility only, and you should use the `dbOpenForwardOnly` constant in the `Type` argument instead of this option.

Constant	Description
dbReadOnly	Creates a read-only recordset, preventing users from making changes to the data (Microsoft Access only). You can use dbReadOnly in either the Options argument or the LockEdits argument, but not both. If you attempt to do so, a runtime error occurs. This option is provided for backward compatibility only, and you should use the dbReadOnly constant in the LockEdits argument instead of this option.
dbInconsistent	Allows inconsistent updates (Microsoft Access dynaset and snapshot recordsets only). An inconsistent update is one in which you can update all the columns in a multi-table recordset unless referential integrity rules prevent it.
dbConsistent	Allows only consistent updates (Microsoft Access dynaset-type and snapshot-type Recordset objects only). A consistent update is one in which you can perform only those updates that result in a consistent view of the data. For example, you cannot update the many side of a one-to-many relationship unless a matching record exists in the one side.

The following table lists the constants that can be specified for the LockEdits argument.

> You cannot supply a LockEdits argument on a recordset whose Options argument is set to dbReadOnly. If you attempt to do so, a runtime error occurs.

Constant	Description
dbReadOnly	Creates a read-only recordset, preventing users from making changes to the data. You can use dbReadOnly in either the Options argument or the LockEdits argument, but not both. If you attempt to do so, a runtime error occurs. Setting dbReadOnly in the Options argument is provided for backward compatibility only. You should use it in the LockEdits argument instead.
dbPessimistic	Uses pessimistic locking for changes made to the recordset in a multi-user environment. Pessimistic locking is where the entire data page that contains the record you're editing is locked (made unavailable to other users) as soon as you issue the Edit method, and remains locked until you issue the Update method (this is the default setting for Microsoft Access workspaces).
dbOptimistic	Uses optimistic locking for changes made to the recordset in a multi-user environment. Optimistic locking is where the entire data page that contains the record you're editing is locked (made unavailable to other users) as soon as you issue the Update method and remains locked until the data is written to the table (this is the default setting for Microsoft Access workspaces). You use optimistic locking when manipulating ODBC databases or when the LockEdits property is set to False.

ADO Object Model Reference

When using VBA to access data in ODBC compliant databases, you can choose from DAO or ADO. To use either technique, you'll need to understand the object model for the appropriate technology. The ADO object model isn't overly complicated, but understanding the details of all the various ADO objects will help ensure that you use the proper object for the designated task.

This appendix lists all of the major objects needed when using ADO to access data within VBA. For each of the major objects, properties, methods, events, and associated collections are provided. Keep this appendix handy when programming ADO and refer to it when you have questions about the specific property, method, or event to use in your code.

Connection Object

The Connection object represents a unique session with a data source. The Connection object has collections, methods, and properties associated with it. The availability of these collections, methods, and properties is dependent on the functionality supported by the provider.

Properties of the Connection Object

The following table describes each of the properties of the Connection object.

Property	DataType	Description
Attributes	Long	Generic property indicating one or more characteristics of the connection object.
CommandTimeout	Long	Configures the timeout value for the Execute method on the Connection object.

Table continues on the next page

Property	DataType	Description
ConnectionString	String	The default property value. Specifies a data source. Pass in a connection string containing a series of argument = value statements separated by semi-colons.
ConnectionTimeout	Long	Indicates how long to wait while establishing a connection before terminating the attempt and generating an error.
CursorLocation	Long	Allows the developer to choose between various cursor locations (usually either client or server).
DefaultDatabase	String	Sets or returns a string that resolves to the name of a database available from the provider.
IsolationLevel	Long	Sets or returns an IsolationLevelEnum value. The default is adXactReadCommitted.
Mode	Long	Indicates the level of permissions available for modifying data in a connection, record, or stream object.
Provider	String	Sets or returns a string value representing the provider name. If no provider is specified, the property will default to MSDASQL (Microsoft OLE DB Provider for ODBC).
State	Long	Describes whether the connection is open or closed.
Version	String	Reads the version from the ADO implementation.

Methods of the Connection Object

The Connection object also provides a number of methods to use when working with a connection object. Those methods are described in the following table.

Method	Description
BeginTrans	Begins a new transaction.
Cancel	Cancels the execution of a pending Open or Execute method.
Close	Closes the connection to the data source.
CommitTrans	Saves any changes and ends the current transaction.
Execute	Executes a command on the connection. This method can pass a query string to the execute method to use without a Command object or can use the Command object to persist the command text and re-execute it. A Command object is also required to use query parameters.

Method	Description
Open	Establishes the connection to the data source.
OpenSchema	Obtains database schema information from the provider.
RollbackTrans	Cancels any changes made in the current transaction and ends the transaction.

Collections of the Connection Object

The Connection object has exactly two collections, Errors and Properties, which are described in the following table.

Collection	Description
Errors	Contains all of the error objects related to the current Connection object.
Properties	Contains all the Property objects for the current connection.

Errors Collection and Error Object

The Errors collection contains all Error objects created by a response to a provider-related failure. The Error object contains the details about the error; it also has properties and methods you can use within your code. Any operation that involves an ADO object can generate errors. Every time another error occurs for the same object, an additional Error object is added to the Errors collection.

One caveat of error processing is that when a new ADO operation generates an error, the Errors collection is cleared and a new set of Error objects can be added to the Errors collection. It is common to use error-handling routines to examine the Error objects in the Errors collection to react to possible errors. This allows you to display helpful error messages in plain language rather than relying on the system to generate errors that are incomprehensible to inexperienced users.

Properties of the Errors Collection

The various properties of the Errors collection are summarized in the following table.

Property	Data Type	Description
Count	Long	Returns the number of error objects stored in the Errors collection.
Item	String or Long	References a specific member of the Errors collection by name or ordinal number.

Methods for the Errors Collection

The following table describes the methods available for the `Errors` collection.

Method	Description
Clear	Removes all `Error` objects from the `Errors` collection.
Refresh	Updates the `Errors` collection to encompass all current `Error` objects.

Properties of the Error Object

Each `Error` object in an `Errors` collection provides information about a specific error that has occurred through its properties. The following table describes each of the properties of the `Error` object.

Property	DataType	Description
Description	String	The default property value. Contains the text of the error.
HelpContext	Long	Context ID of a topic in the Help file.
HelpFile	String	Name and location of the Help file.
NativeError	Long	Returns a long value used to retrieve the database-specific error information for an `Error` object.
Number	Long	Long integer value of the error constant.
Source	String	Identifies the object that raised the error.
SQLState	Variant	Returns a five character error code from the provider when an error occurs during the processing of a SQL statement.

There are no methods for the `Error` object.

Properties Collection and Property Object

The `Properties` collection contains all of the `Property` objects for a specific instance of any given object. The previous statement may be somewhat confusing, but what it really means is that every object contains properties. All of those properties are stored in a `Properties` collection for that particular object. The `Properties` collection for the `Error` object contains the `Description`, `Number`, `Source`, `SQLState`, and `NativeError` properties. There are two types of properties: dynamic and built-in. Neither type of property can be deleted.

Properties of the Property Object

Every `Property` object has four properties of its own, which are detailed in the following table.

Property	DataType	Description
Attributes	Long	Long value that indicates characteristics of the property that are provider specific.
Name	String	String that identifies the property.
Type	Integer	Integer that specifies the property data type.
Value	Variant	The default property value. A variant that contains the property setting.

No methods are associated with the `Property` object.

Command Object

The `Command` object provides a lot of useful functionality for working with the data source. Examples of common operations include retrieving records in a recordset, executing bulk operations, and even manipulating the structure of a database. The flexibility of the `Command` object is specific to the provider used. Depending on the provider, some properties or methods may generate errors when referenced if the object is not supported.

Properties of the Command Object

The following table lists the various properties of the `Command` object.

Property	DataType	Description
ActiveConnection	String or Connection	Indicates which `Connection` object the `Command` object uses.
CommandStream	Stream object	Stream used as the input for the `Command` object.
CommandText	String	Indicates the text of the `Command` being executed.
CommandTimeout	Long	Sets the number of seconds a provider will wait for a command to execute.
CommandType	CommandTypeEnum	Specifies the type of command executed. Values include: adCmdUnspecified, adCmdText, adCmdTable, adCmdStoredProc, adCmdUnknown, adCmdFile, adCmdTableDirect.

Table continues on the next page

Property	DataType	Description
Dialect	GUID	Contains a GUID that represents the dialect of the command text or stream.
Name	String	Identifies the Command object as a method on the associated Connection object.
NamedParameters	Boolean	Indicates whether parameter names are passed to the provider.
Prepared	Boolean	True if the provider should save a compiled version of a Command before execution.
State	Long	Value that represents if the Command object is open, closed, or in the process of connecting, executing, or retrieving information.

Methods of the Command Object

Methods of the Command objects are used to work with a particular command that will be executed on the Connection object. To execute a Command object, just call it by its Name property on the associated Connection object.

Method	Description
Cancel	Cancels the execution of an asynchronous call before it has completed.
CreateParameter	Creates a parameter for the Command object with the specified settings, which are five optional parameters: Name, Type, Direction, Size, and Value.
Execute	Executes the particular command stored in the CommandText property.

Collections of the Command Object

Collection	Description
Parameters	Contains all the Parameter objects used for stored queries and stored procedures.
Properties	Contains all the Property objects for the current command object.

Parameters Collection

The Command object has a Parameters collection associated with it that contains all of the Parameter objects of the Command object. The actual Parameters collection does not contain any properties or collections, only methods.

Methods of the Parameters Collection

There are exactly three methods for the Parameters collection. They are described in the following table.

Method	Arguments	Description
Append	Parameter object	Used to add a Parameter object to the collection.
Refresh	None	Updates all of the Parameter objects in the collection with the latest information from the provider.
Delete	Index	Deletes a Parameter object from the collection. The Index value is either the name or ordinal position of the Parameter in the collection.

Properties of the Parameter Object

Each Parameter object in the Parameters collection contains the actual data for the parameter. The following table describes the various properties of the Parameter objects.

Property	DataType	Description
Attributes	Long	A read/write property that is the sum of any one or more ParameterAttributesEnum values. The default value is adParamSigned.
Direction	ParameterDirectionEnum	Indicates if the Parameter represents an input parameter, an output parameter, an input and an output parameter, or if the parameter is the return value from a stored procedure.
Name	String	Sets or returns the name of the Parameter.
NumericScale	Byte	Sets or returns a byte value that indicates the number of decimal places to which numeric values are resolved.
Precision	Byte	Indicates the degree of precision for a Parameter object. This sets or returns a Byte field to represent the maximum number of digits used to represent values.

Table continues on the next page

Property	DataType	Description
Size	Long	Indicates the maximum size in either bytes or characters of the `Parameter` object.
Type	DataTypeEnum	Indicates the data type of the `Parameter`.
Value	Variant	The default property value. Sets or returns the value of the `Parameter`.

Method of the Parameter Object

The only method available for the `Parameter` object is `AppendChunk`. It simply appends data to the `Parameter` object. Use the `CreateParameter` method of the `Command` object to create a `Parameter` with a specific name and properties. Then use the `Append` method to add the newly created `Parameter` to the `Parameters` collection.

Method	Description
AppendChunk	Adds a `Parameter` to the `Parameters` collection.

Collections of the Parameter Object

There is exactly one collection for the `Parameter` object — `Properties`.

Collection	Description
Properties	Contains all the `Property` objects for the current `Parameter` object.

Recordset Object

The `Recordset` object is used to read or manipulate data in an ADO data source. It represents the set of records from a table or the results of an executed command. All recordsets consist of records (rows) and fields (columns). Depending on the functionality supported by the provider, some `Recordset` methods or properties may not be available.

Properties of the Recordset Object

The `Recordset` object has a variety of properties and methods you'll use in your programming. The following table describes the properties.

Property	DataType	Description
AbsolutePage	Long	Identifies the page the current record of the Recordset is on.
AbsolutePosition	Long	Identifies the position of the current record in the Recordset.
ActiveCommand	Variant	Pointer to the Command object that created the Recordset.
ActiveConnection	String or Connection	Specifies the Connection object used to retrieve the Recordset.
BOF	Boolean	True if you're currently at the beginning of the file, the position before the first record.
Bookmark	Variant	Allows you to return to a specific record in the Recordset.
CacheSize	Long	The number of records ADO caches from the server.
CursorLocation	Long	Lists whether the cursor service that maintain the results of the query is client-side or server-side.
CursorType	CursorTypeEnum	Specifies the type of cursor used to access the query results (dynamic, keyset, status, forward-only).
DataMember	String	Specifies which Recordset in the data source you're referring to.
DataSource	Object	Allows you to associate the Recordset with a data source.
EditMode	EditModeEnum	Specifies the editing status for the current record.
EOF	Boolean	True if you're currently at the end of file, the position after the last record in your Recordset.
Filter	Variant	Allows you to filter your Recordset for particular values.
Index	String	Controls the index currently applied in your Recordset.
LockType	LockTypeEnum	Controls how the contents of the Recordset are locked and updated.
MarshalOptions	MarshalOptionEnum	Specifies which records are transferred back to the server.

Table continues on the next page

Property	DataType	Description
MaxRecords	Long	Long value representing the maximum number of records returned by the query.
PageCount	Long	The number of pages in your Recordset.
PageSize	Long	Specifies the number of records per page in the Recordset.
RecordCount	Long	Long value representing the number of records in the Recordset.
Sort	String	Allows you to specify a sort order in your Recordset.
Source	String or command	String value or command object that contains the query string used for the Recordset.
StayInSync	Boolean	True if the child record needs to be kept updated.
State	Long	Returns the current state of the Recordset.
Status	RecordStatusEnum	Stores the update status of the current record.

There are two common properties used when working with a Recordset object. The first, and probably most important, is the Fields collection. This collection stores all of the fields that contain the results of a given query. The second is the Properties collection, a collection of dynamic properties associated with Recordset.

Methods of the Recordset Object

You'll use a number of methods when manipulating your Recordset object as well. Those methods are listed in the following table.

Method	Description
AddNew	Adds a new record to the Recordset.
Cancel	Cancels the execution of an asynchronous query.
CancelBatch	Cancels pending changes in a Recordset that uses batch optimistic updates.
CancelUpdate	Cancels pending changes currently being edited.
Clone	Creates a new reference to the Recordset that allows navigation independently from the original Recordset.
Close	Closes the Recordset object and releases its contents.
CompareBookmarks	Compares two bookmarks in the same Recordset.

Method	Description
Delete	Deletes the current record in the Recordset.
Find	Searches the Recordset for a record based on the string criteria.
GetRows	Returns the record data in a two-dimensional Variant array.
GetString	Returns the record data in a String format.
Move	Moves the position of the current record.
MoveFirst	Moves to the first record in the Recordset.
MoveLast	Moves to the last record in the Recordset.
MoveNext	Moves to the next record in the Recordset.
MovePrevious	Moves to the previous record in the Recordset.
NextRecordset	Clears any previously existing records and returns the next Recordset. The record returned is the result of the next command in a compound command statement.
Open	Opens the Recordset.
Requery	Re-executes the query that generated the Recordset.
Resync	Retrieves the current data for the records in the Recordset.
Save	Writes the Recordset contents to a file.
Seek	Searches the Recordset for a specific string.
Supports	Returns a Boolean value indicating whether the Recordset supports a particular type of functionality.
Update	Writes pending changes to the Recordset.
UpdateBatch	Submits pending changes in a Recordset that uses batch optimistic updating.

Collections of the Recordset Object

The Recordset object contains two collections: Fields and Properties. The Fields collection is useful for retrieving information about the fields contained in the Recordset object.

Collection	Description
Fields	Contains all the Field objects for the current data contained in the Recordset object.
Properties	Contains all the Property information for the Recordset object.

Fields Collection

The `Fields` collection contains all the `Field` objects of a `Recordset` or `Record` object. It allows you to retrieve information about the field as well as data within the field. The following sections describe the properties and methods for the `Fields` collection. There are no collections for the `Fields` collection.

Properties of the Fields Collection

The `Fields` collection supplies only two properties: `Count` and `Item`, which are detailed in the following table.

Property	DataType	Description
Count	Long	The number of `Field` objects in the `Record` or `Recordset` object.
Item	Field	Identifies the position of the current record in the `Recordset`.

Methods of the Fields Collection

Methods for the `Fields` collection are described in the following table.

Method	Description
Append	Creates and adds a field object to the `Fields` collection.
Update	Finalizes any additions or deletions to the `Fields` collection.
CancelUpdate	Cancels any pending changes for a record.
Delete	Deletes a `Field` from the collection.
Refresh	Refreshes the `Fields` collection.
Resync	Resynchronizes the current record.

Field Object

The `Fields` collection contains `Field` objects. Each object represents an individual field within a `Fields` collection from an ADO `Record` or `Recordset` object.

Properties of the Field Object

The properties for the `Field` object are described in the following table.

Property	DataType	Description
ActualSize	Long	Returns the actual size of the value of the field.
Attributes	Long	Describes certain characteristics of the field.
DataFormat	Object	Can be used to format your data.
DefinedSize	Long	Describes the defined size for the field.
Name	String	Contains the name of the field.
NumericScale	Byte	Number of digits allowed to the right of the decimal point for a numeric field.
OriginalValue	Variant	Stores the original value for the field.
Precision	Byte	Indicates the precision for numeric data.
Status	FieldStatusEnum	Determines whether the field has been successfully added to the collection.
Type	Byte	Lists the data type for the field.
UnderlyingValue	Variant	Lists the most recently retrieved value for the field.
Value	Variant	Contains the field's current value.

Methods of the Field Object

The Field object has two methods, which are detailed in the following table. These methods apply only to string or binary field types and may not be supported by all ADO providers.

Method	Description
AppendChunk	Allows data to be appended to a string or binary field type.
GetChunk	Allows retrieval of data from a string or binary field type.

Collection of the Field Object

The only collection of the Field object is the standard Properties collection.

Collection	Description
Properties	Contains all the property objects for the current Command object.

Record Object

The Record object represents a row from a Recordset or any object returned by a data provider. A Record object contains data from the row and allows the user to easily access that data.

Properties of the Record Object

The following table describes the properties associated with a Record object.

Property	DataType	Description
ActiveConnection	Variant	The Connection object used to retrieve the data for the Record object.
Mode	ConnectModeEnum	Specifies the permissions for modifying the Record object.
ParentURL	String	The Parent URL for the Record object.
RecordType	RecordTypeEnum	Specifies the type of the Record object.
Source	Variant	Specifies the source of the data contained in the Record object.
State	ObjectStateEnum	Indicates the state of the Record object.

Methods of the Record Object

The Record object has seven methods, defined in the following table.

Method	Description
Cancel	Cancels an asynchronous action on the Record object.
Close	Closes an open Record object.
CopyRecord	Copies the Record object to another location.
DeleteRecord	Deletes the current record.
GetChildren	Retrieves the child data associated with the Record object.
MoveRecord	Moves the Record to another location.
Open	Opens an existing Record or creates a new Record.

Collections of the Record Object

The Record object has two collections, just like the Recordset object. These collections are described in the following table.

Collection	Description
Fields	Contains all the Field objects for the data contained in the Record object.
Properties	Contains all the Property information for the Record object.

Stream Object

The Stream object in ADO represents a stream of binary data or text. Although the Stream object was not covered in the chapter for ADO, it is included here for reference. Be aware that not all ADO providers support the Stream object.

Properties for the Stream Object

The following table lists the various properties of the Stream object.

Property	DataType	Description
Charset	String	Specifies the character set for the stream.
EOS	Boolean	True if the current position is at the end of stream (EOS).
LineSeparator	LineSeparatorEnum	Specifies the character or combination of characters used as the line separator in the stream.
Mode	ConnectModeEnum	Specifies the permissions for modifying data in the Stream object.
Position	Long	The current position in the stream.
Size	Long	Specifies the current size of the stream of data.
State	ObjectStateEnum	Specifies the current state of the Stream object.
Type	StreamTypeEnum	Specifies the type of data stored in the Stream object.

Methods for the Stream Object

The methods you can use with the `Stream` object are described in the following table.

Method	Description
Cancel	Cancels a pending asynchronous call to a `Stream` object.
Close	Closes an open `Stream` object.
CopyTo	Copies data from the `Stream` object to another `Stream` object.
Flush	Flushes the contents stored in the Stream's buffer.
LoadFromFile	Loads the contents of a file into the `Stream` object.
Open	Opens the `Stream` object.
Read	Reads binary data from the stream.
ReadText	Reads text data from the stream.
SaveToFile	Writes data from the `Stream` object to a file.
SetEOS	Sets the current position as the end of the `Stream` object.
SkipLine	Moves to the beginning of the next line of data in the text stream.
Write	Appends binary data to the stream.
WriteText	Appends text data to the stream.

ADO Object Argument Enumeration Information

The methods supplied by the various ADO objects often have parameters that require enumeration options. This appendix provides information about common enumerations for common ADO object methods. The information in this appendix relates to both Chapter 7 and Appendix E, and can be used in conjunction with both.

Connection.Execute Method Options

The following tables list the enumeration values that you can specify for the Command.Execute method's options argument.

CommandTypeEnum Members

The CommandType enumeration specifies how the Connection.CommandText argument is to be interpreted.

Member	Value	Description
adCmdUnspecified	-1	Hidden. No command type is specified.
adCmdText	1	The CommandText argument is a command or the name of a stored procedure.
adCmdTable	2	The CommandText argument is the name of a table.
adCmdStoredProc	4	The CommandText argument is the name of a stored procedure.

Table continues on the next page

Member	Value	Description
adCmdUnknown	8	Default. The type of command in the CommandType argument is unknown.
adCmdFile	256	The CommandText argument is the name of a stored recordset (Recordset.Open or Requery methods only).
adCmdTableDirect	512	The CommandText argument is the name of a table (Recordset.Open or Requery methods only). This option cannot be combined with adAsyncExecute.

ExecuteOptionEnum Members

The ExecuteOption enumeration specifies how the provider is to execute the Connection.CommandText argument.

Member	Value	Description
adOptionUnspecified	-1	Hidden. The command is not specified.
adAsyncExecute	16	The command executes asynchronously. This option cannot be combined with adCmdTableDirect.
adAsyncFetch	32	The rows that remain to be retrieved after those specified by the CacheSize property are to be retrieved asynchronously.
adAsyncFetchNonBlocking	64	The main thread never blocks while retrieving data, so if the requested row has not been retrieved, the current row automatically moves to the end of the file. This setting is ignored if the adCmdTableDirect option is used, or if you open a recordset from a stream that contains a persistently stored recordset.
adExecuteNoRecords	128	The CommandText argument is a command or stored procedure that does not return records.
adExecuteStream	1024	Return the results of a command operation as a stream (Command.Execute only).
adExecuteRecord	2048	Hidden. The CommandText argument is a command or stored procedure that returns a single row as a Record object.

For information about how to view hidden objects in the Object Browser, refer to Chapter 2.

Recordset.Open Method Options

The Open method of the Recordset Object can take several different enumerations, the details of which are described in the following tables.

CursorTypeEnum Members

Member	Value	Description
adOpenUnspecified	-1	Hidden. No cursor type is specified.
adOpenForwardOnly	0	Default. Specifies a forward-only cursor. This is similar to a static cursor, except that you can only scroll forward through the records.
adOpenKeyset	1	Specifies a keyset cursor. This is similar to a dynamic cursor, except that records added by other users are not reflected in your recordset; however, records that other users delete are inaccessible in your recordset.
adOpenDynamic	2	Specifies a dynamic cursor. In this cursor type, all additions, deletions, and modifications made by other users are visible in your recordset, and all types of row movement are allowed. If the provider supports bookmarks, they too are allowed.
adOpenStatic	3	Specifies a static cursor. This cursor type is read-only, and additions, deletions, and modifications made by other users are invisible in your recordset.

LockTypeEnum Members

Member	Value	Description
adLockUnspecified	-1	. A lock type is not specified. Clones are created with the same lock type as their original.
adLockReadOnly	1	Specifies a read-only recordset.
adLockPessimistic	2	Specifies pessimistic locking at record-level.
adLockOptimistic	3	Specifies pessimistic locking at record-level. The record is locked only when you call the Update method.
adLockBatchOptimistic	4	Specifies optimistic locking for batch updated.

Options Argument

Options arguments can be one or more of the following enumeration members.

CommandTypeEnum Members

Member	Value	Description
adCmdUnspecified	-1	Hidden. No command type is specified.
adCmdText	1	The Source argument is a command or the name of a stored procedure.
adCmdTable	2	The Source argument is the name of a table.
adCmdStoredProc	4	The Source argument is the name of a stored procedure.
adCmdUnknown	8	Default. The type of command in the Source argument is unknown.
adCmdFile	256	The Source argument is the name of a stored Recordset.
adCmdTableDirect	512	The Source argument is the name of a table. This option cannot be combined with adAsyncExecute.

ExecuteOptionEnum Members

Member	Value	Description
adOptionUnspecified	-1	Hidden. The command is not specified.
adAsyncExecute	16	The command executes asynchronously. This option cannot be combined with adCmdTableDirect.
adAsyncFetch	32	The rows that remain to be retrieved after those specified by the CacheSize property are to be retrieved asynchronously.
adAsyncFetchNonBlocking	64	The main thread never blocks while retrieving data, so if the requested row has not been retrieved, the current row automatically moves to the end of the file. This setting is ignored if the adCmdTableDirect option is used, or if you open a recordset from a stream that contains a persistently stored recordset.
adExecuteNoRecords	128	The Source argument is a command or stored procedure that does not return records.
adExecuteStream	1024	Hidden. Specifies the result of the command execution be returned as a stream. Can be used only with the Command.Execute method.
adExecuteRecord	2048	Hidden. The Source argument is a command or stored procedure that returns a single row as a Record object.

Connection.OpenSchema Method Options

The tables in this section describe the values that can be specified for the Command.OpenSchema method's Schema and Restrictions arguments.

Schema Argument Members

The Schema argument specifies the type of information to return, the members of which are defined in the following table.

Only those values that have meaning in Access are included. The four remaining unlisted values, adSchemaActions, adSchemaCommands, adSchemaFunctions, and adSchemaSets relate specifically to the Microsoft OLE DB Provider for OLAP Services library. For more information about these enumeration members, please refer to the Microsoft Knowledge Base.

SchemaEnum Members

Member	Value	Description
adSchemaAsserts	0	Returns the constraints defined in the catalog. Unsupported by the Jet provider.
adSchemaCatalogs	1	Returns the catalogs that are accessible from the database. Unsupported by the Jet provider.
adSchemaCharacterSets	2	Returns the character sets defined in the catalog. Unsupported by the Jet provider.
adSchemaCheckConstraints	4	Returns the check constraints (validation rules) defined in the catalog.
adSchemaCollations	3	Returns the sort orders defined in the catalog. Unsupported by the Jet provider.
adSchemaColumnPrivileges	13	Returns the privileges on columns that are available to, or granted by, a given user. Unsupported by the Jet provider.
adSchemaColumns	4	Returns the columns of tables and views that are accessible to a given user.
adSchemaColumnsDomainUsage	11	Returns the columns that are dependent on a domain that is owned by a given user. Unsupported by the Jet provider.
adSchemaConstraintColumnUsage	6	Returns the columns used by referential constraints, unique constraints, check constraints, and assertions.

Table continues on the next page

SchemaEnum Members (continued)

Member	Value	Description
adSchemaConstraintTableUsage	7	Returns the tables that are used by referential constraints, unique constraints, check constraints, and assertions for a given user. Unsupported by the Jet provider.
adSchemaCubes	32	Returns information about the available cubes (multi-dimensional data) in a schema (or the catalog, if the provider does not support schemas). Unsupported by the Jet provider.
adSchemaDBInfoKeywords	30	Returns a list of provider-specific keywords.
adSchemaDBInfoLiterals	31	Returns a list of provider-specific literals (quotes and escape characters) used in text commands.
adSchemaDimensions	33	Returns information about the dimensions in a cube; one row per dimension. Unsupported by the Jet provider.
adSchemaForeignKeys	27	Returns the foreign key columns defined in the catalog.
adSchemaHierarchies	34	Returns information about the hierarchies available in a cube dimension. Unsupported by the Jet provider.
adSchemaIndexes	12	Returns the indexes defined in the catalog.
adSchemaKeyColumnUsage	8	Returns the columns that are defined in the catalog as keys.
adSchemaLevels	35	Returns information about the levels available in a cube dimension. Unsupported by the Jet provider.
adSchemaMeasures	36	Returns information about the available cube measures. Unsupported by the Jet provider.
adSchemaMembers	38	Returns information about the available cube members. Unsupported by the Jet provider.
adSchemaPrimaryKeys	28	Returns the primary key columns defined in the catalog.

SchemaEnum Members (continued)

Member	Value	Description
adSchemaProcedureColumns	29	Returns information about the columns in stored procedures. Unsupported by the Jet provider.
adSchemaProcedureParameters	26	Returns information about the parameters and return codes of stored procedures. Unsupported by the Jet provider.
adSchemaProcedures	16	Returns the procedures defined in the catalog. Unsupported by the Jet provider.
adSchemaProperties	37	Returns information about the available properties for each level of the cube dimension. Unsupported by the Jet provider.
adSchemaProviderSpecific	-1	Returns schema information for a provider that defines its own non-standard schema queries.
adSchemaProviderTypes	22	Returns the base data types supported by the provider.
adSchemaReferentialConstraints	9	Returns the referential constraints (relationships) defined in the catalog.
adSchemaSchemata	17	Returns the schemas (database objects) that are owned by a given user. Unsupported by the Jet provider.
adSchemaSQLLanguages	18	Returns the levels of ANSI SQL conformance, options, and dialects supported in the catalog. Unsupported by the Jet provider.
adSchemaStatistics	19	Returns the catalog statistics.
adSchemaTableConstraints	10	Returns the table constraints (validation rules) defined in the catalog.
adSchemaTablePrivileges	14	Returns the privileges on tables that are available to, or granted by, a given user. Unsupported by the Jet provider.
adSchemaTables	20	Returns the tables and views defined in the catalog.
adSchemaTranslations	21	Returns the character translations defined in the catalog. Unsupported by the Jet provider.

Table continues on the next page

SchemaEnum Members

Member	Value	Description
adSchemaTrustees	39	Returns the users and groups defined in the catalog.
adSchemaUsagePrivileges	15	Returns the USAGE privileges on objects that are available to, or granted by, a given user. Unsupported by the Jet provider.
adSchemaViewColumnUsage	24	Returns the columns included in views. Unsupported by the Jet provider.
adSchemaViews	23	Returns the views defined in the catalog.
adSchemaViewTableUsage	25	Returns the tables included in views. Unsupported by the Jet provider.

Restrictions Argument Members

The optional Restrictions parameter allows the output to be filtered by specifying a member of the SchemaEnum enumeration. For example, a Recordset object can be filtered to return only a single table or view. The available members and their constraints as described in the following table.

SchemaEnum Member Restrictions

Member	Constraint Columns
adSchemaAsserts	CONSTRAINT_CATALOG CONSTRAINT_SCHEMA CONSTRAINT_NAME
adSchemaCatalogs	CATALOG_NAME
adSchemaCharacterSets	CHARACTER_SET_CATALOG CHARACTER_SET_SCHEMA CHARACTER_SET_NAME
adSchemaCheckConstraints	CONSTRAINT_CATALOG CONSTRAINT_SCHEMA CONSTRAINT_NAME
adSchemaCollations	COLLATION_CATALOG COLLATION_SCHEMA COLLATION_NAME
adSchemaColumnPrivileges	TABLE_CATALOG TABLE_SCHEMA TABLE_NAME COLUMN_NAME GRANTOR GRANTEE

SchemaEnum Member Restrictions (continued)

Member	Constraint Columns
adSchemaColumns	TABLE_CATALOG TABLE_SCHEMA TABLE_NAME COLUMN_NAME
adSchemaColumnsDomainUsage	DOMAIN_CATALOG DOMAIN_SCHEMA DOMAIN_NAME COLUMN_NAME
adSchemaConstraintColumnUsage	TABLE_CATALOG TABLE_SCHEMA TABLE_NAME COLUMN_NAME
adSchemaConstraintTableUsage	TABLE_CATALOG TABLE_SCHEMA TABLE_NAME
adSchemaCubes	CATALOG_NAME SCHEMA_NAME CUBE_NAME
adSchemaDBInfoKeywords	None
adSchemaDBInfoLiterals	None
adSchemaDimensions	CATALOG_NAME SCHEMA_NAME CUBE_NAME DIMENSION_NAME DIMENSION_UNIQUE_NAME
adSchemaForeignKeys	PK_TABLE_CATALOG PK_TABLE_SCHEMA PK_TABLE_NAME FK_TABLE_CATALOG FK_TABLE_SCHEMA FK_TABLE_NAME
adSchemaHierarchies	CATALOG_NAME SCHEMA_NAME CUBE_NAME DIMENSION_UNIQUE_NAME HIERARCHY_NAME HIERARCHY_UNIQUE_NAME

Table continues on the next page

SchemaEnum Member Restrictions (continued)

Member	Constraint Columns
adSchemaIndexes	TABLE_CATALOG TABLE_SCHEMA INDEX_NAME TYPE TABLE_NAME
adSchemaKeyColumnUsage	CONSTRAINT_CATALOG CONSTRAINT_SCHEMA CONSTRAINT_NAME TABLE_CATALOG TABLE_SCHEMA TABLE_NAME COLUMN_NAME
adSchemaLevels	CATALOG_NAME SCHEMA_NAME CUBE_NAME DIMENSION_UNIQUE_NAME HIERARCHY_UNIQUE_NAME LEVEL_NAME LEVEL_UNIQUE_NAME
adSchemaMeasures	CATALOG_NAME SCHEMA_NAME CUBE_NAME MEASURE_NAME MEASURE_UNIQUE_NAME
adSchemaMembers	CATALOG_NAME SCHEMA_NAME CUBE_NAME DIMENSION_UNIQUE_NAME HIERARCHY_UNIQUE_NAME LEVEL_UNIQUE_NAME LEVEL_NUMBER MEMBER_NAME MEMBER_UNIQUE_NAME MEMBER_CAPTION MEMBER_TYPE Tree operator (For more information, see the OLE DB for OLAP documentation.)
adSchemaPrimaryKeys	PK_TABLE_CATALOG PK_TABLE_SCHEMA PK_TABLE_NAME
adSchemaProcedureColumns	PROCEDURE_CATALOG PROCEDURE_SCHEMA PROCEDURE_NAME COLUMN_NAME

SchemaEnum Member Restrictions (continued)

Member	Constraint Columns
adSchemaProcedureParameters	PROCEDURE_CATALOG PROCEDURE_SCHEMA PROCEDURE_NAME PARAMETER_NAME
adSchemaProcedures	PROCEDURE_CATALOG PROCEDURE_SCHEMA PROCEDURE_NAME PROCEDURE_TYPE
adSchemaProperties	CATALOG_NAME SCHEMA_NAME CUBE_NAME DIMENSION_UNIQUE_NAME HIERARCHY_UNIQUE_NAME LEVEL_UNIQUE_NAME MEMBER_UNIQUE_NAME PROPERTY_TYPE PROPERTY_NAME
adSchemaProviderSpecific	Provider specific
adSchemaProviderTypes	DATA_TYPE BEST_MATCH
adSchemaReferentialConstraints	CONSTRAINT_CATALOG CONSTRAINT_SCHEMA CONSTRAINT_NAME
adSchemaSchemata	CATALOG_NAME SCHEMA_NAME SCHEMA_OWNER
adSchemaSQLLanguages	None
adSchemaStatistics	TABLE_CATALOG TABLE_SCHEMA TABLE_NAME
adSchemaTableConstraints	CONSTRAINT_CATALOG CONSTRAINT_SCHEMA CONSTRAINT_NAME TABLE_CATALOG TABLE_SCHEMA TABLE_NAME CONSTRAINT_TYPE

Table continues on the next page

SchemaEnum Member Restrictions (continued)

Member	Constraint Columns
adSchemaTablePrivileges	TABLE_CATALOG TABLE_SCHEMA TABLE_NAME GRANTOR GRANTEE
adSchemaTables	TABLE_CATALOG TABLE_SCHEMA TABLE_NAME TABLE_TYPE
adSchemaTranslations	TRANSLATION_CATALOG TRANSLATION_SCHEMA TRANSLATION_NAME
adSchemaTrustees	None
adSchemaUsagePrivileges	OBJECT_CATALOG OBJECT_SCHEMA OBJECT_NAME OBJECT_TYPE GRANTOR GRANTEE
adSchemaViewColumnUsage	VIEW_CATALOG VIEW_SCHEMA VIEW_NAME
adSchemaViews	TABLE_CATALOG TABLE_SCHEMA TABLE_NAME
adSchemaViewTableUsage	VIEW_CATALOG VIEW_SCHEMA VIEW_NAME

Group or User SetPermissions Method Options

The SetPermssions method of both the Group and User objects allows you to specify the permissions a group or user has to a database object. As noted in Chapter 7, these method options are specific to MDB database files only. SetPermissions() has no effect on the Access 2007 file format (ACCDB database files).

ObjectTypeEnum Members

The ObjectType option specifies the type of object to which the permission will be applied.

Member	Value	Description
adPermObjColumn	2	A Column object.
adPermObjDatabase	3	A Database object.
adPermObjProcedure	4	A Procedure object.
adPermObjProviderSpecific	-1	The object type is defined by the provider. If this value is specified, an ObjectTypeID must also be specified.
adPermObjTable	1	A Table object.
adPermObjView	5	A View object.

ActionEnum Members

The Action option specifies how the permission should be applied to the specified object.

Member	Value	Description
adAccessDeny	3	Deny the specified permissions.
adAccessGrant	1	Grant the specified permissions. The permissions specified are added to those that have already been granted.
adAccessRevoke	4	Revoke all permissions.
adAccessSet	2	Set the specified permissions. Only the specified permissions will be in force.

RightsEnum Members

The Rights option specifies the actual rights, or permissions, for denying, granting, revoking, or setting.

Members	Value	Description
adRightCreate	16384	The user/group has permission to create a new object of the specified type.
adRightDelete	65536	The user/group has permission to delete data from the specified object. For objects such as tables, the user also has permission to delete data.

Table continues on the next page

Appendix F: ADO Object Argument Enumeration Information

Members	Value	Description
adRightDrop	256	The user/group has permission to remove objects from the catalog.
adRightExclusive	512	The user/group has permission to access the object exclusively.
adRightExecute	536870912	The user/group has permission to execute the object.
adRightFull	268435456	The user/group has all permissions on the object.
adRightInsert	32768	The user/group has permission to insert the object. For objects such as tables, the user also has permission to insert data.
adRightMaximumAllowed	33554432	The user/group has the maximum number of permissions allowed by the provider.
adRightNone	0	The user/group has no permissions for the object.
adRightRead	-2147483648	The user/group has permission to read the object. For objects such as tables, the user also has permission to read its data.
adRightReadDesign	1024	The user/group has permission to read the object's design.
adRightReadPermissions	131072	The user/group can view, but not change, the specific permissions for an object in the catalog.
adRightReference	8192	The user/group has permission to reference the object.
adRightUpdate	1073741824	The user/group has permission to update the object. For objects such as tables, the user also has permission to update its data.
adRightWithGrant	4096	The user/group has permission to grant permissions on the object to other users.
adRightWriteDesign	2048	The user/group has permission to modify the object's design.
adRightWriteOwner	524288	The user/group has permission to modify the object's owner.
adRightWritePermissions	262144	The user/group has permission to modify the specific permissions for an object in the catalog.

InheritTypeEnum Members

The Inherit option specifies how an object inherits permissions.

Constant	Value	Description
adInheritBoth	3	The objects and containers contained by the primary object inherit the permissions.
adInheritContainers	2	Other objects contained by the primary object also inherit the permissions.
adInheritNone	0	Default. Do not inherit permissions.
adInheritNoPropagate	4	The adInheritObjects and adInheritContainers flags are not inherited.
adInheritObjects	1	Objects outside the container inherit the permissions.

The Access Object Model

By now you've probably read at least a few of the chapters in this book and have realized that there are a lot of tasks you can accomplish by programming in VBA. One concept that should be abundantly clear is that to use VBA to manipulate Access, you need some knowledge about the Access object model. It was discussed briefly in Chapter 4, but as a refresher, an object model is a set of objects and collections that programmers use to manipulate a program. Microsoft Access has a rich object model. You'll use that to manipulate forms, reports, queries, macros, and other components of the Access interface.

Much of the information in this appendix can also be found in some form within the Access Visual Basic Reference Help file.

The Application Object

All of the Access objects you'll manipulate within code are children of the Application object, which is the parent object for all objects and collections in the Access object model. Every object and collection is related to the Application object through either a direct parent/child relationship or multiple parent/child relationships. Figure G-1 shows the Access objects and collections that are the direct children of the Application object. The Office 12.0 object library exposes objects from the Application object for each Office application. Because those objects are part of the Office object model, they aren't listed here.

The Application object refers to the currently active Access application. It contains all Microsoft Access objects and collections. You can use the Application object to apply methods or set properties for the entire Access application. For example, you can use the object's SetOption method to control just about all the settings visible in the Access Options dialog box. The various settings you can use with SetOption are listed a little later in this appendix. The following code displays hidden objects in the navigation pane:

```
Application.SetOption "Show Hidden Objects", True
```

Figure G-1

Nearly all code you write in Access utilizes the `Application` object somewhere within the code.

Application Object Properties

The following table lists the various properties of the `Application` object. It contains not only string and Boolean properties, but also properties that refer to other objects within the Access object model. Those objects are discussed later in this appendix.

Property	Data Type	Description
AnswerWizard	AnswerWizard object	Used to reference the current AnswerWizard object.
Application	Application object	Returns the current Access Application object. For example, Me.Application on a form or report.
Assistance	IAssistance object	Returns an IAssistance object that can be used for programmatic searching of Access help.
Assistant	Assistant object	Returns the Office Assistant object. This object has been deprecated in Office 2007.
AutoCorrect	AutoCorrect object	Returns an AutoCorrect object that represents the AutoCorrect settings for the specified control.
AutomationSecurity	MsoAutomationSecurity	Returns or sets an MsoAutomationSecurity constant that represents the security mode Access uses when opening files.
BrokenReference	Boolean	True if the current database has any broken references to databases or type libraries.

Property	Data Type	Description
Build	Long	Build number of the currently installed copy of Access.
CodeContextObject	Object	Determines the object in which a macro or VBA code is executing
CodeData	CodeData	Accesses the CodeData object.
CodeProject	CodeProject	Accesses the CodeProject object.
COMAddIns	COMAddIns collection	References the current COMAddIns collection object.
CommandBars	CommandBars collection	References the CommandBars collection.
CurrentData	CurrentData object	Used to access the CurrentData object.
CurrentObjectName	String	Name of the active database object.
CurrentObjectType	AcObjectType Enum	Intrinsic constant used to determine the type of the active database object. See the Object Browser for possible values.
CurrentProject	CurrentProject object	Accesses the CurrentProject object.
DBEngine	DBEngine object	Returns the instance of the Access database engine and its related properties and collections.
DoCmd	DoCmd object	Returns the DoCmd object that contains many methods commonly used in Access.
FeatureInstall	MsoFeatureInstall	Determines or specifies how Access handles calls to methods or properties not yet installed.
FileDialog	FileDialog object	Represents a common File dialog box such as the Open, Save As, or Browse Folder dialog box.
FileSearch	FileSearch object	This object has been deprecated in Office 2007. You should use the FileSystemObject instead.
Forms	Forms collection	Returns the collection of open forms in a database.
IsCompiled	Boolean	True if the current Visual Basic project is in a compiled state.
LanguageSettings	LanguageSettings object	Returns a reference to the LanguageSettings object. Can be used to determine the user-interface language for the running instance of Access.
MacroError	MacroError object	Returns an instance of the MacroError object. Represents errors raised from Access macros.
MenuBar	String	Specifies the MenuBar to use for an Access database.

Table continues on the next page

Property	Data Type	Description
Modules	Modules collection	Returns the collection of open modules in a database.
Name	String	Returns the name of the application: Microsoft Access.
NewFileTaskPane	NewFile object	Returns a NewFile object listed in the NewFile task pane.
Parent	Application object	Because the Application object is the highest object in the hierarchy, Parent returns the current Application object.
Printer	Printer object	Returns or sets a Printer object representing the default printer on the current computer.
Printers	Printers collection	Returns the printers installed on the current computer.
ProductCode	String	Returns the globally unique identifier (GUID) for the Access application.
References	References collection	Returns the collection of References for the current database.
Reports	Reports collection	Returns the collection of open reports in a database.
Screen	Screen object	Returns the Screen object.
ShortcutMenuBar	String	Specifies the shortcut menu that appears when you right-click on a form, report, or control.
TempVars	TempVars collection	Returns an instance of the TempVars collection. Can be used to maintain temporary data in a collection and pass data between Access macros and VBA code.
UserControl	Boolean	Determines whether the current Access instance was launched via automation.
VBE	VBE object	Returns an instance of the Visual Basic Editor.
Version	String	Returns the current version of Access.
Visible	Boolean	Returns True if the Access window is visible.

Application Object Methods

The following table lists all of the methods available from the Application object. Any arguments for the methods are also listed. For example, you can use the CompactRepair method of the Application object with the following code:

```
Application.CompactRepair "C:\DB\Samples.mdb", "C:\DB\SamplesCompacted.mdb"
```

Method	Arguments	Description
AccessError	ErrorNumber	Returns the error message associated with an Access or DAO error number.
AddToFavorites	None	Adds the name of the current database as a hyperlink address to the Favorites folder.
BuildCriteria	Field, FieldType, Expression	Returns a parsed criteria string as it would appear in the query design grid, in Filter By Form or Server Filter By Form mode.
CloseCurrentDatabase	None	Closes the current database.
CodeDb	None	Returns a DAO.Database object for a library database or add-in.
ColumnHistory	TableName, ColumnName, QueryString	Returns the column history for an Append-Only memo field. Valid for ACCDB files only.
CompactRepair	SourceFile, DestinationFile, LogFile	Compacts and repairs the specified database. Set LogFile to True to record any corruption found to a log file.
ConvertAccessProject	SourceFileName, DestinationFileName, DestinationFileFormat	Converts the specified database from one version to another.
CreateAccessProject	FilePath, Connect	Creates a new Access Data Project (ADP). Specify the Connect argument to set the ConnectionString for the project.
CreateAdditionalData	None	Creates an AdditionalData object that can be used to export related data to XML with the ExportXML method.
CreateControl	FormName, ControlType, Section, Parent, ColumnName, Left, Top, Width, Height	Creates a control on a form that is currently open in Design view. Returns a Control object.
CreateForm	Database, FormTemplate	Creates a new form in Design view and returns a Form object.
CreateGroupLevel	ReportName, Expression, Header, Footer,	Creates a grouping level on a report.
CreateNewWorkgroupFile	Path, Name, Company, WorkgroupID, Replace	Creates a new workgroup information file (MDW).

Table continues on the next page

Method	Arguments	Description
CreateReport	Database, ReportTemplate	Creates a new report in design view and returns a Report object.
CreateReportControl	ReportName, ControlType, Section, Parent, ColumnName, Left, Top, Width, Height	Creates a control on a report that is currently open in design view.
CurrentDb	None	Returns a DAO.Database object that represents the currently open database.
CurrentUser	None	Returns the name of the current user in the database. Used with user-level security in MDB files.
DAvg	Expr, Domain, Criteria	Calculates the average of a set of values in a specified set of records (Domain).
DCount	Expr, Domain, Criteria	Determines the number of records within a set of records.
DDEExecute	ChanNum, Command	Sends a command from a client application to a server application.
DDEInitiate	Application, Topic	Opens a DDE (Dynamic Data Exchange) channel between two applications.
DDEPoke	ChanNum, Item, Data	Supplies text data from a client application to a server application over an open DDE channel.
DDERequest	ChanNum, Item	Requests information over a DDE channel.
DDETerminate	ChanNum	Closes a specified DDE channel.
DDETerminateAll	None	Closes all open DDE channels.
DefaultWorkspaceClone	None	Creates a new Workspace object without requiring the user to log on again.
DeleteControl	FormName, ControlName	Deletes a control on a specified form.
DeleteReportControl	ReportName, ControlName	Deletes a control on a specific report.
DFirst	Expr, Domain, Criteria	Returns the first record from a particular field in a table or query. Because sort order can change, the first record is typically not guaranteed.
DLast	Expr, Domain, Criteria	Returns the first record from a particular field in a table or query. Because sort order can change, the last record is typically not guaranteed.

Method	Arguments	Description
DLookup	Expr, Domain, Criteria	Gets the value from a particular field from a specified set of records.
DMax	Expr, Domain, Criteria	Determines the maximum value in a specified set of records.
DMin	Expr, Domain, Criteria	Determines the minimum value in a specified set of records.
DStDev	Expr, Domain, Criteria	Estimates the standard deviation across a set of values in a set of records. The standard deviation is calculated for a sample.
DStDevP	Expr, Domain, Criteria	Estimates the standard deviation across a set of values in a set of records. The standard deviation is calculated for the population.
DSum	Expr, Domain, Criteria	Calculates the sum of a set of values in a set of records.
DVar	Expr, Domain, Criteria	Estimates the variance across a set of values in a set of records. The variation is calculated for a sample.
DVarP	Expr, Domain, Criteria	Estimates variance across a set of values in a set of records. The variance is calculated for the population.
Echo	EchoOn, bstrStatusBarText	Specifies whether Access repaints the display screen.
EuroConvert	Number, SourceCurrency, TargetCurrency, FullPrecision, TriangulationPrecision	Converts a number to Euro or from Euro to a participating currency. You can also use it to convert a number from one participating currency to another by using the Euro as an intermediary (triangulation).
Eval	StringExpr	Evaluates an expression that results in a text string or numeric value.
ExportNavigationPane	Path	Exports all data associated with the navigation pane to XML. Includes custom categories and groups.
ExportXML	ObjectType, DataSource, DataTarget, SchemaTarget, PresentationTarget, ImageTarget, Encoding, OtherFlags, WhereCondition, AdditionalData	Allows for export of XML data, schemas, and presentation information.

Table continues on the next page

Method	Arguments	Description
FollowHyperlink	Address, SubAddress, NewWindow, AddHistory, ExtraInfo, Method, HeaderInfo	Opens the document or Web page specified by a hyperlink.
GetHiddenAttribute	ObjectType, ObjectName	Determines whether the specified object is hidden in the navigation pane.
GetOption	OptionName	Returns the current value of an option in the Options dialog box.
GUIDFromString	String	Converts a string to a GUID.
HTMLEncode	PlainText, Length	Returns HTML encoded text for data. Can be used to set data in Rich Text memo fields.
hWndAccessApp	None	Determines the handle assigned to the main Access window by Microsoft Windows.
HyperlinkPart	Hyperlink, Part	Returns information about data stored as a hyperlink data type.
ImportNavigationPane	Path, fAppendOnly	Imports navigation pane data that was exported with ExportNavigationPane.
ImportXML	DataSource, ImportOptions	Allows import of XML data and/or schema information.
LoadCustomUI	CustomUIName, CustomUIXML	Loads custom ribbon extensibility XML.
LoadPicture	FileName	Loads a graphic into an ActiveX control.
NewAccessProject	FilePath, Connect	Creates and sets a new ADP as the active data project.
NewCurrentDatabase	Filepath, FileFormat, Template, SiteAddress, ListID	Creates a new Access database (ACCDB or MDB) in the Access window. Can also create a new database from an Access template.
Nz	Value, ValueIfNull	Returns zero, a zero-length string, or another value when a value is null.
OpenAccessProject	FilePath, Exclusive	Opens an ADP as the current Access project.
OpenCurrentDatabase	FilePath, Exclusive, bstrPassword	Opens an MDB file as the current database.

Method	Arguments	Description
`PlainText`	`RichText, Length`	Returns unformatted text for the specified rich text.
`Quit`	`Option`	Quits Microsoft Access.
`RefreshDatabaseWindow`	None	Updates the database window after an object has been created.
`RefreshTitleBar`	None	Refreshes the Access title bar after the `AppTitle` or `AppIcon` has been changed via code.
`Run`	`Procedure` (up to 30 optional arguments can also follow)	Can be used to carry out a sub or function.
`RunCommand`	`Command`	Runs a built-in menu or toolbar command.
`SetDefaultWorkgroupFile`	`Path`	Sets the default Workgroup file to the file specified in the `Path` argument.
`SetHiddenAttribute`	`ObjectType, ObjectName, fHidden`	Sets the hidden attribute of the specified object in the navigation pane.
`SetOption`	`OptionName, Setting`	Sets the current value of an option in the Options dialog box. The various `OptionName` arguments are detailed at the end of this appendix.
`StringFromGUID`	`GUID`	Converts a GUID to a string.
`SysCmd`	`Action, Argument2, Argument3`	Can (1) display a progress meter or specified text in the status bar, (2) return information about Access and its associated files, or (3) return the state of a current database object.
`TransformXML`	`DataSource, TransformSource, OutputTarget, WellFormedXMLOutput, ScriptOption`	Applies an Extensible Stylesheet Language (XSL) stylesheet to an XML data file and writes the XML to an XML data file.

AllObjects Collection

Access contains a hidden collection called the AllObjects collection. Chances are you'll never use this collection directly, but it happens to be the parent object of several collections that are commonly used. These collections are:

Collection	Description
AllDatabaseDiagrams	Contains an object for each database diagram in a SQL Server database. Applies to ADP files only.
AllForms	Contains an object for each form in a database or project file.
AllFunctions	Contains an object for each user-defined function in a SQL Server database. Applies to ADP files only.
AllMacros	Contains an object for each macro in a database or project file.
AllModules	Contains an object for each module in a database or project file.
AllQueries	Contains an object for each query in an Access database (ACCDB or MDB).
AllReports	Contains an object for each report in a database or project file.
AllStoredProcedures	Contains an object for each stored procedure in a SQL Server database. Applies to ADP files only.
AllTables	Contains an object for each table in a database or project file.
AllViews	Contains an object for each view in a SQL Server database. Applies to ADP files only.

Each of these collections contains AccessObject objects that are described in a later section. Because these collections all derive from the AllObjects collection, they have the same properties and methods. For example, take a closer look at the AllForms collection.

As its name implies, the AllForms collection contains an Access object for each form in the CurrentProject or CodeProject object. It contains the typical collection properties of Application, Count, Item, and Parent. Many of the other collections listed in this appendix have the same set of properties, which are described in the following table.

Property	Data Type	Description
Application	Application object	Returns the Application object associated with the current collection.
Count	Long	Returns the number of items in the collection.
Item	AccessObject	Returns a specific member of the collection by position or index.
Parent	Object	Returns the parent object of the current collection.

The CurrentData Object

The CurrentData object is used to refer to objects stored within the current database by the server application (Access database engine or SQL). It has a variety of properties, described in the following table, that you can manipulate as well as several collections of its own.

Property	Data Type	Description
AllDatabaseDiagrams	AllDatabaseDiagrams collection	Represents the collection of database diagrams in the SQL Server database.
AllFunctions	AllFunctions collection	Represents all the user-defined functions in the SQL Server database.
AllQueries	AllQueries collection	Represents all of the queries defined in the database. This collection is empty in ADP files.
AllStoredProcedures	AllStoredProcedures collection	References all of the stored procedures in the database.
AllTables	AllTables collection	References all the tables in the database.
AllViews	AllViews collection	References all views in the database.

The CurrentProject Object

The CurrentProject object represents the Access project for the database or project that is currently open in Access. The Access project consists of the non-data items such as Forms, Reports, Macros, and Modules. The CurrentProject object has several collections and a number of properties you can use within your application. Here are descriptions of those properties:

Property	Data Type	Description
AccessConnection	Connection	Returns a reference to the currently active ADO Connection object.
AllForms	AllForms collection	Returns a reference to the AllForms collection and its associated properties.
AllMacros	AllMacros collection	Returns a reference to the AllMacros collection and its associated properties.
AllModules	AllModules collection	Returns a reference to the AllModules collection and its associated properties.
AllReports	AllReports collection	Returns a reference to the AllReports collection and its associated properties.

Table continues on the next page

Property	Data Type	Description
Application	Application object	Returns a reference to the current Application object.
BaseConnectionString	String	Returns the base Connection String for the CurrentProjector CodeProject object.
Connection	Connection object	Returns the currently active ADO Connection object.
FileFormat	AcFileFormat Enum	Returns a constant representing the Microsoft Access version of the specified project.
FullName	String	Returns the full path and name for the CurrentProject object.
ImportExport Specifications	ImportExport-Specifications collection	Returns the collection of import and export specifications in the database.
IsConnected	Boolean	Determines if the CurrentProject is currently connected to a data source.
IsTrusted	Boolean	Returns True if the current database is opened in enabled mode and can execute code.
Name	String	Returns the name of the current CodeProject.
Parent	Application object	For the CodeProject object, the Parent property returns the associated Application object.
Path	String	Returns the path to the data location for the Access database (.mdb) or Access project (.adp).
ProjectType	AcProjectType Enum	Determines the type of project currently open through the CurrentProject object.
Properties	Properties collection	Returns a reference to the entire Properties collection for the CurrentProject object.
RemovePersonal Information	Boolean	True if user information is removed from the specified project. False if user information is stored within the project.

The following table describes the CurrentProject object's methods.

Method	Arguments	Description
CloseConnection	None	Closes the current connection between the CurrentProject object and the database specified in the project's base connection string.

Method	Arguments	Description
OpenConnection	BaseConnection-String, UserID, Password	Opens an ADO Connection to an existing Access project (.adp) or Access database (.accdb, .mdb) as the current Access project or database.
UpdateDependencyInfo	None	Updates the dependency information for the database.

You've probably noticed that there is some overlap between several objects or methods in the Access and DAO object models, specifically CurrentProject and CodeProject, CurrentData and CodeData, and CurrentDb and CodeDb. Each pair of objects contains the same properties and methods so that they are interchangeable.

Given that they have the same interfaces, how do you know which one to use and when? The short answer is that the Code objects and methods are used to refer to objects in a referenced or add-in database, which are also known as *library* databases because you can call code from them like a code library. Naturally, the Current objects are used to refer to objects in the file that is open in the Access user interface. For example, if you have a database called Samples.mdb, and that database contains a reference to a database called VBASamples.mdb, the current database would be Samples.mdb and the code database would be VBASamples.mdb while code is executing in VBASamples.mdb. When code is running in Samples.mdb, the current and the code database both refer to Samples.mdb.

The following table summarizes some of the differences.

Object/Method	Return Type	AllObjects Collections	Database Usage
CurrentDb	DAO.Database	None	Accesses tables, queries, and record-sets in the current database.
CodeDb	DAO.Database	None	Accesses tables, queries, and record-sets in a library database.
CurrentProject	CurrentProject object	AllForms, AllMacros, AllModules, AllReports	Retrieves AccessObject objects for Access project items in the current database.
CodeProject	CodeProject object	AllForms, AllMacros, AllModules, AllReports	Retrieves AccessObject objects for Access project items in a library database.

Table continues on the next page

Object/Method	Return Type	AllObjects Collections	Database Usage
CurrentData	CurrentData object	ACCDB and MDB: AllQueries, AllTables ADP: AllDatabaseDiagrams, AllFunctions, AllStoredProcedures, AllTables, AllViews	Retrieves AccessObject objects for tables and queries in the current database.
CodeData	CodeData object	ACCDB and MDB: AllQueries, AllTables ADP: AllDatabaseDiagrams, AllFunctions, AllStoredProcedures, AllTables, AllViews	Retrieves AccessObject objects for tables and queries in a library database.

To reiterate, the CurrentProject object or CurrentDb method always returns the database or project file that is currently open in Access. Therefore, you can use these objects to refer to objects in the currently open database from a library database. However, the reverse is not true — in the current database, CurrentProject and CodeProject refer to the same file.

AccessObject

The AccessObject object refers to a particular object within any of the following collections: AllDatabaseDiagrams, AllForms, AllFunctions, AllMacros, AllModules, AllQueries, AllReports, AllStoredProcedures, AllTables, and AllViews. This is an all-purpose object that can be used to determine whether an object is dependent upon another object or whether an object is open in the database.

It has its own properties, described in the following table, that you can implement within your code.

Property	Data Type	Description
CurrentView	AcCurrentView Enum	Returns the current view for the specified Access object.
DateCreated	Date	Returns the date the AccessObject was created.
DateModified	Date	Returns the date the AccessObject was modified.
FullName	String	Sets or returns the full path of the object.
IsLoaded	Boolean	Determines whether the object is currently loaded.
Name	String	Returns the name of the object.

Property	Data Type	Description
Parent	Object	Returns the collection of which the object is a member.
Properties	AccessObjectProperties collection	Returns the AccessObjectProperties collection for the object.
Type	AcObjectType Enum	Returns the type of the AccessObject.

AccessObject has two methods you can use:

Method	Arguments	Description
GetDependencyInfo	None	Returns a DependencyInfo object that represents the database objects that are dependent upon the specified object.
IsDependentUpon	ObjectType, ObjectName	Returns a Boolean value that indicates whether the specified object is dependent upon the database object specified in the ObjectName argument.

The DoCmd Object

In many regards, the DoCmd object is the workhorse of the Access object model. It carries out tasks such as exporting objects to different formats, opening objects, and manipulating the size of the Access window. It has no properties, but it does have a variety of methods you can utilize within your Access application.

All of the methods carry out an action with the same name as the method, so the following table provides descriptions of those actions, rather than of the methods (which merely call the actions).

Method	Arguments	Description
AddMenu	MenuName, MacroName, StatusBarText	Creates a custom menu bar, shortcut bar, or shortcut menu.
ApplyFilter	FilterName, WhereCondition	Applies a filter, a query, or a SQL WHERE clause to a table, form, or report.
Beep	None	Causes the system to beep.
CancelEvent	None	Used to cancel the event that caused Access to run the macro or module containing this action.
ClearMacroError	None	Clears the MacroError object and resets it to the default state.

Table continues on the next page

Appendix G: The Access Object Model

Method	Arguments	Description
Close	ObjectType, ObjectName, Save	Closes the object specified in the ObjectName argument.
CloseDatabase	None	Closes the current database.
CopyDatabaseFile	DatabaseFileName, OverwriteExistingFile, DisconnectAllUsers	Copies the database connected to the current project to a SQL Server database for export.
CopyObject	DestinationDatabase, NewName, SourceObjectType, SourceObjectName	Copies the specified object to another database (.mdb) or Access project (.adp).
DeleteObject	ObjectType, ObjectName	Deletes the specified object.
DoMenuItem	MenuBar, MenuName, Command, SubCommand, Version	Executes the specified menu item. (Note: This is a legacy method from Access 97. In later versions of Access, it was replaced by the RunCommand method. It is included only for backward compatibility.)
Echo	EchoOn, StatusBarText	Turns Echo on or off.
FindNext	None	Finds the next record that meets the criteria specified in the FindRecord action.
FindRecord	FindWhat, Match, MatchCase, Search, SearchAsFormatted, OnlyCurrentField, FindFirst	Finds the first instance of a record that meets the criteria specified by the FindWhat argument.
GoToControl	ControlName	Moves focus to the specified control.
GoToPage	PageNumber, Right, Down	Moves the focus in a form to the first control on the specified page.
GoToRecord	ObjectType, ObjectName, Record, Offset	Makes the specified record the current record in a table, form, or result set.
Hourglass	HourglassOn	Changes the mouse pointer to an hourglass while the macro or code is running.
LockNavigationPane	Lock	Locks or unlocks the navigation pane for updating.
Maximize	None	Maximizes the entire Access Application window.
Minimize	None	Minimizes the entire Access Application window.
MoveSize	Right, Down, Width, Height	Moves or resizes the active window.

Method	Arguments	Description
NavigateTo	Category, Group	Controls the display of categories and groups in the navigation pane.
OpenDiagram	DiagramName	Opens the specified database diagram in design view.
OpenForm	FormName, View, FilterName, WhereCondition, DataMode, WindowMode, OpenArgs	Opens the specified form in the specified view. Can also be used to filter the data displayed on the form.
OpenFunction	FunctionName, View, DataMode	Opens a user-defined function in SQL Server for viewing in Access.
OpenModule	ModuleName, ProcedureName	Opens the specified module at the specified procedure.
OpenQuery	QueryName, View, DataMode	Opens the specified query with the specified type of view.
OpenReport	ReportName, View, FilterName, WhereCondition, WindowMode, OpenArgs	Opens the specified report in the specified view. Can also be used to filter the data displayed on the report.
OpenStoredProcedure	ProcedureName, View, DataMode	Opens the specified stored procedure.
OpenTable	TableName, View, DataMode	Opens the specified table in the specified view.
OpenView	ViewName, View, DataMode	Opens the specified view in datasheet view, design view, or print preview.
OutputTo	ObjectType, ObjectName, OutputFormat, OutputFile, AutoStart, TemplateFile, Encoding, OutputQuality	Outputs the specified object in the specified file formats.
PrintOut	PrintRange, PageFrom, PageTo, PrintQuality, Copies, CollateCopies	Prints the active object.
Quit	Options	Quits the active Access application.
Rename	NewName, ObjectType, OldName	Renames the specified object.
RepaintObject	ObjectType, ObjectName	Completes any pending screen updates for the specified object.
Requery	ControlName	Updates the data in the specified control by requerying the source of the control.

Table continues on the next page

Method	Arguments	Description
Restore	None	Restores a maximized or minimized window to its previous state.
RunCommand	Command	Runs a built-in ribbon command.
RunMacro	MacroName, RepeatCount, RepeatExpression	Runs the specified macro.
RunSavedImportExportSpec	SavedImportExportName	Runs the named import or export specification in the database.
RunSQL	SQLStatement, UseTransaction	Runs an Access action query by using the corresponding SQL statement.
Save	ObjectType, ObjectName	Saves the specified object.
SearchForRecord	ObjectType, ObjectName, Record, WhereCondition	Allows searching of records including a WHERE clause.
SelectObject	ObjectType, ObjectName, InDatabaseWindow	Selects the specified database object.
SendObject	ObjectType, ObjectName, OutputFormat, To, Cc, Bcc, Subject, MessageText, EditMessage, TemplateFile	Sends the specified Access datasheet, form, report, module, or data access page via e-mail.
SetDisplayedCategories	Show, Category	Displays categories in a customized navigation pane.
SetMenuItem	MenuIndex, CommandIndex, SubCommandIndex, Flag	Enables, disables, checks, or unchecks the specified menu item.
SetProperty	ControlName, Property, Value	Sets the property to the specified value for a given control. Intended as a safe way to do SetValue in disabled mode.
SetWarnings	WarningsOn	Turns system messages on or off.
ShowAllRecords	None	Removes any applied filter for the table, query, or form.
ShowToolbar	ToolbarName, Show	Displays or hides a built-in toolbar.
SingleStep	None	Puts an Access macro into single step mode. Has no effect in VBA.
TransferDatabase	TransferType, DatabaseType, DatabaseName, ObjectType, Source, Destination, StructureOnly, StoreLogin	Used to import or export data between the current database (.mdb) or Access project (.adp) and another database.

Method	Arguments	Description
TransferSharePointList	TransferType, SiteAddress, ListID, ViewID, TableName, GetLookupDisplayValues	Imports or links data from a SharePoint site into Access.
TransferSpreadsheet	TransferType, SpreadsheetType, TableName, FileName, HasFieldNames, Range, UseOA	Used to import or export data between the current database (.mdb) or Access project (.adp) and a spreadsheet.
TransferSQLDatabase	Server, Database, UsedTrustedConnection, Login, Password, TransferCopyData	Transfers the entire SQL Server database to another SQL Server database.
TransferText	TransferType, SpecificationName, TableName, FileName, HasFieldNames, HTMLTableName, CodePage	Used to import or export data between a database (.mdb) or Access project (.adp) and a text file.

The Form Object

The Forms collection contains all of the open forms associated with the current database. Forms in the database that are not currently open are not in this collection.

Form Object Properties

The Form object has a variety of properties, which are described in the following table.

Property	Data Type	Description
ActiveControl	Control object	Used with the Screen object to determine the control that has the focus.
AfterDelConfirm	String	Indicates which macro, event procedure, or user-defined function runs when the AfterDelConfirm event occurs.
AfterFinalRender	String	Indicates which macro, event procedure, or user-defined function runs when the AfterFinalRender event occurs.
AfterInsert	String	Indicates which macro, event procedure, or user-defined function runs when the AfterInsert event occurs.
AfterLayout	String	Indicates which macro, event procedure, or user-defined function runs when the AfterLayout event occurs.

Table continues on the next page

Property	Data Type	Description
AfterRender	String	Indicates which macro, event procedure, or user-defined function runs when the AfterRender event occurs.
AfterUpdate	String	Indicates which macro, event procedure, or user-defined function runs when the event AfterUpdate event occurs.
AllowAdditions	Boolean	Determines whether a user can add a record when using a form.
AllowDataSheetView	Boolean	Determines whether the form can be switched to datasheet view.
AllowDeletions	Boolean	Determines whether a user can delete a record when using a form.
AllowEdits	Boolean	Determines whether a user can edit save records when using a form.
AllowFilters	Boolean	Determines whether a user can filter the records when using a form.
AllowFormView	Boolean	Determines whether a form can be viewed in Form view.
AllowLayoutView	Boolean	Determines whether a form can be viewed in Layout view.
AllowPivotChartView	Boolean	Determines whether a form can be viewed in Pivot Chart view.
AllowPivotTableView	Boolean	Determines whether a form can be viewed in Pivot Table view.
Application	Application object	Returns the currently active application object.
AutoCenter	Boolean	Determines whether the form will be automatically centered within the Application window.
AutoResize	Boolean	Determines whether the form will be automatically resized to display complete records.
BeforeDelConfirm	String	Indicates which macro, event procedure, or user-defined function runs when the BeforeDelConfirm event occurs.
BeforeInsert	String	Indicates which macro, event procedure, or user-defined function runs when the BeforeInsert event occurs.

Property	Data Type	Description
BeforeQuery	String	Indicates which macro, event procedure, or user-defined function runs when the BeforeQuery event occurs.
BeforeRender	String	Indicates which macro, event procedure, or user-defined function runs when the BeforeRender event occurs.
BeforeScreenTip	String	Indicates which macro, event procedure, or user-defined function runs when the BeforeScreenTipevent occurs.
BeforeUpdate	String	Indicates which macro, event procedure, or user-defined function runs when the BeforeUpdate event occurs.
Bookmark	Variant	Used to set a bookmark that identifies a particular record in the form's underlying recordset.
BorderStyle	Byte	Specifies the type of border and border elements for the form.
Caption	String	Specifies text that appears in the Form's title bar.
ChartSpace	ChartSpace object	Returns a ChartSpace object.
CloseButton	Boolean	Specifies whether the Close button on a form is enabled.
CommandBeforeExecute	String	Indicates which macro, event procedure, or user-defined function runs when the CommandBeforeExecute event occurs.
CommandChecked	String	Indicates which macro, event procedure, or user-defined function runs when the CommndChecked event occurs.
CommandEnabled	String	Indicates which macro, event procedure, or user-defined function runs when the CommandEnabled event occurs.
CommandExecute	String	Indicates which macro, event procedure, or user-defined function runs when the CommandExecute event occurs.
ControlBox	Boolean	Specifies whether the form has a control menu (in Form and Datasheet view only).
Controls	Controls collection	Returns the collection of all controls on the form.

Table continues on the next page

Property	Data Type	Description
Count	Integer	Determines the number of items in a collection.
CurrentRecord	Long	Used to identify the current record being viewed on a form.
CurrentSectionLeft	Integer	The distance in twips from the left side of the current section to the left side of the form.
CurrentSectionTop	Integer	The distance in twips from the top of the current section to the top of the form.
CurrentView	Integer	Determines how a form is displayed (design, form, layout, pivot, or datasheet view).
Cycle	Byte	Specifies what happens when you press the Tab key while the last control on the form has the focus.
DataChange	String	Indicates which macro, event procedure, or user-defined function runs when the DataChange event occurs.
DataEntry	Boolean	Specifies whether a bound form only allows data entry (if true the form opens showing only a blank record).
DataSetChange	String	Indicates which macro, event procedure, or user-defined function runs when the DataSetChange event occurs.
DataSheetBackColor	Long	Specifies the background color of a table, query, or form in datasheet view.
DataSheetBorderLineStyle	Byte	Indicates the style used for the border of the datasheet.
DataSheetCellsEffect	Byte	Indicates whether special effects are applied to cells in a datasheet.
DatasheetColumnHeader-UnderlineStyle	Byte	Indicates the style to use for the bottom edge of the column headers on the datasheet.
DatasheetFontHeight	Integer	Indicates the font point size used to display and print field names and data on the form's datasheet.
DatasheetFontItalic	Boolean	Indicates whether the font used on the form's datasheet is italicized.

Property	Data Type	Description
DatasheetFontName	String	Specifies the font used in the datasheet of the form.
DatasheetFontUnderline	Boolean	Indicates whether the font used on the form's datasheet is underlined.
DatasheetFontWeight	Integer	Used to indicate the line width for the font used in the form's datasheet view.
DatasheetForeColor	Long	Used to indicate the default font color for a form's datasheet view.
DatasheetGridlinesBehavior	Byte	Used to specify which gridlines appear in a form's datasheet view.
DatasheetGridlinesColor	Long	Used to determine the color of gridlines in a form's datasheet view.
DefaultControl	Control object	Can be used to specify the properties of a particular type of control on a form.
DefaultView	Integer	Used to specify the opening view for a form.
Dirty	Boolean	True if data has been entered but not saved on a form.
DisplayOnSharePointSite	Byte	Specifies whether the form can be made as a view on a SharePoint site.
DividingLines	Boolean	Specifies whether dividing lines separate sections on a form.
FastLaserPrinting	Boolean	Specifies whether lines and rectangles are replaced by text character lines to speed printing.
FetchDefaults	Boolean	Indicates whether Access shows default values for new rows on the form before the row is saved.
Filter	String	Used to specify a subset of records to be displayed when a filter is applied to a form.
FilterOn	Boolean	Specifies whether the Filter property of a form is applied.
FilterOnLoad	Boolean	Indicates that a filter should be loaded with the form when the form loads.
FitToScreen	Boolean	Gets or sets whether the width of the form should be reduced to fit the width of the screen.

Table continues on the next page

Property	Data Type	Description
Form	Form object	Used to refer to the form.
FrozenColumns	Integer	Determines how many columns in a datasheet are frozen.
GridX	Integer	Specifies the horizontal divisions of the alignment grid in the form's design view.
GridY	Integer	Specifies the vertical divisions of the alignment grid in the form's design view.
HasModule	Boolean	Determines whether the form has a class module.
HelpContextID	Long	Specifies the context ID of a topic in the custom help file.
HelpFile	String	Returns the name of the help file associated with the form.
HorizontalDatasheet-GridlineStyle	Byte	Indicates the horizontal gridline style for a form's datasheet.
Hwnd	Long	Determines the handle of the current window.
InputParameters	String	Specifies the input parameters passed to a SQL statement in the RecordSource property of a form.
InsideHeight	Long	Height in twips of the window containing the form.
InsideWidth	Long	Width in twips of the window containing the form.
KeyPreview	Boolean	Specifies whether the form level keyboard event procedures are invoked before a control's keyboard event procedures.
LayoutForPrint	Boolean	Specifies whether the form uses printer (True) or screen (False) fonts.
MaxRecButton	Boolean	Determines if the maximum record limit button is available on the navigation bar of a form.
MaxRecords	Long	Specifies the maximum number of records returned.
MenuBar	String	Specifies the menu bar to use for a form.
MinMaxButtons	Byte	Specifies whether the Maximize and Minimize buttons are visible on the form.

Property	Data Type	Description
Modal	Boolean	Specifies whether a form opens as a modal window.
Module	Module object	Used to specify a form module.
MouseWheel	String	Indicates which macro, event procedure, or user-defined function runs when the MouseWheel event occurs.
Movable	Boolean	True if a form can be moved by the user.
Name	String	Name of the current form.
NavigationButtons	Boolean	Indicates whether navigation buttons and the record number box are displayed on a form.
NavigationCaption	String	Sets or gets the caption for the navigation bar in the form.
NewRecord	Integer	Determines whether the current record is a new record.
OnActivate	String	Indicates which macro, event procedure, or user-defined function runs when the OnActivate event occurs.
OnApplyFilter	String	Indicates which macro, event procedure, or user-defined function runs when the OnApplyFilter event occurs.
OnClick	String	Indicates which macro, event procedure, or user-defined function runs when the OnClick event occurs.
OnClose	String	Indicates which macro, event procedure, or user-defined function runs when the OnClose event occurs.
OnConnect	String	Indicates which macro, event procedure, or user-defined function runs when the OnConnect event occurs.
OnCurrent	String	Indicates which macro, event procedure, or user-defined function runs when the OnCurrent event occurs.
OnDblClick	String	Indicates which macro, event procedure, or user-defined function runs when the OnDblClick event occurs.
OnDeactivate	String	Indicates which macro, event procedure, or user-defined function runs when the OnDeactivate event occurs

Table continues on the next page

Property	Data Type	Description
OnDelete	String	Indicates which macro, event procedure, or user-defined function runs when the OnDelete event occurs.
OnDirty	String	Indicates which macro, event procedure, or user-defined function runs when the OnDirty event occurs.
OnDisconnect	String	Indicates which macro, event procedure, or user-defined function runs when the OnDisconnect event occurs.
OnError	String	Indicates which macro, event procedure, or user-defined function runs when the OnError event occurs.
OnFilter	String	Indicates which macro, event procedure, or user-defined function runs when the OnFilterevent occurs.
OnGotFocus	String	Indicates which macro, event procedure, or user-defined function runs when the OnGotFocus event occurs.
OnInsert	String	Indicates which macro, event procedure, or user-defined function runs when the BeforeInsert event occurs.
OnKeyDown	String	Indicates which macro, event procedure, or user-defined function runs when the OnKeyDown event occurs.
OnKeyPress	String	Indicates which macro, event procedure, or user-defined function runs when the OnKeyPress event occurs.
OnKeyUp	String	Indicates which macro, event procedure, or user-defined function runs when the OnKeyUp event occurs.
OnLoad	String	Indicates which macro, event procedure, or user-defined function runs when the OnLoad event occurs.
OnLostFocus	String	Indicates which macro, event procedure, or user-defined function runs when the OnLostFocus event occurs.
OnMenu	String	Indicates which macro, event procedure, or user-defined function runs when the OnMenu event occurs.

Property	Data Type	Description
OnMouseDown	String	Indicates which macro, event procedure, or user-defined function runs when the OnMouseDown event occurs.
OnMouseMove	String	Indicates which macro, event procedure, or user-defined function runs when the OnMouseMove event occurs.
OnMouseUp	String	Indicates which macro, event procedure, or user-defined function runs when the OnMouseUp event occurs.
OnOpen	String	Indicates which macro, event procedure, or user-defined function runs when the OnOpen event occurs.
OnResize	String	Indicates which macro, event procedure, or user-defined function runs when the OnResize event occurs.
OnTimer	String	Indicates which macro, event procedure, or user-defined function runs when the OnTimer event occurs.
OnUndo	String	Indicates which macro, event procedure, or user-defined function runs when the OnUndo event occurs.
OnUnload	String	Indicates which macro, event procedure, or user-defined function runs when the OnUnload event occurs.
OpenArgs	Variant	Determines the string expression specified by the OpenArgs argument of the OpenForm method.
OrderBy	String	Specifies how records on a form should be shortened.
OrderByOn	Boolean	Specifies whether a form's OrderBy property is applied
OrderByOnLoad	Boolean	Indicates that a sort should be loaded with the form when the form loads.
Orientation	Byte	Specifies the form's orientation (left to right or right to left).
Page	Long	Specifies the current page number when a form is being printed.
Pages	Integer	Returns information needed to print page numbers on a form.

Table continues on the next page

Property	Data Type	Description
Painting	Boolean	Specifies whether forms are repainted.
PaintPalette	Variant	Specifies the palette used by a form.
PaletteSource	String	Specifies the palette for the form.
Parent	Object	For subforms, returns the main Form object where the subform resides. Throws a run-time error for top-level forms.
Picture	String	Can be used to specify a bitmap on a form.
PictureAlignment	Byte	Specifies where a background picture appears in an image control on a form.
PictureData	Variant	Can be used to copy the picture in a form to another object.
PicturePalette	Variant	Contains the palette information.
PictureSizeMode	Byte	Specifies how a picture on a form is sized.
PictureTiling	Boolean	Specifies whether a background picture is tiled across the entire form.
PictureType	Byte	Used to specify if the picture is stored as a linked (1) or embedded (0) object.
PivotTable	PivotTable object	Returns a specific PivotTable on the form.
PivotTableChange	String	Indicates which macro, event procedure, or user-defined function runs when the PivotTableChange event occurs.
PopUp	Boolean	Specifies whether a form opens in a pop-up window.
Printer	Printer object	Represents the default printer on the current system.
Properties	Properties collection	Collection of all properties of the form.
PrtDevMode	Variant	Sets or returns the printing device mode information for the form in the Print dialog box.
PrtDevNames	Variant	Sets or returns information about the printer selected in the Print dialog box.
PrtMip	Variant	Sets or returns the printing device mode information for the form in the Print dialog box.
Query	String	Indicates which macro, event procedure, or user-defined function runs when the Query event occurs.

Property	Data Type	Description
RecordLocks	Byte	Determines how records are locked and what happens when two users try to edit the same record at the same time.
RecordSelectors	Boolean	Determines whether a form displays record selectors in form view.
Recordset	Recordset object	Returns the recordset object for the form.
RecordsetClone	Recordset object	Can be used to refer to a form's recordset specified by the form's RecordSource property.
RecordsetType	Byte	Specifies the type of recordset is used within the form.
RecordSource	String	Used to specify the source of the data for the form.
RecordSourceQualifier	String	Returns or sets a string indicating the SQL Server owner name of the record source for the form.
ResyncCommand	String	Used to specify the SQL statement or stored procedure used in an update snapshot of a table.
RibbonName	String	Name of a custom ribbon to load for the form.
RowHeight	Integer	Specifies the height of rows in a form's datasheet view.
ScrollBars	Byte	Specifies whether scrollbars appear on a form.
Section	Section object	Used to identify a section of a form.
SelectionChange	String	Indicates which macro, event procedure, or user-defined function runs when the SelectionChange event occurs.
SelHeight	Long	Specifies the number of selected rows or records in the current selection rectangle in a form's datasheet.
SelLeft	Long	Specifies which column is leftmost in the current selection rectangle in the form's datasheet.
SelTop	Long	Specifies which row is topmost in the current selection rectangle in the form's datasheet.

Table continues on the next page

Property	Data Type	Description
SelWidth	Long	Specifies the number of selected columns in the current selection rectangle in the form's datasheet.
ServerFilter	String	Used to specify a subset of records displayed when a server filter is applied.
ServerFilterByForm	Boolean	Specifies whether a form is opened in the Server Filter By Form window.
ShortcutMenu	Boolean	Specifies whether a shortcut menu is displayed when you right-click an object on a form.
ShortcutMenuBar	String	Specifies the shortcut menu that appears when you right-click a form.
SplitFormDatasheet	AcSplitFormDatasheet Enum	Specifies whether to allow edits in the datasheet portion of a split form.
SplitFormOrientation	AcSplitForm-Orientation Enum	Specifies the location of the datasheet in a split form.
SplitFormPrinting	AcSplitFormPrinting Enum	Specifies whether the form or datasheet portion of a split form will be printed.
SplitFormSize	Long	Indicates the size of the form portion of a split form.
SplitFormSplitterBar	Boolean	Indicates whether the splitter bar is visible between the form and datasheet portions of a split form.
SplitFormSplitterBarSave	Boolean	Specifies whether the location of the splitter bar is saved for a split form.
SubdatasheetExpanded	Boolean	Specifies the saved state of all subdatasheets within a form.
SubdatasheetHeight	Integer	Determines the display height of a subdatasheet when expanded.
Tag	String	Stores extra information about a form.
TimerInterval	Long	Specifies the interval (in milliseconds) between Timer events on a form.
Toolbar	String	Specifies the toolbar used for a form.
UniqueTable	String	Identifies the "most many" table of a join of a data source of a form.
UseDefaultPrinter	Boolean	Determines whether the form uses the system's default printer.

Property	Data Type	Description
VerticalDatasheet-GridlineStyle	Byte	Specifies the line style to use for vertical gridlines within the form's datasheet.
ViewChange	String	Indicates which macro, event procedure, or user-defined function runs when the ViewChange event occurs.
ViewsAllowed	Byte	Specifies whether users can switch between form and datasheet views.
Visible	Boolean	True when the form isn't minimized.
Width	Integer	Width of the form in twips.
WindowHeight	Integer	Specifies the height of a form in twips.
WindowLeft	Integer	Indicates the screen position in twips of the left edge of the form relative to the left edge of the Access window.
WindowTop	Integer	Specifies the screen position in twips of the top edge of the form relative to the top edge of the Access window.
WindowWidth	Integer	Sets the width of the form in twips.

Form Object Methods

The Form object also has a number of methods you can use within your code. They're described in the following table.

Method	Arguments	Description
GoToPage	PageNumber, Right, Down	Moves the focus to the first control on a specified page in the current form.
Move	Left, Top, Width, Height	Moves the form to the specified coordinates.
Recalc	None	Immediately updates the calculated controls on a form.
Refresh	None	Immediately updates the records in the underlying record source for a form.
Repaint	None	Completes any pending screen updates for the current form.
Requery	None	Updates the data in the form from the underlying recordset.
SetFocus	None	Sets the focus to the current form.
Undo	None	Resets the value of a form when it has been changed.

Form Object Events

Events are at the core of programming Windows applications. As such, there are a large number of events you'll use within your code behind forms. You probably will only use a handful of these events, but they are all available to you. A Form's events are summarized in the following table.

Event	Occurs
Activate	When the form receives focus and becomes the active window.
AfterDelConfirm	After the user confirms the delete and the records are actually deleted.
AfterFinalRender	After all elements in the PivotChart have been rendered.
AfterInsert	After a new record is added.
AfterLayout	After all charts in the PivotChart have been laid out but before they have been rendered.
AfterRender	After an object represented by the ChartObject has been rendered.
AfterUpdate	After changed data in a control or record is updated.
ApplyFilter	When a filter is applied to a form.
BeforeDelConfirm	After the user deletes records but before the delete confirmation dialog box is displayed.
BeforeInsert	When the user types the first character in a new record.
BeforeQuery	When the specified PivotTable queries its data source.
BeforeRender	Before any object in the specified PivotChart has been rendered.
BeforeScreenTip	Before a screen tip is displayed for an element in a PivotChart or PivotTable view.
BeforeUpdate	Before changed data in a control is updated.
Click	When a user presses and releases the mouse button over an object.
Close	When a form is closed and removed from the screen.
CommandBeforeExecute	Before a specified command is executed.
CommandChecked	When the specified Microsoft Office Web Component determines whether the specified command is checked.
CommandEnabled	When the specified Microsoft Office Web Component determines whether the specified command is enabled.
CommandExecute	After the specified command is executed.
Current	When the focus moves to a record or when the form is refreshed or requeried.
DataChange	When certain properties are changed or when certain methods are executed in a PivotTable view.
DataSetChange	Whenever the specified PivotTable view is data-bound and the dataset changes.

Event	Occurs
DblClick	When a user presses and releases the mouse button twice in rapid succession over an object.
Deactivate	When a form loses focus to another object.
Delete	When the user presses the Delete key, but before the record is actually deleted.
Dirty	When data has changed on the form, but the current record hasn't been saved.
Error	When a runtime error occurs when the form has the focus.
Filter	When a user chooses the Filter by Form or Advanced Filter/Sort option on the ribbon.
GotFocus	When the form receives the focus.
KeyDown	When a key is pressed.
KeyPress	When a key is pressed and released.
KeyUp	When a key is released.
Load	When a form is opened and records are displayed.
LostFocus	When the form loses focus to another object.
MouseDown	When the mouse button is pressed.
MouseMove	When the user moves the mouse.
MouseUp	When the mouse button is released.
MouseWheel	When the mouse wheel is moved.
OnConnect	When the PivotTable view connects to a data source.
OnDisconnect	When a PivotTable view disconnects from a data source.
Open	When a form is opened but before the first record is displayed.
PivotTableChange	Whenever the specified PivotTable view field, field set, or total is added or deleted.
Query	Whenever the specified PivotTable view query becomes necessary.
Resize	When a form opens and any time it is resized.
SelectionChange	Whenever a user makes a new selection in a PivotChart or PivotTable view.
Timer	At regular intervals controlled by the form's TimerInterval property.
Undo	When the user undoes a change to a control on a form.
Unload	After a form is closed but before it's removed from the screen.
ViewChange	Whenever the specified PivotChart view or PivotTable view is redrawn.

The Control Object

Within a form, you can have a variety of different controls. You use them to display data from tables, queries, and other data sources such as ADO recordsets. Every control in Access derives from the `Control` object.

Control Object Properties

The `Control` object has quite a few properties, which are described in the following table.

Property	Data Type	Description
Application	Application object	Returns the currently active `Application` object.
BottomPadding	Integer	Specifies the amount of space between a control and its bottom gridline.
Column	Variant	Refers to a specific column in a combo box or listbox.
Controls	Controls collection	Refers to the collection of all the controls on the form.
Form	Form object	Refers to the current form object.
GridlineColor	Long	Specifies the color for control gridlines in a stacked or tabular layout.
GridlineStyleBottom	Byte	Specifies the style for the bottom gridline for a control.
GridlineStyleLeft	Byte	Specifies the style for the left gridline for a control.
GridlineStyleRight	Byte	Specifies the style for the right gridline for a control.
GridlineStyleTop	Byte	Specifies the style for the top gridline for a control.
GridlineWidthBottom	Byte	Specifies the width of the bottom gridline for a control.
GridlineWidthLeft	Byte	Specifies the width of the left gridline for a control.
GridlineWidthRight	Byte	Specifies the width of the right gridline for a control.
GridlineWidthTop	Byte	Specifies the width of the top gridline for a control.
HorizontalAnchor	AcHorizontalAnchor Enum	Specifies how a control is horizontally anchored.
Hyperlink	Hyperlink object	Accesses the properties and methods of a hyperlink object associated with a control.
ItemData	Variant	Returns the data in the bound column for the specified row in a combo box or list box.
ItemsSelected	ItemsSelected collection	Returns a reference to the `ItemsSelected` collection.
Layout	AcLayoutType Enum	Specifies the type of layout for a control.

Property	Data Type	Description
LayoutID	Long	Returns the unique identifier for a layout for the specified control on a form or report. Returns 0 if the control is not in a stacked or tabular layout.
LeftPadding	Integer	Specifies the amount of space between a control and its left gridline.
Name	String	Specifies the name of the control.
Object	ActiveX object	Returns a reference to the ActiveX object associated with a linked or embedded OLE object in a control.
ObjectVerbs	String	Determines the list of verbs an OLE object supports.
OldValue	Variant	Determines the unedited value of a bound control.
Pages	Integer	Returns the number of pages in a control that supports tabbed pages.
Parent	Object	For controls, usually a form object.
Properties	Properties collection	Returns a reference to the entire collection of properties for the object.
Report	Report object	Refers to a report or the report associated with a sub-report control.
RightPadding	Integer	Specifies the amount of space between a control and its right gridline.
Selected	Long	Determines if an item in a list box is selected.
SmartTags	SmartTags collection	Returns the collection of SmartTags that have been added to a control.
TopPadding	Integer	Specifies the amount of space between a control and its top gridline.
VerticalAnchor	AcVerticalAnchor Enum	Specifies how a control is vertically anchored.

Control Object Methods

The methods you can use with a control object are explained in the following table. For all of these methods, the specified object is the control whose method is being called.

Method	Arguments	Description
Dropdown	None	Forces the list in the specified combo box to drop down.
Move	Left, Top, Width, Height	Moves the specified object to the coordinates specified.

Table continues on the next page

Method	Arguments	Description
Requery	None	Updates the data behind a control by requerying the source data for the control.
SetFocus	None	Moves the focus to the specified control.
SizeToFit	None	Sizes the control to fit the text or image it contains.
Undo	None	Resets a control whose value has been changed.

The ImportExportSpecification Object

Access 2007 introduces a new technique for creating and managing import and export specifications. If you worked with specifications in previous versions of Access, you'll be glad to know that you can create a specification for each of the supported file types for import and export! No longer are specifications limited to text files. With the addition of this new feature, Microsoft has added the ImportExport-Specification object and ImportExportSpecifications collection. Obviously, this collection contains ImportExportSpecification objects and consists of the standard collection members: Add, Item, Count.

ImportExportSpecification Object Properties

The following table describes the properties of the ImportExportSpecification object.

Property	Data Type	Description
Application	Application object	Returns the current Application object for the specification.
Description	String	Specifies a friendly description for the specification.
Name	String	Specifies the name of the specification.
Parent	Object	the CurrentProject or CodeProject object for the specification.
XML	String	Specifies the XML representation of the specification.

ImportExportSpecification Object Methods

The ImportExportSpecification object's methods are described here:

Method	Arguments	Description
Delete	None	Deletes the current specification.
Execute	Prompt	Executes the import or export specification.

The Module Object

The Module object refers to either a standard module or a class module within your database.

Module Object Properties

The Module object's properties are described in the following table.

Property	Data Type	Description
Application	Application object	Returns the currently active Application object.
CountOfDeclaration-Lines	Long	Count of the number of lines in the General Declarations section of a standard or class module.
CountOfLines	Long	Count of lines of code in a standard or class module.
Lines	String	Contains the contents of a specified line or lines in a standard or class module.
Name	String	Returns the name of the standard or class module.
Parent	Object	Usually the Application object.
ProcBodyLine	Long	Contains the number of the line at which the body of the specified procedure begins.
ProcCountLines	Long	Contains the number of lines in a specified procedure of a standard of class module.
ProcOfLine	String	Contains the name of the procedure that contains the specified line in a standard or class module.
ProcStartLine	Long	Identifies the line at which a specified procedure begins in a standard or class module.
Type	AcModuleType Enum	Indicates whether a module is a standard module or a class module

Module Object Methods

The methods for the Module object are listed in the following table.

Method	Arguments	Description
AddFromFile	FileName	Adds the contents of the text file to a module.
AddFromString	String	Adds the contents of the string to a module.

Table continues on the next page

Method	Arguments	Description
CreateEventProc	EventName, ObjectName	Creates an event procedure in a class module.
DeleteLines	StartLine, Count	Deletes lines from a module.
Find	Target, StartLine, StartColumn, EndLine, EndColumn, WholeWord, MatchCase, PatternSearch	Finds the specified text in a class module.
InsertLines	Line, String	Inserts a line or group of lines of code in a module.
InsertText	Text	Inserts a string of text into a module.
ReplaceLine	Line, String	Replaces the specified line with a string value.

The Printer Object

Access VBA enables you to manipulate the printers available on your system through code. All available printers are members of the Printers collection. You can access an individual printer through the Printer object.

Printer Object Properties

The properties of the Printer object are explained in the following table.

Properties	Data Type	Specifies
BottomMargin	Long	Bottom margin for the printed page.
ColorMode	AcPrintColor Enum	Whether the printer should output in color or monochrome mode.
ColumnSpacing	Long	Vertical space between detail sections (in twips).
Copies	Long	Number of copies to be printed.
Dataonly	Boolean	True if Access prints only the data and not the labels, borders, gridlines, and graphics.
DefaultSize	Boolean	True when the size of the detail section in design view is used for printing. False if the ItemSizeHeight and ItemSizeWidth properties are used.
DeviceName	String	Name of the printer.
DriverName	String	Name of the driver used by the specified printer.
Duplex	AcPrintDuplex Enum	How the printer handles duplex printing.
ItemLayout	AcPrintItemLayout Enum	Whether the printer lays out columns across, then down, or down, then across.

Properties	Data Type	Specifies
ItemsAcross	Long	Number of columns to print across a page.
ItemSizeHeight	Long	Height of the detail section in twips.
ItemSizeWidth	Long	Width of the detail section in twips.
LeftMargin	Long	Left margin for the printed page.
Orientation	AcPrintOrientation Enum	Print orientation.
PaperBin	AcPrinterBin Enum	Which paper bin the printer should use.
PaperSize	AcPrintPaperSize Enum	Paper size to use when printing.
Port	String	Port name for the specified printer.
PrintQuality	AcPrintObjQuality Enum	Resolution the printer uses to print jobs.
RightMargin	Long	Right margin for the printed page.
RowSpacing	Long	Horizontal space between detail sections (in twips).
TopMargin	Long	Top margin for the printed page.

The References Collection and Reference Object

In addition to the various Access objects detailed in this appendix, you can use objects from other applications such as Excel, Word, Outlook, and non-Microsoft programs such as AutoCad and Peachtree Accounting to program in Access. To use these other object models, set a reference to their type libraries. The References collection contains a reference for every external type library you add to the References dialog box within your code.

The properties of the Reference object are described in the following table.

Property	Data Type	Description
BuiltIn	Boolean	Specifies whether a reference points to a default Reference necessary for Access to function properly.
Collection	References object	Returns a reference to the collection that contains an object.
FullPath	String	Specifies the path and filename of the referenced type library.
Guid	String	Returns a GUID that identifies the type library in the Registry.
IsBroken	Boolean	Specifies whether a Reference object points to a valid reference in the Registry.

Table continues on the next page

Property	Data Type	Description
Kind	Vbext_RefKind Enum	Specifies the type of reference that a Reference object represents.
Major	Long	Specifies the major version number of an application you're referencing.
Minor	Long	Specifies the minor version of the application you're referencing.
Name	String	The name of the Reference object.

The Reports Collection and Report Object

Microsoft Access contains a Reports collection that contains a Report object for every open report within your database. Reports that are not currently open in the database are not in the Reports collection.

Report Object Properties

The properties of the Report object are listed in the following table.

Property	Data Type	Description
ActiveControl	Control object	Used with the Screen object to determine the control that has the focus.
AllowLayoutView	Boolean	Determines whether a report can be viewed in Layout view.
AllowReportView	Boolean	Determines whether a report can be viewed in report view.
Application	Application object	Returns the currently active application object.
AutoCenter	Boolean	Determines whether the report will be automatically centered within the Application window.
AutoResize	Boolean	Determines whether the report will be automatically resized to display complete records.
BorderStyle	Byte	Specifies the type of border and border elements for the report.
Caption	String	Specifies the caption in the title bar for the report.
CloseButton	Boolean	Specifies whether the Close button on a report is enabled.
ControlBox	Boolean	Specifies whether the form has a control menu (in Form and Datasheet view only).
Controls	Controls collection	Specifies the collection of all controls on the report.
Count	Integer	Specifies the number of items within the Reports collection.

Property	Data Type	Description
CurrentRecord	Long	Identifies the current record being viewed on a report.
CurrentView	Integer	Determines how a report is displayed (Design view, Report view, Layout view, or Print Preview).
CurrentX	Single	Specifies the horizontal coordinates for the starting position of the next printing and drawing method on a report.
CurrentY	Single	Specifies the vertical coordinates for the starting position of the next printing and drawing method on a report.
Cycle	Byte	Specifies what happens when you press the Tab key while the last control on the report has the focus.
DateGrouping	Byte	Specifies how you want to group dates on a report.
DefaultControl	Control object	Can be used to specify the properties of a particular type of control on a report.
DefaultView	Byte	Used to specify the opening view for a report (report view or print preview).
Dirty	Boolean	True if data has been entered but not saved on a form.
DisplayOnShare PointSite	Byte	Specifies whether the report can be made as a view on a SharePoint site.
DrawMode	Integer	Specifies how the pen interacts with existing background colors on a report when the Line, Circle, or Pset method is used when printing.
DrawStyle	Integer	Specifies the line style when using the Line and Circle methods to print lines on reports.
DrawWidth	Integer	Specifies the line width for the Line, Circle, and Pset methods to print lines on reports.
FastLaserPrinting	Boolean	Specifies whether lines and rectangles are replaced by text character lines to speed printing.
FillColor	Long	Specifies the color that fills in boxes and circles drawn on reports with the Line and Circle methods.
FillStyle	Integer	Specifies whether circles and lines are transparent, opaque, or filled with a pattern.
Filter	String	Specifies a subset of records to be displayed when a filter is applied to a report.
FilterOn	Boolean	Specifies whether the Filter property of a report is applied.
FilterOnLoad	Boolean	Indicates that a filter should be loaded with the report when the report loads.

Table continues on the next page

Property	Data Type	Description
FitToPage	Boolean	Gets or sets whether the width of the report should be reduced to fit the width of the page.
FontBold	Boolean	Specifies whether a font appears in bold on a form or report.
FontItalic	Boolean	Specifies whether a font appears in italics on a form or report.
FontName	String	Specifies the font for printing controls on reports.
FontSize	Integer	Specifies the font size for printing controls on reports.
FontUnderline	Integer	Specifies whether a font appears underlined on a form or report.
ForeColor	Long	Specifies the color for text in a control.
FormatCount	Integer	Specifies the number of times the OnFormat property has been evaluated for the current section on a report.
GridX	Integer	Specifies the horizontal divisions of the alignment grid in report design view.
GridY	Integer	Specifies the vertical divisions of the alignment grid in report design view.
GroupLevel	GroupLevel object	Refers to a particular group level you're grouping or sorting in a report.
GrpKeepTogether	Byte	Specifies whether groups in a multiple column report that have the KeepTogether property set to Whole Group or With First Detail will be kept together by page or by column.
HasData	Long	Specifies if a report is bound to an empty recordset.
HasModule	Boolean	Specifies whether a report has a class module associated with it.
Height	Long	Specifies the height of the report in twips.
HelpContextID	Long	Specifies the context ID of a topic in the custom help file.
HelpFile	String	Returns the name of the help file associated with the report.
Hwnd	Long	Used to determine the handle of the current report window.
InputParameters	String	Can be used to specify the input parameters passed to a SQL statement in the RecordSource property of a report.
KeyPreview	Boolean	Specifies whether the form level keyboard event procedures are invoked before a control's keyboard event procedures.

Property	Data Type	Description
LayoutForPrint	Boolean	Specifies whether the report uses printer (True) or screen (False) fonts.
Left	Long	Specifies the object's location on a report.
MenuBar	String	Specifies the menu bar to use for a report.
MinMaxButtons	Byte	Specifies whether the Maximize and Minimize buttons are visible on the report.
Modal	Boolean	Specifies whether a report opens as a modal window.
Module	Module object	Specifies a module for the report.
MouseWheel	String	Indicates which macro, event procedure, or user-defined function runs when the MouseWheel event occurs.
Moveable	Boolean	True if a report can be moved by the user.
MoveLayout	Boolean	Specifies if Access should move to the next printing location on the page.
Name	String	Specifies the name of the report.
NextRecord	Boolean	Specifies whether a section should advance to the next record.
OnActivate	String	Indicates which macro, event procedure, or user-defined function runs when the OnActivate event occurs.
OnApplyFilter	String	Indicates which macro, event procedure, or user-defined function runs when the OnApplyFilter event occurs.
OnClick	String	Indicates which macro, event procedure, or user-defined function runs when the OnClick event occurs.
OnClose	String	Indicates which macro, event procedure, or user-defined function runs when the OnClose event occurs.
OnCurrent	String	Indicates which macro, event procedure, or user-defined function runs when the OnCurrent event occurs.
OnDblClick	String	Indicates which macro, event procedure, or user-defined function runs when the OnDblClick event occurs.
OnDeactivate	String	Indicates which macro, event procedure, or user-defined function runs when the OnDeactivate event occurs.
OnError	String	Indicates which macro, event procedure, or user-defined function runs when the OnError event occurs.
OnFilter	String	Indicates which macro, event procedure, or user-defined function runs when the OnFilter event occurs.
OnGotFocus	String	Indicates which macro, event procedure, or user-defined function runs when the OnGotFocus event occurs.

Table continues on the next page

Property	Data Type	Description
OnKeyDown	String	Indicates which macro, event procedure, or user-defined function runs when the OnKeyDown event occurs.
OnKeyPress	String	Indicates which macro, event procedure, or user-defined function runs when the OnKeyPress event occurs.
OnKeyUp	String	Indicates which macro, event procedure, or user-defined function runs when the OnKeyUp event occurs.
OnLoad	String	Indicates which macro, event procedure, or user-defined function runs when the OnLoad event occurs.
OnLostFocus	String	Indicates which macro, event procedure, or user-defined function runs when the OnLostFocus event occurs.
OnMenu	String	Indicates which macro, event procedure, or user-defined function runs when the OnMenu event occurs.
OnMouseDown	String	Indicates which macro, event procedure, or user-defined function runs when the OnMouseDown event occurs.
OnMouseMove	String	Indicates which macro, event procedure, or user-defined function runs when the OnMouseMove event occurs.
OnMouseUp	String	Indicates which macro, event procedure, or user-defined function runs when the OnMouseUp event occurs.
OnNoData	String	Indicates which macro, event procedure, or user-defined function runs when the OnNoData event occurs.
OnOpen	String	Indicates which macro, event procedure, or user-defined function runs when the OnOpen event occurs.
OnPage	String	Indicates which macro, event procedure, or user-defined function runs when the OnPage event occurs.
OnResize	String	Indicates which macro, event procedure, or user-defined function runs when the OnResize event occurs.
OnTimer	String	Indicates which macro, event procedure, or user-defined function runs when the OnTimer event occurs.
OnUnload	String	Indicates which macro, event procedure, or user-defined function runs when the OnUnload event occurs.
OpenArgs	Variant	Determines the string expression specified by the OpenArgs method of the OpenReport method.
OrderBy	String	Specifies how records on a report should be shortened.
OrderByOn	Boolean	Specifies whether the OrderBy property is applied.
OrderByOnLoad	Boolean	Indicates that a sort should be loaded with the form when the form loads.

Property	Data Type	Description
Orientation	Byte	Specifies the report's orientation (left to right or right to left).
Page	Long	Specifies the current page number when a report is printed.
PageFooter	Byte	Specifies whether a report's page footer is printed on the same page as the report footer.
PageHeader	Byte	Specifies whether a report's page header is printed on the same page as the report header.
Pages	Integer	Returns information needed to print page numbers on a report.
Painting	Boolean	Specifies whether reports are repainted.
PaintPalette	Variant	Specifies the palette used by a report.
PaletteSource	String	Used to specify the palette for the report.
Parent	Object	For subreports, returns the main Report object where the subreport resides. Throws a runtime error for top-level reports.
Picture	String	Specifies a bitmap on a report.
PictureAlignment	Byte	Specifies where a background picture appears in an image control on a report.
PictureData	Variant	Can be used to copy the picture in a report to another object.
PicturePages	Byte	Specifies on which page or pages of a report a picture is displayed.
PicturePalette	Variant	Contains information about the palette for the object.
PictureSizeMode	Byte	Specifies how a picture on a report is sized.
PictureTiling	Boolean	Specifies whether a background picture is tiled across the entire report.
PictureType	Byte	Specifies whether Access stores a report's picture as a linked or embedded object.
PopUp	Boolean	Specifies whether a report opens in a pop-up window.
PrintCount	Integer	Specifies the number of times the OnPrint property has been evaluated for the current section of the report.
Printer	Printer object	Represents the default printer on the current system.
PrintSection	Boolean	Specifies whether a section of a report should be printed.
Properties	Properties collection	Represents the collection of all properties for the report.

Table continues on the next page

Property	Data Type	Description
PrtDevMode	Variant	Sets or returns the printing device mode information for the report in the Print dialog box.
PrtDevNames	Variant	Sets or returns information about the printer selected in the Print dialog box.
PrtMip	Variant	Sets or returns the printing device mode information for the report in the Print dialog box.
RecordLocks	Integer	Determines how records are locked and what happens when two users try to edit the same record at the same time.
Recordset	Recordset object	Returns the Recordset object for the report.
RecordSource	String	Used to specify the source of the data for the report.
RecordSource Qualifier	String	Returns or sets a string indicating the SQL Server owner name of the record source for the report.
Report	Report object	Used to refer to the report associated with a subreport.
RibbonName	String	Name of a custom ribbon to load for the report.
ScaleHeight	Single	Specifies the number of units for the vertical measurement of the page when the Circle, Line, Pset, or Print methods are used when a report is printed.
ScaleLeft	Single	Specifies the units for the horizontal coordinates that reference the location of the left edge of the page when the Circle, Line, Pset, or Print methods are used when a report is printed.
ScaleMode	Integer	Specifies the unit of measurement for coordinates on a page when the Circle, Line, Pset, or Print methods are used when a report is printed.
ScaleTop	Single	Specifies the units for the vertical coordinates that reference the location of the top edge of a page when the Circle, Line, Pset, or Print methods are used on a report.
ScaleWidth	Single	Specifies the number of units for the horizontal measurement of the page when the Circle, Line, Pset, or Print methods are used when a report is printed.
ScrollBars	Byte	Specifies whether scrollbars appear on a report.
Section	Section object	Identifies a section of a report.
ServerFilter	String	Specifies a subset of records displayed when a server filter is applied.
Shape	String	Specifies the shape command corresponding to the sorting and grouping of the report.

Property	Data Type	Description
ShortcutMenuBar	String	Specifies the shortcut menu that appears when you right-click a report.
ShowPageMargins	Boolean	Specifies whether page margins are visible on a report open in report view.
Tag	String	Stores extra information about a report.
TimerInterval	Long	Specifies the interval (in milliseconds) between Timer events on a report.
Toolbar	String	Specifies the toolbar used for a report.
Top	Long	Specifies the report's top coordinates.
UseDefaultPrinter	Boolean	Determines whether the report uses the system's default printer.
Visible	Boolean	True when the report isn't minimized.
Width	Integer	Width of the report in twips.
WindowHeight	Integer	Specifies the height of a report in twips.
WindowLeft	Integer	Indicates the screen position in twips of the left edge of the report relative to the left edge of the Access window.
WindowTop	Integer	Specifies the screen position in twips of the top edge of the report relative to the top edge of the Access window.
WindowWidth	Integer	Sets the width of the report in twips.

Report Object Methods

The methods of the Report object are listed in the following table.

Method	Arguments	Description
Circle	flags, X, Y, radius, color, start, end, aspect	Draws a circle, ellipse, or an arc on a report when the Print event occurs.
Line	Flags, x1, y1, x2, y2, color	Draws lines and rectangles on a report when the Print event occurs.
Move	Left, Top, Width, Height	Moves the report to the specified coordinates on the screen.
Print	Expr	Prints text on a Report object using the current color and font.
PSet	flags, X, Y, color	Sets a point on a report object to the specified color when the Print event occurs.

Table continues on the next page

Method	Arguments	Description
Requery	None	Updates the data in the report from the underlying recordset.
Scale	flags, x1, y1, x2, y2	Defines the coordinate system for a Report object.
TextHeight	Expr	Returns the height of a text string as it would be printed in the current font of a report.
TextWidth	Expr	Returns the width of a text string as it would be printed in the current font of a report.

Report Object Events

Access 2007 introduces a new interactive view for reports called Report View. As a result, many of the events that have existed on forms over the years are now available in reports! The events of the Report object are listed in the following table.

Event	Occurs
Activate	When a report receives the focus and becomes the active window.
ApplyFilter	When a filter is applied to a report.
Click	When a user presses and releases the mouse button over an object.
Close	When a report is closed but before it is removed from the screen.
Current	When the focus moves to a record or when the form is refreshed or requeried.
DblClick	When a user presses and releases the mouse button.
Deactivate	When a report loses focus to another object.
Error	When a runtime error occurs when the report has the focus.
Filter	When a user chooses the Advanced Filter/Sort option on the ribbon.
GotFocus	When the report receives the focus.
KeyDown	When a key is pressed.
KeyPress	When a key is pressed and released.
KeyUp	When a key is released.
Load	When a report is opened and records are displayed.
LostFocus	When the report loses focus to another object.
MouseDown	When the mouse button is pressed.
MouseMove	When the user moves the mouse.
MouseUp	When the mouse button is released.

Event	Occurs
MouseWheel	When the mouse wheel is moved.
NoData	After a report with no data is formatted for printing but before the report is printed.
Open	When a report is opened but before it is displayed on the screen.
Page	After a page is formatted for printing but before the page is printed.
Resize	When a form opens and any time it is resized.
Timer	At regular intervals controlled by the form's TimerInterval property.
Unload	After a form is closed but before it's removed from the screen.

The Screen Object

The Screen object refers to whatever form, report, or control currently has the focus within the application. You can use the Screen object and its properties to manipulate the active window no matter which form, report, or control is currently displayed.

The properties of the Screen object are listed in the following table.

Property	Data Type	Description
ActiveControl	Control object	Specifies the control that has the focus.
ActiveDatasheet	Form object	Specifies the datasheet that has the focus.
ActiveForm	Form object	Specifies the form that has the focus.
ActiveReport	Report object	Specifies the report that has the focus.
Application	Application object	References the current Access application.
MousePointer	Integer	Specifies the type of mouse pointer currently displayed.
Parent	Object	Parent of the object that currently has the focus.
PreviousControl	Control object	Specifies the control that previously had the focus.

The Section Object

Every form or report contains several Section objects including the header, footer, and detail sections. Each section has a number of properties and methods you can use within your code.

A Section object has only one method: SetTabOrder. It enables you to programmatically set the tab order for all controls in a section. Calling this method is the equivalent of using the Auto Order button in the Tab Order dialog box.

Section Object Properties

The properties of the Section object are described in the following table.

Property	Data Type	Description
AlternateBackColor	Long	Specifies the alternating row color for a section. It is now easy to change the row color for every other section on a form or report!
Application	Application object	Returns the currently active application.
AutoHeight	Boolean	Indicates whether a section should grow automatically when controls are resized.
BackColor	Long	Specifies the color for the interior of a section.
CanGrow	Boolean	True if you want the section to automatically grow to print or preview all data within the section.
CanShrink	Boolean	True if you want the section to automatically shrink to print or preview only the data within the section (with no extra space).
Controls	Controls collection	References all of the controls within the section.
DisplayWhen	Byte	Controls which sections you want displayed on screen and in print.
EventProcPrefix	String	Used to get the prefix portion of an event procedure name.
ForceNewPage	Byte	Specifies when sections print on a separate page.
HasContinued	Boolean	Determines if part of the current section begins on the previous page.
Height	Integer	Height (in twips) of the current section.
InSelection	Boolean	Determines if a control on a form is selected.
KeepTogether	Boolean	True if the entire section should print on one page.
Name	String	Name of the current section.
NewRowOrCol	Byte	Specifies whether a section is printed within a new row or column within a multicolumn report or form.
OnClick	String	Indicates which macro, event procedure, or user-defined function runs when the OnClick event occurs.
OnDblClick	String	Indicates which macro, event procedure, or user-defined function runs when the OnDblClick event occurs.
OnFormat	String	Indicates which macro, event procedure, or user-defined function runs when the OnFormat event occurs.
OnMouseDown	String	Indicates which macro, event procedure, or user-defined function runs when the OnMouseDown event occurs.

Property	Data Type	Description
OnMouseMove	String	Indicates which macro, event procedure, or user-defined function runs when the OnMouseMove event occurs.
OnMouseUp	String	Indicates which macro, event procedure, or user-defined function runs when the OnMouseUp event occurs.
OnPaint	String	Indicates which macro, event procedure, or user-defined function runs when the OnPaint event occurs.
OnPrint	String	Indicates which macro, event procedure, or user-defined function runs when the OnPrint event occurs.
OnRetreat	String	Indicates which macro, event procedure, or user-defined function runs when the OnRetreat event occurs.
Parent	Object	Refers to the parent of the section (usually either a form, report, or data access page).
Properties	Properties collection	Refers to the entire collection of properties for the section.
RepeatSection	Boolean	Specifies whether the group header is repeated on the next page of column (when the group spans more than one page or column).
SpecialEffect	Byte	Specifies whether any special formatting applies to a section (such as shadow, sunken lines, or highlight).
Tag	String	Stores extra information about a section.
Visible	Boolean	Specifies whether a section is visible on a form or report.
WillContinue	Boolean	Specifies if the current section continues on the next page.

Section Object Events

There are nine events you can use in your code for the Section object. They're described in the following table.

Event	Occurs When
Click	The user presses and releases the mouse button.
DblClick	The user presses and releases the mouse button twice in rapid succession.
Format	A section is formatted. Does not fire in report view.
MouseDown	The user presses the mouse button.
MouseMove	The user moves the mouse.
MouseUp	The user releases the mouse button.

Table continues on the next page

Event	Occurs When
Paint	A section is redrawn on the screen. Does not fire in Print Preview.
Print	A section is printed. Does not fire in report view.
Retreat	Access must move back to a section that has already been formatted. Allows you to undo a change to a control that was made in the Format event for the section.

The SmartTag Object

All of Microsoft Office 2007 has the capability to use SmartTags. You can programmatically manipulate the SmartTag object by accessing its properties and methods.

The properties of the SmartTag object are listed in the following table.

Property	Data Type	Description
Application	Application object	Represents the currently active Access application.
IsMissing	Boolean	Returns true if the SmartTag isn't installed or isn't correctly installed.
Name	String	Returns the name of the SmartTag.
Parent	Object	Refers to the parent object of the SmartTag.
Properties	SmartTagProperties collection	Returns the collection of all properties for a particular SmartTag.
SmartTagActions	SmartTagActions collection	Returns the collection of all actions available for a specific SmartTag.
XML	String	Represents the XML code for a SmartTag.

The SmartTag object has only one method: Delete.

The SmartTagActions collection and the SmartTagProperties collection have the standard properties associated with any collection (Application, Count, Item, and Parent). The individual SmartTagAction object has one method, Execute, which performs the specified SmartTag action. The SmartTagProperty object also has only one method: Delete.

The SubForm Object

When designing Access forms, you can embed a subform within your main form. The SubForm object includes the same properties as the Control object. In addition, some of the SubForm object's properties are the same as other Access form objects. As a convenience, however, all of the SubForm object properties are described in the following table.

SubForm Object Properties

Property	Data Type	Description
AddColon	Boolean	Specifies whether a colon follows the text in labels for new controls.
Application	Application object	Returns the currently active application object.
AutoLabel	Boolean	Specifies whether labels are automatically created and attached to new controls.
BorderColor	Long	Specifies the color of a control's border.
BorderStyle	Byte	Specifies the type of border and border elements for the form.
BorderWidth	Byte	Specifies the width of a control's border.
BottomPadding	Integer	Specifies the amount of space between a control and its bottom gridline.
CanGrow	Boolean	Specifies whether the subform can grow to accommodate all the data.
CanShrink	Boolean	Specifies if the subform can shrink to avoid empty space with no data.
Controls	Controls collection	Returns the collection of all controls on the subform.
ControlType	Byte	Specifies the type of control on a subform.
DisplayWhen	Byte	Specifies which of a subform's sections or controls you want displayed on the screen or in print.
Enabled	Boolean	Returns the status of the conditional format in the FormatCondition object.
EventProcPrefix	String	Specifies the prefix portion of an event procedure name.
FilterOnEmptyMaster	Boolean	Specifies whether all records are displayed in a subform when the value in the master field in the main form is null.
Form	Form object	Returns the form associated with the current subform.
GridlineColor	Long	Specifies the color for control gridlines in a stacked or tabular layout.
GridlineStyleBottom	Byte	Specifies the style for the bottom gridline for a control.
GridlineStyleLeft	Byte	Specifies the style for the left gridline for a control.
GridlineStyleRight	Byte	Specifies the style for the right gridline for a control.
GridlineStyleTop	Byte	Specifies the style for the top gridline for a control.

Table continues on the next page

Property	Data Type	Description
GridlineWidthBottom	Byte	Specifies the width of the bottom gridline for a control.
GridlineWidthLeft	Byte	Specifies the width of the left gridline for a control.
GridlineWidthRight	Byte	Specifies the width of the right gridline for a control.
GridlineWidthTop	Byte	Specifies the width of the top gridline for a control.
Height	Integer	Specifies the height of the subform in twips.
HorizontalAnchor	AcHorizontalAnchor Enum	Specifies how a control is horizontally anchored.
InSelection	Boolean	Specifies whether a control on a subform in design mode is selected.
IsVisible	Boolean	Specifies whether a control on a subform is visible.
LabelAlign	Byte	Specifies text alignment within labels on new controls.
LabelX	Integer	Specifies the horizontal placement of the label for a new control.
LabelY	Integer	Specifies the vertical placement of the label for a new control.
Layout	AcLayoutType Enum	Specifies the type of layout for a control.
LayoutID	Long	Returns the unique identifier for a layout for the specified control on a form or report. Returns 0 if the control is not in a stacked or tabular layout.
Left	Integer	Specifies the subform's location on a form.
LeftPadding	Integer	Specifies the amount of space between a control and its left gridline.
LinkChildFields	String	Specifies field on subform that links the subform with the master form.
LinkMasterFields	String	Specifies field on master form that links the subform with the master form.
Locked	Boolean	Specifies whether you can enter data in a subform.
Name	String	Specifies the name of the subform.
OldBorderStyle	Byte	Specifies the unedited value of the BorderStyle property for a subform.
OnEnter	String	Indicates which macro, event procedure, or user-defined function runs when the OnEnter event occurs.
OnExit	String	Indicates which macro, event procedure, or user-defined function runs when the OnExit event occurs.

Property	Data Type	Description
Parent	Form object	The parent of a subform is the master form.
Properties	Properties collection	Represents the entire properties collection for the subform.
Report	Report object	Refers to the report associated with a subreport control.
RightPadding	Integer	Specifies the amount of space between a control and its right gridline.
Section	Integer	Identifies a section on a subform.
SourceObject	String	Specifies the form that is the source of the subform.
SpecialEffect	Byte	Specifies whether special formatting applies to a subform.
StatusBarText	String	Specifies the text displayed in the status bar when a subform is selected.
TabIndex	Integer	Specifies a subform's place in the tab order on a form.
TabStop	Boolean	Specifies whether you can use the Tab key to set the focus to a subform.
Tag	String	Stores extra information about the subform.
Top	Integer	Specifies the subform's location within a form.
VerticalAnchor	AcVerticalAnchor Enum	Specifies how a control is vertically anchored.
Visible	Boolean	True if the subform is displayed on the screen.
Width	Integer	Specifies the width of the subform in twips.

SubForm Object Events and Methods

A subform also has its own methods and events, which are detailed in the following tables.

Method	Argument	Description
Move	Left, Top, Width, Height	Moves the subform to the coordinates specified.
Requery	None	Updates the controls on the subform by requerying the data source.
SetFocus	None	Moves the focus to the subform.
SizeToFit	None	Sizes the subform to fit the data it contains.

Event	Description
Enter	Occurs immediately before the subform receives the focus.
Exit	Occurs immediately before the subform loses the focus to another control or subform.

The SubReport Object

Much like forms and subforms, reports can also contain subreports. The SubReport object has no methods, and its events are the same as the events for the SubForm object.

The SubReport object has four properties, described in the following table.

Property	Data Type	Description
Application	Application object	Returns the currently active application object.
Form	Form object	Refers to the form associated with a SubReport object.
Parent	Various	Refers to the parent of the selected subform.
Report	Report object	Refers to the report associated with a SubReport object.

Other Helpful Information

There's a lot of information about the Access object model in this appendix. In addition to the basic objects you'll manipulate on a daily basis, there are many other areas of the object model with which you should be familiar. You need to know some of the myriad arguments you can use with some of these objects, as well as the order in which events fire in the different objects. The following sections detail some additional information about programming in Access that may be helpful.

Order of Events

Knowing the order in which events fire is an important aspect of programming with VBA in Access. These order lists can help you decide which events you should choose for your applications. It's also essential to recognize that events do not necessarily fire when actions are triggered using VBA code. For example, if you set a value for a control programmatically, the AfterUpdate event for the control does not fire.

Events that begin with the prefix Before can typically be cancelled by setting the Cancel argument of the event to True.

Forms, Controls, and Subforms

Here's the order of events for the opening sequence of a form with controls:

```
Open->Load->Resize->Activate->Current->Enter (control)->GotFocus (control)
```

If there are no controls on the form, the `GotFocus` event will fire after the `Current` event. If there is an `Attachment` control on the form, the `OnAttachmentCurrent` event will fire before the `Form_Current` event (as long as it is the first control in the tab order).

The following shows the order of events for the closing sequence of a form:

```
Exit (control)->LostFocus (control)->Unload->Deactivate->Close
```

Subform events fire before main form events because records for a subform are loaded first. Because subforms do not have a form window, they do not fire the `Activate` event. The following shows the order of events for the opening sequence of a form with a subform:

```
Open (subform)->Load (subform)->Resize (subform)->Current (subform)->
Open->Load->Resize->Activate->Current
```

Reports and Sections

With the introduction of Report View in Access 2007, many of the events that are available to forms are now available to reports. The events that fire, however, are different for a report open in Report View than in Print Preview.

Report View and Layout View

Here's the order in which events fire for the opening sequence of a report in Report View or Layout View:

```
Open->Load->Resize->Activate->GotFocus->Paint (ReportHeader)->Paint (PageHeader)
->Paint (Detail)->Paint (ReportFooter)->Paint (PageFooter)
```

Notice that neither the `Current` event nor control events fire when a report is opened. That's because unlike a form, objects on a report do not receive focus when the report opens. To trigger the `Current` event for a report, click in the Detail section.

The `Paint` event was added in Access 2007 and fires every time Access draws the section in the report. As such, the Paint event can fire multiple times for a given section. The `Format`, `Print`, and `Retreat` events do not fire in report view or layout view.

When you close a report in Report view or Layout view, events are fired in the following order:

```
Unload->LostFocus->Deactivate->Close
```

Print Preview

The order of events for a report opened in Print Preview is similar to that for report view. The primary difference between the two views is the `Format`, `Print`, and `Paint` events. `Paint` does not fire for sections in print preview.

```
Open->Load->Resize->Activate->GotFocus->Format (Report Header)->Print (Report
Header)->Format (Page Header)->Print (Page Header)->Format (Detail)->Print
(Detail)->Format (ReportFooter)->Print (ReportFooter)->Format (PageFooter)->Print
(PageFooter)->Page
```

As you can see, a lot of events fire for the given sections on a report! If you try to handle events in Print Preview, you might also notice that the Format event can fire for all the sections before the first Print event is fired. That's because reports in Access are actually formatted twice on some occasions. Generally speaking, this can occur when a calculation requires other sections further down the page, or even the report itself to be formatted before the calculation is complete. A good example is the expression that returns the current page and page count in the page footer section: ="Page " & [Page] & " of " & [Pages].

When you close a report in print preview, events are fired in the following order:

    Unload->LostFocus->Deactivate->Close

Records

There are data-related events on forms as well.

Adding Records

There are several events that fire when you add a record using a form:

    BeforeInsert->Dirty->BeforeUpdate->AfterUpdate->AfterInsert

Editing Records

The order of events for editing existing data on a form is:

    Dirty->Dirty (control)->BeforeUpdate (control)->AfterUpdate (control)
    ->BeforeUpdate->AfterUpdate

Deleting Records

When you delete records, the following events are raised:

    Delete->BeforeDelConfirm->AfterDelConfirm

Application.SetOption Method

The SetOption method of the Application object allows you to control all of the options in the Access Options dialog box which is available from the Office button. The following tables detail the string arguments for the options available on each group. For example, to control the visibility of the Status Bar within your Access application, you'd use the following code.

    Application.SetOption "Show Status Bar", True

The arguments you need to manipulate the SetOption method are broken down by the tab of the Access Options dialog box on which they appear.

In previous versions of Access, certain settings were available in the Startup dialog box under the Tools menu. In Access 2007, these settings are included in the Access Options dialog box, but are not set using Application.SetOption. Instead, they can be set or retrieved using the Properties collection of the DAO.Database object for an ACCDB or MDB file. These properties are described in the following tables.

Popular Options

Section	Option Text	String Argument
Top options for working with Access	Always use ClearType	None
	ScreenTip style	None
	Show shortcut keys in ScreenTips	None
	Color scheme	None
Creating databases	Default file format	Default File Format
Directory	Default database folder	Default Database
	New database sort order	New Database Sort Order

Current Database Options

Section	Option Text	String Argument
Application Options	Use as Form and Report icon	`UseAppIconForFrmRpt` (set using Properties collection)
	Display Form	`StartupForm` (set using Properties collection)
	Display Status Bar	`Show Status Bar`
	Document Window Options	`UseMDIMode` (set to False to use Tabbed Documents)
	Display Document Tabs	`ShowDocumentTabs` (set using Properties collection)
	Compact on Close	`Auto Compact`
	Remove personal information from file properties on save	`Remove Personal Information`
	Use Windows-themed Controls on Forms	`Themed Form Controls`
	Enable Layout View for this Database	None
	Enable design changes for tables in Datasheet view (for this database)	`AllowDatasheetSchema` (set using Properties collection)
	Check for truncated number fields	`CheckTruncatedNumFields`
	Picture Property Storage Format	`Picture Property Storage Format`
Navigation	Display Navigation Pane	`StartupShowDBWindow` (set using Properties collection)

Table continues on the next page

Current Database Options

Section	Option Text	String Argument
Ribbon and Toolbar Options	Ribbon Name	`CustomRibbonID` (set using Properties collection)
	Menu Bar	`StartupMenuBar` (set using Properties collection)
	Shortcut Menu Bar	`StartupShortcutMenuBar` (set using Properties collection)
	Allow Full Menus	`AllowFullMenus` (set using Properties collection)
	Allow Default Shortcut Menus	`AllowShortcutMenus` (set using Properties collection)
	Allow Built-in Toolbars	`AllowBuiltInToolbars` (set using Properties collection)
Name AutoCorrect Options	Track name AutoCorrect info	`Track Name AutoCorrect Info`
	Perform name AutoCorrect	`Perform Name AutoCorrect`
	Log name AutoCorrect changes	`Log Name AutoCorrect Changes`
Filter lookup options for Database	Show list of values in Local indexed fields	`Local Show Values in Indexed`
	Show list of values in Local non-indexed fields	`Local Show Values in Non-Indexed`
	Show list of values in ODBC fields	`Show Values in Remote`
	Show list of values in, Records in local snapshot	`Show Values in Snapshot` (ADP files only)
	Show list of values in, Records at server	`Show Values in Server` (ADP files only)
	Don't display lists where more of this number of records read	`Show Values in Limit`

Datasheet Options

Section	Option Text	String Argument
Default colors	Font color	`Default Font Color`
	Background color	`Default Background Color`

Datasheet Options

Section	Option Text	String Argument
	Alternate background color	None
	Gridlines color	`Default Gridlines Color`
Gridline and cell effects	Default gridlines showing horizontal	`Default Gridlines Horizontal`
	Default gridlines showing vertical	`Default Gridlines Vertical`
	Default cell effect	`Default Cell Effect`
	Default column width	`Default Column Width`
Default font	Font	`Default Font Name`
	Size	`Default Font Size`
	Weight	`Default Font Weight`
	Underline	`Default Font Underline`
	Italic	`Default Font Italic`

Object Designers Options

Section	Option Text	String Argument
Table design	Default field type	`Default Field Type`
	Default text field size	`Default Text Field Size`
	Default number field size	`Default Number Field Size`
	AutoIndex on Import/Create	`AutoIndex on Import/Create`
	Show Property Update Options button	`Show Property Update Options buttons`
Query design	Show table names	`Show Table Names`
	Output all fields	`Output All Fields`
	Enable AutoJoin	`Enable AutoJoin`
	Query design font	`Query Design Font Name`
	Query design font size	`Query Design Font Size`
	Run Permissions	`Run Permissions` (MDB files only)
	SQL Server Compatible Syntax (ANSI92) This database	`ANSI Query Mode`
	SQL Server Compatible Syntax (ANSI92) Default for new databases	`ANSI Query Mode Default`

Table continues on the next page

Object Designers Options

Section	Option Text	String Argument
Forms/Reports	Selection behavior	`Selection Behavior`
	Form template	`Form Template`
	Report template	`Report Template`
	Always use event procedures	`Always Use Event Procedures`
Error checking	Enable error checking	`Enable Error Checking`
	Check for unassociated label and control	`Unassociated Label and Control Error Checking`
	Check for new unassociated labels	`New Unassociated Label Error Checking`
	Check for keyboard shortcut errors	`Keyboard Shortcut Errors Error Checking`
	Check for invalid control properties	`Invalid Control Properties Error Checking`
	Check for common report errors	`Common Report Errors Error Checking`
	Error indicator color	`Error Checking Indicator Color`

Proofing Options

Section	Option Text	String Argument
When correcting spelling in Office programs	Ignore words in UPPERCASE	`Spelling ignore words in UPPERCASE`
	Ignore words that contain numbers	`Spelling ignore words with number`
	Ignore Internet and file addresses	`Spelling ignore Internet and file addresses`
	Flag repeated words	None
	Enforce accented uppercase in French	None
	Suggest from main dictionary only	`Spelling suggest from main dictionary only`
	French modes	None

Proofing Options

Section	Option Text	String Argument
	Dictionary language	Spelling dictionary language
	Hebrew modes (Hebrew language only)	Spelling Hebrew modes
	Arabic modes (Arabic language only)	Spelling Arabic modes
	Use post-reform rules (German language only)	Spelling use German post-reform rules
	Combine aux verb/adj (Korean language only)	Spelling combine aux verb/adj
	Search misused word list (Korean language only)	Spelling use auto-change list
	Process compound nouns (Korean language only)	Spelling process compound nouns

Advanced Options

Section	Option Text	String Argument
Editing	Move after enter	Move After Enter
	Behavior entering field	Behavior Entering Field
	Arrow key behavior	Arrow Key Behavior
	Cursor stops at first/last field	Cursor Stops at First/Last Field
	Default find/replace behavior	Default Find/Replace Behavior
	Confirm Record changes	Confirm Record Changes
	Confirm Document deletions	Confirm Document Deletions
	Confirm Action queries	Confirm Action Queries
	Default direction	Default direction
	General alignment	General alignment
	Cursor movement	Cursor movement
	Datasheet IME control	Datasheet Ime Control
	Auto commit	IME Autocommit (East Asian locales only)
	Use Hijri Calendar	Use Hijri Calendar

Table continues on the next page

Section	Option Text	String Argument
Display	Show this number of Recent Documents	Size of MRU File List
	Status bar	Show Status Bar
	Show animations	Show Animations
	Show Smart Tags on Datasheets	Show SmartTags on Datasheets
	Show Smart Tags on Forms and Reports	Show SmartTags on Forms and Reports
	Show Names column in Macro Design	Show Macro Names Column
	Show Conditions column in Macro Design	Show Conditions Column
Printing	Left margin	Left Margin
	Right margin	Right Margin
	Top margin	Top Margin
	Bottom margin	Bottom Margin
General	Show add-in user interface errors	None
	Provide feedback with sound	Provide Feedback with Sound
	Use four-digit year formatting – This database	Four-Digit Year Formatting
	Use four-digit year formatting – All databases	Four-Digit Year Formatting All Databases
Advanced	Default Max Records (applies to ADP files only)	Row Limit
	Open last used database when Access starts	Open Last Used Database When Access Starts
	Default open mode	Default Open Mode for Databases
	Default record locking	Default Record Locking
	Open databases by using record-level locking	Use Row Level Locking
	OLE/DDE Timeout (sec)	OLE/DDE Timeout (sec)
	Refresh interval (sec)	Refresh Interval (sec)
	Number of update retries	Number of Update Retries
	ODBC refresh interval (sec)	ODBC Refresh Interval (sec)
	Update retry interval (msec)	Update Retry Interval (msec)
	Ignore DDE requests	Ignore DDE Requests
	Enable DDE refresh	Enable DDE Refresh
	Command-line arguments	Command-Line Arguments

Others not in the dialog box

Certain options that were available in Access 2003 have been moved to other locations or no longer apply to Access 2007 and do not appear in the Access Options dialog box. Specifically, options related to Data Access Pages are no longer supported.

Option Text	String Argument	Access 2007 Location
Show, Startup Task Pane	`Show Startup Dialog Box`	Not applicable in Access 2007
Show, New object shortcuts	`Show New Object Shortcuts`	Not applicable in Access 2007
Show, Hidden objects	`Show Hidden Objects`	Navigation Options dialog box
Show, System objects	`Show System Objects`	Navigation Options dialog box
Show, Windows in Taskbar	`ShowWindowsInTaskbar`	Not applicable in Access 2007
Click options in database window	`Database Explorer Click Behavior`	Not applicable in Access 2007
Recently used file list	`Enable MRU File List`	Not applicable in Access 2007

Useful Access Enums

As mentioned in Chapter 13, an *enum* or enumeration is a group of related constant values. The Access object model contains many enums that you can use in your applications. There are so many in fact that there are too many to list here! For example, the `AcCommand` enum contains more than 600 values of its own! Obviously we can't list them all here, but the following table introduces you to some enums built in to Access that we think you'll run across quite frequently. Using enums and constants is a big step toward making code more readable, so it's recommended that you use them where possible.

Enum	Members	Usage
AcCloseSave	`acSaveNo`	`DoCmd.Close`
	`acSavePrompt`	
	`acSaveYes`	
AcCommand	`acCmdAddFromOutlook`	`Application.RunCommand`
	`acCmdCloseAll`	`DoCmd.RunCommand`
	`acCmdCompileAndSaveAllModules`	
	`acCmdConnection`	
	`acCmdCopy`	
	`acCmdCreateShortcut`	
	`acCmdCut`	
	`acCmdDeleteRecord`	

Table continues on the next page

Enum	Members	Usage
	acCmdDuplicate	
	acCmdEncryptDecryptDatabase	
	acCmdFind	
	acCmdLinkedTableManager	
	acCmdPaste	
	acCmdPasteSpecial	
	acCmdRunMacro	
	acCmdSave	
	acCmdSaveAsOutlookContact	
	acCmdSavedImports	
	acCmdSaveRecord	
	acCmdSetDatabasePassword	
	acCmdShowColumnHistory	
	acCmdSpelling	
	acCmdStartupProperties	
	acCmdWorkgroupAdministrator	
AcDataObjectType	acActiveDataObject	DoCmd.GoToRecord
	acDataForm	
	acDataFunction	
	acDataQuery	
	acDataReport	
	acDataServerView	
	acDataStoredProcedure	
	acDataTable	
AcFileFormat	acFileFormatAccess2	CurrentProject.FileFormat
	acFileFormatAccess2000	
	acFileFormatAccess2002	
	acFileFormatAccess2007	
	acFileFormatAccess95	
	acFileFormatAccess97	

Enum	Members	Usage
AcFormOpenDataMode	acFormAdd	DoCmd.OpenForm
	acFormEdit	
	acFormPropertySettings	
	acFormReadOnly	
AcObjectType	acDefault	AccessObject.Type
	acDiagram	Application.CurrentObjectType
	acForm	Application.GetHiddenAttribute
	acFunction	Application.SetHiddenAttribute
	acMacro	DoCmd.Close
	acModule	DoCmd.CopyObject
	acQuery	DoCmd.DeleteObject
	acReport	DoCmd.Rename
	acServerView	DoCmd.RepaintObject
	acStoredProcedure	DoCmd.SelectObject
	acTable	DoCmd.TransferDatabase
AcOutputObjectType	acOutputForm	DoCmd.OutputTo
	acOutputFunction	
	acOutputModule	
	acOutputQuery	
	acOutputReport	
	acOutputServerView	
	acOutputStoredProcedure	
	acOutputTable	
AcProjectType	acADP	CurrentProject.ProjectType
	acMDB	
	acNull	
AcQuitOption	acQuitPrompt	Application.Quit
	acQuitSaveAll	DoCmd.Quit
	acQuitSaveNone	
AcRecord	acFirst	DoCmd.GoToRecord

Table continues on the next page

Appendix G: The Access Object Model

Enum	Members	Usage
	acGoTo	
	acLast	
	acNewRec	
	acNext	
	acPrevious	
AcSendObjectType	acSendForm	DoCmd.SendObject
	acSendModule	
	acSendNoObject	
	acSendQuery	
	acSendReport	
	acSendTable	
AcTextTransferType	acExportDelim	DoCmd.TransferText
	acExportFixed	
	acExportHTML	
	acExportMerge	
	acImportDelim	
	acImportFixed	
	acImportHTML	
	acLinkDelim	
	acLinkFixed	
	acLinkHTML	
AcWindowMode	acDialog	DoCmd.OpenForm
	acHidden	DoCmd.OpenReport
	acIcon	
	acWindowNormal	

Windows API Reference Information

So now you probably know enough about using the Win32 API to get yourself into some serious trouble. The trick is to find information about the APIs that are available for use, and learn how to use them with VBA.

Unlike programming languages, information about the Windows API is somewhat harder to find. There are literally hundreds of API functions included in the Windows operating system, and the information that is available is mostly incomplete. There are also quite a few API functions that Microsoft hasn't publicly documented, for whatever reason. We haven't yet found a single resource that includes everything, so this appendix presents several resources that we recommend.

API Viewer

Microsoft Office 2000 and XP offered a Developer Edition that contained many resources specifically aimed at the developer. In versions prior to that, developer tools were packaged in a separate product called the Developer Toolkit. These products included a utility called the API Viewer, which provided detailed information about the Windows APIs, including function, type, and constant declarations. With the release of Office 2007, Microsoft provides the Access Developer Extensions Toolkit, which unfortunately does not include the API Viewer. You can use the API Viewer from previous versions, or from Visual Basic 6.0.

Finding information about the API is difficult, especially detailed information about how to use it with Visual Basic. There are only two Win32 API viewers that we recommend for download from the Internet, and at the time of this writing, both of them are free. There are probably others around, but these two seem to be the best:

❑ The DX21 website provides a free online API viewer at:

   www.dx21.com/VISSTUDIO/WIN32API/INDEX.ASP?ST=Declarations

❑ The AllAPI website provides a good range of information, but the noteworthy point as far as this section is concerned, is that it offers a good (and free) API Viewer for download at:

`www.mentalis.org/agnet/apiviewer.shtml`

Be advised that, as with many websites, you can never guarantee how long a site will remain in existence.

Websites

There are many websites dedicated to the Win32 API, each of which has its good and bad points. Most, however, do not provide a complete API list.

The Microsoft MSDN website is, in our opinion, difficult to use when you don't know what you're looking for. If you know the exact name of the API function you want, you can find excellent references to it on the MSDN site, including information and how-to articles. But finding a complete list of all Windows API functions is nearly impossible. The general consensus is that even Microsoft does not publish documentation for the entire API.

The following short list represents Internet-based resources that are worth a look:

❑ **MSDN:** Search for "Win32 API" or the specific API function name:

`http://search.microsoft.com/search/search.aspx?st=a&View=en-us`

❑ **Microsoft DLL Help Database:**

`http://support.microsoft.com/dllhelp`

❑ **MSDN:** Win32 API declarations download:

`www.microsoft.com/downloads/details.aspx?displaylang=en&familyid=1DB32433-87DD-45D9-A4EC-7C7973D7C94B`

❑ **The ALLAPI Network:**

`www.allapi.net/apilist/apilist.php`

❑ **VBNet Visual Basic Developers Resource Centre:**

`http://vbnet.mvps.org`

❑ **The Access Web:**

`www.mvps.org/access/`

Books

In addition to the extremely fine book you're currently reading, we recommend three other API-related books:

❑ Dan Appleman's *Visual Basic Programmer's Guide to the Win32 API*, ISBN 0-672-31590-4, SAMS.

❏   Steven Roman's *Win32 API Programming with Visual Basic*, ISBN 1-56592-631-5, O'Reilly.

❏   Dan Appleman's *Win32 API Puzzle Book and Tutorial for Visual Basic Programmers*, ISBN 1-893115-01-1, Apress.

Some Useful API Functions

Apart from the `SetFormIcon` function described in Chapter 14, this section is devoted to demonstrating how to use some useful API functions.

Play a Sound in Access

Rather than accept the default `DoCmd.Beep` to notify users of some event, you can offer something a bit more interesting and perhaps meaningful by playing a sound file of your choosing.

```
Public Declare Function sndPlaySound Lib "winmm.dll" Alias "sndPlaySoundA" _
    (ByVal lpszSoundName As String, ByVal uFlags As long) As Long

' The sound is played asynchronously and the function returns immediately
' after beginning the sound. To terminate a sound called with SND_ASYNC, call
' sndPlaySound with lpszSoundName set to NULL
Public Const SND_ASYNC = &H1

' The sound plays repeatedly until sndPlaySound is called again with the
' lpszSoundName parameter set to NULL. You must also specify SND_ASYNC with this
'flag
Public Const SND_LOOP = &H8

' The parameter specified by lpszSoundName points to an image of a waveform
' sound in memory
Public Const SND_MEMORY = &H4

' If the sound cannot be found, the function returns silently without
' playing the default sound
Public Const SND_NODEFAULT = &H2

' If a sound is currently playing, the function immediately returns FALSE without
' playing the requested sound
Public Const SND_NOSTOP = &H10

' The sound is played synchronously and the function does not return
' until the sound ends
Public Const SND_SYNC = &H0

Public Sub PlayAnySound(lpszSoundName As String)
    Dim retVal As Long
    On Error Resume Next
    retVal = sndPlaySound(lpszSoundName, SND_NODEFAULT)
End Sub
```

Find the Position of a Form

The `Form` object in Access includes four properties that would appear to give an indication as to the location of a form onscreen: `WindowHeight`, `WindowLeft`, `WindowTop`, and `WindowWidth`. These properties actually return values based on the client workspace within the Access application window. Because these values can change based on the location of the Access window itself, there is no built-in mechanism to expose the current xy position of a form. The following example demonstrates how to use the `GetWindowRect` API to return the form's screen position in pixels.

Create a small form containing a single command button, and add the following code:

```
Option Compare Database
Option Explicit

Private Type RECT
    left As Long
    top As Long
    right As Long
    bottom As Long
End Type

Private Declare Function GetWindowRect Lib "user32" _
(ByVal hwnd As Long, lpRect As RECT) As Long

Private Sub cmdShow_Click()
    Dim FormDims As RECT

    If GetWindowRect(Me.hwnd, FormDims) Then
        MsgBox "The form is located at:" & _
                vbCrLf & "Left: " & vbTab & FormDims.left & _
                vbCrLf & "Top: " & vbTab & FormDims.top & _
                vbCrLf & "Right: " & vbTab & FormDims.right & _
                vbCrLf & "Bottom: " & vbTab & FormDims.bottom
    End If
End Sub
```

Now open the form and click the button. A message box displays the form's location.

Find the Temp Directory

The Temp directory (typically `C:\Windows\Temp`) is the place where Windows stores temporary files. The `GetTempPath` function returns the path of the Temp directory on the computer. You can also use the `Environ` function in VBA to read the `TEMP` environment variable to return the Temp directory.

```
Private Declare Function GetTempPath _
        Lib "kernel32" Alias "GetTempPathA" ( _
        ByVal nBufferLength As Long, _
        ByVal lpBuffer As String) As Long

Private Const MAXLEN = 255
```

```
Public Function TempPath() As String
    Dim strPath As String
    Dim lngSize As Long
    Dim lngReturn As Long

    strPath = Space(MAXLEN) & Chr(0)
    lngSize = MAXLEN + 1

    lngReturn = GetTempPath(lngSize, strPath)
    If lngReturn <> 0 Then
        TempPath = left(strPath, lngReturn)
    Else
        TempPath = ""
    End If
End Function
```

Generate a Unique Temp Filename

The GetTempFileName function generates a unique temporary filename with a .tmp extension:

```
Private Declare Function GetTempFileName _
    Lib "kernel32" Alias "GetTempFileNameA" ( _
    ByVal lpPathName As String, _
    ByVal lpPrefixString As String, _
    ByVal uUnique As Long, _
    ByVal lpTempFileName As String) As Long

Private Const MAXLEN = 255

Public Function GetTemporaryFile( _
  Optional strDirectory As String, _
  Optional strPrefix As String) As String

    Dim strPath As String
    Dim lngReturn As Long

    strPath = Space(255)

    ' Default to the folder where the database resides
    If Len(strDirectory) = 0 Then
        strDirectory = CurrentProject.Path
    End If

    lngReturn = GetTempFileName(strDirectory, strPrefix, 0, strPath)
    If lngReturn <> 0 Then
        GetTemporaryFile = Left(strPath, InStr(strPath, Chr(0)) - 1)
    Else
        GetTemporaryFile = ""
    End If
End Function
```

Find the Login Name of the Current User

The GetUserName function returns the name of the user currently logged on to the computer. It returns only the login name for the user — it does not return the name of the domain.

```
Private Declare Function GetUserName _
    Lib "advapi32.dll" Alias "GetUserNameA" _
    (ByVal lpBuffer As String, _
    nSize As Long) As Long

Private Const MAXLEN = 255

Function GetLoginName() As String
    Dim strUserName As String
    Dim lngSize As Long

    strUserName = Space(MAXLEN) & Chr(0)
    lngSize = MAXLEN + 1

    If GetUserName(strUserName, lngSize) <> 0 Then
        GetLoginName = Left(strUserName, lngSize -1)
    Else
        GetLoginName = ""
    End If
End Function
```

Find the Computer Name

The GetComputerName function returns the name of the computer. It does not return the fully qualified domain name (FQDN) for computers that are joined to a domain.

```
Private Declare Function GetComputerName _
    Lib "kernel32.dll" Alias "GetComputerNameA" _
    (ByVal lpBuffer As String, _
    nSize As Long) As Long

Private Const MAX_COMPUTERNAME_LENGTH = 31

Function GetMachineName() As String
    Dim strComputerName As String
    Dim lngSize As Long

    strComputerName = Space(MAX_COMPUTERNAME_LENGTH) & Chr(0)
    lngSize = MAX_COMPUTERNAME_LENGTH + 1

    If GetComputerName(strComputerName, lngSize) <> 0 Then
        GetMachineName = Left(strComputerName, lngSize)
    Else
        GetMachineName = ""
    End If
End Function
```

Open or Print Any File

The following procedure enables you to open or print any file, without your needing to know what its executable program is. For example, this same procedure can be used to open or print a Word or PDF document, an Excel spreadsheet, or an ASCII text file. It can even be used to generate e-mail with the default e-mail client if you use the `mailto:` protocol followed by an e-mail address, or to open a Web page with the default Internet browser if you specify a Web address that includes the HTTP protocol.

```
Public Const SW_HIDE = 0
Public Const SW_MINIMIZE = 6

Public Const SW_RESTORE = 9
Public Const SW_SHOW = 5
Public Const SW_SHOWMAXIMIZED = 3
Public Const SW_SHOWMINIMIZED = 2
Public Const SW_SHOWMINNOACTIVE = 7
Public Const SW_SHOWNA = 8
Public Const SW_SHOWNOACTIVATE = 4
Public Const SW_SHOWNORMAL = 1

Public Declare Function ShellExecute Lib "shell32.dll" Alias "ShellExecuteA" _
    (ByVal hWnd As Long, ByVal lpOperation As String, ByVal lpFile As String, _
    ByVal lpParameters As String, ByVal lpDirectory As String, _
    ByVal nShowCmd As Long) As Long

Public Sub ExecuteFile(sFileName As String, sAction As String)
    Dim vReturn As Long
    'sAction can be either "Open" or "Print".

    If ShellExecute(Access.hWndAccessApp, sAction, _
            sFileName, vbNullString, "", SW_SHOWNORMAL) < 33 Then
        DoCmd.Beep
        MsgBox "File not found."
    End If
End Sub
```

Delay Code Execution

The following procedure enables you to make your code pause for a specified amount of time. Appropriately enough, the API used is called Sleep.

```
Declare Sub Sleep Lib "kernel32.dll" (ByVal lngMilliseconds As Long)

Public Sub Pause(lngSeconds As Long)
    'Convert seconds to milliseconds
    Sleep lngSeconds * 1000
End Sub
```

Windows Registry Information

This appendix provides information about the Windows Registry to support the tutorials in Chapter 21, including Windows Registry data types, functions, and constant and user-defined Type declarations.

Windows Registry Data Types

In the same way that database table fields, variables, and API parameters require data of specific types, the kind of data the Registry can store is also defined in terms of data types. The data types in the table that follows are supported under Windows 2000, Windows XP, and Windows Vista.

Data Type	Description
REG_BINARY	Specifies raw binary data. Most hardware information is stored with this data type, which can be displayed and entered in binary or hexadecimal format.
REG_DWORD	A 32-bit (4-byte) number, which is used to store Boolean or other numeric values and information about many device drivers and services. REG_DWORD values can be displayed and edited as binary, hexa-decimal, or decimal format.
REG_DWORD_LITTLE_ENDIAN	Same as REG_DWORD, a 32-bit number, but it is used to store values in a specific way. In REG_DWORD_LIT-TLE_ENDIAN, the most significant byte contains the high-order byte (leftmost). This is the most common format for storing numbers in Windows.

Table continues on the next page

Data Type	Description
REG_DWORD_BIG_ENDIAN	The only difference between this data type and REG_DWORD_LITTLE_ENDIAN is that this data type stores the most-significant byte as the low-order byte (rightmost).
REG_EXPAND_SZ	A variable-length text string used to store variables that are resolved when an application or service uses the data. For example, some values include the variable System root. When a service or application references the data in this data type, it is replaced by the name of the directory containing the Windows system files.
REG_LINK	Stores a symbolic link between system or application data, and a Registry value. REG_LINK supports both ANSI and Unicode characters.
REG_MULTI_SZ	Stores multiple strings that are formatted as an array of null-terminated strings, the last of which is terminated by an extra null character. This means the entire array is terminated by two null characters. The values in this data type can be separated by spaces, commas, or other characters.
REG_QWORD	A 64-bit (8-byte) number that's used to store Boolean or other numeric values and information about many device drivers and services. REG_QWORD values can be displayed and edited as binary, hexadecimal, or decimal format.
REG_QWORD_LITTLE_ENDIAN	The same as REG_QWORD, a 64-bit number.
REG_SZ	A null terminated string. Boolean values and short-text strings are usually stored with this data type.
REG_FULL_RESOURCE_DESCRIPTOR	Stores a series of nested arrays, for resource lists (often for hardware components or drivers). These data types are declared as constants using the VBA Const keyword. For convenience, the constant declarations are included later in this appendix.

Registry Root Key Hives

In the Registry, a *hive* is a node that often contains other keys and values. There are several root keys that you can use for functions that require that a root key be supplied for one of the parameters. These keys are defined as follows:

```
Const HKEY_CLASSES_ROOT As Long = &H80000000
Const HKEY_CURRENT_CONFIG As Long = &H80000005
Const HKEY_CURRENT_USER As Long = &H80000001
Const HKEY_DYN_DATA As Long = &H80000006
```

```
Const HKEY_LOCAL_MACHINE As Long = &H80000002
Const HKEY_PERF_ROOT As Long = HKEY_LOCAL_MACHINE
Const HKEY_PERFORMANCE_DATA As Long = &H80000004
Const HKEY_USERS As Long = &H80000003
```

Registry Function Declarations

There are 45 Win32 Registry functions that you can use from VBA. Some of these functions are included for 16-bit compatibility or requires special knowledge of Windows security and are not listed in this book. As such, this section describes only 34 of the 45 functions. In addition, many new Registry functions were added in Windows XP Professional x64 Edition, Windows Server 2003 SP1, and Windows Vista. These functions are also described in the following pages. The functions are arranged in alphabetical order and a brief description of what each function does is given. It also lists the functions declarations, and describes each of their parameters and their return values.

The following API functions are not included in this section:

❑ RegCreateKey: Creates the specified Registry key. Supported for 16-bit compatibility. Applications should use RegCreateKeyEx.

❑ RegDisablePredefinedCache: Disables the specified handle table for a process's HKEY_CURRENT_USER key.

❑ RegDisablePredefinedCacheEx: Disables the specified handle table for a process's HKEY_CURRENT_USER key. This function requires Windows Vista or later.

❑ RegEnumKey: Enumerates subkeys of the specified Registry key. Supported for 16-bit compatibility. Applications should use RegEnumKeyEx.

❑ RegOpenCurrentUser: Returns a handle to HKEY_CURRENT_USER for the user for whom the current thread is impersonating.

❑ RegOpenKey: Opens the specified Registry key. Supported for 16-bit compatibility. Applications should use RegOpenKeyEx.

❑ RegOpenUserClassesRoot: Returns a handle to HKEY_CLASSES_ROOT for the specified user.

❑ RegOverrridePredefKey: Maps one key to another.

❑ RegQueryMultipleValues: Returns the type and data of the values of an open key.

❑ RegQueryValue: Returns data for the named or default value for the specified Registry key. Supported for 16-bit compatibility. Applications should use RegQueryValueEx.

❑ RegSetValue: Sets the data for the named or default value for the specified Registry key. Supported for 16-bit compatibility. Applications should use RegSetValueEx.

Some functions have been extended to provide more programming flexibility over their predecessors. Such functions are preferred in 32-bit and 64-bit Windows and are distinguished from the former version by a trailing Ex in their name, for example, RegCreateKeyEx.

GetSystemRegistryQuota

Description	Retrieves the current size of the Registry as well as the maximum amount of size that the Registry is allowed to reach.
| Declaration | ```
Declare Function GetSystemRegistryQuota _
    Lib "kernel32.dll" ( _
    dwQuotaAllowed As Long, _
    pdwQuotaUsed As Long) As Long
``` |
| Parameters | pdwQuotaAllowed – Long Integer: Maximum size in bytes that the Registry is allowed to reach.

pdwQuotaUsed – Long Integer — Current size of the Registry in bytes. |
| Return value | Long Integer: Zero on failure.
Non-zero values equal the size of the Registry if the function succeeds.
All other values are the specific error code. |

RegCloseKey

Description	Closes a handle to a Registry key.
| Declaration | ```
Declare Function RegCloseKey Lib "advapi32.dll" _
    (ByVal hKey As Long) As Long
``` |
| Parameter | hKey – Long Integer: The handle of the key to close. |
| Return value | Long Integer: Zero (ERROR_SUCCESS) on success. All other values are the specific error code. |

RegConnectRegistry

Description	Connects to one of five specific Registry keys on a remote computer.
| Declaration | ```
Declare Function RegConnectRegistry _
    Lib "advapi32.dll" _
    Alias "RegConnectRegistryA" ( _
    ByVal lpMachineName As String, _
    ByVal hKey As Long, _
    phkResult As Long) As Long
``` |
| Parameters | lpMachineName – String: Name of the system to connect to. This is in the form \\computername.

hKey – Long Integer: Handle of the hive to connect to. This can only be HKEY_CLASSES_ROOT, HKEY_CURRENT_USER, HKEY_LOCAL_MACHINE, HKEY_PERFORMANCE_DATA, or HKEY_USERS.

phkResult – Long Integer: A variable that is loaded with a handle to the specified key. |
| Return value | Long Integer: Zero (ERROR_SUCCESS) on success.
All other values are the specific error code. |
```

RegCopyTree

Description	Copies values and subkeys from the specified key to the specified destination key. Requires Windows Vista and administrator privileges to copy the key.
| Declaration | ```
Private Declare Function RegCopyTree _
   Lib "advapi32.dll" Alias "RegCopyTreeA" ( _
   ByVal hKeySrc As Long, _
   ByVal lpSubKey As String, _
   ByVal hKeyDest As Long) As Long
``` |
| Parameters | hKeySrc — Long Integer: Handle of the open key, or one of the hive constants listed earlier.

lpSubKey — String: Name of a subkey to copy under the key specified by hKeySrc. You can also specify vbNullString to copy all subkeys.

hKeyDest — Long Integer: Handle to the destination key. The key must be opened with KEY_CREATE_SUB_KEY. |
| Return Value | Long Integer: Zero (ERROR_SUCCESS) on success. All other values are the specific error code. |

RegCreateKeyEx

Description	Creates a new Registry key under the one you specify, but if the key already exists, it opens that key. This is a more sophisticated function than RegCreateKey, and is recommended for use on Win32.
| Declaration | ```
Declare Function RegCreateKeyEx _
   Lib "advapi32.dll" _
   Alias "RegCreateKeyExA" ( _
   ByVal hKey As Long, _
   ByVal lpSubKey As String, _
   ByVal Reserved As Long, _
   ByVal lpClass As String, _
   ByVal dwOptions As Long, _
   ByVal samDesired As Long, _
   lpSecurityAttributes As SECURITY_ATTRIBUTES, _
   phkResult As Long, _
   lpdwDisposition As Long) As Long
``` |
| Parameters | hKey — Long Integer: Handle of the open key, or one of the hive constants listed earlier.

lpSubKey — String: Name of the new subkey to create.

Reserved — Long Integer: A reserved parameter. Set it to zero.

lpClass — String: A class name for the key. This can be vbNullString.

dwOptions — Long Integer: Set to either zero or REG_OPTION_VOLATILE. |

Table continues on the next page

samDesired — `Long Integer`: One or more `KEY_` constants that combine to define the operations that are allowed for this key. You can find these constants at the end of this appendix.

lpSecurityAttributes — `SECURITY_ATTRIBUTES`: A user-defined Type that defines the security attributes for this key. Security attributes are quite a complex subject and most of its features only work on Windows NT and later. In any case, they are rarely used, so the examples provided at the end of this chapter re-declare this parameter as `ByVal lpSecurityAttributesas Long`, and pass a Null (`0&`). For more information about security, refer to the Microsoft Win32 SDK.

phkResult — `Long Integer`: A variable that is loaded with a handle to the new subkey.

lpdwDisposition — `Long Integer`: A variable that is loaded with one of the following constants. `REG_CREATED_NEW_KEY` or `REG_OPENED_EXISTING_KEY`.

Return value	`Long Integer`: Zero (`ERROR_SUCCESS`) on success. All other values are the specific error code.

RegDeleteKey

Description	Deletes the specified subkey.

Declaration	```Declare Function RegDeleteKey Lib "advapi32.dll" _```
	``` Alias "RegDeleteKeyA" (_```
	``` ByVal hKey As Long, _```
	``` ByVal lpSubKey As String) As Long```

Parameters	hKey — `Long Integer`: Handle of the open key, or one of the hive constants listed earlier. lpSubKey — `String`: Name of the subkey to delete.
Return value	`Long Integer`: Zero (`ERROR_SUCCESS`) on success. All other values are the specific error code.

RegDeleteKeyEx

Description	Deletes a key from a specific platform view of the Registry. Requires Windows Server 2003 SP1, Windows XP Professional x64 Edition, or Windows Vista.

Declaration	```Declare Function RegDeleteKeyEx _```
	``` Lib "advapi32.dll" _```
	``` Alias "RegDeleteKeyExA" (_```
	``` ByVal hKey As Long, _```
	``` ByVal lpSubKey As String, _```
	``` ByVal samDesired As Long, _```
	``` ByVal Reserved As Long) As Long```

Parameters	hKey — Long Integer: Handle of the open key, or one of the hive constants listed earlier in the appendix.
	lpSubKey — String: Name of the subkey to delete.
	samDesired — Long Integer: One or more KEYconstants that combine to define the operations that are allowed for this key. Include KEY_WOW64_32KEY or KEY_WOW64_64KEY to delete from a specific platform view of the Registry.
	Reserved — Long Integer: Reserved for future use. Set this value to zero.
Return value	Long Integer: Zero (ERROR_SUCCESS) on success. All other values are the specific error code.

RegDeleteKeyValue

Description	Removes the named value from the specified key. Requires Windows Vista or later.

Declaration	```Private Declare Function RegDeleteKeyValue _```
	``` Lib "advapi32.dll" _```
	``` Alias "RegDeleteKeyValueA" (_```
	``` ByVal hKey As Long, _```
	``` ByVal lpSubKey As String, _```
	``` ByVal lpValueName As String) As Long```

Parameters	hKey — Long Integer: Handle of the open key, or one of the hive constants listed earlier.
	lpSubKey — String: Name of the subkey containing the value to remove. Set to vbNullString to delete the value in the specified key.
	lpValueName — String: Name of the value to remove. Set to vbNullString to clear the (Default) value for the specified key or subkey.
Return Value	Long Integer: Zero (ERROR_SUCCESS) on success. All other values are the specific error code.

RegDeleteTree

Description	Deletes the subkeys and values from the specified Registry key. Requires Windows Vista or later.

Declaration	```Private Declare Function RegDeleteTree _```
	``` Lib "advapi32.dll" _```
	``` Alias "RegDeleteTreeA" (_```
	``` ByVal hKey As Long, _```
	``` ByVal lpSubKey As String) As Long```

Table continues on the next page

Parameters	hKey — Long Integer: Handle of the open key, or one of the hive constants listed earlier.
	lpSubKey — String: Name of the subkey to delete. Set to vbNullString to delete all subkeys under the specified key.
Return value	Long Integer: Zero (ERROR_SUCCESS) on success. All other values are the specific error code.

RegDeleteValue

Description	Deletes a value under the specified subkey.
| Declaration | ```
Declare Function RegDeleteValue _
    Lib "advapi32.dll" _
    Alias "RegDeleteValueA" ( _
    ByVal hKey As Long, _
    ByVal lpValueName As String) As Long
``` |
Parameters	hKey — Long Integer: Handle of the open key, or one of the hive constants listed earlier.
	lpValueName — String: Name of the value to delete. To delete the key's default value, use vbNullString or an empty string.
Return value	Long Integer: Zero (ERROR_SUCCESS) on success. All other values are the specific error code.

RegDisableReflectionKey

Description	Disables Registry reflection for the specified Registry key. Disabling reflection for a key does not affect reflection for any subkeys. Requires Windows XP Professional x64 Edition or Windows Vista.
| Declaration | ```
Declare Function RegDisableReflectionKey _
    Lib "advapi32.dll" ( _
    ByVal hBase As Long) As Long
``` |
| Parameter | hBase — Long Integer: Handle of the open key, or one of the hive constants listed earlier. |
| Return value | Long Integer: Zero (ERROR_SUCCESS) on success. All other values are the specific error code. |

RegEnableReflectionKey

Description	Enables Registry reflection for the specified Registry key. Restoring Registry reflection does not restore reflection on any subkeys. Requires Windows XP Professional x64 Edition or Windows Vista.
| Declaration | ```
Declare Function RegEnableReflectionKey _
    Lib "advapi32.dll" ( _
    ByVal hBase As Long) As Long
``` |
```

Parameter	hBase — Long Integer: Handle of the open key, or one of the hive constants listed earlier.
Return value	Long Integer: Zero (ERROR_SUCCESS) on success. All other values are the specific error code.

RegEnumKeyEx

Description	Enumerates the subkeys for a given key (hive). This is a more sophisticated function than RegEnumKey, and is recommended for use on Win32.
| Declaration | ```
Declare Function RegEnumKeyEx Lib "advapi32.dll" _
    Alias "RegEnumKeyExA" ( _
    ByVal hKey As Long, _
    ByVal dwIndex As Long, _
    ByVal lpName As String, _
    lpcbName As Long, _
    lpReserved As Long, _
    ByVal lpClass As String, _
    lpcbClass As Long, _
    lpftLastWriteTime As FILETIME) As Long
``` |
Parameters	hKey — Long Integer: Handle of the open key, or one of the hive constants listed earlier.
	dwIndex — Long Integer: Index of the subkey to retrieve. This value is zero-based (that is, the first subkey index is zero).
	lpName — String: A null-terminated buffer that is loaded with the name of the key whose index is specified by dwIndex.
	lpcbName — Long Integer: A variable that you load with the length of lpName (including the terminating Null character). When the function returns, this variable contains the number of characters actually loaded into lpName.
	lpReserved — Long Integer: A reserved parameter. Set it to zero.
	lpClass — String: A null-terminated variable that will be loaded with the class name for the key. This can be vbNullString.
	lpcbClass — Long Integer: A variable that you load with the length of lpClass (including the terminating Null character). When the function returns, this variable contains the number of characters actually loaded into lpClass.
	lpftLastWriteTime — FILETIME: A user-defined Type that will contain the last time that the specified subkey was modified.
Return value	Long Integer: Zero (ERROR_SUCCESS) on success. All other values are the specific error code.
```

RegEnumValue

Description	Enumerates the values for a given subkey.
| Declaration | ```
Declare Function RegEnumValue Lib "advapi32.dll" _
    Alias "RegEnumValueA" ( _
    ByVal hKey As Long, _
    ByVal dwIndex As Long, _
    ByVal lpValueName As String, _
    lpcbValueName As Long, _
    ByVal lpReserved As Long, _
    lpType As Long, _
    lpData As Byte, _
    lpcbData As Long) As Long
``` |

Parameters

hKey — Long Integer: The handle of the open key, or one of the hive constants listed earlier.

dwIndex — Long Integer: The index of the value to retrieve. This value is zero-based; that is, the first value index is zero.

lpValueName — String: A null-terminated buffer that is loaded with the name of the value whose index is specified by dwIndex.

lpcbValueName — Long Integer: A variable that you load with the length of lpValueName (including the terminating Null character). When the function returns, this variable contains the number of characters actually loaded into lpValueName.

lpReserved — Long Integer: This is a reserved parameter. Set it to zero.

lpType — Long Integer: The key value type (from the constant list earlier).

lpData — Byte: A buffer that is loaded with the data for the specified value.

lpcbData — Long Integer: A variable that you load with the length of lpData. When the function returns, this variable contains the number of bytes actually loaded into lpData.

Return value

Long Integer: Zero (ERROR_SUCCESS) on success.
All other values are the specific error code.
```

RegFlushKey

Description	Writes the changes made to a key and its subkeys to disk.
Declaration	`Declare Function RegFlushKey Lib "advapi32.dll" _` `    (ByVal hKey As Long) As Long`
Parameters	hKey — `Long Integer`: Handle of the key to flush, or one of the hive constants listed earlier.
Return value	`Long Integer`: Zero (ERROR_SUCCESS) on success. All other values are the specific error code.
Comment	To improve performance, some operating systems delay writing changes to disk; instead, the changes are held in a cache, to be written to disk (flushed) later. The problem with this approach is that in the event of a power failure, all the cached changes are lost. This function forces the operating system to immediately write those changes to disk, but doing so may degrade system performance.

RegGetKeySecurity

Description	Retrieves security information about the specified key.

Declaration	`Declare Function RegGetKeySecurity _`
	`    Lib "advapi32.dll" ( _`
	`    ByVal hKey As Long, _`
	`    ByVal SecurityInformation As Long, _`
	`    pSecurityDescriptor As SECURITY_DESCRIPTOR, _`
	`    lpcbSecurityDescriptor As Long) As Long`

Parameters	hKey — `Long Integer`: Handle of the key whose security information is to be retrieved, or one of the hive constants listed earlier. SecurityInformation — `Long Integer`: A flag that indicates the security information to retrieve. pSecurityDescriptor — `SECURITY_DESCRIPTOR`: A user-defined Type that will contain the security information for the specified key. lpcbSecurityDescriptor — `Long Integer`: A variable that you load with the length of pSecurityDescriptor. When the function returns, this variable contains the number of bytes actually loaded into pSecurityDescriptor.
Return value	`Long Integer`: Zero (ERROR_SUCCESS) on success. All other values are the specific error code.

RegGetValue

Description	Retrieves the data and type for the specified value in the Registry. Requires Windows XP Professional x64 Edition or Windows Vista.

Declaration	

```
' String declaration for pvData
Private Declare Function RegGetValueString _
  Lib "advapi32.dll" _
  Alias "RegGetValueA" ( _
  ByVal hkey As Long, _
  ByVal lpSubKey As String, _
  ByVal lpValue As String, _
  ByVal dwFlags As Long, _
  pdwType As Long, _
  ByVal pvData As String, _
  pcbData As Long) As Long

' Numeric declaration for pvData
Private Declare Function RegGetValueLong _
  Lib "advapi32.dll" _
  Alias "RegGetValueA" ( _
  ByVal hkey As Long, _
  ByVal lpSubKey As String, _
  ByVal lpValue As String, _
  ByVal dwFlags As Long, _
  pdwType As Long, _
  pvData As Long, _
  pcbData As Long) As Long
```

Parameters	hKey — Long Integer: Handle of the open key, or one of the hive constants listed earlier.

lpSubKey — String: Name of a subkey under the key specified in hKey. May also be vbNullString.

lpValue — String: Name of the value to retrieve. Set this to vbNullString to retrieve the (Default) value for the key.

dwFlags — Long Integer: One or more RRF_ constants to restrict the data type of the value queried by the API. You can find these constants at the end of this appendix.

pdwType — Long Integer: Retrieves the type of the value. This is returned to you by the function. Pass zero if you do not wish to retrieve the type.

pvData — String or Long Integer: The data to retrieve from the value. For strings, you must pass a string large enough to contain the value returned by the function. You can call RegGetValue once to get the size in pcbData, then call it a second time to pass a string of the necessary size.

pcbData — Long Integer: Retrieves the size of the data in pvData in bytes. You can pass zero if you do not wish to retrieve the size, unless you are retrieving data in pvData.

Return value	Long Integer: Zero (ERROR_SUCCESS) on success. The function will return ERROR_MORE_DATA if the data passed to pvData is not large enough to hold the data retrieved in the value. All other values are the specific error code.

RegLoadAppKey

Description	Loads a Registry hive from a file that was saved from the Registry or with RegSaveKey.

Declaration	```Declare Function RegLoadAppKey Lib "advapi32.dll" Alias "RegLoadAppKeyW" _```
	 ```(ByVal lpFile As String, _```
	 ` ByRef phkResult As Long, _`
	 ` ByVal samDesired As Long, _`
	 ` ByVal dwOptions As Long, _`
	 ` ByVal Reserved As Long) As Long`

Parameters	lpFile — String: Name of the file that contains the Registry information. phkResult — Long Integer: Variable to receive the handle to the Registry key that is opened with RegLoadAppKey. samDesired — Long Integer: One or more KEY_ constants that combine to define the operations that are allowed for this key. You can find these constants at the end of this appendix. dwOptions — Long Integer: If set to REG_PROCESS_APPKEY, indicates that this hive can only be loaded by the calling process. Cannot be loaded by other processes if it is currently loaded. Reserved — Long Integer: Reserved for future use. Set to zero.
Return value	Long Integer: Zero (ERROR_SUCCESS) on success. All other values are the specific error code.

RegLoadKey

Description	Creates a new subkey (whose information is loaded from a file that was created using the RegSaveKey function) under the specified key.

Declaration	```Declare Function RegLoadKey Lib "advapi32.dll" _```
	 ` Alias "RegLoadKeyA" ( _`
	 ` ByVal hKey As Long, _`
	 ` ByVal lpSubKey As String, _`
	 ` ByVal lpFile As String) As Long`

Table continues on the next page

Parameters	hKey — Long Integer: HKEY_LOCAL_MACHINE, HKEY_USERS, or the handle of a key returned by the RegConnectRegistry function.
	lpSubKey — String: Name of the new subkey to create.
	lpFile — String: Path and name of the file to load.
Return value	Long Integer: Zero (ERROR_SUCCESS) on success. All other values are the specific error code.

RegLoadMUIString

Description	Reads the specified string from the specified key and subkey.
| Declaration | ```
Public Declare Function RegLoadMUIString Lib
"advapi32.dll" Alias "RegLoadMUIStringW" _
 (ByVal hKey As Long, _
  ByVal pszValue As String, _
  ByVal pszOutBuf As String, _
  ByVal cbOutBuf As Long, _
  ByRef pcbData As Long, _
  ByVal Flags As Long, _
  ByVal pszDirectory As String) As Long
``` |
Parameters	hKey — Long Integer: Handle to an open Registry key.
	pszValue — String: Name of the value for the key or subkey to retrieve.
	pszOutBuf — String: Buffer that will receive the string from the function.
	cbOutBuf — Long Integer: Length of pszOutBuff.
	pcbData — Long Integer: Receives the length of the data that is returned into pszOutBuff.
	Flags — Long Integer: When set to REG_MUI_STRING_TRUNCATE, indicates that the string that is returned is truncated to fit in pszOutBuf. pcbData must be set to NULL when this flag is set.
	pszDirectory — String: Path to a directory (optional).
Return value	Long Integer: Zero (ERROR_SUCCESS) on success. All other values are the specific error code.
```

RegNotifyChangeKeyValue

Description	Provides the mechanism to be notified when a Registry key or any of its subkeys is changed.

Declaration	`Declare Function RegNotifyChangeKeyValue _`
	`    Lib "advapi32.dll" ( _`
	`    ByVal hKey As Long, _`
	`    ByVal bWatchSubtree As Long, _`
	`    ByVal dwNotifyFilter As Long, _`
	`    ByVal hEvent As Long, _`
	`    ByVal fAsynchronus As Long) As Long`

Parameters	`hKey` — `Long Integer`: The handle of the key to watch, or one of the hive constants listed earlier. `lpWatchSubTree` — `Long Integer`: Boolean flag that indicates whether to watch the subkeys for change. Zero: Do not watch subkeys. True (nonzero): Watch subkeys. `dwNotifyFilter` — `Long Integer`: One of the following constants: `REG_NOTIFY_CHANGE_ATTRIBUTES` (to detect changes to a key's attributes); `REG_NOTIFY_CHANGE_LAST_SET` (to detect changes to a key's last modification time); `REG_NOTIFY_CHANGE_NAME` (to detect changes to a key's name, or the creation or deletion of keys); `REG_NOTIFY_CHANGE_SECURITY` (to detect changes to a key's security information). `hEvent` — `Long Integer`: A handle to an event. This parameter is ignored if `fAsynchronus` = False (zero). `fAsynchronous` — `Long Integer`: Boolean flag that indicates whether the function returns immediately when a change is detected. True (nonzero): The function returns immediately, but the event specified by `hEvent` is signaled when a change is detected. False (zero): The function does not return until a change is detected.
Return value	`Long Integer`: Zero (`ERROR_SUCCESS`) on success. All other values are the specific error code.
Comment	To use this function, you must understand how to detect and act upon system events, a topic which is beyond the scope of this book.

RegOpenKeyEx

Description	Opens an existing key. This is a more sophisticated function than `RegOpenKey`, and is recommended for use on Win32.

Table continues on the next page

Appendix I: Windows Registry Information

| Declaration | ```
Declare Function RegOpenKeyEx Lib "advapi32.dll" _
    Alias "RegOpenKeyExA" ( _
    ByVal hKey As Long, _
    ByVal lpSubKey As String, _
    ByVal ulOptions As Long, _
    ByVal samDesired As Long, _
    phkResult As Long) As Long
``` |
| Parameters | hKey — Long Integer: Handle of the key to open, or one of the hive constants listed earlier.

lpSubKey — String: Name of the key to open.

ulOptions — Long Integer: A reserved parameter. Set it to zero.

samDesired — Long Integer: One or more KEY_ constants that combine to define the operations that are allowed for this key. You can find these constants at the end of this appendix.

phkResult — Long Integer: A variable that is loaded with a handle to the opened key. |
| Return value | Long Integer: Zero (ERROR_SUCCESS) on success.
All other values are the specific error code. |

RegQueryInfoKey

Description	Retrieves information about an existing key.
| Declaration | ```
Declare Function RegQueryInfoKey _
    Lib "advapi32.dll" _
    Alias "RegQueryInfoKeyA" ( _
    ByVal hKey As Long, _
    ByVal lpClass As String, _
    lpcbClass As Long, _
    lpReserved As Long, _
    lpcSubKeys As Long, _
    lpcbMaxSubKeyLen As Long, _
    lpcbMaxClassLen As Long, _
    lpcValues As Long, _
    lpcbMaxValueNameLen As Long, _
    lpcbMaxValueLen As Long, _
    lpcbSecurityDescriptor As Long, _
    lpftLastWriteTime As FILETIME) As Long
``` |
| Parameters | hKey — Long Integer: The handle of an open key, or one of the hive constants listed earlier.

lpClass — String: A null-terminated variable that will be loaded with the class name for the key. This can be vbNullString. |

lpcbClass — Long Integer: A variable that you load with the length of lpClass (including the terminating Null character). When the function returns, this variable contains the number of characters actually loaded into lpClass.

lpReserved — Long Integer: This is a reserved parameter. Set it to zero.

lpcSubKeys — Long Integer: A variable that will be loaded with the number of subkeys under the selected key.

lpcbMaxSubKeyLen — Long Integer: A variable that will be loaded with the length of the longest subkey under the selected key, excluding the terminating Null character.

lpcbMaxClassLen — Long Integer: A variable that will be loaded with the length of the longest class name for the subkeys under the selected key, excluding the terminating Null character.

lpcValues — Long Integer: A variable that will be loaded with the number of values for the selected key.

lpcbMaxValueNameLen — Long Integer: A variable that will be loaded with the length of the longest value name for the subkeys under the selected key, excluding the terminating Null character.

lpcbMaxValueLen — Long Integer: A variable that will be loaded with the buffer size required to hold the largest value data for this key.

lpcbSecurityDescriptor — Long Integer: A variable that will be loaded with the length of the selected key's Security Descriptor. When the function returns, this variable contains the number of bytes actually loaded into pSecurityDescriptor.

lpftLastWriteTime — FILETIME: A user-defined Type that will contain the last time that the specified subkey was modified.

Return value	Long Integer: Zero (ERROR_SUCCESS) on success. All other values are the specific error code.

RegQueryKeyFlags

Description	Retrieves key flags that are set for the specified Registry key. Requires Windows Vista or later.

Declaration	`Private Declare Function RegQueryKeyFlags _`
	`    Lib "advapi32.dll" ( _`
	`    ByVal hKey As Long, _`
	`    ByVal dwAttribMask As Long, _`
	`    pdwAttribute As Long) As Long`

Table continues on the next page

Parameters	hKey — Long Integer: Handle of the open key, or one of the hive constants listed earlier.
	dwAttribMask — Long Integer: Combine one or more KEY_FLAG_ constants to specify which attribute values to query. You can find these constants at the end of this appendix.
	pdwAttribute — Long Integer: Returns the attribute mask for the specified key.
Return Value	Long Integer: Zero (ERROR_SUCCESS) on success. All other values are the specific error code.

RegQueryReflectionKey

Description	Determines whether Registry reflection is enabled for the specified key. Requires Windows XP Professional x64 Edition or Windows Vista or later.

Declaration	Declare Function RegQueryReflectionKey _
	    Lib "advapi32.dll" (_
	    ByVal hBase As Long, _
	    bIsReflectionDisabled As Long) As Long

Parameters	hBase — Long Integer: Handle to the Registry key to query.
	bIsReflectionDisabled — Long Integer: A value that determines whether Registry reflection is enabled or disabled for the specified key.
Return value	Long Integer: Zero (ERROR_SUCCESS) on success. All other values are the specific error code.

RegQueryValueEx

Description	Retrieves both the type and the value for the specified key. This is a more sophisticated function that RegQueryValue, and is recommended for use on Win32.

Declaration	Declare Function RegQueryValueEx _
	    Lib "advapi32.dll" _
	    Alias "RegQueryValueExA" (_
	    ByVal hKey As Long, _
	    ByVal lpValueName As String, _
	    ByVal lpReserved As Long, _
	    lpType As Long, _
	    lpData As Any, _
	    lpcbData As Long) As Long

Parameters	`hKey` — `Long Integer`: Handle of an open key, or one of the hive constants listed earlier.
	`lpValueName` — `String`: Name of the value to retrieve.
	`lpReserved` — `Long Integer`: A reserved parameter. Set it to zero.
	`lpType` — `Long Integer`: Key value type (from the constants listed earlier).
	`lpData` — `Any`: A buffer that is loaded with the data for the specified value.
	`lpcbData` — `Long Integer`: A variable that is loaded with the length of `lpData`. When the function returns, this variable contains the number of bytes actually loaded into `lpData`.
Return value	`Long Integer`: Zero (`ERROR_SUCCESS`) on success. All other values are the specific error code.

RegReplaceKey

Description	Replaces a subkey with information contained in a file, and creates a backup of the original subkey.
| Declaration | ```
Declare Function RegReplaceKey _
    Lib "advapi32.dll" _
    Alias "RegReplaceKeyA" ( _
    ByVal hKey As Long, _
    ByVal lpSubKey As String, _
    ByVal lpNewFile As String, _
    ByVal lpOldFile As String) As Long
``` |
Parameters	`hKey` — `Long Integer`: Handle of an open key, or one of the hive constants listed earlier.
	`lpValueName` — `String`: Name of the subkey to replace. This subkey must be directly under `HKEY_LOCAL_MACHINE` or `HKEY_USERS`.
	`lpNewFile` — `String`: Name of the file (created using `RegSaveKey`) that contains the information with which to replace the selected subkey.
	`lpOldFile` — `String`: Name of the file to which the existing subkey will be backed up.
Return value	`Long Integer`: Zero (`ERROR_SUCCESS`) on success. All other values are the specific error code.
```

RegRestoreKey

Description	Restores a subkey with information contained in a file.
| Declaration | ```
Declare Function RegRestoreKey _
    Lib "advapi32.dll" _
    Alias "RegRestoreKeyA" ( _
    ByVal hKey As Long, _
    ByVal lpFile As String, _
    ByVal dwFlags As Long) As Long
``` |
| Parameters | hKey — Long Integer: The handle of an open key to restore from disk, or one of the hive constants listed earlier.

lpFile — String: Name of the file that contains the information to restore.

dwFlags — Long Integer: Use zero for a regular restore. Use REG_WHOLE_HIVE_VOLATILE for a temporary restore (which is not saved when the system is restarted), in which case, hKey must point to HKEY_LOCAL_MACHINE or HKEY_USERS. |
| Return value | Long Integer: Zero (ERROR_SUCCESS) on success. All other values are the specific error code. |

RegSaveKey

Description	Saves a key and all its subkeys to a disk file.
| Declaration | ```
Declare Function RegSaveKey Lib "advapi32.dll" _
    Alias "RegSaveKeyA" ( _
    ByVal hKey As Long, _
    ByVal lpFile As String, _
    lpSecurityAttributes As SECURITY_ATTRIBUTES) _
    As Long
``` |
| Parameters | hKey — Long Integer: Handle of an open key, or one of the hive constants listed earlier.

lpFile — String: Name of the file into which the key (and its subkeys) will be saved.

lpSecurityAttributes — SECURITY_ATTRIBUTES: A user-defined Type that defines the security attributes for this key. Security attributes are quite a complex subject and most of their features only work on Windows NT. In any case, they are rarely used, so the examples provided at the end of this chapter re-declare this parameter ByVal SecurityAttributesas Long, and pass a Null (0&). For more information about security, refer to the Microsoft Win32 SDK. |
| Return value | Long Integer: Zero (ERROR_SUCCESS) on success. All other values are the specific error code. |

RegSaveKeyEx

Description	Saves the specified key and its subkeys and values to a file in the specified format.
| Declaration | ```
Private Declare Function RegSaveKeyEx _
  Lib "advapi32.dll" _
  Alias "RegSaveKeyExA" ( _
  ByVal hKey As Long, _
  ByVal lpFile As String, _
  lpSecurityAttributes As SECURITY_ATTRIBUTES, _
  ByVal Flags As Long) As Long
``` |
Parameters	hkey — Long Integer: Handle of an open key, or one of the hive constants listed earlier.
	lpFile — String: Name of the file into which the key (and its subkeys) will be saved.
	lpSecurityAttributes — SECURITY_ATTRIBUTES: A user-defined Type that defines the security attributes for this key. Security attributes are quite a complex subject and most of its features only work on Windows NT. In any case, they are rarely used, so the examples provided at the end of this chapter re-declare this parameter ByVal SecurityAttributes as Long, and pass a Null (0&). For more information about security, refer to the Microsoft Win32 SDK.
	Flags — Long Integer: The format used to save the key or hive.
Return value	Long Integer: Zero (ERROR_SUCCESS) on success. All other values are the specific error code.

RegSetKeyFlags

Description	Sets or clears Registry key flags on the specified key. Requires Windows Vista or later.
| Declaration | ```
Private Declare Function RegSetKeyFlags _
  Lib "advapi32.dll" ( _
  ByVal hKey As Long, _
  ByVal dwAttribMask As Long, _
  ByVal dwAttribute As Long) As Long
``` |
Parameters	hKey — Long Integer: Handle of the open key, or one of the hive constants listed earlier.
	dwAttribMask — Long Integer: Combine one or more KEY_FLAG_ constants to specify which attribute values to set for the key. You can find these constants at the end of this appendix.
	dwAttribute — Long Integer: Combine one or more KEY_FLAG_ constants to set the value for the key. Pass zero to clear the specified attributes.
Return value	Long Integer: Zero (ERROR_SUCCESS) on success. All other values are the specific error code.

RegSetKeySecurity

Description	Sets the security information for the specified key.
| Declaration | ```
Declare Function RegSetKeySecurity _
    Lib "advapi32.dll" ( _


    ByVal hKey As Long, _
    ByVal SecurityInformation As Long, _
    pSecurityDescriptor As SECURITY_DESCRIPTOR) _
    As Long
``` |
| Parameters | hKey − Long Integer: Handle of a key, or one of the hive constants listed earlier.

SecurityInformation − Long Integer: A flag that defines the security information to save.

pSecurityDescriptor − SECURITY_DESCRIPTOR: A user-defined Type that contains the security information to save for the specified key. |
| Return value | Long Integer: Zero (ERROR_SUCCESS) on success.
All other values are the specific error code. |

RegSetKeyValue

Description	Sets a value in the specified Registry key and subkey. Requires Windows Vista or later.
| Declaration | ```
' String declaration of lpData
Private Declare Function RegSetKeyValueString _
    Lib "advapi32.dll" _
    Alias "RegSetKeyValueA" ( _
    ByVal hKey As Long, _
    ByVal lpSubKey As String, _
    ByVal lpValueName As String, _
    ByVal dwType As Long, _
    ByVal lpData As String, _
    ByVal cbData As Long) As Long

' Numeric declaration of lpData
Private Declare Function RegSetKeyValueLong _
    Lib "advapi32.dll" _
    Alias "RegSetKeyValueA" ( _
    ByVal hKey As Long, _
    ByVal lpSubKey As String, _
    ByVal lpValueName As String, _
    ByVal dwType As Long, _
    lpData As Long, _
    ByVal cbData As Long) As Long
``` |

Parameters	hKey — Long Integer: Handle of the open key, or one of the hive constants listed earlier.
	lpSubKey — String: Name of a subkey under the key specified in hKey. May also be vbNullString.
	lpValueName — String: Name of the value to set. Set this to vbNullString to set the (default) value for the key.
	dwType — Long Integer: The value type from the list of data types in the "Windows Registry Data Types" section, at the beginning of this appendix.
	lpData — String or Long Integer: The data to set in the value.
	cbData — Long Integer: Size of the data in bytes. Use the Len function to pass the length of a String.
Return value	Long Integer: Zero (ERROR_SUCCESS) on success. All other values are the specific error code.

RegSetValueEx

Description	Sets the value for the specified key. A more sophisticated function than RegSetValue, and is recommended for use on Win32.
| Declaration | ```
Declare Function RegSetValueEx _
    Lib "advapi32.dll" _
    Alias "RegSetValueExA" ( _

    ByVal hKey As Long, _
    ByVal lpValueName As String, _
    ByVal Reserved As Long, _
    ByVal dwType As Long, _
    lpData As Any, _
    ByVal cbData As Long) As Long
``` |
Parameters	hKey — Long Integer: Handle of an open key, or one of the hive constants listed earlier.
	lpSubKey — String: Name of the subkey whose value is to be set. To set the (Default) value, specify vbNullString. If the value does not exist, it is created.
	Reserved — Long Integer: A reserved parameter. Set it to zero.
	dwType — Long Integer: REG_SZ.
	lpData — Any: Data to be written to the specified key.

Table continues on the next page
```

	cbData — Long Integer: A variable that you load with the length of lpData, including the terminating Null character when used with REG_SZ, REG_EXPAND_SZ, or REG_MULTI_SZ.
Return value	Long Integer: Zero (ERROR_SUCCESS) on success. All other values are the specific error code.

RegUnloadKey

Description	Unloads the specified key and all its subkeys.

Declaration	Declare Function RegUnLoadKey Lib "advapi32.dll" _
	    Alias "RegUnLoadKeyA" (_
	    ByVal hKey As Long, _
	    ByVal lpSubKey As String) As Long

Parameters	hKey — Long Integer: HKEY_LOCAL_MACHINE, HKEY_USERS, or the handle of a key returned by the RegConnectRegistry function. lpSubKey — String: Name of the subkey (loaded using the RegLoadKey function) to unload.
Return value	Long Integer: Zero (ERROR_SUCCESS) on success. All other values are the specific error code.

Registry API Constant and User-Defined Type Declarations

To help you with this book, and so that you won't have to go searching for them, the following is a list of all the Constant and User-Defined Type declarations you'll need when using the Registry APIs.

```
'Key declarations
Const HKEY_CLASSES_ROOT As Long = &H80000000
Const HKEY_CURRENT_CONFIG As Long = &H80000005
Const HKEY_CURRENT_USER As Long = &H80000001
Const HKEY_DYN_DATA As Long = &H80000006
Const HKEY_LOCAL_MACHINE As Long = &H80000002
Const HKEY_PERF_ROOT As Long = HKEY_LOCAL_MACHINE
Const HKEY_PERFORMANCE_DATA As Long = &H80000004
Const HKEY_USERS As Long = &H80000003

'Parameter declarations
Const REG_NOTIFY_CHANGE_ATTRIBUTES As Long = &H2
Const REG_NOTIFY_CHANGE_LAST_SET As Long = &H4
Const REG_NOTIFY_CHANGE_NAME As Long = &H1
Const REG_NOTIFY_CHANGE_SECURITY As Long = &H8
Const REG_CREATED_NEW_KEY As Long = &H1
Const REG_OPENED_EXISTING_KEY As Long = &H2
```

```
Const REG_OPTION_BACKUP_RESTORE As Long = &H4
Const REG_OPTION_VOLATILE As Long = &H1
Const REG_OPTION_NON_VOLATILE As Long = &H0
Const STANDARD_RIGHTS_ALL As Long = &H1F0000

Const SYNCHRONIZE As Long = &H100000
Const READ_CONTROL As Long = &H20000
Const STANDARD_RIGHTS_READ As Long = (READ_CONTROL)
Const STANDARD_RIGHTS_WRITE As Long = (READ_CONTROL)
Const KEY_CREATE_LINK As Long = &H20
Const KEY_CREATE_SUB_KEY As Long = &H4
Const KEY_ENUMERATE_SUB_KEYS As Long = &H8
Const KEY_NOTIFY As Long = &H10
Const KEY_QUERY_VALUE As Long = &H1
Const KEY_SET_VALUE As Long = &H2

Const KEY_READ As Long = (( _
    STANDARD_RIGHTS_READ _
    Or KEY_QUERY_VALUE _
    Or KEY_ENUMERATE_SUB_KEYS _
    Or KEY_NOTIFY) _
    And (Not SYNCHRONIZE))

Const KEY_WRITE As Long = (( _
    STANDARD_RIGHTS_WRITE _
    Or KEY_SET_VALUE _
    Or KEY_CREATE_SUB_KEY) _
    And (Not SYNCHRONIZE))

Const KEY_EXECUTE As Long = (KEY_READ)

Const KEY_ALL_ACCESS As Long = (( _
    STANDARD_RIGHTS_ALL _
    Or KEY_QUERY_VALUE _
    Or KEY_SET_VALUE _
    Or KEY_CREATE_SUB_KEY _
    Or KEY_ENUMERATE_SUB_KEYS _
    Or KEY_NOTIFY _
    Or KEY_CREATE_LINK) _
    And (Not SYNCHRONIZE))

REG_PROCESS_APPKEY = &H1
REG_MUI_STRING_TRUNCATE = &H1

'Key value types
Const REG_BINARY As Long = 3
Const REG_DWORD As Long = 4
Const REG_DWORD_BIG_ENDIAN As Long = 5
Const REG_DWORD_LITTLE_ENDIAN As Long = 4
Const REG_EXPAND_SZ As Long = 2
Const REG_LINK As Long = 6
Const REG_MULTI_SZ As Long = 7
Const REG_NONE As Long = 0
Const REG_RESOURCE_LIST As Long = 8
Const REG_QWORD As Long = 11
```

```
          Const REG_QWORD_LITTLE_ENDIAN As Long = 11
          Const REG_SZ As Long = 1

          'API return codes
          Const ERROR_ACCESS_DENIED As Long = 5&
          Const ERROR_BADDB As Long = 1009&
          Const ERROR_BADKEY As Long = 1010&
          Const ERROR_CANTOPEN As Long = 1011&
          Const ERROR_CANTREAD As Long = 1012&

          Const ERROR_CANTWRITE As Long = 1013&
          Const ERROR_INSUFFICIENT_BUFFER As Long = 122&
          Const ERROR_INVALID_HANDLE As Long = 6&
          Const ERROR_INVALID_PARAMETER As Long = 87&
          Const ERROR_KEY_DELETED As Long = 1018&
          Const ERROR_KEY_HAS_CHILDREN As Long = 1020&
          Const ERROR_MORE_DATA As Long = 234&
          Const ERROR_NO_MORE_ITEMS As Long = 259&
          Const ERROR_OUTOFMEMORY As Long = 14&
          Const ERROR_REGISTRY_CORRUPT As Long = 1015&
          Const ERROR_REGISTRY_IO_FAILED As Long = 1016&
          Const ERROR_REGISTRY_RECOVERED As Long = 1014&
          Const ERROR_SUCCESS As Long = 0&

          'Platform specific view of the Registry
          Const KEY_WOW64_32KEY As Long = &H200
          Const KEY_WOW64_64KEY As Long = &H100

          'Registry restriction flags
          Const RRF_RT_ANY As Long = &HFFFF
          Const RRF_RT_DWORD As Long = &H18
          Const RRF_RT_QWORD As Long = &H48
          Const RRF_RT_REG_BINARY As Long = &H8
          Const RRF_RT_REG_DWORD As Long = &H10
          Const RRF_RT_REG_EXPAND_SZ As Long = &H4
          Const RRF_RT_REG_MULTI_SZ As Long = &H20
          Const RRF_RT_REG_NONE As Long = &H1
          Const RRF_RT_REG_QWORD As Long = &H40
          Const RRF_RT_REG_SZ As Long = &H2
          Const RRF_NOEXPAND As Long = &H10000000
          Const RRF_ZEROONFAILURE As Long = &H20000000

          'Registry key flags
          Const KEY_FLAG_DISABLE_REDIRECTION As Long = &H10
          Const KEY_FLAG_EXEMPT_REFLECTION As Long = &H4
          Const KEY_FLAG_OWNERSHIP_REFLECTION As Long = &H8

          'Registry format flags
          Const REG_STANDARD_FORMAT As Long = &H1
          Const REG_LATEST_FORMAT As Long = &H2
          Const REG_NO_COMPRESSION As Long = &H4

          'SECURITY_INFORMATION constants
          Const OWNER_SECURITY_INFORMATION As Long = &H1
```

```
Const GROUP_SECURITY_INFORMATION As Long = &H2
Const DACL_SECURITY_INFORMATION As Long = &H4
Const SACL_SECURITY_INFORMATION As Long = &H8
Const UNPROTECTED_SACL_SECURITY_INFORMATION As Long = &H10000000
Const UNPROTECTED_DACL_SECURITY_INFORMATION As Long = &H20000000
Const PROTECTED_SACL_SECURITY_INFORMATION As Long = &H40000000
Const PROTECTED_DACL_SECURITY_INFORMATION As Long = &H80000000
'User-defined Types
Type SECURITY_ATTRIBUTES
    nLength As Long
    lpSecurityDescriptor As Long
    bInheritHandle As Long
End Type

Type FILETIME
    dwLowDateTime As Long
    dwHighDateTime As Long
End Type

Type ACL
    AclRevision As Byte
    Sbz1 As Byte
    AclSize As Integer
    AceCount As Integer
    Sbz2 As Integer
End Type

Type SECURITY_DESCRIPTOR
    Revision As Byte
    Sbz1 As Byte
    Control As Long
    Owner As Long
    Group As Long
    Sacl As ACL
    Dacl As ACL
End Type
```

Access Wizards, Builders, and Managers

Access provides many tools that do a lot of work for developers. These tools not only save you time and prevent or minimize errors, but they are also a great resource for teaching yourself how to do things. But many developers may not even know that some of the wizards exist, and if you don't know about them, you aren't likely to be using them to your advantage.

This appendix briefly describes the wizards, builders, and managers in Access 2007. Because you might be looking for a familiar favorite, items are noted as having been added, enhanced or relocated. Although there isn't an official list, our best count is that Access 2007 includes 46 wizards, 9 builders, and 5 managers — that's 60 tools designed to streamline and automate common processes for developers and users.

Access Wizards

As you can tell from the extensive list of enhanced wizards, Access is more user-friendly and automated with each version. The following table describes 57 wizards, including 11 that were replaced or removed from Access 2007. The status column indicates changes between Access 2003 and 2007. Although there is some overlap, the main difference between enhanced and improved is that enhanced is used to denote changes to the wizard including the user interface while improved denotes that the target feature/process — such as the import or export process — has improved. The Replaced status indicates that, although the particular wizard is no longer available, its function is provided elsewhere, as explained in the description.

Wizard	Description	Status
AutoDialer	Adds an AutoDialer to a control on a form, datasheet, or toolbar. It incorporates modem information and dials the number.	Enhanced so that the auto-dialer function can be called from an embedded macro instead of using VBA.
AutoForm	The AutoForm was replaced by the selection of forms available in the Forms group of the create tab, as shown in Figure J-1. Any of the forms are automatically created based on the selected record source. The traditional form wizard is also available.	Replaced.
AutoFormat	Applies a predefined style and format to a form or report, and allows creation of custom styles. This has been enhanced by additional auto formats (displayed as styles in the Form and Report wizards).	Enhanced with additional formats.
AutoPage	DAPs cannot be created in Access 2007 so this wizard is no longer needed. In prior versions, it creates a data access page that can be used on the Web or intranet. A DAP can also get data from other sources, such as Excel.	Removed.
AutoReport	Replaced by the selection of reports available in the Reports group of the create tab, as shown in Figure J-1. These reports are automatically created based on the selected record source. The traditional report wizard is also available.	Replaced.
Chart/Graph	Adds a chart to a form or report based on the data in a table or query.	Unchanged.
Collect Data Through Email Messages	Works with Outlook, Outlook Express, or InfoPath to create an e-mail message to collect data. The body of the e-mail provides an opportunity for an introductory statement above a form that is based on fields selected from a table or query.	New.
Combo Box	Creates a combo box control on a form. This has additional options and now defaults to use embedded macros for the ACCDB file format.	Enhanced to use embedded macros for the ACCDB format.
Command Button	Creates a command button control on a form.	Enhanced to use embedded macros for the ACCDB format. There have also been changes to some of the VBA commands to be in concert with the new controls such as the Ribbon instead of a menu.

Wizard	Description	Status
Conflict Resolver	Resolves conflicts between replicated databases at synchronization time. Works with 2000 and 2002-2003 format MDB files.	Unchanged.
Create Outlook Task	Creates an Outlook Task and includes the details of the process, how to initiate it, and the associated objects and destination locations. Outlook allows these to be recurring tasks.	New.
Crosstab Query	Creates a query that summarizes data in a compact, spreadsheet-like format.	Unchanged.
Database	Created databases for a variety of uses. Replaced by custom templates in 2007.	Replaced by templates.
Database Splitter	Splits databases into data and interface portions, so that one or more users can have local copies of the interface connected to the data on a server. Text added to address database passwords.	Unchanged.
Documenter	Generates an Access report that displays the design characteristics of database objects, including the tables, queries, forms, reports, macros, modules, and attachments.	Enhanced to handle complex data types.
Export Text	Exports data to a text file and allows specifications to be saved. It can also be added to Outlook as a Task. Text export is improved.	Improved to allow scheduling an Outlook Task.
Export to Windows SharePoint Services	Exports to Windows SharePoint Services. There is added functionality to work with attachments and multi-value fields. As with other import and export processes, the specifications can be saved and reused or modified.	Improved to accommodate complex data types.
Find Duplicates Query	Creates a query that finds records that have duplicate field values and are in a single table or query.	Unchanged.
Find Unmatched Query	Creates a query that finds records in one table that have no related records in another table.	Unchanged.
Form	Creates a new form based on the pre-selected record source. The basic form wizard is unchanged, but it now offers more than 20 styles (aka AutoFormats) to select from. The Forms group on the Create tab allows user to create specific types of forms, such as a Split Form or a PivotChart.	Improved

Table continues on the next page

Wizard	Description	Status
Import Exchange/ Outlook	Imports an Exchange or Outlook folder to a table in a Microsoft Access database. Importing is improved.	Improved import.
Import HTML	Imports HTML tables and lists from an Internet or intranet site into an Access table. A great way to start building interfaces with Web-based databases. Importing is improved.	Improved import.
Import from Windows SharePoint Services	Imports from Windows SharePoint Services.	Improved to accommodate complex data types.
Import Spreadsheet	Imports a Microsoft Excel or other spreadsheet into a Microsoft Access table. Significant enhancements, including ability to specify field types. Can also be scheduled as an Outlook Task.	Enhanced Import.
Import Text	Imports a text file into a Microsoft Access table. Importing is improved and it now allows scheduling as an Outlook Task.	Improved import
Input Mask	Creates an input mask for a field that you choose in a table.	Unchanged.
Label	Creates mailing labels in standard and custom sizes.	Unchanged.
Link Exchange/ Outlook	Links an Exchange or Outlook folder to a table in a Microsoft Access database.	Unchanged.
Link HTML	Links an HTML table or list on the Internet or an intranet to a Microsoft Access table.	Unchanged.
Link to Windows SharePoint Services	Links to Windows SharePoint Services list. Linking will accommodate complex data types. 2007 does not allow linking to a view of a SharePoint list.	Improved to accommodate complex data types.
Link Spreadsheet	Links spreadsheet data to a Microsoft Access table. Can pull in SmartTags. The wizard is unchanged, but the process benefits from improvements to importing.	Improved.
Link Table	Linked to tables in Access projects. Now replaced with features in the new ribbon's External Data tab.	Replaced.
Link Text	Links a text file to a Microsoft Access table. The wizard is unchanged, although the process benefits from improvements in data type recognition and can be scheduled as an Outlook Task.	Improved.

Wizard	Description	Status
List Box	Creates a list box control on a form, now includes sort options.	Enhanced.
Lookup	Creates a lookup column in a table, which displays a list of values the user can choose from. Includes a sort option. Enhanced to support complex data.	Enhanced.
Macro To Module Converter	Converts macros to Visual Basic code, including saved macros as well as embedded macros on forms and reports. Enhanced with new macro actions and now supports TempVars.	Enhanced.
Microsoft SQL Server Database	Creates a new Microsoft SQL Server Database connected to a new Microsoft Access project.	Unchanged.
Microsoft Word Mail Merge	Uses an Access table or query as the record course for Microsoft Word letters and e-mails. The wizard can be found in the Export group of the Ribbon's External Data tab by clicking on More to see the last item in the drop-down list.	Unchanged.
Move To SharePoint Site	Simultaneously moves the data from all the tables, maintains the relationships, and manages the complex data types.	New.
Option Group	Creates a group of option buttons on a form.	Unchanged.
Page	Created new data access pages, allowing distinct recordsource determination. DAPs cannot be created in Access 2007 so this wizard is no longer needed.	Removed.
Page Combo Box	Created a drop-down control on a data access page. DAPs cannot be created in Access 2007 so this wizard is no longer needed.	Removed.
Page Command Button	Created a command button control on a data access page. DAPs cannot be created in Access 2007 so this wizard is no longer needed.	Removed.
Page List Box	Created a list box control on a data access page. DAPs cannot be created in Access 2007 so this wizard is no longer needed.	Removed.
Partial Replica	Creates or modifies a partial replica. Builds a replica that contains only a subset of the records that a full replica would have. In Access 2007, this is used only by the MDB file format.	Unchanged.

Table continues on the next page

Wizard	Description	Status
Performance Analyzer	Analyzes the efficiency of a database and produces a list of suggestions for improving its performance.	Unchanged.
PivotTable	Places a Microsoft Excel PivotTable on a Microsoft Access form. PivotTables and PivotCharts are now optional views for tables, queries, forms, views, and stored procedures.	Removed.
Publish as PDF or XPS	Exports files data and formatting to a PDF or XPS file. A PDF viewer, such as the free ADOBE Acrobat Reader viewer, is required to open the files.	New.
Print Relationships	Creates a report that diagrams the relationships in a Microsoft Access database.	Unchanged.
Report	Creates a report based on a table or query. The basic report wizard is unchanged; however it now offers more than 20 styles (aka AutoFormats) to choose from.	Improved.
Simple Query	Creates a select query from the fields that you pick.	Unchanged.
Subform/Subreport	Creates a new subform or subreport on a form or report.	Unchanged.
Subform/Subreport Field Linker	Links fields in a main form and a subform or in a main report and a subreport, based on shared fields or established relationships.	Unchanged.
Table	Table and Field Templates replace this wizard for creating a new table.	Replaced.
Table Analyzer	Takes a table with a lot of duplicate data and splits it into related tables for more efficient storage.	Unchanged.
Upsizing	Upsizes a Microsoft Access database to a Microsoft SQL Server database.	Unchanged.
User-Level Security	In Access 2007, this is available only with the MDB file format. Based on the existing database, the wizard creates a new, encoded database that controls user access and permissions. It also leaves an unsecured backup copy of the database.	Unchanged.

Access Builders

Access 2007 offers nine builders that will guide developers through a process. You're familiar with the Query Builder. There are also some builders, such as the Color Builder, that are available in other Office programs. In Access 2007, the Field Builder is replaced by table templates and the Color Builder is enhanced to provide the color picker used by other programs.

Builder	Description
Color	Enhanced to use the color picker used by other programs. In addition to a larger selection of color swatches, it also displays a palette for selecting customized colors.
Edit List Items	Builds and edits value lists that are the row source for combo box and list box controls or for lookup fields in tables.
Expression	Creates expressions for macros, queries, and property sheets.
Field	Creates fields in tables in previous versions. Replaced by table templates in Access 2007.
Macro	Creates and edits macros, such as those created when a command button is added to a form or report. Builds both embedded and standalone macros.
ODBC Connection String	Creates the correct syntax for a connection to an ODBC database. Walks users through the process to establish a connection to an external data source.
Picture	Creates bitmap images for forms and reports.
Query	Creates the correct syntax for a query.
Smart Tags	Displays a list of available smart tags and their actions. Smart tags enable you to perform tasks within Access that you otherwise would have needed to open other programs to handle. Smart tags can be attached to a file in a table or a query or to controls on a form, report, or data access page.

Access Managers

In addition to builders and wizards, Access has five very powerful managers. Granted, there are times that it works well to create your own tools or use add-ins to provide these functions, but for the most part, the managers do an incredible job. The beauty of managers is that they work right out of the box. They are quick and easy to use, and they provide consistency. There are no changes to the managers in Access 2007, so if you've been using the managers, they will be like old friends.

Manager	Description	Location
Add-In	In addition to installing and uninstalling wizards, builders, and add-ins, the Add-In Manager helps create wizards and helps you to install your own add-ins.	Database Tools Ribbon tab; select Add-ins in the Database Tools group.
Linked Table	Allows linking and changing links to tables in external databases as well as through some ODBC connections, such as with Excel.	Database Tools Ribbon tab; select Linked Table Manager in the Database Tools group.
Manage Data Collection Messages	Tracks the status and allows changes to settings of e-mails used for data collections. Allows messages to be resent or deleted.	External Data ribbon tab, on Collect Data, click Manage Replies.
Manage Data Tasks	View and manage saved import and export specifications. Allows changes to general aspects such as the specification name and file path, but does not allow changes to details, such as the tables, fields, and worksheets. Can create an Outlook Task.	External Data Ribbon tab; click either the Saved Imports or the Saved Exports button.
Switchboard	Creates and manages switchboard forms for applications.	Database Tools Ribbon tab; select Switchboard Manager in the Database Tools group.

Reserved Words and Special Characters

There are numerous words that should not be used to name fields, objects, and variables. For the most part, these are called *reserved words*. Reserved words have a specific meaning to Microsoft Access, the Jet database engine, and the new Access database engine (ACE). We also list reserved words that have specific meaning to SQL Server or ODBC drivers. Depending on how your application interfaces with other programs, it may be prudent to avoid using words that have specific programmatic meanings to those as well. If you want to start a list of reserved words, begin with the list of all the properties of database objects, all Visual Basic keywords, and all third-party and user-defined names and functions.

Access 2007 creates an error message when select reserved words are used as field names. For the most part, however, using reserved words often creates error messages that do not indicate the source of the problem. For example, it is far from intuitive that the following error message:

```
The wizard was unable to preview your report, possibly because
a table needed by your report is exclusively locked
```

may have been triggered by the use of a reserved word. Consequently, a developer may unnecessarily spend time troubleshooting the wrong problem. When you are working with an application that uses reserved words, particularly as the name of tables or fields, rename the database objects if it is at all possible and feasible to do so. If it isn't possible to rename them, then be sure to enclose the names in brackets when they are called in code or in queries. Here's an example showing the name of the table in brackets because the term tableName is a reserved word:

```
SELECT fieldX

FROM [tableName]
```

When writing code, it is often handy to use the IntelliSense feature and just select from the available list of objects and actions. This requires the use of Me. rather than Me! However, if the name of a field is a reserved word that could also be the object's property, the code will not compile. The debugger will stop and highlight the problem object, as shown in Figure K-1. In this instance, merely changing the syntax to use `Me!` (bang) instead of `Me.` (dot) will allow the code to compile. You cannot avoid the problem simply by not compiling the code, because that merely ensures that the code will break and stop the application from running.

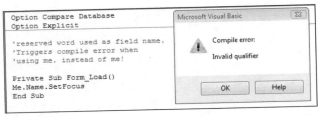

Figure K-1

We recommend that you develop the practice of debugging promptly after making changes to any code. This enables you to catch errors promptly and prevent them from being repeated or compounding. Considering all the things that can go wrong, and the propensity for something to go wrong at the worst times, why tempt fate by not doing everything you can to ensure that your code will run smoothly?

Additionally, search and replace utilities such as Speed Ferret are designed to find and replace the offending word(s) throughout the application, including the code project or VBA. In the past, a couple of products were consistently recommended by developers, but it will likely be a while before similar tools are released for the new file format. The Access news groups and MVP sites are great resources for learning about these types of tools. Some are free, but even a purchased program typically pays for itself with its first use.

It is clear that if reserved words are causing a problem with a database, it is worth enforcing naming conventions. Implementing a comprehensive naming policy can help you avoid most of the problems associated with reserved words. Appendix L discusses some of the well-accepted naming conventions.

What Are the Sources of Reserved Words?

In addition to the lists of reserved words that are directly associated with Access, ACE, and Visual Basic, there are also words that have special meaning to ActiveX Data Objects (ADO), OLE DB, Open Database Connectivity (ODBC), and any DLL (dynamic-link library) referenced in your application. These, too, should be treated as reserved words for your application. Just by setting a reference to a type library, an object library, or an ActiveX control, all the reserved words for the referenced items become reserved words for the Access application. And the list keeps growing because built-in function names and user-defined names also become reserved words. As you create interfaces to work with other programs and development languages, such as SharePoint, Excel, and .NET, you will want to be cautious about their reserved words as well.

It can get even hairier. The reserved words for a given application vary depending on what mode the ACE is running in. This is determined by whether ACE is called from Microsoft Access, the Microsoft OLE DB Provider for ACE, a Data Access Object, or the Microsoft Access ODBC driver. Whether ACE is running in ANSI mode or non-ANSI (traditional) mode also has an effect on the list, such that a query that works under one scenario may fail when the database application is opened in a different mode.

You can find lists of reserved words by using the online help feature in Access, by searching for reserved words on the Internet, and by pouring through reference books. Regretfully, no list will be comprehensive or tailored to your needs and interfaces. Even the lists published by authoritative sources cannot be assumed to be complete. This is another obvious endorsement for implementing naming conventions.

The potential lists of reserved words can seem a bit overwhelming. That is why this appendix not only contains a table of reserved words but also lists some of the words that we think should have been included in the original lists. The table is a compilation of words from a variety of sources, including the reserved words for ANSI mode, and should significantly reduce your research time. Please keep in mind that it is not an exhaustive list and that it does not include additional words associated with third-party add-ins. Allen Browne's Access MVP website (http://allenbrowne.com/AppIssueBadWord.html) has a compilation of reserved words that generously includes the source, such as SQL, Access, Jet, and so forth. Allen also offers a utility that will check your application for usage of reserved words.

Reserved Words with Error Messages

You might wonder why you can't simply use a tool that will check against your custom list of reserved words and give you a timely and specific error message as you are creating your tables and adding fields. Although that seems like a great idea, it wouldn't be easy to implement. The Access team recognizes the merit in the concept, though, and has instituted an automatic check for a limited number of terms that are commonly used in both VBA and as field names. At this time, the list contains only six words:

Name	Value	Text
Date	Year	Month

Nonetheless, the seed has been planted, so to speak.

Keep in mind that you might circumvent this built-in check if you are creating a table in code. Access performs the check and generates the appropriate error message when you are creating a new table in the Access UI (see Figure K-2). However, you won't trigger the error if you create a table using `CreateTableDef` or the `CREATE TABLE` statement.

Figure K-2

Reserved Word List

If you're ambitious, you might be tempted to try to compile your own list of reserved words by combining lists from the most common sources. Be aware, however, that some of the lists were incomplete when initially published, and that additional words should be included in the lists as new objects or actions are added. Given those caveats, you'd still want a list that is a compilation of words from Access, ACE, MS Query SQL, and ANSI-92.

In the past, there were two lists, but with the ease of integration, there's no longer differentiation between Access reserved words and those from other sources. Of course, it is perfectly understandable to prefer to work against Access's list of 200+ terms instead of the compiled list of more than 500 words and terms. Searching Access help for Reserved Words leads you to an explanation and list of Access reserved words and the list of words that should not be used as identifiers. So you're already checking two sources, and there are still the lists of special characters and ASCII characters and their names.

As you can see, there is no easy way to consolidate everything into one tidy list, especially if there is any hope of understanding why you should avoid certain words and characters or knowing how to use them. So you're still stuck with multiple lists: the compilation of words to avoid (reserved words) and the lists of special characters and other ASCII characters.

Following is the list of words and terms that are reserved by Access or by programs and languages commonly used with Access. We've included a few words that have been reported to cause problems, so that you can avoid using them, too.

ABSOLUTE	ACTION	ACK
ADD	ALLOCATE	ALPHANUMERIC
ALTER	ALTER TABLE	AND
ANY	APPLICATION	ARE
AS	ASC	ASSERTION
ASSISTANT	AT	AUTHORIZATION
AUTOINCREMENT	AVG	BAND
BEGIN	BEL	BETWEEN
BINARY	BIT	BIT_LENGTH
BNOT	BOOLEAN	BOR
BOTH	BS	BXOR
BY	BYTE	CAN
CASCADE	CASCADED	CASE
CAST	CATALOG	CHAR
CHAR_LENGTH	CHARACTER	CHARACTER_LENGTH
CHECK	CLOSE	CLUSTERED
COALESCE	COLLATE	COLLATION
COLUMN	COMMIT	COMP
COMPACTDATABASE	COMPRESSION	CONNECT
CONNECTION	CONSTRAINT	CONSTRAINTS
CONTAINER	CONTAINS	CONTINUE
CONVERT	CORRESPONDING	COUNT
COUNTER	CRCREATE	CREATEDATABASE
CREATEDB	CREATEFIELD	CREATEGROUP
CREATEINDEX	CREATEOBJECT	CREATEPROPERTY
CREATERELATION	CREATETABLEDEF	CREATEUSER
CREATEWORKSPACE	CROSS	CURRENCY
CURRENT	CURRENT_DATE	CURRENT_TIME
CURRENT_TIMESTAMP	CURRENT_USER	CURRENTUSER
CURSOR	DATABASE	DATE
DATETIME	DAY	DC1
DC2	DC3	DC4

DEALLOCATE	DEC	DECIMAL
DECLARE	DEFAULT	DEFERRABLE
DEFERRED	DELETE	DESC
DESCRIBE	DESCRIPTION	DESCRIPTOR
DIAGNOSTICS	DISALLOW	DISCONNECT
DISTINCT	DISTINCTROW	DLE
DOCUMENT	DOMAIN	DOUBLE
DROP	ECHO	ELSE
EM	END	END-EXEC
ENQ	EOT	EQV
ERROR	ESC	ESCAPE
ETB	ETX	EXCEPT
EXCEPTION	EXCLUSIVECONNECT	EXCLUSIVECONNECT
EXEC	EXECUTE	EXISTS
EXIT	EXTERNAL	EXTRACT
FALSE	FETCH	FF
FIELD	FIELDS	FILLCACHE
FIRST	FLOAT	FLOAT4
FLOAT8	FOR	FOREIGN
FORM	FORMS	FOUND
FROM	FS	FULL
FUNCTION	GENERAL	GET
GETOBJECT	GETOPTION	GLOBAL
GO	GOTO	GOTOPAGE
GRANT	GROUP	GROUP BY
GS	GUID	HAVING
HOUR	IDENTITY	IDLE
IEEEDOUBLE	IEEESINGLE	IF
IGNORE	IMAGE	IMMEDIATE
IMP	IN	INDEX
INDEXCREATEDB	INDEXES	INDICATOR
INHERITABLE	ININDEX	INITIALLY
INNER	INPUT	INSENSITIVE
INSERT	INSERTTEXT	INT
INTEGER	INTEGER1	INTEGER2
INTEGER4	INTERSECT	INTERVAL
INTO	IS	ISOLATION
JOIN	KEY	LANGUAGE
LAST	LASTMODIFIED	LEADING
LEFT	LEVEL	LEVEL* MIN
LF	LIKE	LOCAL
LOGICAL	LOGICAL1	LONG
LONGBINARY	LONGCHAR	LONGTEXT
LOWER	MACRO	MATCH
MAX	MEMO	MIN
MINUTE	MOD	MODULE
MONEY	MONTH	MOVE
NAK	NAME	NAMES
NATIONAL	NATURAL	NCHAR
NEWPASSWORD	NEXTNO	NONCLUSTERED
NOT	NOTE	NTEXT
NUL	NULL	NULLIF
NUMBER	NUMERIC	NVARCHAR
OBJECT	OCTET_LENGTH	OFF

Appendix K: Reserved Words and Special Characters

OFOLEOBJECT	OLEOBJECT	ON
ONLY	OPEN	OPENRECORDSET
OPTION	OR	ORDER
ORIENTATION	ORORDEROUTER	OUTPUT
OVERLAPS	OWNERACCESS	PAD
PARAMETER	PARAMETERS	PARTIAL
PASSWORD	PERCENT	PIVOT
POSITION	PRECISION	PREPARE
PRESERVE	PRIMARY	PRIOR
PRIVILEGES	PROC	PROCEDURE
PROPERTY	PUBLIC	QUERIES
QUERY	QUIT	READ
REAL	RECALC	RECORDSET
REFERENCES	REFRESH	REFRESHLINK
REGISTERDATABASE	RELATION	RELATIVE
REPAINT	REPAIRDATABASE	REPLICATION
REPORT	REPORTS	REQUERY
RESTRICT	REVOKE	RIGHT
RIGHT SPACE	ROLLBACK	ROWS
RS	SCHEMA	SCREEN
SCROLL	SECOND	SECTION
SELECT	SELECTSCHEMA	SELECTSECURITY
SESSION	SESSION_USER	SET
SET SUM	SETFOCUS	SETOPTION
SHORT	SI	SINGLE
SIZE	SMALLDATETIME	SMALLINT
SMALLMONEY	SO	SOH
SOME	SPACE	SQL
SQLCODE	SQLERROR	SQLSTATE
STDEV	STDEVP	STRING
STX	SUB	SUBSTRING
SUM	SYN	SYSNAME
SYSTEM_USER	TAB	TABLE
TABLEDEF	TABLEDEFS	TABLEID
TABLEID*	TEMPORARY	TEXT
THEN	TIME	TIMESTAMP
TIMEZONE_HOUR	TIMEZONE_MINUTE	TINYINT
TO	TOP	TRAILING
TRANSACTION	TRANSFORM	TRANSLATE
TRANSLATION	TRIM	TRUE
TYPE	UNION	UNIQUE
UNIQUEIDENTIFIER	UNKNOWN	UPDATE
UPDATEIDENTITY	UPDATEOWNER	UPDATESECURITY
UPPER	US	USAGE
USER	USING	VALUE
VALUES	VAR	VARBINARY
VARCHAR	VARP	VARYING
VIEW	VT	WHEN
WHENEVER	WHERE	WITH
WORK	WORKSPACE	WRITE
XOR	YEAR	YES
YESNO	ZONE	

What Are Special Characters?

Special characters are those that are interpreted by Access, SQL Server, and VBA as field type delimiters, as the introduction of a comparison function, or other instructions. Therefore, special characters and control characters (ASCII values 0 through 31) should not be used as part of the name of a database field, object, variable, procedure, or constant. (Okay, we do concede that there are different guidelines for naming VB procedures, variables, and constants than for database objects and field names. But it seems sensible to combine the two sets of rules and apply them to both situations.)

Looking at the list of special characters, it is obvious why some should be avoided. For example, the . (period) can return unexpected results when used with a reserved word. For example, given a field `Name` in table `Students`, the syntax `Students.Name` would return the value of the table's `Name` property instead of the value in the `Name` field.

Similarly, putting an apostrophe in a field name causes the VBA to choke as it interprets the single quote as the beginning or end of a string. Because the ' is being used as an apostrophe, there is nothing to close the string until VBA comes to the next apostrophe (which is likely meant to start another string).

In addition to the following two lists of characters to avoid, there are a couple more seemingly innocent things that can turn into gotchas:

❏ Do not put spaces in field names. For example, field names such as `2ndPhoneand Area Code` could cause unexpected hiccups. If you insist on separating words, use the underscore (a grudgingly acceptable option).

❏ Do not start field or column names with numeric characters.

Remember that an object or field name cannot begin with a space. Access immediately advises you of the error if you try to put certain special characters in a field name. Figure K-3 shows the error message generated by trying to create a field name with a leading space. Notice, however, that Access accepted other special characters within the field name. This may create a false sense of well-being because, as pointed out earlier, a name containing a special character requires special treatment throughout the application.

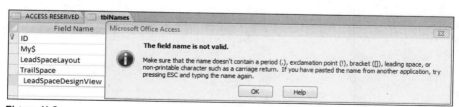

Figure K-3

Special characters not only wreak havoc in code, they can cause problems if they are in text and memo fields. Most of these special characters put the breaks on a word search. An application that has been working smoothly for months may suddenly throw error messages when the user runs a search on a text field. For example, Kim's Curry House, as the name of a business will likely stop a search. The apostrophe causes the SQL interpreter to "think" that a string has been initiated or ended. Solution: Use code to prevent users from entering special characters into text and memo fields. See the code example at the end of this appendix.

Special Characters to Avoid

Key	ASCII	Name
,	44	Comma
.	46	Period
;	59	Semicolon
:	58	Colon
`	96	Grave (open single quote, backtick)
'	39	Apostrophe (single quote)
"	34	Quote (double quote)
?	63	Question mark
/	47	Solidus (slash)
>	62	Greater than
<	60	Less than
[	91	Left square bracket
]	93	Right square bracket
{	123	Left curly brace
}	125	Right curly brace
\	92	Reverse solidus (backslash, whack)
|	124	Vertical bar (pip, pipe)
~	126	Tilde
!	33	Exclamation mark
@	64	Commercial at
#	35	Number sign (pound, hash)
$	36	Dollar sign
%	37	Percent
^	94	Caret
&	38	Ampersand
*	42	Asterisk
(	40	Open parenthesis
)	41	Close parenthesis
=	61	Equal sign
+	43	Plus sign

ASCII Characters to Avoid

You often see the term ASCII, but its full name is seldom spelled out, so here it is in plain English: American Standard Code for Information Interchange. Computers are number-driven, and ASCII code is the numeric representation of characters or actions. The first 32 ASCII characters are actions or non-printing characters, which is why using any of these characters as the name of an object or function would be interpreted as an instruction and could initiate unexpected actions. Most developers recognize ESC, CAN, NUL, LF, CR, and TAB as commands, but many of the other ASCII characters have been forgotten. The following table, then, has a dual purpose. It's a handy reference for knowing what characters to avoid, and it's a useful resource for when you want to include an action such as inserting a carriage return and line feed in your VBA. The character names have been incorporated into the list of words to avoid.

ASCII Characters 0 Through 31

DEC	Hx	Oct	Char	Function
0	0	000	NUL	Null
1	1	001	SOH	Start of heading
2	2	002	STX	Start of text
3	3	003	ETX	End of text
4	4	004	EOT	End of transmission
5	5	005	ENQ	Enquiry
6	6	006	ACK	Acknowledge
7	7	007	BEL	Bell
8	8	010	BS	Backspace
9	9	011	TAB	Horizontal tab
10	A	012	LF	NL line feed, new line
11	B	013	VT	Vertical tab
12	C	014	FF	NP form feed, new page
13	D	015	CR	Carriage return
14	E	016	SO	Shift out
15	F	017	SI	Shift in
16	10	020	DLE	Data link escape
17	11	021	DC1	Device control 1
18	12	022	DC2	Device control 2
19	13	023	DC3	Device control 3

Table continues on the next page

ASCII Characters 0 Through 31 (continued)

DEC	Hx	Oct	Char	Function
20	14	024	DC4	Device control 4
21	15	025	NAK	Negative acknowledgement
22	16	026	SYN	Synchronous idle
23	17	027	ETB	End of transmission block
24	18	030	CAN	Cancel
25	19	031	EM	End of medium
26	1A	032	SUB	Substitute
27	1B	033	ESC	Escape
28	1C	034	FS	File separator
29	1D	035	GS	Group separator
30	1E	036	RS	Record separator
31	1F	037	US	Unit separator

Bonus Code Example

It's sometimes beneficial to prevent users from entering certain characters in data via a form. By setting the form's KeyPreview property to Yes, an event procedure can be used to essentially ignore the entry of selected character. This is accomplished by using an event procedure on the control's OnKeyPress property.

The following example prevents the database from entering a period, apostrophe, or ampersand in the text box txtBusinessName.

```
Private Sub txtBusinessName_KeyPress(KeyAscii As Integer)

   Select Case KeyAscii
      Case 46, 39, 38 ' Period, apostrophe, ampersand
      KeyAscii = 0
   End Select
End Sub
```

If the user entered Kim & John's Cafe, the table would actually store Kim Johns Cafe. The specified ASCII characters are essentially eliminated because the ASCII character 0 is null. (Only the character is eliminated, so unless some other code is included, this will result in two spaces between the words.) This code example can be modified to fit many situations and an infinite combination of characters. Obviously, error trapping needs to be added, but it was left out here for the sake of simplicity. You can use the ASCII character numbers listed in the "Special Characters to Avoid" table earlier in the appendix to write code that will prevent characters from being stored in the database.

Naming Conventions

The logic of using a naming convention is about as easy to grasp as the logic of standardizing an alphabet or language. Both structures are intended to make communication easier. In addition to providing standards, they also allow plenty of opportunities for customization. Adopting a naming convention provides for consistency, can avoid conflicts with reserved words, and sets the framework for building strong code that is more easily read and interpreted by the original developer (yes, you will likely forget why you wrote what you did) and by other developers. You may as well count on someone else trying to interpret your code, whether it is someone on your team, a technical consultant, or someone who inherits your project.

Using a naming convention also helps prevent conflicts due to multiple uses of the same name because, in most cases, a name should have only one meaning within an application.

If you are new to Access or to writing code, this is the perfect time to become familiar with the most common naming conventions and to start developing your own protocols. This appendix includes some guidance for naming objects and provides tables of the most commonly accepted names used in VBA. Now that macros have come into their own, complete with error handling, the appendix also tackles their naming considerations. Adopt, adapt, or create, it's up to you. People who choose to create their own naming conventions still benefit from being familiar with standard naming conventions. After all, they still need to read and interpret code used in Access and VBA help files, books, and sample applications, and at some point, they are likely to collaborate with others on some level.

Why Implement Naming Conventions?

As previously indicated, the use of naming conventions is voluntary, and developers can and do write applications without applying (or enforcing) naming conventions. However, conventions can save a lot of time and money, and can prevent needless frustrations by making it easier and faster to read and interpret code, whether it is code that you wrote last week or last year, or code from another developer.

Naming conventions offer many benefits in that they are like sharing a common language. Typically, that is important if the application is shared, but it's also essential to the individual developer who has to work with a program that he hasn't seen for a couple of years. Following are some of the most common benefits of using a naming convention:

- ❑ They make object names more informative so developers can quickly understand an application's structure and code.

- ❑ They provide a standardized vocabulary for team efforts.

- ❑ They minimize conflicts when adding third-party products.

- ❑ They allow code, tools, and code libraries to be shared across various VBA platforms.

- ❑ They group objects and facilitate various sort options.

- ❑ They can provide self-documenting program code.

- ❑ They enhance search and replace capabilities.

- ❑ They enable you to learn, modify, and incorporate code from others, including from magazines, reference books, the Internet, and peers.

Naming conventions need to be an integral part of the basic design, and they should be fully adopted before one stroke is committed to the database. In addition to establishing rules for objects within your Access application, you also need to manage the path and filenames for objects with which your application will interface. Establishing naming conventions takes a little extra time upfront, but the payoff is fast and it just keeps paying. The benefits are compounded as the application grows, becomes more complicated, interfaces with other applications, and is used by other developers.

Many developers are careful about naming tables, forms, fields, and even the controls that they build. But all too often, the controls that a wizard builds are left with their original names such as `Command65` or `Text58`. Because those names do not indicate what the control really does, they can create confusion and unnecessary conflicts, particularly if code is added to one of the control's events. One solution is to let the wizards do their stuff, and then promptly rename the object so that all future references to it will automatically use the correct name. Please remember that if the wizard generated the code, the name of the object needs to be changed both in the object's property and in VBA. That means you need to open the VBA Editor and update the name of the control within the code created by the wizard.

A Brief History

Currently, the most common naming conventions used in Access applications, Microsoft product documentation, and reference books are based on the Hungarian notation. That notation was created by a Hungarian, Charles Simonyi, while working at Microsoft in the 1980s. In the Access world, Greg Reddick and Stan Leszynski further developed and popularized the naming convention. Greg published the Reddick VBA (RVBA) Naming Conventions at `www.xoc.net/standards/rvbanc.asp`. The Leszynski Naming Conventions (LNC) and development style continue to be referenced in several books and have been incorporated in various websites. Because URLs frequently change, a search is probably the best bet for finding a publication of the LNC.

So much for the history. The critical part is to recognize that the Hungarian notation is pretty much universally recognized, if not adopted, and that it continues to be adapted to keep up with technology. Some tags are becoming obsolete and new ones are continuously added. Although some tags may be retired, there are still programs using them, so it is handy to know where to find a translator, which, in this case, is a table of tag definitions.

The Fundamentals of the Hungarian Convention

The Hungarian convention has a very straightforward design. It dictates that a name may contain up to five parts, and that the parts are combined in the order of prefix(es), tag, base name, qualifier, and suffix:

❑ A *prefix* precedes a tag to provide clarification. It can describe one or more important properties with one or two lowercase characters.

❑ A *tag* is considered by some to be the critical, non-optional element. A tag should be unique and easily differentiated from similarly named tags. A tag is typically three (occasionally four) lowercase characters that identify what the object is — a table, form, or text box, for example. The tag is usually a mnemonic abbreviation, such as tbl, frm, and txt or the first letter of each word from multiword items. Exceptions are often due to the tag already being assigned for a different purpose, adopting a tag from another program, and, of course, that it isn't always easy to create an intuitive three-letter abbreviation.

❑ The *base name* is a descriptive name that defines the particular object. This could be the layman's term used to concisely identify the subject. Use proper case and be brief but clear.

❑ A *qualifier* is an extension that indicates how the object is being used. Qualifiers should be title case and as short as practical, without sacrificing comprehension. For example, the qualifier Avg may be added to a query name to indicate that the query calculated the qryStudentGradeAvg (or qsumStudentGradeAvg).

❑ A *suffix* is rarely needed. Its purpose is to differentiate object names that could otherwise be identical. The suffix is written in title case or as a number and should be as short as practical. For example, a series of queries that calculate the average grade for each grade (see the need to make a distinction?) could be named qryStudentGradeAvg4, qryStudentGradeAvg5, and qryStudentGradeAvg6, indicating the average for the fourth grade, the fifth grade, and the sixth grade class, respectively. And, although many developers avoid using the underscore, some developers like to separate the suffix by using one, as in qryStudentGradeAvg_4.

Although it isn't necessary for an object name to contain all of the parts, nearly every name will contain a tag and a base name. For example, here's the name for a table: tblStudent. You can quickly see that it conforms to the rules — there are no spaces, the tag is all lowercase, and the base name is title case. That is a fairly universally accepted format. Remember, object names should never include special characters or spaces. Other guidelines that you may want to follow are covered in the "Rules for Creating Names — Adding the Personal Touch" section later in this appendix.

The flag is the optional sixth part to a name. A flag affects where an object appears in lists and is effective for grouping items at the beginning or the end of a list. The following table describes common flags.

Flag	Description
_ (underscore)	Causes the item to be listed before numbers and letters. Often used for items under development.
zh	Indicates a system object used for development and maintenance, but it is a hidden object.
zs	Indicates a system object used for development and maintenance but should not be seen by the end user, but not hidden.
zt	Indicates a temporary object that is created programmatically, such as a query built by code, and not preserved after it has been run.
zz	Denotes an object that you are no longer using and that is waiting to be deleted.

> Remember that object names should never include special characters or spaces.

Rules for Creating Names — Adding the Personal Touch

Developers tend to have an independent streak, which often means that we like to do things our own way. Thankfully, development is a creative process so typically there are multiple ways to achieve the desired results. That's also the case with naming conventions. Even if you choose to adopt existing standards, there are plenty of opportunities to incorporate your own preferences and come up with a system that is easy for you to remember, implement, and share. But before you start customizing things, it's still a good idea to understand the basic rules and principles of naming conventions. The following sections provide information to help you to both work with existing standards and create your own. You may find that a combination works best.

Starting with the Basics

Naming conventions apply to application objects, such as forms, reports, controls, queries, and user-defined objects, as well as to Access database engine (ACE) (and Jet) objects such as containers, databases, fields, queryDefs, tableDefs, and workspaces.

Consistency is the key. As stated earlier, it's best to determine your naming conventions before you create the first object in your database so that you can apply them consistently throughout your application. Remember that even when following an established naming convention, there will be plenty of situations that challenge your interpretation of how to apply it.

Next, think KISS (Keep It Short and Simple). Although Access allows up to 64 characters for each object name, no one wants to type or read names that are that long. Plus, your application may need to interface with other programs that are more restrictive in name length. (If your object names aren't compatible with those programs, you could be in for a lot of extra work.) For example, prior to SQL Server 6.0, field names needed to be lowercase for upsizing from Access to the SQL Server. Prior to SQL Server 7.0, field and table names were limited to 30 characters and required an underscore instead of allowing an embedded space. As you can see, just because Access allows 64 characters doesn't mean it is a good thing to create 64-character names.

> *There have been situations with Access 2003 and WindowsXP where an excessively long path to a table name caused Access to close. If you are using Windows XP and your database is in a folder in MyDocuments, for example, that automatically adds about 50 characters to the file path.*

Periods do not belong in names. Periods are a special character that can cause your code to break.

The following are some basic rules and guidelines that apply to both the name and the elements of objects:

❑ Names can contain up to 64 characters (but shorter is better, as previously discussed).

❑ Use complete words in names. If you absolutely must use an abbreviation, ensure that it's a standard, easy-to-interpret one. You might use FName and LName for FirstName and LastName, for example, or in a table with company details you might have field names of CoName, CoAddress, and so on.

❑ Names can consist of any combination of letters and numbers. For example, in tables with multiple address lines, it's common to see Address1 and Address2.

❑ Be aware: While spaces and special characters — except period (.), exclamation point (!), accent grave (`), and brackets ([ ]) — are all technically acceptable, they are known to create problems in table and field names. Do not use them. (We strongly advise you to remove the spaces and characters if you are going to customize and add code to work with these objects.)

> **If you change the name of an object, remember that the name also needs to be updated in any code, modules, or other objects that reference it.**

❑ Don't begin a name with a leading space. (Just don't use spaces. If readability is an issue, use case — capitalize the first letter of each word, like this: June07MarketingOutlook.)

❑ Do not include control characters ASCII values 0–31 (remember that special character thing). See Appendix K to learn about special characters.

❑ Don't duplicate the name of a property or other element used by DAO.

❑ Avoid a series of uppercase letters — these are reserved for formal abbreviations, such as USA.

❑ Names are typically singular rather than plural, for example LastName for a field or txtState for a text box.

❑ Include the base name of the object(s) that it is built on, when practical and logical, such as EventCity for the field City in the table tblEvent.

- ❑ List multiple base objects left-to-right in descending order of importance, such as `tblStudentClass` for a table that joins records from `tblStudents` with records from `tblClass`.

- ❑ A name should use title case construction for the base. It is preceded by a lowercase, three-letter tag, such as in `tblStudentClass`, `lblClassDate`, or `intLattePrice`.

Some Additional Thoughts About Other Objects

If you are going to customize existing conventions or create your own, there are several other things that you will want to consider. The following are some of the more common objects that you'll want to have rules for handling.

Variables and Routines

The body of a variable or routine name should use mixed case and should be only long enough to describe its purpose. For example, `Dim intFormCount As Integer` returns the number of open forms.

Functions

Function names should begin with a verb, and it may add clarity to prefix them with an f for fnc. This can make functions easier to locate and identify when you are perusing through code. Avoid using fn_ because that is the prefix that SQL Server uses for functions. `fDisplayUnexpectedError`, for example, is clearly a function and not the name of a field that contains captured error messages.

Stored procedure names should begin with a verb. Having a tag precede the *base name* facilitates sorting — `ins` for insert and `arc` for archive, for example. When applying tags, avoid sp_, dt_, and xp_ because, again, they are used by SQL Server. `fCloseAllForms` is a good example of a clear and concise name.

Constants

The base name of a constant is often `UPPERCASE_WORDS` with underscores (_) between words. Prefixes such as i, s, g, and m can be very useful in understanding the value and the scope of a constant. For example, in the new line character string `gsNEW_LINE`, the g indicates that it is global to entire application and the s indicates that it's a string.

Constants should be prefixed by the scope prefixes m or g for module or global, respectively. A constant is indicated by appending the letter c to the end of the data type, or it can have the generic tag `con`. For the constant `gintcDiscount`, g is the scope, `int` indicates the data type, c means it's a constant, and the base name is `Discount`. `conDiscount` names the same constant, but conveys less information because it uses the generic tag. `mdblcPi` indicates module level (m), double (dbl) constant (c) with the base name `Pi`.

Classes

A class defines a user-defined object. Because this invents a new data type, you need to invent a new tag for the object. You can add a base name to the tag to spell out the abbreviation indicated by the tag. Chapter 13, for example, used the class module `clsClassroom`.

Arrays and Collections

An array is a variable that can store multiple values. In a *fixed array*, the number of rows and columns are specified; in a *dynamic array*, the dimensions can be established in the procedure calling the array. Arrays often use an a tag, such as `aintFontSizes` or `astrFields`.

Collections are groups of objects, such as the forms collection or a collection established to allow multiple instances of a single form. `col` is often used as prefix to indicate a collection. For example, `mcolFormInstances` is a module-level collection allowing multiple form instances.

Attachments

You can leverage Access's powerful sorting and reporting tools through the use of attachments. This also means that you need to have some control over the path and name of the attachment. Although the rules are more lenient, we still recommend following the KISS principles. Given that advice, here are the rules:

❑ Names of attached files can contain any Unicode character supported by the NTFS file system used in Microsoft Windows NT or later.

❑ The filename must not exceed 255 characters, including the extension.

❑ The filename cannot contain paragraph marks or any of the following special characters: ?, ", /, \, <, >, *, |, and :. Although the other characters are not prohibited, we strongly recommend not using them.

Macros

A macro automates a task. It can be used alone or in a macro group, also called a macro. Macro is one of the objects listed in the Navigation pane. Each macro and macro group should have a unique name that clearly describes the action that it performs. We recommend following standard naming procedures, including avoiding reserved words and special characters.

A good example of a macro name is `AutoExec`. Because it's often employed at start-up, it is the most commonly used macro for an Access database. You learn more about macros in Chapter 2.

More Do's and Don'ts

By now, you'd think that all the basics have been covered, but of course, there is always more. So, just for good measure, here are a few more do's and don'ts:

❑ When creating a new tag, stick to existing rules and styles for length, case, and so forth.

❑ Don't redefine an existing tag. Either create a new unique tag or find an existing tag that fits the purpose.

❑ Before creating a new tag, review existing tags. There is likely already a tag that covers the situation.

❑ Don't use ID as a prefix or suffix.

❏ Because ADO, ADOX, and DAO share some of the same tags, it is a good idea to specify the library name. In addition to avoiding confusion, explicitly naming the library will make the code run faster. For example, to specify that it is an ADO record set, you might write:

```
Dim rst As ADODB.Recordset
```
And to specify that you are using ADOX, you might write:

```
Dim idx As ADOX.Index
```

Tables of Tags

The following tables are a compilation of terms and tags from a multitude of sources. They are by no means all-inclusive listings of all the tags currently in use or that have been used, and new tags will continue to be generated as programs evolve and as developers create their own objects. That being said, the hope is that having this reasonably comprehensive list will save you valuable research time while you are trying to select the right tag or trying to decipher the meaning of an existing tag.

In your work and reading, you'll notice that tags can represent different things at different times. And because it is helpful to know what a tag could mean, you might think of these tables as interpreters, to help you translate other people's code. Therefore, the lists include multiple tags for some objects and a tag may appear more than one time. This isn't to encourage you to vacillate in your usage, but rather to help you interpret the writings of others.

The following table is a compilation of tags and the objects that they represent. It is in alphabetical order by tag. Although a few developers like to use an s to indicate plural, generally only the singular forms are listed in this table.

Object Tags

Tag	Object	Tag	Object
ani	Animated Button	BMP	Windows Bitmap
aob	AccessObject	brk	Page break
aop	AccessObjectProperty	byt	Byte
app	Application	cat	Catalog
bac	Backup	cbo	Combo box
bas	Module	chg	Change
bed	Pen Bedit	chk	Check Box
bfr	BoundObjectFrame	chr	Text (character)
bin	Binary	cht	Chart
bln/tf	Boolean (Yes/No)	clm	Columns

Tag	Object	Tag	Object
clms	Column	dyn/ds	Dynaset
clp	Picture clip	EMF	Enhanced Metafile
cmd	Command button	err	Error
cnn/cnx	Connection	EXIF	Exchangeable File Format
cnt/con	Container	exp	Export
col	Collection	f	Flag
com	Communications	fcd	FormatCondition
ctr/ctl	Control (generic)	fd	Field object
cur	Currency	fdc	Field collection
dap	DataAccessPage	fdlg	Form (dialog)
dat	Data control	fil	File list box
dat/dtm/dt*	Date/Time	fld	Field
db	Database	fld2	Field 2 (for multi-valued fields)
dbc/dbcbo	Data-bound combo box	flt	Filter
dbe	DBEngine	fmnu	Form (menu)
dbg/dbgrd	Data-bound grid	fmsg	Form (message)
dbl	Double	fra	Frame
dcm	DoCmd	frm	Form
ddl	Data definition	fsb	FlatScrollBar
ddn	Drop down list	fsfr/sfrm/sfr	Form (subform)
dec	Decimal	gal	Gallery control
del	Delete	gau	Gauge
DIB	Device Independent Bitmap	GIF	Graphics Interchange Format
dir	Directory list box	glb	Global
dlg/cdl	Common dialog	gra/gph	Graph
dls/dblst	Data-bound list box	grd	Grid
doc	Document	grl	GroupLevel
drv	Drive list box	grp	Option group
Dtp	DTPicker (date picker control)	grp/gru	Group

Table continues on the next page

Tag	Object	Tag	Object
hed	Pen Hedit	mmnu	Macro (menu)
hsb	Horizontal scroll bar	mnu	Menu
hyp	Hyperlink	mpm/msg *	MAPI message
ICON, ICO	Icon	mps/ses	MAPI session
ID	AutoNumber	msg *	MS Flex Grid
idx	Index	mst	MS Tab
ils/iml	ImageList	new	New
Img	ImageCombo	Nod	Node (TreeView)
img	Image	Nods	Nodes (TreeView)
imp	Import	obj	Object
ink	Pen ink	ocx	CustomControl
int	Integer	old	Old
itt	Internet Transfer Control	ole	OLE
ix	Index Object	opt	Option button
ixc	Index collection	out	Outline
JPEG, JPG, JPE	Joint Photographic Experts Group	pal	PaletteButton
key	Key status	pcl	Picture clip or Picture Clip Control
keys	Keys	pic	Picture
lbl	Label	pl3d	Panel 3D
lin	Line	PNG	Portable Network Graphics
lkp	Lookup	prb/prg	ProgressBar
lng	Long	prc	Procedure
lst	List box	prm	Parameter
lvw	ListView	prp	Property
mak	Make table	prt	Printer
mci	MCI	qapp	Query (append)
mcr	Macro	qd	QueryDef Ojbect
mdi	MDI child form	qddl	Query (DDL)
mem	Memo	qdel	Query (delete)

Tag	Object	Tag	Object
qdf	QueryDef	sfr/sfrm	SubForm
qflt	Query (filter)	shp	Shape
qlkp	Query (lookup)	sld	Slider
qmak	Query (make table)	sng	Single
qry	Query	snp	Snapshot
qsel	Query (select)	sok	Winsock
qspt	Query (SQL pass-through)	spn	Spin
qtot	Query (totals)	spt	Pass through (SQL pass through)
qty	Quantity	srp/srpt	SubReport
quni	Query (union)	stf	String (fixed length)
qupd	Query (update)	str	String
qxtb	Query (crosstab)	sys	System
rdyn	Recordset (dynaset)	tab	Tab or TabStrip
r2dyn	Recordset 2 (dynaset for multi-valued fields)	Tabs	Tabs or TabStrips
ref	Reference	tb	Table Object
rel	Relation	tbl	Table
rle	Run Length Encoded Bitmap	Tbr	Toolbar
rpt	Report	td	TableDef Object
rsnp	Recordset (snapshot)	tdf/tbd	TableDef
rsrp/srpt/srp	Report (subreport)	tvr	TempVar
rst	Recordset	tgl	Toggle button
Rst2	Recordset 2 (for multi-valued fields)	TIFF, TIF	Tagged Image File Format
rtbl	Recordset (table)	tlb	Toolbar
rtf	RichTextBox	tlkp	Table (lookup)
sbr/sta	StatusBar	tmr	Timer
scr	Screen	Tre/tvw	TreeView
sec	Section	trx	transaction
sel	Select	txt	Text box
		typ	Type-User-Defined

Table continues on the next page

Tag	Object	Tag	Object
uctl	Control (user)	var/vnt	Variant
udoc	Document (user)	vsb	Vertical scroll bar
udt	User-defined type	vw	View
uni	Union	WMF	Windows Metafile
upd	UpDown	wrk/wsp	Workspace
usr	User	xtb	Crosstab
val	Validate	ysn	Yes/No

* msg is a good example of a tag that can mean two different things: a message box or an MS flex grid. Also, dt can represent a date field or a drill-through function or procedure.

Personally, I like sfrm for subForms and srpt for SubReports. They aren't on the "official lists" but they seem clear to me. As we've been saying, use a system that works for you.

The following table lists the Access Object Variables and their most common tags. Keep in mind that many developers prefer to use only the singular form for tags. This table is alphabetical by the Object Variable name.

Access Object Variable Tags

Tag	Object Variable	Tag	Object Variable
aob	AccessObject	xtb	Crosstab
aops	AccessObjectProperties	ocx	CustomControl
aop	AccessObjectProperty	ddl	Data definition
apd	Append	dat	Data entry
app	Application	dap	DataAccessPage
att	Attachment	del	Delete
bac	Backup	dcm	DoCmd
bfr	BoundObjectFrame	exp	Export
chg	Change	flt	Filter
chk	CheckBox	frm	Form
cbo	ComboBox	fcd	FormatCondition
cmd	CommandButton	fcds	FormatConditions
ctl	Control	frms	Forms

Tag	Object Variable	Tag	Object Variable
grl	GroupLevel	prps	Properties
hyp	Hyperlink	qty	Quantity
img	Image	shp	Rectangle
imp	Import	ref	Reference
lbl	Label	refs	References
lin	Line	rpt	Report
lst	ListBox	scr	Screen
lkp	Look up	sec	Section
mcr	Macro	sel	Select
mak	Make table	sfr	SubForm
bas	Module	srp	SubReport
new	New	sys	System
ole	ObjectFrame	tab	TabControl
old	Old	tbl	Table
opt	OptionButton	tlkp	Table (lookup)
fra	OptionGroup (frame)	txt	TextBox
pag/tab	Page (TabControl)	tgl	ToggleButton
brk	PageBreak	trx	Transaction
pal	PaletteButton	uni	Union
spt	Pass through (SQL pass through)	usr	User
		val	Validate

The following table lists the common ADOX tags. This includes the plural forms although most developers stick with singular. The list is ordered by ADOX object.

ADOX Object Tags

Tag	Object	Tag	Object
cat	Catalog	cmd	Command
clm	Column	grp	Group
clms	Columns	grps	Groups

Table continues on the next page

Tag	Object	Tag	Object
idx	Index	prp	Property
idxs	Indexes	tbl	Table
key	Key	tbls	Tables
keys	Keys	usr	User
prc	Procedure	usrs	Users
prcs	Procedures	vw	View
prps	Properties	vws	Views

The following table lists the common ADO tags. Again, these include plural forms although most developers stick to singular forms. The list is in order by ADO object.

ADO Object Tags

Tag	Object	Tag	Object
cmd	Command	prm	Parameter
cnn/cnx	Connection	prms	Parameters
err	Error	prps	Properties
errs	Errors	prp	Property
fld	Field	rst	Recordset
flds	Fields		

The following table lists the common DAO object tags. Again, these include the plural forms although most developers stick to singular forms. The list is in order by DAO object.

DAO Object Tags

Tag	Object	Tag	Object
cnt/con	Container	err	Error
db	Database	fld	Field
dbe	DBEngine	fdc	Field collection
doc	Document	fd	Field Object
ds	Dynaset	grp/gru	Group

Tag	Object	Tag	Object
idx	Index	rsnp	Recordset (snapshot)
ixc	Index collection	rtbl	Recordset (table)
ix	Index Object	rel	Relation
int	Integer	sng	Single
lng	Long	snp	Snapshot
obj	Object	str	String
prm	Parameter	tbl	Table
prp	Property	tb	Table Object
qry	Query	tdf	TableDef
qdf	QueryDef	td	TableDev Object
qd	QueryDef Object	usr	user
rst	Recordset	var	Variant
rdyn	Recordset (dynaset)	wsp	Workspace

The following table lists the common VB Object tags. Again, these include the plural forms although most developers stick to singular forms. The list is in order by VB object.

VB Object Tags

Tag	Object	Tag	Object
app	App	fra	Frame
chk	CheckBox	glb	Global
clp	Clipboard	hsb	HScrollBar
cbo	ComboBox	img	Image
cmd	CommandButton	lbl	Label
ctl	Control	lics	Licenses
dat	Data	lin	Line
dir	DirListBox	lst	ListBox
drv	DriveListBox	mdi	MDIForm
fil	FileListBox	mnu	Menu
frm	Form	ole	OLE

Table continues on the next page

Tag	Object	Tag	Object
opt	OptionButton	txt	TextBox
pic	PictureBox	tmr	Timer
prt	Printer	uctl	UserControl
prp	PropertyPage	udoc	UserDocument
scr	Screen	vsb	VscrollBar
shp	Shape		

The following table lists the common Data Type tags in order by data type.

Data Type Tags

Tag	Object	Tag	Object
ID	AutoNumber	lng	Long
bin	Binary	mem	Memo
bln/tf	Boolean (Yes/No)	obj	Object
byt	Byte	ole	Ole
col	Collection	sng	Single
cur	Currency	str	String
dat/dtm/dt	Date/Time	stf	String (fixed length)
dec	Decimal	chr	Text (character)
dbl	Double	udt	User-defined type
err	Error	var/vnt	Variant
int	Integer		

The following table lists the common scope prefixes. A scope prefix typically precedes the tags on functions and constants.

Prefix	Scope
(none)	Local, procedural level lifetime
c	Constants
g	Global (public) object lifetime
m	Module-level, private object lifetime
s	Static variable, static object lifetime

Field tags are truly optional. They provide the extra bit of detail when added to an otherwise complete name. Think "self-documenting." Notice in the following table that many of the field tags are the same as the data type tags for other objects.

Tag	Field Object Type
lng	Autoincrementing (either sequential or random) Long (used with the suffix Cnt)
bin	Binary
byte	Byte
cur	Currency
date	Date/time
dbl	Double
guid	Globally unique identifier (GUID) used for replication Autoincrement fields
int	Integer
lng	Long
mem	Memo
ole	OLE
sng	Single
str	Text
bool	Yes/No

Tag suffixes, listed in the following table, are another optional detail. They explicitly identify the type of object.

Tag Suffixes with Objects

Tag	Suffix	Object
tlkp	Lookup	Table (lookup)
qsel	(none)	Query (select)
qapp	Append	Query (append)
qxtb	Xtab	Query (crosstab)
qddl	DDL	Query (DDL)
qdel	Delete	Query (delete)
qflt	Filter	Query (filter)

Table continues on the next page

Tag Suffixes with Objects

Tag	Suffix	Object
qlkp	Lookup	Query (lookup)
qmak	MakeTable	Query (make table)
qspt	PassThru	Query (SQL pass-through)
qtot	Totals	Query (totals)
quni	Union	Query (union)
qupd	Update	Query (update)
fdlg	Dlg	Form (dialog)
fmnu	Mnu	Form (menu)
fmsg	Msg	Form (message)
fsfr	SubForm	Form (subform)
rsrp	SubReport	Report (subreport)
mmnu	Mnu	Macro (menu)

Standards

Throughout the book, we've pulled together reference material, sharing our expertise and experiences, and encouraging you to take the try-it, like-it, modify-as-appropriate approach. That methodology is particularly fitting for the lists and guidelines in these appendixes. With that in mind, here are a few reminders:

❑ Rules and guidelines change over time, so your naming conventions may need to be updated as you work with new versions and additional programs.

❑ There's an overwhelming supply of reference material with varying degrees of quality and applicability.

Some of the more reliable sources for additional or updated information on naming conventions, reserved words and special characters will likely be found by searching Microsoft and www.mvps.org. Although it might seem that the preponderance of Microsoft's articles is related to .NET, there are several that are relevant to Access development.

The most critical factor is that you consistently implement and follow some standard.

Tips and Tricks

This appendix provides a selection of tips, tricks, techniques, and advice to help you build better, stronger, and cooler Access applications. There's a lot of sample code here; you can avoid typing it yourself by downloading the Chamber application files from this book's website.

Visual Interface Standards

No matter how good your application is under the covers, people won't believe it if it doesn't look good. On the other hand, if your application looks great, people may believe it is great. While a user's perception of your Access application might not be fair, you are going to have to deal with it. Luckily, it isn't too hard to make your application look as great on the outside as you made it inside.

Use Businesslike Colors

Don't use a lot of colors on your Access forms. If you want your applications to look like they fit right into the Windows environment, use the venerable Windows Standard color scheme, meaning gray. You should actually make the colors of your forms adapt to the Windows scheme automatically.

For the background color of almost everything (forms, buttons, read-only text boxes, and so on), use the Windows default Background Form color. The numeric color value is –2147483633. Use white for the background of changeable fields. In Access 2007, you can now see the names of the Windows colors in the drop-down list instead of their numbers.

> *Magic numbers: Access color properties use regular, positive numbers for normal static colors. All the "Windows" colors (that change automatically when the Windows scheme changes) are negative numbers.*

To test your colors and make sure they aren't hard-coded to a certain color, change your Windows color scheme to something completely different and look through your screens to make sure all the colors remain consistent.

Use red sparingly. You can use red (255) for the Fore Color of the Exit button and any dangerous buttons you might have, but don't use it anywhere else. If you overuse it, it loses its special purpose as a warning or danger color.

Provide a Well-Marked Exit

Provide an easy but safe exit from most of your screens. Put an Exit button on most screens, always in the same place, such as the lower-right corner. It should call a function that asks users if they really want to exit the application. Users seem to like this a lot because it gives them a quick way to exit the application without the sense that they are circumventing something. Do not put this button on a screen where users haven't completed a particular action, such as in the middle of a wizard or in a pop-up screen where they can modify detailed information.

Here is some code you can call from the On Click event of the Exit button in any form. It can be placed in any Module.

```
Sub ExitProgram()
On Error GoTo Error_Handler

Dim response As Variant
If MsgBox("Are you sure you want to exit " & "My Application" _
   & "?", vbOKCancel, "My Application") = vbOK Then

   DoCmd.Quit
End If

Exit_Procedure:
   Exit Sub

Error_Handler:
   DisplayUnexpectedError Err.Number, Err.Description
   Resume Exit_Procedure
   Resume

End Sub
```

The function DisplayUnexpectedError is described in Chapter 9.

With this code, you can give your users a chance to stay in the application in case they didn't mean to exit. Because applications often take several seconds to start backup, users appreciate an opportunity to reconsider exiting.

Watch Your Punctuation

Most Access applications are used in a business setting, so it's best to keep a professional tone in your application. Proper punctuation is especially important because it shows a level of polish and thoroughness.

For example, use exclamation points very sparingly. Don't kid yourself; it's unlikely that anything in your application is exciting enough to warrant one. Don't let the user think you excite easily.

It's much more professional to say: "All product records were imported successfully." (with a period) than it is to say "All product records were imported successfully!"

Also, always end sentences and statements with periods. It looks more polished to say: "Products sales forecast calculations have been completed." than to say "Products sales forecasts have been completed" (looks rather incomplete without the period, doesn't it?).

If you keep your punctuation correct and your tone businesslike, your users will perceive your application as a competent business tool.

Use Consistent Button Placement

Be consistent with button placement, size, and color. Close and Exit buttons should always be in the same places on the screen. The "drill-down" form the user opens by double-clicking on a row should also be available by clicking the left-most button (Detail) at the bottom of the screen (see Figure M-1).

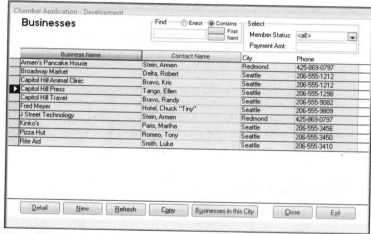

Figure M-1

Also, provide Alt keys for your buttons. It's easy: In the `Caption` property of each button, add an ampersand (&) before the letter you want to use for the Alt key combination. Try to make them consistent across all your forms, and make sure that you don't use the same letter for two different buttons.

Hide Higher-Level Forms

Hide previous forms as you drill down, unless the next one is directly related to the previous one and you open the next one in Dialog mode. Be careful if you let the user click between multiple open forms; the user may get lost or take actions you didn't plan for in your code. This is even more important with Access 2007's new default tabbed form interface because simply maximizing a form won't hide the tabs for the other visible forms. See the daisy-chaining topic later in this appendix for a method that displays only one form at a time.

Use Read-Only "Index" Forms

When your user needs to open a table or recordset to modify data, don't just dump the user straight into the detail form in which the first record is always displayed. It is unprofessional, and it forces the user to navigate to the desired record. In the meantime, the user can mistakenly change the wrong record.

Instead, build an in-between index form showing all the records in continuous form view. The form should be read-only with the Windows Background color instead of a white background. When the user double-clicks on a row or clicks the Detail button, show only that particular detail record by setting the Where Condition on the OpenForm command to the key of the selected record, like this:

```
DoCmd.OpenForm FormName:="frmBusiness", _
   WhereCondition:="BusinessKey = " & Me!BusinessKey
```

If you allow double-clicks on a row, make sure that the user can click on any field in the row, plus the record selector itself. The technique for this is shown in Chapter 8, in the section "Drilling Down with Double-Click."

A good way to distinguish between your index form and the detail form is this: Name the index form with the plural form, and the detail with the singular form. For example, you can have frmBusinesses (read-only index form showing multiple records) and frmBusiness (editable detail form showing only one record).

Another advantage of using an index form (in case you need another one) is that you can get some performance improvements by showing a few fields on the index form and only opening up the whole editable record (often with performance-costly combo boxes, and so on) when the user drills down on it. This is especially noticeable if you are building a client/server application using SQL Server for the back-end database.

Check Your Table Linkage

You already have a database that has a separate front-end application and back-end database, right? Well, don't let the user see an invalid table message if the back-end database isn't in the location that it was last time. Check your table links every time you start your application. There are some common routines on the Internet or in other books to check table links, or you can write your own. Either way, if you handle your linked tables before your user sees a problem, your application will look a lot more professional.

Translate Default Delete Messages

Depending on how slick you want your application to be, you may want to replace the messages Access gives you when you delete records with a friendlier version of your own. You can confirm deletions for each record or for a whole group, and you can prevent the default Access messages from appearing. This takes a bit more work, but it's more professional. (See Chapter 8 for more information about using the Delete and Before Delete Confirm events.) Use wording such as: Are you sure you want to delete product Widget125?

Showing your own message before deleting a record is especially helpful when you have enabled cascade deletes in back-end relationships. You may want to use wording such as:

```
Are you sure you want to delete business Joe's Tire Shop? This will also delete all
the payments made by this business.
```

By using your own friendly warning messages instead of the default Access messages, your application will look more professional and will be easier for your users to understand.

Looking Good

Remember that your users can't see your great code or beautiful database structure. They can see only your user interface — the forms and reports in your application. Much of their perception of your application will be determined by how it looks, so it's important to pay special attention to these areas.

Now that you have your applications looking good, explore some techniques that you can use to make your applications more powerful and easy to use.

Daisy Chain Your Forms

When your user navigates from one form to another, one of your jobs as an application developer is to keep things simple. When users have the ability to click between multiple open forms, they can lose track of their current form, or perform actions that you fail to handle properly. A safer approach is to carefully control which forms are visible at any one time.

Controlling the visibility and flow of one form to another is often called "daisy chaining." There are a few different types of daisy chaining. They involve two main choices: whether to hide the calling form, and whether to open the called form in Dialog mode. For this example, say the calling form is Form A and the called form is Form B.

If Form A needs to be requeried after Form B is closed, then open Form B in Dialog mode to have Form A's code wait until the user is finished with Form B. This often occurs when Form A is an index form showing multiple records, and Form B is a detail form where the user can create, change, or even delete one of the records.

If Form A provides some contextual information that would be handy for the user to see while Form B is open (such as which record he's currently working with), then you can leave Form A visible while Form B is open. To prevent the user from clicking between the two and possibly obscuring Form B, use your old friend Dialog mode to prevent him from clicking on Form A.

If Form A does not need to be visible while Form B is open or requeried when Form B closes, then the easiest form of daisy chaining is to hide Form A when Form B is opened, and make it visible again when Form B closes. This is the most common form of daisy chaining and it works well when traversing menu or "switchboard" forms.

> Dialog mode — the end of the line: When you daisy chain a form and use Dialog mode, you are committed to using Dialog mode for each level thereafter unless you hide the calling form. That's because a form opened in Dialog mode does not allow any non–Dialog mode form to come to the forefront or to accept input. Also, if you open a report while a form is open and visible in Dialog mode, the report will appear behind the Dialog mode form, and also will not accept any input. One way around this is to open the report using Dialog mode. However, then another issue occurs: the report will not be maximized even if you specify `DoCmd.Maximize` in its `On Activate` event.

The main VBA components of the "hiding and showing" aspects of daisy chaining code are described in the following sections.

Form A Opens Form B

When Form A opens Form B, Form A also needs to "hide itself." However, to make Form A visible again, Form B needs to remember which form opened it. To remember this, Form A uses a global variable to "pass in" its own name (see the example Form A in Figure M-2). In this example, the user can drill down on a particular business by double-clicking the record or clicking the Detail button.

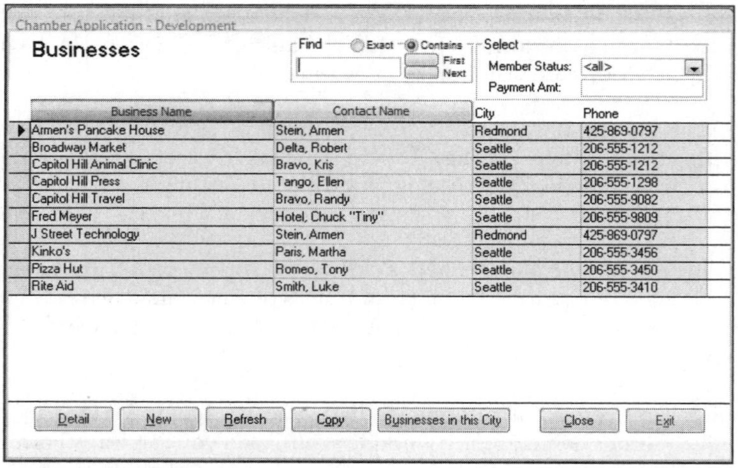

Figure M-2

> Alternatives to globals: Most professional developers avoid using global variables, which don't always retain their values when the code stops due to an error condition or during debugging. However, if globals are used for a short time (for example, to bridge the gap between Form A and Form B), they are an acceptable choice. Alternatives include using `OpenArgs` (but this is one text property that needs to be parsed if more than one value must be passed), and a hidden form to store these global values as text boxes.

A new feature in Access 2007 is the `TempVars` collection. This `Application` collection can store values that persist while the Access database remains open, and the values are not cleared when code is stopped during debugging. You use `TempVars` like this:

```
Application.TempVars.Add ("MyGlobalVariableName", "MyGlobalValue")
```

Then, when you need to retrieve the value, you can load it into a VBA variable like this:

```
MyVariableName = Application.TempVars("MyGlobalVariableName")
```

One handy feature of the `TempVars` collection is that you don't need to check if the particular item is already added to set its value. When you use the `.Add` method for a `TempVars` item that already exists, the new value just replaces the old value.

The following examples employ a global variable for compatibility with earlier versions of Access, but if you know your application will be running in Access 2007 or later, you could switch to using `TempVars`.

Here is some example code in `frmBusinesses` (an index form showing many businesses) to open `frmBusiness` (a detail form to modify a single business).

```
Private Sub cmdDetail_Click()
On Error GoTo Error_Handler

Dim stLinkCriteria As String

If IsNull(Me!BusinessKey) Then
  EnableDisableControls
  GoTo Exit_Procedure
End If

gstrCallingForm = Me.Name
stLinkCriteria = "[BusinessKey]=" & Me![BusinessKey]
DoCmd.OpenForm FormName:="frmBusiness", _
WhereCondition:=stLinkCriteria
Me.Visible = False

Exit_Procedure:
  On Error Resume Next
  Exit Sub

Error_Handler:
  DisplayUnexpectedError Err.Number, Err.Description
  Resume Exit_Procedure
  Resume

End Sub
```

Note that before `frmBusiness` is opened, the name of the current form (`Me.Name`) is loaded into the global variable `gstrCallingForm`.

```
gstrCallingForm = Me.Name
```

Then, after the line to open `frmBusiness`, the current form is hidden using:

```
Me.Visible = False
```

At this point, the first form is hidden and only the second form is visible, as shown in Figure M-3.

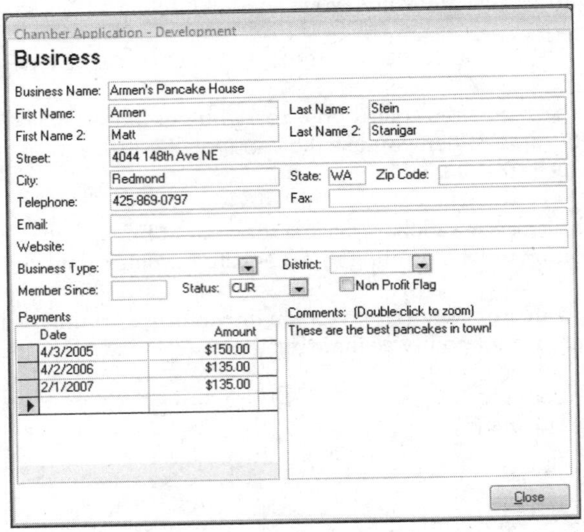

Figure M-3

Form B Opens

When Form B wakes up, it has a little housekeeping to do before anything else happens. In the On Open event, it needs to remember the name of the form that called it. Later, when Form B closes, it will use that name to make Form A visible again.

```
Private Sub Form_Open(Cancel As Integer)
On Error GoTo Error_Handler

Me.Caption = AppGlobal.ApplicationNameAndDB()
mstrCallingForm = gstrCallingForm
gstrCallingForm = ""

Exit_Procedure:
  Exit Sub

Error_Handler:
  DisplayUnexpectedError Err.Number, Err.Description
  Resume Exit_Procedure
  Resume

End Sub
```

To remember the name, the value in `gstrCallingForm` is placed safely into `mstrCallingForm`:

```
mstrCallingForm = gstrCallingForm
```

This module-level variable (indicated by the m prefix) is declared at the top of the Form B's module, like this:

```
Option Compare Database
Option Explicit
Dim mstrCallingForm As String
```

Notice that `gstrCallingForm` is set to an empty string right after its contents are saved into `mstrCallingForm`:

```
gstrCallingForm = ""
```

There is no programming logic reason for doing this; it's really just a message to other programmers that you are completely done using the global variable, so you are clearing its value. It has done its job well (for the last few milliseconds) and can go back to being an empty string now that it has transferred its contents to the local module variable.

At this point, Form B is ready to continue opening and perform whatever functions it is designed to do. It will remember the name of the calling Form A until it closes.

Form B Closes

During the whole time that Form B (`frmBusiness`) is open, Form A (`frmBusinesses`) remains hidden. However, when the user closes Form B, you need to make sure that Form A becomes visible again. The following code is in the On Close event of Form B:

```
Private Sub Form_Close()
On Error GoTo Error_Handler

If mstrCallingForm <> "" Then
  Forms(mstrCallingForm).Visible = True
End If

Exit_Procedure:
  Exit Sub

Error_Handler:
If Err = 2450 Then
  ' ignore error if calling form is no longer loaded
  Resume Next
Else
  DisplayUnexpectedError Err.Number, Err.Description
  Resume Exit_Procedure
  Resume
End If

End Sub
```

The operative code here is:

```
Forms(mstrCallingForm).Visible = True
```

This code uses the `Forms` collection (a collection of all currently open forms in the database) to locate the form with the name stored in `mstrCallingForm` and make it visible.

However, two other sections of code are there just for you, the developer. The first is a check to make sure that `mstrCallingForm` actually has a value before attempting to make it visible. This enables you to open Form B directly during development (instead of from Form A), and not have to deal with the resulting error every time Form B closes.

```
If mstrCallingForm <> "" Then
   Forms(mstrCallingForm).Visible = True
End If
```

Along the same lines, the error handler code contains an exception for `Error 2450`, which will occur if the calling form is no longer loaded. Again, this is to allow you, in development mode, to close Form A while Form B is open without seeing an error when Form B closes.

```
If Err = 2450 Then
   ' ignore error if calling form is no longer loaded
   Resume Next
```

When Form B closes and makes Form A visible again, Form B's link in the daisy chain is complete.

When Form A Is a Subform

Sometimes Form A is a subform. In this case, you cannot send `Me.Name` into Form B because a subform cannot be made visible or hidden directly. Instead, the parent form name needs to be specified.

This is easy to do. Instead of setting the global variable and making the current form hidden, like this:

```
gstrCallingForm = Me.Name

Me.Visible = False
```

you need to use the name of the parent form, like this:

```
gstrCallingForm = Me.Parent.Name

Me.Parent.Visible = False
```

Form B will never know the difference. When it closes, Form A's parent form will be made visible again.

Find Records

Access provides some built-in ways to search for records, but they can be confusing for users that are running your application. The binoculars button pops up a dialog box with several search options, but most users don't know how to use it properly. The problem is that it is has too many options for users who probably just want to find a record containing a certain text value.

Instead, you can include a quick and easy way for your user to find records. Figure M-4 shows a form with a built-in technique to find records.

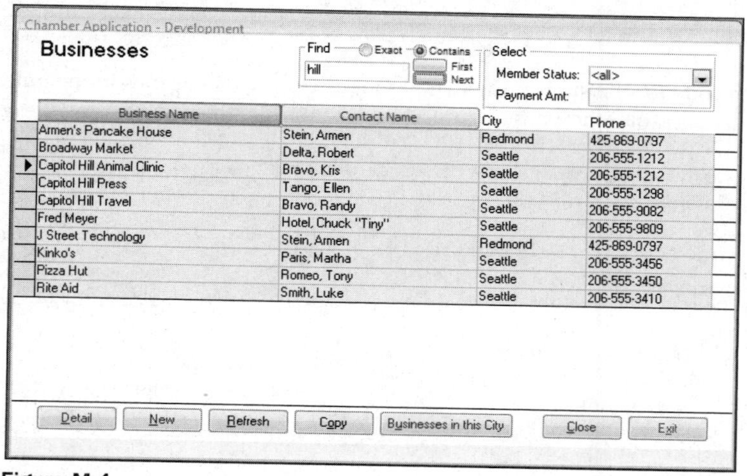

Figure M-4

This record-finding technique allows any phrase to be entered in the text box, then finds the first (or next) record that contains that phrase anywhere in the displayed fields. Alternatively, the user may change the radio buttons to switch to an Exact match instead of a Contains search, where the entire field must match the phrase. Exact mode is not used very often, but it can be handy in searching for exact codes or numbers (such as membership or account numbers).

Calling the Record Finder Code

The On Click event of the First button (shown in Figure M-4) includes this code:

```
Private Sub cmdFirst_Click()
On Error GoTo Error_Handler

FindRecordLike "first"

Exit_Procedure:
  On Error Resume Next
  Exit Sub

Error_Handler:
  DisplayUnexpectedError Err.Number, Err.Description
  Resume Exit_Procedure
  Resume

End Sub
```

The code really has only one operative line:

```
FindRecordLike "first"
```

The code behind cmdNext_Click() is almost identical. Instead of using "first" as the parameter for FindRecordLike, it sends in "next":

```
FindRecordLike "next"
```

Now here's the code for the subroutine FindRecordLike. It also resides in the index form that contains the record finder controls (shown in Figure M-4). It looks like this:

```
Private Sub FindRecordLike(strFindMode As String)
On Error GoTo Error_Handler

Call ww_FindRecord(frmCallingForm:=Me, _
  ctlFindFirst:=Me!cmdFirst, _
  ctlFindNext:=Me!cmdNext, _
  ctlSearchText:=Me!txtFind, _
  ctlSearchOption:=Me!optFind, _
  strFindMode:=strFindMode, _
  strField1:="BusinessName", _
  strField2:="LastName", _
  strField3:="FirstName", _
  strField4:="City")

Exit_Procedure:
  On Error Resume Next
  Exit Sub

Error_Handler:
  DisplayUnexpectedError Err.Number, Err.Description
  Resume Exit_Procedure
  Resume

End Sub
```

This Sub accepts a parameter strFindMode of "first" or "next", which it passes directly to the ww_FindRecord procedure. In fact, pretty much all this procedure does is call ww_FindRecord. The interesting part is the set of parameters that is passed to ww_FindRecord, many of which are explained in the next section. First, take a look at the parameters strField1, strField2, strField3, and strField4.

For the record finder routine to know which fields to search for your user's phrase, you need to make it known. You can do this by sending in up to ten field names. These must be names of fields that appear in the Recordsource for the form. Although they don't technically have to appear on the form itself, it will seem strange to the user to find records containing a phrase that he can't see.

Why not automate the list of fields? It would be possible to use VBA to cycle through all of the fields displayed on the form, using the form's Controls collection, and send their names to the ww_FindRecord procedure automatically. However, that wouldn't necessarily be desirable because you may not want all the fields to be searchable. By sending them yourself using this simple code, you can carefully control which fields are searched.

This example sends only four field names to be searched, but it could have specified up to ten. Fields 2 through 10 are optional parameters, and are explained later in this chapter.

Record Finder Code

To make this code easy to implement, you want to reuse as much code as possible. The key is to pass references to the controls on this form (the text box, buttons, even the form itself) to a reusable Record Finder function. Note that this code has a ww prefix (for Wiley-Wrox) to reduce conflicts with any other public procedures.

```
Option Compare Database
Option Explicit

'Record Finder

'Accepts references from a continuous form with Record Finder
'controls, finds the first/next record containing the search
'text in one of the passed-in field names, and repositions the
'form to that record.

Public Function ww_FindRecord(frmCallingForm As Form, _
  ctlFindFirst As Control, _
  ctlFindNext As Control, _
  ctlSearchText As Control, _
  ctlSearchOption As Control, _
  strFindMode As String, _
  strField1 As String, _
  Optional strField2 As String, _
  Optional strField3 As String, _
  Optional strField4 As String, _
  Optional strField5 As String, _
  Optional strField6 As String, _
  Optional strField7 As String, _
  Optional strField8 As String, _
  Optional strField9 As String, _
  Optional strField10 As String)

On Error GoTo Error_Handler

Dim recClone As Recordset
Dim intBookmark As String
Dim strAllFields As String
Dim strSelection As String

' Field delimiter is used to separate concatenated
' field values below. This prevents text from being
' matched across adjacent fields. It may be changed
' to any text value that is unlikely to appear in the fields.
Const FIELDDELIMITER = "@%%@"
```

```
' If there is no string to search for set the focus back to
' the text box.
If ctlSearchText & "" = "" Or strField1 & "" = "" Then
  ctlSearchText.SetFocus
  Exit Function
End If

DoCmd.Hourglass True

ww_FindRecord = False
```

The next section of code handles the search if the user has specified the Contains mode. It is the default search and the most flexible because it will find the phrase anywhere in any of the specified fields.

```
'Test search option
If ctlSearchOption = 1 Then 'Contains search

  ' build string to concatenate all fields together
  strAllFields = "[" & strField1 & "]"
  If strField2 <> "" Then
    strAllFields = strAllFields & " & """ & FIELDDELIMITER & _
    """ & [" & strField2 & "]"
  End If

  If strField3 <> "" Then
    strAllFields = strAllFields & " & """ & FIELDDELIMITER & _
    """ & [" & strField3 & "]"
  End If

  If strField4 <> "" Then
    strAllFields = strAllFields & " & """ & FIELDDELIMITER & _
    """ & [" & strField4 & "]"
  End If

  If strField5 <> "" Then
    strAllFields = strAllFields & " & """ & FIELDDELIMITER & _
    """ & [" & strField5 & "]"
  End If

  If strField6 <> "" Then
    strAllFields = strAllFields & " & """ & FIELDDELIMITER & _
    """ & [" & strField6 & "]"
  End If

  If strField7 <> "" Then
    strAllFields = strAllFields & " & """ & FIELDDELIMITER & _
    """ & [" & strField7 & "]"
  End If

  If strField8 <> "" Then
    strAllFields = strAllFields & " & """ & FIELDDELIMITER & _
    """ & [" & strField8 & "]"
  End If
```

```
        If strField9 <> "" Then
          strAllFields = strAllFields & " & """ & FIELDDELIMITER & _
          """ & [" & strField9 & "]"
        End If

        If strField10 <> "" Then
          strAllFields = strAllFields & " & """ & FIELDDELIMITER & _
          """ & [" & strField10 & "]"
        End If

        Set recClone = frmCallingForm.RecordsetClone

        ' if find First button was used
        If strFindMode = "first" Then
          recClone.FindFirst strAllFields & " Like ""*" & _
          Replace(ctlSearchText, """", """""") & "*"""
          If recClone.NoMatch Then
            MsgBox "No matches found.", vbOKOnly, "Record Finder"
            ctlSearchText.SetFocus
          Else
            frmCallingForm.Bookmark = recClone.Bookmark
            ctlFindNext.SetFocus
            ww_FindRecord = True
          End If

      Else
        ' if find Next button was used
        If strFindMode = "next" Then
          recClone.Bookmark = frmCallingForm.Bookmark
          recClone.FindNext strAllFields & " Like ""*" & _
          Replace(ctlSearchText, """", """""") & "*"""

          If recClone.NoMatch Then
            MsgBox "No more matches found.", vbOKOnly, _
            "Record Finder"
            ctlFindFirst.SetFocus
          Else
            frmCallingForm.Bookmark = recClone.Bookmark
            ctlFindNext.SetFocus
            ww_FindRecord = True
          End If
        End If
      End If
    End If
  Else
```

Following is the code for the search if the user specifies Exact mode. It checks the exact contents of each of the specified fields to see if they equal the user's search phrase.

```
'ctlSearchOption = 2 'Exact Search
strSelection = "CStr(" & strField1 & " & """") = """ & _
Replace(ctlSearchText, """", """""") & """"

If strField2 <> "" Then
  strSelection = strSelection & _
```

```
         " OR CStr(" & strField2 & " & """") = """ & _
         Replace(ctlSearchText, """", """""") & """"
End If

If strField3 <> "" Then
   strSelection = strSelection & _
   " OR CStr(" & strField3 & " & """") = """ & _
   Replace(ctlSearchText, """", """""") & """"
End If

If strField4 <> "" Then
   strSelection = strSelection & _
   " OR CStr(" & strField4 & " & """") = """ & _
   Replace(ctlSearchText, """", """""") & """"
End If

If strField5 <> "" Then
   strSelection = strSelection & _
   " OR CStr(" & strField5 & " & """") = """ & _
   Replace(ctlSearchText, """", """""") & """"
End If

If strField6 <> "" Then
   strSelection = strSelection & _
   " OR CStr(" & strField6 & " & """") = """ & _
   Replace(ctlSearchText, """", """""") & """"
End If

If strField7 <> "" Then
   strSelection = strSelection & _
   " OR CStr(" & strField7 & " & """") = """ & _
   Replace(ctlSearchText, """", """""") & """"
End If

If strField8 <> "" Then
   strSelection = strSelection & _
   " OR CStr(" & strField8 & " & """") = """ & _
   Replace(ctlSearchText, """", """""") & """"
End If

If strField9 <> "" Then
   strSelection = strSelection & _
   " OR CStr(" & strField9 & " & """") = """ & _
   Replace(ctlSearchText, """", """""") & """"
End If

If strField10 <> "" Then
   strSelection = strSelection & _
   " OR CStr(" & strField10 & " & """") = """ & _
   Replace(ctlSearchText, """", """""") & """"
End If

Set recClone = frmCallingForm.RecordsetClone
```

```
    If strFindMode = "first" Then
      recClone.FindFirst strSelection
      If recClone.NoMatch Then
        MsgBox "No matches found.", vbOKOnly, "Record Finder"
        ctlSearchText.SetFocus
      Else
        frmCallingForm.Bookmark = recClone.Bookmark
        ctlFindNext.SetFocus
        ww_FindRecord = True
      End If

    Else
      ' if find Next button was used
      If strFindMode = "next" Then
        recClone.Bookmark = frmCallingForm.Bookmark
        recClone.FindNext strSelection
        If recClone.NoMatch Then
          MsgBox "No more matches found.", vbOKOnly, _
          "Record Finder"
          ctlFindFirst.SetFocus
        Else
          frmCallingForm.Bookmark = recClone.Bookmark
          ctlFindNext.SetFocus
          ww_FindRecord = True
        End If
      End If
    End If
End If

DoCmd.Hourglass False

Exit_Procedure:
  Exit Function

Error_Handler:
  DoCmd.Hourglass False
  DisplayUnexpectedError Err.Number, Err.Description
  Resume Exit_Procedure
  Resume

End Function
```

There are several techniques in this code that are worth a closer look. They are explained in the next few sections.

Passing Control and Form References to a Function

This function does not reside behind any form, but rather in a separate module. For it to be usable from any index form in the application, it needs to be able to interact with that form, so you pass object references from your form in addition to actual parameter values. Those reference parameters are:

❑ frmCallingForm: The actual form itself, to build a RecordsetClone and to set the Bookmark.

❑ ctlFindFirst: The First button, to set focus.

- ❑   `ctlFindNext`: The Next button, to set focus.

- ❑   `ctlSearchText`: The text box with the search phrase, to use for searching and to set focus.

- ❑   `ctlSearchOption`: The radio button group of Exact/Contains, to determine which kind of search to perform.

The key thing to remember is that these are not values themselves; they are pointers to the controls on the original form, so they give you direct access to those controls as if this code were in that form itself.

The rest of the parameters are values, such as the Find mode (first or next matching record) and the names of up to ten fields to search.

Optional Parameters

This function uses *optional parameters*, meaning that when you call this function, you can choose whether to specify them. In this example, the optional parameters are `strField2` through `strField10`. Optional parameters are very useful in this case because they give you the flexibility to specify any number of fields to search, from 1 to 10. If you didn't use optional parameters in this procedure, you'd have to specify all ten field names every time you called it, sending in empty strings for the ones you didn't need.

Using the RecordsetClone

A `RecordsetClone` is a recordset based on a form's recordset, but with full search capabilities and a different record cursor. You use a `RecordsetClone` of the form to find a matching record, and then use its `Bookmark` property to position the form to the matching record. You do all this with the passed-in `Form` reference:

```
Set recClone = frmCallingForm.RecordsetClone
frmCallingForm.Bookmark = recClone.Bookmark
```

Remember that the reference was passed in as a parameter to this procedure, so the `RecordsetClone` being searched is the same as the recordset currently displayed on the index form that called the record finder procedure.

Searching Multiple Fields Using Concatenation

To search multiple fields, the function takes a different approach than you might be familiar with. Instead of building a complex SQL string that searches each specified field in the recordset with OR statements, it concatenates all the desired fields from the recordset into one large string (`strAllFields`). Then it searches the large text field for the search phrase.

There's one problem with this approach. The search phrase may be discovered using the end of one field and the beginning of another. For example, if the fields for City and State are concatenated together, they may look like this:

```
SeattleWA
```

If your user searches for the phrase `lew`, this record will be found, even though `lew` doesn't appear in any one field.

To avoid this problem, use the FIELDDELIMETER constant. It is set to "@%%@", a value that's unlikely to occur in any search phrase. When you concatenate the desired fields together into the one big field, they are separated by this delimiter value, like this:

```
Seattle@%%@WA
```

By doing this, you separate the two words and prevent a search for lew from finding this record.

Handling Quotes in the Search Phrase

There's a potential problem when the user types a quote (") in the search phrase, as shown in Figure M-5.

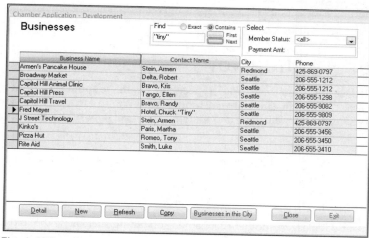

Figure M-5

Because you build strings using quotes in the code, these "extra" quotes supplied by the user can cause errors. To guard against that, replace each quote in the user's search phrase with two quotes (a full discussion of string handling techniques is included in Chapter 15).

To perform the quote replacement, use the VBA Replace function in this rather strange-looking line of code:

```
Replace(ctlSearchText, """", """""")
```

This takes every instance of a quote (") in ctlSearchText and replaces it with two quotes (""). Then, when you build search strings with it, those doubled-up quotes will "collapse" back into solo quotes. It looks weird, but it works.

Setting Focus from Afar

To help the user use the Find routine efficiently, control the focus so that keystrokes make sense. For example, if the user clicks the First button and no match is found, you know that he's probably going to want to change the search phrase to something else. To help him, set the focus to the Search Text control:

```
If recClone.NoMatch Then
   MsgBox "No matches found.", vbOKOnly, "Record Finder"
   ctlSearchText.SetFocus
```

Remember that this code is not in the form the user is viewing — you are controlling focus from this procedure using a reference to the control on the index form that called ww_FindRecord.

Similarly, to facilitate cycling through all the matching records, set focus to the Next button when a record is found, and to the First button after no more records are found. That allows the user to continue to press the Enter key on the keyboard to repeatedly loop through all the matching records. This feature is convenient, adding a lot of polish to your applications.

Split Your Application

You've probably heard it many times: Your application should be split into a front-end application and a back-end database. The benefits are many, including the ability to easily switch back-end databases (for example, between Production and Test) and to deliver new versions of the application without disturbing the user's data.

Access provides a wizard to split databases, but it's easy to do yourself if you follow these steps. Also, it will improve your understanding of what splitting a database really does.

1. Make a backup.

2. Copy your database to another file, named something such as MyApp Data.accdb.

3. Rename the first file to something like MyApp Application.accdb.

4. In the data file, delete all objects except the tables. You can also delete configuration tables that you know will be in the front-end database.

5. In the application file, delete the tables (except any local configuration tables). Then, on the Ribbon's External Data tab, use Import group ➪ Access, and then choose Link To The Data Source By Creating A Linked Table to link all the tables from the data file. (In earlier versions of Access you use File ➪ Get External Data ➪ Link Tables.)

Now that your database is split, you can relink tables using the Linked Table Manager (located in the Database Tools group on the Ribbon's Database Tools tab), or you can install one of the many Access table relinker functions available on the Internet or in other books. (In previous versions of Access, the Linked Table Manager can be found under Tools ➪ Database Utilities.)

Display Informative Form Captions

If you don't set your own form captions, Access just displays the form name there, as shown in Figure M-6.

Figure M-6

This is a sure sign of a novice developer. You need to, at least, replace the caption with the name of your application. One nice additional touch for the caption is to indicate which back-end database you are currently using. That way, your users know instantly whether they're in the Production or Test database, for example.

You'll need a table in the back-end database to store systemwide configuration values. In this example, it is named tsysConfig_System, and it has a field containing the name of the database (see Figure M-7).

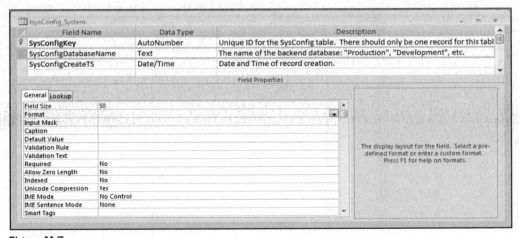

Figure M-7

You also need a local table in the front-end to store static values for the application itself, as shown in Figure M-8. In the example, one of the fields is the name (title) of the application, suitable for showing on various forms throughout the system.

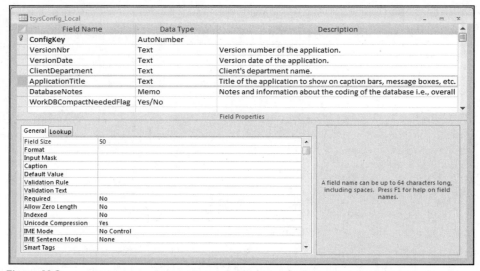

Figure M-8

The code to set the caption is easy. It belongs in the Open event code behind every form:

```
Me.Caption = DLookup("ApplicationTitle", "tsysConfig_Local") _
&" - "& DLookup("SysConfigDatabaseName", "tsysConfig_System")
```

Now, when each form opens, you can set Caption to the title of the application, concatenated with the name of the back-end database, as in Figure M-9.

Figure M-9

By setting the caption of every form, you avoid the rookie move of showing an internal form name such as `frmBusinesses`. And by using a configuration table to supply the application name, you avoid hard-coding it in every form. This makes your job a lot easier for each application you develop because you won't have to change the code in every form — only the value in the one configuration table.

Preload Records

Sometimes, you'll have a problem when you open a detail form for a new record. If there is a subform with child records on the detail form, users will encounter an error if they try to create a child record before entering any data for the parent (master) record, as shown in Figure M-10.

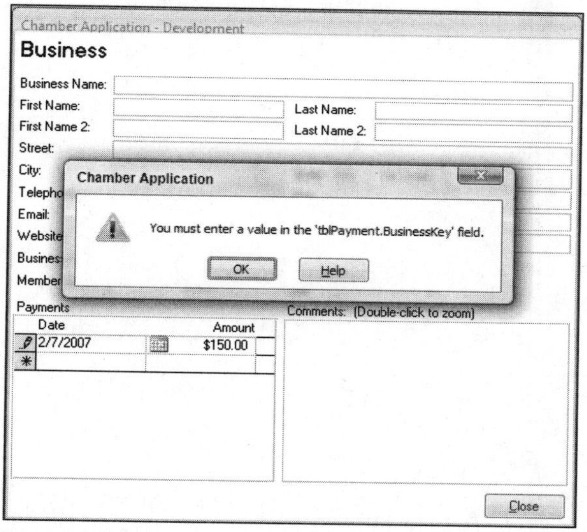

Figure M-10

The error occurs because the parent key still contains a Null, and the child record has a required foreign key for the parent Business record. Even if the foreign parent key in the child record isn't set to Required, another problem occurs: The child record will have a Null foreign parent key, making it an orphan record with no parent.

One way to prevent this error is to create an empty record before opening the Detail form. That way the parent record already has a primary key and can accept related child records. During this preloading operation, you can specify a default name for the new record, such as <New Business>, giving your user a clear indicator that she has just created a new record and allowing her to add child records immediately. Figure M-11 shows the new record.

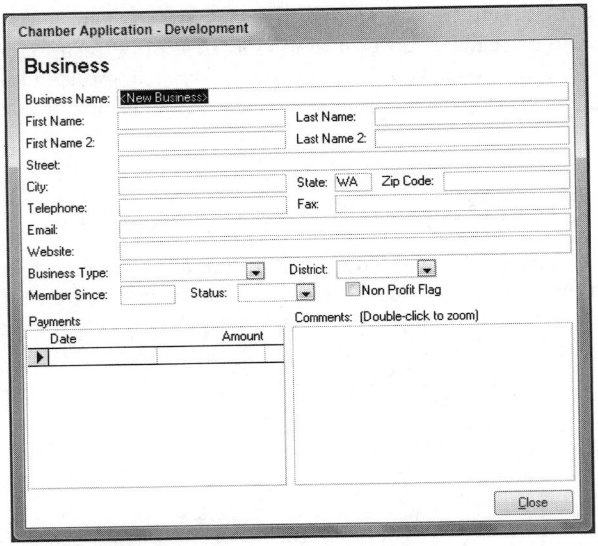

Figure M-11

The code to preload the record is in the index form `frmBusinesses` (refer to Figure M-5), in the `Click` event of the New button:

```
Private Sub cmdNew_Click()
On Error GoTo Error_Handler

Dim rs As Recordset
Dim strDocName As String
Dim strLinkCriteria As String

'Open form to new record

gstrCallingForm = Me.Name
strDocName = "frmBusiness"
strLinkCriteria = "[BusinessKey]=" & NewBusinessKey()
Me.Visible = False
DoCmd.OpenForm FormName:=strDocName, _
    WhereCondition:=strLinkCriteria, WindowMode:=acDialog

'Requery index form to pick up the new record, then
'set the bookmark to this new record.
Me.Requery
Set rs = Me.RecordsetClone
If Me.RecordsetClone.RecordCount > 0 Then

    'If first new record was cancelled, would fail.
    rs.FindFirst strLinkCriteria
    If Not rs.EOF Then
      Me.Bookmark = rs.Bookmark
    End If
```

```
    End If

Exit_Procedure:
  On Error Resume Next
  rs.Close
  Set rs = Nothing
  Exit Sub

Error_Handler:
  DisplayUnexpectedError Err.Number, Err.Description
  Resume Exit_Procedure
  Resume

End Sub
```

Notice that after the Business detail form is closed, the Businesses index form is requeried, and then positioned to the new business record so the user gets visual feedback that the newly added record is indeed now in the list.

Also note that the Business form is opened with a key specified as NewBusinessKey(). The function to generate the new Business record looks like this:

```
Public Function NewBusinessKey() As Long
On Error GoTo Error_Handler
'This function creates a new Business record and returns the key.

Dim db As Database
Dim rec As Recordset
Set db = CurrentDb
Set rec = db.OpenRecordset("tblBusiness")

'Add the record, storing new key value as variable and
'passing it out as the function name
With rec
  .AddNew
  NewBusinessKey = rec!BusinessKey
  !BusinessName = "<New Business>"
  .Update
  .Close
End With

Set rec = Nothing

Exit_Procedure:
  Exit Function

Error_Handler:
  DisplayUnexpectedError Err.Number, Err.Description
  Resume Exit_Procedure
  Resume

End Function
```

Now, there's only one more issue to handle. If the user tries to leave the Business Name as `<New Business>`, you need to prompt her to see whether you should clean up the record, as shown in Figure M-12.

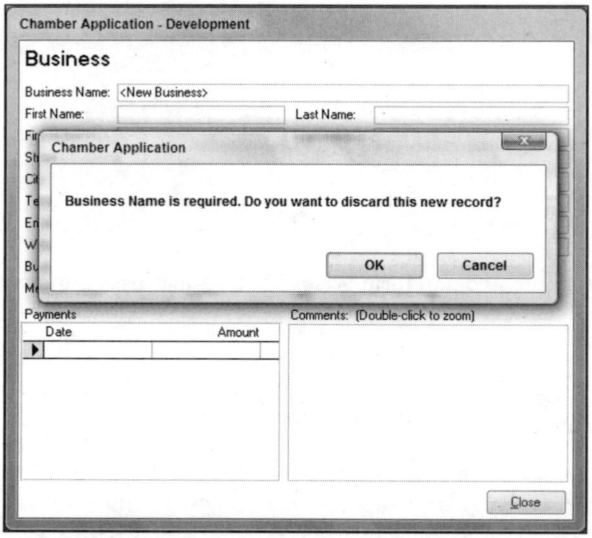

Figure M-12

Notice that the word `discard` is used instead of `delete`. Although you're aware that you've already created a new empty record, the user isn't, so using the word "delete" may be confusing.

The code for this cleanup is in the `Unload` event of the `Business` form:

```
Private Sub Form_Unload(Cancel As Integer)
On Error GoTo Error_Handler

Dim strSQL As String
Dim bDelete As Boolean

bDelete = False

'If user has not changed preloaded record, or if there is no name,
'delete the record.
If (Me!BusinessName = "<New Business>") Then

  If MsgBox("Business Name is required. Do you want to " _
    & "discard this new record?", vbOKCancel, _
  DLookup("ApplicationTitle", "tsysConfig_Local")) = vbOK Then

  'Delete the record
  bDelete = True

  Else
    'Yes delete the record, return to the form
```

```
         Cancel = True
      End If
   End If

   If Me!BusinessName & "" = "" Then

      If MsgBox("Business Name is required. Would you like to " _
         & "delete this record?", vbOKCancel, _
         DLookup("ApplicationTitle", "tsysConfig_Local")) = vbOK Then
      \
         'Delete the record
         bDelete = True

      Else
         Cancel = True
      End If
   End If

   If bDelete = True Then
      strSQL = "DELETE * FROM tblBusiness WHERE BusinessKey = " _
         & Me!BusinessKey
      DoCmd.SetWarnings False
      DoCmd.RunSQL strSQL
      DoCmd.SetWarnings True
   End If

Exit_Procedure:
   Exit Sub

Error_Handler:
   DoCmd.SetWarnings True
   DisplayUnexpectedError Err.Number, Err.Description
   Resume Exit_Procedure
   Resume

End Sub
```

If the user clicks OK, delete the record and close the form. If he clicks Cancel, cancel the Unload event and return to this record.

This code actually does use the word delete instead of discard if the Business Name is blank because some users are unsure how to delete a record, and will try to do so by clearing out the main name field. If you discover records with blank values in a table, that may be what happened. This code recognizes the situation and offers to delete the record.

Use a Splash Screen

You can display a custom logo (instead of the Access logo) while your Access program loads. Name a bitmap the same name as your database file (YourAppName.tif) and put it in the same folder as the database (.mdb or .accdb). The bitmap image will be displayed instead of the Access startup logo when you launch your application.

If you just want to remove the Access startup logo, you can create a bitmap image with just one pixel. Here's how: start Paint, select Image ⇨ Attributes, specify Width = 1 and Height = 1, make sure Pixels is selected in the Units pane, and save the image. It doesn't really matter what color the pixel is because it will hardly be noticeable.

Now, with a fast computer, you probably won't notice your custom logo (or pixel) because it will only be displayed for a fraction of a second. So, you need another splash screen inside your application. The first screen of your application should always be a splash screen that shows at least the application name, client's company name, version number, and your company name. This single feature says, "This is a professional application." You could use a logo (either yours or your client's) and some basic application information, as shown in Figure M-13.

Example code for displaying the Splash screen for a specified number of seconds (3 or 4 seconds seems like a good duration) can be found in the Microsoft Knowledge Base article 101374.

Figure M-13

Pop-Up Memo Workspace Form with Spell Check

Sometimes you want to give your user more room to enter long text into a memo field. Instead of using the built-in Access zoom feature, you can include a "workspace" feature to zoom into a memo field, allow the user to OK or Cancel his changes, and even spell-check the text. This zoom feature is shown on the Comments memo field in Figure M-14.

The following code in the double-click event of the memo field on `frmBusiness` is simple:

```
Private Sub BusinessComments_DblClick(Cancel As Integer)
On Error GoTo Error_Handler

Workspace Me.ActiveControl, Me

Exit_Procedure:
  Exit Sub

Error_Handler:
  DoCmd.SetWarnings True
  DisplayUnexpectedError Err.Number, Err.Description
  Resume Exit_Procedure
  Resume

End Sub
```

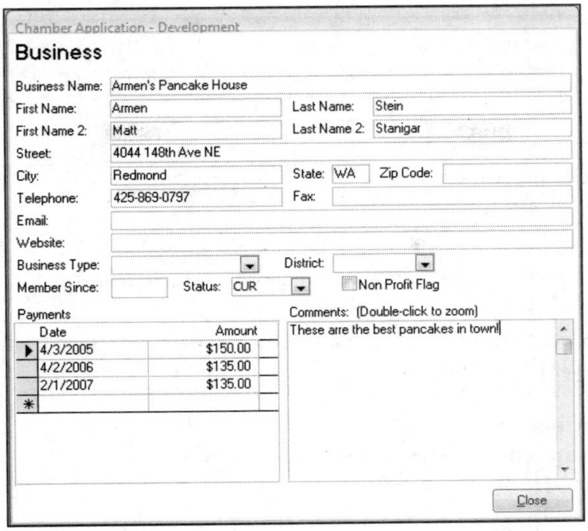

Figure M-14

The code in the Workspace procedure (which is in a standalone module such as basGlobal) looks like this:

```
Sub Workspace(ctl As Control, CallingForm As Form)
On Error GoTo Err_Workspace

CallingForm.Refresh
'Save any data which may have been entered into memo field

Set gctlWorkspaceSource = ctl

If ctl.Locked Or Not ctl.Enabled Then
  DoCmd.OpenForm "frmWorkspace", WindowMode:=acDialog, _
    OpenArgs:="ReadOnly"

Else
  DoCmd.OpenForm "frmWorkspace", WindowMode:=acDialog
End If

If IsLoaded("frmWorkspace") Then
  gctlWorkspaceSource = Forms.frmWorkspace.txtWorkspace
  DoCmd.Close acForm, "frmWorkspace"
End If

Exit_Workspace:
  Exit Sub

Err_Workspace:
  Select Case Err
    Case 3163 'Too much data for field
      MsgBox "The field is too small to accept the amount " _
```

```
                & "of data you attempted to insert. As a result, " _
                & "the operation has been cancelled.", vbExclamation, _
            DLookup("ApplicationTitle", "tsysConfig_Local")
            Resume Next

        Case Else
            MsgBox Err.Number & ", " & Err.Description
            Resume Exit_Workspace

    End Select
End Sub
```

If the original text box control is locked, the `Workspace` form is passed `OpenArgs` of `"ReadOnly"`, which causes the form to display the data in a grayed out, locked text box.

Also, the text on the original form is updated by the `Workspace` text if the `Workspace` form is still open. After that, the `Workspace` form is closed. Figure M-15 shows the `Workspace` form open.

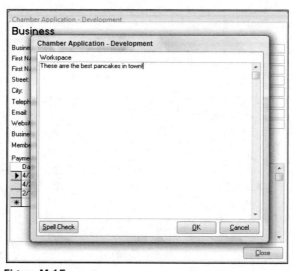

Figure M-15

Following is the code in the `Workspace` form. Note that if the Cancel button is clicked, the `Workspace` form is closed, which prevents any changes from making it back to the calling form.

```
Option Compare Database
Option Explicit

'Note: Uncomment the spell check mode you want to support:
'Const conSpellCheckOption = 0 'No Spell Checking
Const conSpellCheckOption = 1 'Spell Checking
```

```
Private Sub cmdCancel_Click()
On Error GoTo Error_Handler

  DoCmd.Close ObjectType:=acForm, ObjectName:=Me.Name

Exit_Procedure:
  Exit Sub
Error_Handler:
  DisplayUnexpectedError Err.Number, Err.Description
  Resume Exit_Procedure
  Resume
End Sub
```

Options, options: This code is written so that you, the programmer, can decide whether spell-checking will be available. You can turn it off entirely using a value of 0.

If OK is clicked, the `Workspace` form is merely hidden, as the following code shows. It was opened in Dialog mode, so the calling code was paused until now.

```
Private Sub cmdOK_Click()
On Error GoTo Error_Handler

  Me.Visible = False

Exit_Procedure:
  Exit Sub
Error_Handler:
  DisplayUnexpectedError Err.Number, Err.Description
  Resume Exit_Procedure
  Resume
End Sub
```

If the spell-checking option is enabled, the spell check may be performed:

```
Private Sub cmdSpellCheck_Click()
On Error GoTo Error_Handler

  Dim intTemp As Integer

  intTemp = fnCheckSpelling(Me!txtWorkspace)

Exit_Procedure:
  Exit Sub
Error_Handler:
  DisplayUnexpectedError Err.Number, Err.Description
  Resume Exit_Procedure
  Resume
End Sub
```

To support the standard usage of the F7 key to check spelling, this code traps the F7 keystroke and, if the spell-checking button is enabled, runs its code:

```
Private Sub Form_KeyDown(KeyCode As Integer, Shift As Integer)
On Error GoTo Error_Handler

  If KeyCode = vbKeyF7 Then
    KeyCode = 0
    If Me!cmdSpellCheck.Visible And Me!cmdSpellCheck.Enabled Then
      Me.cmdSpellCheck.SetFocus
      Call cmdSpellCheck_Click
    End If
  End If

Exit_Procedure:
  Exit Sub
Error_Handler:
  DisplayUnexpectedError Err.Number, Err.Description
  Resume Exit_Procedure
  Resume
End Sub
```

When the `Workspace` form loads, the option constant determines whether the Spell Check button is visible. Then the text from the original form is loaded into the `Workspace` text box, and the whole thing is locked down if the original text box was locked. Here's the code:

```
Private Sub Form_Load()
On Error GoTo Error_Handler

  Dim ctl As Control

  'Setup SpellChecker Options
  If conSpellCheckOption = 0 Then
    'Spell Checker is OFF
    Me!cmdSpellCheck.Visible = False
  Else
    'Spell Checker is ON
    Me!cmdSpellCheck.Visible = True
  End If

  'Import data into workspace form
  Me!txtWorkspace = gctlWorkspaceSource

  If Me.OpenArgs = "ReadOnly" Then
    Set ctl = Me!txtWorkspace
    With ctl
      .EnterKeyBehavior = False 'Sets to Default / No new line
      .Locked = True
      .BackColor = vbButtonFace
    End With
    Set ctl = Nothing

    Me!cmdSpellCheck.Enabled = False
  End If
```

```
Exit_Procedure:
  Exit Sub
Error_Handler:
  DisplayUnexpectedError Err.Number, Err.Description
  Resume Exit_Procedure
  Resume
End Sub
```

This is just the normal form caption setting as described earlier in this appendix:

```
Private Sub Form_Open(Cancel As Integer)
On Error GoTo Error_Handler

  Me.Caption = DLookup("ApplicationTitle", "tsysConfig_Local") _
  & " - " & DLookup("SysConfigDatabaseName", "tsysConfig_System")

Exit_Procedure:
  Exit Sub
Error_Handler:
  DisplayUnexpectedError Err.Number, Err.Description
  Resume Exit_Procedure
  Resume
End Sub
```

When the Workspace text box receives focus, you make sure that the insertion point jumps to the end of the text, instead of highlighting the whole field. This prevents the user from inadvertently changing the entire field.

```
Private Sub txtWorkspace_GotFocus()
On Error GoTo Error_Handler

  Dim varX As Variant

  ' jump to end of existing text instead of leaving it
  'all highlighted.
  varX = Len(Me!txtWorkspace.Text & "")
  If Not IsNull(varX) And varX > 0 Then
    Me!txtWorkspace.SelStart = Len(Me!txtWorkspace)
    Me!txtWorkspace.SelLength = 0
  End If

Exit_Procedure:
  Exit Sub
Error_Handler:
  DisplayUnexpectedError Err.Number, Err.Description
  Resume Exit_Procedure
  Resume
End Sub
```

When the Spell button is clicked, the text on the Workspace form is checked for spelling errors, as shown in Figure M-16.

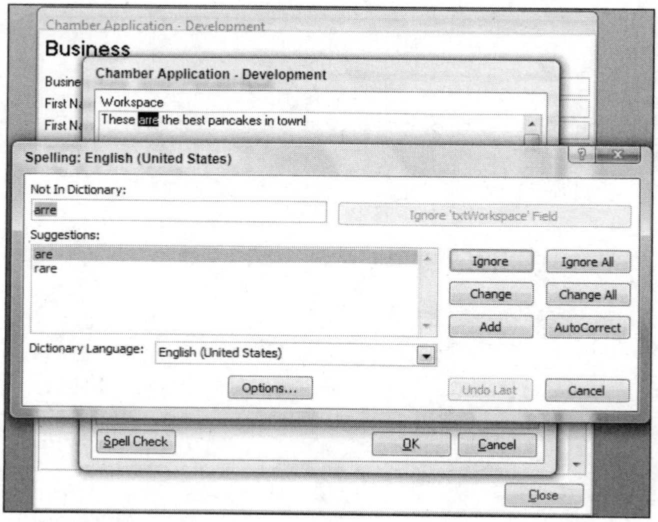

Figure M-16

Here's the code in the Spell Checking module:

```
Option Compare Database
Option Explicit

Public Function fnCheckSpelling(ctl As Control) As Boolean
On Error GoTo Error_Handler

  'This procedure checks the spelling of the text in the
  'passed-in control ctl.

  DoCmd.Hourglass True
  'This function is meant for textbox controls only.
  Select Case ctl.ControlType
    Case acTextBox
      If Not ctl.Enabled Or ctl.Locked Then
        'Text in control cannot be updated.
        GoTo Exit_Procedure
      ElseIf IsNull(ctl) Then
        'Nothing to check
        GoTo Exit_Procedure
      End If
    Case Else
      GoTo Exit_Procedure
  End Select

  ctl.SetFocus
  ctl.SelStart = 0
  ctl.SelLength = Len(ctl.Text & "")
  If ctl.SelLength <> 0 Then
    DoCmd.Hourglass False
```

```
      RunCommand acCmdSpelling
      ctl.SelLength = 0
      fnCheckSpelling = True
   End If

Exit_Procedure:
   On Error Resume Next
   DoCmd.Hourglass False
   Exit Function
Error_Handler:
   DoCmd.Hourglass False
   DisplayUnexpectedError Err.Number, Err.Description
   Resume Exit_Procedure
   Resume
End Function
```

By adding an area for users to enter text in a larger window and check the spelling, you make your application more powerful and easy to use. Plus, when you add this capability, you don't have to make memo field text boxes as large, which saves valuable real estate on your forms.

Determine the User Name

Often, you'll need to know the current user of the application. This might be to determine what activities they are allowed to do or to stamp records with change logging information. There are two user names that you'll be concerned with: the current Access user and the current Windows user.

The Current Access User

The current Access user is determined using the built-in `CurrentUser` function. However, if you are not using Access security and requiring the user to log in with a User Name and Password, this user name will always be the default Access user of Admin. Because this isn't too descriptive, you may need to know the name of the user that is currently using this PC.

The Current Windows User

To determine the currently logged in Windows user, you can use this code. First, in the module declaration section, include this code:

```
Global Const ERRORMOREDATA = 234
Global Const ERR_SUCCESS = 0

Private Declare Function WNetGetUser Lib "mpr" Alias _
    "WNetGetUserA" (ByVal lpName As String, _
    ByVal lpUserName As String, lpnLength As Long) As Long
```

Then, create a function with this code:

```
Public Function WinUserName() As String
Dim lUserNameLen As Long
```

```
Dim stTmp As String
Dim lReturn As Long

Do
    ' Set up the buffer
    stTmp = String$(lUserNameLen, vbNullChar)

    lReturn = WNetGetUser(vbNullString, stTmp, lUserNameLen)

' Continue looping until the call succeeds or the buffer
' can't fit any more data
Loop Until lReturn <> ERRORMOREDATA

If lReturn = ERR_SUCCESS Then
    WinUserName = Left$(stTmp, InStr(1, stTmp, vbNullChar, _
        vbBinaryCompare) -1)
End If

End Function
```

You can use this Windows username anywhere you like, including displaying it on forms, using it to allow or disallow certain features, or including the username whenever a record is changed or created.

Index